T0190001

Lecture Notes in Computer Science   8559

Commenced Publication in 1973
Founding and Former Series Editors:
Gerhard Goos, Juris Hartmanis, and Jan van Leeuwen

Armin Biere   Roderick Bloem (Eds.)

Computer Aided Verification

26th International Conference, CAV 2014
Held as Part of the Vienna Summer of Logic, VSL 2014
Vienna, Austria, July 18-22, 2014
Proceedings

Volume Editors

Armin Biere
Johannes Kepler University Linz
Altenbergerstr. 69, 4040 Linz, Austria
E-mail: biere@jku.at

Roderick Bloem
IAIK, Graz University of Technology
Inffeldgasse 16a, 8010 Graz, Austria
E-mail: roderick.bloem@iaik.tugraz.at

ISSN 0302-9743   e-ISSN 1611-3349
ISBN 978-3-319-08866-2   e-ISBN 978-3-319-08867-9
DOI 10.1007/978-3-319-08867-9
Springer Cham Heidelberg New York Dordrecht London

Library of Congress Control Number: 2014942534

LNCS Sublibrary: SL 1 – Theoretical Computer Science and General Issues

Typesetting: Camera-ready by author, data conversion by Scientific Publishing Services, Chennai, India

Printed on acid-free paper

Springer is part of Springer Science+Business Media (www.springer.com)

logic n. **1** the science of reasoning.
– ORIGIN from Greek *logikē tekhnē*
'art of reason'.

Foreword

VIENNA
SUMMER
OF LOGIC
2014

In the summer of 2014, Vienna hosted the largest scientific conference in the history of logic. The Vienna Summer of Logic (VSL, http://vsl2014.at) consisted of twelve large conferences and 82 workshops, attracting more than 2000 researchers from all over the world. This unique event was organized by the Kurt Gödel Society and took place at Vienna University of Technology during July 9 to 24, 2014, under the auspices of the Federal President of the Republic of Austria, Dr. Heinz Fischer.

The conferences and workshops dealt with the main theme, logic, from three important angles: logic in computer science, mathematical logic, and logic in artificial intelligence. They naturally gave rise to respective streams gathering the following meetings:

Logic in Computer Science / Federated Logic Conference (FLoC)

- 26th International Conference on Computer Aided Verification (CAV)
- 27th IEEE Computer Security Foundations Symposium (CSF)
- 30th International Conference on Logic Programming (ICLP)
- 7th International Joint Conference on Automated Reasoning (IJCAR)
- 5th Conference on Interactive Theorem Proving (ITP)
- Joint meeting of the 23rd EACSL Annual Conference on Computer Science Logic (CSL) and the 29th ACM/IEEE Symposium on Logic in Computer Science (LICS)
- 25th International Conference on Rewriting Techniques and Applications (RTA) joint with the 12th International Conference on Typed Lambda Calculi and Applications (TLCA)
- 17th International Conference on Theory and Applications of Satisfiability Testing (SAT)
- 76 FLoC Workshops
- FLoC Olympic Games (System Competitions)

Mathematical Logic

- Logic Colloquium 2014 (LC)
- Logic, Algebra and Truth Degrees 2014 (LATD)
- Compositional Meaning in Logic (GeTFun 2.0)
- The Infinity Workshop (INFINITY)
- Workshop on Logic and Games (LG)
- Kurt Gödel Fellowship Competition

Logic in Artificial Intelligence

- 14th International Conference on Principles of Knowledge Representation and Reasoning (KR)
- 27th International Workshop on Description Logics (DL)
- 15th International Workshop on Non-Monotonic Reasoning (NMR)
- 6th International Workshop on Knowledge Representation for Health Care 2014 (KR4HC)

The VSL keynote talks which were directed to all participants were given by Franz Baader (Technische Universität Dresden), Edmund Clarke (Carnegie Mellon University), Christos Papadimitriou (University of California, Berkeley) and Alex Wilkie (University of Manchester); Dana Scott (Carnegie Mellon University) spoke in the opening session. Since the Vienna Summer of Logic contained more than a hundred invited talks, it would not be feasible to list them here.

The program of the Vienna Summer of Logic was very rich, including not only scientific talks, poster sessions and panels, but also two distinctive events. One was the award ceremony of the Kurt Gödel Research Prize Fellowship Competition, in which the Kurt Gödel Society awarded three research fellowship prizes endowed with 100.000 Euro each to the winners. This was the third edition of the competition, themed Logical Mind: Connecting Foundations and Technology this year.

The 1st FLoC Olympic Games formed the other event and were hosted by the Federated Logic Conference (FLoC) 2014. Intended as a new FLoC element, the Games brought together 12 established logic solver competitions by different research communities. In addition to the competitions, the Olympic Games facilitated the exchange of expertise between communities, and increased the visibility and impact of state-of-the-art solver technology. The winners in the competition categories were honored with Kurt Gödel medals at the FLoC Olympic Games award ceremonies.

Organizing an event like the Vienna Summer of Logic was a challenge. We are indebted to numerous people whose enormous efforts were essential in making this vision become reality. With so many colleagues and friends working with us, we are unable to list them individually here. Nevertheless, as representatives of the three streams of VSL, we would like to particularly express our gratitude to all people who helped to make this event a success: the sponsors and the Honorary Committee; the Organization Committee and the local organizers; the conference and workshop chairs and Program Committee members; the reviewers and authors; and of course all speakers and participants of the many conferences, workshops and competitions.

The Vienna Summer of Logic continues a great legacy of scientific thought that started in Ancient Greece and flourished in the city of Gödel, Wittgenstein and the Vienna Circle. The heroes of our intellectual past shaped the scientific world-view and changed our understanding of science. Owing to their achievements, logic has permeated a wide range of disciplines, including computer science, mathematics, artificial intelligence, philosophy, linguistics, and many more. Logic is everywhere – or in the language of Aristotle, πάντα πλήρη λογικῆς τέχνης.

July 2014   Matthias Baaz
                                                                          Thomas Eiter
                                                                          Helmut Veith

Preface

This volume contains the papers presented at CAV 2014: International Conference on Computer Aided Verification held during July 18–22, 2014 in Vienna, Austria.

CAV 2014 was the 26th in a series dedicated to the advancement of the theory and practice of computer-aided formal analysis methods for hardware and software systems.

As part of the Federated Logic Conference (FLoC) and the Vienna Summer of Logic, CAV 2014 was collocated with many other conferences in logic. CAV considers it vital to continue spurring advances in hardware and software verification while expanding to new domains such as biological systems and computer security.

The conference covered the spectrum from theoretical results to concrete applications, with an emphasis on practical verification tools and the algorithms and techniques that are needed for their implementation. The proceedings of the conference will have been the Springer-Verlag Lecture Notes in Computer Science series. A selection of papers was invited to a special issue of Formal Methods in System Design and the Journal of the ACM.

There were 229 paper submissions, 175 regular papers and 54 short papers. Each submission was reviewed by at least three, and on average 4 Program Committee members. The Program Committee decided to accept 57 papers which is an acceptance rate of 25%, consisting of 46 regular papers (26%) and 11 short papers (20%).

There were 293 abstract submissions originally and a couple of papers, not included in the number of 229 papers above, immediately rejected due to excessively exceeding the page limit. Among the 172 rejected papers considered for computing the acceptance rate, there were 7 regular and one short paper withdrawn on behalf of the authors after first versions of reviews had been sent out during the rebuttal phase.

Regarding paper format, CAV 2014 saw some important changes compared to previous versions. Beside long papers, e.g., regular papers, there were also short papers, but short papers were not restricted to be tool papers anymore. It was also encouraged to submit high quality tool papers and empirical evaluations as long papers. These regular papers with mostly only empirical results, and not necessarily new theory, produced some reservations on the side of the reviewers and was an import topic during the discussion of the Program Committee. Further, references did not count towards the page limit.

Beside the presentations of the accepted papers, and shared FLoC sessions, the program of CAV 2014 featured two tutorials, two CAV invited talks, three competition presentations and last but not least the presentation of the CAV award.

The first tutorial was given by David Monniaux, Verimag, Grenoble, France, on "How Do We Get Inductive Invariants?" and the second tutorial by Fabio Somenzi, University of Colorado at Boulder, USA, on "Hardware Model Checking".

The first invited talk by Erik Winfree, Caltech, Pasadena, California, USA, had "Designing and Verifying Molecular Circuits and Systems Made of DNA" as the title. The second invited talk by Rance Cleaveland, University of Maryland and Fraunhofer, USA, discussed "Automated Testing".

The CAV 2014 affiliated competitions consisted of the first "Syntax-Guided Synthesis Competition", organized by Rajeev Alur, Dana Fisman, Rishabh Singh and Armando Solar-Lezama. Then there was the presentation of the results of the first Synthesis Competition for Reactive Systems "SYNTCOMP" organized by Swen Jacobs, Roderick Bloem, Rüdiger Ehlers and the 7th incarnation of the "Hardware Model Checking Competition", which was organized by Armin Biere and Keijo Heljanko.

The CAV award was presented by the CAV Award Committee, which consisted of Moshe Vardi, Ahmed Bouajjani, Tom Ball, and headed by Marta Kwiatkowska.

The FLoC 2014 Interconference Topics on Security and SAT/SMT/QBF are a FLoC 2014 initiative by CAV, CSF, and IJCAR to foster exchange and discussion between conferences. The Interconference Topics consist of sessions from the participating conferences with a joint thematic focus. They provide a special opportunity for FLoC participants with particular interest in these topics.

We would like to thank our workshop and competition chair Martina Seidl, for caring about 21 CAV workshops, including 4 workshops affiliated with other FLoC conferences too. As publication chair Swen Jacobs did an excellent job setting up the web-pages and producing the proceedings.

Of course without the tremendous effort put in the reviewing process by our Program Committee members this conference would not have been possible. We would further thank the Steering Committee for support and guidance during the whole conference process as well as Andrei Voronkov for providing the EasyChair service in general and excellent support during using EasyChair for CAV 2014.

May 2014

Armin Biere
Roderick Bloem

Organization

Program Chairs

Armin Biere   Johannes Kepler University of Linz, Austria
Roderick Bloem   Graz University of Technology, Austria

Program Committee

Rajeev Alur	University of Pennsylvania, USA
Domagoj Babic	Google, USA
Gogul Balakrishnan	University of Wisconsin, USA
Nikolaj Bjorner	Microsoft Research, USA
Ahmed Bouajjani	LIAFA, University Paris Diderot, France
Aaron Bradley	University of Colorado Boulder, USA
Pavol Cerny	University of Colorado Boulder, USA
Koen Claessen	Chalmers University of Technology, Sweden
Byron Cook	Microsoft Research, UK
Azadeh Farzan	University of Toronto, Canada
Bernd Finkbeiner	Saarland University, Germany
Jasmin Fisher	Microsoft Research, UK
Mike Gordon	University of Cambridge, UK
Orna Grumberg	Technion - Israel Institute of Technology, Israel
Leopold Haller	University of Oxford, UK
Keijo Heljanko	Aalto University, Finland
William Hung	Synopsys Inc, USA
Somesh Jha	University of Wisconsin, USA
Susmit Jha	Intel, USA
Barbara Jobstmann	EPFL, Jasper DA, CNRS-Verimag, Switzerland/France
Bengt Jonsson	Uppsala University, Sweden
Laura Kovacs	Chalmers University of Technology, Sweden
Daniel Kroening	University of Oxford, UK
Marta Kwiatkowska	University of Oxford, UK
Kim Guldstrand Larsen	Aalborg University, Denmark
Joao Marques-Silva	University College Dublin, Ireland
Kedar Namjoshi	Bell Labs, USA
Corina Pasareanu	CMU and NASA Ames Research Center, USA
Doron Peled	Bar Ilan University, Israel
Pavithra Prabhakar	IMDEA Software Institute, Spain
Jean-Francois Raskin	Université Libre de Bruxelles, Belgium

Koushik Sen	University of California Berkeley, USA
Natasha Sharygina	Università della Svizzera Italiana, Switzerland
Nishant Sinha	IBM Research, India
Anna Slobodova	Centaur Technology, USA
Fabio Somenzi	University of Colorado Boulder, USA
Cesare Tinelli	University of Iowa, USA
Thomas Wahl	Northeastern University, USA
Georg Weissenbacher	Vienna University of Technology, Austria
Eran Yahav	Technion - Israel Institute of Technology, Israel

Organization Committee

Swen Jacobs	Graz University of Technology, Austria
Martina Seidl	Johannes Kepler University Linz, Austria

Steering Committee

Michael Gordon	University of Cambridge, UK
Orna Grumberg	Technion - Israel Institute of Technology, Israel
Aarti Gupta	NEC Laboratories, USA
Kenneth McMillan	Microsoft Research, USA

Additional Reviewers

Abate, Alessandro
Abd Elkader, Karam
Adzkiya, Dieky
Albarghouthi, Aws
Alberti, Francesco
Alglave, Jade
Alt, Leonardo
Althoff, Matthias
Aronis, Stavros
Atig, Mohamed Faouzi
Avigad, Jeremy
Bacci, Giorgio
Bacci, Giovanni
Bandhakavi, Sruthi
Bansal, Kshitij
Basler, Gerard
Basset, Nicolas
Bastani, Osbert
Basu, Samik

Batty, Mark
Belov, Anton
Ben Sassi, Mohamed Amin
Bingham, Jesse
Birgmeier, Johannes
Blackshear, Sam
Bogomolov, Sergiy
Boker, Udi
Boldo, Sylvie
Botincan, Matko
Boudjadar, A. Jalil
Boulmé, Sylvain
Bozianu, Rodica
Brain, Martin
Brenguier, Romain
Brockschmidt, Marc
Bucheli, Samuel
Bultan, Tevfik
Cabodi, Gianpiero

Cassel, Sofia
Cassez, Franck
Ceska, Milan
Chadha, Rohit
Chakarov, Aleksandar
Chen, Hong-Yi
Chen, Hongyi
Chen, Xin
Chen, Yu-Fang
Chockler, Hana
Choi, Wontae
Chowdhury, Omar
Christodorescu, Mihai
Ciardo, Gianfranco
Clemente, Lorenzo
Cordeiro, Lucas
D'Amorim, Marcelo
D'Antoni, Loris
D'Silva, Vijay
D'Souza, Deepak
Daca, Przemyslaw
Dalsgaard, Andreas Engelbredt
Dang, Thao
David, Alexandre
David, Cristina
Davidson, Drew
Davis, Jared
De Carli, Lorenzo
De Moura, Leonardo
Dehnert, Christian
Delahaye, Benoit
Delaune, Stephanie
Delzanno, Giorgio
Dhawan, Mohan
Dillig, Isil
Dodds, Mike
Donaldson, Alastair
Doyen, Laurent
Drachsler, Dana
Dragoi, Cezara
Duret-Lutz, Alexandre
Een, Niklas
Emmi, Michael
Enea, Constantin
Falcone, Ylies

Faymonville, Peter
Fedyukovich, Grigory
Feng, Lu
Ferrara, Pietro
Filieri, Antonio
Filiot, Emmanuel
Fisman, Dana
Forejt, Vojtech
Fredrikson, Matt
Fränzle, Martin
Fu, Hongfei
Fuhs, Carsten
Furia, Carlo A.
Galenson, Joel
Ganai, Malay
Ganty, Pierre
Gerke, Michael
Girard, Antoine
Gopan, Denis
Greaves, David
Greenstreet, Mark
Griesmayer, Andreas
Griggio, Alberto
Groce, Alex
Grosu, Radu
Grundy, Jim
Gupta, Ashutosh
Gurfinkel, Arie
Haase, Christoph
Hadarean, Liana
Haddad, Axel
Hahn, Ernst Moritz
Hall, Ben
Hao, Kecheng
Harris, William
Hassan, Zyad
He, Fei
Hendriks, Martijn
Herbreteau, Frédéric
Hermanns, Holger
Hoare, Tony
Hochreiter, Sepp
Holik, Lukas
Holzer, Andreas
Hunter, Paul

Hyvärinen, Antti
Ignatiev, Alexey
Iosif, Radu
Itzhaky, Shachar
Ivancic, Franjo
Jacobs, Swen
Jaeger, Manfred
Janota, Mikolas
Jansen, Nils
Jha, Sumit Kumar
Jin, Hoon Sang
Johansson, Moa
Joshi, Saurabh
Jovanovic, Aleksandra
Kahlon, Vineet
Kahsai, Temesghen
Kannan, Jayanthkumar
Katz, Omer
Khlaaf, Heidy
Kiefer, Stefan
Kim, Chang Hwan Peter
Kim, Hyondeuk
Kincaid, Zachary
Klein, Felix
Komuravelli, Anvesh
Konev, Boris
Konnov, Igor
Kotek, Tomer
Kuismin, Tuomas
Kuncak, Viktor
Kupferman, Orna
Kupriyanov, Andrey
Kähkönen, Kari
Lal, Akash
Landsberg, David
Lee, Wonchan
Leino, Rustan
Leonardsson, Carl
Leue, Stefan
Liang, Tianyi
Liu, Jun
Liu, Lingyi
Liu, Peizun
Liu, Wanwei
Loginov, Alexey

Logozzo, Francesco
Lopes, Nuno
Lopes, Nuno P.
Luchaup, Daniel
Luckow, Kasper
Malik, Sharad
Mangal, Ravi
Manquinho, Vasco
Markey, Nicolas
Mauborgne, Laurent
McCamant, Stephen
McClurg, Jedidiah
Mereacre, Alexandru
Meshman, Yuri
Meyer, Roland
Mikucionis, Marius
Minea, Marius
Mitra, Sayan
Moarref, Salar
Monmege, Benjamin
Morgado, Antonio
Moses, Yoram
Mukherjee, Rajdeep
Mukund, Madhavan
Myers, Andrew
Nadel, Alexander
Natraj, Ashutosh
Navarro Perez, Juan Antonio
Navas, Jorge
Nghiem, Truong
Nickovic, Dejan
Niebert, Peter
Nimkar, Kaustubh
Norman, Gethin
Nyman, Ulrik
Olesen, Mads Chr.
Omari, Adi
Ozay, Necmiye
Pajic, Miroslav
Palikareva, Hristina
Paoletti, Nicola
Papavasileiou, Vasilis
Parker, David
Parkinson, Matthew
Parlato, Gennaro

Partush, Nimrod
Passmore, Grant
Pavlogiannis, Andreas
Payer, Mathias
Perez, Guillermo
Peter, Isabelle
Pichon, Jean
Piskac, Ruzica
Podelski, Andreas
Poetzl, Daniel
Prabhu, Prakash
Pradel, M.
Pradel, Michael
Putot, Sylvie
Qian, Kairong
Rabe, Markus N.
Radhakrishna, Arjun
Raghothaman, Mukund
Ramachandran, Jaideep
Raman, Vishwanath
Ranise, Silvio
Ratschan, Stefan
Ravanbakhsh, Hadi
Ray, Sandip
Rezine, Ahmed
Rezine, Othmane
Rinetzky, Noam
Rodriguez, Cesar
Rogalewicz, Adam
Rollini, Simone Fulvio
Rubio-Gonzalez, Cindy
Ruemmer, Philipp
Rybalchenko, Andrey
Saarikivi, Olli
Šafránek, David
Sagonas, Konstantinos
Saha, Indranil
Sanchez, Cesar
Sangnier, Arnaud
Sankaranarayanan, Sriram
Sarkar, Susmit
Schrammel, Peter
Sezgin, Ali
Shacham, Ohad
Sharma, Subodh

Sheinvald, Sarai
Shoham, Sharon
Siirtola, Antti Tapani
Singhania, Nimit
Sinha, Rohit
Sinha, Saurabh
Sorrentino, Francesco
Sosnovich, Adi
Srba, Jiri
Stainer, Amelie
Stenman, Jari
Stergiou, Christos
Sticksel, Christoph
Strichman, Ofer
Sturm, Thomas
Su, Kaile
Sznajder, Nathalie
Tarrach, Thorsten
Tasiran, Serdar
Tautschnig, Michael
Tentrup, Leander
Terauchi, Tachio
Thachuk, Chris
Tiwari, Ashish
Tonetta, Stefano
Topcu, Ufuk
Torfah, Hazem
Totla, Nishant
Trefler, Richard
Trinh, Cong Quy
Tripakis, Stavros
Trivedi, Ashutosh
Tschantz, Michael Carl
Tsiskaridze, Nestan
Tsitovich, Aliaksei
Turrini, Andrea
Udupa, Abhishek
Ujma, Mateusz
Urban, Caterina
Vafeiadis, Viktor
Vardi, Moshe
Veanes, Margus
Vechev, Martin
Villard, Jules
Viswanathan, Mahesh

Viswanathan, Ramesh
Vizel, Yakir
Von Essen, Christian
Wachter, Björn
Widder, Josef
Wieringa, Siert
Wiltsche, Clemens
Wintersteiger, Christoph
Wintersteiger, Christoph M.
Worrell, James

Wrigstad, Tobias
Xia, Bican
Xue, Bingtian
Yi, Wang
Zheng, Feijun
Zhou, Min
Zhu, Yunyun
Zielonka, Wieslaw
Zimmermann, Martin
Zwirchmayr, Jakob

Invited Tutorials and Talks

How Do We Get Inductive Invariants?

David Monniaux

CNRS, Verimag, Grenoble, France

Verifying the correctness of loop-free programs (or of general programs, up to bounded depth) is difficult: the state space explodes exponentially as the depth increases. Yet, the difficulty increases as we allow unboundedly many execution steps; proof approaches then generally rely on finding inductive invariants (properties shown to hold initially, then to remain true by induction).

Abstract interpretation attempts finding inductive invariants within a given domain, e.g. conjunctions of linear inequalities. The classical approach iterates a transformer until the property becomes inductive. In general, this approach may not terminate; thus termination is often enforced with a "widening" operator, which attempts at generalizing the iterates into an inductive property. Unfortunately, widening operators are brittle, with non-monotonic behaviors (supplying more information about a system may result in worse analysis outcomes!). Therefore, other approaches have been developed (policy iteration,...), which avoid this pitfall.

Finally, we shall discuss possible combinations of abstract interpretation and SMT-solving.

Hardware Model Checking

Fabio Somenzi

University of Colorado at Boulder, USA

This tutorial described the state-of-the art in Hardware-Model Checking using SAT and BDD-based techniques, including a discussion of the overall architecture of modern, multi-engine model checkers.

Designing and Verifying Molecular Circuits and Systems Made of DNA

Erik Winfree

California Institute of Technology, Pasadena, CA, USA

Inspired by the information processing core of biological organisms and its ability to fabricate intricate machinery from the molecular scale up to the macroscopic scale, research in synthetic biology, molecular programming, and nucleic acid nanotechnology aims to create information-based chemical systems that carry out human-defined molecular programs that input, output, and manipulate molecules and molecular structures. For chemistry to become the next information technology substrate, we will need improved tools for designing, simulating, and analyzing complex molecular circuits and systems. Using DNA nanotechnology as a model system, I will discuss how programming languages can be devised for specifying molecular systems at a high level, how compilers can translate such specifications into concrete molecular implementations, how both high-level and low-level specifications can be simulated and verified according to behavioral logic and the underlying biophysics of molecular interactions, and how Bayesian analysis techniques can be used to understand and predict the behavior of experimental systems that, at this point, still inevitably contain many ill-characterized components and interactions.

Automated Testing

Rance Cleaveland

University of Maryland, USA

In model-based testing, (semi-)formal models of systems are used to drive the derivation of test cases to be applied to the system-under-test (SUT). The technology has long been a part of the traditional hardware-design workflows, and it is beginning to find application in embedded-software development processes also. In automotive and land-vehicle control-system design in particular, models in languages such as MATLAB(r) / Simulink(r) / Stateflow(r) are used to drive the testing of the software used to control vehicle behavior, with tools like Reactis(r), developed by a team including the speaker, providing automated test-case generation support for this endeavor.

This talk will discuss how test-case generation capabilities may also be used to help verify that models meet formal specifications of their behavior. The method we advocate, Instrumentation-Based Verification (IBV), involves the formalizaton of behavior specifications as models that are used to instrument the model to be verified, and the use of coverage testing of the instrumented model to search for specification violations. The presentation will discuss the foundations of IBV, the test-generation approach and other features in Reactis that are used to support IBV, and the results of several case studies involving the use of the methods.

Competition Presentations

The First Syntax-Guided Synthesis Competition (SyGuS-COMP 2014)

Rajeev Alur[1], Dana Fisman[1], Rishabh Singh[2], and Armando Solar-Lezama[2,*]

[1] University of Pennsylvania
[2] Massachusetts Institute of Technology

Abstract. *Syntax-Guided Synthesis (SyGuS)* is the computational problem of finding an implementation f that meets both a semantic constraint given by a logical formula φ in a background theory T, and a syntactic constraint given by a grammar G, which specifies the allowed set of candidate implementations [1]. Such a synthesis problem can be formally defined in SyGuS-IF [2], a language that is built on top of SMT-LIB.

The *Syntax-Guided Synthesis Competition (SyGuS-COMP)* is an effort to facilitate, bring together and accelerate research and development of efficient solvers for SyGuS by providing a platform for evaluating different synthesis techniques on a comprehensive set of benchmarks. The benchmarks for the first competition are restricted to the theories of bitvector and integer linear arithmetic, yet their origin spans a variety of domains including bitvector algorithms, concurrency, robotics, and invariant generation. The solvers are scored primarily on the number of benchmark solved and the solving time, and secondarily on the succinctness of the synthesized solution.

References

1. Alur, R., Bodík, R., Juniwal, G., Martin, M.M.K., Raghothaman, M., Seshia, S.A., Singh, R., Solar-Lezama, A., Torlak, E., Udupa, A.: Syntax-Guided Synthesis. In: FMCAD, pp. 1–17. IEEE (2013)
2. Raghothaman, M., Udupa, A.: Language to Specify Syntax-Guided Synthesis Problems (May 2014), http://arxiv.org/abs/1405.5590

* This research was supported by NSF Expeditions in Computing award CCF-1138996 and the competition awards were sponsored by Microsoft Research and FLoC.

Hardware Model Checking Competition
CAV 2014 Edition

Armin Biere[1] and Keijo Heljanko[2]

[1] Johannes Kepler University Linz, Austria
[2] Aalto University, Finland

The results of the 7th International Hardware Model Checking Competition were presented at CAV 2014. Model checkers were required to produce witnesses for single safety properties. The traces were checked by the AIGSIM tool, which is part of the AIGER tools. Otherwise, the competition was run in almost the same way as in the previous two years. The competition was run on a cluster at Aalto University with exclusive access to 32 nodes of 2x Six-Core AMD Opteron 2435 2.6GHz with at least 16 GB of RAM. This meant 12 cores for each solver per benchmark, memory limit of 15 GB and time limit of 900 seconds. As fall back we had the cluster at JKU with the same characteristics as in previous years. Beside the requirement to produces witnesses, rules, input and output format did not change.

During the FLoC Olympic Games ceremony in the second week, three real silver medals were handed out to the winners of the three tracks of the competition. These three tracks in the CAV 2014 edition of the competitHardwaion consisted of: the single safety, the liveness and the deep bound track. There was no multiple property track for the CAV edition. It was considered to be the technically most challenging track, particularly while moving to new hardware, and further, only three medals were available. The winner of the deep bound track received both a medal and check, sponsored again by Oski technology. The competition further relied on support by the national research network on Rigorous System Engineering (RiSE) funded by the Austrian Science Fund (FWF) and also used resources made available through the Science-IT project at Aalto University.

SYNTCOMP -
Synthesis Competition for Reactive Systems

Roderick Bloem[1], Rüdiger Ehlers[2,3], and Swen Jacobs[1]

[1] Graz University of Technology
Austria
[2] University of Bremen
Germany
[3] DFKI GmbH
Bremen, Germany

We present results of the first competition for reactive synthesis tools. For this first iteration, we focused on safety specifications, which are given as sequential circuits in an extension of the AIGER format for and-inverter graphs [1]. In the extended format, input signals of the circuit can be declared as controllable or uncontrollable. The synthesized implementation can read the uncontrollable input signals, and uses this information to drive the controllable signals such that the circuit never emits a **true** value at its error output signal.

The setting allows to encode a wide range of synthesis problems, and benchmarks for the first competition ranged from machine and robot controllers to hardware components like on-chip bus arbiters, and translations of LTL properties in general. Liveness properties are encodable in the form of *bounded* liveness properties, and the competition featured both benchmarks that make and that do not make use of this approach.

Tools were ranked with respect to the time needed for realizability checks and the size of circuits produced. Particular focus has been put on the verification of the synthesized implementations. Tools had to output the resulting controller in a format that is suitable as input to tools from the hardware model checking competition (HWMCC), i.e., as another and-inverter-graph circuit. Solutions had to be verifiable by current model checking tools in order to count for the competition. The competition also featured a track in which only the realizability of a specification needed to be checked, i.e., whether some controller exists or not.

SYNTCOMP was part of the FLoC 2014 Olympic Games and relied on support by the Austrian national research network on Rigorous Systems Engineering (RiSE), funded by the Austrian Science Fund (FWF).

Reference

1. Jacobs, S.: Extended AIGER Format for Synthesis. arXiv:1405.5793 (May 2014)

Table of Contents

Software Verification

Security

Automata

Model Checking and Testing

Biology and Hybrid Systems

Games and Synthesis

Concurrency

SMT and Theorem Proving

Bounds and Termination

Abstraction

The Spirit of Ghost Code*

Jean-Christophe Filliâtre[1,2], Léon Gondelman[1], and Andrei Paskevich[1,2]

[1] Lab. de Recherche en Informatique, Univ. Paris-Sud, CNRS, Orsay, F-91405
[2] INRIA Saclay – Île-de-France, Orsay, F-91893

Abstract. In the context of deductive program verification, ghost code
is part of the program that is added for the purpose of specification.
Ghost code must not interfere with regular code, in the sense that it
can be erased without observable difference in the program outcome. In
particular, ghost data cannot participate in regular computations and
ghost code cannot mutate regular data or diverge. The idea exists in the
folklore since the early notion of auxiliary variables and is implemented
in many state-of-the-art program verification tools. However, a rigorous
definition and treatment of ghost code is surprisingly subtle and few
formalizations exist.

In this article, we describe a simple ML-style programming language
with mutable state and ghost code. Non-interference is ensured by a type
system with effects, which allows, notably, the same data types and functions to be used in both regular and ghost code. We define the procedure
of ghost code erasure and we prove its safety using bisimulation. A similar type system, with numerous extensions which we briefly discuss, is
implemented in the program verification environment Why3.

1 Introduction

A common technique in deductive program verification consists in introducing
data and computations, traditionally named *ghost code*, that only serve to facilitate specification. Ghost code can be safely erased from a program without
affecting its final result. Consequently, a ghost expression cannot be used in a
regular (non-ghost) computation, it cannot modify a regular mutable value, and
it cannot raise exceptions that would escape into regular code. However, a ghost
expression can use regular values and its result can be used in program annotations: preconditions, postconditions, loop invariants, assertions, etc. A classical
use case for ghost code is to equip a data structure with ghost fields containing
auxiliary data for specification purposes. Another example is ghost step counters
to prove the time complexity of an algorithm.

When it comes to computing verification conditions, for instance using a weakest precondition calculus, there is no need to make a distinction between ghost
and regular code. At this moment, ghost code is just a computation that supplies
auxiliary values to use in specification and to simplify proofs. This computation,

---

* This work is partly supported by the Bware (ANR-12-INSE-0010, http://bware.
lri.fr/) project of the French national research organization (ANR).

A. Biere and R. Bloem (Eds.): CAV 2014, LNCS 8559, pp. 1–16, 2014.
© Springer International Publishing Switzerland 2014

however, is not necessary for the program itself and thus should be removed when we compile the annotated source code. Therefore we need a way to ensure, by static analysis, that ghost code does not interfere with the rest of the program.

Despite that the concept of ghost code exists since the early days of deductive program verification, and is supported in most state-of-the-art tools [1–4], it is surprisingly subtle. In particular, a sound non-interference analysis must ensure that every ghost sub-expression terminates. Otherwise, one could supply such a sub-expression with an arbitrary postcondition and thus be able to prove anything about the program under consideration. Another non-obvious observation is that structural equality cannot be applied naively on data with ghost components. Indeed, two values could differ only in their ghost parts and consequently the comparison would yield a different result after the ghost code erasure.

There is a number of design choices that show up when conceiving a language with ghost code. First, how explicit should we be in our annotations? For example, should every ghost variable be annotated as such, or can we infer its status by looking at the values assigned to it? Second, how much can be shared between ghost and regular code? For instance, can a ghost value be passed to a function that does not specifically expect a ghost argument? Similarly, can we store a ghost value in a data structure that is not specifically designed to hold ghost data, e.g. an array or a tuple? Generally speaking, we should decide where ghost code can appear and what can appear in ghost code.

In this article, we show that, using a tailored type system with effects, we can design a language with ghost code that is both expressive and concise. As a proof of concept, we describe a simple ML-style programming language with mutable state, recursive functions, and ghost code. Notably, our type system allows the same data types and functions to be used in both regular and ghost code. We give a formal proof of the soundness of ghost code erasure, using a bisimulation argument. A type system based on the same concepts is implemented in the verification tool Why3 [4]. The language presented is this paper is deliberately simplified. The more exciting features, listed in Section 4 and implemented in Why3, only contribute to more complex effect tracking in the type system, which is mostly orthogonal to the problem of ghost code non-interference.

Outline. This paper is organized as follows. Section 2 introduces an ML-like language with ghost code. Section 3 defines the operation of ghost code erasure and proves its soundness. Section 4 describes the actual implementation in Why3. We conclude with related work in Section 5 and perspectives in Section 6. An extended version of this paper containing proofs is available at http://hal.archives-ouvertes.fr/hal-00873187/.

2   GhostML

We introduce GhostML, a mini ML-like language with ghost code. It features global references (that is, mutable variables), recursive functions, and integer and Boolean primitive types.

2.1   Syntax

The syntax of GhostML is given in Fig. 1. Terms are either values or compound expressions like application, conditional, reference access and modification. We assume a fixed finite set of global references. All the language constructions are standard ML, except for the keyword ghost which turns a term t into ghost code.

$t ::=$	TERMS	$v ::=$	VALUES
$\mid v$	value	$\mid c$	constant
$\mid t\ v$	application	$\mid x^\beta$	variable
$\mid$ let $x^\beta = t$ in t	local binding	$\mid \lambda x^\beta : \tau.\ t$	anonymous function
$\mid$ if v then t else t	conditional	$\mid$ rec $x^\beta : \tau^\beta \overset{\epsilon}{\Rightarrow} \tau.\ \lambda x^\beta : \tau.\ t$	
$\mid r^\beta := v$	assignment		recursive function
$\mid !r^\beta$	dereference		
$\mid$ ghost t	ghost code	$c ::=$	CONSTANTS
		$\mid ()$	unit
$\tau ::=$	TYPES	$\mid ..., -1, 0, 1, ...$	integers
$\mid \kappa$	primitive type	$\mid$ true, false	Boolean
$\mid \tau^\beta \overset{\epsilon}{\Rightarrow} \tau$	functional type	$\mid +, \vee, =, ...$	operators
$\kappa ::=$	PRIMITIVE TYPES	$\beta \in \{\perp, \top\}$	GHOST STATUS
$\mid$ int $\mid$ bool $\mid$ unit	primitive types	$\epsilon \in \{\perp, \top\}$	EFFECT

Fig. 1. Syntax

Every variable is tagged with a ghost status β, which is $\top$ for ghost variables and $\perp$ for regular ones (here and below, "regular" stands for "non-ghost"). Similarly, references and formal function parameters carry their ghost status. Consider the following example:

$$\text{let } upd^\top = \lambda x^\perp : \text{int. } g^\top := x^\perp \text{ in } upd^\top\ !r^\perp$$

Here, function $upd^\top$ takes one regular parameter $x^\perp$ and assigns it to a ghost reference $g^\top$. Then $upd^\top$ is applied to the contents of a regular reference $r^\perp$.

Note that compound terms obey a variant of *A-normal* form [5]. That is, in application, conditional, and reference assignment, one of the sub-expressions must be a value. This does not reduce expressiveness, since a term such as $(t_1\ (t_2\ v))$ can be rewritten as let $x^\beta = t_2\ v$ in $t_1\ x^\beta$, where β depends on the ghost status of the first formal parameter of t_1.

Types are either primitive data-types (int, bool, unit) or function types. A function type is an arrow $\tau_2^\beta \overset{\epsilon}{\Rightarrow} \tau_1$ where β stands for the function argument's ghost status, and ϵ is the *latent* effect of the function. An effect ϵ is a Boolean value that indicates presence of regular side effects such as modification of a regular reference or possible non-termination.

MiniML Syntax. The syntax of traditional MiniML can be obtained by omitting all ghost indicators β (on references, variables, parameters, and types) and excluding the ghost construct. Equivalently, we could define MiniML as the subset of GhostML where all ghost indicators β are $\bot$ and where terms of the form ghost t do not appear.

2.2   Semantics

Fig. 2 gives a small-step operational semantics to GhostML which corresponds to a deterministic call-by-value reduction strategy. Each reduction step defines a relation between states. A state is a pair $t \mid \mu$ of a term t and a store μ. A store μ maps global references of t to constants. The regular part of a store μ, written $\mu_\bot$, is the restriction of μ to regular references. Rules indicate the store μ only when relevant.

A reduction step can take place directly at the top of a term t. Such a step is called a head reduction and is denoted $t \mid \mu \xrightarrow{\alpha} t' \mid \mu'$. Rule (E-GHOST) expresses that, from the point of view of operational semantics, there is no difference between regular and ghost code. Other head reduction rules are standard. For instance, rules (E-OP-λ) and (E-OP-δ) evaluate the application of a constant c_0 to constants $c_1...c_m$. Such an application is either partial ($1 \leq m < \text{arity}(c_0)$), and then turned into a function $\lambda x^\bot : \kappa.\ c_0\ c_1\ ...\ c_m\ x^\bot$, or total ($m = \text{arity}(c_0)$), and then some oracle function δ gives the result $\delta(c_0, c_1, \ldots, c_m)$. For instance, $\delta(\text{not}, \text{true}) = \text{false}$, $\delta(+, 47, -5) = 42$, etc.

A reduction step can also be contextual, *i.e.* it takes place in some sub-expression. Since our language is in A-normal form, there are only two contextual rules, (E-CONTEXT-APP) and (E-CONTEXT-LET).

As usual, $\rightarrow^*$ denotes the reflexive, transitive closure of $\rightarrow$. We say that a closed term t evaluates to v in a store μ if there is a μ' such that $t \mid \mu \rightarrow^* v \mid \mu'$. Note that, since t is closed, v is not a variable. Finally, the divergence of a term t in a store μ is defined co-inductively as follows:

$$\frac{t \mid \mu \rightarrow^1 t' \mid \mu' \qquad t' \mid \mu' \rightarrow \infty}{t \mid \mu \rightarrow \infty}\text{(E-DIV)}$$

MiniML Semantics. Since ghost statuses do not play any role in the semantics of GhostML, dropping them (or, equivalently, marking all β as $\bot$) and removing the rule (E-GHOST) results in a standard call-by-value small-step operational semantics for MiniML. For the sake of clarity, we use a subscript m when writing MiniML reduction steps: $t \mid \mu \rightarrow_m t' \mid \mu'$.

2.3   Type System

The purpose of the type system is to ensure that "well-typed terms do not go wrong". In our case, "do not go wrong" means not only that well-typed terms verify the classical type soundness property, but also that ghost code *does not*

$$\text{ghost } t \xrightarrow{\alpha} t \qquad\qquad\qquad\qquad\qquad (\text{E-Ghost})$$

$$\frac{1 \le m < \text{arity}(c_0)}{c_0\ c_1\ \dots\ c_m \xrightarrow{\alpha} \lambda x^\perp : \kappa.\ c_0\ c_1\ \dots\ c_m\ x^\perp} \qquad (\text{E-Op-}\lambda)$$

$$\frac{m = \text{arity}(c_0) \qquad \delta(c_0, c_1, \dots, c_m) \text{ is defined}}{c_0\ c_1\ \dots\ c_m \xrightarrow{\alpha} \delta(c_0, c_1, \dots, c_m)} \qquad (\text{E-Op-}\delta)$$

$$(\lambda x^\beta : \tau.\ t)\ v \xrightarrow{\alpha} t[x^\beta \leftarrow v] \qquad\qquad (\text{E-App-}\lambda)$$

$$(\text{rec } f^\beta : \tau^\beta \xRightarrow{\epsilon} \tau.\ \lambda x^\beta : \tau.\ t)\ v \xrightarrow{\alpha} t[x^\beta \leftarrow v, f^\beta \leftarrow \text{rec } f^\beta : \tau^\beta \xRightarrow{\epsilon} \tau.\ \lambda x^\beta : \tau.\ t]$$
$$(\text{E-App-Rec})$$

$$\text{let } x^\beta = v_1 \text{ in } t_2 \xrightarrow{\alpha} t_2[x^\beta \leftarrow v_1] \qquad\qquad (\text{E-Let})$$

$$\text{if true then } t_1 \text{ else } t_2 \xrightarrow{\alpha} t_1 \qquad\qquad (\text{E-If-True})$$

$$\text{if false then } t_1 \text{ else } t_2 \xrightarrow{\alpha} t_2 \qquad\qquad (\text{E-If-False})$$

$$!r^\beta \mid \mu \xrightarrow{\alpha} \mu(r^\beta) \mid \mu \qquad\qquad\qquad (\text{E-Deref})$$

$$r^\beta := c \mid \mu \xrightarrow{\alpha} () \mid \mu[r^\beta \mapsto c] \qquad\qquad (\text{E-Assign})$$

$$\frac{t \mid \mu \xrightarrow{\alpha} t' \mid \mu'}{t \mid \mu \rightarrow t' \mid \mu'} \qquad\qquad\qquad (\text{E-Head})$$

$$\frac{t_1 \mid \mu \rightarrow t_1' \mid \mu'}{(t_1\ v) \mid \mu \rightarrow (t_1'\ v) \mid \mu'} \qquad\qquad (\text{E-Context-App})$$

$$\frac{t_2 \mid \mu \rightarrow t_2' \mid \mu'}{\text{let } x^\beta = t_2 \text{ in } t_1 \mid \mu \rightarrow \text{let } x^\beta = t_2' \text{ in } t_1 \mid \mu'} \qquad (\text{E-Context-Let})$$

Fig. 2. Semantics

interfere with regular code. More precisely, non-interference means that ghost code never modifies regular references and that it always terminates. For that purpose, we introduce a type system with effects, where the typing judgment is

$$\Sigma, \Gamma \vdash t : \tau, \beta, \epsilon.$$

Here, τ is the type of term t. Boolean indicators β and ϵ indicate, respectively, the ghost status of t and its regular side effects. Γ is a typing environment that binds variables to types. Σ is a store typing that binds each reference r^β to the primitive type of the stored value. We restrict types of stored values to primitive types to avoid a possible non-termination via Landin's knot (that is,

$$\frac{\mathsf{Typeof}(c) = \tau}{\Sigma, \Gamma \vdash c : \tau, \bot, \bot} \tag{T-Const}$$

$$\frac{(x^\beta : \tau) \in \Gamma}{\Sigma, \Gamma \vdash x^\beta : \tau, \beta, \bot} \tag{T-Var}$$

$$\frac{\Sigma, \Gamma, x^\beta : \tau \vdash t : \tau_0, \beta_0, \epsilon}{\Sigma, \Gamma \vdash (\lambda x^\beta : \tau. t) : \tau^\beta \overset{\epsilon}{\Rightarrow} \tau_0, \beta_0, \bot} \tag{T-λ}$$

$$\frac{\Sigma, \Gamma, f^\bot : \tau_2^\beta \overset{\top}{\Rightarrow} \tau_1 \vdash (\lambda x^\beta : \tau_2. t) : \tau_2^\beta \overset{\epsilon}{\Rightarrow} \tau_1, \bot, \bot}{\Sigma, \Gamma \vdash (\mathsf{rec}\ f^\bot : \tau_2^\beta \overset{\top}{\Rightarrow} \tau_1.\ \lambda x^\beta : \tau_2. t) : \tau_2^\beta \overset{\top}{\Rightarrow} \tau_1, \bot, \bot} \tag{T-Rec}$$

$$\frac{\Sigma, \Gamma \vdash v : \mathsf{bool}, \beta_0, \bot \quad \Sigma, \Gamma \vdash t_1 : \tau, \beta_1, \epsilon_1 \quad \Sigma, \Gamma \vdash t_2 : \tau, \beta_2, \epsilon_2}{\Sigma, \Gamma \vdash (\mathsf{if}\ v\ \mathsf{then}\ t_1\ \mathsf{else}\ t_2) : \tau, \beta_0 \vee \beta_1 \vee \beta_2, \epsilon_1 \vee \epsilon_2} \tag{T-If}$$

$$\frac{\Sigma, \Gamma, x^\bot : \tau_2 \vdash t_1 : \tau_1, \beta_1, \epsilon_1 \quad \Sigma, \Gamma \vdash t_2 : \tau_2, \beta_2, \epsilon_2}{\Sigma, \Gamma \vdash (\mathsf{let}\ x^\bot = t_2\ \mathsf{in}\ t_1) : \tau_1, \beta_1 \vee \beta_2, \epsilon_1 \vee \epsilon_2} \tag{T-Let-Regular}$$

$$\frac{\Sigma, \Gamma, x^\top : \tau_2 \vdash t_1 : \tau_1, \beta_1, \epsilon_1 \quad \Sigma, \Gamma \vdash t_2 : \tau_2, \beta_2, \bot}{\Sigma, \Gamma \vdash (\mathsf{let}\ x^\top = t_2\ \mathsf{in}\ t_1) : \tau_1, \beta_1, \epsilon_1} \tag{T-Let-Ghost}$$

$$\frac{\Sigma, \Gamma \vdash t : \tau_2^\bot \overset{\epsilon_1}{\Rightarrow} \tau_1, \beta_1, \epsilon_2 \quad \Sigma, \Gamma \vdash v : \tau_2, \beta_2, \bot}{\Sigma, \Gamma \vdash (t\ v) : \tau_1, \beta_1 \vee \beta_2, \epsilon_1 \vee \epsilon_2} \tag{T-App-Regular}$$

$$\frac{\Sigma, \Gamma \vdash t : \tau_2^\top \overset{\epsilon_1}{\Rightarrow} \tau_1, \beta_1, \epsilon_2 \quad \Sigma, \Gamma \vdash v : \tau_2, \beta_2, \bot}{\Sigma, \Gamma \vdash (t\ v) : \tau_1, \beta_1, \epsilon_1 \vee \epsilon_2} \tag{T-App-Ghost}$$

$$\frac{(r^\beta : \kappa) \in \Sigma}{\Sigma, \Gamma \vdash !r^\beta : \kappa, \beta, \bot} \tag{T-Deref}$$

$$\frac{\Sigma, \Gamma \vdash v : \kappa, \beta', \bot \quad (r^\beta : \kappa) \in \Sigma \quad \beta \geq \beta'}{\Sigma, \Gamma \vdash (r^\beta := v) : \mathsf{unit}, \beta, \neg\beta} \tag{T-Assign}$$

$$\frac{\Sigma, \Gamma \vdash t : \tau, \beta, \bot}{\Sigma, \Gamma \vdash (\mathsf{ghost}\ t) : \tau, \top, \bot} \tag{T-Ghost}$$

Fig. 3. Typing rules

recursion encoded using a mutable variable containing a function), which would be undetected in our type system.

Typing rules are given in Fig. 3. To account for non-interference, each rule whose conclusion is a judgement $\Sigma, \Gamma \vdash t : \tau, \beta, \epsilon$ is added the implicit extra side condition

$$(\beta = \top) \Rightarrow (\epsilon \vee \epsilon^+(\tau) = \bot) \tag{1}$$

where $\epsilon^+(\tau)$ is defined recursively on τ as follows:

$$\epsilon^+(\kappa) \triangleq \bot$$
$$\epsilon^+(\tau_2 \overset{\epsilon}{\underset{\beta}{\Rightarrow}} \tau_1) \triangleq \epsilon \vee \epsilon^+(\tau_1)$$

In other words, whenever t is ghost code, it must terminate and must not modify any regular reference. In particular, a ghost function whose body is possibly non-terminating or possibly modifies a regular reference is rejected by the type system.

Let us explain some rules in detail. The rule (T-CONST) states that any constant c is regular code, (i.e. $\beta = \bot$) yet is pure and terminating (i.e. $\epsilon = \bot$). Moreover, we assume that if c is some constant operation, then its formal parameters are all regular. The type of each constant is given by some oracle function $\mathsf{Typeof}(c)$. For instance, $\mathsf{Typeof}(+) = \mathsf{int}^\bot \overset{}{\Rightarrow} \mathsf{int}^\bot \overset{}{\Rightarrow} \mathsf{int}$.

Recursive functions are typed as follows. For simplicity, we assume that whenever a recursive function is used, we may have non-termination. Therefore, we enforce the latent effect ϵ of any recursive function to be $\top$. Consequently, no recursive function can be used or even occur in ghost code. In practice, however, we do not have to assign a latent non-termination effect to recursive functions whose termination can be established by static analysis (e.g. by a formal proof).

The rule (T-IF) shows how ghost code is propagated through conditional expressions: if at least one of the branches or the Boolean condition is ghost code, then the conditional itself becomes ghost. Note, however, that the typing side-condition (1) will reject conditionals where one part is ghost and another part has some effect, as in

$$\text{if true then } r^\bot := 42 \text{ else ghost } ().$$

The rule (T-GHOST) turns any term t into ghost code, with ghost status $\top$, whatever the ghost status of t is, provided that t is pure and terminating. Thus, terms such as $\mathsf{ghost}\ (r^\bot := 42)$ or $\mathsf{ghost}\ (\mathsf{fact}\ 3)$ are ill-typed, since their evaluation would interfere with the evaluation of regular code.

The side condition $(\beta \geq \beta')$ of the rule (T-ASSIGN) ensures that regular references cannot be assigned ghost code. (Boolean values are ordered as usual, with $\top > \bot$.) Additionally, the rule conclusion ensures that, if the assigned reference is regular $(\beta = \bot)$, then ϵ is $\top$; on the contrary, if the assigned reference is ghost $(\beta = \top)$, then ϵ is $\bot$, since ghost reference assignments are not part of regular effects.

The most subtle rules are those for local bindings and application. Rule (T-LET-GHOST) states that, whatever the ghost status of a term t_2 is, as long as

t_2 is pure and terminating, we can bind a ghost variable $x^\top$ to t_2. Similarly, by rule (T-App-Ghost) a function that expects a ghost parameter can be applied to both ghost and regular values.

Rule (T-Let-Regular) is somewhat dual to (T-Let-Ghost): it allows us to bind a regular variable $x^\perp$ to a ghost term. The difference with the previous case is that, now, the ghost status of the let expression depends on the ghost status of t_2: if t_2 is ghost code, then the "contaminated" let expression becomes ghost itself. Consequently, if t_2 is ghost, then by the implicit side-condition, as $\epsilon_1 \vee \epsilon_2$ must be equal to $\perp$, both t_1 and t_2 must be pure and terminating. Similarly, rule (T-App-Regular) allows us to pass a ghost value to a function expecting a regular parameter, in which case the application itself becomes ghost. In other words, the goal of rules (T-Let-Regular) and (T-App-Regular) is to allow ghost code to use regular code. This was one of our motivations.

It is worth pointing out that there is no sub-typing in our system. That is, in rules for application, the formal parameter and the actual argument must have *exactly* the same type τ_2. In particular, all latent effects and ghost statuses in function types must be the same. For instance, a function expecting an argument of type $\mathsf{int}^\perp \xrightarrow{\epsilon} \mathsf{int}$ cannot be applied to an argument of type $\mathsf{int}^\top \xrightarrow{\epsilon} \mathsf{int}$.

Type System of MiniML. Similarly to operational semantics, if we drop all ghost statuses (or, equivalently, if we consider them marked as $\perp$) and get rid of typing rule (T-Ghost), we get a standard typing system with effects for MiniML with simple types. For clarity, we add a subscript m when we write typing judgments for MiniML terms: $\Sigma, \Gamma \vdash_m t : \tau, \epsilon$.

2.4 Type Soundness

The type system of GhostML enjoys the standard soundness property. Any well-typed program either diverges or evaluates to a value. This property is well established in the literature for ML with references [6, 7], and we can easily adapt the proof in our case. Due to lack of space, we only give the main statements.

As usual, we decompose type soundness into *preservation* and *progress* lemmas. First, we define well-typedness of a store with respect to a store typing.

Definition 1. *A store μ is well-typed with respect to a store typing Σ, written $\Sigma \vdash \mu$, if $dom(\mu) \subseteq dom(\Sigma)$ and $\mu(r^\beta)$ has type $\Sigma(r^\beta)$ for every $r^\beta \in dom(\mu)$.*

With this definition, the *preservation* lemma is stated as follows:

Lemma 1 (Preservation). *If $\Sigma, \Gamma \vdash t : \tau, \beta, \epsilon$ and $\Sigma \vdash \mu$, then $t \mid \mu \to t' \mid \mu'$ implies that $\Sigma, \Gamma \vdash t' : \tau, \beta', \epsilon'$ and $\Sigma \vdash \mu'$, where $\beta \geq \beta'$ and $\epsilon \geq \epsilon'$.*

The only difference with respect to the standard statement is that ghost statuses and effect indicators can decrease during evaluation.

Lemma 2 (Progress). *If $\Sigma, \emptyset \vdash t : \tau, \beta, \epsilon$, then either t is a value or, for any store μ such that $\Sigma \vdash \mu$, there exists a reduction step $t \mid \mu \to t' \mid \mu'$.*

Additionally, we have the following results for effect-less programs.

Lemma 3 (Store Preservation). *If* $\Sigma, \emptyset \vdash t : \tau, \beta, \bot$ *and* $\Sigma \vdash \mu$, *then* $t \mid \mu \rightarrow t' \mid \mu'$ *implies* $\mu_\bot = \mu'_\bot$.

Lemma 4 (Program Termination). *If* $\Sigma, \emptyset \vdash t : \tau, \beta, \bot$ *and* $\Sigma \vdash \mu$, *then evaluation of* t *in store* μ *terminates, that is, there is a value* v *and a store* μ' *such that* $t \mid \mu \rightarrow^* v \mid \mu'$.

A consequence of the previous lemmas and the side condition (1) is that ghost code does not modify the regular store and is terminating.

3 From GhostML to MiniML

This section describes an erasure operation that turns a GhostML term into a MiniML term. The goal is to show that ghost code can be erased from a regular program without observable difference in the program outcome.

The erasure is written either $\mathcal{E}_\beta(.)$, when parameterized by some ghost status β, and simply $\mathcal{E}(.)$ otherwise. First, we define erasure on types and terms. The main idea is to preserve the structure of regular terms and types, and to replace any ghost code by a value of type unit.

Definition 2 (τ-erasure). *Let* τ *be some GhostML type. The erasure* $\mathcal{E}_\beta(\tau)$ *of type* τ *with respect to* β *is defined by induction on the structure of* τ *as follows:*

$$
\begin{aligned}
\mathcal{E}_\top(\tau) &\triangleq \mathsf{unit} \\
\mathcal{E}_\bot(\tau_2^{\beta_2} \xrightarrow{\epsilon} \tau_1) &\triangleq \mathcal{E}_{\beta_2}(\tau_2) \Rightarrow \mathcal{E}_\bot(\tau_1) \\
\mathcal{E}_\bot(\kappa) &\triangleq \kappa
\end{aligned}
$$

In other words, the structure of regular types is preserved and all ghost types are turned into type unit. Now we can define erasure on terms.

Definition 3 (t-Erasure). *Let* t *be such that* $\Sigma, \Gamma \vdash t : \tau, \beta, \epsilon$ *holds. The erasure* $\mathcal{E}_\beta(t)$ *is defined by induction on the structure of* t *as follows:*

$$
\begin{aligned}
\mathcal{E}_\top(t) &\triangleq () \\
\mathcal{E}_\bot(c) &\triangleq c \\
\mathcal{E}_\bot(x^\bot) &\triangleq x \\
\mathcal{E}_\bot(\lambda x^\beta : \tau.\, t) &\triangleq \lambda x : \mathcal{E}_\beta(\tau).\, \mathcal{E}_\bot(t) \\
\mathcal{E}_\bot(\mathsf{rec}\ f^\bot : \tau_2^{\beta_2} \xrightarrow{\top} \tau_1.\, t) &\triangleq \mathsf{rec}\ f : \mathcal{E}_\bot(\tau_2^{\beta_2} \xrightarrow{\top} \tau_1).\, \mathcal{E}_\bot(t) \\
\mathcal{E}_\bot(r^\bot := v) &\triangleq r := \mathcal{E}_\bot(v) \\
\mathcal{E}_\bot(!r^\bot) &\triangleq !r \\
\mathcal{E}_\bot(\mathsf{if}\ v\ \mathsf{then}\ t_1\ \mathsf{else}\ t_2) &\triangleq \mathsf{if}\ \mathcal{E}_\bot(v)\ \mathsf{then}\ \mathcal{E}_\bot(t_1)\ \mathsf{else}\ \mathcal{E}_\bot(t_2) \\
\mathcal{E}_\bot(t\ v) &\triangleq \mathcal{E}_\bot(t)\ \mathcal{E}_{\beta'}(v) \quad \text{where } t \text{ has type } \tau_2^{\beta'} \xrightarrow{\epsilon} \tau_1 \\
\mathcal{E}_\bot(\mathsf{let}\ x^{\beta'} = t_2\ \mathsf{in}\ t_1) &\triangleq \mathsf{let}\ x = \mathcal{E}_{\beta'}(t_2)\ \mathsf{in}\ \mathcal{E}_\bot(t_1)
\end{aligned}
$$

Note that ghosts variables and ghost references do not occur anymore in $\mathcal{E}_\perp(t)$. Note also that a regular function (recursive or not) with a ghost parameter remains a function, but with an argument of type unit. Similarly, a let expression that binds a ghost variable inside a regular code remains a let, but now binds a variable to (). More generally, $\mathcal{E}_\perp(t)$ is a value if and only if t is a value.

Leaving unit values and arguments in the outcome of erasure may seem unnecessary. However, because of latent effects, full erasure of ghost code is not possible. Consider for instance the function

$$\lambda x^\perp : \text{int}.\, \lambda y^\top : \text{int}.\, r^\perp := x$$

where r is a regular reference. Then a partial application of this function to a single argument should not trigger the modification of r. Our solution is to keep a second argument y of type unit.

3.1   Well-Typedness Preservation

We prove that erasure preserves well-typedness of terms. To do so, we first define the erasure of a typing context and of a store typing by a straightforward induction on their size:

Definition 4 (Γ-erasure and Σ-erasure).

$$
\begin{aligned}
\mathcal{E}(\emptyset) &\triangleq \emptyset & \mathcal{E}(\emptyset) &\triangleq \emptyset \\
\mathcal{E}(\Gamma, x^\top : \tau) &\triangleq \mathcal{E}(\Gamma), x : \text{unit} & \mathcal{E}(\Sigma, r^\top : \kappa) &\triangleq \mathcal{E}(\Sigma) \\
\mathcal{E}(\Gamma, x^\perp : \tau) &\triangleq \mathcal{E}(\Gamma), x : \mathcal{E}_\perp(\tau) & \mathcal{E}(\Sigma, r^\perp : \kappa) &\triangleq \mathcal{E}(\Sigma), r : \kappa
\end{aligned}
$$

With these definitions, we prove well-typedness preservation under erasure:

Theorem 1 (Well-typedness Preservation). *If $\Sigma, \Gamma \vdash t : \tau, \perp, \epsilon$ holds, then $\mathcal{E}(\Sigma), \mathcal{E}(\Gamma) \vdash_m \mathcal{E}_\perp(t) : \mathcal{E}_\perp(\tau), \epsilon$ holds.*

3.2   Correctness of Erasure

Finally, we prove correctness of erasure, that is, evaluation is preserved by erasure. To turn this into a formal statement, we first define the erasure of a store μ by a straightforward induction on the store size:

Definition 5 (μ-erasure).

$$
\begin{aligned}
\mathcal{E}(\emptyset) &\triangleq \emptyset \\
\mathcal{E}(\mu \uplus \{r^\top \mapsto c\}) &\triangleq \mathcal{E}(\mu) \\
\mathcal{E}(\mu \uplus \{r^\perp \mapsto c\}) &\triangleq \mathcal{E}(\mu) \uplus \{r \mapsto c\}
\end{aligned}
$$

Notice that $\mathcal{E}(\mu)$ removes ghost annotations, and thus is not the same that $\mu_\perp$. The correctness of erasure means that, for any evaluation $t \mid \mu \rightarrow^* v \mid \mu'$ in GhostML, we have $\mathcal{E}_\perp(t) \mid \mathcal{E}(\mu) \rightarrow_m^* \mathcal{E}_\perp(v) \mid \mathcal{E}(\mu')$ in MiniML and that, for any diverging evaluation $t \mid \mu \rightarrow \infty$ in GhostML, we have $\mathcal{E}_\perp(t) \mid \mathcal{E}(\mu) \rightarrow_m \infty$ in MiniML. We prove these two statements using a bisimulation argument. First, we need the substitution lemma below, which states that substitution and erasure commute.

Lemma 5 (Substitution Under Erasure). *Let t be a GhostML term and v a GhostML value such that $\Sigma, \Gamma, x^\beta : \tau \vdash t : \tau_0, \perp, \epsilon$ and $\Sigma, \Gamma \vdash v : \tau, \beta', \perp$, with $\beta \geq \beta'$, hold. Then the following holds:*

$$\mathcal{E}_\perp(t)[x \leftarrow \mathcal{E}_\beta(v)] = \mathcal{E}_\perp(t[x^\beta \leftarrow v]).$$

Note that if $\Sigma \vdash \mu$ then $\mathcal{E}(\Sigma) \vdash_m \mathcal{E}(\mu)$. To prove erasure correctness for terminating programs, we use the following forward simulation argument:

Lemma 6 (Forward Simulation of GhostML). *If $\Sigma, \emptyset \vdash t : \tau, \perp, \epsilon$ and, for some store μ such that $\Sigma \vdash \mu$, we have $t \mid \mu \rightarrow t' \mid \mu'$, then the following holds in MiniML: $\mathcal{E}_\perp(t) \mid \mathcal{E}(\mu) \rightarrow_m^{0|1} \mathcal{E}_\perp(t') \mid \mathcal{E}(\mu')$.*

We are now able to prove the first part of the main theorem:

Theorem 2 (Terminating Evaluation Preservation). *If typing judgment $\Sigma, \emptyset \vdash t : \tau, \perp, \epsilon$ holds and $t \mid \mu \rightarrow^* v \mid \mu'$, for some value v and some store μ such that $\Sigma \vdash \mu$, then $\mathcal{E}_\perp(t) \mid \mathcal{E}(\mu) \rightarrow_m^* \mathcal{E}_\perp(v) \mid \mathcal{E}(\mu')$.*

To prove the second part of the erasure correctness (non-termination preservation), we use the following simulation argument.

Lemma 7 (Forward Simulation of MiniML). *If $\Sigma, \emptyset \vdash t : \tau, \perp, \epsilon$ holds, then, for any store μ such that $\Sigma \vdash \mu$, if $\mathcal{E}_\perp(t) \mid \mathcal{E}(\mu) \rightarrow_m q \mid \nu$ for some term q and some store ν, then $t \mid \mu \rightarrow^{\geq 1} t' \mid \mu'$ where $\mathcal{E}_\perp(t') = q$ and $\mathcal{E}(\mu') = \nu$.*

Finally, we establish non-termination preservation:

Theorem 3 (Non-termination Preservation). *If $\Sigma, \emptyset \vdash t : \tau, \perp, \epsilon$ holds and $t \mid \mu \rightarrow \infty$, for some store μ such that $\Sigma \vdash \mu$, then $\mathcal{E}_\perp(t)$ also diverges, that is, $\mathcal{E}_\perp(t) \mid \mathcal{E}(\mu) \rightarrow_m \infty$.*

4   Implementation

Our method to handle ghost code is implemented in the verification tool Why3[1]. With respect to GhostML, the language and the type system of Why3 have the following extensions:

Type Polymorphism. The type system of Why3 is first-order and features ML-style type polymorphism. Our approach to associate ghost status with variables and expressions, and not with types, makes this extension straightforward.

---

[1] Why3 is freely available from http://why3.lri.fr/

Local References. Another obvious extension of GhostML is the support of non-global references. As long as such a reference cannot be an alias for another one, the type system of GhostML requires practically no changes. In a system where aliases are admitted, the type system and, possibly, the verification condition generator must be adapted to detect modifications made by a ghost code in locations accessible from regular code. In Why3, aliases are tracked statically, and thus non-interference is ensured purely by type checking.

Data Structures with Ghost Fields. Why3 supports algebraic data types (in particular, records), whose fields may be regular or ghost. Pattern matching on such structures requires certain precautions. Any variable bound in the ghost part of a pattern must be ghost. Moreover, pattern matching over a ghost expression that has at least two branches must make the whole expression ghost, whatever the right-hand sides of the branches are, just as in the case of a conditional over a ghost Boolean expression.

That said, ghost code can use the same data types as regular code. A ghost variable may be a record with regular, mutable fields, which can be accessed and modified in ghost code. Similarly, Why3 has a unique type of arrays and admits both regular and ghost arrays.

Exceptions. Adding exceptions is rather straightforward, since in Why3 exceptions are introduced only at the top level. Indeed, it suffices to add a new effect indicator, that is the set of exceptions possibly raised by a program expression. We can use the same exceptions in ghost and regular code, provided that the ghost status of an expression that raises an exception is propagated upwards until the exception is caught.

Provable Termination. For the sake of simplicity, GhostML forbids the use of recursive functions in ghost code. In Why3, the use of recursive functions and loops in ghost code is allowed. The system requires that such constructs are supplied with a "variant" clause, so that verification conditions for termination are generated.

Example. Let us illustrate the use of ghost code in Why3 on a simple example. Fig. 4 contains an implementation of a mutable queue data type, in Baker's style. A queue is a pair of two immutable singly-linked lists, which serve to amortize push and pop operations. Our implementation additionally stores the pure logical view of the queue as a list, in the third, ghost field of the record. Notice that we use the same list type both for regular and ghost data.

We illustrate propagation in function push (lines 27–30), where a local variable v is used to hold some intermediate value, to be stored later in the ghost field of the structure. Despite the fact that variable v is not declared ghost, and the fact that function append is a regular function, Why3 infers that v is ghost. Indeed, the ghost value q.view contaminates the result of append. It would therefore generate an error if we tried to store v in a non-ghost field of an existing regular structure. Since the expression append q.view (Cons x Nil)

```
1  module Queue
2
3    type elt
4
5    type list = Nil | Cons elt list
6
7    let rec append (l1 l2: list) : list
8      variant { l1 }
9    = match l1 with
10     | Nil → l2
11     | Cons x r1 → Cons x (append r1 l2)
12     end
13
14   let rec rev_append (l1 l2: list) : list
15     variant { l1 }
16   = match l1 with
17     | Nil → l2
18     | Cons x r1 → rev_append r1 (Cons x l2)
19     end
20
21   type queue = {
22             mutable front: list;
23             mutable rear:  list;
24       ghost mutable view:  list;
25   }
26
27   let push (x: elt) (q: queue) : unit
28   = q.rear ← Cons x q.rear;
29     let v = append q.view (Cons x Nil) in
30     q.view ← v
31
32   exception Empty
33
34   let pop (q: queue): elt
35     raises { Empty }
36   = match q.front with
37     | Cons x f →
38         q.front ← f;
39         q.view ← append f (rev_append q.rear Nil);
40         x
41     | Nil →
42         match rev_append q.rear Nil with
43         | Nil →
44             raise Empty
45         | Cons x f →
46             q.front ← f;
47             q.rear ← Nil;
48             q.view ← f;
49             x
50         end
51     end
52 end
```

Fig. 4. Queue implementation in Why3

is ghost, it must not diverge. Thus Why3 requires function **append** to be terminating. This is ensured by the **variant** clause on line 8. In function **pop** (lines 34–52), the regular function **rev_append** is used both in regular code (line 42) and ghost code (line 39).

The online gallery of verified Why3 programs contains several other examples of use of ghost code[2], in particular, ghost function parameters and ghost functions to supply automatic induction proofs (also known as lemma functions).

5   Related Work

The idea to use ghost code in a program to ease specification exists since the early days (late sixties) of deductive program verification, when so-called auxiliary variables became a useful technique in the context of concurrent programming. According to Jones [8] and Reynolds [9], the notion of auxiliary variable was first introduced by Lucas in 1968 [10]. Since then, numerous authors have adapted this technique in various domains.

It is worth pointing out that some authors, in particular Kleymann [11] and Reynolds [9], make a clear distinction between non-operational variables used in program annotations and specification-purpose variables that can appear in the program itself. The latter notion has gradually evolved into the wider idea that ghost code can be arbitrary code, provided it does not interfere with regular code. For example, Zhang *et al.* [12] discuss the use of auxiliary code in the context of concurrent program verification. They present a simple WHILE language with parallelism and auxiliary code, and prove that the latter does not interfere with the rest of the program. In their case, non-interference is ensured by the stratified syntax of the language. For instance, loops can contain auxiliary code, but auxiliary code cannot contain loops, which ensures termination. They also define auxiliary code erasure and prove that a program with ghost code has no less behaviors than its regular part. Schmaltz [13] proposes a rigorous description of ghost code for a large fragment of C with parallelism, in the context of the VCC verification tool [2]. VCC includes ghost data types, ghost fields in regular structures, ghost parameters in regular functions, and ghost variables. In particular, ghost code is used to manipulate ownership information. A notable difference w.r.t. our work is that VCC does not perform any kind of inference of ghost code. Another difference is that VCC *assumes* that ghost code terminates, and the presence of constructions such as **ghost(goto l)** makes it difficult to reason about ghost code termination.

Another example of a modern deductive verification tool implementing ghost code is the program verifier Dafny [1]. In Dafny, "the concept of ghost versus non-ghost declarations is an integral part of the Dafny language: each function, method, variable, and parameter can be declared as either ghost or non-ghost." [14]. In addition, a class can contain both ghost fields and regular fields. Dafny ensures termination of ghost code. Ghost code can update ghost fields, but is not allowed to allocate memory or update non-ghost fields. Consequently, ghost

---

[2] http://toccata.lri.fr/gallery/ghost.en.html

code cannot obtain full reuse of libraries that allocate and mutate classes or arrays. However, on the fragment of Dafny's language corresponding to GhostML, Dafny provides a semantics of ghost code similar to what is presented here.

The property of non-interference of ghost code is a special case of information flow non-interference [15]. Indeed, one can see ghost code as high-security information and regular code as low-security information, and non-interference precisely means that high-security information does not leak into low-security computations. Information flow properties can be checked using a type system [16] and proofs in that domain typically involve a bisimulation technique (though not necessarily through an erasure operation). Notice that applying an information flow type system to solve our problem is not straightforward, since termination of ghost code is a crucial requirement. For instance, the type system described by Simonet and Pottier [17] simply assumes termination of secret code. To the best of our knowledge, this connection between information flow and ghost code has not been made before, and mainstream deductive verification tools employ syntactical criteria of non-interference instead of type-based ones. In this paper, we develop such a type-based approach, specifically tailored for program verification.

6   Conclusion and Perspectives

In this paper, we described an ML-like language with ghost code. Non-interference between ghost code and regular code is ensured using a type system with effects. We formally proved the soundness of this type system, that is, ghost code can be erased without observable difference. Our type system results in a highly expressive language, where the same data types and functions can be reused in both ghost and regular code.

We see two primary directions of future work on ghost code and Why3. First, ghost code, especially ghost fields, plays an important role in program refinement. Indeed, ghost fields that give sufficient information to specify a data type are naturally shared between the interface and the implementation of this data type. In this way, the glue invariant becomes nothing more than the data type invariant linking regular and ghost fields together. Our intention is to design and implement in Why3 a module system with refinement that makes extensive use of ghost code and data. Second, since ghost code does not have to be executable, it should be possible to use in ghost code various constructs which, up to now, may only appear in specifications, such as quantifiers, inductive predicates, non-deterministic choice, or infinitely parallel computations (cf. the aggregate `forall` statement in Dafny).

Acknowledgments. We are grateful to Sylvain Conchon, Rustan Leino, and François Pottier for comments and discussions regarding earlier versions of this paper.

References

1. Leino, K.R.M.: Dafny: An Automatic Program Verifier for Functional Correctness. In: Clarke, E.M., Voronkov, A. (eds.) LPAR-16 2010. LNCS, vol. 6355, pp. 348–370. Springer, Heidelberg (2010)
2. Cohen, E., Dahlweid, M., Hillebrand, M., Leinenbach, D., Moskal, M., Santen, T., Schulte, W., Tobies, S.: VCC: A practical system for verifying concurrent C. In: Berghofer, S., Nipkow, T., Urban, C., Wenzel, M. (eds.) TPHOLs 2009. LNCS, vol. 5674, pp. 23–42. Springer, Heidelberg (2009)
3. Jacobs, B., Piessens, F.: The VeriFast program verifier. CW Reports CW520, Department of Computer Science, K.U. Leuven (August 2008)
4. Filliâtre, J.C., Paskevich, A.: Why3 — where programs meet provers. In: Felleisen, M., Gardner, P. (eds.) ESOP 2013. LNCS, vol. 7792, pp. 125–128. Springer, Heidelberg (2013)
5. Flanagan, C., Sabry, A., Duba, B.F., Felleisen, M.: The essence of compiling with continuations. SIGPLAN Not. 28(6), 237–247 (1993)
6. Wright, A.K., Felleisen, M.: A syntactic approach to type soundness. Information and Computation 115, 38–94 (1992)
7. Pierce, B.C.: Types and Programming Languages. MIT Press (2002)
8. Jones, C.B., Roscoe, A., Wood, K.R.: Reflections on the Work of C.A.R. Hoare, 1st edn. Springer Publishing Company, Incorporated (2010)
9. Reynolds, J.C.: The craft of programming. Prentice Hall International series in computer science. Prentice Hall (1981)
10. Lucas, P.: Two constructive realizations of the block concept and their equivalence. Technical Report 25.085, IBM Laboratory, Vienna (June 1968)
11. Kleymann, T.: Hoare logic and auxiliary variables. Formal Asp. Comput. 11(5), 541–566 (1999)
12. Zhang, Z., Feng, X., Fu, M., Shao, Z., Li, Y.: A structural approach to prophecy variables. In: Agrawal, M., Cooper, S.B., Li, A. (eds.) TAMC 2012. LNCS, vol. 7287, pp. 61–71. Springer, Heidelberg (2012)
13. Schmaltz, S.: Towards the Pervasive Formal Verification of Multi-Core Operating Systems and Hypervisors Implemented in C. PhD thesis, Saarland University, Saarbrcken (2013)
14. Leino, K.R.M., Moskal, M.: Co-induction simply. In: Jones, C., Pihlajasaari, P., Sun, J. (eds.) FM 2014. LNCS, vol. 8442, pp. 382–398. Springer, Heidelberg (2014)
15. Denning, D.E., Denning, P.J.: Certification of programs for secure information flow. Communications of the ACM 20(2), 504–513 (1977)
16. Pottier, F., Conchon, S.: Information flow inference for free. In: Proceedings of the Fifth ACM SIGPLAN International Conference on Functional Programming (ICFP 2000), Montréal, Canada, pp. 46–57 (September 2000)
17. Pottier, F., Simonet, V.: Information flow inference for ML. ACM Transactions on Programming Languages and Systems 25(1), 117–158 (2003) ACM

SMT-Based Model Checking
for Recursive Programs

Anvesh Komuravelli, Arie Gurfinkel, and Sagar Chaki

Carnegie Mellon University, Pittsburgh, PA, USA

Abstract. We present an SMT-based symbolic model checking algorithm for safety verification of recursive programs. The algorithm is modular and analyzes procedures individually. Unlike other SMT-based approaches, it maintains both *over-* and *under-approximations* of procedure summaries. Under-approximations are used to analyze procedure calls without inlining. Over-approximations are used to block infeasible counterexamples and detect convergence to a proof. We show that for programs and properties over a decidable theory, the algorithm is guaranteed to find a counterexample, if one exists. However, efficiency depends on an oracle for quantifier elimination (QE). For Boolean Programs, the algorithm is a polynomial decision procedure, matching the worst-case bounds of the best BDD-based algorithms. For Linear Arithmetic (integers and rationals), we give an efficient instantiation of the algorithm by applying QE *lazily*. We use existing interpolation techniques to over-approximate QE and introduce *Model Based Projection* to under-approximate QE. Empirical evaluation on SV-COMP benchmarks shows that our algorithm improves significantly on the state-of-the-art.

1 Introduction

We are interested in the problem of *safety* of recursive programs, *i.e.*, deciding whether a assertion always holds. The first step in Software Model Checking is to approximate the input program by a program model where the program operations are terms in a first-order theory $\mathcal{D}$. Many program models exist today, e.g., *Boolean Programs* [6] of SLAM [5], GOTO programs of CBMC [14], BOO-GIEPL of BOOGIE [7], and, indirectly, internal representations of many tools such as UFO [1], HSF [21], etc. Given a safety property and a program model over $\mathcal{D}$, it is possible to analyze bounded executions using an oracle for *Satisfiability Modulo Theories* (SMT) for $\mathcal{D}$. However, in the presence of unbounded recursion, safety is undecidable in general. Throughout this paper, we assume that procedures cannot be passed as parameters.

There exist several program models where safety is efficiently decidable[1], e.g., Boolean Programs with unbounded recursion and the unbounded use of stack [36,6]. The general observation behind these algorithms is that one can *summarize* the input-output behavior of a procedure. A summary of a procedure is an input-output relation describing what is currently known about its behavior. Thus,

---

[1] This is no longer true when we allow procedures as parameters [12].

A. Biere and R. Bloem (Eds.): CAV 2014, LNCS 8559, pp. 17–34, 2014.
© Springer International Publishing Switzerland 2014

a summary can be used to analyze a procedure call without inlining or analyzing the body of the callee [11,37]. For a Boolean Program, the number of states is finite and hence, a summary can only be updated finitely many times. This observation led to a number of efficient algorithms that are polynomial in the number of states, e.g., the RHS framework [36], recursive state machines [4], and symbolic BDD-based algorithms of BEBOP [6] and MOPED [19]. When safety is undecidable (e.g., when $\mathcal{D}$ is Linear Rational Arithmetic (LRA) or Linear Integer Arithmetic (LIA)), several existing software model checkers work by iteratively obtaining Boolean Program abstractions using Predicate Abstraction [13,5]. In this paper, we are interested in an alternative algorithm that works directly on the original program model without an explicit step of Boolean abstraction. Despite the undecidability, we are interested in an algorithm that is guaranteed to find a counterexample to safety, if one exists.

Several algorithms have been recently proposed for verifying recursive programs without predicate abstraction. Notable examples are WHALE [2], HSF [21], GPDR [27], Ultimate Automizer [24,25] and Duality [33]. With the exception of GPDR, these algorithms are based on a combination of Bounded Model Checking (BMC) [8] and Craig Interpolation [16]. First, they use an SMT-solver to check for a bounded counterexample, where the bound is on the depth of the call stack (*i.e.*, the number of nested procedure calls). Second, they use (tree) interpolation to over-approximate procedure summaries. This is repeated with increasing values of the bound until a counterexample is found or the approximate summaries are inductive. The reduction to BMC ensures that the algorithms are guaranteed to find a counterexample. However, the size of the SMT instance grows exponentially with the bound on the call-stack (*i.e.*, linear in the size of the call tree). Therefore, for Boolean Programs, these algorithms are at least worst-case exponential in the number of states.

On the other hand, GPDR follows the approach of IC3 [9] by solving BMC incrementally without unrolling the call-graph. Interpolation is used to over-approximate summaries and caching is used to indirectly under-approximate them. For some configurations, GPDR is worst-case polynomial for Boolean Programs. However, even for LRA, GPDR might fail to find a counterexample [28].

In this paper, we introduce RECMC, the first SMT-based algorithm for model checking safety of recursive programs that is worst-case polynomial (in the number of states) for Boolean Programs while being a co-semidecision procedure for programs over decidable theories (see Section 4). Our main insight is to maintain not only over-approximations of procedure summaries (which we call *summary facts*), but also their under-approximations (which we call *reachability facts*). While summary facts are used to block spurious counterexamples, reachability facts are used to analyze a procedure call without inlining or analyzing the body of the callee. Our use of reachability facts is similar to that of *summary edges* of the RHS [36] algorithm. This explains our complexity result for Boolean Programs. However, our summary facts make an important difference. While the use of summary facts is an interesting heuristic for Boolean Programs that does not improve the worst-case complexity, it is crucial for richer theories.

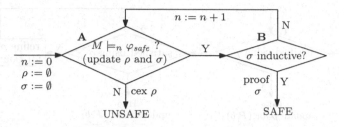

Fig. 1. Flow of the algorithm RECMC to check if $M \models \varphi_{safe}$

Almost every step of RECMC results in existential quantification of variables. RECMC tries to eliminate these variables, as otherwise, they would accumulate and the size of an inferred reachability fact, for example, grows exponentially in the bound on the call-stack. But, a naïve use of quantifier elimination (QE) is expensive. Instead, we develop an alternative approach that under-approximates QE. However, obtaining arbitrary under-approximations can lead to divergence of the algorithm. We introduce the concept of *Model Based Projection* (MBP), for *covering* $\exists \overline{x} \cdot \varphi(\overline{x}, \overline{y})$ by *finitely-many* quantifier-free under-approximations obtained using models of $\varphi(\overline{x}, \overline{y})$. We developed efficient MBPs (see Section 5) for Linear Arithmetic based on the QE methods by Loos-Weispfenning [31] for LRA and Cooper [15] for LIA. We use MBP to under-approximate reachability facts in RECMC. In the best case, only a partial under-approximation is needed and a complete quantifier elimination can be avoided.

We have implemented RECMC as part of our tool SPACER using the framework of Z3 [17] and evaluated it on 799 benchmarks from SV-COMP [38]. SPACER significantly outperforms the implementation of GPDR in Z3 (see Section 6).

In summary, our contributions are: (a) an efficient SMT-based algorithm for model checking recursive programs, that analyzes procedures individually using under- and over-approximations of procedure summaries, (b) MBP functions for under-approximating quantifier elimination for LRA and LIA, (c) a new, complete algorithm for Boolean Programs, with complexity polynomial in the number of states, similar to the best known method [6], and (d) an implementation and an empirical evaluation of the approach.

2 Overview

In this section, we give an overview of RECMC and illustrate it on an example. Let $\mathcal{A}$ be a recursive program. For simplicity of presentation, assume no loops, no global variables and that arguments are passed by reference. Let $P(\overline{v}) \in \mathcal{A}$ be a procedure with parameters $\overline{v}$ and let $\overline{v}_0$ be fresh variables not appearing in P with $|\overline{v}| = |\overline{v}_0|$. A safety property for P is an assertion $\varphi(\overline{v}_0, \overline{v})$. We say that P satisfies φ, denoted $P(\overline{v}) \models \varphi(\overline{v}_0, \overline{v})$, iff the Hoare-triple $\{\overline{v} = \overline{v}_0\} P(\overline{v}) \{\varphi(\overline{v}_0, \overline{v})\}$ is valid. Note that every Hoare-triple corresponds to a safety property in this sense, as shown by Clarke [11], using a *Rule of Adaptation*. Given a safety property φ and a natural number $n \geq 0$, the problem of *bounded safety* is to determine

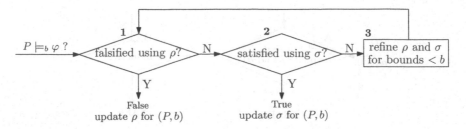

Fig. 2. Flow of the algorithm BNDSAFETY to check $P \models_b \varphi$

```
M (m) {          T (t) {                    D (d) {
    T (m);           if (t>0) {                 d := d-1;
    D (m);               t := t-2;          }
    D (m); }             T (t);
                         t := t+1; } }
```

Fig. 3. A recursive program with 3 procedures

whether all executions of P using a call-stack bounded by n satisfy φ. We use $P(\overline{v}) \models_n \varphi(\overline{v}_0, \overline{v})$ to denote bounded safety.

The key steps of RECMC are shown in Fig. 1. RECMC decides safety for the main procedure M of $\mathcal{A}$. RECMC maintains two *assertion maps* ρ and σ. The *reachability* map ρ maps each procedure $P(\overline{v}) \in \mathcal{A}$ to a set of assertions over $\overline{v}_0 \cup \overline{v}$ that under-approximate its behavior. Similarly, the *summary* map σ maps a procedure P to a set of assertions that over-approximate its behavior. Given P, the maps are partitioned according to the bound on the call-stack. That is, if $\delta(\overline{v}_0, \overline{v}) \in \rho(P, n)$ for $n \geq 0$, then for every model m of δ, there is an execution of P that begins in $m(\overline{v}_0)$ and ends in $m(\overline{v})$, using a call-stack bounded by n. Similarly, if $\delta(\overline{v}_0, \overline{v}) \in \sigma(P, n)$, then $P(\overline{v}) \models_n \delta(\overline{v}_0, \overline{v})$.

RECMC alternates between two steps: (**A**) deciding bounded safety (that also updates ρ and σ maps) and (**B**) checking whether the current proof of bounded safety is inductive (*i.e.*, independent of the bound). It terminates when a counterexample or a proof is found.

Bounded safety, $P \models_b \varphi$, is decided using BNDSAFETY shown in Fig. 2. Step **1** checks whether φ is falsified by current reachability facts in ρ of the callees of P. If so, it infers a new reachability fact for P at bound b witnessing the falsification of φ. Step **2** checks whether φ is satisfied using current summary facts in σ of the callees. If so, it infers a new summary fact for P at bound b witnessing the satisfaction of φ. If the prior two steps fail, there is a potential counterexample π in P with a call to some procedure R such that the reachability facts of R are too strong to witness π, but the summary facts of R are too weak to block it. Step **3** updates ρ and σ by creating (and recursively deciding) a new bounded safety problem for R at bound $b - 1$.

We conclude this section with an illustration of RECMC on the program in Fig. 3 (adapted from [11]). The program has 3 procedures: the main procedure M, and procedures T and D. M calls T and D. T modifies its argument t and calls itself recursively. D decrements its argument d. Let the property be $\varphi = m_0 \geq 2m + 4$.

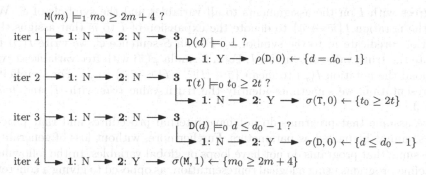

Fig. 4. A run of BNDSAFETY on program in Fig. 3 and a bound 1 on the stack depth. Numbers in bold refer to the steps in Fig. 2.

The first iteration of RECMC is trivial. The bound $n = 0$ and since M has no call-free executions it vacuously satisfies any bounded safety property. Fig. 4 shows the four iterations of BNDSAFETY for the second iteration of RECMC where $n = 1$. For this bound, the maps ρ and σ are initially empty. The first iteration of BNDSAFETY finds a potential counterexample path in M and the approximation for D is updated with a new reachability fact: $d = d_0 - 1$. In the second iteration, the approximation for T is updated. Note that the two calls to D are "jumped over" using the reachability fact for D computed in the first iteration. The new summary fact for T is: $t_0 \geq 2t$. In the third iteration, the approximation for D is updated again, now with a summary fact $d \leq d_0 - 1$. Finally, the summary facts for T and D at bound 0 are sufficient to establish bounded safety at $n = 1$. At this point, the summary map σ is:

$$\sigma(\text{M}, 1) = \{m_0 \geq 2m + 4\} \qquad \sigma(\text{T}, 0) = \{t_0 \geq 2t\} \qquad \sigma(\text{D}, 0) = \{d \leq d_0 - 1\}$$

Ignoring the bounds, σ is inductive. For example, we can prove that the body of T satisfies $t_0 \geq 2t$, assuming that the calls do. Thus, step **B** of RECMC succeeds and the algorithm terminates declaring the program SAFE. In the rest of the paper, we show how to automate RECMC using an SMT-oracle.

3   Preliminaries

Consider a first-order language with equality and let $\mathcal{S}$ be its signature, *i.e.*, the set of non-logical function and predicate symbols (including equality). An $\mathcal{S}$-*structure* I consists of a domain of interpretation, denoted $|I|$, and assigns elements of $|I|$ to variables, and functions and predicates on $|I|$ to the symbols of $\mathcal{S}$. Let φ be a formula. We assume the usual definition of satisfaction of φ by I, denoted $I \models \varphi$. I is called a *model* of φ iff $I \models \varphi$ and this can be extended to a set of formulas. A first-order $\mathcal{S}$-*theory Th* is a set of deductively closed $\mathcal{S}$-sentences. I satisfies φ modulo *Th*, denoted $I \models_{Th} \varphi$, iff $I \models Th \cup \{\varphi\}$. φ is *valid* modulo *Th*, denoted $\models_{Th} \varphi$, iff every model of *Th* is also a model of φ.

Let I be an $\mathcal{S}$-structure and $\overline{w}$ be a list of fresh function/predicate symbols not in $\mathcal{S}$. A $(\mathcal{S} \cup \overline{w})$-structure J is called an *expansion* of I to $\overline{w}$ iff $|J| = |I|$ and

J agrees with I on the assignments to all variables and the symbols of $\mathcal{S}$. We use the notation $I\{\overline{w} \mapsto \overline{u}\}$ to denote the expansion of I to $\overline{w}$ that assigns the function/predicate u_i to the symbol w_i. For an $\mathcal{S}$-sentence φ, we write $I(\varphi)$ to denote the truth value of φ under I. For a formula $\varphi(\overline{x})$ with free variables $\overline{x}$, we overload the notation $I(\varphi)$ to mean $\{\overline{a} \in |I|^{|\overline{x}|} \mid I\{\overline{x} \mapsto \overline{a}\} \models \varphi\}$. For simplicity of presentation, we sometimes identify the truth value *true* with $|I|$ and *false* with $\emptyset$.

We assume that programs do not have internal procedures and that procedures cannot be passed as parameters. Furthermore, without loss of generality, we assume that programs do not have loops or global variables. In the following, we define programs using a logical representation, as opposed to giving a concrete syntax. A *program* $\mathcal{A}$ is a finite list of procedures with a designated *main* procedure M where the program begins. A *procedure* P is a tuple $\langle \overline{\iota}_P, \overline{o}_P, \Sigma_P, \overline{\ell}_P, \beta_P \rangle$, where (a) $\overline{\iota}_P$ is the finite list of variables denoting the input values of the parameters, (b) $\overline{o}_P$ is the finite list of variables denoting the output values of the parameters, (c) Σ_P is a fresh predicate symbol of arity $|\overline{\iota}_P| + |\overline{o}_P|$, (d) $\overline{\ell}_P$ is the finite list of local variables, and (e) β_P is a quantifier-free sentence over the signature $(\mathcal{S} \cup \{\Sigma_Q \mid Q \in \mathcal{A}\} \cup \overline{\iota}_P \cup \overline{o}_P \cup \overline{\ell}_P)$ in which a predicate symbol Σ_Q appears only positively. We use $\overline{v}_P$ to denote $\overline{\iota}_P \cup \overline{o}_P$.

Intuitively, for a procedure P, Σ_P is used to denote its semantics and β_P encodes its body using the predicate symbol Σ_Q for a call to the procedure Q. We require that a predicate symbol Σ_Q appears only positively in β_P to ensure a fixed-point characterization of the semantics as shown later on. For example, for the signature $\mathcal{S} = \langle 0, Succ, -, +, \leq, >, = \rangle$, the program in Fig. 3 is represented as $\langle M, T, D \rangle$ with $M = \langle m_0, m, \Sigma_M, \langle \ell_0, \ell_1 \rangle, \beta_M \rangle$, $T = \langle t_0, t, \Sigma_T, \langle \ell_0, \ell_1 \rangle, \beta_T \rangle$ and $D = \langle d_0, d, \Sigma_D, \emptyset, \beta_D \rangle$, where

$$\beta_M = \Sigma_T(m_0, \ell_0) \wedge \Sigma_D(\ell_0, \ell_1) \wedge \Sigma_D(\ell_1, m) \qquad \beta_D = (d = d_0 - 1)$$
$$\beta_T = (t_0 \leq 0 \wedge t_0 = t) \ \vee \ (t_0 > 0 \wedge \ell_0 = t_0 - 2 \wedge \Sigma_T(\ell_0, \ell_1) \wedge t = \ell_1 + 1) \tag{1}$$

Here, we abbreviate $Succ^i(0)$ by i and (m_0, t_0, d_0) and (m, t, d) denote the input and the output values of the parameters of the original program, respectively. For a procedure P, let $Paths(P)$ denote the set of all prime-implicants of β_P. Intuitively, each element of $Paths(P)$ encodes a path in the procedure.

Let $\mathcal{A} = \langle P_0, \ldots, P_n \rangle$ be a program and I be an $\mathcal{S}$-structure. Let $\overline{X}$ be a list of length n such that each X_i is either (i) a truth value if $|\overline{v}_{P_i}| = 0$, or (ii) a subset of $|I|^{|\overline{v}_{P_i}|}$ if $|\overline{v}_{P_i}| \geq 1$. Let $J(I, \overline{X})$ denote the expansion $I\{\Sigma_{P_0} \mapsto X_0\} \ldots \{\Sigma_{P_n} \mapsto X_n\}$. The *semantics* of a procedure P_i given I, denoted $[\![P_i]\!]_I$, characterizes all the terminating executions of P_i and is defined as follows. $\langle [\![P_0]\!]_I, \ldots, [\![P_n]\!]_I \rangle$ is the (pointwise) least $\overline{X}$ such that for all $Q \in \mathcal{A}$, $J(I, \overline{X}) \models \forall \overline{v}_Q \cup \overline{\ell}_Q \cdot (\beta_Q \Rightarrow \Sigma_Q(\overline{v}_Q))$. This has a well-known least fixed-point characterization [11].

For a bound $b \geq 0$ on the call-stack, the *bounded semantics* of a procedure P_i given I, denoted $[\![P_i]\!]_I^b$, characterizes all the executions using a stack of depth bounded by b and is defined by induction on b:

$$[\![P_i]\!]_I^0 = J(I, \langle \emptyset, \ldots, \emptyset \rangle)(\exists \overline{\ell}_{P_i} \cdot \beta_{P_i}), \quad [\![P_i]\!]_I^b = J(I, \langle [\![P_0]\!]_I^{b-1}, \ldots, [\![P_n]\!]_I^{b-1} \rangle)(\exists \overline{\ell}_{P_i} \cdot \beta_{P_i})$$

An *environment* is a function that maps a predicate symbol Σ_P to a formula over $\bar{v}_P$. Given a formula τ and an environment E, we abuse the notation $[\![\cdot]\!]$ and write $[\![\tau]\!]_E$ for the formula obtained by instantiating every predicate symbol Σ_P by $E(\Sigma_P)$ in τ.

Let Th be an $\mathcal{S}$-theory. A *safety property* for a procedure $P \in \mathcal{A}$ is a formula over $\bar{v}_P$. P satisfies a safety property φ w.r.t Th, denoted $P \models_{Th} \varphi$, iff for all models I of Th, $[\![P]\!]_I \subseteq I(\varphi)$. A *safety property* ψ of the program $\mathcal{A}$ is a safety property of its main procedure. A *safety proof* for $\psi(\bar{v}_M)$ is an environment Π that is both safe and inductive:

$$\models_{Th} [\![\forall \bar{x} \cdot \Sigma_M(\bar{x}) \Rightarrow \psi(\bar{x})]\!]_\Pi, \quad \forall P \in \mathcal{A} \cdot \models_{Th} [\![\forall \bar{v}_P \cup \bar{\ell}_P \cdot (\beta_P \Rightarrow \Sigma_P(\bar{v}_P))]\!]_\Pi$$

Given a formula $\varphi(\bar{v}_P)$ and $b \geq 0$, a procedure P satisfies *bounded safety* w.r.t Th, denoted $P \models_{b,Th} \varphi$, iff for all models I of Th, $[\![P]\!]_I^b \subseteq I(\varphi)$. In this case, we also call φ a *summary fact* for $\langle P, b \rangle$. We call φ a *reachability fact* for $\langle P, b \rangle$ iff $I(\varphi) \subseteq [\![P]\!]_I^b$, for all models I of Th. Intuitively, *summary facts* and *reachability facts* for $\langle P, b \rangle$, respectively, over- and under-approximate $[\![P]\!]_I^b$ for every model I of Th.

A *bounded assertion map* maps a procedure P and a natural number $b \geq 0$ to a set of formulas over $\bar{v}_P$. Given a bounded assertion map m and $b \geq 0$, we define two special environments U_m^b and O_m^b as follows.

$$U_m^b : \Sigma_P \mapsto \bigvee \{\delta \in m(P, b') \mid b' \leq b\} \qquad O_m^b : \Sigma_P \mapsto \bigwedge \{\delta \in m(P, b') \mid b' \geq b\}$$

We use U_m^b and O_m^b to under- and over-approximate the bounded semantics. For convenience, let U_m^{-1} and O_m^{-1} be environments that map every symbol to $\perp$.

4   Model Checking Recursive Programs

In this section, we present our algorithm $\mathrm{RECMC}(\mathcal{A}, \varphi_{safe})$ that determines whether a program $\mathcal{A}$ satisfies a safety property φ_{safe}. Let $\mathcal{S}$ be the signature of the first-order language under consideration and assume a fixed $\mathcal{S}$-theory Th. To avoid clutter, we drop the subscript Th from the notation $\models_{Th}$ and $\models_{b,Th}$. We also establish the soundness and complexity of RECMC. An efficient instantiation of RECMC to Linear Arithmetic is presented in Section 5.

Main Loop. RECMC maintains two *bounded assertion maps* ρ and σ for reachability and summary facts, respectively. For brevity, for a first-order formula τ, we write $[\![\tau]\!]_\rho^b$ and $[\![\tau]\!]_\sigma^b$ to denote $[\![\tau]\!]_{U_\rho^b}$ and $[\![\tau]\!]_{O_\sigma^b}$, respectively, where the environments U_ρ^b and O_σ^b are as defined in Section 3. Intuitively, $[\![\tau]\!]_\rho^b$ and $[\![\tau]\!]_\sigma^b$, respectively, under- and over-approximate τ using ρ and σ.

The pseudo-code of the main loop of RECMC (corresponding to the flow diagram in Fig. 1) is shown in Fig. 5. RECMC follows an *iterative deepening* strategy. In each iteration, $\mathrm{BNDSAFETY}$ (described below) checks whether all executions of $\mathcal{A}$ satisfy φ_{safe} for a bound $n \geq 0$ on the call-stack, *i.e.*, if $M \models_n$

```
RecMC(A, φ_safe)
 1  n ← 0 ; ρ ← ∅ ; σ ← ∅
 2  while true do
 3  │   res, ρ, σ ← BndSafety(A, φ_safe, n, ρ, σ)
 4  │   if res is UNSAFE then
 5  │   │   └ return UNSAFE, ρ
    │   else
 6  │   │   │   ind, σ ← CheckInductive(A, σ, n)
 7  │   │   │   if ind then
 8  │   │   │   └ return SAFE, σ
 9  │   └   n ← n + 1
```

```
CheckInductive(A, σ, n)
10  ind ← true
11  foreach P ∈ A do
12  │   foreach δ ∈ σ(P, n) do
13  │   │   if ⊨ ⟦β_P⟧^n_σ ⇒ δ then
14  │   │   └ σ ← σ ∪ (⟨P, n + 1⟩ ↦ δ)
    │   else
15  │   └   ind ← false
16  return (ind, σ)
```

Fig. 5. Pseudo-code of RecMC

φ_{safe}. BndSafety also updates the maps ρ and σ. Whenever BndSafety returns $UNSAFE$, the reachability facts in ρ are sufficient to construct a counterexample and the loop terminates. Whenever BndSafety returns $SAFE$, the summary facts in σ are sufficient to prove the absence of a counterexample for the current bound n on the call-stack. In this case, if σ is also inductive, as determined by CheckInductive, O^n_σ is a safety proof and the loop terminates. Otherwise, the bound on the call-stack is incremented and a new iteration of the loop begins. Note that, as a side-effect of CheckInductive, some summary facts are propagated to the bound $n + 1$. This is similar to *push generalization* in IC3 [9].

Bounded Safety. We describe the routine BndSafety$(A, \varphi_{safe}, n, \rho_{Init}, \sigma_{Init})$ as an abstract transition system [34] defined by the inference rules shown in Fig. 6. Here, n is the current bound on the call-stack and ρ_{Init} and σ_{Init} are the maps of reachability and summary facts input to the routine. A state of BndSafety is a triple $\mathcal{Q} \parallel \rho \parallel \sigma$, where ρ and σ are the current maps and $\mathcal{Q}$ is a set of triples $\langle P, \varphi, b \rangle$ for a procedure P, a formula φ over $\overline{v}_P$, and a number $b \geq 0$. A triple $\langle P, \varphi, b \rangle \in \mathcal{Q}$ is called a *bounded reachability query* and asks whether $P \not\models_b \neg\varphi$, *i.e.*, whether there is an execution in P using a call-stack bounded by b where the values of $\overline{v}_P$ satisfy φ.

BndSafety starts with a single query $\langle M, \neg\varphi_{safe}, n \rangle$ and initializes the maps of reachability and summary facts (rule Init). It checks whether $M \models_n \varphi_{safe}$ by inferring new summary and reachability facts to answer existing queries (rules Sum and Reach) and generating new queries (rule Query). When there are no queries left to answer, *i.e.*, $\mathcal{Q}$ is empty, it terminates with a result of either $UNSAFE$ or $SAFE$ (rules Unsafe and Safe).

Sum infers a new summary fact when a query $\langle P, \varphi, b \rangle$ can be answered negatively. In this case, there is an over-approximation of the bounded semantics of P at b, obtained using the summary facts of callees at bound $b - 1$, that is unsatisfiable with φ. That is, $\models \llbracket \beta_P \rrbracket^{b-1}_\sigma \Rightarrow \neg\varphi$. The inference of the new fact is by interpolation [16] (denoted by Itp in the side-condition of the rule). Thus, the new summary fact ψ is a formula over $\overline{v}_P$ such that $\models (\llbracket \beta_P \rrbracket^{b-1}_\sigma \Rightarrow \psi(\overline{v}_P)) \wedge (\psi(\overline{v}_P) \Rightarrow \neg\varphi)$. Note that ψ over-approximates the bounded semantics of P at b. Every query $\langle P, \eta, c \rangle \in \mathcal{Q}$ such that η is unsatisfiable with the updated environment $O^c_\sigma(\Sigma_P)$ is immediately answered and removed.

$$\text{Init} \; \frac{}{\{\langle M, \neg\varphi_{safe}, n\rangle\} \parallel \rho_{Init} \parallel \sigma_{Init}}$$

$$\text{Sum} \; \frac{\mathcal{Q} \parallel \rho \parallel \sigma \qquad \langle P, \varphi, b\rangle \in \mathcal{Q} \qquad \models [\![\beta_P]\!]_\sigma^{b-1} \Rightarrow \neg\varphi}{\mathcal{Q} \setminus \{\langle P, \eta, c\rangle \mid c \le b, \models [\![\Sigma_P]\!]_\sigma^c \wedge \psi \Rightarrow \neg\eta\} \parallel \rho \parallel \sigma \cup \{\langle P, b\rangle \mapsto \psi\}}$$

$$\text{where } \psi = \text{Itp}([\![\beta_P]\!]_\sigma^{b-1}, \neg\varphi)$$

$$\text{Reach} \; \frac{\mathcal{Q} \parallel \rho \parallel \sigma \qquad \langle P, \varphi, b\rangle \in \mathcal{Q} \qquad \pi \in Paths(P) \qquad \not\models [\![\pi]\!]_\rho^{b-1} \Rightarrow \neg\varphi}{\mathcal{Q} \setminus \{\langle P, \eta, c\rangle \mid c \ge b, \not\models \psi \Rightarrow \neg\eta\} \parallel \rho \cup \{\langle P, b\rangle \mapsto \psi\} \parallel \sigma}$$

$$\text{where } \psi = \exists \bar{\ell}_P \cdot [\![\pi]\!]_\rho^{b-1}$$

$$\text{Query} \; \frac{\begin{array}{c} \mathcal{Q} \parallel \rho \parallel \sigma \qquad \langle P, \varphi, b\rangle \in \mathcal{Q} \qquad \models [\![\beta_P]\!]_\sigma^{b-1} \Rightarrow \neg\varphi \qquad \pi \in Paths(P) \\ \pi = \pi_u \wedge \Sigma_R(\bar{a}) \wedge \pi_v \qquad \models [\![\pi_u]\!]_\sigma^{b-1} \wedge [\![\Sigma_R(\bar{a})]\!]_\rho^{b-1} \wedge [\![\pi_v]\!]_\rho^{b-1} \Rightarrow \neg\varphi \\ \not\models [\![\pi_u]\!]_\sigma^{b-1} \wedge [\![\Sigma_R(\bar{a})]\!]_\sigma^{b-1} \wedge [\![\pi_v]\!]_\rho^{b-1} \Rightarrow \neg\varphi \end{array}}{\mathcal{Q} \cup \{\langle R, \psi, b-1\rangle\} \parallel \rho \parallel \sigma}$$

$$\text{where } \begin{cases} \psi = (\exists (\bar{v}_P \cup \bar{\ell}_P) \setminus \bar{a} \cdot [\![\pi_u]\!]_\sigma^{b-1} \wedge [\![\pi_v]\!]_\rho^{b-1} \wedge \varphi) [\bar{a} \leftarrow \bar{v}_R] \\ \text{for all } \langle R, \eta, b-1\rangle \in \mathcal{Q}, \models \psi \Rightarrow \neg\eta \end{cases}$$

$$\text{Unsafe} \; \frac{\emptyset \parallel \rho \parallel \sigma \qquad \not\models [\![\Sigma_M]\!]_\rho^n \Rightarrow \varphi_{safe}}{UNSAFE} \qquad \text{Safe} \; \frac{\emptyset \parallel \rho \parallel \sigma \qquad \models [\![\Sigma_M]\!]_\sigma^n \Rightarrow \varphi_{safe}}{SAFE}$$

Fig. 6. Rules defining $\text{BndSafety}(\mathcal{A}, \varphi_{safe}, n, \rho_{Init}, \sigma_{Init})$

Reach infers a new reachability fact when a query $\langle P, \varphi, b\rangle$ can be answered positively. In this case, there is an under-approximation of the bounded semantics of P at b, obtained using the reachability facts of callees at bound $b-1$, that is satisfiable with φ. That is, $\not\models [\![\beta_P]\!]_\rho^{b-1} \Rightarrow \neg\varphi$. In particular, there exists a path π in $Paths(P)$ such that $\not\models [\![\pi]\!]_\rho^{b-1} \Rightarrow \neg\varphi$. The new reachability fact ψ is obtained by choosing such a π non-deterministically and existentially quantifying all local variables from $[\![\pi]\!]_\rho^{b-1}$. Note that ψ under-approximates the bounded semantics of P at b. Every query $\langle P, \eta, c\rangle \in \mathcal{Q}$ such that η is satisfiable with the updated environment $U_\rho^c(\Sigma_P)$ is immediately answered and removed.

Query creates a new query when a query $\langle P, \varphi, b\rangle$ cannot be answered using current ρ and σ. In this case, the current over-approximation of the bounded semantics of P at b is satisfiable with φ while its current under-approximation is unsatisfiable with φ. That is, $\not\models [\![\beta_P]\!]_\rho^{b-1} \Rightarrow \neg\varphi$ and $\models [\![\beta_P]\!]_\rho^{b-1} \Rightarrow \neg\varphi$. In particular, there exists a path π in $Paths(P)$ such that $\not\models [\![\pi]\!]_\sigma^{b-1} \Rightarrow \neg\varphi$ and $\models [\![\pi]\!]_\rho^{b-1} \Rightarrow \neg\varphi$. Intuitively, π is a potential counterexample path that needs to be checked for feasibility. Such a π is chosen non-deterministically. π is guaranteed to have a call $\Sigma_R(\bar{a})$ to a procedure R such that the under-approximation $[\![\Sigma_R(\bar{a})]\!]_\rho^{b-1}$ is too strong to witness π but the over-approximation $[\![\Sigma_R(\bar{a})]\!]_\sigma^{b-1}$

	π_i	$[\![\pi_i]\!]^0_\rho$	$[\![\pi_i]\!]^0_\sigma$
$i = 1$	$\Sigma_T(m_0, \ell_0)$	$\perp$	$\top$
$i = 2$	$\Sigma_D(\ell_0, \ell_1)$	$\ell_1 = \ell_0 - 1$	$\top$
$i = 3$	$\Sigma_D(\ell_1, m)$	$m = \ell_1 - 1$	$\top$

Fig. 7. Approximations of the only path π of the procedure M in Fig. 3

is too weak to block it. That is, π can be partitioned into a prefix π_u, a call $\Sigma_R(\bar{a})$ to R, and a suffix π_v such that the following hold:

$$\models [\![\Sigma_R(\bar{a})]\!]^{b-1}_\rho \Rightarrow (([\![\pi_u]\!]^{b-1}_\sigma \wedge [\![\pi_v]\!]^{b-1}_\rho) \Rightarrow \neg\varphi)$$

$$\not\models [\![\Sigma_R(\bar{a})]\!]^{b-1}_\sigma \Rightarrow (([\![\pi_u]\!]^{b-1}_\sigma \wedge [\![\pi_v]\!]^{b-1}_\rho) \Rightarrow \neg\varphi)$$

Note that the prefix π_u and the suffix π_v are over- and under-approximated, respectively. A new query $\langle R, \psi, b - 1 \rangle$ is created where ψ is obtained by existentially quantifying all variables from $[\![\pi_u]\!]^{b-1}_\sigma \wedge [\![\pi_v]\!]^{b-1}_\rho \wedge \varphi$ except the arguments $\bar{a}$ of the call, and renaming appropriately. If the new query is answered negatively (using SUM), all executions along π where the values of $\bar{v}_P \cup \bar{\ell}_P$ satisfy $[\![\pi_v]\!]^{b-1}_\rho$ are spurious counterexamples. An additional side-condition requires that ψ "does not overlap" with η for any other query $\langle R, \eta, b - 1 \rangle$ in $\mathcal{Q}$. This is necessary for termination of BNDSAFETY (Theorem 2). In practice, the side-condition is trivially satisfied by always applying the rule to $\langle P, \varphi, b \rangle$ with the smallest b.

For example, consider the program in Fig. 3 represented by (1) and the query $\langle M, \varphi, 1 \rangle$ where $\varphi \equiv m_0 < 2m + 4$. Let $\sigma = \emptyset$, $\rho(D, 0) = \{d = d_0 - 1\}$ and $\rho(T, 0) = \emptyset$. Let $\pi = (\Sigma_T(m_0, \ell_0) \wedge \Sigma_D(\ell_0, \ell_1) \wedge \Sigma_D(\ell_1, m))$ denote the only path in the procedure M. Fig. 7 shows $[\![\pi_i]\!]^0_\rho$ and $[\![\pi_i]\!]^0_\sigma$ for each conjunct π_i of π. As the figure shows, $[\![\pi]\!]^0_\sigma$ is satisfiable with φ, witnessed by the execution $e \equiv \langle m_0 = 3, \ell_0 = 3, \ell_1 = 2, m = 1 \rangle$. Note that this execution also satisfies $[\![\pi_2 \wedge \pi_3]\!]^0_\rho$. But, $[\![\pi_1]\!]^0_\rho$ is too strong to witness it, where π_1 is the call $\Sigma_T(m_0, \ell_0)$. To create a new query for T, we first existentially quantify all variables other than the arguments m_0 and ℓ_0 from $\pi_2 \wedge \pi_3 \wedge \varphi$, obtaining $m_0 < 2\ell_0$. Renaming the arguments by the parameters of T results in the new query $\langle T, t_0 < 2t, 0 \rangle$. Further iterations of BNDSAFETY would answer this query negatively making the execution e spurious. Note that this would also make all other executions where the values to $\langle m_0, \ell_0, \ell_1, m \rangle$ satisfy $[\![\pi_2 \wedge \pi_3]\!]^0_\rho$ spurious.

Soundness and Complexity. Soundness of RECMC follows from that of BNDSAFETY, which can be shown by a case analysis on the inference rules[2].

Theorem 1. BNDSAFETY *and* RECMC *are sound.*

BNDSAFETY is complete relative to an oracle for satisfiability modulo Th. Even though the number of reachable states of a procedure is unbounded in general, the number of reachability facts inferred by BNDSAFETY is finite. This is because a reachability fact corresponds to a path (see REACH) and given a bound on the call-stack, the number of such facts is bounded. This further bounds the number of queries that can be created.

---

[2] Proofs of all of the theorems can be found in the extended version of the paper [28].

Theorem 2. *Given an oracle for Th,* BNDSAFETY$(\mathcal{A}, \varphi, n, \emptyset, \emptyset)$ *terminates.*

As a corollary of Theorem 2, RECMC is a co-semidecision procedure for safety, *i.e.*, RECMC is guaranteed to find a counterexample if one exists. In contrast, the closest related algorithm GPDR [27] is not a co-semidecision procedure [28]. Finally, for Boolean Programs RECMC is a complete decision procedure. Unlike the general case, the number of reachable states of a Boolean Program, and hence the number of reachability facts, is finite and independent of the bound on the call-stack. Let $N = |\mathcal{A}|$ and $k = \max\{|\overline{v}_P| \mid P \in \mathcal{A}\}$.

Theorem 3. *Let* $\mathcal{A}$ *be a Boolean Program. Then* RECMC$(\mathcal{A}, \varphi)$ *terminates in* $O(N^2 \cdot 2^{2k})$-*many applications of the rules in Fig. 6.*

Note that due to the iterative deepening strategy of RECMC, the complexity is quadratic in the number of procedures (and not linear as in [6]). In contrast, other SMT-based algorithms, such as WHALE [2], are worst-case exponential in the number of states of a Boolean Program.

In summary, RECMC checks safety of a recursive program by inferring the necessary under- and over-approximations of procedure semantics and using them to analyze procedures individually.

5   Model Based Projection

RECMC, as presented in Section 4, can be used as-is, when Th is Linear Arithmetic. But, note that the rules REACH and QUERY introduce existential quantifiers in reachability facts and queries. Unless eliminated, these quantifiers accumulate and the size of the formulas grows exponentially in the bound on the call-stack. Eliminating them using quantifier elimination (QE) is expensive. Instead, we suggest an alternative approach that under-approximates existential quantification with quantifier-free formulas *lazily* and efficiently. We first introduce a model-based under-approximation of QE, called *Model Based Projection* (MBP). Second, we give an efficient (linear in the size of formulas involved) MBP procedure for Linear Rational Arithmetic (LRA). Due to space limitations, MBP for Linear Integer Arithmetic (LIA) is described in the extended version [28]. Finally, we show a modified version of BNDSAFETY that uses MBP instead of existential quantification and show that it is sound and terminating.

Model Based Projection (*MBP*). Let $\lambda(\overline{y})$ be the existentially quantified formula $\exists \overline{x} \cdot \lambda_m(\overline{x}, \overline{y})$ where λ_m is quantifier free. A function $Proj_\lambda$ from models (modulo Th) of λ_m to quantifier-free formulas over $\overline{y}$ is a *Model Based Projection* (for λ) iff it has a finite image, $\lambda \equiv \bigvee_{M \models \lambda_m} Proj_\lambda(M)$, and for every model M of λ_m, $M \models Proj_\lambda(M)$.

In other words, $Proj_\lambda$ covers the space of all models of $\lambda_m(\overline{x}, \overline{y})$ by a finite set of quantifier-free formulas over $\overline{y}$. MBP exists for any theory that admits quantifier elimination, because one can first obtain an equivalent quantifier-free formula and map every model to it.

MBP for Linear Rational Arithmetic. We begin with a brief overview of Loos-Weispfenning (LW) method [31] for quantifier elimination in LRA. We borrow our presentation from Nipkow [35] to which we refer the reader for more details. Let $\lambda(\overline{y}) = \exists \overline{x} \cdot \lambda_m(\overline{x}, \overline{y})$ as above. Without loss of generality, assume that $\overline{x}$ is singleton, λ_m is in Negation Normal Form, and x only appears in the literals of the form $\ell < x$, $x < u$, and $x = e$, where ℓ, u, and e are x-free. Let $lits(\lambda)$ denote the literals of λ. The LW-method states that

$$\exists x \cdot \lambda_m(x) \equiv \left(\bigvee_{(x=e) \in lits(\lambda)} \lambda_m[e] \vee \bigvee_{(\ell<x) \in lits(\lambda)} \lambda_m[\ell + \epsilon] \vee \lambda_m[-\infty] \right) \quad (2)$$

where $\lambda_m[\cdot]$ denotes a *virtual substitution* for the literals containing x. Intuitively, $\lambda_m[e]$ covers the case when a literal $(x = e)$ is true. Otherwise, the set of ℓ's in the literals $(\ell < x)$ identify intervals in which x can lie which are covered by the remaining substitutions. We omit the details of the substitution and instead illustrate it on an example. Let λ_m be $(x = e \wedge \phi_1) \vee (\ell < x \wedge x < u) \vee (x < u \wedge \phi_2)$, where $\ell, e, u, \phi_1, \phi_2$ are x-free. Then,

$$\exists x \cdot \lambda_m(x) \equiv \lambda_m[e] \vee \lambda_m[\ell + \epsilon] \vee \lambda_m[-\infty]$$
$$\equiv \big(\phi_1 \vee (\ell < e \wedge e < u) \vee (e < u \wedge \phi_2)\big) \vee \big(\ell < u \vee (\ell < u \wedge \phi_2)\big) \vee \phi_2$$
$$\equiv \phi_1 \vee (\ell < u) \vee \phi_2$$

We now define an MBP $LRAProj_\lambda$ for LRA as a map from models of λ_m to disjuncts in (2). Given $M \models \lambda_m$, $LRAProj_\lambda$ picks a disjunct that covers M based on values of the literals of the form $x = e$ and $\ell < x$ in M. Ties are broken by a syntactic ordering on terms (e.g., when $M \models \ell' = \ell$ for two literals $\ell < x$ and $\ell' < x$).

$$LRAProj_\lambda(M) = \begin{cases} \lambda_m[e], & \text{if } (x = e) \in lits(\lambda) \wedge M \models x = e \\ \lambda_m[\ell + \epsilon], & \text{else if } (\ell < x) \in lits(\lambda) \wedge M \models \ell < x \wedge \\ & \quad \forall (\ell' < x) \in lits(\lambda) \cdot M \models ((\ell' < x) \Rightarrow (\ell' \leq \ell)) \\ \lambda_m[-\infty], & \text{otherwise} \end{cases}$$

Theorem 4. *$LRAProj_\lambda$ is a Model Based Projection.*

Note that $LRAProj_\lambda$ is linear in the size of λ. An MBP for LIA can be defined similarly [28] based on Cooper's method [15].

Bounded Safety with MBP. Intuitively, each quantifier-free formula in the image of $Proj_\lambda$ under-approximates λ. As above, we use λ_m for the quantifier-free matrix of λ. We modify the side-condition $\psi = \lambda$ of REACH and QUERY to use quantifier-free under-approximations as follows: (i) for REACH, the new side-condition is $\psi = Proj_\lambda(M)$ where $M \models \lambda_m \wedge \varphi$, (ii) for QUERY, the new side-condition is $\psi = Proj_\lambda(M)$ where $M \models \lambda_m \wedge [\![\Sigma_R(a)]\!]_\sigma^{b-1}$. Note that to avoid redundant applications of the rules, we require M to satisfy a formula stronger than λ_m. Intuitively, (i) ensures that the newly inferred reachability

	SLAM		SVCOMP-1		SVCOMP-2		SVCOMP-3	
	SAFE	UNSAFE	SAFE	UNSAFE	SAFE	UNSAFE	SAFE	UNSAFE
SPACER	1,721	985	249	509	213	497	234	482
Z3	1,722	997	245	509	208	493	234	477
VBS	1,727	998	252	509	225	500	240	482

Fig. 8. Number of programs verified by SPACER, Z3 and the Virtual Best Solver

fact answers the current query and (ii) ensures that the new query cannot be immediately answered by known facts. In both cases, the required model M can be obtained as a side-effect of discharging the premises of the rules. Soundness of BNDSAFETY is unaffected and termination of BNDSAFETY follows from the image-finiteness of $Proj_\lambda$.

Theorem 5. *Assuming an oracle and an MBP for Th,* BNDSAFETY *is sound and terminating with the modified rules.*

Thus, BNDSAFETY with a linear-time MBP (such as $LRAProj_\lambda$) keeps the size of the formulas small by efficiently inferring only the necessary under-approximations of the quantified formulas.

6 Implementation and Experiments

We have implemented RECMC for analyzing C programs as part of the tool SPACER. The back-end is based on Z3 [18] which is used for SMT-solving and interpolation. It supports propositional logic, linear arithmetic, and bit-vectors (via bit-blasting). The front-end is based on UFO [3]. It converts C programs to the Horn-SMT format of Z3, which corresponds to the logical program representation of Section 3. The implementation and benchmarks are available online[3].

We evaluated SPACER on two sets of benchmarks. The first set contains 2,908 Boolean Programs obtained from the SLAM toolkit[4]. The second contains 799 C programs from the Software Verification Competition (SVCOMP) 2014 [38]. We call this set SVCOMP-1. We also evaluated on two variants of SVCOMP-1, which we call SVCOMP-2 and SVCOMP-3, obtained by factoring out parts of the program into procedures and introducing more modularity. We compared SPACER against the implementation of GPDR in Z3. We used a time limit of 30 minutes and a memory limit of 16GB, on an Ubuntu machine with a 2.2 GHz AMD Opteron(TM) Processor 6174 and 516GB RAM. The results are summarized in Fig. 8. Since there are programs verified by only one of the tools, Fig. 8 also reports the number of programs verified by at least one, *i.e.*, the Virtual Best Solver (VBS).

Boolean Program Benchmarks. On most of the SLAM benchmarks, the runtimes of SPACER and Z3 are similar (within 2 minutes). We then evaluated on a Boolean Program from [6] in which the size of the call-tree grows exponentially

---

[3] http://www.cs.cmu.edu/~akomurav/projects/spacer/home.html
[4] https://svn.sosy-lab.org/software/sv-benchmarks/trunk/clauses/BOOL/slam.zip

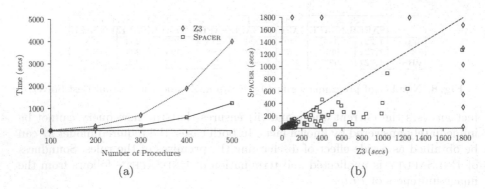

Fig. 9. SPACER vs. Z3 for (a) BEBOP example and (b) SVCOMP-1 benchmarks

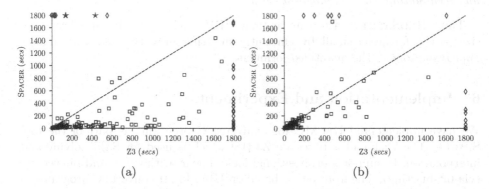

Fig. 10. SPACER vs. Z3 for the benchmarks (a) SVCOMP-2 and (b) SVCOMP-3

in the number of procedures. As Fig. 9(a) shows, SPACER handles the increasing complexity in the example significantly better than Z3.

SVCOMP 2014 Benchmarks. Fig. 9(b), 10(a) and 10(b) show the scatter plots for SVCOMP-1, SVCOMP-2 and SVCOMP-3 benchmarks. A diamond indicates a time-out and a star indicates a mem-out. The plots show that SPACER is significantly better on most of the programs. This shows the practical advantage of the approximations and MBP of RECMC.

7   Related Work

There is a large body of work on interprocedural program analysis. It was pointed out early on that verification of recursive programs is reducible to the computation of a fixed-point over relations (called *summaries*) representing the input-output behavior of each procedure [11,37]. Such procedure summaries are called *partial correctness relations* in [11], and are part of the *functional approach* of [37]. Reps, Horwitz, and Sagiv [36] showed that for a large class of finite interprocedural dataflow problems the summaries can be computed in time polynomial in the number of *facts* and procedures. Ball and Rajamani [6] adapted the

RHS algorithm to the verification of Boolean Programs. Following the SLAM project, other software model checkers – such as BLAST [26] and MAGIC [10] – also implemented the CEGAR loop with predicate abstraction. None used under-approximations of procedure semantics as we do.

Recently, several SMT-based algorithms have been proposed for safety verification of recursive programs, including WHALE [2], HSF [21], Duality [33], Ultimate Automizer [24], and Corral [30]. While these algorithms have been developed independently, they share a similar structure. They use SMT-solvers to look for counterexamples and interpolation to over-approximate summaries. Corral is an exception, which relies on user input and heuristics to supply the summaries. The algorithms differ in the SMT encoding and the heuristics used. However, in the worst-case, they completely unroll the call graph into a tree.

The work closest to ours is Generalized Property Driven Reachability (GPDR) of Hoder and Bjørner [27]. GPDR extends the hardware model checking algorithm IC3 of Bradley [9] to SMT-supported theories and recursive programs. Unlike RECMC, GPDR does not maintain reachability facts. In the context of Fig. 6, this means that ρ is always empty and there is no REACH rule. Instead, the QUERY rule is modified to use a model M that satisfies the premises (instead of our use of the path π when creating a query). Furthermore, the answers to the queries are cached. In the context of Boolean Programs, this ensures that every query is asked at most once (and either cached or blocked by a summary fact). Since there are only finitely many models, the algorithm always terminates. However, in the case of Linear Arithmetic, a formula can have infinitely many models and GPDR might end up applying the QUERY rule indefinitely. In contrast, RECMC creates only finitely many queries for a given bound on the call-stack and is guaranteed to find a counterexample if one exists.

Combination of over- and under-approximations for analysis of procedural programs has also been explored in [23,20]. However, our notion of an under-approximation is very different. Both [23,20] under-approximate summaries by *must transitions*. A must transition is a pair of formulas $\langle \varphi, \psi \rangle$ that under-approximates the summary of a procedure P iff for every state that satisfies φ, P has an execution that ends in a state satisfying ψ. In contrast, our reachability facts are similar to *summary edges* of RHS [36]. A reachability fact is a single formula φ such that every satisfying assignment to φ captures a terminating execution of P.

8   Conclusion

We presented RECMC, a new SMT-based algorithm for model checking safety properties of recursive programs. For programs and properties over decidable theories, RECMC is guaranteed to find a counterexample if one exists. To our knowledge, this is the first SMT-based algorithm with such a guarantee while being polynomial for Boolean Programs. The key idea is to use a combination of under- and over-approximations of the semantics of procedures, avoiding re-exploration of parts of the state-space. We described an efficient instantiation of RECMC for Linear Arithmetic (over rationals and integers) by introducing *Model-Based Projection* to under-approximate the expensive quantifier elimination. We have implemented it in our tool SPACER and shown empirical evidence that it significantly improves on the state-of-the-art.

In the future, we would like to explore extensions to other theories. Of particular interest are the theory EUF of uninterpreted functions with equality and the theory of arrays. The challenge is to deal with the lack of quantifier elimination. Another direction of interest is to combine RECMC with *Proof-based Abstraction* [32,22,29] to explore a combination of the approximations of procedure semantics with transition-relation abstraction.

Acknowledgment. We thank Edmund M. Clarke and Nikolaj Bjørner for many helpful discussions. Our definition of MBP is based on the idea of projected implicants co-developed with Nikolaj. We thank Cesare Tinelli and the anonymous reviewers for insightful comments. This research was sponsored by the National Science Foundation grants no. DMS1068829, CNS0926181 and CNS0931985, the GSRC under contract no. 1041377, the Semiconductor Research Corporation under contract no. 2005TJ1366, the Office of Naval Research under award no. N000141010188 and the CMU-Portugal Program. This material is based upon work funded and supported by the Department of Defense under Contract No. FA8721-05-C-0003 with Carnegie Mellon University for the operation of the Software Engineering Institute, a federally funded research and development center. Any opinions, findings and conclusions or recommendations expressed in this material are those of the author(s) and do not necessarily reflect the views of the United States Department of Defense. This material has been approved for public release and unlimited distribution. DM-0000973.

References

1. Albarghouthi, A., Gurfinkel, A., Chechik, M.: From Under-Approximations to Over-Approximations and Back. In: Flanagan, C., König, B. (eds.) TACAS 2012. LNCS, vol. 7214, pp. 157–172. Springer, Heidelberg (2012)
2. Albarghouthi, A., Gurfinkel, A., Chechik, M.: WHALE: An Interpolation-Based Algorithm for Inter-procedural Verification. In: Kuncak, V., Rybalchenko, A. (eds.) VMCAI 2012. LNCS, vol. 7148, pp. 39–55. Springer, Heidelberg (2012)
3. Albarghouthi, A., Gurfinkel, A., Li, Y., Chaki, S., Chechik, M.: UFO: Verification with Interpolants and Abstract Interpretation. In: Piterman, N., Smolka, S.A. (eds.) TACAS 2013 (ETAPS 2013). LNCS, vol. 7795, pp. 637–640. Springer, Heidelberg (2013)
4. Alur, R., Benedikt, M., Etessami, K., Godefroid, P., Reps, T., Yannakakis, M.: Analysis of Recursive State Machines. TOPLAS 27(4), 786–818 (2005)
5. Ball, T., Majumdar, R., Millstein, T., Rajamani, S.K.: Automatic Predicate Abstraction of C Programs. SIGPLAN Not. 36(5), 203–213 (2001)
6. Ball, T., Rajamani, S.K.: Bebop: A Symbolic Model Checker for Boolean Programs. In: Havelund, K., Penix, J., Visser, W. (eds.) SPIN 2000. LNCS, vol. 1885, pp. 113–130. Springer, Heidelberg (2000)

7. Barnett, M., Chang, B.-Y.E., DeLine, R., Jacobs, B., Leino, K.R.M.: Boogie: A Modular Reusable Verifier for Object-Oriented Programs. In: de Boer, F.S., Bonsangue, M.M., Graf, S., de Roever, W.-P. (eds.) FMCO 2005. LNCS, vol. 4111, pp. 364–387. Springer, Heidelberg (2006)
8. Biere, A., Cimatti, A., Clarke, E.M., Strichman, O., Zhu, Y.: Bounded Model Checking. Advances in Computers 58, 117–148 (2003)
9. Bradley, A.R.: SAT-Based Model Checking without Unrolling. In: Jhala, R., Schmidt, D. (eds.) VMCAI 2011. LNCS, vol. 6538, pp. 70–87. Springer, Heidelberg (2011)
10. Chaki, S., Clarke, E.M., Groce, A., Jha, S., Veith, H.: Modular Verification of Software Components in C. IEEE Trans. Software Eng. 30(6), 388–402 (2004)
11. Clarke, E.M.: Program Invariants as Fixed Points. Computing 21(4), 273–294 (1979)
12. Clarke, E.M.: Programming Language Constructs for Which It Is Impossible To Obtain Good Hoare Axiom Systems. JACM 26(1), 129–147 (1979)
13. Clarke, E.M., Grumberg, O., Jha, S., Lu, Y., Veith, H.: Counterexample-Guided Abstraction Refinement. In: CAV (2000)
14. Clarke, E., Kroning, D., Lerda, F.: A Tool for Checking ANSI-C Programs. In: Jensen, K., Podelski, A. (eds.) TACAS 2004. LNCS, vol. 2988, pp. 168–176. Springer, Heidelberg (2004)
15. Cooper, D.C.: Theorem Proving in Arithmetic without Multiplication. In: Machine Intelligence, pp. 91–100 (1972)
16. Craig, W.: Three uses of the Herbrand-Gentzen theorem in relating model theory and proof theory. Symbolic Logic 22(3), 269–285 (1957)
17. de Moura, L., Bjørner, N.: Z3: An Efficient SMT Solver. In: Ramakrishnan, C.R., Rehof, J. (eds.) TACAS 2008. LNCS, vol. 4963, pp. 337–340. Springer, Heidelberg (2008)
18. de Moura, L., Bjørner, N.S.: Z3: An Efficient SMT Solver. In: Ramakrishnan, C.R., Rehof, J. (eds.) TACAS 2008. LNCS, vol. 4963, pp. 337–340. Springer, Heidelberg (2008)
19. Esparza, J., Hansel, D., Rossmanith, P., Schwoon, S.: Efficient Algorithms for Model Checking Pushdown Systems. In: Emerson, E.A., Sistla, A.P. (eds.) CAV 2000. LNCS, vol. 1855, pp. 232–247. Springer, Heidelberg (2000)
20. Godefroid, P., Nori, A.V., Rajamani, S.K., Tetali, S.: Compositional May-Must Program Analysis: Unleashing the Power of Alternation. In: POPL, pp. 43–56 (2010)
21. Grebenshchikov, S., Lopes, N.P., Popeea, C., Rybalchenko, A.: Synthesizing Software Verifiers from Proof Rules. In: PLDI, pp. 405–416 (2012)
22. Gupta, A., Ganai, M.K., Yang, Z., Ashar, P.: Iterative Abstraction using SAT-based BMC with Proof Analysis. In: ICCAD, pp. 416–423 (2003)
23. Gurfinkel, A., Wei, O., Chechik, M.: Model checking recursive programs with exact predicate abstraction. In: Cha, S(S.), Choi, J.-Y., Kim, M., Lee, I., Viswanathan, M. (eds.) ATVA 2008. LNCS, vol. 5311, pp. 95–110. Springer, Heidelberg (2008)
24. Heizmann, M., Christ, J., Dietsch, D., Ermis, E., Hoenicke, J., Lindenmann, M., Nutz, A., Schilling, C., Podelski, A.: Ultimate Automizer with SMTInterpol. In: Piterman, N., Smolka, S.A. (eds.) TACAS 2013 (ETAPS 2013). LNCS, vol. 7795, pp. 641–643. Springer, Heidelberg (2013)
25. Heizmann, M., Hoenicke, J., Podelski, A.: Nested Interpolants. SIGPLAN Not. 45(1), 471–482 (2010)
26. Henzinger, T.A., Jhala, R., Majumdar, R., Sutre, G.: Lazy abstraction. In: Proc. of POPL, pp. 58–70 (2002)

27. Hoder, K., Bjørner, N.: Generalized Property Directed Reachability. In: Cimatti, A., Sebastiani, R. (eds.) SAT 2012. LNCS, vol. 7317, pp. 157–171. Springer, Heidelberg (2012)
28. Komuravelli, A., Gurfinkel, A., Chaki, S.: SMT-based Model Checking for Recursive Programs. CoRR, abs/1405.4028 (2014)
29. Komuravelli, A., Gurfinkel, A., Chaki, S., Clarke, E.M.: Automatic Abstraction in SMT-Based Unbounded Software Model Checking. In: Sharygina, N., Veith, H. (eds.) CAV 2013. LNCS, vol. 8044, pp. 846–862. Springer, Heidelberg (2013)
30. Lal, A., Qadeer, S., Lahiri, S.K.: A solver for reachability modulo theories. In: Madhusudan, P., Seshia, S.A. (eds.) CAV 2012. LNCS, vol. 7358, pp. 427–443. Springer, Heidelberg (2012)
31. Loos, R., Weispfenning, V.: Applying Linear Quantifier Elimination. Computing 36(5), 450–462 (1993)
32. McMillan, K.L., Amla, N.: Automatic Abstraction without Counterexamples. In: Garavel, H., Hatcliff, J. (eds.) TACAS 2003. LNCS, vol. 2619, pp. 2–17. Springer, Heidelberg (2003)
33. McMillan, K.L., Rybalchenko, A.: Solving Constrained Horn Clauses using Interpolation. Technical Report MSR-TR-2013-6, Microsoft Research (2013)
34. Nieuwenhuis, R., Oliveras, A., Tinelli, C.: Solving SAT and SAT Modulo Theories: From an abstract Davis–Putnam–Logemann–Loveland procedure to DPLL(T). J. ACM 53(6), 937–977 (2006)
35. Nipkow, T.: Linear Quantifier Elimination. J. Autom. Reason. 45(2), 189–212 (2010)
36. Reps, T.W., Horwitz, S., Sagiv, S.: Precise Interprocedural Dataflow Analysis via Graph Reachability. In: POPL, pp. 49–61 (1995)
37. Sharir, M., Pnueli, A.: Two Approaches to Interprocedural Data Flow Analysis. In: Program Flow Analysis: Theory and Applications, pp. 189–233. Prentice-Hall (1981)
38. Software Verification Competition. TACAS (2014), http://sv-comp.sosy-lab.org

Property-Directed Shape Analysis

Shachar Itzhaky[1], Nikolaj Bjørner[2], Thomas Reps[3,4],
Mooly Sagiv[1], and Aditya Thakur[3]

[1] Tel Aviv University, Tel Aviv, Israel
[2] Microsoft Research, USA
[3] University of Wisconsin–Madison, USA
[4] GrammaTech, Inc., USA

Abstract. This paper addresses the problem of automatically generating quantified invariants for programs that manipulate singly and doubly linked-list data structures. Our algorithm is *property-directed*—i.e., its choices are driven by the properties to be proven. The algorithm is able to establish that a correct program has no memory-safety violations—e.g., null-pointer dereferences, double frees—and that data-structure invariants are preserved. For programs with errors, the algorithm produces concrete counterexamples.

More broadly, the paper describes how to integrate IC3 with full predicate abstraction. The analysis method is complete in the following sense: if an inductive invariant that proves that the program satisfies a given property is expressible as a Boolean combination of a given set of predicates, then the analysis will find such an invariant. To the best of our knowledge, this method represents the first shape-analysis algorithm that is capable of (i) reporting concrete counterexamples, or alternatively (ii) establishing that the predicates in use are not capable of proving the property in question.

1 Introduction

The goal of our work is to automatically generate quantified invariants for programs that manipulate singly-linked and doubly-linked list data structures. For a correct program, the invariant generated ensures that the program has no memory-safety violations, such as null-pointer dereferences, and that data-structure invariants are preserved. For a program in which it is possible to have a memory-safety violation or for a data-structure invariant to be violated, the algorithm produces a concrete counterexample. Although in this paper we mainly discuss memory-safety properties and data-structure invariants, the technique can be easily extended to other correctness properties (see §5).

To the best of our knowledge, our method represents the first shape-analysis algorithm that is capable of (i) reporting concrete counterexamples, or alternatively (ii) establishing that the abstraction in use is not capable of proving the property in question. This result is achieved by combining several existing ideas in a new way:

- The algorithm uses a predicate-abstraction domain [12] in which quantified predicates express properties of singly and doubly linked lists. In contrast to most recent work, which uses restricted forms of predicate abstraction—such as Cartesian abstraction [1]—our algorithm uses full predicate abstraction (i.e., the abstraction uses arbitrary Boolean combinations of predicates).

A. Biere and R. Bloem (Eds.): CAV 2014, LNCS 8559, pp. 35–51, 2014.
© Springer International Publishing Switzerland 2014

- The abstraction predicates and language semantics are expressed in recently developed *reachability logics*, AF^R and EA^R, respectively, which are decidable using a reduction to SAT [17].
- The algorithm is property-directed—i.e., its choices are driven by the memory-safety properties to be proven. In particular, the algorithm is based on IC3 [3], which we here refer to as *property-directed reachability* (PDR).

PDR integrates well with full predicate abstraction: in effect, the analysis obtains the same precision as the best abstract transformer for full predicate abstraction, without ever constructing the transformers explicitly. In particular, we cast PDR as a *framework* that is parameterized on

- the logic $\mathcal{L}$ in which the semantics of program statements are expressed, and
- the finite set of predicates that define the abstract domain $\mathcal{A}$ in which invariants can be expressed. An element of $\mathcal{A}$ is an arbitrary Boolean combination of the predicates.

Furthermore, our PDR framework is *relatively complete with respect to the given abstraction*. That is, the analysis is guaranteed to terminate and either (i) verifies the given property, (ii) generates a concrete counterexample to the given property, or (iii) reports that the abstract domain is not expressive enough to establish the proof. Outcome (ii) is possible because the "frame" structure maintained during PDR can be used to build a trace formula; if the formula is satisfiable, the model can be presented to the user as a concrete counterexample. Moreover, if the analysis fails to prove the property or find a concrete counterexample (outcome (iii)), then there is no way to express an inductive invariant that establishes the property in question using a Boolean combination of the abstraction predicates. Note that outcome (iii) is a much stronger guarantee than what other approaches provide in such cases when they neither succeed nor give a concrete counterexample.

Key to instantiating the PDR framework for shape analysis was a recent development of the AF^R and EA^R logics for expressing properties of linked lists [17]. AF^R is used to define abstraction predicates, and EA^R is used to express the language semantics. AF^R is a decidable, alternation-free fragment of first-order logic with transitive closure (FO^{TC}). When applied to list-manipulation programs, atomic formulas of AF^R can denote reachability relations between memory locations pointed to by pointer variables, where reachability corresponds to repeated dereferences of *next* or *prev* fields. One advantage of AF^R is that it does not require any special-purpose reasoning machinery: an AF^R formula can be converted to a formula in "effectively propositional" logic, which can be reduced to SAT solving. That is, in contrast to much previous work on shape analysis, our method makes use of *a general purpose SMT solver*, Z3 [5] (rather than specialized tools developed for reasoning about linked data structures, e.g., [25,6,2,11]).

The main restriction in AF^R is that it allows the use of a relation symbol f^* that denotes the transitive closure of a function symbol f, but only limited use of f itself. Although this restriction can be somewhat awkward, it is mainly a concern for the analysis designer (and the details have already been worked out in [17]). As a language

Table 1. Predicates for expressing various properties of linked lists whose elements hold data values. x and y denote program variables that point to list elements or null. f and b are parameters that denote pointer fields. (The mnemonics are referred to in Table 6.).

Name	Description	Mnemonic
$x = y$	equality	
$x\langle f\rangle y$	$x\text{->}f = y$	
$x\langle f^*\rangle y$	an f path from x to y	
$f.ls\,[x, y]$	unshared f linked-list segment between x and y	
$alloc(x)$	x points to an allocated element	St
$f.stable(h)$	any f-path from h leads to an allocated element	St
$f/b.rev\,[x, y]$	reversed f/b linked-list segment between x and y	R
$f.sorted\,[x, y]$	sorted f list segment between x and y	S

for expressing invariants, AF^R provides a fairly natural abstraction, which means that analysis *results* should be understandable by non-experts (see §2).[1]

Our work represents the first algorithm for shape analysis that either (i) succeeds, (ii) returns a concrete counterexample, or (iii) returns an abstract trace showing that the abstraction in use is not capable of proving the property in question. The specific contributions of our work include

- A framework, based on the PDR algorithm, for finding an inductive invariant in a certain logic fragment (abstract domain) that allows one to prove that a given pre-/post-condition holds or find a concrete counter-example to the property, or, in the case of a negative result, the information that there is no inductive invariant expressible in the abstract domain (§3).
- An instantiation of the framework for finding invariants of programs that manipulate singly-linked or doubly-linked lists. This instantiation uses AF^R to define a simple predicate-abstraction domain, and is the first application of PDR to establish quantified invariants of programs that manipulate linked lists (§4).
- An empirical evaluation showing the efficacy of the PDR framework for a set of linked-list programs (§5).

2   A Motivating Example

To illustrate the analysis, we use the procedure insert, shown in Fig. 1, that inserts a new element pointed to by e into the non-empty, singly-linked list pointed to by h. insert is annotated with a pre-condition and a post-condition.

Table 1 shows a set of predicates for expressing properties of linked lists whose elements hold data values. The predicates above the horizontal line in Table 1 are inspired by earlier work on shape analysis [13] and separation logic [24].

Given an input procedure, optionally annotated with a pre-condition *Pre* and post-condition *Post* (expressed as formulas over the same vocabulary of predicates); the goal

---

[1] By a "non-expert", we mean someone who has no knowledge of either the analysis algorithm, or the abstraction techniques used inside the algorithm.

```
void insert(List e, List h, List x) {
  Requires: h ≠ null ∧ h⟨n⁺⟩x ∧ x⟨n*⟩null ∧ e ≠ null ∧ e⟨n⟩null ∧ ¬h⟨n*⟩e
  Ensures: h ≠ null ∧ h⟨n*⟩e ∧ e⟨n⟩x ∧ x⟨n*⟩null
  p = h;
  q = null;
  while (p != x && p != null) {
    q = p;
    p = p->n;
  }
  q->n = e;
  e->n = p;
}
```

Fig. 1. A procedure to insert the element pointed to by e into the non-empty, singly-linked list pointed by h

of the analysis is to compute an invariant for the head of each loop[2] expressed as a CNF formula over the predicates given in Table 1 (and their negations).

The task is not trivial because (i) a loop invariant may be more complex than a program's pre-condition or post-condition, and (ii) it is infeasible to enumerate all the potential invariants expressible as CNF formulas over the predicates shown in Table 1. For instance, there are 6 variables in insert (including null), and hence $2^{6 \times 6 \times 6}$ clauses can be created from the 36 possible instantiations of each of the 6 binary predicates in Table 1. Therefore, the number of candidate invariants that can be formulated with these predicates is more than $2^{2^{6 \times 6 \times 6}}$. It would be infeasible to investigate them all explicitly.

Our analysis algorithm is based on *property-directed reachability* [3]. It starts with the trivial invariant **true**, which is repeatedly refined until it becomes inductive.[3] On each iteration, a concrete counterexample to inductiveness is used to refine the invariant by excluding predicates that are implied by that counterexample.

When applied to the procedure in Fig. 1, our analysis algorithm terminated in about 24 seconds, and inferred the following 13-clause loop invariant:

$$
\begin{aligned}
& q \neq e && \wedge\, (h\langle n^*\rangle x \wedge p = x \to h\langle n^*\rangle q) && \wedge\, (p = x \to q\langle n\rangle p) \\
& \wedge\, (\neg e\langle n\rangle e) \wedge (q\langle n^*\rangle p \to q\langle n\rangle p) && && \wedge\, (h\langle n^*\rangle p \vee p = \text{null}) \\
& \wedge\, (e\langle n\rangle\text{null}) \wedge (x = \text{null} \vee p\langle n^*\rangle x) && && \wedge\, (q \neq x \vee p \neq \text{null}) \quad (1) \\
& \wedge\, \neg h\langle n^*\rangle e \wedge (p = \text{null} \to h\langle n^*\rangle q) && && \wedge\, (p = q \vee q\langle n\rangle p) \\
& && \wedge\, (h\langle n^*\rangle q \wedge h\langle n^*\rangle x \to h\langle n\rangle q \vee q\langle n^*\rangle x)
\end{aligned}
$$

This loop invariant also guarantees that the code is memory safe. It is also possible to apply the analysis to infer sufficient conditions for memory safety using true post-conditions.

Our analysis is also capable of finding concrete counterexamples when the procedure violates the specification. For example, when the conjunct "$x \neq h$" is added to

---

[2] The current implementation supports procedures with only a single loop; however, this restriction is not an essential limitation of our technique.

[3] An invariant I is inductive at the entry to a loop if whenever the code of the loop body is executed on an arbitrary state that satisfies both I and the loop condition, the result is a state that satisfies I.

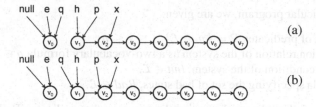

(a)

(b)

Fig. 2. A two-state counterexample trace obtained from the algorithm when it is applied to a version of Fig. 1 in which the conjunct $x \neq h$ was added to the precondition and $e \neq \texttt{null}$ was removed. (a) First state at the loop head; (b) second state at the loop head, at which point the loop exits, and a null-dereference violation subsequently occurs.

Algorithm 1: PDR$_\mathcal{A}$($Init, \rho, Bad$)	**Algorithm 2:** reduce$_\mathcal{A}$(j, A)
1 $R[-1] :=$ **false**	1 $(r, A_1) := Check_\mathcal{A}(Init, A)$
2 $R[0] :=$ **true**	2 **if** $r =$ sat **then**
3 $N := 0$	3 $\sigma := \texttt{Model}(Init \wedge \rho^{N-j} \wedge (Bad)^{j \times (N-j)})$
4 **while true do**	4 **if** σ is None **then error** "abstraction failure"
5 **if there exists** $0 \leq i < N$	5 **else error** "concrete counterexample(σ)"
such that $R[i] = R[i+1]$	6 **while** true **do**
then	7 $(r, A_2) :=$
6 **return valid**	8 $Check_\mathcal{A}((Init)' \vee (R[j-1] \wedge \rho), (A)')$
7 $(r, A) := Check_\mathcal{A}(Bad, R[N])$	9 **if** $r =$ unsat **then break**
8 **if** $r =$ unsat **then**	10 **else** reduce$_\mathcal{A}$($j - 1, A_2$)
9 $N := N + 1$	11 **for** $i = 0 \ldots j$ **do**
10 $R[N] :=$ **true**	12 $R[i] := R[i] \wedge (\neg A_1 \vee \neg A_2)$
11 **else**	
12 reduce$_\mathcal{A}$(N, A)	

the precondition in Fig. 1 and "$e \neq \texttt{null}$" is removed, the algorithm returns the counterexample trace shown in Fig. 2. Not surprisingly, e is $\texttt{null}$ in the first state at the loop head (Fig. 1(a)). The loop body executes once, at which point we reach the loop head in the state shown in Fig. 1(b). The loop then exits, and there is a null-dereference violation on e in the statement $\texttt{e->next = p}$.

3   Property-Directed Reachability

In this section, we present an adaptation of the IC3 algorithm that uses predicate abstraction. In this paper, by *predicate abstraction* we mean the technique that performs verification using a given *fixed* set of abstraction predicates [9], and not techniques that incorporate automatic refinement of the abstraction predicates; e.g. CEGAR. The PDR algorithm shown in Alg. 1 is parameterized by a given finite set of predicates $\mathcal{P}$ expressed in a logic $\mathcal{L}$. The requirements on the logic $\mathcal{L}$ are:

R1 $\mathcal{L}$ is decidable (for satisfiability).
R2 The transition relation for each statement of the programming language can be
     expressed as a two-vocabulary $\mathcal{L}$ formula.

Then for a particular program, we are given:

- A finite set of predicates $\mathcal{P} = \{p_i \in \mathcal{L}\}, 1 \leq i \leq n$.
- The transition relation of the system as a two-vocabulary formula $\rho \in \mathcal{L}$.
- The initial condition of the system, $Init \in \mathcal{L}$.
- The formula specifying the set of bad states, $Bad \in \mathcal{L}$.

Let $\mathcal{A}$ be the full predicate abstraction domain over the predicates $\mathcal{P}$. That is, each element $A \in \mathcal{A}$ is an *arbitrary* Boolean combination of the predicates $\mathcal{P}$. $A \in \mathcal{A}$ is inductive with respect to $Init$ and ρ if and only if $Init \to A$ and $A \wedge \rho \to (A)'$. $(\varphi)'$ renames the vocabulary of constant symbols and relation symbols occurring in φ from $\{c, \ldots, r, \ldots\}$ to $\{c', \ldots, r', \ldots\}$. φ is $(\varphi)'$ stripped of primes.

If the logic $\mathcal{L}$ is propositional logic, then Alg. 1 is an instance of IC3 [3]. Our presentation is a simplification of more advanced variants [3,7,14]. For instance, the presentation omits inductive generalization, although our implementation does implement inductive generalization (see §5). Furthermore, this simplified presentation brings out the fact that the PDR algorithm is really an analysis *framework* that is parameterized on the set of abstraction predicates $\mathcal{P}$.

The algorithm employs an unbounded array R, where each *frame* $R[i] \in \mathcal{A}$ over-approximates the set of concrete states after executing the loop at most i times. The algorithm maintains an integer N, called the *frame counter*, such that the following invariants hold for all $0 \leq i < N$:

1. $Init$ is a subset of all $R[i]$, i.e., $Init \to R[i]$.
2. The safety requirements are satisfied, i.e., $R[i] \to \neg Bad$.
3. Each of the $R[i + 1]$ includes the states in $R[i]$, i.e., $R[i] \to R[i + 1]$.
4. The successors of $R[i]$ are included in $R[i + 1]$, i.e., for all σ, σ' if $\sigma \models R[i]$ and $\langle \sigma, \sigma' \rangle \models \rho$, then $\sigma' \models R[i + 1]$.

We illustrate the workings of the algorithm using a simple example, after which we explain the algorithm in detail.

Example 1. Consider the program while (x != y) x = x.n; with precondition $Init \stackrel{\text{def}}{=} y \neq \text{null} \wedge x \langle n^+ \rangle y$. We wish to prove absence of null-dereference; that is, $Bad \stackrel{\text{def}}{=} x \neq y \wedge x = \text{null}$.

Table 2 shows a trace of PDR running with this input; each line represents a SAT query carried out by PDR$_\mathcal{A}$ (line 7) or by reduce$_\mathcal{A}$ (line 8). At each stage, if the result (r) is "unsat", then either we unfold one more loop iteration ($N := N + 1$) or we learn a new clause to add to $R[j]$ of the previous step, as marked by the "↗" symbol. If the result is "sat", the resulting model is used to further refine an earlier clause by recursively calling reduce$_\mathcal{A}$.

On the first row, we start with $R[0] = \textbf{true}$, so definitely $R[0] \wedge Bad$ is satisfiable, for example with a model where $x = y = \text{null}$. The algorithm checks if this model represents a reachable state at iteration 0 (see the second row), and indeed it is not—the result is "unsat" and the unsat-core is $y = \text{null}$ ($Init \wedge y = \text{null}$ is not satisfiable). Therefore, we infer the negation, $y \neq \text{null}$, and add that to $R[0]$. The algorithm progresses in the same manner—e.g., after two more lines, $R[0] = (y \neq \text{null} \wedge x \neq \text{null})$, and so on. Eventually, the loop terminates when $R[i] = R[i + 1]$ for some i; in this example, the algorithm

Table 2. Example run with $Init \overset{\text{def}}{=} y \neq \text{null} \wedge x\langle n^+\rangle y$, $Bad \overset{\text{def}}{=} x \neq y \wedge x = \text{null}$, and $\rho \overset{\text{def}}{=} (x' = n(x))$. The output invariant is $I := x\langle n^*\rangle y$.

j	Formula	Model	$A := \beta_A(Model)$	Inferred
0	$R[0] \wedge Bad$	$(\text{null}, 1)\ 1 \mapsto \text{null}$	$A := x = \text{null} \wedge x \neq y \wedge \neg x\langle n^*\rangle y \wedge y\langle n^*\rangle x$	$x \neq \text{null}$
-1	$((Init)' \vee (R[-1] \wedge \rho)) \wedge (A)'$	unsat		↗
0	$R[0] \wedge Bad$	unsat		
1	$R[1] \wedge Bad$	$(\text{null}, 1)\ 1 \mapsto \text{null}$	$A := x = \text{null} \wedge x \neq y \wedge \neg x\langle n^*\rangle y \wedge y\langle n^*\rangle x$	–
0	$((Init)' \vee (R[0] \wedge \rho)) \wedge (A)'$	$(1,1)\ 1 \mapsto \text{null}$	$A := x = y \neq \text{null} \wedge x\langle n^*\rangle y \wedge y\langle n^*\rangle x$	$x \neq y$
-1	$((Init)' \vee (R[-1] \wedge \rho)) \wedge (A)'$	unsat		↗
1	$R[1] \wedge Bad$	$(\text{null}, 1)\ 1 \mapsto \text{null}$	$A := x = \text{null} \wedge x \neq y \wedge \neg x\langle n^*\rangle y \wedge y\langle n^*\rangle x$	–
0	$((Init)' \vee (R[0] \wedge \rho)) \wedge (A)'$	$(1,2)\ 1, 2 \mapsto \text{null}$	$A := x \neq y \wedge x, y \neq \text{null} \wedge \neg x\langle n^*\rangle y \wedge \neg y\langle n^*\rangle x$	$x\langle n^*\rangle y$
-1	$((Init)' \vee (R[-1] \wedge \rho)) \wedge (A)'$	unsat		↗
1	$R[1] \wedge Bad$	$(\text{null}, 1)\ 1 \mapsto \text{null}$	$A := x = \text{null} \wedge x \neq y \wedge \neg x\langle n^*\rangle y \wedge y\langle n^*\rangle x$	$x\langle n^*\rangle y$
0	$((Init)' \vee (R[0] \wedge \rho)) \wedge (A)'$	unsat		↗
1	$R[1] \wedge Bad$	unsat		
2	$R[2] \wedge Bad$	$(\text{null}, 1)\ 1 \mapsto \text{null}$	$A := x = \text{null} \wedge x \neq y \wedge \neg x\langle n^*\rangle y \wedge y\langle n^*\rangle x$	$x\langle n^*\rangle y$
1	$((Init)' \vee (R[1] \wedge \rho)) \wedge (A)'$	unsat		↗
	$R[1] = R[2]$	valid		

terminates because $R[1] = R[2]$. The resulting invariant is $R[2] \equiv (y \neq \text{null} \wedge x\langle n^*\rangle y)$, a slight generalization of Pre in this case.   □

Some terminology used in the PDR algorithm:

- $\text{Model}(\varphi)$ returns a model σ satisfying φ if it exists, and **None** if it doesn't.
- The abstraction of a model σ, denoted by $\beta_A(\sigma)$, is the cube of predicates from $\mathcal{P}$ that hold in σ: $\beta_A(\sigma) = \bigwedge\{p \mid \sigma \models p, p \in \mathcal{P}\} \wedge \bigwedge\{\neg q \mid \sigma \models \neg q, q \in \mathcal{P}\}$.
- Let $\varphi \in \mathcal{L}$ is a formula in the unprimed vocabulary, $A \in \mathcal{A}$ is a value in the unprimed or primed vocabulary. $Check_A(\varphi, A)$ returns a pair (r, A_1) such that
  - if $\varphi \wedge A$ is satisfiable, then $r = \text{sat}$ and A_1 is the abstraction of a concrete state in the unprimed vocabulary. That is, if the given A is in the unprimed vocabulary, then $\beta_A(\sigma)$ for some $\sigma \models \varphi \wedge A$; else if A is in the primed vocabulary, then $A_1 = \beta_A(\sigma)$ for some $(\sigma, \sigma') \models \varphi \wedge A$.
  - if $\varphi \wedge A$ is unsatisfiable, then $r = \text{unsat}$, and A_1 is a predicate such that $A \rightarrow A_1$ and $\varphi \wedge A_1$ is unsatisfiable. The vocabulary of A_1 is the same as that of A. If A is in the primed vocabulary (as in line 8 of Alg. 2), $Check_A$ drops the primes from A_1 before returning the value.
  A valid choice for A_1 in the unsatisfiable case would be $A_1 = A$ (and indeed the algorithm would still be correct), but ideally A_1 should be the weakest such predicate. For instance, $Check_A(\text{false}, A)$ should return $(\text{unsat}, \text{true})$. In practice, when $\varphi \wedge A$ is unsatisfiable, the A_1 returned is an unsat core of $\varphi \wedge A$ constructed exclusively from conjuncts of A. Such an unsat core is a Boolean combination of predicates in $\mathcal{P}$, and thus is an element of $\mathcal{A}$.

We now give a more detailed explanation of Alg. 1. Each $R[i]$, $i \geq 0$ is initialized to **true** (lines 2 and 10), and $R[-1]$ is **false**. N is initialized to 0 (line 3). At line 5, the algorithm checks whether $R[i] = R[i+1]$ for some $0 \leq i < N$. If true, then an inductive invariant proving unreachability of Bad has been found, and the algorithm returns **valid** (line 6).

At line 7, the algorithm checks whether $R[N] \wedge Bad$ is satisfiable. If it is unsatisfiable, it means that $R[N]$ excludes the states described by Bad, and the frame counter N is incremented (line 9). Otherwise, $A \in \mathcal{A}$ represents an abstract state that satisfies $R[N] \wedge Bad$. PDR then attempts to reduce $R[N]$ to try and exclude this abstract counterexample by calling $reduce_{\mathcal{A}}(N, A)$ (line 12).

The reduce algorithm (Alg. 2) takes as input an integer $j, 0 \leq j \leq N$, and an abstract state $A \in \mathcal{A}$ such that there is a path starting from A of length $N - j$ that reaches Bad. Alg. 2 tries to strengthen $R[j]$ so as to exclude A. At line 1, reduce first checks whether $Init \wedge A$ is satisfiable. If it is satisfiable, then there is an abstract trace of length $N - j$ from $Init$ to Bad, using the transition relation ρ. The call to Model at line 3 checks whether there exists a concrete model corresponding to the abstract counterexample. ρ^k denotes k unfoldings of the transition relation ρ; ρ^0 is **true**. $(Bad)^{\prime \times k}$ denotes k applications of the renaming operation $(\cdot)'$ to Bad. If no such concrete model is found, then the abstraction was not precise enough to prove the required property (line 4); otherwise, a concrete counterexample to the property is returned (line 5).

Now consider the case when $Init \wedge A$ is unsatisfiable on line 1. $A_1 \in \mathcal{A}$ returned by the call to $Check_{\mathcal{A}}$ is such that $Init \wedge A_1$ is unsatisfiable; that is, $Init \to \neg A_1$.

The while-loop on lines 6–10 checks whether the $(N - j)$-length path to Bad can be extended backward to an $(N - j + 1)$-length path. In particular, it checks whether $R[j - 1] \wedge \rho \wedge (A)'$ is satisfiable. If it is satisfiable, then the algorithm calls reduce recursively on $j - 1$ and A_2 (line 10). If no such backward extension is possible, the algorithm exits the while loop (line 9). Note that if $j = 0$, $Check_{\mathcal{A}}(R[j - 1] \wedge \rho, A)$ returns (**unsat, true**), because $R[-1]$ is set to **false**.

The conjunction of $(\neg A_1 \vee \neg A_2)$ to $R[i], 0 \leq i \leq j$, in the loop on lines 11–12 eliminates abstract counterexample A while preserving the required invariants on R. In particular, the invariant $Init \to R[i]$ is maintained because $Init \to \neg A_1$, and hence $Init \to (R[i] \wedge (\neg A_1 \vee \neg A_2))$. Furthermore, A_2 is the abstract state from which there is a (spurious) path of length $N - j$ to Bad. By the properties of $Check_{\mathcal{A}}$, $\neg A_1$ and $\neg A_2$ are each disjoint from A, and hence $(\neg A_1 \vee \neg A_2)$ is also disjoint from A. Thus, conjoining $(\neg A_1 \vee \neg A_2)$ to $R[i], 0 \leq i \leq j$ eliminates the spurious abstract counterexample A. Lastly, the invariant $R[i] \to R[i + 1]$ is preserved because $(\neg A_1 \vee \neg A_2)$ is conjoined to all $R[i], 0 \leq i \leq j$, and not just $R[j]$.

Formally, the output of $PDR_{\mathcal{A}}(Init, \rho, Bad)$ is captured by the following theorem:

Theorem 1. *Given (i) the set of abstraction predicates* $\mathcal{P} = \{p_i \in \mathcal{L}\}, 1 \leq i \leq n$ *where* $\mathcal{L}$ *is a decidable logic, and the full predicate abstraction domain* $\mathcal{A}$ *over* $\mathcal{P}$, *(ii) the initial condition Init* $\in \mathcal{L}$, *(iii) a transition relation* ρ *expressed as a two-vocabulary formula in* $\mathcal{L}$, *and (iv) a formula Bad* $\in \mathcal{L}$ *specifying the set of bad states*, $PDR_{\mathcal{A}}(Init, \rho, Bad)$ *terminates, and reports either*

1. valid *if there exists* $A \in \mathcal{A}$ *s.t. (i) Init* $\to A$, *(ii) A is inductive, and (iii) A* $\to \neg Bad$,
2. *a concrete counterexample trace, which reaches a state satisfying Bad, or*
3. *an abstract trace, if the inductive invariant required to prove the property cannot be expressed as an element of* $\mathcal{A}$.   □

The proof of Theorem 1 in [18] is based on the observation that, when "abstraction failure" is reported by $reduce_{\mathcal{A}}(j, A)$, the set of models $\sigma_i \models R[i]$ $(j \leq i < N)$ represents an abstract error trace.

Inductive Generalization. Each $R[i]$ is a conjunction of clauses $\varphi_1 \wedge \cdots \wedge \varphi_m$. If we detect that some ψ_j comprising a subset of literals of φ_j, it holds that $R[i] \wedge \rho \wedge \psi_j \models (\psi_j)'$, then ψ_j is *inductive relative to* $R[i]$. In this case, it is safe to conjoin ψ_j to $R[k]$ for $k \leq i + 1$. Spurious counter-examples can also be purged if they are inductively blocked. The advantages of this method are explained thoroughly by Bradley [3].

4 Property-Directed Reachability for Linked-List Programs

In this section, we describe how $PDR_{\mathcal{A}}(Init, \rho, Bad)$ described in Alg. 1 can be instantiated for verifying linked-list programs. The key insight is the use of the recently developed reachability logics for expressing properties of linked lists [17].

4.1 Reachability Logics

We use two related logics for expressing properties of linked data structures:

- AF^R is a decidable fragment of first-order logic with transitive closure (FO^{TC}), which is an alternation-free quantified logic. This logic is used to express the abstraction predicates $\mathcal{P}$, and pre- and post-conditions. It is closed under negation, and decidable for both satisfiability and validity.
- EA^R allows there to be universal quantifiers inside of existential ones. It is used to define the transition formulas of statements that allocate new nodes and dereference pointers. This logic is not closed under negation, and is only decidable for satisfiability. We count on the fact that transition formulas are only used in a positive form in the satisfiability queries in Alg. 1.

Although AF^R is used as the language for defining the predicates in $\mathcal{P}$, the *wlp* rules go slightly outside of AF^R, producing EA^R formulas (see Table 5 below).

Definition 1. *(EA^R) A **term**, t, is a variable or constant symbol. An **atomic formula** is one of the following: (i) $t_1 = t_2$; (ii) $r(t_1, t_2, \ldots, t_a)$ where r is a relation symbol of arity a (iii) A **reachability constraint** $t_1 \langle f^* \rangle t_2$, where f is a function symbol. A **quantifier-free formula** (QF^R) is a boolean combination of atomic formulas. A **universal formula** begins with zero or more universal quantifiers followed by a quantifier-free formula. An **alternation-free formula** (AF^R) is a boolean combination of universal formulas. EA^R consists of formulas with quantifier-prefix $\exists^* \forall^*$.*
   In particular, $QF^R \subset AF^R \subset EA^R$. □

Technically, EA^R forbids *any* use of an individual function symbol f; however, when f defines an acyclic linkage chain—as in acyclic singly linked and doubly linked lists—f can be defined in terms of f^* by using universal quantification to express that an element is the closest in the chain to another element. This idea is formalized by showing that for all α and β, $f(\alpha) = \beta \leftrightarrow E_f(\alpha, \beta)$ where E_f is defined as follows:

$$E_f(\alpha, \beta) \stackrel{\text{def}}{=} \alpha \langle f^+ \rangle \beta \wedge \forall \gamma : \alpha \langle f^+ \rangle \gamma \rightarrow \beta \langle f^* \rangle \gamma, \tag{2}$$

where $\alpha \langle f^+ \rangle \beta \stackrel{\text{def}}{=} \alpha \langle f^* \rangle \beta \wedge \alpha \neq \beta$. However, because of the quantifier in Eqn. (2), the right-hand side of Eqn. (2) can only be used in a context that does not introduce a quantifier alternation (so that the formula remains in a decidable fragment of FO^{TC}).

Table 3. AF^R formulas for the derived predicates shown in Table 1. f and b denote pointer fields. dle is an uninterpreted predicate that denotes a total order on the data values. The intention is that $\mathrm{dle}(\alpha, \beta)$ holds whenever $\alpha\text{-}{>}d \leq \beta\text{-}{>}d$, where d is the data field. We assume that the semantics of dle are enforced by an appropriate total-order background theory.

Name	Formula
$x\langle f\rangle y$	$E_f(x, y)$
$f.ls\,[x, y]$	$\forall \alpha, \beta : x\langle f^*\rangle\alpha \wedge \alpha\langle f^*\rangle y \wedge \beta\langle f^*\rangle\alpha \to (\beta\langle f^*\rangle x \vee x\langle f^*\rangle\beta)$
$f.stable(h)$	$\forall \alpha : h\langle f^*\rangle\alpha \to alloc(\alpha)$
$f/b.rev\,[x, y]$	$\forall \alpha, \beta : \left(\begin{array}{c} \alpha \neq \texttt{null} \wedge \beta \neq \texttt{null} \\ \wedge\ x\langle f^*\rangle\alpha \wedge \alpha\langle f^*\rangle y \wedge x\langle f^*\rangle\beta \wedge \beta\langle f^*\rangle y \end{array} \right) \to (\alpha\langle f^*\rangle\beta \leftrightarrow \beta\langle b^*\rangle\alpha)$
$f.sorted\,[x, y]$	$\forall \alpha, \beta : \left(\begin{array}{c} \alpha \neq \texttt{null} \wedge \beta \neq \texttt{null} \\ \wedge\ x\langle f^*\rangle\alpha \wedge \alpha\langle f^*\rangle\beta \wedge \beta\langle f^*\rangle y \end{array} \right) \to \mathrm{dle}(\alpha, \beta)$

A Predicate Abstraction Domain that Uses AF^R. The abstraction predicates used for verifying properties of linked list programs were introduced informally in Table 1. Table 3 gives the corresponding formal definition of the predicates as AF^R formulas. Note that all four predicates defined in Table 3 are quantified. (The quantified formula for E_f is given in Eqn. (2).) In essence, we use a template-based approach for obtaining quantified invariants: the discovered invariants have a quantifier-free structure, but the atomic formulas can be quantified AF^R formulas.

We now show that the EA^R logic satisfies requirements R1 and R2 for the PDR algorithm stated in §3.

Decidability of EA^R. To satisfy requirement R1 stated in §3, we have to show that EA^R is decidable for satisfiability.

EA^R is decidable for satisfiability because any formula in this logic can be translated into the "effectively propositional" decidable logic of $\exists^*\forall^*$ formulas described by Piskac et al. [22]. EA^R includes relations of the form f^* (the reflexive transitive closure of a function symbol f), but only allows limited use of f itself.

Every EA^R formula can be translated into an $\exists^*\forall^*$ formula using the following steps [17]: (i) add a new uninterpreted relation R_f, which is intended to represent reflexive transitive reachability via f; (ii) add the consistency rule Γ_{linOrd} shown in Table 4, which asserts that R_f is a partial order, i.e., reflexive, transitive, acyclic, and linear;[4] and (iii) replace all occurrences of $t_1\langle f^*\rangle t_2$ by $R_f(t_1, t_2)$. (By means of this translation step, acyclicity is built into the logic.)

Proposition 1 (Simulation of EA^R). *Consider EA^R formula φ over vocabulary $\mathcal{V} = \langle \mathcal{C}, \mathcal{F}, \mathcal{R}\rangle$. Let $\varphi' \stackrel{\mathrm{def}}{=} \varphi[R_f(t_1, t_2)/t_1\langle f^*\rangle t_2]$. Then φ' is a first-order formula over vocabulary $\mathcal{V}' = \langle \mathcal{C}, \emptyset, \mathcal{R} \cup \{R_f : f \in \mathcal{F}\rangle$, and $\Gamma_{\mathrm{linOrd}} \wedge \varphi'$ is satisfiable if and only if the original formula φ is satisfiable.*

This proposition is the dual of [16, Proposition 3, Appendix A.1] for validity of $\forall^*\exists^*$ formulas.

---

[4] Note that the order is a partial order and not a total order, because not every pair of elements must be ordered.

Table 4. A universal formula, Γ_{linOrd}, which asserts that all points reachable from a given point are linearly ordered

$\forall \alpha : R_f(\alpha, \alpha)$	reflexivity
$\land\, \forall \alpha, \beta, \gamma : R_f(\alpha, \beta) \land R_f(\beta, \gamma) \to R_f(\alpha, \gamma)$	transitivity
$\land\, \forall \alpha, \beta : R_f(\alpha, \beta) \land R_f(\beta, \alpha) \to \alpha = \beta$	acyclicity
$\land\, \forall \alpha, \beta, \gamma : R_f(\alpha, \beta) \land R_f(\alpha, \gamma) \to (R_f(\beta, \gamma) \lor R_f(\gamma, \beta))$	linearity

Table 5. Rules for *wlp* for atomic commands. *alloc* stands for a memory location that has been allocated and not subsequently freed. $E_f(y, \alpha)$ is the universal formula defined in Eqn. (2). $Q[y/x]$ denotes Q with all occurrences of atomic formula x replaced by y.

Command C	$wlp(C, Q)$
assume φ	$\varphi \to Q$
x = y	$Q[y/x]$
x = y->f	$y \neq \texttt{null} \land \exists \alpha : (E_f(y, \alpha) \land Q[\alpha/x])$
x->f = null	$x \neq \texttt{null} \land Q[\alpha\langle f^*\rangle\beta \land (\neg\alpha\langle f^*\rangle x \lor \beta\langle f^*\rangle x)/\alpha\langle f^*\rangle\beta]$
x->f = y	$x \neq \texttt{null} \land Q[\alpha\langle f^*\rangle\beta \lor (\alpha\langle f^*\rangle x \land y\langle f^*\rangle\beta)/\alpha\langle f^*\rangle\beta]$
x = malloc()	$\exists\alpha : \neg alloc(\alpha) \land Q[(alloc(\beta) \lor (\beta = \alpha \land \beta = x))/alloc(\beta)]$
free(x)	$alloc(x) \land Q[(alloc(\beta) \land \beta \neq x)/alloc(\beta)]$

Axiomatic Specification of Concrete Semantics in EA^R. To satisfy requirement R2 stated in §3, we have to show that the transition relation for each statement *Cmd* of the programming language can be expressed as a two-vocabulary formula $\rho \in EA^R$. Let $wlp(Cmd, Q)$ be the weakest liberal precondition of command *Cmd* with respect $Q \in EA^R$. Then, the transition formula for command *Cmd* is $wlp(Cmd, Id)$, where *Id* is a two-vocabulary formula that specifies that the input and the output states are identical, i.e.,

$$Id \stackrel{\text{def}}{=} \bigwedge_{c \in C} c = c' \land \bigwedge_{f \in F} \forall \alpha, \beta : \alpha\langle f^*\rangle\beta \Leftrightarrow \alpha\langle f'^*\rangle\beta.$$

To show that the concrete semantics of linked list programs can be expressed in EA^R, we have to prove that EA^R is closed under *wlp*; that is, for all commands *Cmd* and $Q \in EA^R$, $wlp(Cmd, Q) \in EA^R$.

Table 5 shows rules for computing *wlp* for atomic commands. Note that pointer-related rules in Table 5 each include a memory-safety condition to detect null-dereferences. For instance, the rule for "x->f = y" includes the conjunct "$x \neq$ null"; if, in addition, we wish to detect accesses to unallocated memory, the rule would be extended with the conjunct "$alloc(x)$".

The following lemma establishes the soundness and completeness of the *wlp* rules.

Lemma 1. *Consider a command C of the form defined in Table 5 and postcondition Q. Then, $\sigma \models wlp(C, Q)$ if and only if the execution of C on σ can yield a state σ' such that $\sigma' \models Q$.*

This lemma is the dual of [16, Prop. 1, App. A.1] for validity of $\forall^*\exists^*$ formulas.

Weakest liberal preconditions of compound commands $C_1; C_2$ (sequencing) and $C_1 | C_2$ (nondeterministic choice) are defined in the standard way, i.e.,

Table 6. Experimental results. Column $\mathcal{A}$ signifies the set of predicates used (blank = only the top part of Table 1; S = with the addition of the *sorted* predicate family; R = with the addition of the *rev* family; St = with the addition of the *stable* family, where *alloc* conjuncts are added in *wlp* rules). Running time is measured in seconds. N denotes the highest index for a generated element $R[i]$. The number of clauses refers to the inferred loop invariant.

Benchmark		Memory-safety + data-structure integrity				Additional properties			
	$\mathcal{A}$	Time	N	# calls to Z3	# clauses	$\mathcal{A}$	Time	N	# calls to Z3	# clauses
create		1.37	3	28	3		8.19	4	96	7
delete		14.55	4	61	6		9.32	3	67	7
deleteAll	St	6.77	3	72	6	St	37.35	7	308	12
filter		2.37	3	27	4		55.53	5	94	5
insert		26.38	5	220	16		25.25	4	155	13
prev		0.21	2	3	0		11.64	4	118	6
last		0.33	2	3	0		7.49	3	41	4
reverse		5.35	5	128	4		146.42	6	723	11
sorted insert	S	41.07	3	48	7	S	51.46	4	134	10
sorted merge		26.69	4	87	10	S	256.41	5	140	14
make doubly-linked		18.91	3	44	5	R	1086.61	5	112	8

$$wlp(C_1; C_2, Q) \overset{\text{def}}{=} wlp(C_1, wlp(C_2, Q)) \qquad wlp(C_1 | C_2, Q) \overset{\text{def}}{=} wlp(C_1, Q) \wedge wlp(C_2, Q)$$

Consider a program with a single loop "while *Cond* do *Cmd*". Alg. 1 can be used to prove whether or not a precondition $Pre \in AF^R$ before the loop implies that a postcondition $Post \in AF^R$ holds after the loop, if the loop terminates: we supply Alg. 1 with $Init \overset{\text{def}}{=} Pre$, $\rho \overset{\text{def}}{=} Cond \wedge wlp(Cmd, Id)$ and $Bad \overset{\text{def}}{=} \neg Cond \wedge \neg Post$. Furthermore, memory safety can be enforced on the loop body by setting $Bad \overset{\text{def}}{=} (\neg Cond \wedge \neg Post) \vee (Cond \wedge \neg wlp(Cmd, \mathbf{true}))$.

5 Experiments

To evaluate the usefulness of the analysis algorithm, we applied it to a collection of sequential procedures that manipulate singly and doubly-linked lists (see Table 6). For each program, we report the predicates used, the time (in seconds), the number of PDR frames, the number of calls to Z3, and the size of the resulting inductive invariant, in terms of the number of clauses. All experiments were run on a 1.7GHz Intel Core i5 machine with 4GB of RAM, running OS X 10.7.5. We used version 4.3.2 of Z3 [5], compiled for a 64-bit Intel architecture (using gcc 4.2 and LLVM).

For each of the benchmarks, we verified that the program avoids null-dereferences, as well as that it preserves the data-structure invariant that the inputs and outputs are acyclic linked-lists. In addition, for some of the benchmarks we were also able to verify some additional correctness properties. While full functional correctness, or even partial correctness, is hard to achieve using predicate abstraction, we were able to use simple formulas to verify several interesting properties that go beyond memory-safety properties and data-structure invariants. Table 7 describes the properties we checked for the various examples. As seen from columns 3, 4, 8, and 9 of the entries for delete and insert in Table 6, trying to prove *stronger* properties can sometimes result in *fewer*

Table 7. Some correctness properties that can be verified by the analysis procedure. For each of the programs, we have defined suitable *Pre* snf *Post* formulas in AF^R.

Benchmark	Property checked
create	Some memory location pointed to by x (a global variable) that was allocated prior to the call, is not reachable from the list head, h.
delete	The argument x is no longer reachable from h.
deleteAll	An arbitrary non-null element x of the list becomes non-allocated.
filter	Two arbitrary elements x and y that satisfy the filtering criterion and have an n-path between them, maintain that path.
insert	The new element e is reachable from h and is the direct predecessor of the argument x.
last	The function returns the last element of the list.
prev	The function returns the element just before x, if one exists.
reverse	If x comes before y in the input, then x should come after y in the output.
sorted insert	The list rooted at h remains sorted.
make doubly-linked	The resulting p is the inverse of n within the list rooted at h.

Table 8. Results of experiments with buggy programs. Running time is measured in seconds. N denotes the highest index for a generated element $R[i]$. "C.e. size" denotes the largest number of individuals in a model in the counterexample trace.

Benchmark	Bug description	Automatic bug finding			
		Time	N	# calls to Z3	c.e. size
insert	Precondition is too weak (omitted $e \neq$ null)	4.46	1	17	8
filter	Potential null dereference	6.30	1	21	3
	Typo: list head used instead of list iterator	103.10	3	79	4
reverse	Corrupted data structure: a cycle is created	0.96	1	9	2

iterations being needed, resulting in a *shorter* running time. In the remainder of the examples, handling additional properties beyond memory-safety properties and data-structure invariants required more processing effort, which can be attributed mainly to the larger set of symbols (and hence predicates) in the computation.

Bug Finding. We also ran our analysis on programs containing deliberate bugs, to demonstrate the utility of this approach to bug finding. In all of the cases, the method was able to detect the bug and generate a concrete trace in which the safety or correctness properties are violated. The output in that case is a series of concrete states $\sigma_0..\sigma_N$ where each σ_i contains the set of heap locations, pointer references, and program variables at step i. The experiments and their results are shown in Table 8. We found both the length of the trace and the size of the heap structures to be very small. Their small size makes the traces useful to present to a human programmer, which can help in locating and fixing the bug.

Observations. It is worth noting that for programs where the proof of safety is trivial— because every access is guarded by an appropriate conditional check, such as in prev and last—the algorithm terminates almost immediately with the correct invariant true. This behavior is due to the property-directedness of the approach, in contrast with abstract interpretation, which always tries to find the least fixed point, regardless of the desired property.

We experimented with different refinements of inductive-generalization (§12). Our algorithm could in many cases succeed without it, but without the most basic version that just pushes each clause (without removing literals), we observed runs with up to $N = 40$ iterations. On the other hand, the more advanced versions of inductive generalization did not help us: trying to remove literals resulted in a large number of expensive (and useless) solver calls; and blocking spurious counter-examples using inductive generalization also turned out to be quite expensive in our setting.

We also noticed that the analysis procedure is sensitive to the number of abstraction predicates used. In particular, using predicates whose definitions involve quantifiers can affect the running time considerably. When the predicate families $f.sorted\ [x, y]$ and $f/b.rev\ [x, y]$ are added to $\mathcal{A}$, running times can increase substantially (about 20-60 times). This effect occurred even in the case of sorted merge, where we did not attempt to prove an additional correctness property beyond safety and integrity—and indeed there were no occurrences of the added predicates in the loop invariant obtained. As can be seen from Table 6, the PDR algorithm *per se* is well-behaved, in the sense that the number of calls to Z3 increased only modestly with the additional predicates. However, each call to Z3 took a lot more time.

6 Related Work

The literature on program analysis is vast, and the subject of shape analysis alone has an extensive literature. Thus, in this section we are only able to touch on a few pieces of prior work that relate to the ideas used in this paper.

Predicate Abstraction. Houdini [8] is the first algorithm of which we are aware that aims to identify a loop invariant, given a set of predicates as candidate ingredients. However, Houdini only infers *conjunctive* invariants from a given set of predicates. Santini [29,28] is a recent algorithm for discovering invariants expressed in terms of a set of candidate predicates. Like our algorithm, Santini is based on full predicate abstraction (i.e., it uses arbitrary Boolean combinations of a set of predicates), and thus is strictly more powerful than Houdini. Santini could make use of the predicates and abstract domain described in this paper; however, unlike our algorithm, Santini would not be able to report counterexamples when verification fails. Other work infers quantified invariants [27,15] but does not support the reporting of counterexamples. Templates are used in many tools to define the abstract domains used to represent sets of states, by fixing the form of the constraints permitted. Template Constraint Matrices [26] are based on inequalities in linear real arithmetic (i.e., polyhedra), but leave the linear coefficients as symbolic inputs to the analysis. The values of the coefficients are derived in the course of running the analysis. In comparison, a coefficient in our use of EA^R corresponds to one of the finitely many constants that appear in the program, and we instantiated our templates prior to using PDR.

As mentioned in §1, PDR meshes well with full predicate abstraction: in effect, the analysis obtains the benefit of the precision of the abstract transformers for full predicate abstraction, without ever constructing the abstract transformers explicitly. PDR also allows a predicate-abstraction-based tool to create concrete counterexamples when verification fails.

Abstractions Based on Linked-list Segments. In this paper, our abstract domain is based on formulas expressed in AF^R, which has very limited capabilities to express properties of stretches of data structures that are not pointed to by a program variable. This feature is similar to the self-imposed limitations on expressibility used in a number of past approaches, including (a) canonical abstraction [25]; (b) a prior method for applying predicate abstraction to linked lists [21]; (c) an abstraction method based on "must-paths" between nodes that are either pointed to by variables or are list-merge points [19]; and (d) domains based on separation logic's list-segment primitive [6,2] (i.e., "ls$[x, y]$" asserts the existence of a possibly empty list segment running from the node pointed to by x to the node pointed to by y). Decision procedures have been used in previous work to compute the best transformer for individual statements that manipulate linked lists [30,23].

STRAND and Elastic Quantified Data Automata. Recently, Garg et al. developed methods for obtaining quantified invariants for programs that manipulate linked lists via an abstract domain of *quantified data automata* [10,11]. To create an abstract domain with the right properties, they use a weakened form of automaton—so-called *elastic* quantified data automata—that is unable to observe the details of stretches of data structures that are not pointed to by a program variable. (Thus, an elastic automaton has some of the characteristics of the work based on linked-list segments described above.) An elastic automaton can be converted to a formula in the decidable fragment of STRAND over lists [20].

Other Work on IC3/PDR. Our work represents the first application of PDR to programs that manipulate dynamically allocated storage. We chose to use PDR because it has been shown to work extremely well in other domains, such as hardware verification [3,7]. Subsequently, it was generalized to software model checking for program models that use linear real arithmetic [14] and linear rational arithmetic [4]. Cimatti and Griggio [4] employ a quantifier-elimination procedure for linear rational arithmetic, based on an approximate pre-image operation. Our use of a predicate-abstraction domain allows us to obtain an approximate pre-image as the unsat core of a single call to an SMT solver (line 8 of Alg. 2).

7 Conclusion

Compared to past work on shape analysis, our approach (i) is based on full predicate abstraction, (ii) makes use of standard theorem proving techniques, (iii) is capable of reporting concrete counterexamples, and (iv) is based on property-directed reachability. The experimental evaluation in §5 illustrates these four advantages of our approach. The algorithm is able to establish memory-safety and preservation of data-structure invariants for all of the examples, using only the simple predicates given in Table 1. This result is surprising because earlier work on shape analysis that employed the same predicates [13] failed to prove these properties. One reason is that [13] only uses positive and negative combinations of these predicates, whereas our algorithm uses arbitrary Boolean combinations of predicates.

References

1. Ball, T., Podelski, A., Rajamani, S.K.: Boolean and cartesian abstraction for model checking C programs. In: Margaria, T., Yi, W. (eds.) TACAS 2001. LNCS, vol. 2031, pp. 268–283. Springer, Heidelberg (2001)
2. Berdine, J., Calcagno, C., Cook, B., Distefano, D., O'Hearn, P.W., Wies, T., Yang, H.: Shape analysis for composite data structures. In: Damm, W., Hermanns, H. (eds.) CAV 2007. LNCS, vol. 4590, pp. 178–192. Springer, Heidelberg (2007)
3. Bradley, A.R.: SAT-based model checking without unrolling. In: Jhala, R., Schmidt, D. (eds.) VMCAI 2011. LNCS, vol. 6538, pp. 70–87. Springer, Heidelberg (2011)
4. Cimatti, A., Griggio, A.: Software model checking via IC3. In: Madhusudan, P., Seshia, S.A. (eds.) CAV 2012. LNCS, vol. 7358, pp. 277–293. Springer, Heidelberg (2012)
5. de Moura, L., Bjørner, N.S.: Z3: An efficient SMT solver. In: Ramakrishnan, C.R., Rehof, J. (eds.) TACAS 2008. LNCS, vol. 4963, pp. 337–340. Springer, Heidelberg (2008)
6. Distefano, D., O'Hearn, P.W., Yang, H.: A local shape analysis based on separation logic. In: Hermanns, H., Palsberg, J. (eds.) TACAS 2006. LNCS, vol. 3920, pp. 287–302. Springer, Heidelberg (2006)
7. Eén, N., Mishchenko, A., Brayton, R.: Efficient implementation of property directed reachability. In: FMCAD (2011)
8. Flanagan, C., Leino, K.R.M.: Houdini, an annotation assistant for ESC/Java. In: Oliveira, J.N., Zave, P. (eds.) FME 2001. LNCS, vol. 2021, pp. 500–517. Springer, Heidelberg (2001)
9. Flanagan, C., Qadeer, S.: Predicate abstraction for software verification. In: POPL (2002)
10. Garg, P., Löding, C., Madhusudan, P., Neider, D.: Learning universally quantified invariants of linear data structures. In: Sharygina, N., Veith, H. (eds.) CAV 2013. LNCS, vol. 8044, pp. 813–829. Springer, Heidelberg (2013)
11. Garg, P., Madhusudan, P., Parlato, G.: Quantified data automata on skinny trees: An abstract domain for lists. In: Logozzo, F., Fähndrich, M. (eds.) SAS 2013. LNCS, vol. 7935, pp. 172–193. Springer, Heidelberg (2013)
12. Graf, S., Saïdi, H.: Construction of abstract state graphs with PVS. In: Grumberg, O. (ed.) CAV 1997. LNCS, vol. 1254, pp. 72–83. Springer, Heidelberg (1997)
13. Hendren, L.: Parallelizing Programs with Recursive Data Structures. PhD thesis, Cornell Univ., Ithaca, NY (January 1990)
14. Hoder, K., Bjørner, N.: Generalized property directed reachability. In: Cimatti, A., Sebastiani, R. (eds.) SAT 2012. LNCS, vol. 7317, pp. 157–171. Springer, Heidelberg (2012)
15. Hoder, K., Kovács, L., Voronkov, A.: Invariant generation in vampire. In: Abdulla, P.A., Leino, K.R.M. (eds.) TACAS 2011. LNCS, vol. 6605, pp. 60–64. Springer, Heidelberg (2011)
16. Itzhaky, S., Banerjee, A., Immerman, N., Nanevski, A., Sagiv, M.: Effectively-propositional reasoning about reachability in linked data structures. Technical report, IMDEA, Madrid, Spain (2011), http://software.imdea.org/~ab/Publications/cav2013tr.pdf
17. Itzhaky, S., Banerjee, A., Immerman, N., Nanevski, A., Sagiv, M.: Effectively-propositional reasoning about reachability in linked data structures. In: Sharygina, N., Veith, H. (eds.) CAV 2013. LNCS, vol. 8044, pp. 756–772. Springer, Heidelberg (2013)
18. Itzhaky, S., Bjørner, N., Reps, T., Sagiv, M., Thakur, A.: Property-directed shape analysis. TR 1807, Comp. Sci. Dept., Univ. of Wisconsin, Madison, WI (May 2014)
19. Lev-Ami, T., Immerman, N., Sagiv, M.: Abstraction for shape analysis with fast and precise transformers. In: Ball, T., Jones, R.B. (eds.) CAV 2006. LNCS, vol. 4144, pp. 547–561. Springer, Heidelberg (2006)

20. Madhusudan, P., Qiu, X.: Efficient decision procedures for heaps using STRAND. In: Yahav, E. (ed.) Static Analysis. LNCS, vol. 6887, pp. 43–59. Springer, Heidelberg (2011)
21. Manevich, R., Yahav, E., Ramalingam, G., Sagiv, M.: Predicate abstraction and canonical abstraction for singly-linked lists. In: Cousot, R. (ed.) VMCAI 2005. LNCS, vol. 3385, pp. 181–198. Springer, Heidelberg (2005)
22. Piskac, R., de Moura, L., Bjørner, N.: Deciding effectively propositional logic using DPLL and substitution sets. J. Autom. Reasoning 44(4), 401–424 (2010)
23. Podelski, A., Wies, T.: Counterexample-guided focus. In: POPL (2010)
24. Reynolds, J.: Separation logic: A logic for shared mutable data structures. In: LICS (2002)
25. Sagiv, M., Reps, T., Wilhelm, R.: Parametric shape analysis via 3-valued logic. TOPLAS 24(3), 217–298 (2002)
26. Sankaranarayanan, S., Sipma, H.B., Manna, Z.: Scalable analysis of linear systems using mathematical programming. In: Cousot, R. (ed.) VMCAI 2005. LNCS, vol. 3385, pp. 25–41. Springer, Heidelberg (2005)
27. Srivastava, S., Gulwani, S.: Program verification using templates over predicate abstraction. In: PLDI, pp. 223–234 (2009)
28. Thakur, A., Lal, A., Lim, J., Reps, T.: PostHat and all that: Attaining most-precise inductive invariants. TR-1790, Comp. Sci. Dept., Univ. of Wisconsin, Madison, WI (April 2013)
29. Thakur, A., Lal, A., Lim, J., Reps, T.: PostHat and all that: Automating abstract interpretation. Electr. Notes Theor. Comp. Sci (2013)
30. Yorsh, G., Reps, T., Sagiv, M.: Symbolically computing most-precise abstract operations for shape analysis. In: Jensen, K., Podelski, A. (eds.) TACAS 2004. LNCS, vol. 2988, pp. 530–545. Springer, Heidelberg (2004)

Shape Analysis via Second-Order Bi-Abduction

Quang Loc Le[1], Cristian Gherghina[2], Shengchao Qin[3], and Wei-Ngan Chin[1]

[1] Department of Computer Science, National University of Singapore
[2] Singapore University of Design and Technology
[3] Teesside University

Abstract. We present a new modular shape analysis that can synthesize heap memory specification on a per method basis. We rely on a *second-order bi-abduction* mechanism that can give interpretations to unknown shape predicates. There are several novel features in our shape analysis. Firstly, it is grounded on second-order bi-abduction. Secondly, we distinguish unknown pre-predicates in pre-conditions, from unknown post-predicates in post-condition; since the former may be strengthened, while the latter may be weakened. Thirdly, we provide a new *heap guard* mechanism to support more precise preconditions for heap specification. Lastly, we formalise a set of derivation and normalization rules to give concise definitions for unknown predicates. Our approach has been proven sound and is implemented on top of an existing automated verification system. We show its versatility in synthesizing a wide range of intricate shape specifications.

1 Introduction

An important challenge for automatic program verifiers lies in inferring shapes describing abstractions for data structures used by each method. In the context of heap manipulating programs, determining the shape abstraction is crucial for proving memory safety and is a precursor to supporting functional correctness.

However, discovering shape abstractions can be rather challenging, as linked data structures span a wide variety of forms, from singly-linked lists, doubly-linked lists, circular lists, to tree-like data structures. Previous shape analysis proposals have made great progress in solving this problem. However, the prevailing approach relies on using a predefined vocabulary of shape definitions (typically limited to singly-linked list segments) and trying to determine if any of the pre-defined shapes fit the data structures used. This works well with programs that use simpler shapes, but would fail for programs which use more intricate data structures. An example is the method below (written in C and adapted from [19]) to build a tree whose leaf nodes are linked as a list.

```
struct tree { struct tree* parent; struct tree* l; struct tree* r; struct tree* next}
struct tree* tll(struct tree* x, struct tree* p, struct tree* t)
{ x->parent = p;
  if (x->r==NULL) { x->next=t; return x; }
  else{ struct tree* lm = tll(x->r, x, t); return tll(x->l, x, lm); } }
```

Our approach to modular shape analysis would introduce an unknown pre-predicate H (as the pre-condition), and an unknown post-predicate G (as the post-condition), as shown below, where res is the method's result.

$$\text{requires} \quad H(x, p, t) \qquad \text{ensures} \quad G(x, p, res, t)$$

A. Biere and R. Bloem (Eds.): CAV 2014, LNCS 8559, pp. 52–68, 2014.
© Springer International Publishing Switzerland 2014

Using Hoare-style verification and a new second-order bi-abduction entailment procedure, we would derive a set of relational assumptions for the two unknown predicates. These derived assumptions are to ensure memory safety, and can be systematically transformed into concise predicate definitions for the unknown predicates, such as:

$$H(x,p,t) \equiv x \mapsto tree(\mathcal{D}_p,\mathcal{D}_l,r,\mathcal{D}_n) \wedge r=NULL$$
$$\vee\ x \mapsto tree(\mathcal{D}_p,l,r,\mathcal{D}_n)*H(l,x,lm)*H(r,x,t) \wedge r \neq NULL$$

$$G(x,p,res,t) \equiv x \mapsto tree(p,\mathcal{D}_l,r,t) \wedge res=x \wedge r=NULL$$
$$\vee\ x \mapsto tree(p,l,r,\mathcal{D}_n)*G(l,x,res,lm)*G(r,x,lm,t) \wedge r \neq NULL$$

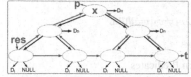

Fig. 1. An example of $G(x,p,res,t)$

The derived pre-predicate H captures a binary tree-like shape that would be traversed by the method. $x \mapsto tree(\mathcal{D}_p,\mathcal{D}_l,r,\mathcal{D}_n)$ denotes that x refers to a tree node with its parent,l,r and next fields being $\mathcal{D}_p$, $\mathcal{D}_l$, r and $\mathcal{D}_n$, respectively. We use dangling references, such as $\mathcal{D}_l, \mathcal{D}_p, \mathcal{D}_n$, as generic markers that denote field pointers that are not traversed by the method. Thus no assertion can be made on any of the $\mathcal{D}$ pointers. The post-predicate G, illustrated in Fig 1, adds parent field links for all nodes, and next field links for just the leaves. [1]

Current shape analysis mechanisms [12,4,6] are unable to infer pre/post specifications that ensure memory-safety for such complex examples. In this paper, we propose a fresh approach to shape analysis that can synthesize, from scratch, a set of shape abstractions that ensure memory safety. The central concept behind our proposal is the use of *unknown predicates* (or *second-order variables*) as place holders for shape predicates that are to be synthesized directly from proof obligations gathered by our verification process. Our proposal is based on a novel *bi-abductive entailment* that supports *second-order* variables. The core of the new entailment procedure generates a set of relational assumptions on unknown predicates to ensure memory safety. These assumptions are then refined into predicate definitions, by predicate *derivation* and *normalization* steps.

By building the generation of the required *relational assumptions* over unknown predicates directly into the new entailment checker, we were able to integrate our shape analysis into an existing program verifier with changes made only to the entailment process, rather than the program verification/analysis itself. Our proposed shape analysis thus applies an almost standard set of Hoare rules in constructing proof obligations which are discharged through the use of a new *second-order* bi-abductive entailment.

This paper makes the following four primary contributions.

- A novel *second-order bi-abduction* guided by an annotation scheme to infer relational assumptions (over unknown predicates) as part of Hoare-style verification.
- A set of formal rules for *deriving* and *normalizing* each unknown predicate definition from the relational assumptions with heap guard conditions.
- A *sound* and *modular* shape analysis, that is applied on a per method basis[2].
- Our implementation and experiments on *shape inference*, closely integrated into an automated verification system. The report [21] contains more details of our tool.

---

[1] Note that new links formed by the method are colored in red.

[2] Most existing shape analyses require either global analyses or re-verification after analysis. For example, bi-abduction in [6] requires its method's inferred pre-condition to be re-verified due to its use of over-approximation on heap pre-condition which can be unsound.

2 Logic Syntax for Shape Specification

Separation logic is an extension of Hoare logic for reasoning with heap-based programs [20,28]. We outline below the fragment underlying the proposed analysis:

$$
\begin{array}{llll}
\text{Disj. formula} & \varPhi & ::= & \Delta \mid \varPhi_1 \vee \varPhi_2 \\
\text{Guarded Disj.} & \varPhi^g & ::= & \Delta \mid (\Delta \,@\, (\kappa \wedge \pi)) \mid \varPhi^g{}_1 \vee \varPhi^g{}_2 \\
\text{Conj. formula} & \Delta & ::= & \exists \bar{v} \cdot (\kappa \wedge \pi) \\
\text{Spatial formula} & \kappa & ::= & \text{emp} \mid \top \mid v {\mapsto} c(\bar{v}) \mid \text{P}(\bar{v}) \mid \text{U}(\bar{v}) \mid \kappa_1 {*} \kappa_2 \\
\text{Pure formula} & \pi & ::= & \alpha \mid \neg \alpha \mid \pi_1 \wedge \pi_2 \\
\text{Var (Dis)Equality} & \alpha & ::= & v \mid v_1 {=} v_2 \mid v {=} \text{NULL} \mid v_1 {\neq} v_2 \mid v {\neq} \text{NULL} \\
\text{Pred. Defn.} & \text{P}^{\text{def}} & ::= & \text{P}(\bar{v}) \equiv \varPhi^g \\
\text{Pred. Dict.} & \Gamma & ::= & \{\text{P}_1^{\text{def}}, \ldots, \text{P}_n^{\text{def}}\} \\
\end{array}
$$

$$
\begin{array}{ll}
\text{P} \in \text{Known Predicates} & \text{U} \in \text{Unknown Predicates} \\
c \in \text{Data Nodes} & v \in \text{Variables} \quad \bar{v} \equiv v_1 \ldots v_n
\end{array}
$$

We introduce $\Delta \,@\, (\kappa \wedge \pi)$, a special syntactic form called *guarded heap* that capture a heap context $\kappa \wedge \pi$ in which Δ holds. Thus, $\Delta \,@\, (\kappa \wedge \pi)$ holds for heap configurations that satisfy Δ and that can be extended such that they satisfy $\Delta * \kappa \wedge \pi$. In Sec.5 we will describe its use in allowing our shape inference to incorporate path sensitive information in the synthesized predicates. The assertion language is also extended with the following formula for describing heaps: emp denoting the empty heap; $\top$ denoting an arbitrary heap (pointed by dangling reference); points-to assertion, $x {\mapsto} c(\bar{v})$, specifying the heap in which x points to a data structure of type c whose fields contain the values $\bar{v}$; known predicate, $\text{P}(\bar{v})$, which holds for heaps in which the shape of the memory locations reachable from $\bar{v}$ can be described by the P predicate; unknown predicates, $\text{U}(\bar{v})$, with no prior given definitions. Separation conjunction $\kappa_1 {*} \kappa_2$ holds for heaps that can be partitioned in two disjoint components satisfying κ_1 and κ_2, respectively. The pure formula captures only pointer equality and disequality. We allow a special constant NULL to denote a pointer which does not point to any heap location. Known predicates $\text{P}(\bar{v})$ are defined inductively through disjunctive formulas $\varPhi^g$. Their definitions are either user-given or synthesised by our analysis. We will use Γ to denote the repository (or set) of available predicate definitions. Through our analysis, we shall construct an inductive definition for each unknown predicate, where possible. Unknown predicates that have *not* been instantiated would not have any definition. They denote data fields that are not accessed by their methods, and would be marked as *dangling pointers*.

3 Overview of Our Approach

Our approach comprises three main steps: (i) inferring relational assumptions for unknown predicates via Hoare-style verification, (ii) deriving predicates from relational assumptions, (iii) normalizing predicates. For (i), a key machinery is the entailment procedure that must work with second-order variables (unknown predicates). Previous bi-abduction entailment proposals, pioneered by [6], would take an antecedent Δ_{ante} and a consequent Δ_{conseq} and return a frame residue Δ_{frame} and the precondition Δ_{pre}, such that the following holds: $\Delta_{\text{pre}} * \Delta_{\text{ante}} \vDash \Delta_{\text{conseq}} * \Delta_{\text{frame}}$. Here, all four components use separation logic formulas based on known predicates with prior definitions.

Taking a different tact, we start with an existing entailment procedure for separation logic with user-defined predicates, and extend it to accept formulas with second-order variables such that given an antecedent Δ_{ante} and a consequent Δ_{conseq} the resulting entailment procedure infers both the frame residue Δ_{frame} and a set (or conjunction) of relational assumptions (on unknowns) of the form $\mathcal{R} = \bigwedge_{i=1}^{n}(\Delta_i \Rightarrow \Phi^g{}_i)$ such that:

$$\mathcal{R} \wedge \Delta_{\text{ante}} \vDash \Delta_{\text{conseq}} * \Delta_{\text{frame}}$$

The inferred $\mathcal{R}$ ensures the entailment's validity. We shall use the following notation $\Delta_{\text{ante}} \vdash \Delta_{\text{conseq}} \rightsquigarrow (\mathcal{R}, \Delta_{\text{frame}})$ for this second-order bi-abduction process.

There are two scenarios to consider for unknown predicates: (1) Δ_{ante} contains an *unknown* predicate instance that matched with a points-to or known predicate in Δ_{conseq}; (2) Δ_{conseq} contains an *unknown* predicate instance. An example of the first scenario is:

$$U(x) \vdash x \mapsto snode(n) \rightsquigarrow (U(x) \Rightarrow x \mapsto snode(n) * U_0(n), \ U_0(n))$$

Here, we generated a relational assumption to denote an *unfolding* (or instantiation) for the unknown predicate U to a heap node $snode$ followed by another unknown $U_0(n)$ predicate. The data structure $snode$ is defined as struct snode { struct snode* next}. A simple example of the second scenario is shown next.

$$x \mapsto snode(NULL) * y \mapsto snode(NULL) \vdash U_1(x) \rightsquigarrow (x \mapsto snode(NULL) \Rightarrow U_1(x), \ y \mapsto snode(NULL))$$

The generated relational assumption depicts a *folding* process for unknown $U_1(x)$ which captures a heap state traversed from the pointer x. Both folding and unfolding of unknown predicates are crucial for second-order bi-abduction. To make it work properly for unknown predicates with multiple parameters, we shall later provide a novel #-annotation scheme to guide these processes. For the moment, we shall use this annotation scheme implicitly. Consider the following method which traverses a singly-linked list and converts it to a doubly-linked list (let us ignore the states $\alpha_1, .., \alpha_5$ for now):

```
struct node { struct node* prev; struct node* next}
void sll2dll(struct node* x, struct node* q)
{(α₁) if (x==NULL) (α₂) return; (α₃) x->prev = q; (α₄) sll2dll(x->next, x); (α₅)}
```

To synthesize the shape specification for this method, we introduce two unknown predicates, H for the pre-condition and G for the post-condition, as below.

$$\text{requires} \quad H(x, q) \qquad \text{ensures} \quad G(x, q)$$

We then apply code verification using these pre/post specifications with unknown predicates and attempt to collect a set of relational assumptions (over the unknown predicates) that must hold to ensure memory-safety. These assumptions would also ensure that the pre-condition of each method call is satisfied, and that the coresponding post-condition is ensured at the end of the method body. For example, our analysis can infer four relational assumptions for the sll2dll method as shown in Fig. 2(a).

These relational assumptions include two new unknown predicates, H_p and H_n, created during the code verification process. All relational assumptions are of the form $\Delta_{\text{lhs}} \Rightarrow \Delta_{\text{rhs}}$, except for (A3) which has the form $\Delta_{\text{lhs}} \Rightarrow \Delta_{\text{rhs}} @ \Delta_g$ where Δ_g denotes a heap guard condition. Such heap guard condition allows more precise pre-conditions to be synthesized (e.g. H_n in (A3)), and is shorthand for $\Delta_{\text{lhs}} * \Delta_g \Rightarrow \Delta_{\text{rhs}} * \Delta_g$.

Let us look at how relational assumptions are inferred. At the start of the method, we have (α_1), shown in Fig. 2 (b), as our program state. Upon exit from the then branch, the

(A1).$H(x,q) \wedge x{=}\text{NULL} \Rightarrow G(x,q)$ (α_1). $H(x,q)$

(A2).$H(x,q) \wedge x{\neq}\text{NULL} \Rightarrow$ (α_2). $H(x,q) \wedge x{=}\text{NULL}$

      $x{\mapsto}\text{node}(x_p,x_n){*}H_p(x_p,q){*}H_n(x_n,q)$ (α_3). $x{\mapsto}\text{node}(x_p,x_n){*}H_p(x_p,q){*}H_n(x_n,q) \wedge x{\neq}\text{NULL}$

(A3).$H_n(x_n,q) \Rightarrow H(x_n,x) @ x{\mapsto}\text{node}(q,x_n)$ (α_4). $x{\mapsto}\text{node}(q,x_n){*}H_p(x_p,q){*}H_n(x_n,q) \wedge x{\neq}\text{NULL}$

(A4).$x{\mapsto}\text{node}(q,x_n){*}G(x_n,x) \Rightarrow G(x,q)$ (α_5). $x{\mapsto}\text{node}(q,x_n){*}H_p(x_p,q){*}G(x_n,x) \wedge x{\neq}\text{NULL}$

(a)   (b)

Fig. 2. Relational assumptions (a) and program states (b) for sll2dll

verification requires that the postcondition $G(x,q)$ be established by the program state (α_2), generating the relational assumption (A1) via the following entailment:

$$(\alpha_2) \vdash G(x,q) \rightsquigarrow (\text{A1, emp} \wedge x{=}\text{NULL}) \tag{E1}$$

To get ready for the field access x->prev, the following entailment is invoked to unfold the unknown H predicate to a heap node, generating the relational assumption (A2):

$$H(x,q) \wedge x{\neq}\text{NULL} \vdash x{\mapsto}\text{node}(x_p,x_n) \rightsquigarrow (\text{A2}, H_p(x_p,q){*}H_n(x_n,q) \wedge x{\neq}\text{NULL}) \tag{E2}$$

Two new unknown predicates H_p and H_n are added to capture the prev (x_p) and next (x_n) fields of x (i.e. they represent heaps referred to by x_p and x_n respectively). After binding, the verification now reaches the state (α_3), which is then changed to (α_4) by the field update x->prev = q. Relational assumption (A3) is inferred from proving the precondition $H(x_n,x)$ of the recursive call sll2dll(x->next, x) at the program state (α_4):

$$(\alpha_4) \vdash H(x_n,x) \rightsquigarrow (\text{A3}, x{\mapsto}\text{node}(q,x_n){*}H_p(x_p,q) \wedge x{\neq}\text{NULL}) \tag{E3}$$

Note that the heap guard $x{\mapsto}\text{node}(q,x_n)$ from (α_4) is recorded in (A3), and is crucial for predicate derivation. The program state at the end of the recursive call, (α_5), is required to establish the post-condition $G(x,q)$, generating the relational assumption (A4):

$$(\alpha_5) \vdash G(x,q) \rightsquigarrow (\text{A4}, H_p(x_p,q) \wedge x{\neq}\text{NULL}) \tag{E4}$$

These relational assumptions are automatically inferred symbolically during code verification. Our next step (ii) uses a predicate derivation procedure to transform (by either equivalence-preserving or abductive steps) the set of relational assumptions into a set of predicate definitions. Sec. 5 gives more details on predicate derivation. For our sll2dll example, we initially derive the following predicate definitions (for H and G):

$$H(x,q) \equiv \text{emp} \wedge x{=}\text{NULL} \vee x{\mapsto}\text{node}(x_p,x_n) * H_p(x_p,q) * H(x_n,x)$$
$$G(x,q) \equiv \text{emp} \wedge x{=}\text{NULL} \vee x{\mapsto}\text{node}(q,x_n) * G(x_n,x)$$

In the last step (iii), we use a normalization procedure to simplify the definition of predicate H. Since H_p is discovered as a dangling predicate, the special variable $\mathcal{D}_p$ corresponds to a *dangling reference* introduced: $H(x,q) \equiv \text{emp} \wedge x{=}\text{NULL} \vee x{\mapsto}\text{node}(\mathcal{D}_p,x_n) * H(x_n,x)$. Furthermore, we can synthesize a more concise H_2 from H by eliminating its useless q parameter: $H(x,q) \equiv H_2(x)$ and $H_2(x) \equiv \text{emp} \wedge x{=}\text{NULL} \vee x{\mapsto}\text{node}(\mathcal{D}_p,x_n) * H_2(x_n)$.

Our approach currently works only for shape abstractions of tree-like data structures with forward and back pointers. (We are unable to infer specifications for graph-like or overlaid data structures yet.) These abstractions are being inferred *modularly* on a per method basis. The inferred preconditions are typically the weakest ones that would ensure memory safety, and would be applicable to all contexts of use. Furthermore, the normalization step aims to ensure concise and re-useable predicate definitions. We shall next elaborate and formalise on our second-order bi-abduction process.

4 Second-Order Bi-Abduction with an Annotation Scheme

We have seen the need for a bi-abductive entailment procedure to systematically handle unknown predicates. To cater to predicates with multiple parameters, we shall use an automatic #-*annotation* scheme to support both unfolding and folding of unknown predicates. Consider a predicate $U(v_1, .., v_n, w_1\#, .., w_m\#)$, where parameters $v_1, .., v_n$ are unannotated and parameters $w_1, .., w_m$ are #-annotated. From the perspective of unfolding, we permit each variable from $v_1, .., v_n$ to be instantiated at most once (we call them *instantiable*), while variables $w_1, .., w_m$ are *disallowed* from instantiation (we call them *non-instantiable*). This scheme ensures that each pointer is instantiated at most once, and avoids formulae, like $U_3(y, y)$ or $U_2(r, y)*U_3(y, x\#)$, from being formed. Such formulae, where a variable may be repeatedly instantiated, may cause a trivial FALSE pre-condition to be inferred. Though sound, it is imprecise. From the perspective of folding, we allow heap traversals to start from variables $v_1, .., v_n$ and would stop whenever references to $w_1, .., w_m$ are encountered. This allows us to properly infer segmented shape predicates and back pointers. Our annotation scheme is fully automated, as we would infer the #-annotation of pre-predicates based on which parameters could be field accessed; while parameters of post-predicates are left unannotated. For our running example, since q parameter is not field accessed (in its method's body), our automatic annotation scheme would start with the following pre/post specification:

$$\text{requires} \quad H(x, q\#) \qquad \text{ensures} \quad G(x, q)$$

Unfold. The entailment below results in an unfolding of the unknown H predicate. It is essentially (E2) in Sec 3, except that q is marked explicitly as non-instantiable.

$$H(x, q\#) \wedge x{\neq}NULL \vdash x{\mapsto}node(x_p, x_n) \rightsquigarrow (A2, \Delta_1) \qquad (E2')$$

With non-instantiable variables explicitly annotated, the assumption (A2) becomes:

$$A2 \equiv H(x, q\#) \wedge x{\neq}NULL \Rightarrow x{\mapsto}node(x_p, x_n)*H_p(x_p, q\#)*H_n(x_n, q\#)$$

As mentioned earlier, we generated a new unknown predicate for each pointer field (H_p for x_p, and H_n for x_n), so as to allow the full recovery of the shape of the data structure being traversed or built. Note that each x, x_p, x_n appears only once in unannotated forms, while the annotated $q\#$ remains annotated throughout to prevent the pointer from being instantiated. If we allow q to be instantiable in (E2') above, we will instead obtain:

$$H(x, q) \wedge x{\neq}NULL \vdash x{\mapsto}node(x_p, x_n) \rightsquigarrow (A2', \Delta_1')$$

We get $A2' \equiv H(x, q) \wedge x{\neq}NULL \Rightarrow x{\mapsto}node(x_p, x_n)*H_p(x_p, q\#)*H_n(x_n, q\#)*\underline{U_2(q, x\#)}$, where the unfolding process creates extra unknown predicate $U_2(q, x\#)$ to capture shape for q.

Our proposal for instantiating unknown predicates is also applicable when known predicates appear in the RHS. These known predicates may have parameters that act as *continuation fields* for the data structure. An example is the list segment $lseg(x, p)$ predicate where the parameter p is a continuation field.

$$ll(x) \equiv emp \wedge x{=}NULL \vee x{\mapsto}snode(n) * ll(n)$$
$$lseg(x, p) \equiv emp \wedge x{=}p \vee x{\mapsto}snode(n) * lseg(n, p)$$

Where `snode` (defined in the previous section) denotes singly-linked list node. Note that continuation fields play the same role as fields for data nodes. Therefore, for such parameters, we also generate new unknown parameters to capture the connected data structure that may have been traversed. We illustrate this with two examples:

$$U(x) \vdash ll(x) \rightsquigarrow (U(x) \Rightarrow ll(x), \; emp) \quad U(x) \vdash lseg(x,p) \rightsquigarrow (U(x) \Rightarrow lseg(x,q) * U_2(q), \; U_2(p))$$

The first predicate $ll(x)$ did not have a continuation field. Hence, we did not generate any extra unknown predicate. The second predicate $lseg(x,p)$ did have a continuation field p, and we generated an extra unknown predicate $U_2(p)$ to capture a possible extension of the data structure beyond this continuation field.

Fold. A second scenario that must be handled by second-order entailment involves unknown predicates in the consequent. For each unknown predicate $U_1(\bar{v}, \bar{w}\#)$ in the consequent, a corresponding assumption $\Delta \Rightarrow U_1(\bar{v}, \bar{w}\#) @ \Delta_g$ is inferred where Δ contains unknown predicates with at least one instantiatable parameters from $\bar{v}$, or heaps *reachable* from $\bar{v}$ (via either any data fields or parameters of known predicates) but stopping at non-instantiatable variables $\bar{w}\#$; a residual frame is also inferred from the antecedent (but added with pure approximation of footprint heaps [9]). For example, consider the following entailment:

$$x \mapsto snode(q) * q \mapsto snode(NULL) \land q \neq NULL \vdash U_1(x, q\#) \rightsquigarrow (A_{f1}, \; \Delta_1)$$

The output of this entailment is:

$$A_{f1} \equiv x \mapsto snode(q) \land q \neq NULL \Rightarrow U_1(x, q\#) \quad \Delta_1 \equiv q \mapsto snode(NULL) \land x \neq NULL \land x \neq q$$

As a comparison, let us consider the scenario where q is unannotated, as follows:

$$x \mapsto snode(q) * q \mapsto snode(NULL) \land q \neq NULL \vdash U_1(x, q) \rightsquigarrow (A_{f2}, \; \Delta_2)$$

In this case, the output of the entailment becomes:

$$A_{f2} \equiv x \mapsto snode(q) * q \mapsto snode(NULL) \Rightarrow U_1(x, q) \quad \Delta_2 \equiv x \neq NULL \land q \neq NULL \land x \neq q$$

Moreover, the folding process also captures *known* heaps that are reachable from #-parameters as *heap guard conditions*, e.g. $x \mapsto node(q, x_n)$ in our running example (E3):

$$x \mapsto node(q, x_n) * H_p(x_p, q\#) * H_n(x_n, q\#) \land x \neq NULL \vdash H(x_n, x\#)$$
$$\rightsquigarrow (H_n(x_n, q\#) \Rightarrow H(x_n, x\#) @ x \mapsto node(q, x_n), \; x \mapsto node(q, x_n) * H_p(x_p, q\#) \land x \neq NULL) \quad (E3')$$

Such heap guards help with capturing the relations of heap structures and recovering those relationships when necessary (e.g. back-pointer $x\#$).

Formalism. Bi-abductive unfold is formalized in Fig. 3. Here, $slice(\bar{w}, \pi)$ is an auxiliary function that existentially quantifies in π all free variables that are not in the set $\bar{w}$.

Thus it eliminates from π all subformulas not related to $\bar{w}$ (*e.g.* $slice(\{x, q\}, q = NULL \land y > 3)$ returns $q = NULL$). In the first line, a RHS assertion, either a points-to assertion $r \mapsto c(\bar{p})$ or a known predicate instance $P(r, \bar{p})$ is paired through the parameter r with the unknown predicate U. Second, the unknown predicates

$$[\text{SO-ENT-UNFOLD}]$$
$$\kappa_s \equiv r \mapsto c(\bar{p}) \text{ or } \kappa_s \equiv P(r, \bar{p})$$
$$\kappa_{fields} = *_{p_j \in \bar{p}} \, U_j(p_j, \bar{v}_i\#, \bar{v}_n\#), \text{ where } U_j: \text{fresh preds}$$
$$\kappa_{rem} = U_{rem}(\bar{v}_i, \bar{v}_n\#, r\#), \text{ where } U_{rem}: \text{a fresh pred}$$
$$\pi_a = slice(\{r, \bar{v}_i, \bar{v}_n, \bar{p}\}, \pi_1) \quad \pi_c = slice(\{\bar{p}\}, \pi_2)$$
$$\sigma \equiv (U(r, \bar{v}_i, \bar{v}_n\#) \land \pi_a \Rightarrow \kappa_s * \kappa_{fields} * \kappa_{rem} \land \pi_c)$$
$$\frac{\kappa_1 * \kappa_{fields} * \kappa_{rem} \land \pi_1 \vdash \kappa_2 \land \pi_2 \rightsquigarrow (\mathcal{R}, \Delta_R)}{U(r, v_i, v_n\#) * \kappa_1 \land \pi_1 \vdash \kappa_s * \kappa_2 \land \pi_2 \rightsquigarrow (\sigma \land \mathcal{R}, \Delta_R)}$$

Fig. 3. Bi-Abductive Unfolding

U_j are generated for the data fields/parameters of κ_s. Third, the unknown predicate U_{rem} is generated for the instantiatable parameters $\bar{v}_i$ of U. The fourth and fifth lines compute relevant pure formulas and generate the assumption, respectively. Finally, the unknown predicates κ_{fields} and κ_{rem} are combined in the residue of LHS to continue discharging the remaining formula in RHS.

Bi-abductive fold is formalized in Fig. 4. The function $reach(\bar{w}, \kappa_1 \wedge \pi_1, \bar{z}\#)$ extracts portions from the antecedent heap (κ_1) that are (1) unknown predicates containing at least one instantiatable parameter from $\bar{w}$; or (2) point-to or known predicates reachable from $\bar{w}$, but not reachable from $\bar{z}$. In our running example (the entailment (E3') on last page), the function $reach(\{x_n\}, x \mapsto node(q, x_n) * H_p(x_p, q\#) * H_n(x_n, q\#) \wedge x \neq NULL, \{x\#\})$ is used to obtain $H_n(x_n, q\#)$. More detail on this function is in the report [21]. The $heaps(\Delta)$ function enumerates all known predicate instances (of the form $P(\bar{v})$) and points-to instances (of the form $r \mapsto c(\bar{v})$) in Δ. The function $root(\kappa)$ is defined as: $root(r \mapsto c(\bar{v})) = \{r\}$, $root(P(r, \bar{v})) = \{r\}$. In the first line, heaps of LHS are separated into the assumption κ_{11} and the residue κ_{12}. Second, heap guards (and their root pointers) are inferred based on κ_{12} and the #-annotated parameters $\bar{z}$. The assumption is generated in the third line and finally, the residual heap is used to discharge the remaining heaps of RHS.

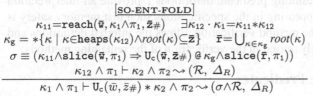

$$[\text{SO-ENT-FOLD}]$$
$$\kappa_{11} = reach(\bar{w}, \kappa_1 \wedge \pi_1, \bar{z}\#) \quad \exists \kappa_{12} \cdot \kappa_1 = \kappa_{11} * \kappa_{12}$$
$$\kappa_g = *\{\kappa \mid \kappa \in heaps(\kappa_{12}) \wedge root(\kappa) \subseteq \bar{z}\} \quad \bar{r} = \bigcup_{\kappa \in \kappa_g} root(\kappa)$$
$$\sigma \equiv (\kappa_{11} \wedge slice(\bar{w}, \pi_1) \Rightarrow U_c(\bar{w}, \bar{z}\#) @ \kappa_g \wedge slice(\bar{r}, \pi_1))$$
$$\frac{\kappa_{12} \wedge \pi_1 \vdash \kappa_2 \wedge \pi_2 \rightsquigarrow (\mathcal{R}, \Delta_R)}{\kappa_1 \wedge \pi_1 \vdash U_c(\bar{w}, \bar{z}\#) * \kappa_2 \wedge \pi_2 \rightsquigarrow (\sigma \wedge \mathcal{R}, \Delta_R)}$$

Fig. 4. Bi-Abductive Folding

Hoare Rules. We shall now present Hoare rules to show how second-order entailment is used there. For simplicity, we consider a core imperative language (Fig. 5) that supports heap-based data structures (*datat*) and methods (*meth*).

Prog ::= *datat** *meth**   *datat* ::= data c { *field** }
field ::= $t\ v$ t ::= int | bool | void | c | ...
meth ::= $t\ mn\ (([ref]\ t\ v)^*)\ \Phi_{pr}\ \Phi_{po};\ \{e\}$
e ::= NULL | k^τ | v | $v.f$ | $v = e$ | $v.f = e$ | new $c(v^*)$
     | $e_1; e_2$ | $t\ v;\ e$ | $mn(v^*)$ | if v then e_1 else e_2

Fig. 5. The Core Language

A method declaration includes a header with pre-/post-condition and its body. Methods can have call-by-reference parameters (prefixed with ref). Loops, including nested loops, are transformed to tail-recursive methods with ref parameters to capture mutable variables. To support shape analysis, code verification is formalized as a proof of quadruple: $\vdash \{\Delta_{pre}\}\ e\ \{\mathcal{R}, \Delta_{post}\}$, where $\mathcal{R}$ accumulates the set of relational assumptions generated by the entailment procedure. The specification may contain unknown predicates in preconditions and postconditions. We list in Fig. 6 the rules for field access, method calls and method declaration. Note that primed variable (e.g. x') denotes the latest value (of the program variable x). The formula $\Delta_1 *_{\bar{v}} \Delta_2$ denotes $\exists \bar{r} \cdot ([\bar{r}/\bar{v}']\Delta_1) * ([\bar{r}/\bar{v}]\Delta_2)$ (see [9]).

The key outcome is that if a solution for the set of relational assumptions $\mathcal{R}$ can be found, the program is memory-safe and all the methods abide by their specifications. Furthermore, we propose a bottom-up verification process which is able to incrementally build suitable predicate instantiations one method at a time by solving the collected

$$[\text{SA-CALL}]$$
$$t_0 \; mn \; ((\texttt{ref } t_i \; v_i)_{i=1}^{m-1}, (t_j \; v_j)_{j=m}^{n}) \; \Phi_{pr} \; \Phi_{po}; \{e\} \in \texttt{Prog}$$
$$\rho = [v_k'/v_k]_{k=1}^{n} \quad \Phi_{pr}' = \rho(\Phi_{pr}) \quad \texttt{W} = \{v_1, .., v_{m-1}\} \quad \texttt{V} = \{v_m, .., v_n\}$$
$$\dfrac{\Delta \vdash \Phi_{pr}' \leadsto (\mathcal{R}, \Delta_2) \quad \Delta_3 = (\Delta_2 \wedge \bigwedge_{i=m}^{n}(v_i' = v_i)) \; *_{\texttt{V} \cup \texttt{W}} \; \Phi_{po}}{\vdash \{\Delta\} \; mn(v_1, .., v_{m-1}, v_m, .., v_n) \; \{\mathcal{R}, \Delta_3\}}$$

$$[\text{SA-FLD-RD}]$$
$$\texttt{data c } \{t_1 \; f_1, .., t_n \; f_n\} \in \texttt{Prog}$$
$$\Delta_1 \vdash x' \mapsto c(v_1..v_n) \leadsto (\mathcal{R}, \Delta_3)$$
$$\Delta_4 = \exists v_1..v_n \cdot (\Delta_3 * x' \mapsto c(v_1..v_n) \wedge \texttt{res} = v_i)$$
$$\dfrac{}{\vdash \{\Delta_1\} \; x.f_i \; \{\mathcal{R}, \Delta_4\}}$$

$$[\text{SA-METH}]$$
$$\vdash \{\Phi_{pr} \wedge \bigwedge (u' = u)^*\} \; e \; \{\mathcal{R}_1, \Delta_1\}$$
$$\Delta_1 \vdash \Phi_{po} \leadsto (\mathcal{R}_2, \Delta_2)$$
$$\Gamma = \texttt{solve}(\mathcal{R}_1 \cup \mathcal{R}_2)$$
$$\dfrac{}{t_0 \; mn \; ((t \; u)^*) \; \Phi_{pr} \; \Phi_{po} \; \{e\}}$$

Fig. 6. Several Hoare Rules

relational assumptions $\mathcal{R}$ progressively. The predicate definition synthesis (`solve`) consists of two separate operations : predicate synthesis, `PRED_SYN`, and predicate normalization, `PRED_NORM`. That is $\texttt{solve}(\mathcal{R}) = \texttt{PRED\_NORM}(\texttt{PRED\_SYN}(\mathcal{R}))$. After the method is successfully verified, the resulting predicate definitions Γ provide an interpretation for the unknown predicates appearing in the specifications such that memory safety is guaranteed. By returning Γ, the method verification allows the inferred definitions and specifications to be consistently reused in the verification of the remaining methods.

5   Derivation of Shape Predicates

Once the relational assumptions have been inferred, we proceed to apply a series of refinement steps to derive predicate definitions for each pre- and post-predicate. Fig. 7 outlines our strategy for predicate synthesis. We use the [syn-*] notation to name refinement rules. For space reasons, we describe some rules and leave the rest to the report [21]. Steps that are left out include: (i) *sort-group* to decide on the transformation order of relational assumptions; (ii) rules to process some relational assumptions as proof obligations. For example, if the result of the recursive method is field-accessed after the recursive call, the post-predicate would appear as an unknown predicate for heap instantiation. This must be processed as an entailment obligation, after the definition of its post-predicate has been derived; (iii) *inline* to unfold synthesized predicates in the remaining assumptions.

```
function PRED_SYN( R)
  Γ ← ∅
  R ← exhaustively apply [syn-base] on R
  R_pre, R_post ← sort-group(R)
  while R_pre ≠ ∅ do
    U^pre, σ ← pick unknown & assumption in R_pre
    U^pre_def ← apply [syn-case], [syn-group-pre], and
        [syn-pre-def] on σ
    R_pre, R_post ← inline U^pre_def in (R_pre \ σ), R_post
    discharge U^pre obligations
    Γ ← Γ ∪ {U^pre_def}
  end while
  while R_post ≠ ∅ do
    U^post, σ ← pick unknown & assumption in R_post
    U^post_def ← apply [syn-group-post], [syn-post-def] on σ
    discharge U^post obligations
    R_post ← R_post \ σ    Γ ← Γ ∪ {U^post_def}
  end while
  return Γ
end function
```

Fig. 7. Shape Derivation Outline

5.1 Base Splitting of Pre/Post-Predicates

We first deal with relational assumptions of the form $U^{pre}(\ldots)*\Delta \Rightarrow U^{post}(\ldots)$, which capture constraints on both a pre-predicate and a post-predicate. To allow greater flexibility in applying specialized techniques for pre-predicates or post-predicates, we split the assumption into two assumptions such that pre-predicate U^{pre} is separated from post-predicate U^{post}. Base splitting can be formalized as follows:

$$\frac{\boxed{\text{syn-base}}}{\sigma : U^{pre}(\bar{x})*\kappa\wedge\pi \Rightarrow U^{post}(\bar{y}) \quad \sigma_1 : U^{pre}(\bar{x})\wedge\text{slice}(\bar{x},\pi)\Rightarrow\text{emp} \quad \sigma_2 : \kappa\wedge\pi \Rightarrow U^{post}(\bar{y})}$$

$$\kappa_g = *\{\kappa_1 \mid \kappa_1 \in \text{heaps}(\kappa)\wedge pars(\kappa_1)\cap\bar{x}\neq\emptyset\} \qquad \bar{w} = \bigcup\{pars(\kappa_1) \mid \kappa_1 \in \kappa_g\}$$

$$\sigma_3 : U^{pre}(\bar{x})\Rightarrow U^{fr}(\bar{x}) @ \kappa_g\wedge\text{slice}(\bar{x}\cup\bar{w},\pi) \qquad \sigma_4 : U^{fr}(\bar{x}) \Rightarrow \top$$

$$\text{if is\_base}(\bar{x},\pi)=\text{true then } (\sigma_1\wedge\sigma_2) \text{ else } (\sigma\wedge\sigma_3\wedge\sigma_4)$$

The premise contains an assumption (σ) which could be split. The conclusion captures the new relational assumptions. There are two scenarios:
(1) The first scenario takes place when the test $\text{is\_base}(\bar{x},\pi)$ holds. It signifies that π contains a base case formula for some pointer(s) in $\bar{x}$. Note that $\text{is\_base}(\bar{x},\pi)$ holds if and only if $(\exists \text{ v}\in\bar{x}. \pi\vdash \text{v=NULL})$ or $(\exists \text{v}_1,\text{v}_2\in\bar{x}.\pi\vdash \text{v}_1=\text{v}_2)$. In such a situation, the assumption σ is split into σ_1 and σ_2. This reflects the observation that a pre-predicate guard will likely constrain the pre-predicate to a base-case with empty heap. This scenario happens in our running example where the assumption (A1) is split to:

(A1a). $H(x,q) \wedge x=\text{NULL} \Rightarrow \text{emp}$ \qquad (A1b). $\text{emp} \wedge x=\text{NULL} \Rightarrow G(x,q)$

(2) If the test $\text{is\_base}(\bar{x},\pi)$ fails, there is no base case information available for us to instantiate $U^{pre}(\bar{x})$. The assumption σ is not split and kept in the result. To have a more precise derivation, we would also record the fact that $U^{pre}(\bar{x})$ has no instantiation under the current context. To do this, in the second line we record in κ_g such a heap context (related to $\bar{x}$), extract in $\bar{w}$ related pointers from the context, and introduce a fresh unknown predicate U^{fr} as the instantiation for U^{pre}, as indicated by the assumption σ_3 in the third line. Note the heap guard specifies the context under which such an assumption holds. We also add σ_4 into the result, where the new predicate U^{fr} is instantiated to the aforementioned memory locations (encapsulated by $\top$). Assumptions of the form $U^{fr}(p) \Rightarrow \top$ are being used to denote dangling pointers. We also note that introducing the dangling predicate U^{fr} into the guarded assumption σ_3 is essential to help relate non-traversed pointer fields between the pre-predicate U^{pre} and the post-predicate U^{post}. The function $pars(\kappa)$ (the 2nd line) retrieves parameters: $pars(r\mapsto c(\bar{v}))) = \bar{v}, pars(P(r,\bar{v})) = \bar{v}$.

As an example, consider splitting $(\sigma_5) : U^{pre}(p)*x\mapsto\text{node}(p,n)\wedge n=\text{NULL} \Rightarrow U^{post}(x)$. The test $\text{is\_base}(\{p\}, n=\text{NULL})$ fails. In addition to (σ_5), the splitting returns also

$$(\sigma_6) : U^{pre}(p) \Rightarrow U^{fr}(p) @ (x\mapsto\text{node}(p,n)\wedge n=\text{NULL}) \qquad (\sigma_7) : U^{fr}(p) \Rightarrow \top$$

5.2 Deriving Pre-Predicates

Pre-predicates typically appear in relational assumptions under pure guards π, of the form $U^{pre}(\ldots)\wedge\pi \Rightarrow \Delta$. To derive definitions for these pre-predicates, the first step is to transform relational assumptions that overlap on their guards by forcing a case analysis that generates a set of relational assumptions with disjoint guard conditions:

$$\frac{\boxed{\text{syn-case}}}{U(\bar{x})\wedge\pi_1\Rightarrow\Delta_1 @ \Delta_{1g} \quad U(\bar{x})\wedge\pi_2\Rightarrow\Delta_2 @ \Delta_{2g} \quad \pi_1\wedge\pi_2\not\Rightarrow\text{FALSE}}$$

$$\Delta_1\wedge\Delta_2\Rightarrow^{\bar{x}}_{\wedge}\Delta_3 \quad \Delta_{1g}\wedge\Delta_{2g}\Rightarrow^{\bar{x}}_{\wedge}\Delta_{3g} \quad \text{SAT}(\Delta_{3g})$$

$$U(\bar{x})\wedge\pi_1\wedge\neg\pi_2\Rightarrow\Delta_1 @ \Delta_{3g} \quad U(\bar{x})\wedge\pi_2\wedge\neg\pi_1\Rightarrow\Delta_2 @ \Delta_{3g} \quad U(\bar{x})\wedge\pi_1\wedge\pi_2\Rightarrow\Delta_3 @ \Delta_{3g}$$

For brevity, we assume a renaming of free variables to allow $\bar{x}$ to be used as arguments in both assumptions. Furthermore, we use the $\Rightarrow_{\wedge}^{\bar{x}}$ operator to denote a normalization of overlapping conjunction, $\Delta_1 \wedge \Delta_2$ [28]. Informally, in order for $\Delta_1 \wedge \Delta_2$ to hold, it is necessary that the shapes described by Δ_1 and Δ_2 agree when describing the same memory locations. Normalization thus determines the overlapping locations, Δ_c such that $\Delta_1 = \Delta_c * \Delta_1'$ and $\Delta_2 = \Delta_c * \Delta_2'$ and returns $\Delta_c * \Delta_1' * \Delta_2'$. We leave a formal definition of $\Rightarrow_{\wedge}^{\bar{x}}$ to the technical report [21]. Once all the relational assumptions for a given pre-predicate have been transformed such that the pure guards do not overlap, we may proceed to combine them using the rule [syn-group-pre] shown below. We shall perform this exhaustively until a single relational assumption for U is derived. If the assumption RHS is independent of any post-predicate, it becomes the unknown pre-predicate definition, as shown in the rule [syn-pre-def] below.

$$\frac{\text{[syn-group-pre]}}{\text{U}(\bar{x}) \wedge \pi_1 \Rightarrow \Phi_1^g \quad \text{U}(\bar{x}) \wedge \pi_2 \Rightarrow \Phi_2^g \quad \pi_1 \wedge \pi_2 \Rightarrow \text{FALSE}} {\text{U}(\bar{x}) \wedge (\pi_1 \vee \pi_2) \Rightarrow \Phi_1^g \wedge \pi_1 \vee \Phi_2^g \wedge \pi_2} \qquad \frac{\text{[syn-pre-def]}}{\text{U}^{\text{pre}}(\bar{x}) \Rightarrow \Phi^g \quad \text{no\_post}(\Phi^g)}{\text{U}^{\text{pre}}(\bar{x}) \equiv \Phi^g}$$

For the sll2dll example, applying the [syn-group-pre] rule to (A2) and (A1a) yields:

$$(\text{A5}). \ \text{H}(\text{x}, \text{q}) \Rightarrow \text{x} \mapsto \text{node}(\text{x}_\text{p}, \text{x}_\text{n}) * \text{H}_\text{p}(\text{x}_\text{p}, \text{q}) * \text{H}_\text{n}(\text{x}_\text{n}, \text{q}) \vee \text{emp} \wedge \text{x} = \text{NULL}$$

This is then trivially converted into a definition for its pre-predicate, without any weakening, thus ensuring soundness of our pre-conditions.

5.3 Deriving Post-Predicates

We start the derivation for a post-predicate after all pre-predicates have been derived. We can incrementally group each pair of relational assumptions on a post-predicate via the [syn-group-post] rule shown below. By exhaustively applying [syn-group-post] rule all assumptions relating to predicate U^{post} get condensed into an assumption of the form: $\Delta_1 \vee \ldots \vee \Delta_n \Rightarrow \text{U}^{\text{post}}(\bar{x})$. This may then be used to confirm the post-predicate by generating the predicate definition via the [syn-post-def] rule.

$$\frac{\text{[syn-group-post]}}{\Delta_a \Rightarrow \text{U}^{\text{post}}(\bar{x}) \quad \Delta_b \Rightarrow \text{U}^{\text{post}}(\bar{x})}{\Delta_a \vee \Delta_b \Rightarrow \text{U}^{\text{post}}(\bar{x})} \qquad \frac{\text{[syn-post-def]}}{\Delta_1 \vee \ldots \vee \Delta_n \Rightarrow \text{U}^{\text{post}}(\bar{x})}{\text{U}^{\text{post}}(\bar{x}) \equiv \Delta_1 \vee \ldots \vee \Delta_n}$$

Using these rules, we can combine (A4) and (A1b) in the sll2dll example to obtain:

$$\text{G}(\text{x}, \text{q}) \equiv \text{emp} \wedge \text{x} = \text{NULL} \vee \text{x} \mapsto \text{node}(\text{q}, \text{x}_\text{n}) * \text{G}(\text{x}_\text{n}, \text{x})$$

5.4 Predicate Normalization for More Concise Definitions

After we have synthesized suitable predicate definitions, we proceed with predicate normalization to convert each predicate definition to its most concise form. Our current method, PRED_NORM, uses four key steps: (i) eliminate dangling predicates, (ii) eliminate useless parameters, (iii) re-use predicate definitions and (iv) perform predicate splitting. We briefly explain the normalization steps and leave details in the report [21]. The first step deals with dangling predicates which do not have any definition. Though it is safe to drop such predicates (by frame rule), our normalization procedure replaces them by special variables, to help capture linking information between pre- and post-conditions. The second step eliminates predicate arguments that are not used in their synthesized definitions, with the help of second-order entailment. The third step leverage on our entailment procedure to conduct an equivalence proof to try to match a newly inferred definition with a definition previously provided or inferred. Lastly, to increase the chance for such predicate reuse, we allow predicates to be split into smaller predicates. This is again done with the help of second-order entailment procedure, allowing us to undertake such normalization tasks soundly and easily.

6   Soundness Lemmas and Theorem

Here we briefly state several key soundness results, and leave the proof details to the report [21]. For brevity, we introduce the notation $\mathcal{R}(\Gamma)$ to denote a set of predicate instantiations $\Gamma=\{U_1(\bar{v}_1)\equiv\Delta_1, ..U_n(\bar{v}_n)\equiv\Delta_n\}$ satisfying the set of assumptions $\mathcal{R}$. That is, for all assumptions $\Delta \Rightarrow \Phi^g \in \mathcal{R}$, (i) Γ contains a predicate instantiation for each unknown predicate appearing in Δ and Φ^g; (ii) by interpreting all unknown predicates according to Γ, then it is provable that Δ implies Φ^g, written as $\Gamma : \Delta \vdash \Phi^g$.

Soundness of Bi-abductive Entailment. Abduction soundness requires that if all the relational assumptions generated are satisfiable, then the entailment is valid.

Lemma 1. *Given the entailment judgement $\Delta_a \vdash \Delta_c \leadsto (\mathcal{R}, \Delta_f)$, if there exists Γ such that $\mathcal{R}(\Gamma)$, then the entailment $\Gamma : \Delta_a \vdash \Delta_c * \Delta_f$ holds.*

Derivation Soundness. For derivation soundness, if a set of predicate definitions is constructed then those definitions must satisfy the initial set of assumptions. We argue that (i) assumption refinement does not introduce spurious instantiations, (ii) the generated predicates satisfy the refined assumptions, (iii) normalization is meaning preserving.

Lemma 2. *Given a set of relational assumptions $\mathcal{R}$, let $\mathcal{R}'$ be the set obtained by applying any of the refinement steps, then for any Γ such that $\mathcal{R}'(\Gamma)$, we have $\mathcal{R}(\Gamma)$.*

Lemma 3. *If $\mathcal{R}$ contains only one pre-assumption on predicate $U^{pre}, U^{pre}(\bar{v})\Rightarrow\Phi^g$ and if our algorithm returns a solution Γ, then $(U^{pre}(\bar{v})\equiv\Phi^g)\in \Gamma$. Similarly, if $\mathcal{R}$ has a sole post-assumption on U^{post}, $\Phi\Rightarrow U^{post}$ and if solution Γ is returned, then $(U^{post}(\bar{v})\equiv\Phi)\in \Gamma$.*

Lemma 4. *Given a set of assumptions $\mathcal{R}$, if PRED_SYN($\mathcal{R}$) returns a solution Γ then $\mathcal{R}(\Gamma)$. Furthermore, if PRED_NORM(Γ) returns a solution Γ' then $\mathcal{R}(\Gamma')$.*

Theorem 6.1 (Soundness) *If $\Delta_a \vdash \Delta_c \leadsto (\mathcal{R}, \Delta_f)$ and Γ=PRED_NORM(PRED_SYN($\mathcal{R}$)) then $\Gamma : \Delta_a \vdash \Delta_c * \Delta_f$.*

7   Implementation and Experimental Results

We have implemented the proposed shape analysis within HIP [9], a separation logic verification system. The resulting verifier, called S2, uses an available CIL-based [27] translator [3] from C to the expression-oriented core language. Our analysis modularly infers the pre/post specification for each method. It attempts to provide the weakest possible precondition to ensure memory safety (from null dereferencing and memory leaks), and the strongest possible post-condition on heap usage patterns, where possible.

Expressivity. We have explored the generality and efficiency of the proposed analy-

---

[3] Our translation preserves the semantics of source programs, subject to CIL's limitations.

Table 1. Experimental Results (**c** for *check* and **t** for *traverse*)

Example	w/o norm. size	w/o norm. Syn.	w/ norm. size	w/ norm. Syn.	Veri.	Example	w/o norm. size	w/o norm. Syn.	w/ norm. size	w/ norm. Syn.	Veri.
SLL (delete)	9	0.23	2	0.29	0.22	CSLL (t)	8	0.22	5	0.23	0.24
SLL (reverse)	20	0.21	8	0.22	0.2	CSLL of CSLLs (c)	18	0.24	4	0.23	0.22
SLL (insert)	13	0.2	11	0.21	0.2	SLL2DLL	18	0.19	2	0.2	0.18
SLL (setTail)	7	0.16	2	0.18	0.16	DLL (check)	8	0.21	2	0.23	0.19
SLL (get-last)	20	0.7	17	0.75	0.21	DLL (append)	11	0.2	8	0.2	0.2
SLL-sorted (c)	11	0.26	2	0.27	0.22	CDLL (c)	23	0.22	8	0.26	0.21
SLL (bubblesort)	13	0.28	9	0.36	0.26	CDLL of 5CSLLs (c)	28	0.39	4	0.66	1.3
SLL (insertsort)	15	0.3	11	0.3	0.27	CDLL of CSLLs$_2$ (c)	29	0.33	4	0.44	0.29
SLL (zip)	20	0.27	2	0.32	0.24	btree (search)	33	0.23	2	0.24	0.23
SLL-zip-leq	20	0.27	2	0.27	0.25	btree-parent (t)	11	0.23	2	0.29	0.24
SLL + head (c)	12	0.24	2	0.71	0.2	rose-tree (c)	14	0.28	14	0.3	0.23
SLL + tail (c)	10	0.19	2	0.72	0.18	swl (t)	19	0.23	13	0.27	22
skip-list$_2$ (c)	9	0.28	1	0.32	0.25	mcf (c)	19	0.26	17	0.28	0.26
skip-list$_3$ (c)	9	0.36	1	0.46	0.3	tll (t)	21	0.23	2	0.25	0.21
SLL of 0/1 SLLs	8	0.25	1	0.26	0.23	tll (c)	21	0.29	2	0.32	0.19
CSLL (c)	17	0.18	2	0.23	0.21	tll (set-parent)	39	0.24	2	0.35	0.24

sis through a number of small but challenging examples. We have evaluated programs which manipulate lists, trees and combinations (e.g. `tll`: trees whose leaves are chained in a linked list). The experiments were performed on a machine with the Intel i7-960 (3.2GHz) processor and 16 GB of RAM. Table 1 presents our experimental results. For each test, we list the name of the manipulated data structure and the effect of the verified code under the `Example` column. Here we used SLL,DLL,CLL,CDLL for singly-, doubly-, cyclic-singly-, cyclic-doubly- linked lists. SLL + head/tail for an SLL where each element points to the SLL's head/tail. SLL of 0/1 SLLs uses an SLL nested in a SLL of size 0 or 1, CSLL of CSLLs for CSLL nested in CSLL, CDLL of 5CSLLs for an CDLL where each node is a source of five CSLL, and CDLL of CSLLs$_2$ for CDLL where each node is a nested CSLL. The skip lists subscript denotes the number of skip pointers. The swl procedure implements list traversal following the DeutschSchorr-Waite style. `rose-trees` are trees with nodes that are allowed to have variable number of children, typically stored as linked lists, and `mcf` trees [16] are rose-tree variants where children are stored in doubly-linked lists with sibling and parent pointers. In order to evaluate the performance of our shape synthesis, we re-verified the source programs against the inferred specifications and listed the verification time (in seconds) in the `Veri.` column and the synthesis times in column `Syn.`. In total, the specification inference took 8.37s while the re-verification[4] took 8.25s.

The experiments showed that our tool can handle fairly complex recursive methods, like trees with linked leaves. It can synthesize shape abstractions for a large variety of

---

[4] Due to our use of sound inference mechanisms, re-verification is not strictly required. We perform it here to illustrate the benefit of integrating inference within a verification framework.

data structures; from list and tree variants to combinations. Furthermore, the tool can infer shapes with mutual-recursive definitions, like the rose-trees and mcf trees.

The normalization phase aims to simplify inferred shape predicates. To evaluate its effectiveness, we performed the synthesis on two scenarios: without (w/o) and with (w/) normalization. The number of conjuncts in the synthesized shapes is captured with *size* column. The results show that normalization is helpful; it reduces by 68% (169/533) the size of synthesized predicates with a time overhead of 27% (8.37s/10.62s).

Larger Experiments. We evaluated S2 on real source code from the Glib open source library [1]. Glib is a cross-platform C library including non-GUI code from the GTK+ toolkit and the GNOME desktop environment. We focused our experiments on the files which implemented heap data structures, i.e. SLL (gslist.c), DLL (glist.c), balanced binary trees (gtree.c) and N-ary trees (gnode.c). In Fig.8 we list for each file number of lines of code (excluding comments) LOC, number of procedures (while/for loops) #Proc (#Loop). #√ describes the number of procedures and loops for which S2 inferred specifications that guarantee memory safety. S2

	LOC	#Proc	#Loop	#√	Syn. (sec)
gslist.c	698	33	18	47	11.73
glist.c	784	35	19	49	7.43
gtree.c	1204	36	14	44	3.69
gnode.c	1128	37	27	52	16.34

Fig. 8. Experiments on Glib Programs

can infer specifications that guarantee memory safety for 89% of procedures and loops (192/216).[5]

Limitations. Our present proposal cannot handle graphs and overlaid data structures since our instantiation mechanism always expands into tree-like data structures with back pointers. This is a key limitation of our approach. For an example, see the report [21]. For future work, we also intend to combine shape analysis with other analyses domains, in order to capture more expressive specifications, beyond memory safety.

8 Related Work and Conclusion

A significant body of research has been devoted to shape analysis. Most proposals are orthogonal to our work as they focus on determining shapes based on a fixed set of shape domains. For instance, the analysis in [26] can infer shape and certain numerical properties but is limited to the linked list domain. The analyses from [32,11,4,15,3,24] are tailored to variants of lists and a fixed family of list interleavings. Likewise, Calcagno et al. [7] describes an analysis for determining lock invariants with only linked lists. Lee et al. [22] presents a shape analysis specifically tailored to overlaid data structures. In the matching logic framework, a set of predicates is typically assumed for program verification [31]. The work [2] extends this with specification inference. However, it currently does not deal with the inference of inductive data structure abstractions.

The proposal by Magill et al. [26] is able to infer numerical properties, but it is still parametric in the shape domain. Similarly, the separation logic bi-abduction described in [6,17] assumes a set of built-in or user-defined predicates. Xisa, a tool presented

---

[5] Our current implementation does not support array data structures. Hence, some procedures like g_tree_insert_internal cannot be verified.

by Rival et. al. [8], works on programs with more varied shapes as long as structural invariant checkers, which play the role of shape definitions, are provided. A later extension [30] also considers shape summaries for procedures with the additional help of global analysis. Other similarly parameterized analysis includes [13]. In comparison, our approach is built upon the foundation of second-order bi-abductive entailment, and is able to infer unknown predicates from scratch or guided by user-supplied assertions. This set-up is therefore highly flexible, as we could support a mix of inference and verification, due to our integration into an existing verification system.

With respect to fully automatic analyses, there are [5], [16] and the Forester system [18]. Although very expressive in terms of the inferred shape classes, the analysis proposed by Guo et al. [16] relies on a heavy formalism and depends wholly on the shape construction patterns being present in the code. They describe a global analysis that requires program slicing techniques to shrink the analyzed code and to avoid noise on the analysis. Furthermore, the soundness of their inference could not be guaranteed; therefore a re-verification of the inferred invariants is required. Brotherston and Gorogiannis [5] propose a novel way to synthesize inductive predicates by ensuring both memory safety and termination. However, their proposal is currently limited to a simple imperative language without methods. A completely different approach is presented in the Forrester system [18] where a fully automated shape synthesis is described in terms of graph transformations over forest automata. Their approach is based on learning techniques that can discover suitable forest automata by incrementally constructing shape abstractions called boxes. However, their proposal is currently restricted both in terms of the analysed programs, e.g. recursion is not yet supported, and in terms of the inferred shapes, as recursive nested boxes (needed by tll) are not supported.

In the TVLA tradition, [29] describes an interprocedural shape analysis for cut-free programs. The approach explores the interaction between framing and the reachability-based representation. Other approaches to shape analysis include grammar-based inference, e.g. [23] which relies on inferred grammars to define the recursive backbone of the shape predicates. Although [23] is able to handle various types of structures, e.g. trees and dlls, it is limited to structures with only one argument for back pointers. [25] employs inductive logic programming (ILP) to infer recursive pure predicates. While, it might be possible to apply a similar approach to shape inference, there has not yet been any such effort. Furthermore, we believe a targeted approach would be able to easily cater for the more intricate shapes. Since ILP has been shown to effectively synthesize recursive predicates, it would be interesting to explore an integration of ILP with our proposal for inferring recursive predicates of both shape and pure properties. A recent work [14] that aims to automatically construct verification tools has implemented various proof rules for reachability and termination properties however it does not focus on the synthesis of shape abstractions. In an orthogonal direction, [10] presents an analysis for constructing precise and compact method summaries. Unfortunately, both these works lack the ability to handle recursive data structures.

Conclusion. We have presented a novel approach to *modular* shape analysis that can automatically synthesize, from scratch, a set of shape abstractions that are needed for ensuring memory safety. This capability is premised on our decision to build *shape predicate inference* capability directly into a new second-order bi-abductive entailment procedure. Second-order variables are placeholders for unknown predicates that can be synthesized from proof obligations gathered by Hoare-style verification. Thus, the soundness of our inference is based on the soundness of the entailment procedure itself, and is not subjected to a re-verification process. Our proposal for shape analysis has been structured into three key stages: (i) gathering of relational assumptions on unknown shape predicates; (ii) synthesis of predicate definitions via derivation; and (iii) normalization steps to provide concise shape definitions. We have also implemented a prototype of our inference system into an existing verification infrastructure, and have evaluated on a range of examples with complex heap usage patterns.

Acknowledgement. We thank Quang-Trung Ta for his C front-end integration. We gratefully acknowledge the support of research grant MOE2013-T2-2-146.

References

1. Glib-2.38.2 (2013), https://developer.gnome.org/glib/ (accessed November 13, 2013)
2. Alpuente, M., Feliú, M.A., Villanueva, A.: Automatic inference of specifications using matching logic. In: PEPM, pp. 127–136 (2013)
3. Berdine, J., Calcagno, C., Cook, B., Distefano, D., O'Hearn, P.W., Wies, T., Yang, H.: Shape analysis for composite data structures. In: Damm, W., Hermanns, H. (eds.) CAV 2007. LNCS, vol. 4590, pp. 178–192. Springer, Heidelberg (2007)
4. Berdine, J., Cook, B., Ishtiaq, S.: SLAYER: Memory safety for systems-level code. In: Gopalakrishnan, G., Qadeer, S. (eds.) CAV 2011. LNCS, vol. 6806, pp. 178–183. Springer, Heidelberg (2011)
5. Brotherston, J., Gorogiannis, N.: Cyclic abduction of inductively defined safety and termination preconditions. Technical Report RN/13/14, University College London (2013)
6. Calcagno, C., Distefano, D., O'Hearn, P.W., Yang, H.: Compositional shape analysis by means of bi-abduction. In: POPL, pp. 289–300 (2009)
7. Calcagno, C., Distefano, D., Vafeiadis, V.: Bi-abductive resource invariant synthesis. In: Hu, Z. (ed.) APLAS 2009. LNCS, vol. 5904, pp. 259–274. Springer, Heidelberg (2009)
8. Chang, B.-Y.E., Rival, X.: Relational inductive shape analysis. In: POPL, pp. 247–260 (2008)
9. Chin, W.N., David, C., Nguyen, H.H., Qin, S.: Automated verification of shape, size and bag properties via user-defined predicates in separation logic. Sci. Comput. Program. 77(9), 1006–1036 (2012)
10. Dillig, I., Dillig, T., Aiken, A., Sagiv, M.: Precise and compact modular procedure summaries for heap manipulating programs. In: PLDI, pp. 567–577 (2011)
11. Distefano, D., O'Hearn, P.W., Yang, H.: A local shape analysis based on separation logic. In: Hermanns, H., Palsberg, J. (eds.) TACAS 2006. LNCS, vol. 3920, pp. 287–302. Springer, Heidelberg (2006)
12. Dudka, K., Peringer, P., Vojnar, T.: Predator: A practical tool for checking manipulation of dynamic data structures using separation logic. In: Gopalakrishnan, G., Qadeer, S. (eds.) CAV 2011. LNCS, vol. 6806, pp. 372–378. Springer, Heidelberg (2011)
13. Gotsman, A., Berdine, J., Cook, B.: Interprocedural Shape Analysis with Separated Heap Abstractions. In: Yi, K. (ed.) SAS 2006. LNCS, vol. 4134, pp. 240–260. Springer, Heidelberg (2006)
14. Grebenshchikov, S., Lopes, N.P., Popeea, C., Rybalchenko, A.: Synthesizing software verifiers from proof rules. In: PLDI, pp. 405–416 (2012)

15. Gulavani, B.S., Chakraborty, S., Ramalingam, G., Nori, A.V.: Bottom-up shape analysis. In: Palsberg, J., Su, Z. (eds.) SAS 2009. LNCS, vol. 5673, pp. 188–204. Springer, Heidelberg (2009)

16. Guo, B., Vachharajani, N., August, D.I.: Shape analysis with inductive recursion synthesis. In: PLDI, pp. 256–265 (2007)

17. He, G., Qin, S., Chin, W.-N., Craciun, F.: Automated specification discovery via user-defined predicates. In: Groves, L., Sun, J. (eds.) ICFEM 2013. LNCS, vol. 8144, pp. 397–414. Springer, Heidelberg (2013)

18. Holik, L., Lengál, O., Rogalewicz, A., Šimáček, J., Vojnar, T.: Fully automated shape analysis based on forest automata. In: Sharygina, N., Veith, H. (eds.) CAV 2013. LNCS, vol. 8044, pp. 740–755. Springer, Heidelberg (2013)

19. Iosif, R., Rogalewicz, A., Simacek, J.: The tree width of separation logic with recursive definitions. In: Bonacina, M.P. (ed.) CADE 2013. LNCS (LNAI), vol. 7898, pp. 21–38. Springer, Heidelberg (2013)

20. Ishtiaq, S., O'Hearn, P.W.: BI as an Assertion Language for Mutable Data Structures. In: ACM POPL, London (January 2001)

21. Le, Q.L., Gherghina, C., Qin, S., Chin, W.N.: Shape analysis via second-order bi-abduction. In Technical Report, Soc, NUS (February 2014), http://loris-7.ddns.comp.nus.edu.sg/~project/s2/beta/src/TRs2.pdf

22. Lee, O., Yang, H., Petersen, R.: Program analysis for overlaid data structures. In: Gopalakrishnan, G., Qadeer, S. (eds.) CAV 2011. LNCS, vol. 6806, pp. 592–608. Springer, Heidelberg (2011)

23. Lee, O., Yang, H., Yi, K.: Automatic verification of pointer programs using grammar-based shape analysis. In: Sagiv, M. (ed.) ESOP 2005. LNCS, vol. 3444, pp. 124–140. Springer, Heidelberg (2005)

24. Lev-Ami, T., Sagiv, M., Reps, T., Gulwani, S.: Backward analysis for inferring quantified preconditions. Technical Report TR-2007-12-01, Tel Aviv University (2007)

25. Loginov, A., Reps, T., Sagiv, M.: Abstraction Refinement via Inductive Learning. In: Etessami, K., Rajamani, S.K. (eds.) CAV 2005. LNCS, vol. 3576, pp. 519–533. Springer, Heidelberg (2005)

26. Magill, S., Tsai, M.-H., Lee, P., Tsay, Y.-K.: Automatic numeric abstractions for heap-manipulating programs. In: POPL, pp. 211–222 (2010)

27. Necula, G., McPeak, S., Rahul, S., Weimer, W.: CIL: Intermediate Language and Tools for Analysis and Transformation of C Programs. In: Horspool, R.N. (ed.) CC 2002. LNCS, vol. 2304, pp. 213–228. Springer, Heidelberg (2002)

28. Reynolds, J.: Separation Logic: A Logic for Shared Mutable Data Structures. In: IEEE LICS, pp. 55–74 (2002)

29. Rinetzky, N., Sagiv, M., Yahav, E.: Interprocedural shape analysis for cutpoint-free programs. In: Hankin, C., Siveroni, I. (eds.) SAS 2005. LNCS, vol. 3672, pp. 284–302. Springer, Heidelberg (2005)

30. Rival, X., Chang, B.-Y.E.: Calling context abstraction with shapes. In: POPL, pp. 173–186 (2011)

31. Rosu, G., Stefanescu, A.: Checking reachability using matching logic. In: OOPSLA, pp. 555–574. ACM (2012)

32. Yang, H., Lee, O., Berdine, J., Calcagno, C., Cook, B., Distefano, D., O'Hearn, P.W.: Scalable shape analysis for systems code. In: Gupta, A., Malik, S. (eds.) CAV 2008. LNCS, vol. 5123, pp. 385–398. Springer, Heidelberg (2008)

ICE: A Robust Framework for Learning Invariants

Pranav Garg[1], Christof Löding[2], P. Madhusudan[1], and Daniel Neider[2]

[1] University of Illinois at Urbana-Champaign
[2] RWTH Aachen University

Abstract. We introduce ICE, a robust learning paradigm for synthesizing invariants, that learns using examples, counter-examples, and *implications*, and show that it admits honest teachers and strongly convergent mechanisms for invariant synthesis. We observe that existing algorithms for black-box abstract interpretation can be interpreted as ICE-learning algorithms. We develop new strongly convergent ICE-learning algorithms for two domains, one for learning Boolean combinations of numerical invariants for scalar variables and one for *quantified* invariants for arrays and dynamic lists. We implement these ICE-learning algorithms in a verification tool and show they are robust, practical, and efficient.

1 Introduction

The problem of generating adequate inductive invariants to prove a program correct is at the heart of automated program verification. Synthesizing invariants is in fact the *hardest* aspect of program verification—once adequate inductive invariants are synthesized [1–5], program verification reduces to checking validity of verification conditions obtained from finite loop-free paths [6–8], which is a logic problem that has been highly automated over the years.

Invariant generation techniques can be broadly classified into two kinds: white-box techniques where the synthesizer of the invariant is acutely aware of the precise program and property that is being proved and black-box techniques where the synthesizer is largely agnostic to the structure of the program and property, but works with a partial view of the requirements of the invariant. Abstract interpretation [1], counter-example guided abstraction refinement, predicate abstraction [9, 10], the method of Craig interpolants [11, 12], IC3 [13], etc. all fall into the white-box category. In this paper, we are interested in the newly emerging black-box techniques for invariant generation.

Learning Invariants: One prominent black-box technique for invariant generation is the emerging paradigm of *learning*. Intuitively (see picture on the right), we have two components in the verification tool: a white-box *teacher* and a black-box *learner*. The 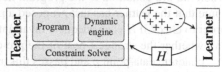 learner synthesizes suggestions for the invariants in each round. The teacher is completely aware of the program and the property being verified, and is responsible for two things: (a) to check if a purported invariant H (for hypothesis) supplied by the learner is indeed an invariant and is adequate in proving the property of the program (typically using a constraint solver), and (b) if the invariant is not adequate, to come up with concrete program configurations that need to be added or removed from the invariant

A. Biere and R. Bloem (Eds.): CAV 2014, LNCS 8559, pp. 69–87, 2014.

(denoted by + and − in the figure). The learner, who comes up with the invariant H is completely agnostic of the program and property being verified, and aims to build a simple formula that is consistent with the sample.

When learning an invariant, the teacher and learner talk to each other in rounds, where in each round the teacher comes up with additional constraints involving new data-points and the learner replies with some set satisfying the constraints, until the teacher finds the set to be an adequate inductive invariant. The above learning approach for invariants has been explored for quite some time in various contexts [14–16], and is gaining considerable excitement and traction in recent years [17–20].

Advantages of Learning: There are many advantages the learning approach has over white-box approaches. First, a synthesizer of invariants that works cognizant of the program and property is very hard to build, simply *due* to the fact that it has to deal with the complex logic of the program. When a program manipulates complex data-structures, pointers, objects, etc. with a complex memory model and semantics, building a set that is guaranteed to be an invariant gets extremely complex. However, the invariant for a loop in such a program may be much simpler, and hence a black-box technique that uses a "guess and check" approach guided by a finite set of configurations is much more light-weight and has better chances of finding the invariant. (See [4] where a similar argument is made for black-box generation of the abstract post in an abstract interpretation setting.) Second, learning, which typically concentrates on finding the *simplest* concept that satisfies the constraints, implicitly provides a tactic for generalization, while white-box techniques (like interpolation) need to build in tactics to generalize. Finally, the black-box approach allows us to seamlessly integrate highly scalable machine-learning techniques into the verification framework [21, 22].

ICE-learning: The problem with the learning approach described above is that it is *broken*, as we show in this paper! Approaches to learning invariants have been unduly influenced by algorithmic learning theory, automata learning, and machine learning techniques, which have traditionally offered learning from positive and negative examples. *As we show in this paper, learning using examples and counter-examples does not form a robust learning framework for synthesizing invariants.* To see why, consider the following simple program—

$$pre; \ S; \ \textbf{while} \ (b) \ \textbf{do} \ L; \ \textbf{od} \ S'; post$$

with a single loop body for which we want to synthesize an invariant that proves that when the pre-condition to the program holds, the post-condition holds upon exit. Assume that the learner has just proposed a particular set H as a hypothesis invariant. In order to check if H is an adequate invariant, the teacher checks three things:

(a) whether the strongest-post of the pre-condition across S implies H; if not finds a concrete data-point p and passes this as a positive example to the learner.

(b) whether the strongest-post of $(H \wedge \neg b)$ across S' implies the post-condition; if not, pass a data-point p in H that shouldn't belong to the invariant as a *negative* example.

(c) whether H is inductive; i.e., whether the strongest post of $H \wedge b$ across loop body L implies H; if not, finds two concrete configurations p and p', with $p \in H$, $p' \notin H$.

In the last case above, the teacher is *stuck*. Since she does not *know* the precise invariant (there are after all many), she has no way of knowing whether p should be excluded from H or whether p' should be included. In many learning algorithms in the literature

[14–16, 20], the teacher cheats: she arbitrarily makes one choice and goes with that, hoping that it will result in an invariant. However, this makes the entire framework non-robust, causing divergence, blocking the learner from learning the simplest concepts, and introducing arbitrary bias that is very hard to control. If learning is to be seriously developed for synthesizing invariants, we need to fix this foundationally in the framework itself.

The main contribution of this paper is a new learning framework called ICE-learning, which stands for *learning using Examples, Counter-examples, and Implications*. We propose that we should build learning algorithms that do not take just examples and counter-examples, as most traditional learning algorithms do, but instead also handle *implications*. The teacher, when faced with non-inductiveness of the current conjecture H in terms of a pair (p, p'), simply communicates this implication pair to the learner, demanding that the learnt set satisfies the property that if p is included in H, then so is p'. The learner makes the choice, based on considerations of simplicity, generalization, etc., whether it would include both p and p' in its set or leave p out.

We show that ICE-learning is a *robust* learning model, in the sense that the teacher can always communicate to a learner precisely why a conjecture is not an invariant (even for programs with multiple loops, nested loops, etc.). This robustness then leads to new questions that we can formulate about learning, which we cannot ask in the setting of learning with only examples and counter-examples. In particular, we can ask whether the iterative learning process, for a particular learner, *strongly converges*— whether the learner will eventually learn the invariant, provided one exists expressible as a concept, no matter how the teacher gives examples, counter-examples, and implications to refute the learner's conjectures.

We emphasize that earlier works in the literature have indeed seen *inductiveness* as an important aspect of synthesizing invariants, and several mechanisms for guiding the search towards an inductive property are known [13, 23–26]. Our work here is however the first that we know that develops a robust learning model that explicitly incorporates the search for inductive sets in black-box invariant generation.

Our main contributions are as follows:

- We propose the ICE-learning framework as a robust learning framework for synthesizing invariants. We study ICE-learning algorithms at two levels: ICE-learning for a particular sample as well as the *iterative* ICE-model in which the teacher and learner iteratively interact to find the invariant. The complexity of the ICE-learner for a sample, strong convergence of iterative learning, and the number of rounds of iteration required to learn are pertinent questions.
- We show that when the class of concepts forms a *lattice*, ICE learning can be often achieved, and in fact methods that already exist in the literature can be seen as ICE-learning algorithms. In particular, the abstract Houdini algorithm [3,4] and the work reported in [27] for invariant synthesis over abstract numerical domain lattices are in fact ICE-learning algorithms. However, these algorithms are not typically *strongly convergent* and moreover, cannot learn from negative examples at all. We hence concentrate on strongly convergent ICE-learning algorithms for two different domains in this paper that do use negative examples and implications effectively.

- We develop a new ICE-learning algorithm for *Boolean combinations of numerical invariants*, which does not form a complete lattice. Given an ICE-sample, we show how to find the *simplest* expressible formula that satisfies the sample. Our algorithm *iterates* over all possible template formulas, growing in complexity, till it finds an appropriate formula, and adapts template-based synthesis techniques that use constraint solvers [28–31] to build a black-box ICE-learning algorithm. We prove that the resulting iterative ICE-algorithm is strongly convergent. Note that the user only specifies the logic for the invariants, and does not need to give templates. We build a tool over Boogie [8] for synthesizing invariants over scalar variables and show that it is extremely effective: it mostly outperforms other techniques, and furthermore gives guarantees of simplicity and strong convergence that other algorithms do not.

- As a second instantiation of the ICE-framework, we develop a new strongly convergent ICE-learning algorithm for *quantified* invariants. We develop a general technique of reducing ICE-learning of quantified properties to ICE-learning of quantifier-free properties, but where the latter is generalized to *sets of configurations* rather than single configurations. We instantiate this technique to build an ICE-learner for quantified properties of arrays and lists. This new learning algorithm (which is the most involved technical contribution of this paper) extends the classical RPNI learning algorithm for automata [32] to learning in the ICE-model and further learns *quantified data automata* [20], which can be converted to quantified logical formulas over arrays/lists. We build a prototype verifier by building this learner and the teacher as well, and show that this results in extremely efficient and robust learning of quantified invariants.

Related Work: Prominent white-box techniques for invariant synthesis include abstract interpretation [1], interpolation [11, 12] and IC3 [13]. Abstract interpretation has been used for generating invariants over mostly convex domains [2, 33], some non-convex domains [34, 35] and more recently even over non-lattice abstract domains [36]. Template based approaches to synthesizing invariants using constraint solvers have been explored in a white-box setting in [28–31], and we adapt these techniques in Section 4 for developing an ICE-learning algorithm for numerical invariants. Several white-box techniques for synthesizing quantified invariants are also known. Most of them are based on abstract interpretation or on interpolation theorems for array theories [37–45].

Turning to black-box learning-based techniques for synthesizing invariants, Daikon [46] was a prominent early technique proposed for conjunctive Boolean learning to find *likely* invariants from configurations recorded along test runs. Learning was introduced in the context of verification by Cobleigh et al. [14], which was followed by applications of Angluin's L* algorithm [47] to finding rely-guarantee contracts [15] and stateful interfaces for programs [16]. Houdini [3] uses essentially conjunctive Boolean learning (which can be achieved in polynomial time) to learn conjunctive invariants over templates of atomic formulas. In Section 3, we show that the Houdini algorithm along with its generalization by Thakur et al. [4] and [27] to arbitrary abstract domains like intervals, octagons, polyhedrons, linear equalities, etc. are in fact ICE-learning algorithms.

Recently, there is renewed interest in the application of learning to program verification, in particular to synthesize invariants [17–19] by using scalable machine learning techniques [21, 22] to find classifiers that can separate good states that the program can reach (positive examples) from the bad states the program is forbidden from reaching (counter-examples). Quantified *likely* invariants for linear data-structures and arrays are found from dynamic executions using learning in [20], but these aren't necessarily adequate. Boolean formula learning has also been applied recently for learning quantified invariants in [48]. In addition, learning has been applied towards inductive program synthesis [49, 50] and model extraction and testing of software [51, 52].

Counterexamples to inductiveness of an invariant have been handled in the past [24–26], but only in the context of lattice domains where the learned concepts grow monotonically and implications essentially yield positive examples. Recently, [23] tries to find inductive invariants by finding *common* interpolants for same program locations. Though [18] mentions a heuristic for handling implication samples in their algorithm for learning invariants their tool does not implement that heuristic. As far as we know, our work here is the first to explicitly incorporate the search for inductive sets in black-box invariant generation.

2 Illustrative Example

Consider the C program on the right. This program requires a scalar loop invariant ($i > p \Rightarrow j = 1$) for its verification using VCC [53]. Even in order to synthesize such a scalar invariant, white-box techniques would need to reason about the array a[] in the program, and in general have to deal with complex language features like objects, pointers, a complex memory model and its semantics, etc. A black-box approach can however learn such an invariant from a small set of program configurations restricted to scalars.

```
#include <vcc.h>
int foo(int a[], int p)
_(requires (p>=25 && p<75))
_(requires a[p]==1)
_(requires \thread_local_array
                  (a, 100))
{
    int i=0, j=0;
    while (i<100)
    _(invariant (i>p ==> j==1))
    {
        if (a[i]==1)
            j = 1;
        i = i+1;
    }
    _(assert j==1);
}
```

Consider a black-box engine that calls foo with the values for p— $25, 26, \ldots$ and that unrolls the loop a few times to find positive examples for (i, j, p) in the kind $(0, 0, 25), (1, 0, 25), (1, 1, 25), \ldots$ for a small number of values of i, and counter-examples of the form $(100, 0, 25)$, $(100, 2, 25)$, $\ldots (99, 0, 25), (99, 2, 25), \ldots$ (values close to 100 for i and different from 1 for j). From these positive and negative examples, the learner could naturally come up with a conjecture such as ($i > 50 \Rightarrow j = 1$) (machine learning algorithms tend to come up with such invariants).

Now notice that the teacher is *stuck* as all positive and negative examples are satisfied by the conjecture, though it is not inductive. Consequently, when using a learner from only positive and negative samples, the teacher cannot make progress. However, in ICE-learning, the teacher can give an implication pair, say of the form $((50, 0, 25), (51, 0, 25))$, and proceed with the learning. Hence we can make progress in learning, and a learner that produces the simplest conjectures satisfying the samples would eventually generalize a large enough sample to come up with a correct invariant. Our tool from Section 4 precisely learns the above mentioned invariant for this program.

3 The ICE-Learning Framework

When defining a (machine) learning problem, one usually specifies a domain D (like points in the real plane or finite words over an alphabet), and a class of concepts C (like rectangles in the plane or regular languages), which is a class of subsets of the domain. In classical learning frameworks (see [22]), the teacher provides a set of positive examples in D that are part of the target concept, and a set of counter-examples (or negative examples) in D that are not part of the target concept. Based on these, the learner must construct a hypothesis that approximates the target concept the teacher has in mind.

ICE-learning: In our setting, the teacher does *not* have a precise target concept from C in mind, but is looking for an inductive set which meets certain additional constraints. Consequently, we extend this learning setting with a third type of information that can be provided by the teacher: implications. Formally, let D be some domain and $C \subseteq 2^D$ be a class of subsets of D, called the concepts. The teacher knows a triple (P, N, R), where $P \subseteq D$ is an (infinite) set of positive examples, $N \subseteq D$ is an (infinite) set of counter-examples (or negative examples), and $R \subseteq D \times D$ is a relation interpreted as an (infinite) set of implications. We call (P, N, R) the *target description*, and these sets are typically *infinite* and are obtained from the program, but the teacher has the ability to query these sets effectively.

The learner is given a finite part of this information (E, C, I) with $E \subseteq P$, $C \subseteq N$, and $I \subseteq R$. We refer to (E, C, I) as an (ICE) *sample*. The task of the ICE-learner is to construct *some* hypothesis $H \in C$ such that $P \subseteq H$, $N \cap H = \emptyset$, and for each pair $(x, y) \in R$, if $x \in H$, then $y \in H$. A hypothesis with these properties is called a *correct hypothesis*. Note that a target description (P, N, R) may have several correct hypotheses (while H must include P, exclude N, and be R-closed, there can be several such sets).

Iterative ICE-learning: The above ICE-learning corresponds to a passive learning setting, in which the learner does not interact with the teacher. In general, the quality of the hypothesis will heavily depend on the amount of information contained in the sample. However, when the hypothesis is wrong, we would like the learner to gain information from the teacher using new samples. Since such a learning process proceeds in rounds, we refer to it as *iterative ICE-learning*.

The iterative ICE-learning happens in rounds, where in each round, the learner starts with some sample (E, C, I) (from previous rounds or an initialization) and constructs a hypothesis $H \in C$ from this information, and asks the teacher whether this is correct. If the hypothesis is correct (i.e., if $P \subseteq H$, $H \cap N = \emptyset$, and for every $(x, y) \in R$, if $x \in H$, then $y \in H$ as well), then the teacher answers "correct" and the learning process terminates. Otherwise, the teacher returns either some element $d \in D$ with $d \in P \setminus H$ or $d \in H \cap N$, or an implication $(x, y) \in R$ with $x \in H$ and $y \notin H$. This new information is added to the sample of the learner.

The learning proceeds in rounds and when the learning terminates, the learner has learnt *some* R-closed concept that includes P and excludes N.

Using ICE-Learning to Synthesize Invariants: Honesty and Progress
Given an ICE-learning algorithm for a concept class, we can build algorithms for synthesizing invariants by building the required (white-box) teacher. We can apply such learning for finding invariants in programs with multiple loops, nested loops, etc.

The learning will simultaneously learn all these invariant annotations. The teacher can check the hypotheses by generating verification conditions for the hypothesized invariants and by using automatic theorem provers to check their validity.

The two salient features of ICE-learning is that it facilitates *progress* and *honesty*. The teacher can always make progress by adding an example/counter-example/implication such that H (and any other previous hypothesis) does not satisfy it. Furthermore, while augmenting the sample, the teacher can answer honestly, not precluding *any* possible adequate inductive invariant of the program. Honesty and progress are impossible to achieve when learning just from positive and negative examples (when the hypothesis is not inductive, there is no way to make progress without making a dishonest choice).

Convergence: The setting of iterative ICE-learning naturally raises the question of convergence of the learner, that is, does the learner find a correct hypothesis in a finite number of rounds? We say that a learner *strongly converges*, if for every target description (P, N, R) it reaches a correct hypothesis (from the empty sample) after a finite number of rounds, no matter what information is provided by the teacher (of course, the teacher has to answer correctly according to the target description (P, N, R)).

Note that the definition above demands convergence for arbitrary triples (P, N, R), and allows the teacher in each round to provide *any* information that contradicts the current hypothesis, and is hence a very strong property.

Observe now that for a *finite* class C of concepts, a learner strongly converges if it never constructs the same hypothesis twice. This assumption on the learner is satisfied if it only produces hypotheses H that are consistent with the sample (E, C, I), that is, if $E \subseteq H, C \cap H = \emptyset$, and for each pair $(x, y) \in I$, if $x \in H$, then $y \in H$. Such a learner is called a *consistent learner*. Since the teacher always provides a witness for an incorrect hypothesis, the next hypothesis constructed by a consistent learner must be different from all the previous ones.

Lemma 1. *For a finite class C of concepts, every consistent learner strongly converges.*

For various iterative ICE-algorithm classes, where class of concepts may be infinite, we will study strong convergence.

ICE-Learning over Lattice Domains: It turns out that ICE-algorithms are especially easy to build when the class of concepts forms a lattice, as typical in an abstract interpretation setting.

Consider an abstract domain that is a lattice. Then given any sample (E, C, I), we can compute the *best* (smallest) abstract element that satisfies the constraints (E, C, I) as follows. First, we take the least upper bound of the set of all $\alpha(e)$, for each $e \in E$. Then we see if these satisfy the implication constraints; if not, then for every pair $(p, p') \in I$ that is not satisfied, we know that p' *must* be added to the set (since p belongs to every set that includes E). Hence all these elements p' can be added by applying α to them, and we can take the lub with respect to the existing set. We continue in this fashion till we converge to an abstract element that is the smallest satisfying E and I. Now, we can check if C is excluded from it; if yes, we have computed the best set, else there is no set satisfying the constraints. The above is an ICE-algorithm for any abstract domain.

We can, using this argument, establish polynomial-time (non-iterative) ICE-learning algorithms for conjunctive formulas (in fact, this is what the classical Houdini algorithm does [3,22]), k-CNF formulas [22], and for abstract domains such as octagons, polyhedra, etc. as in [24,25]

However, note that the iterative extension of the above ICE-algorithm may not halt (unless the domain has finite height). One can of course use a widening heuristically after some rounds to halt, but then clearly the iterative ICE algorithm will not be necessarily *strongly convergent*. The iterative ICE-algorithm with widening is, in fact, precisely the *abstract Houdini* algorithm proposed recently in [4], and is similar to another recent work in [27], and are not *strongly convergent*.

The iterative ICE-learning algorithms we develop in this paper *are strongly convergent*. While the above derived iterative ICE-algorithms essentially ignore counter-examples, and fail to use counter-examples and implications as a way to *come down* the lattice after a widening/over-generalization, the algorithms we propose in the next two sections are more general schemes that truly utilize examples, counter-examples, and implications to find succinct expressions.

4   An ICE-Learning Algorithm for Numerical Invariants

In this section, we describe a learning algorithm for synthesizing invariants that are arbitrary Boolean combinations of numerical atomic formulas. Since we want the learning algorithm to generalize the sample (and not capture precisely the finite set of implication-closed positive examples), we would like it to learn a formula with the *simplest* Boolean structure. In order to do so, we iterate over templates over the Boolean structure of the formulas, and learn a formula in the given template.

Note that the domain is a join-semilattice (every pair of elements has a least upper bound) since formulas are closed under disjunction. Hence we can employ the generic abstract Houdini algorithm [4] to obtain a passive ICE-learning algorithm. However, using the vanilla algorithm will learn only the precise set of positive and implication-closed set, and hence not generalize without a widening. Widening for disjunctive domains is not easy, as there are several ways to generalize disjunctive sets [54]. Furthermore, even with a widening, we will not get a *strongly convergent* iterative ICE-algorithm that we desire (see experiments in this section where abstract Houdini diverges even on conjunctive domains on some programs for this reason). The algorithm we build in this section will not only be strongly convergent but also will produce the *simplest* expressible invariant.

Let $Var = \{x_1, \cdots, x_n\}$ be the set of (integer) variables in the scope of the program. For simplicity, let us restrict atomic formulas in our concept class to octagonal constraints, over program configurations, of the general form:
$$s_1 v_1 + s_2 v_2 \leq c, \quad s_1, s_2 \in \{0, +1, -1\}, \quad v_1, v_2 \in Var, \quad v_1 \neq v_2, \quad c \in \mathbb{Z}.$$
(We can handle more general atomic formulas as well; we stick to the above for simplicity and effectiveness.)

Our ICE-learning algorithm will work by iterating over more and more complex *templates* till it finds the simplest formula that satisfies the sample. A *template* fixes the Boolean structure of the desired invariants and also restricts the constants $c \in \mathbb{Z}$ appearing in the atomic formulas to lie within a finite range $[-M, +M]$, for some $M \in \mathbb{Z}^+$. Bounding the constants leads to strong convergence as we show below. For a given template $\bigvee_i \bigwedge_j \alpha^{ij}$, the iterative ICE-learning algorithm we describe below learns an adequate invariant φ, of the form:

$$\varphi(x_1, \cdots, x_n) = \bigvee_i \bigwedge_j (s_1^{ij} v_1^{ij} + s_2^{ij} v_2^{ij} \le c^{ij}), \quad |c^{ij}| \le M.$$

Given a sample (E, C, I), the learner iterates through templates, and for each template, tries to find concrete values for s_k^{ij}, v_k^{ij} ($k \in \{1, 2\}$) and c^{ij} such that the formula φ is consistent with the sample; i.e., for every data-point $p \in E$, $\varphi(p)$ holds; for $p \in C$, $\varphi(p)$ does not hold; and for every implication pair $(p, p') \in I$, $\varphi(p')$ holds if $\varphi(p)$ holds. Unfortunately, finding these values in the presence of implications is hard; classifying each implication pair (p, p') as both positive or p as negative tends to create an exponential search space that is hard to search efficiently. Our ICE-learner uses a constraint solver to search this exponential space in a reasonably efficient manner. It does so by checking the satisfiability of the formula Ψ (below), over free variables s_k^{ij}, v_k^{ij} and c^{ij}, which precisely captures all the ICE-constraints. In this formula, b_p is a Boolean variable which tracks $\varphi(p)$; the Boolean variables b_p^{ij} represent the truth value of $(s_1^{ij} v_1^{ij} + s_2^{ij} v_2^{ij} \le c^{ij})$ on point p, r_{kp}^{ij} encode the value of $s_k^{ij} \cdot v_k^{ij}$ (line 2); and d_{kp}^{ij} encode the value of v_k^{ij} (line 3).

$$\Psi(s_k^{ij}, v_k^{ij}, c^{ij}) \equiv \left(\bigwedge_{p \in E} b_p \right) \wedge \left(\bigwedge_{p \in C} \neg b_p \right) \wedge \left(\bigwedge_{(p,p') \in I} b_p \Rightarrow b_{p'} \right) \wedge \left(\bigwedge_p \left(b_p \Leftrightarrow \bigvee_i \bigwedge_j b_p^{ij} \right) \right) \wedge$$

$$\left(\bigwedge_{p,i,j} \left(b_p^{ij} \Leftrightarrow \left(\sum_{k \in \{1,2\}} r_{kp}^{ij} \le c^{ij} \right) \right) \right) \wedge \left(\bigwedge_{i,j} \left(-M \le c^{ij} \le M \right) \right) \wedge \left(\bigwedge_{\substack{p,i,j \\ k \in \{1,2\}}} \begin{pmatrix} s_k^{ij} = 0 \Rightarrow r_{kp}^{ij} = 0 \\ s_k^{ij} = 1 \Rightarrow r_{kp}^{ij} = d_{kp}^{ij} \\ s_k^{ij} = -1 \Rightarrow r_{kp}^{ij} = -d_{kp}^{ij} \end{pmatrix} \right) \wedge$$

$$\left(\bigwedge_{\substack{p,i,j \\ k \in \{1,2\}}} \bigwedge_{l \in [1,n]} (v_k^{ij} = l \Rightarrow d_{kp}^{ij} = p(l)) \right) \wedge \left(\bigwedge_{\substack{i,j \\ k \in \{1,2\}}} \left(-1 \le s_k^{ij} \le 1 \right) \right) \wedge \left(\bigwedge_{\substack{i,j \\ k \in \{1,2\}}} (1 \le v_k^{ij} \le n) \right) \wedge \left(\bigwedge_{i,j} (v_1^{ij} \ne v_2^{ij}) \right)$$

Note that Ψ falls in the theory of quantifier-free linear integer arithmetic, the satisfiability of which is decidable. A satisfying assignment for Ψ gives a *consistent* formula that the learner conjectures as an invariant. If Ψ is unsatisfiable, then there is no invariant for the current template consistent with the given sample. In this case we iterate by increasing the complexity of the template. For a given template, the class of formulas conforming to the template is finite. Our enumeration of templates *dovetails* between the Boolean structure and the range of constants in the template, thereby progressively increasing the complexity of the template. Consequently, the ICE-learning algorithm always synthesizes a consistent hypothesis if there is one, and furthermore synthesizes a hypothesis of the simplest template.

A similar approach can be used for learning invariants over linear constraints, and even more general constraints if there is an effective solver for the resulting theory.

Convergence: Our iterative ICE-algorithm conjectures a consistent hypothesis in each round, and hence ensures that we do not repeat hypotheses. Furthermore, the enumeration of templates using dovetailing ensures that all templates are eventually considered, and together with the fact that there are a finite number of formulas conforming to any template ensures strong convergence.

Theorem 1. *The above ICE-learning algorithm always produces consistent conjectures and the corresponding iterative ICE-algorithm strongly converges.*

Our learning algorithm is quite different from earlier white-box constraint based approaches to invariant synthesis [28–31]. These approaches directly encode the adequacy of the invariant (encoding the entire program's body) into a constraint, and use Farkas' lemma to reduce the problem to satisfiability of quantifier-free non-linear arithmetic formulas, which is harder and in general undecidable. We, on the other hand, split the task between a white-box teacher and a black-box learner, communicating only through ICE-constraints on concrete data-points. This greatly reduces the complexity of the problem, leading to a simple teacher and a much simpler learner. Our idea is more similar to [19] which use algebraic techniques to guess the coefficients.

Table 1. Results for ICE-learning numerical invariants. ICE is the total time taken by our tool. All times reported are in seconds. × means an adequate invariant was not found.

| Program | Invariant | White Box | | Black Box | | ICE | Program | Invariant | White Box | | Black Box | | ICE |
		InvGen [31]	CPA [55]	absH [4]	ML [18]				InvGen [31]	CPA [55]	absH [4]	ML [18]	
w1[29]	$x \leq n$	0.1	×	0.1	0.2	0.0	w2[29]	$x \leq n - 1$	0.1	×	0.2	0.1	0.0
fig6[56]	true	0.1	1.3	0.1	0.1	0.0	fig1[29]	$x \leq -1 \vee y \geq 1$	×	4.5	×	×	0.1
fig8[56]	true	0.0	1.4	0.0	0.0	0.0	fig3[56]	$lock = 1 \vee x \leq y - 1$	0.1	1.4	×	0.1	0.0
ex14[57]	$x \geq 1$	×	1.5	0.2	0.2	0.0	fig9[56]	$x = 0 \wedge y \geq 0$	0.1	1.4	0.0	0.2	0.0
finf1	$x = 0$	0.1	1.5	0.1	0.4	0.0	ex23[57]	$0 \leq y \leq z \wedge$ $z \leq c + 4572$	×	90.5	0.2	×	14.2
finf2	$x = 0$	0.1	1.4	0.0	0.1	0.0
sum3	$sn = x$	0.1	1.5	0.1	0.1	0.0	ex7 [57]	$0 \leq i \wedge y \leq len$	×	1.6	0.2	0.4	0.0
term2	true	0.0	1.6	0.0	0.0	0.0	sum1	$sn = i - 1 \wedge$ $(sn = 0 \vee sn \leq n)$	×	×	×	×	1.8
term3	true	0.0	1.4	0.0	0.0	0.0
trex1	$z >= 1$	0.1	1.5	0.1	0.4	0.0	sum4	$sn = i - 1 \wedge sn \leq 8$	0.1	2.8	×	×	2.6
trex2	true	0.0	1.4	0.0	0.0	0.0	tcs [12]	$i \leq j - 1 \vee i \geq j + 1 \vee$ $x = y$	0.1	1.4	×	0.5	1.4
trex4	true	0.0	1.4	0.0	0.0	0.0
winf1	$x = 0$	0.0	1.4	0.0	0.0	0.0	trex3	$0 \leq x1 \wedge 0 \leq x2 \wedge$ $0 \leq x3 \wedge d1 = 1 \wedge$ $d2 = 1 \wedge d3 = 1$	0.5	×	×	×	2.2
winf2	$x = 0$	0.0	1.4	0.0	0.0	0.0
winf3	$x = 0$	×	1.4	0.3	0.1	0.1
vmail	$i \geq 0$	×	1.4	0.1	0.3	0.0	matrix	$a[0][0] \leq m \vee j \leq 0;$ $a[0][0] \leq m \vee j+k \leq 0$	×	×	×	×	5.8
lucmp	$n = 5$	×	77.0	0.0	0.1	0.0
n.c11	$0 \leq len$ ≤ 4	0.1	2.2	×	0.2	0.6	cgr2[29]	$N \leq 0 \vee (x \geq 0 \wedge$ $0 \leq m \leq N - 1)$	×	1.8	×	×	7.3
cgr1[29]	$x - y \leq 2$	0.1	1.5	0.1	0.2	0.0	array	$j \leq 0 \vee m \leq a[0]$	×	×	×	0.2	0.3
oct	$x + y \leq 2$	0.0	1.3	0.2	0.1	0.2	vbsd	$pathlim \leq tmp$	×	1.6	0.5	×	0.0

Experimental Results: We have implemented our learning algorithm as an invariant synthesis tool [1] in Boogie [8]. In our tool we enumerate templates in an increasing order of their complexity. For a given Boolean structure of the template B_i, we fix the range of constants M in the template to be the greater value out of i and the maximum integer in the program. If an adequate invariant is not found, we increase i. If an adequate invariant is found, we use binary search on M to find an invariant that has the same Boolean structure but the smallest constants. This enumeration of templates is complete and it ensures that we learn the *simplest* invariant. In our tool, ICE-samples discovered while learning an invariant belonging to a simpler template are not wasted but used in subsequent rounds. As already mentioned, our learner uses an incremental Z3 [58] solver that adds a new constraint for every ICE-sample discovered by the Boogie based teacher.

---

[1] Available at http://www.cs.uiuc.edu/~madhu/cav14/

We evaluate our tool on SV-COMP benchmarks[2] and several other programs from the literature (see Table 1). We use SMACK [59] to convert C programs to Boogie and use our tool to learn loop invariants for the resulting Boogie programs. We use inlining to infer invariants for programs with multiple procedures. In Table 1 we compare our tool to invariant synthesis using abstract Houdini [4] (called absH in Table 1), [18] (called ML), Invgen [31] and interpolation based Impact algorithm [60] implemented in CPAchecker (called CPA) [55]. We implemented the octagonal domain in abstract Houdini for a comparison with our tool. As mentioned in Section 3, abstract Houdini is an ICE-learning algorithm but is not strongly convergent. Unlike our tool, abstract Houdini is not able to learn disjunctive octagonal invariants. In addition, it is unable to prove programs like trex3 and n.c11 where it loses precision due to widening. InvGen [31] uses a white-box constraint-based approach to invariant synthesis. Unlike our tool that enumerates all templates, InvGen requires the user to specify a template for the invariants. Being white-box, it cannot handle programs with arrays and pointers, even if the required invariants are numerical constraints over scalar variables. Being incomplete, it is also unable to prove several scalar programs like fig1 and cegar2. Finally, [18] is a machine learning algorithm for inferring numerical invariants. From our experience, the inference procedure in [18] is very sensitive to the test harness used to obtain the set of safe/unsafe program configurations. For several programs, we could not learn an adequate invariant using [18] despite many attempts with different test harnesses.

The experiments show that our tool outperforms [4, 18, 31, 55] on most programs, and learns an adequate invariant for all programs in reasonable time. Though we use the more complex but more robust framework of ICE-learning that promises to learn the simplest invariants and is strongly convergent, it is generally faster than other learning algorithms like [17, 18] that learn invariants from just positive and negative examples, and lack any such promises.

5 Learning Universally Quantified Properties

In this section we describe a setting of ICE-learning for *universally quantified* concepts over linear data-structures like arrays and lists. A configuration of a program can be described by the heap structure (locations, the various field-pointers, etc.), and a finite set of pointer variables pointing into the heap. Since the heap is unbounded, typical invariants for programs manipulating heaps require universally quantified formulas. For example, a list is sorted if the data at all pairs y_1, y_2 of successive positions is sorted correctly. We consider synthesis of universal properties of the form $\psi = \forall y_1, \ldots, y_k \varphi(y_1, \ldots, y_k)$, where φ is a quantifier-free formula. We now describe how to modify the ICE-learning framework so that we can use a learner for the quantifier-free property described by $\varphi(y_1, \ldots, y_k)$.

We consider for each concrete program configuration c the set S_c of *valuation configurations* of the form (c, val), where val is a valuation of the variables $y_1, \ldots, y_k$. For example, if the configurations are heaps, then the valuation maps each quantified variable y_i to a cell in the heap, akin to a scalar pointer variable. Then $c \models \psi$ if $(c, val) \models \varphi$ for all valuations val, and $c \not\models \psi$ if $(c, val) \not\models \varphi$ for some valuation val.

---

[2] https://svn.sosy-lab.org/software/sv-benchmarks/tags/svcomp13/loops/

This leads to the setting of *data-set based ICE-learning*. In this setting, the target description is of the form $(\hat{P}, \hat{N}, \hat{R})$ where $\hat{P}, \hat{N} \subseteq 2^D$ and $\hat{R} \subseteq 2^D \times 2^D$. A hypothesis $H \subseteq D$ is correct if $P \subseteq H$ for each $P \in \hat{P}$, $N \nsubseteq H$ for each $N \in \hat{N}$, and for each pair $(X, Y) \in \hat{R}$, if $X \subseteq H$, then also $Y \subseteq H$. The sample is a finite part of the target description, that is, it is of the form $(\hat{E}, \hat{C}, \hat{I})$, where $\hat{E}, \hat{C} \subseteq 2^D$, and $\hat{I} \subseteq 2^D \times 2^D$.

An ICE-learner for the data-set based setting corresponds to an ICE-learner for universally quantified concepts in the original data-point based setting using the following connection. Given a standard target description (P, N, R) over D, we now consider the domain D_{val} extended with valuations of the quantified variables $y_1, \ldots, y_k$ as described above. Replacing each element c of the domain by the set $S_c \subseteq D_{val}$ transforms (P, N, R) into a set-based target description. Then a hypothesis H (described by a quantifier-free formula $\varphi(y_1, \ldots, y_k)$) is correct w.r.t. the set-based target description iff the hypothesis described by $\forall y_1, \ldots, y_k \varphi(y_1, \ldots, y_k)$ is correct w.r.t. the original target description. Unlike [40] that uses "Skolem constants", learning over data-sets allows us to learn from not only examples, but also from counter-examples and implications (where simple Skolem constants will not work).

Recap of Quantified Data Automata and Related Results [20]:
We will develop ICE-learning algorithms for universally quantified invariants over arrays and lists that can be expressed by an automaton model called quantified data automata (QDA) introduced by Garg et al. in [20]. We here briefly recall the main ideas concerning this model and refer the reader to [20] for more detailed definitions.

For example, consider a typical invariant in a sorting program over an array A: $\forall y_1, y_2.((0 \leq y_1 \land y_2 = y_1 + 1 \land y_2 \leq i) \Rightarrow A[y_1] \leq A[y_2])$. This says that for all successive cells y_1, y_2 that occur somewhere in the array A before the cell pointed to by a scalar pointer variable i, the data stored at y_1 is no larger than the data stored at y_2.

We model arrays (or other linear data structures) by *data words*, in which each position corresponds to an element or cell in the data structure. Each position in such a word is labeled with a tuple of a set of pointer variables of the program that indicates their position in the data structure and a data value from some data domain (e.g., integers) that indicates the value contained in the cell of the data structure. A QDA defines a set of data words. However, to capture the idea of expressing universally quantified properties, a QDA reads *valuation words*, which are additionally annotated with universally quantified variables. The alphabet of a QDA is a pair in which the first component corresponds to the pointer variables, and the second component contains the universally quantified variable at that position (if any).

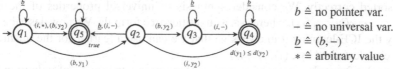

$$b \,\hat{=}\, \text{no pointer var.}$$
$$- \,\hat{=}\, \text{no universal var.}$$
$$\underline{b} \,\hat{=}\, (b, -)$$
$$* \,\hat{=}\, \text{arbitrary value}$$

Fig. 1. An example QDA representing an invariant of a sorting routine

The sortedness invariant above is captured by the QDA in Figure 1. The QDA accepts a valuation word if the data values at the positions of y_1 and y_2 satisfy the formula at the final state it reaches. Moreover, the automaton accepts a data word w if for *all* possible valuations of y_1 and y_2, the automaton accepts the corresponding valuation word.

We assume that the set of formulas used to label the final states of a QDA forms a finite lattice in which the order $\sqsubseteq$ is compatible with implication of formulas, that is, if $\varphi_1 \sqsubseteq \varphi_2$, then $\varphi_1 \Rightarrow \varphi_2$.

In [20] the subclass of elastic QDAs (EQDAs) is considered because they have a decidable emptiness problem and can be translated into decidable logics, like the array property fragment (APF) [61] for arrays, or a decidable fragment of the logic STRAND [62] for lists. The key property of these logics is their inability to express that quantified variables are only a bounded distance away from each other. This is captured at the automaton level by only allowing self loops on $\underline{b}$ in EQDAs. The example QDA in Figure 1 is *not* an elastic QDA because there is a $\underline{b}$-transition from q_2 to q_5. However, there is an EQDA for an equivalent invariant in which the sortedness property is checked for every pair of cells y_1, y_2 such that $y_1 \leq y_2$. Note that since each variable can occur only once, the blank symbol is the only one that can appear arbitrarily often in an input word. Therefore, there are only finitely many EQDAs for a fixed alphabet (set of variables). We refer the reader to [20] for more details on EQDAs.

ICE-Learning Algorithms for EQDAs. The goal of this section is to develop an iterative ICE-learner for concepts represented by EQDAs. The first relevant question is whether there is a *polynomial time* iterative ICE-learner. We show that this is *impossible* when the set of pointers and quantified variables is unbounded (see the technical report [63] for a proof sketch).

Theorem 2. *There is no polynomial time iterative ICE-learner for EQDAs, when the alphabet size is unbounded.*

The theorem is proved by adapting a result from [64], namely that there is no polynomial time learning algorithm for DFAs that only uses equivalence queries. This shows that there is no hope of obtaining an iterative ICE-learner for EQDAs (or even QDAs) in the style of the well-known L^* algorithm of Angluin, which learns DFAs in polynomial time using equivalence and membership queries.

Though we cannot hope for a polynomial time iterative ICE-learner, we develop a (non-iterative) ICE-learner that constructs an EQDA from a given sample in polynomial time. In the iterative setting this yields a learner for which each round is polynomial, while the number of rounds is not polynomial, in general. Our ICE-learning algorithm is adapted from the classical RPNI passive learning algorithm [32], which takes as input a sample (E, C) of positive example words E and counter-example words C, and constructs a DFA that DFA accepts all words in E and rejects all words in C.

RPNI can be viewed as an instance of an abstract state merging algorithm that is sketched as Algorithm 1. In this general setting, the algorithm takes a finite collection S of data, called a *sample*, as input and produces a *Moore machine* (i.e., a DFA with output) that is consistent with the sample (we define this formally later). In the case of classical RPNI, $S = (E, C)$ consists of two finite sets of example and counter-example words, the resulting Moore machine is interpreted as a DFA, and we require that all words in E be accepted whereas all words in C be rejected by the DFA.

Algorithm 1 proceeds in two consecutive phases. In Phase 1 (Lines 1 and 2), it calls init(S) to construct an initial Moore machine $\mathcal{A}_{\text{init}}$ from S that satisfies the sample (assuming that this is possible). Then, it picks a total order $q_0 < \ldots < q_n$ on the states of

$\mathcal{A}_{init}$, which determines the order in which the states are to be merged in the subsequent phase. The actual state merging then takes place in Phase 2 (Lines 3 to 14). According to the given order, Algorithm 1 tries to merge each state q_i with a "smaller" state q_j (i.e., $j < i$) and calls test on the resulting Moore machine to check whether this machine still satisfies the sample; since a merge can cause nondeterminism, it might be necessary to merge further states in order to restore determinism. A merge is kept if the Moore machine passes test; otherwise the merge is discarded, guaranteeing that the final Moore machine still satisfies sample. Note that we represent merging of states by means of a congruence relation $\sim \subseteq Q \times Q$ over the states (i.e., $\sim$ is an equivalence relation that is compatible with the transitions) and the actual merging operation as constructing the quotient Moore machine $\mathcal{A}_{init}/\sim$ in the usual way. Note that in the case of DFAs, each merge increases the language and thus can be seen as a generalization step in the learning algorithm.[3]

Algorithm 1: Generic State Merging algorithm.

Input: A sample S

Output: A Moore machine $\mathcal{A}$ that passes test($\mathcal{A}$)

1 $\mathcal{A}_{init} = (Q, \Sigma, \Gamma, q_0, \delta, f) \leftarrow$ init(S);
2 $(q_0, \ldots, q_n) \leftarrow$ order(Q);
3 $\sim_0 \leftarrow \{(q, q) \mid q \in Q\}$;
4 **for** $i = 1, \ldots, n$ **do**
5   **if** $q_i \not\sim_{i-1} q_j$ for all $j \in \{0, \ldots, i-1\}$ **then**
6          $j \leftarrow 0$;
7   **repeat**
8   Let $\sim$ be the smallest congruence that contains $\sim_{i-1}$ and the pair (q_i, q_j);
9              $j \leftarrow j + 1$;
10   **until** test($\mathcal{A}_{init}/\sim$);
11         $\sim_i \leftarrow \sim$;
12   **else**
13         $\sim_i \leftarrow \sim_{i-1}$;
14 **end**
15 **return** $\mathcal{A}_{init}/\sim_n$;

We are now ready to describe our new ICE-learning algorithm for EQDAs that extends the above Algorithm 1, handling both EQDAs and implication samples. In our setting, a sample is of the form $(\hat{E}, \hat{C}, \hat{I})$ where $\hat{E}, \hat{C}$ are sets of sets of valuation words and $\hat{I}$ contains pairs of sets of valuation words. From [20] we know that EQDAs can be viewed as Moore machines that read valuation words and output data formulas. Hence we can adapt the RPNI algorithm to learn EQDAs, as explained below.

For the initialization init(S) we construct an EQDA whose language is the smallest (w.r.t. inclusion) EQDA-definable language that is consistent with the sample S. To do this, we consider the set of all positive examples, i.e., the set $E := \bigcup \hat{E}$. This is a set of valuation words, from which we strip off the data part, obtaining a set E' of symbolic words only made up of pointers and universally quantified variables. We start with the prefix tree of E' using the prefixes of words in E' as states (as the original RPNI does). The final states are the words in E'. Each such word $w \in E'$ originates from a set of valuation words in E (all the extensions of w by data that result in a valuation word in E). If we denote this set by E_w, then we label the state corresponding to w with the least formula that is satisfied in all valuation words in E_w (recall that the formulas form a lattice). This defines the smallest QDA-definable set that contains all words in E. If this QDA is not consistent with the sample, then either there is no such QDA, or the QDA is not consistent with an implication, that is, for some $(X, Y) \in \hat{I}$ it accepts everything in

---

[3] We refer the reader to the technical report [63] more details.

X but not everything in Y. In this case, we add X and Y to $\hat{E}$ and restart the construction (since every QDA consistent with the sample must accept all of X and all of Y).

To make this QDA $\mathcal{A}$ elastic, all states that are connected by a $\underline{b}$-transition are merged. This defines the smallest EQDA-definable set that contains all words accepted by $\mathcal{A}$ (see [20]). Hence, if this EQDA is not consistent with the sample, then either there is no such EQDA, or an implication $(X, Y) \in \hat{I}$ is violated, and we proceed as above by adding X and Y to $\hat{E}$ and restarting the computation. This adapted initialization results in an EQDA whose language is the *smallest EQDA-definable language that is consistent with the sample*.

Once Phase 1 is finished, our algorithm proceeds to Phase 2, in which it successively merges states of $\mathcal{A}_{\text{init}}$, to obtain an EQDA that remains consistent with the sample but has less states. When merging accepting states, the new formula at the combined state is obtained as the lub of the formulas of the original states. Note that merging states of an EQDA preserves the self-loop condition for $\underline{b}$-transitions. Finally, the test routine simply checks whether the merged EQDA is consistent with the sample.

It follows that the hypothesis constructed by this adapted version of RPNI is an EQDA that is consistent with the sample. Hence we have described a consistent learner. For a fixed set of pointer variables and universally quantified variables there are only a finite number of EQDAs. Therefore by Lemma 1 we conclude that the above learning is strongly convergent (though the number of rounds need not be polynomial).

Table 2. RPNI-based ICE-learning for quantified array invariants. R: # rounds of iterative-ICE; $|Q|$: # states in final EQDA. $\times$ means timeout of 5 min.

Program	White-Box	Black-Box		
	SAFARI (s)	R	$|Q|$	ICE(s)
copy	0.0	4	8	**0.7**
copy-lt-key	$\times$	5	13	**1.2**
init	0.7	4	8	**0.6**
init-partial	$\times$	8	12	**1.5**
compare	0.1	9	8	**1.3**
find	0.2	9	8	**1.2**
max	0.1	3	8	**0.4**
increment	$\times$	5	8	**0.7**
sorted-find	$\times$	8	17	**5.1**
sorted-insert	$\times$	6	21	**2.0**
sorted-reverse	$\times$	18	17	**9.4**
devres [48]	0.1	3	8	**0.7**
rm_pkey [48]	0.3	3	8	**0.7**

Theorem 3. *The adaption of the RPNI algorithm for iterative set-based ICE-learning of EQDAs strongly converges.*

Experiments: We built a prototype tool implementing the set-based ICE-learning algorithm for EQDAs, consisting of both a learner and a teacher. The ICE-learner is implemented by extending the classical RPNI algorithm from the LIBALF library [65]. Given an EQDA conjectured by the learner, the teacher we build converts it to a quantified formula in the APF [61] or decidable STRAND for lists [62], and uses a constraint solver to check adequacy of invariants. Since there is no tool implementing the decision procedure for STRAND, we evaluate our prototype on array programs only.

Table 2 presents the results of our prototype on typical programs manipulating arrays[4]. We compare our results to SAFARI [44], a verification tool based on interpolation in array theories. SAFARI, in general, cannot handle list programs, and also array

---

[4] Available at http://www.cs.uiuc.edu/~madhu/cav14/

programs like *sorted-find* that have quantified pre-conditions. On the others, SAFARI diverges for some programs, and probably needs manually provided term abstractions to achieve convergence. The results show that our ICE-learning algorithm for quantified invariants is effective, in addition to promising polynomial-per-round efficiency, promising invariants that fall in decidable theories, and promising strong convergence.

Acknowledgements. This work was partially funded by NSF CAREER award #0747041 and NSF Expeditions in Computing ExCAPE Award #1138994.

References

1. Cousot, P., Cousot, R.: Abstract interpretation: A unified lattice model for static analysis of programs by construction or approximation of fixpoints. In: POPL, ACM, pp. 238–252. ACM (1977)
2. Miné, A.: The octagon abstract domain. In: WCRE, pp. 310–319 (2001)
3. Flanagan, C., Leino, K.R.M.: Houdini, an annotation assistant for eSC/Java. In: Oliveira, J.N., Zave, P. (eds.) FME 2001. LNCS, vol. 2021, pp. 500–517. Springer, Heidelberg (2001)
4. Thakur, A., Lal, A., Lim, J., Reps, T.: PostHat and all that: Attaining most-precise inductive invariants. Technical Report TR1790, University of Wisconsin, Madison, WI (April 2013)
5. Fähndrich, M., Logozzo, F.: Static contract checking with abstract interpretation. In: Beckert, B., Marché, C. (eds.) FoVeOOS 2010. LNCS, vol. 6528, pp. 10–30. Springer, Heidelberg (2011)
6. Floyd, R.: Assigning meaning to programs. In: Schwartz, J.T. (ed.) Mathematical Aspects of Computer Science. Proceedings of Symposia in Applied Mathematics, vol. 19, pp. 19–32. AMS (1967)
7. Hoare, C.A.R.: An axiomatic basis for computer programming. Commun. ACM 12(10), 576–580 (1969)
8. Barnett, M., Chang, B.-Y.E., DeLine, R., Jacobs, B., M. Leino, K.R.: Boogie: A modular reusable verifier for object-oriented programs. In: de Boer, F.S., Bonsangue, M.M., Graf, S., de Roever, W.-P. (eds.) FMCO 2005. LNCS, vol. 4111, pp. 364–387. Springer, Heidelberg (2006)
9. Ball, T., Rajamani, S.K.: The SLAM project: debugging system software via static analysis. In: POPL, pp. 1–3. ACM (2002)
10. Henzinger, T.A., Jhala, R., Majumdar, R., Sutre, G.: Lazy abstraction. In: POPL, pp. 58–70. ACM (2002)
11. McMillan, K.L.: Interpolation and SAT-based model checking. In: Hunt Jr., W.A., Somenzi, F. (eds.) CAV 2003. LNCS, vol. 2725, pp. 1–13. Springer, Heidelberg (2003)
12. Jhala, R., McMillan, K.L.: A practical and complete approach to predicate refinement. In: Hermanns, H., Palsberg, J. (eds.) TACAS 2006. LNCS, vol. 3920, pp. 459–473. Springer, Heidelberg (2006)
13. Bradley, A.R.: SAT-based model checking without unrolling. In: Jhala, R., Schmidt, D. (eds.) VMCAI 2011. LNCS, vol. 6538, pp. 70–87. Springer, Heidelberg (2011)
14. Cobleigh, J.M., Giannakopoulou, D., Păsăreanu, C.S.: Learning assumptions for compositional verification. In: Garavel, H., Hatcliff, J. (eds.) TACAS 2003. LNCS, vol. 2619, pp. 331–346. Springer, Heidelberg (2003)
15. Alur, R., Madhusudan, P., Nam, W.: Symbolic compositional verification by learning assumptions. In: Etessami, K., Rajamani, S.K. (eds.) CAV 2005. LNCS, vol. 3576, pp. 548–562. Springer, Heidelberg (2005)

16. Alur, R., Cerný, P., Madhusudan, P., Nam, W.: Synthesis of interface specifications for java classes. In: POPL, pp. 98–109. ACM (2005)
17. Sharma, R., Nori, A.V., Aiken, A.: Interpolants as classifiers. In: Madhusudan, P., Seshia, S.A. (eds.) CAV 2012. LNCS, vol. 7358, pp. 71–87. Springer, Heidelberg (2012)
18. Sharma, R., Gupta, S., Hariharan, B., Aiken, A., Nori, A.V.: Verification as learning geometric concepts. In: Logozzo, F., Fähndrich, M. (eds.) Static Analysis. LNCS, vol. 7935, pp. 388–411. Springer, Heidelberg (2013)
19. Sharma, R., Gupta, S., Hariharan, B., Aiken, A., Liang, P., Nori, A.V.: A data driven approach for algebraic loop invariants. In: Felleisen, M., Gardner, P. (eds.) ESOP 2013. LNCS, vol. 7792, pp. 574–592. Springer, Heidelberg (2013)
20. Garg, P., Löding, C., Madhusudan, P., Neider, D.: Learning universally quantified invariants of linear data structures. In: Sharygina, N., Veith, H. (eds.) CAV 2013. LNCS, vol. 8044, pp. 813–829. Springer, Heidelberg (2013)
21. Mitchell, T.M.: Machine learning. McGraw-Hill (1997)
22. Kearns, M.J., Vazirani, U.V.: An introduction to computational learning theory. MIT Press, Cambridge (1994)
23. Albarghouthi, A., McMillan, K.L.: Beautiful interpolants. In: Sharygina, N., Veith, H. (eds.) CAV 2013. LNCS, vol. 8044, pp. 313–329. Springer, Heidelberg (2013)
24. Reps, T., Sagiv, M., Yorsh, G.: Symbolic implementation of the best transformer. In: Steffen, B., Levi, G. (eds.) VMCAI 2004. LNCS, vol. 2937, pp. 252–266. Springer, Heidelberg (2004)
25. Yorsh, G., Ball, T., Sagiv, M.: Testing, abstraction, theorem proving: better together! In: ISSTA, pp. 145–156 (2006)
26. van Eijk, C.A.J.: Sequential equivalence checking without state space traversal. In: DATE, pp. 618–623 (1998)
27. Garoche, P.-L., Kahsai, T., Tinelli, C.: Incremental invariant generation using logic-based automatic abstract transformers. In: Brat, G., Rungta, N., Venet, A. (eds.) NFM 2013. LNCS, vol. 7871, pp. 139–154. Springer, Heidelberg (2013)
28. Colón, M., Sankaranarayanan, S., Sipma, H.: Linear invariant generation using non-linear constraint solving. In: Hunt Jr., W.A., Somenzi, F. (eds.) CAV 2003. LNCS, vol. 2725, pp. 420–432. Springer, Heidelberg (2003)
29. Gulwani, S., Srivastava, S., Venkatesan, R.: Program analysis as constraint solving. In: PLDI, pp. 281–292. ACM (2008)
30. Gupta, A., Majumdar, R., Rybalchenko, A.: From tests to proofs. In: Kowalewski, S., Philippou, A. (eds.) TACAS 2009. LNCS, vol. 5505, pp. 262–276. Springer, Heidelberg (2009)
31. Gupta, A., Rybalchenko, A.: Invgen: An efficient invariant generator. In: Bouajjani, A., Maler, O. (eds.) CAV 2009. LNCS, vol. 5643, pp. 634–640. Springer, Heidelberg (2009)
32. Oncina, J., Garcia, P.: Inferring regular languages in polynomial update time. Pattern Recognition and Image Analysis, 49–61 (1992)
33. Cousot, P., Halbwachs, N.: Automatic discovery of linear restraints among variables of a program. In: POPL, pp. 84–96. ACM (1978)
34. Filé, G., Ranzato, F.: The powerset operator on abstract interpretations. Theor. Comput. Sci. 222(1-2), 77–111 (1999)
35. Sankaranarayanan, S., Ivančić, F., Shlyakhter, I., Gupta, A.: Static analysis in disjunctive numerical domains. In: Yi, K. (ed.) SAS 2006. LNCS, vol. 4134, pp. 3–17. Springer, Heidelberg (2006)
36. Gange, G., Navas, J.A., Schachte, P., Søndergaard, H., Stuckey, P.J.: Abstract interpretation over non-lattice abstract domains. In: Logozzo, F., Fähndrich, M. (eds.) SAS 2013. LNCS, vol. 7935, pp. 6–24. Springer, Heidelberg (2013)
37. Cousot, P., Cousot, R., Logozzo, F.: A parametric segmentation functor for fully automatic and scalable array content analysis. In: POPL, pp. 105–118. ACM (2011)

38. Gulwani, S., McCloskey, B., Tiwari, A.: Lifting abstract interpreters to quantified logical domains. In: POPL, pp. 235–246. ACM (2008)
39. Bouajjani, A., Dragoi, C., Enea, C., Sighireanu, M.: On inter-procedural analysis of programs with lists and data. In: PLDI, pp. 578–589 (2011)
40. Flanagan, C., Qadeer, S.: Predicate abstraction for software verification. In: POPL, pp. 191–202 (2002)
41. Lahiri, S.K., Bryant, R.E.: Predicate abstraction with indexed predicates. ACM Trans. Comput. Log. 9(1) (2007)
42. Jhala, R., McMillan, K.L.: Array abstractions from proofs. In: Damm, W., Hermanns, H. (eds.) CAV 2007. LNCS, vol. 4590, pp. 193–206. Springer, Heidelberg (2007)
43. McMillan, K.L.: Quantified invariant generation using an interpolating saturation prover. In: Ramakrishnan, C.R., Rehof, J. (eds.) TACAS 2008. LNCS, vol. 4963, pp. 413–427. Springer, Heidelberg (2008)
44. Alberti, F., Bruttomesso, R., Ghilardi, S., Ranise, S., Sharygina, N.: SAFARI: SMT-based abstraction for arrays with interpolants. In: Madhusudan, P., Seshia, S.A. (eds.) CAV 2012. LNCS, vol. 7358, pp. 679–685. Springer, Heidelberg (2012)
45. Seghir, M.N., Podelski, A., Wies, T.: Abstraction refinement for quantified array assertions. In: Palsberg, J., Su, Z. (eds.) SAS 2009. LNCS, vol. 5673, pp. 3–18. Springer, Heidelberg (2009)
46. Ernst, M.D., Czeisler, A., Griswold, W.G., Notkin, D.: Quickly detecting relevant program invariants. In: ICSE, pp. 449–458. ACM (2000)
47. Angluin, D.: Learning regular sets from queries and counterexamples. Inf. Comput. 75(2), 87–106 (1987)
48. Kong, S., Jung, Y., David, C., Wang, B.-Y., Yi, K.: Automatically inferring quantified loop invariants by algorithmic learning from simple templates. In: Ueda, K. (ed.) APLAS 2010. LNCS, vol. 6461, pp. 328–343. Springer, Heidelberg (2010)
49. Alur, R., Bodík, R., Juniwal, G., Martin, M.M.K., Raghothaman, M., Seshia, S.A., Singh, R., Solar-Lezama, A., Torlak, E., Udupa, A.: Syntax-guided synthesis. In: FMCAD, pp. 1–17 (2013)
50. Solar-Lezama, A., Tancau, L., Bodík, R., Seshia, S.A., Saraswat, V.A.: Combinatorial sketching for finite programs. In: ASPLOS, pp. 404–415 (2006)
51. Ackermann, C., Cleaveland, R., Huang, S., Ray, A., Shelton, C., Latronico, E.: Automatic requirement extraction from test cases. In: Barringer, H., et al. (eds.) RV 2010. LNCS, vol. 6418, pp. 1–15. Springer, Heidelberg (2010)
52. Choi, W., Necula, G.C., Sen, K.: Guided gui testing of android apps with minimal restart and approximate learning. In: OOPSLA, pp. 623–640 (2013)
53. Cohen, E., Dahlweid, M., Hillebrand, M., Leinenbach, D., Moskal, M., Santen, T., Schulte, W., Tobies, S.: VCC: A practical system for verifying concurrent C. In: Berghofer, S., Nipkow, T., Urban, C., Wenzel, M. (eds.) TPHOLs 2009. LNCS, vol. 5674, pp. 23–42. Springer, Heidelberg (2009)
54. Bagnara, R., Hill, P.M., Zaffanella, E.: Widening operators for powerset domains. In: Steffen, B., Levi, G. (eds.) VMCAI 2004. LNCS, vol. 2937, pp. 135–148. Springer, Heidelberg (2004)
55. Beyer, D., Keremoglu, M.E.: CPAchecker: A tool for configurable software verification. In: Gopalakrishnan, G., Qadeer, S. (eds.) CAV 2011. LNCS, vol. 6806, pp. 184–190. Springer, Heidelberg (2011)
56. Gulavani, B.S., Henzinger, T.A., Kannan, Y., Nori, A.V., Rajamani, S.K.: Synergy: a new algorithm for property checking. In: SIGSOFT FSE, pp. 117–127. ACM (2006)
57. Ivancic, F., Sankaranarayanan, S.: NECLA Benchmarks, http://www.nec-labs.com/research/system/systems_SAV-website/small_static_bench-v1.1.tar.gz
58. de Moura, L., Bjørner, N.S.: Z3: An efficient SMT solver. In: Ramakrishnan, C.R., Rehof, J. (eds.) TACAS 2008. LNCS, vol. 4963, pp. 337–340. Springer, Heidelberg (2008)

59. Rakamaric, Z., Emmi, M.: SMACK: Static Modular Assertion Checker, https://github.com/smackers/smack

60. McMillan, K.L.: Lazy abstraction with interpolants. In: Ball, T., Jones, R.B. (eds.) CAV 2006. LNCS, vol. 4144, pp. 123–136. Springer, Heidelberg (2006)

61. Bradley, A.R., Manna, Z., Sipma, H.B.: What's decidable about arrays? In: Emerson, E.A., Namjoshi, K.S. (eds.) VMCAI 2006. LNCS, vol. 3855, pp. 427–442. Springer, Heidelberg (2006)

62. Madhusudan, P., Parlato, G., Qiu, X.: Decidable logics combining heap structures and data. In: POPL, pp. 611–622. ACM (2011)

63. Garg, P., Löding, C., Madhusudan, P., Neider, D.: Ice: A robust framework for learning invariants. Technical report, University of Illinois (October 2013), http://hdl.handle.net/2142/45973

64. Angluin, D.: Negative results for equivalence queries. Machine Learning 5, 121–150 (1990)

65. Bollig, B., Katoen, J.-P., Kern, C., Leucker, M., Neider, D., Piegdon, D.R.: libalf: The Automata Learning Framework. In: Touili, T., Cook, B., Jackson, P. (eds.) CAV 2010. LNCS, vol. 6174, pp. 360–364. Springer, Heidelberg (2010)

From Invariant Checking to Invariant Inference Using Randomized Search

Rahul Sharma and Alex Aiken

Stanford University, USA
{sharmar,aiken}@cs.stanford.edu

Abstract. We describe a general framework C2I for generating an invariant inference procedure from an invariant checking procedure. Given a checker and a language of possible invariants, C2I generates an inference procedure that iteratively invokes two phases. The search phase uses randomized search to discover candidate invariants and the validate phase uses the checker to either prove or refute that the candidate is an actual invariant. To demonstrate the applicability of C2I, we use it to generate inference procedures that prove safety properties of numerical programs, prove non-termination of numerical programs, prove functional specifications of array manipulating programs, prove safety properties of string manipulating programs, and prove functional specifications of heap manipulating programs that use linked list data structures.

1 Introduction

In traditional program verification, a human annotates the loops of a given program with invariants and a decision procedure checks these invariants by proving some *verification conditions* (VCs). We explore whether decision procedures can also be used to infer the loop invariants; doing so helps automate one of the core problems in verification (discovering appropriate invariants) and relieves programmers from a significant annotation burden.

The idea of using decision procedures for invariant inference is not new [28,16]. However, this approach has been applied previously only in domains with some special structure, e.g., when the VCs belong to theories that admit quantifier elimination, such as linear rational arithmetic (Farkas' lemma) or linear integer arithmetic (Cooper's method). For general inference tasks, such theory-specific techniques do not apply, and the use of decision procedures for such tasks has been restricted to invariant checking: to prove or refute a given manually provided candidate invariant.

We describe a general framework C2I that, given a procedure for checking invariants, uses that checker to produce an invariant inference engine for a given language of possible invariants. We apply C2I to various classes of invariants; we use it to generate inference procedures that prove safety properties of numerical programs, prove non-termination of numerical programs, prove functional specifications of array manipulating programs, prove safety properties of string

A. Biere and R. Bloem (Eds.): CAV 2014, LNCS 8559, pp. 88–105, 2014.

manipulating programs, and prove functional specifications of heap manipulating programs that use linked list data structures. The two main characteristics of C2I are

- The decision procedure is only used to check a program annotated with candidate invariants (in contrast to approaches that use the decision procedure directly to infer an invariant).
- C2I uses a randomized search algorithm to search for candidate invariants. Empirically, the search technique is effective for generating good candidates for various classes of invariants.

The use of a decision procedure as a checker for candidate invariants is also not novel [34,36,45,46,42,20,19]. The main contribution of this paper is a general and effective search procedure that makes a framework like C2I feasible. The use of randomized search is motivated by its recent success in program synthesis [44,2] and recognizing that invariant inference is also a synthesis task. More specifically, our contributions are:

- We describe a framework C2I that iteratively invokes randomized search and a decision procedure to perform invariant inference. The randomized search combines random walks with hill climbing and is an instantiation of the well-known Metropolis Hastings MCMC sampler [11].
- We empirically demonstrate the generality of our search algorithm. We use randomized search for finding numerical invariants, *recurrent sets* [27], universally quantified invariants over arrays, invariants over string operators, and invariants involving reachability predicates for linked list manipulating programs. These studies show that invariant inference is amenable to randomized search.
- Even though we expect the general inference engines based on randomized search to be significantly inferior in performance to the domain-specific invariant inference approaches, our experiments show that randomized search has competitive performance with the more specialized techniques.
- Randomized search is effective only when done efficiently. We describe optimizations that allow us to obtain practical randomized search algorithms for invariant inference.

The rest of the paper is organized as follows. We describe our search algorithm in Section 2. Next, we describe inference of numerical invariants in Section 3, universally quantified invariants over arrays in Section 4, string invariants in Section 5, and invariants over linked lists in Section 6. Finally, we discuss related work in Section 7 and conclude in Section 8.

2   Preliminaries

An imperative program annotated with invariants can be verified by checking some *verification conditions* (VCs), which must be discharged by a decision procedure. As an example, consider the following program:

$$\texttt{assume } P; \texttt{while } B \texttt{ do } S \texttt{ od}; \texttt{assert } Q$$

The loop has a pre-condition P. The entry to the loop is guarded by the predicate B and S is the loop body (which, for the moment, we assume to be loop-free). We assert that the states obtained after execution of the loop satisfy Q. Given a loop invariant I, we can prove that the assertion holds if the following three VCs are valid:

$$P \Rightarrow I; \quad \{I \wedge B\}S\{I\}; \quad I \wedge \neg B \Rightarrow Q \qquad (1)$$

In this paper, we explore finding such an invariant I by randomized search. Given a candidate invariant, a decision procedure checks the conditions of Eqn. 1. Since there are three conditions for a predicate to be an invariant, there are three queries that need to be discharged to check a candidate. Each query, if it fails, generates a different kind of counterexample; we discuss these next.

Let C be a candidate invariant. The first condition states that for any invariant I, any state that satisfies P also satisfies I. However, if $P \wedge \neg C$ has a satisfying assignment g, then $P(g)$ is *true* and $C(g)$ is *false* and hence g proves C is not an invariant. We call any state that must be satisfied by an actual invariant, such as g, a *good* state. Now consider the second condition of Eqn. 1. A *pair* (s, t) satisfies the property that s satisfies B and if the execution of S is started in state s then S can terminate in state t. Since an actual invariant I is inductive, it should satisfy $I(s) \Rightarrow I(t)$. Hence, a pair (s, t) satisfying $C(s) \wedge \neg C(t)$ proves C is not an invariant. Finally, consider the third condition. A satisfying assignment b of $C \wedge \neg B \wedge \neg Q$ proves C is inadequate to discharge the post-condition. For an adequate invariant I, $I(b)$ should be *false*. We call a state that must not be satisfied by an adequate invariant, such as b, a *bad* state. Hence, given an incorrect candidate invariant and a decision procedure that can produce counterexamples, the decision procedure can produce either a good state, a pair, or a bad state as a counterexample to refute the candidate.

Problems other than invariant inference can also be reduced to finding some unknown predicates to satisfy some VCs [21]. Consider the following problem: prove that the loop `while` B `do` S `od` fails to terminate if executed with input i. One can obtain such a proof by demonstrating a *recurrent set* [9,27] I which makes the following VCs valid.

$$I(i); \quad \{I \wedge B\}S\{I\}; \quad I \Rightarrow B \qquad (2)$$

Our inference algorithm consumes VCs with some unknown predicates. We use the term *invariant* for any such unknown predicate that we want to infer. In the rest of this section, we focus on the case when we need to infer a single predicate. The development here generalizes easily to inferring multiple predicates.

2.1 Metropolis Hastings

We denote the verification conditions by V, the unknown invariant by I, a candidate invariant by C, the set of predicates that satisfy V by $\mathcal{I}$ (more than one predicate can satisfy V), and the set of all possible candidate invariants by $\mathcal{S}$.

We view inference as a cost minimization problem. For each predicate $P \in \mathcal{S}$ we assign a non-negative cost $c_V(P)$ where the subscript indicates that the cost depends on the VCs. Suppose the cost function is designed to obey $C \in \mathcal{I} \Leftrightarrow c_V(C) = 0$. Then by minimizing c_V we can find an invariant. In general, c_V is highly irregular and not amenable to exact optimization techniques. In this paper, we use a MCMC sampler to minimize c_V.

Search(J: Initial candidate)
Returns: A candidate C with $c_V(C) = 0$.

1. $C := J$
2. **while** $c_V(C) \neq 0$ **do**
3. $m := SampleMove(rand())$
4. $C' := m(C)$
5. $c_o := c_V(C)$, $c_n := c_V(C')$
6.   **if** $c_n < c_o$ or $e^{-\gamma(c_n - c_o)} > \frac{rand()}{RANDMAX}$ **then**
7. $C := C'$
8.   **end if**
9. **end while**
10. **return** C

Fig. 1. Metropolis Hastings for cost minimization

The basic idea of a Metropolis Hastings sampler is given in Figure 1. The algorithm maintains a current candidate C. It also has a set of *moves*. A move, $m : \mathcal{S} \mapsto \mathcal{S}$, *mutates* a candidate to a different candidate. The goal of the search is to sample candidates with low cost. By applying a randomly chosen move, the search transitions from a candidate C to a new candidate C'. If C' has lower cost than C we keep it and C' becomes the current candidate. If C' has higher cost than C, then with some probability we still keep C'. Otherwise, we undo this move and apply another randomly selected move to C. Using these random mutations, combined with the use of the cost function, the search moves towards low cost candidates. We continue proposing moves until the search *converges*: the cost reduces to zero.

The algorithm in Figure 1, when instantiated with a suitable proposal mechanism (*SampleMove*) and a cost function (c_V), can be used for a variety of optimization tasks. If the proposal mechanism is designed to be *symmetric* and *ergodic* then Figure 1 has interesting theoretical guarantees.

A proposal mechanism is *symmetric* if the probability of proposing a transition from C_1 to C_2 is equal to the probability of proposing a transition from C_2 to C_1. Note that the cost is not involved here: whether the proposal is accepted or rejected is a different matter. Symmetry just talks about the probability that a particular transition is proposed from the available transitions.

A proposal mechanism is *ergodic* if there is a non-zero probability of reaching every possible candidate C_2 starting from any arbitrary candidate C_1. That is, there is a sequence of moves, $m_1, m_2, \ldots, m_k$, such that the probability of sampling each m_i is non-zero and $C_2 = m_k(\ldots (m_1(C_1) \ldots)$. This property is desirable because it says that it is not impossible to reach $\mathcal{I}$ starting from a bad initial guess. If the proposal mechanism is symmetric and ergodic then the following theorem holds [4]:

Theorem 1. *In the limit, the algorithm in Figure 1 samples candidates in inverse proportion to their cost.*

Intuitively, this theorem says that the candidates with lower cost are sampled more frequently. A corollary of this theorem is that the search always converges. The proof of this theorem relies on the fact that the *search space S* should be finite dimensional. Note that MCMC sampling has been shown to be effective in practice for extremely large search spaces and, with good cost functions, is empirically known to converge well before the limit is reached [4]. Hence, we design our search space of invariants to be a large but finite dimensional space that contains most useful invariants by using templates. For example, our search space of disjunctive numerical invariants restricts the boolean structure of the invariants to be a DNF formula with ten disjuncts where each disjunct is a conjunction of ten linear inequalities. This very large search space is more than sufficient to express all the invariants in our numerical benchmarks.

Theorem 1 has limitations. The guarantee is only asymptotic and convergence could require more than the remaining lifetime of the universe. However, if the cost function is arbitrary then it is unlikely that any better guarantee can be made. In practice, for a wide range of cost functions with domains ranging from protein alignment [40] to superoptimization [44], MCMC sampling has been demonstrated to converge in reasonable time. Empirically, cost functions that provide feedback to the search have been found to be useful [44]. If the search makes a move that takes it closer to the answer then it should be rewarded with a decrease in cost. Similarly, if the search transitions to something worse then the cost should increase. We next present our cost function.

2.2 Cost Function

Consider the VCs of Eqn. 1. One natural choice for the cost function is

$$c_V(C) = 1 - \mathit{Validate}(V[C/I])$$

where $\mathit{Validate}(X)$ is 1 if predicate X is valid and 0 otherwise. We substitute the candidate C for the unknown predicate I in the VCs and if the VCs are valid then the cost is zero and otherwise the cost is one. This cost function has the advantage that a candidate with cost zero is an invariant. However, this cost function is a poor choice for two reasons:

1. Validation is slow. A decision procedure takes several milliseconds in the best case to discharge a query. For a random search to be effective we need to be able to explore a large number of proposals quickly.
2. This cost function does not give any incremental feedback. The cost of all incorrect candidates is one, although some candidates are clearly closer to the correct invariant than others.

Empirically, search based on this cost function times out on even the simplest of our benchmarks. Instead of using a decision procedure in the inner loop of the search, we use a set of concrete program states that allows us to quickly identify incorrect candidates. As we shall see, concrete states also give us a straightforward way to measure how close a candidate is to a true invariant.

Recall from the discussion of Eqn. 1 that there are three different kinds of interesting concrete states. Assume we have a set of good states G, a set of bad states B, and a set of pairs Z. The data elements encode constraints that a true invariant must satisfy. A good candidate C is should satisfy the following constraints:

1. It should separate all the good states from all the bad states: $\forall g \in G. \forall b \in B. \neg(C(g) \Leftrightarrow C(b))$.
2. It should contain all good states: $\forall g \in G. C(g)$.
3. It should exclude all bad states: $\forall b \in B. \neg C(b)$.
4. It should satisfy all pairs: $\forall (s,t) \in Z. C(s) \Rightarrow C(t)$.

For most classes of predicates it is easy to check whether a candidate satisfies these constraints for given sets G, B, and Z without using decision procedures. For every violated constraint, we assign a penalty cost. In general, we can assign different weights to different constraints, but for simplicity, we weight them equally. The reader may notice that the first constraint is subsumed by constraints 2 and 3. However, we keep it as a separate constraint as it encodes the amount of data that justifies a candidate. If a move causes a candidate to satisfy a bad state (which it did not satisfy before) then intuitively the increase in cost should be higher if the initial candidate satisfied many good states than if it satisfied only one good state. The third constraint penalizes equally in both scenarios (the cost increases by 1) and in such situations the first constraint is useful. The result is a cost function that does not require decision procedure calls, is fast to evaluate, and can give incremental credit to the search: the candidates that violate more constraints are assigned a higher cost than those that violate only a few constraints.

$$c_V(C) = \sum_{g \in G} \sum_{b \in B} \left(\neg C(g) * \neg C(b) + C(g) * C(b) \right) + \\ \sum_{g \in G} \neg C(g) + \sum_{b \in B} C(b) + \sum_{(s,t) \in Z} C(s) * \neg C(t) \tag{3}$$

In evaluating this expression, we interpret *false* as zero and *true* as one.

This cost function has one serious limitation: Even if a candidate has zero cost, still the candidate might not be an invariant. Once a zero cost candidate C is found, we check whether C is an invariant using a decision procedure; note this decision procedure call is made only if C satisfies all the constraints and therefore has at least some chance of actually being an invariant. If C is not an invariant one of the three parts of Eqn. 1 will fail and if the decision procedure can produce counterexamples then the counterexample will also be one of three possible kinds. If the candidate violates the first condition of Eqn. 1 then the counterexample is a good state and we add it to G. If the candidate violates the second condition then the counter example is a pair that we add to

Z, and finally if the candidate violates the third condition then we get a bad state that we add to B. We then search again for a candidate with zero cost according to the updated data. Thus our inference procedure can be thought of as a counterexample guided inductive synthesis (CEGIS) procedure [49], in particular, as an ICE learner [20]. Note that a pair (s,t) can also contribute to G or B. If $s \in G$ then t can be added to G. Similarly, if $t \in B$ then s can be added to B. If a state is in both G and B then we abort the search. Such a state is both a certificate of the invalidity of the VCs and of a bug in the program.

Not all decision procedures can produce counterexamples; in fact, in many more expressive domains of interest (e.g., the theory of arrays) generating counterexamples is impossible in general. In such situations the data we need can also be obtained by running the program. Consider the program point η where the invariant is supposed to hold. Good states are generated by running the program with inputs that satisfy the pre-conditions and collecting the states that reach η. Next, we start the execution of the program from η with an arbitrary state σ; i.e., we start the execution of the program "in the middle". If an assertion violation happens during the execution then all the states reaching η, including σ, during this execution are bad states. Otherwise, including the case when the program does not terminate (the loop is halted after a user-specified number of iterations), the successive states reaching η can be added as pairs. Note that successive states reaching the loop head are always pairs and may also be pairs of good states, bad states, or even neither.

The cost function of Eqn. 3 easily generalizes to the case when we have multiple unknown predicates. Suppose there are n unknown predicates $I_1, I_2, \ldots I_n$ in the VCs. We associate a set of good states G_i and bad states B_i with every predicate I_i. For pairs, we observe that VCs in our benchmarks have at most one unknown predicate symbol to the right of the implication and one unknown predicate symbol to the left (both occurring positively), implying that commonly n^2 sets of pairs suffices: a set of pairs $Z_{i,j}$ is associated with every pair of unknown predicates I_i and I_j. A candidate $C_1, \ldots, C_n$ satisfies the set of pairs $Z_{i,j}$ if $\forall (s,t) \in Z_{i,j}.C_i(s) \Rightarrow C_j(t)$. For the pair $(s,t) \in Z_{i,j}$, if $s \in G_i$ then we add t to G_j and if $t \in B_j$ then we add s to B_i. Each of G_i, B_i, and $Z_{i,j}$ induces constraints and a candidate is penalized by each constraint it fails to satisfy.

In subsequent sections we use the cost function in Eqn. 3 and the search algorithm in Figure 1, irrespective of the type of program (numeric, array, string, or list) under consideration. What differs is the instantiation of C2I with different decision procedures and search spaces of invariants. Since a proposal mechanism dictates how a search space is traversed, different search spaces require different proposal mechanisms. In general, when C2I is instantiated with a search space, the user must provide a proposal mechanism and a function *eval* that evaluates a predicate in the search space on a concrete state, returning *true* or *false*. The function *eval* is used to evaluate the cost function; for the search spaces discussed in this paper, the implementation of *eval* is straightforward and we omit it. We discuss the proposal mechanisms for each of the search spaces in some detail in the subsequent sections.

3 Numerical Invariants

We describe the proposal mechanism for inferring numerical invariants. Suppose $x_1, x_2, \ldots, x_n$ are the variables of the program, all of type $\mathbb{Z}$. A program state σ is a valuation of these variables: $\sigma \in \mathbb{Z}^n$. For each unknown predicate of the given VCs, the search space $\mathcal{S}$ is formulas of the following form:

$$\bigvee_{i=1}^{\alpha} \bigwedge_{j=1}^{\beta} \left(\sum_{k=1}^{n} w_k^{(i,j)} x_k \leq d^{(i,j)} \right)$$

Hence, predicates in $\mathcal{S}$ are boolean combinations of linear inequalities. We refer to w's as *coefficients* and d's as *constants*. The possible values that w's and d's can take are restricted to a finite bag of coefficients $W = \{w_1, w_2, \ldots, w_{|W|}\}$ and a finite bag of constants $D = \{d_1, d_2, \ldots, d_{|D|}\}$ respectively. These bags contain all of the statically occurring constants in the program as well as their sums and differences, which has sufficed in our experience. If needed, heuristics to mine relevant constants from concrete states, as described in [46], can be used.

For our experiments, for the benchmarks that require conjunctive invariants we set $\alpha = 1$ and $\beta = 10$ and for those that require disjunctive invariants we set $\alpha = \beta = 10$. This search space, $\mathcal{S}$, is sufficiently large to contain invariants for all of our benchmarks.

3.1 Proposal Mechanism

We use $y \sim Y$ to denote that y is selected uniformly at random from the set Y and $[a : b]$ to denote the set of integers in the range $\{a, a+1, \ldots, b-1, b\}$. Unless stated otherwise, all random choices are derived from uniform distributions. Before a move we make the following random selections: $i \sim [1 : \alpha]$, $j \sim [1 : \beta]$, and $k \sim [1 : n]$ .We have the following three moves, each of which is selected with probability $\frac{1}{3}$:

- Coefficient move: select $l \sim [1 : |W|]$ and update $w_k^{(i,j)}$ to W_l.
- Constant move: select $m \sim [1 : |D|]$ and update $d^{(i,j)}$ to D_m.
- Inequality move: With probability $1 - \rho$, apply constant move to $d^{(i,j)}$ and coefficient move to $w_h^{(i,j)}$ for all $h \in [1 : n]$. Otherwise (with probability ρ) remove the inequality by replacing it with *true*.

These moves are motivated by the fact that prior empirical studies of MCMC have found that a proposal mechanism that has a bias towards simple solutions and a good mixture of moves that make minor and major changes to a candidate leads to good results [44]. This proposal mechanism is symmetric and ergodic. Combining this proposal mechanism with the cost function in Eqn. 3 and the procedure in Figure 1 provides us a search procedure for numerical invariants. We call this procedure MCMC in the empirical evaluation of Section 3.3. The user can also restrict the constituent inequalities of the candidate invariants to a given abstract domain. This variation is called Templ in the evaluation in Section 3.3.

Table 1. Inference of numerical invariants for proving safety properties

Program	Z3-H	ICE	[46]	[28]	MCMC	Templ	Program	Z3-H	ICE	[46]	[28]	MCMC	Templ
cgr1 [25]	0.0	0.0	0.2	0.1	0.0	0.0	ex7 [32]	0.0	0.0	0.4	?	0.0	0.0
cgr2 [25]	0.0	7.3	?	?	1.5	1.2	ex14 [32]	0.0	0.0	0.2	?	0.0	0.0
fig1 [25]	0.0	0.1	?	?	0.9	1.4	array [5]	0.0	0.3	0.2	?	0.2	0.3
w1 [25]	0.0	0.0	0.2	0.1	0.0	0.0	fil1 [5]	0.0	0.0	0.4	0.1	0.0	0.0
fig3 [22]	0.0	0.0	0.1	0.1	0.0	0.0	ex11 [5]	0.0	0.6	0.2	0.1	0.0	0.0
fig9 [22]	0.0	0.0	0.2	0.1	0.0	0.0	trex01 [5]	0.0	0.0	0.4	0.1	0.0	0.0
tacas [33]	TO	1.4	0.5	0.1	0.5	0.0	monniaux	5.14	0.0	1.0	0.2	0.0	0.0
ex23 [32]	?	14.2	?	?	0.1	0.1	nested	0.0	?	1.0	0.0	0.3	2.1

3.2 Example

We now give a simple example to illustrate the moves. Suppose we have two variables x_1 and x_2, $\alpha = \beta = 1$, the initial candidate is $C \equiv 0 * x_1 + 0 * x_2 \leq 0$, $W = \{0, 1\}$, and $D = \{0, 1\}$. Then a coefficient move leaves C unchanged with probability 0.5 and mutates it to $1 * x_1 + 0 * x_2 \leq 0$ or $0 * x_1 + 1 * x_2 \leq 0$ with probability 0.25 each. A constant move leaves C unchanged with probability 0.5 and mutates it to $0 * x_1 + 0 * x_2 \leq 1$ with probability 0.5. A predicate move (for $\rho = 0$) leaves C unchanged with probability 0.125 and mutates it to $x_1 \leq 0$, $x_2 \leq 0$, $0 \leq 1$, $x_1 \leq 1$, $x_2 \leq 1$, $x_1 + x_2 \leq 0$, or $x_1 + x_2 \leq 1$ with probability 0.125 each.

3.3 Evaluation

We start with no data: $G = B = Z = \emptyset$. The initial candidate invariant J is the predicate in $\mathcal{S}$ that has all the coefficients and the constants set to zero: $\forall i, j, k.w_k^{(i,j)} = 0 \wedge d^{(i,j)} = 0$. The cost is evaluated using Eqn. 3 and when a candidate with cost zero is found then the decision procedure Z3 [38] is called. If Z3 proves that the candidate is indeed an invariant then we are done. Otherwise, Z3 provides a counterexample that is incorporated in the data and the search is restarted with J as the initial candidate. A *round* consists of one search-and-validate iteration: finding a predicate with zero cost and asking Z3 to prove/refute it.

For each benchmark in Table 1, the problem is to find an invariant strong enough to discharge assertions in the program. The Z3-H column shows the time taken by Z3-HORN [30]. Z3-HORN is a decision procedure inside Z3 for solving VCs with unknown predicates. ICE shows the search-and-validate approach of [20]. The next column evaluates a geometric machine learning algorithm [46] to search for candidate invariants and the next column is INVGEN [28] a symbolic invariant inference engine that uses concrete data for constraint simplification. Columns ICE, [46], and [28] have been copied verbatim from [20] and the reader is referred to [20] for details. The MCMC column shows for MCMC search the total time of all the rounds including the time for both search and validation. The Templ column shows the time when we manually provide abstract domains (octagons/octahedra) to the search. All of our experiments were performed on a

Table 2. Results on non-termination benchmarks

Program	Z3-H	MCMC	Templ
term1	0.01	0.02	0.01
term2	TO	0.04	0.05
term3	TO	0.04	0.06
term4	0.01	0.04	0.06
term5	0.01	0.01	0.02
term6	TO	0.12	0.07

2.2 GHz Intel i7 with 4GB of memory. The experiments we compare to in Table 1 and in the rest of the paper were performed on a variety of machines. Our goal in reporting performance numbers is not to make precise comparisons, but only to show that C2I has competitive performance with other techniques. Indeed, we observe that the time measurements of the C2I searches in Table 1 are competitive with previous techniques.

We consider the benchmarks for proving non-termination from TNT [27] and LOOPER in Table 2. Since these papers do not include performance results, we compare randomized search with Z3-HORN. In Table 2, Z3-HORN is fast on half of the benchmarks and times out after thirty minutes on the other half. This observation suggests the sensitivity of symbolic inference engines to the search heuristics and the usefulness of Theorem 1. Randomized search, with an asymptotic convergence guarantee, successfully handles all the benchmarks in less than a second.

4 Arrays

We consider the inference of universally quantified invariants over arrays. A program state for an array manipulating program contains the values of all the numerical variables and the arrays in scope. Given an invariant, existing decision procedures are robust enough to check that it indeed is an actual invariant, but generally fail to find concrete counterexamples to refute incorrect candidates. This situation is a real concern, because if our technique is to be generally applicable then it must deal with the possibility that the decision procedures might not always be able to produce counterexamples to drive the search. As outlined in Section 2.2, the good states, the bad states, and the pairs required for search can also be obtained from program executions.

We use an approach similar to [46,19] to generate data. Let Σ_k denote all states in which all numerical variables are assigned values $\leq k$, all arrays have sizes $\leq k$, and all elements of these arrays are also $\leq k$. We generate all states in Σ_0, then Σ_1, and so on. To generate data, we run the loop with these states (see Section 2.2). To refute a candidate invariant, states from these runs are returned to the search. For our benchmarks, we did not need to enumerate beyond Σ_4 (at most 150 states) before an invariant was discovered. Note that [46,19] test only on reachable states. We additionally test on unreachable states to obtain bad states and pairs. Better testing approaches are certainly possible [29].

Table 3. Results on array manipulating programs

Program	[15]	Z3-H	ARMC	Dual	MCMC	Templ
init	0.01	0.06	0.15	0.72	0.02	0.01
init-nc	0.02	0.08	0.48	6.60	0.15	0.02
init-p	0.01	0.03	0.14	2.60	0.01	0.01
init-e	0.04	TO	TO	TO	TO	TO
2darray	0.04	0.18	?	TO	0.41	0.02
copy	0.01	0.04	0.20	1.40	0.80	0.02
copy-p	0.01	0.04	0.21	1.80	0.13	0.01
copy-o	0.04	TO	?	4.50	TO	0.50
reverse	0.03	0.12	2.28	8.50	3.48	0.03
swap	0.12	0.41	3.0	40.60	TO	0.21

Program	[15]	Z3-H	ARMC	Dual	MCMC	Templ
d-swap	0.16	1.37	4.4	TO	TO	0.51
strcpy	0.07	0.05	0.15	0.62	0.02	0.01
strlen	0.02	0.07	0.02	0.20	0.01	0.01
memcpy	0.04	0.20	16.30	0.20	0.03	0.01
find	0.02	0.01	0.08	0.38	0.30	0.02
find-n	0.02	0.01	0.08	0.39	0.95	0.01
append	0.02	0.04	1.76	1.50	TO	0.12
merge	0.09	0.04	?	1.50	TO	0.41
alloc-f	0.02	0.02	0.09	0.69	0.10	0.01
alloc-nf	0.03	0.03	0.13	0.42	0.14	0.07

We now define a search space of invariants to simulate the fluid updates abstraction for reasoning about arrays [15]. If $x_1, \ldots, x_n$ are the numerical variables of the program and f and g are array variables, then we are interested in array invariants of the following form:

$$\forall u, v. T(x_1, x_2, \ldots, x_n, u, v) \Rightarrow f[u] = g[v] \qquad (4)$$

The variables u and v are universally quantified variables and T is a numerical predicate in the quantified variables and the variables of the program. Using this template, we reduce the search for array invariants to numerical predicates $T(x_1, x_2, \ldots, x_n, u, v)$. The search for T proceeds as described in Section 3.

4.1 Evaluation

We evaluate the randomized search algorithms on the benchmarks of [15] in Table 3. The VCs for these benchmarks were obtained from the repository of the competition on software verification.[1] We have omitted benchmarks with bugs from the original benchmark set; these bugs are triggered during data generation. The second column shows the time taken to analyze these benchmarks using the fluid updates abstraction in [15]. Using a specialized abstract domain leads to a very efficient analysis, but the scope of the analysis is limited to array manipulating programs that have invariants given by Eqn. 4.

In [8], the authors use templates to reduce the task of inferring universally quantified invariants for array manipulating programs to numerical invariants and show results using three different back-ends: Z3-HORN [30], ARMC [21], and DUALITY [37]. These are reproduced verbatim as columns Z3-H, ARMC, and Dual of Table 3. Details about these columns can be found in the original text [8]. Note that the benchmark init-e requires a divisibility constraint that none of these back-ends or our search algorithms currently support.

Columns MCMC and Templ describe our randomized searches: the total time to search (with sufficient data) and validate an invariant. Again the results are

---

[1] https://svn.sosy-lab.org/software/sv-benchmarks/trunk/clauses/QALIA/

```
i := 0; x := "a";
while(non_det()){ i++; x := "(" + x + ")"; }
assert( x.length == 2*i+1 );
if(i>0) assert( x.contains( "(a)" ) );
```

Fig. 2. A string manipulating program

competitive with previous domain-specific approaches. Also, a comparison of MCMC and Templ shows that convergence depends crucially on the proposal mechanism.

5 Strings

Consider the string manipulating program in Figure 2. To validate its assertions, the invariants must express facts about the contents of strings, integers, and lengths of strings; we are unaware of any previous inference technique that can infer such invariants. The string operations such as *length* (compute the length of a string), *indexof* (find the position of a string in another string), *substr* (extract a substring between given indices), etc., intermix integers and strings and pose a challenge for invariant inference. However, the decision procedure Z3-STR [51] can decide formulas over strings and integers. We use C2I to construct an invariant inference procedure from Z3-STR.

A program state contains the values of all the numerical and the string variables. The search space S consists of boolean combinations of predicates that belong to a given bag $\mathcal{P}$ of predicates: $\bigvee_{j=1}^{\alpha} \left(\bigwedge_{k=1}^{\beta} P_k^j \right)$ where $P_k^j \in \mathcal{P}$. The bag $\mathcal{P}$ is constructed using the constants and the predicates occurring in the program. We set $\alpha = 5, \beta = 10$, and for Figure 2, $\mathcal{P}$ has predicates $x.contains(y)$, $y_1 = y_2$, $w_1 i + w_2 x.length + w_3 \leq 0$ where $y \in \{x, \text{"a"}, \text{"("}, \text{")"}, \text{"(a)"}\}$ and $w \in [-2:2]$. A move replaces a randomly selected P_k^j with a randomly selected predicate from $\mathcal{P}$. The current counterexample generation capabilities of Z3-STR are unreliable and we generate data using the process explained in Section 4. (At most 25 data elements are sufficient to obtain an invariant.) For the program in Figure 2, randomized search discovers the following invariant:

$$\left(x = \text{"a"} \wedge i = 0\right) \vee \left(x.contains(\text{"(a)"}) \wedge x.length = 2i + 1\right)$$

We consider some additional examples in Table 4 and the name indicates the string operations they use. Due to the absence of an existing benchmark suite for string-manipulating programs, our evaluation is limited to a few handwritten examples.

One alternative to C2I for proving these examples involves designing a new abstract interpretation [14,13], which requires designing an abstract domain that incorporates both strings and integers, an abstraction function, a widening operator, and abstract transfer functions that are precise enough to find disjunctive invariants like the one shown above. Such an alternative requires significantly greater effort than instantiating C2I. In our implementation, both the proposal mechanism and the *eval* function required to instantiate C2I are under 50 lines of C++ each.

6   Relations

In this section we define a proposal mechanism to find invariants over relations. We are given a program with variables $x_1, x_2, \ldots, x_n$ and some relations $R_1, R_2, \ldots, R_m$. A program state is an evaluation of these variables and these relations. The search space consists of predicates F given by the following grammar:

$$
\begin{aligned}
Predicate\ F &::= \bigwedge_{i=1}^{\theta} F^i \\
Formula\ F^i &::= \bigwedge_{j=1}^{\delta} G_j^i \\
Subformula\ G^i &::= \forall u_1, u_2, \ldots, u_i.T \\
QF\ Predicate\ T &::= \bigvee_{k=1}^{\alpha} \bigwedge_{l=1}^{\beta} L_l^k \\
Literal\ L &::= A \mid \neg A \\
Atom\ A &::= R(V_1, \ldots, V_a) \quad a = arity(R) \\
Argument\ V &::= x \mid u \mid \kappa
\end{aligned}
\tag{5}
$$

A predicate in the search space is a conjunction of formulas. The superscript of F^i denotes the number of quantified variables in its subformulas. A subformula G^i is a quantified predicate with its quantifier free part T expressed in DNF. Each atomic proposition of this DNF formula is a relation whose arguments can be a variable of the program (x), a quantified variable (u), or some constant (κ) like *null*. The variables *in scope* of a relation in a predicate are the program variables and the quantified variables in the associated subformula.

Next we define the moves of our proposal mechanism. We select a move uniformly at random from the list below and apply it to the current candidate C. As usual, we write "at random" to mean "uniformly at random".

1. Variable move: Select an atom of C at random. Next, select one of the arguments and replace it with an argument selected at random from the variables in scope and the constants.
2. Relation move: Select an atom of C at random and replace its relation with a relation selected at random from the set of relations of the same arity. The arguments are unaffected.
3. Atom move: Select an atom of C at random and replace its relation with a relation selected at random from all available relations. Perform variable moves to fill the arguments of the new relation.
4. Flip polarity: Negate a literal selected at random from the literals of C.
5. Literal move: Perform an atom move and flip polarity.

These moves are symmetric and ergodic. Next, we evaluate the MCMC algorithm in Figure 1 with this proposal mechanism and the cost function of Eqn. 3.

We instantiate the relational proposal mechanism with reachability relations: The reachability relation $n^*(i, j)$ holds if the cell pointed to by j can be reached from i using zero or more pointer dereferences. A recently published decision procedure is complete for such candidates via a reduction of such formulas to boolean satisfiability [31]. We use this decision procedure as our validator and randomized search to find invariants for some standard singly linked list manipulating programs (described in [31]) in Table 5.

Table 4. Results on string manipulating programs. The time taken (in seconds) by MCMC search and by Z3-STR (for proving the correctness of the invariants) are shown.

	Figure 2	replace	index	substring
Search	0.8	0.02	0.06	0.05
Z3-STR	0.03	TO	114.6	0.01

Table 5. Results for list manipulating programs

Program	#G	#R	Search	Valid
delete	50	2	0.20	0.04
delete-all	20	7	1.03	0.13
find	50	9	0.42	0.04
filter	50	26	10.41	0.11
last	50	3	0.90	0.04
reverse	20	54	55.11	0.08

6.1 Evaluation

For defining the search space using Eqn. 5 we set $\alpha = \beta = \delta = 5$ and $\theta = 2$, which is sufficient to express the invariants for benchmarks in Table 5. We run our benchmarks on lists of length up to five to generate an initial set of good states, the size of which is shown in the column **#G**. Starting from a non-empty set of good states results in faster convergence than starting from an empty set. Next, we start our search with zero bad states and zero pairs and generate candidate invariants. The number of rounds for the search to converge to an invariant is shown in the column **#R**. Later rounds take more time than the initial rounds. Columns **Search** and **Valid** describe the time to search (with sufficient data) and to validate an invariant respectively.

During our evaluation of various verification tasks, we observe that the decision procedures for advanced logics are not able to accept all formulas in their input language. Hence, sometimes we must perform some equality-preserving simplifications on the candidate invariants our search discovers. Currently we perform this step manually when necessary, but the simplifications could be automated.

7 Related Work

The goal of this paper is a framework to obtain inference engines from decision procedures. C2I is parametrized by the language of possible invariants. This characteristic is similar to TVLA [43]. TVLA requires specialized heuristics (focus, coerce, etc.) to maintain precision. We do not require these heuristics and this generality aids us in obtaining inference procedures for verification tasks beyond shape analysis. C2I is a template-based analysis that does not use decision procedures to instantiate the templates and limits their use to checking an annotated program. We do not rely on decision procedures to compute a predicate cover [26], or for fixpoint iterations [18,50], or on Farkas' lemma [25,28,12,7]. Hence, C2I is applicable to various decision procedures, including incomplete procedures (Section 4 and Section 5).

The literature on invariant inference is huge. Most techniques for invariant inference are symbolic analyses that trade generality for effective techniques in specific domains [35,28,16,10,6,1]. We are not aware of any symbolic inference technique that has been successfully demonstrated to infer invariants for the various types of programs that we consider (numeric, array, string, and list). Daikon [17] and Houdini [18] use conjunctive learning, [45,41] use equation solving, and [47] uses SVMs: these fail to infer disjunctive invariants over inequalities. The underlying machine learning algorithm of [46] uses geometry and hence is applicable to numerical predicates only.

Algorithmic learning [36,34] approaches also iteratively invoke search and validate phases. They use a CDNF learning algorithm that requires membership queries, "is a conjunction of atomic predicates contained in the invariant?", that are resolved heuristically. We do not require membership queries. Other techniques that use concrete data to guide verification include [22,3,24,39].

We are unaware of the any previous work that uses Metropolis Hastings for invariant inference. In a related work, [23] uses Gibbs sampling for inference of numerical invariants. However, the inference does not use concrete states and the resulting cost function is expensive to evaluate. Handling programs with pointers and arrays is left as an open problem by [23].

We use efficiency to guide the choice of parameters for randomized search. E.g., in our evaluations, we set γ in Figure 1 to $log_e 2$. Systematic approaches described in [48] can also be used for setting such parameters.

8   Conclusion

We have demonstrated a general procedure for generating an inference procedure from a checking procedure and applied it to a variety of programs. The inference procedure uses randomized search for generating candidate invariants that are proven or refuted by the checker. While C2I is general and can handle many classes of useful invariants, its performance is still competitive with state of the art tools that are specialized for specific domains.

Acknowledgements. We thank Eric Schkufza, Manolis Papadakis, and the anonymous reviewers for their comments. This work was supported by NSF grant CCF-1160904, a Microsoft fellowship, and the Air Force Research Laboratory under agreement number FA8750-12-2-0020. The U.S. Government is authorized to reproduce and distribute reprints for Governmental purposes notwithstanding any copyright notation thereon.

References

1. Alberti, F., Bruttomesso, R., Ghilardi, S., Ranise, S., Sharygina, N.: SAFARI: SMT-based abstraction for arrays with interpolants. In: Madhusudan, P., Seshia, S.A. (eds.) CAV 2012. LNCS, vol. 7358, pp. 679–685. Springer, Heidelberg (2012)

2. Alur, R., Bodík, R., Juniwal, G., Martin, M.M.K., Raghothaman, M., Seshia, S.A., Singh, R., Solar-Lezama, A., Torlak, E., Udupa, A.: Syntax-guided synthesis. In: FMCAD (2013)
3. Amato, G., Parton, M., Scozzari, F.: Discovering invariants via simple component analysis. J. Symb. Comput. 47(12) (2012)
4. Andrieu, C., de Freitas, N., Doucet, A., Jordan, M.I.: An Introduction to MCMC for Machine Learning. Machine Learning 50(1) (2003)
5. Beyer, D.: Competition on Software Verification (SV-COMP) benchmarks, https://svn.sosy-lab.org/software/svbenchmarks/tags/svcomp13/loops/
6. Beyer, D., Henzinger, T.A., Jhala, R., Majumdar, R.: The software model checker Blast. STTT 9(5-6) (2007)
7. Beyer, D., Henzinger, T.A., Majumdar, R., Rybalchenko, A.: Invariant synthesis for combined theories. In: Cook, B., Podelski, A. (eds.) VMCAI 2007. LNCS, vol. 4349, pp. 378–394. Springer, Heidelberg (2007)
8. Bjørner, N., McMillan, K., Rybalchenko, A.: On solving universally quantified horn clauses. In: Logozzo, F., Fähndrich, M. (eds.) SAS 2013. LNCS, vol. 7935, pp. 105–125. Springer, Heidelberg (2013)
9. Burnim, J., Jalbert, N., Stergiou, C., Sen, K.: Looper: Lightweight detection of infinite loops at runtime. In: ASE (2009)
10. Calcagno, C., Distefano, D., O'Hearn, P.W., Yang, H.: Compositional shape analysis by means of bi-abduction. In: POPL (2009)
11. Chib, S., Greenberg, E.: Understanding the Metropolis-Hastings Algorithm. The American Statistician 49(4) (1995)
12. Colón, M.A., Sankaranarayanan, S., Sipma, H.B.: Linear invariant generation using non-linear constraint solving. In: Hunt Jr., W.A., Somenzi, F. (eds.) CAV 2003. LNCS, vol. 2725, pp. 420–432. Springer, Heidelberg (2003)
13. Costantini, G., Ferrara, P., Cortesi, A.: Static analysis of string values. In: Qin, S., Qiu, Z. (eds.) ICFEM 2011. LNCS, vol. 6991, pp. 505–521. Springer, Heidelberg (2011)
14. Cousot, P., Cousot, R.: Abstract interpretation: A unified lattice model for static analysis of programs by construction or approximation of fixpoints. In: POPL (1977)
15. Dillig, I., Dillig, T., Aiken, A.: Fluid updates: Beyond strong vs. Weak updates. In: Gordon, A.D. (ed.) ESOP 2010. LNCS, vol. 6012, pp. 246–266. Springer, Heidelberg (2010)
16. Dillig, I., Dillig, T., Li, B., McMillan, K.L.: Inductive invariant generation via abductive inference. In: OOPSLA (2013)
17. Ernst, M.D., Perkins, J.H., Guo, P.J., McCamant, S., Pacheco, C., Tschantz, M.S., Xiao, C.: The Daikon system for dynamic detection of likely invariants. Sci. Comput. Program. 69(1-3) (2007)
18. Flanagan, C., Leino, K.R.M.: Houdini, an annotation assistant for ESC/Java. In: Oliveira, J.N., Zave, P. (eds.) FME 2001. LNCS, vol. 2021, pp. 500–517. Springer, Heidelberg (2001)
19. Garg, P., Löding, C., Madhusudan, P., Neider, D.: Learning universally quantified invariants of linear data structures. In: Sharygina, N., Veith, H. (eds.) CAV 2013. LNCS, vol. 8044, pp. 813–829. Springer, Heidelberg (2013)
20. Garg, P., Löding, C., Madhusudan, P., Neider, D.: ICE: A Robust Framework for Learning Invariants. In: Biere, A., Bloem, R. (eds.) CAV 2014. LNCS, vol. 8559, pp. 69–86. Springer, Heidelberg (2014)
21. Grebenshchikov, S., Lopes, N.P., Popeea, C., Rybalchenko, A.: Synthesizing software verifiers from proof rules. In: PLDI (2012)

22. Gulavani, B.S., Henzinger, T.A., Kannan, Y., Nori, A.V., Rajamani, S.K.: Synergy: a new algorithm for property checking. In: FSE (2006)
23. Gulwani, S., Jojic, N.: Program verification as probabilistic inference. In: POPL (2007)
24. Gulwani, S., Necula, G.C.: Discovering affine equalities using random interpretation. In: POPL (2003)
25. Gulwani, S., Srivastava, S., Venkatesan, R.: Program analysis as constraint solving. In: PLDI (2008)
26. Gulwani, S., Srivastava, S., Venkatesan, R.: Constraint-based invariant inference over predicate abstraction. In: Jones, N.D., Müller-Olm, M. (eds.) VMCAI 2009. LNCS, vol. 5403, pp. 120–135. Springer, Heidelberg (2009)
27. Gupta, A., Henzinger, T.A., Majumdar, R., Rybalchenko, A., Xu, R.-G.: Proving non-termination. In: POPL (2008)
28. Gupta, A., Majumdar, R., Rybalchenko, A.: From tests to proofs. In: Kowalewski, S., Philippou, A. (eds.) TACAS 2009. LNCS, vol. 5505, pp. 262–276. Springer, Heidelberg (2009)
29. Harder, M., Mellen, J., Ernst, M.D.: Improving test suites via operational abstraction. In: ICSE (2003)
30. Hoder, K., Bjørner, N.: Generalized property directed reachability. In: Cimatti, A., Sebastiani, R. (eds.) SAT 2012. LNCS, vol. 7317, pp. 157–171. Springer, Heidelberg (2012)
31. Itzhaky, S., Banerjee, A., Immerman, N., Nanevski, A., Sagiv, M.: Effectively-propositional reasoning about reachability in linked data structures. In: Sharygina, N., Veith, H. (eds.) CAV 2013. LNCS, vol. 8044, pp. 756–772. Springer, Heidelberg (2013)
32. Ivancic, F., Sankaranarayanan, S.: NECLA Static Analysis Benchmarks, http://www.neclabs.com/research/system/systems_SAV-website/small_static_bench-v1.1.tar.gz
33. Jhala, R., McMillan, K.L.: A practical and complete approach to predicate refinement. In: Hermanns, H., Palsberg, J. (eds.) TACAS 2006. LNCS, vol. 3920, pp. 459–473. Springer, Heidelberg (2006)
34. Jung, Y., Kong, S., Wang, B.-Y., Yi, K.: Deriving invariants by algorithmic learning, decision procedures, and predicate abstraction. In: Barthe, G., Hermenegildo, M. (eds.) VMCAI 2010. LNCS, vol. 5944, pp. 180–196. Springer, Heidelberg (2010)
35. Kannan, Y., Sen, K.: Universal symbolic execution and its application to likely data structure invariant generation. In: ISSTA (2008)
36. Kong, S., Jung, Y., David, C., Wang, B.-Y., Yi, K.: Automatically inferring quantified loop invariants by algorithmic learning from simple templates. In: Ueda, K. (ed.) APLAS 2010. LNCS, vol. 6461, pp. 328–343. Springer, Heidelberg (2010)
37. McMillan, K., Rybalchenko, A.: Combinatorial approach to some sparse-matrix problems. Tech. rep., Microsoft Research (2013)
38. de Moura, L., Bjørner, N.S.: Z3: An efficient SMT solver. In: Ramakrishnan, C.R., Rehof, J. (eds.) TACAS 2008. LNCS, vol. 4963, pp. 337–340. Springer, Heidelberg (2008)
39. Naik, M., Yang, H., Castelnuovo, G., Sagiv, M.: Abstractions from tests. In: POPL (2012)
40. Neuwald, A.F., Liu, J.S., Lipman, D.J., Lawrence, C.E.: Extracting protein alignment models from the sequence database. Nucleic Acids Research 25 (1997)
41. Nguyen, T., Kapur, D., Weimer, W., Forrest, S.: Using dynamic analysis to discover polynomial and array invariants. In: ICSE (2012)

42. Nori, A.V., Sharma, R.: Termination proofs from tests. In: ESEC/SIGSOFT FSE (2013)
43. Sagiv, S., Reps, T.W., Wilhelm, R.: Parametric shape analysis via 3-valued logic. ACM Trans. Program. Lang. Syst. 24(3) (2002)
44. Schkufza, E., Sharma, R., Aiken, A.: Stochastic superoptimization. In: ASPLOS (2013)
45. Sharma, R., Gupta, S., Hariharan, B., Aiken, A., Liang, P., Nori, A.V.: A data driven approach for algebraic loop invariants. In: Felleisen, M., Gardner, P. (eds.) ESOP 2013. LNCS, vol. 7792, pp. 574–592. Springer, Heidelberg (2013)
46. Sharma, R., Gupta, S., Hariharan, B., Aiken, A., Nori, A.V.: Program verification as learning geometric concepts. In: SAS (2013)
47. Sharma, R., Nori, A.V., Aiken, A.: Interpolants as classifiers. In: Madhusudan, P., Seshia, S.A. (eds.) CAV 2012. LNCS, vol. 7358, pp. 71–87. Springer, Heidelberg (2012)
48. Sharma, R., Nori, A.V., Aiken, A.: Bias-variance tradeoffs in program analysis. In: POPL (2014)
49. Solar-Lezama, A.: The sketching approach to program synthesis. In: Hu, Z. (ed.) APLAS 2009. LNCS, vol. 5904, pp. 4–13. Springer, Heidelberg (2009)
50. Srivastava, S., Gulwani, S.: Program verification using templates over predicate abstraction. In: PLDI (2009)
51. Zheng, Y., Zhang, X., Ganesh, V.: Z3-str: a Z3-based string solver for web application analysis. In: ESEC/SIGSOFT FSE (2013)

SMACK: Decoupling Source Language Details from Verifier Implementations*

Zvonimir Rakamarić[1] and Michael Emmi[2]

[1] School of Computing, University of Utah, USA
zvonimir@cs.utah.edu
[2] IMDEA Software Institute, Spain
michael.emmi@imdea.org

Abstract. A major obstacle to putting software verification research into practice is the high cost of developing the infrastructure enabling the application of verification algorithms to actual production code, in all of its complexity. Handling an entire programming language is a huge endeavor that few researchers are willing to undertake; even fewer could invest the effort to implement a verification algorithm for many source languages. To decouple the implementations of verification algorithms from the details of source languages, and enable rapid prototyping on production code, we have developed SMACK. At its core, SMACK is a translator from the LLVM intermediate representation (IR) into the Boogie intermediate verification language (IVL). Sourcing LLVM exploits an increasing number of compiler front ends, optimizations, and analyses. Targeting Boogie exploits a canonical platform which simplifies the implementation of algorithms for verification, model checking, and abstract interpretation. Our initial experience in verifying C-language programs is encouraging: SMACK is competitive in SV-COMP benchmarks, is able to translate large programs (100 KLOC), and is being used in several verification research prototypes.

1 Introduction

A major obstacle to putting software verification research into practice is the high cost of developing the infrastructure enabling the application of verification algorithms to actual production code, in all of its complexity. Each high-level programming language brings a diverse assortment of statements and expressions with varying semantics. Handling an entire language is a huge effort which few researchers are willing to undertake; even fewer could invest the effort required to implement their verification algorithms for multiple source languages.

To address this problem, we introduce SMACK: a translator from the LLVM compiler's popular *intermediate representation* (IR) [27,24] into the Boogie *intermediate verification language* (IVL) [19,26]. SMACK's primary function is to precisely and efficiently translate the rich set of LLVM-IR features, including dynamic memory allocation and pointer arithmetic, to the comparatively-simple

---

* Partially supported by NSF award CCF 1346756.

A. Biere and R. Bloem (Eds.): CAV 2014, LNCS 8559, pp. 106–113, 2014.

Boogie IVL, which does not include such features. SMACK thus promotes the development of verification algorithms on simple IVLs, effectively decoupling the implementations of verification algorithms from the details of source languages, and enabling rapid prototyping on production code. Sourcing LLVM IR exploits a rapidly-growing frontier of LLVM frontends, encompassing a diverse set of languages including C/C++, Java, Haskell, Erlang, Python, Ruby, Ada, and Fortran. In addition, SMACK benefits from code simplifications made by LLVM's optimizer, including constant propagation and dead-code elimination, as well as readily-available analyses, including LLVM's pointer analyses. Targeting Boogie IVL exploits a canonical platform which simplifies the implementation of verification algorithms due to Boogie's minimal syntax and mathematically-focused expression language, which is easily rendered into the satisfiability modulo theories (SMT) format of automated theorem provers [6]. By embracing Boogie IVL as a canonical program representation, SMACK not only simplifies the development of program verification technology, but also fosters the development of interoperable technology in which verification backends can be easily swapped.

Our initial experience in verifying C-language programs with SMACK, using Microsoft Research's Boogie and Corral [23] as backends, is encouraging. SMACK has eased the development of our research prototypes by enabling IVL-level, rather than C-level or LLVM-level, implementations. In doing so, it appears that our approach does not significantly compromise performance, as SMACK (with Boogie and Corral backends) is competitive on SV-COMP [33] benchmarks. Furthermore, SMACK translates large, full-featured programs — including the entire Contiki operating system [15], at around 100 KLOC of C code — and has been used on intricate implementations which make extensive use of features such as dynamic memory allocation.

While our experience with SMACK has thus far been centered on SMT-based *bounded verification*, i.e., validation of program assertions up to recursion-depth and loop-unroll bounds, our prior experience [10,30] suggests that SMACK can also be applied straightforwardly to *deductive verification*, i.e., validation of assertions in programs adequately annotated with loop invariants and procedure pre- and post-conditions. While in theory SMACK is equally applicable for fully automatic unbounded verification methods (e.g., based on computing fixed points), in practice such applications may require powerful reasoning engines capable of generating quantified invariants over the unbounded maps which SMACK uses to model dynamically-allocated memory; it remains to be seen whether such applications are feasible.

SMACK is an open source project available on GitHub[1] implemented in roughly 4K lines of C++ code, and is integrated into the **rise4fun** website.[2] Currently, SMACK is supported on Linux, OSX, and Windows, and is used in several projects, including Microsoft Research's Q program verifier.[3]

---

[1] http://github.com/smackers/smack
[2] http://rise4fun.com/SMACK
[3] http://research.microsoft.com/en-us/projects/verifierq

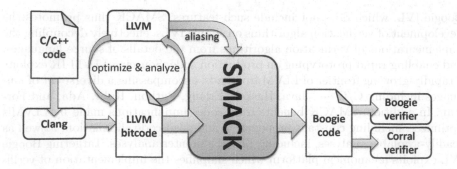

Fig. 1. Design of the SMACK modular software verification ecosystem

Related Work. Automatic verification using automated theorem provers, and in particular SMT solvers, is an active area of research. Many tools are available with various capabilities, features, and trade-offs, including Caduceus [21], Calysto [4], Cascade [34], CBMC [13], CPAchecker [7], ESBMC [16], Frama-C [17], GraVy [2], HAVOC [10], Joogie [3], KLEE [9], LLBMC [28], SATABS [12], Symbolic PathFinder [29], TASS [32], UFO [1], and VCC [14]. Our SMACK effort stands alone, since none of these tools combine the language independence of leveraging a popular IR with the ease of implementation provided by IVLs. Furthermore, SMACK has been designed to accommodate a diverse set of extensions, from supporting new source language features to generating alternate IVL encodings.

2   Translation from LLVM IR to Boogie IVL

We have developed SMACK as one essential component of the software verification ecosystem depicted in Fig. 1. Currently, the other components include the Clang compiler [11], the LLVM compiler infrastructure [27,24], and the Boogie [19,26] and Corral [23] verification engines. Beginning from a program written in C/C++, we use Clang to emit LLVM bitcode in an intermediate representation (IR) used by LLVM. LLVM IR is a typed, static single assignment (SSA), and platform-independent assembly language, and an ideal representation for LLVM's code optimizer/analyzer.

Following LLVM code optimizations, such as constant propagation and dead-code elimination, SMACK translates LLVM bitcode to code in Boogie's intermediate verification language (IVL). Boogie IVL is typed, imperative, and procedural, includes a rich mathematical expression language, and is an ideal representation for program verifiers. The Boogie programs which SMACK generates are essentially control-flow graphs with very few statements — they have goto, assignment, procedure call & return, and assume/assert statements — which manipulate global and procedure-local variables over very few types — only integers and maps from integers to integers. For the most part, SMACK's translation is tight, in the sense that LLVM data and instructions correspond closely to Boogie data and instructions, modulo representing fixed-width integers with mathematical integers.[4]

While there are many syntactic differences between LLVM IR and Boogie IVL, a key fundamental difference which SMACK addresses is memory representation: while LLVM IR performs dynamic allocation on the memory heap, programs in Boogie IVL have only a fixed number of global variables, albeit over unbounded types including mathematical integers and maps (i.e., arrays). Although in theory the entire heap could be represented with one single map, experience indicates that this strategy is not efficient; a verifier which represents map-type variables with array-theory expressions would suffer as the map is updated across many addresses. Instead, SMACK uses static analyses in LLVM to infer a set of memory regions which are *disjoint*, in the sense that two distinct regions are never accessed by the same program expression; each region of the heap is then given its own map, and each heap access translates to an expression using the accessed region's map [31]. SMACK's modular design facilitates the implementation of alternate memory models by, for example, redefining: (1) the Boogie-code implementations of malloc and free to describe alternate allocation policies (which does not require recompiling SMACK), or (2) the translation of load and store operations to model heap accesses at byte-sized granularity (currently requires recompilation).

SMACK passes the resulting Boogie-IVL program to either the Boogie or Corral verifier; both function by generating verification conditions [5] which are discharged using satisfiability modulo theories (SMT) solvers, such as Z3 [18].

3   An Example Translation

We illustrate our verification workflow step-by-step on the program listed in Fig. 2. The C program (top left) is first compiled with Clang into the LLVM IR program shown on the right. In the process, calls to malloc in C are compiled into the respective invocations in the LLVM IR. Structure field accesses are compiled into a combination of getelementptr and load/store instructions, where getelementptr performs the structure field address computation that is subsequently accessed using load/store. Note that while the LLVM IR is a simple representation, it does include dynamic memory allocation, pointer arithmetic, and complex data types — none of which are included in the Boogie IVL.

From the LLVM IR program, SMACK generates the Boogie IVL program by leveraging LLVM's static *data structure analysis* (DSA) [25] to split memory into a set of disjoint regions so that pointers to two distinct regions can never alias [31]. Each such region is then statically assigned its own map, and each memory access translates to an expression using the accessed region's map. In Fig. 2, based on the fact that DSA accurately reported that LLVM IR pointer variables %5 and {%6, %7} cannot alias, SMACK statically introduced memory

---

[4] While our current implementation uses *unbounded* integers and maps thereof, in principle we could also use bit-vectors to model, e.g., 32-bit integers precisely.

```
// original C code
typedef struct { int f; int g; } S;

void main() {
  S *x = malloc(sizeof(S));
  S *y = malloc(sizeof(S));
  x->f = 1;
  y->f = 2;
  y->g = 3;
  assert(x->f == 1);
}


// Boogie IVL code from SMACK
var $M.0, $M.1: [int] int;

procedure main() {
  var $p, $p1, $p2, .., $p6: int;
$bb0:
  call $p := $malloc(8);
  call $p1 := $malloc(8);
  $p2 := $pa($pa($p, 0, 8), 0, 1);
  $M.0[$p2] := 1;
  $p3 := $pa($pa($p1, 0, 8), 0, 1);
  $M.1[$p3] := 2;
  $p4 := $pa($pa($p1, 0, 8), 4, 1);
  $M.1[$p4] := 3;
  $p5 := $pa($pa($p, 0, 8), 0, 1);
  $p6 := $M.0[$p5];
  assert($p6 == 1);
  return;
}
```

```
// LLVM IR code from Clang/LLVM
define void @main() #0 {
  %1 = call i8* @malloc(i64 8)
  %2 = bitcast i8* %1 to %struct.S*
  %3 = call i8* @malloc(i64 8)
  %4 = bitcast i8* %3 to %struct.S*
  %5 = getelementptr inbounds
         %struct.S* %2, i32 0, i32 0
  store i32 1, i32* %5, align 4
  %6 = getelementptr inbounds
         %struct.S* %4, i32 0, i32 0
  store i32 2, i32* %6, align 4
  %7 = getelementptr inbounds
         %struct.S* %4, i32 0, i32 1
  store i32 3, i32* %7, align 4
  %8 = getelementptr inbounds
         %struct.S* %2, i32 0, i32 0
  %9 = load i32* %8, align 4
  %10 = icmp eq i32 %9, 1
  ... assertion omitted ...
  ret void
}
```

Fig. 2. An example program in C, along with its LLVM IR and Boogie IVL translations

maps $M.0 and $M.1 in Boogie code, respectively. While not shown, our translation defines the $pa function to model **getelementptr**, and the $malloc procedure to model memory allocation, by keeping track precisely of allocated and unallocated sections of memory. The **load** and **store** instructions are then translated as accesses into the appropriate region's map. Finally, assertions in C are ultimately translated into Boogie assertions, and checked using our backend verifiers.

4   Our Experience with SMACK

Our experience in using SMACK for developing research prototype verification tools has benefited from increased productivity without prohibitive performance sacrifices. One example is the c2s project[5] which implements various concurrent-to-sequential Boogie code translations — so called "sequentializations" — for delay-bounded verification [20], and which has been used in several of the authors' research projects. The authors of the CSeq tool [22], which implements a related sequentialization directly in C code rather than in a simple IVL, admit a telling limitation:

---

[5] http://github.com/michael-emmi/c2s

Table 1. Comparison of SMACK, CPAchecker, CBMC, and UFO on SV-COMP bench-marks. #B is the number of benchmarks (both correct and buggy) in a suite. No-Reuse and Reuse correspond to two distinct memory models currently provided by SMACK. Experiments were performed on an Intel Core i7-3930K 3.20 GHz machine with 32 GB of memory running Ubuntu 12.04. All runtimes are in seconds.

Benchmark Suite	#B	KLOC	SMACK				SV-COMP 2014		
			No-Reuse		Reuse				
			Boogie	Corral	Boogie	Corral	CPAchecker	CBMC	UFO
locks	13	2.3	9.1	9.3	9.0	9.3	365.1	1.4	2.9
ntdrivers-simpl	10	18.1	12.3	85.7	12.3	86.4	43.5	4.6	3.4

"CSeq does not support [heap-allocated memory] yet. Lifting these re-strictions, and in particular supporting dynamic memory . . . will require significant efforts."

In contrast, the Boogie IVL-based c2s tool was simple to implement, and has been used for the analysis of intricate C-language concurrent data structure implementations which make extensive use of dynamic memory allocation [8].

Despite the threat to performance incurred by separating backend verifiers from source languages, SMACK-based tools are competitive with state-of-the-art verifiers. While a truly-meaningful comparison is difficult, since different veri-fiers generally provide different guarantees, Table 1 makes an attempt, comparing SMACK with 3 competitive verifiers (CPAchecker [7], CBMC [13], UFO [1]) on 2 benchmark suites from the SV-COMP [33] annual software verification compe-tition. Both suites contain both correct and buggy benchmarks, and all verifiers categorize them correctly: neither false positives nor negatives are reported.[6]

Note that since these are preliminary results mixing tools aimed at bug-finding (SMACK, CBMC) with those aimed at verification (CPAchecker, UFO), a direct comparison of runtimes is somewhat unfair. However, the table does illustrate that even though SMACK has not been optimized for SV-COMP benchmarks — thus far we have spent minimal effort in optimization — its performance is comparable to established verifiers which regularly participate in SV-COMP. As future work, we plan to expand these preliminary results with more benchmarks, and enroll SMACK in a future SV-COMP.

As expected, the current version of SMACK does have some limitations. First, integer datatypes are modeled with unbounded mathematical integers; this lim-itation can be lifted by leveraging Boogie's support for bit-vectors. Floating point datatypes pose a more serious challenge, as they are not widely supported by current software verifiers and automated theorem provers. Finally, SMACK currently precisely handles word-aligned memory accesses only.

---

[6] To make our results readily reproducible, we created a virtual machine profile in the Apt testbed facility containing all used tools, scripts, and benchmarks. It is available at https://www.aptlab.net/p/fmr/smack-cav2014.

References

1. Albarghouthi, A., Li, Y., Gurfinkel, A., Chechik, M.: UFO: A framework for abstraction- and interpolation-based software verification. In: Madhusudan, P., Seshia, S.A. (eds.) CAV 2012. LNCS, vol. 7358, pp. 672–678. Springer, Heidelberg (2012)
2. Arlt, S., Rubio-González, C., Rümmer, P., Schäf, M., Shankar, N.: The gradual verifier. In: Badger, J.M., Rozier, K.Y. (eds.) NFM 2014. LNCS, vol. 8430, pp. 313–327. Springer, Heidelberg (2014)
3. Arlt, S., Rümmer, P., Schäf, M.: Joogie: From Java through Jimple to Boogie. In: ACM SIGPLAN International Workshop on State of the Art in Java Program Analysis (SOAP), pp. 3–8 (2013)
4. Babić, D., Hu, A.J.: Calysto: Scalable and precise extended static checking. In: International Conference on Software Engineering (ICSE), pp. 211–220 (2008)
5. Barnett, M., Leino, K.R.M.: Weakest-precondition of unstructured programs. In: ACM SIGPLAN-SIGSOFT Workshop on Program Analysis For Software Tools and Engineering (PASTE), pp. 82–87 (2005)
6. Barrett, C., Stump, A., Tinelli, C.: The SMT-LIB standard: Version 2.0. In: International Workshop on Satisfiability Modulo Theories (SMT) (2010)
7. Beyer, D., Keremoglu, M.E.: CPAchecker: A tool for configurable software verification. In: Gopalakrishnan, G., Qadeer, S. (eds.) CAV 2011. LNCS, vol. 6806, pp. 184–190. Springer, Heidelberg (2011)
8. Bouajjani, A., Emmi, M., Enea, C., Hamza, J.: Verifying concurrent programs against sequential specifications. In: Felleisen, M., Gardner, P. (eds.) ESOP 2013. LNCS, vol. 7792, pp. 290–309. Springer, Heidelberg (2013)
9. Cadar, C., Dunbar, D., Engler, D.: KLEE: Unassisted and automatic generation of high-coverage tests for complex systems programs. In: USENIX Conference on Operating Systems Design and Implementation (OSDI), pp. 209–224 (2008)
10. Chatterjee, S., Lahiri, S.K., Qadeer, S., Rakamarić, Z.: A reachability predicate for analyzing low-level software. In: Grumberg, O., Huth, M. (eds.) TACAS 2007. LNCS, vol. 4424, pp. 19–33. Springer, Heidelberg (2007)
11. Clang: A C language family frontend for LLVM, http://clang.llvm.org
12. Clarke, E., Kroning, D., Sharygina, N., Yorav, K.: SATABS: SAT-based predicate abstraction for ANSI-C. In: Halbwachs, N., Zuck, L.D. (eds.) TACAS 2005. LNCS, vol. 3440, pp. 570–574. Springer, Heidelberg (2005)
13. Clarke, E., Kroning, D., Lerda, F.: A tool for checking ANSI-C programs. In: Jensen, K., Podelski, A. (eds.) TACAS 2004. LNCS, vol. 2988, pp. 168–176. Springer, Heidelberg (2004)
14. Cohen, E., Dahlweid, M., Hillebrand, M., Leinenbach, D., Moskal, M., Santen, T., Schulte, W., Tobies, S.: VCC: A practical system for verifying concurrent C. In: Berghofer, S., Nipkow, T., Urban, C., Wenzel, M. (eds.) TPHOLs 2009. LNCS, vol. 5674, pp. 23–42. Springer, Heidelberg (2009)
15. Contiki: The open source OS for the Internet of things, http://www.contiki-os.org
16. Cordeiro, L., Fischer, B., Marques-Silva, J.: SMT-based bounded model checking for embedded ANSI-C software. In: IEEE/ACM International Conference on Automated Software Engineering (ASE), pp. 137–148 (2009)
17. Cuoq, P., Kirchner, F., Kosmatov, N., Prevosto, V., Signoles, J., Yakobowski, B.: Frama-C: A software analysis perspective. In: Eleftherakis, G., Hinchey, M., Holcombe, M. (eds.) SEFM 2012. LNCS, vol. 7504, pp. 233–247. Springer, Heidelberg (2012)

18. de Moura, L., Bjørner, N.S.: Z3: An efficient SMT solver. In: Ramakrishnan, C.R., Rehof, J. (eds.) TACAS 2008. LNCS, vol. 4963, pp. 337–340. Springer, Heidelberg (2008)
19. DeLine, R., Leino, K.R.M.: BoogiePL: A typed procedural language for checking object-oriented programs. Technical Report MSR-TR-2005-70, Microsoft Research (2005)
20. Emmi, M., Qadeer, S., Rakamarić, Z.: Delay-bounded scheduling. In: ACM SIGPLAN-SIGACT Symposium on Principles of Programming Languages (POPL), pp. 411–422 (2011)
21. Filliâtre, J.-C., Marché, C.: Multi-prover verification of C programs. In: Davies, J., Schulte, W., Barnett, M. (eds.) ICFEM 2004. LNCS, vol. 3308, pp. 15–29. Springer, Heidelberg (2004)
22. Fischer, B., Inverso, O., Parlato, G.: Cseq: A sequentialization tool for C (competition contribution). In: Piterman, N., Smolka, S.A. (eds.) TACAS 2013. LNCS, vol. 7795, pp. 616–618. Springer, Heidelberg (2013)
23. Lal, A., Qadeer, S., Lahiri, S.K.: A solver for reachability modulo theories. In: Madhusudan, P., Seshia, S.A. (eds.) CAV 2012. LNCS, vol. 7358, pp. 427–443. Springer, Heidelberg (2012)
24. Lattner, C., Adve, V.: LLVM: A compilation framework for lifelong program analysis & transformation. In: International Symposium on Code Generation and Optimization (CGO), pp. 75–86 (2004)
25. Lattner, C., Lenharth, A., Adve, V.S.: Making context-sensitive points-to analysis with heap cloning practical for the real world. In: ACM SIGPLAN Conference on Programming Language Design and Implementation (PLDI), pp. 278–289 (2007)
26. Leino, K.R.M.: This is Boogie 2 (2008)
27. The LLVM compiler infrastructure, http://llvm.org
28. Merz, F., Falke, S., Sinz, C.: LLBMC: Bounded model checking of C and C++ programs using a compiler IR. In: Joshi, R., Müller, P., Podelski, A. (eds.) VSTTE 2012. LNCS, vol. 7152, pp. 146–161. Springer, Heidelberg (2012)
29. Păsăreanu, C.S., Mehlitz, P.C., Bushnell, D.H., Gundy-Burlet, K., Lowry, M., Person, S., Pape, M.: Combining unit-level symbolic execution and system-level concrete execution for testing NASA software. In: International Symposium on Software Testing and Analysis (ISSTA), pp. 15–26 (2008)
30. Rakamarić, Z., Hu, A.J.: Automatic inference of frame axioms using static analysis. In: IEEE/ACM International Conference on Automated Software Engineering (ASE), pp. 89–98 (2008)
31. Rakamarić, Z., Hu, A.J.: A scalable memory model for low-level code. In: Jones, N.D., Müller-Olm, M. (eds.) VMCAI 2009. LNCS, vol. 5403, pp. 290–304. Springer, Heidelberg (2009)
32. Siegel, S.F., Zirkel, T.K.: TASS: The toolkit for accurate scientific software. Mathematics in Computer Science 5(4), 395–426 (2011)
33. International competition on software verification (SV-COMP), http://sv-comp.sosy-lab.org
34. Wang, W., Barrett, C., Wies, T.: Cascade 2.0. In: McMillan, K.L., Rival, X. (eds.) VMCAI 2014. LNCS, vol. 8318, pp. 142–160. Springer, Heidelberg (2014)

Synthesis of Masking Countermeasures against Side Channel Attacks

Hassan Eldib and Chao Wang

Department of ECE, Virginia Tech, Blacksburg, VA 24061, USA
{heldib,chaowang}@vt.edu

Abstract. We propose a new synthesis method for generating countermeasures for cryptographic software code to mitigate power analysis based side channel attacks. Side channel attacks may arise when computers and microchips leak sensitive information about the software code and data that they process, e.g., through power dissipation or electromagnetic radiation. Such information leaks have been exploited in commercial systems in the embedded space. Our new method takes an unprotected C program as input and returns a functionally equivalent but side channel leak free new program as output. The new program is guaranteed to be *perfectly masked* in that all intermediate computation results are made statistically independent from the secret data. We have implemented our new method in a tool based on the LLVM compiler and the Yices SMT solver. Our experiments on a set of cryptographic software benchmarks show that the new method is both effective and scalable for applications of realistic size.

1 Introduction

When cryptographic algorithms are proved to be secure against thousands of years of brute force cryptanalysis attacks, the assumption is that sensitive information can be manipulated in a closed computing environment. Unfortunately, real computers and microchips leak information about the software code and data that they process, e.g. through power dissipation or electromagnetic radiation. For example, the power consumption of a typical embedded device executing instruction a=t⊕k may depend on the value of the secret variable k [21]. Such information can be exploited by an adversary through statistical post-processing such as differential power analysis (DPA [19]), leading to successful attacks in linear time. In recent years, many commercial systems in the embedded space have shown weakness against such attacks [25,22,4].

In this paper, we propose a new synthesis method, which takes an unprotected software program as input and returns a functionally equivalent but side channel leak free new program as output. By leveraging a new verification procedure that we developed recently, called *SC Sniffer* [14,15], we can guarantee that the synthesized new program is secure by construction. That is, all intermediate computations of the program are *perfectly masked* [9] in that their computation results are statistically independent from the secret data. Masking is a popular and relatively low-cost mitigation strategy for removing the statistical dependency between sensitive data and side channel emissions. For example, Boolean masking [4,26] uses an XOR operation of a random bit r with variable a to obtain a masked variable: $a_m = a \oplus r$. The original value can be restored by a second XOR operation: $a_m \oplus r = a$. Since a_m no longer depends on the sensitive data a statistically, subsequent computations based on a_m will not leak information about the value of a.

A. Biere and R. Bloem (Eds.): CAV 2014, LNCS 8559, pp. 114–130, 2014.

When a computation $f(z)$ is in the linear domain in terms of $\oplus$ and with respect to the sensitive input z, masking can be implemented as $f(z \oplus r) \oplus f(r)$ since it is equivalent to $f(z) \oplus f(r) \oplus f(r) = f(z)$. That is, we mask z using an XOR with random bit r before the computation and de-mask using an XOR with $f(r)$ afterward. However, when $f(z)$ is a non-linear function, the computation $f(z)$ often needs to be completely redesigned, e.g., by splitting $f()$ into $f'()$ and $f''()$ such that $f'(z \oplus r) \oplus f''(r) = f(z)$. Finding the proper $f'()$ and $f''()$ is a highly creative process currently performed by cryptographic experts. Indeed, designing a new masking countermeasure for algorithms such as AES and SHA-3 would be publishable work in cryptographic venues.

Our new synthesis method relies on *inductive synthesis* and satisfiability modulo theory (SMT) solvers to search for masking countermeasures within a bounded design space. More specifically, given the software code to be masked, we use a set of quantifier-free first-order logic formulas to encode the two requirements of the synthesized new code – that it must be perfectly masked and that it must be functionally equivalent to the original code. The resulting formulas can be decided by an off-the-shelf SMT solver. Based on this formal analysis, we can guarantee that the synthesized program is provably secure against power analysis based side channel attacks even on devices with physical emissions.

In recent years, there is a growing interest in using compilers to automate the application of side-channel countermeasures [1,5,7,23]. However, these existing methods rely on matching known code patterns and applying predefined code transformations. They do not employ SMT solver based exhaustive search or the notion of *perfect masking* during the process. As a result, they cannot guarantee to find the leakage free new program even if such program exists, or formally prove that the generated code is leakage free. Our new method provides both guarantees. Although inductive synthesis has enjoyed remarkable success recently (e.g., [17,16,20,3,27]), this is the first time that it is applied to mitigating side channel attacks.

We have implemented our new method in a software tool called *SC Masker*, which builds upon the LLVM compiler [11] and the Yices SMT solver [12]. We have conducted experiments on a set of cryptographic software benchmarks, including both AES and MAC-Keccak. Our experiments show that the new method is both effective in eliminating side channel leaks and scalable for handling cryptographic software code of practical size.

To sum up, we have made the following contributions:

- We propose a new method for synthesizing *masking* countermeasures to protect cryptographic software code against power analysis attacks.
- We implement the method in a software tool, which takes an unprotected C program as input and returns a perfectly masked new program as output.
- We conduct experiments on a set of cryptographic software benchmarks to demonstrate the effectiveness and scalability of the new method.

The remainder of this paper is organized as follows. We will establish notation and define the synthesis problem in Section 2. We will illustrate the overall flow of our method using an example in Section 3. The detailed algorithms will be presented in Section 4, which include both inductively computing the candidate program and formally verifying the candidate program. We will present a partitioned synthesis procedure in Section 5 to further improve the runtime performance. Our experimental results will be presented in Section 6. Finally, we will give our conclusions in Section 7.

2   Preliminaries

Following the notation used by Blömer *et al.* [9], we assume that a sensitive computation $c \leftarrow f(x, k)$ takes a plaintext x and a secret key k as input and returns a ciphertext c as output. The implementation of function $f(x, k)$ consists of a sequence of intermediate operations. Each intermediate operation is referred to as a function $I_i(x, k)$, where i is the index of that operation.

Side Channel Attacks. We assume that the plaintext x and the ciphertext c may be observed by an adversary, whereas the secret key k is hidden in the computing device. The goal of the adversary is to deduce k based on observing x, c, and the power leakage of the device. Based on the widely used Hamming Weight (HW) model, we assume that the power leakage of the device correlates to the values involved in the sensitive operations $I_1(x, k) \ldots I_n(x, k)$. Here, $I_i(x, k)$ refers to the i-th instruction whose result is a function of both x and k. Given two different key values k and k', for instance, the power consumption of $k \oplus x$ and $k' \oplus x$ may differ. The information leak may be exploited by techniques such as differential power analysis (DPA [19]).

To eliminate side channel leaks, a countermeasure called *masking* can be implemented to randomize the instantaneous power consumption to make it statistically independent from the secret data. For example, when the computation $f(z)$ is a linear function of variable z in the $\oplus$ domain, meaning that $f(z_1 \oplus z_2) = f(z_1) \oplus f(z_2)$, masking requires no modification of the original implementation of function $f(z)$.

$$f(z \oplus r) \oplus f(r) = f(z) \oplus f(r) \oplus f(r) = f(z) .$$

Here, the random bit r is generated internally on the cryptographic device so the adversary cannot access its value. Due to commutativity of the XOR operation, we can mask z with r before the computation on the device and de-mask with $f(r)$ afterward.

However, when $f(z)$ is a non-linear function, the implementation of $f(z)$ often needs to be completely redesigned. Depending on the order of attacks to be mitigated, for instance, z may have to be divided into n chunks by using XOR operations with n random bits $r_1 \ldots r_n$. Then, each chunk is fed to a newly designed cryptographic function $f_i'(z \oplus r_i, r_i)$, where $1 \leq i \leq n$. At the end, these results are combined to reconstruct $f(z)$ by using XOR operations with another function $f_i''(z \oplus r_i, r_i)$. Consider $n=1$ as an example. We require the new functions $f'()$ and $f''()$ to satisfy the following constraint:

$$f'(z \oplus r, r) \oplus f''(z \oplus r, r) = f(z) .$$

However, the design of such cryptographic functions f' and f'' is a highly creative manual process currently undertaken by experts – it is labor intensive and error prone. Furthermore, even if the masking algorithm is provably secure, bugs introduced during the software coding process may still cause information leaks.

Iterative Inductive Synthesis. To overcome these problems, we propose using inductive synthesis to generate implementations of perfect masking countermeasures. We follow the iterative synthesis procedure shown in Fig. 1, which consists of three steps:

1. Given an unprotected program as input, we first compute a candidate new program that is masked and is functionally equivalent to the original program, at least for a small set of test inputs.

2. We try to prove that the candidate program is perfectly masked and is functionally equivalent to the original program under all possible test inputs.
3. If the verification succeeds, we are done. Otherwise, the candidate program is invalid. In the latter case, we block this solution, go back to Step 1, and try again.

The reason why we choose not to generate, in one step, a candidate program that is valid for all possible test inputs is because of performance concerns. A candidate program valid for all possible test inputs would be prohibitively more expensive for an SMT solver to compute. By separating the synthesis task

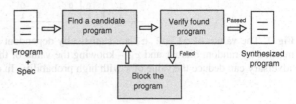

Fig. 1. The iterative inductive synthesis procedure

into three subtasks, namely the inductive synthesis of candidate programs, the formal verification of candidate programs, and the iterative refinement step, we can make all three substeps practically feasible to complete.

In this work, the verification step will consist of two substeps. First, we prove that the candidate program is functionally equivalent to the original program under all possible inputs. Second, we prove that all intermediate computations in the candidate program are perfectly masked. Toward this end, we leverage a verification procedure that we developed recently, called *SC Sniffer* [14,15], which can check whether an intermediate computation result of the program is statistically dependent on the secret data.

Verifying Perfect Masking. Given a pair (x, k) of plaintext and key for the function $f(x, k)$ and an intermediate computation result $I_i(x, k, r)$ masked by the random variable r, we use $D_{x,k}(R)$ to denote the distribution of $I(x, k, r)$. Here, r is an s-bit random variable uniformly distributed in the domain $R = \{0, 1\}^s$; it is meant to be used to remove the information leakage of $I_i(x, k, r)$ while maintaining the input-output relation of function $f(x, k)$. If $D_{x,k}(R)$ is statistically independent from k, we say that the function is perfectly masked [9]. Otherwise, the function has side channel leaks.

Definition 1. *Given an implementation of function $f(x, k)$ and a set of its intermediate results $\{I_i(x, k, r)\}$, we say that the function is perfectly masked if for each $I_i(x, k, r)$,*

$$D_{x,k}(R) = D_{x,k'}(R) \quad \text{for any two pairs } (x, k) \text{ and } (x, k') .$$

As an example, consider Fig. 2 where ciphertexts c1,c2,c3,c4 are results of four different masking schemes for plaintext bit x and key bit k using random bits r1 and r2. According to the truth tables on the right-hand side, all of these four outputs are logically dependent on r1,r2. However, this does not imply statistical independence from the secret k. Indeed, c1,c2,c3 all leak sensitive information. Specifically, when x is logical 0, and when c1 is 1, we know for sure that the secret k is also 1, regardless of the values of the random variables. Similarly, when c2 is logical 0, we know for sure that k is also 0. When c3 is logical 1 (or 0), there is a 75% chance that k is logical 1 (or 0). In contrast, c4 is the only leak-free output because it is statistically independent of k – when k is logical 1 (or 0), there is 50% chance that c4 is logical 1 (or 0).

Our method in *SC Sniffer* [14,15] relies on translating the verification problem into a set of satisfiability (SAT) problems, each of which is encoded as a logical formula.

$c_1 = x \oplus k \wedge (r_1 \wedge r_2)$

$c_2 = x \oplus k \vee (r_1 \wedge r_2)$

$c_3 = x \oplus k \oplus (r_1 \wedge r_2)$

$c_4 = x \oplus k \oplus (r_1 \oplus r_2)$

x	k	r1	r2	c1	c2	c3	c4	x	k	r1	r2	c1	c2	c3	c4
0	0	0	0	0	0	0	0	1	0	0	0	0	1	1	1
0	0	0	1	0	0	0	1	1	0	0	1	0	1	1	0
0	0	1	0	0	0	0	1	1	0	1	0	0	1	1	0
0	0	1	1	0	1	1	0	1	0	1	1	1	1	0	1
0	1	0	0	0	1	1	1	1	1	0	0	0	0	0	0
0	1	0	1	0	1	1	0	1	1	0	1	0	0	0	1
0	1	1	0	0	1	1	0	1	1	1	0	0	0	0	1
0	1	1	1	1	1	0	1	1	1	1	1	0	1	1	0

Fig. 2. The values of c_1, c_2, c_3 are statistically dependent on the key bit k although they are masked by random bits r_1 and r_2 – knowing the value of these ciphertexts and plaintext x, an adversary can deduce the value of k with high probability. In contrast, c_4 is perfectly masked.

These formulas can be decided using an off-the-shelf SMT solver. More specifically, we start by marking all the plaintext bits in x as public, the key bits in k as secret, and the mask bits in r as random. Then, we traverse the entire program and for each intermediate computation $I(x, k, r)$, check the satisfiability of the following formula:

$$\exists x, k, k' . \left(\sum_{r \in R} I(x, k, r) \neq \sum_{r \in R} I(x, k', r) \right)$$

Here, k and k' are two different values of the secret key and R is the set of values of random variable r. The summation $\sum_{r \in R} I(x, k, r)$ represents the number of values of r that can make $I(x, k, r)$ evaluate to logical 1, and the summation $\sum_{r \in R} I(x, k', r)$ represents the number of values of r that can make $I(x, k', r)$ evaluate to logical 1. Assume that random variable r is uniformly distributed in the domain R, the above two summations represent the probabilities of I being logical 1 under key values k and k', respectively. If the above formula is satisfiable, then we have found a plaintext x and two values (k, k') such that the distributions of $I(x, k, r)$ and $I(x, k', r)$ differs – it means that the value of the secret key bit is leaked. In contrast, if the formula is unsatisfiable, it is a formal proof that $I(x, k, r)$ is perfectly masked by r. We will present the detailed SMT encoding in Section 4.2.

3 Motivating Example

In this section, we illustrate the overall flow of our synthesis method using an example. Our example is part of the implementation of MAC-Keccak, the newly standardized SHA-3 cryptographic hashing algorithm [24], after three rounds of competitions by cryptographic experts worldwide. The MAC-Keccak code [8] consists of five main functions that are repeated for 24 rounds on the input bits (plaintext and key) in order to compute the output (ciphertext). The computation in a single round can be represented by $out = \iota.\chi.\pi.\rho.\theta(in)$, where $\iota(), \pi(), \rho()$ and $\theta()$ are linear functions in the domain of $\oplus$, consisting of operations such as XOR, SHIFT and ROTATE, whereas $\chi()$ is a nonlinear function, containing nonlinear operations such as AND.

Our synthesis procedure takes the MAC-Keccak code as input and returns a perfectly masked version of the code as output. It starts by transforming the original program into an intermediate representation (IR) using the LLVM compiler front-end. Since we focus on cryptographic software, not general purpose software, we can assume that all

```
1 : Chi(bool i1, bool i2, bool i3) {          1 : mChi(bool i1, bool i2, bool i3) {
2 :   bool n1, n2, n3;                        2 :   bool r1, r2, r3;  //random bits added
3 :   n3 = ¬i2;                               3 :   bool b1, b2, b3, n1, n2, n3, n4, n5, n6, n7, n8, n9;
4 :   n2 = n3 ∧ i3;                           4 :   b1 = i1 ⊕ r1;
5 :   n1 = n2 ⊕ i1;                           5 :   b2 = i2 ⊕ r2;
6 :   return n1;                              6 :   b3 = i3 ⊕ r3;
7 : }                                         7 :   n9 = b3 ∧ r2;
                                              8 :   n8 = r3 ∧ r2;
                                              9 :   n7 = r3 ∨ b2;
                                             10 :   n6 = r1 ⊕ n9;
                                             11 :   n5 = n7 ⊕ n8;
                                             12 :   n4 = b2 ∨ b3;
                                             13 :   n3 = n5 ⊕ n6;
                                             14 :   n2 = n4 ⊕ b1;
                                             15 :   n1 = n2 ⊕ n3;
                                             16 :   return n1;
                                             17 : }
```

i1	i2	i3	n3	n2	n1
0	0	0	1	0	0
0	0	1	1	1	1
0	1	0	0	0	0
0	1	1	0	0	0
1	0	0	1	0	1
1	0	1	1	0	1
1	1	0	0	0	1
1	1	1	0	0	1

Fig. 3. The original χ function in MAC-Keccak, its truth table, and the synthesized χ function. Here ¬ denotes NOT, ∧ denotes AND, ∨ denotes OR, and ⊕ denotes XOR.

program variables are bounded integers and there is no input-dependent control flow. (Cryptographic software typically do not have input-dependent control flow because it is vulnerable to timing attacks.) Therefore, it is relatively straightforward to transform the input program into a Boolean program, e.g., by merging if-else conditions, unwinding loops, inlining functions, and bit-blasting the integer operations. Thus, from now on, we are only concerned with an IR where all instructions operate on bits. Focusing on the bit-level analysis allows us to detect leaks at the finest granularity possible.

The next step is traversing the abstract syntax tree of the Boolean program in a topological order, starting at the input nodes and ending at the output node. For each internal node, we first check whether its function is linear in the domain of ⊕. As we have shown earlier, for a linear function $f(z)$, we can mask the input z with an XOR of a random bit r before the computation and demask with an XOR of $f(r)$ afterward. Furthermore, to make sure that all intermediate nodes stay masked, we need to chain the mask-demask segments together, by masking the output of a function with a new random variable before demasking it with the previous random variable.

For nonlinear functions, such as $\chi()$, there are no easy ways of generating the countermeasures. In this work, we rely on the iterative inductive synthesis and SMT solvers to search for a valid countermeasure in a bounded design space. Given the $\chi()$ function in Fig. 3 (left), our method will produce the new code in Fig. 3 (right). Our method ensures that these two versions have the same input-output relation, and at the same time, all the intermediate computation results in the new program are perfectly masked with random bits r1, r2 and r3. Our method has two main advantages over the state of the art. First, it is more economical and sustainable than the manual mitigation approach, especially when considering the rapid increase in the application size and platform variety. Second, it eliminates both the design errors and the implementation errors while guaranteeing that the synthesized program is secure by construction. That is, by assuming that each of r1, r2 and r3 in Fig. 3 (right) is randomly distributed, our method guarantees that the probability of each intermediate result being logical 1 (or 0) is statistically independent from the values of i1, i2 and i3.

4   Synthesis of Masking Countermeasures

In this section, we present our basic algorithm for iteratively synthesizing a masked version of the input Boolean program. We leave performance optimizations to the next section. The pseudocode is shown in Algorithm 1, where P is the original program, *inputs* is the set of inputs, and *output* is the output. The input variables also have annotations indicating whether they are plaintext bits, key bits, or random bits. The synthesis procedure returns a new program $newP$ whose input-output relation is equivalent to that of P. At the same time, all internal nodes of $newP$ are perfectly masked. New random bits may be added by the synthesis procedure gradually, on a *need-to* basis.

Algorithm 1. Inductive synthesis of a masked version of the input program P.

```
1. SYNTHESIZEMASKING (P, inputs, output) {
2.    blocked ← { };
3.    testSet ← { };
4.    size ← 1;
5.    while (size < MAX_CODE_SIZE) {
6.       newP ← COMPUTECANDIDATE(P, inputs, output, size, blocked, testSet);
7.       if (newP does not exist)
8.          size ← size + 1;
9.       else {
10.         test1 ← CHECKEQUIVALENCE(newP, P);
11.         test2 ← CHECKINFOLEAKAGE(newP);
12.         if ( {test1, test2} == { } )
13.            return newP;
14.         blocked ← blocked ∪{newP};
15.         testSet ← testSet ∪{test1, test2};
16.      }
17.   }
18.   return no_solution;
19. }
```

The synthesis procedure iterates through three elementary steps: (1) compute a candidate program $newP$ which is functionally equivalent to the original program P, at least for a selected set of test inputs; (2) verify that $newP$ is functionally equivalent to P for all possible inputs and is perfectly masked; (3) if any of the two verification substeps fails, we block this solution, add the failure triggering inputs to *testSet*, and repeat. The synthesis procedure iteratively searches for a new candidate program with increasing code size, until the size reaches MAX_CODE_SIZE. We record the bad solutions in the set *blocked* to avoid repeating them in the future. We record in *testSet* all the test cases that led to failures at some previous verification steps.

In the remainder of this section, we present the detailed algorithms for two elementary steps: computing the candidate program and verifying the candidate program.

4.1   Computing the Candidate Program

The first step in computing $newP$ from P is to create a parameterized AST that captures all possible masked Boolean programs up to a bounded size. Following the notation used in [13], we call this parameterized AST as a *skeleton*. An example is shown in Fig. 4, which has 11 nodes. Each node is either an *Op* node or a *V* node. The internal node *Op* can be instantiated to any bit-level operation such as ⊕, &, |, or !. The *V* node can be instantiated to any variable in the original program, or fresh random bit added by the synthesis procedure, or constant (logical 0 or 1). The instantiation of *Op* nodes and *V* nodes is controlled by a set of auxiliary variables, whose values will be assigned by the SMT solver.

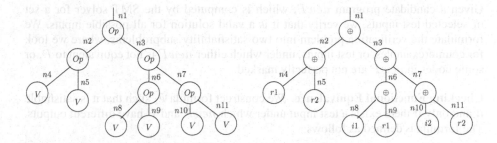

Fig. 4. A candidate program skeleton consisting of 11 parameterized AST nodes

Fig. 5. The synthesized candidate program with instantiated Boolean masking

As an example, consider node n_8 in Fig. 4. The corresponding logical constraint may be ((N8==V1)&&bV1)||(N8==V2)&&bV2), where N8 denotes the output of n_8 and V1 and V2 are two variables in the input program. Auxiliary variables bV1 and bV2 are added to decide which of the node types are chosen – we would add another constraint saying that one and only one of bV1 and bV2 must be true. Based on which variable is set to true by the SMT solver, the output of node n_8 is determined. For node n_1, the constraint may be ((N1==(N2&N3))&&bAND1)||((N1==(N2|N3))&&bOR1) ||((N1==(N2⊕N3))&&bXOR1) ||((N1==(⊕N2))&&bNOT1 where N1, N2 and N3 denote the output of node n_1, n_2, and n_3, respectively. Auxiliary variables bAND1, bOR1, bXOR1, and bNOT1 are constrained such that one and only one of them must be true. Fig. 5 shows a masked candidate program synthesized by the SMT solver, which represents $n_1 = i_1 \oplus i_2$.

The next step is to build an SMT formula Φ that imposes two additional requirements: (1) the input-output relation of the candidate program *skeleton* is equivalent to the original program P, and (2) the internal nodes of the candidate program are all masked by some random variables. More formally, the formula Φ is defined as follows:

$$\Phi = \Phi_P \wedge \Phi_{skel} \wedge \Phi_{iEqv} \wedge \Phi_{oEqv} \wedge \Phi_{masked} \wedge \Phi_{testSet} \wedge \Phi_{blocked},$$

where the subformulas are defined as follows:

- Φ_P encodes the program logic of P.
- Φ_{skel} encodes the program logic of the *skeleton*.
- Φ_{iEqv} asserts that the input variables of P and *skeleton* have the same values.
- Φ_{oEqv} asserts that the outputs of P and *skeleton* have the same value.
- Φ_{masked} asserts that all internal nodes are masked by some random bits – some random bit must appear in the support of the function of each node.

- $\Phi_{testSet}$ asserts that the input variables should take values only from *testSet*.
- $\Phi_{blocked}$ asserts that the previously failed solutions should not be selected.

If formula Φ is satisfiable, a candidate solution is found, and it will be verified for equivalence and perfect masking in the following step. Otherwise, the skeleton *size* will be incremented and the SMT solver will be invoked again on the new formula.

4.2 Verifying the Candidate Program

Given a candidate program $newP$, which is computed by the SMT solver for a set of selected test inputs, we verify that it is a valid solution for all possible inputs. We formulate the verification problem into two satisfiability subproblems, where we look for counterexamples, or test inputs, under which either $newP$ is not equivalent to P, or some nodes in $newP$ are not perfectly masked.

Checking Functional Equivalence. We construct formula Ψ_1 such that it is satisfiable if and only if there exists a test input under which $newP$ and P have different outputs. The formula is defined as follows:

$$\Psi_1 = \Phi_P \wedge \Phi_{newP} \wedge \Phi_{iEqv} \wedge \Phi_{oDiff},$$

where Φ_P and Φ_{newP} encode the input-output relations of the two programs, Φ_{iEqv} asserts that they have the same input values, and Φ_{oDiff} asserts that they have different outputs. If Ψ_1 is satisfiable, we find a test case showing that $newP$ is a bad solution. If Ψ_1 is unsatisfiable, then $newP$ and P are functional equivalent.

Checking for Information Leakage. We construct formula Ψ_2 such that it is satisfiable if and only if there exists an intermediate node in $newP$ that leaks sensitive information. Toward this end, we leverage our recently developed verification procedure [14,15] to check, for each intermediate node $I(x, k, r)$, whether there exist a plaintext x and two key values k, k' such that $\sum_{r \in R} I(x, k, r) \neq \sum_{r \in R} I(x, k', r)$. As we have explained in Section 2, this inequality means that the probabilistic distributions of $I(x, k, r)$ and $I(x, k', r)$ differ for the two key values k and k'. The formula Ψ_2 is defined as follows:

$$\Psi_2 := \left(\bigwedge_{r \in R} \Phi_{I(x,k,r)} \right) \wedge \left(\bigwedge_{r \in R} \Phi_{I(x,k',r)} \right) \wedge \Phi_{b2i} \wedge \Phi_{sum} \wedge \Phi_{sumDiff},$$

where the subformulas are defined as follows:

- *Program logic* ($\Phi_{I(x,k,r)}$): Each subformula $\Phi_{I(x,k,r)}$ encodes the input-output relation of $I(x, k, r)$ with a fixed value $r \in R$ and variable k. Each subformula $\Phi_{I(x,k',r)}$ encodes the input-output relation of $I(x, k', r)$ with a fixed value $r \in R$ and variable k'. All subformulas share the same plaintext variable x.
- *Boolean-to-int* (Φ_{b2i}): This subformula encodes the conversion of the bit output of each $I(x, k, r)$ to an integer (true becomes 1 and false becomes 0), which will be summed up later to compute $\sum_{r \in R} I(x, k, r)$ and $\sum_{r \in R} I(x, k', r)$.
- *Sum-up-the-1s* (Φ_{sum}): This subformula encodes the two summations of the logical 1's in the outputs of the $|R|$ copies of $I(x, k, r)$ and the $|R|$ copies of $I(x, k', r)$.
- *Different sums* ($\Phi_{sumDiff}$): It asserts that the two summations have different results.

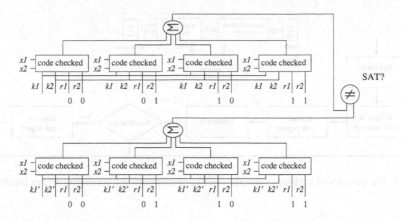

Fig. 6. SMT encoding for checking the statistical dependence of an output on secret data $(k1, k2)$

If Ψ_2 is unsatisfiable, then the intermediate result I is perfectly masked. If Ψ_2 is satisfiable, then I has information leakage.

Fig. 6 provides a pictorial illustration of our SMT encoding for an intermediate result $I(k1, k2, r1, r2)$, where $k1, k2$ are the key bits and $r1, r2$ are the random bits. The first four boxes encode the program logic of $\Phi_{I(x,k,0)} \cdots \Phi_{I(x,k,3)}$ for key bits $(k1k2)$, with the random bits set to $00, 01, 10$, and 11, respectively. The other four boxes encode the program logic of $\Phi_{I(x,k',0)} \cdots \Phi_{I(x,k',3)}$ for key bits $(k1'k2')$, with the random bits set to $00, 01, 10$, and 11, respectively. The entire formula checks whether there exist two sets of key values $(k1k2$ and $k1'k2')$ under which the probabilities of I being logical 1 are different.

As a more concrete example, consider the computation $c2 = x \oplus k \vee (r1 \wedge r2)$ in Fig. 2. The SMT solver may return the solution $x=0$, $k=0$ and $k'=1$ because, according to the truth table in Fig. 2, $\sum_{r\in R} c2(0,0,r) = 1$ whereas $\sum_{r\in R} c2(0,1,r) = 4$. Consider $c4 = x \oplus k \oplus (r1 \oplus r2)$ in Fig. 2 as another example. The SMT solver will not be able to find any solution because it is perfectly masked. For instance, when $x=0$, $k=0$ and $k'=1$, we have $\sum_{r\in R} c4(0,0,r) = 2$ and $\sum_{r\in R} c4(0,1,r) = 2$.

5 Partitioned Synthesis to Improve Performance

SMT solver based inductive synthesis has the advantage of being exhaustive during the search of countermeasures within a bounded design space. With the help of the verification subprocedure, our method also guarantees that the resulting program is secure by construction. However, its main disadvantage is the limited scalability, since the SMT solver slows down quickly as the program size increases. Although we expect SMT solvers to continue improving in the coming years, it is unlikely that a monolithic SMT based synthesis procedure will scale up to large programs (this is consistent with what others in the field have observed [3,2]). In this section, we propose a *partitioned* synthesis procedure to combine static code analysis with judicious use of inductive synthesis so that the combined method can handle cryptographic software code of realistic size.

The partitioned synthesis procedure (Fig. 7) starts by traversing the AST nodes of the program in a topological order, from the inputs to the output. Depending on whether the

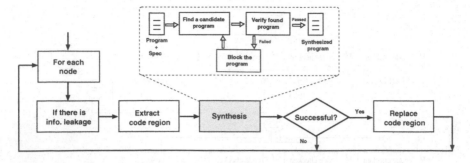

Fig. 7. The partitioned synthesis procedure for applying masking countermeasures locally

AST node n is linear or nonlinear as shown in Algorithm 2, it invokes either MASKLIN-EAR or SYNTHESIZEMASKING (presented in the previous section). When n is a linear function, we mask its input variables and demask the output with random variables, without modifying the linear function itself, as explained in Section 2. When n is a nonlinear function, instead of invoking SYNTHESIZEMASKING for the entire fan-in cone of n, we partition it into small code regions, and synthesize a masked version for each region. Then, we substitute the original code region reg in program P with the new code region new_reg. The entire synthesis procedure terminates when all small code regions of all nonlinear AST nodes in program P are perfectly masked.

Algorithm 2. Partitioned synthesis algorithm for masking the program P.

1. PARTITIONEDSYNTHESIS $(P, inputs, output)$ {
2.   **for each** (AST node $n \in P$) {
3.   **if** (n represents a linear function)
4. $new\_n \leftarrow$ MASKLINEAR$(P, inputs, n)$;
5.   replace n in program P with new_n;
6.   **else** {
7.   **while** ($\exists$ unprotected code region $reg \in FanIn(n)$) {
8.   Let (reg_ins, reg_out) be the inputs and output of reg;
9. $new\_reg \leftarrow$ SYNTHESIZEMASKING(P, reg_ins, reg_out);
10.   replace reg in program P with new_reg;
11.   }
12.   }
13. }
14. **return** P;
15. }

Selecting a Code Region. While selecting a code region in $FanIn(n)$ of a nonlinear node n, we first start from an AST node $m \in FanIn(n)$ that is not yet perfectly masked, and then include a number of its connected unprotected nodes. The exact number of fan-in nodes to be included in the code region of node m is controlled by a user specified bound. Choosing the right bound, and hence the size of the code region, is a tradeoff between the compactness of the synthesized program and the computational overhead.

On the one hand, if we set the bound to positive infinity, the *partitioned* synthesis procedure would degenerate to the *monolithic* approach. On the other hand, if we set the bound to a small number, the synthesized solution may be suboptimal in that some of the masking operations are unnecessary.

For illustration purposes only, we consider an extreme case where the region size is set to 1, meaning that each nonlinear AST node is masked separately. Under this assumption, in Fig. 3, we illustrate the process of masking the $\chi()$ function from Fig. 8. The first code region involves the NOT operation at Line 3, whose masked version is shown in the middle column. The second code region involves the AND operation at Line 4, whose masked version is shown in the middle column. The third code region involves the XOR of $n2$ and $i1$ at Line 5, whose masked version is shown in the middle column. It is worth pointing out that, in this extreme case, the resulting program will be suboptimal. However, the actual implementation of our partitioned synthesis procedure was able to obtain a perfectly masked countermeasure whose size is more compact.

```
                    b1  = i2  ⊕ r1;              b1  = i2  ⊕ r1;
L3:  n3 = ¬ i2;  →  t1  = ¬ b1;           →     t1  = ¬ b1;
                    n3  = t1  ⊕ r1;              n3  = t1  ⊕ r2;  //swap with r1

                    b3  = i3  ⊕ r3;              b3  = i3  ⊕ r3;
                    b2  = n3  ⊕ r2;              b2  = n3  ⊕ r1;  //swap with r2
                    t10 = ¬ b2;                  t10 = ¬ b2;
                    t9  = b3  ∧ r2;              t9  = b3  ∧ r2;
L4:  n2 = n3 ∧ i3; →  t8  = ¬ r3;         →     t8  = ¬ r3;
                    t7  = t10 ∧ r3;              t7  = t10 ∧ r3;
                    t6  = b2  ∧ b3;              t6  = b2  ∧ b3;
                    t5  = ¬ t9;                  t5  = ¬ t9;
                    t4  = t8  ∨ r2;              t4  = t8  ∨ r2;
                    t3  = t6  ∨ t7;              t3  = t6  ∨ t7;
                    t2  = t4  ⊕ t5;              t2  = t4  ⊕ t5;
                    n2  = t2  ⊕ t3;              n2  = t2  ⊕ r4;  //swap with t3

                    b4  = n2  ⊕ r4;              b4  = n2  ⊕ t3;  //swap with r4
                    b5  = i1  ⊕ r1;              b5  = i1  ⊕ r1;
L5:  n1 = n2 ⊕ i1; →  t12 = b4  ⊕ b5;     →     t12 = b4  ⊕ b5;
                    t11 = r1  ⊕ r4;              t11 = r1  ⊕ r4;
                    n1  = t11 ⊕ t12;             n1  = t11 ⊕ t12;
```

Fig. 8. Example: the process of masking individual code regions and composing them together

Replacing the Code Region. Continue with the above *extreme case* exercise, we now explain how to use the newly synthesized code region (new_reg) to replace the original code region (reg) in program P. The replacement process is mostly straightforward, due to the fact that our partitioned synthesis procedure traverses regions in a bottom-up topological order. However, there is one caveat – before demasking the output of the new region new_reg, we need to mask it with another random variable; otherwise, the output of new_reg would become unmasked.

We solve this problem by asserting, while computing the candidate program in procedure SYNTHESIZEMASKING, that the output and all inputs must be an XOR operation with some random variables. Due to the associativity of XOR operations, and the fact that now two adjacent code regions are connected through two XOR operations, we can switch the order of the two XOR operations during region replacement, without modifying the functionality of the final output.

In Fig. 8, the right-hand-side column shows an example for chaining the three new code regions of the χ function obtained in the middle column, by swapping their adjacent XOR operations with random bits.

Reusing Random Variables. To further reduce the size of the synthesized program, we reuse random variables as much as possible while masking the non-adjacent code regions. Specifically, while building the candidate program *skeleton* for a code region *reg* (see Section 4.1), we first need to create a list of random variables to be used in the *V* nodes. The number of random variables is at most as large as the number of input variables in *reg*. However, we do not have to create fresh random variables every time they are needed. Instead, we can reuse existing random variables in the program, as long as they are not used in the code regions adjacent to *reg*. This optimization can significantly reduce the number of random bits required in the masked new program, while at the same time soundly maintaining the statistical independence of the masked nodes.

6   Experiments

We have implemented our new synthesis method in a software tool called *SC Masker*, which builds upon the LLVM compiler front-end and the Yices SMT solver. Our tool runs in two modes: the monolithic mode and the partitioned mode, to facilitate experimental comparison of the two approaches. We have evaluated our method on a set of cryptographic software benchmarks. Our experimental evaluation was designed to answer the following questions:

- How effective is the new synthesis method in eliminating side channel leaks? Is the synthesized program as compact as the countermeasures handcrafted by experts?
- How scalable is the tool in handling code of realistic size? Our partitioned synthesis procedure is designed to address the scalability problem. Is it effective in practice?

Our benchmarks fall into three categories. The first set, from P1 to P8, are medium sized cryptographic functions that are partially masked. Specifically, P1 and P2 are taken from Bayrak *et al.* [6], which are incorrectly masked computations due to code motion in compiler optimization. P3 and P4 are from Herbst *et al.* [18], which are gate-level implementations of partially masked AES. P5 and P6 are masked versions of the χ function from Bertoni *et al.* [8], after integer to Boolean compilation with optimizations. P7 and P8 are two modified versions of the MAC-Keccak nonlinear χ functions. The second set, from P9 to P12, are small to medium sized cryptographic functions that are completely unmasked. Specifically, P9 is the original MAC-Keccak χ function taken from the reference implementation [8] (Equation 5.2 on Page 46). P10 and P11 are two nonlinear functions, *mul4* and *invg4*, from an implementation of AES in [10]. P12 is a single-round complete implementation of AES found in [10]. The third set, from P13 to P18, are partially masked large programs with a significant number of instructions not yet masked. These programs are generated by us from the MAC-Keccak reference code [24] after converting it from an integer program to a Boolean program. In each case, the whole program has been transformed into a single function to test the scalability of our new methods.

Table 1 shows the experimental results obtained on a machine with a 3.4 GHz Intel i7-2600 CPU, 4 GB RAM, and a 32-bit Linux OS. Columns 1-6 show the statistics

Table 1. Comparing performance of the monolithic and partitioned methods in *SC Masker*

Program					Monolithic			Partitioned		
Name	LoC	Keys	Plains	Rands	Nodes	Rands	Nodes	Time	Rands	Nodes	Time
P1	79	16	16	16	47	16	85	2.9s	16	85	2.9s
P2	67	8	8	16	31	16	55	1.5s	16	55	1.5s
P3	32	2	2	2	9	4	15	8.3s	4	15	8.1s
P4	32	2	2	2	6	6	9	0.2s	6	9	0.2s
P5	59	3	3	4	18	8	24	19m17s	8	27	8.3s
P6	60	3	3	4	18	8	24	0.5s	8	24	0.5s
P7	66	3	3	4	22	8	25	0.3s	8	25	0.3s
P8	66	3	3	4	22	8	25	0.3s	8	25	0.3s
P9	9	3	0	0	3	-	-	TO	4	14	3.1s
P10	57	8	0	0	37	-	-	TO	8	264	4m36s
P11	82	8	0	0	48	-	-	TO	4	485	13m10s
P12	365	8	0	0	182	-	-	TO	8	1072	22m10s
P13	56k	58	161	58	19k	-	-	TO	58	20k	24m7s
P14	56k	58	161	58	19k	-	-	TO	58	21k	41m37s
P15	56k	58	161	58	19k	-	-	TO	58	21k	36m21s
P16	56k	58	161	58	19k	-	-	TO	58	21k	35m42s
P17	56k	58	161	58	19k	-	-	TO	58	21k	48m15s
P18	56k	58	161	58	19k	-	-	TO	58	20k	23m41s

of each benchmark, including the name, the lines of code, the number of key bits, the number of plaintext bits, the number of random bits, and the number of operations (Nodes). Columns 7-9 show the results of the monolithic synthesis algorithm, including the number of random bits and the number of operations (Nodes) in the synthesized program, as well as the run time. Columns 10-12 show the results of the partitioned synthesis algorithm, including the number of random bits and the number of operations (Nodes) in the synthesized program, as well as the run time. Here, TO means that the *SC Masker* tool ran out of the time limit of 4 hours.

The experimental results show that our new synthesis method, especially when it runs in the partitioned mode, is scalable in handling cryptographic software of realistic size. On the first set of test cases, where the programs are small, both monolithic and partitioned procedures can complete quickly, and the differences in run time and compactness of the new program are small. However, on large programs such as AES and MAC Keccak, the monolithic method can not finish within four hours, whereas the partitioned method can finish in a reasonably small amount of time. Furthermore, we can see that most of the existing random bits in the original programs were reused.

As far as the compactness of the new program is concerned, we know of only one benchmark (P9) that has a previously published masking countermeasure. The countermeasure [8] handcrafted by cryptographic engineering experts has 14 operations. The countermeasure synthesized by our own tool (using the partitioned approach) also has 14 operations. Therefore, at least for this example, it is as compact than the handcrafted countermeasure. However, recall that our method has the additional advantages of being fully automated and at the same time guaranteeing that the synthesized new program is provably secure. Furthermore, when given more CPU time – for example, by setting the time limit to 10 hours and using a larger region size – our synthesis procedure in *SC Masker* was able to produce a countermeasure with only 12 operations, which is more compact than the countermeasure handcrafted by experts. We can also show that this is the smallest possible solution because reducing the skeleton size further causes the SMT solver to report unsatisfiability.

As another measurement of the scalability of our new methods, we conducted experiments on a parameterized version of test program P1 by expanding it from 1 encryption round up to 10 rounds. In each program, the input for one round is the output from the previous round. We ran the *SC Masker* tool twice, once with the monolithic approach and once with the partitioned approach. The results are plotted in Fig. 9, where the x-axis shows the program size in terms of the number of encryption rounds and the y-axis shows the run time in seconds. Also note that the y-axis is in logarithmic scale. Whereas the monolithic approach quickly ran out of time for programs with ≥ 5 rounds, the execution time increase of the partitioned approach remains modest – this demonstrates the capability of our *partitioned* method in handling large programs.

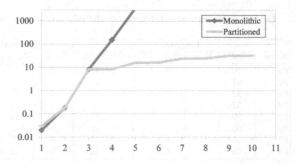

Fig. 9. Comparing the run time of the two synthesis methods in *SC Masker* (the time is in seconds)

7   Conclusions

We have presented a new synthesis method for automatically generating perfect masking countermeasures for cryptographic software to defend against power analysis based side channel attacks. Our method guarantees that the resulting software code is secure by construction. We have implemented our method in the *SC Masker* tool and evaluated it on a set of cryptographic software benchmarks. Our experiments show that the new method is effective in eliminating side channel leaks and at the same time is scalable for handling programs of practical size. For future work, we plan to continue optimizing our SMT based encoding and at the same time extending it to handle other masking schemes, including additive masking, multiplicative masking, as well as application specific masking such as RSA blinding.

Acknowledgments. This work is supported in part by the NSF grant CNS-1128903 and the ONR grant N00014-13-1-0527.

References

1. Agosta, G., Barenghi, A., Pelosi, G.: A code morphing methodology to automate power analysis countermeasures. In: ACM/IEEE Design Automation Conference, pp. 77–82 (2012)
2. Akiba, T., Imajo, K., Iwami, H., Iwata, Y., Kataoka, T., Takahashi, N., Moskal, M., Swamy, N.: Calibrating research in program synthesis using 72,000 hours of programmer time. Technical report, Microsoft Research (2013)
3. Alur, R., Bodík, R., Juniwal, G., Martin, M.M.K., Raghothaman, M., Seshia, S.A., Singh, R., Solar-Lezama, A., Torlak, E., Udupa, A.: Syntax-guided synthesis. In: International Conference on Formal Methods in Computer-Aided Design, pp. 1–17 (2013)

4. Balasch, J., Gierlichs, B., Verdult, R., Batina, L., Verbauwhede, I.: Power analysis of Atmel CryptoMemory – recovering keys from secure EEPROMs. In: RSA Conference Cryptographers' Track, pp. 19–34 (2012)
5. Bayrak, A., Regazzoni, F., Brisk, P., Standaert, F.-X., Ienne, P.: A first step towards automatic application of power analysis countermeasures. In: ACM/IEEE Design Automation Conference, pp. 230–235 (2011)
6. Bayrak, A.G., Regazzoni, F., Novo, D., Ienne, P.: Sleuth: Automated verification of software power analysis countermeasures. In: Bertoni, G., Coron, J.-S. (eds.) CHES 2013. LNCS, vol. 8086, pp. 293–310. Springer, Heidelberg (2013)
7. Bayrak, A., Velickovic, N., Ienne, P., Burleson, W.: An architecture-independent instruction shuffler to protect against side-channel attacks. ACM Transactions on Architecture and Code Optimization 8(4), 20 (2012)
8. Bertoni, G., Daemen, J., Peeters, M., Assche, G.V., Keer, R.V.: Keccak implementation overview, http://keccak.neokeon.org/Keccak-implementation-3.2.pdf
9. Blömer, J., Guajardo, J., Krummel, V.: Provably secure masking of AES. In: Handschuh, H., Hasan, M.A. (eds.) SAC 2004. LNCS, vol. 3357, pp. 69–83. Springer, Heidelberg (2004)
10. Boyar, J., Peralta, R.: A small depth-16 circuit for the AES S-Box. In: International Workshop on Security, pp. 287–298 (2012)
11. Lattner, C., Adve, V.: The LLVM Instruction Set and Compilation Strategy. Tech. report, CS Dept., Univ. of Illinois at Urbana-Champaign (August 2002)
12. Dutertre, B., de Moura, L.: A fast linear-arithmetic solver for DPLL(T). In: Ball, T., Jones, R.B. (eds.) CAV 2006. LNCS, vol. 4144, pp. 81–94. Springer, Heidelberg (2006)
13. Eldib, H., Wang, C.: An SMT based method for optimizing arithmetic computations in embedded software code. In: International Conference on Formal Methods in Computer-Aided Design (2013)
14. Eldib, H., Wang, C., Schaumont, P.: SMT-based verification of software countermeasures against side-channel attacks. In: Ábrahám, E., Havelund, K. (eds.) TACAS 2014 (ETAPS). LNCS, vol. 8413, pp. 62–77. Springer, Heidelberg (2014)
15. Eldib, H., Wang, C., Taha, M., Schaumont, P.: QMS: Evaluating the side-channel resistance of masked software from source code. In: ACM/IEEE Design Automation Conference (2014)
16. Gulwani, S., Jha, S., Tiwari, A., Venkatesan, R.: Synthesis of loop-free programs. In: ACM SIGPLAN Conference on Programming Language Design and Implementation, pp. 62–73 (2011)
17. Gulwani, S., Srivastava, S., Venkatesan, R.: Program analysis as constraint solving. In: ACM SIGPLAN Conference on Programming Language Design and Implementation, pp. 281–292 (2008)
18. Herbst, C., Oswald, E., Mangard, S.: An AES smart card implementation resistant to power analysis attacks. In: Zhou, J., Yung, M., Bao, F. (eds.) ACNS 2006. LNCS, vol. 3989, pp. 239–252. Springer, Heidelberg (2006)
19. Kocher, P.C., Jaffe, J., Jun, B.: Differential power analysis. In: Wiener, M. (ed.) CRYPTO 1999. LNCS, vol. 1666, pp. 388–397. Springer, Heidelberg (1999)
20. Kuncak, V., Mayer, M., Piskac, R., Suter, P.: Software synthesis procedures. Commun. ACM 55(2), 103–111 (2012)
21. Mangard, S., Oswald, E., Popp, T.: Power Analysis Attacks – Revealing the Secrets of Smart Sards, pp. 1–337. Springer (2007)
22. Moradi, A., Barenghi, A., Kasper, T., Paar, C.: On the vulnerability of FPGA bitstream encryption against power analysis attacks – extracting keys from Xilinx Virtex-II FPGAs. IACR Cryptology (2011)
23. Moss, A., Oswald, E., Page, D., Tunstall, M.: Compiler assisted masking. In: Prouff, E., Schaumont, P. (eds.) CHES 2012. LNCS, vol. 7428, pp. 58–75. Springer, Heidelberg (2012)
24. NIST. Keccak reference implementation code submission to the SHA-3 competition, http://csrc.nist.gov/groups/ST/hash/sha-3/Round3/documents/Keccak_FinalRnd.zip

25. Paar, C., Eisenbarth, T., Kasper, M., Kasper, T., Moradi, A.: Keeloq and side-channel analysis – evolution of an attack. In: International Workshop on Fault Diagnosis and Tolerance in Cryptography, pp. 65–69 (2009)
26. Prouff, E., Rivain, M.: Masking against side-channel attacks: A formal security proof. In: Johansson, T., Nguyen, P.Q. (eds.) EUROCRYPT 2013. LNCS, vol. 7881, pp. 142–159. Springer, Heidelberg (2013)
27. Solar-Lezama, A.: Program sketching. International Journal on Software Tools for Technology Transfer 15(5-6), 475–495 (2013)

Temporal Mode-Checking for Runtime Monitoring of Privacy Policies

Omar Chowdhury[1], Limin Jia[1], Deepak Garg[2], and Anupam Datta[1]

[1] Carnegie Mellon University,
[2] Max Planck Institute for Software Systems
{omarc,liminjia,danupam}@cmu.edu, dg@mpi-sws.org

Abstract. Fragments of first-order temporal logic are useful for representing many practical privacy and security policies. Past work has proposed two strategies for checking event trace (audit log) compliance with policies: online monitoring and offline audit. Although online monitoring is space- and time-efficient, existing techniques insist that satisfying instances of all subformulas of the policy be amenable to caching, which limits expressiveness when some subformulas have infinite support. In contrast, offline audit is brute force and can handle more policies but is not as efficient. This paper proposes a new online monitoring algorithm that caches satisfying instances when it can, and falls back to the brute force search when it cannot. Our key technical insight is a new flow- and time-sensitive static check of variable groundedness, called the *temporal mode check*, which determines subformulas for which such caching is feasible and those for which it is not and, hence, guides our algorithm. We prove the correctness of our algorithm and evaluate its performance over synthetic traces and realistic policies.

Keywords: Mode checking, runtime monitoring, metric first-order temporal logic, privacy policy.

1 Introduction

Many organizations routinely collect sensitive personal information like medical and financial records to carry out business operations and to provide services to clients. These organizations must handle sensitive information in compliance with applicable privacy legislation like the Health Insurance Portability and Accountability Act (HIPAA) [1] and the Gramm-Leach-Bliley Act (GLBA) [2]. Violations attract substantial monetary and even criminal penalties [3]. Hence, developing mechanisms and automatic tools to check privacy policy compliance in organizations is an important problem.

The overarching goal of this paper is to improve the state of the art in checking whether an event trace or audit log, which records relevant events of an organization's data handling operations, is compliant with a given privacy policy. At a high-level, this problem can be approached in two different ways. First, logs may be recorded and compliance may be checked *offline*, when demanded by an audit authority. Alternatively, an *online* program may monitor privacy-relevant events, check them against the prevailing privacy policy and report

A. Biere and R. Bloem (Eds.): CAV 2014, LNCS 8559, pp. 131–149, 2014.
© Springer International Publishing Switzerland 2014

violations on the fly. Both approaches have been considered in literature: An algorithm for offline compliance checking has been proposed by a subset of the authors [4], whereas online monitoring has been the subject of extensive work by other researchers [5–11].

These two lines of work have two common features. First, they both assume that privacy policies are represented in first-order temporal logic, extended with explicit time. Such extensions have been demonstrated adequate for representing the privacy requirements of both HIPAA and GLBA [12]. Second, to ensure that only finitely many instances of quantifiers are tested during compliance checking, both lines of work use static policy checks to restrict the syntax of the logic. The specific static checks vary, but always rely on assumptions about finiteness of predicates provided by the policy designer. Some work, e.g. [5, 8–11], is based on the *safe-range check* [5], which requires syntactic subformulas to have finite support independent of each other; other work, e.g. [4, 7], is based on the *mode check* from logic programming [13–15], which is more general and can propagate variable groundedness information across subformulas.

Both lines of work have their relative advantages and disadvantages. An online monitor can cache policy-relevant information from logs on the fly (in so-called *summary structures*) and discard the remaining log immediately. This saves space. It also saves time because the summary structures are organized according to the policy formula so lookups are quicker than scans of the log in the offline method. However, online monitoring algorithms proposed so far require that all subformulas of the policy formula be amenable to caching. Furthermore, many real policies, including several privacy requirements of HIPAA and GLBA, are not amenable to such caching. In contrast, the offline algorithm proposed in our prior work [4] uses brute force search over a stored log. This is inefficient when compared to an online monitor, but it can handle all privacy requirements of HIPAA and GLBA. In this work, we combine the space- and time-efficiency of online monitoring with the generality of offline monitoring: We extend existing work in online monitoring [5] for privacy policy violations with a brute force search fallback based on offline audit for subformulas that are not amenable to caching. Like the work of Basin *et al.* [5], our work uses policies written in metric first-order temporal logic (MFOTL) [16].

Our key technical innovation is what we call the *temporal mode check*, a new static check on formulas to ensure finiteness of quantifier instantiation in our algorithm. Like a standard mode check, the temporal mode check is flow-sensitive: It can propagate variable groundedness information across subformulas. Additionally, the temporal mode check is *time-sensitive*: It conservatively approximates whether the grounding substitution for a variable comes from the future or the past. This allows us to classify all subformulas into those for which we build summary structures during online monitoring (we call such formulas buildable or B-formulas) and those for which we do not build summary structures and, hence, use brute force search.

As an example, consider the formula $\Box\exists x, y, z.(\mathsf{p}(x) \wedge \diamondsuit\mathsf{q}(x, y) \wedge \diamondsuit\mathsf{r}(x, z))$, which means that in all states, there exist x, y, z such that $\mathsf{p}(x)$ holds and in some past states $q(x,y)$ and $r(x,z)$ hold. Assume that p and q are finite predicates and that r is infinite, but given a ground value for its first argument, the second argument has finite computable support. One possible efficient strategy for monitoring this formula is to build summary structures for p and q and in each state where an x satisfying p exists, to quickly *lookup* the summary structure for q to find a past state and a y such that $\diamondsuit q(x,y)$ holds, and to *scan* the log brute force to find a past state and z such that $\diamondsuit r(x,z)$ holds. Note that doing so requires marking p and q as B-formulas, but r as not a B-formula (because z can be computed only after x is known, but x is known from satisfaction of p, which happens in the *future* of r). Unlike the safe-range check or the standard mode check, our new temporal mode check captures this information correctly and our monitoring algorithm, **précis**, implements this strategy. No existing work on online monitoring can handle this formula because r cannot be summarized [5–11]. The work on offline checking can handle this formula [4], it does not build summary structures and is needlessly inefficient on q.

We prove the correctness of **précis** over formulas that pass the temporal mode check and analyze its asymptotic complexity. We also empirically evaluate the performance of **précis** on synthetically generated traces, with respect to privacy policies derived from HIPAA and GLBA. The goal of our experiment is to demonstrate that incrementally maintaining summary structures for B-formulas of the policy can improve the performance of policy compliance checking relative to a baseline of pure brute force search. This baseline algorithm is very similar to the offline monitoring algorithm of [4], called **reduce**. In our experiments, we observe marked improvements in running time over **reduce**, e.g., up to 2.5x-6.5x speedup for HIPAA and up to 1.5x speed for GLBA, even with very conservative (unfavorable) assumptions about disk access. Even though these speedups are not universal (online monitoring optimistically constructs summary structures and if those structures are not used later then computation is wasted), they do indicate that temporal mode checking and our monitoring algorithm could have substantial practical benefit for privacy policy compliance.

Due to space restrictions, we defer the correctness proof of **précis** and several other details to a technical report [17].

2   Policy Specification Logic

Our policy specification logic, $\mathcal{GMP}$, is a fragment of MFOTL [16, 18] with restricted universal quantifiers. The syntax of $\mathcal{GMP}$ is shown below.

(**Policy formula**) $\varphi ::= p(t) \mid \top \mid \bot \mid \varphi_1 \wedge \varphi_2 \mid \varphi_1 \vee \varphi_2 \mid \exists x.\varphi \mid \forall x.(\varphi_1 \rightarrow \varphi_2)$
$\qquad \varphi_1 \, \mathcal{S}_{\mathbb{I}} \varphi_2 \mid \diamondsuit_{\mathbb{I}} \varphi \mid \boxminus_{\mathbb{I}} \varphi \mid \ominus_{\mathbb{I}} \varphi \mid \varphi_1 \, \mathcal{U}_{\mathbb{I}} \varphi_2 \mid \diamondsuit_{\mathbb{I}} \varphi \mid \square_{\mathbb{I}} \varphi \mid \bigcirc_{\mathbb{I}} \varphi$

The letter t denotes terms, which are *constants* or *variables* (x, y, etc.). Bold-faced roman letters like t denote sequences or vectors. Policy formulas are denoted by φ, α, and β. Universal quantifiers have a restricted form $\forall x.\varphi_1 \rightarrow \varphi_2$. A *guard* [19] φ_1 is required as explained further in Section 3.

Policy formulas include both past temporal operators ($\diamondsuit$, $\boxminus$, $\mathcal{S}$, $\ominus$) and future temporal operators ($\diamondsuit$, $\square$, $\mathcal{U}$, $\bigcirc$). Each temporal operator has an associated time interval $\mathbb{I}$ of the form $[lo, hi]$, where $lo, hi \in \mathbb{N}$ and $lo \le hi$. The interval selects a sub-part of the trace in which the immediate subformula is interpreted. For example, $\diamondsuit_{[2,6]}\varphi$ means that at some point between 2 and 6 time units in the past, φ holds. For past temporal operators, we allow the higher limit (hi) of $\mathbb{I}$ to be ∞. We omit the interval when it is $[0,\infty]$. Policies must be *future-bounded*: both limits $(lo$ and $hi)$ of intervals associated with future temporal operators must be finite. $\mathcal{GMP}$ is not closed under negation due to the absence of the duals of operators $\mathcal{S}$ and $\mathcal{U}$. However, these operators do not arise in the practical privacy policies we have investigated.

Formulas are interpreted over a timed event trace (or, log) $\mathcal{L}$. Given a possibly-infinite domain of terms $\mathcal{D}$, each element of $\mathcal{L}$—the ith element is denoted $\mathcal{L}_i$—maps each ground atom $\mathsf{p}(t)$ for $t \in \mathcal{D}$ to either true or false. Each position $\mathcal{L}_i$ is associated with a time stamp, $\tau_i \in \mathbb{N}$, which is used to interpret intervals in formulas. We use τ to represent the sequence of time stamps, each of which is a natural number. For any arbitrary $i,j \in \mathbb{N}$ with $i > j$, $\tau_i > \tau_j$ (monotonicity). The environment η maps free variables to values in $\mathcal{D}$. Given an execution trace $\mathcal{L}$ and a time stamp-sequence τ, a position $i \in \mathbb{N}$ in the trace, an environment η, and a formula φ, we write $\mathcal{L}, \tau, i, \eta \models \varphi$ to mean that φ is satisfied in the ith position of $\mathcal{L}$ with respect to η and τ. The definition of $\models$ is standard and can be found in the technical report [17].

Example policy. The following $\mathcal{GMP}$ formula represents a privacy rule from clause §6802(a) of the U.S. privacy law GLBA [2]. It states that a financial institution can disclose to a non-affiliated third party any non-public personal information (*e.g.*, name, SSN) if such financial institution provides (within 30 days) or has provided, to the consumer, a notice of the disclosure.

$$\forall p_1, p_2, q, m, t, u, d. \, (\, \mathsf{send}(p_1^-, p_2^-, m^-) \wedge \mathsf{contains}(m^+, q^-, t^-) \wedge \mathsf{info}(m^+, d^-, u^-) \rightarrow$$
$$\mathsf{inrole}(p_1^-, institution^+) \wedge \mathsf{nonAffiliate}(p_2^+, p_1^-) \wedge \mathsf{consumerOf}(q^-, p_1^+) \wedge \mathsf{attrIn}(t, npi)$$
$$\wedge \diamondsuit (\exists m_1.\mathsf{send}(p_1^-, q^-, m_1^-) \wedge \mathsf{noticeOfDisclosure}(m_1^+, p_1^+, p_2^+, q^+, t^+)) \,) \vee$$
$$\diamondsuit_{[0,30]} \exists m_2.\mathsf{send}(p_1^-, q^-, m_2^-) \wedge \mathsf{noticeOfDisclosure}(m_2^+, p_1^+, p_2^+, q^+, t^+) \,)$$

3   Temporal Mode Checking

We review mode-checking and provide an overview of our key insight, temporal mode-checking. Then, we define temporal mode-checking for $\mathcal{GMP}$ formally.

Mode-checking. Consider a predicate $\mathsf{addLessEq}(x, y, a)$, meaning $x + y \leq a$, where x, y, and a range over $\mathbb{N}$. If we are given ground values for x and a, then the number of substitutions for y for which $\mathsf{addLessEq}(x, y, a)$ holds is finite. In this case, we may say that $\mathsf{addLessEq}$'s argument position 1 and 3 are input positions (denoted by '$+$') and argument position 2 is an output position (denoted by '$-$'), denoted $\mathsf{addLessEq}(x^+, y^-, a^+)$. Such a specification of inputs and outputs is called a *mode-specification*. The meaning of a mode-specification for a predicate is that if we are given ground values for arguments in the input positions, then the number of substitutions for the variables in the output positions that result in a satisfied relation is finite. For instance, $\mathsf{addLessEq}(x^+, y^+, a^-)$ is not a valid mode-specification. Mode analysis (or mode-checking) lifts input-output specifications on predicates to input-output specification on formulas. It is commonly formalized as a judgment $\chi_{in} \vdash \varphi : \chi_{out}$, which states that given a grounding substitution for variables in χ_{in}, there is at most a finite set of substitutions for variables in χ_{out} that could together satisfy φ. For instance, consider the formula $\varphi \equiv p(x) \wedge q(x, y)$. Given the mode-specification $p(x^-)$ and $q(x^+, y^-)$ and a left-to-right evaluation order for conjunction, φ passes mode analysis with $\chi_{in} = \{\}$ and $\chi_{out} = \{x, y\}$. Mode analysis guides an algorithm to obtaining satisfying substitutions. In our example, we first obtain substitutions for x that satisfy $p(x)$. Then, we plug ground values for x in $q(x, y)$ to get substitutions for y. However, if the mode-specification is $p(x^+)$ and $q(x^+, y^-)$, then φ will fail mode analysis unless x is already ground (i.e., $x \in \chi_{in}$).

Mode analysis can be used to identify universally quantified formulas whose truth is finitely checkable. We only need to restrict universal quantifiers to the form $\forall \boldsymbol{x}.(\varphi_1 \to \varphi_2)$, and require that $\boldsymbol{x}$ be in the output of φ_1 and that φ_2 be well-moded (x may be in its input). To check that $\forall \boldsymbol{x}.(\varphi_1 \to \varphi_2)$ is true, we first find the values of $\boldsymbol{x}$ that satisfy φ_1. This is a finite set because $\boldsymbol{x}$ is in the output of φ_1. We then check that for each of these $\boldsymbol{x}$'s, φ_2 is satisfied.

Overview of temporal mode-checking. Consider the policy $\varphi_p \equiv p(x^-) \wedge \diamondsuit q(x^+, y^-)$ and consider the following obvious but inefficient way to monitor it: We wait for $p(x)$ to hold for some x, then we look back in the trace to find a position where $q(x, y)$ holds for some y. This is mode-compliant (we only check q with its input x ground) but requires us to traverse the trace backward whenever $p(x)$ holds for some x, which can be slow.

Ideally, we would like to incrementally build a summary structure for $\diamondsuit q(x, y)$ containing all the substitutions for x and y for which the formula holds as the monitor processes each new trace event. When we see $p(x)$, we could quickly look through the summary structure to check whether a relation of the form $q(x, y)$ for the specific x and any y exists. However, note that building such a structure may be *impossible* here. Why? The mode-specification $q(x^+, y^-)$ tells us only that we will obtain a finite set of satisfying substitutions when x is already ground. However, in this example, the ground x comes from p, which holds in the *future* of q, so the summary structure may be infinite and, hence, unbuildable. In contrast, if the mode-specification of q is $q(x^-, y^-)$, then we can build the summary structure because, independent of whether or not x is ground, only a finite number of substitutions can satisfy q. In this example, we would label $\diamondsuit q(x, y)$ *buildable* or a B-formula when the mode-specification is $q(x^-, y^-)$ and a non-B-formula when the mode-specification is $q(x^+, y^-)$.

With conventional mode analysis, φ_p is well-moded under both mode-specifications of q. Consequently, in order to decide whether φ_p is a B-formula, we need a refined analysis which takes into account the fact that, with the mode-specification $q(x^+, y^-)$, information about grounding of x flows *backward* in time from p to q and, hence, $\diamondsuit q(x, y)$ is not a B-formula. This is precisely what our temporal mode-check accomplishes: It tracks whether an input substitution comes from the past/current state, or from the future. By doing so, it provides enough information to determine which subformulas are B-formulas.

$$\boxed{\chi_C \vdash_{\mathbf{B}} \varphi : \chi_O}$$

$$\dfrac{\forall k \in I(\mathsf{p}).fv(t_k) \subseteq \chi_C \qquad \chi_O = \displaystyle\bigcup_{j \in O(\mathsf{p})} fv(t_j)}{\chi_C \vdash_{\mathbf{B}} \mathsf{p}(t_1, \ldots, t_n) : \chi_O} \text{ B-PRE}$$

$$\dfrac{\chi_C \vdash_{\mathbf{B}} \varphi_1 : \chi_1 \qquad \chi_C \cup \chi_1 \vdash_{\mathbf{B}} \varphi_2 : \chi_2 \qquad \chi_O = \chi_1 \cup \chi_2}{\chi_C \vdash_{\mathbf{B}} \varphi_1 \wedge \varphi_2 : \chi_O} \text{ B-AND}$$

$$\dfrac{\{\} \vdash_{\mathbf{B}} \varphi_2 : \chi_1 \qquad \chi_1 \vdash_{\mathbf{B}} \varphi_1 : \chi_2 \qquad \chi_O = \chi_1}{\chi_C \vdash_{\mathbf{B}} \varphi_1 \, \mathcal{S}_{\mathbb{I}} \varphi_2 : \chi_O} \text{ B-SINCE}$$

$$\boxed{\chi_C, \chi_F \vdash \varphi : \chi_O}$$

$$\dfrac{\forall k \in I(\mathsf{p}).fv(t_k) \subseteq (\chi_C \cup \chi_F) \qquad \chi_O = \displaystyle\bigcup_{j \in O(\mathsf{p})} fv(t_j)}{\chi_C, \chi_F \vdash \mathsf{p}(t_1, \ldots, t_n) : \chi_O} \text{ PRE}$$

$$\dfrac{\{\} \vdash_{\mathbf{B}} \varphi_2 : \chi_1 \qquad \chi_1, \chi_C \cup \chi_F \vdash \varphi_1 : \chi_2 \qquad \chi_O = \chi_1}{\chi_C, \chi_F \vdash \varphi_1 \, \mathcal{S}_{\mathbb{I}} \varphi_2 : \chi_O} \text{ SINCE-1}$$

$$\dfrac{\chi_C \vdash_{\mathbf{B}} \varphi_2 : \chi_1 \qquad \chi_C, \chi_F \cup \chi_1 \vdash \varphi_1 : \chi_2 \qquad \chi_O = \chi_1}{\chi_C, \chi_F \vdash \varphi_1 \, \mathcal{U}_{\mathbb{I}} \varphi_2 : \chi_O} \text{ UNTIL-1}$$

$$\dfrac{\begin{array}{cc} \chi_C, \chi_F \vdash \varphi_1 : \chi_1 \qquad \{x\} \subseteq \chi_1 \\ fv(\varphi_1) \subseteq \chi_C \cup \chi_F \cup \{x\} \qquad fv(\varphi_2) \subseteq (\chi_C \cup \chi_1 \cup \chi_F) \\ \chi_C, \chi_F \cup \chi_1 \vdash \varphi_2 : \chi_2 \end{array}}{\chi_C, \chi_F \vdash \forall x.(\varphi_1 \rightarrow \varphi_2) : \{\}} \text{ UNIV-1}$$

Fig. 1. Selected rules of temporal mode-checking

Formally, our temporal mode-checking has two judgments: $\chi_C \vdash_{\mathbf{B}} \varphi : \chi_O$ and $\chi_C, \chi_F \vdash \varphi : \chi_O$. The first judgment assumes that substitutions for χ_C are available from the past or at the current time point; any subformula satisfying such a judgment is labeled as a B-formula. The second judgment assumes that substitutions for χ_C are available from the past or at current time point, but those for χ_F will be available in future. A formula satisfying such a judgment is not a B-formula but can be handled by brute force search. Our implementation of temporal mode analysis first tries to check a formula by the first judgment, and falls back to the second when it fails. The formal rules for mode analysis (described later) allow for both possibilities but do not prescribe a preference. At the top-level, φ is *well-moded* if $\{\}, \{\} \vdash \varphi : \chi_O$ for some χ_O.

To keep things simple, we do not build summary structures for future formulas such as $\alpha \mathcal{U}_{\mathbb{I}} \beta$, and do not allow future formulas in the judgment form $\chi_C \vdash_{\mathbf{B}} \varphi : \chi_O$ (however, we do build summary structures for nested past-subformulas of future formulas). To check $\alpha \mathcal{U}_{\mathbb{I}} \beta$, we wait until the upper limit of $\mathbb{I}$ is exceeded and then search backward. As an optimization, one may build conservative summary structures for future formulas, as in some prior work [5].

Recognizing B-formulas. We list selected rules of temporal mode-checking in Figure 1. Rule B-PRE, which applies to an atom $p(t_1, \ldots, t_n)$, checks that all variables in input positions of p are in χ_C. The output χ_O is the set of variables in output positions of p. ($I(p)$ and $O(p)$ are the sets of input and output positions of p, respectively.) The rule for conjunctions $\varphi_1 \wedge \varphi_2$ first checks φ_1 and then checks φ_2, propagating variables in the output of φ_1 to the input of φ_2. These two rules are standard in mode-checking. The new, interesting rule is B-SINCE for the formula $\varphi_1 \mathcal{S}_I \varphi_2$. Since structures for φ_1 and φ_2 could be built at time points earlier than the current time, the premise simply ignores the input χ_C. The first premise of B-SINCE checks φ_2 with an empty input. Based on the semantics of temporal logic, φ_1 needs to be true on the trace after φ_2, so all variables ground by φ_2 (i.e., χ_1) are available as "current" input in φ_1. As an example, $\{\} \vdash_B \top \mathcal{S} q(x^-, y^-) : \{x, y\}$.

Temporal mode-checking judgement. In the mode-checking judgment χ_C, $\chi_F \vdash \varphi : \chi_O$, we separate the set of input variables for which substitutions are available at the current time point or from the past (χ_C) from the set of variables for which substitutions are available from the future (χ_F). The distinction is needed because sub-derivations of the form $\chi_C' \vdash_B \varphi' : \chi_O'$ should be passed only the former variables as input.

Rule PRE for atoms checks that variables in input positions are in the union of χ_C and χ_F. There are four rules for $\varphi_1 \mathcal{S}_I \varphi_2$, accounting for the buildability/non-buildability of each of the two subformulas. We show only one of these four rules, SINCE-1, which applies when φ_2 is a B-formula but φ_1 is not. In this case, φ_2 will be evaluated (for creating the summary structure) at time points earlier than $\varphi_1 \mathcal{S} \varphi_2$ and, therefore, cannot use variables in χ_C or χ_F as input (see Figure 2). When checking φ_1, variables in the output of φ_2 (called χ_1), χ_C and χ_F are all inputs, but those in χ_C or χ_F come from the future. The entire formula is not a B-formula as φ_1 is not.

Similarly, there are four rules for $\varphi_1 \mathcal{U}_I \varphi_2$, of which we show only one, UNTIL-1. This rule applies when φ_2 is a B-formula, but φ_1 is not. Its first premise checks that φ_2 is a B-formula with input χ_C. Our algorithm checks φ_1 only when φ_2 is true, so the outputs χ_1 of φ_2 are available as input for φ_1. In checking φ_1, both χ_1 and χ_F may come from the future.

The first premise of rule UNIV-1 checks that the guard φ_1 is well-moded with some output χ_1. The second premise, $\{x\} \subseteq \chi_1$, ensures that the guard φ_1 can be satisfied only for a finite number of substitutions for x, which is necessary to feasibly check φ_2. The third premise, $fv(\varphi_1) \subseteq (\chi_C \cup \chi_F \cup \{x\})$,

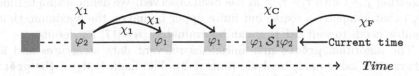

Fig. 2. Example: Temporal information in mode checking $\varphi_1 \mathcal{S}_I \varphi_2$

ensures that no variables other than x are additionally grounded by checking φ_1. The fourth premise, $fv(\varphi_2) \subseteq (\chi_C \cup \chi_F \cup \chi_1)$, ensures that all free variables in φ_2 are already grounded by the time φ_2 needs to be checked. The final premise ensures the well-modedness of φ_2. The third and fourth premises are technical conditions, needed for the soundness of our algorithm.

4 Runtime Monitoring Algorithm

Our policy compliance algorithm **précis** takes as input a well-moded $\mathcal{GMP}$ policy φ, monitors the system trace as it grows, builds summary structures for nested B-formulas and reports a violation as soon as it is detected.

We write σ to denote a substitution, a finite map from variables to values in the domain $\mathcal{D}$. The identity substitution is denoted $\bullet$ and $\sigma_\perp$ represents an invalid substitution. For instance, the result of joining ($\bowtie$) two substitutions σ_1 and σ_2 that do not agree on the values of shared variables is $\sigma_\perp$. We say that σ' extends σ, written $\sigma' \geq \sigma$, if the domain of σ' is a superset of the domain of σ and they agree on mappings of variables that are in the domain of σ. We summarize relevant algorithmic functions below.

précis(φ) is the top-level function (Algorithm 1).

checkCompliance$(\mathcal{L}, i, \tau, \pi, \varphi)$ checks whether events in the ith position of the trace $\mathcal{L}$ satisfy φ, given the algorithm's internal state π and the time stamps τ. State π contains up-to-date summary structures for all B-formulas of φ.

uSS$(\mathcal{L}, i, \tau, \pi, \varphi)$ incrementally updates summary structures for B-formula φ when log position i is seen. It assumes that the input π is up-to-date w.r.t. earlier log positions and it returns the state with the updated summary structure for φ. (**uSS** abbreviates **updateSummaryStructures**).

sat$(\mathcal{L}, i, \tau, \mathsf{p}(t), \sigma)$ returns the set of all substitutions σ_1 for free variables in $\mathsf{p}(t)$ that make $\mathsf{p}(t)\sigma_1$ true in the ith position of $\mathcal{L}$, given σ that grounds variables in the input positions of p. Here, $\sigma_1 \geq \sigma$.

ips$(\mathcal{L}, i, \tau, \pi, \sigma, \varphi)$ generalizes **sat** from atomic predicates to policy formulas. It takes the state π as an input to look up summary structures when B-formulas are encountered.

Top-level monitoring algorithm. Algorithm 1 (**précis**), the top-level monitoring process, uses two pointers to log entries: *curPtr* points to the last entry in the log $\mathcal{L}$, and *evalPtr* points to the position at which we next check whether φ is satisfied. Naturally, *curPtr* $\geq$ *evalPtr*. The gap between these two pointers is determined by the intervals occurring in future temporal operators in φ. For example, with the policy $\Diamond_{[lo,hi]}\beta$, β can be evaluated at log position i only after a position $j \geq i$ with $\tau_j - \tau_i \geq hi$ has been observed. We define a simple function $\Delta(\varphi)$ that computes a coarse but finite upper bound on the maximum time the monitor needs to wait before φ can be evaluated (see [17] for details).

The algorithm **précis** first initializes relevant data structures and labels B-formulas using mode analysis (lines 1-2). The main body of the **précis** is a trace-event triggered loop. In each iteration of the loop, **précis**: (1) updates the summary structures in π based on the newly available log entries (lines 6-7),

---

Algorithm 1. The **precis** algorithm

Require: A $\mathcal{GMP}$ policy φ

1: $\pi \leftarrow \emptyset$; $curPtr \leftarrow 0$; $evalPtr \leftarrow 0$; $\mathcal{L} \leftarrow \emptyset$; $\tau \leftarrow \emptyset$;

2: `Mode-check` φ. `Label all B-formulas of` φ.

3: **while** $(true)$ **do**

4:    `Wait until new events are available`

5:    `Extend` $\mathcal{L}$ `and` τ `with new entries`

6:    **for all** (B-formulas φ_s of φ in ascending formula size) **do**

7:      $\pi \leftarrow \text{uSS}(\mathcal{L}, curPtr, \tau, \pi, \varphi_s)$ `//update summary structures`

8:    **while** $(evalPtr \leq curPtr)$ **do**

9:      **if** $(\tau_{curPtr} - \tau_{evalPtr} \geq \Delta(\varphi))$ **then**

10:        $tVal \leftarrow \text{checkCompliance}(\mathcal{L}, evalPtr, \tau, \pi, \varphi)$

11:        **if** $tVal = false$ **then**

12:          `Report violation on` $\mathcal{L}$ `position` $evalPtr$

13:        $evalPtr \leftarrow evalPtr + 1$

14:      **else**

15:        break

16:     $curPtr \leftarrow curPtr + 1$

---

and (2) evaluates the policy at positions where it can be fully evaluated, i.e., where the difference between the entry's time point and the current time point ($curPtr$) exceeds the maximum delay $\Delta(\varphi)$. Step (1) uses the function **uSS** and step (2) uses the function **checkCompliance**. **checkCompliance** is a wrapper for **ips** that calls **ips** with • as the input substitution. If **ips** returns an empty set of satisfying substitutions, **checkCompliance** returns false, signaling a violation at the current time point, else it returns true.

Finding substitutions for policy formulas. The recursive function **ips** returns the set of substitutions that satisfy a formula at a given log position, given a substitution for the formula's input variables. Selected clauses of the definition of **ips** are shown in Figure 3. When the formula is an atom, **ips** invokes **sat**, an abstract wrapper around specific implementations of predicates. When the policy is a universally quantified formula, **ips** is called on the guard φ_1 to find the guard's satisfying substitutions Σ_1. Then, **ips** is called to check that φ_2 is true for all substitutions in Σ_1. If the latter fails, **ips** returns the empty set of substitutions to signal a violation, else it returns $\{\sigma_{in}\}$.

When a B-formula $\alpha\, \mathcal{S}_{\mathbb{I}}\beta$ is encountered, all its satisfying substitutions have already been computed and stored in π. Therefore, **ips** simply finds these substitutions in π (expression $\pi.\mathcal{A}(\alpha\, \mathcal{S}_{\mathbb{I}}\beta)(i).\mathbb{R}$), and discards those that are inconsistent with σ_{in} by performing a join ($\bowtie$). For the non-B-formula $\alpha\, \mathcal{S}_{\mathbb{I}}\beta$, **ips** calls itself recursively on the sub-formulas α and β, and computes the substitutions brute force.

Incrementally updating summary structures. We explain how we update summary structures for formulas of the form $\varphi_1\, \mathcal{S}_{\mathbb{I}}\varphi_2$ here. Updates for $\ominus_{\mathbb{I}}\varphi$, $\boxminus_{\mathbb{I}}\varphi$, and $\diamondsuit_{\mathbb{I}}\varphi$ are similar and can be found in the technical report [17].

$$\mathbf{ips}(\mathcal{L}, i, \tau, \pi, \sigma_{\mathrm{in}}, \mathbf{p}(t)) \quad = \mathbf{sat}(\mathcal{L}, i, \tau, \mathbf{p}(t), \sigma_{\mathrm{in}})$$

$$\mathbf{ips}(\mathcal{L}, i, \tau, \pi, \sigma_{\mathrm{in}}, \forall x.(\varphi_1 \to \varphi_2)) \quad = \quad \begin{aligned}\mathrm{let} \quad & \Sigma_1 \leftarrow \mathbf{ips}(\mathcal{L}, i, \tau, \pi, \sigma_{\mathrm{in}}, \varphi_1) \\ \mathrm{return} \quad & \begin{cases} \emptyset & \text{if } \exists \sigma_c \in \Sigma_1.(\mathbf{ips}(\mathcal{L}, i, \tau, \pi, \sigma_c, \varphi_2) = \emptyset) \\ \{\sigma_{\mathrm{in}}\} & \text{otherwise} \end{cases}\end{aligned}$$

$$\mathbf{ips}(\mathcal{L}, i, \tau, \pi, \sigma_{\mathrm{in}}, \alpha \, \mathcal{S}_{\mathrm{I}}\beta) = \begin{cases} \textbf{If } \alpha \, \mathcal{S}_{\mathrm{I}}\beta \text{ is a B-formula then} \\ \quad \textbf{return } \sigma_{\mathrm{in}} \bowtie \pi.\mathcal{A}(\alpha \, \mathcal{S}_{\mathrm{I}}\beta)(i).\mathbb{R} \\ \textbf{Else} \\ \mathrm{let} \quad S_\beta \leftarrow \{\langle \sigma, k \rangle | k = \max l.((0 \leq l \leq i) \wedge ((\tau_i - \tau_l) \in \mathbb{I}) \\ \qquad\qquad \wedge \sigma \in \mathbf{ips}(\mathcal{L}, l, \tau, \pi, \sigma_{\mathrm{in}}, \beta))\} \\ \qquad S_{R_1} \leftarrow \{\sigma | \langle \sigma, i \rangle \in S_\beta \wedge 0 \in \mathbb{I}\} \\ \qquad S_{R_2} \leftarrow \{\bowtie \sigma_l^\alpha \neq \sigma_\perp | \exists \langle \sigma_\beta, k \rangle \in S_\beta.k < i \wedge \\ \qquad\qquad \forall l.(k < l \leq i \to \sigma_l^\alpha \in \mathbf{ips}(\mathcal{L}, l, \tau, \pi, \sigma_\beta, \varphi_1))\} \\ \quad \textbf{return } S_{R_1} \cup S_{R_2} \end{cases}$$

Fig. 3. Definition of the **ips** function, selected clauses

For each **B-formula** of the form $\alpha \, \mathcal{S}_{[lo,hi]}\beta$, we build three structures: $\mathbb{S}_\beta$, $\mathbb{S}_\alpha$, and $\mathbb{R}$. The structure $\mathbb{S}_\beta$ contains a set of pairs of form $\langle \sigma, k \rangle$ in which σ represents a substitution and $k \in \mathbb{N}$ is a position in $\mathcal{L}$. Each pair of form $\langle \sigma, k \rangle \in \mathbb{S}_\beta$ represents that for all $\sigma' \geq \sigma$, the formula $\beta\sigma'$ is true at position k of $\mathcal{L}$. The structure $\mathbb{S}_\alpha$ contains a set of pairs of form $\langle \sigma, k \rangle$, each of which represents that for all $\sigma' \geq \sigma$ the formula $\alpha\sigma'$ has been true from position k until the current position in $\mathcal{L}$. The structure $\mathbb{R}$ contains a set of substitutions, which make $(\alpha \, \mathcal{S}_{[lo,hi]}\beta)$ true in the current position of $\mathcal{L}$. We use $\mathbb{R}^i$ (similarly for other structures too) to represent the structure $\mathbb{R}$ at position i of $\mathcal{L}$. We also assume $\mathbb{S}_\beta^{(-1)}$, $\mathbb{S}_\alpha^{(-1)}$, and $\mathbb{R}^{(-1)}$ to be empty (the same applies for other structures too). We show here how the structures $\mathbb{S}_\beta$ and $\mathbb{R}$ are updated. We defer the description of update of $\mathbb{S}_\alpha$ to the technical report [17].

To update the structure $\mathbb{S}_\beta$, we first calculate the set Σ_β of substitutions that make β true at i by calling **ips**. Pairing all these substitutions with the position i yields S_{new}^β. Next, we compute the set $S_{\mathrm{remove}}^\beta$ of all old $\langle \sigma, k \rangle$ pairs that do not satisfy the interval constraint $[lo, hi]$ (i.e., for which $\tau_i - \tau_k > hi$). The updated structure $\mathbb{S}_\beta^i$ is then obtained by taking a union of S_{new}^β and the old structure $\mathbb{S}_\beta^{(i-1)}$, and removing all the pairs in the set $S_{\mathrm{remove}}^\beta$.

$$\Sigma_\beta \quad \leftarrow \mathbf{ips}(\mathcal{L}, i, \tau, \pi, \bullet, \beta) \quad \Big| \quad S_{\mathrm{remove}}^\beta \leftarrow \{\langle \sigma, k \rangle \mid \langle \sigma, k \rangle \in \mathbb{S}_\beta^{(i-1)} \wedge (\tau_i - \tau_k) > hi\}$$
$$S_{\mathrm{new}}^\beta \leftarrow \{\langle \sigma, i \rangle \mid \sigma \in \Sigma_\beta\} \quad \Big| \quad \mathbb{S}_\beta^i \quad \leftarrow (\mathbb{S}_\beta^{(i-1)} \cup S_{\mathrm{new}}^\beta) \setminus S_{\mathrm{remove}}^\beta$$

To compute the summary structure $\mathbb{R}$ for $\alpha \, \mathcal{S}_{\mathrm{I}}\beta$ at i, we first compute the set S_{R_1} of all substitutions for which the formula β is true in the ith position and the interval constraint is respected by the position i. Then we compute S_{R_2} as the join $\sigma \bowtie \sigma_1$ of substitutions σ for which β was satisfied at some prior position k, and substitutions σ_1 for which α is true from position $k+1$ to i. The updated structure $\mathbb{R}^i$ is the union of S_{R_1} and S_{R_2}.

$$S_{R_1} \leftarrow \{\sigma \mid \langle\sigma, i\rangle \in \mathbb{S}_\beta^i \wedge 0 \in [lo, hi]\}$$
$$S_{R_2} \leftarrow \{\sigma \bowtie \sigma_1 \mid \exists k, j.\langle\sigma, k\rangle \in \mathbb{S}_\beta^i \wedge (k \neq i) \wedge (\tau_i - \tau_k \in [lo, hi]) \wedge \langle\sigma_1, j\rangle \in \mathbb{S}_\alpha^i \wedge$$
$$(j \leq (k+1)) \wedge \sigma \bowtie \sigma_1 \neq \sigma_\perp\}$$
$$\mathbb{R}^i \leftarrow S_{R_1} \cup S_{R_2}$$

Optimizations. When all temporal sub-formulas of φ are B-formulas, $curPtr$ and $evalPtr$ proceed in synchronization and only the summary structure for position $curPtr$ needs to be maintained. When φ contains future temporal formulas but all past temporal sub-formulas of φ are B-formulas, then we need to maintain only the summary structures for positions in $[evalPtr, curPtr]$, but the rest of the log can be discarded immediately. When φ contains at least one past temporal subformula that is not a B-formula we need to store the slice of the trace that contains all predicates in that non-B-formula.

The following theorem states that on well-moded policies, **précis** terminates and is correct. The theorem requires that the internal state π be *strongly consistent* at $curPtr$ with respect to the log $\mathcal{L}$, time stamp sequence τ, and policy φ. Strong consistency means that the state π contains sound and complete substitutions for all B-formulas of φ for all trace positions in $[0, curPtr]$ (see [17]).

Theorem 1 (Correctness of précis). *For all $\mathcal{GMP}$ policies φ, for all $evalPtr$, $curPtr \in \mathbb{N}$, for all traces $\mathcal{L}$, for all time stamp sequences τ, for all internal states π, for all empty environments η_0 such that (1) π is strongly consistent at $curPtr$ with respect to $\mathcal{L}$, τ, and φ, (2) $curPtr \geq evalPtr$ and $\tau_{curPtr} - \tau_{evalPtr} \geq \Delta(\varphi)$, and (3) $\{\}, \{\} \vdash \varphi : \chi_O$ where $\chi_O \subseteq fv(\varphi)$, it is the case that* $\mathbf{checkCompliance}(\mathcal{L}, evalPtr, \tau, \pi, \varphi)$ *terminates and if* $\mathbf{checkCompliance}(\mathcal{L}, evalPtr, \tau, \pi, \varphi) = tVal$, *then* $(tVal = true) \leftrightarrow \exists\sigma.(\mathcal{L}, \tau, evalPtr, \eta_0 \models \varphi\sigma)$.

Proof. By induction on the policy formula φ (see [17]). $\qed$

Complexity of précis. The runtime complexity of one iteration of **précis** for a given policy φ is $|\varphi| \times$ (complexity of the uSS function) + (complexity of ips function), where $|\varphi|$ is the policy size. We first analyze the runtime complexity of ips. Suppose the maximum number of substitutions returned by a single call to sat (for any position in the trace) is $\mathbb{F}$ and the maximum time required by sat to produce one substitution is $\mathbb{A}$. The worst case runtime of ips occurs when all subformulas of φ are non-B-formulas of the form $\varphi_1 \mathcal{S} \varphi_2$ and in that case the complexity is $\mathcal{O}((\mathbb{A} \times \mathbb{F} \times \mathbb{L})^{\mathcal{O}(|\varphi|)})$ where $\mathbb{L}$ denotes the length of the trace. uSS is invoked only for B-formulas. From the definition of mode-checking, all sub-formulas of a B-formula are also B-formulas. This property of B-formulas ensures that when uSS calls ips, the worst case behavior of ips is not encountered. The overall complexity of uSS is $\mathcal{O}(|\varphi| \times (\mathbb{A} \times \mathbb{F})^{\mathcal{O}(|\varphi|)})$. Thus, the runtime complexity of each iteration of the **précis** function is $\mathcal{O}((\mathbb{A} \times \mathbb{F} \times \mathbb{L})^{\mathcal{O}(|\varphi|)})$.

5   Implementation and Evaluation

This section reports an experimental evaluation of the **précis** algorithm. All measurements were made on a 2.67GHz Intel Xeon CPU X5650 running Debian

GNU/Linux 7 (Linux kernel 3.2.48.1.amd64-smp) on 48GB RAM, of which at most 2.2GB is used in our experiments. We store traces in a SQLite database. Each n-ary predicate is represented by a $n+1$ column table whose first n columns store arguments that make the predicate true on the trace and the last column stores the trace position where the predicate is true. We index each table by the columns corresponding to input positions of the predicate. We experiment with randomly generated synthetic traces. Given a $\mathcal{GMP}$ policy and a target trace length, at each trace point, our synthetic trace generator randomly decides whether to generate a policy-compliant action or a policy violating action. For a compliant action, it recursively traverses the syntax of the policy and creates trace actions to satisfy the policy. Disjunctive choices are resolved randomly. Non-compliant actions are handled dually. The source code and traces used in the experiments are available from the authors' homepages.

Our goal is to demonstrate that incrementally maintaining summary structures for B-formulas can improve the performance of policy compliance checking. Our baseline for comparison is a variant of **précis** that does not use any summary structures and, hence, checks temporal operators by brute force scanning. This baseline algorithm is very similar to the **reduce** algorithm of prior work [4] and, indeed, in the sequel we refer to our baseline as **reduce**. For the experimental results reported here, we deliberately hold traces in an in-memory SQLite database. This choice is conservative; using a disk-backed database improves **précis**' performance relative to **reduce** because **reduce** accesses the database more intensively (our technical report contains comparative evaluation using a disk-backed database and confirms this claim [17]). Another goal of our experiment is to identify how **précis** scales when larger summary structures must be maintained. Accordingly, we vary the upper bound hi in intervals $[lo, hi]$ in past temporal operators.

We experiment with two privacy policies that contain selected clauses of HIPAA and GLBA, respectively. As **précis** and **reduce** check compliance of non-B-formulas similarly, to demonstrate the utility of building summary structures, we ensure that the policies contain B-formulas (in our HIPAA policy, 7 out of 8 past temporal formulas are B-formulas; for GLBA the number is 4 out of 9). Our technical report [17] lists the policies we used. Figure 4 show our evaluation times for the HIPAA privacy policy for the following upper bounds on the past temporal operators: 100, 1000, 3000, and ∞. Points along the x-axis are the size of the trace and also the number of privacy-critical events checked. The y-axis represents the *average* monitoring time per event. We plot four curves for each bound: (1) The time taken by **précis**, (2) The time taken by **reduce**, (3) The time spent by **précis** in building and accessing summary structures for B-formulas, and (4) The time spent by **reduce** in evaluating B-formulas. For all trace positions $i \in \mathbb{N}$, $\tau_{i+1} - \tau_i = 1$.

The difference between (1) and (3), and (2) and (4) is similar at all trace lengths because it is the time spent on non-buildable parts of the policy, which is similar in **précis** and **reduce**. For the policy considered here, **reduce** spends most time on B-formulas, so construction of summary structures improves per-

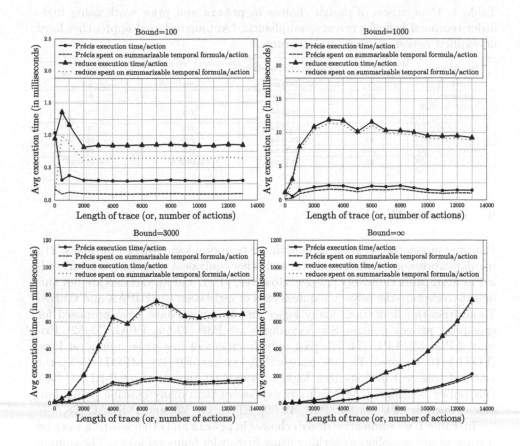

Fig. 4. **Experimental results (HIPAA)**

formance. For trace lengths greater than the bound, the curves flatten out, as expected. As the bound increases, the average execution time for **reduce** increases as the algorithm has to look back further on the trace, and so does the relative advantage of **précis**. Overall, **précis** achieves a speedup up of 2.5x-6.5x over **reduce** after the curves flatten out in the HIPAA policy. The results for GLBA, not shown here but discussed in our technical report [17] are similar, with speedups of 1.25x to 1.5x. The technical report also describes the amount of memory needed to store summary structures in **précis**. Briefly, this number grows proportional to the minimum of trace length and policy bound. The maximum we observe (for trace length 13000 and bound ∞) is 2.2 GB, which is very reasonable. This can be further improved by compression.

Table 1. Comparison of design choices in **précis** and prior work using first-order temporal logic for privacy compliance. *Automata-based approaches have no explicit notion of summary structures.

Algorithms	Incomplete states allowed?	Mode of operation	Summary structures (past formulas)	Summary structures (future formulas)
précis	no	online	yes	no
reduce [4]	yes	offline	no	no
Chomicki [8, 9] Krukow et al. [10]	no	online	yes	no
Bauer et al. [11]	yes	online	yes	no
Basin et al. [5, 7]	no	online	yes	yes
Basin et al. [6]	yes	online	yes	yes
Bauer et al. [20]	no	online	(automata)*	(automata)*

6 Related Work

Runtime monitoring of *propositional* linear temporal logic (pLTL) formulas [21], regular expressions, finite automata, and other equivalent variants has been studied in literature extensively [22–48]. However, pLTL and its variants are not sufficient to capture the privacy requirements of legislation like HIPAA and GLBA. To address this limitation, many logics and languages have been proposed for specifying privacy policies. Some examples are P3P [49,50], EPAL [51,52], Privacy APIs [53], LPU [54, 55], past-only fragment of first-order temporal logic (FOTL) [10,11], predLTL [56], pLogic [57], PrivacyLFP [12], MFOTL [5–7], the guarded fragment of first-order logic with explicit time [4], and P-RBAC [58]. Our policy language, $\mathcal{GMP}$, is more expressive than many existing policy languages such as LPU [54,55], P3P [49,50], EPAL [51,52], and P-RBAC [58].

In Table 1, we summarize design choices in **précis** and other existing work on privacy policy compliance checking using first-order temporal logics. The column "Incomplete states allowed?" indicates whether the work can handle some form of incompleteness in observation about states. Our own prior work [4] presents the algorithm **reduce** that checks compliance of a mode-checked fragment of FOL policies with respect to potentially incomplete logs. This paper makes the mode check time-aware and adds summary structures to **reduce**, but we assume that our event traces have complete information in all observed states.

Bauer et al. [11] present a compliance-checking algorithm for the (non-metric) past fragment of FOTL. $\mathcal{GMP}$ can handle both past and future (metric) temporal operators. However, Bauer et al. allow counting operators, arbitrary computable functions, and partial observability of events, which we do not allow. They allow a somewhat simplified guarded universal quantification where the guard is a single predicate. In $\mathcal{GMP}$, we allow the guard of the universal quantification to be a complex $\mathcal{GMP}$ formula. For instance, the following formula cannot be expressed in the language proposed by Bauer et al. but $\mathcal{GMP}$ mode checks it: $\forall x, y. (\mathsf{q}(x^+, y^+) \, \mathcal{S} \, \mathsf{p}(x^-, y^-)) \rightarrow \mathsf{r}(x^+, y^+)$. Moreover, Bauer et al. only consider closed formulas and also assume that each predicate argument position is output. We do not insist on these restrictions. In further development, Bauer et al. [20], propose an automata-based, incomplete monitoring algorithm for a fragment of FOTL called LTL^{FO}. They consider non-safety policies (unbounded future operators), which we do not consider.

Basin *et al.* [5] present a runtime monitoring algorithm for a fragment of MFOTL. Our summary structures are directly inspired by this work and the work of Chomicki [8,9]. We improve expressiveness through the possibility of brute force search similar to [4], when subformulas are not amenable to summarization. Basin *et al.* build summary structures for future operators, which we do not (such structures can be added to our monitoring algorithm). In subsequent work, Basin *et al.* [6] extend their runtime monitoring algorithm to handle incomplete logs and inconsistent logs using a three-valued logic, which we do not consider. In more recent work, Basin *et al.* [7] extend the monitoring algorithm to handle aggregation operators and function symbols, which $\mathcal{GMP}$ does not include. These extensions are orthogonal to our work.

Our temporal mode check directly extends mode checking from [4] by adding time-sensitivity, although the setting is different— [4] is based on first-order logic with an explicit theory of linear time whereas we work with MFOTL. The added time-sensitivity allows us to classify subformulas into those that can be summarized and those that must be brute forced. Some prior work, e.g. [5–11], is based on the safe-range check instead of the mode check. The safe-range check is less expressive than a mode check. For example, the safe-range check does not accept the formula $q(x^+, y^+, z^-)\,\mathcal{S}\,p(x^-, y^-)$, but our temporal mode check does (however, the safe-range check will accept the formula $q(x^-, y^-, z^-)\,\mathcal{S}\,p(x^-, y^-)$). More recent work [7] uses a static check intermediate in expressiveness between the safe-range check and a full-blown mode check.

7   Conclusion

We have presented a privacy policy compliance-checking algorithm for a fragment of MFOTL. The fragment is characterized by a novel temporal mode-check, which, like a conventional mode-check, ensures that only finitely many instantiations of quantifiers are tested but is, additionally, time-aware and can determine which subformulas of the policy are amenable to construction of summary structures. Using information from the temporal mode-check, our algorithm **précis** performs best-effort runtime monitoring, falling back to brute force search when summary structures cannot be constructed. Empirical evaluation shows that summary structures improve performance significantly, compared to a baseline without them.

Acknowledgement. This work was partially supported by the AFOSR MURI on "Science of Cybersecurity", the National Science Foundation (NSF) grants CNS 1064688, CNS 0964710, and CCF 0424422, and the HHS/ONC grant HHS90TR0003/01. The authors thank anonymous reviewers, Sagar Chaki, Andreas Gampe, and Murillo Pontual for their helpful comments and suggestions.

References

1. Health Resources and Services Administration: Health insurance portability and accountability act, Public Law 104-191 (1996)
2. Senate Banking Committee: Gramm-Leach-Bliley Act, Public Law 106-102 (1999)
3. Roberts, P.: HIPAA Bares Its Teeth: $4.3m Fine For Privacy Violation, https://threatpost.com/en_us/blogs/hipaa-bares-its-teeth-43m-fine-privacy-violation-022311
4. Garg, D., Jia, L., Datta, A.: Policy auditing over incomplete logs: Theory, implementation and applications. In: Proceedings of the 18th ACM Conference on Computer and Communications Security, CCS 2011, pp. 151–162. ACM, New York (2011)
5. Basin, D., Klaedtke, F., Müller, S.: Monitoring security policies with metric first-order temporal logic. In: Proceedings of the 15th ACM Symposium on Access Control Models and Technologies, SACMAT 2010, pp. 23–34. ACM, New York (2010)
6. Basin, D., Klaedtke, F., Marinovic, S., Zălinescu, E.: Monitoring compliance policies over incomplete and disagreeing logs. In: Qadeer, S., Tasiran, S. (eds.) RV 2012. LNCS, vol. 7687, pp. 151–167. Springer, Heidelberg (2013)
7. Basin, D., Klaedtke, F., Marinovic, S., Zălinescu, E.: Monitoring of temporal first-order properties with aggregations. In: Legay, A., Bensalem, S. (eds.) RV 2013. LNCS, vol. 8174, pp. 40–58. Springer, Heidelberg (2013)
8. Chomicki, J.: Efficient checking of temporal integrity constraints using bounded history encoding. ACM Trans. Database Syst. 20(2), 149–186 (1995)
9. Chomicki, J., Niwiński, D.: On the feasibility of checking temporal integrity constraints. In: Proceedings of the Twelfth ACM SIGACT-SIGMOD-SIGART Symposium on Principles of Database Systems, PODS 1993, pp. 202–213. ACM, New York (1993)
10. Krukow, K., Nielsen, M., Sassone, V.: A logical framework for history-based access control and reputation systems. J. Comput. Secur. 16(1), 63–101 (2008)
11. Bauer, A., Goré, R., Tiu, A.: A first-order policy language for history-based transaction monitoring. In: Leucker, M., Morgan, C. (eds.) ICTAC 2009. LNCS, vol. 5684, pp. 96–111. Springer, Heidelberg (2009)
12. DeYoung, H., Garg, D., Jia, L., Kaynar, D., Datta, A.: Experiences in the logical specification of the hipaa and glba privacy laws. In: Proceedings of the 9th Annual ACM Workshop on Privacy in the Electronic Society, WPES 2010, pp. 73–82. ACM, New York (2010)
13. Apt, K., Marchiori, E.: Reasoning about prolog programs: From modes through types to assertions. Formal Aspects of Computing 6(1), 743–765 (1994)
14. Dembinski, P., Maluszynski, J.: And-parallelism with intelligent backtracking for annotated logic programs. In: Proceedings of the 1985 Symposium on Logic Programming, Boston, Massachusetts, USA, July 15-18, pp. 29–38. IEEE-CS (1985)
15. Mellish, C.S.: The automatic generation of mode declarations for Prolog programs. Department of Artificial Intelligence, University of Edinburgh (1981)
16. Koymans, R.: Specifying real-time properties with metric temporal logic. Real-Time Systems 2(4), 255–299 (1990)
17. Chowdhury, O., Jia, L., Garg, D., Datta, A.: Temporal mode-checking for run-time monitoring of privacy policies. Technical Report CMU-CyLab-14-005, Cylab, Carnegie Mellon University, Pittsburgh, Pennsylvania (May 2014)

18. Alur, R., Henzinger, T.: Logics and models of real time: A survey. In: de Bakker, J.W., Huizing, C., de Roever, W.-P., Rozenberg, G. (eds.) REX 1991. LNCS, vol. 600, pp. 74–106. Springer, Heidelberg (1992)
19. Andréka, H., Németi, I., van Benthem, J.: Modal languages and bounded fragments of predicate logic. Journal of Philosophical Logic 27(3), 217–274 (1998)
20. Bauer, A., Küster, J.-C., Vegliach, G.: From propositional to first-order monitoring. In: Legay, A., Bensalem, S. (eds.) RV 2013. LNCS, vol. 8174, pp. 59–75. Springer, Heidelberg (2013)
21. Pnueli, A.: The temporal logic of programs. In: Proceedings of the 18th Annual Symposium on Foundations of Computer Science, SFCS 1977, pp. 46–57. IEEE Computer Society, Washington, DC (1977)
22. Roşu, G.: On Safety Properties and Their Monitoring. Technical Report UIUCDCS-R-2007-2850, Department of Computer Science, University of Illinois at Urbana-Champaign (2007)
23. Büchi, J.R.: On a Decision Method in Restricted Second-Order Arithmetic. In: International Congress on Logic, Methodology, and Philosophy of Science, pp. 1–11. Stanford University Press (1962)
24. Hussein, S., Meredith, P.O., Roşu, G.: Security-policy monitoring and enforcement with JavaMOP. In: ACM SIGPLAN Seventh Workshop on Programming Languages and Analysis for Security (PLAS 2012), pp. 3:1–3:11 (2012)
25. Meredith, P., Roşu, G.: Runtime verification with the RV system. In: Barringer, H., et al. (eds.) RV 2010. LNCS, vol. 6418, pp. 136–152. Springer, Heidelberg (2010)
26. Meredith, P., Roşu, G.: Efficient parametric runtime verification with deterministic string rewriting. In: Proceedings of 28th IEEE/ACM International Conference. Automated Software Engineering (ASE 2013). IEEE/ACM, NA (May 2013)
27. Pellizzoni, R., Meredith, P., Caccamo, M., Roşu, G.: Hardware runtime monitoring for dependable cots-based real-time embedded systems. In: Proceedings of the 29th IEEE Real-Time System Symposium (RTSS 2008), pp. 481–491 (2008)
28. Meredith, P., Jin, D., Chen, F., Roşu, G.: Efficient monitoring of parametric context-free patterns. In: Proceedings of the 23rd IEEE/ACM International Conference on Automated Software Engineering (ASE 2008), pp. 148–157. IEEE/ACM (2008)
29. Roşu, G., Havelund, K.: Synthesizing dynamic programming algorithms from linear temporal logic formulae. Technical report, Research Institute for Advanced Computer Science (2001)
30. Roşu, G., Havelund, K.: Rewriting-based techniques for runtime verification. Automated Software Engineering 12(2), 151–197 (2005)
31. Havelund, K., Roşu, G.: Efficient monitoring of safety properties. Int. J. Softw. Tools Technol. Transf. 6(2), 158–173 (2004)
32. Roşu, G., Chen, F., Ball, T.: Synthesizing monitors for safety properties: This time with calls and returns. In: Leucker, M. (ed.) RV 2008. LNCS, vol. 5289, pp. 51–68. Springer, Heidelberg (2008)
33. Leucker, M., Schallhart, C.: A brief account of runtime verification. The Journal of Logic and Algebraic Programming 78(5), 293–303 (2009); The 1st Workshop on Formal Languages and Analysis of Contract-Oriented Software (FLACOS 2007)
34. Roşu, G., Bensalem, S.: Allen Linear (Interval) Temporal Logic –Translation to LTL and Monitor Synthesis. In: Ball, T., Jones, R.B. (eds.) CAV 2006. LNCS, vol. 4144, pp. 263–277. Springer, Heidelberg (2006)
35. D'Amorim, M., Roşu, G.: Efficient monitoring of ω-languages. In: Etessami, K., Rajamani, S.K. (eds.) CAV 2005. LNCS, vol. 3576, pp. 364–378. Springer, Heidelberg (2005)

36. Basin, D., Jugé, V., Klaedtke, F., Zălinescu, E.: Enforceable security policies revisited. ACM Trans. Inf. Syst. Secur. 16(1), 3:1–3:26 (2013)
37. Bauer, L., Ligatti, J., Walker, D.: More enforceable security policies. In: Cervesato, I., ed.: Foundations of Computer Security: Proceedings of the FLoC 2002 Workshop on Foundations of Computer Security, Copenhagen, Denmark, DIKU Technical Report, July 25–26, 95–104 (2002)
38. Schneider, F.B.: Enforceable security policies. ACM Trans. Inf. Syst. Secur. 3(1), 30–50 (2000)
39. Giannakopoulou, D., Havelund, K.: Automata-based verification of temporal properties on running programs. In: Proceedings of the 16th Annual International Conference on Automated Software Engineering, ASE 2001, pp. 412–416 (November 2001)
40. Martinell, F., Matteucci, I.: Through modeling to synthesis of security automata. Electron. Notes Theor. Comput. Sci. 179, 31–46 (2007)
41. Huisman, M., Tamalet, A.: A formal connection between security automata and jml annotations. In: Chechik, M., Wirsing, M. (eds.) FASE 2009. LNCS, vol. 5503, pp. 340–354. Springer, Heidelberg (2009)
42. Ligatti, J., Bauer, L., Walker, D.: Run-time enforcement of nonsafety policies. ACM Trans. Inf. Syst. Secur. 12(3), 19:1–19:41 (2009)
43. Ligatti, J., Bauer, L., Walker, D.: Edit automata: Enforcement mechanisms for run-time security policies. Int. J. Inf. Sec. (2005)
44. Bauer, A., Leucker, M., Schallhart, C.: Monitoring of real-time properties. In: Arun-Kumar, S., Garg, N. (eds.) FSTTCS 2006. LNCS, vol. 4337, pp. 260–272. Springer, Heidelberg (2006)
45. Bauer, A., Leucker, M., Schallhart, C.: The good, the bad, and the ugly, but how ugly is ugly? In: Sokolsky, O., Taşıran, S. (eds.) RV 2007. LNCS, vol. 4839, pp. 126–138. Springer, Heidelberg (2007)
46. Bauer, A., Leucker, M., Schallhart, C.: Comparing LTL semantics for runtime verification. Logic and Computation 20(3), 651–674 (2010)
47. Bauer, A., Leucker, M., Schallhart, C.: Runtime verification for LTL and TLTL. ACM Trans. Softw. 20(4), 14:1–14:64 (2011)
48. Bauer, A., Falcone, Y.: Decentralised LTL monitoring. In: Giannakopoulou, D., Méry, D. (eds.) FM 2012. LNCS, vol. 7436, pp. 85–100. Springer, Heidelberg (2012)
49. Cranor, L., Langheinrich, M., Marchiori, M., Presler-Marshall, M., Reagle, J.M.: The platform for privacy preferences 1.0 (p3p1.0) specification. World Wide Web Consortium, Recommendation REC-P3P-20020416 (April 2002)
50. Reagle, J., Cranor, L.F.: The platform for privacy preferences. Commun. ACM 42(2), 48–55 (1999)
51. Ashley, P., Hada, S., Karjoth, G., Powers, C., Schunter, M.: Enterprise Privacy Authorization Language (EPAL). Technical report, IBM Research, Rüschlikon (2003)
52. Karjoth, G., Schunter, M.: A privacy policy model for enterprises. In: Proceedings of the 15th IEEE Workshop on Computer Security Foundations, CSFW 2002, pp. 271–281. IEEE Computer Society, Washington, DC (2002)
53. May, M.J., Gunter, C.A., Lee, I.: Privacy apis: Access control techniques to analyze and verify legal privacy policies. In: Proceedings of the 19th IEEE Workshop on Computer Security Foundations, CSFW 2006, pp. 85–97. IEEE Computer Society, Washington, DC (2006)
54. Barth, A., Datta, A., Mitchell, J.C., Nissenbaum, H.: Privacy and contextual integrity: Framework and applications. In: Proceedings of the 2006 IEEE Symposium on Security and Privacy, SP 2006, pp. 184–198. IEEE Computer Society, Washington, DC (2006)

55. Barth, A., Mitchell, J., Datta, A., Sundaram, S.: Privacy and utility in business processes. In: Proceedings of the 20th IEEE Computer Security Foundations Symposium, CSF 2007, pp. 279–294. IEEE Computer Society, Washington, DC (2007)
56. Dinesh, N., Joshi, A., Lee, I., Sokolsky, O.: Checking traces for regulatory conformance. In: Leucker, M. (ed.) RV 2008. LNCS, vol. 5289, pp. 86–103. Springer, Heidelberg (2008)
57. Lam, P.E., Mitchell, J.C., Sundaram, S.: A formalization of hipaa for a medical messaging system. In: Fischer-Hübner, S., Lambrinoudakis, C., Pernul, G. (eds.) TrustBus 2009. LNCS, vol. 5695, pp. 73–85. Springer, Heidelberg (2009)
58. Ni, Q., Bertino, E., Lobo, J., Brodie, C., Karat, C.M., Karat, J., Trombeta, A.: Privacy-aware role-based access control. ACM Trans. Inf. Syst. Secur. 13(3), 24:1–24:31 (2010)

String Constraints for Verification*

Parosh Aziz Abdulla[1], Mohamed Faouzi Atig[1], Yu-Fang Chen[2], Lukáš Holík[3],
Ahmed Rezine[4], Philipp Rümmer[1], and Jari Stenman[1]

[1] Department of Information Technology, Uppsala University, Sweden
[2] Institute of Information Science, Academia Sinica, Taiwan
[3] Faculty of Information Technology, Brno University of Technology, Czech Republic
[4] Department of Computer and Information Science, Linköping University, Sweden

Abstract. We present a decision procedure for a logic that combines
(i) word equations over string variables denoting words of arbitrary
lengths, together with (ii) constraints on the length of words, and on
(iii) the regular languages to which words belong. Decidability of this
general logic is still open. Our procedure is sound for the general logic,
and a decision procedure for a particularly rich fragment that restricts
the form in which word equations are written. In contrast to many existing procedures, our method does not make assumptions about the
maximum length of words. We have developed a prototypical implementation of our decision procedure, and integrated it into a CEGAR-based
model checker for the analysis of programs encoded as Horn clauses. Our
tool is able to automatically establish the correctness of several programs
that are beyond the reach of existing methods.

1 Introduction

Software model checking is an active research area that has witnessed a remarkable success in the past decades [15,8]. Model checking tools are already used in
industrial applications [2]. One reason for this success is recent developments in
SMT technology [5,7,3], which allow efficient symbolic representations of different data types in programs. This dependence encompasses, however, that model
checking tools are inherently limited by the data types that can be handled by
the underlying SMT solver. A data type for which satisfying decision procedures have been missing is that of *strings*. Our work proposes a rich string logic
together with a decision procedure targeting model checking applications.

String data types are present in programming and scripting languages. In fact,
it is impossible to capture the essence of many programs, for instance in database
and web applications, without the ability to precisely represent and reason about
string data types. The control flow of programs can depend on words denoted
by string variables, on the length of words, or on regular languages to which
they belong. For example, a program allowing users to choose a username and

---

* Supported by the Uppsala Programming for Multicore Architectures Research Center (UPMARC), the Czech Science Foundation (13-37876P), Brno University of
Technology (FIT-S-12-1, FIT-S-14-2486), and the Linköping CENIIT Center (12.04).

A. Biere and R. Bloem (Eds.): CAV 2014, LNCS 8559, pp. 150–166, 2014.
© Springer International Publishing Switzerland 2014

a password may require the password to be of a minimal length, to be different from the username, and to be free from invalid characters. Reasoning about such constraints is also crucial when verifying that database and web applications are free from SQL injections and other security vulnerabilities.

Existing solvers for programs manipulating string variables and their length are either unsound, not expressive enough, or lack the ability to provide counterexamples. Many solvers [9,23,24] are unsound since they assume an a priori fixed upper bound on the length of the possible words. Others [9,17,26] are not expressive enough as they do not handle word equations, length constraints, or membership predicates. Such solvers are mostly aimed at performing symbolic executions, i.e., establishing feasibility of paths in a program. The solver in [25] performs sound over-approximation, but without supplying counterexamples in case the verification fails. In contrast, our decision procedure specifically targets model checking applications. In fact, we use it in a prototype model checker in order to automatically establish program correctness for several examples.

Our decision procedure establishes satisfiability of formulae written as Boolean combinations of: (i) word (dis)equalities such as $(a \cdot u = v \cdot b)$ or $(a \cdot u \neq v \cdot b)$, where a, b are letters and u, v are string variables denoting words of arbitrary lengths, (ii) length constraints such as $(|u| = |v| + 1)$, where $|u|$ refers to the length of the word denoted by string variable u, and (iii) predicates representing membership in regular expressions, e.g., $u \in c \cdot (a + b)^*$. Each of these predicates can be crucial for capturing the behavior and establishing the correctness of a string-manipulating program (cf. the program in Section 2). The analysis is not trivial as it needs to capture subtle interactions between different types of predicates. For instance, the formulae $\phi_1 = (a \cdot u = v \cdot b) \wedge (|u| = |v| + 1)$ and $\phi_2 = (a \cdot u = v \cdot b) \wedge v \in c \cdot (a + b)^*$ are unsatisfiable, i.e., there is no possible assignment of words to u and v that makes the conjunctions evaluate to true. The analysis then needs to propagate facts from one type of predicates to another; e.g., in ϕ_1 the analysis deduces from $(a \cdot u = v \cdot b)$ that $|u| = |v|$, which results in an unsatisfiable formula $(|u| = |v| \wedge |u| = |v| + 1))$. The general decidability problem is still open. We guarantee termination of our procedure for a fragment of the logic including the three types of predicates. The fragment we consider is rich enough to capture all the practical examples we have encountered.

We have integrated our decision procedure in a prototype model checker and used it to verify properties of implementations of common string manipulating functions such as the Hamming and Levenshtein distances. Predicates required for verification can be provided by hand; to achieve automation, in addition we propose a constraint-based interpolation procedure for regular word constraints. In combination with our decision procedure for words, this enables us to automatically analyze programs that are currently beyond the reach of state-of-the-art software model checkers.

Related Work. The pioneering work by Makanin [18] proposed a decision procedure for word equations (i.e., Boolean combinations of (dis)equalities) where the variables can denote words of arbitrary lengths. The decidability problem is already open [4] when word equations are combined with length constraints of the form $|u| = |v|$. Our logic adds predicates representing membership in regular languages to word equations and length constraints. This means that decidability is still an open problem. A contribution of our work is the definition of a rich sub-logic for which we guarantee the termination of our procedure.

In a work close to ours, the authors in [10] show decidability of a logic that is strictly weaker than the one for which we guarantee termination. For instance, in [10], membership predicates are allowed only under the assumption that no string variables can appear in the right hand sides of the equality predicates. This severely restricts the expressiveness of the logic. In [26], the authors augment the Z3 [7] SMT solver in order to handle word equations with length constraints. However, they do not support regular membership predicates. In our experience, these are crucial during model checking based verification.

Finally, in addition to considering more general equations, our work comes with an interpolation-based verification technique adapted for string programs. Notice that neither of [10,26] can establish correctness of programs with loops.

Outline. In the next section, we use a simple program to illustrate our approach. In Section 3 we introduce a logic for word equations with arithmetic and regular constraints, and then describe in Section 4 a procedure for deciding satisfiability of formulae in the logic. In Section 5 we define a class formulae for which we guarantee the termination of our decision procedure. We describe the verification procedure in Section 6 and the implementation effort in Section 7. Finally in Section 8 we give some conclusions and directions for future work.

2   A Simple Example

In this section, we use the simple program listed in Fig. 1 to give a flavor of our verification approach. The listing makes use of features that are common in string manipulating programs. We will argue that establishing correctness for such programs requires: (i) the ability to refer to string variables of arbitrary lengths, (ii) the ability to express combinations of constraints, like that the words denoted by the variables belong to regular expressions, that their lengths obey arithmetic inequalities, or that the words themselves are solutions to word equations, and (iii) the ability for a decision procedure to precisely capture the subtle interaction between the different kinds of involved constraints.

In the program of Fig. 1, a string variable s is initialized with the empty word. A loop is then executed an arbitrary number of times. At each iteration of the loop, the instruction s= 'a' + s + 'b' appends the letter 'a' at the beginning of variable s and the letter 'b' at its end. After the loop, the program asserts that s does not have the word 'ba' as a substring (denoted by !s.contains('ba'), and that its length (denoted by s.length()) is even.

Observe that the string variable s does not assume a maximal length. Any verification procedure that requires an a priori fixed bound on the length of the string variables is necessarily unsound and will fail to establish correctness.

Moreover, establishing correctness requires the ability to express and to reason about predicates such as those mentioned in the comments of the code in Fig. 1.

```
// Pre = (true)
String s= '';
// P₁ = (s ∈ ε)
while(*){
    // P₂ = (s = u · v ∧ u ∈ a* ∧ v ∈ b* ∧ |u| = |v|)
    s= 'a' + s + 'b';
}
// P₃ = P₂
assert(!s.contains('ba') && (s.length() % 2) == 0);
// Post = P₃
```

Fig. 1. A simple program manipulating a string variable s. Our logic allows to precisely capture the word equations, membership predicates and length constraints that are required for validating the assertion is never violated. Our decision procedure can then automatically validate the required verification conditions described in Fig. 2.

$vc_1 : post(Pre, \mathtt{s} = "") \implies P_1$ $vc_2 : P_1 \implies P_2$

$vc_3 : post(P_2, \mathtt{s} = "a" \cdot \mathtt{s} \cdot "b") \implies P_2$ $vc_4 : P_2 \implies P_3$

$vc_5 : post(P_3, \mathtt{assume(s.contains("ba")} \;||\; \mathtt{!(s.length()\%2 ==0)))} \implies false$

$vc_6 : post(P_3, \mathtt{assume(!s.contains("ba")} \;\&\&\; \mathtt{(s.length()\%2 ==0)))} \implies Post$

Fig. 2. Verification conditions for the simple program of Fig. 1

For instance, the loop invariant P_2 states that: (i) the variable s denotes a finite word w_s of arbitrary length, (ii) that w_s equals the concatenation of two words w_u and w_v, (iii) that $w_u \in a^*$ and $w_v \in b^*$, and (iv) that the length $|w_u|$ of word w_u equals the length $|w_v|$ of word w_v.

Using the predicates in Fig. 1, we can formulate program correctness in terms of the validity of each of the implications listed in Fig. 2. For instance, validity of the verification condition vc_5 amounts to showing that $\neg vc_5 = (s = u \cdot v \wedge u \in a^* \wedge v \in b^* \wedge |u| = |v|) \wedge (s = s_1 \cdot b \cdot a \cdot s_2 \vee \neg(|s| = 2n))$ is unsatisfiable. To establish this result, our decision procedure generates the two proof obligations $\neg vc_{51} : (s = u \cdot v \wedge u \in a^* \wedge v \in b^* \wedge |u| = |v| \wedge s = s_1 \cdot b \cdot a \cdot s_2)$ and $\neg vc_{52} : (s = u \cdot v \wedge u \in a^* \wedge v \in b^* \wedge |u| = |v| \wedge \neg(|s| = 2n))$.

In order to check vc_{51}, the procedure symbolically matches all the possible ways in which a word denoted by $u \cdot v$ can also be denoted by $s_1 \cdot b \cdot a \cdot s_2$. For instance, $u = s_1 \cdot b \wedge v = a \cdot s_2$ is one possible matching. In order to be able to show unsatisfiability, the decision procedure has to also consider the other possible matchings. For instance, the case where the word denoted by u is a strict prefix of the one denoted by s_1 has also to be considered. For this reason, the matching process might trigger new matchings. In general, there is no guarantee that the sequence of generated matchings will terminate. However, we show that this sequence terminates for an expressive fragment of the logic. This fragment includes the predicates of mentioned in this section and all predicates we encountered in practical programs, The procedure then checks satisfiability of each such a matching. For instance, the matching $u = s_1 \cdot b \wedge v = a \cdot s_2$

is shown to be unsatisfiable due the the membership predicate $v \in b^*$. In fact our procedure automatically proves that $\neg v_{51}$ is not satisfiable after checking all possible matchings.

So for $\neg vc_5$ to be satisfiable, $\neg vc_{52}$ needs to be satisfiable. Our procedure deduces that this would imply that $|u| = |v| \wedge \neg(|u| + |v| = 2n)$ is satisfiable. We leverage on existing standard decision procedures for linear arithmetic in order to show that this is not the case. Hence $\neg vc_5$ is unsatisfiable and vc_5 is valid. For this example, and those we report on in Section 6, our procedure can establish correctness fully automatically given the required predicates.

Observe that establishing validity requires the ability to capture interactions among the different types of predicates. For instance, establishing validity of vc_5 involves the ability to combine the word equations ($s = u \cdot v \wedge s = s_1 \cdot b \cdot a \cdot s_2$) with the membership predicates ($u \in a^* \wedge v \in b^*$) for vc_{51}, and with the length constraints ($|u| = |v| \wedge \neg(|s| = 2n)$) for vc_{52}. Capturing such interactions is crucial for establishing correctness and for eliminating false positives.

3   Defining the String Logic $\mathcal{E}_{e,r,l}$

In this section we introduce a logic, which we call $\mathcal{E}_{e,r,l}$, for word equations, regular constraints (short for membership constraints in regular languages) and length and arithmetic inequalities. We assume a finite alphabet Σ and write Σ^* to mean the set of finite words over Σ. We work with a set U of string variables denoting words in Σ^* and write $\mathcal{Z}$ for the set of integer numbers.

Syntax. We let variables u, v range over the set U. We write $|u|$ to mean the length of the word denoted by variable u, k to mean an integer in $\mathcal{Z}$, c to mean a letter in Σ and w to mean a word in Σ^*. The syntax of formulae in $\mathcal{E}_{e,r,l}$ is defined as follows:

$$
\begin{array}{lll}
\phi & ::= \phi \wedge \phi \mid \neg \phi \mid \varphi_e \mid \varphi_l \mid \varphi_r & \text{formulae} \\
\varphi_e & ::= tr = tr \mid tr \neq tr & \text{(dis)equalities} \\
\varphi_l & ::= e \leq e & \text{arithmetic inequalities} \\
\varphi_r & ::= tr \in \mathcal{R} & \text{membership predicates} \\
tr & ::= \epsilon \mid c \mid u \mid tr \cdot tr & \text{terms} \\
\mathcal{R} & ::= \emptyset \mid \epsilon \mid c \mid w \mid \mathcal{R} \cdot \mathcal{R} \mid \mathcal{R} + \mathcal{R} \mid \mathcal{R} \cap \mathcal{R} \mid \mathcal{R}^C \mid \mathcal{R}^* & \text{regular expressions} \\
e & ::= k \mid |tr| \mid k * e \mid e + e & \text{integer expressions}
\end{array}
$$

Assume variables $\{u_i\}_{i=1}^n$, terms $\{tr_i\}_{i=1}^n$ and integer expressions $\{e_i\}_{i=1}^n$. We write $\phi[u_1/tr_1] \ldots [u_n/tr_n]$ (resp. $\phi[|u_1|/e_1] \ldots [|u_n|/e_n]$) to mean the formula obtained by syntactically substituting in ϕ each occurrence of u_i by term tr_i (resp. each occurrence of $|u_i|$ by expression e_i). Such a substitution is said to be well-defined if no variable u_i (resp. $|u_i|$) appears in any tr_i (resp. e_i).

The set of word variables appearing in a term is defined as follows: $Vars(\epsilon) = \emptyset$, $Vars(c) = \emptyset$, $Vars(u) = \{u\}$ and $Vars(tr_1 \cdot tr_2) = Vars(tr_1) \cup Vars(tr_2)$.

Semantics. The semantics of $\mathcal{E}_{e,r,l}$ is mostly standard. We describe it using a mapping η (called *interpretation*) that assigns words in Σ^* to string variables in U. We extend η to terms as follows: $\eta(\epsilon) = \epsilon$, $\eta(c) = c$ and $\eta(tr_1.tr_2) = \eta(tr_1).\eta(tr_2)$. Every regular expression $\mathcal{R}$ is evaluated to the language $\mathcal{L}(\mathcal{R})$ it represents. Given an interpretation η, we define another mapping β_η that associates a number in $\mathcal{Z}$ to integer expressions as follows: $\beta_\eta(k) = k$, $\beta_\eta(|u|) = |\eta(u)|$, $\beta_\eta(|tr|) = |\eta(tr)|$, $\beta_\eta(k * e) = k * \beta_\eta(e)$, and $\beta_\eta(e_1 + e_2) = \beta_\eta(e_1) + \beta(e_2)$. A formula in $\mathcal{E}_{e,r,l}$ is then evaluated to a value in $\{ff, tt\}$ as follows:

$$
\begin{aligned}
val_\eta(\phi_1 \wedge \phi_2) &= tt \quad \text{iff} \quad val_\eta(\phi_1) = tt \text{ and } val_\eta(\phi_2) = tt \\
val_\eta(\neg\phi_1) &= tt \quad \text{iff} \quad val_\eta(\phi_1) = ff \\
val_\eta(tr \in \mathcal{R}) &= tt \quad \text{iff} \quad \eta(tr) \in \mathcal{L}(\mathcal{R}) \\
val_\eta(tr_1 = tr_2) &= tt \quad \text{iff} \quad \eta(tr_1) = \eta(tr_2) \\
val_\eta(tr_1 \neq tr_2) &= tt \quad \text{iff} \quad \neg(\eta(tr_1) = \eta(tr_2)) \\
val_\eta(e_1 \leq e_2) &= tt \quad \text{iff} \quad \beta_\eta(e_1) \leq \beta_\eta(e_2)
\end{aligned}
$$

A formula ϕ is said to be *satisfiable* if there is an interpretation η such that $val_\eta(\phi) = tt$. It is said to be *unsatisfiable* otherwise.

4   Inference Rules

In this section, we describe our set of inference rules for checking the satisfiability of formulae in the logic $\mathcal{E}_{e,r,l}$ of Section 3. Given a formula ϕ, we build a proof tree rooted at ϕ by repeatedly applying the inference rules introduced in this Section. We can assume, without loss of generality, that the formula is given in Disjunctive Normal Form. An inference rule is of the form:

$$
\text{NAME} : \frac{B_1 \ B_2 \ ... \ B_n}{A} \ cond
$$

In this inference rule, NAME is the name of the rule, *cond* is a side condition on A for the application of the rule, $B_1 \ B_2 \ ... \ B_n$ are called premises, and A is called the conclusion of the rule. (We omit the side condition *cond* from NAME when it is *tt*.) The premises and conclusion are formulae in $\mathcal{E}_{e,r,l}$. Each application consumes a conclusion and produces the set of premises. The inference rule is said to be *sound* if the satisfiability of the conclusion implies the satisfiability of one of the premises. It is said to be *locally complete* if the satisfiability of one of the premises implies the satisfiability of the conclusion. If all inference rules are locally complete, and if ϕ or one of the produced premises turns out to be satisfiable, then ϕ is also satisfiable. If all the inference rules are sound and none of the produced premises is satisfiable, then ϕ is also unsatisfiable.

We organize the inference rules in four groups. We use the rules of the first group to eliminate disequalities. The rules of the second group are used to simplify equalities. The rules of the third group are used to eliminate membership predicates. The rules of the last group are used to propagate length constraints. In addition, we assume standard decision procedures [3] for integer arithmetic.

Lemma 1. *The inference rules of this section are sound and locally complete.*

4.1 Removing Disequalities

We use rules NOT-EQ and DISEQ-SPLIT in order to eliminate disequalities. In rule NOT-EQ, we establish that $tr \neq tr \wedge \phi$ is not satisfiable and close this branch of the proof. In the second rule DISEQ-SPLIT, we eliminate disequalities involving arbitrary terms. For this, we make use of the fact that the alphabet Σ is finite and replace any disequality with a finite set of equalities. More precisely, assume a formula $tr \neq tr' \wedge \phi$ in $\mathcal{E}_{e,r,l}$. We observe that the disequality $tr \neq tr'$ holds iff the words w_{tr} and $w_{tr'}$ denoted by the terms tr and tr' are different. This corresponds to one of three cases. Assume three fresh variables u, v and v'. In the first case, the words w_{tr} and $w_{tr'}$ contain different letters $c \neq c'$ after a common prefix w_u. They are written as the concatenations $w_u \cdot c \cdot w_v$ and $w_u \cdot c' \cdot w_{v'}$ respectively. We capture this case using the set $\text{SPLIT}_{\text{DISEQ-SPLIT}} = \{tr = u \cdot c \cdot v \wedge tr' = u \cdot c' \cdot v' \wedge \phi \mid c, c' \in \Sigma \text{ and } c \neq c'\}$. In the second case, the word $w_{tr'} = w_u$ is a strict prefix of $w_{tr} = w_u \cdot c \cdot w_v$. We capture this with $\text{SPLIT}'_{\text{DISEQ-SPLIT}} = \{tr = u \cdot c \cdot v \wedge tr' = u \wedge \phi \mid c \in \Sigma\}$. In the third case, the word $w_{tr} = w_u$ is a strict prefix of $w_{tr'} = w_u \cdot c \cdot w'_v$, and we capture this case using the set $\text{SPLIT}''_{\text{DISEQ-SPLIT}} = \{tr = u \wedge tr' = u \cdot c \cdot v' \wedge \phi \mid c \in \Sigma\}$.

$$\text{NOT-EQ} : \frac{*}{tr \neq tr \wedge \phi} \qquad\qquad \text{EQ} : \frac{\phi}{tr = tr \wedge \phi}$$

$$\text{DISEQ-SPLIT} : \frac{\text{SPLIT}_{\text{DISEQ-SPLIT}} \cup \text{SPLIT}'_{\text{DISEQ-SPLIT}} \cup \text{SPLIT}''_{\text{DISEQ-SPLIT}}}{tr \neq tr' \wedge \phi}$$

4.2 Simplifying Equalities

We introduce rules EQ, EQ-VAR, and EQ-WORD to manipulate equalities. Rule applications take into account symmetry of the equality operator (i.e., if a rule can apply to $w \cdot tr_1 = tr_2 \wedge \phi$ then it can also apply to $tr_2 = w \cdot tr_1 \wedge \phi$). Rule EQ eliminates trivial equalities of the form $tr = tr$.

Rule EQ-VAR eliminates variable u from the equality $u \cdot tr_1 = tr_2 \wedge \phi$. Let w_u be some word denoted by u. For the equality to hold, w_u must be a prefix of the word denoted by tr_2. There are two cases. The first case, represented by $\text{SPLIT}_{\text{EQ-VAR}}$ in EQ-VAR, captures situations where w_u coincides with a word denoted by a prefix tr_3 of tr_2. The second case, represented by $\text{SPLIT}'_{\text{EQ-VAR}}$, captures situations where w_u does not coincide with a word denoted by a prefix of tr_2. Instead, tr_2 can be written as $tr_3 \cdot v \cdot tr_4$ and the word w_u is written as the concatenation of two words, one that is denoted by tr_3 and another that is prefix of the word denoted by v.

$$\text{EQ-VAR} : \frac{\text{SPLIT}_{\text{EQ-VAR}} \cup \text{SPLIT}'_{\text{EQ-VAR}}}{u \cdot tr_1 = tr_2 \wedge \phi}$$

The set $\text{SPLIT}_{\text{EQ-VAR}}$ captures the first case, when w_u coincides with a word denoted by a prefix tr_3 of tr_2. The premises for this case are partitioned into two sets, namely $\text{SPLIT}_{\text{EQ-VAR-1}}$ and $\text{SPLIT}_{\text{EQ-VAR-2}}$:

$$\text{SPLIT}_{\text{EQ-VAR-1}} = \begin{cases} (tr_1 = tr_4 \wedge \phi)[u/tr_3] \mid \\ tr_2 = tr_3 \cdot tr_4 \text{ and } u \text{ does not syntactically appear in } tr_3 \end{cases}$$

$$\text{SPLIT}_{\text{EQ-VAR-2}} = \begin{cases} tr_1 = tr_4 \wedge tr_5 \cdot tr_6 \in \epsilon \wedge \phi \mid \\ tr_2 = tr_3 \cdot tr_4 \text{ and } tr_3 = tr_5 \cdot u \cdot tr_6 \end{cases}$$

Variable u is eliminated from the premises contained in the set $\text{SPLIT}_{\text{EQ-VAR-1}}$. The second set $\text{SPLIT}_{\text{EQ-VAR-2}}$ captures cases where u does syntactically appear in tr_3. Variable u might still appear in some of the premises of $\text{SPLIT}_{\text{EQ-VAR-2}}$.

The set $\text{SPLIT}'_{\text{EQ-VAR}}$ in EQ-VAR captures the second case, namely when w_u does not coincide with a word denoted by a prefix of tr_2, written $tr_3 \cdot v \cdot tr_4$ for some variable v. The premises in $\text{SPLIT}'_{\text{EQ-VAR}}$ are partitioned into two sets, namely $\text{SPLIT}'_{\text{EQ-VAR-1}}$ and $\text{SPLIT}'_{\text{EQ-VAR-2}}$:

$$\text{SPLIT}'_{\text{EQ-VAR-1}} = \begin{cases} ((tr_1 = v_2 \cdot tr_4 \wedge \phi)[u/tr_3 \cdot v_1])[v/v_1 \cdot v_2] \mid \\ tr_2 = tr_3 \cdot v \cdot tr_4 \text{ and } u \text{ appears neither in } tr_3 \text{ nor in } v \end{cases}$$

$$\text{SPLIT}'_{\text{EQ-VAR-2}} = \begin{cases} (tr_1 = u_2 \cdot tr_4 \wedge u_1 \cdot u_2 = tr_3 \cdot u_1 \wedge \phi)[u/tr_3 \cdot u_1] \mid \\ tr_2 = tr_3 \cdot u \cdot tr_4 \text{ and } u \text{ does not appear in } tr_3 \end{cases}$$

The premises in $\text{SPLIT}'_{\text{EQ-VAR-1}}$ mention neither u nor v. The set $\text{SPLIT}'_{\text{EQ-VAR-2}}$ captures cases where u in the left-hand side overlaps with its occurrence on the right-hand side. Cases where u appears in tr_3 are captured in $\text{SPLIT}_{\text{EQ-VAR}}$.

Rule EQ-WORD eliminates the word w from the equality $w \cdot tr_1 = tr_2 \wedge \phi$:

$$\text{EQ-WORD} : \frac{\text{SPLIT}_{\text{EQ-WORD}} \cup \text{SPLIT}'_{\text{EQ-WORD}}}{w \cdot tr_1 = tr_2 \wedge \phi}$$

Again, we define two sets representing the premises of the rule:

$$\text{SPLIT}_{\text{EQ-WORD}} = \{ tr_3 \in w \wedge tr_4 = tr_1 \wedge \phi \mid tr_2 = tr_3 \cdot tr_4 \}$$

$$\text{SPLIT}'_{\text{EQ-WORD}} = \{ (tr_3 \cdot v_1 \in w \wedge v_2 \cdot tr_4 = tr_1 \wedge \phi)[v/v_1 \cdot v_2] \mid tr_2 = tr_3 \cdot v \cdot tr_4 \}$$

To simplify the presentation, we do not present suffix versions for rules EQ-VAR and EQ-WORD. Such rules match suffixes instead of prefixes and simply mirror the rules described above.

4.3   Removing Membership Predicates

We use rules REG-NEG, MEMB, NOT-MEMB, REG-SPLIT and REG-LEN to simplify and eliminate membership predicates. We describe them below.

Rule REG-NEG replaces the negation of a membership predicate in a regular expression $\mathcal{R}$ with a membership predicate in its complement $\mathcal{R}^C$.

$$\text{REG-NEG} : \frac{tr \in \mathcal{R}^C \wedge \phi}{\neg(tr \in \mathcal{R}) \wedge \phi}$$

Rule MEMB eliminates the predicate $w \in \mathcal{R}$ in case the word w belongs to the language $\mathcal{L}(\mathcal{R})$ of the regular expression $\mathcal{R}$. If w does not belong to $\mathcal{L}(\mathcal{R})$ then rule NOT-MEMB closes this branch of the proof.

$$\textsc{Memb}: \frac{\phi}{w \in \mathcal{R} \wedge \phi} \; w \in \mathcal{L}(\mathcal{R}) \qquad \textsc{Not-Memb}: \frac{*}{w \in \mathcal{R} \wedge \phi} \; w \notin \mathcal{L}(\mathcal{R})$$

Rule $\textsc{Reg-Split}$ simplifies membership predicates of the form $tr \cdot tr' \in \mathcal{R}$. Given such a predicate, the rule replaces it with a disjunction $\bigvee_{i=1}^{n} \left(tr \in \mathcal{R}_i \wedge tr' \in \mathcal{R}_i' \right)$ where the set $\{(\mathcal{R}_i, \mathcal{R}_i')\}_{i=1}^{n}$ is finite and only depends on the regular expression $\mathcal{R}$. To define this set, represent $\mathcal{L}(\mathcal{R})$ using some arbitrary but fixed finite automaton (S, s_0, δ, F). Assume $S = \{s_0, \ldots, s_n\}$. Choose the regular expressions $\mathcal{R}_i, \mathcal{R}_i'$ such that : (1) $\mathcal{R}_i$ has the same language as the automaton $(S, s_0, \delta, \{s_i\})$, and (2) $\mathcal{R}_i'$ has the same language as the automaton (S, s_i, δ, F). For any word $w_{tr} \cdot w_{tr'}$ denoted by $tr \cdot tr'$ and accepted by $\mathcal{R}$, there will be a state s_i in S such that w_{tr} is accepted by $\mathcal{R}_i$ and $w_{tr'}$ is accepted by $\mathcal{R}_i'$. Given a regular expression $\mathcal{R}$, we let $\mathcal{F}(\mathcal{R})$ denote the set $\{(\mathcal{R}_i, \mathcal{R}_i')\}_{i=1}^{n}$ above.

$$\textsc{Reg-Split}: \frac{\{tr \in \mathcal{R}' \wedge tr' \in \mathcal{R}'' \wedge \phi \mid (\mathcal{R}', \mathcal{R}'') \in \mathcal{F}(\mathcal{R})\}}{tr \cdot tr' \in \mathcal{R} \wedge \phi}$$

Rule $\textsc{Reg-Len}$ can only be applied in certain cases. To identify these cases, we define the condition $\Gamma(\phi, u)$ which states, given a formula ϕ and a variable u, that u is not used in any membership predicate or in any (dis)equation in ϕ. In other words, the condition states that if u occurs in ϕ then it occurs in a length predicate. The rule $\textsc{Reg-Len}$ replaces, in one step, all the membership predicates $\{u \in \mathcal{R}_i\}_{i=1}^{n}$ with an arithmetic constraint $Len(\mathcal{R}_1 \cap \ldots \cap \mathcal{R}_m, u)$. This arithmetic constraint expresses that the length $|u|$ of variable u belongs to the semi-linear set corresponding to the Parikh image of the intersection of all regular expressions $\{\mathcal{R}_i\}_{i=1}^{n}$ appearing in membership predicates of variable u. It is possible to determine a representation of this semi linear set by starting from a finite state automaton representing the intersection $\cap_i \mathcal{R}_i$ and replacing all letters with a unique arbitrary letter. The obtained automaton is determinized and the semi linear set is deduced from the length of the obtained lasso if any (notice that since the automaton is deterministic and its alphabet is a singleton, its form will be either a lasso or a simple path.) After this step, there will be no membership predicates involving u.

$$\textsc{Reg-Len}: \frac{Len(\mathcal{R}_1 \cap \ldots \cap \mathcal{R}_m, u) \wedge \phi}{u \in \mathcal{R}_1 \wedge \ldots \wedge u \in \mathcal{R}_m \wedge \phi} \; \Gamma(\phi, u)$$

4.4 Propagating Term Lengths

The rule $\textsc{Term-Leng}$ is the only inference rule in the fourth group. It substitutes the expression $|tr| + |tr'|$ for every occurrence in ϕ of the expression $|tr \cdot tr'|$.

$$\textsc{Term-Leng}: \frac{\phi[|tr \cdot tr'|/|tr| + |tr'|]}{\phi} \; |tr \cdot tr'| \text{ appears in } \phi$$

We can also add rules to systematically add the length predicate $|tr| = |tr'|$ each time an equality $tr = tr'$ appears in a formula; however, such rules are not necessary for the completeness of our procedure, as shown in the next section.

5   Completeness of the Procedure

In this section, we define a class of formulae of *acyclic form* (we say a formula is in acyclic form, or acyclic for short) for which the decision procedure in Section 4 is guaranteed to terminate. For simplicity, we assume w.l.o.g that the formula is a conjunction of predicates and negated predicates.

Non-termination may be caused by an infinite chain of applications of rule EQ-VAR of Section 4.2 for removing equalities. Consider for instance the equality $u \cdot v = v \cdot u$. One of the cases generated within the disjunct $\text{SPLIT}'_{\text{EQ-VAR-1}}$ of EQ-VAR is $v_1 \cdot v_2 = v_2 \cdot v_1$. This is the same as the original equality up to renaming of variables. In this case, the process of removing equalities clearly does not terminate. To prevent this, we will require that no variable can appear on both sides of an equality. We also need to prevent the repetition of a variable inside one side of an equality. This is needed in cases like $u \cdot u = v \cdot v$ where $\text{SPLIT}'_{\text{EQ-VAR-1}}$ includes $v_1 = v_2 \cdot v_1 \cdot v_2$, with a variable v_1 on both sides of the equality, which is the situation which we wanted to prevent at the first place. These restrictions must hold initially and must be preserved by applications of any of the rules presented in Sections 4. Attention must be given to rules that modify equalities. Rules such as EQ-VAR involve substitution of a variable from one side of an equality by a term from the other side. We need to prevent *chains* of such substitutions that cause variables to appear several times in a (dis)equality. Acyclic formulae must also guarantee that the undesired cases cannot appear after a use of DISEQ-SPLIT of Section 4.1 that transforms a disequality to equalities. We respectively state preservation of these restriction and termination of the procedure of Section 4 in theorems 1 and 2 at the end of this Section. First, we need some definitions.

Linear formulae. A formula in $\mathcal{E}_{e,r,l}$ is said to be *linear* if it contains no equality or disequality where a variable appears more than once.

Given a conjunction ϕ in $\mathcal{E}_{e,r,l}$ involving m (dis)equalities, we can build a *dependency graph* $G_\phi = (N, E, \text{label}, \text{map})$ in the following way. We order the (dis)equalities from e_1 to e_m, where each e_j is of the form $\text{lhs}(j) \approx \text{rhs}(j)$ for $j : 1 \leq j \leq m$ and $\approx \in \{=, \neq\}$. For each $j : 1 \leq j \leq m$, a node n_{2j-1} is used to refer to the left-hand side of the jth (dis)equality, and n_{2j} to its right-hand side. For example, two different nodes are used even in the case of the simple equality $u = u$, one to refer to the left-hand side, and the other to refer the right-hand side. N is then the set of $2 \times m$ nodes $\{n_i | i : 1 \leq i \leq 2 \times m\}$. The mapping label associates the term $\text{lhs}(j)$ (resp. $\text{rhs}(j)$) to each node n_{2j-1} (resp. n_{2j}) for $j : 1 \leq j \leq m$. label is not necessarily a one to one mapping. The mapping $\text{map} : E \to \{\text{rel}, \text{var}\}$ labels edges as follows: $\text{map}(n, n') = \text{rel}$ for each $(n, n') = (n_{2j-1}, n_{2j})$ for each $j : 1 \leq j \leq m$, and $\text{map}(n, n') = \text{var}$ iff $n \neq n'$, and $\text{label}(n)$ and $\text{label}(n')$ have some common variables. By construction, map is defined to be total, i.e., E contains only edges that are labeled by map.

A *dependency cycle* in $G_\phi = (N, E, \text{label}, \text{map})$ is a cycle where successive edges have alternating labels. Formally, a dependency cycle is a sequence of distinct nodes $n_0, n_1, \ldots, n_k$ in N with $k \geq 1$ such that 1) for every $i : 0 \leq i \leq k$,

$\text{map}(n_i, n_{i+1\%(k+1)})$ is defined, and 2) for each $i : 0 \leq i < k$, $\text{map}(n_i, n_{i+1}) \neq \text{map}(n_{i+1}, n_{i+2\%(k+1)})$.

Acyclic graph. A conjunction ϕ in $\mathcal{E}_{e,r,l}$ is said to be acyclic iff it is linear and its dependency graph does not contain any dependency cycle.

Theorem 1. *Application of rules of Section 4 preserves acyclicity.*

An *ordered procedure* is any procedure that applies the rules of Section 4 on a formula in $\mathcal{E}_{e,r,l}$ in the four following phases. In the first phase, all disequalities are eliminated using DISEQ-SPLIT and NOT-EQ. In the second phase, the procedure eliminates one equality at a time by repeatedly applying EQ-VAR, EQ-WORD and EQ. In the third phase, membership predicates are eliminated by repeatedly applying REG-NEG, MEMB, NOT-MEMB, REG-SPLIT and REG-LEN. In the last phase, arithmetic predicates are solved using a standard decision procedure [3].

Theorem 2. *Ordered procedures terminate on acyclic formulae.*

6   Complete Verification of String-Processing Programs

The analysis of string-processing programs has gained importance due to the increased use of string-based APIs and protocols, for instance in the context of databases and Web programming. Much of the existing work has focused on the detection of bugs or the synthesis of attacks; in contrast, the work presented in this paper primarily targets verification of *functional correctness.* The following sections outline how we use our logic $\mathcal{E}_{e,r,l}$ for this purpose. On the one hand, our solver is designed to handle the satisfiability checks needed when constructing finite abstractions of programs, with the help of predicate abstraction [11,13] or Impact-style algorithms [19]; since $\mathcal{E}_{e,r,l}$ can express both length properties and regular expressions, it covers predicates sufficient for a wide range of verification applications. On the other hand, we propose a constraint-based Craig interpolation algorithm for the automatic refinement of program abstractions (Section 6.2), leading to a completeness result in the style of [16]. We represent programs in the framework of Horn clauses [20,12], which make it easy to handle language features like recursion; however, our work is in no way restricted to this setting.

6.1   Horn Constraints with Strings

In our context, a *Horn clause* is a formula $H \leftarrow C \wedge B_1 \wedge \cdots \wedge B_n$ where C is a formula (constraint) in $\mathcal{E}_{e,r,l}$; each B_i is an application $p(t_1, \ldots, t_k)$ of a relation symbol $p \in \mathcal{R}$ to first-order terms; H is either an application $p(t_1, \ldots, t_k)$ of $p \in \mathcal{R}$ to first-order terms, or the constraint *false.* H is called the *head* of the clause, $C \wedge B_1 \wedge \cdots \wedge B_n$ the *body.* A set $\mathcal{HC}$ of Horn clauses is called *solvable* if there is an assignment that maps every n-ary relation symbol p to a word formula $C_p[x_1, \ldots, x_n]$ with n free variables, such that every clause in $\mathcal{HC}$ is valid. Since Horn clauses can capture properties such as initiation and consecution of invariants, programs can be encoded as sets of Horn clauses in such a way that the clauses are solvable if and only if the program is correct.

Example 1. The example from Section 2 is represented by the following set of Horn clauses, encoding constraints on the intermediate assertions Pre, P_1, P_2, P_3. Note that the clauses closely correspond to the verification conditions given in Fig. 2. Any solution of the Horn clauses represents a set of mutually inductive invariants, and witnesses correctness of the program.

$$Pre(s) \leftarrow true$$
$$P_1(s') \leftarrow s' = \epsilon \land Pre(s)$$
$$P_2(s) \leftarrow P_1(s)$$
$$P_2("a" \cdot s \cdot "b") \leftarrow P_2(s)$$

$$P_3(s) \leftarrow P_2(s)$$
$$false \leftarrow s \in (a|b)^* \cdot ba \cdot (a|b)^* \land P_3(s)$$
$$false \leftarrow \forall k.\, 2k \neq |s| \land P_3(s)$$

Algorithms to construct solutions of Horn clauses with the help of *predicate abstraction* have been proposed for instance in [12]; in this context, automatic solving is split into two main steps: 1) the synthesis of *predicates* as building blocks for solutions, and 2) the construction of solutions as Boolean combinations of the predicates. The second step requires a solver to decide consistency of sets of predicates, as well as implication between predicates (a set of predicates implies some other predicate); our logic is designed for this purpose.

$\mathcal{E}_{e,r,l}$ covers a major part of the string operations commonly used in software programs; further operations can be encoded elegantly, including:

- *extraction of substring* v of length *len* from a string u, starting at position *pos*, which is defined by the formula:

$$u = p \cdot v \cdot s \land |v| = len \land |p| = pos$$

- *replacement* of the substring v (of length *len*, starting at position *pos*) by v', resulting in the new overall string u':

$$u = p \cdot v \cdot s \land u' = p \cdot v' \cdot s \land |v| = len \land |p| = pos$$

- *search* for the first occurrence of a string, using either equations or regular expression constraints.

6.2 Constraint-Based Craig Interpolation

In order to synthesize new predicates for verification, we propose a constraint-based *Craig interpolation* algorithm [6]. We say that a formula $I[\bar{s}]$ is an interpolant of a conjunction $A[\bar{s}], B[\bar{s}]$ over common variables $\bar{s} = s_1, \ldots, s_n$ (and possibly including further local variables), if the conjunctions $A[\bar{s}] \land \neg I[\bar{s}]$ and $B[\bar{s}] \land I[\bar{s}]$ are unsatisfiable. In other words, an interpolant $I[\bar{s}]$ is an over-approximation of $A[\bar{s}]$ that is disjoint from $B[\bar{s}]$. It is well-known that interpolants are suitable candidates for predicates in software model checking; for a detailed account on the use of interpolants for solving Horn clauses, we refer the reader to [22].

Our interpolation procedure is shown in Alg. 1, and generates interpolants in the form of regular constraints separating $A[\bar{s}]$ and $B[\bar{s}]$. This means that

---

Algorithm 1. Constraint-based interpolation of string formulae

Input: Interpolation problem $A[\bar{s}] \wedge B[\bar{s}]$ with common variables $\bar{s}$; bound L.
Output: Interpolant $s_1|s_2|\cdots|s_n \in \mathcal{R}$; or result **Inseparable**.

1 $Aw \leftarrow \emptyset$; $Bw \leftarrow \emptyset$;
2 **while** *there is RE* $\mathcal{R}$ *of size* $\leq L$ *such that* $Aw \subseteq \mathcal{L}(\mathcal{R})$ *and* $Bw \cap \mathcal{L}(\mathcal{R}) = \emptyset$ **do**
3 $\quad$ **if** $A[\bar{s}] \wedge \neg(s_1|s_2|\cdots|s_n \in \mathcal{R})$ *is satisfiable with assignment* η **then**
4 $\quad\quad|\quad Aw \leftarrow Aw \cup \{\eta(s_1)|\cdots|\eta(s_n)\}$;
5 $\quad$ **else if** $B[\bar{s}] \wedge (s_1|s_2|\cdots|s_n \in \mathcal{R})$ *is satisfiable with assignment* η **then**
6 $\quad\quad|\quad Bw \leftarrow Bw \cup \{\eta(s_1)|\cdots|\eta(s_n)\}$;
7 $\quad$ **else**
8 $\quad\quad|\quad$ **return** $s_1|s_2|\cdots|s_n \in \mathcal{R}$;
9 $\quad$ **end**
10 **end**
11 **return** *Inseparable*;

---

interpolants are not arbitrary formulae in the logic $\mathcal{E}_{e,r,l}$, but are restricted to the form $s_1|s_2|\cdots|s_n \in \mathcal{R}$, where "|" $\in \Sigma$ is a distinguished separating letter, and $\mathcal{R}$ is a regular expression. In addition, only interpolants up to a *bound L* are considered; L can limit, for instance, the length of the regular expression $\mathcal{R}$, or the number of states in a finite automaton representing $\mathcal{R}$.

Alg. 1 maintains finite sets Aw and Bw of words representing solutions of $A[\bar{s}]$ and $B[\bar{s}]$, respectively. In line 2, a candidate interpolant of the form $s_1|s_2|\cdots|s_n \in \mathcal{R}$ is constructed, in such a way that $\mathcal{L}(\mathcal{R})$ is a superset of Aw but disjoint from Bw. The concrete construction of candidate interpolants of size $\leq L$ can be implemented in a number of ways, for instance via an encoding as a SAT or SMT problem (as done in our implementation), or with the help of learning algorithms like L^* [1]. It is then checked whether $s_1|s_2|\cdots|s_n \in \mathcal{R}$ satisfies the properties of an interpolant (lines 3, 5), which can be done using the string solver developed in this paper. If any of the properties is violated, the constructed satisfying assignment η gives rise to a further word to be included in Aw or Bw.

Lemma 2 (Correctness). *Suppose bound* L *is chosen such that it is only satisfied by finitely many formulae* $s_1|s_2|\cdots|s_n \in \mathcal{R}$. *Then Alg. 1 terminates and either returns a correct interpolant* $s_1|s_2|\cdots|s_n \in \mathcal{R}$, *or reports* **Inseparable**.

By iteratively increasing bound L, eventually a regular interpolant for any (unsatisfiable) conjunction $A[\bar{s}] \wedge B[\bar{s}]$ can be found, provided that such an interpolant exists at all. This scheme of bounded interpolation is suitable for integration in the complete model checking algorithm given in [16]: since only finitely many predicates can be inferred for every value L, divergence of model checking is impossible for any fixed L. By globally increasing L in an iterative manner, eventually every predicate that can be expressed in the form $s_1|s_2|\cdots|s_n \in \mathcal{R}$ will be found.

7 Implementation

We have implemented our algorithm in a tool called NORN[1] The tool takes as input a formula in the logic described in Section 3, and returns either *Sat* together with a witness of satisfiability (i.e., concrete string values for all variables), or *Unsat*. NORN first converts the given formula to DNF, after which each disjunct goes through the following steps:

1. Recursively split equalities, backtracking if necessary, until no equality constraints are left.
2. Recursively split membership constraints, again backtracking if necessary, and compute the language of each variable. From the language, we extract length constraints which we add to the formula.
3. Solve the remaining length constraints using PRINCESS [3].

We will now explain the second step in more detail. Assume that we have a membership constraint $tr \in A$, where A is an automaton (NORN makes use of DK.BRICS.AUTOMATON [21] for all automata operations). We can remove a sequence of trailing constants $a_1 a_2 \cdots a_k$ in $tr = tr' \cdot a_1 a_2 \cdots a_n$ by replacing the constraint with $tr' \in rev(\delta_{a_k \cdots a_2 a_1}(rev(A)))$, where $\delta_s(A)$ denotes the derivative of A w.r.t. the string s, and $rev(A)$ denotes the reverse of A. We now have a membership constraint $s_1 \cdots s_n \in A'$ where the term consists of a number of segments s_i, each of the form $a_1 \cdots a_{n_i} X_i$, i.e., a number of constants followed by a variable. The procedure keeps, at each step, a mapping m that maps each variable to an automaton representing the language it admits. For the constraint to be satisfiable, the constraints $s_1 \in A'_1$ and $s_2 \cdots s_n \in A'_2$ must be satisfiable for some pair (A_1, A_2) in the splitting of A'. This means that we can update our mapping by $m(X_i) = m(X_i) \cap \delta_{a_1 \cdots a_n}(A_1)$ and recurse on $s_2 \cdots s_n \in A'_2$. If at any point any automaton in the mapping becomes empty, the membership constraint is unsatisfiable, and we backtrack.

If, in the third step, PRINCESS tells that the given formula is satisfiable, it gives concrete lengths for all variables. By restricting each variable to the solution given by PRINCESS and reversing the substitutions performed in step 1, we can compute witnesses for the variables in the original formula.

NORN can be used both as a library and as a command line tool. In addition to the logic in Section 3, NORN supports character ranges (e.g. $[a - c]$) and the wildcard character (.) in regular expressions. It also supports the divisibility predicate $x \ div \ y$, which says that x divides y. This translates to the arithmetic constraint $x = y * n$, where n is a free variable.

Model Checking. We have integrated NORN into the predicate abstraction-based model checker ELDARICA [14], on the basis of the algorithm and interpolation procedure from Section 6. We use the regular interpolation procedure from Section 6.2 in combination with an ordinary interpolation procedure for Presburger arithmetic to infer predicates about word length. Table 1 gives an overview

---

[1] Available at http://user.it.uu.se/~jarst116/norn/.

Table 1. Verification runtime for a set of string-processing programs. Experiments were done on an Intel Core i5 machine with 3.2GHz, running 64 bit Linux.

Program	Property	Time
$a^n b^n$ (Fig. 1)	$s \notin (a+b)^* \cdot ba \cdot (a+b)^* \wedge \exists k.\ 2k = \|s\|$	8.0s
StringReplace	pre: $s \in (a+b+c)^*$; post: $s \in (a+c)^*$	4.5s
ChunkSplit	pre: $s \in (a+b)^*$; post: $s \in (a+b+c)^*$	5.5s
Levenshtein	$dist \leq \|s\| + \|t\|$	5.3s
HammingDistance	$dist = \|v\|$ if $u \in 0^*, v \in 1^*$	27.1s

of preliminary results obtained when analyzing a set of hand-written string-processing programs. Although the programs are quite small, the presence of string operations makes them intricate to analyze using automated model checking techniques; most of the programs require invariants in form of regular expressions for verification to succeed. Our implementation is able to verify all programs fully automatically within a few seconds; since performance has not been the main focus of our implementation work so far, further optimization will likely result in much reduced runtimes. To the best of our knowledge, all of the programs are beyond the scope of other state-of-the-art software model checkers.

8   Conclusions and Future Work

In contrast to much of the existing work that has focused on the detection of bugs or the synthesis of attacks for string-manipulating programs; the work presented in this paper primarily targets verification of *functional correctness*. To achieve this goal, we have made several key contributions. First, we have presented a decision procedure for a rich logic of strings. Although the problem in its generality remains open, we are able to identify an expressive fragment for which our procedure is both sound and complete. We are not aware of any decision procedure with a similar expressive power. Second, we leverage on the fact that our logic is able to reason both about length properties and regular expressions in order to capture and manipulate predicates sufficient for a wide range of verification applications. Future works include experimenting with better integrations of the different theories, exploring different Craig interpolation techniques, and exploring the applicability of our framework to more general classes of string processing applications.

References

1. Angluin, D.: Learning regular sets from queries and counterexamples. Inf. Comput. 75(2), 87–106 (1987)
2. Ball, T., Levin, V., Rajamani, S.K.: A decade of software model checking with slam. Commun. ACM 54(7), 68–76 (2011)
3. Brillout, A., Kroening, D., Rümmer, P., Wahl, T.: An interpolating sequent calculus for quantifier-free Presburger arithmetic. Journal of Automated Reasoning 47, 341–367 (2011)

4. Büchi, J.R., Senger, S.: Definability in the existential theory of concatenation and undecidable extensions of this theory. Z. Math. Logik Grundlagen Math. 34(4) (1988)

5. Cimatti, A., Griggio, A., Schaafsma, B.J., Sebastiani, R.: The mathSAT5 SMT solver. In: Piterman, N., Smolka, S.A. (eds.) TACAS 2013. LNCS, vol. 7795, pp. 93–107. Springer, Heidelberg (2013)

6. Craig, W.: Linear reasoning. A new form of the Herbrand-Gentzen theorem. The Journal of Symbolic Logic 22(3) (1957)

7. de Moura, L., Bjørner, N.S.: Z3: An Efficient SMT Solver. In: Ramakrishnan, C.R., Rehof, J. (eds.) TACAS 2008. LNCS, vol. 4963, pp. 337–340. Springer, Heidelberg (2008)

8. D'Silva, V., Kroening, D., Weissenbacher, G.: A survey of automated techniques for formal software verification. IEEE Trans. on CAD of Integrated Circuits and Systems 27(7), 1165–1178 (2008)

9. Ganesh, V., Dill, D.L.: A decision procedure for bit-vectors and arrays. In: Damm, W., Hermanns, H. (eds.) CAV 2007. LNCS, vol. 4590, pp. 519–531. Springer, Heidelberg (2007)

10. Ganesh, V., Minnes, M., Solar-Lezama, A., Rinard, M.: Word equations with length constraints: What's decidable? In: Biere, A., Nahir, A., Vos, T. (eds.) HVC. LNCS, vol. 7857, pp. 209–226. Springer, Heidelberg (2013)

11. Graf, S., Saidi, H.: Construction of abstract state graphs with PVS. In: Grumberg, O. (ed.) CAV 1997. LNCS, vol. 1254, pp. 72–83. Springer, Heidelberg (1997)

12. Grebenshchikov, S., Lopes, N.P., Popeea, C., Rybalchenko, A.: Synthesizing software verifiers from proof rules. In: PLDI, pp. 405–416 (2012)

13. Henzinger, T.A., Jhala, R., Majumdar, R., McMillan, K.L.: Abstractions from proofs. In: 31st POPL (2004)

14. Hojjat, H., Konečný, F., Garnier, F., Iosif, R., Kuncak, V., Rümmer, P.: A verification toolkit for numerical transition systems. In: Giannakopoulou, D., Méry, D. (eds.) FM 2012. LNCS, vol. 7436, pp. 247–251. Springer, Heidelberg (2012)

15. Jhala, R., Majumdar, R.: Software model checking. ACM Comput. Surv. 41(4) (2009)

16. Jhala, R., McMillan, K.L.: A practical and complete approach to predicate refinement. In: Hermanns, H., Palsberg, J. (eds.) TACAS 2006. LNCS, vol. 3920, pp. 459–473. Springer, Heidelberg (2006)

17. Kieżun, A., Ganesh, V., Artzi, S., Guo, P.J., Hooimeijer, P., Ernst, M.D.: HAMPI: A solver for word equations over strings, regular expressions, and context-free grammars. ACM Transactions on Software Engineering and Methodology 21(4) (2012)

18. Makanin, G.S.: The problem of solvability of equations in a free semigroup. Mathematics of the USSR-Sbornik 32(2), 129–198 (1977)

19. McMillan, K.L.: Lazy abstraction with interpolants. In: Ball, T., Jones, R.B. (eds.) CAV 2006. LNCS, vol. 4144, pp. 123–136. Springer, Heidelberg (2006)

20. Méndez-Lojo, M., Navas, J., Hermenegildo, M.V.: A flexible (C)LP-based approach to the analysis of object-oriented programs. In: King, A. (ed.) LOPSTR 2007. LNCS, vol. 4915, pp. 154–168. Springer, Heidelberg (2008)

21. Møller, A.: dk.brics.automaton – finite-state automata and regular expressions for Java (2010), http://www.brics.dk/automaton/

22. Rümmer, P., Hojjat, H., Kuncak, V.: Classifying and solving horn clauses for verification. In: Cohen, E., Rybalchenko, A. (eds.) VSTTE 2013. LNCS, vol. 8164, pp. 1–21. Springer, Heidelberg (2014)

23. Saxena, P., Akhawe, D., Hanna, S., Mao, F., McCamant, S., Song, D.: A Symbolic Execution Framework for JavaScript. In: IEEE Symposium on Security and Privacy, pp. 513–528. IEEE Computer Society (2010)
24. Saxena, P., Hanna, S., Poosankam, P., Song, D.: FLAX: Systematic discovery of client-side validation vulnerabilities in rich web applications. In: NDSS. The Internet Society (2010)
25. Yu, F., Alkhalaf, M., Bultan, T.: Stranger: An automata-based string analysis tool for PHP. In: Esparza, J., Majumdar, R. (eds.) TACAS 2010. LNCS, vol. 6015, pp. 154–157. Springer, Heidelberg (2010)
26. Zheng, Y., Zhang, X., Ganesh, V.: Z3-str: A Z3-based string solver for web application analysis. In: Proceedings of the 2013 9th Joint Meeting on Foundations of Software Engineering, ESEC/FSE 2013, pp. 114–124. ACM, New York (2013)

A Conference Management System
with Verified Document Confidentiality

Sudeep Kanav, Peter Lammich, and Andrei Popescu

Fakultät für Informatik, Technische Universität München, Germany

Abstract. We present a case study in verified security for realistic systems: the implementation of a conference management system, whose functional kernel is faithfully represented in the Isabelle theorem prover, where we specify and verify confidentiality properties. The various theoretical and practical challenges posed by this development led to a novel security model and verification method generally applicable to systems describable as input–output automata.

1 Introduction

Information-flow security is concerned with preventing or facilitating (un)desired flow of information in computer systems, covering aspects such as confidentiality, integrity, and availability of information. Dieter Gollmann wrote in 2005 [15]: "Currently, information flow and noninterference models are areas of research rather than the bases of a practical methodology for the design of secure systems." The situation has improved somewhat in the past ten years, with mature software systems such as Jif [1] offering powerful and scalable information flow technology integrated with programming.

However, the state of the art in information-flow security models [24] is still far from finding its way towards applications to real-world systems. If we further restrict attention to *mechanically verified* work, the situation is even more dramatic, with examples of realistic system verification [3,8,28] being brave exceptions. This is partly explained by the complexity of information-flow properties, which is much greater than that of traditional functional properties [23]. However, this situation is certainly undesirable, in a world where confidentiality and secrecy raise higher and higher challenges.

In this paper, we take on the task of implementing, and verifying the confidentiality of, a realistic system: CoCon,[1] a full-fledged conference system, featuring multiple users and conferences and offering much of the functionality of widely used systems such as EasyChair [10] and HotCRP [11].

Conference systems are widely used in the scientific community—EasyChair alone claims one million users. Moreover, the information flow in such systems possesses enough complexity so that errors can sneak inside implementations, sometimes with bitter–comical consequences. Recently, Popescu, as well as the authors of 267 papers submitted to a major security conference, initially received an acceptance notification, followed by a retraction [19]: "We are sorry to inform you that your paper was not accepted for this year's conference. We received 307 submissions and only accepted 40 of them ... We apologize for an earlier acceptance notification, due to a system error."[2]

---

[1] A running version of CoCon, as well as the formal proof sources, are available at [20].

[2] After reading the initial acceptance notification, Popescu went out to celebrate; it was only hours later when he read the retraction.

A. Biere and R. Bloem (Eds.): CAV 2014, LNCS 8559, pp. 167–183, 2014.
© Springer International Publishing Switzerland 2014

WARNING: HotCRP version 2.47 (commit range 94ca5a0e43bd7dd0565c2c8dc7d8f710a206ab49 through
9c1b45475411ecb85d46bad1f76064881792b038) was subject to an information exposure where some
authors could see PC comments. Users of affected versions should upgrade or set the following option in
Code/options.inc: $Opt["disableCapabilities"] = true;

Fig. 1. Confidentiality bug in HotCRP

The above is an information-integrity violation (a distorted decision was initially communicated to the authors) and could have been caused by a human error rather than a system error—but there is the question whether the system should not prevent even such human errors. The problem with a past version of HotCRP [11] shown in Fig. 1 is even more interesting: it describes a genuine confidentiality violation, probably stemming from the logic of the system, giving the authors capabilities to read confidential comments by the program committee (PC).

Although our methods would equally apply to integrity violations, guarding against confidentiality violations is the focus of this verification work. We verify properties such as the following (where DIS addresses the problem in Fig. 1):

PAP$_1$: A group of users learn nothing about a paper unless one of them becomes an author of that paper or a PC member at the paper's conference

PAP$_2$: A group of users learn nothing about a paper *beyond the last submitted version* unless one of them becomes an author of that paper

REV: A group of users learn nothing about the content of a review *beyond the last submitted version before the discussion phase and the later versions* unless one of them is that review's author

DIS: The authors learn nothing about the discussion of their paper

We will be concerned with properties restricting the information flow from the various documents maintained by the system (papers, reviews, comments, decisions) towards the users of the system. The restrictions refer to certain conditions (e.g., authorship, PC membership) as well as to upper bounds (e.g., at most the last submitted version) for information release.

We specify CoCon's kernel using the proof assistant Isabelle [29, 30], with which we formulate and verify confidentiality. The functional implementation of this kernel is automatically synthesized from the specification and wrapped into a web application offering the expected behavior of a conference system as a menu-based interface.

A first contribution of this paper is the engineering approach behind the system specification and implementation (§2). To keep the Isabelle specification (§3) manageable, yet faithful to the implementation and therefore reach a decent balance between trust and usability, we employ state-of-the-art theorem proving and code synthesis technology towards a security-preserving layered architecture.

A second contribution is a novel security model called *bounded-deducibility* (BD) security, born from confronting notions from the literature with the challenges posed by our system (§4). The result is a reusable framework, applicable to any IO automaton. Its main novelty is wide flexibility: it allows the precise formulation of role-based and time-based declassification triggers and of declassification upper bounds. We endow this framework with a declassification-oriented unwinding proof technique (§5).

Our third and last contribution is the verification itself: the BD security framework, its general unwinding theorem, and the unwinding proofs for CoCon's confidentiality properties expressed as instances of BD security are all mechanized in Isabelle.

2   Overall Architecture and Security Guarantees

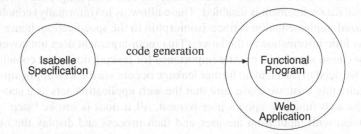

The architecture of our system follows the paradigm of security by design:

- We formalize and verify the kernel of the system in the Isabelle proof assistant
- The formalization is automatically translated in a functional programming language
- The translated program is wrapped in a web application

Isabelle Specification. We specify the system as an input–output automaton (Mealy machine), with the inputs called "actions". We first define, using Isabelle's records, the notions of state (holding information about users, conferences, and papers) and user action (representing user requests for manipulating documents and rights in the system: upload/download papers, edit reviews, assign reviewers, etc.). Then we define the step function that takes a state and an action and returns a new state and an output.

Scala Functional Program. The specification was designed to fall within the executable fragment of Isabelle. This allows us to automatically synthesize, using Isabelle's code generator [17], a program in the functional fragment of Scala [2] isomorphic to the specification. The types of data used in the specification (numbers, strings, tuples, records) are mapped to the corresponding Scala types. An exception is the Isabelle type of paper contents, which is mapped to the Scala/JVM file type.

Web Application. Finally, the Scala program is wrapped in a web application, offering a menu-based user interface. Upon login, a user sees his conferences and his roles for each of them; the menus offer role-sensitive choices, e.g., assign reviewers (for chairs) or upload papers (for authors).

Overall Security Guarantees. Our Isabelle verification targets information-flow properties. These properties express that for any possible trace of the system, there is no way to infer from certain observations on that trace (e.g., actions performed by designated users), certain values extracted from that trace (e.g., the paper uploads by other users). The question arises as to what guarantees we have that the properties we verified formally for the specification also hold for the overall system. E.g., if we prove in Isabelle that users never learn the content of other users' papers, how can we be sure that this is actually the case when using the web interface? We do not have a formal answer to this, but only an informal argument in terms of the trustworthiness of two trusted steps.

First, we need to trust Isabelle's code generator. Its general-purpose design is very flexible, supporting program and data refinement [17]. In the presence of these rich features, the code generator is only known to preserve partial correctness, hence safety properties [16, 17]. However, here we use the code generator in a very restrictive manner, to "refine" an already deterministic specification which is an implementation in its own right—the code generator simply translates it from the functional language of Isabelle to that of Scala. In addition, all the used Isabelle functions are proved to terminate, and nontrivial data refinement is disabled. These allow us to (informally) conclude that the synthesized implementation is trace-isomorphic to the specification, hence the former leaks as little information as the latter. (This meta-argument does not cover timing channels, but these seem to be of little importance for leaking document content.)

Second, we need to trust that no further leakage occurs via the web application wrapper. To acquire this trust, we make sure that the web application acts as a stateless interface to the step function: upon a user request, all it does is invoke "step" (one or multiple times) with input from the user and then process and display the output of the step function. The third-party libraries used by our web application also have to be trusted to not be vulnerable to exploits.

In summary, the formal guarantees we provide in Isabelle have to be combined with a few trusted steps to apply to the whole system. Our verification targets only the system's implementation logic—lower-level attacks such as browser-level forging are out of its reach, but are orthogonal issues that could in principle be mitigated separately.

3   System Specification

The system behaves similarly to EasyChair [10], a popular conference system created by Andrei Voronkov. It hosts multiple users and conferences, allowing the creation of new users and conferences at any time. The system has a superuser, which we call *voronkov* as a tribute to EasyChair. The voronkov is the first user of the system, and his role is to approve new-conference requests. A conference goes through several phases.

No-Phase. Any user can apply for a new conference, with the effect of registering it in the system with "No-Phase". After approval from the voronkov, the conference moves to the setup phase, with the applicant becoming a conference chair.

Setup. A conference chair can add new chairs and new regular PC members. From here on, moving the conference to successor phases can be done by the chairs.

Submission. A user can list the conferences awaiting submissions (i.e., being in submission phase). He can submit a paper, upload new versions, or indicate other users as coauthors thereby granting them reading and editing rights.

Bidding. Authors are no longer allowed to upload or register new papers and PC members are allowed to view the submitted papers. PC members can place bids, indicating for each paper one of the following preferences: "want to review", "would review", "no preference", "would not review", and "conflict". If the preference is "conflict", the PC member cannot be assigned that paper, and will not see its discussion. "Conflict" is assigned automatically to papers authored by a PC member.

Reviewing. Chairs can assign papers to PC members for reviewing either manually or by invoking an external program to establish fair assignment based on some parameters: preferences, number of papers per PC member, and number of reviewers per paper.

Discussion. All PC members having no conflict with a paper can see its reviews and can add comments. Also, chairs can edit the decision.

Notification. The authors can read the reviews and the accept/reject decision, which no one can edit any longer.

3.1   State, Actions, and Step Function

The state stores the lists of registered conference, user, and paper IDs and, for each ID, actual conference, user, or paper information. Each paper ID is assigned a paper having title, abstract, content, and, in due time, a list of reviews, a discussion text, and a decision: Paper $=$ String $\times$ String $\times$ Paper_Content $\times$ List(Review) $\times$ Dis $\times$ Dec

We keep different versions of the decision and of each review, as they may transparently change during discussion: Dec $=$ List(String) and Review $=$ List(Review_Content) where Review_Content consists of triples (expertise, text, score).

In addition, the state stores: for each conference, the list of (IDs of) papers submitted to that conference, the list of news updated by the chairs, and the current phase; for each user and paper, the preferences resulted from biddings; for each user and conference, a list of roles: chair, PC member, paper author, or paper reviewer (the last two roles also containing paper IDs).

record State $=$

conflDs : List(ConflD)   conf : ConflD $\rightarrow$ Conf   userlDs : List(UserID)

pass : UserID $\rightarrow$ Pass   user : UserID $\rightarrow$ User   roles : ConflD $\rightarrow$ UserID $\rightarrow$ List(Role)

paperlDs : ConflD $\rightarrow$ List(PaperID)   paper : PaperID $\rightarrow$ Paper

pref : UserID $\rightarrow$ PaperID $\rightarrow$ Pref   news : ConflD $\rightarrow$ List(String)   phase : ConflD $\rightarrow$ Phase

Actions are parameterized by user IDs and passwords. There are 45 actions forming five categories: creation, update, undestructive update (u-update), reading and listing.

The **creation actions** register new objects (users, conferences, chairs, PC members, papers, authors), assign reviewers (by registering new review objects), and declare conflicts. E.g., cPaper *cid uid pw pid title abs* is an action by user *uid* with password *pw* attempting to register to conference *cid* a new paper *pid* with indicated title and abstract.

The **update actions** modify the various documents of the system: user information and password, paper content, reviewing preference, review content, etc. For example, uPaperC *cid uid pw pid ct* is an attempt to upload a new version of paper *pid* by modifying its content to *ct*. The **u-update actions** are similar, but also record the history of a document's versions. E.g., if a reviewer decides to change his review during the discussion phase, then the previous version is still stored in the system and visible to the other PC members (although never to the authors). Other documents subject to u-updates are the news, the discussion, and the accept-reject decision.

The **reading actions** access the content of the system's documents: papers, reviews, comments, decisions, news. The **listing actions** produce lists of IDs satisfying various filters—e.g., all conferences awaiting paper submissions, all PC members of a conference, all the papers submitted by a given user, etc.

Note that the first three categories of actions are aimed at *modifying* the state, and the last two are aimed at *observing* the state through outputs. However, the modification actions also produce a simple output, since they may succeed or fail. Moreover, the observation actions can also be seen as changing the state to itself. Therefore we can assume that both types produce a pair consisting of a new state and an action.

We define the function step : State $\rightarrow$ Act $\rightarrow$ Out $\times$ State that operates by determining the type of the action and dispatching specialized handler functions. The initial state of the system, istate $\in$ State, is the one with a single user, the voronkov, and a dummy password (which can be changed immediately). The step function and the initial state are the only items exported by our specification to the outside world.

4   Security Model

Here we first analyze the literature for possible inspiration concerning a suitable security model for our system. Then we introduce our own notion, which is an extension of Sutherland's nondeducibility [38] that factors in declassification triggers and bounds.

4.1   Relevant Literature

There is a vast amount of literature on information-flow security, with many variants of formalisms and verification techniques. An important distinction is between notions that completely forbid information flow (between designated sources and sinks) and notions that only restrict the flow, allowing some declassification. Historically, the former were introduced first, and the latter were subsequently introduced as generalizations.

Absence of Information Flow. The information-flow security literature starts in the late 1970s and early 1980s [7, 13, 32], motivated by the desire to express the absence of information leaks of systems more abstractly and more precisely than by means of access control [4, 21]. Very influential were Goguen and Meseguer's notion of noninterference [13] and its associated proof by unwinding [14]. Unwinding is essentially a form of simulation that allows one to construct incrementally, from a perturbed trace of the system, an alternative "corrected" trace that "closes the leak". Many other notions were introduced subsequently, either in specialized programming-language-based [36] or process-algebra-based [12,35] settings or in purely semantic, event-system-based settings [25,26,31,38]. (Here we are mostly interested in the last category.) These notions are aimed at extending noninterference to nondeterministic systems, closing Trojan-horse channels, or achieving compositionality. The unwinding technique has been generalized for some of these variants—McLean [27] and Mantel [23] give overviews.

Even ignoring our aimed declassification aspect, most of these notions do not adequately model our properties of interest exemplified in the introduction. One problem is that they are not flexible enough w.r.t. the observations. They state nondetectability of absence or occurrence of certain events anywhere in a system trace. By contrast, we are interested in a very controlled positioning of such undetectable events: in the property PAP_2 from the introduction, the unauthorized user should not learn of preliminary (non-final) uploads of a paper. Moreover, we are not interested in whole events, but rather in certain relevant values extracted from the events: e.g., the content of the paper, and not the ID of one of the particular authors who uploads it.

A fortunate exception to the above flexibility problems is Sutherland's early notion of *nondeducibility* [38]. One considers a set of worlds World and two functions $F :$ World $\to J$ and $H :$ World $\to K$. For example, the worlds could be the valid traces of the system, F could select the actions of certain users (potential attackers), and H could select the actions of other users (intended as being secret). *Nondeducibility of H from F* says that the following holds for all $w \in$ World: for all k in the image of H, there exists $w_1 \in$ World such that $F\ w_1 = F\ w$ and $H\ w_1 = k$. Intuitively, from what the attacker (modeled as F) knows about the actual world w, the secret actions (the value of H) could be anything (in the image of H)—hence cannot be "deduced". The generality of this framework allows one to fine-tune both the location of the relevant events in the trace and their values of interest. But generality is no free lunch: it is no longer clear how to provide an unwinding-like incremental proof method.

Halpern and O'Neill [18] recast nondeducibility as a property called secrecy maintenance, in a multi-agent framework of "runs-and-systems" [33] based on epistemic logic. Their formulation enables general-purpose epistemic logic primitives for deducing absence of leaks, but no unwinding or any other inductive reasoning technique.

On the practical verification side, Arapinis et al. [3] introduce ConfiChair, a conference system that improves on standard systems such as EasyChair by guaranteeing that "the cloud", consisting of the system provider/administrator, cannot learn the content of the papers and reviews and cannot link users with their written reviews. This is achieved by a cryptographic protocol based on key translations and mixes. They encode the desired properties as strong secrecy (a property similar to Goguen-Meseguer noninterference) and verify them using the ProVerif [5] tool specialized in security protocols. Our work differs from theirs in three major aspects. First, they propose a cryptography-based enhancement, while we focus on a traditional conference systems not involving cryptography. Second, they manage to encode and verify the desired properties automatically, while we use interactive theorem proving. While their automatic verification is an impressive achievement, we cannot hope for the same with our targeted properties which, while having a similar nature, are more nuanced and complex. E.g., properties like PAP_2 and REV, with such flexible indications of declassification bounds, go far beyond strong secrecy and require interactive verification. Finally, we synthesize functional code isomorphic to the specification, whereas they provide a separate implementation, not linked to the specification which abstracts away from many functionality aspects.

Restriction of Information Flow. A large body of work on declassification was pursued in a language-based setting. Sabelfeld and Sands [37] give an overview of the state of the art up to 2009. Although they target language-based declassification, they phrase some generic dimensions of declassification most of which apply to our case:

- What information is released? Here, document content, e.g., of papers, reviews, etc.
- Where in the system is information released? In our case, the relevant "where" is a "from where" (referring to the source, not to the exit point): from selected places in the system trace, e.g., the last submitted version before the deadline.
- When can information be released? After a certain trigger occurs, e.g., authorship.

Sabelfeld and Sands consider another interesting instance of the "where" dimension, namely intransitive noninterference [22, 34]. This is an extension of noninterference that allows downgrading of information, say, from High to Low, via a controlled Declassifier level. It could be possible to encode aspects of our properties of interest as intransitive noninterference—e.g., we could encode the act of a user becoming an author as a declassifying action for the target paper. However, such an encoding would be rather technical and somewhat artificial for our system; additionally, it is not clear how to factor in our aforementioned specific "where" dimension.

Recently, the "when" aspect of declassification has been included as first-class citizen in customized temporal logics [6, 9], which can express aspects of our desired properties, e.g., "unless/until he becomes an author". Their work is focused on efficiently model-checking finite systems, whereas we are interested in verifying an infinite system. Combining model checking with infinite-to-finite abstraction is an interesting prospect, but reflecting information-flow security properties under abstraction is difficult problem.

4.2 Bounded-Deducibility Security

We introduce a novel notion of information-flow security that:

- retains the precision and versatility of nondeducibility
- factors in declassification as required by our motivating examples
- is amenable to a general unwinding technique

We shall formulate security in general, not only for our concrete system from §3.1, but for any IO automaton indicated by the following data. We fix sets of states, State, actions, Act, and outputs, Out, an initial state istate $\in$ State, and a step function step : State $\to$ Act $\to$ Out $\times$ State. We let Trans, the set of *transitions*, be State $\times$ Act $\times$ Out $\times$ State. Thus, a transition *trn* is a tuple, written (s, a, o, s'); s indicates the source, a the action, o the output, and s' the target. *trn* is called valid if it is induced by the step function, namely step $s\ a = (o, s')$.

A *trace tr* $\in$ Trace is any list of transitions: Trace = List (Trans). For any $s \in$ State, the set of valid traces starting in s, Valid$_s \subseteq$ Trace, consists of the traces of the form $[(s_1, a_1, o_1, s_2), (s_2, a_2, o_2, s_3), \ldots, (s_{n-1}, a_{n-1}, o_n, s_n)]$ for some n where $s_1 = s$ and each transition (s_i, a_i, o_i, s_i) is valid. We will be interested in the valid traces starting in the initial state istate—we simply call these *valid traces* and write Valid for Valid$_{istate}$.

Besides the IO automaton, we assume that we are given the following data:

- a *value domain* Val, together with a *value filter* φ : Trans $\to$ Bool and a *value producer f* : Trans $\to$ Val
- an *observation domain* Obs, together with an *observation filter* γ : Trans $\to$ Bool and an *observation producer g* : Trans $\to$ Obs

We define the *value function* V : Trace $\to$ List(Val) componentwise, filtering out values not satisfying φ and applying f:

$$V\ [] \equiv [] \qquad\qquad V([trn] \cdot tr) \equiv \text{if } \varphi\ trn \text{ then } (f\ trn) \cdot (V\ tr) \text{ else } V\ tr$$

We also define the *observation function* O : Trace $\to$ List(Obs) just like V, but using γ as a filter and g as a producer.

We think of the above as an instantiation of the abstract framework for nondeducibility recalled in §4.1, where World = Valid, $F = $ O, and $H = $ V. Thus, nondeducibility states that the observer O may learn nothing about V. Here we are concerned with a more fine-grained analysis, asking ourselves *what* may the observer O learn about V.

Using the idea underlying nondeducibility, we can answer this precisely: Given a trace $tr \in$ Valid, the observer sees O tr and therefore can infer that V tr belongs to the set of all values V tr_1 for some $tr_1 \in$ Valid such that O $tr_1 = $ O tr. In other words, he can infer that the value is in the set V $(O^{-1}(O\ tr) \cap \text{Valid})$, and nothing beyond this. We call this set the *declassification* associated to tr, written Dec$_{tr}$.

We want to establish, under certain conditions, *upper* bounds for declassification, or in set-theoretic terms, *lower* bounds for Dec$_{tr}$. To this end, we further fix:

- a *declassification bound* B : List(Val) $\to$ List(Val) $\to$ Bool
- a *declassification trigger* T : Trans $\to$ Bool

The system is called *bounded-deducibility-secure* (*BD-secure*) if for all $tr \in$ Trace such that never T tr, it holds that $\{vl_1 \mid$ B (V tr) $vl_1\} \subseteq$ Dec$_{tr}$ (where "never T tr" means "T holds for no transition in tr"). Informally, BD security expresses the following:

If the trigger T *never holds (i.e., unless* T *eventually holds, i.e., until* T *holds),*
the observer O *can learn nothing about the values* V *beyond* B

We can think of B positively, as an upper bound for declassification, or negatively, as a lower bound for uncertainty. On the other hand, T is a trigger removing the bound B— as soon as T becomes true, the containment of declassification is no longer guaranteed. In the extreme case of B being everywhere true and T everywhere false, we have no declassification, i.e., total uncertainty—in other words, standard nondeducibility.

Unfolding some definitions, we can alternatively express BD security as the following being true for all $tr \in$ Valid and $vl, vl_1 \in$ List(Val):

$$\text{never } T \ tr \wedge V \ tr = vl \wedge B \ vl \ vl_1 \rightarrow (\exists tr_1 \in \text{Valid}. \ O \ tr_1 = O \ tr \wedge V \ tr_1 = vl_1) \quad (*)$$

4.3 Discussion

BD security is a natural extension of nondeducibility. If one considers the latter as reasonably expressing the *absence* of information leak, then one is likely to accept the former as a reasonable means to indicate *bounds* on the leak. Unlike previous notions in the literature, BD security allows to express the bounds *as precisely as desired*.

As an extension of nondeducibility, BD security is subject to the same criticism. The problem with nondeducibility [25, 27, 35] is that in some cases it is too weak, since it takes as *plausible* each possible explanation for an observation: if the observation sequence is *ol*, then any trace *tr* such that O *tr* = *vl* is plausible. But what if the low-level observers can synchronize their actions and observations with the actions of other entities, such as a high-level user or a Trojan horse acting on his behalf, or even a third-party entity that is neither high nor low? Even without synchronization, the low-level observer may learn from outside the system, of certain behavior patterns of the high-level users. Then the set of plausible explanations can be reduced, leading to information leak.

In our case, the low-level observers are a group of users assumed to never acquire a certain status (e.g., authorship of a paper). The other users of the system are either "high-level" (e.g., the authors of the paper) or "third-party" (e.g., the non-author users not in the group of observers). Concerning the high-level users, it does not make sense to assume that they would cooperate to leak information *through the system*, since they certainly have better means to do that outside the system, e.g., via email. Users also do not have to trust external software, since everything is filtered through the system kernel—e.g., a chair can run an external linear-programming tool for assigning reviewers, but each assignment is still done through the verified step function. As for the possible third-party cooperation towards leaks of information, this is bypassed by our consideration of arbitrary groups of observers: in the worst case, all the unauthorized users can be placed in this group. However, the possibility to learn and exploit behavior patterns from outside the system is not explicitly addressed by BD security—it would be best dealt with by a probabilistic analysis.

4.4 Instantiation to Our Running Examples

Recall that BD security involves the following parameters:
- an IO automaton (State, Act, Out, istate, step)
- infrastructures for values (Val, φ, f) and observations (Obs, γ, g)
- a declassification specification: trigger T and bound B

In particular, this applies to our conference system automaton. BD security then captures our examples by suitably instantiating the observation and declassification parameters. For all our examples, we have the same observation infrastructure. We fix UIDs, the set of IDs of the observing users. We let Obs = Act × Out. Given a transition, γ holds iff the action's subject is a user in UIDs, and g returns the pair (action,output). O tr thus purges tr keeping only actions of users in UIDs.

The value infrastructure depends on the considered type of document. For PAP_1 and PAP_2 we fix PID, the ID of the paper of interest. We let Val = List(Paper_Content). Given a transition, φ holds iff the action is an upload of paper PID, and f returns the uploaded content. V tr thus returns the list of all uploaded paper contents for PID.

The declassification triggers and bounds are specific to each example. For PAP_1, we define $T(s, a, o, s')$ as "in state s', some user in UIDs is an author of PID or a PC member of some conference cid where PID is registered," formally:

$$\exists uid \in \text{UIDs. isAut } s' \text{ } uid \text{ PID } \vee (\exists cid. \text{ PID} \in \text{paperIDs } s' \text{ } cid \wedge \text{isPC } s' \text{ } uid \text{ } cid)$$

Intuitively, the intent with PAP_1 is that, provided T never holds, users in UIDs learn nothing about the various consecutive versions of PID. But is it true that they can learn *absolutely nothing*? There is a remote possibility that a user could infer that no version was submitted (by probing the current phases of the conferences in the system and noticing that none has reached the submission phase). But indeed, nothing beyond this quite harmless information should leak: any nonempty value sequence vl might as well have been any other (possibly empty!) sequence vl_1. Hence we define B vl vl_1 as $vl \neq []$.

For PAP_2, the trigger involves only authorship, ignoring PC membership at the paper's conference—we take $T(s, a, o, s')$ to be $\exists uid \in \text{UIDs. isAut } s' \text{ } uid \text{ PID}$. Here we have a genuine example of nontrivial declassification bound—since a PC member can learn the paper's content but only as its last submitted version, we define B vl vl_1 as $vl \neq [] \neq vl_1 \wedge \text{last } vl = \text{last } vl_1$, where the function last returns the last element of a list.

For REV, the value infrastructure refers not only to the review's content but also to the conference phase: Val = List (Phase × Review_Content). The functions φ and f are defined similarly to those for paper contents, mutatis mutandis; in particular, f returns a pair (ph, rct) consisting of the conference's current phase and the updated review's content; hence V returns a list of such pairs. The trigger T is similar to that of PAP_2 but refers to review authorship rather than paper authorship. The bound B is more complex. Any user can infer that the only possiblities for the phase are Reviewing and Discussion, in this order—i.e., that vl has the form $ul \cdot wl$ such that the pairs in ul have Reviewing as first component and the pairs in wl have Discussion. Moreover, any PC member having no conflict with PID can learn last ul (the last submitted version before Discussion), and wl (the versions updated during Discussion, public to non-conflict PC members); but (until T holds) nothing beyond these. So B vl vl_1 states that vl decomposes as $ul \cdot wl$ as indicated above, vl_1 decomposes similarly as $ul_1 \cdot wl$, and last $ul = \text{last } ul_1$.

DIS needs rephrasing to be captured as BD security. It can be decomposed into:

DIS_1: An author always has conflict with his papers

DIS_2: A group of users learn nothing about a paper's discussion unless one of them becomes a PC member at the paper's conference *having no conflict with the paper*

DIS_1 is a safety property. DIS_2 is an instance of BD security defined as expected.

	Source	Declassification Trigger	Declassification Bound
1	Paper Content	Paper Authorship	Last Uploaded Version
2		Paper Authorship or PC Membership^B	Absence of Any Upload
3	Review	Review Authorship	Last Edited Version Before Discussion and All the Later Versions
4		Review Authorship or Non-Conflict PC Membership^D	Last Edited Version Before Notification
5		Review Authorship or Non-Conflict PC Membership^D or PC Membership^N or Paper Authorship^N	Absence of Any Edit
6	Discussion	Non-Conflict PC Membership	Absence of Any Edit
7	Decision	Non-Conflict PC Membership	Last Edited Version
8		Non-Conflict PC Membership or PC Membership^N or Paper Authorship^N	Absence of Any Edit
9	Reviewer Assignment	Non-Conflict PC Membership^R	Non-Conflict PC Membership of Reviewers and No. of Reviews
10		Non-Conflict PC Membership^R or Paper Authorship^N	Non-Conflict PC Membership of Reviewers

Phase Stamps: B = Bidding, D = Discussion, N = Notification, R = Review

4.5 More Instances

The above table shows an array of confidentiality properties formulated as BD security. They provide a classification of relevant roles, statuses and conference phases that are necessary conditions for degrees of information release. The observation infrastructure is always the same, given by the actions and outputs of a fixed group of users as in §4.4.

The table lists several information sources, each yielding a different value infrastructure. In rows 1–8, the sources are actual documents: paper content, review, discussion, decision. The properties PAP_1, PAP_2, REV and DIS_2 form the rows 2, 1, 3, and 6. In rows 9 and 10, the sources are the identities of the reviewers assigned to the paper.

The declassification triggers express paper or review authorship (being or becoming an author of the indicated document) or PC membership at the paper's conference, with or without the requirement of lack of conflict with the paper. Some triggers are also listed with "phase stamps" that strengthens the statements. E.g., row 2 contains a strengthening of the trigger discussed so far for PAP_1: "PC membership^B" should be read as "PC membership and paper's conference phase being at least bidding." Some of the triggers require lack of conflict with the paper, which is often important for the security statement to be strong enough. This is the case of DIS_2 (row 6), since without the non-conflict assumption DIS_2 and DIS_1 would no longer imply DIS. By contrast, lack of conflict cannot be added to PC membership in PAP_1 (row 2), since such a stronger version would not hold: even if a PC member decides to indicate conflict with a paper, this happens after he had the opportunity to see the paper's content.

Most of the declassification bounds are similar to those from §4.4. The row 10 property states that, unless one becomes a PC member having no conflict with a paper in the reviewing phase or a paper's author in the notification phase, one can't learn anything about the paper's assigned reviewers beyond what everyone knows: that reviewers are non-conflict PC members. If we remove the non-authorship restriction, then the user may also infer the number of reviewers—but, as row 9 states, nothing beyond this.

5 Verification

To cope with general declassification bounds, BD security speaks about system traces in conjunction with value sequences that must be produced by these traces. We extend the unwinding proof technique to this situation and employ the result to the verification of our confidentiality properties.

5.1 Unwinding Proof Method

We see from definition (∗) that to prove BD security, one starts with a valid tr (starting in s and having value sequence vl) and an "alternative" value sequence vl_1 such that B vl vl_1 and one needs to produce an "alternative" trace tr_1 starting in s whose value sequence is vl_1 and whose observation sequence is the same as that of tr.

In the tradition of unwinding for noninterference [14, 34], we wish to construct tr_1 from tr *incrementally*: as tr grows, tr_1 should grow nearly synchronously. In order for tr_1 to have the same observation sequence (produced by O) as tr, we need to require that the observable transitions of tr_1 (i.e., for which γ holds) be *identical* to those of tr.

As for the value sequences (produced by V), we face the following problem. In contrast to the unwinding relations studied so far in the literature, we must consider an additional parameter, namely the *a priori given* value sequence vl_1 that needs to be produced by tr_1. In fact, it appears that one would need to maintain, besides an unwinding relation on states θ : State $\to$ State $\to$ Bool, also an "evolving" generalization of the declassification trigger B; then θ and B would certainly need to be synchronized. We resolve this by enlarging the domain of the unwindings to quaternary relations Δ : State $\to$ List(Val) $\to$ State $\to$ List(Val) $\to$ Bool that generalize both θ and B. Intuitively, Δ s vl s_1 vl_1 keeps track of the current state of tr, the remaining value sequence of tr, the current state of tr_1, and the remaining value sequence of tr_1.

Let the predicate consume trn vl vl' mean that the transition trn either produces a value that is consumed from vl yielding vl' or produces no value and $vl = vl'$. Formally:

$$\text{if } \varphi \text{ } trn \text{ then } (vl \neq [] \wedge f \text{ } trn = \text{head } vl \wedge vl' = \text{tail } vl) \text{ else } (vl' = vl)$$

In light of the above discussion, we are tempted to define an unwinding as a relation Δ such that Δ s vl s_1 vl_1 implies *either* of the following conditions:

- REACTION: For any valid transition (s, a, o, s') and lists of values vl, vl' such that consume (s, a, o, s') vl vl' holds, either of the following holds:
  - IGNORE: The transition yields no observation ($\neg \gamma \, a \, o$) and Δ s' vl' s_1 vl_1 holds
  - MATCH: There exist a valid transition (s_1, a_1, o_1, s_1') and a list of values vl_1' such that consume (s, a, o, s') vl_1 vl_1' and Δ s_1 vl' s_1' vl_1' hold
- INDEPENDENT ACTION: There exist a valid transition (s_1, a_1, o_1, s_1') that yields no observation ($\neg \gamma \, a_1 \, o_1$) and a list of values vl_1' such that consume $a_1 \, o_1 \, vl_1 \, vl_1'$ and Δ s vl s_1' vl_1' hold

The intent is that BD security should hold if there exists an unwinding Δ that "initially includes" B. A trace tr_1 could then be constructed incrementally from tr, vl and vl_1, applying REACTION or INDEPENDENT ACTION until the three lists become empty.

Progress. However, such an argument faces difficulties. First, INDEPENDENT ACTION is not guaranteed to decrease any of the lists. To address this, we strengthen INDEPENDENT ACTION by adding the requirement that $\varphi\,(s_1, a_1, o_1, s_1')$ holds—this ensures that vl_1 decreases (i.e., vl_1' is strictly shorter then vl_1). This way, we know that each RE-ACTION and INDEPENDENT ACTION decreases at least one list: the former tr and the latter vl_1; and since vl is empty whenever tr is, the progress problem seems resolved.

Yet, there is a second, more subtle difficulty: after tr has become empty, how can we know that vl_1 will start decreasing? With the restrictions so far, one may still choose REACTION with parameters that leave vl_1 unaffected. So we need to make sure that the following implication holds: if $tr = []$ and $vl_1 \neq []$, then vl_1 will be consumed. Since from inside the unwinding relation we cannot (and do not want to!) see tr, but only vl, we weaken the assumption of this implication to "if $vl = []$ and $vl_1 \neq []$;" more-over, we strengthen its conclusion to requiring that only the INDEPENDENT ACTION choice (guaranteed to shorten vl_1) be available. Equivalently, we condition the alternative choice of REACTION by the negation of the above, namely $vl \neq [] \lor vl_1 = []$.

Exit Condition. The third observation is not concerned with a difficulty, but with an optimization. We note that BD security holds trivially if the original trace tr cannot saturate the value list vl, i.e., if $V\,tr \neq vl$—this happens if and only if, at some point, an element v of vl can no longer be saturated, i.e., for some decompositions $tr = tr' \cdot tr''$ and $vl = vl' \cdot [v] \cdot vl''$ of tr and vl, it holds that $V\,tr' = vl'$ and $\forall trn \in tr''.\,\varphi\,trn \rightarrow f\,trn \neq v$. Can we detect such a situation from within Δ? The answer is (an over-approximated) yes: after $\Delta\,s\,vl\,s_1\,vl_1$ evolves by REACTION and INDEPENDENT ACTION to $\Delta\,s'\,([v] \cdot vl'')\,s_1'\,vl_1'$ for some s', s_1' and vl_1' (presumably consuming tr' and saturating the vl' prefix of vl), then one can safely exit the game if one proves that no valid trace tr'' starting from s' can ever saturate v, in that it satisfies $\forall trn \in tr''.\,\varphi\,trn \rightarrow f\,trn \neq v$.

The final definition of BD unwinding is given below, where reach : State $\rightarrow$ Bool is the state reachability predicate and reach $_{\neg T}$: State $\rightarrow$ Bool is its strengthening to reachability by transitions that do not satisfy T:

$$\text{unwind}\,\Delta \;\equiv\; \forall s\,vl\,s_1\,vl_1.\,\text{reach}_{\neg T}\,s \,\wedge\, \text{reach}\,s_1 \,\wedge\, \Delta\,s\,vl\,s_1\,vl_1 \,\rightarrow$$
$$((vl \neq [] \,\vee\, vl_1 = []) \,\wedge\, \text{reaction}\,\Delta\,s\,s\,vl\,s_1\,vl_1) \,\vee$$
$$\text{iaction}\,\Delta\,s\,s\,vl\,s_1\,vl_1 \,\vee$$
$$(vl \neq [] \,\wedge\, \text{exit}\,s\,(\text{head}\,vl))$$

The predicates iaction and reaction formalize INDEPENDENT ACTION (with its afore-mentioned strengthening) and REACTION, the latter being a disjunction of predicates formalizing IGNORE and MATCH. The predicate exit $s\,v$ is defined as $\forall\,tr\,trn.\,(tr \cdot [trn]) \in \text{Valid}_s \,\wedge\, \varphi\,trn \rightarrow f\,trn \neq v$. It expresses a safety property, and therefore can be verified in a trace-free manner. We can now prove that indeed any unwinding relation constructs an "alternative" trace tr_1 from any trace tr starting in a P-reachable state:

Lemma. unwind $\Delta \,\wedge\, \text{reach}_{\neg T}\,s \,\wedge\, \text{reach}\,s_1 \,\wedge\, \Delta\,s\,vl\,s_1\,vl_1 \,\wedge\, tr \in \text{Valid}_s \,\wedge\, \text{never}\,T\,tr \,\wedge\, V\,tr = vl \,\rightarrow\, (\exists tr_1.\,tr_1 \in \text{Valid}_{s_1} \,\wedge\, O\,tr_1 = O\,tr \,\wedge\, V\,tr_1 = vl_1)$

Unwinding Theorem. If unwind Δ and $\forall vl\,vl_1.\,\text{B}\,vl\,vl_1 \rightarrow \Delta$ istate vl istate vl_1, then the system is BD-secure.

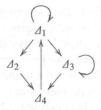

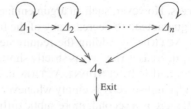

Fig. 3. A network of unwinding components   Fig. 4. A linear network with exit

Proof ideas. The lemma follows by induction on length tr + length vl_1 (as discussed above about progress). The theorem follows from the lemma taking $s_1 = s = $ istate.

According to the theorem, BD unwinding is a *sound proof method for BD security*: to check BD security it suffices to define a relation Δ and prove that it coincides with B on the initial state and that it is a BD unwinding.

5.2 Compositional Reasoning

To keep each reasoning step manageable, it is convenient to allow decomposing the single unwinding relation Δ into relations $\Delta_1, \ldots, \Delta_n$. Unlike Δ, a component Δ_i may unwind not only to itself but to any combination of Δ_j's. Technically, we define the predicate unwind_to just like unwind but taking two arguments instead of one: a first relation and a second relation to which the first one unwinds. We replace the single requirement unwind Δ with a set of requirements unwind_to Δ_i (disj (next Δ_i)), where next Δ_i is a chosen subset of $\{\Delta_1, \ldots, \Delta_n\}$ and disj takes the disjunction of a set of predicates. This enables a form of sound compositional reasoning: if we verify a condition as above for each component Δ_i, we obtain an overall unwinding relation disj $\{\Delta_1, \ldots, \Delta_n\}$.

The network of components can form any directed graph —Fig. 3 shows an example. However, our unwinding proofs will be phase-directed, and hence the following linear network will suffice (Fig. 4): each Δ_i unwinds either to itself, or to Δ_{i+1} (if $i \neq n$), or to an exit component Δ_e that invariably chooses the "exit" unwinding condition. For the first component, Δ_1, we need to verify that it extends B on the initial state.

5.3 Verification of Concrete Instances

We have verified all the BD security instances listed in §4.5. For each of them we defined a suitable chain of unwinding components Δ_i as in Fig. 4.

Recall from the definition of BD security that one needs to construct an alternative trace tr_1 (which produces the value sequence vl_1) from the original trace tr (which produces the value sequence vl). A chain of Δ_i's witnesses the strategy for such a construction, although it does not record the whole traces tr_1 and tr but only the states they have reached so far, s and s_1. The separation between Δ_i's is guided by milestones in the journey of tr and tr_1, such as: a paper's registration to a conference, conference phases, the registration of a relevant agent like a chair, a non-conflicted PC member, or a reviewer. E.g., Fig. 5 shows the unwinding components in the proof of PAP$_2$, where B vl vl_1 is the declassification bound ($vl \neq [] \neq vl_1 \wedge$ last $vl = $ last vl_1) and the changes from Δ_i to Δ_{i+1} are emphasized.

$\Delta_1\ s\ vl\ s_1\ vl_1$	$\neg\,(\exists cid.\ \mathsf{PID} \in \mathsf{paperIDs}\ s\ cid)\ \wedge\ s = s_1\ \wedge\ \mathsf{B}\ vl\ vl_1$
$\Delta_2\ s\ vl\ s_1\ vl_1$	$(\exists cid.\ \mathsf{PID} \in \mathsf{paperIDs}\ s\ cid\ \wedge\ \mathsf{phase}\ s\ cid = \mathsf{Submission}\ )\wedge\ s =_{\mathsf{PID}} s_1\ \wedge \mathsf{B}\ vl\ vl_1$
$\Delta_3\ s\ vl\ s_1\ vl_1$	$(\exists cid.\ \mathsf{PID} \in \mathsf{paperIDs}\ s\ cid)\ \wedge\ s = s_1\ \wedge\ vl = vl_1 = []$
$\Delta_{\mathsf{e}}\ s\ vl\ s_1\ vl_1$	$(\exists cid.\ \mathsf{PID} \in \mathsf{paperIDs}\ s\ cid\ \wedge\ \mathsf{phase}\ s\ cid > \mathsf{Submission})\ \wedge\ vl \neq []$

Fig. 5. The unwinding components for the proof of PAP_2

Each property has one or more critical phases, the only phases when vl and vl_1 can be produced. E.g., for PAP_2, paper uploading is only available in Submission (while for REV, there is an update action in Reviewing, and an u-update one in Discussion). Until those phases, tr_1 proceeds synchronously to tr taking the same actions—consequently, the states s and s_1 are equal in Δ_1. In the critical phases, the traces tr and tr_1 will diverge, due to the need of producing different (but B-related) value sequences. As a result, the equality between s and s_1 is replaced with the weaker relation of *equality everywhere except on certain components of the state*, e.g., the content of a given paper (written $=_{\mathsf{PID}}$ for PAP_2), or of a given review, or of the previous versions of a given review, etc.

At the end of the critical phases, tr_1 will usually need to resynchronize with tr and hereafter proceed with identical actions. Consequently, s and s_1 will become connected by a stronger "equality everywhere except" relation or even plain equality again. The smooth transition between consecutive components Δ_i and Δ_{i+1} that impose different state equalities is ensured by a suitable INDEPENDENT-ACTION/REACTION strategy. For PAP_2, such a strategy for transitioning from Δ_2 to Δ_3 (with emptying vl and vl_1 at the same time) is the following: by INDEPENDENT ACTION, tr_1 will produce all values in vl_1 save for the last one, which will be produced by REACTION in sync with tr when tr reaches the last value in vl; this is possible since B guarantees last $vl =$ last vl_1. The exit component Δ_{e} witnesses situations (s, vl) not producible from any system trace tr in order to exclude them via Exit. For PAP_2, such a situation is the paper's conference phase exceeding Submission with values vl still to be produced. Δ_{e} is reached from Δ_2 when a change-phase action occurs.

Several safety properties are needed in the unwinding proofs. For PAP_2, we use that there is at most one conference to which a paper can be registered—this ensures that no value can be produced (i.e., φ (head vl) does not hold) from within Δ_1 or Δ_2, since no paper upload is possible without prior registration.

The verification took us two person months, during which we also developed reusable proof infrastructure and automation. Eventually, we could prove the auxiliary safety properties automatically. The unwinding proofs still required some interaction for indicating the INDEPENDENT-ACTION/REACTION strategy—we are currently exploring the prospect of fully automating the strategy part too, based on a suitable security-preserving abstraction in conjunction with an external model checker.

Conclusion. Most of the information-flow security models proposed by theoreticians have not been confronted with the complexity of a realistic application, and therefore fail to address, or abstract away from, important aspects of the conditions for information release or restraint. In our verification case study, we approached the problem bottom-up: we faithfully formalized a realistic system, on which we identified, formulated and verified confidentiality properties. This experience led to the design of a flexible verification infrastructure for restricted information flow in IO automata.

Acknowledgement. Tobias Nipkow encouraged us to pursue this work. Several people made helpful comments and/or indicated related work: the CAV reviewers, Jasmin Blanchette, Manuel Eberl, Lars Hupel, Fabian Immler, Steffen Lortz, Giuliano Losa, Tobias Nipkow, Benedikt Nordhoff, Martin Ochoa, Markus Rabe, and Dmitriy Traytel. The research was supported by the DFG project Security Type Systems and Deduction (grant Ni 491/13-2), part of Reliably Secure Software Systems (RS^3). The authors are listed in alphabetical order.

References

1. Jif: Java + information flow (2014), http://www.cs.cornell.edu/jif
2. The Scala Programming Language (2014), http://www.scala-lang.org
3. Arapinis, M., Bursuc, S., Ryan, M.: Privacy supporting cloud computing: Confichair, a case study. In: Degano, P., Guttman, J.D. (eds.) POST 2012. LNCS, vol. 7215, pp. 89–108. Springer, Heidelberg (2012)
4. Bell, E.D., La Padula, J.L.: Secure computer system: Unified exposition and multics interpretation, Technical Report MTR-2997, MITRE, Bedford, MA (1975)
5. Blanchet, B., Abadi, M., Fournet, C.: Automated verification of selected equivalences for security protocols. In: LICS, pp. 331–340 (2005)
6. Clarkson, M.R., Finkbeiner, B., Koleini, M., Micinski, K.K., Rabe, M.N., Sánchez, C.: Temporal logics for hyperproperties. In: Abadi, M., Kremer, S. (eds.) POST 2014. LNCS, vol. 8414, pp. 265–284. Springer, Heidelberg (2014)
7. Cohen, E.S.: Information transmission in computational systems. In: SOSP, pp. 133–139 (1977)
8. de Amorim, A.A., Collins, N., DeHon, A., Demange, D., Hritcu, C., Pichardie, D., Pierce, B.C., Pollack, R., Tolmach, A.: A verified information-flow architecture. In: POPL, pp. 165–178 (2014)
9. Dimitrova, R., Finkbeiner, B., Kovács, M., Rabe, M.N., Seidl, H.: Model checking information flow in reactive systems. In: Kuncak, V., Rybalchenko, A. (eds.) VMCAI 2012. LNCS, vol. 7148, pp. 169–185. Springer, Heidelberg (2012)
10. The EasyChair conference system (2014), http://easychair.org
11. The HotCRP conference management system (2014), http://read.seas.harvard.edu/~kohler/hotcrp
12. Focardi, R., Gorrieri, R.: Classification of security properties (part i: Information flow). In: Focardi, R., Gorrieri, R. (eds.) FOSAD 2000. LNCS, vol. 2171, pp. 331–396. Springer, Heidelberg (2001)
13. Goguen, J.A., Meseguer, J.: Security policies and security models. In: IEEE Symposium on Security and Privacy, pp. 11–20 (1982)
14. Goguen, J.A., Meseguer, J.: Unwinding and inference control. In: IEEE Symposium on Security and Privacy, pp. 75–87 (1984)
15. Gollmann, D.: Computer Security, 2nd edn. Wiley (2005)
16. Haftmann, F.: Code Generation from Specifications in Higher-Order Logic. Ph.D. thesis, Technische Universität München (2009)
17. Haftmann, F., Nipkow, T.: Code generation via higher-order rewrite systems. In: Blume, M., Kobayashi, N., Vidal, G. (eds.) FLOPS 2010. LNCS, vol. 6009, pp. 103–117. Springer, Heidelberg (2010)

18. Halpern, J.Y., O'Neill, K.R.: Secrecy in multiagent systems. ACM Trans. Inf. Syst. Secur. 12(1) (2008)
19. IEEE Symposium on Security and Privacy. Email notification (2012)
20. Kanav, S., Lammich, P., Popescu, A.: The CoCon website, http://www21.in.tum.de/~popescua/rs3/GNE.html
21. Lampson, B.W.: Protection. Operating Systems Review 8(1), 18–24 (1974)
22. Mantel, H.: Information flow control and applications - bridging a gap -. In: Oliveira, J.N., Zave, P. (eds.) FME 2001. LNCS, vol. 2021, pp. 153–172. Springer, Heidelberg (2001)
23. Mantel, H.: A Uniform Framework for the Formal Specification and Verification of Information Flow Security. PhD thesis, University of Saarbrücken (2003)
24. Mantel, H.: Information flow and noninterference. In: Encyclopedia of Cryptography and Security, 2nd edn., pp. 605–607 (2011)
25. McCullough, D.: Specifications for multi-level security and a hook-up property. In: IEEE Symposium on Security and Privacy (1987)
26. McLean, J.: A general theory of composition for trace sets closed under selective interleaving functions. In: Proc. IEEE Symposium on Security and Privacy, pp. 79–93 (1994)
27. McLean, J.: Security models. In: Encyclopedia of Software Engineering (1994)
28. Murray, T., Matichuk, D., Brassil, M., Gammie, P., Klein, G.: Noninterference for operating system kernels. In: Hawblitzel, C., Miller, D. (eds.) CPP 2012. LNCS, vol. 7679, pp. 126–142. Springer, Heidelberg (2012)
29. Nipkow, T., Klein, G.: Concrete Semantics. With Isabelle/HOL, p. 310. Springer (forthcoming), http://www.in.tum.de/~nipkow/Concrete-Semantics
30. Nipkow, T., Paulson, L.C., Wenzel, M.T. (eds.): Isabelle/HOL. LNCS, vol. 2283. Springer, Heidelberg (2002)
31. O'Halloran, C.: A calculus of information flow. In: ESORICS, pp. 147–159 (1990)
32. Popek, G.J., Farber, D.A.: A model for verification of data security in operating systems. Commun. ACM 21(9), 737–749 (1978)
33. Ronald Fagin, Y.M., Halpern, J.Y., Vardi, M.: Reasoning about knowledge. MIT Press (2003)
34. Rushby, J.: Noninterference, transitivity, and channel-control security policies. Tech. report (December 1992)
35. Ryan, P.Y.A.: Mathematical models of computer security. In: Focardi, R., Gorrieri, R. (eds.) FOSAD 2000. LNCS, vol. 2171, pp. 1–62. Springer, Heidelberg (2001)
36. Sabelfeld, A., Myers, A.C.: Language-based information-flow security. IEEE Journal on Selected Areas in Communications 21(1), 5–19 (2003)
37. Sabelfeld, A., Sands, D.: Declassification: Dimensions and principles. Journal of Computer Security 17(5), 517–548 (2009)
38. Sutherland, D.: A model of information. In: 9th National Security Conference, pp. 175–183 (1986)

VAC - Verifier of Administrative Role-Based Access Control Policies

Anna Lisa Ferrara[1], P. Madhusudan[2], Truc L. Nguyen[3], and Gennaro Parlato[3]

[1] University of Bristol, UK
[2] University of Illinois, USA
[3] University of Southampton, UK

Abstract. In this paper we present VAC, an automatic tool for verifying security properties of administrative Role-based Access Control (RBAC). RBAC has become an increasingly popular access control model, particularly suitable for large organizations, and it is implemented in several software. Automatic security analysis of administrative RBAC systems is recognized as an important problem, as an analysis tool can help designers check whether their policies meet expected security properties. VAC converts administrative RBAC policies to imperative programs that simulate the policies both precisely and abstractly and supports several automatic verification back-ends to analyze the resulting programs. In this paper, we describe the architecture of VAC and overview the analysis techniques that have been implemented in the tool. We also report on experiments with several benchmarks from the literature.

1 Introduction

Access control models allow to restrict access to shared resources by selectively assigning permissions to users. Role-based Access Control (RBAC) has become an increasingly popular access control model [5], it is standardized by NIST and is implemented in several software, such as Microsoft SQL Servers, Microsoft Active Directory, SELinux, and Oracle DBMS. RBAC reduces the complexity of user permissions administration by grouping users into roles and assigning permissions to each role. An *Administrative* RBAC User-Role Assignment (ARBAC-URA) policy defines a set of administrative roles and rules which specify how administrators *can assign* or *can revoke* roles to users [27].

Automatic security analysis of ARBAC systems is recognized as an important problem, as an analysis tool can help designers check whether their policies meet the expected security properties [25]. This is particularly desirable whenever policies need to be correct by design, for instance when accesses are not mediated by a monitor [6]. Most interesting security properties, such as privilege escalation and separation of duties, can be phrased as the *role-reachability problem* (i.e., is there a reachable configuration where some user can eventually be assigned to a target role?) [19, 7]. The role-reachability problem is known to be PSPACE-complete and hard to solve on real-world policies having hundreds of roles and rules and thousands of users [28].

A. Biere and R. Bloem (Eds.): CAV 2014, LNCS 8559, pp. 184–191, 2014.
© Springer International Publishing Switzerland 2014

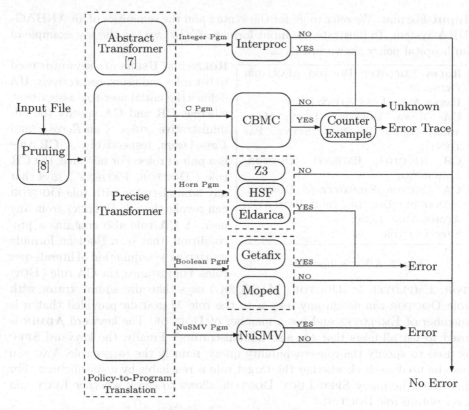

Fig. 1. Vac's Architecture

In this paper, we present Vac (*Verifier of Access Control*), an automatic and scalable tool for solving the role-reachability problem of ARBAC-URA policies. The main components of Vac are a pruning module that aims at simplifying the state space by reducing a policy to a smaller one that preserves the reachability of the target role, and a policy-to-program translation module that converts a policy to an imperative program that simulates the policy both precisely and abstractly. Vac supports a plethora of automatic verification back-ends for the analysis of the resulting programs and has a built-in counterexample generator.

In the rest of the paper, we describe the architecture of Vac and overview the analysis techniques implemented in the tool. Finally, we present experimental results showing the effectiveness of Vac on analyzing realistic and complex benchmarks from the literature.

2 Software Architecture and Verification Approaches

The high-level architecture of Vac is shown in Fig. 1. We first describe the input format of Vac and then its components.

Input Format. We refer to [8] for the syntax and the semantics of an ARBAC-URA system. To illustrate the input format of VAC[1] we use the toy example of an hospital policy shown in Fig. 2.

ROLES EMPLOYEE DOCTOR MANAGER PATIENT;
USERS ANNA LUKE STEVE LUCY;
UA ⟨ANNA, DOCTOR⟩ ⟨LUCY, MANAGER⟩ ⟨LUKE, DOCTOR⟩ ⟨STEVE, PATIENT⟩;
CR ⟨DOCTOR, PATIENT⟩ ⟨DOCTOR, MANAGER⟩;
CA ⟨DOCTOR, EMPLOYEE & -DOCTOR, MANAGER⟩ ⟨DOCTOR, TRUE, PATIENT⟩;
ADMIN ANNA LUKE;
SPEC DOCTOR;

Fig. 2. A VAC's input file

ROLES and USERS are keywords used to list roles and users, respectively. **UA** defines the initial user-role assignment, whereas **CR** and **CA** specify the administrative rules *Can-Revoke* and *Can-Assign*, respectively. A **CR** rule is a pair of roles. For instance, the **CR** rule ⟨ DOCTOR, PATIENT ⟩ says that any administrator with role DOCTOR can revoke the role PATIENT from any user. A **CA** rule also contains a precondition, that is, a Boolean formula written as a conjunction of literals over roles. For instance, the **CA** rule ⟨ DOCTOR, EMPLOYEE & -DOCTOR, MANAGER ⟩ says that any administrator with role DOCTOR can assign any user u to the role MANAGER provided that u is member of EMPLOYEE and not a member of DOCTOR. The keyword **ADMIN** is used to list all users that are also administrators[2]. Finally, the keyword **SPEC** is used to specify the role-reachability query, namely the target role. VAC can also be used to check whether the target role is reachable by a specific user. For instance, the query **SPEC** LUCY DOCTOR allows to check whether LUCY can ever obtain role DOCTOR.

Pruning Module. This module takes as input a policy, which we refer as the original policy, and outputs a simplified one (in the same format as the input) that preserves the reachability of the target role. The module implements the pruning heuristic from [8] which is crucial for scalability. It eliminates roles, rules and users with the aim of reducing the state space to explore. This heuristic relies upon a fundamental theorem which states that the role-reachability problem can be solved by tracking only $k+1$ users, where k is the number of administrative roles [8]. Thus, the heuristic exploits sufficient conditions to eliminate administrative roles that are not relevant for the analysis. The effectiveness of the above method is amplified by a static pruning algorithm consisting of six pruning actions: the first three aim at discarding roles that are irrelevant to the reachability of the target role while the remaining ones identify administrative rules that can be combined or eliminated. Furthermore, whenever the target role is reachable within two steps in the intermediate policy, the pruning procedure terminates immediately returning the counterexample.

Policy-to-Program Translation. This module takes as input a policy and translates it into a program that simulates the evolution of the system. VAC provides the following two policy-to-program translations:

---

[1] VAC's input format is compatible with that of Mohawk [16].
[2] The list of administrators can be obtained from **CA** and **CR** rules. However, we include the keyword **ADMIN** to be consistent with Mohawk's input format [16].

Abstract Transformer. This module implements the policy-to-program translation proposed in [7]. A policy P is translated into an imperative non-deterministic while-program P' with an error location. P' uses only integer variables to capture the number of users in a subset of role combinations and abstractly simulates the evolution of the system in such a way that if the error location is not reachable then the role reachability problem has a negative answer on P. On the contrary, if the error location is reachable in P', this may correspond to a false positive as P' over-approximates the behaviour of P. P' is then analyzed by VAC using Interproc [18] with the box abstract domain.

Precise Transformer. This module translates a policy P into a Boolean program P' that precisely simulates the evolution of the system tracking at most $k+1$ users picked non-deterministically, where k is the number of administrative roles. The correctness of this approach relies on a fundamental theorem proven in [8]. The program uses $k+1$ blocks of n Boolean variables, where n is the number of roles in the policy. Each block tracks the role-membership of a selected user. The rest of the program consists of an infinite loop in which the administrative rules are non-deterministically simulated on a non-deterministically chosen user. The loop contains also an error location that is reachable whenever a tracked user reaches the target role. The role-reachability problem admits a positive answer on P if and only if the error location is reachable in P'. The reachability problem for Boolean programs is decidable and VAC supports several automated tools as back-ends for the analysis of P'. In particular, a complete analysis can be performed by using either (1) one of the following tools for Horn clauses: Z3 (μZ) [4, 13], HSF [11, 12], and Eldarica [15, 14], or (2) Moped [20, 29] and Getafix [23, 24] which are model checkers for Boolean Programs based on BDDs, or (3) NuSMV a model checker based on BDDs and SAT solvers [2, 3]. VAC uses the C bounded model checker CBMC [21, 22] for under-approximate analysis, particularly effective to find errors. If CBMC finds an error, it returns a counterexample showing how the error location can be reached in the program. Otherwise, VAC reports Unknown.

Counterexample Module. VAC implements an involved built-in counterexample generation module that takes as input the counterexample of the pruned policy returned by CBMC along with some information collected during the execution of the pruning, and outputs a counterexample (attack) of the original policy.

3   Implementation and Availability

Implementation. VAC is implemented in C and has dependencies with ANTLR (v3.2 for C), ROXML, and CCL libraries[3].

Availability. The source code, a set of benchmarks and static Linux binaries are available at: http://users.ecs.soton.ac.uk/gp4/VAC.

Usage. The shell command ./vac.sh <InputFile> runs VAC with the default setting: (1) runs the abstract transformer and Interproc to prove correctness;

---

[3] ANTLR, ROXML and CCL are respectively available at http://www.antlr.org/, http://www.libroxml.net, and https://code.google.com/p/ccl/.

Table 1. VAC's results on realistic case studies

	name	ARBAC Policy #roles	#rules	#admin	#users	Pruning #roles	#rules	#admin	#users	Time	Reach Answer	Time
1	Hospital1	13	37	5	1092	4	5	3	6	0.009s	No	0.029s
	Hospital2	13	37	5	1092	4	5	3	6	0.009s	No	0.023s
	Hospital3	13	37	5	1092	3	2	1	4	0.009s	Yes	0.103s
	Hospital4	13	37	5	1092	4	4	1	4	0.009s	Yes	0.110s
2	University1	32	449	9	943	6	7	3	13	0.009s	No	0.034s
	University2	32	449	9	943	6	8	3	13	0.004s	Yes	0.192s
	University3	32	449	9	943	4	5	1	6	0.006s	No	0.021s
	University4	32	449	9	943	12	37	4	31	0.004s	Yes	1.571s
3	Bank1	343	2225	1	2	3	2	1	2	0.007s	Yes	0.112s
	Bank2	683	4445	1	2	3	2	1	2	0.019s	Yes	0.139s
	Bank3	1023	6665	1	2	3	2	1	2	0.024s	Yes	0.167s
	Bank4	1363	8885	1	2	3	2	1	2	0.030s	Yes	0.168s
	Bank5	343	2225	1	2	3	2	1	2	0.044s	Yes	0.138s
	Bank6	683	4445	1	2	3	2	1	2	0.155s	Yes	0.247s
	Bank7	1023	6665	1	2	3	2	1	2	0.300s	Yes	0.435s
	Bank8	1363	8885	1	2	3	2	1	2	0.522s	Yes	0.663s
	Bank9	531	5126	1	2000	2	0	1	2	0.244s	No	0.253s
	Bank10	531	5126	1	2000	2	0	1	2	0.248s	No	0.254s
	Bank11	531	5126	1	2000	3	2	1	2	0.245s	Yes	0.396s
	Bank12	531	5126	1	2000	6	5	1	2	0.066s	Yes	0.223s

(2) if a proof cannot be provided, VAC runs the precise transformer and CBMC (with unwind set to 2) to find a counterexample; (3) if CBMC does not find an error, VAC runs μZ for complete analysis. VAC has options to print the translated programs and the simplified policies, and select the back-end for the analysis.

4 Experimental Results

We evaluate VAC, using the default setting, on several benchmarks from the literature. All experiments have been performed on a Linux 64-bit machine with Intel Core i7-3770 CPU and 16GB of RAM.

Table 1 shows the results on three sets of benchmarks based on realistic case studies. The first two case studies are carried out by Stoller at al. [30] and represent policies for a university and for an hospital, respectively. The third case study, conducted by Jayaraman et al. [16], models a bank with several branches[4]. While the first eight bank policies are from [16], we have built the last four from [16] by slightly modifying their policies to add more users and to make two of them correct. Table 1 reports the number of roles, rules, administrative roles and users of both the original policy and that after pruning. It also reports the tool's answer, the time taken by the pruning, and the overall analysis time.

Table 1 shows that the pruning module significantly reduces the size of these policies. Furthermore, VAC is extremely efficient in verifying these policies, regardless of whether the target role is reachable or not. More precisely, all benchmarks with a negative answer can be proved correct in less than a second. Similarly, on benchmarks with a reachable target the analysis takes less than 2 seconds including the time to generate the counterexample.

---

[4] The number of roles and rules depends on the number of branches considered. For instance, 343 roles corresponds to 10 branches and 1363 to 40 branches.

Table 2. Vac' s results on complex test suites

Size Policy		Vac							
		First Suite			Second Suite			Third Suite		
#roles	#rules	Pruning		Verification	Pruning		Verification	Pruning		Verification
		#roles	#rules	Time	#roles	#rules	Time	#roles	#rules	Time
4	10	3	1	0.080s	3	1	0.084s	2	1	0.085s
5	25	4	2	0.087s	4	2	0.096s	2	1	0.092s
20	100	3	1	0.099s	3	1	0.089s	3	2	0.087s
40	200	4	2	0.099s	4	2	0.096s	2	1	0.091s
200	1000	2	1	0.101s	2	1	0.088s	2	1	0.096s
500	2500	3	1	0.100s	3	1	0.104s	3	2	0.128s
4000	20000	2	1	0.239s	2	1	0.198s	4	3	0.252s
20000	80000	2	1	0.844s	2	1	0.579s	3	2	0.922s
30000	120000	2	1	1.288s	2	1	0.849s	2	1	1.285s
40000	200000	2	1	1.586s	2	1	1.100s	4	3	1.646s

Table 2 shows the results on three sets of complex test suites, synthetically generated by Jayaraman et al. [16], with the aim of capturing the complexity of real systems. Each suite consists of ten policies where the number of roles and rules ranges respectively from 4 to 40k and 10 to 200k. The role-reachability problem has a positive answer on all these benchmarks. Vac is very effective on these policies as well. The analysis takes less than 2 seconds on all policies and the pruning module reduces the policies to equivalent systems with a handful of roles and rules.

5   Conclusions

We have presented Vac an automatic and efficient tool for verifying security properties of administrative role-based access control policies. The main components of Vac are a pruning module which is essential for scalability, and a policy-to-program translation module that reduces the role-reachability problem to program verification problems. It supports several tools for the analysis, such as CBMC, Eldarica, Getafix, Interproc, Moped, NuSMV, HSF, and Z3 (μZ). Furthermore, it can provide counterexamples.

Related Work. Among the state-of-the-art tools for the analysis of ARBAC-URA systems, Vac is the only tool that simultaneously has the following features: (1) complete analysis (2) counterexample generation, and (3) scalable analysis on large policies. Mohawk [16] performs only under-approximate analysis, though it now considers thresholds for completeness [17]; RBAC-PAT [10] is unable to handle large policies. They also can only analyze policies with *separate administration* where administrators cannot change their role-membership; this is not realistic, but simplifies analysis as only a single user needs to be tracked.

asaspXL is the latest tool developed by Ranise et al. for the analysis of ARBAC policies [26]. A previous version (asasp [1]) was not able to scale on large policies. asaspXL is mainly designed to handle large policies and does so by encoding the instances to MCMT [9] which is a model checker for infinite state systems based on SMT solvers and backward reachability. In contrast, Vac does not target any specific kind of instances, and handles large policies by carrying out an effective pruning that is independent of the verification technique used for the analysis. VAC and ASASPXL can potentially handle the same kind of instances though they have different input formats.

All tools above do not generate counterexamples. Furthermore, VAC, on the policies of Section 4, has either the same performances or outperforms the tools mentioned above. VAC has also been used for the analysis of *temporal* RBAC [31].

Acknowledgements. Research was partially supported by ERC Advanced Grant ERC-2010-AdG-267188-CRIPTO and NSF CCF #1018182.

References

[1] Alberti, F., Armando, A., Ranise, S.: ASASP: Automated Symbolic Analysis of Security Policies. In: Bjørner, N., Sofronie-Stokkermans, V. (eds.) CADE 2011. LNCS, vol. 6803, pp. 26–33. Springer, Heidelberg (2011)

[2] Cimatti, A., Clarke, E.M., Giunchiglia, E., Giunchiglia, F., Pistore, M., Roveri, M., Sebastiani, R., Tacchella, A.: NuSMV: A New Symbolic Model Checker, http://nusmv.fbk.eu

[3] Cimatti, A., Clarke, E.M., Giunchiglia, E., Giunchiglia, F., Pistore, M., Roveri, M., Sebastiani, R., Tacchella, A.: NuSMV 2: An OpenSource Tool for Symbolic Model Checking. In: Brinksma, E., Larsen, K.G. (eds.) CAV 2002. LNCS, vol. 2404, pp. 359–364. Springer, Heidelberg (2002)

[4] de Moura, L., Berdine, J., Bjorner, N.: Z3 High-performance Theorem Prover, http://z3.codeplex.com

[5] Ferraiolo, D., Kuhn, R.: Role-Based Access Control. In: 15th NIST-NCSC National Computer Security Conference, pp. 554–563. Springer (1992)

[6] Ferrara, A.L., Fuchsbauer, G., Warinschi, B.: Cryptographically Enforced RBAC. In: CSF, pp. 115–129. IEEE (2013)

[7] Ferrara, A.L., Madhusudan, P., Parlato, G.: Security Analysis of Role-Based Access Control through Program Verification. In: CSF, pp. 113–125 (2012)

[8] Ferrara, A.L., Madhusudan, P., Parlato, G.: Policy Analysis for Self-administrated Role-Based Access Control. In: Piterman, N., Smolka, S.A. (eds.) TACAS 2013 (ETAPS 2013). LNCS, vol. 7795, pp. 432–447. Springer, Heidelberg (2013)

[9] Ghilardi, S., Ranise, S.: MCMT: A Model Checker Modulo Theories. In: Giesl, J., Hähnle, R. (eds.) IJCAR 2010. LNCS, vol. 6173, pp. 22–29. Springer, Heidelberg (2010)

[10] Gofman, M.I., Luo, R., Solomon, A.C., Zhang, Y., Yang, P., Stoller, S.D.: RBAC-PAT: A Policy Analysis Tool for Role Based Access Control. In: Kowalewski, S., Philippou, A. (eds.) TACAS 2009. LNCS, vol. 5505, pp. 46–49. Springer, Heidelberg (2009)

[11] Grebenshchikov, S., Gupta, A., Lopes, N.P., Popeea, C., Rybalchenko, A.: HSF(C): A Software Verifier based on Horn Clauses, http://www7.in.tum.de/tools/hsf

[12] Grebenshchikov, S., Gupta, A., Lopes, N.P., Popeea, C., Rybalchenko, A.: HSF(C): A Software Verifier Based on Horn Clauses. In: Flanagan, C., König, B. (eds.) TACAS 2012. LNCS, vol. 7214, pp. 549–551. Springer, Heidelberg (2012)

[13] Hoder, K., Bjørner, N., de Moura, L.: μZ– An Efficient Engine for Fixed Points with Constraints. In: Gopalakrishnan, G., Qadeer, S. (eds.) CAV 2011. LNCS, vol. 6806, pp. 457–462. Springer, Heidelberg (2011)

[14] Hojjat, H., Konečný, F., Garnier, F., Iosif, R., Kuncak, V., Rümmer, P.: A Verification Toolkit for Numerical Transition Systems. In: Giannakopoulou, D., Méry, D. (eds.) FM 2012. LNCS, vol. 7436, pp. 247–251. Springer, Heidelberg (2012)

[15] Hojjat, H., Rümmer, P., Konecny, F.: A Predicate Abstraction Engine, http://lara.epfl.ch/w/eldarica

[16] Jayaraman, K., Ganesh, V., Tripunitara, M.V., Rinard, M.C., Chapin, S.J.: Automatic Error Finding in Access-Control Policies. In: CCS, pp. 163–174 (2011)

[17] Jayaraman, K., Tripunitara, M.V., Ganesh, V., Rinard, M.C., Chapin, S.J.: Mohawk: Abstraction-Refinement and Bound-Estimation for Verifying Access Control Policies. ACM Trans. Inf. Syst. Secur. 15(4), 18 (2013)

[18] Jeannet, B., Lalire, G., Argoud, M.: The Interproc Analyzer, http://pop-art.inrialpes.fr/interproc/interprocweb.cgi

[19] Jha, S., Li, N., Tripunitara, M., Wang, Q., Winsborough, W.: Towards Formal Verification of Role-Based Access Control Policies. IEEE Transactions on Dependable and Secure Computing 5(4), 242–255 (2008)

[20] Kiefer, S., Schwoon, S., Suwimonteerabuth, D.: A Model Checker for Pushdown Systems, http://www2.informatik.uni-stuttgart.de/fmi/szs/tools/moped

[21] Kroening, D., Clarke, E.: CBMC - Bounded Model Checking for ANSI-C, http://www.cprover.org/cbmc

[22] Kroening, D., Tautschnig, M.: CBMC – C Bounded Model Checker - (Competition Contribution). In: Ábrahám, E., Havelund, K. (eds.) TACAS 2014. LNCS, vol. 8413, pp. 389–391. Springer, Heidelberg (2014)

[23] La Torre, S., Madhusudan, P., Parlato, G.: Getafix: A Symbolic Model-checker for Recursive Programs, http://www.cs.uiuc.edu/~madhu/getafix

[24] La Torre, S., Madhusudan, P., Parlato, G.: Analyzing Recursive Programs using a Fixed-point Calculus. In: Hind, M., Diwan, A. (eds.) PLDI, pp. 211–222. ACM (2009)

[25] Li, N., Tripunitara, M.V.: Security Analysis in Role-Based Access Control. ACM Trans. Inf. Syst. Secur. 9(4), 391–420 (2006)

[26] Ranise, S., Truong, A., Armando, A.: Boosting Model Checking to Analyse Large ARBAC Policies. In: Jøsang, A., Samarati, P., Petrocchi, M. (eds.) STM 2012. LNCS, vol. 7783, pp. 273–288. Springer, Heidelberg (2013)

[27] Sandhu, R.S., Bhamidipati, V., Munawer, Q.: The ARBAC97 Model for Role-Based Administration of Roles. ACM Trans. Inf. Syst. Secur. 2(1), 105–135 (1999)

[28] Sasturkar, A., Yang, P., Stoller, S.D., Ramakrishnan, C.: Policy analysis for Administrative Role-Based Access Control. Theoretical Computer Science 412(44), 6208–6234 (2011)

[29] Schwoon, S.: Model-Checking Pushdown Systems. Ph.D. Thesis, Technische Universität München (June 2002)

[30] Stoller, S.D., Yang, P., Ramakrishnan, C.R., Gofman, M.I.: Efficient Policy Analysis for Administrative Role Based Access Control. In: CCS, pp. 445–455 (2007)

[31] Uzun, E., Atluri, V., Sural, S., Vaidya, J., Parlato, G., Ferrara, A.L., Madhusudan, P.: Analyzing temporal role based access control models. In: Atluri, V., Vaidya, J., Kern, A., Kantarcioglu, M. (eds.) SACMAT, pp. 177–186. ACM (2012)

From LTL to Deterministic Automata: A Safraless Compositional Approach

Javier Esparza and Jan Křetínský*

Institut für Informatik, Technische Universität München, Germany
IST Austria

Abstract. We present a new algorithm to construct a (generalized) deterministic Rabin automaton for an LTL formula φ. The automaton is the product of a master automaton and an array of slave automata, one for each **G**-subformula of φ. The slave automaton for **G**ψ is in charge of recognizing whether **FG**ψ holds. As opposed to standard determinization procedures, the states of all our automata have a clear logical structure, which allows for various optimizations. Our construction subsumes former algorithms for fragments of LTL. Experimental results show improvement in the sizes of the resulting automata compared to existing methods.

1 Introduction

Linear temporal logic (LTL) is the most popular specification language for linear-time properties. In the automata-theoretic approach to LTL verification, formulae are translated into ω-automata, and the product of these automata with the system is analyzed. Therefore, generating small ω-automata is crucial for the efficiency of the approach.

In quantitative probabilistic verification, LTL formulae need to be translated into *deterministic* ω-automata [BK08, CGK13]. Until recently, this required to proceed in two steps: first translate the formula into a non-deterministic Büchi automaton (NBA), and then apply Safra's construction [Saf88], or improvements on it [Pit06, Sch09] to transform the NBA into a deterministic automaton (usually a Rabin automaton, or DRA). This is also the approach adopted in PRISM [KNP11], a leading probabilistic model checker, which reimplements the optimized Safra's construction of ltl2dstar [Kle].

In [KE12] we presented an algorithm that *directly* constructs a generalized DRA (GDRA) for the fragment of LTL containing only the temporal operators **F** and **G**. The GDRA can be either (1) degeneralized into a standard DRA, or (2) used directly in the probabilistic verification process [CGK13]. In both cases

* This research was funded in part by the European Research Council (ERC) under grant agreement 267989 (QUAREM) and by the Austrian Science Fund (FWF) project S11402-N23 (RiSE). The author is on leave from Faculty of Informatics, Masaryk University, Czech Republic, and partially supported by the Czech Science Foundation, grant No. P202/12/G061.

A. Biere and R. Bloem (Eds.): CAV 2014, LNCS 8559, pp. 192–208, 2014.

we get much smaller automata for many formulae. For instance, the standard approach translates a conjunction of three fairness constraints into an automaton with over a million states, while the algorithm of [KE12] yields a GDRA with one single state (when acceptance is defined on transitions), and a DRA with 462 states. In [GKE12, KLG13] our approach was extended to larger fragments of LTL containing the **X** operator and restricted appearances of **U**, but a general algorithm remained elusive.

In this paper we present a novel approach able to handle full LTL, and even the alternation-free linear-time μ-calculus. The approach is *compositional*: the automaton is obtained as a parallel composition of automata for different parts of the formula, running in lockstep[1]. More specifically, the automaton is the parallel composition of a *master automaton* and an array of *slave automata*, one for each **G**-subformula of the original formula, say φ. Intuitively, the master monitors the formula that remains to be fulfilled (for example, if $\varphi = (\neg a \wedge \mathbf{X}a) \vee \mathbf{XX}\mathbf{G}a$, then the remaining formula after $\emptyset\{a\}$ is **tt**, and after $\{a\}$ it is **XG**a), and takes care of checking safety and reachability properties. The slave for a subformula **G**ψ of φ checks whether **G**ψ *eventually* holds, i.e., whether **FG**ψ holds. It also monitors the formula that remains to be fulfilled, but only partially: more precisely, it does not monitor any **G**-subformula of ψ, as other slaves are responsible for them. For instance, if $\psi = a \wedge \mathbf{G}b \wedge \mathbf{G}c$, then the slave for **G**ψ only checks that eventually a always holds, and "delegates" checking **FG**b and **FG**c to other slaves. Further, and crucially, the slave may provide the information that not only **FG**ψ, but a stronger formula holds; the master needs this to decide that, for instance, not only **FG**φ but even **XG**φ holds.

The acceptance condition of the parallel composition of master and slaves is a disjunction over all possible subsets of **G**-subformulas, and all possible stronger formulas the slaves can check. The parallel composition accepts a word with the disjunct corresponding to the subset of formulas which hold in it.

The paper is organized incrementally. In Section 3 we show how to construct a DRA for a formula **FG**φ, where φ has no occurrence of **G**. This gives the DRA for a bottom-level slave. Section 4 constructs a DRA for an arbitrary formula **FG**φ, which gives the DRA for a general slave, in charge of a formula that possible has **G**-subformulas. Finally, Section 5 constructs a DRA for arbitrary formulas by introducing the master and its parallel composition with the slaves. Full proofs can be found in [EK14].

Related work. There are many constructions translating LTL to NBA, e.g., [Cou99, DGV99, EH00, SB00, GO01, GL02, Fri03, BKRS12, DL13]. The one recommended by ltl2dstar and used in PRISM is LTL2BA [GO01]. Safra's construction with optimizations described in [KB07] has been implemented in ltl2dstar [Kle], and reimplemenetd in PRISM [KNP11]. A comparison of LTL translators into deterministic ω-automata can be found in [BKS13].

---

[1] We could also speak of a product of automata, but the operational view behind the term parallel composition helps to convey the intuition.

2 Linear Temporal Logic

In this paper, $\mathbb{N}$ denotes the set of natural numbers including zero. "For almost every $i \in \mathbb{N}$" means for all but finitely many $i \in \mathbb{N}$.

This section recalls the notion of linear temporal logic (LTL). We consider the negation normal form and we have the future operator explicitly in the syntax:

Definition 1 (LTL Syntax). *The formulae of the linear temporal logic (LTL) are given by the following syntax:*

$$\varphi ::= \mathbf{tt} \mid \mathbf{ff} \mid a \mid \neg a \mid \varphi \wedge \varphi \mid \varphi \vee \varphi \mid \mathbf{X}\varphi \mid \mathbf{F}\varphi \mid \mathbf{G}\varphi \mid \varphi\mathbf{U}\varphi$$

over a finite fixed set Ap of atomic propositions.

Definition 2 (Words and LTL Semantics). *Let $w \in (2^{Ap})^\omega$ be a word. The ith letter of w is denoted $w[i]$, i.e. $w = w[0]w[1]\cdots$. We write w_{ij} for the finite word $w[i]w[i+1]\cdots w[j]$, and $w_{i\infty}$ or just w_i for the suffix $w[i]w[i+1]\cdots$.*

The semantics of a formula on a word w is defined inductively as follows:

$w \models \mathbf{tt}$

$w \not\models \mathbf{ff}$

$w \models a \iff a \in w[0]$

$w \models \neg a \iff a \notin w[0]$

$w \models \varphi \wedge \psi \iff w \models \varphi \text{ and } w \models \psi$

$w \models \varphi \vee \psi \iff w \models \varphi \text{ or } w \models \psi$

$w \models \mathbf{X}\varphi \iff w_1 \models \varphi$

$w \models \mathbf{F}\varphi \iff \exists k \in \mathbb{N} : w_k \models \varphi$

$w \models \mathbf{G}\varphi \iff \forall k \in \mathbb{N} : w_k \models \varphi$

$w \models \varphi\mathbf{U}\psi \iff \exists k \in \mathbb{N} : w_k \models \psi \text{ and } \forall 0 \le j < k : w_j \models \varphi$

Definition 3 (Propositional implication). *Given two formulae φ and ψ, we say that φ propositionally implies ψ, denoted by $\varphi \models_p \psi$, if we can prove $\varphi \models \psi$ using only the axioms of propositional logic. We say that φ and ψ are propositionally equivalent, denoted by $\varphi \equiv_p \psi$, if φ and ψ propositionally imply each other.*

Remark 4. We consider formulae up to propositional equivalence, i.e., $\varphi = \psi$ means that φ and ψ are propositionally equivalent. Sometimes (when there is risk of confusion) we explicitly write $\equiv_p$ instead of $=$.

2.1 The Formula $af(\varphi, w)$

Given a formula φ and a finite word w, we define a formula $af(\varphi, w)$, read "φ after w". Intuitively, it is the formula that any infinite continuation w' must satisfy for ww' to satisfy φ.

Definition 5. *Let φ be a formula and $\nu \in 2^{Ap}$. We define the formula $af(\varphi, \nu)$ as follows:*

$af(\mathbf{tt}, \nu) = \mathbf{tt}$

$af(\mathbf{ff}, \nu) = \mathbf{ff}$

$af(a, \nu) = \begin{cases} \mathbf{tt} & \text{if } a \in \nu \\ \mathbf{ff} & \text{if } a \notin \nu \end{cases}$

$af(\neg a, \nu) = \neg af(a, \nu)$

$af(\varphi \wedge \psi, \nu) = af(\varphi, \nu) \wedge af(\psi, \nu)$

$af(\varphi \vee \psi, \nu) = af(\varphi, \nu) \vee af(\psi, \nu)$

$af(\mathbf{X}\varphi, \nu) = \varphi$

$af(\mathbf{G}\varphi, \nu) = af(\varphi, \nu) \wedge \mathbf{G}\varphi$

$af(\mathbf{F}\varphi, \nu) = af(\varphi, \nu) \vee \mathbf{F}\varphi$

$af(\varphi\mathbf{U}\psi, \nu) = af(\psi, \nu) \vee (af(\varphi, \nu) \wedge \varphi\mathbf{U}\psi)$

We extend the definition to finite words as follows: $af(\varphi, \epsilon) = \varphi$ *and* $af(\varphi, \nu w) = af(af(\varphi, \nu), w)$. *Finally, we define* $Reach(\varphi) = \{af(\varphi, w) \mid w \in (2^{Ap})^*\}$.

Example 6. Let $Ap = \{a, b, c\}$, and consider the formula $\varphi = a \vee (b \ \mathbf{U} \ c)$. For example, we have $af(\varphi, \{a\}) = \mathbf{tt}$ $af(\varphi, \{b\}) = (b \ \mathbf{U} \ c)$, $af(\varphi, \{c\}) = \mathbf{tt}$, and $af(\varphi, \emptyset) = \mathbf{ff}$. $Reach(\varphi) = \{\varphi, \alpha \wedge \varphi, \beta \vee \varphi, \mathbf{tt}, \mathbf{ff}\}$, and $Reach(\varphi) = \{a \vee (b \ \mathbf{U} \ c), (b \ \mathbf{U} \ c), \mathbf{tt}, \mathbf{ff}\}$.

Lemma 7. *Let* φ *be a formula, and let* $ww' \in (2^{Ap})^\omega$ *be an arbitrary word. Then* $ww' \models \varphi$ *iff* $w' \models af(\varphi, w)$.

Proof. Straightforward induction on the length of w.   □

3   DRAs for Simple FG-Formulae

We start with formulae $\mathbf{FG}\varphi$ where φ is G-free, i.e., contains no occurrence of $\mathbf{G}$. The main building block of our paper is a procedure to construct a DRA recognizing $L(\mathbf{FG}\varphi)$. (Notice that even the formula $\mathbf{FG}a$ has no deterministic Büchi automaton.) We proceed in two steps. First we introduce Mojmir automata and construct a Mojmir automaton that clearly recognizes $L(\mathbf{FG}\varphi)$. We then show how to transform Mojmir automata into equivalent DRAs.

A Mojmir automaton[2] is a deterministic automaton that, at each step, puts a fresh token in the initial state, and moves all older tokens according to the transition function. The automaton accepts if all but finitely many tokens eventually reach an accepting state.

Definition 8. *A Mojmir automaton* $\mathcal{M}$ *over an alphabet* Σ *is a tuple* (Q, i, δ, F), *where* Q *is a set of states,* $i \in Q$ *is the initial state,* $\delta \colon Q \times \Sigma \to Q$ *is a transition function, and* $F \subseteq Q$ *is a set of accepting states satisfying* $\delta(F, \Sigma) \subseteq F$, *i.e., states reachable from final states are also final.*

The run *of* $\mathcal{M}$ *over a word* $w[0]w[1] \cdots \in (2^{Ap})^\omega$ *is the infinite sequence* $(q_0^0)(q_0^1, q_1^1)(q_0^2, q_1^2, q_2^2) \cdots$ *such that*

$$q_{token}^{step} = \begin{cases} i & \text{if token} = step, \\ \delta(q_{token}^{step-1}, w[step-1]) & \text{if token} < step \end{cases}$$

A run is accepting if for almost every token $\in \mathbb{N}$ *there exists* $step \geq token$ *such that* $q_{token}^{step} \in F$.

Notice that if two tokens reach the same state at the same time point, then from this moment on they "travel together".

The Mojmir automaton for a formula φ has formulae as states. The automaton is constructed so that, when running on a word w, the i-th token "tracks" the formula that must hold for w_i to satisfy φ. That is, after j steps the i-th token is on the formula $af(\varphi, w_{ij})$. There is only one accepting state here, namely the one propositionally equivalent to $\mathbf{tt}$. Therefore, if the i-th token reaches an accepting state, then w_i satisfies φ.

---

[2] Named in honour of Mojmír Křetínský, father of one of the authors.

196   J. Esparza and J. Křetínský

Definition 9. *Let φ be a $\mathbf{G}$-free formula. The Mojmir automaton for φ is $\mathcal{M}(\varphi) = (Reach(\varphi), \varphi, af, \{\mathbf{tt}\})$.*

Example 10. Figure 1 on the left shows the Mojmir automaton for the formula $\varphi = a \vee (b \, \mathbf{U} \, c)$. The notation for transitions is standard: $q_1 \xrightarrow{a + \bar{a}c} q_3$ means that there is a transitions from q_1 to q_3 for each subset of 2^{Ap} that contains a, or does not contain a and contains c.

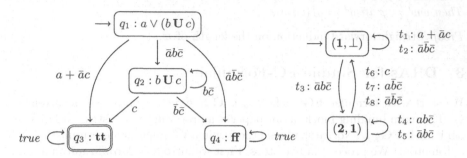

Fig. 1. A Mojmir automaton for $a \vee (b \, \mathbf{U} \, c)$ and its corresponding DRA

Since $\mathcal{M}(\varphi)$ accepts iff almost every token eventually reaches an accepting state, $\mathcal{M}(\varphi)$ accepts a word w iff $w \models \mathbf{FG}\varphi$.

Lemma 11. *Let φ be a $\mathbf{G}$-free formula and let w be a word. Then $w \models \varphi$ iff $af(\varphi, w_{0i}) = \mathbf{tt}$ for some $i \in \mathbb{N}$.*

Theorem 12. *Let φ be a $\mathbf{G}$-free formula. Then $\mathsf{L}(\mathcal{M}(\varphi)) = \mathsf{L}(\mathbf{FG}\varphi)$.*

3.1 From Mojmir Automata to DRAs

Given a Mojmir automaton $\mathcal{M} = (Q, i, \delta, F)$ we construct an equivalent DRA. We illustrate all steps on the Mojmir automaton on the left of Figure 1. It is convenient to use shorthands q_a to q_e for state names as shown in the figure.

We label tokens with their dates of birth (token i is the token born at "day" i). Initially there is only one token, token 0, placed on the initial state i. If, say, $\delta(i, \nu) = q$, then after $\mathcal{M}$ reads ν token 0 moves to q, and token 1 appears on i.

A state of a Mojmir automaton is a *sink* if it is not the initial state and all its outgoing transitions are self-loops. For instance, q_3 and q_4 are the sinks of the automaton on the left of Figure 1. We define a *configuration* of $\mathcal{M}$ as a mapping $C \colon Q \setminus S \to 2^{\mathbb{N}}$, where S is the set of sinks and $C(q)$ is the set of (dates of birth of the) tokens that are currently at state q. Notice that we do not keep track of tokens in sinks.

We extend the transition function to configurations: $\delta(C)$ is the configuration obtained by moving all tokens of C according to δ. Let us represent a configuration C of our example by the vector $(C(q_1), C(q_2))$. For instance, we have $\delta((\{1, 2\}, \{0\}), \bar{a}b\bar{c})) = (\{3\}, \{0, 1, 2\})$. We represent a run as an infinite sequence of configurations starting at $(\{0\}, \emptyset)$. The run $(q_1) \xrightarrow{ab\underline{c}} (q_3, q_1) \xrightarrow{\bar{a}b\bar{c}} (q_3, q_2, q_1) \xrightarrow{\bar{a}b\bar{c}} (q_3, q_2, q_2, q_1) \cdots$ is represented by $(0, \emptyset) \xrightarrow{ab\underline{c}} (1, \emptyset) \xrightarrow{\bar{a}b\bar{c}} (2, 1) \xrightarrow{\bar{a}b\bar{c}} (3, \{1, 2\}) \cdots$ where for readability we identify the singleton $\{n\}$ and the number n.

We now define a finite abstraction of configurations. A *ranking* of Q is a partial function $r: Q \to \{1, \ldots, |Q|\}$ that assigns to some states q a *rank* and satisfies: (1) the initial state is ranked (i.e., $r(i)$ is defined) and all sinks are unranked; (2) distinct ranked states have distinct ranks; and (3) if some state has rank $\mathbf{j}$, then some state has rank $\mathbf{k}$ for every $1 \le \mathbf{k} \le \mathbf{j}$. For $\mathbf{i} < \mathbf{j}$, we say that $\mathbf{i}$ is *older than* $\mathbf{j}$. The *abstraction* of a configuration C is the ranking $\alpha[C]$ defined as follows for every non-sink q. If $C(q) = \emptyset$, then q is unranked. If $C(q) \ne \emptyset$, then let $x_q = \min\{C(q)\}$ be the oldest token in $C(q)$. We call x_q the *senior token* of state q, and $\{x_q \in \mathbb{N} \mid q \in Q\}$ the set of *senior tokens*. We define $\alpha[C](q)$ as the *seniority rank* of x_q: if x_q is the oldest senior token, then $\alpha[C](q) = 1$; if it is the second oldest, then $\alpha[C](q) = 2$, and so on. For instance, the senior tokens of $(2, \{0, 1\}, \emptyset)$ are 2 and 0, and so $\alpha(2, \{0, 1\}, \emptyset) = (\mathbf{2}, \mathbf{1}, \perp)$ (recall that sinks are unranked). Notice that there are only finitely many rankings, and so only finitely many abstract configurations.

The transition function δ can be lifted to a transition function δ' on abstract configurations by defining $\delta'(\alpha[C], \nu) = \alpha[\delta(C, \nu)]$. It is easy to see that $\delta'(\alpha[C], \nu)$ can be computed directly from $\alpha[C]$ (even if C is not known). We describe how, and at the same time illustrate by computing $\delta'((\mathbf{2}, \mathbf{1}), \bar{a}b\bar{c})$ for our running example.

(i) Move the senior tokens according to δ. (Tokens with ranks $\mathbf{1}$ and $\mathbf{2}$ move to q_2.)

(ii) If a state holds more than one token, keep only the most senior token. (Only the token with rank $\mathbf{1}$ survives.)

(iii) Recompute the seniority ranks of the remaining tokens. (In this case unnecessary; if, for instance, the token of rank $\mathbf{3}$ survives and the token of rank $\mathbf{2}$ does not, then the token of rank $\mathbf{3}$ gets its rank upgraded to $\mathbf{2}$.)

(iv) If there is no token on the initial state, add one with the next lowest seniority rank. (Add a token to q_1 of rank $\mathbf{2}$.)

Example 13. Figure 1 shows on the right the transition system generated by the function δ' starting at the abstract configuration $(\mathbf{1}, \perp)$.

It is useful to think of tokens as companies that can buy other companies: at step (2), the senior company buys all junior companies; they all get the rank of the senior company, and from this moment on travel around the automaton together with the senior company. So, at every moment in time, every token in a non-sink state has a rank (the rank of its senior token). The rank of a token can age as it moves along the run, for two different reasons: its senior token can be bought by another senior token of an older rank, or all tokens of an older rank reach a sink. However, ranks can never get younger.

Further, observe that in any run, the tokens that never reach any sink eventually get the oldest ranks, i.e., ranks $\mathbf{1}$ to $\mathbf{i} - \mathbf{1}$ for some $i \ge 1$. We call these tokens *squatters*. Each squatter either enters the set of accepting states (and stays there by assumption on Mojmir automata) or never visits any accepting state. Now, consider a run in which almost every token succeeds. Squatters that never visit accepting states eventually stop buying other tokens, because otherwise infinitely many tokens would travel with them, and thus infinitely many tokens would never reach final states. So the run satisfies these conditions:

(1) Only finitely many tokens reach a non-accepting sink ("fail").
(2) There is a rank **i** such that
   (2.1) tokens of rank older than **i** buy other tokens in non-accepting states only
       finitely often, and
   (2.2) infinitely many tokens of rank **i** reach an accepting state ("succeed").

Conversely, we prove that if infinitely many tokens never succeed, then (1) or (2) does not hold. If infinitely many tokens fail, then (1) does not hold. If only finitely many tokens fail, but infinitely many tokens squat in non-accepting non-sinks, then (2) does not hold. Indeed, since the number of states is finite, infinitely many squatters get bought in non-accepting states and, since ranks can only improve, their ranks eventually stabilize. Let **j** − 1 be the youngest rank such that infinitely many tokens stabilize with that rank. Then the squatters are exactly the tokens of ranks $1, \ldots, \mathbf{j} - 1$, and infinitely many tokens of rank **j** reach (accepting) sinks. But then (2.2) is violated for every $\mathbf{i} < \mathbf{j}$, and (2.1) is violated for every $\mathbf{i} \geq \mathbf{j}$ as, by the pigeonhole principle, there is a squatter (with rank older than **j**) residing in non-accepting states and buying infintely many tokens.

So the runs in which almost every token succeeds are exactly those satisfying (1) and (2). We define a Rabin automaton having rankings as states, and accepting exactly these runs. We use a Rabin condition with pairs of sets of transitions, instead of states.[3] Let *fail* be the set of transitions that move a token into a non-accepting sink. Further, for every rank **j** let *succeed*(**j**) be the set of transitions that move a token of rank **j** into an accepting state, and *buy*(**j**) the set of transitions that move a token of rank older than **j** and another token into the same non-accepting state, causing one of the two to buy the other.

Definition 14. *Let* $\mathcal{M} = (Q, i, \delta, F)$ *be a Mojmir automaton with a set S of sinks. The deterministic Rabin automaton* $\mathcal{R}(\mathcal{M}) = (Q_{\mathcal{R}}, i_{\mathcal{R}}, \delta_{\mathcal{R}}, \bigvee_{i=1}^{|Q|} P_i)$ *is defined as follows:*

- $Q_{\mathcal{R}}$ *is the set of rankings* $r: Q \to \{1, \ldots, |Q|\}$;
- $i_{\mathcal{R}}$ *is the ranking defined only at the initial state i (and so $i_{\mathcal{R}}(i) = 1$);*
- $\delta_{\mathcal{R}}(r, \nu) = \alpha[\delta(r, \nu)]$ *for every ranking r and letter ν;*
- $P_j = (fail \cup buy(\mathbf{j}), succeed(\mathbf{j}))$, *where*

$$fail = \{(r, \nu, s) \in \delta_{\mathcal{R}} \mid \exists q \in Q : r(q) \in \mathbb{N} \wedge \delta(q, \nu) \in S \setminus F\}$$

$$succeed(\mathbf{j}) = \{(r, \nu, s) \in \delta_{\mathcal{R}} \mid \exists q \in Q : r(q) = \mathbf{j} \wedge \delta(q, \nu) \in F\}$$

$$buy(\mathbf{j}) = \{(r, \nu, s) \in \delta_{\mathcal{R}} \mid \exists q, q' \in Q : r(q) < \mathbf{j} \wedge r(q') \in \mathbb{N}$$
$$\wedge \left(\delta(q, \nu) = \delta(q', \nu) \notin F \vee \delta(q, \nu) = i \notin F\right)\}$$

---

[3] It is straightforward to give an equivalent automaton with a condition on states, but transitions are better for us.

We say that a word $w \in L(\mathcal{R}(\mathcal{M}))$ is accepted at rank $\mathbf{j}$ if P_j is the accepting pair in the run of $\mathcal{R}(\mathcal{M})$ on w with smallest index. The rank at which w is accepted is denoted by $rk(w)$.

By the discussion above, we have

Theorem 15. *For every Mojmir automaton $\mathcal{M}$: $L(\mathcal{M}) = L(\mathcal{R}(\mathcal{M}))$.*

Example 16. Let us determine the accepting pairs of the DRA on the right of Figure 1. We have $fail = \{t_2, t_7, t_8\}, buy(1) = \emptyset, succeed(1) = \{t_1, t_6\}$, and $buy(2) = \{t_5, t_8\}, succeed(2) = \{t_4, t_6, t_7\}$.

It is easy to see that the runs accepted by the pair P_1 are those that take t_2, t_7, t_8 only finitely often, and visit $(\mathbf{1}, \perp)$ infinitely often. They are accepted at rank $\mathbf{1}$. The runs accepted at rank $\mathbf{2}$ are those accepted by P_2 but not by P_1. They take $t_1, t_2, t_5, t_6, t_7, t_8$ finitely often, and so they are exactly the runs with a t_4^ω suffix.

3.2   The Automaton $\mathcal{R}(\varphi)$

Given a **G**-free formula φ, we define $\mathcal{R}(\varphi) = \mathcal{R}(\mathcal{M}(\varphi))$. By Theorem 12 and Theorem 15, we have $L(\mathcal{R}(\varphi)) = L(\mathbf{FG}\varphi)$.

If w is accepted by $\mathcal{R}(\varphi)$ at rank $rk(w)$, then we not only know that w satisfies $\mathbf{FG}\varphi$. In order to explain exactly what else we know, we need the following definition.

Definition 17. *Let $\delta_\mathcal{R}$ be the transition function of the DRA $\mathcal{R}(\varphi)$ and let $w \in L(\varphi)$ be a word. For every $j \in \mathbb{N}$, we denote by $\mathcal{F}(w_{0j})$ the conjunction of the formulae of rank younger than or equal to $rk(w)$ at the state $\delta_\mathcal{R}(i_\mathcal{R}, w_{0j})$.*

Intuitively, we also know that w_j satisfies $\mathcal{F}(w_{0j})$ for almost every index $j \in \mathbb{N}$, a fact we will use for the accepting condition of the Rabin automaton for general formulae in Section 5. Before proving this, we give an example.

Example 18. Consider the Rabin automaton on the right of Figure 1. Let $w = (\{b\}\{c\})^\omega$. Its corresponding run is $(t_3 t_6)^\omega$, which is accepted at rank $\mathbf{1}$. For every even value j, $\mathcal{F}(w_{0j})$ is the conjunction of the formulae of rank $\mathbf{1}$ and $\mathbf{2}$ at the state $(\mathbf{2}, \mathbf{1})$. So we get $\mathcal{F}(w_{0j}) = (a \vee (b \mathbf{U} c)) \wedge (b \mathbf{U} c) \equiv_p (b \mathbf{U} c)$, and therefore we know that infinitely many suffixes of w satisfy $(b \mathbf{U} c)$. In other words, the automaton tells us not only that $w \models \mathbf{FG}(a \vee (b \mathbf{U} c))$, but also that $w \models \mathbf{FG}(b \mathbf{U} c)$.

We now show this formally. If $w \models \mathbf{FG}\varphi$, there is a smallest index $ind(w, \varphi)$ at which φ "starts to hold". For every index $j \geq ind(w, \varphi)$, we have $w_j \models \bigwedge_{k=ind(w,\varphi)}^{j} af(\varphi, w_{kj})$. Intuitively, this formula is the conjunction of the formulae "tracked" by the tokens of $\mathcal{M}(\varphi)$ born on days $ind(w, \varphi), ind(w, \varphi)+1, \ldots, j$. These are the "true" tokens of $\mathcal{M}(\varphi)$, that is, those that eventually reach an accepting state. We get:

Lemma 19. *Let φ be a **G**-free formula and let $w \in L(\mathcal{R}(\varphi))$. Then*

(1) $\mathcal{F}(w_{0j}) \equiv \bigwedge_{k=ind(w,\varphi)}^{j} af(\varphi, w_{kj})$ for almost every $j \in \mathbb{N}$; and

(2) $w_j \models \mathcal{F}(w_{0j})$ for almost every $j \in \mathbb{N}$.

4   DRAs for Arbitrary FG-Formulae

We construct a DRA for an arbitrary formula **FG**-formula **FG**φ. It suffices to construct a Mojmir automaton, and then apply the construction of Section 3.1. We show that the Mojmir automaton can be defined compositionally, as a parallel composition of Mojmir automata, one for each **G**-subformula.

Definition 20. *Given a formula φ, we denote by $\mathbb{G}(\varphi)$ the set of **G**-subformulae of φ, i.e., the subformulae of φ of the form **G**ψ.*

More precisely, for every $\mathcal{G} \subseteq \mathbb{G}(\mathbf{FG}\varphi)$ and every $\mathbf{G}\psi \in \mathcal{G}$, we construct a Mojmir automaton $\mathcal{M}(\psi, \mathcal{G})$. Automata $\mathcal{M}(\psi, \mathcal{G})$ and $\mathcal{M}(\psi, \mathcal{G}')$ for two different sets $\mathcal{G}, \mathcal{G}'$ have the same transition system, i.e., they differ only on the accepting condition. The automaton $\mathcal{M}(\psi, \mathcal{G})$ checks that $\mathbf{FG}\psi$ holds, under the assumption that $\mathbf{FG}\psi'$ holds for all the subformulae $\mathbf{G}\psi'$ of ψ that belong to $\mathcal{G}$. Circularity is avoided, because automata for ψ only rely on assumptions about proper subformulae of ψ. Loosely speaking, the Rabin automaton for $\mathbf{FG}\varphi$ is the parallel composition (or product) of the Rabin automata for the $\mathcal{M}(\psi, \mathcal{G})$ (which are independent of $\mathcal{G}$), with an acceptance condition obtained from the acceptance conditions of the $\mathcal{M}(\psi, \mathcal{G})$.

We only need to define the automaton $\mathcal{M}(\varphi, \mathcal{G})$, because the automata $\mathcal{M}(\psi, \mathcal{G})$ are defined inductively in exactly the same way. Intuitively, the automaton for $\mathcal{M}(\varphi, \mathcal{G})$ does not "track" **G**-subformulae of φ, it delegates that task to the automata for its subformulae. This is formalized with the help of the following definition.

Definition 21. *Let φ be a formula and $\nu \in 2^{Ap}$. The formula $af_{\mathbf{G}}(\varphi, \nu)$ is inductively defined as $af(\varphi, \nu)$, with only this difference:*

$$af_{\mathbf{G}}(\mathbf{G}\varphi, \nu) = \mathbf{G}\varphi \qquad \text{(instead of } af(\mathbf{G}\varphi, \nu) = af(\varphi, \nu) \wedge \mathbf{G}\varphi\text{).}$$

We define $Reach_{\mathbf{G}}(\varphi) = \{af_{\mathbf{G}}(\varphi, w) \mid w \in (2^{Ap})^*\}$ (up to $\equiv_p$).

Example 22. Let $\varphi = \psi\mathbf{U}\neg a$, where $\psi = \mathbf{G}(a \wedge \mathbf{X}\neg a)$. We have

$$af_{\mathbf{G}}(\varphi, \{a\}) = af_{\mathbf{G}}(\psi, \{a\}) \wedge \varphi \equiv_p \psi \wedge \varphi$$
$$af(\varphi, \{a\}) \quad = af(\psi, \{a\}) \wedge \varphi \quad \equiv_p \neg a \wedge \psi \wedge \varphi$$

Definition 23. *Let φ be a formula and let $\mathcal{G} \subseteq \mathbb{G}(\varphi)$. The Mojmir automaton of φ with respect to $\mathcal{G}$ is the quadruple $\mathcal{M}(\varphi, \mathcal{G}) = (Reach_{\mathbf{G}}(\varphi), \varphi, af_{\mathbf{G}}, F_{\mathcal{G}})$, where $F_{\mathcal{G}}$ contains the formulae $\varphi' \in Reach_{\mathbf{G}}(\varphi)$ propositionally implied by $\mathcal{G}$, i.e. the formulae satisfying $\bigwedge_{\mathbf{G}\psi \in \mathcal{G}} \mathbf{G}\psi \models_p \varphi'$.*

Observe that only the set of accepting states of $\mathcal{M}(\varphi, \mathcal{G})$ depends on $\mathcal{G}$. The following lemma shows that states reachable from final states are also final.

Lemma 24. *Let φ be a formula and let $\mathcal{G} \subseteq \mathbb{G}(\varphi)$. For every $\varphi' \in Reach_{\mathbf{G}}(\varphi)$, if $\bigwedge_{\mathbf{G}\psi \in \mathcal{G}} \mathbf{G}\psi \models_p \varphi'$ then $\bigwedge_{\mathbf{G}\psi \in \mathcal{G}} \mathbf{G}\psi \models_p af_{\mathbf{G}}(\varphi', \nu)$ for every $\nu \in 2^{Ap}$.*

Proof. Follows easily from the definition of $\models_p$ and $af_\mathbf{G}(\mathbf{G}\psi) = \mathbf{G}\psi$.

Example 25. Let $\varphi = (\mathbf{G}\psi)\mathbf{U}\neg a$, where $\psi = a \wedge \mathbf{X}\neg a$. We have $\mathbb{G}(\varphi) = \{\mathbf{G}\psi\}$, and so two automata $\mathcal{M}(\varphi, \emptyset)$ and $\mathcal{M}(\varphi, \{\mathbf{G}\psi\})$, whose common transition system is shown on the left of Figure 2. We have one single automaton $\mathcal{M}(\psi, \emptyset)$, shown on the right of the figure. A formula φ' is an accepting state of $\mathcal{M}(\psi, \emptyset)$ if $\mathbf{tt} \models_p \varphi'$; and so the only accepting state of the automaton on the right is $\mathbf{tt}$. On the other hand, $\mathcal{M}(\varphi, \{\mathbf{G}\psi\})$ has both $\mathbf{G}\psi$ and $\mathbf{tt}$ as accepting states, but the only accepting state of $\mathcal{M}(\varphi, \emptyset)$ is $\mathbf{tt}$.

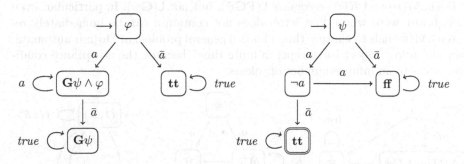

Fig. 2. Mojmir automata for $\varphi = (\mathbf{G}\psi)\ \mathbf{U}\neg a$, where $\psi = a \wedge \mathbf{X}\neg a$

Theorem 26. *Let φ be a formula and let w be a word. Then $w \models \mathbf{FG}\varphi$ iff there is $\mathcal{G} \subseteq \mathbb{G}(\varphi)$ such that (1) $w \in \mathsf{L}(\mathcal{M}(\varphi, \mathcal{G}))$, and (2) $w \models \mathbf{FG}\psi$ for every $\mathbf{G}\psi \in \mathcal{G}$.*

Using induction on the structure of $\mathbf{G}$-subformulae we obtain:

Theorem 27. *Let φ be a formula and let w be a word. Then $w \models \mathbf{FG}\varphi$ iff there is $\mathcal{G} \subseteq \mathbb{G}(\mathbf{FG}\varphi)$ such that $w \in \mathsf{L}(\mathcal{M}(\psi, \mathcal{G}))$ for every $\mathbf{G}\psi \in \mathcal{G}$.*

4.1 The Product Automaton

Theorem 27 allows us to construct a Rabin automaton for an arbitrary formula of the form $\mathbf{FG}\varphi$. For every $\mathbf{G}\psi \in \mathbb{G}(\mathbf{FG}\varphi)$ and every $\mathcal{G} \subseteq \mathbb{G}(\mathbf{FG}\varphi)$ let $\mathcal{R}(\psi, \mathcal{G}) = (Q_\psi, i_\psi, \delta_\psi, Acc_\psi^\mathcal{G})$ be the Rabin automaton obtained by applying Definition 14 to the Mojmir automaton $\mathcal{M}(\psi, \mathcal{G})$. Since $Q_\psi, i_\psi, \delta_\psi$ do not depend on $\mathcal{G}$, we define the product automaton $\mathcal{P}(\varphi)$ as

$$\mathcal{P}(\varphi) = \left(\prod_{\mathbf{G}\psi \in \mathbb{G}(\varphi)} Q_\psi, \prod_{\mathbf{G}\psi \in \mathbb{G}(\varphi)} \{i_\psi\}, \prod_{\mathbf{G}\psi \in \mathbb{G}(\varphi)} \delta_\psi, \bigvee_{\mathcal{G} \subseteq \mathbb{G}_\varphi} \bigwedge_{\mathbf{G}\psi \in \mathbb{G}(\varphi)} Acc_\psi^\mathcal{G} \right)$$

Since each of the $Acc_\psi^\mathcal{G}$ is a Rabin condition, we obtain a generalized Rabin condition. This automaton can then be transformed into an equivalent Rabin automaton [KE12]. However, as shown in [CGK13], for many applications it is better to keep it in this form. By Theorem 27 we immediately get:

Theorem 28. *Let φ be a formula and let w be a word. Then $w \models \mathbf{FG}\varphi$ iff there is $\mathcal{G} \subseteq \mathbb{G}(\mathbf{FG}\varphi)$ such that $w \in L(\mathcal{P}(\varphi))$.*

5   DRAs for Arbitrary Formulae

In order to explain the last step of our procedure, consider the following example.

Example 29. Let $\varphi = b \wedge \mathbf{X}b \wedge \mathbf{G}\psi$, where $\psi = a \wedge \mathbf{X}(b\mathbf{U}c)$ and let $Ap = \{a, b, c\}$. The Mojmir automaton $\mathcal{M}(\psi)$ is shown in the middle of Figure 3. Its corresponding Rabin automaton $\mathcal{R}(\psi)$ is shown on the right, where the state $(\mathbf{i}, \mathbf{j})$ indicates that ψ has rank $\mathbf{i}$ and $b\mathbf{U}c$ has rank $\mathbf{j}$. We have $fail = \{t_1, t_5, t_6, t_7, t_8\}$, $buy(\mathbf{1}) = \emptyset$, $succeed(\mathbf{1}) = \{t_4, t_7\}$ and $buy(\mathbf{2}) = \{t_3\}$, $succeed(\mathbf{2}) = \emptyset$.

Both $\mathcal{M}(\psi)$ and $\mathcal{R}(\psi)$ recognize $\mathsf{L}(\mathbf{FG}\psi)$, but not $\mathsf{L}(\mathbf{G}\psi)$. In particular, even though any word whose first letter does not contain a can be immediately rejected, $\mathcal{M}(\psi)$ fails to capture this. This is a general problem of Mojmir automata: they can never "reject (or accept) in finite time" because the acceptance condition refers to an infinite number of tokens.

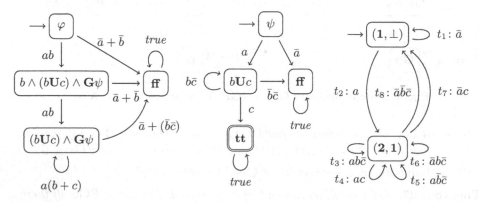

Fig. 3. Automata $\mathcal{T}(\varphi)$, $\mathcal{M}(\psi)$, and $\mathcal{R}(\psi)$ for $\varphi = b \wedge \mathbf{X}b \wedge \mathbf{G}\psi$ and $\psi = a \wedge \mathbf{X}(b\mathbf{U}c)$

5.1   Master Transition System

The "accept/reject in finite time" problem can be solved with the help of the *master transition system* (an automaton without an accepting condition).

Definition 30. *Let φ be a formula. The* master transition system *for φ is the tuple* $\mathcal{T}(\varphi) = (Reach(\varphi), \varphi, af)$.

The master transition system for the formula of Example 29 is shown on the left of Figure 3. Whenever we enter state $\mathbf{ff}$, we have $af(\varphi, w) = \mathbf{ff}$ for the word w read so far, and so the run is not accepting.

Consider now the word $w = \{a, b, c\}^\omega$, which clearly satisfies φ. How do master $\mathcal{T}(\varphi)$ and slave $\mathcal{M}(\psi)$ decide together that $w \models \varphi$ holds? Intuitively, $\mathcal{M}(\psi)$ accepts, and tells the master that $w \models \mathbf{FG}\psi$ holds. The master reaches the state $(b \mathbf{U} c) \wedge \mathbf{G}\psi$ and stays there forever. Since she knows that $\mathbf{FG}\psi$ holds, the master deduces that $w \models \varphi$ holds if $w \models \mathbf{FG}(b \mathbf{U} c)$. But where can it get this information from?

At this point the master resorts to Lemma 19: the slave $\mathcal{M}(\psi)$ (or, more precisely, its Rabin automaton $\mathcal{R}(\psi)$) not only tells the master that w satisfies $\mathbf{FG}\psi$, but also at which rank, and so that w_j satisfies $\mathcal{F}(w_{0j})$ for almost every $j \in \mathbb{N}$. In our example, during the run $w = \{a, b, c\}^\omega$, all tokens flow down the path $a \wedge \mathbf{X}(b\,\mathbf{U}\,c) \xrightarrow{a} b\,\mathbf{U}\,c \xrightarrow{c} \mathbf{tt}$ "in lockstep". No token buys any other, and all tokens of rank 1 succeed. The corresponding run of $\mathcal{R}(\psi)$ executes the sequence $t_2 t_4^\omega$ of transitions, stays in $(2, 1)$ forever, and accepts at rank 1. So we have $\mathcal{F}(w_{0j}) = (b\,\mathbf{U}\,c) \wedge \psi$ for every $j \geq 0$, and therefore the slave tells the master that $w_j \models (b\,\mathbf{U}\,c)$ for almost every $j \in \mathbb{N}$.

So in this example the information required by the master is precisely the additional information supplied by $\mathcal{M}(\psi)$ due to Lemma 19. The next theorem shows that this is always the case.

Theorem 31. *Let φ be a formula and let w be a word. Let $\mathcal{G}$ be the set of formulae $\mathbf{G}\psi \in \mathbb{G}(\varphi)$ such that $w \models \mathbf{FG}\psi$. We have $w \models \varphi$ iff for almost every $i \in \mathbb{N}$:*

$$\bigwedge_{\mathbf{G}\psi \in \mathcal{G}} (\mathbf{G}\psi \wedge \mathcal{F}(\psi, w_{0i})) \models_p af(\varphi, w_{0i}) .$$

The automaton recognizing φ is a product of the automaton $\mathcal{P}(\varphi)$ defined in Section 4.1, and $\mathcal{T}(\varphi)$. The run of $\mathcal{P}(\varphi)$ of a word w determines the set $\mathcal{G} \subseteq \mathbb{G}(\varphi)$ such that $w \models \mathbf{FG}\psi$ iff $\psi \in \mathcal{G}$. Moreover, each component of $\mathcal{P}(\varphi)$ accepts at a certain rank, and this determines the formula $\mathcal{F}(\psi, w_{0i})$ for every $i \geq 0$ (it suffices to look at the state reached by the component of $\mathcal{P}(\varphi)$ in charge of the formula ψ). By Theorem 31, it remains to check whether eventually

$$\bigwedge_{\mathbf{G}\psi \in \mathcal{G}} (\mathbf{G}\psi \wedge \mathcal{F}(\psi, w_{0i})) \models_p af(\varphi, w_{0i})$$

holds. This is done with the help of $\mathcal{T}(\varphi)$, which "tracks" $af(\varphi, w_{0i})$. To check the property, we turn the accepting condition into a disjunction not only on the possible $\mathcal{G} \subseteq \mathbb{G}(\varphi)$, but also on the possible rankings that assign to each formula $\mathbf{G}\psi \in \mathcal{G}$ a rank. This corresponds to letting the product guess which G-subformulae will hold, and at which rank they will be accepted. The slaves check the guess, and the master checks that it eventually only visits states implied by the guess.

5.2   The GDRA $\mathcal{A}(\varphi)$

We can now formally define the final automaton $\mathcal{A}(\varphi)$ recognizing φ. Let $\mathcal{P}(\varphi) = (Q_\mathcal{P}, i_\mathcal{P}, \delta_\mathcal{P}, Acc_\mathcal{P})$ be the product automaton described in Section 4.1, and let $\mathcal{T}(\varphi) = (Reach(\varphi), \varphi, af)$. We let

$$\mathcal{A}(\varphi) = (Reach(\varphi) \times Q_\mathcal{P}, (\varphi, i_\mathcal{P}), af \times \delta_\mathcal{P}, Acc)$$

where the accepting condition Acc is defined top-down as follows:

– Acc is a disjunction containing a disjunct $Acc_\pi^\mathcal{G}$ for each pair $(\mathcal{G}, \pi)$, where $\mathcal{G} \subseteq \mathbb{G}(\varphi)$ and π is a mapping assigning to each $\psi \in \mathcal{G}$ a rank, i.e., a number between 1 and the number of Rabin pairs of $\mathcal{R}(\varphi, \mathcal{G})$.

– The disjunct $Acc_\pi^{\mathcal{G}}$ is a conjunction of the form $Acc_\pi^{\mathcal{G}} = M_\pi^{\mathcal{G}} \wedge \bigwedge_{\psi \in \mathcal{G}} Acc_\pi(\psi)$.

– Condition $Acc_\pi(\psi)$ states that $\mathcal{R}(\psi, \mathcal{G})$ accepts with rank $\pi(\psi)$ for every $\psi \in \mathcal{G}$. It is therefore a Rabin condition with only one Rabin pair.

– Condition $M_\pi^{\mathcal{G}}$ states that $\mathcal{A}(\varphi)$ eventually stays within a subset F of states defined as follows. Let $(\varphi', r_{\psi_1}, \ldots, r_{\psi_k}) \in Reach(\varphi) \times Q_P$, where r_ψ is a ranking of the formulae of $Reach_{\mathbf{G}}(\psi)$ for every $\mathbf{G}\psi \in \mathbb{G}(\varphi)$, and let $\mathcal{F}(r_\psi)$ be the conjunction of the states of $\mathcal{M}(\psi)$ to which r_ψ assigns rank $\pi(\psi)$ or higher. Then

$$(\varphi', r_{\psi_1}, \ldots, r_{\psi_k}) \in F \quad \text{iff} \quad \bigwedge_{\mathbf{G}\psi \in \mathcal{G}} \mathbf{G}\psi \wedge \mathcal{F}(r_\psi) \models_p \varphi' .$$

Notice that $M_\pi^{\mathcal{G}}$ is a co-Büchi condition, and so a Rabin condition with only one pair.

Theorem 32. *For any LTL formula φ, $\mathsf{L}(\mathcal{A}(\varphi)) = \mathsf{L}(\varphi)$.*

6   The Alternation-Free Linear-Time μ-Calculus

The linear-time μ-calculus is a linear-time logic with the same expressive power as Büchi automata and DRAs (see e.g. [Var88, Dam92]). It extends propositional logic with the next operator $\mathbf{X}$, and least and greatest fixpoints. This section is addressed to readers familiar with this logic. We take as syntax

$$\varphi ::= \mathbf{tt} \mid \mathbf{ff} \mid a \mid \neg a \mid y \mid \varphi \wedge \varphi \mid \varphi \vee \varphi \mid \mathbf{X}\varphi \mid \mu x.\varphi \mid \nu x.\varphi$$

where y ranges over a set of variables. We assume that if $\sigma y.\varphi$ and $\sigma z.\psi$ are distinct subformulae of a formula, then y and z are also distinct. A formula is *alternation-free* if for every subformula $\mu y.\varphi$ ($\nu y.\varphi$) no path of the syntax tree leading from μy (νy) to y contains an occurrence of νz (μz) for some variable z. For instance, $\mu y.(a \vee \mu z.(y \vee \mathbf{X}z)$ is alternation-free, but $\nu y.\mu z.((a \wedge y) \vee \mathbf{X}z)$ is not. It is well known that the alternation-free fragment is strictly more expressive than LTL and strictly less expressive than the full linear-time μ-calculus. In particular, the property "a holds at every even moment" is not expressible in LTL, but corresponds to $\nu y.(a \wedge \mathbf{XX}y)$.

Our technique extends to the alternation-free linear-time μ-calculus. We have refrained from presenting it for this more general logic because it is less well known and formulae are more difficult to read. We only need to change the definition of the functions af and $af_{\mathbf{G}}$. For the common part of the syntax (everything but the fixpoint formulae) the definition is identical. For the rest we define

$$af(\mu y.\varphi, \nu) = af(\varphi, \nu) \vee \mu y.\varphi \qquad af_{\mathbf{G}}(\mu y.\varphi, \nu) = af_{\mathbf{G}}(\varphi, \nu) \vee \mu y.\varphi$$
$$af(\nu y.\varphi, \nu) = af(\varphi, \nu) \wedge \nu y.\varphi \qquad af_{\mathbf{G}}(\nu y.\varphi, \nu) = \nu y.\varphi$$

The automaton $\mathcal{A}(\varphi)$ is a product of automata, one for every ν-subformula of φ, and a master transition system. Our constructions can be reused, and the proofs require only technical changes in the structural inductions.

7   Experimental Results

We compare the performance of the following tools and methods:

(T1) ltl2dstar [Kle] implements and optimizes [KB07] Safra's construction
     [Saf88]. It uses LTL2BA [GO01] to obtain the non-deterministic Büchi
     automata (NBA) first. Other translators to NBA may also be used, such
     as Spot [DL13] or LTL3BA [BKRS12] and in some cases may yield better
     results (see [BKS13] for comparison thereof), but LTL2BA is recommended
     by ltl2dstar and is used this way in PRISM [KNP11].
(T2) Rabinizer [GKE12] and Rabinizer 2 [KLG13] implement a direct construc-
     tion based on [KE12] for fragments LTL($\mathbf{F}, \mathbf{G}$) and LTL$_{\backslash \mathbf{GU}}$, respectively.
     The latter is used only on formulae not in LTL($\mathbf{F}, \mathbf{G}$).
(T3) LTL3DRA [BBKS13] which implements a construction via alternating au-
     tomata, which is "inspired by [KE12]" (quoted from [BBKS13]) and per-
     forms several optimizations.
(T4) Our new construction. Notice that we produce a state space with a logical
     structure, which permits many optimizations; for instance, one could in-
     corporate the suspension optimization of LTL3BA [BBDL^{+}13]. However,
     in our prototype implementation we use only the following optimization:
     In each state we only keep track of the slaves for formulae ψ that are still
     "relevant" for the master's state φ, i.e. $\varphi[\psi/\mathbf{tt}] \not\equiv_p \varphi[\psi/\mathbf{ff}]$. For instance,
     after reading $\emptyset$ in $\mathbf{GF}a \vee (b \wedge \mathbf{GF}c)$, it is no longer interesting to track if c
     occurs infinitely often.

Table 1 compares these four tools. For T1 and T2 we produce DRAs (although
Rabinizer 2 can also produce GDRAs). For T3 and T4 we produce GDRAs with
transition acceptance (tGDRAs), which can be directly used for probabilistic
model checking without blow-up [CGK13]. The table shows experimental results
on four sets of formulae (see the four parts of the table)

1. Formulae of the LTL($\mathbf{F}, \mathbf{G}$) fragment taken from (i) BEEM (BEnchmarks
   for Explicit Model checkers) [Pel07] and from [SB00] on which ltl2dstar was
   originally tested [KB06] (see [EK14]); and (ii) fairness-like formulae. All the
   formulae were used already in [KE12, BBKS13]. Our method usually achieves
   the same results as the optimized LTL3DRA, outperforming the first two
   approaches.
2. Formulae of LTL$_{\backslash \mathbf{GU}}$ taken from [KLG13] and [EH00]. They illustrate the
   problems of the standard approach to handle (i) $\mathbf{X}$ operators inside the scope
   of other temporal operators and (ii) conjunctions of liveness properties.
3. Some further formulae illustrating teh same phenomenon.
4. Some complex LTL formulae expressing "after Q until R" properties, taken
   from SPEC PATTERN [DAC99] (available at [spe]) .

All automata were constructed within a few seconds, with the exception
of the larger automata generated by ltl2dstar: it took several minutes for automata over ten thousand states and hours for hundreds of thousands of states.

Formula	T1	T2	T3	T4
$\mathbf{FG}a \vee \mathbf{GF}b$	4	4	1	1
$(\mathbf{FG}a \vee \mathbf{GF}b) \wedge (\mathbf{FG}c \vee \mathbf{GF}d)$	11 324	18	1	1
$\bigwedge_{i=1}^{3}(\mathbf{GF}a_i \to \mathbf{GF}b_i)$	1 304 706	462	1	1
$\bigwedge_{i=1}^{2}(\mathbf{GF}a_i \to \mathbf{GF}a_{i+1})$	572	11	1	1
$\bigwedge_{i=1}^{3}(\mathbf{GF}a_i \to \mathbf{GF}a_{i+1})$	290 046	52	1	1
$(\mathbf{X}(\mathbf{G}r \vee r\mathbf{U}(r \wedge s\mathbf{U}p)))\mathbf{U}(\mathbf{G}r \vee r\mathbf{U}(r \wedge s))$	18	9	8	8
$p\mathbf{U}(q \wedge \mathbf{X}(r \wedge (\mathbf{F}(s \wedge \mathbf{X}(\mathbf{F}(t \wedge \mathbf{X}(\mathbf{F}(u \wedge \mathbf{XF}v))))))))$	9	13	13	13
$(\mathbf{GF}(a \wedge \mathbf{XX}b) \vee \mathbf{FG}b) \wedge \mathbf{FG}(c \vee (\mathbf{X}a \wedge \mathbf{XX}b))$	353	73	–	12
$\mathbf{GF}(\mathbf{XXX}a \wedge \mathbf{XXXX}b) \wedge \mathbf{GF}(b \vee \mathbf{X}c) \wedge \mathbf{GF}(c \wedge \mathbf{XX}a)$	2 127	169	–	16
$(\mathbf{GF}a \vee \mathbf{FG}b) \wedge (\mathbf{GF}c \vee \mathbf{FG}(d \vee \mathbf{X}e))$	18 176	80	–	2
$(\mathbf{GF}(a \wedge \mathbf{XX}c) \vee \mathbf{FG}b) \wedge (\mathbf{GF}c \vee \mathbf{FG}(d \vee \mathbf{X}a \wedge \mathbf{XX}b))$	?	142	–	12
$a\mathbf{U}b \wedge (\mathbf{GF}a \vee \mathbf{FG}b) \wedge (\mathbf{GF}c \vee \mathbf{FG}d) \vee$	640 771	210	8	7
$\quad \vee a\mathbf{U}c \wedge (\mathbf{GF}a \vee \mathbf{FG}d) \wedge (\mathbf{GF}c \vee \mathbf{FG}b)$				
$\mathbf{FG}((a \wedge \mathbf{XX}b \wedge \mathbf{GF}b)\mathbf{U}(\mathbf{G}(\mathbf{XX}!c \vee \mathbf{XX}(a \wedge b))))$	2 053	–	–	11
$\mathbf{G}(\mathbf{F}!a \wedge \mathbf{F}(b \wedge \mathbf{X}!c) \wedge \mathbf{GF}(a\mathbf{U}d)) \wedge \mathbf{GF}((\mathbf{X}d)\mathbf{U}(b \vee \mathbf{G}c))$	283	–	–	7
φ_{35} : 2 cause-1 effect precedence chain	6	–	–	6
φ_{40} : 1 cause-2 effect precedence chain	314	–	–	32
φ_{45} : 2 stimulus-1 response chain	1 450	–	–	78
φ_{50} : 1 stimulus-2 response chain	28	–	–	23

Table 1. Some experimental results

The automaton for $\bigwedge_{i=1}^{3}(\mathbf{GF}a_i \to \mathbf{GF}b_i)$ took even more than a day and ? denotes a time-out after one day. Not applicability of the tool to the formula is denoted by $-$. Additional details and more experimental results can be found in [EK14].

8 Conclusions

We have presented the first direct translation from LTL formulae to deterministic Rabin automata able to handle arbitrary formulae. The construction generalizes previous ones for LTL fragments [KE12, GKE12, KLG13]. Given φ, we compute (1) the master, the slaves for each $\mathbf{G}\psi \in \mathbb{G}(\varphi)$, and their parallel composition, and (2) the acceptance condition: we first guess $\mathcal{G} \subseteq \mathbb{G}(\varphi)$ which are true (this yields the accepting states of slaves), and then guess the ranks (this yields the information for the master's co-Büchi acceptance condition).

The compositional approach opens the door to many possible optimizations. Since slave automata are typically very small, we can aggressively try to optimize them, knowing that each reduced state in one slave potentially leads to large savings in the final number of states of the product. So far we have only implemented the simplest optimizations, and we think there is still much room for improvement.

We have conducted a detailed experimental comparison. Our construction outperforms two-step approaches that first translate the formula into a Büchi automaton and then apply Safra's construction. Moreover, despite handling full LTL, it is at least as efficient as previous constructions for fragments. Finally, we produce a (often much smaller) generalized Rabin automaton, which can be directly used for verification, without a further translation into a standard Rabin automaton.

References

[BBDL+13] Babiak, T., Badie, T., Duret-Lutz, A., Křetínský, M., Strejček, J.: Compositional approach to suspension and other improvements to LTL translation. In: Bartocci, E., Ramakrishnan, C.R. (eds.) SPIN 2013. LNCS, vol. 7976, pp. 81–98. Springer, Heidelberg (2013)

[BBKS13]   Babiak, T., Blahoudek, F., Křetínský, M., Strejček, J.: Effective translation of LTL to deterministic Rabin automata: Beyond the (F,G)-fragment. In: Van Hung, D., Ogawa, M. (eds.) ATVA 2013. LNCS, vol. 8172, pp. 24–39. Springer, Heidelberg (2013)

[BK08]   Baier, C., Katoen, J.-P.: Principles of model checking. MIT Press (2008)

[BKRS12]   Babiak, T., Křetínský, M., Řehák, V., Strejček, J.: LTL to Büchi automata translation: Fast and more deterministic. In: Flanagan, C., König, B. (eds.) TACAS 2012. LNCS, vol. 7214, pp. 95–109. Springer, Heidelberg (2012)

[BKS13]   Blahoudek, F., Křetínský, M., Strejček, J.: Comparison of LTL to deterministic Rabin automata translators. In: McMillan, K., Middeldorp, A., Voronkov, A. (eds.) LPAR-19 2013. LNCS, vol. 8312, pp. 164–172. Springer, Heidelberg (2013)

[CGK13]   Chatterjee, K., Gaiser, A., Křetínský, J.: Automata with generalized Rabin pairs for probabilistic model checking and LTL synthesis. In: Sharygina, N., Veith, H. (eds.) CAV 2013. LNCS, vol. 8044, pp. 559–575. Springer, Heidelberg (2013)

[Cou99]   Couvreur, J.-M.: On-the-fly verification of linear temporal logic. In: World Congress on Formal Methods, pp. 253–271 (1999)

[DAC99]   Dwyer, M.B., Avrunin, G.S., Corbett, J.C.: Patterns in property specifications for finite-state verification. In: ICSE, pp. 411–420 (1999)

[Dam92]   Dam, M.: Fixed points of Büchi automata. In: FSTTCS, pp. 39–50 (1992)

[DGV99]   Daniele, M., Giunchiglia, F., Vardi, M.Y.: Improved automata generation for linear temporal logic. In: Halbwachs, N., Peled, D.A. (eds.) CAV 1999. LNCS, vol. 1633, pp. 249–260. Springer, Heidelberg (1999)

[DL13]   Duret-Lutz, A.: Manipulating LTL formulas using spot 1.0. In: Van Hung, D., Ogawa, M. (eds.) ATVA 2013. LNCS, vol. 8172, pp. 442–445. Springer, Heidelberg (2013)

[EH00]   Etessami, K., Holzmann, G.J.: Optimizing Büchi automata. In: Palamidessi, C. (ed.) CONCUR 2000. LNCS, vol. 1877, pp. 153–167. Springer, Heidelberg (2000)

[EK14]   Esparza, J., Křetínský, J.: From LTL to deterministic automata: A safraless compositional approach. Technical Report abs/1402.3388, arXiv.org (2014)

[Fri03]   Fritz, C.: Constructing Büchi automata from linear temporal logic using simulation relations for alternating Büchi automata. In: Ibarra, O.H., Dang, Z. (eds.) CIAA 2003. LNCS, vol. 2759, pp. 35–48. Springer, Heidelberg (2003)

[GKE12]   Gaiser, A., Křetínský, J., Esparza, J.: Rabinizer: Small deterministic automata for LTL(F,G). In: Chakraborty, S., Mukund, M. (eds.) ATVA 2012. LNCS, vol. 7561, pp. 72–76. Springer, Heidelberg (2012)

[GL02]   Giannakopoulou, D., Lerda, F.: From states to transitions: Improving translation of LTL formulae to Büchi automata. In: FORTE, pp. 308–326 (2002)

[GO01]   Gastin, P., Oddoux, D.: Fast LTL to Büchi automata translation. In: Berry, G., Comon, H., Finkel, A. (eds.) CAV 2001. LNCS, vol. 2102, pp. 53–65. Springer, Heidelberg (2001); Tool accessible at http://www.lsv.ens-cachan.fr/~gastin/ltl2ba/

[KB06]   Klein, J., Baier, C.: Experiments with deterministic ω-automata for formulas of linear temporal logic. Theor. Comput. Sci. 363(2), 182–195 (2006)

[KB07]   Klein, J., Baier, C.: On-the-fly stuttering in the construction of deterministic ω-automata. In: Holub, J., Žďárek, J. (eds.) CIAA 2007. LNCS, vol. 4783, pp. 51–61. Springer, Heidelberg (2007)

[KE12]   Křetínský, J., Esparza, J.: Deterministic automata for the (F,G)-fragment of LTL. In: Madhusudan, P., Seshia, S.A. (eds.) CAV 2012. LNCS, vol. 7358, pp. 7–22. Springer, Heidelberg (2012)

[Kle]   Klein, J.: ltl2dstar - LTL to deterministic Streett and Rabin automata, http://www.ltl2dstar.de/

[KLG13]   Křetínský, J., Garza, R.L.: Rabinizer 2: Small deterministic automata for LTL\GU. In: Van Hung, D., Ogawa, M. (eds.) ATVA 2013. LNCS, vol. 8172, pp. 446–450. Springer, Heidelberg (2013)

[KNP11]   Kwiatkowska, M., Norman, G., Parker, D.: PRISM 4.0: Verification of probabilistic real-time systems. In: Gopalakrishnan, G., Qadeer, S. (eds.) CAV 2011. LNCS, vol. 6806, pp. 585–591. Springer, Heidelberg (2011)

[Pel07]   Pelánek, R.: Beem: Benchmarks for explicit model checkers. In: Bošnački, D., Edelkamp, S. (eds.) SPIN 2007. LNCS, vol. 4595, pp. 263–267. Springer, Heidelberg (2007)

[Pit06]   Piterman, N.: From nondeterministic Büchi and Streett automata to deterministic parity automata. In: LICS, pp. 255–264 (2006)

[Saf88]   Safra, S.: On the complexity of ω-automata. In: FOCS, pp. 319–327. IEEE Computer Society (1988)

[SB00]   Somenzi, F., Bloem, R.: Efficient Büchi automata from LTL formulae. In: Emerson, E.A., Sistla, A.P. (eds.) CAV 2000. LNCS, vol. 1855, pp. 248–263. Springer, Heidelberg (2000)

[Sch09]   Schewe, S.: Tighter bounds for the determinisation of Büchi automata. In: FOSSACS, pp. 167–181 (2009)

[spe]   Spec Patterns: Property pattern mappings for LTL, http://patterns.projects.cis.ksu.edu/documentation/patterns/ltl.shtml

[Var88]   Vardi, M.Y.: A temporal fixpoint calculus. In: POPL, pp. 250–259 (1988)

Symbolic Visibly Pushdown Automata[*]

Loris D'Antoni and Rajeev Alur

University of Pennsylvania
{lorisdan,alur}@seas.upenn.edu

Abstract. Nested words model data with both linear and hierarchical structure such as XML documents and program traces. A nested word is a sequence of positions together with a matching relation that connects open tags (calls) with the corresponding close tags (returns). Visibly Pushdown Automata are a restricted class of pushdown automata that process nested words, and have many appealing theoretical properties such as closure under Boolean operations and decidable equivalence. However, like any classical automata models, they are limited to finite alphabets. This limitation is restrictive for practical applications to both XML processing and program trace analysis, where values for individual symbols are usually drawn from an unbounded domain. With this motivation, we introduce Symbolic Visibly Pushdown Automata (SVPA) as an executable model for nested words over infinite alphabets. In this model, transitions are labeled with predicates over the input alphabet, analogous to symbolic automata processing strings over infinite alphabets. A key novelty of SVPAs is the use of binary predicates to model relations between open and close tags in a nested word. We show how SVPAs still enjoy the decidability and closure properties of Visibly Pushdown Automata. We use SVPAs to model XML validation policies and program properties that are not naturally expressible with previous formalisms and provide experimental results for our implementation.

Keywords: visibly pushdown automata, symbolic automata, XML.

1 Introduction

Nested words model data with both linear and hierarchical structure such as XML documents and program traces. A nested word is a sequence of positions together with a matching relation that connects open tags (calls) with the corresponding close tags (returns). Visibly Pushdown Languages operate over nested words, and are defined as the languages accepted by Visibly Pushdown Automata (VPA) [1,2]. It can be shown that this class is closed under Boolean operations and enjoys decidable equivalence. The model of VPA has been proven to be useful in many computational tasks, from streaming XML processing [11,13,18] to verification of recursive programs [5,12]. As many classical models, VPAs build on two basic assumptions: there is a finite state space; and there is a finite alphabet.

---

[*] This research was supported by NSF Expeditions in Computing award CCF 1138996.

A. Biere and R. Bloem (Eds.): CAV 2014, LNCS 8559, pp. 209–225, 2014.
© Springer International Publishing Switzerland 2014

While finiteness of the state-space is a key aspect that enables many decidable properties, the finite alphabet assumption is in general not necessary. Moreover, practical applications such as XML processing and program trace analysis, use values for individual symbols that are typically drawn from an infinite domain. This paper focuses on this limitation and proposes a way to extend VPAs to infinite domains based on the recently proposed idea of symbolic automata.

Symbolic Finite Automata (SFAs) [3,9,19] are finite state automata in which the alphabet is given by a Boolean algebra that may have an infinite domain, and transitions are labeled with predicates over such algebra. In order for SFAs to be closed under Boolean operations and preserve decidability of equivalence, it should be decidable to check whether predicates in the algebra are satisfiable. SFAs accept languages of strings over a potentially infinite domain. Although strictly more expressive than finite-state automata, Symbolic Finite Automata are closed under Boolean operations and admit decidable equivalence.

We introduce Symbolic Visibly Pushdown Automata (SVPA) as an executable model for nested words over infinite alphabets. In SVPAs transitions are labeled with predicates over the input alphabet, analogous to symbolic automata for strings over infinite alphabets. A key novelty of SVPAs is the use of binary predicates to model relations between open and close tags in a nested word. Even though SVPAs completely subsume VPAs, we show how SVPAs still enjoy the decidability and closure properties of VPAs. This result is quite surprising since previous extensions of Symbolic Automata with binary predicates have undecidable equivalence and are not closed under Boolean operations [7].

We finally investigate potential applications of SVPAs in the context of analysis of XML documents and monitoring of recursive programs over infinite domains. We show how SVPAs can model XML validation policies and program properties that are not naturally expressible with previous formalisms and provide experimental results on the performance of our implementation. For example SVPAs can naturally express the following properties: an XML document is well-matched (every close tag is the same as the corresponding open tag), every person has age greater than 5, and every person's name starts with a capital letter. Using the closure properties of SVPAs, all these properties can then be expressed as a single deterministic SVPAs that can be efficiently executed.

Contributions: In summary, our contributions are:

- the new model of Symbolic Visibly Pushdown Automata (Section 3);
- new algorithms for intersecting, complementing, and determinizing SVPAs, and for checking emptiness of SVPAs, that extend classical algorithms to the symbolic setting (Section 4); and
- a prototype implementation of SVPAs and its evaluation using XML processing and program monitoring as case-studies (Section 5).

2   Motivating Example: Dynamic Analysis of Programs

In dynamic analysis program properties are monitored at runtime. Automata theory has come handy in specifying monitors. Let x be a global variable of a program P. We can use Finite State Automata (FSA) to describe "correct" values of x during the execution of P. For example if x has type $bool$, an FSA can specify that x starts with value $true$ and has value $false$ when P terminates.

Infinite Domains. In the previous example, x has type $bool$. In practice, one would want to express properties about variables of any type. If x is of type int and has infinitely many possible values, FSAs do not suffice any more. For example no FSA can express the property φ_{ev} stating that x remains even throughout the whole execution of P. One solution to this problem is that of using predicate abstraction and create an alphabet of two symbols $even(x)$ and $\neg even(x)$. However, this solution causes the input alphabet to be different from the original one ($\{even(x), \neg even(x)\}$ instead of the set of integers), and requires to choose a priori which abstraction to use.

Symbolic Finite Automata (SFA) [9,19] solve this problem by allowing transitions to be labeled with predicates over a decidable theory. Despite this, SFAs enjoy all the closure and decidability properties of finite state automata. The SFA A_{ev} for the property φ_{ev} has one state looping on an edge labeled with the predicate $even(x)$ expressible in Presburger arithmetic. Unlike predicate abstraction, SFAs do not change the underlying alphabet and allow predicates to be combined. For example, let A_{pos} be the SFA accepting all the sequences of positive integers. When intersecting A_{pos} and A_{ev} the transitions predicates will be combined, and we will obtain an SFA accepting all the sequences containing only integers that are both even and positive. An important restriction is that the underlying theory of the predicates needs to be decidable. For example, the property φ_{pr}, which states that x is a prime number at some point in P, cannot be expressed by an SFA.

SFAs allow only unary predicates and cannot relate values at different positions. Extended Symbolic Finite Automata (ESFA) [8] allow binary predicates for comparing adjacent positions, but this extension causes the model to lose closure and decidability properties [7]. Other models for comparing values over infinite alphabets at different positions are Data Automata (DA) [4] and Register Automata (RA) [6] where one can for example check that all the symbols in an input sequence are equal. This property is not expressible by an SFA or an ESFA, however Data Automata can only use equality and cannot specify properties such as $even(x)$.

Procedure Calls. Let x be of type $bool$ and let's assume that the program P contains a procedure q. The following property $\varphi_=$ can be specified by neither an FSA nor a SFA: every time q is called, the value of x at the call is the same as the value of x when q returns. The problem is that none of the previous model is able to "remember"' which call corresponds to which return. Visibly Pushdown Automata (VPA) [2] solve this problem by storing the value of x on a stack at a call and then retrieve it at the corresponding return. Unlike classical pushdown automata, this model still enjoys closure under Boolean operations and decidable equivalence. This is achieved by making calls and returns visible in the input and allowing the stack to push only at calls and to pop only at returns.

Table 1. Properties of different automata models

Model	Bool. Closure and Decidable Equiv.	Determinizability	Hierarchical Inputs	Infinite Alphabets	Binary Predicates
FSA	✓	✓	✗	✗	—
SFA	✓	✓	✗	✓	—
ESFA	✗	✗	✗	✓	Adjacent Positions
DA, RA	some variants	✗	trees	✓	Only Equality
VPA	✓	✓	✓	✗	—
SVPA (this paper)	✓	✓	✓	✓	Calls/Returns

Procedure Calls and Infinite Domains. Let x be of type *int* and let's assume that the program P contains a procedure q. No VPA can express the property $\psi_<$ requiring that, whenever q is called the value of x at the call is smaller than the value of x at the corresponding return. Expressing this kind of property in a decidable automaton model is the topic of this paper.

We introduce Symbolic Visibly Pushdown Automata (SVPA) that combine the features of SFAs and VPAs by allowing transitions to be labeled with predicates over any decidable theory and values to be stored on a stack at calls and retrieved at the corresponding returns. The property $\psi_<$ can then be expressed by an SVPA $A_<$ as follows. At a procedure call of q, $A_<$ will store the value c of x on the stack. When reading the value r of x at a procedure return of q, the value c of x at the corresponding call will be on top of the stack. Using the predicate $c < r$, the transition assures that the property $\psi_<$ is met. SVPAs still enjoy closure under Boolean operations, determinizability, and decidable equivalence, and the key to decidability is that binary predicates can only be used to compare values at matching calls and returns (unlike ESFAs). Data Automata and Register Automata have been extended to trees and grammars [4,6,14] but their expressiveness, for the same reason we discussed for strings, is orthogonal to that of SVPAs. Table 1 summarizes the properties of all the models we discussed.

3   Symbolic Visibly Pushdown Automata

In this section we formally define Symbolic Visibly Pushdown Automata (SVPA). We first provide some preliminary definitions for symbolic alphabets. Next we recall the basic definition of tagged alphabet and nested words, and we extend such definition to infinite alphabets. Last, we define SVPAs and their semantics.

3.1   Preliminaries

We use standard first-order logic and follow the notational conventions that are consistent with the original definition of symbolic transducers [21]. We write Σ for the input alphabet. A *label theory* is given by a recursively enumerable set Ψ of formulas that is closed under Boolean operations. We use $\mathbb{P}_x(\Psi)$ and $\mathbb{P}_{x,y}(\Psi)$ to denote the set of unary and binary predicates in Ψ respectively. We assume that every unary predicate in $\mathbb{P}_x(\Psi)$ contains x as the only free variable (similarly

$\mathbb{P}_{x,y}(\Psi)$ with x and y). It is easy to observe that given two unary predicates $\varphi_1, \varphi_2 \in \mathbb{P}_x(\Psi)$, the predicates $\varphi_1 \wedge \varphi_2$ and $\neg\varphi_1$ are also unary predicates in $\mathbb{P}_x(\Psi)$, and given a predicate $\varphi_1 \in \mathbb{P}_x(\Psi) \cup \mathbb{P}_{x,y}(\Psi)$ and a binary predicate $\varphi_2 \in \mathbb{P}_{x,y}(\Psi)$ the predicates $\varphi_1 \wedge \varphi_2$ and $\neg\varphi_2$ are also binary predicates in $\mathbb{P}_{x,y}(\Psi)$. A predicate $\varphi \in \mathbb{P}_x$ (resp. $\varphi \in \mathbb{P}_{x,y}$) is satisfiable, $IsSat(\varphi)$, if there exists a *witness* $a \in \Sigma$ (resp. $(a,b) \in \Sigma \times \Sigma$) that when substituted to x makes φ true, $[\![\varphi[a/x]]\!] = true$ (resp. $[\![\varphi[a/x, b/y]]\!] = true$). A label theory Ψ is *decidable* when, for any $\varphi \in \Psi$, checking whether $IsSat(\varphi)$ is true is decidable.

Nested words. Data with both linear and hierarchical structure can be encoded using nested words [2]. Given a set Σ of symbols, the *tagged alphabet* $\hat{\Sigma}$ consists of the symbols a, $\langle a$, and $a\rangle$, for each $a \in \Sigma$. A *nested word* over Σ is a finite sequence over $\hat{\Sigma}$. For a nested word $a_1 \cdots a_k$, a position j, for $1 \leq j \leq k$, is said to be a *call* position if the symbol a_j is of the form $\langle a$, a *return* position if the symbol a_j is of the form $a\rangle$, and an *internal* position otherwise. The tags induce a matching relation between call and return positions. Nested words can naturally encode strings and ordered trees.

3.2 Model

We can now formally define the model of symbolic visibly pushdown automata.

Definition 1 (SVPA). *A (nondeterministic) symbolic visibly pushdown automaton over an alphabet Σ is a tuple $A = (Q, Q_0, P, \delta_i, \delta_c, \delta_r, Q_F)$, where*

- *Q is a finite set of states,*
- *$Q_0 \subseteq Q$ is a set of initial states,*
- *P is a finite set of stack symbols,*
- *$\delta_i \subseteq Q \times \mathbb{P}_x \times Q$ is a finite set of internal transitions*
- *$\delta_c \subseteq Q \times \mathbb{P}_x \times Q \times P$, is a finite set of call transitions,*
- *$\delta_r \subseteq Q \times \mathbb{P}_{x,y} \times P \times Q$, is a finite set of return transitions,*
- *$\delta_b \subseteq Q \times \mathbb{P}_x \times Q$, is a finite set of empty-stack return transitions, and*
- *$Q_F \subseteq Q$ is a set of accepting states.*

A transition $(q, \varphi, q') \in \delta_i$, where $\varphi \in \mathbb{P}_x$, when reading a symbol a such that $a \in [\![\varphi]\!]$, starting in state q, updates the state to q'. A transition $(q, \varphi, q', p) \in \delta_c$, where $\varphi \in \mathbb{P}_x$, and $p \in P$, when reading a symbol $\langle a$ such that $a \in [\![\varphi]\!]$, starting in state q, pushes the symbol p on the stack along with the symbol a, and updates the state to q'. A transition $(q, \varphi, p, q') \in \delta_r$, where $\varphi \in \mathbb{P}_{x,y}$, is triggered when reading an input $b\rangle$, starting in state q, and with $(p, a) \in P \times \Sigma$ on top of the stack such that $(a, b) \in [\![\varphi]\!]$; the transition pops the element on the top of the stack and updates the state to q'. A transition $(q, \varphi, q') \in \delta_b$, where $\varphi \in \mathbb{P}_x$, is triggered when reading a tagged input $a\rangle$ such that $a \in [\![\varphi]\!]$, starting in state q, and with the current stack being empty; the transition updates the state to q'.

A stack is a finite sequence over $P \times \Sigma$. We denote by Γ the set of all stacks. Given a nested word $w = a_1 \ldots a_k$ in Σ^*, a run of M on w starting in state q is a sequence $\rho_q(w) = (q_1, \theta_1), \ldots, (q_{k+1}, \theta_{k+1})$, where $q = q_1$, each $q_i \in Q$, each

$\theta_i \in \Gamma$, the initial stack θ_1 is the empty sequence ε, and for every $1 \leq i \leq k$ the following holds:

Internal if a_i is internal, there exists $(q, \varphi, q') \in \delta_i$, such that $q = q_i$, $q' = q_{i+1}$, $a_i \in [\![\varphi]\!]$, and $\theta_{i+1} = \theta_i$;

Call if $a_i = \langle a$, for some a, there exists $(q, \varphi, q', p) \in \delta_c$, such that $q = q_i$, $q' = q_{i+1}$, $a \in [\![\varphi]\!]$, and $\theta_{i+1} = \theta_i(p, a)$; and

Return if $a_i = a \rangle$, for some a, there exists $(q, \varphi, p, q') \in \delta_r$, $b \in \Sigma$, and $\theta' \in \Gamma$, such that $q = q_i$, $q' = q_{i+1}$, $\theta_i = \theta'(p, b)$, $\theta_{i+1} = \theta'$, and $(b, a) \in [\![\varphi]\!]$.

Bottom if $a_i = a \rangle$, for some a, there exists $(q, \varphi, q') \in \delta_b$, such that $q = q_i$, $q' = q_{i+1}$, $\theta_i = \theta_{i+1} = \varepsilon$, and $a \in [\![\varphi]\!]$.

A run is *accepting* if q_1 is an initial state in Q_0 and q_{k+1} is a final state in F. A nested word w is accepted by A if there exists an accepting run of A on w. The language $L(A)$ accepted by A is the set of nested words accepted by A.

Definition 2 (Deterministic SVPA). *A symbolic visibly pushdown automaton A is deterministic iff $|Q_0| = 1$ and*

- *for each two transitions $t_1 = (q_1, \varphi_1, q_1'), t_2 = (q_2, \varphi_2, q_2') \in \delta_i$, if $q_1 = q_2$ and IsSat$(\varphi_1 \wedge \varphi_2)$, then $q_1' = q_2'$;*
- *for each two transitions $t_1 = (q_1, \varphi_1, q_1', p_1), t_2 = (q_2, \varphi_2, q_2', p_2) \in \delta_c$, if $q_1 = q_2$ and IsSat$(\varphi_1 \wedge \varphi_2)$, then $q_1' = q_2'$ and $p_1 = p_2$;*
- *for each two transitions $t_1 = (q_1, \varphi_1, p_1, q_1'), t_2 = (q_2, \varphi_2, p_2, q_2') \in \delta_r$, if $q_1 = q_2$, $p_1 = p_2$, and IsSat$(\varphi_1 \wedge \varphi_2)$, then $q_1' = q_2'$; and*
- *for each two transitions $t_1 = (q_1, \varphi_1, q_1'), t_2 = (q_2, \varphi_2, q_2') \in \delta_b$, if $q_1 = q_2$, and IsSat$(\varphi_1 \wedge \varphi_2)$, then $q_1' = q_2'$.*

For a deterministic SVPA A we use q_0 to denote the only initial state of A.

Definition 3 (Complete SVPA). *A deterministic symbolic visibly pushdown automaton A is complete iff for each $q \in Q$, $a, b \in \Sigma$, and $p \in P$, there exist 1) a transition $(q, \varphi, q') \in \delta_i$, such that $a \in [\![\varphi]\!]$; 2) a transition $(q, \varphi, q', p') \in \delta_c$, such that $a \in [\![\varphi]\!]$; 3) a transition $(q, \varphi, p, q') \in \delta_r$, such that $(a, b) \in [\![\varphi]\!]$; and 4) a transition $(q, \varphi, q') \in \delta_b$, such that $a \in [\![\varphi]\!]$.*

4   Closure Properties and Decision Procedures

In this section we describe the closure and decidability properties of SVPAs. We first introduce few preliminary concepts and then show how SVPAs are equivalent in expressiveness to deterministic SVPAs, and complete SVPAs. We then prove that SVPAs are closed under Boolean operations. Last, we provide an algorithm for checking emptiness of SVPAs over decidable label theories and use it to prove the decidability of SVPA language equivalence. For each construction we provide a complexity parameterized by the underlying theory, and we assume that transitions are only added to a construction when satisfiable.

4.1   Closure Properties

Before describing the determinization algorithm we introduce the concept of a minterm. The notion of a minterm is fundamental for determinizing symbolic automata, and it captures the set of equivalence classes of the input alphabet for a given symbolic automaton. Intuitively, for every state q of the symbolic automaton, a minterm is a set of input symbols that q will always treat in the same manner. Given a set of predicates Φ a *minterm* is a minimal satisfiable Boolean combination of all predicates that occur in Φ. We use the notation $Mt(\Phi)$ to denote the set of minterms of Φ. For example the set of predicates $\Phi = \{x > 2, x < 5\}$ over the theory of linear integer arithmetic has minterms $Mt(\Phi) = \{x > 2 \wedge x < 5, \ \neg x > 2 \wedge x < 5, \ x > 2 \wedge \neg x < 5\}$. While in the case of symbolic finite automata this definition is simpler (see [9]), in our setting we need to pay extra attention to the presence of binary predicates. We need therefore to define two types of minterms, one for unary predicates and one for binary predicates. Given an SVPA A we define

- the set Φ_1^A of unary predicates of A as the set $\{\varphi \mid \exists q, q', p.(q, \varphi, q') \in \delta_i \vee (q, \varphi, q', p) \in \delta_c \vee (q, \varphi, q') \in \delta_b\}$;
- the set Φ_2^A of binary predicates of A as the set $\{\varphi \mid \exists q, q', p.(q, \varphi, p, q') \in \delta_r\}$;
- the set Mt_1^A as the set $Mt(\Phi_1^A)$ of unary predicate minterms of A; and
- the set Mt_2^A as the set $Mt(\Phi_2^A)$ of binary predicate minterms of A.

The goal of minterms is that of capturing the equivalence classes of the label theory in the current SVPA. Let Φ be the set of minterms of an SVPA A. Consider two nested words $s = a_1 \ldots a_n$ and $t = b_1 \ldots b_n$ of equal length and such that for every i, a_i has the same tag as b_i (both internals, etc.). Now assume the following is true: for every $1 \leq i \leq n$, if a_i is internal there exists a minterm $\varphi \in Mt_1^A$ such that both a_i and b_i are models of φ, and, if a_i is a call with corresponding return a_j, then there exists a minterm $\psi \in Mt_2^A$ such that both (a_i, a_j) and (b_i, b_j) are models of ψ. If the previous condition holds, the two nested words will be indistinguishable in the SVPA A, meaning that they will have exactly the same set of runs. Following, this intuition we have that even though the alphabet might be infinite, only a finite number of predicates is *interesting*. We can now discuss the determinization construction.

Theorem 1 (Determinization). *For every SVPA A there exists a deterministic SVPA B accepting the same language.*

Proof. The main difference between the determinization algorithm in [2] and the symbolic version is in the use of minterms. Similarly to the approach presented in [9], we use the minterm computation to generate a finite set of relevant predicates. After we have done so, we can generalize the determinization construction shown in [2].

We now describe the intuition behind the construction. Given a nested word n, A can have multiple runs over n. Thus, at any position, the state of B needs to keep track of all possible states of A, as in case of classical subset construction for determinization of nondeterministic word automata. However, keeping only a set of states of A is not enough: at a return position, B needs to use the information on the top of the stack and in the state to figure out which pairs of states (starting in state q you can reach state q') belong to the same run. The main idea behind the construction is to do a subset construction over summaries (pairs of states) but postpone handling the call-transitions by storing the set of summaries before the call, along with the minterm containing the call symbol, in the stack, and simulate the effect of the corresponding call-transition at the time of the matching return for every possible minterm.

The components of the deterministic automaton B equivalent to $A = (Q, Q_0, P, \delta_c, \delta_i, \delta_r, Q_F)$ are the following. The states of B are $Q' = 2^{Q \times Q}$. The initial state is the set $Q_0 \times Q_0$ of pairs of initial states. A state $S \in Q'$ is accepting iff it contains a pair of the form (q, q') with $q' \in Q_f$. The stack symbols of B are $P' = Q' \times Mt_1^A$. The internal transition function δ_i' is given by: for $S \in Q'$, and $\varphi \in Mt_1^A$, $\delta_i'(S, \varphi)$ consists of pairs (q, q'') such that there exists $(q, q') \in S$ and an internal transition $(q', \varphi', q'') \in \delta_i$ such that $IsSat(\varphi \wedge \varphi')$. The call transition function δ_c' is given by: for $S \in Q'$ and $\varphi \in Mt_1^A$, $\delta_c'(S, \varphi) = (S', (S, \varphi))$, where S' consists of pairs (q'', q'') such that there exists $(q, q') \in S$, a stack symbol $p \in P$, and a call transition $(q', \varphi', q'', p) \in \delta_c$ such that $IsSat(\varphi \wedge \varphi')$. The return transition function δ_r' is given by: for $S, S' \in Q'$ and $\varphi_1 \in Mt_1^A, \varphi_2 \in Mt_2^A$, the state $\delta_r'(S, (S', \varphi_1), \varphi_2)$ consists of pairs (q, q'') such that there exists $(q, q') \in S'$, $(q_1, q_2) \in S$, a stack symbol $p \in P$, a call transition $(q', \varphi_1', q_1, p) \in \delta_c$, and a return transition $(q_2, p, \varphi_2', q'') \in \delta_r$ such that $IsSat(\varphi_1 \wedge \varphi_1')$ and $IsSat(\varphi_2 \wedge \varphi_2')$. The empty-stack return transition function δ_b' is given by: for $S \in Q'$ and $\varphi \in Mt_1^A$, the state $\delta_b'(S, \varphi)$ consists of pairs (q, q'') such that there exists $(q, q') \in S$ and a return transition $(q', \varphi', q'') \in \delta_b$ such that $IsSat(\varphi \wedge \varphi')$. Our construction differs from the one in [2] in two aspects:

- in [2] each stack symbol contains an element from Σ. This technique cannot be used in our setting and in our construction each stack symbol contains a predicate from the set of unary minterms.
- the construction in [2] builds on the notion of reachability and looks for matching pairs of calls and returns. In our construction, this operation has to be performed symbolically, by checking whether the unary predicate stored by the call on the stack and the binary predicate at the return are not disjoint.

We finally discuss the complexity of the determinization procedure. Assume A has n states, m stack symbols, and p different predicates of size at most ℓ. We first observer that the number of minterms is at most 2^p and each minterm has size $O(p\ell)$.[1] If $f(a)$ is the cost of checking the satisfiability of a predicate of size a, then the minterm computation has complexity $O(2^p f(\ell p))$. The resulting automaton B has $O(2^{n^2})$ states, and $O(2^p 2^{n^2})$ stack symbols. The determinization procedure has worst complexity $O(2^p 2^{n^2} m + 2^p f(p\ell))$.

Theorem 2 (Completeness). *For every SVPA A there exists a complete SVPA B accepting the same language.*

---

[1] If the alphabet is finite the number of minterms is bounded by $min(2^p, |\Sigma|)$.

Proof. Since the procedure is trivial we only discuss its complexity. Assume A has n states, m stack symbols, and p different predicates of size at most ℓ. Let $f(a)$ be the cost of checking the satisfiability of a predicate of size a. The procedure has complexity $O(nmf(\ell p))$. ☒

Theorem 3 (Boolean Closure). *SVPAs are closed under Boolean operations.*

Proof. We prove that SVPAs are closed under complement and intersection. We first prove that SVPAs are closed under complement. Given an SVPA A we construct a complete SVPA C such that C accepts a nested word n iff n is not accepted by A. First, we use Theorem 2 to construct an equivalent deterministic SVPA $B = (Q, q_0, P, \delta_i, \delta_c, \delta_r, Q_F)$. We can now construct the SVPA $C = (Q, q_0, P, \delta_i, \delta_c, \delta_r, Q \setminus Q_F)$ in which the set of accepting states is complemented.

We next prove that SVPAs are closed under intersection. Given two deterministic SVPAs $A_1 = (Q^1, q_0^1, P^1, \delta_i^1, \delta_c^1, \delta_r^1, Q_F^1)$ and $A_2 = (Q^2, q_0^2, P^2, \delta_i^2, \delta_c^2, \delta_r^2, Q_F^2)$ (using Theorem 1) we construct an SVPA B such that B accepts a nested word n iff n is accepted by both A_1 and A_2. The construction of B is a classical product construction. The SVPA B will have state set $Q' = Q^1 \times Q^2$, initial state $q_0' = (q_0^1, q_0^2)$, stack symbol set $P' = P^1 \times P^2$, and final state set $Q_F' = Q_F^1 \times Q_F^2$. The transition function will simulate both A_1 and A_2 at the same time.

- for each $(q_1, \varphi_1, q_1') \in \delta_i^1$, and $(q_2, \varphi_2, q_2') \in \delta_i^2$, δ_i' will contain the transition $((q_1, q_2), \varphi_1 \wedge \varphi_2, (q_1', q_2'))$;
- for each $(q_1, \varphi_1, q_1', p_1) \in \delta_c^1$, and $(q_2, \varphi_2, q_2', p_2) \in \delta_c^2$, and δ_c' will contain the transition $((q_1, q_2), \varphi_1 \wedge \varphi_2, (q_1', q_2'), (p_1, p_2))$;
- for each $(q_1, \varphi_1, p_1, q_1') \in \delta_r^1$, and $(q_2, \varphi_2, p_2, q_2') \in \delta_r^2$, δ_r' will contain the transition $((q_1, q_2), \varphi_1 \wedge \varphi_2, (p_1, p_2), (q_1', q_2'))$; and
- for each $(q_1, \varphi_1, q_1') \in \delta_b^1$, and $(q_2, \varphi_2, q_2') \in \delta_b^2$, δ_b' will contain the transition $((q_1, q_2), \varphi_1 \wedge \varphi_2, (q_1', q_2'))$;

Assume each SVPA A_i has n_i states, m_i stack symbols, and p_i different predicates of size at most ℓ_i. Let $f(a)$ be the cost of checking the satisfiability of a predicate of size a. The intersection procedure has complexity $O(n_1 n_2 m_1 m_2 + p_1 p_2 f(\ell_1 + \ell_2))$.

4.2   Decision Procedures

We conclude this section with an algorithm for checking emptiness of SVPAs over decidable label theories, which we finally use to prove the decidability of SVPA equivalence.

Theorem 4 (Emptiness). *Given an SVPA A over a decidable label theory it is decidable whether $L(A) = \emptyset$.*

Proof. The algorithm for checking emptiness is a symbolic variant of the algorithm for checking emptiness of a pushdown automaton. We are given an SVPA $A = (Q, q_0, P, \delta_i, \delta_c, \delta_r, Q_F)$ over a decidable theory Ψ. First, for every two states $q, q' \in Q$ we compute the reachability relation $R_{wm} \subseteq Q \times Q$ such that $(q, q') \in R_{wm}$ iff there exists a run $\rho_q(w)$ that, staring in state q, after reading a well matched nested word w, ends in state q'. We define R_{wm} as follows:

- for all $q \in Q$, $(q, q) \in R_{wm}$;
- if $(q_1, q_2) \in R_{wm}$, and there exists $q, q' \in Q$, $p \in P$, $\varphi_1 \in \mathbb{P}_x(\Psi), \varphi_2 \in \mathbb{P}_{x,y}(\Psi)$, such that $(q, \varphi_1, q_1, p) \in \delta_c$, $(q_2, \varphi_2, p, q') \in \delta_r$, and $IsSat(\varphi_1 \wedge \varphi_2)$, then $(q, q') \in R_{wm}$. Observe that unary and binary predicates unify on the first variable x;
- if $(q_1, q_2) \in R_{wm}$, and there exists $q \in Q$, $\varphi \in \mathbb{P}_x(\Psi)$, such that $(q, \varphi, q_1) \in \delta_i$, and $IsSat(\varphi)$, then $(q, q_2) \in R_{wm}$; and
- if $(q_1, q_2) \in R_{wm}$ and $(q_2, q_3) \in R_{wm}$, then $(q_1, q_3) \in R_{wm}$.

The above reachability relation captures all the runs over well-matched nested words. Unmatched calls and returns can be handled using a similar set of rules. We can then compute therefore the reachability relation $R \subseteq Q \times Q$ such that $(q, q') \in R$ iff there exists a run $\rho_q(w)$ that ends in state q' after reading a nested word w. The SVPA A is empty iff $(Q_0 \times Q_F) \cap R = \emptyset$.

Assume A has n states, m stack symbols, t transitions, and p predicates of size at most ℓ. Let $f(a)$ be the cost of checking the satisfiability of a predicate of size a. The emptiness procedure has complexity $O(n^3 mt + p^2 f(\ell))$.

We can now combine the closure under Boolean operations and the decidability of emptiness to show that equivalence of SVPAs is decidable.

Corollary 1 (Equivalence). *Given two SVPAs A and B over a decidable label theory it is decidable whether $L(A) \subseteq L(B)$ and whether $L(A) = L(B)$.*

Complexity: In [2] it is shown that the VPA universality, inclusion, and equivalence problems are ExpTime-hard. If the function $IsSat()$ can be computed in polynomial time the same complexity bounds hold for SVPAs.   ⊠

5   Applications and Evaluation

In this section we present potential applications of SVPAs together with experimental results. First, we illustrate how the presence of symbolic alphabets and closure properties enables complex XML validation, HTML sanitization, and runtime monitoring of recursive programs. Finally, we present some experimental results on SVPA's execution and algorithms.[2]

5.1   XML Validation

XML (and HTML) documents are ubiquitous. Validating an XML document is the task of checking whether such a document meets a given specification. XML Schema is the most common language for writing XML specifications and their properties have been studied in depth [17,22]. The XML schema S shown in

---

[2]   All the experiments were run on a 4 Cores Intel i7-2600 CPU 3.40GHz, with 8GB of RAM. The library is configured for 32 bits architecture.

```
<xs:schema>
<xs:element name="people"  type="PeopleType"/>
<xs:complexType name="PeopleType"><xs:sequence>
 <xs:element name="person" minOccurs="0" maxOccurs="unbounded">
  <xs:complexType><xs:sequence>
   <xs:element name="firstname">
    <xs:simpleType><xs:restriction base="xs:string">
     <xs:pattern value="[A-Z]([a-z])*"/>
    </xs:restriction></xs:simpleType>
   </xs:element>
   <xs:element name="lastname">
    <xs:simpleType><xs:restriction base="xs:string">
     <xs:pattern value="[A-Z]([a-z])*"/>
    </xs:restriction></xs:simpleType>
   </xs:element>
  </xs:sequence></xs:complexType>
 </xs:element>
</xs:sequence></xs:complexType>
</xs:schema>
```

```
<people>
 <person>
  <firstname>
   Mark
  </firstname>
  <lastname>
   Red
  </lastname>
 </person>
 <person>
  <firstname>
   Mario
  </firstname>
  <lastname>
   Rossi
  </lastname>
 </person>
</people>
```

(1) XML Schema S   (2) Document Example

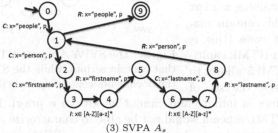

(3) SVPA A_s

Fig. 1. (1) XML Schema S describing documents containing a person with a first and last name, (2) an XML document accepted by S, and 3) an SVPA A_S accepting the same XML documents as S.

Figure 1 describes the format of XML documents containing first and last names. In words the document should start with the tag **people** and then contain a sequence of **person** each of which has a first and last name. First and last name should be both strings belonging to the regular expression [A-Z]([a-z])*.

Dealing with infinite alphabets. Although the XML Schema in Figure 1 only uses a finite set of possible nodes (**people**, **firstname**, etc.), it allows the content of the leaves to be any string accepted by the regular expression [A-Z]([a-z])*. This kind of constraints can be easily captured using an SVPA over the theory of strings. Such a SVPA A_S is depicted in Figure 1.3.[3] The letters I, C, and R on each transition respectively stand for internal, call, and return transitions.

Although in this particular setting the alphabet could be made finite by linearizing each string, such encoding would not be natural and would cause the corresponding VPA to be very complex. Moreover previous models that use such an encoding, such as [16,17], require the parser to further split each node value into separate characters. In the case of SVPAs, as it can be observed in Figure 1,

---

[3] We encode each XML document as a nested word over the theory of strings. For each open tag, close tag, attribute, attribute value, and text node the nested word contains one input symbol with the corresponding value.

there is a clear separation between the constraints on the tree structure (captured by the states), and the constraints on the leaves (captured by the predicates). This natural representation makes the model more succinct and executable since it reflects the typical representation of XML via events (SAX parser, etc.).

5.2   HTML Filters

A central concern for secure web application is untrusted user inputs. These lead to cross-site scripting (XSS) attacks, which may echo an untrusted input verbatim back to the browser. HTML filters aim at blocking potentially malicious user HTML code from being executed on the server. For example, a security sensitive application might want to discard all documents containing `script` nodes which might contain malicious JavaScript code (this is commonly done in HTML sanitization). Since HTML5 allows to define custom tags, the set of

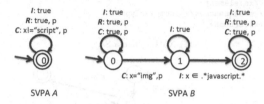

SVPA A   SVPA B

Fig. 2. The SVPA A rejects HTML documents that contain scripts, while the SVPA B accepts the documents containing malicious images

possible node names is infinite and cannot be known a priori. In this particular setting, an HTML schema would not be able to characterize such an HTML filter. This simple property can be checked using an SVPA over the theory of strings. Such an SVPA A is depicted on the left of Figure 2. The SVPA A only accepts nested words that do not contain `script` nodes. Notice that the call transition is triggered by any string different from `script` and the alphabet is therefore infinite.

Since SVPAs can be intersected, complemented, and determinized, we can take advantage of these properties to make the design of HTML filters modular. We now consider an example for which it is much simpler to specify what it means for a document to be malicious rather than to be safe. On the right of Figure 2 it is shown a non-deterministic SVPA B for checking whether a `img` tag may call JavaScript code in one of its attributes. To compute our filter (the set of safe inputs) we can now compute the complement B' of B that only accepts HTML documents that do not contain malicious `img` tags.

We can now combine A and B' into a single filter. This can be easily done by computing the intersection $F = A \cap B'$. If necessary, the SVPA F can then be determinized, obtaining an executable filter that can efficiently process HTML documents with a single left-to-right pass.

Fig. 3. SVPA W accepting HTML documents with matching open and close tags

The power of binary predicates. The previous HTML filter is meant to process only well-formed HTML documents. A well-formed HTML document is one in which all the open tags are correctly matched (every open tag is closed by a close tag containing the same symbol). In practice the input documents goes first through a well-formedness checker and then through a filter. This causes the input HTML to be processed multiple times and in performance critical applications this is not feasible. This check can however be performed by the SVPA W in Figure 3.

5.3 Runtime Program Monitors

We already discussed in Section 2 how SVPAs are useful for defining monitors for dynamic analysis of programs. In this section we present an example of how SVPAs can be used to express complex properties about programs over infinite domains such as integers. Consider the recursive implementation of Fibonacci on the right. Let's assume we are interested into monitoring the values of x at every call of Fib, and the values returned by Fib. For

```
function Fib(int x)
  if x < 2 then return x
  return Fib(x − 1) + Fib(x − 2)
```

example for the input 5, our monitored nested word will be $\langle 2 \langle 1 \ 1 \rangle \ \langle 0 \ 0 \rangle \ 1 \rangle$. The following properties can all be expressed using SVPAs:

1. if the input of Fib is greater or equal than 0, then the same hold for all the subsequent inputs of Fib;
2. if the output of Fib is negative, than Fib was called exactly once in the whole execution and with a negative input;
3. the output of Fib is greater or equal than the corresponding input.

We can then intersect the SVPAs corresponding to each property and generate a single pass linear time monitor for Fib. As we discussed in Section 2, SVPAs cannot express properties that relate all the values in the computation such as: the value of a variable x increases monotonically throughout the computation. However, thanks to the presence of binary predicates at returns, SVPAs provide a model for describing pre and post conditions of programs over decidable theories (see property 3). In particular, SVPAs can describe post conditions that relate the values of the inputs and the outputs of a function.

5.4 Experimental Results

Execution performance. We implemented the filter $F = A \cap \bar{B} \cap W$ and analyzed the performance of filtering HTML documents with size between 8 and 1293 KB, depth between 3 and 11, number of tokens between 1305 and 84242, and average token length between 11 and 14

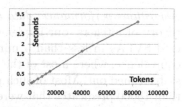

characters.[4] Constructing the SVPA F took 435 milliseconds. The running times

---

[4] To solve the underlying theory of equality plus regular constraints, we implemented a solver on top of the Microsoft Automata library [20]. We decided not to use a full blown solver such as Hampi [15], since it was not necessary in our setting.

per number of tokens (in seconds) are shown in the figure on the right. We observed that the depth of the input does not affect the running time, while the length affects it linearly. Surprisingly, the running time is also not affected by the average length of the tokens. This is due to the fact that most tokens can be rejected by partially reading them.

Algorithms performance: data. We evaluated the determinization and equivalence algorithms on a representative set of SVPAs over three different alphabet theories: strings, integers, and bitvectors (characters).[5] For each theory t we generated an initial set of SVPAs S_1^t containing 5 nondeterministic SVPAs for properties of the following form: 1) the input contains a call and matching return with different symbols; 2) the input contains an internal symbol satisfying a predicate φ_0; 3) the input contains a subword $\langle a\, b\, c \rangle$ such that $a \in [\![\varphi_1]\!]$, $b \in [\![\varphi_2]\!]$, and $a = c$; 4) the input contains a subword $\langle a\, \langle b$ such that $a \in [\![\varphi_3]\!]$, $b \in [\![\varphi_4]\!]$; and 5) for every internal symbol a in the input, $a \in [\![\varphi_4]\!]$, or $a \in [\![\varphi_5]\!]$. The predicates $\Phi = \{\varphi_0, \ldots, \varphi_5\}$ vary for each theory and are all different. For each theory we then computed the set $S_2^t = \{A \cap B \mid A, B \in S_1^t\} \cup \{A \cap B \cap C \mid A, B, C \in S_1^t\}$. We then used the sets S_2^t to evaluate the determinization algorithm, and computed the corresponding set of deterministic SVPAs D_2^t. Finally we checked equivalence of any two SVPAs A and B in D_2^t.

The results of our experiments are shown in Figure 4: the left column shows the size of each test set and the number of instances for which the algorithms timed out (5 minutes). The right column shows the running time for the instances in which the algorithms did not time out. For both algorithms we plot against number of states and number of transitions. For the determinization, the sizes refer to the automaton before determinization, while in the case of equivalence, the sizes refer to the sum of the corresponding metrics of the two input SVPAs. The distribution of the sizes of the SVPAs differed slightly when varying the theories, but since the differences are very small we show the average sizes. For each theory we determinized a total of 65 SVPAs and checked for equivalence 241 pairs of SVPAs. For both operation, on average, 96% of the time is spent in the theory solver. For the theory of characters we also compared our tool to the VPALib library, a Java implementation of VPAs.[6] The application timed out for all the inputs considered in our experiments.

Algorithms performance: data analysis. Except for few instances involving the theory of integers, our implementation was able to determinize all the considered SVPAs in less than 5 minuets. The situation was different in the case of equivalence, where most of the input pairs with more than 250 transitions or 13 states timed out. Most of such pairs were required to check satisfiability of more than 15000 predicates that were generated when building the intersected SVPAs necessary to check equivalence. We could observe that the theory of characters is

---

[5] The characters and strings solver are implemented on top of the Automata library [20] which is based on BDDs, while the integer solver is Z3 [10].

[6] Available http://www.emn.fr/z-info/hnguyen/vpa/

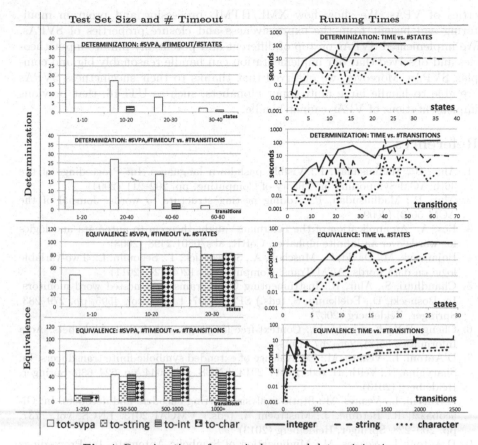

Fig. 4. Running times for equivalence and determinization

on average 6 times faster than the theory of strings and 10 times faster than the theory of integers. However, we did observe that the theory of integers timed out less often in the case of equivalence. We believe that this is due to the different choices of predicates in Φ and to the fact that Z3 uses a caching mechanism that avoids checking for satisfiability of the same predicate twice. While during the determinization such a technique is not very beneficial due to the limited number of different minterms, in the case of equivalence, especially for bigger inputs, many of the predicates are repeated making caching useful in practice.

When comparing against an existing implementation of VPAs, we observed that the benefit of using SVPA is immense: due to the large size of the alphabet (2^{16} characters), VPALib timed out for each input we considered.

6   Conclusion

We introduce Symbolic Visibly Pushdown Automata that extend VPAs with predicates over a decidable input theory, while preserving the closure properties of VPAs. We show how XML/HTML processing and program monitoring can benefit from the expressiveness and closure properties of SVPAs. We implemented SVPAs on top of different and potentially infinite input theories and observed that our implementation can handle reasonably big and complex SVPAs. Moreover, we observed that thanks to their succinctness SVPAs are able to handle large finite input alphabets, such as UTF16, that previous implementations of VPAs cannot handle.

References

1. Alur, R., Madhusudan, P.: Visibly pushdown languages. In: Proceedings of the 36th ACM Symposium on Theory of Computing, pp. 202–211 (2004)
2. Alur, R., Madhusudan, P.: Adding nesting structure to words. Journal of the ACM 56(3) (2009)
3. Bès, A.: An application of the Feferman-Vaught theorem to automata and logics for words over an infinite alphabet. CoRR, abs/0801.2498 (2008)
4. Bojanczyk, M., David, C., Muscholl, A., Schwentick, T., Segoufin, L.: Two-variable logic on data words. ACM Trans. Comput. Log. 12(4), 27 (2011)
5. Chaudhuri, S., Alur, R.: Instrumenting C programs with nested word monitors. In: Bošnački, D., Edelkamp, S. (eds.) SPIN 2007. LNCS, vol. 4595, pp. 279–283. Springer, Heidelberg (2007)
6. Cheng, E.Y., Kaminski, M.: Context-free languages over infinite alphabets. Acta Informatica 35(3), 245–267 (1998)
7. D'Antoni, L., Veanes, M.: Equivalence of extended symbolic finite transducers. In: Sharygina, N., Veith, H. (eds.) CAV 2013. LNCS, vol. 8044, pp. 624–639. Springer, Heidelberg (2013)
8. D'Antoni, L., Veanes, M.: Static analysis of string encoders and decoders. In: Giacobazzi, R., Berdine, J., Mastroeni, I. (eds.) VMCAI 2013. LNCS, vol. 7737, pp. 209–228. Springer, Heidelberg (2013)
9. D'Antoni, L., Veanes, M.: Minimization of Symbolic Automata. In: Proceedings of the 41st ACM SIGPLAN-SIGACT Symposium on Principles of Programming Languages (2014)
10. de Moura, L., Bjørner, N.S.: Z3: An efficient SMT solver. In: Ramakrishnan, C.R., Rehof, J. (eds.) TACAS 2008. LNCS, vol. 4963, pp. 337–340. Springer, Heidelberg (2008)
11. Debarbieux, D., Gauwin, O., Niehren, J., Sebastian, T., Zergaoui, M.: Early nested word automata for xPath query answering on XML streams. In: Konstantinidis, S. (ed.) CIAA 2013. LNCS, vol. 7982, pp. 292–305. Springer, Heidelberg (2013)
12. Driscoll, E., Thakur, A., Reps, T.: Opennwa: A nested-word automaton library. In: Madhusudan, P., Seshia, S.A. (eds.) CAV 2012. LNCS, vol. 7358, pp. 665–671. Springer, Heidelberg (2012)
13. Gauwin, O., Niehren, J.: Streamable fragments of forward xPath. In: Bouchou-Markhoff, B., Caron, P., Champarnaud, J.-M., Maurel, D. (eds.) CIAA 2011. LNCS, vol. 6807, pp. 3–15. Springer, Heidelberg (2011)
14. Kaminski, M., Tan, T.: Tree automata over infinite alphabets. In: Avron, A., Dershowitz, N., Rabinovich, A. (eds.) Pillars of Computer Science. LNCS, vol. 4800, pp. 386–423. Springer, Heidelberg (2008)
15. Kieżun, A., Ganesh, V., Guo, P.J., Hooimeijer, P., Ernst, M.D.: HAMPI: A solver for string constraints. In: Proceedings of the 2009 International Symposium on Software Testing and Analysis, ISSTA 2009, Chicago, IL, USA, July 21-23 (2009)

16. Kumar, V., Madhusudan, P., Viswanathan, M.: Visibly pushdown automata for streaming XML. In: WWW 2007: Proceedings of the 16th International Conference on World Wide Web, pp. 1053–1062. ACM, New York (2007)
17. Martens, W., Neven, F., Schwentick, T.: Complexity of decision problems for XML schemas and chain regular expressions. SIAM J. Comput. 39(4), 1486–1530 (2009)
18. Mozafari, B., Zeng, K., D'Antoni, L., Zaniolo, C.: High-Performance Complex Event Processing over Hierarchical Data. In: ACM TODS's Special Issue on Best of SIGMOD (2013)
19. Veanes, M.: Applications of symbolic finite automata. In: Konstantinidis, S. (ed.) CIAA 2013. LNCS, vol. 7982, pp. 16–23. Springer, Heidelberg (2013)
20. Veanes, M., Bjørner, N.: Symbolic automata: The toolkit. In: Flanagan, C., König, B. (eds.) TACAS 2012. LNCS, vol. 7214, pp. 472–477. Springer, Heidelberg (2012)
21. Veanes, M., Hooimeijer, P., Livshits, B., Molnar, D., Bjorner, N.: Symbolic finite state transducers: Algorithms and applications. In: Proceedings of the Symposium on Principles of Programming Languages (POPL) (January 2012)
22. Zilio, S.D., Lugiez, D.: XML schema, tree logic and sheaves automata. In: Nieuwenhuis, R. (ed.) RTA 2003. LNCS, vol. 2706, pp. 246–263. Springer, Heidelberg (2003)

Engineering a Static Verification Tool for GPU Kernels

Ethel Bardsley[1], Adam Betts[1], Nathan Chong[1], Peter Collingbourne[2],
Pantazis Deligiannis[1], Alastair F. Donaldson[1],
Jeroen Ketema[1], Daniel Liew[1], and Shaz Qadeer[3]

[1] Imperial College London
[2] Google*
[3] Microsoft Research

Abstract. We report on practical experiences over the last 2.5 years related to the engineering of GPUVerify, a static verification tool for OpenCL and CUDA GPU kernels, plotting the progress of GPUVerify from a prototype to a fully functional and relatively efficient analysis tool. Our hope is that this experience report will serve the verification community by helping to inform future tooling efforts.

1 Introduction

Graphics processing units (GPUs) are now a mainstay technology with which to accelerate computationally intensive applications. The OpenCL [25] and CUDA [33] programming models allow general-purpose computations to be offloaded to run on a variety of GPU platforms. In these programming models, a computation to run on the GPU is described using a *kernel* function, a template describing the behaviour of a single thread. Threads are organized into a set of groups, threads in the same group can synchronize with each other using *barriers*, and each thread has a unique id which it can use to access distinct data and follow distinct control paths from other threads.

A challenge in GPU programming is to avoid *data races*, where distinct threads access a common memory location, at least one access is a write, and there is no intervening barrier synchronization. Data races tend to arise due to a combination of intricate data access patterns necessary to achieve high memory performance, which can be hard to write correctly, and the desire to minimize expensive barrier synchronization operations, also to maximize performance. Data races lead to nondeterministically occurring bugs that can be hard to diagnose and fix, and since performance is the *sole* motivation for GPU offloading, race-prone programming styles are not likely to go away.

In response to the GPU programming paradigm and the problem of data races, a variety of formal and semi-formal methods for finding, or proving absence, of defects in GPU kernels have been proposed [27,8,26,23,28,14,29,10,4,12,5]. Over the last 2.5 years, our contribution to this area has been GPUVerify,[1] an open source tool for static verification of race-freedom for OpenCL and CUDA kernels.

Our research papers [8,15,11] have presented the top-level ideas that underpin the GPUVerify approach, and focus on arguing soundness of the approach with respect to

---

* Peter Collingbourne was at Imperial College London when he contributed to this work.
[1] http://multicore.doc.ic.ac.uk/tools/GPUVerify

A. Biere and R. Bloem (Eds.): CAV 2014, LNCS 8559, pp. 226–242, 2014.
© Springer International Publishing Switzerland 2014

an operational semantics for a core GPU kernel programming language. Embedding these ideas in a tool that can be applied directly to the source code of real-world examples with a reasonable degree of efficiency and automation has required a significant optimization effort and a number of important engineering decisions. This has been guided by a growing set of GPU kernel benchmarks which now counts 564 examples. In this tool paper we aim to communicate this engineering experience and insight, not reflected in the aforementioned research papers, to the verification community in the hope that it will be of general interest and may help inform future tooling efforts.

We provide an overview of GPUVerify (Sect. 2) and describe how we have evolved the front-end capabilities of the tool in order to handle a large set of benchmarks (Sect. 3). We then describe and evaluate several methods for improving the verification performance of the tool (Sect. 4). Our aim is for GPUVerify to be useful to industry, motivating steps for minimizing false positives and presenting clear error messages, which we describe (Sect. 5); we also discuss steps taken to ease uptake of the tool by industrial partners (Sect. 6). We conclude with a summary of lessons learned and the identification of *invariant generation* as a key challenge for future work (Sect. 7).

Related Work. A number of other works on GPU kernel analysis have appeared recently and can be categorized into methods for verification [27,26,23,12,4] and bug-finding via symbolic execution [28,14,29,10]. Our research papers provide a detailed discussion of how these works relate to GPUVerify, including experimental comparisons [8,11]. We do *not* compare GPUVerify with related tools here: the aim of this work is not to promote GPUVerify as "the colonel of kernel verification tools," but rather to communicate the insights into verification tool development that have emerged from the project.

2   Overview of the GPUVerify Technique

The key idea behind GPUVerify is that a massively parallel GPU kernel can be proven free from data races by deriving a *sequential* program from the kernel and verifying that this program is free from assertion failures. This avoids reasoning about thread interleavings and allows existing verification techniques for sequential programs to be reused. If verification of the sequential program fails, the proof failure may shed light on a defect in the original kernel, if one exists. Alternatively, the failure may be a false positive arising due to the abstractions employed while constructing the sequential program, or due to limitations of the method used to verify the sequential program; in practice, the main limitation relates to loop invariant generation.

The method GPUVerify uses to transform a kernel into a sequential program is presented in detail in [8,15]. The transformation proceeds in three steps. First, thread id-sensitive control flow is eliminated by *predicating* each statement [1]. For example, the if-statement shown to the right will be turned `if (tid > 0) s₁;` | `(tid > 0) ⇒ s₁;`
into the code on the far right, where a state- `else s₂;` | `!(tid > 0) ⇒ s₂;`
ment of the form $p \Rightarrow s$ is a predicated statement which behaves as a no-op if p is *false*, and has the same effect as s if p is *true*. Predication is semantics-preserving and ensures that every thread follows the same control path through the kernel.

Second, each access to a shared memory array is instrumented to allow data races to be detected. For each thread t and each array A two sets are introduced: one to track

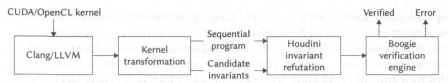

Fig. 1. The GPUVerify architecture, which draws on the Clang/LLVM and Boogie frameworks

reads from and one to track writes to A by t. Upon an access, the offset at which the access occurs is recorded in the appropriate set, and occurrence of a data race is checked by considering overlap between relevant sets.

The third and final step applies a *two-thread reduction*. This is an abstraction that removes all but two *arbitrary* threads and then combines the two threads into a single sequential program by applying a round-robin schedule. The effects of additional unmodeled threads on the shared state are over-approximated using abstraction. That the reduction is sound is explained in detail in [8,15], and hinges on the observation that if barriers are the only mechanism for synchronization then a race-free kernel behaves *deterministically* when applied to a given input; thus, as long as data races are detected, analysis can focus on the single round-robin schedule. The method is incomplete due to the shared state abstraction which over-approximates the effects of additional threads, and may include error-inducing behaviours that are infeasible during concrete execution. The two-thread reduction has been used in other works on GPU kernel analysis [27], and the idea of reducing verification complexity through pairwise reasoning is well-known and has been employed, for example, in model checking of cache coherence protocols [13,30,39].

Architecture. The architecture of GPUVerify is depicted in Fig. 1, and leverages the mature and widely used Clang/LLVM[2] and Boogie [6] tool chains. Clang/LLVM is used to parse CUDA and OpenCL kernels and lower them into LLVM intermediate representation (IR). This removes all complex syntactic features (including C++ templates), yielding a simple representation of a kernel. The kernel transformation process first invokes Bugle, our custom-built LLVM IR-to-Boogie translator, to translate the obtained LLVM IR into a Boogie program, giving a Boogie representation of the kernel. Predication, race instrumentation and two-thread reduction are then applied, as outlined above, to yield the sequential Boogie program to be verified. Kernel transformation also speculates candidate loop invariants based on a number of custom-designed templates, which attempt to capture data access idioms we observed in many kernels.

After kernel transformation, GPUVerify uses the Houdini algorithm [20] (implemented as part of the Boogie framework) to compute the largest conjunctive invariant over the set of speculated loop invariants, discarding any candidate invariants that cannot be proven.[3] The sequential program and synthesized invariant are then passed to the Boogie verification engine for the actual verification. Boogie in turn invokes an SMT solver: the Z3 solver is the default [32], and we have added support for the CVC4 solver [7], as discussed further in Sect. 4. The result of this stage is either successful verification of the sequential program, which implies race-freedom of the original kernel, or an error indicating that the original kernel may exhibit a defect.

---

[2] http://llvm.org/

[3] That we obtain the *largest* conjunction is a property of the Houdini algorithm [20].

3 Applying GPUVerify to a Large Set of Benchmarks

We have applied GPUVerify to 564 kernels gathered from nine sources:

- *AMD Accelerated Parallel Processing SDK* v2.6 [2] (78 OpenCL kernels)
- *NVIDIA GPU Computing SDK* v5.0 [34] (166 CUDA kernels); we also include a further 8 CUDA kernels from a previous version of the SDK (v2.0)
- Microsoft *C++ AMP Sample Projects* [31] (20 kernels, hand translated to CUDA)
- The *gpgpu-sim* benchmarks [3] (33 CUDA kernels)
- The *Parboil* benchmarks v2.5 [38] (25 OpenCL kernels)
- The *Rodinia* benchmark suite v2.4 [9] (36 OpenCL kernels)
- The *SHOC* benchmark suite [16] (87 OpenCL kernels)
- The *PolyBench/GPU* benchmark suite [21] (49 OpenCL kernels)
- Rightware *Basemark CL* v1.1 [37] (62 OpenCL kernels)

Each suite is publicly available except for *Basemark CL* which was provided to us under an academic license. This collection covers all the publicly available GPU benchmark suites that we are aware of. The kernel counts above do not include 41 kernels that we manually removed from our study: (i) 16 kernels are trivially race-free as they are run by a single thread, (ii) 8 kernels use features that are currently unsupported by GPUVerify, such as CUDA *surfaces*, and (iii) 17 kernels require refinements of the GPUVerify verification method that cannot currently be applied automatically [11].

Our default assumption is that these benchmarks are free from defects, thus our aim is verification. However, in the process of applying GPUVerify we have identified, reported and fixed several data race bugs. At the time of writing, running with full optimizations on our experimental platform (described in Sect. 4), and with a timeout of 10 minutes per benchmark, GPUVerify can verify 422 kernels and reports possible defects for 115. We know that some of these failures are (and expect most to be) false positives that demand improved invariant inference, but some may correspond to further bugs that we have not yet identified. The timeout is reached in 27 cases.

We now explain how we have managed the evolution of GPUVerify's front-end capabilities from a simple prototype applied to hand-crafted examples to a tool with wide applicability to GPU kernel benchmarks. In Sect. 4 we discuss engineering decisions related to the performance of verification.

Incremental Front-End Support. The starting point for GPUVerify was the idea of using sequential program verification technology to analyse GPU kernels, but it took several iterations to arrive at the method described in Sect. 2. To allow us to experiment with example kernels while our ideas were in flux, we first devised a manual process for translating GPU kernels into Boogie. Starting with Boogie mitigated the risk of investing in a CUDA or OpenCL front-end and subsequently discovering that our ideas would not be practical. Using our Boogie-based GPU kernel language we implemented a prototype of the kernel transformation step from Fig. 1 and manually encoded a number of kernels into Boogie to evaluate the prototype. After encoding around 20 examples it became clear that our technique had promise, but that we would need to invest in a front-end for OpenCL and/or CUDA to study a larger set of examples.

We first designed a translator that mapped OpenCL and CUDA kernels (subject to various restrictions) into our Boogie kernel language. This translator used Clang to parse kernels, and performed translation at the level of the Clang abstract syntax tree (AST). The structured nature of the Clang AST allowed for a relatively simple transformation into structured Boogie. This was essential as we did not know how to apply predication (a key part of our method, see Sect. 2) to unstructured programs. We were able to process a fairly large set of benchmarks using this front-end, facilitating our first publication on GPUVerify [8] which presents an evaluation using 163 kernels. However, the "structured" limitation eliminated kernels exhibiting unstructured control-flow (arising e.g. from switch statements and short-circuit evaluation of Boolean operators). Working at the Clang AST level also meant that we had to directly deal with syntactic features ranging from the difference between `while` and `for` loops (easy but annoying), through details of struct accesses (medium difficulty), to handling of C++ templates arising in CUDA code (fiendishly difficult, and not attempted).

We realized that to apply the tool widely it would be beneficial to work at the level of LLVM intermediate representation (IR), by which point complex syntactic features have been desugared. Because LLVM IR is unstructured, we focused on solving the problem of applying predication to unstructured control-flow-graphs [15] and implemented Bugle, our custom LLVM-to-Boogie translator (see Sect. 2), which produces unstructured Boogie code to which the new predication method can be applied. We considered leveraging an existing LLVM-to-Boogie translator, SMACK [35], but opted to build a custom translator that could take direct advantage of the relatively simple nature of the GPU programming model.

Environment Modeling for OpenCL and CUDA Significant further engineering effort was required to model built-in functions provided by OpenCL and CUDA. For OpenCL and CUDA, respectively, this included 164 and 231 built-in math functions and 136 and 30 atomic operations. For OpenCL we benefited from `libclc`,[4] an open source OpenCL library implementation. In addition, we have equipped GPUVerify with support for OpenCL image types, CUDA textures and an abstraction of a widely used CUDA random number generation library. Our environment modeling is not complete (e.g. we do not yet support CUDA *surfaces*) and it is a moving target as OpenCL and CUDA continue to evolve. Nevertheless, our modeling effort so far allows GPUVerify to process many practical examples.

4　Engineering Issues for Efficient Verification

Our first implementation of GPUVerify worked for small examples, but did not perform well on more complex kernels involving multiple loops and many shared memory accesses. We now describe the steps we have taken to improve verification performance through efficient memory modeling, uniformity analysis to reduce the need for predication, supporting multiple SMT solvers, and optimizations to produce formulas that can be efficiently processed by SMT solvers.

Experimental Setup. Throughout this section we report experimental results over the 564 kernels in our benchmark collection (see Sect. 3). All experiments were conducted on a compute cluster using nodes with Intel Xeon EP-2620 cores at 2GHz with 16GB

---

[4] http://libclc.llvm.org/

RAM running RedHat Linux 6.3, using Z3 v4.3.1, CVC4 v1.4-prerelease from 29-01-2014 and Clang/LLVM v3.4. Times reported are averages over three runs.

We use *baseline* to refer to GPUVerify equipped with the efficient memory model and uniformity analysis described below, but without any of the additional optimizations we go on to discuss. We use the *responsive* set to refer to the 492 kernels for which verification completes (in 391 with "success", in 101 with "possible defect") for *baseline* and all more highly optimized configurations. We report speedup results with respect to the *responsive* set. We do not further discuss 12 kernels for which GPUVerify reached the timeout with every optimization configuration. In 60 cases, GPUVerify reached the timeout for some optimization configurations but not others. We do not include these cases when discussing speedups afforded by optimizations.

Our tool chain, non-commercial benchmarks and experimental data (in the form of interactive graphs) are available online.[5]

Modeling Memory. The C language rules for pointer casting apply to CUDA and OpenCL, meaning that it is legitimate to cast an expression e of type $T*$, where T is some type, to an expression of type char*, after which offsets from e can be addressed with byte-level granularity. An example of casting in practical GPU code appears in a histogram kernel shipped with the CUDA SDK. The kernel works on an array of char data and starts by initializing the array to be uniformly zero. During initialization the array is cast from char* to int* to allow zero-initialization to be performed word-by-word, which is more efficient than working byte-by-byte.

For GPUVerify to work "out-of-the-box" we must handle this kind of pointer usage even though it is uncommon. We initially let our Bugle front-end model memory at byte-level granularity. To illustrate this, consider an array A with elements of type short, and a write instruction $A[i] = x$. In the Boogie code generated by Bugle with byte-level memory modeling, A is declared as a map from 32-bit offsets to bytes, and the single write is translated into two byte-level writes ('bv' stands for bitvector):

```
var A : [bv32]bv8;      // Map from addresses to bytes
A[i*2+0] := x[8:0];     // The write to A is modeled by two byte-level writes.
A[i*2+1] := x[16:8];    // We use *, + and integer literals for brevity.
```

This representation is problematic, especially for data types with large widths such as double: it leads to many loads and stores that need to be instrumented when performing race analysis and complicates the loop invariants necessary to prove race-freedom. Both issues place significant demands on the underlying SMT solver. In practice we found that verification with this simple memory model was unacceptably slow.

To overcome this problem we have developed a unification algorithm that conservatively determines whether an array A with element type T may ever be accessed at a granularity that is not a multiple of sizeof(T). If such an access may be possible, A is modeled with byte-level granularity as described above. Otherwise A is modeled with "type-level" granularity as a map from addresses to bitvectors of size $8 * \text{sizeof}(T)$: accessing an element of A leads to a single read or write in the generated Boogie code.

With this analysis, byte-level modeling is avoided in all but 40 of our 564 kernels and in 39 of these cases at least one array is still modeled with type-level granularity. We evaluated the impact of byte- vs. type-level modeling using the 365 kernels in our

---

[5] http://multicore.doc.ic.ac.uk/tools/GPUVerify/CAV2014

collection for which *baseline* GPUVerify responds within 60 seconds. Turning off the memory analysis described above, forcing byte-level memory modeling everywhere, we find that 31 kernels reach the 10 minute timeout and 12 kernels flip from verifying to failing (due to more complex invariants that can be necessary when reasoning at the byte level). Overall, analysis took 6.6× longer, but this is not a fully fair comparison because (a) the 31 kernels that timeout might in practice take much longer to verify, and (b) comparing times for a kernel where the verification result differs has limited meaning. Nevertheless, the slow-down associated with byte-level modeling indicates that our memory analysis is necessary in making GPUVerify practically useful.

Our experience supports existing evidence that, in the context of verification, modeling memory at the lowest common denominator level of bytes does not scale [36].

Uniformity Analysis. The kernel transformation performed by GPUVerify involves *predicating* a kernel and applying the *two-thread reduction* (see Sect. 2). Predication is essential for handling fragments of a kernel where threads might take different control flow paths, and because distinct threads may operate on distinct data the two-thread reduction must in general introduce a pair of variables for each private variable appearing in a kernel, one copy for each thread being modeled.

We have observed that in practical kernels, some or all control flow is often *uniform* across threads: the guards of conditional and loop statements do not depend (directly or indirectly) on thread ids. In fact, to achieve high performance when writing code for mainstream GPUs it is important to *minimize* thread divergence, and have threads follow the same control flow path whenever possible [22]. We found it often necessary to provide loop invariants to *recover* uniformity between the two threads under consideration, by asserting equality between predicates guarding execution and between id-insensitive private variables.

To avoid the overhead of generating such invariants and the duplication of private variables that are guaranteed to be uniform, we have designed and implemented a *uniformity analysis*. This is a taint analysis working at the control-flow graph level that uses the program dependence graph [18] to determine which variables and basic blocks are *non-uniform* because they are (transitively) control- or data-dependent on the thread ids. The analysis initially sets every variable and block to be *uniform*, except the `tid` variable which is *non-uniform*. Uniformity information is then updated repeatedly until a fixpoint is reached: a variable becomes *non-uniform* if it is assigned an expression that contains a non-uniform variable, or if it is updated inside a non-uniform block; a block becomes non-uniform if it is found to be (transitively) control-dependent on a condition that contains a non-uniform variable. Predication need only be applied to non-uniform blocks, and only non-uniform private variables need to be duplicated when the two-thread reduction is applied. This reduces the burden of loop invariant generation and leads to smaller SMT formulas due to the reduction in private variables.

To illustrate uniformity analysis, consider the example code snippet of Fig. 2(a), contrived for purposes of illustration, where private variables x, y and z are assumed to be initially uniform between threads. Fig. 2(b) shows the result of applying predication to the kernel according to the scheme discussed in Sect. 2, and then duplicating the statements according to the two-thread reduction so that each of the two threads has its own copy v_i of each private variable v ($i \in \{1, 2\}$) and every statement is executed

```
if (x > 0) {          (x₁ > 0 ∧ tid₁ < x₁) ⇒ y₁++;     if (x > 0) {
  if (tid < x)        (x₂ > 0 ∧ tid₂ < x₂) ⇒ y₂++;       (tid₁ < x) ⇒ y₁++;
    y++;              (x₁ > 0) ⇒ z₁ += y₁;               (tid₂ < x) ⇒ y₂++;
  z += y;             (x₂ > 0) ⇒ z₂ += y₂;               z₁ += y₁;
  x /= 2;             (x₁ > 0) ⇒ x₁ /= 2;                z₂ += y₂;
}                     (x₂ > 0) ⇒ x₂ /= 2;                x /= 2;
                                                        }

      (a)                        (b)                         (c)
```

Fig. 2. Uniformity analysis: (a) original code with the outer conditional uniform and the inner conditional non-uniform; (b) after predication and two-threaded duplication, without uniformity analysis; (c) after predication and two-threaded duplication, with uniformity analysis

separately by each thread. Uniformity analysis determines that the condition $tid <$ x is non-uniform, because it refers to tid. As a result, y is non-uniform because the statement $y++$ is control-dependent on the condition $tid < x$. Because y is non-uniform, z is also deemed non-uniform because it is updated by the statement $z += y$ which involves y on the right-hand side. The variable x and thus the condition $x < 0$ remain uniform. With the results of uniformity analysis, GPUVerify is free to perform less aggressive predication and duplication of the kernel, illustrated by Fig. 2(c). Only the inner conditional is predicated, the private variable x is not duplicated, and there is thus only one assignment to x.

As in the byte-level modeling experiment described above, we evaluated the impact of uniformity analysis using the 365 kernels in the *responsive* set for which *baseline* GPUVerify responds within 60 seconds. Turning off uniformity analysis, 6 kernels reach the 10 minute timeout and 33 flip from verifying to failing; the latter is due to the lack of loop invariants required to recover uniformity when the analysis is disabled. Overall, analysis took $1.9\times$ longer with uniformity analysis disabled, but this is not a fully fair comparison for the same reasons as in the byte-level modeling experiment.

A similar analysis has been proposed for optimizing OpenCL kernels for CPU (rather than GPU) performance [24]. The analyses were developed independently.

Support for CVC4. Boogie uses the Z3 solver [32] by default. We added support to Boogie for CVC4 [7], which also provides the theories used by GPUVerify (bitvectors, arrays, and uninterpreted functions). Our main motivation here was CVC4's permissive license: shipping GPUVerify with CVC4 in place of Z3 would make it easier for industrial users to try the tool (see Sect. 6). Two by-products of this effort are that we found and reported several bugs in CVC4 which were promptly fixed, and that our CVC4 support has been committed to Boogie, making CVC4 available to other Boogie users. It is also useful for us to have two solvers available for evaluation, to help determine when poor performance on a kernel is due to a solver quirk vs. a fundamental issue.

Fig. 3 presents log scale scatter plots comparing the performance of GPUVerify using CVC4 vs. Z3 with (a) baseline (no optimizations) and (b) all optimizations described below enabled, over the *responsive* benchmarks. A point (x, y) corresponds to a kernel for which end-to-end verification took x and y seconds, using Z3 and CVC4 respectively. Points above/below the diagonal correspond to kernels where Z3 performed better/worse than CVC4. We distinguish between kernels for which verification succeeds ($+$) and fails ($\circ$). The total time for analysis using Z3 and CVC4 with all optimizations was 5774 sec-

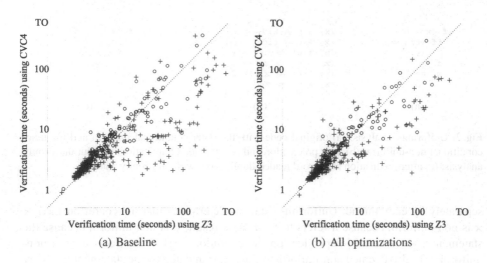

Fig. 3. Scatter plots comparing the performance of Z3 and CVC4 over the *responsive* benchmarks. A symbol +, respectively o, represents a kernel for which verification succeeds, respectively fails.

onds and 3448 seconds respectively, indicating that CVC4 was $1.7\times$ faster than Z3 over the *responsive* set. Going beyond this set and with optimizations enabled, verification for 15 kernels timed out using Z3 but completed using CVC4, and the converse was true for 8 kernels.

Optimizing for Verification Performance. We now describe four methods for optimizing the Boogie programs generated by GPUVerify so that they lead to SMT formulas that are easier to decide. The optimizations preserve the result of verification (precisely the same assertions can fail).[6] Each optimization was motivated by one or more challenging examples, for which the optimization led to an encouraging speedup. We evaluate the optimizations experimentally across our benchmark suite using Z3 and CVC4, and comment on the performance that could be gained through portfolio verification.

Eliminating redundant read instrumentation. The first optimization is extremely simple: when we can deduce statically that an array is never written to, we do not perform race analysis for the array. This is a common situation, as GPU kernels often read data from one or more input arrays, and write results to separate output arrays. The optimization may seem trivial, but we mention it because we only considered it after two years' work on GPUVerify. Our efforts and attention were focused on more sophisticated challenges, and this "low hanging fruit" escaped our attention. Our results below show that the optimization is effective overall, serving as a reminder that, when optimizing a program analysis method, it is worth exploring easy optimization avenues first.

Optimizing within barrier intervals. The idea of redundant read instrumentation led us to devise a refinement of this optimization. Define a *barrier interval* to be a call-

---

[6] An exception to this is that in some cases the "redundant reads" optimization actually aids in verification, because shared state abstraction is unnecessary for read-only arrays.

free, single-entry single-exit region of a control flow graph which starts and ends with a barrier [28]. If shared array A is never written to in a barrier interval $\mathcal{I}$ then there is no need to check for races on A during $\mathcal{I}$: in the absence of writes, there is no possibility for races between instructions in $\mathcal{I}$, and the barriers guarding entry to and exit from $\mathcal{I}$ eliminate the possibility of races between reads inside and writes outside $\mathcal{I}$.[7]

Private array removal. Vector data types and operations are widely used in GPU code. In LLVM IR, thread-private vector data is represented as residing in *memory*, rather than in virtual registers. Our Bugle front-end translates each private memory region in LLVM IR into a separate Boogie map, and vector element access are represented at the Boogie level via indexing operations into these maps. Because a vector has a fixed number of elements (e.g. x, y, z and w for a 4D vector), the map indexing expressions are always taken from a small set of literal values. We implemented a pass in GPUVerify which identifies when a map is indexed exclusively using a set of k distinct literals. In such cases, the map and associated indexing expressions are replaced by k distinct scalar variables, each representing an element of the original map. This reduces the extent to which array reasoning is required; our hypothesis was that this would improve solver performance.

Watchdog race checking. Recall from Sect. 2 that data race detection is performed by introducing sets containing the offsets of array accesses. In practice, such sets can be modeled via their characteristic functions using maps. However, this requires quantifiers to express invariants relating to the contents of sets, such as emptiness.

To avoid quantifiers and the associated theorem proving burden, we originally devised a non-deterministic representation of sets [8], based on [17]. Let s and t denote the arbitrary threads considered by the two-thread reduction. For an array A, we introduce variables allowing at most one read from and at most one write to A to be tracked. We then instrument each read operation issued by thread s with a nondeterministic choice between updating the instrumentation variables to record the offset that was read from, or leaving the instrumentation variables untouched. Write operations are instrumented similarly. On kernel entry, and at each barrier, the instrumentation variables are set to indicate that no accesses are tracked. Races between s and t are detected by checking whether offsets accessed by thread t conflict with the offsets tracked by the instrumentation variables. The nondeterministic encoding is sound for race detection because proving correctness of the sequential program generated by GPUVerify involves showing that a conflict between threads on an array is impossible for *all* resolutions of nondeterminism [8]. Treating the two threads under consideration asymmetrically is also sound because verification involves considering *all* possible ordered pairs of distinct threads, so for any pair of distinct threads s and t, analysis will be performed with respect to the ordered pair (s, t) as well as the ordered pair (t, s).

The above encoding avoids quantifiers, but each array access leads to a nondeterministic choice so that the number of paths through the instrumented program grows exponentially with the number of accesses. For kernels that exhibit hundreds of syntactically distinct reads and writes, this leads to prohibitively slow verification.

---

[7] For brevity, this description of the optimization focusses on the situation where all threads executing a kernel are in a single work group; GPUVerify is sensitive to the multi-group case.

Table 1. Summary of optimization results for different solvers. Each speedup is reported with respect to the baseline results for the relevant solver.

Solver	Configuration	Total Time (secs)			Total Speedup			Aggregate Speedups			
		All	Pass	Fail	All	Pass	Fail	Min	Max	Med	Avg
z3	baseline	11882	9070	2812							
	rr	10464	8074	2389	1.1	1.1	1.2	0.5	15.7	1.0	1.2
	rr+bi	10016	7629	2387	1.2	1.2	1.2	0.6	18.5	1.0	1.3
	rr+bi+pa	8206	5973	2232	1.4	1.5	1.3	0.6	77.1	1.1	1.8
	rr+bi+pa+wd	5774	3966	1807	2.1	2.3	1.6	0.5	86.9	1.1	2.5
cvc4	baseline	6080	3616	2464							
	rr	5000	3116	1884	1.2	1.2	1.3	0.1	4.4	1.2	1.3
	rr+bi	5002	3094	1907	1.2	1.2	1.3	0.1	4.3	1.1	1.3
	rr+bi+pa	4450	2611	1838	1.4	1.4	1.3	0.1	16.6	1.1	1.4
	rr+bi+pa+wd	3448	1921	1526	1.8	1.9	1.6	0.3	16.5	1.2	1.5

This led us to devise an alternative race detection method which we call *watchdog* race checking. Watchdog race checking uses a single, unconstrained constant representing an offset with respect to which races should be checked: the "watched offset". Verification involves proving for every array that a data race at the watched offset is impossible. Because the watched offset is arbitrary, this implies that every offset of each array is race-free. For each array, two Booleans are introduced to record whether a read from or write to the watched offset has occurred. Initially these Booleans are false, and they are reset at each barrier. Thread s sets the "read" Boolean to true whenever it reads from the watched offset, and similarly for the "write" Boolean. A race between s and t is reported if thread t reads from the watched offset and the "write" Boolean is *true*, or if thread t writes to the watched offset and either the "read" or "write" Boolean is *true*. The non-deterministic choice per array access is eliminated.

In practice we have adapted the watchdog method so that at each barrier we nondeterministically choose whether to check for data races until the next barrier. This allows the Boolean variables to be set to *false* at barriers by simply *assuming* that they are false. This removes these variables from the modifies sets (modsets) of loops, simplifying invariant generation. We thus reduce blow-up from being exponential in the number of array accesses to exponential in the number of barriers, typically a much smaller number.

Effect of Optimizations on the Benchmarks. Table 1 shows the effects of our optimizations over the *responsive* set of kernels. We show results with Z3 and CVC4 being used for SMT solving. Recall that *baseline* refers to GPUVerify with type-level memory modeling and uniformity analysis but without further optimizations. We use **rr, bi, pa** and **wd** to refer to the redundant read, barrier interval, private array and watchdog race checking optimizations, respectively. We consider applying these optimizations on top of *baseline* in this order; this was the order in which we added the optimizations to GPUVerify, so it illustrates the evolution of the tool. The *Total Time* columns show the

Table 2. Summary of theoretical optimization results using portfolio solving

Portfolio Configuration	Total Time (secs)		
	All	Pass	Fail
Z3 and CVC4, baseline	4875	3031	1843
Z3 and CVC4, all optimizations	2900	1696	1203
All solver and optimization configurations	2825	1659	1166

total time for analysis, summed over all benchmarks (*All*), and also restricted to benchmarks for which verification passes (*Pass*) and fails (*Fail*). For each configuration except *baseline*, the *Speedup* columns show the speedup of an optimization configuration over baseline, for each solver. The *Aggregate Speedups* columns show the minimum (*Min*), maximum (*Max*), median (*Med*) and mean (*Avg*) speedups over *baseline*.

The key message from Table 1 is that our optimizations are increasingly effective, and effective overall, but that the overall speedups afforded by our efforts are modest: $2.1\times$ with Z3 and a $1.8\times$ with CVC4. The maximum and minimum speedups per benchmark show that the effects of an "optimization" can be dramatic, both positively and negatively: an $86.9\times$ speedup is observed for one benchmark with Z3 and full optimizations (543 seconds to 6 seconds); with CVC the worst speedup is $0.3\times$ (a $3.3\times$ *slowdown*) with full optimizations. The median and mean results suggest that our optimizations have little impact on a significant number of the benchmarks. With the exception of watchdog race checking (a change in race instrumentation is relevant to *all* benchmarks) this is not surprising: many kernels do not exhibit read-only arrays (thus **rr** cannot help), many do not use vectors (thus **pa** cannot help) and we have already argued that the **bi** optimization is rather specialized. We find it counter-intuitive that the **rr** optimization, which simplifies the Boogie program generated by GPUVerify, has such a negative impact in the worst case with CVC4. The associated kernel has a single read-only array and went from 4 seconds using *baseline* to 49 seconds using **rr**. The unpredictable nature of SMT solvers motivates using multiple solvers during analysis.

The potential for portfolio verification. Our combination of solvers and optimizations opens the door for "portfolio verification": running multiple instances of GPUVerify completely independently using different solver and optimization configurations, reporting the first analysis result yielded by a configuration. Table 2 shows the lowest total time for analysis over the *responsive* benchmarks that could be expected using portfolio verification with multiple solver and optimization configurations. Comparing the best total time in Table 1 (3448 seconds for CVC4) with the total time for full portfolio verification in Table 2 (2825 seconds) the best further speedup portfolio verification could give is a modest $1.2\times$ overall. We see the main potential of portfolio verification to be minimizing the response time of GPUVerify.

5   False Positives and Error Reporting

Although GPUVerify performs sound verification, we envisage the tool being useful in practice for bug-finding, where failed proof attempts shed light on genuine defects. Feedback from GPU programmers elicited through talks and tutorials at industry-focused events appear to support this usage mode. We have taken several steps to reduce false positives and improve the quality of error messages reported by the tool.

Aliasing Assumptions on Kernel Entry. A GPU kernel operates on a number of shared arrays, provided as pointer arguments. According to the OpenCL and CUDA documentation, there is nothing to stop these pointers from aliasing one another. In practice we have not encountered a single case of such aliasing across our set of 564 benchmarks. To be truly sound, GPUVerify should assume that pointers could overlap arbitrarily. This would lead to false positive race reports for practically *all* array accesses, rendering the tool unusable. To avoid this, we took the pragmatic decision to have GPUVerify silently assume that distinct pointer parameters to a kernel refer to disjoint arrays.

While validating GPUVerify, an engineer at our industrial partner Rightware identified this source of unsoundness: *"I have probably uncovered a minor bug in GPUVerify ... if we have a kernel like* [the slightly simplified example on the right] *GPUVerify happily says it's all right. However the user can ... set the same memory object as an argument for both a and b ...* [w]*hich has a clear race condition"*. When asked whether this scenario is likely in practice, the engineer confirmed: *"We don't have any kernels where it would be wise to pass the same pointer value in multiple arguments"*, but suggested that GPUVerify could emit a warning about its aliasing assumptions if the developer has not used the C99 `restrict` qualifier to indicate explicitly that pointer arguments refer to disjoint data: *"I'd recommend a warning when not using restrict, because in probably all the practical cases the kernel arguments are separate"*.

```
__kernel void
aliasing(__global int* a,
         __global int* b) {
  b[get_global_id(0)+1]
    = a[get_global_id(0)];
}
```

In response to this advice we added a pass to GPUVerify which emits a warning if a kernel has multiple `__global` pointer arguments that are not restrict-annotated.

Auto-inlining. Although GPUVerify supports a modular analysis mode, automatic generation of procedure specifications is challenging, and imprecise specifications lead to false positives. Typical GPU kernels are free from recursion and function pointers (both are forbidden in OpenCL and only recently allowed in CUDA as part of CUDA 3.1) and are presented in whole-program form. To avoid false positives we automatically apply aggressive inlining to kernels that do not use recursion or function pointers, repeatedly inlining calls until no calls remain. All non-kernel functions are then discarded, and verification is attempted on the now monolithic kernel functions. One downside to this pragmatic approach is that if a source file contains a function that is never invoked, but which would exhibit a data race if it were to be invoked, GPUVerify will not analyse the function and thus will not report a possible defect. Across the *responsive* set, in *baseline* mode, we find that disabling auto-inlining leads to false positives being reported for 31 kernels where verification succeeds with auto-inlining enabled.

KernelInterceptor: Verifying Dynamically Collected Kernel Instances. A GPU kernel is typically designed to work correctly only for certain thread counts and input values, and GPUVerify requires preconditions specifying constraints on these parameters to avoid false positive error reports. Providing these preconditions can be a barrier to using the tool: preliminary experience with engineers at Rightware and ARM suggest that even the developer of a kernel may not be able to immediately identify suitable constraints on kernel parameters. To help overcome this we have designed KernelInterceptor [5], a tool to accompany GPUVerify for analysis of OpenCL kernels. KernelInterceptor is a shim which intercepts calls to the OpenCL host API used to specify thread counts and input parameters, gathering this data for all kernel instances launched during the running of an application. GPUVerify can then be automatically invoked using preconditions corresponding to each kernel instance that was observed, eliminating false positives arising due to unrealistic parameter values.

Error Reporting. Our initial GPUVerify prototype reported verification failures by printing a trace for the Boogie program generated by the tool; this information was of limited use even to us as the tool's developers. To allow clear error reports referring to the original source code of a kernel we have extended our Bugle front-end so that source information, available from LLVM IR if Clang is invoked appropriately, is embedded in the generated Boogie code via Boogie attributes.

Meaningfully reporting data races proved more difficult than we anticipated, because a data race involves *two* access operations: a *first* access is logged, and subsequently a race is detected due to a conflicting *second* access. At the Boogie level, an assertion corresponding to the *second* access fails. Source information for this access is available from attributes attached to the assertion, but source information for the *first* access is *not* directly available. Furthermore, the race report may stem from an abstract trace that jumps over a loop by replacing the loop with a summary computed using an invariant. In this case it may be that no specific *first* access is responsible for the race report; instead, it may be that GPUVerify could not find a strong enough invariant to prove race-freedom between the loop and the *second* access. To overcome this reporting problem we use Boogie's *state capture* facility to ask the SMT solver to provide a valuation of all program variables after each logging operation and at the head of each loop. This allows us to walk an abstract counterexample trace and determine whether the possible race is due to a specific *first* access or instead stems from the abstraction of a loop. In the former case we can provide a specific race report, otherwise we report all relevant array accesses in the loop as possibly racing with the *second* access.

6   Engagement With Industry

We briefly summarize our efforts to make it easy for industrial users to access and learn about GPUVerify, and discuss preliminary feedback from two industrial partners.

Industry-Friendly Licenses. The licenses associated with the Clang/LLVM and Boogie frameworks mean that they can be used freely in a commercial context. This is not true of the Z3 solver. Providing support for CVC4, with a license attractive to industry, has been vital in allowing industrial partners to try out GPUVerify.

Web Access. We have made GPUVerify available as a web service through Microsoft's rise4fun site,[8] allowing interested users to try the tool with no installation overhead.

Tutorial Videos. To give potential users in industry a practical overview of GPUVerify we have recorded a series of tutorial videos, available on YouTube. We have also given in-person tutorials at industry-focussed conferences and OpenCL vendor sites.

Preliminary Industrial Feedback. Feedback from our industrial contacts at Rightware and ARM on GPUVerify has been encouraging. Rightware have used GPUVerify

---

[8] http://rise4fun.com/GPUVerify-OpenCL and http://rise4fun.com/GPUVerify-CUDA

to verify race-freedom across their Basemark CL suite, discovering one defect in the process. We are collaborating with engineers at ARM on adapting GPUVerify to provide tailored analysis support for OpenCL kernels targeting ARM's Mali GPU series.

7   Lessons Learned and Future Problems

We summarize the principal take-aways from our experience building GPUVerify, and pose what in our view is the main challenge associated with future work in this area.

Lessons Learned. We hope the following may be informative for future projects.

Target a tractable problem. GPUVerify's goals are modest: attempt to verify race-freedom (not full functional correctness) for GPU kernels (not arbitrary C programs). With this tight scope we have been able to exploit the relative simplicity of GPU kernels to achieve a fairly high degree of automation and efficiency.

Re-use infrastructure. We cannot overstate how much we have gained by exploiting Clang/LLVM, Boogie, Z3 and CVC4. When considering infrastructure re-use, it is worth paying attention to licensing issues if the ultimate goal is industrial uptake.

Evolve front-end capabilities. All software verification tools have to face the "front-end" problem. Restricting to a toy language simplifies front-end development but dooms a tool to only academic use; working with a full-fledged compiler infrastructure can blur implementation difficulty with the essence of a new idea. We advocate a staged approach to this problem as outlined in Sect. 3, which is aided by intermediate verification languages such as Boogie [6] and Why3 [19].

Beware of outliers. We optimized GPUVerify in response to kernels for which performance was particularly bad. We achieved massive speedups for some outliers, but were brought down to earth by the modest overall speedups and new *negative* outliers resulting from our optimizations (see Table 1). Evaluating the general effectiveness of verification optimizations requires a large set of benchmarks.

Challenge: Flexible Invariant Generation. The main weakness of GPUVerify is its invariant generation capabilities. We use Houdini for invariant generation in GPUVerify because, though somewhat brute force, it is *flexible* and applicable to arbitrary programs. At present we are unable to exploit advanced invariant generation techniques because they restrict the form of programs to which they can be applied. We offer our large set of publicly available benchmarks as a challenge for invariant generation researchers interested in lifting restrictions on program form.

Acknowledgments. This work was supported by the EU FP7 project CARP, EPSRC grant EP/K011499/1, a PhD studentship partly sponsored by ARM Ltd., a gift from Intel Corporation, and the Imperial College London UROP scheme. The project benefited from discussions at Dagstuhl seminar 13142. We are grateful to Teemu Virolainen at Rightware and Anton Lokhmotov at ARM for their feedback on GPUVerify.

References

1. Allen, J., Kennedy, K., Porterfield, C., Warren, J.: Conversion of control dependence to data dependence. In: POPL, pp. 177–189 (1983)
2. AMD: AMD Accelerated Parallel Processing (APP) SDK, http://developer.amd.com/sdks/amdappsdk
3. Bakhoda, A., Yuan, G.L., Fung, W.W.L., Wong, H., Aamodt, T.M.: Analyzing CUDA workloads using a detailed gpu simulator. In: ISPASS, pp. 163–174 (2009)
4. Bardsley, E., Donaldson, A.F.: Warps and atomics: Beyond barrier synchronization in the verification of GPU kernels. In: Badger, J.M., Rozier, K.Y. (eds.) NFM 2014. LNCS, vol. 8430, pp. 230–245. Springer, Heidelberg (2014)
5. Bardsley, E., Donaldson, A.F., Wickerson, J.: KernelInterceptor: Automating gpu kernel verification by intercepting kernels and their parameters. In: IWOCL (2014)
6. Barnett, M., Chang, B.-Y.E., DeLine, R., Jacobs, B., M. Leino, K.R.: Boogie: A modular reusable verifier for object-oriented programs. In: de Boer, F.S., Bonsangue, M.M., Graf, S., de Roever, W.-P. (eds.) FMCO 2005. LNCS, vol. 4111, pp. 364–387. Springer, Heidelberg (2006)
7. Barrett, C., Conway, C.L., Deters, M., Hadarean, L., Jovanović, D., King, T., Reynolds, A., Tinelli, C.: CVC4. In: Gopalakrishnan, G., Qadeer, S. (eds.) CAV 2011. LNCS, vol. 6806, pp. 171–177. Springer, Heidelberg (2011)
8. Betts, A., Chong, N., Donaldson, A.F., Qadeer, S., Thomson, P.: GPUVerify: a verifier for GPU kernels. In: OOPSLA, pp. 113–132 (2012)
9. Che, S., et al.: Rodinia: A benchmark suite for heterogeneous computing. In: Workload Characterization, pp. 44–54 (2009)
10. Chiang, W.-F., Gopalakrishnan, G., Li, G., Rakamarić, Z.: Formal analysis of GPU programs with atomics via conflict-directed delay-bounding. In: Brat, G., Rungta, N., Venet, A. (eds.) NFM 2013. LNCS, vol. 7871, pp. 213–228. Springer, Heidelberg (2013)
11. Chong, N., Donaldson, A.F., Kelly, P., Ketema, J., Qadeer, S.: Barrier invariants: a shared state abstraction for the analysis of data-dependent GPU kernels. In: OOPSLA (2013)
12. Chong, N., Donaldson, A.F., Ketema, J.: A sound and complete abstraction for reasoning about parallel prefix sums. In: POPL, pp. 397–410 (2014)
13. Chou, C.-T., Mannava, P.K., Park, S.: A simple method for parameterized verification of cache coherence protocols. In: Hu, A.J., Martin, A.K. (eds.) FMCAD 2004. LNCS, vol. 3312, pp. 382–398. Springer, Heidelberg (2004)
14. Collingbourne, P., Cadar, C., Kelly, P.H.J.: Symbolic crosschecking of data-parallel floating-point code. IEEE Trans. Software Eng. (to appear, 2014)
15. Collingbourne, P., Donaldson, A.F., Ketema, J., Qadeer, S.: Interleaving and lock-step semantics for analysis and verification of GPU kernels. In: Felleisen, M., Gardner, P. (eds.) Programming Languages and Systems. LNCS, vol. 7792, pp. 270–289. Springer, Heidelberg (2013)
16. Danalis, A., et al.: The scalable heterogeneous computing (SHOC) benchmark suite. In: GPGPU 2010, pp. 63–74 (2010)
17. Donaldson, A.F., Kroening, D., Rümmer, P.: Automatic analysis of DMA races using model checking and k-induction. Formal Methods in System Design 39(1), 83–113 (2011)
18. Ferrante, J., Ottenstein, K.J., Warren, J.D.: The program dependence graph and its use in optimization. ACM Trans. Program. Lang. Syst. 9(3), 319–349 (1987)
19. Filliâtre, J.-C., Paskevich, A.: Why3 — where programs meet provers. In: Felleisen, M., Gardner, P. (eds.) Programming Languages and Systems. LNCS, vol. 7792, pp. 125–128. Springer, Heidelberg (2013)

20. Flanagan, C., M. Leino, K.R.: Houdini, an annotation assistant for eSC/Java. In: Oliveira, J.N., Zave, P. (eds.) FME 2001. LNCS, vol. 2021, pp. 500–517. Springer, Heidelberg (2001)

21. Grauer-Gray, S., Xu, L., Searles, R., Ayalasomayajula, S., Cavazos, J.: Auto-tuning a high-level language targeted to GPU codes. In: InPar (2012)

22. Harris, M., Buck, I.: GPU flow-control idioms. In: GPU Gems 2. Addison-Wesley (2005)

23. Huisman, M., Mihelčić, M.: Specification and verification of GPGPU programs using permission-based separation logic. In: BYTECODE (2013)

24. Karrenberg, R., Hack, S.: Improving performance of openCL on cPUs. In: O'Boyle, M. (ed.) CC 2012. LNCS, vol. 7210, pp. 1–20. Springer, Heidelberg (2012)

25. Khronos OpenCL Working Group: The OpenCL specification, version 2.0 (2013)

26. Leung, A., Gupta, M., Agarwal, Y., et al.: Verifying GPU kernels by test amplification. In: PLDI, pp. 383–394 (2012)

27. Li, G., Gopalakrishnan, G.: Scalable SMT-based verification of GPU kernel functions. In: FSE, pp. 187–196 (2010)

28. Li, G., Li, P., Sawaya, G., Gopalakrishnan, G., Ghosh, I., Rajan, S.P.: GKLEE: Concolic verification and test generation for GPUs. In: PPoPP, pp. 215–224 (2012)

29. Li, P., Li, G., Gopalakrishnan, G.: Parametric flows: Automated behavior equivalencing for symbolic analysis of races in CUDA programs. In: SC, pp. 29:1–29:10 (2012)

30. McMillan, K.L.: Verification of infinite state systems by compositional model checking. In: Pierre, L., Kropf, T. (eds.) CHARME 1999. LNCS, vol. 1703, pp. 219–237. Springer, Heidelberg (1999)

31. Microsoft Corporation: C++ AMP sample projects for download (MSDN blog), http://blogs.msdn.com/b/nativeconcurrency/archive/2012/01/30/c-amp-sample-projects-for-download.aspx

32. de Moura, L., Bjørner, N.S.: Z3: An efficient SMT solver. In: Ramakrishnan, C.R., Rehof, J. (eds.) TACAS 2008. LNCS, vol. 4963, pp. 337–340. Springer, Heidelberg (2008)

33. NVIDIA: CUDA C programming guide, version 5.5 (2013)

34. NVIDIA: GPU Computing SDK (accessed 2013), https://developer.nvidia.com/gpu-computing-sdk

35. Rakamaric, Z., Hu, A.J.: Automatic inference of frame axioms using static analysis. In: ASE, pp. 89–98 (2008)

36. Rakamarić, Z., Hu, A.J.: A scalable memory model for low-level code. In: Jones, N.D., Müller-Olm, M. (eds.) VMCAI 2009. LNCS, vol. 5403, pp. 290–304. Springer, Heidelberg (2009)

37. Rightware Oy: Basemark CL, http://www.rightware.com/benchmarking-software/basemark-cl/

38. Stratton, J., et al.: Parboil: A revised benchmark suite for scientific and commercial throughput computing. Tech. Rep. IMPACT-12-01, UIUC (2012)

39. Talupur, M., Tuttle, M.R.: Going with the flow: Parameterized verification using message flows. In: FMCAD, pp. 1–8 (2008)

Lazy Annotation Revisited

Kenneth L. McMillan

Microsoft Research, Redmond, WA, USA

Abstract. Lazy Annotation is a method of software model checking that performs a backtracking search for a symbolic counterexample. When the search backtracks, the program is annotated with a learned fact that constrains future search. In this sense, the method is closely analogous to conflict-driven clause learning in SAT solvers.

In this paper, we develop several improvements to the basic Lazy Annotation approach. The resulting algorithm is compared both conceptually and experimentally to two approaches based on similar principles but using different learning strategies: unfolding-based Bounded Model Checking and Property-Driven Reachability.

1 Introduction

Lazy Annotation is a method of software model checking motivated by conflict-driven clause learning (CDCL) in Boolean satisfiability (SAT) solvers. It performs a backtracking search for a symbolic execution of a program that violates a safety property. When the search reaches a conflict, it backtracks, annotating the program with a learned fact that constrains future search. As in CDCL, the learned fact is derived as a Craig interpolant.

In this paper, we develop several improvements to the basic Lazy Annotation approach. Among other things, we adapt Lazy Abstraction to large-block encodings [6], allowing us to exploit the power of modern satisfiability modulo theories (SMT) solvers. We compare the resulting algorithm to unfolding-based Bounded Model Checking and to Property-Driven Reachability. These methods share the general approach of conflict-driven learning, but differ in their search and learning strategies. Our goal will be to clarify these distinctions conceptually, and to test empirically the relative strengths of the different strategies. In particular, we will try to answer two questions:

1. Whether structured or unstructured search is more effective, and
2. What characterizes an effective conflict learning strategy, in terms of reducing bounded search and converging to an unbounded solution.

Related Work. The basic idea of Lazy Annotation was introduced by Jaffar *et al.* [17] in the context of Constraint Logic Programming (CLP). A more general approach, handling richer theories and recursive procedures, was introduced by the author [21], along with the name Lazy Annotation. Here, we adopt the latter approach, in particular its use of proof-based interpolants and its method of inferring unbounded proofs from bounded proofs. Following Jaffar *et al.*,

A. Biere and R. Bloem (Eds.): CAV 2014, LNCS 8559, pp. 243–259, 2014.
© Springer International Publishing Switzerland 2014

we work within the CLP framework, but generalize from simple linear arithmetic constraints to constraints in full first-order logic, exploiting the strength of modern SMT solvers. Moreover, we will allow clauses with multiple sub-goals (called the *nonlinear case* in [16]). Thus we can verify, for example, recursive procedural programs.

The IC3 method of Bradley [9] is similar at a high level to Lazy Annotation. Both methods perform bounded verification for increasing bounds, until an inductive invariant can be inferred from the bounded proof. Both methods generate symbolic goal states that are known to reach an error. These are refuted in a bounded sense by computing interpolants (in a sense we will define). Apart from various optimizations, the primary difference is in the particular strategy for computing these interpolants, an issue we will study in detail.

The class of algorithms based on IC3 has been called Property-Driven Reachability [12]. Although PDR originally applied only to propositional logic and the linear case, the approach was later extended to the non-linear case and richer logics [16] making it suitable for software model checking. Cimatti and Griggio give a hybrid approach applying PDR to software model checking [10]. Propositional PDR can also be applied to software via predicate abstraction [16,11].

Another related approach was introduced recently by Bayless *et al.* [5] for the propositional linear case. In addition, there are various other CDCL-like methods [15,24] to which the conclusions of this study may be relevant.

2 Informal Discussion of Lazy Annotation

To give an intuitive explanation of the basic search and learning strategy of Lazy Annotation (LA in the sequel) we first consider the special case of transition systems (equivalently, imperative programs with a single loop). This will allow us to use the familiar vocabulary of transition systems, and to compare approaches more easily.

We model a transition system using the following *constrained Horn clauses*:

$$I(\bar{x}) \Rightarrow R(\bar{x}) \tag{1}$$
$$R(\bar{x}) \wedge T(\bar{x}, \bar{x}') \Rightarrow R(\bar{x}') \tag{2}$$

Here, $\bar{x}$ is a vector of variables representing the program state. The free variables are considered to be universally quantified in these clauses (a convention we will use in the remainder of the paper). The predicate I is a fixed set of initial states, while T is a fixed transition relation. Predicate R represents an *unknown* inductive invariant for which we wish to solve. The solution must satisfy the *query* formula $R(\bar{x}) \Rightarrow S(\bar{x})$, where S is a fixed set of safe states. Any such R constitutes a proof that our transition system is safe (that is, no initial state can reach a non-safe state via any sequence of transitions).

Our strategy for finding a solution for R will be to search for a refutation. A refutation takes the form of path in the transition system from an initial state to a non-safe state. As we will see, such a path corresponds to a ground derivation of a contradiction using our clauses.

As in bounded model checking, we search for a refutation path by *unwinding* the system k steps. This gives the following set of clauses:

$$I(\bar{x}) \Rightarrow R_0(\bar{x})$$
$$R_0(\bar{x}) \wedge T(\bar{x}, \bar{x}') \Rightarrow R_1(\bar{x}')$$
$$\ldots$$
$$R_{k-1}(\bar{x}) \wedge T(\bar{x}, \bar{x}') \Rightarrow R_k(\bar{x}')$$
$$R_k(\bar{x}) \Rightarrow S(\bar{x})$$

A refutation for this acyclic (or non-recursive) set of clauses is a transition sequence that violates safety after exactly k steps. Correspondingly, a solution for $R_0 \ldots R_k$ represents a proof that there is no such path. If we find a solution of the k-step unwound system, we can then attempt to derive from it a solution for the original cyclic system.

During our search for a refutation path, we maintain a candidate solution for $R_0 \ldots R_k$ called the *annotation*. The annotation of R_i is an over-approximation of the set of reachable states of the system after i steps. We require that the annotation be inductive. That is, it must satisfy all the Horn clauses, but not necessarily the query (unlike in PDR, we don't require that the annotation be an expanding chain).

Our search takes the unsafe states as an initial goal and symbolically executes the system backward from this goal. At each step we narrow the search by making a *decision*. A decision is simply an arbitrary constraint on our symbolic path. The search reaches a *conflict* when the goal (the symbolic path) becomes unsatisfiable. In this case, we backtrack, undoing the most recent decision. In the process we *learn* an annotation that prevents us from making the same decision in the future. The learned annotation is computed as an interpolant.

A *search goal* is a conjunction of facts to be derived and constraints to be satisfied. Our initial goal is $R_k(\bar{x}_k) \wedge \neg S(\bar{x}_k)$. That is, we wish to derive an unsafe state reachable in k steps. A backward step in the search corresponds to *resolution* of the goal with a clause. Thus, in the first step, we resolve the goal with the clause $R_{k-1}(\bar{x}) \wedge T(\bar{x}, \bar{x}') \Rightarrow R_k(\bar{x}')$ to obtain the new goal $R_{k-1}(\bar{x}_{k-1}) \wedge T(\bar{x}_{k-1}, \bar{x}_k) \wedge \neg S(\bar{x}_k)$. This goal represents a state reachable in $k-1$ steps that can reach an unsafe state in one step. As we perform resolution steps, our goal represents execution paths of increasing length.

Now suppose a goal is satisfiable in the current annotation. That is, when we substitute the annotation for R_i into the goal, the resulting formula is satisfiable. This means we can reach the error from R_i. We then make a decision, adding an arbitrary constraint to the goal. Decisions prevent the goal from becoming overly complex as we perform resolution steps. A decision typically constrains the most recent execution step. Thus, if our goal is $R_i(\bar{x}_i) \wedge T(\bar{x}_i, \bar{x}_{i+1}) \wedge \cdots \neg S(\bar{x}_k)$, it becomes $R_i(\bar{x}_i) \wedge D_i(\bar{x}_i, \bar{x}_{i+1}) \wedge T(\bar{x}_i, \bar{x}_{i+1}) \wedge \cdots \neg S(\bar{x}_k)$. Here D_i is a fixed predicate representing the i-th decision. The choice is D_i is arbitrary, but we require that the goal remain satisfiable.

Because decisions constrain the search, we may find after making a resolution step that the goal is unsatisfiable. At this point we are in conflict, and must backtrack to the previous goal, undoing one resolution step and one decision. In the process, we strengthen the annotation so that the last decision becomes infeasible. Our strengthening must be a value of R_{i+1} such that the resolved clause is true, that is,

$$R_i(\bar{x}_i) \wedge T(\bar{x}_i, \bar{x}_{i+1}) \Rightarrow R_{i+1}(\bar{x}_{i+1}) \tag{3}$$

and such that the prior decision is infeasible, that is, such that

$$R_{i+1}(\bar{x}_{i+1}) \wedge D_{i+1}(\bar{x}_{i+1}, \bar{x}_{i+2}) \wedge T(\bar{x}_{i+1}, \bar{x}_{i+2}) \wedge \cdots \neg S(\bar{x}_k) \tag{4}$$

is unsatisfiable. The reader may recognize that the formula $R_{i+1}(\bar{x}_{i+1})$ is an *interpolant* between two parts of the infeasible goal. We can compute such an interpolant from a proof of unsatisfiability of the goal, provided the proof system admits feasible interpolation [20]. The new annotation forces a different decision after backtracking.

LA can terminate in one of two ways. After resolving on R_0, the goal contains no facts to derive. In this case, it is a feasible BMC formula representing a path from initial to unsafe states. On the other hand, if the initial goal becomes unsatisfiable (that is, if R_k implies S under the annotation) then we have a proof that no unsafe state is reachable in k steps.

We can then use the annotation of the bounded unwinding as a hint in constructing a solution of the original cyclic problem. We will will refer to this as the *convergence phase*. In [21], the convergence approach was to start with all of the conjuncts of annotations R_i of the bounded problem and apply the Houdini algorithm [13] to reduce these to their maximal inductive subset. If this yields a solution, we are done, otherwise we increase the unfolding depth k. The convergence phase in PDR is similar: annotations are propagated forward until a fixed point is reached. There are many other possibilities, however, including Lazy Abstraction with Interpolants (LAWI) and predicate abstraction. Here, we will focus on solving the bounded problem and leave aside the largely orthogonal question of convergence.

3   Formal Description of Lazy Annotation

We will now formalize LA as an algorithm, extending it from simple transition systems to the general case of constrained Horn clauses.

We use standard first-order logic over a signature Σ of function and predicate symbols of defined arities. We use ϕ, ψ for formulas, P, Q, R for predicate symbols, x, y, z for individual variables t, u for terms and $\bar{x}$ for a vector of variables. Truth of a formula is relative to a background theory $\mathcal{T}$. A subset of the signature $\Sigma_I \subseteq \Sigma$ is *interpreted* by the theory. We assume the symbol $=$ has the usual interpretation. We assume theory $\mathcal{T}$ is *complete* in that it has at most one model. Thus, every sentence over Σ_I has a defined truth value. This assumption can be removed, in which case many of the definitions that follow become relative to a choice of theory model. Unless otherwise stated, we assume that $\mathcal{T}$ is decidable.

The *vocabulary* of ϕ, denoted $L(\phi)$, consists of its free variables and the subset of $\Sigma \setminus \Sigma_I$ occurring in ϕ. An *interpolant* for $A \wedge B$ is a formula I such that $A \Rightarrow I$ and $B \Rightarrow \neg I$ are valid, and $L(I) \subseteq L(A) \cap L(B)$. We will write $\phi[X]$ for a formula with free variables in X. A *P-fact* is a formula of the form $P(t_1, \ldots, t_n)$. A formula or term is *ground* if it contains no variables. When a set of formulas appears as a formula, it represents the conjunction of the set. If ϕ is a formula and σ a symbol substitution, $\phi\sigma$ is the result of performing substitution σ on ϕ.

Definition 1. *Relative to a vocabulary of predicate symbols $\mathcal{R}$, we say*

1. *A fact is a P-fact for some $P \in \mathcal{R}$,*
2. *A constraint is a formula ϕ s.t. $L(\phi) \cap \mathcal{R} = \emptyset$,*
3. *A goal is a set of facts and constraints.*
4. *A rule is a sentence of the form $\forall X.B[X] \Rightarrow H[X]$ where the body $B[X]$ is a goal and the head $H[X]$ is a fact.*

We will also write goals in the form $F[X] \mid C[X]$ and rules in the form $F[X] \Rightarrow H[X] \mid C[X]$, where $F[X]$ is the set of facts (the subgoals*) and $C[X]$ is the set of constraints.*

Definition 2. *A ground instance of a rule $F[X] \Rightarrow H[X] \mid C[X]$ (respectively a goal $F[X] \mid C[X]$) is $F\sigma \Rightarrow H\sigma$ (respectively $F\sigma$) for any ground substitution σ on X such that $C\sigma$ is true in $\mathcal{T}$.*

Definition 3. *A ground derivation from a set of rules $\mathcal{C}$ is a sequence of ground instances of rules in $\mathcal{C}$ in which each subgoal is the head of a preceding clause. A ground derivation of a goal G is a ground derivation of all the subgoals of some ground instance of G.*

Definition 4. *A Horn reachability problem is a triple $(\mathcal{R}, \mathcal{C}, G)$ where $\mathcal{R}$ is a vocabulary of predicate symbols, $\mathcal{C}$ is a set of rules over $\mathcal{R}$ and G is a goal over $\mathcal{R}$. It is* satisfiable *if there is a ground derivation of G from $\mathcal{C}$. A dual solution of the problem is a model of $\mathcal{C}$ in which G is unsatisfiable.*

Definition 5. *A Horn reachability problem $(\mathcal{R}, \mathcal{C}, G)$ is acyclic if there is a total order $<$ on $\mathcal{R}$ such that for all rules $F \Rightarrow P(\bar{x}) \mid C$ in $\mathcal{C}$ and all subgoals $Q(\bar{y})$ in F, $Q < P$.*

A set of Horn clauses has a least model, which is the set of derivable facts. Thus, a Horn reachability problem has a dual solution *iff* it is unsatisfiable.

We assume that the predicates in $\mathcal{R}$ occur only in the form $P(\bar{x})$ where $\bar{x}$ is a vector of distinct variables. We can enforce this by introducing new variables and equalities, for example rewriting $B[X] \Rightarrow P(f(x))$ to $B[X] \wedge y = f(x) \Rightarrow P(y)$. We represent the interpretation of a predicate $P(\bar{x})$ symbolically by a characteristic formula $\phi[\bar{x}]$. We write $\alpha(P) = \lambda\bar{x}.\ \phi[\bar{x}]$ to mean that, in the interpretation α, $P(\bar{x})$ holds iff ϕ holds. Given relations P and Q, we write $P \wedge Q$ for the intersection of P and Q and $P \vee Q$ for their union. Further, we will write $\top$ for $\lambda\bar{x}.\ \text{TRUE}$ and $\bot$ for $\lambda\bar{x}.\ \text{FALSE}$ (where the arity of $\bar{x}$ is understood from context).

The procedure maintains a model α of the rules $\mathcal{C}$ called the *annotation*. This model over-approximates the derivable facts (*i.e.* reachable program states). Initially, $\alpha(P) = \top$ for all $P \in \mathcal{R}$. The LA procedure is shown in Figure 1. As Jaffar *et al.* observe [17], it is essentially Prolog execution with a form of tabling using interpolants. We assume a procedure $\text{Itp}(A, B)$ that takes two inconsistent formulas A and B and returns an interpolant for $A \wedge B$.

The main procedure is SEARCH, which takes a goal G and searches for a ground derivation of it. It assumes that the goal is satisfiable in the current annotation, that is, $G\alpha$ is satisfiable. If not, the problem is trivially unsatisfiable. If there are no subgoals in G, the problem is trivially *satisfiable*, and we return SAT. Else we arbitrarily choose a subgoal $P(\bar{x})$ to derive. We then loop over all rules C with head matching $P(\bar{x})$. For each such C, we call the procedure RSTEP to continue the search using C to derive $P(\bar{x})$ (procedure REN renames the variables in C to avoid clashes with the goal). If the search succeeds, we return SAT. Else RSTEP returns a value for P that contains all facts derivable using C and rules out the goal. After the loop, the disjunction of the returned values over-approximates P. Thus, we strengthen $\alpha(P)$ by this disjunction, maintaining α as a model of $\mathcal{C}$ and making $G\alpha$ unsatisfiable.

Procedure RSTEP takes a goal G, a subgoal $P(\bar{x})$ of G to be satisfied, and a rule C of the form $B \Rightarrow P(\bar{y})$ to be used to derive the subgoal (where the free variables of the goal G and clause C are distinct). First we resolve the rule with the goal. Since $\bar{y}$ is a vector of variables, the most general unifier is trivial: we just map $\bar{y}$ to $\bar{x}$. We produce the *prefix* by applying the unifier to the body of the rule and the *suffix* by removing the subgoal from G. The *resolvent* G' is the union of the prefix and suffix. This is our new goal.

Now we test whether the new goal G' is satisfiable in the current annotation, using decision procedure for theory $\mathcal{T}$ (for example, an SMT solver). If it is unsatisfiable, we compute an interpolant $\phi[\bar{x}]$ between the prefix and suffix. Because $\phi[\bar{x}]$ is implied by the prefix, we know that the assignment $P = \lambda\bar{x}. \phi$ satisfies rule C in the current annotation. Moreover, since $\phi[\bar{x}]$ is inconsistent with the suffix, we know that this interpretation is inconsistent with the original goal G. We therefore return the symbolic relation $\lambda\bar{x}. \phi$ as an over-approximation of P showing that the subgoal cannot be derived using rule C.

On the other hand, suppose the new goal is satisfiable in the current annotation. We now make a *decision*. The decision is chosen from a finite language $\mathcal{L}_D(G')$ using only the variables of the new goal G'. Though the decision is arbitrary, it must at least be consistent with G' so that the resulting goal is satisfiable. This means that the disjunction of formulas in language $\mathcal{L}_D(G')$ must be valid. In our implementation, our decision language is the set of truth assignments to the atoms of G'. Thus, we can construct a decision consistent with G' by using the satisfying assignment returned by our decision procedure. Having made a decision, we now have a satisfiable goal, which we attempt to solve by calling the main procedure SEARCH recursively.

Theorem 1 (Total correctness). *Given an acyclic Horn reachability problem* $\Pi = (\mathcal{R}, \mathcal{C}, G)$, *such that* G *is satisfiable,* SEARCH(G) *terminates and:*

Procedure RSTEP($G, P(\bar{x}), C = (B \Rightarrow P(\bar{y}))$)
Input: goal G, subgoal $P(\bar{x})$, rule C
Output: SAT, or a bound on P refuting the goal

1   Let pref $= B\langle \bar{x}/\bar{y} \rangle$ and suff $= G \setminus \{P(\bar{x})\}$
2   Let $G' = $ pref $\cup$ suff
3   While TRUE do:
4   if $G'\alpha$ is unsatisfiable, return $\lambda\bar{x}$. Itp(pref, suff)
5   choose D in $\mathcal{L}_D(G')$ s.t. $(D \wedge G')\alpha$ is satisfiable
6   if SEARCH($G' \cup \{D\}$) = SAT return SAT
7   Done.

Procedure SEARCH($G = (F \mid C)$)
Input: goal G s.t. $G\alpha$ satisfiable
Output: SAT or UNSAT and $G\alpha$ unsatisfiable

1   If F (the subgoal set) is empty, return SAT
2   Choose a subgoal $P(\bar{x})$ in F
3   Let $R = \emptyset$
3   For each rule $C = (B \Rightarrow P(\bar{y}))$ in C do:
4   Let $R_C = $ RSTEP($G, P(\bar{x}),$ REN(C))
5   If $R_C = $ SAT return SAT
6   Let $R = R \cup \{R_C\}$
7   Done
8   Let $\alpha(P) = \alpha(P) \wedge (\vee R)$
9   Return UNSAT.

Fig. 1. Basic unwinding algorithm

- *if it returns* SAT, *Π is satisfiable*
- *if it returns* UNSAT, *Π is unsatisfiable and α is a dual solution of Π.*

The proof can be found in [23].

3.1 Comparison to BMC

We will use BMC to refer to Bounded Model Checking by unfolding and applying a decision procedure, as in [7]. In the transition system case, a completed search goal in LA is precisely a k-step BMC formula. If we make no decisions, LA reduces to BMC followed by interpolation. The difference between BMC and LA is therefore in the decision and learning strategies. Decision-making in BMC is *unstructured* in the sense that the decision procedure may make decisions on any variables in the goal formula in any order. In LA, decision making is *structured*. That is, we alternate resolution (unfolding) and decision steps. Similarly, learning in BMC is unstructured. The decision procedure may learn clauses that span the entire BMC formula. In LA, learning is structured. Each learned annotation is a set of facts describing a single program state.

It is not clear *a priori* what the most effective strategy is. The unstructured approach allows greater flexibility and more opportunities for heuristic optimization. On the other hand, a more structured approach may guide us to learn more general facts, reducing the search space more rapidly. In section 5.2 we will try to resolve this question empirically.

3.2   Comparison to PDR

Like LA, PDR has structured search and learning strategies. The fundamental differences are in the form of the goals and the interpolation approach.

The Variable Elimination Trade-Off. In PDR, the goal is restricted to the form $R(\bar{x}) \wedge C(\bar{x})$ where $R(\bar{x})$ is an atom to be derived, and the constraint $C(\bar{x})$ is a (quantifier-free) conjunction of literals. Thus, after resolving we must approximate the goal in some way that uses only the variables $\bar{x}$. For example, suppose we resolve the goal $R_k(\bar{x}_k) \wedge C_k(\bar{x}_k)$ with the clause $R_{k-1}(\bar{x}_{k-1}) \wedge T(\bar{x}_{k-1}, \bar{x}_k) \Rightarrow R_k(\bar{x}_k)$ to obtain $R_{k-1}(\bar{x}_{k-1}) \wedge T(\bar{x}_{k-1}, \bar{x}_k) \wedge C_k(\bar{x}_k)$. To obtain a new goal, we must somehow eliminate $\bar{x}_k$. The weakest such goal would be equivalent to $\exists \bar{x}_k. \ R_{k-1}(\bar{x}_{k-1}) \wedge T(\bar{x}_{k-1}, \bar{x}_k) \wedge C_k(\bar{x}_k)$. However, it may not be possible or desirable to eliminate this quantifier precisely.

Instead, we may compute a *stronger* goal in the right vocabulary. This is, in effect, decision making. As an example, if we constrain each unwanted variable to have a specific concrete value, then eliminating those variables becomes trivial. However, this may result in too-specific goal, and hence weak or irrelevant annotations. An alternative would be to use quantifier elimination for those variables for which it is inexpensive, and to use concrete values otherwise. In any event, there is an inherent trade-off to be made between the generality of a goal and its cost. We will refer to this as the *variable elimination trade-off*. LA avoids this trade-off by simply not eliminating variables from the goals. A disadvantage of this as that the goals grow syntactically larger as the search deepens.

Interpolation in PDR. The most important difference between PDR and LA is in the computation of interpolants. For simplicity, consider the transition system case. In LA, the interpolant is computed by dividing the goal into two parts (Equations 3 and 4). The prefix is a single step from R_i to R_{i+1}, while the suffix is a path from R_{i+1} to a safety violation at R_k. By contrast, in PDR the interpolant is between a *prefix path* from R_0 to R_{i+1} and a cube $C_{i+1}[\bar{x}_{i+1}]$ (a conjunction of literals). In other words, the clause learned by PDR is an interpolant for $A \wedge B$, where

$$A \equiv I(\bar{x}_k) \wedge \bigwedge_{k=0\ldots i} T(\bar{x}_k, \bar{x}_{k+1})$$
$$B \equiv C_{i+1}[\bar{x}_{i+1}]$$

In fact, it is not *any* such interpolant, but an interpolant that is inductive *relative* to the current annotation. This means that if P is the interpolant, we have $R_k(x_k) \wedge P(\bar{x}_k) \wedge T(\bar{x}_k, \bar{x}_{k+1}) \Rightarrow P(\bar{x}_{k+1})$, for $k = 0 \ldots i$. Intuitively, a simple relatively inductive interpolant might be likely to participate in an eventual inductive invariant. We may construct such an interpolant as a clause using a

subset of (the negations of) the literals in the goal. Bradley gives an approach
to finding such a clause that is relative inductive [9]. We may also apply generalization rules specific to theories [16].

This approach to interpolation has advantages and disadvantages. The form
of the goal makes it possible to search effectively for a relatively inductive interpolant. On the other hand, because of the variable elimination trade-off, the goal
may be more specialized than necessary. The resulting weak or irrelevant annotation may provide little reduction in the search space. This is another question
that must be answered empirically, and we will attempt to do this in Section 5.1.

Goal Preservation. Implementations of PDR typically carry the refutation of
each goal all the way to the depth bound, prioritizing goals by depth. We will
call this method "goal preservation". This tends to speed the bounded refutation
process and also can produce counterexamples longer than the depth bound [9].
Goal preservation is equally applicable to LA, though we will not use it here.

4   Improvements to Lazy Annotation

In this section, we introduce a number of improvements within the basic LA
framework, relative to the implementation described in [21].

Decision Space. In the implementation of [21], a decision is simply a choice of
basic block exiting a control location in the control-flow graph. This is effective
for simple basic blocks, but in a "large block" encoding [6] the resulting goals are
too complex. We require a more fine-grained decision space to sufficiently narrow
the search. To achieve this, we use truth assignments to the atomic formulas of
the goal (*i.e.*, minterms) as decisions. Such a minterm is easily extracted from
a satisfying assignment. In a large-block encoding, a minterm of the transition
relation corresponds roughly to an execution path. If the code has disjunctive
guards, a minterm also fixes a disjunct that is true. However, we do not fix the
values of data variables. This reduces the combinatorial complexity of the problem while allowing a large space of data values.

Back-Jumping. In a CDCL SAT solver, many decisions are not actually used
in the proof of a conflict. In such a case, we backtrack over the decision to an
earlier decision that is actually used, and learn an interpolant at that point. The
same situation can occur in LA in the case of multiple sub-goals. It will help to
think of a goal in LA as a tree in which the leaves are sub-goals and the interior
vertices are constraints. Each resolution step expands one leaf of the tree. Now
suppose we expand leaf Q, followed by leaf R on a different branch, and reach a
conflict. Suppose further that the proof of unsatisfiability does not use any formulas introduced in the expansion of Q. After backtracking from the expansion
of R (strengthening R using an interpolant) we can immediately backtrack from
the expansion of Q without any additional annotation (put another way, since
this step is not used in the proof, its interpolant is TRUE). We may continue to

back-jump in this way until we reach an expansion that is in the proof core of the conflict, eliminating unneeded calls to the decision procedure.

Resolution Heuristic. Each time we make a resolution step, we must choose a sub-goal to expand and a rule to derive it. We can use a heuristic for this choice that is closely related to variable scoring heuristics in CDCL SAT solvers. We maintain a *relevance score* for each rule, initially zero. When we backtrack from a resolution without strengthening the annotation (for example, by back-jumping) we decrement the relevance score of the rule. When choosing a rule to resolve with, we select first the rule with the highest score.

Interpolant Generalization. Given a proof of a conflict produced by an SMT solver, we can compute an interpolant for the resolution step using methods of feasible interpolation [20]. However, these interpolants may be both syntactically complex and weaker than necessary, depending on the proof actually obtained by the decision procedure. We can borrow an idea from PDR to improve the result. First, notice the asymmetry between the prefix and suffix in the interpolation. The suffix has fixed truth values assigned to each atom by decision making. The prefix on the other hand contains propositionally complex formulas from the annotation and the transition relation. The interpolant thus tends to be a disjunction at the top level, as most case splitting in the proof will occur on the prefix side. We therefore attempt to strengthen it by greedily dropping disjuncts as long as it remains implied by the prefix. Often this leads to a simple interpolant in clause form. If the interpolant is still syntactically complex, we can use more aggressive interpolation methods as in [2]. A simple approach is to sample prime implicants of the prefix. The interpolant is the disjunction of the interpolants for the prime implicants.

Eager Propagation. In IC3, before increasing the unwinding depth, annotations are propagated forward. That is, we copy annotations from earlier to later predicates in the unwinding while the annotation remains a model of the rules. More frequent propagation is also possible and was found to be effective by Suda [25]. In experiments with LA, propagation after completing a bound was found to strengthen the annotation infrequently. A somewhat more effective approach is to propagate eagerly, during the search. When backtracking to a sub-goal with predicate R_i that is an instance of R in the unwinding, we attempt to propagate annotations of earlier instances of R. If any propagation succeeds in strengthening the annotation of R, we backtrack again, in the hope that the strengthening will rule out an earlier sub-goal.

5   Experiments

We will now consider some experiments comparing the performance of PDR, traditional BMC and our improved LA for large-block encodings. We wish to determine experimentally (1) whether structured or unstructured search is more effective, and (2) which interpolation approach is more effective in reducing the bounded search and in converging to an unbounded solution.

As a representative implementation of PDR, we will use the PDR engine implemented in the Z3 theorem prover [16]. This implementation supports linear integer arithmetic (LIA) and has limited support for other theories, such as the theory of arrays. Z3/PDR computes interpolants for linear arithmetic using Farkas' lemma and inductive generalization. To represent BMC, we will use Stratified Inlining (SI) in Corral [18]. This tool inlines procedures until either a complete error path is found (using Z3), or the problem becomes unsatisfiable (indicating the program is safe) or until a given recursion bound is reached (in which case the result is inconclusive). Inlining a procedure is equivalent to performing a resolution step on the procedure's summary. The author has implemented LA within Z3. It is used as a non-recursive Horn solver in Duality [19]. Bounded solving is done using LA, while convergence is achieved using LAWI. Duality supports full (quantified) first-order logic with linear integer arithmetic and arrays using an interpolation procedure for proofs in this theory implemented in Z3 [22]. Neither Z3/PDR nor Duality use goal preservation in the experiments. This is the default setting in Z3/PDR, as the authors report the method does not produce a clear benefit [8].

Details of the experimental setup can be found in an extended version of this paper [23]. It includes details on obtaining the benchmarks, source code of the tools, and addition data.

5.1 First Experiment

Our first experiment uses benchmark problems from the SV-COMP 2013 software model checking competition. We use an encoding of these problems into a Horn clause representation available in the SV-COMP repository, provided by Gurfinkel [14]. These are linear cyclic problems that are obtained by inlining all procedures. For the experiment, two subsets of the benchmark problems were chosen: the "Control Flow and Integer Variables" subset and the "Product Lines" subset. These were chosen because they do not rely on complex pointer reasoning and can be encoded using only the theory of linear arithmetic, allowing them to be handled by PDR. This choice was made in advance and was not expanded after obtaining and analyzing data to avoid the possibility of bias due to "benchmark shopping".

For additional context, we include the tool UFO [1]. This tool was the winner of the SV-COMP 2013 in both of the chosen categories. Fortuitously, the Horn clause versions of the problems were generated by UFO. Thus we can be fairly confident that UFO, Z3/PDR and Duality/LA are using the same logical representation of the problem, giving a direct comparison. On the other hand, since Corral cannot use this problem representation (and thus would require a different language front-end) we omit it from this experiment. An additional difficulty in comparison arises because the competition version of UFO is not a single algorithm, but a portfolio of seven algorithms run in parallel. To make a fair comparison against the other algorithms, we use the two most successful

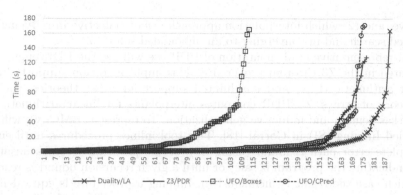

Fig. 2. Cactus plot of run times on SV-COMP 2013 problems

of these seven (those that most frequently had the least run time). The first we will call BOXES. It augments LAWI with a multiple-interval abstract domain. The second we will call CPRED. It augments LAWI with a Cartesian predicate abstraction domain.

The four chosen tool configurations were run on a 4-core 64-bit 2.67GHz Intel Xeon CPU with 24GB of main memory. The tools were run on all benchmark problems with a time-out of 180 seconds. Time for compilation and optimization of the C language source code is not included. The benchmark problems completed by all tools in under one second were discarded. The run times for the remaining problems are plotted in Figure 2. Each line shows the run times for all completed benchmarks sorted in increasing order. Thus, a lower line is better. We observe that overall CPRED and Z3/PDR are roughly comparable, while Duality solves a larger subset of problems (in fact, all but one).

The are several possible reasons for the difference between LA and PDR. One possibility is that the outer convergence loop is generating different unwindings. To eliminate this possibility, we will focus on the subset of benchmarks in the "ssh" and "ssh-simplified" sub-categories. These benchmarks are simple loops (*i.e.* transition systems) and therefore have only one possible unwinding. For simple loops, we may compare the quality of the annotations generated by the two methods in terms of the number of resolutions and the depth of the unwinding at convergence.

Figure 3 shows scatter plots comparing the unwinding depth at convergence and the number of resolutions steps for Z3/PDR and Duality/LA. Points on the boundary are time-outs. Both measures are substantially lower for Duality/LA, indicating more effective conflict learning. The greater convergence depth for Z3/PDR could be explained by learning many annotations that are true only to a bounded depth. To obtain an inductive invariant in PDR, the search must exceed the depth at which these annotations fail to propagate. The greater search depth may be sufficient to explain the higher number of resolution steps.

From this, it appears that inductive generalization is not able to fully remedy the over-specialization resulting from the variable elimination trade-off in PDR, though it is crucial to the performance of PDR in this benchmark [23].

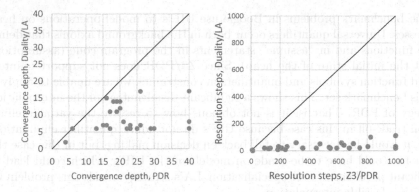

Fig. 3. Comparison of Duality/LA and PDR on SV-COMP 2013 ssh benchmarks

We may conjecture two possible reasons for the greater convergence depth in PDR: over-specialization producing irrelevant learned clauses or too-aggressive propagation of these clauses. In [23] we observe that propagation only weakly affects performance while generalization strongly affects convergence, providing some evidence for the former hypothesis.

5.2 Second Experiment

In our second experiment, we consider a broader class of Horn reachability problems. We use procedural programs modeled using unknown relations as procedure summaries. Each procedure is represented by a single rule. For example, procedure P that calls Q twice on its input and then increments the result would be modeled by the clause $Q(x, y) \land Q(y, z) \land x' = z + 1 \Rightarrow P(x, x')$. Because one procedure may call many procedures, we will have multiple sub-goals. Further, we expand the constraint language to include uninterpreted function symbols (UIF's), arrays and quantifiers, and we allow user-specified background axioms.

Our benchmark examples come from the Static Device Driver (SDV) tool [3]. They are safety properties of example device drivers for the Microsoft Windows kernel. SDV translates these problems into the Boogie programming language [4]. Corral then checks the required properties using a field abstraction. Global variables and fields of structures are added to the abstraction on a counter-example driven basis until the property is proved, or a counterexample is successfully concretized. We translate the verification of each abstract model into a Horn reachability problem using the Boogie verification condition generator, after converting program loops into tail-recursive procedures.

We compare the performance of SI with Stratified Inlining (SI). To make a fair comparison, we check only bounded safety properties (that is, we assume each loop is executed up to k times for fixed k). We effect this bound in Duality by simply terminating the unwinding if and when it reaches the recursion bound (as it happens, such termination does not occur, so Duality/LA performs unbounded verification).

The benchmark problems in Boogie use UIF's to model operations on heap addresses. Universal quantifiers occur both in the background axioms that define these functions and in "assume" statements in the program code (assumptions about the initial state of the heap). Since Z3/PDR does not support uninterpreted function symbols and quantifiers in constraints, we are unable to apply it to this benchmark set. This shows a significant disadvantage of the interpolation strategy of PDR. That is, it is not obvious how to resolve the variable elimination trade-off in this case because UIF's do not admit quantifier elimination. Thus, it would be necessary to fall back on decision making, but in this case the decisions would have to be made on models of the UIF's, which could lead to significant problems of over-specialization. LA's strategy avoids this problem by exploiting feasible interpolation.

Both LA and SI may fail due to the undecidability of the theory. This means that both methods may produce "false alarms" caused by a failure of Z3's quantifier instantiation heuristics. The comparison is fair, however, since the correctness of counterexamples is in both cases determined by Corral, using Z3 for concretization (in no case did either tool produce a counterexample that Corral determined to be incorrect).

A scatter plot comparing the run times of LA and SI is shown in Figure 4. Each point represents the full verification time for one property, including the time for Corral to compute abstraction refinements. We observe that in some cases SI is approximately two times faster. This can be accounted for by the overhead of running Z3 in proof-generating mode in order to produce interpolants. On the other hand, on a significant number problems LA is substantially faster, by up to two orders of magnitude.

We note several important overheads in LA relative to SI. First, the learning phase in LA is orders-of-magnitude more costly than clause learning in an SMT solver. Further, because of backtracking, LA may add and remove a given constraint in the goal many times (while SI never removes constraints). Thus we must attribute the overall better performance of LA on bounded problems to more effective learning. In fact, inspection shows that LA often learns concise and relevant procedure summaries, even in the presence of quantifiers. For example, we see summaries of the form $\forall i.a'[i] = a[i] \vee p(a'[i])$, where p is a simple predicate. This says the procedure preserves elements of array a except where it establishes property p.

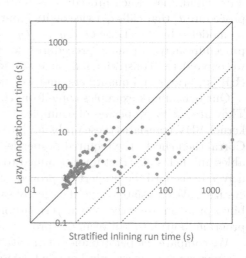

Fig. 4. Lazy Annotation *vs* Stratified Inlining

An aspect of these problems that may help to explain better learning performance of LA is the fact that some procedures are called at many sites. Whenever an annotation of such a procedure is learned, it simultaneously strengthens the summaries of all of the instances of the procedure in the current goal. Thus the learned annotations are re-usable in a way that is not possible in an unstructured search.

Finally, we consider the effects of the individual improvements to LA introduced here. To briefly summarize, minterm decision making may help or hurt, but with interpolant generalization it helps significantly. Generalization seems to be needed in the case when convergence depth is an issue. The heuristic for sub-goal choice is not very effective, while back-jumping provides a modest speed-up. Eager propagation is effective in the limited case (simple loops) for which it was implemented. Details of the experiments supporting these conclusions can be found in [23].

6   Conclusion

We have observed that traditional BMC, LA and PDR can all be viewed as back-tracking search with conflict-driven learning. The methods differ fundamentally in two aspects: search strategy (structured *vs.* unstructured) and interpolation strategy (relative induction *vs.* proof-based). Comparing LA with PDR on software model checking problems, we found that PDR's interpolation strategy as implemented in Z3 produced less effective learned annotations. We conjectured that this is due to over-specialized goals resulting from the *variable elimination trade-off*. This is illustrative of a general tension in CDCL-like methods relating the generality and cost of decisions and interpolants. Comparing LA with BMC, we found that structured conflict learning in LA was more effective than unstructured learning in an SMT solver, even on bounded problems (consistent with the results of [5] in the propositional case). The high overhead of learning in LA was more than compensated by the resulting reduction in search. We found that decision making does in fact lead to improved performance for large-block encodings by reducing the decision problems. However, it requires some form of interpolant generalization to prevent over-specialized goals from producing weak annotations. An interesting remaining question is whether some form of inductive generalization would helpful in LA, or whether the cost outweighs the benefit.

Acknowledgments. The author would like to thank Akash Lal for assistance in using SDV and corral.

References

1. Albarghouthi, A., Gurfinkel, A., Li, Y., Chaki, S., Chechik, M.: UFO: Verification with interpolants and abstract interpretation. In: Piterman, N., Smolka, S.A. (eds.) TACAS 2013. LNCS, vol. 7795, pp. 637–640. Springer, Heidelberg (2013)

2. Albarghouthi, A., McMillan, K.L.: Beautiful interpolants. In: Sharygina, N., Veith, H. (eds.) CAV 2013. LNCS, vol. 8044, pp. 313–329. Springer, Heidelberg (2013)

3. Ball, T., Cook, B., Levin, V., Rajamani, S.K.: SLAM and Static Driver Verifier: Technology Transfer of Formal Methods inside Microsoft. In: Boiten, E.A., Derrick, J., Smith, G.P. (eds.) IFM 2004. LNCS, vol. 2999, pp. 1–20. Springer, Heidelberg (2004)

4. Barnett, M., Chang, B.-Y.E., DeLine, R., Jacobs, B., M. Leino, K.R.: Boogie: A modular reusable verifier for object-oriented programs. In: de Boer, F.S., Bonsangue, M.M., Graf, S., de Roever, W.-P. (eds.) FMCO 2005. LNCS, vol. 4111, pp. 364–387. Springer, Heidelberg (2006)

5. Bayless, S., Val, C.G., Ball, T., Hoos, H.H., Hu, A.J.: Efficient modular SAT solving for IC3. In: FMCAD, pp. 149–156. IEEE (2013)

6. Beyer, D., Cimatti, A., Griggio, A., Keremoglu, M.E., Sebastiani, R.: Software model checking via large-block encoding. In: FMCAD, pp. 25–32. IEEE (2009)

7. Biere, A., Clarke, E., Raimi, R., Zhu, Y.: Verifying safety properties of a powerPC^{TM} microprocessor using symbolic model checking without BDDs. In: Halbwachs, N., Peled, D.A. (eds.) CAV 1999. LNCS, vol. 1633, pp. 60–71. Springer, Heidelberg (1999)

8. Bjørner, N.: private communication (2014)

9. Bradley, A.R.: SAT-based model checking without unrolling. In: Jhala, R., Schmidt, D. (eds.) VMCAI 2011. LNCS, vol. 6538, pp. 70–87. Springer, Heidelberg (2011)

10. Cimatti, A., Griggio, A.: Software model checking via IC3. In: Madhusudan, P., Seshia, S.A. (eds.) CAV 2012. LNCS, vol. 7358, pp. 277–293. Springer, Heidelberg (2012)

11. Cimatti, A., Griggio, A., Mover, S., Tonetta, S.: IC3 modulo theories via implicit predicate abstraction. In: Ábrahám, E., Havelund, K. (eds.) TACAS 2014. LNCS, vol. 8413, pp. 46–61. Springer, Heidelberg (2014)

12. Eén, N., Mishchenko, A., Brayton, R.K.: Efficient implementation of property directed reachability. In: FMCAD, pp. 125–134. FMCAD Inc. (2011)

13. Flanagan, C., M. Leino, K.R.: Houdini, an annotation assistant for eSC/Java. In: Oliveira, J.N., Zave, P. (eds.) FME 2001. LNCS, vol. 2021, pp. 500–517. Springer, Heidelberg (2001)

14. Gurfinkel, A. (2013), https://svn.sosy-lab.org/software/sv-benchmarks/trunk/clauses/LRA/svcomp13/

15. Harris, W.R., Sankaranarayanan, S., Ivancic, F., Gupta, A.: Program analysis via satisfiability modulo path programs. In: Hermenegildo, M.V., Palsberg, J. (eds.) POPL, pp. 71–82. ACM (2010)

16. Hoder, K., Bjørner, N.: Generalized property directed reachability. In: Cimatti, A., Sebastiani, R. (eds.) SAT 2012. LNCS, vol. 7317, pp. 157–171. Springer, Heidelberg (2012)

17. Jaffar, J., Santosa, A.E., Voicu, R.: An interpolation method for CLP traversal. In: Gent, I.P. (ed.) CP 2009. LNCS, vol. 5732, pp. 454–469. Springer, Heidelberg (2009)

18. Lal, A., Qadeer, S., Lahiri, S.K.: Corral: A solver for reachability modulo theories. Technical Report MSR-TR-2012-9, Microsoft Research (April 2012)

19. McMillan, K., Rybalchenko, A.: Computing relational fixed points using interpolation. Technical Report MSR-TR-2013-6, Microsoft Research (January 2013)

20. McMillan, K.L.: An interpolating theorem prover. In: Jensen, K., Podelski, A. (eds.) TACAS 2004. LNCS, vol. 2988, pp. 16–30. Springer, Heidelberg (2004)

21. McMillan, K.L.: Lazy annotation for program testing and verification. In: Touili, T., Cook, B., Jackson, P. (eds.) CAV 2010. LNCS, vol. 6174, pp. 104–118. Springer, Heidelberg (2010)
22. McMillan, K.L. (2013), http://z3.codeplex.com
23. McMillan, K.L.: Lazy annotation revisited. Technical Report MSR-TR-2014-65, Microsoft Research (May 2014)
24. McMillan, K.L., Kuehlmann, A., Sagiv, M.: Generalizing DPLL to richer logics. In: Bouajjani, A., Maler, O. (eds.) CAV 2009. LNCS, vol. 5643, pp. 462–476. Springer, Heidelberg (2009)
25. Suda, M.: Triggered clause pushing for IC3. CoRR, abs/1307.4966 (2013)

Interpolating Property Directed Reachability[*]

Yakir Vizel[1] and Arie Gurfinkel[2]

[1] Computer Science Department, The Technion, Haifa, Israel
[2] Carnegie Mellon Software Engineering Institute, Pittsburgh, USA

Abstract. Current SAT-based Model Checking is based on two major approaches: Interpolation-based (IMC) (global, with unrollings) and Property Directed Reachability/IC3 (PDR) (local, without unrollings). IMC generates candidate invariants using interpolation over an unrolling of a system, without putting any restrictions on the SAT-solver's search. PDR generates candidate invariants by a local search over a single instantiation of the transition relation, effectively guiding the SAT solver's search. The two techniques are considered to be orthogonal and have different strength and limitations. In this paper, we present a new technique, called AVY, that effectively combines the key insights of the two approaches. Like IMC, it uses unrollings and interpolants to construct an initial candidate invariant, and, like PDR, it uses local inductive generalization to keep the invariants in compact clausal form. On the one hand, AVY is an incremental IMC extended with a local search for CNF interpolants. On the other, it is PDR extended with a global search for bounded counterexamples. We implemented the technique using ABC and have evaluated it on the HWMCC benchmark-suite from 2012 and 2013. Our results show that the prototype significantly outperforms PDR and McMillan's interpolation algorithm (as implemented in ABC) on the industrial sub-category of the benchmark.

1 Introduction

SAT-based (unbounded) Model Checking (MC) is an extremely successful technique for both Hardware [12,4,10] and Software [13,2,11] verification. Current state-of-the-art techniques are Interpolation-based Model Checking (IMC) [12,15] and Property Directed Reachability/IC3 (PDR) [4,10]. PDR and IMC are able to either verify a property by generating a safe inductive invariant, or falsify a property by finding a counterexample. Conceptually, both work by repeatedly *generalizing* bounded proofs of correctness, until either a safe inductive invariant

---

[*] This material is based upon work funded and supported by the Department of Defense under Contract No. FA8721-05-C-0003 with Carnegie Mellon University for the operation of the Software Engineering Institute, a federally funded research and development center. Any opinions, findings and conclusions or recommendations expressed in this material are those of the author(s) and do not necessarily reflect the views of the United States Department of Defense. This material has been approved for public release and unlimited distribution. DM-0001263.

A. Biere and R. Bloem (Eds.): CAV 2014, LNCS 8559, pp. 260–276, 2014.
© Springer International Publishing Switzerland 2014

is synthesized or a counterexample is found. They scale to systems with an enormous number of states, are considered orthogonal, and have different strength and weaknesses.

IMC works by searching for a counterexample via repeatedly posing Bounded Model Checking [3] (BMC) queries to a SAT-solver. If a BMC query Q is satisfied, a counterexample is found. Otherwise, the SAT-solver generates a proof of unsatisfiability of Q. An interpolation procedure is then used to generalize the proof to a candidate safe invariant using sequence interpolants [15]. If the invariant is also inductive (checked by an additional SAT query), the procedure stops and returns SAFE to the user, indicating the validity of the checked property. Otherwise, the process repeats with another, longer, BMC query.

IMC leverages both advances in BMC and in interpolation. It can be seen as a simple addition to BMC that turns it into a complete Model Checking procedure. Other than proof-logging which is necessary for interpolation, it poses no restrictions on the SAT-solver's search. However, IMC does not offer much control over generalization. It is at the mercy of both the SAT-solver that provides a particular resolution proof, and of the procedure used to generate the interpolant. For example, attempts to improve IMC by using interpolation algorithms with different strength have not been very successful [9]. Furthermore, the interpolants tend to be large, which poses additional limitation on their use.

PDR is similar to IMC, but approaches the process in a completely different manner. Instead of blindly relying on the SAT-solver, it manages both the search for the counterexample and the generalization phases. Conceptually, PDR is based on a backward search. Starting with a bad (UNSAFE) state, it uses a SAT-solver to repeatedly find a one-step predecessor state. Thus, all SAT-queries are local, involving only one instance of the transition relation, and no BMC-unrolling is used. If the bad suffix can be extended all the way to the initial state, a counterexample is found. Otherwise, when a suffix cannot be extended further, a process called *inductive generalization* [4], is used to learn a consequence that blocks the current suffix (and possibly many others). The conjunction of all such learned consequences is used to synthesize an inductive invariant. While this description omits many important aspects of PDR, it is sufficient for now.

PDR offers many advantages compared to IMC, including incremental solving and fine-grained control over generalization. However, it is limited to a fixed *local* search strategy that can be inefficient. In fact, it is not difficult to construct examples in which backward search is ineffective and PDR does not perform well.

In this paper, we present a new algorithm, AVY, that strives to overcome these deficiencies by combining both *global* interpolant-driven generalization with *local* inductive generalization. AVY can be seen as a combination of PDR and IMC. On the one hand, it extends IMC with PDR-like local reasoning in the form of local search and inductive generalization. On the other hand, it extends PDR with the use of unrolling and proof-based interpolation. More interestingly, it allows the combination of IMC and PDR strategies inside a single solver.

The first step of AVY is similar to IMC: it unrolls the system and searches for a counterexample. If none is found, it generates a candidate invariant using sequence interpolants [15]. This is the global generalization phase. Next, it enters the local generalization phase and uses PDR-style inductive generalization to strengthen the candidate invariant and to put it into CNF. If the candidate is inductive, the process stops. Otherwise, the next global phase is entered.

Maintaining the candidate invariant in CNF allows AVY to use it as "learned clauses" in the next global phase. When a new global phase starts, AVY adds the clauses from the previously computed candidate invariant into the checked BMC formula, thus making the global phase incremental. This significantly reduces the search space for the SAT-solver to explore. It also reduces the size of the resulting resolution proof and the computed interpolants. This addresses the main problem with IMC: lack of incrementality as already learned interpolants are not used in successive iterations and interpolant growth.

Adding the learned clauses to the BMC problem at a given iteration N, makes it, in a way, equivalent to the problem PDR tries to solve at iteration N. Though, unlike PDR, AVY handles this problem globally, with one SAT-solver instance that can roam over the entire search space, and does not break it to local checks as part of a backward search. This kind of strategy addresses the main weakness of PDR: no use of "global" knowledge during the search.

The combination of interpolation and inductive reasoning allows AVY to benefit from the advantages of both methods. It uses the SAT-solver without guiding it during the search, but it does guide its proof construction. The advantage of this combination is evident in our experiments. We have implemented AVY on top of ABC [5] and compared it against PDR and McMillan's interpolation (ITP), as implemented in ABC, on the HWMCC'12/13 benchmarks. Our experiments indicate that AVY can solve a considerable number of test cases, especially on the industrial sub-category, that are not solved by either PDR nor ITP.

Related work. This paper builds on Interpolation-based Model Checking [12,15], IC3 [4], and PDR [10]. We describe them in detail in Section 3. Some of the techniques used in AVY have appeared before, but not in the way AVY combines them. Like [6], we use sequence interpolants, but we show that they can be more efficient than the original algorithm in [12]. Like [1], we re-use previously computed interpolants, but we combine re-use with inductive generalization. Our approach can be seen as an efficient extension of [7] to sequence interpolation.

As stated above, AVY is a synergy between an interpolation-based approach and PDR. Ideas for combining the two have also appeared in [16,17]. In [16], the authors suggest to use both forward and backward reachable sets of states. This allows them to try and block a set of all bad states in a local manner that resembles the blocking of a bad state applied by PDR. Unlike [16], in this work we only use the forward reachable states that are derived by means of interpolation, and use specific PDR functionality to transform these sets into CNF and use them to simplify the successive BMC invocations. In [17], the authors show how to compute interpolants in CNF and create a variant of the algorithm that appears in [12], which uses the fact that interpolants are in CNF in order to apply PDR-style reasoning. There are two major differences between AVY and the approach that appear in [17]. First, in [17], the resolution refutation is used to derive a "near interpolant" in CNF, which is then strengthened and transformed into an interpolant by applying inductive generalization on the (A, B) pair, while AVY derives a sequence interpolant, and then uses PDR to transform it to CNF. Second, like in [17], AVY also uses the fact that interpolants are in CNF and tries to push clauses between different interpolants. But, while [17] uses pushing only to learn clauses that may appear in later interpolants that were not computed yet, AVY, as stated, uses the pushed clauses to simplify the BMC formula.

The rest of the paper is structured as follows. After describing the necessary background and notation in Section 2, we give an overview of SAT-based Model Checking in Section 3. Section 4 presents two versions of AVY, a basic and an optimized one. We describe our experimental results in Section 5, and conclude in Section 6.

2 Preliminaries

In this section, we present notations and background that is required for the description of our algorithm.

Safety verification. A transition system T is a tuple $(\mathcal{V}, Init, Tr, Bad)$, where $\mathcal{V}$ is a set of variables that defines the states of the system (i.e., $2^{\mathcal{V}}$), $Init$ and Bad are formulas with variables in $\mathcal{V}$ denoting the set of initial states and bad states, respectively, and Tr is a formula with free variables in $\mathcal{V} \cup \mathcal{V}'$, denoting the transition relation. A state $s \in 2^{\mathcal{V}}$ is said to be reachable in T if and only if (iff) there exists a state $s_0 \in Init$, and $(s_i, s_{i+1}) \in Tr$ for $0 \le i \le N$, and $s = s_N$.

A transition system T is UNSAFE iff there exists a state $s \in Bad$ s.t. s is reachable. Equivalently, T is UNSAFE iff there exists a number N such that the following formula is satisfiable:

$$Init(v_0) \wedge \left(\bigwedge_{i=0}^{N-1} Tr(v_i, v_{i+1}) \right) \wedge Bad(v_N) \tag{1}$$

When T is UNSAFE and $s_N \in Bad$ is the reachable state, the path from $s_0 \in Init$ to s_N is called a *counterexample* (CEX).

A transition system T is SAFE iff all reachable states in T do not satisfy Bad. Equivalently, there exists a formula Inv, called an *inductive safe invariant*[1], that satisfies:

$$Init(v) \rightarrow Inv(v) \qquad Inv(v) \wedge Tr(v, u) \rightarrow Inv(u) \qquad Inv(v) \rightarrow \neg Bad(v) \tag{2}$$

A *safety* verification problem is to decide whether a transition system T is SAFE or UNSAFE, i.e., whether there exists an initial state in $Init$ that can reach a bad state in Bad, or synthesize a safe inductive invariant.

In SAT-based model checking, the verification problem is determined by computing over-approximations of the states reachable in T and, by that, trying to either construct an invariant or find a CEX.

---

[1] The reachable states form an inductive invariant. The inductive invariant is *safe* if the reachable states do not intersect the bad states.

Craig Interpolation. Given a pair of inconsistent formulas (A, B) (i.e., $A \wedge B \models \bot$), a *Craig interpolant* [8] for (A, B) is a formula I such that:

$$A \rightarrow I \qquad I \rightarrow \neg B \qquad \mathcal{L}(I) \subseteq \mathcal{L}(A) \cap \mathcal{L}(B) \qquad (3)$$

where $\mathcal{L}(A)$ denotes the set of all atomic propositions in A. A *sequence (or path) interpolant* extends interpolation to a sequence of formulas. We write $\boldsymbol{F} = [F_1, \ldots, F_N]$ to denote a sequence with N elements, and $\boldsymbol{F}_i$ for the ith element of the sequence. Given an unsatisfiable sequence of formulas $\boldsymbol{A} = [A_1, \ldots, A_N]$, i.e., $A_1 \wedge \cdots \wedge A_N \models \bot$, a *sequence interpolant* $\boldsymbol{I} = \text{SEQITP}(\boldsymbol{A})$ for $\boldsymbol{A}$ is a sequence of formulas $\boldsymbol{I} = [I_1, \ldots, I_{N-1}]$ such that:

$$A_1 \rightarrow I_1 \qquad \forall 1 < i < N \cdot I_{i-1} \wedge A_i \rightarrow I_i \qquad I_{N-1} \wedge A_N \rightarrow \bot \qquad (4)$$

and for all $1 \leq i \leq N$, $\mathcal{L}(I_i) \subseteq \mathcal{L}(A_1 \wedge \cdots \wedge A_i) \cap \mathcal{L}(A_{i+1} \wedge \cdots \wedge A_N)$. We use subscripts on brackets to mark interpolation partitions for a formula. For example, $(A)_0 \wedge (B)_1 \wedge (C)_0$ means that A and C belong to partition 0 and B to partition 1, respectively.

3   SAT-Based Model Checking

In this section, we review two algorithms for SAT-based *unbounded* Model Checking – Interpolation-based Model Checking (IMC), and Property Directed Reachability/IC3 (PDR).

The key insight in both algorithms is to maintain an over-approximation of a set of reachable states in an inductive trace. An *inductive trace*, or simply a trace, is a sequence of formulas $[F_0, \ldots, F_N]$ that satisfy:

$$Init \rightarrow F_0 \qquad \forall 0 \leq i < N \cdot F_i(v) \wedge Tr(v, u) \rightarrow F_{i+1}(u) \qquad (5)$$

A trace is *safe* if each F_i is safe: $\forall i \cdot F_i \rightarrow \neg Bad$; it is *monotone* if $\forall 0 \leq i < N \cdot F_i \rightarrow F_{i+1}$; it is *clausal* if each F_i is in CNF (in this case, we often abuse notation and treat each F_i as a set of clauses). A trace $[F_0, \ldots, F_N]$ is *stronger* than a trace $[G_0, \ldots, G_N]$ if $\forall 0 \leq i \leq N \cdot F_i \rightarrow G_i$. We assume that traces are silently extended as needed, by letting $F_i = \top$ for all $i > N$ for any trace $[F_0, \ldots, F_N]$. Traces are closed under pointwise conjunction.

A trace $[F_0, \ldots, F_N]$ is *closed* if $\exists 1 \leq i \leq N \cdot F_i \rightarrow \left(\bigvee_{j=0}^{i-1} F_j \right)$. There is an obvious relationship between existence of closed traces and safety of a transition system:

Theorem 1. *A transition system T is SAFE iff it admits a safe closed trace.*

Thus, safety verification is reduced to searching for a safe closed trace or finding a CEX.

Input: Transition system $T = (Init, Tr, Bad)$

1   $F_0 \leftarrow Init$; $N \leftarrow 0$

2   **repeat**

3 | $G \leftarrow \text{IMCMKSAFE}([F_0, \dots, F_N], Bad)$

4 | **if** $G = [\,]$ **then return** UNSAFE $\forall 0 \leq i \leq N \cdot F_i \leftarrow G[i]$

       // Invariant: $F_0, \dots, F_N$ is a safe trace

5 | **if** $\exists 1 \leq i \leq N \cdot F_i \rightarrow (\bigvee_{j=0}^{i-1} F_j)$ **then return** SAFE

       $N \leftarrow N + 1$; $F_N \leftarrow \top$

6   **until** ∞;

Algorithm 1. IMC

Input: Transition system $T = (Init, Tr, Bad)$

Input: A trace $F_0, \dots, F_N$

1   $\varphi \leftarrow (Init(v_0))_0 \wedge \bigwedge_{i=0}^{N-1} (Tr(v_i, v_{i+1}))_i \wedge (Bad(v_N))_N$

2   **if** ISSAT(φ) **then return** $[\,]$ $I_1, \dots, I_N \leftarrow \text{SEQITP}(\varphi)$

3   $G_0 \leftarrow Init$; $\forall 1 \leq i \leq N \cdot G_i \leftarrow F_i \wedge I_i$

4   **return** $[G_0, \dots, G_N]$

Algorithm 2. IMCMKSAFE

3.1   Interpolation-Based Model Checking

The original interpolation-based algorithm is due to McMillan [12]. Here, we present its variant from [15], called IMC, based on sequence interpolants. This version is closer to PDR (described in Section 3.2) and is a basis for our algorithm.

IMC is shown in Alg. 1. It maintains a trace $[F_0, \dots, F_N]$. The trace is made safe toward the end of the loop (line 4). In the beginning of each iteration, a candidate trace is made safe using IMCMKSAFE, if possible. The algorithm terminates when either a trace cannot be made safe, or when a closed trace is discovered.

IMCMKSAFE is shown in Alg. 2. The key insight is that a safe trace can be constructed by sequence interpolation. First, a BMC problem is solved to check for absence of a CEX. Second, a sequence interpolant is computed and is used to strengthen the current trace. Note that the sequence interpolant $Init, I_1, \dots, I_N$ itself is a trace. Hence, correctness follows via closure of traces under conjunction.

The main advantage of IMC is that it integrates well with BMC, effectively turning incremental BMC into a complete Model Checking procedure. A main deficiency is that interpolants from one BMC check are not used to help the next one. An obvious improvement is to use the current trace to strengthen the BMC query at line 1 of IMCMKSAFE as follows:

$$\varphi \leftarrow Init(v_0) \wedge \bigwedge_{i=0}^{N-1} Tr(v_i, v_{i+1}) \wedge F_{i+1}(v_{i+1}) \wedge Bad(v_N) \tag{6}$$

This, however, is not effective in practice. The formulas F_i are typically large (as propositional formulas) and adding them significantly slows down BMC.

Input: Transition system $T = (Init, Tr, Bad)$
1 $F_0 \leftarrow Init$; $N \leftarrow 0$
2 **repeat**
3 | $G \leftarrow \text{PDRMKSAFE}([F_0, \ldots, F_N], Bad)$
4 | **if** $G = [\,]$ **then return** UNSAFE $\forall 0 \le i \le N \cdot F_i \leftarrow G[i]$
5 | $F_0, \ldots, F_N \leftarrow \text{PDRPUSH}([F_0, \ldots, F_N])$
   | // $F_0, \ldots, F_N$ is a safe δ-trace
6 | **if** $\exists 0 \le i \le N \cdot F_i = \emptyset$ **then return** SAFE $N \leftarrow N + 1$; $F_N \leftarrow \emptyset$
7 **until** ∞;

Algorithm 3. PDR/IC3

3.2 Property Directed Reachability

In this section, we give an overview of Property Directed Reachability (PDR/IC3) algorithm and its properties. Our presentation of PDR/IC3 is unorthodox, but it highlights the parts necessary for understanding our new algorithm. For more details on PDR/IC3 the reader is referred to [4,10].

Like IMC, PDR computes an inductive trace. Unlike IMC, PDR does not use an unrolling of the transition system during the computation of the trace. Furthermore, the trace is kept monotone and clausal. To better explain the characteristics of the trace computed by PDR, we introduce the notion of a δ-trace: A δ-trace is a sequence of formulas $[F_0, \ldots, F_N]$ such that the sequence $[G_0, \ldots, G_N]$, where $G_i = \bigwedge_{j=i}^{N} F_j$, is a monotone clausal trace. For a δ-trace F, we write $F_i^\uparrow$ for the ith element of the corresponding trace (i.e., G_i above). Note that a δ-trace F is closed if there exists an i such that $F_i = \emptyset$.

PDR is shown in Alg. 3. It maintains a loop invariant that $F_0, \ldots, F_N$ is a safe δ-trace (after line 5). Each iteration starts with a δ-trace that is safe except for the last element F_N. If possible, the trace is made safe via PDRMKSAFE, otherwise the problem is decided UNSAFE. Then, the now safe δ-trace $F_0, \ldots, F_N$ is strengthened using PDRPUSH. PDRPUSH takes a δ-trace $F = [F_0, \ldots, F_N]$ and returns a stronger *pushed* δ-trace $G = [G_0, \ldots, G_N]$ defined as follows:

$$H_0 = F_0 \qquad H_i = F_i \cup \{c \in H_{i-1} \mid (H_{i-1}(u) \wedge Tr(u,v)) \to c(v)\} \quad (7)$$
$$G_N = H_N \qquad G_i = H_i \setminus H_{i+1} \text{ for } 0 \le i < N \quad (8)$$

If this closes the trace, the problem is decided SAFE. Otherwise, N is incremented and the loop is repeated.

PDRMKSAFE takes a δ-trace $F = [F_0, \ldots, F_N]$ that is safe except for F_N and makes it safe (by strengthening it) if possible, and, if not, returns an empty sequence. This is the main procedure of PDR. We only give a high-level description of it here. Intuitively, PDRMKSAFE does a backward search along the given trace F, starting in some state $s_N \in Bad$ (recall, F_N is unsafe, so such s_N always exists). Then, a predecessor s_{N-1} is extracted from a model of $F_{N-1}(v) \wedge Tr(v,u) \wedge s_N(u)$. This is repeated until $Init$ is reached, or, for some i, $F_{i-1}(v) \wedge Tr(v,u) \wedge s_i(u)$ becomes UNSAT. In the latter case,

$F_{i-1}(u) \land Tr(u, v) \rightarrow \neg s_i(u)$, and $\neg s_i$ can be conjoined (added as a clause) to F_i. PDRMKSAFE improves this by a process called *inductive generalization*. Instead of adding $\neg s_i$ directly, it finds a sub-clause $c \rightarrow \neg s_i$ such that

$$Init \rightarrow c \qquad F_i^{\uparrow}(u) \land c(u) \land Tr(u, v) \rightarrow c(v) \qquad (9)$$

Such c is guaranteed to exist, in the worst case $\neg s_i$ is taken as c. Inductive generalization is often argued to be the most important element that contributes to the efficiency of PDR. This process is continued until F_N becomes safe. An important property of PDRMKSAFE is that it is guaranteed to find some safe strengthening of F if a strengthening exists.

PDR offers many advantages, including incrementally (at each iteration only longer paths are explored) and locality of its SAT queries (all queries are over a single transition relation only). However, locality and the backward search strategy are also its Achilles' heel. There are many practical problems for which IMC's global and less directed search is superior.

4   Interpolating Property Directed Reachability

In this section, we introduce AVY, a Model Checking algorithm that, like IMC, uses BMC and sequence interpolants, and furthermore, like PDR it uses backward search and inductive generalization. We first describe the basic building blocks of AVY, and then go into fine-grained details.

4.1   Basic Algortihm

AVY is shown in Alg. 4. Like PDR it maintains a safe δ-trace $F = [F_0, \dots, F_N]$ and has the same high-level structure. However, the main steps for constructing the trace, making it safe (via AVYMKSAFE) and maintaining δ-form (via AVYMKDELTA), are done differently. We first give a high-level description of AVY and then of the two main functions.

Main loop. First, AVYMKSAFE is used to check whether the current trace can be safely extended to the next bound. If possible, it returns a safe trace G that is stronger than F. However, G is not necessarily a δ-trace. Second, AVYMKDELTA strengthens (again) G and makes it a δ-trace. Finally, the algorithm continues as PDR, using PDRPUSH to further strengthen the trace and check for convergence. In each iteration the trace can be incremented by an arbitrary step. But, for simplicity of presentation, assume that $step = 1$ unless stated otherwise. Note that the main loop maintains a safe δ-trace. Hence, in each iteration, the main loop of PDR can be used instead, leading to an interleaved version of the two algorithms.

AVYMKSAFE is presented in Alg. 5. It resembles IMCMKSAFE, but with one key difference: it uses the existing trace to simplify both the BMC and interpolation problems (see line 1, where $F_i^{\uparrow}$ is conjoined to the ith copy of the Tr). If the BMC formula φ is UNSAT, AVYMKSAFE extracts the sequence interpolant and uses it to strengthen and extend the existing trace. Otherwise, φ is SAT and AVYMKSAFE returns an empty trace.

There are multiple ways to partition the BMC formula φ for interpolation. To better understand the choice made in AVYMKSAFE, consider the following example: $T = (\{x\}, x = 0, x' = x + 1, x \geq 6)$. T represents a simple counter that counts from 0, and the bad region is where the counter goes beyond 5. Let us assume that we have the following trace $[x = 0, x \leq 1, \top]$, and consider the BMC problem for bound 2, with the partitioning used by AVYMKSAFE:

$$((x_0 = 0) \wedge (x_1 = x_0 + 1))_0 \wedge ((x_1 \leq 1) \wedge (x_2 = x_1 + 1))_1 \wedge (x_2 \geq 6)_2 \quad (10)$$

An alternative way to partition the formula is to add the ith element of the trace to the $i - 1$ partition (for $i \geq 1$):

$$((x_0 = 0) \wedge (x_1 = x_0 + 1) \wedge (x_1 \leq 1))_0 \wedge (x_2 = x_1 + 1)_1 \wedge (x_2 \geq 6)_2 \quad (11)$$

The choice of the partitioning influences the resulting sequence interpolant. In (10), the sequence interpolant contains only the parts that are needed to strengthen the existing trace. In (11), the interpolant is stronger than the trace (i.e., as if the trace was not added to the BMC formula).

In our example, in (10), since $x_1 \leq 1$ is strong enough, the suffix $((x_1 \leq 1) \wedge (x_2 = x_1 + 1))_1 \wedge (x_2 \geq 6)_2$ is UNSAT. By that we conclude that the first element of the sequence interpolant is $\top$. That is, F_1 in the trace needs no strengthening, which is evident in the resulting interpolant.

The example illustrates the advantage in choosing the partitioning used by AVY: the newly computed sequence interpolant takes into account the existing trace and only strengthens it as needed. This is part of the incrementality in AVY.

AVYMKDELTA is shown in Alg. 6. We first describe the intuition, then the mechanics. AVYMKDELTA converts a safe trace $G = [G_0, \ldots, G_N]$ into a monotone and clausal trace $F = [F_0, \ldots, F_N]$. Note that the result of AVYMKSAFE is safe but neither monotone nor clausal. One alternative to making a trace $[G_0, \ldots, G_N]$ monotone is to replace each element G_i by a disjunction of its predecessors $\{G_j\}_{j < i}$, i.e., by letting $F_i = \bigvee_{j < i} G_j$. But this is inefficient because the resulting formulas are too large.

Another alternative is to use interpolation. For example, let $[Init, G_1, G_2]$ be a safe but non-monotone and non-clausal trace. To make it monotone, we need $Init \rightarrow G_1$ and $G_1 \rightarrow G_2$. For the first implication, create the following problem

$$A = Init(v) \vee (Init(u) \wedge Tr(u, v)) \qquad B = \neg Init(v) \wedge \neg G_1(v) \quad (12)$$

From the definition of a trace, $A \wedge B$ is unsatisfiable. Let F_1 be a corresponding interpolant. By construction, $Init \rightarrow F_1$ and $Init(u) \wedge Tr(u, v) \rightarrow F_1(v)$. For the second implication, we compute an interpolant F_2 between $A = F_1(v) \vee (F_1(u) \wedge Tr(u, v))$ and $B = \neg(F_1(v) \vee G_2(v))$. F_2 satisfies: $F_1 \rightarrow F_2$ and $F_1(v) \wedge Tr(v, v') \rightarrow F_2(v')$. Hence, the trace $[Init, F_1, F_2]$ is safe and monotone.

However, in addition to monotonicity, we require that the trace is a clausal δ-trace. Transforming an arbitrary propositional formula into CNF without adding

Input: Transition system $T = (Init, Tr, Bad)$
1 $F_0 \leftarrow Init$; $N \leftarrow 0$
2 **repeat**
3 $\quad$ $G \leftarrow$ AvyMkSafe($[F_0, \ldots, F_N], Bad$)
4 $\quad$ **if** $G = [\,]$ **then return** UNSAFE $F_0, \ldots, F_N \leftarrow$ AvyMkDelta(G)
5 $\quad$ $F_0, \ldots, F_N \leftarrow$ PdrPush($[F_0, \ldots, F_N]$)
$\quad$ $\quad$ // $F_0, \ldots, F_N$ is a safe δ-trace
6 $\quad$ **if** $\exists 0 \le i \le N \cdot F_i = \emptyset$ **then return** SAFE pick $step \ge 1$
7 $\quad$ $\forall N \le i < N + step \cdot F_i \leftarrow \emptyset$
8 $\quad$ $N \leftarrow N + step$
9 **until** ∞;

Algorithm 4. Avy (simplified)

Input: Transition system $T = (Init, Tr, Bad)$
Input: A δ-trace $\boldsymbol{F} = [F_0, \ldots, F_N]$
1 $\varphi \leftarrow \bigwedge_{i=0}^{N-1} \left(\boldsymbol{F}_i^{\uparrow}(v_i) \wedge Tr(v_i, v_{i+1}) \right)_i \wedge (\boldsymbol{F}_N^{\uparrow}(v_N) \wedge Bad(v_N))_N$
2 **if** isSat(φ) **then return** $[\,]$ $I_1, \ldots, I_N \leftarrow$ seqItp(φ)
3 $G_0 \leftarrow Init$; $\forall 1 \le i \le N \cdot G_i \leftarrow \boldsymbol{F}_i^{\uparrow} \wedge I_i$
4 **return** $[G_0, \ldots, G_N]$

Algorithm 5. AvyMkSafe

new variables is expensive. One possibility is to generate interpolants in CNF by a CNF-producing interpolation procedure (e.g., [17]). While [17] is efficient it does not generate a δ-trace.

Instead, we have chosen to re-use PDR's PdrMkSafe that already maintains a δ-trace. Our unorthodox use of PdrMkSafe is guided towards our purpose. We establish the correctness of this method at the end of the section.

As before, consider a non-monotone non-clausal trace $[Init = G_0, G_1, G_2]$. Recall that PdrMkSafe takes a δ-trace and returns a strengthened safe δ-trace w.r.t. a given property. For the first element of the trace, we define $[Init, \top]$ as the input δ-trace. Then, PdrMkSafe is used to transform this δ-trace into a safe δ-trace w.r.t. the property $Init \vee G_1$. The result of PdrMkSafe is therefore a safe δ-trace $[Init, F_1]$ s.t. $Init \to \boldsymbol{F}_1^{\uparrow}$ and $Init(u) \wedge Tr(u, v) \to \boldsymbol{F}_1^{\uparrow}(v)$. For the second element G_2, the δ-trace $[Init, F_1, \top]$ is used. Now, PdrMkSafe is used to transform w.r.t. the property $\boldsymbol{F}_1^{\uparrow} \vee G_2$. The result is again, a safe δ-trace $[Init, F_1, F_2]$ s.t. the previous holds and in addition, $\boldsymbol{F}_1^{\uparrow} \to \boldsymbol{F}_2^{\uparrow}$ and $\boldsymbol{F}_1^{\uparrow}(u) \wedge Tr(u, v) \to \boldsymbol{F}_2^{\uparrow}(v)$. The general version of this algorithm is shown in Alg. 6.

We conclude with an outline of the correctness argument. To show correctness, it is enough to show that (a) AvyMkSafe always returns a safe trace if possible, and (b) AvyMkDelta returns a safe δ-trace given a safe trace. The rest of the proof (both for soundness and completeness) is the same as for PDR. Part (a) is an immediate consequence of sequence interpolation property, and we do not expand on it further. To show (b), we need to show that (i) the calls to

Input: Transition system $T = (Init, Tr, Bad)$
Input: A safe trace $\boldsymbol{G} = [G_0, \ldots, G_N]$
Output: A safe δ-trace $\boldsymbol{F} = [F_0 \ldots, F_N]$
1 $F_0 \leftarrow Init$
2 $[\_, F_1] \leftarrow \text{PDRMKSAFE}([Init, \top], \neg(Init \vee G_1))$
3 **for** $i \leftarrow 2$ **to** N **do**
4 $\quad | \quad [\_, \_, F_i] \leftarrow \text{PDRMKSAFE}([Init, F_{i-1}, \top], \neg(F_{i-1} \vee G_i))$
5 **end**

Algorithm 6. AVYMKDELTA

PDRMKSAFE always return a safe δ-trace, and (ii) δ-traces can be concatenated together. Part (ii) is an immediate consequence of the δ-trace property:

Lemma 1. *If $\boldsymbol{F} = [Init, F_1, \ldots, F_N]$ and $\boldsymbol{G} = [Init, F_N, G_2]$ are safe δ-traces, then so is $[Init, F_1, \ldots, F_N, G_2]$.*

To establish (i), we only need to show that the input to PDRMKSAFE can be made safe. For the call at line 2 of AVYMKDELTA, by the trace property of $\boldsymbol{G}$, $Init(u) \wedge Tr(u, v) \rightarrow G_1(v)$. For the call at line 4, we show by induction that $(F_{i-1}(u) \wedge Tr(u, v)) \rightarrow (F_{i-1}(v) \vee G_i(v))$. The base case is $i = 2$. We know that $F_1 \rightarrow (Init \vee G_1)$ (the call at line 2). Since both $[G_0, G_1, G_2]$ and $[Init, F_1]$ are traces, we have: $(G_1(u) \wedge Tr(u, v)) \rightarrow G_2(v)$ and $(Init(u) \wedge Tr(u, v)) \rightarrow F_1(v)$. By these three facts we get $(F_1(u) \wedge Tr(u, v)) \rightarrow (F_1(v) \vee G_2(v))$. The inductive case is similar. Using $(F_{i-1}(u) \wedge Tr(u, v)) \rightarrow (F_{i-1}(v) \vee G_i(v))$, we can conclude that each call at line 4 does not change F_{i-1} and thus Lemma 1 is applicable.

Theorem 2. AVY *is sound and complete for step* $= 1$.

When $step > 1$, AVYMKSAFE is not guaranteed to return a safe trace. While the last frame is safe, the intermediate ones might not be. One way around this is to require that Tr gets trapped in the Bad region.

Definition 1 (Stuck-On-Error). *A transition system $T = (Init, Tr, Bad)$ is stuck-on-error iff $\forall s \in Bad \cdot \exists t \in Bad \cdot Tr(s, t)$.*

Note that stuck-on-error can be enforced for any Tr by adding a self-loop on all Bad states. The rest of the proof remains unchanged.

Theorem 3. AVY *is sound and complete for step* > 1 *for any transition system T that satisfies stuck-on-error property of Def. 1.*

4.2   The Whole Picture

In the previous section, we gave a simplified description of AVY. Here, we describe some of its key features. The complete algorithm is shown in Alg. 7. The biggest change is that this version combines all the steps into a single function. In the rest of the section, we explain some features in detail.

Global δ-trace. Unlike the simplified presentation before, this version maintains a single global δ-trace. At every iteration, F is used incrementally by adding missing clauses. This is evident at lines 5–7. Note that both at line 5 and at line 7, the δ-trace that is given to PDRMKSAFE already has clauses that were learned in previous iterations. Hence, when transforming the newly generated interpolant to CNF, only clauses that are missing are added to F. This eliminates an expensive clause re-learning of the simplified version of the algorithm.

Guided Proofs. The upside of relying on interpolation is that AVY does not interfere with the SAT-solver during the BMC step. The downside is that, compared to PDR, there is very little control on the quality of the generated lemmas. A solution we adopt is to "guide" the SAT-solver that is producing the proof for interpolation. This is done by asking the solver to produce Minimal Unsatisfiable Subset (MUS) that excludes as many clauses from Tr and includes as many clauses from F as possible. The choice of a MUS affects the quality of the generated interpolants, and the choice of MUS algorithm affects the efficiency. In our implementation, we use a basic MUS algorithm (cf. [14]), and the MUS strategies described next.

We have tried two strategies for guiding the proof. First, called **min-core**, simply computes the MUS, letting the MUS algorithm pick which clauses to select. While this strategy is very fine grained, it was not effective in practice. It did cause an order of magnitude improvement in one example, but degraded performance overall.

The second strategy, called **min-suffix**, attempts to find a MUS that completely contains a suffix of the BMC problem. That is, it looks for the largest k such that $(\bigwedge_{i=k}^{N-1} F_i^\uparrow(v_i) \wedge Tr(v_i, v_{i+1})) \wedge F_N^\uparrow(v_N) \wedge Bad(v_N)$ is unsatisfiable.

To illustrate, consider the example from the previous section (reproduced here for convenience):

$$((x_0 = 0) \wedge (x_1 = x_0 + 1))_0 \wedge ((x_1 \leq 1) \wedge (x_2 = x_1 + 1))_1 \wedge (x_2 \geq 6)_2 \quad (13)$$

Recall, $x \leq 1$ is sufficient and, therefore, **min-suffix** reduces it to:

$$(\top)_0 \wedge ((x_0 \leq 1) \wedge (x_1 = x_0 + 1))_1 \wedge (x_1 \geq 6)_2 \quad (14)$$

The immediate benefits of **min-suffix** are: (a) the solved BMC formula is simpler (shorter bound); (b) the extracted sequence interpolant is smaller and, therefore, less interpolants need to be transformed to monotone clausal form; and (c) the proof is guided towards the important facts (e.g., to $x \leq 1$ in the case above). This makes generalization more effective.

Shallow Push. At each iteration of trace strengthening, new clauses are added to the global trace F. Therefore, it is possible to push the clauses forward after adding them (line 8) as they might be useful for the next iteration. Note that this is very different from the simplified version of the algorithm. There, the pushing-phase happens only after all of the strengthening. In practice, we push more conservatively, to which we refer as *shallow push*. During shallow push,

Input: Transition system $T = (Init, Tr, Bad)$
Data: A δ-trace $\boldsymbol{F} = [F_0, \ldots, F_N]$

1   $F_0 \leftarrow Init$; $N \leftarrow 0$
2   **repeat**
3      $\varphi \leftarrow \bigwedge_{i=0}^{N-1} \left(\boldsymbol{F}_i^{\uparrow}(v_i) \wedge Tr(v_i, v_{i+1}) \right)_i \wedge (\boldsymbol{F}_N^{\uparrow}(v_N) \wedge Bad(v_N))_N$
4   **if** $\text{ISSAT}(\varphi)$ **then return** UNSAFE $I_1, \ldots, I_N \leftarrow \text{SEQITP}(\varphi)$
5      $[\_, F_1] \leftarrow \text{PDRMKSAFE}([Init, \boldsymbol{F}_1^{\uparrow}], \neg(Init \vee I_1))$
6   **for** $i \leftarrow 2$ **to** N **do**
7         $[\_, \_, F_i] \leftarrow \text{PDRMKSAFE}([Init, \boldsymbol{F}_{i-1}^{\uparrow}, \boldsymbol{F}_i^{\uparrow}], \neg(\boldsymbol{F}_{i-1}^{\uparrow} \vee I_i))$
8         $F_0, \ldots, F_N \leftarrow \text{PDRPUSH}([F_0, \ldots, F_N])$
9   **end**
       // $F_0, \ldots, F_N$ is a safe δ-trace
10   **if** $\exists 0 \leq i \leq N \cdot F_i = \emptyset$ **then return** SAFE pick $step \geq 1$
11     $\forall N \leq i < N + step \cdot F_i \leftarrow \emptyset$
12     $N \leftarrow N + step$
13 **until** ∞;

Algorithm 7. AVY

clauses are only pushed starting from the ith location (where clauses were just added). This way, in the next iteration, when PDRMKSAFE is applied, it may need to find less clauses (or even none at all).

Table 1. Summary of solved instances on HWMCC'12 and HWMCC'13. CNF-ITP appears with (*) since we were not able to run it on the entire HWMCC'13 benchmark due to technical issues.

Status	AVY	PDR	ITP	CNF-ITP	Virtual Best
SAFE	76	72	62	59(*)	112
UNSAFE	24	15	26	25(*)	29

5   Experiments

We have implemented AVY[2] using C++ on top of ABC [5] – a well known open-source verification framework. We have compared it on HWMCC'12 and HWMCC'13 benchmark suites against PDR, McMillan's Interpolation algorithm (ITP) [12] as implemented in ABC, and CNF-ITP [17]. Note that ITP is slightly different from IMC described in Section 3.1. While an efficient implementation of IMC was not available, prior experiments indicate that ITP outperforms IMC on HWMCC benchmarks [6]. All experiments were performed on Intel E5-2697V2 running at 2.7GHz and with 256GB of RAM with a 900 seconds timeout.

---

[2] Available at http://www.cs.technion.ac.il/~yvizel/avy.html

Table 2. Detailed experimental results. D represents the depth of convergence, $\sharp$ Clauses - the number of clauses in the proof, and *Time* is the runtime in seconds. (*) Note that CNF-ITP failed to run on the OSKI cases due to technical issues.

Test	Status	ITP		CNF-ITP			PDR			Avy		
		D	Time[s]	D	$\sharp$ Clauses	Time[s]	D	$\sharp$ Clauses	Time[s]	D	$\sharp$ Clauses	Time[s]
6s102	T	53	TO	46	16,350	111	13	2966	222.22	23	162	61.92
6s121	T	342	TO	42	2,907	13.2	17	–	TO	49	1,713	499.14
6s130	T	14	18.66	18	93,600	856	7	–	TO	9	2,669	114.7
6s144	T	35	TO	23	–	TO	9	–	TO	22	371	449.53
6s159	T	63	11.5	10	280	0.3	45	114	2.7	36	19	10.2
6s189	T	37	TO	23	–	TO	8	–	TO	26	384	793.15
6s194	T	70	TO	80	–	TO	38	4,763	93.32	50	–	TO
6s205b16	T	61	213.01	35	–	TO	43	–	TO	10	–	TO
6s206rb025	T	7	2.51	6	24	2.5	4	8	0.22	4	8	8.28
6s207rb16	F	9	2.52	10	–	TO	5	–	TO	8	–	22.94
6s282b15	T	33	13.38	33	49,025	65	19	1,576	9.99	25	697	116.59
6s288r	T	83	TO	40	3,998	155	19	236	10.38	21	106	170.49
6s131	T	13	19.18	20	–	TO	6	–	TO	8	2,626	96.88
6s162	F	73	217.72	73	–	TO	13	–	TO	72	–	173.63
6s38	T	23	TO	24	4,508	558	9	–	TO	12	1,193	130.15
6s407rb296	T	18	TO	9	–	TO	9	–	TO	12	238	173.18
6s408rb191	T	37	TO	16	33,116	228	6	883	0.97	8	644	199.94
6s8	T	43	TO	38	–	TO	26	–	TO	35	2,021	829.12
6s9	T	14	30.56	10	–	TO	9	–	TO	8	2,727	96.85
intel011	T	72	TO	20	–	TO	27	–	TO	52	572	233.94
intel015	T	72	TO	21	–	TO	51	–	TO	60	726	124.29
intel018	T	78	TO	16	–	TO	50	–	TO	60	328	56.6
intel020	T	90	TO	15	3,975	48	33	–	TO	46	370	56.28
intel021	T	92	TO	18	5,958	115	33	–	TO	52	365	99.62
intel022	T	84	TO	21	–	TO	27	–	TO	38	405	73.18
intel023	T	96	TO	32	9,312	606	30	–	TO	50	243	57.09
intel024	T	96	TO	15	4,395	78	23	–	TO	38	194	23.43
intel025	T	60	TO	17	–	TO	23	–	TO	42	1,204	421.07
intel029	T	84	TO	16	–	TO	47	–	TO	54	230	53.31
intel034	T	86	TO	16	1,344	119	55	–	TO	72	232	603.85
oski1rub03	T	9	4.02	–(*)	–(*)	–(*)	8	169	12.71	6	43	13.96
oski1rub04	F	13	28.46	–(*)	–(*)	–(*)	14	–	112.42	12	–	81.89
oski1rub07	T	4	1.22	–(*)	–(*)	–(*)	7	144	3.51	2	140	6.22

We have joined HWMCC'12 and HWMCC'13 together into a set of benchmarks, excluding BEEM [3] test cases as we put emphasis on the industrial section of the benchmark (which includes 328 test cases).

The results are summarized in Table 1. AVY dominates the benchmark in number of solved instances. In particular, on the INTEL set, AVY and CNF-ITP are the only techniques able to solve safe instances, though AVY solves considerably more instances than CNF-ITP. Inspecting the entire set of solved instances, the instances solved by AVY and PDR are significantly different. The "Virtual Best" column shows the result of a solver that runs all 3 techniques and takes the best result. It shows that AVY is complimentary to PDR. Together, they solve at least a third more benchmarks than either one in isolation.

---

[3] http://paradise.fi.muni.cz/beem

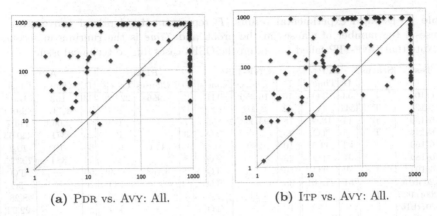

(a) PDR vs. AVY: All.   (b) ITP vs. AVY: All.

Fig. 1. Runtime comparison between AVY (y-axis) and PDR and ITP

More details are shown in Table 2. There are two important parameters to notice: the depth at which a proof (fixpoint) is found and the number of clauses in the proof. On the cases where both PDR and AVY reach to a fixpoint, the number of clauses in the proof AVY finds is smaller than those in the proof found by PDR, even in the cases where PDR converges at a lower depth.

The run-time results for the entire benchmark are shown in Fig. 1. In all plots, AVY is represented by the y-axis. While whenever AVY solves a problem that is solved by another method, it is slower, it solves a large number of problems not solved by other techniques. We believe that the performance issues are in part due to our implementation of interpolation and lack of support for the combination of incremental SAT-solving and interpolation.

We have also evaluated the effect of specific techniques used by AVY and found all of them to be important. AVY is not competitive if any of them are disabled. In particular, maintaining the global δ-trace and guiding the proof towards minimal unsatisfiable suffix are critical to performance. In addition, 3 test cases were only solved with the **min-core** option.

6 Conclusion

We introduce AVY, a new SAT-based model checking algorithm. Like IMC and PDR, AVY constructs a safe inductive invariant to show the validity of a property. It uses BMC-unrolling with sequence interpolants to construct an initial candidate invariant (similar to IMC), but then uses local backward search and inductive generalization to keep the candidate invariant in a compact clausal form. AVY combines the advantages of both IMC and PDR. Our experiments show that AVY is a very capable algorithm that can solve a considerable number of test cases that are not solvable by neither PDR nor ITP and CNF-ITP.

As future directions, we would like to experiment with other methods that can keep the trace in compact clausal form (e.g., using the approach from [17]). In addition, we believe that the concepts that were introduced in this paper extends beyond finite state systems and can be applied in the context of software model checking.

References

1. Albarghouthi, A., Gurfinkel, A., Chechik, M.: Craig Interpretation. In: Miné, A., Schmidt, D. (eds.) SAS 2012. LNCS, vol. 7460, pp. 300–316. Springer, Heidelberg (2012)
2. Albarghouthi, A., Gurfinkel, A., Li, Y., Chaki, S., Chechik, M.: Ufo: Verification with interpolants and abstract interpretation - (competition contribution). In: Piterman, N., Smolka, S.A. (eds.) TACAS 2013. LNCS, vol. 7795, pp. 637–640. Springer, Heidelberg (2013)
3. Biere, A., Cimatti, A., Clarke, E.M., Strichman, O., Zhu, Y.: Bounded model checking. Advances in Computers 58, 117–148 (2003)
4. Bradley, A.R.: SAT-Based Model Checking without Unrolling. In: Jhala, R., Schmidt, D. (eds.) VMCAI 2011. LNCS, vol. 6538, pp. 70–87. Springer, Heidelberg (2011)
5. Brayton, R., Mishchenko, A.: Abc: An academic industrial-strength verification tool. In: Touili, T., Cook, B., Jackson, P. (eds.) CAV 2010. LNCS, vol. 6174, pp. 24–40. Springer, Heidelberg (2010)
6. Cabodi, G., Nocco, S., Quer, S.: Interpolation sequences revisited. In: DATE, pp. 316–322. IEEE (2011)
7. Chockler, H., Ivrii, A., Matsliah, A.: Computing interpolants without proofs. In: Biere, A., Nahir, A., Vos, T. (eds.) HVC. LNCS, vol. 7857, pp. 72–85. Springer, Heidelberg (2013)
8. Craig, W.: Three Uses of the Herbrand-Gentzen Theorem in Relating Model Theory and Proof Theory. J. of Symbolic Logic 22(3), 269–285 (1957)
9. D'Silva, V., Kroening, D., Purandare, M., Weissenbacher, G.: Interpolant strength. In: Barthe, G., Hermenegildo, M. (eds.) VMCAI 2010. LNCS, vol. 5944, pp. 129–145. Springer, Heidelberg (2010)
10. Eén, N., Mishchenko, A., Brayton, R.K.: Efficient implementation of property directed reachability. In: Bjesse, P., Slobodová, A. (eds.) FMCAD, pp. 125–134. FMCAD Inc. (2011)
11. Hoder, K., Bjørner, N.: Generalized property directed reachability. In: Cimatti, A., Sebastiani, R. (eds.) SAT 2012. LNCS, vol. 7317, pp. 157–171. Springer, Heidelberg (2012)
12. McMillan, K.L.: Interpolation and SAT-based model checking. In: Hunt Jr., W.A., Somenzi, F. (eds.) CAV 2003. LNCS, vol. 2725, pp. 1–13. Springer, Heidelberg (2003)
13. McMillan, K.L.: Lazy abstraction with interpolants. In: Ball, T., Jones, R.B. (eds.) CAV 2006. LNCS, vol. 4144, pp. 123–136. Springer, Heidelberg (2006)
14. Nadel, A.: Boosting minimal unsatisfiable core extraction. In: Bloem, R., Sharygina, N. (eds.) FMCAD, pp. 221–229. IEEE (2010)
15. Vizel, Y., Grumberg, O.: Interpolation-sequence based model checking. In: FMCAD, pp. 1–8. IEEE (2009)
16. Vizel, Y., Grumberg, O., Shoham, S.: Intertwined forward-backward reachability analysis using interpolants. In: Piterman, N., Smolka, S.A. (eds.) TACAS 2013. LNCS, vol. 7795, pp. 308–323. Springer, Heidelberg (2013)

17. Vizel, Y., Ryvchin, V., Nadel, A.: Efficient generation of small interpolants in CNF. In: Sharygina, N., Veith, H. (eds.) CAV 2013. LNCS, vol. 8044, pp. 330–346. Springer, Heidelberg (2013)

Verifying Relative Error Bounds Using Symbolic Simulation

Jesse Bingham and Joe Leslie-Hurd

Intel Corporation, Hillsboro, U.S.A
jesse.d.bingham@intel.com
joe.leslie-hurd@intel.com

Abstract. In this paper we consider the problem of formally verifying hardware that is specified to compute reciprocal, reciprocal square root, and power-of-two functions on floating point numbers to within a given *relative error*. Such specifications differ from the common case in which any given input is specified to have *exactly one* correct output. Our approach is based on symbolic simulation with binary decision diagrams, and involves two distinct steps. First, we prove a lemma that reduces the relative error specification to several inequalities that involve reasoning about natural numbers only. The most complex of these inequalities asserts that the product of several naturals is less-than/greater-than another natural. Second, we invoke one of several customized algorithms that decides the inequality, without performing the expensive symbolic multiplications directly. We demonstrate the effectiveness of our approach on a next-generation Intel® processor design and report encouraging time and space metrics for these proofs.

1 Introduction

Formal verification of hardware data path designs is by now standard practice for many design organizations, see e.g. [8,16,12,17]. Typically the specifications for such circuits are *functional*, meaning that there is exactly one correct output for any given input. In principle, verification can be carried out by writing an executable specification and checking that for all inputs, the output of the design is equal to that of the specification. Symbolic simulation allows one to verify this for all inputs in one fell swoop.[1]

In this paper, we consider designs with specifications that are not functional since a given input can correctly produce any one of a *multitude* of possible outputs. These specifications only require that the design result *approximates* the true mathematical result, in the sense that the relative error is less than some bound. Note that this is distinct from many functional specifications that allow approximate results via rounding; in that case the rounding is precisely defined so that there is still exactly one correct answer.

---

[1] Although for some operations, one must employ case splitting and/or decomposition due to exponential blow up.

A. Biere and R. Bloem (Eds.): CAV 2014, LNCS 8559, pp. 277–292, 2014.

We consider three unary operations in this work: reciprocal (RCP), reciprocal square root (RSQRT), and power-of-two (EXP2). The first two take one IEEE floating point number as input, while power-of-two takes a fixed-point number; all three *produce* one IEEE floating point number as output. The common thread in verifying these three operations is summarized by the following two elements:

1. Express the relative error specification as two inequalities, each of the form

$$B \diamond \prod_{i=1}^{n} M_i \tag{1}$$

where $\diamond$ is either $<$ or $>$, along with some simpler conditions also involving only integer reasoning. Here B and $M_1, \ldots, M_n$ are positive integers that are specific to the operation under consideration, and each have tractable symbolic representations. The equivalence of these inequalities to the desired relative error bounds are stated and proven as meta-theorems in this paper.
2. Use one of several custom algorithms for deciding the inequalities (1). These algorithms are optimized for efficient symbolic computation; though $M_1, \ldots, M_n$ have tractable representations, the product typically does not, so directly computing the product and checking the inequality can be prohibitively expensive. The other conditions involving integers are simple enough that they don't require any specially optimized algorithms to decide symbolically.

The general technique of reducing problems involving floating point numbers to problems involving integers is well-known, and for example has been used to find test vectors for floating point units where the outputs are very close to rounding boundaries [11]. The chief novelty of this paper is the specific recipes for reducing the relative error specifications of three families of floating point operations—RCP, RSQRT and EXP2—to a form that can be proved by symbolic computation techniques.

The primary contribution of the paper presents these novel reductions and demonstrates how they can be integrated with standard symbolic simulation tools for RTL. This facilitates formal verification of relative error bounds for our three instruction classes on a next-generation Intel® processor. This is the first verification approach for relative error bounds that uses symbolic simulation instead of theorem proving, which offers the advantage of providing counter-examples whenever the verification fails, shortening debugging time. A secondary contribution of this paper is the technique for verifying the relative error bounds of the EXP2 floating point operation, which computes an approximation to 2^x for an input x. We present a recipe for verifying bounds of this transcendental function using symbolic arithmetic operations.

The rest of the paper is organized as follows. Background notions and notations are given in Sect. 2. The lemmas that reduce the relative error specifications to integer reasoning are give in Sect. 3. Sect. 4 presents the three symbolic decision procedures for (1). Our case study results, paper summary, and a discussion of related work correspond to Sects. 5, 6, and 7, respectively.

2   Background

2.1   Relative Error

Let $\mathbb{B}$, $\mathbb{N}$, $\mathbb{Z}$, and $\mathbb{R}$ represent the set of booleans $\{0,1\}$, naturals $\{0,1,2,\ldots\}$, integers, and reals, respectively. For any $x \in \mathbb{R}$, we use the usual floor and ceiling operations that map $x \in \mathbb{R}$ to $\mathbb{Z}$: $\lfloor x \rfloor$ is the maximum integer n such that $n \leq x$ and $\lceil x \rceil$ is the minimum integer n such that $n \geq x$. We also define $\langle x \rangle = x - \lfloor x \rfloor$, i.e. $\langle x \rangle$ is the "fractional" part of x.

Let y and y^* be reals; here y can be thought of as a mathematically precise result, whereas y^* is an approximation of y. For real $\epsilon > 0$, we say that y^* *approximates y with relative error ϵ* if

$$\left| \frac{y^* - y}{y} \right| < \epsilon$$

For a natural $p \geq 2$, we use the notation $y^* \approx_p y$ to assert that y^* approximates y with relative error 2^{-p}. We make the assumption that $p \geq 2$, and hence the relative error is at most $\frac{1}{4}$, to rule out some pathological cases in our proofs.[2] In this paper we will be interested in establishing

$$\forall x.\ h(x) \approx_p f(x)$$

where $h(x)$ is the output of a hardware design given input x, and f is the mathematical function that the hardware is designed to approximate.

2.2   Floating Point Numbers

A *floating point number* [5], or simply *float*, is a triple (s, e, m) where $s \in \{-1, 1\}$ is called the *sign*, $e \in \mathbb{Z}$ is called the *exponent*, and $m \in \mathbb{N}$ is called the *mantissa*.[3] The mantissa must satisfy a range constraint $2^\ell \leq m < 2^{\ell+1}$ where $\ell \in \mathbb{N}$ is a constant called the *mantissa fraction length*.[4] In this paper we will deal with *single precision* and *double precision* floats, which have $\ell = 23$ and $\ell = 52$, respectively. If x is a floating point number, we write $s(x)$, $e(x)$, and $m(x)$ for the sign, exponent, and mantissa of x, respectively. The real number represented by x is defined to be

$$s(x)m(x)2^{e(x)-\ell}$$

and in a minor abuse of notation we will use x and the represented real interchangeably.

---

[2] The relative errors used in our hardware verification case studies have $p \in \{11, 14, 23, 28\}$.

[3] Here we abstract slightly away from bit-level floating point encodings, e.g. as defined in IEEE Standard 754 [7].

[4] In practice e also satisfies a range constraint $e_{min} \leq e \leq e_{max}$, where e_{min} and e_{max} are maximal and minimal exponents. However, the results in this paper do not depend on exponent range constraints and so we omit them.

2.3   Symbolic Simulation

Let V be a finite set of boolean-valued variables. An *assignment* (to V) is a function $\alpha : V \to \mathbb{B}$. For any set S (which we'll call the *base type*), a function of type $(V \to \mathbb{B}) \to S$ is called a *symbolic S*; if S is unspecified we will simply refer to this as a *symbolic object*. Thus a symbolic S is a function that takes an assignment and produces an element of the base type S. In this paper we will be interested in symbolic booleans (a.k.a *boolean functions*), symbolic integers/naturals, and symbolic floats. To represent and manipulate boolean functions we will use the well-known binary decision diagram (BDD) [2] data structure. One can then represent a symbolic integer b using a finite list of boolean functions $b_n, \ldots, b_0$ and twos-complement encoding; i.e. for an assignment α,

$$b(\alpha) = -b_n(\alpha)2^n + b_{n-1}(\alpha)2^{n-1} + \cdots + b_0(\alpha)2^0$$

Once equipped with symbolic integers, we can represent symbolic floats as (s, e, m), where s is a boolean function indicating the sign, and e and m are symbolic integers. Furthermore, any function involving the various base types of interest can be extended to take and return symbolic objects. In code, this typically involves simply replacing primitive operations with symbolic variants. One fundamental operation that we will use symbolically is if-then-else, explained as follows. Let X_i and X_e be symbolic objects having the same base type, and let c be a boolean function. Then we define

$$\mathbf{ite}(c, X_i, X_e) = \lambda\alpha. \text{ if } c(\alpha) \text{ then } X_i(\alpha) \text{ else } X_e(\alpha)$$

For the rest of the paper, we assume availability of symbolic variants of other fundamental operations, such as addition, subtraction, multiplication, exponentiation, and constants, and will not notationally distinguish the symbolic from the non-symbolic operations.

Symbolic simulation is a well-known approach wherein symbolic objects are propagated through the primitives of a hardware (or software) design [4]. In this paper we employ BDD-based symbolic simulation, e.g. [15]. Here, a hardware description language representation of the design is compiled down to a gate-level implementation, which operates on wires carrying boolean values. Roughly, symbolic simulation involves associating to each input wire a unique boolean variable from V (represented by a BDD), and then propagating the symbolic booleans through the gates according to the gate's function. Symbolic simulation proper completes when the resulting BDDs on the output wires of interest have been computed. These output BDDs are then fed into a specification-checking phase that either proves correctness or returns a counter-example in the form of an assignment to V. In the framework in which we did our work, the specification refers to inputs and output being naturals, integers, or floats; i.e. the BDDs seen by the symbolic simulator are packaged into symbolic objects before evaluating the specification. Hence, even though symbolic simulation works on a "bit-blasted", gate-level representation, we can meaningfully construct a specification that relates the input float to the output float (or other type, as appropriate).

3   Bounded Product Reduction

In this section we present the meta-theorems needed to reduce the relative error verification problem for RCP (Sect. 3.1), RSQRT (Sect. 3.2), and EXP2 (Sect. 3.3) to integer inequalities. Note that the theorem (and proof) for the first two are quite similar, though sufficiently different as to warrant separate theorems, whereas the reduction for EXP2 is somewhat more elaborate. Though the reduction for RSQRT involves reasoning about irrational numbers, these can be eliminated by squaring; however the irrationality of EXP2 cannot be disposed of in such an easy manner and requires more sophisticated techniques.

3.1   Reciprocal

Suppose we wish to establish $y \approx_p 1/x$, where x and y are floating point numbers. To reduce the problem to purely integer reasoning, we invoke the following key lemma.

Lemma 1 (Reduction for RCP).

Let x and y be floating point numbers. Then we have $y \approx_p 1/x$ if and only if all of the following three conditions hold:

(i) $s(x) = s(y)$

(ii) $e(x) + e(y) \in \{-2, -1, 0\}$

(iii) $2^{2\ell+2} - 2^{2\ell+2-p} < m(x)m(y)2^{e(x)+e(y)+2} < 2^{2\ell+2} + 2^{2\ell+2-p}$

Proof. We have

$$
\begin{aligned}
& y \approx_p 1/x \\
\Leftrightarrow & \; |xy - 1| < 2^{-p} \\
\Leftrightarrow & \; \left| \left(s(x)m(x)2^{e(x)-\ell} \right) \left(s(y)m(y)2^{e(y)-\ell} \right) - 1 \right| < 2^{-p} \\
\Leftrightarrow & \; \left| s(x)s(y)m(x)m(y)2^{-2\ell}2^{e(x)+e(y)} - 1 \right| < 2^{-p} \\
\Leftrightarrow & \; 1 - 2^{-p} < s(x)s(y)m(x)m(y)2^{-2\ell}2^{e(x)+e(y)} < 1 + 2^{-p} \\
\Leftrightarrow & \; 2^{2\ell+2}(1 - 2^{-p}) < s(x)s(y)m(x)m(y)2^{e(x)+e(y)+2} < 2^{2\ell+2}(1 + 2^{-p})
\end{aligned}
$$

which is equivalent to

$$
2^{2\ell+2} - 2^{2\ell+2-p} < s(x)s(y)m(x)m(y)2^{e(x)+e(y)+2} < 2^{2\ell+2} + 2^{2\ell+2-p} \quad (2)
$$

Since $2^{2\ell+2} - 2^{2\ell+2-p}$ is positive, we must have $s(x) = s(y)$. Thus, since $s(x)s(y) = 1$, the above is equivalent to Condition (iii) of the lemma statement. Also, from the definition of floating point number, we have $2^{2\ell} \le m(x)m(y) < 2^{2\ell+2}$. If $e(x) + e(y) \le -3$, then

$$
m(x)m(y)2^{e(x)+e(y)+2} \; \le \; m(x)m(y)/2 \; < \; 2^{2\ell+1} \; \le \; 2^{2\ell+2} - 2^{2\ell+2-p}
$$

(since p is a positive integer), contradicting the lower bound of (2). Similarly, if $e(x) + e(y) \ge 1$, then

$$
m(x)m(y)2^{e(x)+e(y)+2} \; \ge \; m(x)m(y)2^3 \; > \; 2^{2\ell+3} \; > \; 2^{2\ell+2} + 2^{2\ell+2-p}
$$

which violates the upper bound of (2).   □

Conditions (i) and (ii) of Lemma 1 clearly only involve integers; furthermore, assuming $p \leq 2\ell + 2$, so too does (iii).[5] Hence, we have reduced $y \approx_p 1/x$ to two instances of (1) with $n = 2$, where $M_1 = m(x)2^{e(x)+e(y)+2}$ and $M_2 = m(y)$, and the bound $B = 2^{2\ell+2}(1 - 2^{-p})$ (resp. $B = 2^{2\ell+2}(1 + 2^{-p})$) in the first (resp. second) instance. Note that we choose to multiply $m(x)$ by $2^{e(x)+e(y)+2}$ to create M_1, rather than have $n = 3$. The BDD complexity introduced by multiplying $m(x)$ by $2^{e(x)+e(y)+2}$ is relatively insignificant, since under condition (ii) the latter ranges over just $\{1, 2, 4\}$.

3.2   Reciprocal Square Root

Reciprocal square root involves a similar derivation as reciprocal, except we can disregard the sign, since the operation is only defined on non-negative floats.

Lemma 2 (Reduction for RSQRT). *Let x and y be positive floating point numbers. Then we have $y \approx_p 1/\sqrt{x}$ if and only if both of the following conditions hold:*

$$(i) \; -3 \leq e(x) + 2e(y) \leq 0$$
$$(ii) \; 2^{3\ell+3} - 2^{3\ell+4-p} + 2^{3\ell+3-2p} < m(x)m(y)^2 2^{e(x)+2e(y)+3}$$
$$< 2^{3\ell+3} + 2^{3\ell+4-p} + 2^{3\ell+3-2p}$$

Proof. We have

$$y \approx_p 1/\sqrt{x}$$
$$\Leftrightarrow |y\sqrt{x} - 1| < 2^{-p}$$
$$\Leftrightarrow -2^{-p} < y\sqrt{x} - 1 < 2^{-p}$$
$$\Leftrightarrow 1 - 2^{-p} < y\sqrt{x} < 1 + 2^{-p}$$
$$\Leftrightarrow (1 - 2^{-p})^2 < xy^2 < (1 + 2^{-p})^2$$
$$\Leftrightarrow (1 - 2^{-p})^2 < \left(m(x)2^{e(x)-\ell}\right)\left(m(y)2^{e(y)-\ell}\right)^2 < (1 + 2^{-p})^2$$
$$\Leftrightarrow (1 - 2^{-p})^2 < m(x)m(y)^2 2^{e(x)+2e(y)-3\ell} < (1 + 2^{-p})^2$$
$$\Leftrightarrow 2^{3\ell+3}(1 - 2^{-p})^2 < m(x)m(y)^2 2^{e(x)+2e(y)+3} < 2^{3\ell+3}(1 + 2^{-p})^2$$
$$\Leftrightarrow 2^{3\ell+3} - 2^{3\ell+4-p} + 2^{3\ell+3-2p} < m(x)m(y)^2 2^{e(x)+2e(y)+3}$$
$$< 2^{3\ell+3} + 2^{3\ell+4-p} + 2^{3\ell+3-2p}$$

Note that since $p \geq 2$, we have $2^{3\ell+2} < 2^{3\ell+3} - 2^{3\ell+4-p} + 2^{3\ell+3-2p}$ and $2^{3\ell+3} + 2^{3\ell+4-p} + 2^{3\ell+3-2p} < 2^{3\ell+4}$, and from the definition of floating point number, we have $2^{3\ell} \leq m(x)m(y)^2 < 2^{3\ell+3}$. If $e(x)+2e(y) \leq -4$, the we get the contradiction

$$2^{3\ell+2} < m(x)m(y)^2 2^{e(x)+2e(y)+3} \leq m(x)m(y)^2 2^{-1} < 2^{3\ell+2}$$

If $e(x) + 2e(y) \geq 1$, then we get the contradiction

$$2^{3\ell+4} > m(x)m(y)^2 2^{e(x)+2e(y)+3} \geq m(x)m(y)^2 2^4 \geq 2^{3\ell+4}$$

$\square$

---

[5] In all our hardware verification case studies we have $p \leq 2\ell + 2$, however if this does not hold, one need only multiply all three quantities by $2^{p-2\ell-2}$ to obtain integers.

3.3   Power-of-Two

In this section, we consider relative error bounds for an instruction EXP2 that takes an input x and returns an approximation of 2^x. Unlike the preceding instructions, EXP2 does not take a floating point number as input, but rather a *fixed point* number. A *fixed point number with precision q* is a real number x such that $x2^q \in \mathbb{Z}$. Though EXP2 takes a fixed point number as input, it produces a floating point number as output.

Lemma 3. *Let x be a fixed point number with precision q and let y be a positive floating point number, and let $p \geq 2$ be an integer. Then we have $y \approx_p 2^x$ if and only if both of the following conditions hold:*

(i) $e(y) - \lfloor x \rfloor \in \{-1, 0, 1\}$

(ii) $2^{\langle x \rangle} 2^\ell (2^p - 1) \; < \; m(y) 2^{p + e(y) - \lfloor x \rfloor} \; < \; 2^{\langle x \rangle} 2^\ell (2^p + 1)$

Proof. Letting $d = e(y) - \lfloor x \rfloor$, we have

$$
\begin{aligned}
& y \approx_p 2^x \\
\Leftrightarrow \; & |y 2^{-x} - 1| < 2^{-p} \\
\Leftrightarrow \; & |m(y) 2^{e(y) - \ell - \lfloor x \rfloor - \langle x \rangle} - 1| < 2^{-p} \\
\Leftrightarrow \; & |m(y) 2^{-\ell} 2^{-\langle x \rangle} 2^d - 1| < 2^{-p} \\
\Leftrightarrow \; & 1 - 2^p < m(y) 2^{-\ell} 2^{-\langle x \rangle} 2^d < 1 + 2^{-p} \\
\Leftrightarrow \; & 2^{\langle x \rangle} 2^\ell (2^p - 1) < m(y) 2^{p+d} < 2^{\langle x \rangle} 2^\ell (2^p + 1)
\end{aligned}
$$

Since $0 \leq \langle x \rangle < 1$, we have $\frac{1}{2} < 2^{-\langle x \rangle} \leq 1$; we also have $1 \leq m(y) 2^{-\ell} < 2$. Thus,

$$
\tfrac{1}{2} \; < \; m(y) 2^{-\ell} 2^{-\langle x \rangle} \; < \; 2
$$

and therefore if $2^d \leq \frac{1}{4}$ or $4 \leq 2^d$, the left-hand side of the inequality becomes strictly greater than $\frac{1}{2}$, and thus the inequality cannot hold since the right-hand side is less than or equal to $\frac{1}{2}$. Thus $d \in \{-1, 0, 1\}$. $\qquad \square$

All quantities involved in the inequalities *(ii)* above are integers, *except* the value $2^{\langle x \rangle}$, which in general is an irrational in $[1, 2)$. Hence we cannot hope to simply scale all values by some power of two to make an equi-satisfiable integer inequality, as was done in Lemmas 1 and 2. However, if we are equipped with a means of computing $\lfloor 2^k 2^{\langle x \rangle} \rfloor$ and $\lceil 2^k 2^{\langle x \rangle} \rceil$ precisely, for any $k \in \mathbb{N}$, we can still obtain an equivalent computable inequality. This is afforded by the following lemma.

Lemma 4. *Let r be a real and m and n be naturals. Then $rm < n$ (resp. $n < rm$) if and only if there exists some natural k such that $\lceil r 2^k \rceil m < n 2^k$ (resp. $n 2^k < \lfloor r 2^k \rfloor m$)*

Proof. The $\Leftarrow$ direction is easy. For the $\Rightarrow$ direction, suppose $rm < n$. Then $rm + q = n$ for some real $q > 0$, and thus $r + q/m = n/m$. Choose k such that $2^{-k} < q/m$. Then $n = rm + q > rm + m2^{-k}$, and thus $n2^k > r2^k m + m = (r2^k + 1)m > \lceil r 2^k \rceil m$. The respective statement is proven analogously. $\qquad \square$

We now exploit Lemma 4 to create a "computable" version of Lemma 3:

Lemma 5. *Let x be a fixed point number with precision q, let y be a positive floating point number, and let $p > 0$ be an integer. Then we have $y \approx_p 2^x$ if and only if $e(y) - \lfloor x \rfloor \in \{-1, 0, 1\}$ and there exists natural k such that*

$$\left\lceil 2^{k+\langle x \rangle} \right\rceil 2^\ell (2^p - 1) < m(y) 2^{k+p+e(y)-\lfloor x \rfloor} < \left\lfloor 2^{k+\langle x \rangle} \right\rfloor 2^\ell (2^p + 1) \quad (3)$$

Proof. Follows from Lemmas 3 and 4   □

Although the condition (3) from Lemma 5 only involves integers, it still requires a means of symbolically computing $\lceil 2^{k+\langle x \rangle} \rceil$ and $\lfloor 2^{k+\langle x \rangle} \rfloor$. Such computations are possible, however we chose to merely compute upper- and lower-bounds, respectively, on these two quantities. We now elaborate on this scheme.

Observe that since x is a fixed-point number with precision q, we have that $\langle x \rangle = \sum_{i=1}^{q} x_i 2^{-i}$, where $x_i \in \mathbb{B}$, and hence

$$2^{k+\langle x \rangle} = 2^k \prod_{i=1}^{q} 2^{x_i 2^{-i}}$$

Now let us suppose we have a pair of functions $sqrt2L, sqrt2U : \mathbb{N} \times \mathbb{N} \to \mathbb{N}$ such that for all $n, i \in \mathbb{N}$ we have $sqrt2L(n, i) \leq 2^{n+2^{-i}} \leq sqrt2U(n, i)$. Here we may think of n as a bit-precision used to approximate the 2^ith-root of 2. Taking $k = nq$ and replacing the exponent x_i with an **ite** operator yields

$$\begin{aligned} \left\lfloor 2^{nq+\langle x \rangle} \right\rfloor &\geq \prod_{i=1}^{q} \mathbf{ite}(x_i, sqrt2L(n, i), 2^n) \\ \left\lceil 2^{nq+\langle x \rangle} \right\rceil &\leq \prod_{i=1}^{q} \mathbf{ite}(x_i, sqrt2U(n, i), 2^n) \end{aligned} \quad (4)$$

The introduction of the ceiling and floor operators on the LHSs of (4) are justified since the RHSs are naturals. Condition (3) is hence implied by

$$\begin{aligned} 2^\ell (2^p - 1) \prod_{i=1}^{q} \mathbf{ite}(x_i, sqrt2U(n, i), 2^n) &< m(y) 2^{k+p+e(y)-\lfloor x \rfloor} \\ 2^\ell (2^p + 1) \prod_{i=1}^{q} \mathbf{ite}(x_i, sqrt2L(n, i), 2^n) &> m(y) 2^{k+p+e(y)-\lfloor x \rfloor} \end{aligned} \quad (5)$$

We have obtained adequate functions for $sqrt2L$ and $sqrt2U$ via some straightforward modifications of a pre-existing function that performs (floor of) square-root on symbolic naturals. Therefore, when verifying EXP2, we need only decide inequalities of the form (5), with the "precision" parameter n selected large enough for the verification to succeed.

4   Deciding Symbolic Product Inequalities

Section 3 showed how the relative error specification for RCP, RSQRT, and EXP2 can be reduced to two inequalities of the form (1): $B \diamond \prod_{i=1}^{n} M_i$, where $\diamond$ is either $<$ or $>$ and each $M_i \in \mathbb{N}$. In this section we describe three algorithms for deciding symbolic inequalities of this form. Technically, these algorithms return the symbolic boolean characterizing the space of assignments for which the inequality holds; verification is successful iff this is the constant function *True*. Let us abbreviate $\prod_{i=1}^{n} M_i$ by Π, and let us refer to our problem as $<$-*bounding* (resp. $>$-*bounding*) when $\diamond$ is $<$ (resp. $>$).

A common feature of the three algorithms is that all involve a loop that iteratively computes closer and closer approximations $a_0, a_1, \ldots$ of Π. When $<$-bounding, this sequence is such that for all i, $a_i \leq a_{i+1} \leq \Pi$; thus if we reach an i such that $B < a_i$, we have proven $B < \Pi$. The analogous statement with all inequalities reversed holds for $>$-bounding. Let sat_i denote the symbolic boolean $B \diamond a_i$. Assuming it exists, let $v \in \mathbb{N}$ be minimal such that $sat_v = True$. Clearly, after iteration v the algorithm can safely return *True*. Furthermore, if $a_v \neq \Pi$, we have proven the bound without computing Π exactly. This *early termination* saves significant time and space, since v can be much smaller than the total number of iterations the algorithm would otherwise execute, and the BDD sizes in the representation of a_v are much smaller than that of Π.

Since the sequence $a_0, a_1, \ldots$ is monotonic, so too is $sat_0, sat_1, \ldots$, in the sense that $sat_i \Rightarrow sat_{i+1}$ for all i. Let $u \in \mathbb{N}$ be minimal such that $sat_u \neq False$. Typically, u is somewhat smaller than v, which implies there are iterations i wherein $False \neq sat_i \neq True$ (i.e., sat_i is a non-constant boolean function). This reveals a certain redundancy in these later iterations; even though we have completed the proof for the space sat_i, we continue to do computationally complex operations to go from a_i to a_{i+1}, which implicitly involve *all* assignments. We hence investigated the use of an optimization called *sat-space restriction* (SSR), in which, at the end of the ith iteration, we replace a_i with $\mathbf{ite}(sat_i, 0, a_i)$. SSR thus zeros out the approximations a_i in the space wherein the bound is already established. Our intuition suggests that SSR might be an impactful optimization, but its efficacy is an empirical question. Experiments have confirmed that it is indeed useful. For instance, for single precision RCP with $p = 28$ and using the algorithm of Sect. 4.3, computing the relative error specification took 8,771 and 7,038 seconds when SSR was off and on respectively, giving a 20% runtime improvement.[6]

The SSR optimization also improves the robustness of our symbolic product algorithms in the presence of hardware bugs, which can cause many more iterations of the Π-approximating loop. SSR ensures that the extra iterations only perform symbolic computations within the space of the buggy inputs. As an extreme example, if this space contains a single input vector, then the extra iterations will involve BDDs that are either constants or the minterm corresponding to the buggy input, and hence are immune to blow-up.

An orthogonal optimization to SSR is *truncation* (Tr), which involves truncating a certain number of lower order "bits" from each a_i. For a natural t and symbolic natural a, define $truncL_t(a) = 2^t \lfloor a2^{-t} \rfloor$ and $truncU_t(a) = 2^t(\lfloor a2^{-t} \rfloor + 1)$. Clearly $truncL_t(a) \leq a \leq truncU_t(a)$; and we may safely apply $truncL$ (resp. $truncU$) when $<$-bounding (resp. $>$-bounding). Truncating can be useful, since

---

[6] These results were averaged over 3 runs.

the lower order t BDDs in intermediate computations might introduce significant complexity, while negligibly contributing to the magnitude of the value.

We now present the three algorithms we use for deciding (1).

4.1 Brute Force

This algorithm does full symbolic multiplications, but can apply Tr on intermediate results. In terms of the above characterization, the approximation sequence is degenerate and has just the single element $a_0 = b_n$, where $b_0 = 1$ and $b_{i+1} = b_i' M_i$ and b_i' is either $truncL_t(b_i)$ or $truncU_t(b_i)$ for $<$-bounding or $>$-bounding, respectively. We then simply symbolically evaluate and return $B \Leftrightarrow b_n$. We call this *brute force* since the individual multiplications $b_i' M_i$ are done with an off-the-shelf symbolic multiplication algorithm that is oblivious to the fact that we only wish to *bound* the final product. This is not the case for the next two algorithms, wherein multiplication is aware of B and $\Leftrightarrow$.

4.2 Partial Product Summation

The partial product summation is only used when $n = 2$; we will write x and y for M_1 and M_2, respectively. Let y_i be the the the ith "bit" of the symbolic natural y, i.e. $y = \sum_{i=1}^{r} y_i 2^i$ where r is selected to be large enough to accommodate all values in y's range. The approximations $a_0, a_1, \ldots$ are based on the "partial product" expansion $xy = \sum_{j=0}^{r} y_j x 2^j$. In particular, a_i involves summing the first $i + 1$ terms of this expansion, and replacing the remaining terms by a (symbolically simpler) natural ϕ_i.

$$a_i = \phi_i + \sum_{j=r-i}^{r} y_j x 2^j$$

When $<$-bounding, we simply use $\phi_i = 0$; while for $>$-bounding, $\phi_i = x 2^{r-i}$.[7]

Fig. 1 depicts the algorithmic expression of the $>$-bounding partial product summation. The approximation a_i is computed on line 6; this is separate from acc, which is simply the sum of the first $i + 1$ term of the partial product summation. Line 7 updates the *sat* space, handling the final iteration (wherein $acc = xy$, but is typically not reached) with a special case. Lines 8-10 check for and do early termination, which invariably happens in our case studies that use this algorithm. Lines 11 and 12 are the optional Tr and SSR optimizations, respectively.

4.3 Polynomial Expansion

Though this approach can be generalized for any n, we only use it for RCP and RSQRT, and hence $n \in \{2, 3\}$. Here we explain the $n = 3$ case and denote our three multiplicands by x, y, and z. Let us fix a natural $b \geq 1$, and assume that

---

[7] One can safely tighten this slightly to $x(2^{r-i} - 1)$, but we used $x 2^k$ since its representation as a symbolic natural is not more complex than that of x.

```
1: function PP_BOUND_UPPER(B, x, y)
2:     acc := 0
3:     sat := false
4:     for i := 0 upto r do
5:         acc := acc + ite(y_{r-i}, x2^{r-i}, 0)
6:         a := acc + x2^{r-i}
7:         sat := sat ∨ ite(i = r, B > acc, B ≥ a)
8:         if sat = True then
9:             return True
10:        end if
11:        acc := truncL_t(acc)
12:        acc := ite(sat, 0, acc)
13:    end for
14:    return sat
15: end function
```

Fig. 1. The partial product summation algorithm (>-bounding)

each of x, y, and z is representable using rb bits; i.e. each of the three symbolic naturals is in the range $[0, 2^{rb})$. Let us express x as $x = \sum_{j=0}^{r} x_j d^j$, where $d = 2^b$ and each x_i is a symbolic natural with range $\{0, \ldots, d-1\}$. Note that in the symbolic natural representation discussed in Sect. 2.3, obtaining the x_i's from x is trivial, since each x_i is represented by a "bit slice" of x. We express y and z similarly, respectively yielding $y_r, \ldots, y_0$ and $z_r, \ldots, z_0$. Our approach is based on the identity $xyz = \sum_{h,j,k} x_h y_j z_k d^{h+j+k}$, where the sum ranges over all triples $(h, j, k) \in \{0, \ldots, r\}^3$.

Let $\tau_0, \tau_1, \ldots$ be a total ordering of the triples $\{0, \ldots, r\}^3$, and let $T_i = \{\tau_j : j \leq i\}$. For <-bounds, we form a_i by simply summing the terms corresponding to the triples of T_i, which clearly is a lower bound, since each term is nonnegative.

$$a_i = \sum_{(h,j,k) \in T_i} x_h y_j z_k d^{h+j+k} \leq xyz \qquad (6)$$

For >-bounds, the analogous a_i is somewhat more involved:

$$a_i = \left(d^{r+1} - 1\right)^3 - \sum_{(h,j,k) \in T_i} \left((d-1)^3 - x_h y_j z_k\right) d^{h+j+k} \qquad (7)$$

$$\geq \left(d^{r+1} - 1\right)^3 - \sum_{h,j,k} \left((d-1)^3 - x_h y_j z_k\right) d^{h+j+k}$$

$$= \sum_{h,j,k} (d-1)^3 d^{h+j+k} - \sum_{h,j,k} \left((d-1)^3 - x_h y_j z_k\right) d^{h+j+k}$$

$$= \sum_{h,j,k} \left((d-1)^3 - (d-1)^3 + x_h y_j z_k\right) d^{h+j+k}$$

$$= xyz$$

The natural choice of $\tau_0, \tau_1, \ldots$ (for either direction of bounding) is one that orders terms with higher powers of d first. In other words, whenever $h + j + k >$

$h' + j' + k'$, the triple (h, j, k) comes before (h', j', k') and triples with equal sums are ordered arbitrarily. Fig 2 gives the $<$-bounding variant of the algorithm; $>$-bounding is similar, but uses (7) instead of (6). In particular, line 3 is replaced with $a := (d^{r+1} - 1)^3$, and line 6 is replaced with $a := a - ((d-1)^3 - x_h y_j z_k) d^\sigma$; lines 7 and 11 are modified in the obvious way. Similar to Fig. 1, lines 11 and 12 are the optional optimizations Tr and SSR, respectively.

```
 1: function POLY_EXPANSION_BOUND_LOWER(B, x, y, z)
 2:     sat := False
 3:     a := 0
 4:     for σ := 3r downto 0 do
 5:         for all (h, j, k) ∈ ℕ³ such that h + j + k = σ do
 6:             a := a + x_h y_j z_k d^σ
 7:             sat := sat ∨ B < a
 8:             if sat = True then
 9:                 return True
10:             end if
11:             a := truncL_t(a)
12:             a := ite(sat, 0, a)
13:         end for
14:     end for
15:     return sat
16: end function
```

Fig. 2. The polynomial expansion algorithm ($<$-bounding)

5   Case Studies

Our method has been implemented in reFLect, the lazy functional language used to program Intel's *Forte* tool suite [14], and sits as a specification layer on top of the *Relational STE* [10] symbolic simulator. The design under verification was from a next-generation many-core CPU under development at Intel®. The RCP and RSQRT instructions analyzed in the paper are used as initial approximations in the implementation of division and squareroot computations; it is therefore crucial that they satisfy the specified relative error for the final result to be correct. Each core on the CPU is equipped with a SIMD unit that implements a fused-multiply-add (FMA) datapath, which computes $x + yz$ with only a single rounding for floats x, y, and z, as well as special-purpose hardware for our three approximate instruction families. The instruction classes RCP and RSQRT have instances for the three relative errors 2^{-11}, 2^{-14} and 2^{-28}; most of which are supported for both single precision (SP) and double-precision (DP) floats, while EXP2 has only relative error 2^{-23}, but has an instance that produce each of SP and DP results. The input for the SP (resp. DP) EXP2 flavor is a fixed-point integer with precision 24 and an 8-bit (resp. 11-bit) integer part, i.e. they fall in the range $[-2^7, 2^7)$ (resp. $[-2^{10}, 2^{10})$). All instructions in our three classes are implemented using a similar method. Roughly, a selection of bits from the input

Table 1. Verification Results

Op.	Tot. Time	Spec. Time.	Mem.	Alg.	Case split
RCP 11S	58	3	1.8	P	No
RCP 14S	103	49	1.8	P	No
RCP 14D	135	51	1.8	P	No
RCP 28S	14,972	7,038	17.4	E(4,0)	No
RCP 28D	2.7 days	1.3 days	3.6	E(5,0)	512-way
RSQRT 11S	68	4	1.8	P	No
RSQRT 14S	124	69	1.8	P	No
RSQRT 14D	139	55	1.8	P	No
RSQRT 28S	18,301	13,173	6.0	E(5,0)	16-way
RSQRT 28D	22.7 days	16.7 days	9.0	E(5,110)	1,024-way
EXP2 23S	72,759	63,428	2.9	B(30)	128-way
EXP2 23D	59,706	51,152	2.8	B(30)	128-way

are used to map into a instruction-specific ROM to obtain coefficients to use in a quadratic approximation. The FMA hardware is then used to perform the operations (multiplication, addition, normalization and rounding) necessary for evaluating the quadratic formula into a floating point result.

Table 1 gives the verification results.[8] The *Op* column gives the instruction type, along with the value of p and an indication of single precision (S) or double precision (P) floats.[9] The *Tot Time* column gives the total (wall clock) run time for the proof; the units are seconds except for the entries measured in days. *Spec Time* is the time for just computing the relative error specification; the time for symbolic simulation is not included.[10] *Mem* is the maximum virtual memory, in GB, the Forte process used during execution. *Alg* indicated which of the decision procedures from Sect. 4 was used: $B(t)$ is the brute force algorithm from Sect. 4.1 with parameter t, P is the "partial product" approach from Sect. 4.2 with SSR enabled, while $E(r,t)$ is the algorithm of Sect. 4.3 with SSR and parameters r and t. Some instructions require *case splitting* [1], which partitions the input space into a number of cases; the *Case split* column indicates if this was used, and if so how many cases. The case splits were obvious and involved holding constant some of the input bits used to index into the coefficient ROMs in the circuit. It is important to note that the multi-day runs were in reality performed by grouping the cases into 10 buckets and running them on different machines

---

[8] All runs used the BDD variable order of sign, exponent, and then mantissa source variables.

[9] The instructions RCP28S and RSQRT28S are oddities since the minimum relative error allowed by the single precision format is 2^{-23}. The specification says to do the computation in the double precision domain, and then round to the nearest single precision. We were able to verify that the relative error bound was 2^{-22} and 2^{-23}, respectively, for these instructions.

[10] The time accounted to symbolic simulation also involves a non-negligible component for a cone-of-influence reduction.

concurrently—case splits are embarrassingly parallelizable—so the real time used for even RSQRT 28D was just over 2 days.

The 2^{-14} flavors of RCP and RSQRT are interesting in that, unlike the others, they support *denormal* inputs and outputs. Denormal floats are very small values that have the minimum possible exponent, and have $m(x) < 2^{\ell}$. Though our theory assumes normal floats, it is still applicable to denormals since we have not assumed any lower bound on the exponent. Our specification code simply "normalizes" the float before doing the relative error check, this means that we map the denormal float (s, e, m) to $(s, e - j, m2^j)$, where $j \in \mathbb{N}$ is selected so that $2^{\ell} \le m2^j < 2^{\ell+1}$. This operation clearly preserves the value represented by the float. This step did not introduce any significant verification complexity.

6   Summary

This paper has presented a novel technique for verifying relative error specifications using symbolic simulation, demonstrated on three operations taken from an industrial case study. For each of the three operations, the relative error specification is reduced to inequalities between products of integers, which is then symbolically evaluated using a custom procedure to avoid BDD blow-up. In addition to verifying an industry hardware design, this technique delivered additional benefits when applied in an industrial setting. We found that the ability of symbolic simulation to deliver counter-examples greatly improved communication between the verification and design teams, and as a consequence the debugging cycle was shortened.

7   Related Work

The most relevant existing work is a paper by Sawada [13] which presents a technique for verifying the relative error of approximate RCP and RSQRT instructions. The technique relies on the manual construction of a high level model of the hardware implementation, expressed in terms of bounded polynomial functions. The high level model is proved to satisfy the relative error bounds by using custom proof strategies in the ACL2 theorem prover. The advantage of this approach is that it mechanizes the high level reasoning needed to reduce the relative error specification to a form suitable for automatic analysis. Our approach currently relies on pen-and-paper meta-theorems to support this reduction, although we are confident they could be mechanized using the Goaled theorem prover integrated with Forte [10]. However, the advantage of our approach is that it works directly on the register transfer level (RTL)—there is no need to construct a high level model of its behaviour—and it can also be applied to verify the relative error bounds of EXP2. Sawada's paper reports results for precisions only up to $p = 14$, at which level a relative error verification of reciprocal required 13,953 seconds on a 2.93GHz processor. Our verification of RCP14 for DP float inputs required only 133 seconds (on a 3.07 GHz machine).

Another related work is a paper by Harrison [6] presenting a verification of relative error bounds for trigonometric functions implemented using software floating point operations. Although this was an interactive proof carried out using the HOL Light theorem prover, it made essential use of a custom automatic proof tactic for proving that the operations implementing the range reduction step are sufficiently accurate for every possible floating point input. This is similar to our relative error verification, although the technique presented in the paper of encoding a tailored real analysis argument as an automatic proof tactic is very different from our technique of reducing floating point numbers to integers followed by symbolic simulation using BDDs.

Our verification approach relies on performing symbolic arithmetic operations on integers represented by lists of BDDs, using a technique introduced by Minato and Somenzi [9]. The chief difficulty of performing symbolic arithmetic in this way is that the representing BDDs tend to blow up in size. For example, it was shown by Bryant [3] that any BDD representing the middle bit of a product of two symbolic integers is necessarily exponential in the number of bits of the multiplicands (regardless of the ordering of the variables). Thatchachar [18] also proves exponential bounds for RCP and square root (but does not cover RSQRT) for a general class of representations that includes BDDs. Hence a possible alternative approach that computes the "exact" RCP result and then shows that the hardware output is within the relative error would be infeasible, and our more sophisticated methods are justified.

Acknowledgement. We extend gratitude to Professor Alan Hu for agreeing to present this paper on our behalf.

References

1. Aagaard, M.D., Jones, R.B., Seger, C.-J.H.: Formal verification using parametric representations of Boolean constraints. In: Design Automation Conference (DAC 1999) (July 1999)
2. Bryant, R.E.: Graph-based algorithms for boolean function manipulation. IEEE Transactions on Computers C-35(8), 677–691 (1986)
3. Bryant, R.E.: On the complexity of VLSI implementations and graph representations of Boolean functions with application to integer multiplication. IEEE Trans. Comput. 40(2), 205–213 (1991)
4. Darringer, J.A.: The application of program verification techniques to hardware verification. In: Proceedings of the 16th Design Automation Conference, DAC 1979, Piscataway, NJ, USA, pp. 375–381. IEEE Press (1979)
5. Goldberg, D.: What every computer scientist should know about floating point arithmetic. ACM Computing Surveys 23(1), 5–48 (1991)
6. Harrison, J.V.: Formal verification of floating point trigonometric functions. In: Johnson, S.D., Hunt Jr., W.A. (eds.) FMCAD 2000. LNCS, vol. 1954, pp. 217–233. Springer, Heidelberg (2000)
7. IEEE. Standard for binary floating-point arithmetic. ANSI/IEEE Standard 754-1985. The Institute of Electrical and Electronic Engineers, Inc., 345 East 47th Street, New York, NY 10017, USA (1985)

8. Kaivola, R., Ghughal, R., Narasimhan, N., Telfer, A., Whittemore, J., Pandav, S., Slobodová, A., Taylor, C., Frolov, V., Reeber, E., Naik, A.: Replacing testing with formal verification in intel® core™ i7 processor execution engine validation. In: Bouajjani, A., Maler, O. (eds.) CAV 2009. LNCS, vol. 5643, pp. 414–429. Springer, Heidelberg (2009)

9. Minato, S.-I., Somenzi, F.: Arithmetic Boolean expression manipulator using BDDs. Formal Methods in System Design 10(2-3), 221–242 (1997)

10. O'Leary, J., Kaivola, R., Melham, T.: Relational STE and theorem proving for formal verification of industrial circuit designs. In: Jobstmann, B., Ray, S. (eds.) Formal Methods in Computer-Aided Design (FMCAD 2013), pp. 97–104. IEEE (October 2013)

11. Parks, M.: Number-theoretic test generation for directed rounding. IEEE Trans. Comput. 49(7), 651–658 (2000)

12. Paruthi, V.: Large-scale application of formal verification: From fiction to fact. In: Formal Methods in Computer-Aided Design (FMCAD 2010), pp. 175–180 (2010)

13. Sawada, J.: Automatic verification of estimate functions with polynomials of bounded functions. In: Formal Methods in Computer-Aided Design (FMCAD 2010), pp. 151–158 (2010)

14. Seger, C.J., Jones, R.B., O'Leary, J.W., Melham, T., Aagaard, M.D., Barrett, C., Syme, D.: An industrially effective environment for formal hardware verification. Trans. Comp.-Aided Des. Integ. Cir. Sys. 24(9), 1381–1405 (2006)

15. Seger, C.-J.H., Bryant, R.E.: Formal verification by symbolic evaluation of partially-ordered trajectories. Formal Methods in System Design 6(2), 147–189 (1995)

16. Slobodová, A., Davis, J., Swords, S., Hunt, W.A.: A flexible formal verification framework for industrial scale validation. In: Singh, S., Jobstmann, B., Kishinevsky, M., Brandt, J. (eds.) MEMOCODE, pp. 89–97. IEEE (2011)

17. Stewart, D.: Formal for everyone - Challenges in achievable multi-core design and verification. In: Cabodi, G., Singh, S. (eds.) Formal Methods in Computer-Aided Design (FMCAD 2012), p. 186. IEEE (October 2012), http://www.cs.utexas.edu/ hunt/FMCAD/FMCAD12/ FormalForEveryone_DStewart _ARM.pdf

18. Thathachar, J.: On the limitations of ordered representations of functions. In: Vardi, M.Y. (ed.) CAV 1998. LNCS, vol. 1427, pp. 232–243. Springer, Heidelberg (1998)

Regression Test Selection
for Distributed Software Histories

Milos Gligoric[1], Rupak Majumdar[2], Rohan Sharma[1], Lamyaa Eloussi[1],
and Darko Marinov[1]

[1] University of Illinois at Urbana-Champaign, USA
[2] Max Planck Institute for Software Systems, Germany
{gliga,sharma27,eloussi2,marinov}@illinois.edu, rupak@mpi-sws.org

Abstract. Regression test selection analyzes incremental changes to a
codebase and chooses to run only those tests whose behavior may be
affected by the latest changes in the code. By focusing on a small subset
of all the tests, the testing process runs faster and can be more tightly
integrated into the development process. Existing techniques for regression test selection consider two versions of the code at a time, effectively
assuming a development process where changes to the code occur in a
linear sequence.

Modern development processes that use *distributed* version-control
systems are more complex. Software version histories are generally modeled as directed graphs; in addition to version changes occurring linearly, multiple versions can be related by other commands, e.g., branch,
merge, rebase, cherry-pick, revert, etc. This paper describes a regression
test-selection technique for software developed using modern distributed
version-control systems. By modeling different branch or merge commands directly in our technique, it computes safe test sets that can be
substantially smaller than applying previous techniques to a linearization
of the software history.

We evaluate our technique on software histories of several large open-
source projects. The results are encouraging: our technique obtained an
average of 10.89× reduction in the number of tests over an existing technique while still selecting all tests whose behavior may differ.

1 Introduction

Regression testing [22, 36, 37] reruns previously completed tests whenever a
change is made to a piece of software, to ensure that the change has not affected the outcome of those tests. Regression testing can be expensive if the test
suite is large and tests take a long time to run. Therefore, substantial research
has focused on speeding up regression testing by selecting an adequate subset of
tests (with several extensive surveys [5,11,37] on the topic). These test-selection
techniques are usually based on computing changes between two program versions[1], the "old" and the "new" versions, and using a fast syntactic algorithm to

---

[1] We use the term "version" for what version-control systems often call "revision".

A. Biere and R. Bloem (Eds.): CAV 2014, LNCS 8559, pp. 293–309, 2014.
© Springer International Publishing Switzerland 2014

identify the subset of tests whose behavior *may* change between the old and new versions. Empirically, these techniques are effective in reducing the set of tests to be run and are widely used in companies such as Google [16] and Microsoft [34].

Existing test-selection techniques view software history as a linear sequence of commits to a centralized version-control system (such as CVS or SVN). However, modern software development processes that use distributed version-control systems (DVCSs) do not match this simplistic view. Software version histories that use DVCSs, such as Git and Mercurial, are complex graphs of branches, merges, and rebases of the code that mirror more complex sharing patterns between developers. For example, Figure 1 shows a part of the Linux Kernel Git repository [25]: this software history is a complex graph, with multiple branches being merged. (There is a case in Linux where 30 branches are merged at once.) We empirically find that such complexities are not isolated to the Linux kernel development: most open-source codebases perform frequent merges. Section 4 reports detailed results for a number of open-source projects; we find about third of the commits to be merge-related.

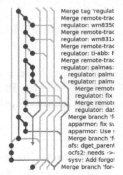

Fig. 1. Linux history

In this paper, we consider the problem of test selection for codebases that use DVCS commands. One possible baseline approach is to apply traditional test selection by picking an arbitrary linearization of the history. While this technique is *safe*, i.e., it does not miss tests whose outcome may be affected by the change, we empirically demonstrate that this approach can be very *imprecise*, i.e., it can select many tests whose outcome cannot be affected by the change. Instead, we propose a test-selection technique that explicitly takes into account the history graph of software versions. We have implemented our technique and show, through an evaluation on several open-source code repositories, that our technique selects on average an order of magnitude fewer tests than the baseline technique while still retaining safety.

We evaluate our technique both on real open-source code repositories that use DVCS and on distributed repositories that we systematically generate from projects that use a linear sequence of commits. We compare several options for selecting tests at each merge version of such repositories. These options have different trade-offs in terms of cost (how many traditional test selections need to be performed to compute the selected tests) and precision (how many tests are selected to be run, while maintaining safety). In particular, we describe a fast test-selection technique for code merges that does not require *any* test selection computation, but still achieves a reduction of 10.89× better than a baseline technique that performs one traditional test selection for a merge point, and only 2.78× worse than an expensive technique that performs one traditional test selection for each branch being merged.

The accompanying technical report [15] provides additional results, visualizations, and proofs.

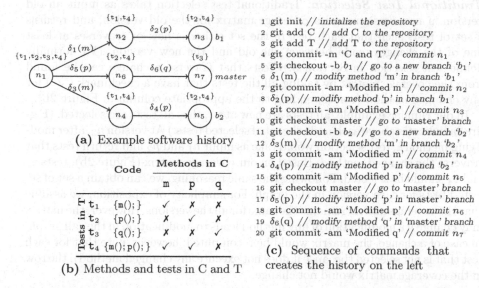

(a) Example software history

Code	Methods in C		
	m	p	q
t_1 {m();}	✓	✗	✗
t_2 {p();}	✗	✓	✗
t_3 {q();}	✗	✗	✓
t_4 {m();p();}	✓	✓	✗

(b) Methods and tests in C and T

1 git init // *initialize the repository*
2 git add C // *add C to the repository*
3 git add T // *add T to the repository*
4 git commit -m 'C and T' // *commit n_1*
5 git checkout -b b_1 // *go to a new branch 'b_1'*
6 δ_1(m) // *modify method 'm' in branch 'b_1'*
7 git commit -am 'Modified m' // *commit n_2*
8 δ_2(p) // *modify method 'p' in branch 'b_1'*
9 git commit -am 'Modified p' // *commit n_3*
10 git checkout master // *go to 'master' branch*
11 git checkout -b b_2 // *go to a new branch 'b_2'*
12 δ_3(m) // *modify method 'm' in branch 'b_2'*
13 git commit -am 'Modified m' // *commit n_4*
14 δ_4(p) // *modify method 'p' in branch 'b_2'*
15 git commit -am 'Modified p' // *commit n_5*
16 git checkout master // *go to 'master' branch*
17 δ_5(p) // *modify method 'p' in 'master' branch*
18 git commit -am 'Modified p' // *commit n_6*
19 δ_6(q) // *modify method 'q' in 'master' branch*
20 git commit -am 'Modified q' // *commit n_7*

(c) Sequence of commands that creates the history on the left

Fig. 2. Example of a software history and one potential sequence of changes and commands to create this history

2   Overview

We motivate regression test selection through an example session using Git [14], a popular DVCS.

Distributed Software Histories. Figure 2a visualizes a version history obtained by performing the sequence of Git commands from Figure 2c. First, we initialize the software history[2], add two files and make a commit n_1 with these files (lines 1-4). Figure 2b shows the abstract representation of the committed files C and T; file C (*"Code"*) defines three methods m, p, and q that are checked by tests t_1, t_2, t_3, and t_4 defined in file T (*"Test"*). Second, we create a new branch b_1 (line 5), make and commit changes to m (lines 6–7) and p (lines 8–9). Third, we create another branch b_2 (lines 10–11) and perform a similar sequence of commands as on the first branch (lines 12–15). Finally, we switch to the *master* branch (line 16) and perform a similar sequence of commands (lines 17–20). Although the sequence of commands is similar for each branch, we assume non-conflicting changes on different branches.

Figure 2b further shows which test executes which method; we will assume that we have available such a *coverage matrix* for every version in the software history. When a method changes, the tests that executed that method are called *modification-traversing* tests. We focus on modifications at a method level for simplicity; one can track coverage of other program elements as well [37].

---

[2] git init creates the initial node not shown in Figure 2a.

Traditional Test Selection. Traditional test selection takes as input an old version, a new version, and a coverage matrix for the old version, and returns a set of tests such that each test in the set either is new or traverses at least one of the changes made between the old and the new version. (We formally define test selection in Section 3.) Tests that traverse a change can be found from the coverage matrix by taking all the tests that have a checkmark ('✓') for any changed method (corresponding to the appropriate column in Figure 2b).

In our running example, all tests are new at n_1, thus all tests are selected. (Figure 2a indicates above each node the set of selected tests.) At version n_2, after modifying method m, test selection would take as input n_1 and n_2 and return tests that traverse the changed method. Based on our coverage matrix (Figure 2b), tests t_1 and t_4 should be selected. Following the same reasoning, we can obtain a set of selected tests for each version in the graph. For simplicity of exposition, we assume that the coverage matrix remains the same for all the versions. However, the matrix may change if a modification of any method leads to modification in the call graph. In case of a change, the matrix would be recomputed; however, note that for each test that is not selected (because it does not execute any changed method), the row in the coverage matrix would not change.

Test Selection for Distributed Software Histories. Test selection for distributed software histories has not been studied previously. We illustrate what the traditional test selection would select when a software history (Figure 2a) is extended by executing some of the commands available in DVCSs. Specifically, we show that a naive application of the traditional test selection leads to safe but imprecise results (i.e., selects too much), or requires several runs of traditional test-selection techniques, which introduces additional overhead and therefore reduces the benefits of test selection. We consider three commands: *merge*, *cherry-pick*, and *revert*.

Command: Merge. The merge command joins two or more development branches together. A merge without conflicts and any additional edits is called *auto-merge* and is the most common case in practice. Auto-merge has a property that the changes between the merge point and its parents are a subset of the changes between the lowest common ancestors [3,10] of the parents and the parents; we exploit this property in our technique and discuss it further in Section 3. If we execute `git merge b₁ b₂` after the sequence shown in Figure 2c, while we are still on the *master* branch, we will merge branches b_1 and b_2 into a new version n_8 on the *master* branch; this version n_8 will have three parents: n_3, n_5, and n_7. The question is what tests to select to run at version n_8.

We propose multiple options (and Section 4 summarizes how to automatically choose between these options). First, we can use traditional test selection between the immediate dominator [1] of the new version (n_1) and the new version (n_8). In our example, the changes between these two versions modify all the methods, so test selection would select all four tests. The advantage of this option is that it runs traditional test selection only once, but there can be many changes, and therefore many tests are selected. Second, we can run the traditional test selection between the new version and each of its parents and take the intersection of the selected tests. In our example, we would run the traditional test selection between the following pairs: (n_3, n_8), (n_5, n_8), (n_7, n_8); the results for each pair would be: $\{t_1, t_2, t_3, t_4\}$, $\{t_1, t_2, t_3, t_4\}$, and $\{t_1, t_2, t_4\}$, respectively. The intersection of these sets gives the final result: $\{t_1, t_2, t_4\}$. The intuition is that the tests not in the intersection, $\{t_3\}$, need not be run because their result for the new version, n_8, can be copied from at least one parent, in this case from n_7. Although the second option selects fewer tests, it requires running traditional test selection three times, which can lead to significant overhead. Third, we can collect tests that were modification-traversing on at least two branches (from the branching version at n_1 to the parents that get merged). In our example, we would select $\{t_1, t_2, t_4\}$. As opposed to previous options, this option requires *zero runs* of the traditional test-selection techniques. However, this option is only safe for *auto merge* and requires that the test selection results be stored for previous versions.

Command: Cherry-Pick. Cherry-pick copies the changes introduced by some existing commit. If we execute `git cherry-pick n`$_2$ after the sequence shown in Figure 2c, we will apply changes (δ_1) made between versions n_1 and n_2 on top of version n_7 in *master* branch (which is extended with a new version n_8). Naively applying the traditional test selection on versions n_7 and n_8 would select the same tests as at version n_2. However, test t_1 does not need to be selected at n_8, as this test is not affected by changes on the *master* branch (on which the cherry-picked commit is applied). Therefore, the outcome of t_1 at n_8 will be the same as at n_2.

Command: Revert. This command reverts some existing commits. If we execute `git revert n`$_6$ after the sequence shown in Figure 2c, we will revert changes made between versions n_1 and n_6. The *master* branch will be extended with a new version n_8. Naively applying traditional test-selection techniques between versions n_7 and n_8 would select the same set of tests as at version n_6. Instead, if we consider the revert command being executed and changes being made, we can reuse the results of a test from version n_1 as long as the test is not modification-traversing for any other change after the version being reverted (n_6). In our example, we can see that the result of all tests can be reused, and therefore no test has to be selected.

To conclude, naively applying traditional test selection may lead to imprecise results and/or spend too much time on analysis. We believe that our technique, which reasons about the history and commands being executed, leads to a good balance between reduction (in terms of the number of tests being executed) and time spent on analysis.

3 Test Selection Technique

3.1 Modeling Distributed Software Histories

We model a distributed software history as a directed acyclic graph $G = \langle N, E \rangle$ with a unique root $n_0 \in N$ corresponding to the initial version. Each node $n \in N$

corresponds to a version, and each edge corresponds to the parent-child relation among versions. Each node is created by applying one of the DVCS commands to a set of parent nodes; we assume the command is known. (While the command that creates a node is definitely known at the point of creation, it is not usually kept in the DVCS and cannot always be uniquely determined from the history.) The functions $\mathsf{pred}(n) = \{n' \in N \mid \langle n', n \rangle \in E\}$ and $\mathsf{succ}(n) = \{n' \in N \mid \langle n, n' \rangle \in E\}$ denote the set of parents and children of version n, respectively. We write $n \preceq n'$ if there exists a directed path from n to n' or the two nodes are the same. We write $n \preceq^* n'$ to denote the set of all nodes between versions n and n': $n \preceq^* n' = \{n'' \mid n \preceq n'' \text{ and } n'' \preceq n'\}$. Similarly, we write $n \preceq^e n'$ to denote the set of all edges between versions n and n': $n \preceq^e n' = \{\langle n'', n''' \rangle \in E \mid n'', n''' \in n \preceq^* n'\}$. The function $\mathsf{sdom}(n) = \{n' \mid n_0 \preceq^e n' \cup n' \preceq^e n = n_0 \preceq^e n \text{ and } n \neq n'\}$ denotes the set of nodes that strictly dominate n. For $n \neq n_0$, the function $\mathsf{imd}(n)$ denotes the unique immediate dominator [1] of n, i.e., $\mathsf{imd}(n) = n'$ such that $n' \in \mathsf{sdom}(n)$ and $\nexists n'' \in \mathsf{sdom}(n)$ such that $n' \in \mathsf{sdom}(n'')$. The function $\mathsf{dom}(n, n')$ denotes the lowest common dominator of n and n', i.e., for a version n'' such that $\mathsf{pred}(n'') \supseteq \{n, n'\}$, $\mathsf{dom}(n, n') = \mathsf{imd}(n'')$. The function $\mathsf{lca}(n, n')$ denotes the lowest common ancestors [3,9,10] (also known as "merge-bases" or "best common ancestors" in Git terminology [13,20]) for two versions, i.e., $\mathsf{lca}(n, n') = \{n'' \mid n'' \preceq n \text{ and } n'' \preceq n' \text{ and } \nexists n''' \neq n'' \text{ such that } n''' \preceq n \text{ and } n''' \preceq n' \text{ and } n'' \preceq n'''\}$. (We illustrate the difference between lca and dom in the technical report [15].) The following property holds for all nodes:

$$\mathsf{dom}(n, n') \preceq \mathsf{lca}(n, n') \tag{1}$$

3.2   Test Selection for Two Versions

We formalize test selection following earlier work in the area [32,37] and also model changes and modification-traversing tests. This section focuses on test selection between *two* software versions. Next sections present our technique for distributed software histories.

Let G be a distributed software history. For a version n, let $\mathcal{A}(n)$ denote the set of tests *available* at the version n. Let n and n' be two versions such that $n \preceq n'$. A *test selection* technique takes as input the versions n and n' and returns a subset $\mathcal{S}_{sel}(n, n')$ of $\mathcal{A}(n')$. Note that new tests, i.e, $\mathcal{A}(n') \setminus \mathcal{A}(n)$ are always in $\mathcal{S}_{sel}(n, n')$. A test-selection technique is *safe* [31] if every test in $\mathcal{A}(n') \setminus \mathcal{S}_{sel}(n, n')$ has the same outcome when run on the versions n and n'.

A trivially safe test-selection technique returns $\mathcal{A}(n')$. However, we are interested in selection techniques that select as small a subset as possible. One way to obtain a minimal set is to run each test in $\mathcal{A}(n')$ on the two versions and keep those that have different outcomes. However, the purpose of the test selection technique is to be more efficient than running all tests. A compromise between minimality and efficiency is provided by the notion of *modification-traversing* tests [32], which syntactically approximate the set of tests that may have a different outcome. Let $\partial(n, n')$ be the set of static code changes between versions n and n' (which need not be parent-child versions). Various techniques compute these changes at various levels of granularity (e.g., basic blocks, statements, methods, or other program elements). By extension, we denote the set of changes on all edges from n to n' as

$$\partial^{\star}(n, n') = \bigcup_{\langle n'', n''' \rangle \in n \preceq^e n'} \partial(n'', n''')$$

We use the following property:

$$\partial(n, n') \subseteq \partial^{\star}(n, n') \tag{2}$$

It is not an equality because some changes can be reverted on a path from n to n', e.g., consider a graph with three versions n_1, n_2, and n_3, where all the changes between n_1 and n_2 are reverted between n_2 and n_3: the code at n_3 is exactly the same as the code at n_1, and therefore $\partial(n_1, n_3) = \{\}$.

A test is called *modification-traversing* if its execution on n executes any code element that is modified in n'. (Note that "modified" includes all the cases where the existing elements from n are *changed or removed* in n' or where new elements are *added* in n'.) We define a predicate $\varsigma(t, \partial)$ that holds if the test t is modification-traversing for any change in the given set of changes ∂. The predicate can be computed by tracking code paths during a test run and intersecting covered program elements with a syntactic difference between the two versions. We define a function $\mathsf{mt}(\mathcal{T}, \partial) = \{t \in \mathcal{T} \mid \varsigma(t, \partial)\}$ that returns every test from the set of tests $\mathcal{T}$ that is modification-traversing for any change in the set of changes ∂. Two properties that we will need later are that mt distributes over changes:

$$\mathsf{mt}(\mathcal{T}, \partial_1 \cup \partial_1) = \mathsf{mt}(\mathcal{T}, \partial_1) \cup \mathsf{mt}(\mathcal{T}, \partial_2) \tag{3}$$

and thus mt is monotonic with respect to the set of changes:

$$\partial \subseteq \partial' \text{ implies } \mathsf{mt}(\mathcal{T}, \partial) \subseteq \mathsf{mt}(\mathcal{T}, \partial') \tag{4}$$

Traditional test selection selects all modification-traversing tests from the old version that remain in the new version and the new tests from the new version:

$$\mathsf{tts}(n, n') = \mathsf{mt}(\mathcal{A}(n) \cap \mathcal{A}(n'), \partial(n, n')) \cup (\mathcal{A}(n') \setminus \mathcal{A}(n)) \tag{5}$$

As $\mathsf{pred}(n')$ is often a singleton $\{n\}$, we also write $\mathsf{tts}(\{n\}, n') = \mathsf{tts}(n, n')$.

Under the assumption that tests execute deterministically, test selection based on modification-traversing tests is provably safe [32, 33].

3.3 Test Selection for Distributed Software Histories

Our technique for test selection takes as inputs (1) the software history $G = \langle N, E \rangle$ optionally annotated with tests selected at each version, (2) a specific version $h \in N$ that represents the latest version (which is usually called HEAD in DVCS), and (3) optionally the DVCS command used to create the version h. It produces as output a set of selected tests $\mathcal{S}_{sel}(h)$ at the given software version.

We define our technique and prove that it guarantees safe test selection.

Command: Commit. The h version has one parent, and the changes between the parent and h can be arbitrary, with no special knowledge of how they were created.

The set of selected tests can be computed by applying the traditional test selection between the h version and its parent:

$$S_{commit}(h) = \text{tts}(\text{pred}(h), h) \tag{6}$$

Command: Merge. *Merge* joins two or more versions and extends the history with a new version that becomes h. We propose two options to compute the set of selected tests at h: the first is fast but possibly imprecise, the second is slower but more precise.

Option 1: This option performs the traditional test selection between the immediate dominator of h and h itself:

$$S_{merge}^1(h) = \text{tts}(\text{imd}(h), h) \tag{7}$$

This option is fast: it computes only one traditional test selection, even if the merge has many parents. However, the number of modifications between the two versions being compared can be large, leading to many tests being selected unnecessarily. Our empirical evaluation in Section 4 shows that this option indeed selects too many tests, discouraging the straightforward use of this option.

Option 2: This option performs one traditional test selection between each parent of the merged version and the merged version h itself, and then intersects the resulting sets:

$$S_{merge}^k(h) = \bigcap_{n \in \text{pred}(h)} \text{tts}(n, h) \tag{8}$$

This option can be more precise, selecting substantially fewer tests. However, it has to run k traditional test selections for k parents.

Theorem 1. *$S_{merge}^1(h)$ and $S_{merge}^k(h)$ are safe for every merge version h.*

Command: Automerge. A common special case of *merge* is *auto merge*, where versions are merged automatically without any manual changes to resolve conflicts. (Using the existing DVCS commands can quickly check if a merge is an auto merge.) Empirically (see Figure 3), auto merge is very common: on average over 90% of versions with more than one parent are auto merges.

The key property of auto merge is that the merged code version has a union of all code changes from all branches but has only those changes (i.e., no other manual changes). Formally, given k parents $p_1, p_2, \ldots p_k$ that get merged into a new version h, the changes from each parent p to the merged version h reflect the changes on all the branches for different parents:

$$\partial(p, h) = \bigcup_{p' \in \text{pred}(h), p' \neq p} \bigcup_{l \in \text{lca}(p, p')} \partial(l, p') \tag{9}$$

The formula uses lca because of the way Git auto merges branches [13, 20].

For auto merge, we give a test-selection technique, S^0_{merge}, that is based entirely on the software history up to the parents being merged and does not require running any traditional test selection between pairs of code versions at the point of merge (although it assumes that test selection was performed on the versions up to the parents of the merge). The set of selected tests consists of (1) existing tests (from the lowest common dominator of two (different) parents of h) affected by changes on at least two different branches being merged (because the interplay of the changes from various branches can flip the test outcome):

$$S_{aff}(h) = \bigcup_{p,p' \in \mathsf{pred}(h), p \neq p', d = \mathsf{dom}(p,p')} (\bigcup_{n \in d \preceq^* p \backslash \{d\}} S_{sel}(n)) \cap (\bigcup_{n \in d \preceq^* p' \backslash \{d\}} S_{sel}(n)) \tag{10}$$

and (2) new tests available at the merge point but not available on all branches:

$$S_{new}(h) = \mathcal{A}(h) \backslash \bigcap_{p'' \in \mathsf{pred}(h)} \mathcal{A}(p'') \tag{11}$$

Finally, $S^0_{merge}(h) = S_{aff}(h) \cup S_{new}(h)$. The advantage of this option is that it runs *zero* traditional test selections. One disadvantage is that it could select more tests than S^k_{merge}. Another disadvantage is that it requires storing tests selected at each version.

Theorem 2. $S^0_{merge}(h)$ *is safe for every* auto *merge version* h.

Intuitively, S^0_{merge} is safe because a test that is affected on only one branch need not be rerun at the merge point: it has the same result at that point as on that one branch. The proof is in the technical report [15].

Command: Cherry-Pick. *Cherry-pick* reapplies the changes that were performed between a commit n_{cp} and one of its parents $n'_{cp} \in \mathsf{pred}(n_{cp})$ (the parent can be implicit for non-merge n_{cp}), and extends the software history (on the branch where the command is applied) with a new version h. We propose two options to determine the set of selected tests at h. The first option uses the general selection for a commit (the traditional test selection between the current node and its parent): $S^1_{cherry}(h) = \mathsf{tts}(\mathsf{pred}(h), h)$.

The second option, called S^0_{cherry}, does not require running traditional test selection, but is safe only for *auto cherry-pick*. This option selects each test that satisfies one of the following three conditions: (1) tests selected between n'_{cp} and n_{cp} as well as between the point p at which cherry-pick is applied ($\{p\} = \mathsf{pred}(h)$) and $d = \mathsf{dom}(p, n'_{cp})$, (2) tests selected between n'_{cp} and n_{cp} and also selected before n'_{cp} up to d, and (3) new tests at n_{cp}.

$$S^0_{cherry}(h) = (S_{sel}(n'_{cp}, n_{cp}) \cap ((\cup_{n \in d \preceq^* p \backslash \{d\}} S_{sel}(n)) \cup (\cup_{n \in d \preceq^* n'_{cp} \backslash \{d\}} S_{sel}(n))))$$
$$\cup (\mathcal{A}(n_{cp}) \backslash \mathcal{A}(n'_{cp})) \tag{12}$$

The intuition for (1) is that the combination of changes that affected tests on both branches, from d to p and from d to n'_{cp}, may lead to different test outcomes. The intuition for (2) is that changes before n_{cp} may not exist in the branch on which the cherry-pick is applied and so the outcome of these tests may change. If neither (1) nor (2) hold, the test result can be copied from n_{cp} itself. The formula for cherry pick is similar to that for auto merge but applies to only one commit being cherry picked rather than to an entire branch being merged.

Command: Revert. *Revert* computes inverse changes of some existing commit n_{re} and extends the software history by applying those inverse changes to create a new version that becomes h. (Reverting a merge creates additional issues that we do not handle specially: one can always run the traditional test selection.) Similar to cherry-pick, we propose two options to determine the set of selected tests. The first option is a naive application of the traditional test selection between h and its parent, i.e., $\mathcal{S}^1_{revert}(h) = \mathsf{tts}(\mathsf{pred}(h), h)$.

The second option, called $\mathcal{S}^0_{revert}$, does not run traditional test selection, but is safe only for *auto revert*. It selects each test that satisfies one of the following three conditions: (1) tests selected between n_{re} and its parent ($\{p'\} = \mathsf{pred}(n_{re})$) as well as before the point to which the revert is applied ($\{p\} = \mathsf{pred}(h)$) up to their dominator ($d = \mathsf{dom}(p, p')$), (2) tests selected between n_{re} and its parent p' and also selected before the point that is being reverted (p') up to d, and (3) tests that were deleted at the point being reverted (such that in the inverse change tests are added):

$$\mathcal{S}^0_{revert}(h) = (S_{sel}(p', n_{re}) \cap ((\cup_{n \in d \preceq^* p \setminus \{d\}} S_{sel}(n)) \cup (\cup_{n \in d \preceq^* p' \setminus \{d\}} S_{sel}(n))))$$
$$\cup (\mathcal{A}(p') \setminus \mathcal{A}(n_{re})) \tag{13}$$

Intuitively, revert is an inverse of cherry-pick and safe for the same reasons: the tests that are not selected would have the same outcome at the h version as at the version prior to n_{re}.

4 Evaluation

We performed several experiments to evaluate the effectiveness of our technique. First, we demonstrate the importance of having a test-selection technique for distributed software histories. Second, we evaluate the effectiveness of our test-selection technique by comparing the number of tests selected using $\mathcal{S}^1_{merge}$, $\mathcal{S}^k_{merge}$, and $\mathcal{S}^0_{merge}$ on a number of software histories (both real and systematically generated), i.e., we consider how much test selection would have saved had it been run on the versions in the history. Third, we compare $\mathcal{S}^1_{cherry}$ and $\mathcal{S}^0_{cherry}$ on a number of real cherry-pick commits.

Real Software Histories are Highly Non-Linear. We collected statistics for software histories of several large open-source projects that use Git. To check whether software histories are non-linear across many project types, we chose

Project	SHA	Size MB	Authors†	(C)ommits	(M)erges	(R)ebases†	Cherrypicks & Reverts (CR)	(M+R+CR) /C	M/C on master	Auto-merges %
Activator	a3bc65e	1.2	14	1499	446	10	29	32.35	93.93	95.73
TimesSquare	d528622	0.31	22	145	50	1	1	35.86	65.71	96.00
Astyanax	ba58831	2.0	59	725	134	3	14	20.82	23.04	94.02
Bootstrap	c75f8a5	3.2	474	6893	1573	21	557	31.20	25.75	83.21
Cucumber	5416686	1.2	145	2495	413	21	148	23.32	15.92	77.48
Graphhopper	e2805e4	7.2	13	1265	59	3	59	9.56	3.64	55.93
JGit	7995d87	9.0	83	2801	615	774	24	50.44	33.35	97.48
LinuxKernel	e62063d	484.5	11133	400479	27472	151569	–	–	30.12	–
LinuxKVM	b796a09	406.2	8542	273639	17483	107768	–	–	8.92	–
Retrofit	5bd3c1e	0.62	61	631	216	4	2	35.18	58.54	99.07
Others (14)	-	231.28	2150	86380	14066	12928	3829	35.68	20.64	85.15
Min	-	0.31	13	145	50	1	0	9.30	3.64	55.93
Max	-	484.5	11133	400479	27472	151569	1973	63.37	93.93	100.00
Median	-	5.20	60.50	2175.00	373.00	19.49	34.50	31.77	27.03	94.62
Ari. mean	-	47.77	945.66	32373.00	2605.29	11379.25	211.95	31.76	34.05	90.25
Geo. mean	-	5.69	79.04	2275.60	415.71	45.60	21.11	18.91	20.49	51.93
Std. Dev.	-	121.71	2717.26	93955.04	6343.27	36281.83	447.38	14.19	26.56	10.30

† We use a heuristic to determine the number of authors and rebases

Fig. 3. Statistics for several projects that use Git

projects from different domains (e.g., Cucumber is a tool for running acceptance tests, JGit is a pure Java implementation of the Git version-control system, etc.), implemented in different languages, of various sizes, having different number of unit tests and developers. Figure 3 shows the collected statistics (in detail for 10 projects and averages for 14 others; we provide an extended table in the technical report [15]). The key column is $(M+R+CR)/C$ that shows the ratio of the number of merges, rebases[3], cherry-picks, and reverts over the total number of commits for the entire software history. The ratio can be as high as 63.37% and is 31.76% on average. Stated differently, we may be able to improve test selection for about a third of the commits in an average DVCS history. Additionally, we collected a similar ratio only for the *master* branch, because most development processes run tests for all commits on that branch but not necessarily on other branches (e.g., see the Google process for testing commits [16]). While this ratio included only merges (and not rebases, cherry-picks, or reverts), its average is even higher for the *master* branch than for the entire repository (34.05% vs. 31.76%), which increases the importance of test selection for distributed software histories. Finally, to confirm that the ratio of merges is independent of the DVCS, we collected statistics on three projects that use Mercurial [27]— OpenJDK, Mercurial, and NetBeans—and the average ratio of merges was 20%, which is slightly lower than the average number for Git but still significant.

---

[3] Note that we approximate the number of rebases by counting commits with different author and committer field.

Subject	Available Tests		Total Execution [sec]	
	min	max	min	max
Cucumber (core)	156	308	10	14
Graphhopper (core)	626	692	14	20
JGit	2231	2232	106	116
Retrofit	181	184	10	10

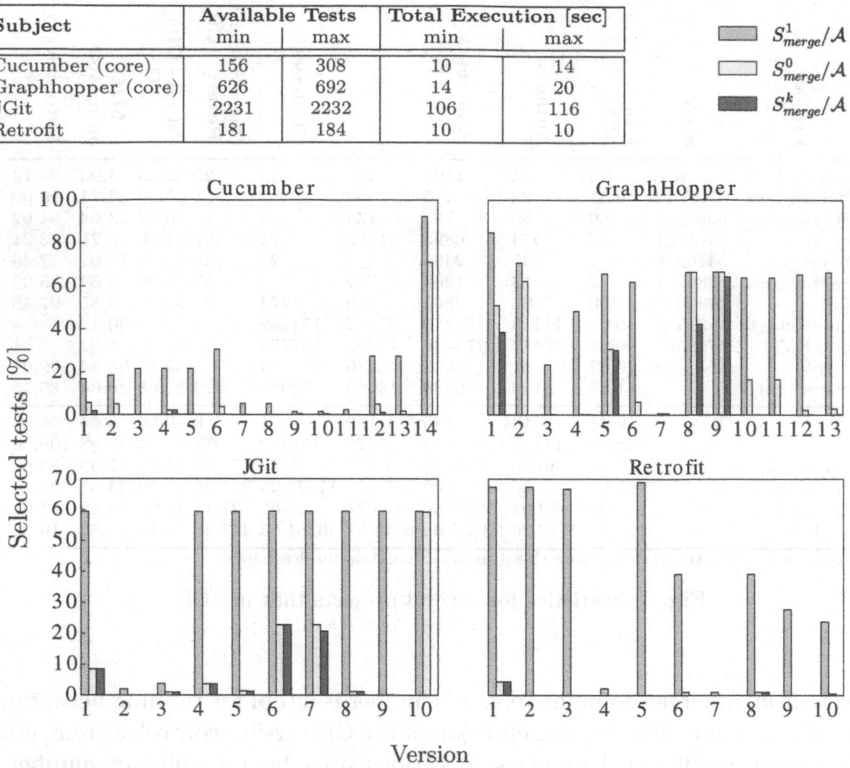

$S^1_{merge}/\mathcal{A}$
$S^0_{merge}/\mathcal{A}$
$S^k_{merge}/\mathcal{A}$

Fig. 4. Percentage of selected tests for real merges using various techniques

Implementation. We implemented a tool in Java to perform test selection proposed in Section 3. The tool is independent of the DVCS being used and scales to quite large projects. Because any test-selection technique for distributed histories would require a traditional test selection between two versions (tts) for linear histories, and because there is no publicly available tool for the traditional test selection that scales to the large projects used in our study, we implemented a simple prototype tool for projects written in Java, following known results [5, 28, 37, 38]. Specifically, our tts computes changes and tracks executed code at the class level but still guarantees safety [28].

Real Merges. Our first set of experiments evaluates our technique on the actual software histories. We used software histories of four large open-source projects (downloaded from GitHub): Cucumber, GraphHopper, JGit, and Retrofit. We selected these projects as their setup was not too complex[4], and they differ in size, number of authors, number of commits, and number of merges. For each project, we identify the last merge commit in the current software history and then run

---

[4] We have to build and run tests over a large number of commits, and dependencies in many real projects make running tests from older commits rather non-trivial.

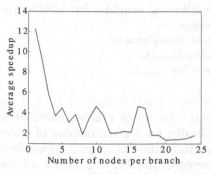

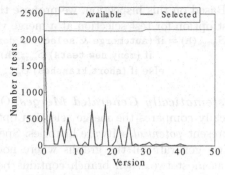

(a) Average speedup across all subjects   (b) JFreeChart history statistics

Fig. 5. (a) $\mathcal{S}^1_{merge}/\mathcal{S}^0_{merge}$ (speedup) for various numbers of commits in each branch constructed from linear software histories, (b) example linear history

our test-selection tool on all the merge commits whose immediate dominator was in the 50 commits before the last merge commit.

At every merge, we run all three options—$\mathcal{S}^1_{merge}$, $\mathcal{S}^k_{merge}$, and $\mathcal{S}^0_{merge}$—and compare the number of tests they select. Testing literature [5,12,33,35,37] commonly measures the speedup of test selection as the ratio of the number of selected tests over the number of available tests $(\mathcal{S}_{sel}/\mathcal{A})^5$. In addition, Figure 4 reports the min and max number of available tests across the considered merge commits, and the min and max total time to execute these tests. All tests in these projects are unit tests and take a similar amount of time to execute, so computing the ratio of the numbers of tests is a decent approximation of the ratio of test execution times.

Figure 4 plots the results for these four projects. In most cases, $\mathcal{S}^k_{merge}$ and $\mathcal{S}^0_{merge}$ achieve substantial saving compared to $\mathcal{S}^1_{merge}$. (Calculated differently, the average speedup of $\mathcal{S}^0_{merge}$ over $\mathcal{S}^1_{merge}$ was 10.89× and $\mathcal{S}^k_{merge}$ over $\mathcal{S}^0_{merge}$ was 2.78×.) Although $\mathcal{S}^0_{merge}$ achieved lower saving than $\mathcal{S}^k_{merge}$ in a few cases (that we discuss below in more detail), it is important to recall that $\mathcal{S}^k_{merge}$ requires k runs of traditional test selection, while $\mathcal{S}^0_{merge}$ requires 0 runs.

We inspected in more detail the cases where $\mathcal{S}^k_{merge}/\mathcal{S}^0_{merge}$ was low. For GraphHopper (versions 2, 10, and 11), two branches have a large number of exactly the same commits (in particular, one branch has 11 commits and another has 10 of those 11 commits, which were created with some cherry-picking); when these branches were merged, the differences between the merged version and parents were rather small, resulting in a few tests being selected by $\mathcal{S}^k_{merge}$, although the changes between the parents and the dominator were rather big, resulting in many tests being selected by $\mathcal{S}^0_{merge}$. For JGit (version 10) and Cucumber (version 14), some new tests were added on one branch before merging it with another; $\mathcal{S}^0_{merge}$ is rather conservative in selecting (all) new tests, but new tests are not added frequently.

---

[5] For space reasons, we omit the set cardinality from the ratios.

Based on this inspection, we propose the following heuristic for choosing the best option for test selection at a merge version:

$\mathcal{S}_{\text{merge}}(h) =$ if (automerge & selection done at every commit)
if (many new tests) $\mathcal{S}_{\text{merge}}^{k}(h)$ else $\mathcal{S}_{\text{merge}}^{0}(h)$
else if (short branches) $\mathcal{S}_{\text{merge}}^{1}(h)$ else $\mathcal{S}_{\text{merge}}^{k}(h)$

Systematically Generated Merges. Our second set of experiments systematically compares the merge selection options on a set of graphs generated to represent *potential* software histories. Specifically, for a given number of nodes k, we generate all the graphs where nodes have the out degree (branching) of at most two, each branch contains between 1 and $k/2 - 2$ nodes, all the branches have the same number of nodes, and there are no linear segments on the master branch (except the last few nodes that remained after generating the branches). In other words, the generated graphs are diamonds of different length. For example for $k = 7$, we have the following two graphs: ·<:>·<:>· and ·<: = :>·—·. The total number of merges for the given number of nodes k is $\lfloor(k-1)/3\rfloor + \lfloor(k-1)/5\rfloor + \ldots + \lfloor(k-1)/(k-1)\rfloor$.

In addition to generating history graphs, we need to assign code and tests to each node of the graph. As random code or tests could produce too unrealistic data, we use the following approach: (1) we took the latest 50 versions of four large open-source projects with *linear* software histories: JFreeChart (SVN: 3021), Goldman Sachs collections (Git: 28070efd), Ivy (SVN: 1550956), and Functor (SVN: 1439120) (as an example, Figure 5b shows the number of available and selected tests for JFreeChart), (2) we assigned a version from the linear history to a node of the graph by preserving the relative ordering of versions such that a linear extension of the generated graph (partial order) matches the given linear history (total order). Using the above formula to calculate the number of merges for generated graph, for 50 versions, there are 68 merges (in 24 graphs); as we have four projects, the total number of merges is 272.

After the software histories are fully generated, we perform test selection on each of the graphs for each of the projects and collect the number of tests selected by all three options at each merge commit. As for the experiments on real software histories, we calculate the speedup as the ratio of the number of tests. Figure 5a shows the average speedup (across all four projects) for various number of nodes per branch. As expected, with more commits per branch, the speedup decreases, because the sets of changes on each branch become bigger and thus their intersection (as computed by our $\mathcal{S}_{merge}^{0}$ option) becomes larger. However, the speedup remains high for quite long branches. In fact, this speedup is likely an under-approximation of what can be achieved in real software projects because the assignment of changes across branches may not be representative of actual software histories: many related changes may be sprinkled across branches, which leads to a smaller speedup. Also, linear software histories are known to include more changes per commit [2]. We can see from the comparison of absolute values of the speedup in Figure 5a and Figure 4 that real software histories have an even higher speedup than our generated histories.

Real Cherry-Picks. We also compared $\mathcal{S}^1_{cherry}$ and $\mathcal{S}^0_{cherry}$ on 7 cherry-picks identified in the `Retrofit` project. (No other version from the other three projects in our experiments used a cherry-pick command.) For 6 cases, $\mathcal{S}^0_{cherry}$ selected 7 tests more than $\mathcal{S}^1_{cherry}$, but all these tests were new. As mentioned, our current technique is rather conservative in selecting new tests; in future, we plan to improve our technique by considering coverage matrices across branches. In the remaining case, $\mathcal{S}^0_{cherry}$ selected 43% fewer tests (42 vs. 73 tests) than $\mathcal{S}^1_{cherry}$.

5 Related Work

Test selection is the most common optimization technique in regression testing [5, 11, 37]. Regression testing in general, and test selection in particular, have been studied for more than three decades [5,11,19,22,36,37] and are quite important in practice [16,34]. Prior research has investigated regression-testing techniques for various languages and domains [5,6,8,11,12,21,26,33–35,37], but all previous techniques considered only two program versions at a time. Most traditional test-selection techniques are safe; the key difference is how they define the coverage matrix and identify differences between software versions. For example, Rothermel and Harrold [33] presented a test-selection technique based on control-flow graphs. Zhang et al. [38] defined the coverage matrix on extended call graphs. Harrold and Soffa [18] and Gupta et al. [17] defined the coverage matrix on definition-use pairs. Several researchers [23, 24, 28] used a coverage matrix on modules (also known as "firewall" approach). Many other approaches have been proposed; for an overview, see the recent surveys [5,11,37].

Our technique for *distributed histories* is compatible with all these traditional techniques for *linear histories* as we abstract them in the core mt and tts functions. We are the first to propose a technique for safe test selection for distributed software histories; we use traditional test selection when a version is created by a commit command, and we reason about software history, modification-traversing tests, and commands being executed when a version is created by other DVCS commands (merge, cherry-pick, and revert).

Others [2, 4, 7, 29, 30] have observed several pitfalls of mining DVCS, e.g., DVCS commands are not recorded. We assume our test-selection technique is run at the time a new version is created (when the executed command is known).

6 Conclusions

We proposed the first test-selection technique that takes into account version histories arising out of distributed development, and proposed several options that trade off computation effort and precision. Our experimental results on real software histories demonstrate that our technique scales to large projects and achieves high effectiveness over a naive application of traditional test selection.

Acknowledgments. We thank Hsien-Chih Chang, Pranav Garg, Alex Gyori, Sarfraz Khurshid, P. Madhusudan, Aleksandar Milicevic, Ben Raichel, August Shi, and Mahesh Viswanathan for discussions, and the anonymous reviewers for comments. This research was partially supported by the US National Science Foundation Grant Nos. CNS-0958199 and CCF-1012759.

References

1. Aho, A.V., Sethi, R., Ullman, J.D.: Compilers: Principles, Techniques, and Tools. Addison-Wesley Longman Publishing Co., Inc., Boston (1986)
2. Alali, A., Kagdi, H., Maletic, J.I.: What's a typical commit? A characterization of open source software repositories. In: International Conference on Program Comprehension, pp. 182–191 (2008)
3. Bender, M.A., Pemmasani, G., Skiena, S., Sumazin, P.: Finding least common ancestors in directed acyclic graphs. In: Symposium on Discrete Algorithms, pp. 845–853 (2001)
4. Bird, C., Rigby, P.C., Barr, E.T., Hamilton, D.J., German, D.M., Devanbu, P.: The promises and perils of mining Git. In: International Working Conference on Mining Software Repositories, pp. 1–10 (2009)
5. Biswas, S., Mall, R., Satpathy, M., Sukumaran, S.: Regression test selection techniques: A survey. Informatica (Slovenia) 35(3), 289–321 (2011)
6. Briand, L., Labiche, Y., He, S.: Automating regression test selection based on UML designs. Information and Software Technology 51(1), 16–30 (2009)
7. Brindescu, C., Codoban, M., Shmarkatiuk, S., Dig, D.: How do centralized and distributed version control systems impact software changes? In: International Conference on Software Engineering (to appear, 2014)
8. Chittimalli, P.K., Harrold, M.J.: Regression test selection on system requirements. In: India Software Engineering Conference, pp. 87–96 (2008)
9. Czumaj, A., Kowaluk, M., Lingas, A.: Faster algorithms for finding lowest common ancestors in directed acyclic graphs. Theor. Comput. Sci. 380(1-2), 37–46 (2007)
10. Eckhardt, S., Mühling, A.M., Nowak, J.: Fast lowest common ancestor computations in dags. In: Arge, L., Hoffmann, M., Welzl, E. (eds.) ESA 2007. LNCS, vol. 4698, pp. 705–716. Springer, Heidelberg (2007)
11. Engström, E., Runeson, P., Skoglund, M.: A systematic review on regression test selection techniques. Inf. Softw. Technol. 52(1), 14–30 (2010)
12. Engström, E., Skoglund, M., Runeson, P.: Empirical evaluations of regression test selection techniques: a systematic review. In: International Symposium on Empirical Software Engineering and Measurement, pp. 22–31 (2008)
13. git-merge-base, https://www.kernel.org/pub/software/scm/git/docs/git-merge-base.html
14. Git home page, http://git-scm.com/
15. Gligoric, M., Majumdar, R., Sharma, R., Eloussi, L., Marinov, D.: Regression test selection for distributed software histories. Technical report (2014), https://www.ideals.illinois.edu/handle/2142/49112
16. Gupta, P., Ivey, M., Penix, J.: Testing at the speed and scale of Google (June 2011), http://google-engtools.blogspot.com/2011/06/testing-at-speed-and-scale-of-google.html

17. Gupta, R., Harrold, M.J., Soffa, M.L.: Program slicing-based regression testing techniques. Softw. Test., Verif. Reliab. 6(2), 83–111 (1996)
18. Harrold, M.J., Soffa, M.L.: Interprocedual data flow testing. In: Third Symposium on Software Testing, Analysis, and Verification, pp. 158–167 (1989)
19. Harrold, M., Soffa, M.: An incremental approach to unit testing during maintenance. In: International Conference on Software Maintenance, pp. 362–367 (1988)
20. How does merging work? http://cbx33.github.io/gitt/afterhours4-1.html
21. Jones, J., Harrold, M.J.: Test-suite reduction and prioritization for modified condition/decision coverage. Transactions on Software Engineering 29, 195–209 (2003)
22. K.F. Fischer, F. Raji, A.C.: A methodology for retesting modified software. In: National Telecommunications Conference (1981)
23. Kung, D.C., Gao, J., Hsia, P., Lin, J., Toyoshima, Y.: Class firewall, test order, and regression testing of object-oriented programs. Journal of Object-Oriented Programming 8(2), 51–65 (1995)
24. Leung, H.K.N., White, L.: Insights into regression testing. In: International Conference on Software Maintenance, pp. 60–69 (1989)
25. LinuxKernel Git repository, //git://git.kernel.org/pub/scm/linux/kernel/git/torvalds/linux.git
26. Memon, A.M., Soffa, M.L.: Regression testing of GUIs. In: International Symposium on Foundations of Software Engineering, pp. 118–127 (2003)
27. Mercurial home page, http://mercurial.selenic.com/
28. Orso, A., Shi, N., Harrold, M.J.: Scaling regression testing to large software systems. In: International Symposium on Foundations of Software Engineering, pp. 241–251 (2004)
29. Perez De Rosso, S., Jackson, D.: What's wrong with Git?: A conceptual design analysis. In: International Symposium on New Ideas, New Paradigms, and Reflections on Programming & Software, pp. 37–52 (2013)
30. Rigby, P., Barr, E., Bird, C., Devanbu, P., German, D.: What effect does distributed version control have on OSS project organization? In: International Workshop on Release Engineering, pp. 29–32 (2013)
31. Rothermel, G., Harrold, M.J.: A safe, efficient algorithm for regression test selection. In: Conference on Software Maintenance, pp. 358–367 (1993)
32. Rothermel, G., Harrold, M.J.: A framework for evaluating regression test selection techniques. In: International Conference on Software Engineering, pp. 201–210 (1994)
33. Rothermel, G., Harrold, M.J.: A safe, efficient regression test selection technique. Trans. Softw. Eng. Methodol. 6(2), 173–210 (1997)
34. Srivastava, A., Thiagarajan, J.: Effectively prioritizing tests in development environment. In: International Symposium on Software Testing and Analysis, pp. 97–106 (2002)
35. Willmor, D., Embury, S.M.: A safe regression test selection technique for database driven applications. In: International Conference on Software Maintenance, pp. 421–430 (2005)
36. Yau, S.S., Kishimoto, Z.: A method for revalidating modified programs in the maintenance phase. In: Signature Conference on Computers, Software, and Applications (1987)
37. Yoo, S., Harman, M.: Regression testing minimization, selection and prioritization: a survey. Software Testing, Verification and Reliability 22(2), 67–120 (2012)
38. Zhang, L., Kim, M., Khurshid, S.: Localizing failure-inducing program edits based on spectrum information. In: International Conference on Software Maintenance, pp. 23–32 (2011)

GPU-Based Graph Decomposition into Strongly Connected and Maximal End Components

Anton Wijs[1,*], Joost-Pieter Katoen[2], and Dragan Bošnački[1]

[1] Eindhoven University of Technology, The Netherlands
[2] RWTH Aachen University, Germany

Abstract. This paper presents parallel algorithms for component decomposition of graph structures on General Purpose Graphics Processing Units (GPUs). In particular, we consider the problem of decomposing sparse graphs into strongly connected components, and decomposing stochastic games (such as Markov decision processes) into maximal end components. These problems are key ingredients of many (probabilistic) model-checking algorithms. We explain the main rationales behind our GPU-algorithms, and show a significant speed-up over the sequential counterparts in several case studies.

1 Introduction

Strongly connected components (SCCs, for short) are sub-graphs in which each pair of states is mutually reachable. Finding maximal SCCs, i.e., SCCs that are not contained in others, is a key ingredient of various model-checking algorithms. To mention a few, this applies to the standard verification algorithms for CTL-formulas of the form $\mathsf{EG}\,\varphi$ as well as for verifying fair CTL [1, Ch. 6] and checking language emptiness [2]. The high relevance of SCCs has led to various dedicated variants of Tarjan's classical algorithm [3] such as symbolic [4] and a plethora of parallel [5–7] algorithms. In the context of probabilistic model checking, a generalisation of SCCs – known as maximal end components (MECs) – play a pivotal role [8, 9]. Determining MECs is a main step in the verification of qualitative and quantitative properties on Markov decision processes (MDPs) and continuous-time variants thereof. MDPs are an important class of models used for the analysis of probabilistic systems consisting of several components running in parallel. Parallelism is modelled by non-determinism whereas the steps within a component may be probabilistic (e.g., modelling a coin flip). MDP model checking is a very active branch of probabilistic model checking with applications in amongst others planning and randomised distributed algorithms. MECs are maximal strongly connected sub-graphs in which the MDP can ensure to reside

---

* This work was sponsored by the NWO Exacte Wetenschappen, EW (NWO Physical Sciences Division) for the use of supercomputer facilities, with financial support from the Nederlandse Organisatie voor Wetenschappelijk Onderzoek (Netherlands Organisation for Scientific Research, NWO), as well as the EU MEALS project and the EU FP7 CARP project.

A. Biere and R. Bloem (Eds.): CAV 2014, LNCS 8559, pp. 310–326, 2014.

when playing against a probabilistic adversary. MEC decomposition of MDPs is typically a pre-processing step of probabilistic model checking to determining almost-sure limiting properties [1, Ch. 10]. Other applications include the analysis of multi-player stochastic games [10] as well as recent approaches to combined worst-case and expected value objectives for mean pay-off games [11]. Improvements of the traditional sequential algorithms for determining MECs [1, 8, 9] have been reported [12] and were tailored to MDPs with low tree-width [13].

In this paper, we provide new algorithms to efficiently decompose graphs into SCCs and MECs by exploiting GPUs (Graphical Processing Units). Our decomposition algorithms build upon three key principles. First, inspired by the Forward-Backward algorithm (FB) [14], each thread combines *a forward and a backward reachability search* so as to identify SCCs. Previous work on GPU-based SCC decomposition [5–7] identified the FB algorithm (combined with a trimming procedure to remove trivial SCCs) as the best performing one for general input graphs. Opposed to these works, we focus on graphs that are commonly observed in model checking, i.e., sparse graphs with a low average out-degree (number of outgoing transitions per state) and tailor our algorithms to treat these graphs efficiently. The backward and forward search are started from some common state, called the pivot. The second main principle is to exploit a *novel pivot selection* strategy which turns out to be simple and efficient. Finally, we optimise the memory management to achieve *coalesced memory access* by the individual threads, i.e., data access can be accomplished in a single memory fetch. Altogether this alleviates memory latency and thread divergence where part of the threads execute one branch of the common code, while others take another branch. The overall memory requirements are significantly lower than for competitive algorithms [5] as besides the input graph $G = (V, E)$, only a single additional integer array of size $|V|$ is needed to store decomposition results. Given the restricted memory size on a GPU, this memory reduction is essential. Our GPU-based MEC decomposition algorithm uses the same principles as the SCC algorithm; it can be viewed as a parallel version of the standard sequential algorithms [1, 8, 9]. To the best of our knowledge, this is the first GPU-based MEC decomposition. We implemented our algorithms using CUDA[1] for NVIDIA GPUs, and ran them on examples of the PRISM benchmark suite [15]. Speed-up factors of 15-30 and 79 have been achieved for SCC and MEC decomposition, respectively. For SCC decomposition, this is a significant improvement over previous results (e.g. [5]) for sparse graphs with a low average out-degree.

Exploiting general purpose GPUs (GPGPUs, for short) in the setting of model checking is not new. Thanks to efforts of several research groups [16–18], GPGPUs have been applied to significantly improve the run times of model checking algorithms. In the context of probabilistic model checking, these improvements usually targeted the numerical part of the algorithms, so as to exploit the inherent advantages of the GPUs [16, 19, 20]. More recently, we presented an on-the-fly search algorithm for standard model checking running entirely on GPUs [21].

---

[1] http://www.nvidia.com/object/cuda_home_new.html.

Organisation of the paper. Section 2 treats the basics of MDPs, MECs and relevant SCC and MEC decomposition algorithms. Section 3 gives a detailed account of our GPU algorithms focussing on our main design choices. Section 4 presents the experimental results, and Section 5 concludes.

2   Preliminaries

This section gives an introduction to the main concepts of MDPs and MECs [1, Ch. 10], presents the parallel FB algorithm for SCC decomposition [14] and the standard sequential algorithm for MEC decomposition [8, 9] of MDPs.

2.1   Markov Decision Processes and Maximal-End Components

Let $\Delta(X)$ denote the set of probability distributions over the countable set X, i.e., the set of functions $\mu : X \to [0,1]$ with $\sum_{x \in X} \mu(x) = 1$.

Definition 1 (Markov Decision Process). *A* Markov decision process (MDP) *is a tuple $M = (S, \hat{s}, T)$, where S is a finite set of states, $\hat{s} \in S$ is the* initial state, *and $T : S \to 2^{\Delta(S)}$ is the* transition function *with $T(s) \neq \emptyset$ and $T(s)$ is finite for all $s \in S$.*

The transition function T maps every state $s \in S$ to a finite, non-empty set of distributions over S. In state s, one of the distributions in $\mu \in T(s)$ is selected non-deterministically, and the MDP evolves to state s' with probability $\mu(s')$. As $T(s)$ is non-empty for every state, this procedure can be repeated *ad infinitum*. For state s, $T(s)$ can be viewed as the set of distributions that are selected in a non-deterministic manner. Alternatively, an MDP can be consider as a single-player game in which the system plays against a random adversary. An MDP naturally induces a digraph in the following sense.

Definition 2 (MDP Graph). *The* induced labelled digraph *of MDP $M = (S, \hat{s}, T)$ is $G = (V, E)$ with $V = S$ is the set of* vertices *and $E \subseteq V \times \Delta(V) \times V$ is the set of* labelled edges *defined by: $(u, \mu, v) \in E$ iff $\mu(v) > 0$ for some $\mu \in T(u)$.*

Intuitively speaking, there is a μ-labelled edge between two vertices (states) u and v whenever v is in the support of distribution μ in $T(u)$. For node u and distribution μ, let $E_\mu(u) = \{v \in V \mid (u, \mu, v) \in E\}$. We call $E_\mu(u)$ the set of *target vertices (states)* of the *source vertex (state)* u under distribution μ. Moreover, let $E(u) = \bigcup_\mu E_\mu(u)$. For labelled digraphs we adopt the standard graph-theoretical notions like paths, cycles, components, etc.. An MDP graph $G = (V, E)$ is strongly connected iff for every two vertices $u, v \in V$ there is a path from u to v and a path from v to u. The set of nodes $C \subseteq V$ is a *strongly connected component* (SCC) of G iff G restricted to C, denoted $G{\uparrow}C$, i.e., the graph $G{\uparrow}C = (C, (C \times \Delta(C) \times C) \cap E)$, is strongly connected. SCC C is *maximal* iff there is no SCC $C' \neq C$ with $C \subset C'$. In the sequel, unless stated otherwise, we use the abbreviation SCC for maximal SCCs. In the following, let $G = (V, E)$ be an MDP graph.

Definition 3 (SCC Decomposition). *An SCC decomposition of graph $G = (V, E)$ is a partitioning of V that consists of all maximal SCCs of G.*

It is convenient to distinguish vertices that are potentially "closed" in the sense that for at least one non-deterministic choice (distribution) all transitions remain within a given set.

Definition 4 (E-Closed Nodes). *Vertex $v \in V$ is existentially closed (e-closed) for $X \subseteq V$ iff $E_\mu(v) \subseteq X$ for some $\mu \in T(v)$.*

Definition 5 (End-Components). *$U \subseteq V$ is an end-component of MDP graph G if $G{\uparrow}U$ is strongly connected and every $u \in U$ is e-closed for U.*

End-components that share common nodes can be merged into a single end-component. A *maximal* end-component (MEC) of G is an end-component C for which there is no end-component $C' \neq C$ such that $C \subset C'$. Observe that every vertex in V belongs to at most one maximal end-component.

Definition 6 (MEC Decomposition). *A MEC decomposition of MDP graph G is the partitioning of V into the MECs of G and the set of vertices that do not belong to any MEC (of G).*

For the description of the MDP algorithms (below) we define the notion of attractor. Stated in words, an attractor is a set of vertices in which the MDP may reside with positive probability no matter which distributions are non-deterministically selected.

Definition 7 (Attractor). *The attractor $Attr(U)$ of $U \subseteq V$ is defined as $Attr(U) = \bigcup_{i \geq 0} U_i$ where U_i is defined inductively by:*

- *$U_0 = U$, and*
- *$U_{i+1} = U_i \cup \{u \in V \mid \forall \mu. E_\mu(u) \cap U_i \neq \emptyset\}$, for $i \geq 0$.*

The attractor $Attr(U)$ contains U plus all vertices from which the vertices in U can be reached via at least one transition regardless of the resolution of the non-deterministic choices by the adversary. The MEC-decomposition algorithm discussed later on exploits the following two results from [22]. The first result identifies the vertices that do not belong to any MEC and thus can be removed without affecting the MEC decomposition of the rest of the MDP graph.

Lemma 1 (Removing Attractor Nodes). *Let $G = (V, E)$ be an MDP graph.*

1. *For SCC C in G, let $U = \{v \in C \mid \forall \mu. E_\mu(v) \not\subseteq C\}$ and $Z = Attr(U) \cap C$. Then: for every MEC X of G it holds that $Z \cap X = \emptyset$.*
2. *Let C be a MEC in G and $Z = Attr(C) \setminus C$. Then: for every MEC $X \neq C$ of G it holds that $Z \cap X = \emptyset$.*

The second result from [22] provides a sufficient criterion for an SCC to be a MEC.

Lemma 2 (Closed SCCs are MECs). *An SCC C of the MDP graph $G = (V, E)$ with $E(v) \subseteq C$ for all $v \in C$, is a MEC.*

A corollary of Lemma 2 is that every bottom SCC, i.e., an SCC C such that all transitions from C lead back to C, is a MEC.

2.2 SCC Decomposition Using Forward-Backward Search

Many algorithms exist to perform SCC decomposition. Linear-time algorithms such as the ones by Tarjan [3] and Dijkstra [23] are based on depth-first search and thus very hard to parallelize, especially when the goal is to run thousands of threads in parallel as is the case with GPUs. An alternative for SCC decomposition is the Forward-Backward algorithm (FB, for short) proposed by Fleischer *et al.* [14]. This algorithm is based on a breadth-first search (BFS) strategy, combining a forward and a backward search. It has worst-case complexity $O(|V|^2 + |V| \cdot |E|)$, but offers great potential for GPU-based parallelization.

The Forward-Backward (FB) algorithm starts by (randomly) selecting a *pivot* vertex p (see Alg. 1, line 3). The SCC to which p belongs is then found by performing both a *forward* BFS and a *backward* BFS starting from p, to determine the forward and backward closure (of p), respectively (Alg. 1, lines 4-5). The intersection of the vertices reached via the forward and backward BFSs

---

Algorithm 1. FB with Trimming (FBT)

Require: graph $G = (V, E)$
Ensure: SCC decomposition of G is given
    $V' \leftarrow$ Trim(V) *produces trivial SCCs*
2: **if** $V' \neq \emptyset$ **then**
      pivot $\leftarrow$ selectPivot(V')
4:    $F \leftarrow$ fwdBfs(*pivot*, (V', E))
      $B \leftarrow$ bwdBfs(*pivot*, (V', E))
6:    *remove SCC $F \cap B$ from V'*
      do in parallel
8:        FBT((($F \setminus B$), E))
        FBT((($B \setminus F$), E))
10:      FBT((($V \setminus (B \cup F)$), E))

---

constitutes an SCC (and is removed, Alg. 1, line 6). The graph vertices are then partitioned into the vertices belonging only to the forward closure, those only in the backward closure, and those outside both closures. These subsets are referred to as *search regions*. Subsequently, FB can be invoked recursively in parallel on the three search regions. This can be done, since all other, not yet detected SCCs, are contained in one of these search regions. The FB algorithm can be improved by *trimming* [24] (see Alg. 1, line 1). This step eliminates the trivial SCCs consisting of only one vertex. The trimming procedure exploits topological sort elimination by starting in a vertex with zero in- or out-degree. As such vertex cannot be a part of a non-trivial SCC, they can be safely removed to avoid using them as pivots in the FB search. Since the removal can create other trimming candidates, the procedure is iterated (in the method Trim(V) in Alg. 1) until there are no vertices for trimming left. Trimming is also used in our parallel SCC algorithm. Several studies [5–7] have shown that parallel SCC decomposition algorithms including Coloring heads off [25] and Recursive OBF [26], show inferior performance compared to the FBT algorithm.

2.3 Sequential MEC Decomposition Algorithms

The basic sequential algorithm for MEC decomposition of MDP graph $G = (V, E)$ is based on iterative SCC decomposition of G followed by transforming the SCCs into MECs [1, 8, 9]. The algorithm consists of the following stages:

1. Compute the SCC decomposition of G. For SCC C, let $U = \{v \in C \mid \forall \mu. E_\mu(v) \not\subseteq C\}$.

2. If $U \neq \emptyset$, remove $\text{Attr}(U) \cap C$ from G. (cf. Lemma 1.)
3. Every SCC C without an outgoing edge is a MEC [2] (cf. Lemma 2). As justified by Lemma 1.2, remove $\text{Attr}(C)$ for every C for which we established that C is a MEC.
4. Recursively compute the MEC-decompositions of the sub-MDP graphs obtained after the removal of the vertices in steps 2 and 3. (This is needed since the removal of the vertices might have destroyed the strong connectivity of some of the components.)

The first step of the algorithm, i.e., the SCC decomposition of the MDP graph, can be done in $O(m)$ time, where $m = |E|$ is the number of edges, e.g., using, e.g., Tarjan's algorithm [3]. The second step can be done in $O(m)$ time. There are at most $n = |V|$ iterations implied by step 3, since in each iteration at least one vertex is removed. This yields an overall time complexity of $O(m \cdot n)$. Recent works [22] and [13] present an adapted MEC-decomposition algorithm with time complexity $O(m \cdot \min(\sqrt{m}, n^{2/3}))$ and $O(n \cdot k^2 . 38 \cdot 2^k)$, respectively, where k is the so-called tree width of G. We base our GPU algorithm on the basic algorithm, since the recent algorithms involve steps that seem very hard to perform within the many-core paradigm of GPUs, like the lock-step search phase of [22].

3   GPU-Based Graph Decomposition Algorithm

3.1   GPU Basics

Harnessing the power of GPUs is facilitated by specific Application Programming Interfaces. In this paper, we assume a concrete NVIDIA GPU architecture and the Compute Unified Device Architecture (CUDA) interface. Nevertheless, the algorithms that we present here can be straightforwardly applied to any architecture which provides massive hardware multithreading, supports the SIMT (Single Instruction Multiple Threads) model, and relies on coalesced access to the memory.

CUDA is an interface by NVIDIA which is used to program GPUs. CUDA extends C and FORTRAN. We use the C extension. GPU-specific features of CUDA include special declarations to explicitly place variables in the various types of memory (see Figure 1), predefined keywords containing the IDs of individual threads and blocks of threads, synchronization statements for cooperation between threads, run time API for memory management (allocation, deallocation), and statements to launch functions, referred to as *kernels*, on a GPU. In this section we give a brief overview of CUDA, adequate for presenting our results in subsequent sections. More details can be found in, for instance, [16, 21].

CUDA Programming Model. A CUDA program consists of a *host* program which runs on the Central Processing Unit (CPU) and a (collection of) CUDA kernels. Kernels, which describe the parallel parts of the program, are executed many times in parallel by different threads on the GPU device, and are launched from

---

[2] Since G has at least one bottom SCC, i.e. at least one SCC satisfies this criterion.

the host. Most GPUs have the restriction that at most one kernel can be launched at a time, but there are also GPUs available that allow to run multiple different kernels on different threads. When launching a kernel, the number of threads that should execute it needs to be specified. All those threads execute the same kernel, i.e. code. Each thread is executed by a streaming processor (SP), see Figure 1. In general, GPU threads are grouped in blocks of a predefined size, usually a power of two. We refer to this size with *BlockSize*. A block of threads is assigned to a multiprocessor. Each thread block is uniquely identifiable by its block ID (referred to with the keyword *BlockId*) and analogously each thread is uniquely identifiable by its thread ID (keyword *ThreadId*) within its block. Using these, it is possible to define other IDs, such as the GPU-global thread ID *Global-ThreadId = (BlockId · BlockSize) + ThreadId*. The total number of threads running is defined by *NrOfThreads*.

CUDA Memory Model. Threads have access to different kinds of memory. Each thread has its own on-chip registers, access to which is very fast. Moreover, threads within a block can communicate via the *shared memory* of a multiprocessor, which is on-chip and also very fast. If multiple blocks are executed in parallel then the shared memory is equally split between them. All blocks have access to the *global memory* which is large (usu-

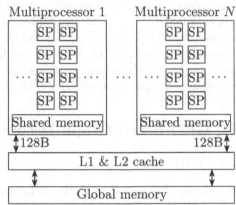

Fig. 1. Hardware model of CUDA GPUs

ally up to 5 GB), but slow, since it is off-chip. Two caches called L1 and L2 are used to cache data read from the global memory. The host has read and write access to the global memory. Thus, the global memory is used for communication between the host and the kernel.

GPU Architecture. As already mentioned, the architecture of a GPU features a set of streaming multiprocessors (SMs). Each of those contains a set of SPs. The NVIDIA KEPLER K20M, which we used for our experiments, has 13 SMs, each consisting of 192 SPs, which gives in total 2496 SPs. Furthermore, it has 5 GB global memory.

CUDA Execution Model. Threads are executed using the SIMT model. This means that each thread is executed independently with its own instruction address and local state (registers and local memory), but their execution is organized in groups of 32 called *warps*. The threads in a warp execute instructions in a synchronous manner, meaning that they move through the code in lockstep. This limits the possibilities for data races, but it also means that so-called *divergence* of thread executions can negatively impact performance of the computation. Consider the if-then-else construct **if C then A else B**. If the threads in a warp start executing this, and there are both threads for which **C** holds and threads for which it does not, then all the threads will together step through both alternatives **A** and **B**. The ones that do not need to execute **A** (or **B**) will have to 'go along' due to the SIMT model, but they will not actually execute it. Avoiding thread divergence is one of the main worries when implementing a program for the GPU.

Similarly, memory accesses of the threads in a single warp are serialized when they need to access separate parts of the global memory. If these accesses can be grouped together physically, i.e. if the accesses are coalesced, then the data can be obtained using a single fetch, thereby greatly improving the runtime. Hence, global memory access should be coalesced as much as possible. This is orthogonal to the fact that in graph decomposition algorithms, accessing transitions is irregular. Thus, achieving coalesced access is non-trivial. For sparse graphs, we propose a technique to reduce irregular memory access later in this section.

3.2   Related GPU Implementations

Sparse graphs are usually stored in the *Compressed Sparse Row* format. An integer array *trans* of size $|E|$ is used to store all the transitions, in order of the source state IDs, and an array *offsets* consisting of $|V| + 1$ integers provides the start and end indices of the outgoing transitions of each source state, e.g. for state i, its outgoing transitions are stored in *trans* from position *offsets*[i] up to and including *offsets*[$i + 1$] $- 1$.

The usual approach to perform a BFS-like search through a CSR description on a GPU involves the threads repeatedly scanning the *offsets* array using their ID, as in [27]; first, they start with reading *offsets*[*ThreadId*] and *offsets*[*ThreadId* + 1], later possibly moving to other offsets depending on the total number of threads running and the size of the graph. Each time that offsets have been read, and the corresponding source state is in the search frontier, the relevant range of transitions can be accessed next, and, in cases that the target states have not yet been visited, these are added to the new frontier.

Li *et al.* [7] remark that a GPU BFS which avoids a one-to-one mapping between threads and nodes is preferable over the standard quadratic approach. In other words, approaches like the one of Merrill et al. [28], which uses a work queue, would be preferable. An important reason is that many threads otherwise idle, and with large differences in the out-degree of nodes, work imbalance tends to occur. With sparse matrices such as those underlying MDPs, however, this is not a big concern. The out-degree of most states tends to be similar, and small. In fact, in [29], an implementation of Merrill's approach does not result in further speedups for model checking problems, but it does require more memory. Therefore, we opt for the standard approach to do BFS on a GPU.

Pivot selection is an important step in SCC decomposition, which is non-trivial to implement efficiently on a GPU, since all threads need to agree on the pivots used for the newly discovered regions before launching new BFSs, and the regions need to be distinguishable by means of unique IDs. Several elaborate schemes for this have been presented. In [5], an additional array of size $|V|$ is used, and all threads assigned to states in regions that need to be searched try to write their ID to a common entry in this array. Determining which entry should be targeted is done using a region counting scheme and renumbering heuristics. Also in [7], such an array is used, but instead of racing to entries, a random number generator is implemented, state IDs are written to designated entries, and a prefix sum is used to count the number of new regions. Finally, Hong et al. [6] maintain set representations while doing the forward and backward BFSs, and use these to select pivots. We claim that our solution, which we explain in this section, is more elegant than earlier attempts, and at least as efficient. Instead of essentially trying to use a region counter, we simply use the pivot IDs themselves to identify regions, and our procedure requires no additional memory, instead using the *results* and *trans* arrays.

In addition to our new pivot selection, we also contribute compared to earlier work by using SM local caching of states, and restructuring the input to increase the number of coalesced memory accesses. Finally, we merge the frontier and explored set representations with the graph representation, thereby being more economic with the memory, and avoiding additional memory lookups.

3.3   SCC Decomposition on the GPU

Data representation. For the encoding of a transition, first of all note that for our problems, the probability distributions in MDP graphs are not relevant, only 1) the target states, and 2) the distribution group a transition belongs to. In our implementations, we desire to work with 32-bit integers, as opposed to 64-bit integers, since CUDA provides special atomic read and write operations for them. Hence, we assume that for each transition, an encoding of the group and the target state together fits in a 32-bit integer. Our program actually checks this: first, it is determined for the input what the maximum number of groups per source state is, say m. Then, the $log(m)$ highest bits of each transition integer are reserved for the group encoding.

To produce the desired output, i.e. the SCC decomposition, we allocate memory for another integer array *results* of size $|V|$. After decomposition, its content indicates which states belong to which SCC. Any two states i, j belong to the same SCC iff $results[i] = results[j]$.

Besides the original input, when memory allows, we also store the transposed MDP graph on the GPU. Since the original representation is tailored for a (forward) BFS, the transposed graph will be for a backward BFS. If there is not enough memory, then a kernel is available for scanning *offsets* and *trans* to perform a backward BFS, which is possible, but requires more memory accesses.

Finally, for bookkeeping purposes, we reserve the three highest bits in each entry of *offsets* and *results*. The highest bit of entry i is used to indicate that state i is no longer involved in the current search iteration, i.e. it is already identified as part of a component. The second and third highest bits in *offsets* and *results* entries are used to keep track of the search frontier and the set of explored states in the forward and the backward BFSs, respectively. We reason that this is acceptable: with this restriction, it is still possible to refer to 2^{29}

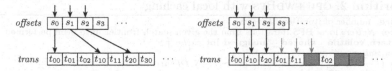

Fig. 2. Fetching transitions before and after restructuring

states, i.e. about 537 million states. For a graph to be decomposed by our GPU implementation, at least $2 \cdot |V| + |E| + 1$ integers are needed. A typical GPU has up to 5 GB global memory, which allows up to 1.3 billion integers to be stored, hence 29 bits is sufficient to refer to all the states of a graph that can be handled.

Restructuring input for coalesced memory access. In a BFS iteration, offsets are read in a coalesced way by the fact that the threads in a warp, with consecutive IDs, access an uninterrupted range of offsets. For the transitions in *trans*, though, this is a different matter, which is illustrated on the left in Figure 2. For the sake of clarity, we assume in this example that the warp size is 3. In the figure, transition t_{00} is the first outgoing transition of state s_0, t_{10} is the first one of state s_1, and so on. Since the transitions are stored in separate blocks in *trans*, it is clear that access to *trans* will not be coalesced.

To fix this, we interleave the transition entries such that for all the states assigned to a warp, their first transitions are stored in an uninterrupted block, followed by all the second transitions, and so on. This allows to fetch transitions in a coalesced way. The drawback of this is that padding might be required to ensure that each thread accesses the same number of entries. On the right of Figure 2, the interleaved version of the example is given. We call a block of transitions ordered in this fashion which is assigned to a warp a *segment*. To avoid extensive padding, though, we use a hybrid representation. For a user-defined out-degree upper-bound u, which we call the segment *interval*, all the states with at most u outgoing transitions are renumbered to appear in the first part of *offsets* and *trans*, and all the other states are placed at the tail end. In the corresponding first part of *trans*, restructuring is applied, but on the tail part it is not. This allows to avoid that states with unusually many transitions cause the introduction of too many padding entries across the whole *trans* array.

Algorithm. To illustrate our implementation of FBT for GPUs, we will discuss some of its more interesting aspects. Essentially, every step of Alg. 1 is parallelised by means of a separate kernel. In addition to this, we also have a kernel for the combination of lines 4 and 5, i.e. the BFSs. In this hybrid kernel, iterations of both BFSs are performed simultaneously during a single scan of the offsets.

Alg. 2 describes the GPU forward BFS. A local cache is allocated in shared memory. The size of this cache is defined in the host code, i.e. externally, as its declaration mentions. Its contents is initialised as empty. At lines 3-7, the offsets entries assigned to the executing thread are read and checked. Note that GPU specific notions such as *NrOfThreads* and *BlockSize* have been defined in

Algorithm 2. GPU-FWDBFS with local caching

Require: number of iterations *NrIters*
Ensure: *NrIters* local BFS iterations from the given search frontier have been performed
    extern volatile _shared_ unsigned int *cache* []
2:   <*initialise cache*>
    for ($i \leftarrow Global\text{-}ThreadId$; $i < |V|$; $i \leftarrow i + NrOfThreads$) **do**
4:     $srcinfo \leftarrow offsets[i]$
      if INFRONTIER(*srcinfo*) **then**
6:         $offsets[i] \leftarrow$ MOVETOEXPLORED(*srcinfo*)
        EXPLORE(*srcinfo*)
8:   **for** ($iter \leftarrow 1$; $iter < NrIters$; $iter\ ++$) **do**
    for $i \leftarrow ThreadId$; $i < cachesize$; $i \leftarrow i + BlockSize$ **do**
10:       $srcinfo \leftarrow cache[i]$
      if $srcinfo \neq$ **empty then**
12:         $cache[i] \leftarrow$ **empty**
        EXPLORE(*srcinfo*)

Section 3.1. Two of the three highest bits in the *offsets* entries indicate whether the corresponding state is 1) in the search frontier or not and 2) has been explored or not. If a state is in the frontier, it is removed and set to explored by the operation MOVETOEXPLORED at line 6. After that, the state is explored.

This approach to BFS requires many complete scans of *offsets* to detect the current frontier and explore states. Since global memory is slow, this is a major performance bottleneck. To mitigate this, we have opted for using SM local state caches residing in the shared memory. The GPU-FWDBFS kernel accepts a given number of iterations *NrIters*. In the first iteration, the usual scanning is performed, but in addition to being added to the frontier in the global memory, newly discovered states are added to the cache. After the first iteration, lines 8-13 are executed, in which the cache is scanned for exploration work.

In Alg. 3, the GPU explore procedure is described, which is in the implementation actually directly integrated with GPU-FWDBFS. First, *stepsize* is defined depending on whether the transitions belonging to state *i* to be explored reside in a segment or not. If so, the variable *thcont* is set, which at line 7, when all the threads in a warp exchange their value of *thcont* (the BROADCAST procedure), results in the entire warp commencing with the exploration, since at least one thread needs to explore. At line 9, *srcregion* stores the FBT search region (see Section 2.2) to which state *i* belongs. Note that at lines 11-12, if the thread is scanning a segment, the upper bound offset can be derived using the segment interval, and reading a second *offsets* entry can actually be avoided. The segment interval indicates the number of transition entries for each source state in a segment. Starting at line 15, the successors of *i* are read. Threads that are only reading entries to assure coalesced accesses do not execute lines beyond line 17. At line 20, ISACTIVE checks if the search region of the target state *j* of transition *t* has already been identified as an SCC in a previous round. This is the case if both the second and third highest bits of *results*[*j*] are set. If it is not part of a detected SCC, and both the source and target state of *t* are part of the same search region (line 22), where *tgtregion* represents the search region of the target state (line 21), then the target state is elligible for addition to the frontier. If its *offsets* entry indicates that the state is newly discovered, then, depending on the current search iteration, the target state is or is not added to the local cache (lines 25-27). Besides this, *nextIter* is set, which is read by the host after each search iteration to determine whether another iteration is required. Also, the target state is added to the search frontier (lines 30-31). Finally, in the final iteration, no states are added to the cache, since after the final iteration, kernel execution will stop anyway, and the contents of the shared memory does not survive once a kernel has terminated.

Similar to GPU-FWDBFS, we also have a backward BFS variant operating on the transposed graph, if present, and a backward BFS variant operating on the original graph, which works different from Alg. 3, since it involves in each iteration checking that from a state, the current frontier can be reached. Keeping track of the contents of the frontier and the set of explored states is done by using the bookkeeping bits in *results*. Besides this, we have a hybrid approach, in which both an iteration of the forward BFS and the backward BFS is performed. All these different versions allow to manage at the host level which searches should be performed in the next iteration, based on the feedback given by the threads.

Finally, the other main challenge is in selecting pivots. After merging the results of the forward and backward BFS in the bookkeeping bits of *results*, we resolve this by hashing the current regions of states to locations in *trans*. Note that state i belongs to search region *results*[i]. For this state, location *results*[i] + REACHEDINBWD(*results*[i]) + 2 · REACHEDINFWD(*results*[i]), will be accessed in *trans*, with REACHEDINBWD and REACHEDINFWD indicating whether the state has been reached in the backward or forward BFS, respectively. Since this location may actually be beyond the bounds of *results*, pivot selection is performed in several iterations, in each iteration j only considering the regions with a hash between $j \cdot |E|$ and $(j + 1) \cdot |E|$. Once a thread has determined the hash h, it will try to 'claim' the corresponding *trans*[h] entry by atomically writing the ID of its state with the highest bit set to lock the entry. Exactly one thread i will be able to do this, after which that thread will store the original *trans*[h] entry temporarily in *results*[i], and all other threads read the new contents of *trans*[h], and write this new region information into their *results* entries. The enforced data races are used to pseudo-randomly choose pivots. Finally, to revert *trans* back to its original content, after pivot selection, thread i swaps *results*[i] and the unlocked *trans*[h]. Note that with this approach, SCCs are actually identified by their pivots, and any number of pivots can be selected in parallel.

3.4   MEC Decomposition on the GPU

Our GPU implementation for MEC decomposition is based on the basic algorithm presented in Section 2. For step 1, we use our GPU SCC decomposition. For step 2, we first reset the second and third highest bookkeeping bits in *results* to reuse them as follows: one bit is used to indicate that a state should be removed, and the other bit is used to mark newly discovered MECs. First, a single scan of the input suffices to identify the sets U of the various SCCs. Whenever a state i in the SCC with ID *pivot* is identified to be in U, we lock entry *trans*[*pivot*] to indicate that this SCC cannot be a MEC, and we mark *results*[i] for removal.

Algorithm 3. EXPLORE with local caching for GPU

Require: offset entry *srcinfo* of a state *i*
Ensure: if *i* is in search frontier, then the successors of *i* are added to search frontier, and *i* is moved
    to the explored set
    thcont = 0
2: **if** $i < 32 \cdot \#segments$ **then**
     stepsize ← 32
4:    *thcont* = 1
   else
6:    *stepsize* ← 1
   BROADCAST(*thcont*)
8: **if** *thcont* **then**
    srcregion ← GETREGION(*results*[*i*])
10:    *offset1* ← GETOFFSET(*srcinfo*)
    if *stepsize* = 32 **then**
12:      *offset2* ← *offset1* + (32 · *segmentinterval*)
    else
14:      *offset2* ← GETOFFSET(*offsets*[*i* + 1])
    for (*j* ← *offset1*; *j* < *offset2*; *j* ← *j* + *stepsize*) **do**
16:      *t* ← *trans*[*j*]
      if INFRONTIER(*srcinfo*) **then**
18:        *k* ← GETTGTSTATE(*t*)
        r ← *results*[*j*]
20:        **if** ISACTIVE(*r*) **then**
          tgtregion ← GETREGION(*r*)
22:          **if** *srcregion* = *tgtregion* **then**
            tgtinfo ← *offsets*[*k*]
24:            **if** ISNEW(*tgtinfo*) **then**
              if *iter* < *NrIters* − 1 **then**
26:                **if** ¬STOREINCACHE(*k*) **then**
                  nextIter ← **true**
28:              **else**
                nextIter ← **true**
30:              ADDTOFRONTIER(*tgtinfo*)
            offsets[*k*] ← *tgtinfo*

After that, we compute the intersections of the attractor sets of the U and the SCCs that they belong to; states in those sets are marked for removal. In step 3, *results* is scanned and all entries with region *pivot* and *trans*[*pivot*] unlocked are marked as being in a MEC. Subsequently, we repeatedly compute the attractor sets of those MECs and mark the entries for removal. Concluding, in a single scan, locked *trans* entries are unlocked, to be removed *results* entries are set to a defined 'empty' value (and their *offsets* entry is locked), and discovered MECs are locked as well. Locking of *offsets* and *results* entries means that the highest bit is set, and those entries are effectively removed from the search.

It is important to note that SCCs discovered in a MEC decomposition iteration must necessarily be subsets of SCCs discovered in the previous iteration. This means that we can reuse earlier results to select multiple pivots at the start of an iteration, thereby starting multiple FBT searches in parallel.

4 Experiments

We conducted experiments to measure the performance of our implementations using a representative set of benchmark models taken from the standard distribution of the PRISM model checker and additional models provided through

Table 1. SCC decomposition results of Tarjan and several GPU configurations

Model	|V|	|E|	out	#CC	Tar	F0,1	F0,7	F3,1	F3,7	F0,1-nh
wlan.2500	12.6M	28.1M	2.23	12.5M	**6.17**	29.16	20.71	119.00	61.90	26.73
phil.7	11.0M	98.5M	8.97	1	23.47	**0.70**	0.71	1.14	1.18	0.73
diningcrypt.t.10.(0.5)	42.9M	279.4M	6.51	42.9M	41.42	1.63	**1.62**	1.74	1.75	2.08
test-and-set.7	51.4M	468.5M	9.12	4672	103.92	30.33	36.04	95.67	92.40	**19.12**
leader.7	68.7M	280.5M	4.08	42.2M	68.08	45.02	**5.35**	110.18	12.27	47.84
phil_lss.5,10	72.9M	425.6M	5.84	1	99.75	3.28	3.30	6.46	6.34	**3.25**
coin.8.3	87.9M	583.0M	6.63	5.4M	135.61	125.94	**9.10**	582.59	42.04	179.00
mutual.7.13	76.2M	653.7M	8.58	1	121.31	4.08	**3.72**	4.97	4.66	4.71
zeroconf_dl.F.200.1k.6	118.6M	273.5M	2.31	118.6M	97.91	28.63	**6.12**	28.98	6.23	28.63
firewire_dl.800.36.(0.2)	129.3M	293.6M	2.27	129.3M	104.07	26.71	**6.71**	26.97	6.87	26.60

its dedicated website.[3] In fact, we have selected all available MDP models that were scalable to interesting proportions while not requiring more memory than our GPU could handle, and were accepted by the latest version of PRISM. All experiments were performed on machines running CENTOS LINUX, with an INTEL E5-2620 2.0 GHz CPU, 64 GB RAM, and an NVIDIA Kepler K20m GPU. This GPU has 2496 cores and 5 GB global memory.

For all GPU experiments, we launched $|V|/512$ blocks of 512 threads each, i.e. one thread per state. This keeps the amount of work per thread minimal, and does not introduce idle threads that keep the scheduler busy.

For comparison, we used a CPU implementation of Tarjan's SCC decomposition. Table 1 presents the graph characteristics of the cases and the runtimes in seconds running the CPU and GPU implementations, the latter in a range of different configurations. The 'out' column provides the average out-degree, while the '#CC' column displays the number of SCCs in the graph. 'Tar' stands for Tarjan, and Fi, j represents GPU FBT with i search iterations per BFS kernel launch using the local cache, and j being the interval (out-degree upperbound) used for restructuring the input. Finally, F0, 1-nh is an FBT search in which we have disabled the hybrid search kernel.

Table 2. MEC dec. results

Model	BM	GM
wlan.2500	32.33	21.46
phil.7	51.22	0.73
diningcrypt.t.10.(0.5)	140.85	1.80
test-and-set.7	203.50	36.70
leader.7	239.80	7.48
phil_lss.5,10	281.32	3.45
coin.8.3	363.07	12.63
mutual.7.13 -N	302.66	3.83
zeroconf_dl.F.200.1k.6	390.05	6.23
firewire_dl.800.36.(0.2)	470.96	6.90

Most graphs have a very particular structure; several consist practically entirely of trivial SCCs, and others are a single SCC. We have not preselected any models, so it is interesting to note this phenomenon. It merits further study whether most MDP problems boil down to MDP graphs of one of these types.

For graphs consisting of only one SCC, speedups of around 30 times can be observed. This is not surprising, since these can be analysed in a single GPU

---

[3] All relevant material is available at http://www.win.tue.nl/~awijs/gpudecompose.

search iteration. When there are many trivial SCCs present, the trimming procedure is very influential. The efficiency of the trimming procedure is bound by the average out-degree of a graph; the more connected a trivial SCC state is to other states, the more potential there is for detecting other trivial SCCs in the next trimming iteration. For this reason, the *diningcrypt* case can be decomposed quickly compared to the *zeroconf* and *firewire* cases.

Concerning the latter two cases and other cases with many non-trivial SCCs, it can be observed that the input restructuring works very well (F0,7). In most cases, speedups of about 15 times can be observed. This is significant when considering that in related work [5], only speedups up to 5-6 times were measured for graphs representing model checking problems. Besides the restructuring, the new pivot selection procedure and the data representation likely also play a role in the improved speedup, but it is hard to determine how much, since these are core aspects of our implementation that we cannot easily disable. An experimental comparison with the work of [5] seems useful, however their implementation cannot handle graphs of similar size, due to the fact that eight bits are used per integer for bookkeeping, whereas we only use three. In addition, their implementation does not accept MDP graphs, so some reimplementation work would be required. It is clear, however, that coalesced data access, which is improved by using the restructuring option, is the main cause for the improved speedups. The controlled experiments in which we disabled the hybrid search kernel (F0,1-*nh*) shows that using the kernel at best only causes a minor speedup. In some cases, disabling it even results in speedups, because it results for those particular graph structures in fewer memory accesses. The contribution of the local caches is minimal (cases F3,1 and F3,7), and in some cases using them causes a slowdown. An overall negative result has been obtained for *wlan*. Its graph has a structure which considerably limits the trimming procedure. It both has a low average out-degree and only a few states from which trimming can be instantiated.

In Table 2, results for MEC decomposition are presented. BM stands for Basic MEC decomposition on the CPU, using Tarjan's SCC decomposition for the first step. GM is GPU MEC decomposition using the overall best setup without caches and with restructuring (F0,7). Speedups up to 79 times were measured. The cause for the increased speedups is that the additional steps after SCC decomposition in BM can be performed extremely efficient in parallel on a GPU, since they require (fully coalesced) scanning of the input arrays.

5   Conclusions

We presented GPU algorithms for finding SCCs and MECs in sparse graphs. The implementations exhibit speedups of 15-30 times for SCC decomposition and up to 79 times for MEC decomposition. A critical improvement for SCC decomposition compared to related work is achieved by improving (coalesced) data access. The extra steps for MEC decomposition are very suitable for GPUs.

For future work, we plan to address similar problems in probabilistic model checking [1], and to integrate the algorithms in model checking tools.

References

1. Baier, C., Katoen, J.P.: Principles of Model Checking. The MIT Press (2008)
2. Wang, C., Bloem, R., Hachtel, G.D., Ravi, K., Somenzi, F.: Compositional SCC analysis for language emptiness. Formal Methods in System Design 28, 5–36 (2006)
3. Tarjan, R.E.: Depth-First Search and Linear Graph Algorithms. SIAM J. Comput. 1(2), 146–160 (1972)
4. Bloem, R., Gabow, H.N., Somenzi, F.: An Algorithm for Strongly Connected Component Analysis in n log n Symbolic Steps. Formal Methods in System Design 28, 37–56 (2006)
5. Barnat, J., Bauch, P., Brim, L., Ceska, M.: Computing Strongly Connected Components in Parallel on CUDA. In: IPDPS, pp. 544–555. IEEE (2011)
6. Hong, S., Rodia, N., Olukotun, K.: On Fast Parallel Detection of Strongly Connected Components (SCC) in Small-World Graphs. In: SC 2013, p. 92. ACM (2013)
7. Li, G., Zhu, Z., Cong, Z., Yang, F.: Efficient Decomposition of Strongly Connected Components on GPUs. Journal of Systems Architecture 60(1), 1–10 (2014)
8. Courcoubetis, C., Yannakakis, M.: The complexity of probabilistic verification. J. ACM 42(4), 857–907 (1995)
9. de Alfaro, L.: How to specify and verify the long-run average behavior of probabilistic systems. In: LICS, 454–465. IEEE Computer Society (1998)
10. Ummels, M., Wojtczak, D.: The Complexity of Nash Equilibria in Stochastic Multiplayer Games. Logical Methods in Computer Science 7 (2011)
11. Bruyère, V., Filiot, E., Randour, M., Raskin, J.-F.: Meet your expectations with guarantees: Beyond worst-case synthesis in quantitative games. In: STACS. LIPIcs, vol. 25, pp. 199–213. Schloss Dagstuhl (2014)
12. Chatterjee, K., Henzinger, M.: Faster and Dynamic Algorithms for Maximal End-Component Decomposition and Related Graph Problems in Probabilistic Verification. In: SODA, pp. 1318–1336. SIAM (2011)
13. Chatterjee, K., Łącki, J.: Faster Algorithms for Markov Decision Processes with Low Treewidth. In: Sharygina, N., Veith, H. (eds.) CAV 2013. LNCS, vol. 8044, pp. 543–558. Springer, Heidelberg (2013)
14. Fleischer, L.K., Hendrickson, B.A., Pinar, A.: On identifying strongly connected components in parallel. In: Rolim, J.D.P. (ed.) IPDPS-WS 2000. LNCS, vol. 1800, pp. 505–511. Springer, Heidelberg (2000)
15. Kwiatkowska, M., Norman, G., Parker, D.: PRISM 4.0: Verification of Probabilistic Real-time Systems. In: Gopalakrishnan, G., Qadeer, S. (eds.) CAV 2011. LNCS, vol. 6806, pp. 585–591. Springer, Heidelberg (2011)
16. Bošnački, D., Edelkamp, S., Sulewski, D., Wijs, A.J.: Parallel Probabilistic Model Checking on General Purpose Graphic Processors. STTT 13(1), 21–35 (2011)
17. Barnat, J., Brim, L., Ceska, M., Lamr, T.: CUDA Accelerated LTL Model Checking. In: ICPADS, 34–41. IEEE (2009)
18. Edelkamp, S., Sulewski, D.: Efficient Explicit-State Model Checking on General Purpose Graphics Processors. In: van de Pol, J., Weber, M. (eds.) SPIN 2010. LNCS, vol. 6349, pp. 106–123. Springer, Heidelberg (2010)
19. Wijs, A.J., Bošnački, D.: Improving GPU Sparse Matrix-Vector Multiplication for Probabilistic Model Checking. In: Donaldson, A., Parker, D. (eds.) SPIN 2012. LNCS, vol. 7385, pp. 98–116. Springer, Heidelberg (2012)
20. Bošnački, D., Edelkamp, S., Sulewski, D., Wijs, A.: GPU-PRISM: An Extension of PRISM for General Purpose Graphics Processing Units. In: PDMC 2010, pp. 17–19. IEEE (2010)

21. Wijs, A., Bošnački, D.: GPUexplore: Many-Core On-The-Fly State Space Exploration. In: Ábrahám, E., Havelund, K. (eds.) TACAS 2014. LNCS, vol. 8413, pp. 233–247. Springer, Heidelberg (2014)
22. Chatterjee, K., Henzinger, M.: An $O(n^2)$ Time Algorithm for Alternating Büchi Games. In: SODA, pp. 1386–1399. SIAM (2012)
23. Dijkstra, E.W., Feijen, W.H.J.: A Method of Programming. Addison-Wesley (1988)
24. McLendon III, W., Hendrickson, B., Plimpton, S., Rauchwerger, L.: Finding Strongly Connected Components in Distributed Graphs. J. Parallel Distrib. Comput. 65, 901–910 (2005)
25. Orzan, S.: On Distributed Verification and Verified Distribution. PhD thesis, Free University of Amsterdam (2004)
26. Barnat, J., Moravec, P.: Parallel Algorithms for Finding SCCs in Implicitly Given Graphs. In: Brim, L., Haverkort, B.R., Leucker, M., van de Pol, J. (eds.) FMICS 2006 and PDMC 2006. LNCS, vol. 4346, pp. 316–330. Springer, Heidelberg (2007)
27. Harish, P., Narayanan, P.J.: Accelerating Large Graph Algorithms on the GPU Using CUDA. In: Aluru, S., Parashar, M., Badrinath, R., Prasanna, V.K. (eds.) HiPC 2007. LNCS, vol. 4873, pp. 197–208. Springer, Heidelberg (2007)
28. Merrill, D., Garland, M., Grimshaw, A.: Scalable GPU Graph Traversal. In: PPoPP, 117–128. ACM (2012)
29. Stuhl, M.: Computing Strongly Connected Components with CUDA. Master's thesis, Masaryk University (2013)

Software Verification
in the Google App-Engine Cloud

Dirk Beyer, Georg Dresler, and Philipp Wendler

University of Passau, Germany

Abstract. Software verification often requires a large amount of computing resources. In the last years, cloud services emerged as an inexpensive, flexible, and energy-efficient source of computing power. We have investigated if such cloud resources can be used effectively for verification. We chose the platform-as-a-service offer Google App Engine and ported the open-source verification framework CPACHECKER to it. We provide our new verification service as a web front-end to users who wish to solve single verification tasks (tutorial usage), and an API for integrating the service into existing verification infrastructures (massively parallel bulk usage). We experimentally evaluate the effectiveness of this service and show that it can be successfully used to offload verification work to the cloud, considerably sparing local verification resources.

1 Introduction

Software verification usually requires a large amount of computation resources. In practice, it is often not only a single verification task that needs to be solved, but a large quantity of individual tasks. This occurs for example in regression verification, where the correctness of all components of a system has to be re-established after some development work. For illustration, let us consider Linux driver verification: there are approximately 1 200 commits per week affecting on average 4 device drivers. Assuming that each changed driver is verified against only 100 safety properties after each commit, and that only 12 s of run time are necessary per verification task, the weekly verification time would sum up to 67 days. Those tasks are usually independent and can be run in parallel to reduce the time until the answers are available to the developers. Instead of buying and maintaining an expensive cluster of machines for occasional peaks of computational load, we can also move the actual verification execution into a computing cloud, where resources are available on demand. This enables a verification process that is less expensive (only actual usage is paid) and faster (higher degree of parallelism).

Two of the different flavors of computing cloud services are suitable for implementing a cloud-service-based verification system: Infrastructure as a Service (IaaS) and Platform as a Service (PaaS). For IaaS, a large number of virtual machines (VMs) is reserved, and expenses incur only for the actual uptime of the machines. Amazon's Elastic Compute Cloud (EC2) is a popular example for IaaS. The customer is responsible for all setup work for the VM, including setup of

A. Biere and R. Bloem (Eds.): CAV 2014, LNCS 8559, pp. 327–333, 2014.
© Springer International Publishing Switzerland 2014

the operating system and applications, and an infrastructure for load-balancing (starting VMs as necessary) needs to be implemented by the customer. For PaaS, the customer is allowed to run own applications on an application server, and expenses incur only for the actual consumption of resources by the application. Google's App Engine is a popular example for PaaS. The PaaS provider operates the application server and will automatically run the application on as many machine instances as necessary depending on the demand. This provides a high degree of scalability without administrative effort by the customer.

We are interested to evaluate the applicability of the Google App Engine as verification infrastructure. There are a number of requirements that an application has to satisfy in order to be runnable on a PaaS. For example, in a typical PaaS environment, the application has no or only limited direct access to external services such as the file system, and the application needs to be integrated using specific APIs for serving user requests. Due to the traditionally high resource consumption of verification tools and the restricted environment, we wanted to investigate if an effective and efficient verification service can be implemented based on the Google App Engine. The convenient scalability and the eliminated administration effort make it a promising approach.

Related Work. Several approaches exist to distribute a single verification task across multiple machines [7, 11, 12], for which IaaS clouds can be used as a source of a high number of virtual machines. Such techniques usually do not scale perfectly with the number of machines due to the communication effort, and require specialized verification algorithms. We focus instead on distributing many independent tasks, which works with any existing automatic verification technique and does not require communication between the worker machines. This concept is used in other areas of computation for a long time, but was not yet evaluated for automatic software verification. Also the applicability of a restricted environment and a PaaS offer for verification was not yet studied.

The idea of providing a web front-end for verification services which is usable with a browser is not new, and several such services are available from different groups[1,2,3,4]. These are intended to serve for demonstration and evaluation purposes, and not as a possibility to offload high-volume verification load.

2 Background

Google App Engine. The Google App Engine [13] is a PaaS offer to run web applications on Google's infrastructure. It provides services that are designed to be scalable, reliable, and highly available under heavy load or huge amounts of data. Scaling and load balancing are automatically adjusted to the needs of the application. The App Engine allows to run applications in JAVA, Python, PHP,

---

[1] Multiple tools from Microsoft and others: http://rise4fun.com

[2] Aprove: http://aprove.informatik.rwth-aachen.de/index_llvm.asp

[3] Divine: http://divine.fi.muni.cz/try.cgi

[4] Interproc: http://pop-art.inrialpes.fr/interproc/interprocweb.cgi

or Go. Applications are executed in a sandbox that abstracts the underlying operating system, and provides a secure and isolated environment.

An App-Engine application provides specialized request handlers, which represent the entry points into the application. To serve requests, an application has a pool of zero or more instances allocated. Instances are long-living containers for request handlers that retain local memory and are initialized ahead of incoming requests. The use of a single instance with the smallest configuration of 128 MB of RAM and a 600 MHz CPU for one hour counts as one 'instance hour' and costs 0.05 USD as of May 2014[5]. There are more powerful instances available (up to 1 GB of RAM and a 4.8 GHz CPU) that consume the instance hours at a higher rate. The App Engine also offers a schema-less data store and a task-queue service, which is used to enqueue tasks for execution in the background independent from user interaction.

Restrictions. To provide abstraction from the operating system and to ensure security, the JAVA run-time environment of the App Engine restricts access to a specific set of classes in the JAVA standard library[6]. The most important of the forbidden actions are file-system writes, starting external processes, and loading native libraries. Data need to be stored using the data-store service or the Google Cloud Storage. For the other operations, no alternatives are possible except implementing all functionality in JAVA code. There are also some restrictions on the resource usage of applications[7]. Request handlers are expected to terminate quickly (in under 60 s), but tasks in the task queue are allowed to take up to 10 minutes. The data store takes entities up to a size of 1 MB, which poses a problem with large log or source-code files.

Billing. The pricing model of the App Engine specifies the cost for each resource in detail, and charges incur only for the resources that were actually used. Most resources are freely available up to a resource-specific quota[8]. For example, 28 instance hours can be used free of charge each day.

CPAchecker. CPACHECKER [3] is an open-source framework for software verification, which is available online[9] under the Apache 2.0 license. It is based on the concept of Configurable Program Analysis [2], which supports the integration of different verification components. CPACHECKER implements a wide range of well-known verification techniques, such as lazy abstraction [10], CEGAR [9], predicate abstraction [4], bounded model checking [6], and explicit-value analysis [5]. It is platform-independent because it is implemented entirely in JAVA (including its libraries, e.g., the JAVA-based SMT solver SMTINTERPOL [8]).

---

[5] https://developers.google.com/appengine/pricing
[6] https://developers.google.com/appengine/docs/java/jrewhitelist
[7] https://developers.google.com/appengine/docs/java/backends/
[8] https://developers.google.com/appengine/docs/quotas
[9] http://cpachecker.sosy-lab.org

3 Verification in the Google App-Engine Cloud

Porting CPAchecker. It is in principle possible to use all analyses of CPACHECKER in the Google App Engine because it is written in JAVA. Due to the above-mentioned restrictions, some adoptions were necessary. Most features of CPACHECKER that rely on disabled JAVA APIs are either optional or non-critical, and could thus be turned off with CPACHECKER's own configuration mechanism. This includes, for example, extended time and memory measurements, and counterexample checks with the external checker CBMC (which is written in C++ and thus not portable to the App Engine). If an SMT solver is needed, we use SMTINTERPOL, which is written in JAVA. The major obstacle for porting CPACHECKER to the App Engine was to re-design file-system writes. CPACHECKER expected the source-code file on the disk and would usually write several output files with information about the analyzed program and perhaps a counterexample. While the output files are optional, they provide helpful information to the user and thus should be available. Thus, we integrated an abstraction layer for all file-system operations of CPACHECKER that re-routes the reading of the input program and the writing of all output files to the data-store service. Apart from minor other adoptions, these were the only changes to CPACHECKER. All of our work was integrated into the CPACHECKER project and is available as open source from its repository.

API for Bulk Usage. The most important application of our cloud-based verification service is solving a large quantity of verification tasks, as in regression verification. We developed an API for automatically submitting tasks and retrieving results. We integrated a client for this API in CPACHECKER's execution infrastructure, such that in terms of user interaction, there is no difference between running the verification tasks locally or using the App Engine. Due to the scalability of the App Engine, the results will be available quickly because many verification tasks can be solved in parallel. Another application of the verification-service API is an integration in situations where verification is needed but resources are limited or a verifier might not be available. For example, using the verification service inside an IDE plug-in would make it easier and faster for developers to verify their code.

Front-End for Tutorial Usage. The second channel of access is provided for users who wish to try out CPACHECKER, or experiment with software verification in general: we provide a web-based user interface that is easy to use in a web browser and requires no installation effort from the user. The user uploads or enters a program, selects a specification that the program should satisfy, and chooses a configuration of the verifier. After starting the verification run, the user is kept informed about the current status of the task, and the result is provided after the run is finished. Further output like log files, statistics, and information about counterexamples are presented and available for download. The front-end that we implemented is available online[10].

---

[10] http://cpachecker.appspot.com

4   Experimental Evaluation

To evaluate the effectiveness and efficiency of the Google App-Engine cloud for verification purposes, we run CPACHECKER in version 1.3.2-cav14 on verification tasks from the International Competition on Software Verification (SV-COMP'14) [1]. We compare the amount of successfully verified programs and the verification time to a local execution of the verifier. To show the applicability of the cloud service, we use two verification approaches that have different characteristics with regard to performance and resource requirements: an explicit-value analysis [5] and a predicate analysis [4] (using the SMT solver SMTINTERPOL).

Setup. We limit the wall time for each verification task to 9 minutes. We did not use any limits for CPU time, because this is not supported by the App Engine. In the App Engine, we used the default of the available instances, which provides 128 MB of RAM and 600 MHz of CPU frequency. For a direct comparison, we also limited the size of the JAVA heap memory to 128 MB for the local executions. For desktop machines, this is a rather low limit as current machines provide much more RAM. Thus, we additionally ran the same analyses with a heap size of 4 096 MB. In both cases, we assigned one CPU core (plus one hyper-threading core) of an Intel Core i7-2600 quad-core CPU with 3.4 GHz. In the App Engine, we reserved 100 instances at the same time. For local execution, we ran 4 tasks in parallel on the same machine. We selected those categories from the SV-COMP repository[11] as benchmark verification tasks that are well-supported by the chosen analyses: ControlFlow, DeviceDrivers64, SequentializedConcurrent, and Simple. We excluded programs whose source code was larger than 1 MB (restriction by the data store). This resulted in 2 458 program files written in C.

Results. Table 1 shows a summary of the results. For each configuration, we list the number of successfully computed answers, and the CPU time that was necessary to compute them. We also show the wall time that elapsed between start and end of the benchmark, i.e., the time the user has to wait for all results. Both times are rounded to two significant digits. In Fig. 1 we show quantile functions for the successful results (i.e., the verifier returned an answer) of all configurations. The results are sorted by their run time, i.e., a data point (x, y) means that the respective configuration has successfully verified x programs in at most y seconds each. The area under a graph represents the sum of the CPU time that is necessary for computing the answers (the lower a graph is, the faster a configuration is). This value can also be seen in the row 'CPU Time' of Table 1. The further to the right a graph stretches, the more answers were returned by a configuration. Dark lines (red, blue) in the plot show executions in the App Engine, the corresponding light lines (orange, cyan) show the local executions.

The plot shows that the App Engine is actually often faster. This is due to the relatively long startup time of a JVM on the local machine (almost 2 s), which is not needed in the App Engine. The table and the graph both show that CPACHECKER running in the App Engine is not able to verify as many programs as locally within the same time limit, and needs more CPU time. Impressively,

---

[11] https://svn.sosy-lab.org/software/sv-benchmarks/trunk/c/

Table 1. Summary of results comparing App-Engine execution with local execution

Analysis	Explicit-Value			Predicate		
Location	App Engine	Local		App Engine	Local	
CPU Frequency	600 MHz	3.4 GHz	3.4 GHz	600 MHz	3.4 GHz	3.4 GHz
Heap Size	128 MB	128 MB	4096 MB	128 MB	128 MB	4096 MB
Successful: No. of Results	1 842	1 920	2 021	1 771	1 952	2 012
CPU Time (s)	16 000	13 000	31 000	41 000	39 000	50 000
Total: Wall Time (s)	11 000	30 000	53 000	9 900	46 000	58 000
Effective Parallelization	25	4	4	30	4	4

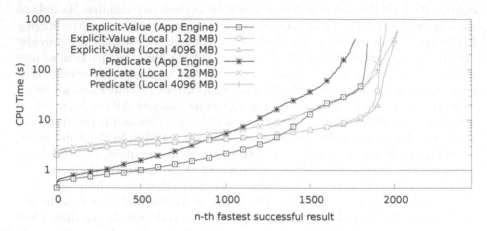

Fig. 1. Quantile functions showing the CPU time for the successful results; symbols at every 100-th data point; linear scale between 0 s and 1 s, logarithmic scale beyond

the difference in the number of results is only about 10 %. Note that we used the rather slow standard instances in the App Engine which provide a much lower CPU speed than our local machine. More powerful instances would be available as well (at a higher price). Furthermore, the row 'Total Wall Time' in Table 1 shows that due to the high scalability of the cloud and the massive parallelism, the total waiting time for the user is much lower (3 hours instead of 8 to 16 hours), even though we ran 4 tasks in parallel locally. The effective parallelization in the App Engine is less than the number of instances (100) due to queue saturation problems which could be fixed with an improved implementation. More details on this issue can be found on the supplementary webpage[12].

Running all 4 916 tasks in the cloud cost 38.09 USD where the explicit-value and predicate analysis consumed 17.78 USD and 20.31 USD, respectively. All experiments that we ran for the preparation of this paper cost only 185.72 USD in total (for obtaining valid results, we had to run the experiments several times). The experiments were done when the prices were still higher, with prices of May 2014 the cost would have been 38 % less.

---

[12] http://www.sosy-lab.org/~dbeyer/cpa-appengine

5 Conclusion

We ported the successful open-source verification framework CPACHECKER to the Google App Engine, and have shown that cloud-based verification is an effective way to gain scalability and a high degree of parallelism, allowing users to receive verification results much faster. This new verification service enables a convenient integration of software verification into development environments that do not support the execution of a verification engine locally. It also provides a convenient way for tutorial-like experiments with a verifier without any installation effort.

References

1. Beyer, D.: Status report on software verification (competition summary SV-COMP 2014). In: Ábrahám, E., Havelund, K. (eds.) TACAS 2014. LNCS, vol. 8413, pp. 373–388. Springer, Heidelberg (2014)
2. Beyer, D., Henzinger, T.A., Théoduloz, G.: Configurable software verification: Concretizing the convergence of model checking and program analysis. In: Damm, W., Hermanns, H. (eds.) CAV 2007. LNCS, vol. 4590, pp. 504–518. Springer, Heidelberg (2007)
3. Beyer, D., Keremoglu, M.E.: CPACHECKER: A tool for configurable software verification. In: Gopalakrishnan, G., Qadeer, S. (eds.) CAV 2011. LNCS, vol. 6806, pp. 184–190. Springer, Heidelberg (2011)
4. Beyer, D., Keremoglu, M.E., Wendler, P.: Predicate abstraction with adjustable-block encoding. In: Bloem, R., Sharygina, N. (eds.) FMCAD 2010, pp. 189–197. FMCAD (2010)
5. Beyer, D., Löwe, S.: Explicit-state software model checking based on CEGAR and interpolation. In: Cortellessa, V., Varró, D. (eds.) FASE 2013. LNCS, vol. 7793, pp. 146–162. Springer, Heidelberg (2013)
6. Biere, A., Cimatti, A., Clarke, E., Zhu, Y.: Symbolic model checking without BDDs. In: Cleaveland, W.R. (ed.) TACAS/ETAPS 1999. LNCS, vol. 1579, pp. 193–207. Springer, Heidelberg (1999)
7. Breuer, P.T., Pickin, S.: Open source verification under a cloud. ECEASST 33 (2010)
8. Christ, J., Hoenicke, J., Nutz, A.: SMTInterpol: An interpolating SMT solver. In: Donaldson, A., Parker, D. (eds.) SPIN 2012. LNCS, vol. 7385, pp. 248–254. Springer, Heidelberg (2012)
9. Clarke, E.M., Grumberg, O., Jha, S., Lu, Y., Veith, H.: Counterexample-guided abstraction refinement for symbolic model checking. J. ACM 50(5), 752–794 (2003)
10. Henzinger, T.A., Jhala, R., Majumdar, R., Sutre, G.: Lazy abstraction. In: Launchbury, J., Mitchell, J. C. (eds.) POPL 2002, pp. 58–70. ACM (2002)
11. Holzmann, G.J., Joshi, R., Groce, A.: Swarm verification. In: Inverardi, P., Ireland, A., Visser, W. (eds.) ASE 2008, pp. 1–6. IEEE (2008)
12. Lerda, F., Sisto, R.: Distributed-memory model checking with SPIN. In: Dams, D., Gerth, R., Leue, S., Massink, M. (eds.) SPIN 1999. LNCS, vol. 1680, pp. 22–39. Springer, Heidelberg (1999)
13. Sanderson, D.: Programming Google App Engine. O'Reilly (2012)

The NUXMV Symbolic Model Checker*

Roberto Cavada, Alessandro Cimatti, Michele Dorigatti, Alberto Griggio,
Alessandro Mariotti, Andrea Micheli, Sergio Mover,
Marco Roveri, and Stefano Tonetta

Fondazione Bruno Kessler

Abstract. This paper describes the NUXMV symbolic model checker for finite-
and infinite-state synchronous transition systems. NUXMV is the evolution of the
NUSMV open source model checker. It builds on and extends NUSMV along
two main directions. For finite-state systems it complements the basic verification
techniques of NUSMV with state-of-the-art verification algorithms. For infinite-
state systems, it extends the NUSMV language with new data types, namely Integers and Reals, and it provides advanced SMT-based model checking techniques.

Besides extended functionalities, NUXMV has been optimized in terms of performance to be competitive with the state of the art. NUXMV has been used in
several industrial projects as verification back-end, and it is the basis for several extensions to cope with requirements analysis, contract based design, model
checking of hybrid systems, safety assessment, and software model checking.

1 Introduction

NUSMV [1] is a symbolic model checker for finite state fair transition systems. It has
been developed jointly by Carnegie Mellon University, the University of Trento and
Fondazione Bruno Kessler (FBK) since 1999. It is distributed as open source under
the LGPL license, and it integrates some of the most successful BDD and SAT based
symbolic model checking algorithms up to 2011 (the year of its last official release).

Since its first release in 1999, the public available version of NUSMV has been
complemented and extended, internally at FBK, with multiple functionalities. This was
done in order to facilitate its deployment in several operational settings, and to take into
account the needs resulting from industrial and research projects. In particular, we integrated functionalities for requirements engineering, safety assessment, contract based
design, and techniques for the analysis of hybrid systems; we also interfaced NUXMV
with SMT engines. The whole set of new functionalities were developed as a single
code-base, referred in several papers as NuSMT and NuSMV3. To better maintain such
features, and to facilitate the deployment, we started a re-engineering process where we
separated all of them in several different tools. In this view, NUSMV is the code-base
that provides basic functionalities and common data structures to all the other tools (e.g.
symbol table, handling of expressions, interface with the CUDD [2] BDD package, interface with the SAT solvers (e.g. MINISAT [3]). NUSMV also provides all the basic
model checking algorithms for the pure Boolean case.

* This work was carried out within the D-MILS project, which is partially funded under the
European Commission's Seventh Framework Programme (FP7).

A. Biere and R. Bloem (Eds.): CAV 2014, LNCS 8559, pp. 334–342, 2014.

In this paper we describe NUXMV, a new symbolic model checker for finite- and infinite-state synchronous fair transition systems. NUXMV is the evolution of NUSMV, as such it builds on NUSMV and extends it along two main directions. For finite-state systems, it complements NUSMV basic verification techniques with a family of new state-of-the-art verification algorithms. For infinite-state systems, it extends the NUSMV language with new data types, namely Integers and Reals, and it provides advanced SMT-based model checking techniques. NUXMV participated in the 2013 hardware model checking competition (HWMCC'13) positioning among the first four in the single and multiple tracks. NUXMV also compares well with other model checkers for infinite-state systems. Finally, NUXMV has been successfully used in several application domains and in industrial settings. It is currently the core verification engine for many other tools (also industrial ones). The tool is distributed in binary code, free to be used for academic research and for non-commercial uses. The latest version of NUXMV can be downloaded from https://nuxmv.fbk.eu.

2 Functionalities

NUXMV inherits, and thus provides to the user, all the functionalities of NUSMV [1]. In this section we describe all the new features distinguishing them in those for the analysis of finite-state domains, those for the analysis of infinite-state domains, and other generic features.

2.1 Analysis of Finite-State Domains

NUXMV complements the NUSMV language with the AIGER [4] format. AIGER is the language adopted in the hardware model checking competition. Once the AIGER file is read, the internal data structures of NUXMV are populated, and it is possible to verify the properties (if any) with any of the available verification algorithms, or specify new properties interactively "playing" with the design.

NUXMV implements a vast portfolio of algorithms for invariant checking. We currently provide an implementation for the McMillan interpolation-based approach [5] and for the interpolation sequence approach [6]. Interpolation based algorithms are complemented with k-induction algorithms [7] and a family of algorithms based on IC3 [8,9,10]. The IC3 algorithm using abstraction refinement [10] comes in two variant depending on the approach to refinement: the original one based on IC3, and a new variant based on BMC. All these techniques, benefit from the use of temporal decomposition [11] and from techniques to discover equivalences to simplify the problem. We remark that, to implement the interpolation based algorithms we extended MINISAT [3] to build a resolution proof.

Still related to the verification of invariants, we also improved the BDD based invariant checking algorithms by allowing the user to specify hints in the spirit of guided reachability [12]. The hints are specified using a restricted fragment of the PSL SERE [13]. The hints can also be used to compute the full set of the reachable states.

For LTL SAT based model checking, we complemented the BMC based algorithms of NUSMV [14,15] with k-liveness [16] integrated within an IC3 framework. K-liveness is based on counting and bounding the number of times a fairness constraint can become true. This is used in conjunction with the construction of a monitor for LTL properties, for which we use the LTL2SMV [17] as provided by NuSMV.

2.2 Analysis of Infinite-State Domains

In order to allow the user to specify infinite-state systems, we extended the language of NuSMV with two new data types, namely Reals and unbounded Integers. This, for instance, enables to specify domains with infinite data types (like e.g. the example in Fig. 1).

To analyze such kind of designs, we integrated in NuXmv several new verification algorithms based on Satisfiability Modulo Theory (SMT) [18] and on abstraction, or combination of abstraction with other techniques.

We lifted Simple Bounded Model Checking (SBMC) [15] from the pure Boolean case to the SMT case. The encoding is the same as that of SBMC, but instead of using a SAT solver we

```
 1  MODULE main
 2  IVAR
 3    d : Real;
 4  VAR
 5    state : {s0, s1};
 6    res   : Real;
 7  ASSIGN
 8    init(state) := s0;
 9    next(state) := case
10      state = s0 & res >= 0.10 : s1;
11      state = s1 & res >= 0.20 : s0;
12      TRUE                     : state;
13    esac;
14    next(t) := case
15      state = s0 & res < 0.10 : res + d;
16      state = s1 & res < 0.20 : res + d;
17      TRUE                    : 0.0;
18    esac;
19  INIT
20    res >= 0.0
21  TRANS
22    (state = s0 -> (d >= 0 & d <= 0.01)) &
23    (state = s1 -> (d >= 0 & d <= 0.02))
24  INVARSPEC res <= 0.3;
```

Fig. 1. Example of the NuXmv language

use an SMT solver. The SBMC SMT based approach for LTL verification is complemented with k-liveness combined with IC3 extended to the infinite-state case [19]. This approach relies on recent results on applying an IC3-based approach to the verification of infinite-state systems [20]. We remark that, although these approaches are in general incomplete, if a lazo-shaped counterexample exists, it is guaranteed to be eventually found. Moreover, for certain designs, they are able to conclude that the property hold.

As far as invariant checking is concerned, we lifted the pure Boolean approaches like BMC, k-induction, interpolation, and IC3 to the infinite-state systems case. Intuitively, we use an SMT solver in place of the SAT solver. Similarly to the finite case, we provide an SMT based implementation for the McMillan approach [5], the interpolation sequence approach [6], k-induction [7] and for algorithms based on IC3 [20,21].

NuXmv also implements several approaches based on abstraction refinement [22]. We provide new algorithms combining abstraction with BMC and k-induction [23]. The algorithms do not rely on quantifier elimination techniques to compute the abstraction, but encode the model checking problem over the abstract state space into SMT problems. The advantage, is that they avoid the possible bottleneck of abstraction computation. The very same approach has been recently lifted and tightly integrated within the IC3 framework [21], with very good results. All these techniques complement the "classical" counterexample guided (predicate) abstraction refinement (CEGAR) [22], also implemented in NuXmv. The CEGAR approach requires the computation of a quantifier-free formula that is equivalent to the abstract transition relation w.r.t. a given set of predicates. This, in turn, requires the solving of an AllSAT problem [24]. For this step, NuXmv implements different techniques: a combination of BDD and SMT [25,26], where BDDs are used as compact Boolean model enumerators within an AllSMT approach; a technique that exploits the structure of the system under verification, to partition the abstraction problem into the combination of several smaller abstraction problems [27]. For the refinement step to discard the spurious counterexample, NUXMV implements three approaches based on the analysis of the unsatisfiable core, on the analysis of the interpolants, and on the weakest preconditions.

2.3 Miscellaneous Functionalities

NUXMV provides novel functionalities that aim at facilitating the modeling and the understanding of complex designs. For instance, it allows for the generation of an explicit state representation (subject to the projection over a set of user specified predicates) in XMI format of the design under verification. The generated XMI can be visualized in any UML based viewer supporting the import from XMI.

LTL and invariant properties have been extended to allow for the use of input signals and next values of state variables. This does not add any expressive power to the language, but facilitates the writing of properties from the user's point of view. Internally, each state formula containing a reference to an input or next signal is replaced with a corresponding monitor allowing for the reuse of off-the-shelf verification engines.

NUXMV also provides several model transformation techniques aiming to reduce the state space of the design. It uses static analysis techniques to extract possible values for variables, and then re-encode the design using such information (e.g. using a word at 32 bit to store 2 values can be re-encoded with just one Boolean variable). These techniques are complemented with others aiming at simplifying the model through constants and free inputs propagation [28].

Finally, in NUXMV we removed the NUSMV limitation that restricted the support to bit vectors with less than 64 bits only.

3 Architecture

NUXMV extends the NUSMV [1] architecture as described here after. NUXMV shares with NUSMV all the basic functionalities, e.g. the symbol table, the flattening of the design, the Boolean encoding of scalar variables, the representation of the finite-state machines at the different abstraction levels (e.g., scalar, BDD). Moreover, it inherits from NUSMV all the basic model checking algorithms for finite domains both using BDDs (using the CUDD [2]) and SAT (e.g. MINISAT [3]). To implement the new functionalities, we added new Boolean reasoning engines. We extended MINISAT with the construction of the resolution proof. On top of this, we built an interface to extract interpolants. In this respect, we extended the standard API in NUSMV to also provide API for extracting and manipulating interpolants. This also enables for the use of different SAT engines in a transparent way.

For IC3 based algorithms, NUXMV provides two modes: execution as a library, or call of an external executable (this was also done to participate to the hardware model checking competition). The use of an external executable also opens to experiment with other engines, and to reuse the results within NUXMV, provided the I/O interface is respected. The model checking problem is dumped into AIGER format, and for violated properties the resulting AIGER trace is converted back into a NUXMV trace.

To reason over infinite-state systems, we created an interface towards SMT engines. We instantiated this interface on the MATHSAT5 [29] SMT solver (although in

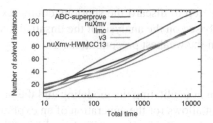 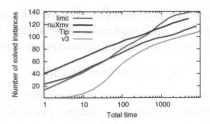

Fig. 2. Results for finite domains on the HWMCC13 samples

principle other SMT solvers could be plugged in). The interface enables for a wide range of queries: satisfiability checking and AllSMT queries; extraction of unsatisfiable cores and of interpolants; and, quantifier elimination. This interface is the basis on top of which the majority of the SMT based algorithms are built. For IC3 based algorithms, a more tight integration with the SMT solver is required, therefore we implemented them directly on top of MATHSAT5. We then interfaced this new engine with NUXMV.

NUXMV has been developed in C and in C++. It compiles and executes on the most widely used Operating Systems (OSs) and architectures; namely, Linux, MS Windows, and MacOS X. Porting to other OSs is also possible (although not tested yet).

4 Performance Evaluation

In order to see where NUXMV is positioned w.r.t. the state-of-the-art, we report in this section some results. In Fig. 2 we plot the comparison of NUXMV against the three best performers at the HWMCC13. The comparison is run on the same benchmarks used in the HWMCC13 in the single safety (left) and in the liveness (right) tracks. We compare two versions of NUXMV, the one that participated in the competition (NUXMV-HWMCC13) and the current one. The results show that, still ABC is the top performer, but the current version of NUXMV is able to solve more problems that the one submitted to the competition. Moreover, it solves more problems than iimc and v3 that are performing better than NUXMV-HWMCC13. Concerning the liveness track, NUXMV did not participate in the competition. Here iimc is still the winner, but NUXMV performs better than v3 and tip (positioned 2nd and 3rd resp. in the HWMCC13).

In Fig. 3 we report some results for the SMT cases. On the left we compare IC3 with implicit abstraction algorithm [21] as available in NUXMV against state-of-the-art engines on a set of bit-vector (BV) benchmarks (we took all the benchmarks used in [20], using BV as background theory instead of LRA, the instances of the bitvector set of the Software Verification Competition [30] and the instances from the test suite of InvGen [31]). For the other solvers, bit-blasting was performed. In Fig. 3 on the right, we compare NUXMV with other model checkers for Linear Integer Arithmetic (LIA). (The label nuXmv-IC3(IA) corresponds to the label IC3+IA(BV) of [21].) We used benchmarks taken from Lustre programs as available from the web page of Kind [32]. These results show that in both cases NUXMV can solve more problems than the other state-of-the-art tools.

These results, clearly show that NUXMV is well positioned in the space of formal verification engines, both for the finite domain case, and for the infinite domain one.

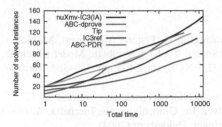 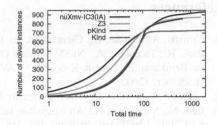

Fig. 3. Results on SMT domains: BV and LIA (taken from [21]

5   Applications

The NUXMV symbolic model checker has been used in a wide range of applications, both at academic and at industrial level.

As far as the industrial settings are concerned, we report that NUXMV is used at Rockwell-Collins as one of the available back-end verification engines [33]. NUXMV has been extended and is daily used by Ales s.r.l., also as a back-end verification engine, for their internal verification flow [34]. Moreover, Ansaldo STS integrated NUXMV within their development environment for the verification of railways interlocking software [35]. We also remark that NUXMV has been widely used in several industrial projects with the European Space Agency (ESA). For instance, it is the back-end of the COMPASS tool [36], developed within the COMPASS [37] and AUTOGEF [38] projects both funded by ESA. It has also been used in the EuRailCheck tool for the validation of a fragment of the ETCS requirements [39]. EuRailCheck was developed in response of an invitation to tender issued by the European Railway Agency.

NUXMV is also the back-end of several other tools. (We remark that, since the development of NUXMV started a long time ago, its functionalities were used already by other tools, often relying on intermediate, non-official versions of NUXMV itself.) It has been integrated in AutoFocus [40]. It is used in the KRATOS [41] software model checker, in RATSY [42] for temporal logic synthesis, and in OCRA [43] for contract based requirements analysis. Finally, it is the basis on top of which we built the safety assessment tool FSAP [44] and the HyCOMP [45] tool for the verification of hybrid systems.

6   Conclusions and Future Work

In this paper we presented NUXMV, a new symbolic model checker for finite- and infinite-state transition systems. We described its functionalities, and we reported some results that compare its performance with the state-of-the-art. The results show that it is well positioned w.r.t. the other possible competitors.

As future work, we would like to add support for arrays, their combination with bit vectors, and uninterpreted functions, and to interface with the BTOR format. We would like to exploit multi-core architecures to further speed-up the analyses. Finally, we would like to wrap the NUXMV functionalities in a scripting language to facilitate the experimentation of new algorithms and the customization w.r.t. user needs.

References

1. Cimatti, A., Clarke, E., Giunchiglia, E., Giunchiglia, F., Pistore, M., Roveri, M., Sebastiani, R., Tacchella, A.: NuSMV 2: An OpenSource Tool for Symbolic Model Checking. In: Brinksma, E., Larsen, K.G. (eds.) CAV 2002. LNCS, vol. 2404, pp. 359–364. Springer, Heidelberg (2002)
2. Somenzi, F.: CUDD: Colorado University Decision Diagram package — release 2.4.1
3. Eén, N., Sörensson, N.: An extensible sat-solver. In: Giunchiglia, E., Tacchella, A. (eds.) SAT 2003. LNCS, vol. 2919, pp. 502–518. Springer, Heidelberg (2004)
4. Biere, A., Heljanko, K., Wieringa, S.: AIGER (2011), http://fmv.jku.at/aiger/
5. McMillan, K.L.: Interpolation and sat-based model checking. In: Hunt Jr., W.A., Somenzi, F. (eds.) CAV 2003. LNCS, vol. 2725, pp. 1–13. Springer, Heidelberg (2003)
6. Vizel, Y., Grumberg, O.: Interpolation-sequence based model checking. In: FMCAD, pp. 1–8. IEEE (2009)
7. Sheeran, M., Singh, S., Stålmarck, G.: Checking safety properties using induction and a sat-solver. In: Johnson, S.D., Hunt Jr., W.A. (eds.) FMCAD 2000. LNCS, vol. 1954, pp. 108–125. Springer, Heidelberg (2000)
8. Bradley, A.R.: Sat-based model checking without unrolling. In: Jhala, R., Schmidt, D. (eds.) VMCAI 2011. LNCS, vol. 6538, pp. 70–87. Springer, Heidelberg (2011)
9. Hassan, Z., Bradley, A.R., Somenzi, F.: Better generalization in ic3. In: FMCAD, pp. 157–164. IEEE (2013)
10. Vizel, Y., Grumberg, O., Shoham, S.: Lazy abstraction and sat-based reachability in hardware model checking. In: Cabodi, G., Singh, S. (eds.) FMCAD, pp. 173–181. IEEE (2012)
11. Case, M.L., Mony, H., Baumgartner, J., Kanzelman, R.: Enhanced verification by temporal decomposition. In: FMCAD, pp. 17–24. IEEE (2009)
12. Thomas, D., Chakraborty, S., Pandya, P.K.: Efficient guided symbolic reachability using reachability expressions. STTT 10(2), 113–129 (2008)
13. Eisner, C., Fisman, D.: A Practical Introduction to PSL. Series on Integrated Circuits and Systems. Springer-Verlag New York, Inc., Secaucus (2006)
14. Biere, A., Cimatti, A., Clarke, E.M., Zhu, Y.: Symbolic model checking without bdds. In: Cleaveland, W.R. (ed.) TACAS/ETAPS 1999. LNCS, vol. 1579, pp. 193–207. Springer, Heidelberg (1999)
15. Biere, A., Heljanko, K., Junttila, T.A., Latvala, T., Schuppan, V.: Linear encodings of bounded ltl model checking. Logical Methods in Computer Science 2(5) (2006)
16. Claessen, K., Sörensson, N.: A liveness checking algorithm that counts. In: Cabodi, G., Singh, S. (eds.) FMCAD, pp. 52–59. IEEE (2012)
17. Clarke, E.M., Grumberg, O., Hamaguchi, K.: Another Look at LTL Model Checking. Formal Methods in System Design 10(1), 47–71 (1997)
18. Barrett, C.W., Sebastiani, R., Seshia, S.A., Tinelli, C.: Satisfiability modulo theories. In: Handbook of Satisfiability, pp. 825–885. IOS Press (2009)
19. Cimatti, A., Griggio, A., Mover, S., Tonetta, S.: Verifying ltl properties of hybrid systems with k-liveness. Technical report. Under review (2014)
20. Cimatti, A., Griggio, A.: Software model checking via ic3. In: Madhusudan, P., Seshia, S.A. (eds.) CAV 2012. LNCS, vol. 7358, pp. 277–293. Springer, Heidelberg (2012)
21. Cimatti, A., Griggio, A., Mover, S., Tonetta, S.: Ic3 modulo theories via implicit predicate abstraction. In: Ábrahám, E., Havelund, K. (eds.) TACAS 2014. LNCS, vol. 8413, pp. 46–61. Springer, Heidelberg (2014)
22. Clarke, E.M., Grumberg, O., Jha, S., Lu, Y., Veith, H.: Counterexample-guided abstraction refinement for symbolic model checking. J. ACM 50(5), 752–794 (2003)
23. Tonetta, S.: Abstract model checking without computing the abstraction. In: Cavalcanti, A., Dams, D.R. (eds.) FM 2009. LNCS, vol. 5850, pp. 89–105. Springer, Heidelberg (2009)

24. Lahiri, S.K., Nieuwenhuis, R., Oliveras, A.: SMT Techniques for Fast Predicate Abstraction. In: Ball, T., Jones, R.B. (eds.) CAV 2006. LNCS, vol. 4144, pp. 424–437. Springer, Heidelberg (2006)

25. Cavada, R., Cimatti, A., Franzén, A., Kalyanasundaram, K., Roveri, M., Shyamasundar, R.K.: Computing Predicate Abstractions by Integrating BDDs and SMT Solvers. In: FMCAD, pp. 69–76. IEEE Computer Society (2007)

26. Cimatti, A., Franzén, A., Griggio, A., Kalyanasundaram, K., Roveri, M.: Tighter integration of BDDs and SMT for Predicate Abstraction. In: DATE, pp. 1707–1712. IEEE (2010)

27. Cimatti, A., Dubrovin, J., Junttila, T.A., Roveri, M.: Structure-aware computation of predicate abstraction. In: FMCAD, pp. 9–16. IEEE (2009)

28. Armoni, R., Fix, L., Fraer, R., Heyman, T., Vardi, M.Y., Vizel, Y., Zbar, Y.: Deeper Bound in BMC by Combining Constant Propagation and Abstraction. In: ASP-DAC, pp. 304–309. IEEE (2007)

29. Cimatti, A., Griggio, A., Schaafsma, B.J., Sebastiani, R.: The MathSAT5 SMT Solver. In: Piterman, N., Smolka, S.A. (eds.) TACAS 2013. LNCS, vol. 7795, pp. 93–107. Springer, Heidelberg (2013)

30. Beyer, D.: Second Competition on Software Verification - (Summary of SV-COMP 2013. In: Piterman, N., Smolka, S.A. (eds.) TACAS 2013. LNCS, vol. 7795, pp. 594–609. Springer, Heidelberg (2013)

31. Gupta, A., Rybalchenko, A.: InvGen: An efficient invariant generator. In: Bouajjani, A., Maler, O. (eds.) CAV 2009. LNCS, vol. 5643, pp. 634–640. Springer, Heidelberg (2009)

32. Hagen, G., Tinelli, C.: Scaling up the formal verification of lustre programs with smt-based techniques. In: Cimatti, A., Jones, R.B. (eds.) FMCAD, pp. 1–9. IEEE (2008)

33. Miller, S.P., Whalen, M.W., Cofer, D.D.: Software model checking takes off. Commun. ACM 53(2), 58–64 (2010)

34. Ferrante, O., Benvenuti, L., Mangeruca, L., Sofronis, C., Ferrari, A.: Parallel NuSMV: A NuSMV Extension for the Verification of Complex Embedded Systems. In: Ortmeier, F., Daniel, P. (eds.) SAFECOMP Workshops 2012. LNCS, vol. 7613, pp. 409–416. Springer, Heidelberg (2012)

35. Cimatti, A., Corvino, R., Lazzaro, A., Narasamdya, I., Rizzo, T., Roveri, M., Sanseviero, A., Tchaltsev, A.: Formal Verification and Validation of ERTMS Industrial Railway Train Spacing System. In: Madhusudan, P., Seshia, S.A. (eds.) CAV 2012. LNCS, vol. 7358, pp. 378–393. Springer, Heidelberg (2012)

36. Bozzano, M., Cimatti, A., Katoen, J.-P., Nguyen, V.Y., Noll, T., Roveri, M., Wimmer, R.: A Model Checker for AADL. In: Touili, T., Cook, B., Jackson, P. (eds.) CAV 2010. LNCS, vol. 6174, pp. 562–565. Springer, Heidelberg (2010)

37. Bozzano, M., Cimatti, A., Katoen, J.-P., Nguyen, V.Y., Noll, T., Roveri, M.: The compass approach: Correctness, modelling and performability of aerospace systems. In: Buth, B., Rabe, G., Seyfarth, T. (eds.) SAFECOMP 2009. LNCS, vol. 5775, pp. 173–186. Springer, Heidelberg (2009)

38. Alaña, E., Naranjo, H., Yushtein, Y., Bozzano, M., Cimatti, A., Gario, M., de Ferluc, E., Garcia, G.: Automated generation of FDIR for the compass integrated toolset (AUTOGEF). DASIA 2012 (2012)

39. Chiappini, A., Cimatti, A., Macchi, L., Rebollo, O., Roveri, M., Susi, A., Tonetta, S., Vittorini, B.: Formalization and validation of a subset of the european train control system. In: Kramer, J., Bishop, J., Devanbu, P.T., Uchitel, S. (eds.) ICSE (2), pp. 109–118. ACM (2010)

40. Autofocus-Team: The AutoFOCUS tool, https://af3.fortiss.org

41. Cimatti, A., Griggio, A., Micheli, A., Narasamdya, I., Roveri, M.: Kratos - A Software Model Checker for SystemC. In: Gopalakrishnan, G., Qadeer, S. (eds.) CAV 2011. LNCS, vol. 6806, pp. 310–316. Springer, Heidelberg (2011)

42. Bloem, R., Cimatti, A., Greimel, K., Hofferek, G., Könighofer, R., Roveri, M., Schuppan, V., Seeber, R.: RATSY - A New Requirements Analysis Tool with Synthesis. In: Touili, T., Cook, B., Jackson, P. (eds.) CAV 2010. LNCS, vol. 6174, pp. 425–429. Springer, Heidelberg (2010)
43. Cimatti, A., Dorigatti, M., Tonetta, S.: OCRA: A tool for checking the refinement of temporal contracts. In: ASE, pp. 702–705. IEEE (2013)
44. Bozzano, M., Villafiorita, A.: The FSAP/NuSMV-SA Safety Analysis Platform. STTT 9(1), 5–24 (2007)
45. Cimatti, A., Mover, S., Tonetta, S.: SMT-Based Verification of Hybrid Systems. In: Hoffmann, J., Selman, B. (eds.) AAAI. AAAI Press (2012)

Analyzing and Synthesizing Genomic Logic Functions

Nicola Paoletti[1,2], Boyan Yordanov[1], Youssef Hamadi[1],
Christoph M. Wintersteiger[1], and Hillel Kugler[1]

[1] Microsoft Research, Cambridge, UK
{yordanov,cwinter,youssefh,hkugler}@microsoft.com
[2] Department of Computer Science, University of Oxford, UK
nicola.paoletti@cs.ox.ac.uk
http://research.microsoft.com/z3-4biology

Abstract. Deciphering the developmental program of an embryo is a
fundamental question in biology. Landmark papers [9,10] have recently
shown how computational models of gene regulatory networks provide
system-level causal understanding of the developmental processes of the
sea urchin, and enable powerful predictive capabilities. A crucial aspect
of the work is empirically deriving plausible models that explain all the
known experimental data, a task that becomes infeasible in practice due
to the inherent complexity of the biological systems. We present a generic
Satisfiability Modulo Theories based approach to analyze and synthesize
data constrained models. We apply our approach to the sea urchin embryo, and successfully improve the state-of-the-art by synthesizing, for
the first time, models that explain all the experimental observations in
[10]. A strength of the proposed approach is the combination of accurate synthesis procedures for deriving biologically plausible models with
the ability to prove inconsistency results, showing that for a given set
of experiments and possible class of models no solution exists, and thus
enabling practical refutation of biological models.

1 Introduction

Understanding the underlying developmental program of an embryo is a fasci-
nating scientific question. How do cells divide and organize to form a body plan,
each one becoming a specific cell type capable of performing specialized functions
and interacting with other nearby cells to form a living organism? Answering
these questions, apart from their significant scientific value, has far reaching applications, for instance in early diagnosis, disease treatment, and regenerative
medicine.

At the heart of understanding the complexity of development is the challenge of understanding the process of biological computation that is performed
within living cells and organisms. The information processing is implemented
via highly concurrent biological machinery determining when to express specific
genes, which in an abstract view is seen as turning these genes on or off. Gene

A. Biere and R. Bloem (Eds.): CAV 2014, LNCS 8559, pp. 343–357, 2014.
© Springer International Publishing Switzerland 2014

regulatory networks (GRNs) control the dynamic (and spatial) patterns of gene expression, which influence the decisions cells make during development. Unraveling the structure and logic of these GRNs is thus a key research challenge.

Landmark papers studying the development of the sea urchin [9,10] have recently shown how computational models of gene regulatory networks provide system-level causal understanding of the embryonic developmental processes, and enable powerful predictive capabilities. The methodology used in that work is based on modeling and simulation of Boolean systems with time delays and discrete time semantics using a form of vector-based equations that determine the dynamics of gene expression. A crucial aspect of this work is deriving biologically plausible models that explain all the known experimental data, a task that becomes infeasible when using simulation based methods, due to the inherent complexity of the biological systems.

We present an SMT-based approach that enables the analysis of realistic GRNs and synthesizes models that accurately explain all known data. Our method significantly extends the framework presented in [14] in order to incorporate time delays, spatial domains and the systematic use of uninterpreted functions. We take a pragmatic approach, and rather than introducing a new language for biological modeling we formalize the vector equation notation introduced in [10] which has been demonstrated to be useful for experimental biologists, shedding light on some of its constructs and features that were previously described informally.

The GRN reconstruction described in [9] is a result of over thirty years of research, and incorporates detailed experimental data from various sources and techniques. The scientific essence of a model is its ability to explain *all* existing data and make new testable predictions. The detailed data of the expression of many relevant genes at different time points and different spatial domains in the embryo make the construction of such a model very hard. We explain how we were able to construct the first model that fully explains all of the data from [9], including perturbation experiments, through the use of formal analysis and synthesis methods. Furthermore, we demonstrate that a subset of vector equations is inconsistent with experimental data, regardless of how the other vector equations are set, which is essential information for experimentalists and which is impossible to obtain through the use of simulation techniques only. The scalability of our methods as shown by analyzing the sea urchin model paves the way for practical usage of formal methods, potentially transforming the way in which computational modeling and experiments enhance our understanding of biology.

2   Background

To establish a formal basis for our analysis, we first define some basic concepts and a succinct notion of Gene Regulatory Networks with spatial and temporal domains, as well as observations and perturbations.

At the most fundamental level we require the set of Boolean values $\mathbb{B} = \{0, 1\}$ and the usual Boolean operations. A *bit-vector* $b \in \mathbb{B}^n$ is a vector of Boolean variables $b_0, b_1, \ldots, b_{n-1}$, where $b_i \in \mathbb{B}$ for each $i = 0, \ldots, n - 1$. We assume the usual bit-wise operations on bit-vectors, including the arithmetic operators $+, -, *, /$. We write $b_i = b_j$ to indicate the logical equivalence $b_i \iff b_j$.

For most of the problems we investigate in this paper, it is convenient to have one compact mathematical object which carries all the information available from the biological context over the formal context. For this reason we define the notion of Gene Regulatory networks with Delays, and spatial Domains:

Definition 1 (GRNDD). *A Gene Regulatory Network with Delays and spatial Domains (GRNDD) is a tuple $(G, D, SR, \mathbb{T}, F)$, where:*

- *G is a finite set of* genes;
- *D is a finite set of* spatial domains;
- *SR is a finite set of* spatial relations *between domains;*
- *$\mathbb{T} = \{0, 1, \ldots, t_{max}\}$ is the discrete time domain; and*
- *F is a finite set of* vector equations.

A GRNDD captures the required information describing the system dynamics which can be represented as a transition system. The components of the transition system are the genes G, the spatial domains D and the vector equations (which implicitly define the transition relation). SR is a set of relations that describes the relationship between spatial domains (e.g., whether they are next to each other, or close to each other, etc). Each element of SR is a function $r : \mathbb{T} \times D \times D \to \mathbb{B}$, and $r(t, d_i, d_j) = 1$ iff the relation r holds between spatial domains d_i and d_j at time t.

Note that our definition of a GRNDD contains a discrete and *bounded* time domain, where t_{max} is the *maximum execution time*. The problems we investigate in the remainder of this paper are always related to a set of observational data, which represent finite executions of the system, often providing experimental measurements for each time step from steps 0 to t_{max}.

A state q of a GRNDD is a valuation of the expression of each gene in each spatial domain, i.e., essentially a bit-vector that describes whether each of the genes is enabled or not in a spatial domain. Thus, we define the set of states $Q := \mathbb{B}^{|G \times D|}$. The expression (valuation) of gene g in domain d in a state q is denoted by $q(g, d)$. A path is a sequence of states and we denote the set of paths as $\Pi := \{< q_0, \ldots, q_i > \mid 0 \le i \le t_{max} \wedge q_i \in Q\}$ and $\pi[i]$ denotes the i-th state in path π.

The set of vector equations F of a GRNDD contains an update function for every gene $g \in G$ which has the signature $f_g : \Pi \times \mathbb{T} \times D \to \mathbb{B}$. In other words, the vector equation of a gene g is a function $f_g(\pi, t, d)$ which determines whether g is expressed at a time t in spatial domain d in a path π. Note that these update functions depend on a whole path through the system, because they may depend not only on a unique previous state, but on a sequence of previously visited states. As pointed out in [10], the term "vector equation" reflects the matrices of gene expression in space and time that these equations generate. We provide a syntax and semantics of these functions in Sec. 2.1.

To incorporate experimental data into our analysis, we define a set of observations as follows:

Definition 2 (Observations). *Observations are sets of tuples* (C, E), *where*

- C *is a set of perturbed vector equations; and*
- E *is a set of predicates* $e : \Pi \times \Pi \to \mathbb{B}$ *describing* effects.

The most basic observation is that of the so-called *wild type*, which means that a system is observed without making changes to the system; such an observation has the form $(\emptyset, \pi)$ where π is a predicate that describes a concrete path (of finite length). Observations with non-empty C are called *perturbation* (or *mutation*) experiments. These describe the system behavior after some change is made to the system. A common experiment is that of a *knock-out* where some gene is repressed, e.g., $C = \{f_g(\pi, t, d) := 0\}$ for some gene g. In Section 3.1, we illustrate how the predicates in E can be defined for expressing perturbation effects.

2.1 Formal Syntax and Semantics of Vector Equations

A formal syntax for vector equations is not strictly required. In practice however, the establishment of a language greatly simplifies the modeling task. In [10] such a language is proposed, but a a formal syntax or semantics is not provided. To establish a fully formal basis, we revisit their operators and prescribe a formal semantics to them.[1]

Definition 3 (Vector equation language). *The syntax of vector equations is given by the following grammar:*

$$V ::= g \mid > t \mid < t \mid \text{In } \bar{d} \mid \neg V \mid V \wedge V \mid V \vee V$$
$$\mid \text{At-}n \ V \mid \text{After-}n \ V \mid \text{Perm-}n \ V \mid \text{In } \bar{d} \ V \mid \text{In } r \ \bar{d} \ V$$

where $g \in G$, $t \in \mathbb{T}$, $n \in \mathbb{N}$, $r \in SR$ *and* $\bar{d} \in D$.

The semantics of a term V within the vector equation language is defined with respect to a path π, a time point i, and a spatial domain d using the Boolean connectors $\neg$, $\wedge$ and $\vee$. The semantics of temporal operators are defined as:

$$g(\pi, i, d) \iff \pi[i](g, d) \qquad \text{(gene expression)}$$

$$> t \ (\pi, i, d) \iff i > t \qquad \text{(time boundary)}$$

$$< t \ (\pi, i, d) \iff i < t \qquad \text{(time boundary)}$$

$$\text{At-}n \ V(\pi, i, d) \iff n \leq i \wedge V(\pi, i - n, d) \quad \text{(delayed temporary effect)}$$

---

[1] It is interesting to note that our formalization turns out to be within a subset of the past fragment of linear temporal logic (details omitted from this version of the paper).

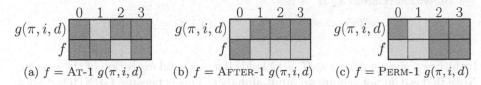

(a) $f = $ AT-1 $g(\pi, i, d)$ (b) $f = $ AFTER-1 $g(\pi, i, d)$ (c) $f = $ PERM-1 $g(\pi, i, d)$

Fig. 1. Examples showing the semantics of temporal operators. Yellow squares correspond to the points where the gene is on, gray squares where the gene is off.

AFTER-n $V(\pi, i, d) \Longleftrightarrow$
$$\exists k.\ 0 \le k \le i - n \wedge V(\pi, k, d) \qquad \text{(permanent activation)}$$

PERM-n $V(\pi, i, d) \Longleftrightarrow$
$$\neg(\exists k.\ 1 \le k \le i - n \ \wedge \ V(\pi, k, d) \wedge \neg V(\pi, k - 1, d)) \quad \text{(permanent repression)}$$

The AT-n $V(\pi, i, d)$ operator corresponds to the evaluation of V at n steps in the past. AFTER-n $V(\pi, i, d)$ evaluates to true and stays true thereafter, if V is true n steps earlier, while PERM-n $V(\pi, i, d)$ evaluates to false, and stays false thereafter, if V becomes true n steps earlier. Note that PERM-n does not simply represent the negation of AFTER-n operator, but instead implies that V has to be false $n - 1$ and *become* true n steps in the past. An illustration of the path-based semantics of the AT-, AFTER- and PERM- operators is provided in Fig. 1.

The semantics of spatial operators are defined as

IN $\bar{d}$ $(\pi, i, d) \Longleftrightarrow d = \bar{d}$ (evaluation at domain $\bar{d}$)

IN $\bar{d}$ $V(\pi, i, \_) \Longleftrightarrow V(\pi, i, \bar{d})$ (evaluation of V at domain $\bar{d}$)

IN r $\bar{d}$ $V(\pi, i, \_) \Longleftrightarrow \exists d.\ r(i, \bar{d}, d) \wedge V(\pi, i, d)$ (eval. of V in a related domain)

While IN $\bar{d}$ and IN $\bar{d}$ $E(\pi, i, \_)$ evaluate whether an atom or formula E holds at a given domain, IN r $\bar{d}$ $E(\pi, i, \_)$ evaluates to 1 when E holds in some domain d related to $\bar{d}$ via the spatial relation r at time t.

3 Gene Expression Computation as a Path Synthesis Problem

We adapt the method presented in [14] for the encoding of Boolean networks as finite transition systems (over bit-vectors), in order to support spatial domains and time delays.

Definition 4 (Dynamics of a GRNDD). *The dynamics of a GRNDD $N = (G, D, SR, \mathbb{T}, F)$ is formally a finite-state automaton with*

- *set of states $Q = \mathbb{B}^{|G \times D|}$;*
- *initial state $q_0 \in Q$; and*

- *transition relation* $\delta : \Pi \to \mathbb{B} =$

$$\delta(\pi) \iff \bigwedge_{0 < i \leq \mathbb{T}, g \in G, d \in D} \pi[i](g, d) = f_g(\pi, i, d)$$

Intuitively, given a path $\pi \in \Pi$, $\delta(\pi)$ holds if π is a valid execution of the system. Note that we do not require an input alphabet. This is because GRNDDs do not have external input. However, non-deterministic behaviour is possible as part of the initial state selection or for update functions with delays beyond the initial time (e.g. $f_g(\pi, i, d) = $ AT-3 $V(\pi, i, d)$, at $i = 2$) or referring to the current time (e.g. $f_g(\pi, i, d) = $ AT-0 $V(\pi, i, d)$). Such non-determinism can be limited by the requirement that the system's dynamics are consistent with certain observations.

Note that our model of dynamics is based on that of a concurrent but *synchronous* execution model, meaning that the expressions of all genes of the network are updated within one step of the execution. In principle, it is possible to integrate asynchronous dynamics, even if for this work we have followed the semantics proposed in [10].

We are now ready to state the computation of the temporal and spatial gene expression in terms of a path synthesis problem:

Problem 1 (Gene expression computation). *Let $N = (G, D, SR, \mathbb{T}, F)$ be a GRNDD. The computation of the temporal and spatial gene expression of network N corresponds to the synthesis of a (set of) path(s) $\{\pi_i\} \subseteq \Pi$ of length $|\mathbb{T}|$ such that for each π_i, $\delta(\pi_i)$ holds.*

In our experiments, we encode this problem into the theory of bit-vector and uninterpreted functions (SMT QF_UFBV). If these constraints are satisfiable, i.e. there exist paths π_i such that $\delta(\pi_i)$ holds, then the SMT solver is able to construct them one by one.

The dynamics of a perturbed GRNDD are defined in a straight-forward way:

Definition 5 (Perturbed Dynamics). *Let $N = (G, D, SR, \mathbb{T}, F)$ be a GRNDD, let $o = (C, E)$ be an observation. Set F' to be F with all functions that have a definition in C replaced with their definition. Then the dynamics of the perturbed system are the dynamics of $(G, D, SR, \mathbb{T}, F')$.*

Finally, we need to be able to check whether a given GRNDD indeed replicates the behavior seen in a set of observations. Formally, we do this by computing gene expressions under all perturbations and checking whether the effects that were observed experimentally are also observed in the GRNDD:

Problem 2 (Adequacy). *Let $N = (G, D, SR, \mathbb{T}, F)$ be a GRNDD and let O be a set of observations. Let Π_N be the computed gene expressions for N. Determine whether for each observation $(C_i, E_i) \in O$ there is a path π_i of length $|\mathbb{T}|$ which is contained in Π_N and a path π_i' of the same length in N perturbed by C_i, such that $E_i(\pi_i, \pi_i')$ holds.*

If a GRNDD N is adequate, i.e., if Problem 2 is answered in the positive, then N does indeed allow executions that perfectly explain all observational data. In the next section we make use of this problem definition to synthesize adequate GRNDDs.

3.1 Comparison Operators

In the biological literature, the effects of perturbation experiments are often only formulated in a qualitative fashion (e.g. 'if gene g_0 is knocked out, then g_1 is over-expressed'), rather than in actual execution traces. For the purposes of formal analysis however, a formal semantics of the effects of perturbations is required. To do so, we characterize the class of comparison operators that can occur in the predicates E_i in observations. We consider predicates of the form

$$(\pi_i, g_i, d_i, [t_i^s, t_i^e]) \bowtie (\pi_j, g_j, d_j, [t_j^s, t_j^e])$$

in order to compare the expression of a gene g_i, in a domain d_i, in a path π_i and in a discrete time interval $[t_i^s, \dots, t_i^e]$, with the expression of a gene g_j, in a domain d_j, in a path π_j and in a time interval $[t_j^s, \dots, t_j^e]$. We consider two types of operators: First, the *weak* operators are $\bowtie \in \{>, <, \leq, \geq, =\}$ and they are used to compare the 'average' expression of the operands in the considered time intervals. We define

$$(\pi_i, g_i, d_i, [t_i^s, t_i^e]) \bowtie (\pi_j, g_j, d_j, [t_j^s, t_j^e]) \iff$$

$$\frac{\sum_{t=t_i^s}^{t_i^e} \pi_i[t](g_i, d_i)}{t_i^e - t_i^s} \bowtie \frac{\sum_{t=t_j^s}^{t_j^e} \pi_j[t](g_j, d_j)}{t_j^e - t_j^s}$$

Second, the *strong* operators are $\bowtie \in \{\gg, \ll, \gg=, =\ll, ==\}$ and they compare gene expressions point-by-point, and not on the basis of their average over a time interval. Hence, they are defined only if $t_i^e - t_i^s = t_j^e - t_j^s$, i.e. if the time intervals of the two operands have the same length. Let us assume that $t_i^s = t_j^s + k$ and that $t_i^e = t_j^e + k$, with $k \in \mathbb{Z}$. Then,

$$(\pi_i, g_i, d_i, [t_i^s, t_i^e]) \bowtie (\pi_j, g_j, d_j, [t_j^s, t_j^e]) \iff$$

$$\bigwedge_{t=t_i^s}^{t_i^e} \pi_i[t](g_i, d_i) \bowtie_w \pi_j[t+k](g_j, d_j)$$

where $\bowtie_w$ denotes the weak version of a strong operator $\bowtie$. Fig. 2 shows two examples of how these operators apply.

4 Synthesis of Vector Equations

In this section we present a procedure for the automated synthesis of vector equations, so that the computed temporal expressions meet the observations, with the aim of answering positively to Problem 2. We extend the vector equation language to enable *synthesis of basic gene interactions*, i.e. simple regulatory interactions from which more complex gene functions are constructed; and the *synthesis of generic Boolean functions*, based on the use of uninterpreted functions for finding admissible logical combinations of vector equation terms.

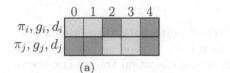
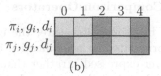

$$(a) \qquad\qquad\qquad\qquad (b)$$

Fig. 2. Comparison of two temporal expression patterns π_i and π_j. Yellow squares indicate time-points where the gene is expressed, gray squares where it is not. Gene g_i in π_i and domain d_i is overexpressed w.r.t. gene g_j in π_j and domain d_j. However, the strong comparison operator $\gg=$ does not hold in the example (a) over the time interval $[0,4]$, while its weak equivalent ($\geq$) does. Contrarily in example (b), $(\pi_i, g_i, d_i, [0,4]) \gg= (\pi_j, g_j, d_j, [0,4])$, because the comparison is verified point-by-point, and thus $(\pi_i, g_i, d_i, [0,4]) \geq (\pi_j, g_j, d_j, [0,4])$ also holds.

Definition 6 (Basic interaction). *Let $N = (G, D, SR, \mathbb{T}, F)$ be a GRNDD. A basic interaction (BI) of N is a tuple $f = (g, b, d, r, t, op)$ where:*

- $g \subseteq G$ *is a set of* input genes;
- $b \subseteq \mathbb{B}$ *is a set of Boolean values indicating whether genes in g are expressed or not;*
- $d \subseteq D^\epsilon = D \cup \{\epsilon\}$ *is a possibly empty set of ($d = \epsilon$) spatial domains;*
- $r \subseteq SR^\epsilon = SR \cup \{\epsilon\}$ *is a possibly empty set of spatial relations;*
- $op \subseteq \{\text{AT-}, \text{AFTER-}, \text{PERM-}\}$ *and $t \in \mathbb{T}$ are a set of temporal operators and a corresponding set of delays, respectively.*

A BI $f = (g, b, d, r, t, op)$ describes a set of interactions where an input gene $g' \in g$ (whose expression depends on a $b' \in b$) affects the target gene according to a temporal operator $op' \in op$ and delay in $t' \in t$, and possibly occurring in a domain $d' \in d$, or in a domain that is in a spatial relation $r' \in r$ with d'. In order to avoid unwanted redundancies and non-determinism, we exclude the empty temporal operator which is semantically equivalent to AT-0. The choice of this particular template for BIs was driven by observing that in the sea urchin model presented in [10], every vector equation takes the form of a logical combination of terms characterized by the same information. On the specification side, we want to allow the modeler to incorporate some degree of flexibility in the declaration of a BI to synthesize, and in turn to include gene regulations that are supported by experimental evidence. Moreover, constraining the set of potential interactions has the added benefit that the resulting functions are easily interpreted by the domain expert who specified the templates, and that the same templates enables the exclusion of unwanted or biologically unlikely interactions. Of course, there is also a performance advantage, because a smaller set of functions is considered by the solver.

Formally, the declaration of a basic interaction is of the form

$$f \subseteq G \times \mathbb{B} \times D^\epsilon \times SR^\epsilon \times \mathbb{T} \times \{\text{AT-}, \text{AFTER-}, \text{PERM-}\} \to \mathbb{B}$$

where f is a symbol from the set $\mathcal{I}$ of declared BI symbols. In practice, we constrain every BI by a declaration of choice of (subsets of) admissible values to each of its elements. For example, $f \stackrel{dec}{=} (\{g\}, \mathbb{B}, \{\epsilon\}, \{\epsilon\}, \{0,1,2\}, \{\text{AFTER-}, \text{PERM-}\})$ describes an interaction with a gene g whose expression is unknown (b can take any Boolean value), where no domain-specific or inter-domain signaling occurs (both d and r are fixed to ϵ), and causing a permanent effect ($op = \{\text{AFTER-}, \text{PERM-}\}$) on the target gene with a maximum delay of 2.

Obviously, for every declaration $f \stackrel{dec}{=} (g, b, d, r, t, op)$, we need to impose the BI f to be evaluated to one of the admissible values specified in its declaration, which imposes the constraint

$$\bigvee_{g' \in g, b' \in b, d' \in d, r' \in r, t' \in t, op' \in op} f = (g', b', d', r', t', op')$$

Apart from basic interactions, we also allow the specification of arbitrary Boolean functions by the use of uninterpreted functions (UF) of the form $uf : \mathbb{B}^n \rightarrow \mathbb{B}$. The only constraint we impose on such functions is whether input variables are allowed to be negated or not. This information depends on domain knowledge, e.g., it may be known that expression of some gene inhibits the expression of another gene, but the precise mechanism of inhibition is unknown.

Indeed the negation of a term radically changes the regulatory input it represents, by turning an activation input into an inhibition (and vice versa). Therefore, if we require that the synthesized function does not contradict known biological hypotheses about the kind of input interaction, for a UF uf of arity n the following constraints are imposed:

$$\bigwedge_{i=1,\ldots,n} uf(b_1, \ldots, b_{i-1}, 0, b_{i+1}, \ldots b_n) \implies uf(b_1, \ldots, b_{i-1}, 1, b_{i+1}, \ldots b_n)$$

We briefly explain the rationale behind this formula. According to the sum-of-products (SoP, DNF) form of uf, if $uf(b_1, \ldots, b_{i-1}, 0, b_{i+1}, \ldots, b_n)$ holds for some choice of $b_1, \ldots, b_n$, then the function translates to a formula of the form

$$uf = (b_1' \wedge \ldots \wedge b_{i-1}' \wedge \neg b_i \wedge b_{i+1}' \wedge \ldots \wedge b_n') \vee \ldots$$

which contains a min-term where the i-th variable is negated and b_j' is either b_j or $\neg b_j$ for $j \neq i$. A way to get rid of the negated term $\neg b_i$ is to enforce that $uf(b_1, \ldots, b_{i-1}, 1, b_{i+1}, \ldots, b_n)$ holds for the same choice of variables $b_1, \ldots, b_{i-1}$, $b_{i+1}, \ldots, b_n$. By doing so, in the SoP representation of uf the negated term would conveniently simplify because

$$(b_1' \wedge \ldots \wedge b_{i-1}' \wedge \neg b_i \wedge b_{i+1}' \wedge \ldots \wedge b_n') \vee$$
$$(b_1' \wedge \ldots \wedge b_{i-1}' \wedge b_i \wedge b_{i+1}' \wedge \ldots \wedge b_n') \vee \ldots$$
$$= (b_1' \wedge \ldots \wedge b_{i-1}' \wedge b_{i+1}' \wedge \ldots \wedge b_n') \vee \ldots$$

We now extend the vector equation language in order to support the specification of BIs and UFs to be synthesized:

Definition 7 (Vector equation language for synthesis). *The syntax of vector equations supporting the synthesis of basic interactions and Boolean functions is given by the following grammar:*

$$V ::= f \mid uf(V, \ldots, V) \mid g \mid >t \mid <t \mid \text{IN } \bar{d} \mid \neg V \mid V \wedge V \mid V \vee V$$
$$\mid \text{AT-}n \ V \mid \text{AFTER-}n \ V \mid \text{PERM-}n \ V \mid \text{IN } \bar{d} \ V \mid \text{IN } r \ \bar{d} \ V$$

where $g \in G$, $t \in \mathbb{T}$, $n \in \mathbb{N}$, $r \in SR$, $\bar{d} \in D$, $f \in \mathcal{I}$ *is a declared BI symbol; and* $uf \in \mathcal{U}$ *is a declared UF symbol.*

The semantics of the expression $uf(V_1, \ldots, V_n)$ simply consists in the application of the UF uf over its arguments:

$$uf(V_1, \ldots, V_n) \ (\pi, i, d) \iff uf(V_1(\pi, i, d), \ldots, V_n(\pi, i, d)) \ .$$

The semantics of a BI f is defined as a conjunction of formulas of the form $f = (g', b', d', r', t', op') \implies V(\pi, i, d)$ which relate any synthesizable evaluation of f to the corresponding vector equation term V:

$$\bigwedge_{\substack{g' \in g, b' \in b, \\ d' \in d, r' \in r, \\ t' \in t, op' \in op}} f = (g', b', d', r', t', op') \implies op' \ t'(IN \ r'd'(b' \iff g')) \ (\pi, i, d)$$

where $IN \ r'd' \ V$ corresponds to $INd' \ V$ if $r' = \epsilon \wedge d' \neq \epsilon$, or to V if $d' = \epsilon$. A BI is naturally mapped to a vector equation term describing the same interaction. For instance, the interaction $(g, 1, d, \epsilon, 2, \text{AT-})$ corresponds to term $\text{AT-2}(\text{IN } d(g))$, while $(g, 0, d, r, 0, \text{PERM-})$ corresponds to $\text{PERM-0}(\text{IN } r \ d(\neg g))$.

Bit-Vector Encoding of Basic Interactions. To make use of specialized simplification and solving procedures in the solver, we use a bit-vector encoding of BIs. Given an interaction $f = (g, b, d, r, t, op)$, let us denote with $\bar{f}$ its bit-vector encoding, and with $\bar{f}(g) \in \mathbb{B}^{\lceil log_2 |G| \rceil}$, $\bar{f}(b) \in \mathbb{B}$, $\bar{f}(d) \in \mathbb{B}^{\lceil log_2 (|D|+1) \rceil}$, $\bar{f}(r) \in \mathbb{B}^{\lceil log_2 (|SR|+1) \rceil}$, $\bar{f}(t) \in \mathbb{B}^{\lceil log_2 |\mathbb{T}| \rceil}$ and $\bar{f}(op) \in \mathbb{B}^2$ the fields of $\bar{f}$ encoding the finite-ranging elements g, b, d, r, t and op, respectively, as subsequences of $\bar{f}$. Thus, the total length of $\bar{f}$ is:

$$N = \lceil log_2 |G| \rceil + 1 + \lceil log_2 (|D|+1) \rceil + \lceil log_2 (|SR|+1) \rceil + \lceil log_2 |\mathbb{T}| \rceil + 2 \ .$$

Note that it is typically unnecessary to allocate $\lceil log_2 |\mathbb{T}| \rceil$ bits to describe a delay t, since in any non-trivial model, it is very unlikely to have delays as long as the total execution time. Hence, in most cases it is worth fixing a maximum delay $\bar{t} < |\mathbb{T}|$ for a more efficient bit-vector representation of the interaction.

5 Predicting Sea Urchin Development

We evaluated our approach by considering one of the most complete models of sea urchin embryonic development [10], which contains *45 genes* (and the vector equations describing their dynamics); *4 spatial domains*; and *2 spatial relations* between domains. The sea urchin is a well established model organism, allowing to study fundamental biological processes in a simpler setting, with mature and powerful experimental methods, and the advantage that many of the underlying mechanisms are conserved in higher level organisms. The model execution spans the discrete time interval $[0, 30]$ hours post fertilization (hpf), corresponding to the early stages of development. We implemented the vector equation language and the synthesis methods in a prototype where we make extensive use of the QF_UFBV support in the Z3 theorem prover [4].

We summarize the procedure followed for synthesizing a set of vector equations that completely explain all experimental data (both wild-type expression and perturbation effects). The resulting equations have been obtained by considerably changing the original formulation of the sea urchin model that explains most but not all the data. Although the synthesis of vector equations in terms of their regulatory logic and input interactions is fully automated, the final model is derived after a number of manual refinement steps, which allows to progressively add assumptions that are both biologically plausible and logically consistent. This semi-automated strategy helps in excluding models able to reproduce experimental observations but that are not biologically meaningful.

Initially, we validated the correctness of our formalization of the language, by showing that the SMT-based implementation of the original model produced the same expression patterns as reported in [10].

1. Removal of Hard-Coded Data Constraints. The original model contains a number of terms formulated in a way that reproduces exactly wild-type observations, of the form $IN\ d \wedge t > t_s \wedge t < t_e$. Such a term basically forces the expression of the output gene to be expressed in a specific domain (d) and time-interval $([t_s + 1, t_e - 1])$, regardless of the initial conditions or interactions with other genes, thus providing just a description of the observation and no predictive capabilities. We removed from the original equations any occurrence of such terms (present in 8 vector equations), and we found that the resulting model still does not admit solutions that meet experimental observations.

2. Exploration of Unsatisfiable Vector Equations. Identifying the components of a biological model which fail in reproducing the expected behavior is a hard task, especially if the system is characterized by a large numbers of interacting components like in our case. We address this problem with the automated extraction of unsatisfiable subsets of vector equations, that are not able to explain experimental data regardless of how the other equations are defined. This kind of analysis points the biologist to the exact source of inconsistency, thus prompting further investigation of the underlying regulatory interactions that make the model contradict experimental data.

In our case, we found that 14 out of the 45 original equations were inconsistent on their own, i.e. solving Problem 2 with a GRNDD model that contains only one among those equations determines inadequacy. Note that the removal of inconsistent equations from the model does not necessarily make it satisfiable.

Indeed, our model was found inconsistent even after excluding all these problematic equations, suggesting that any minimal unsatisfiable subset would include a major part of the original equations. We therefore synthesize a new equation for every gene, as explained in the following step:

3. Reformulation of Vector Equations into Functions to Synthesize. With our framework we are able to synthesize correct models that also incorporate biological knowledge and assumptions. The procedure consists of replacing each vector equation with an uninterpreted Boolean function over a set of basic interactions to synthesize, one for each term of the original equation. The final equations are obtained through an iterative refinement where initially, each term to synthesize is constrained to meet the original specification only in the input gene and in the temporal operator, which are the most fundamental information of a regulatory interaction. Then, we restrict the space of solutions by gradually restoring the satisfiable features of the initial model (and removing hard-coded observations as described in Step 1).

Specifically, consider a general vector equation f of the form:

$$f = \ldots op\ t(IN\ r\ d(b \iff g)) \ldots$$

where op is the temporal operator, t the delay, d and r the (possibly empty) domain and spatial relation, respectively, g the input gene and b the Boolean indicating whether g is on or off. A UF uf is considered in place of the initial logical combination of terms, and each term is replaced by a BI as follows:

$$f = uf(\ldots, (\{g\}, \mathbb{B}, D^\epsilon, SR^\epsilon, \mathbb{T}', \{op\}), \ldots)$$

where only g and op are constrained to their original values, and $\mathbb{T}' = [0, 12]$ hpf is a reasonably large set of admissible delays. The subsequent refinement steps include restoring b and constraining each function uf so that its interpretation does not negate the involved terms; setting back the original spatial relation and domain; and restricting the delay to the interval $[max(0, t - 3), t + 3]$ so that we admit an error of 3 hpf, which is reported in [10] to be the resolution of experimental observations. Using the following procedure we have synthesized a biologically plausible model that fully explains all the experimental data represented in [10]. The proposed SMT-based approach paves the way for new kinds of in silico experiments, infeasible without automated reasoning and synthesis techniques. The biological interpretation of our model is however beyond the scope of this paper.

6   Related Work

6.1   Program Synthesis

In our work synthesis is used to support the abstract reasoning process biologists perform in their research towards deriving mechanistic predictive models.

Our system takes observation data and equations templates as specifications and produces new vector equations which fully reproduce the observations and respect the initial templates. In program synthesis the aim is to automate the process of implementation and ensure that the program is correct by construction. Program synthesis accepts specifications and generates code fulfilling those specifications.

In [12] sketches are used to synthesize programs. A sketch is a program with placeholders. The synthesizer takes a sketch along a working reference implementation and generates an optimized version of the reference implementation. This work has been extended to take into account Boolean constraints and a numerical qualitative objective [3].

Work in [13] introduced a so called proof-theoretic synthesis that interprets program synthesis as generalized program verification. It requires the user to provide an input-output functional specification, a description of the atomic operations in the programming language, and a specification of the synthesized programs looping structure, allowed stack space, and bound on usage of certain operations. Their system works by using the Z3 theorem prover to reconcile constraints that relate unknown statements, guards, inductive invariants, and ranking functions.

These synthesis tools require a higher level of specification effort. This is different from our work which uses less information to start with. In particular, we do not ask the biologist to provide a working set of fully specified vector equations, or fine details on the generated equations. However our approach enables biologists to provide additional constraints that capture information inferred from experimental results or biological intuition, which helps the synthesis methods to derive more realistic models.

6.2 Computational Biology and Synthesis

The use of synthesis as a method to construct models of biological systems has gained interest in the setting of discrete models that capture biological behavior and enable important predictions and understanding. In particular several approaches have been developed and applied to a classical system in developmental biology describing fate specification of Vulval Precursor Cells (VPCs) in the *C. elegans* nematode. In [7] a method that introduces a set of don't care (dc) Boolean variables that must be assigned values in order to obtain a concrete model is presented. When a dc variable is set to 1, this indicates that the information from the corresponding component does not contribute to the observed result. The problem is formulated as maximizing the number of dc variables that are set to 1, while retaining a model solution that is consistent and explains all the given known data. This amounts to solving a QBF formula with a maximization goal for the dc variables. In [5] the question of synthesizing concurrent models with bounded asynchrony satisfying a set of experiments that include genetic mutations is addressed and the developed language and tools are applied to the VPC system. Technically this turns out to be a QBF formula with three levels of alternation, and new algorithms are developed to solve it. Additional work on synthesis from scenario-based specifications and its application to the VPC system is described in [8,6], there the approach considered views the problem as a game between the environment (the experimentalist) and the system (the nematode) and the solution relies on computing fix-points symbolically via compositional methods.

Besides being applicable to the reverse engineering of biological systems, approaches based on the use of formal synthesis and verification are also relevant for their design. For example, in the field of synthetic biology one goal is to engineer genetic networks with specific, useful properties. In [2] temporal logic was used to capture such properties and model-checking was applied to study if a synthetic gene network design was consistent with these specifications. A parameter synthesis strategy was also developed to tune a design in order to achieve the required behavior in [2] and, more recently, similar modular design strategies were proposed in [1].

In [14] we introduce Z34Bio, an SMT-based framework for the automated analysis and design of several classes of biological systems, where a common symbolic representation as transition systems over bit-vectors is used to encode multiple classes of biological models, including Boolean networks and chemical reaction networks. The framework was applied in [14] to the verification of DNA circuit design and to the stability analysis of gene regulatory networks, in particular showing how multiple gene knockouts that affect the stability of the system are automatically identified. Recent extensions to this framework include methods for analyzing probabilistic systems [11].

7   Conclusion

Deciphering and understanding the underlying developmental program of an embryo is a fundamental problem. In particular, biologists have spent several decades detailing how a complex gene regulatory network controls the development of sea urchin embryos. In [10] it is shown how a model of the sea urchin GRN is turned empirically into a predictive dynamic Boolean model. Beyond the mere understanding of a complex process, this result provides a tool with which to test *in silico* regulatory circuitry and developmental perturbations.

In this paper, we present a generic SMT-based approach for analyzing GRNs in order to synthesize predictive dynamic and Boolean GRN. We applied our approach to the sea urchin embryo, and successfully improve the current state-of-the art by providing, for the first time, biologists with models that perfectly explain all known data.

There are several major benefits to our method. First, our approach saves biologists and modelers months or even years of tedious work trying to derive the *best* predictive model. Second, biologists may have greater confidence in silico tests since the provided models perfectly explain all known data. Third, our method enables to determine that part of a model is inconsistent and cannot explain all known experimental data, helping to focus research efforts on specific biological mechanisms and assumptions that require reevaluation.

This last benefit is related to the finding of minimal unsatisfiable cores in verification applications. However, in our context, this represents much more than the discovery of a transient problem with a particular version of a chip design or software component. Instead, it represents a new way to push the boundaries of knowledge, by driving biologists toward new scientific findings and empowering their capacity to *understand life*.

Acknowledgments. Nicola Paoletti is part supported by the ERC Advanced Grant VERIWARE. The research was carried out during his internship at Microsoft Research Cambridge, UK.

References

1. Bartocci, E., Bortolussi, L., Nenzi, L.: A temporal logic approach to modular design of synthetic biological circuits. In: Gupta, A., Henzinger, T.A. (eds.) CMSB 2013. LNCS (LNBI), vol. 8130, pp. 164–177. Springer, Heidelberg (2013)
2. Batt, G., Yordanov, B., Weiss, R., Belta, C.: Robustness analysis and tuning of synthetic gene networks. Bioinformatics 23(18) (2007)
3. Chaudhuri, S., Clochard, M., Solar-Lezama, A.: Bridging Boolean and quantitative synthesis using smoothed proof search. In: POPL. ACM (2014)
4. de Moura, L., Bjørner, N.: Z3: An efficient SMT solver. In: Ramakrishnan, C.R., Rehof, J. (eds.) TACAS 2008. LNCS, vol. 4963, pp. 337–340. Springer, Heidelberg (2008)
5. Koksal, A., Pu, Y., Srivastava, S., Bodik, R., Fisher, J., Piterman, N.: Synthesis of biological models from mutation experimentss. In: SIGPLAN-SIGACT Symposium on Principles of Programming Languages. ACM (2013)
6. Kugler, H., Plock, C., Roberts, A.: Synthesizing Biological Theories. In: Gopalakrishnan, G., Qadeer, S. (eds.) CAV 2011. LNCS, vol. 6806, pp. 579–584. Springer, Heidelberg (2011)
7. Kugler, H., Pnueli, A., Stern, M.J., Hubbard, E.J.A.: "Don't Care" Modeling: A logical framework for developing predictive system models. In: Grumberg, O., Huth, M. (eds.) TACAS 2007. LNCS, vol. 4424, pp. 343–357. Springer, Heidelberg (2007)
8. Kugler, H., Segall, I.: Compositional Synthesis of Reactive Systems from Live Sequence Chart Specifications. In: Kowalewski, S., Philippou, A. (eds.) TACAS 2009. LNCS, vol. 5505, pp. 77–91. Springer, Heidelberg (2009)
9. Peter, I.S., Davidson, E.H.: A gene regulatory network controlling the embryonic specification of endoderm. Nature 474(7353) (2011)
10. Peter, I.S., Faure, E., Davidson, E.H.: Predictive computation of genomic logic processing functions in embryonic development. Proc. of the National Academy of Sciences 109(41) (2012)
11. Rabe, M.N., Wintersteiger, C.M., Kugler, H., Yordanov, B., Hamadi, Y.: Symbolic approximation of the bounded reachability probability in markov chains. In: QEST. LNCS, Springer (to appear, 2014)
12. Solar-Lezama, A., Rabbah, R.M., Bodík, R., Ebcioglu, K.: Programming by sketching for bit-streaming programs. In: PLDI. ACM (2005)
13. Srivastava, S., Gulwani, S., Foster, J.S.: From program verification to program synthesis. In: POPL. ACM (2010)
14. Yordanov, B., Wintersteiger, C.M., Hamadi, Y., Kugler, H.: Z34Bio: An SMT-based framework for analyzing biological computation. In: SMT (2013)

Finding Instability in Biological Models

Byron Cook[1,2], Jasmin Fisher[1,3], Benjamin A. Hall[1],
Samin Ishtiaq[1], Garvit Juniwal[4], and Nir Piterman[5]

[1] Microsoft Research
[2] University College London
[3] University of Cambridge
[4] University of California, Berkeley
[5] University of Leicester

Abstract. The stability of biological models is an important test for establishing their soundness and accuracy. Stability in biological systems
represents the ability of a robust system to always return to homeostasis. In recent work, modular approaches for proving stability have been
found to be swift and scalable. If stability is however not proved, the
currently available techniques apply an exhaustive search through the
unstable state space to find loops. This search is frequently prohibitively
computationally expensive, limiting its usefulness. Here we present a
new modular approach eliminating the need for an exhaustive search
for loops. Using models of biological systems we show that the technique
finds loops significantly faster than brute force approaches. Furthermore,
for a subset of stable systems which are resistant to modular proofs, we
observe a speed up of up to 3 orders of magnitude as the exhaustive
searches for loops which cause instability are avoided. With our new
procedure we are able to prove instability and stability in a number of
realistic biological models, including adaptation in bacterial chemotaxis,
the lambda phage lysogeny/lysis switch, voltage gated channel opening
and cAMP oscillations in the slime mold *Dictyostelium discoideum*. This
new approach will support the development of new tools for biomedicine.

Keywords: Stability, instability, verification, biology.

1 Introduction

Traditional computer science approaches are playing an increasingly important
role in the modeling and analysis of biological systems. Formal verification approaches for biological signaling systems have been successfully applied in a wide
range of different organisms and phenomena [1–3]. In different systems, proofs
of both reachability [4, 5], and stability [6] can give powerful insights into the
mechanisms of cell differentiation and homeostasis. Stability specifically offers
a valuable tool when considering systems which can be reliably considered as
being at equilibrium or homeostatic. We consider stability here in terms of a
guarantee that the system always eventually moves towards a single self-loop
state, regardless of the initial state of the model. In the context of biological

A. Biere and R. Bloem (Eds.): CAV 2014, LNCS 8559, pp. 358–372, 2014.

systems, instability can therefore indicate a developmental switch (e.g. bifurcation) or oscillation (e.g. cycles with lengths greater than 1). In contrast, stability demonstrates that the system is at a robust equilibrium, as any temporary perturbation will eventually converge to the equilibrium state.

The development of formal models of biological systems further offers a new platform for discoveries in the life sciences and medical research. By translating the diagrammatic models typically generated in experimental disciplines into forms which can be explored using verification techniques, we can highlight inadequacies in the model and propose new testable hypotheses. In contrast to models based on precise reproduction of physical or chemical properties of a given biological phenomenum, *executable* models avoid a reliance on highly accurate quantitative data from experimental studies. For questions such as "could a drug targeted to this protein ever kill the cell?" or "does the model accurately represent a robust equilibrium?", the relative independence of formal models from detailed physical constants is a strength of this technique over traditional physico-chemical simulation. Furthermore, this degree of abstraction more closely mimics the qualitative data generated by genetic screens. Boolean and qualitative networks specifically have been successfully used in the study of diverse systems. Initially applied to the study of gene regulation [7] these formalisms have been applied to blood cell differentiation, skin homeostasis and cancer development [8–11]. The ability to analyze models with these approaches has great relevance to clinicians and the biomedical industries. Furthermore, Boolean networks have been used successfully to systematically model drug interactions in tumorigenesis [12], in order to rationally identify new drug targets. This ability to validate drug targets *in silico* offers the potential to avoid costly failures at late stage clinical trials, and as such new model checking techniques have great relevance to clinicans and the biomedical industries.

Existing tools suitable for the analysis of biological qualitative networks, such as GinSim [13] and NuSMV [14], explore stability through the use of efficient representations of the state transitions as binary decision diagrams and multi-valued decision diagrams [15], coupled with simulation. The reliance on exhaustive simulation however limits the size of the models which can practically be analysed, forcing users with large models to reduce the size of the model by a semi-automated process of model reduction (e.g. [10]). Additionally, encoding complex transition functions in these tools is laborious, making expression of realistic biological models difficult.

Proofs of stabilization in biological systems are complicated by the complex temporal relationships between interacting elements which are necessary for stability, and prevent the use of scalable techniques which abstract these details away. These temporal interactions are necessary to describe systems which show adaptation [16], or timed switches [17]. Previous work presented an algorithm for proving stability [6] which is sound and complete, and reverts to an exhaustive search for cycles of increasing length (up to the diameter of the system) if stability cannot be proved rapidly. Failure to find multiple self-loop states or cycles proves the stability of the system. Thus, if a stable model is resistant to quick proofs of stability, the search for cyclic counterexamples can be prohibitive. As a result of the rapid growth in the number and diversity of biological qualitative networks, we have recently identified several realistic, stable models which resist the approach of [6].

In this paper, we tackle the problem of proving instability with a new modular approach. This greatly increases the speed of disproving stability in several systems by rapidly identifying loops arising from cyclic instabilities. Previous techniques proved stability by taking lemmas of the form: $[FG(p1) \wedge \cdots \wedge FG(pk)] \Rightarrow FG(q)$, where $p1 \ldots pk$ are formulae over the inputs of a given component, and q is a formula about the component's output, where F and G denote "eventually" and "always" in linear temporal logic [18]. If this fails to find a single self-loop state, exhaustive searches for multiple self-loop states and loops are performed.

To avoid this costly calculation, our new approach searches for counterexamples using a divide/conquer technique, based around a modular approach for proving stability. If a single or multiple self-loops cannot be found when analyzing the system, the state space is divided into two, and each individually searched for local self-loops. Finally, through an analysis of the cut and a small number of steps of simulation, either counter examples of cycles are found or stability is proved.

Our new approach increases the speed of the proof of instability and stability (in the case that stability cannot be proved easily) by over 2 orders of magnitude compared with previous approaches [6] in addition to being sound and complete.

2   Verifying Stability in Qualitative Networks

Qualitative Networks (QNs) [8] have been extensively used to model biological phenomena. A QN $Q(V, T, N)$, of granularity $N + 1$ consists of n variables: $V = (v_1, v_2, \cdots, v_n)$. The state of the system is a finite map $s : V \to \{0, 1, \cdots N\}$. The set of initial states is the set of all states. Each variable $v_i \in V$ has a *target function* $T_i \in T$ associated with it: $T_i : \{0, 1, \cdots, N\}^n \to \{0, 1, \cdots N\}$. Qualitative networks update the variables using synchronous parallelism.

Target functions in qualitative networks direct the execution of the network from state $s = (d_1, d_2, \cdots, d_n)$. The *next state* $s' = (d'_1, d'_2, \cdots, d'_n)$ is computed by:

$$d'_v = \begin{cases} d_v + 1 & d_v < T_v(s) \text{ and } d_v < N, \\ d_v - 1 & d_v > T_v(s) \text{ and } d_v > 0, \\ d_v & \text{otherwise.} \end{cases} \qquad (1)$$

A target function of a variable v is typically a simple algebraic function, such as sum, over several other variables $w_1, w_2, \cdots w_m$. Variables $w_1, w_2, \cdots, w_m$ are called *inputs* of v and v is an *output* of each one of $w_1, w_2, \cdots, w_m$. The input function induces a *dependency* graph of the network with the variables as nodes, where an edge (u, v) exists iff u is an *input* of v.

A QN $Q(V, T, N)$ defines a state space $\Sigma = \{s : V \to \{0, 1, \cdots N\}\}$ and a transition function $\delta : \Sigma \to \Sigma$, where $\delta(s) = s'$ such that for every $v \in V$, $s'(v)$ depends on $T_v(s)$ as in Eq. 1. For a state $s \in \Sigma$ we denote $s(v)$ also by s_v. Likewise, $\delta(s)_v = \delta(s)(v)$ is the value of v in $\delta(s)$. We say that a state s is *recurring* if it is possible to get back to s after a finite number of applications of δ. That is, if for some $i > 0$, we have $\delta^i(s) = s$. As the state space of a qualitative network is finite, the set of recurring states is never empty. We say that a network is *stabilizing* if there exists a unique recurring state s. That is, there is a unique state s such that $\delta(s) = s$, and for every other state s' and every $i > 0$ we have $\delta^i(s') \neq s'$. Intuitively, this means that starting from an arbitrary state, we always end up in a self-loop state and always the same one. For an *unstable* network, we have two possibilities: (a) *multiple self-loop states*; (b) at most one self-loop state but *non-trivial cycles*.

In [6], the problem of determining whether a network stabilizes or not is solved by proving local lemmas about the range of values a variable can eventually take depending upon already proven lemmas about its inputs. Each newly proven lemma is then used to strengthen the lemmas about its outputs until nothing changes. The order in which variables are picked for strengthening is arbitrary. The proven lemmas can sometimes be enough to determine that a network stabilizes. If not, an explicit search for counter-examples is carried out. First, the existence of multiple self-loops is checked by encoding it as a Boolean satisfiability problem. If this check fails, bounded model-checking (BMC) is used to find non-trivial cycles of increasing length. For stabilizing networks where modular lemmas are not strong enough to show the same (see Fig. 1b), BMC unrolling to a length more than or equal to the system's diameter is required to show non-existence of cycles, which is infeasible even for moderately sized networks.

Here, we revisit the modular proof-based approach from [6], using a technique similar in spirit to abstract interpretation [19, 20]. We present a novel, scalable instability detection algorithm in Sec. 3 that reuses the old algorithm as one of its sub-procedures.

2.1 Over-approximating Recurring States

All states of a QN are considered initial states. Let $\Sigma_i, i \geq 0$ be the set of states of the QN that are reachable in i or more steps starting from some initial state. Note that if a state s of a QN is not reachable in i or more steps, then it is not reachable in i' or more steps for every $i' > i$. Hence, $\Sigma = \Sigma_0 \supseteq \Sigma_1 \supseteq \Sigma_2 \supseteq \cdots$ is a decreasing sequence. Since the state space is finite, there will exist $l \leq \text{diameter}(\Sigma)$, such that $\Sigma_{l'} = \Sigma_l$, for every $l' \geq l$. The set Σ_l is the set of all recurring states of the network, which is a singleton for a *stabilizing* network.

Computing the exact reachability sets is not feasible in practice. Instead we try to over-approximate the set of recurring states by using a layer of abstraction to represent sets of states. Analogous to interval domain from abstract interpretation [19, 20], for each variable v, we just keep track of the range of its possible values. Let $[i, j]$, $i, j \in \mathbb{Z}$, $i \leq j$, denote the interval containing all integers from i to j inclusive. Interval $[i_1, j_1]$ *contains* another interval $[i_2, j_2]$ iff $i_1 \leq i_2$ and

$j_1 \geq j_2$. Let $\mathcal{L}_N$ be the the the set of all intervals contained in $[0, N]$. An element $(I_1, \cdots, I_n)$ of the set $\mathcal{S} = \mathcal{L}_N^n$ represents a sub-space of Σ where variable v can take all values in the interval I_v. We refer to elements of $\mathcal{S}$ as *regions*. A region $\rho_I = (I_1, \cdots, I_n)$ is said to *contain* another region $\rho_J = (J_1, \cdots J_n)$ (written as $\rho_I \sqsupseteq \rho_J$) iff I_k contains J_k for every $1 \leq k \leq n$. $(\mathcal{S}, \sqsupseteq)$ is a finite (hence complete) partial order with $[0, N]^n$ as the $\top$ element. A region $\rho = ([l_1, h_1], \cdots, [l_n, h_n])$ can be equivalently represented by functions V_{lo}^ρ and V_{hi}^ρ s.t. $\forall v \in \{0, \cdots, n\}$, $V_{lo}^\rho(v) = l_v$ and $V_{hi}^\rho(v) = h_v$. The set of states s in ρ s.t. $\delta(s)$ is outside of ρ is denoted by $\rho\bullet = \{s \in \rho \wedge \delta(s) \notin \rho\}$. If $\rho\bullet$ is not empty, we say the region ρ is *open* wrt δ, otherwise it is *closed*.

Let v be a variable and $(w_1, \cdots, w_m)$ be its inputs. We define a function $F : \mathcal{S} \to \mathcal{S}$, which updates the bounds of eventually possible values of v using the bounds on the values of its inputs as restricted to ρ. Let $(w_1, \cdots, w_m) = \text{inputs}(v)$. We compute the set of values of the target function T_v applied to all possible input combinations in ρ and use that to update the interval of v. Formally, $F(\rho) = (f_1(\rho), \cdots f_n(\rho))$, with

$$f_v(\rho) = [\min(\theta_v(\rho)), \max(\theta_v(\rho))], \text{ where} \tag{2}$$

$$\theta_v(\rho) = T_v([V_{lo}^\rho(w_1), V_{hi}^\rho(w_1)] \times \cdots \times [V_{lo}^\rho(w_m), V_{hi}^\rho(w_m)]) \tag{3}$$

by suitably lifting the definition of T_v to sets of states.

Note that F is monotonic because $\rho_1 \sqsupseteq \rho_2$ implies $T_v(\rho_1) \supseteq T_v(\rho_2)$ and thereby $f_v(\rho_1)$ *contains* $f_v(\rho_2)$. By Kleene's fixed point theorem, F will have a greatest fixed point νF, which can be computed by finite number of repeated applications of F on $\top$. Since F is monotonic, repeated applications of F on $\top$ would give rise to a decreasing sequence of regions $\top \sqsupseteq F(\top) \sqsupseteq F^2(\top) \sqsupseteq \cdots$. Every element of this sequence is a closed region, because an outgoing transition from some state s in $F^i(\top)$ would mean that in s, target function of some variable v takes a value not contained in $[V_{lo}^{F^i(\top)}(v), V_{hi}^{F^i(\top)}(v)]$, implying $F^{i+1}(\top) \not\sqsubseteq F^i(\top)$. Using these observations, we claim the following.

Lemma 1. *The greatest fixed point νF is an over-approximation of the set of recurring states in Σ.*

We can prove this by induction on the number of times F is applied. $\top = [0, N]^n = \Sigma$ contains all recurring states, which proves the base case. Assume the inductive hypothesis that for some $i \geq 0$, $F^i(\top)$ contains all recurring states. We show that one more application of F cannot remove even one recurring states from $F^i(\top)$. For some state $s \in F^i(\top) \setminus F^{i+1}(\top)$, there exists a variable v s.t. $f_v(F^i(\top))$ does not contain s_v. For the sake of contradiction, assume s is recurring. Then, there exists $m > 0$ s.t. $\forall i \in \{1, \cdots, m-1\} \cdot \delta^i(s) \neq s$ and $\delta^m(s) = s$. Since all variables can change by at most 1 in each transition according to Eq. 1, there must exist $i, j \in \{0, \cdots, m-1\}$ s.t. $T_v(\delta^i(s)) \geq s_v$ and $T_v(\delta^j(s)) \leq s_v$. Since $F^i(\top)$ is closed, $\delta^i(s), \delta^j(s) \in F^i(\top)$. This means $f_v(F^i(\top))$ must contain s_v which leads to a contradiction. Thus, $F^{i+1}(\top)$ also contains all recurring states, proving our claim.

2.2 Computing the Greatest Fixed Point νF

We refer to one application of some f_v as an *update*. Then, νF is a fixed point of a system of equations, one equation corresponding to each f_v. The simplest algorithm to compute νF is to repeatedly apply F until a fixed point is reached. One application of F corresponds to a parallel application of each f_v. This algorithm is far from optimal since it does not exploit the dependencies in the network. In the worst case, when each application of F changes either lower or upper bounds of exactly one of the variables by 1, it can perform $\mathcal{O}(Nn^2)$ updates. Biological models expressed as QNs are typically expected to have a small granularity, reflecting the high level of abstraction from the underlying physico-chemical nature. Since every f_i is monotonic, every sequential algorithm will find the greatest fixed point as long each f_i is applied a sufficient number of times. Each update can be compared to a lemma generation step (Algorithm 4 in [6]).

Computing νF is often scalable because most variables in a typical QN have a small number of inputs. Each update to a variable means going over all possible combinations of its inputs $w_1, \cdots, w_m$ within the current region ρ, i.e. $([V_{lo}^{\rho}(w_1), V_{hi}^{\rho}(w_1)] \times \cdots \times [V_{lo}^{\rho}(w_m), V_{hi}^{\rho}(w_m)])$, which is feasible when the number of inputs is small. In many cases the target functions are also monotonic in some inputs, which allows for checking only the boundaries of the region (instead of the complete Cartesian product) to get the min/max possible target function value.

In cases where νF is a singleton, we safely conclude that the network stabilizes. We denote such networks as being *trivially stable*. When it is not a singleton, it may still be possible that the network is stable and the over-approximation is too coarse. Such networks are termed as being *non-trivially stable*.

2.3 Example

Fig. 1 shows how the fixed-point computation would proceed on the example transition systems. Each of them are of granularity 3 and have two variables A and B. The target functions corresponding to the transition system in Fig.1a are: $T_A(a, b) = 0$, $T_B(a, b) =$ if $a = 0$ then 0 else b. Target functions of the other two transitions systems are cumbersome to write and are hence omitted in the text. In case of Fig.1a, two updates are enough to determine that the only recurring state is $A = 0, B = 0$. In Fig.1b even though the network is stabilizing, it is not possible to strengthen the intervals of either A or B beyond $[0, 2] \times [0, 2]$. In Fig.1c, the network is unstable due to presence of a cycle, and one update each to intervals of A and B leads to the greatest fixed point region $[0, 1] \times [0, 1]$. We still have to explicitly check for presence of cycles within this smaller region.

3 Finding Instability

If the greatest fixed point νF is not a singleton, we can think of the following disjoint possibilities: (a) the network is unstable due to presence of (a.1) at least

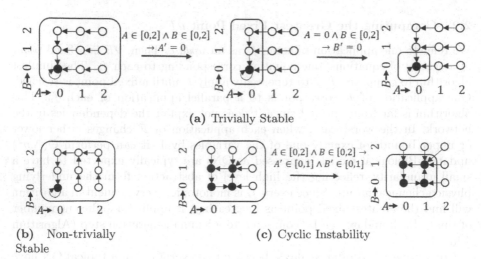

(a) Trivially Stable

(b) Non-trivially Stable

(c) Cyclic Instability

Fig. 1. Computing νF on transition systems of example QNs. Circles denote states and arrows between states denote transitions. Solid circle means that the state is recurring. Rounded rectangles are used to represent regions (interval domain).

two self-loop states, or (a.2) at most one self-loop state but at least one non-trivial cycle; (b) the network stabilizes and νF is too coarse to conclude that, in which case it has exactly one self-loop and no non-trivial cycles. Checking (a.1) can be encoded as a Boolean satisfiability problem. A decision procedure is used to check the existence of two distinct states: u and w such that both are self-loops: $\forall i \in \{1, \cdots, n\} \cdot (\delta(u)_i = u_i) \wedge (\delta(w)_i = w_i)$. This decision procedure usually works very well. On the contrary, as mentioned earlier the check for distinguishing (a.2) and (b) is a brute force call to a decision procedure that searches for loops of increasing length (up to the diameter of the network). Especially in the case that (b) is true, performance is prohibitive. This motivates development of a new algorithm to distinguish between cases (a.2) and (b).

First, we define some terminology. Let ρ be a region of the QN Q. A pair (ρ_1, ρ_2) of disjoint regions such that $\rho_1 \cup \rho_2 = \rho$ is called a *cut* of ρ. As both ρ_1 and ρ_2 are regions and $\rho_1 \cup \rho_2$ must be ρ, it follows that there exists some variable v and a value d such that $\rho_1 = \{s \in \rho \mid s(v) \leq d\}$ and $\rho_2 = \{s \in \rho \mid s(v) > d\}$ without loss of generality. In this case it must also be the case that $\rho_1 \cup \rho_2 = \rho_1 \sqcup \rho_2$ (where $\sqcup$ is the join operation in the lattice of regions). Let $\rho_1 \bullet \rho_2 = \{s \mid s \in \rho_1 \wedge \delta(s) \in \rho_2\}$ be the set of states in ρ_1 that have a transition to some state in ρ_2 and $\delta(\rho_1 \bullet \rho_2)$ is the image of $\rho_1 \bullet \rho_2$ wrt δ. We have $\delta(\rho_1 \bullet \rho_2) \subseteq \rho_2$. A pair of sets of states $\gamma = (\gamma_{\rho_1}, \gamma_{\rho_2})$ is a *frontier* of the cut (ρ_1, ρ_2) iff $\rho_1 \bullet \rho_2 \subseteq \gamma_{\rho_1} \subseteq \rho_1$, $\delta(\rho_2 \bullet \rho_1) \subseteq \gamma_{\rho_1}$ and $\rho_2 \bullet \rho_1 \subseteq \gamma_{\rho_2} \subseteq \rho_2$, $\delta(\rho_1 \bullet \rho_2) \subseteq \gamma_{\rho_2}$. A cut (ρ_1, ρ_2) can have one of three natures:(1) *zero*-way iff there is no transition from a state in ρ_1 to a state in ρ_2 and also the other way;(2)*one*-way iff there are transitions in exactly one direction; (3) *two*-way if there are transitions in both directions. That is, (ρ_1, ρ_2) is: *zero*-way iff both

$\rho_1 \bullet \rho_2$ and $\rho_1 \bullet \rho_1$ are empty; *one*-way iff exactly one of $\rho_1 \bullet \rho_2$ and $\rho_2 \bullet \rho_1$ is empty; *two*-way iff both $\rho_1 \bullet \rho_2$ and $\rho_2 \bullet \rho_1$ are non-empty. The nature of a frontier is also defined similarly, based on directionality of transitions between γ_{ρ_1} and γ_{ρ_2}. Note that all frontiers of a cut have the same nature as the cut, hence determining the nature of some frontier suffices to determine the nature of the cut.

We use (s_0, k) to denote a *simple* cycle $(s_0, \delta(s_0) \neq s_0, \cdots, \delta^{k-1}(s_0) \neq s_0, \delta^k (s_0) = s_0)$ of length $k > 0$. A cycle (s_0, k) is non-trivial iff $k > 1$. We say that (s_0, k) is within a region ρ if $\forall i \in \{0, \cdots, k\} \cdot \delta^i(s_0) \in \rho$. Algorithm 1 guarantees to find a non-trivial cycle (if one exists) within a region ρ by using two generic procedures SHRINK and CUT.

SHRINK: $\mathcal{S} \to \mathcal{S}$. SHRINK takes a region ρ as input and returns a region $\rho' \sqsubseteq \rho$ such that ρ' still contains every cycle that exists within ρ. In particular, SHRINK could ignore transitions that lead from ρ outside of ρ.

CUT: $\mathcal{S} \to (\mathcal{S} \times \mathcal{S}) \times (\mathcal{P}(\Sigma) \times \mathcal{P}(\Sigma))$. CUT takes a region ρ as input and returns a cut (ρ_1, ρ_2) of ρ and a frontier $\gamma = (\gamma_{\rho_1}, \gamma_{\rho_2})$ of the cut.

Later in the section, we describe concrete implementations of these procedures that were used in our experiments, but it should be noted that every implementation that follows the specifications would work as far as correctness of Algorithm 1 is concerned. Algorithm 1 is a recursive procedure that first applies SHRINK to the input region ρ to find a smaller region containing all cycles that exist within ρ. If the smaller region contains a single state, we can conclude that ρ does not have non-trivial cycles. Otherwise, we use CUT to split the shrunk region in two disjoint sub-regions ρ_1 and ρ_2 to which Algorithm 1 can be applied recursively. If a cycle is found within one of the sub-regions, it can be returned as a cycle within ρ. In case no cycle is found within either of the sub-regions, we still have to look for cycles that may exist across the cut (ρ_1, ρ_2). This is done using Algorithm 2.

Algorithm 2 uses a frontier $\gamma = (\gamma_{\rho_1}, \gamma_{\rho_2})$ of the cut (ρ_1, ρ_2) found by CUT. If the cut is *one/zero*-way, there can't exist a non-trivial cycle across this cut (existence of a cycle across (ρ_1, ρ_2) would imply that there is at least one transition from a state in ρ_1 to a state in ρ_2 and also the other way and hence both $\rho_1 \bullet \rho_2$ and $\rho_2 \bullet \rho_1$ would be non-empty). We use a frontier to find the nature of the cut because $\rho_1 \bullet \rho_2$ and $\rho_2 \bullet \rho_1$ can be difficult to compute exactly. How to compute a frontier and determine its nature is described in more detail in Sec. 3.1.

In case the cut is *two*-way, we start an exhaustive search for a cycle across the cut by sequentially running simulations starting at each state in γ_{ρ_1}. Each simulation is run until either the current state in the simulation is outside of region ρ or a lasso is found. If there is cycle across the cut, this search is guaranteed to find it because there would exist a state s_{ρ_1} on the cycle such that $\delta(s_{\rho_1}) = \rho_2$ and hence $s_{\rho_1} \in \rho_1 \bullet \rho_2 \subseteq \gamma_{\rho_1}$.

Lemma 2. FINDINSTABILITY(νF) *returns a simple non-trivial cycle* $(s_0, k > 1)$ *iff there exists at least one non-trivial cycle in Q and returns null otherwise.*

A rigorous proof of this statement can be sketched using structural induction on regions following the reasoning above.

Algorithm 1: FINDINSTABILITY

Input: A region ρ

Output: Either a simple non-trivial cycle $(s_0, k > 1)$ within ρ or null if ρ does not contain a non-trivial cycle

1   $\rho \leftarrow$ SHRINK(ρ)
2   **if** ρ contains a single state **then**
3   **return** null
4   **else**
5     $(\rho_1, \rho_2), \gamma \leftarrow$ CUT(ρ)
6     $res_1 \leftarrow$ FINDINSTABILITY(ρ_1)
7   **if** $res_1 \neq$ null **then return** res_1 $res_2 \leftarrow$ FINDINSTABILITY(ρ_2)
8   **if** $res_2 \neq$ null **then return** res_2 **return**
    FINDCYCLEACROSSCUT$((\rho_1, \rho_2), \gamma)$
9   **end**

Algorithm 2: FINDCYCLEACROSSCUT

Input: A cut (ρ_1, ρ_2) of the region $\rho_1 \cup \rho_2 = \rho$ and frontier $\gamma = (\gamma_{\rho_1}, \gamma_{\rho_2})$ of the cut. The regions ρ_1 and ρ_2 do not have any cycles within them.

Output: Either a simple non-trivial cycle $(s_0, k > 1)$ within ρ s.t.
$\exists i, j \in \{0, \cdots, k\}.\delta^i(s_0) \in \rho_1 \wedge \delta^j(s_0) \in \rho_2$ or null if there is no such cycle

1   **if** γ is *one*-way or *zero*-way **then**
2   **return** null
3   **else**
4     $iter_\gamma \leftarrow$ iterator(γ_{ρ_1})
5     $cyc \leftarrow$ null
6   **while** $cyc =$ null $\wedge \neg$exhausted?$(iter_\gamma)$ **do**
7       $cur \leftarrow$ getElemAndAdvance$(iter_\gamma)$
8       $seen, i \leftarrow$ emptyMap, 0
9   **while** $cur \notin$ keys$(seen) \wedge cur \in \rho$ **do**
10        $seen[cur] \leftarrow i$
11        $cur, i \leftarrow \delta(cur), i + 1$
12   **end**
13   **if** $cur \in \rho$ **then**
14        $len \leftarrow i - seen[cur]$
15   **if** $len > 1$ **then** $cyc \leftarrow (cur, len)$
16
17   **end**
18   **return** cyc
19   **end**

3.1   Concrete Implementations of SHRINK and CUT

In this section we describe the concrete implementation of SHRINK and CUT that we used in our experiments.

SHRINK: Given a region ρ, consider the modified target function T_v^ρ of a variable v:

$$T_v^\rho(s) = \min(V_{hi}^\rho(v), \max(V_{lo}^\rho(v), T_v(s)))$$

The modified transition function δ_ρ is defined using Eq. 1 by replacing T_v by T_v^ρ. The intention with T_v^ρ is to create target functions tailored to ρ so that ρ is closed wrt δ_ρ, while still preserving all transitions that are completely within ρ. This is done by forcing the target function value to be within $[V_{lo}^\rho(v), V_{hi}^\rho(v)]$, truncating to the upper/lower bound if the original value is too large/too small.

The function F_ρ is defined by replacing T_v by T_v^ρ in Eq. 3. Let $\mathcal{S}_\rho$ be the set of all regions contained within ρ and $(\mathcal{S}_\rho, \sqsupseteq)$ be the corresponding partial order. It can be shown that for every state s: (1) $s \in \rho \setminus \rho\bullet \to \delta_\rho(s) = \delta(s)$, and (2) $s \in \rho\bullet \to \delta_\rho(s) \in \rho$. This means ρ is closed wrt to δ_ρ and hence the greatest fixed point $\nu_{\mathcal{S}_\rho} F_\rho$ on $\mathcal{S}_\rho$ is well defined. Thus, $\nu_{\mathcal{S}_\rho} F_\rho$ is an over-approximation of the set of states in ρ that are recurring wrt δ_ρ. Also, if there exists a cycle (wrt δ) within ρ, it will also be a cycle wrt δ_ρ and hence be within $\nu_{\mathcal{S}_\rho} F_\rho$. SHRINK$(\rho) = \nu_{\mathcal{S}_\rho} F_\rho$ can be computed following the approach in Sec. 2.

CUT: The straight-forward way to cut a region ρ is to split the interval of one of the variables into two. Let $\rho|_{[v]=I}$ denote the region obtained from ρ by replacing the interval corresponding to v by I and keeping other intervals unchanged. Upon splitting v at α with $V_{lo}^\rho(v) \leq \alpha < V_{hi}^\rho(v)$, we get the cut (ρ_1, ρ_2) with $\rho_1 = \rho|_{[v]=[V_{lo}^\rho(v),\alpha]}$ and $\rho_2 = \rho|_{[v]=[\alpha+1,V_{hi}^\rho(v)]}$. Since we know that for every state s and variable v, $\delta(s)_v$ differs from s_v by at most 1, we can safely choose $(\gamma_{\rho_1}, \gamma_{\rho_2})$ as a frontier of this cut, where $\gamma_{\rho_1} = \{s|s \in \rho|_{[v]=[\alpha,\alpha]}\}$ and $\gamma_{\rho_2} = \{s|s \in \rho|_{[v]=[\alpha+1,\alpha+1]}\}$. The nature of this cut can be determined by encoding the problem of checking the nature of the frontier as a boolean satisfiability problem. Checking existence of a transition from γ_{ρ_1} to γ_{ρ_2} is equivalent to checking existence of a state w s.t. $w \in \rho_1 \wedge w_v = \alpha \wedge \delta(w) \in \rho_2 \wedge \delta(w)_v = \alpha+1$, where $w \in \rho_1$ would be a conjunction of simple predicates restricting the range of each variable in w to be within ρ_1 and likewise for $\delta(w) \in \rho_2$.

We have n choices for variable v and then $V_{hi}^\rho(v) - V_{lo}^\rho(v)$ choices for the splitting point α for each v. CUT(ρ) enumerates through all these possibilities and returns the first one that has a *zero/one*-way nature. A *zero/one*-way cut saves the effort of finding cycles across it later. If all possibilities are *two*-way, then it returns a balanced cut, one for which ρ_1 and ρ_2 are similar in size.

3.2 Efficiency of FINDINSTABILITY

In the worst case, Algorithm 1 can be equivalent to a brute-force enumeration over all states of the QN that tries to build cycles by running simulations, but the effectiveness of SHRINK to eliminate parts of the state space that do not contain cycles and the existence of *zero/one*-way cuts makes it scale to considerably large QNs. Experiments show that this can be better than a bounded model-checking based approach by a few orders of magnitude. However, a stable system which resisted an initial SHRINK and for which only a *two*-way cut could be found would be expected to require such a brute-force search. One possible approach to reduce the search space would be to search specifically for *two*-way cuts whose frontiers can be bisected into a *two*-way cut and a *zero*-way cut. In the continued development of new models, we hope to discover examples of this behavior, and will be look to address this issue in future. In the absence of such models

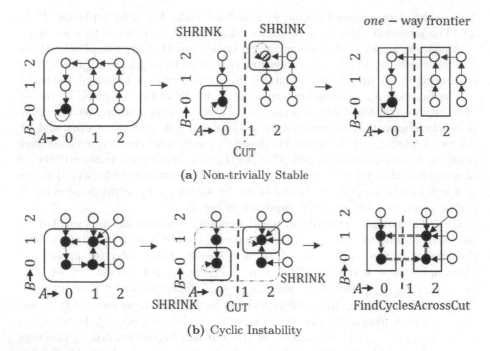

(a) Non-trivially Stable

(b) Cyclic Instability

Fig. 2. Progress of Algorithm 1 on transition systems in Fig.1b,1c. Dotted lines represent the splitting point in CUT. Dotted arrows represent the modifications made to transition functions of sub-regions in order to apply SHRINK. Sharp-edged rectangles denote frontiers. Other notation is the same as in Fig.1.

at present however we have here restricted our testing to implementations of Algorithm 1.

3.3 Example

Fig.2 illustrates how Algorithm 1 makes progress on examples from Fig.1b and Fig.1c. In Fig.2a, for the non-trivially stable system, CUT splits the interval of A at 0 to produce two sub-regions. One SHRINK operation on each of the sub-regions reduces them to singletons, hence confirming non-existence of cycles within them. Owing to the cut being *one*-way, non-existence of cycles across it is also easily checked. In Fig.2b, Algorithm 1 is applied to the fixed point obtained previously ($[0,1] \times [0,1]$). Similar to the previous example, interval of A is split at 0, and the sub-regions get reduced to singletons by SHRINK. However, the cut is *two*-way and Algorithm 2 successfully finds a cycle by running a simulation from a point in the frontier.

4 Benchmarks and Evaluation

We implemented the approach in a tool called BioModelAnalyzer+ (BMA+) and compared directly against the approach from [6] implemented within BioModelAnalyzer (BMA, [18, 21, 22]). For each benchmark, BMA+ first computes the greatest fixed point νF. If stability cannot be proved, it tries to find a counter-example of type multiple self-loops by encoding it as a satisfiability problem. If such a counter-example cannot be found, Algorithm 1 is used to check for existence of a cycle. All calculations were performed single-threaded on a Windows 8 PC with an Intel i7 processor @ 2.1 GHz. There was an upper bound of 2GB on memory usage. Time out was set at 15 mins. We used Z3 [23] version 3 as the decision procedure. All benchmark systems are available at http://www.cs.le.ac.uk/people/npiterman/publications/2014/instability/, and an implementation of the BMA+ algorithm is available through the BioModelAnalyzer website (http://biomodelanalyzer.research.microsoft.com/, right click the proof button to access the tool and select "SCM analysis").

We study the results for models of different nature separately. Comparisons with other available tools are available from [6].

4.1   Trivially Stable Systems and Systems with Multiple Self-Loops

We benchmarked our new approach using a range of well characterized stable and bifurcating (multiple self-loops) systems from previous studies [6, 8, 18, 21, 24]. Both tools run extremely fast and show similar performance for these benchmarks, as would be expected. See Table 1. However, we still see a slowdown for BMA+ arising from changes in the procedure which are not relevant here.

Table 1. Results for trivially stable (TS) and bifurcating (BF) models. N+1 is the granularity, |E| is the number of edges in dependency graph, |V| is the number of variables. BMA and BMA+ denote the running time of the respective tools in milliseconds.

Model	Nature	N+1	|E|	|V|	BMA	BMA+	$\frac{\text{BMA}}{\text{BMA+}}$
Leukaemia	TS	3	81	51	71	94	0.8
Diabetes	TS	3	125	87	66	93	0.7
Budding yeast	TS	5	26	16	55	80	0.7
VPC lin15KO	TS	3	140	85	56	122	0.5
Dicty single cell	TS	2	12	8	47	111	0.4
Skin 1D unstable	BF	5	89	75	2206	1973	1.1
Skin 1D	BF	5	94	75	239	238	1
Skin 1D unstable 2	BF	5	89	75	383	357	1.1
Skin 2D 5x2 TF	BF	5	239	198	337	315	1.1
MCP Array	BF	2	104	45	140	241	0.6

4.2   Systems with cyclic instability

Oscillations occur in a wide range of different biological systems. In nerves under constant stimulation, the patterns of opening and closing of ion channels in an action potential are expected to generate cycles. Oscillations are also widely found in different biological systems as a mechanism for synchronizing populations of cells in organs and whole animals. In *Dictyostelium discoideum*, coordi-

Table 2. Results for models with cyclic instabilities. K is the length of the cycle found by BMA+. TO denotes a time out. In comparing systems where BMA times out, the speed up is calculated relative to the time limit (15 minutes) and noted with ">". Other notation is same as in Table 1

Model	N+1	|E|	|V|	K	BMA	BMA+	$\frac{BMA}{BMA+}$
Dicty population	2	71	35	5	60066	2541	23.6
Firing Neuron	2	21	21	6	218	458	0.5
LModel	4	105	25	5	43934	9865	4.5
Leukaemia unstable	3	92	57	5	4497	446	10.1
SSkin 1D	5	46	30	11	TO	132350	>6.8
SSkin 2D 3 cells 2 layers	5	64	40	18	TO	2706	>322.6

Table 3. Results for non-trivially stable models. TO denotes time out. Other notation is same as in Tables 1 and 2

Model	N+1	|E|	|V|	BMA	BMA+	$\frac{BMA}{BMA+}$
Ion channel	2	7	10	499	173	2.9
Lambda phage	2	13	8	3113	197	15.8
Resting neuron	2	28	21	TO	244949	>3.7
E. coli chemotaxis	5	10	9	TO	250	>3600

nated oscillations in groups of cells signal the transition from unicellular growth to multicellular development [25]. BMA+ consistently performs almost an order of magnitude better than BMA for these benchmarks. See Table 2.

4.3 Non-trivially Stable Systems

The non-trivially stable systems highlight important examples of stable biological systems which cannot be proved to be stable with SHRINK alone. Chemotaxis in *E. coli* is a paradigm for bacterial signaling. Attractants and repellents bind to a receptors at the cell pole, altering the activity of the kinase CheA. This in turn both alters the switching behavior of the flagellar motor and changes the sensitivity of the receptor array to allow for adaptation. The alteration of receptor sensitivity is slower than motor activation, ensuring that the flagellar switching behavior reverts to an equilibrium state in an unchanging environment. Similarly, an action potential passes along a neuron by the opening of ion channels (triggered by changes in the local membrane potential), followed by a delayed closure of the pore. The time delay aspects in both of these models (speed of the adaptation machinery in chemotaxis, and the slow closure of the ion channels) lead to them both being stable systems. However, proving stability is non-trivial because of this property. Table 3 shows the benefit of BMA+ over BMA. We observe significant speed up in all cases.

Particularly noteworthy is the improvement in the calculation of the stable state in the *E. coli* signaling system, as despite being a significantly smaller model than many others presented here (in terms of number of variables and edges), proofs of stability using the previous approach were prohibitively costly.

Through a single application of the cut, the stability of the system was proved comparably quickly to a simple example of the same size.

5 Conclusions

This paper describes a new algorithm for the formal analysis of biological models, which offers a rapid approach for proving instability arising from loops. This technique builds on previous approaches by rapidly searching for cycles in cases where stability cannot be proved trivially. We find a large speed up for proving instability of cyclic systems, but additionally we show that it offers an impressive speed up when considering the behavior of stable systems with timed switches, such as bacterial chemotaxis. By proving stability in these new models our findings further reinforce the importance of inherent biological robustness [6] in signaling systems. In order to build accurate models of chemotaxis signaling in *E. coli* and action potentials in a neuron, we need to include timing effects to reproduce realistic biological behavior. Without these timing effects, the models unnaturally show bifurcation and cycling behavior respectively. Our new approach allows us to better identify loops and pseudo-loops in biological signaling systems observed in this biomedically important class of systems.

Acknowledgments. We thank Dr C Pears and Dr A Watson for insightful comments and advice.

References

1. Fisher, J., Henzinger, T.: Executable cell biology. Nature Biotechnology 25, 1239–1249 (2007)
2. Bonzanni, N., Feenstra, K.A., Fokkink, W., Krepska, E.: What can formal methods bring to systems biology? In: Cavalcanti, A., Dams, D.R. (eds.) FM 2009. LNCS, vol. 5850, pp. 16–22. Springer, Heidelberg (2009)
3. Chabrier-Rivier, N., Danos, M.C., Fages, V., Schächter, F., Modeling, V.: querying biomolecular interaction networks. Theor. Comput. Sci. 325, 25–44 (2004)
4. Bonzanni, N., Krepska, E., Feenstra, K.A., Fokkink, W., Kielmann, T., Bal, H., Heringa, J.: Executing multicellular differentiation: Quantitative predictive modelling of *C.elegans* vulval development. Bioinformatics 25, 2049–2056 (2009)
5. Fisher, J., Piterman, N., Hajnal, A., Henzinger, T.: Predictive modeling of signaling crosstalk during *c. elegans* vulval development. PLoS Computational Biology 3, e92 (2007)
6. Cook, B., Fisher, J., Krepska, E., Piterman, N.: Proving stabilization of biological systems. In: Jhala, R., Schmidt, D. (eds.) VMCAI 2011. LNCS, vol. 6538, pp. 134–149. Springer, Heidelberg (2011)
7. Kauffman, S.: Metabolic stability and epigenesis in randomly constructed genetic nets. Journal of Theoretical Biology 22, 437–467 (1969)
8. Schaub, M., Henzinger, T., Fisher, J.: Qualitative networks: A symbolic approach to analyze biological signaling networks. BMC Systems Biology 1 (2007)

9. Krumsiek, J., Marr, C., Schroeder, T., Theis, F.J.: Hierarchical differentiation of myeloid progenitors is encoded in the transcription factor network. PLoS One 6, e22649 (2011)
10. Grieco, L., Calzone, L., Bernard-Pierrot, I., Radvanyi, F., Kahn-Perlès, B., Thieffry, D.: Integrative modelling of the influence of MAPK network on cancer cell fate decision. PLoS Comput. Biol. 9, e1003286 (2013)
11. Bonzanni, N., Garg, A., Feenstra, K.A., Schütte, J., Kinston, S., Miranda-Saavedra, D., Heringa, J., Xenarios, I., Göttgens, B.: Hard-wired heterogeneity in blood stem cells revealed using a dynamic regulatory network model. Bioinformatics 29, i80–i88 (2013)
12. Huang, S.: Gene expression profiling, genetic networks, and cellular states: An integrating concept for tumorigenesis and drug discovery. Journal of Molecular Medicine 77, 469–480 (1999)
13. Naldi, A., Berenguier, D., Fauré, A., Lopez, F., Thieffry, D., Chaouiya, C.: Logical modelling of regulatory networks with GINsim 2.3. Biosystems 97, 134–139 (2009)
14. Cimatti, A., Clarke, E., Giunchiglia, F., Roveri, M.: Nusmv: A new symbolic model verifier. In: Halbwachs, N., Peled, D. (eds.) CAV 1999. LNCS, vol. 1633, pp. 495–499. Springer, Heidelberg (1999)
15. Naldi, A., Thieffry, D., Chaouiya, C.: Decision diagrams for the representation and analysis of logical models of genetic networks. In: Calder, M., Gilmore, S. (eds.) CMSB 2007. LNCS (LNBI), vol. 4695, pp. 233–247. Springer, Heidelberg (2007)
16. Wadhams, G.H., Armitage, J.P.: Making sense of it all: Bacterial chemotaxis. Nat. Rev. Mol. Cell Biol. 5, 1024–1037 (2004)
17. Hille, B.: Ion Channels of Excitable Membranes, 3rd edn., pp. 2001–2007. Sinauer Associates Inc. (2001-2007)
18. Claessen, K., Fisher, J., Ishtiaq, S., Piterman, N., Wang, Q.: Model-checking signal transduction networks through decreasing reachability sets. In: Sharygina, N., Veith, H. (eds.) CAV 2013. LNCS, vol. 8044, pp. 85–100. Springer, Heidelberg (2013)
19. Cousot, P., Cousot, R.: Abstract interpretation: A unified lattice model for static analysis of programs by construction or approximation of fixpoints. In: Principles of Programming Languages, pp. 238–252 (1977)
20. Cousot, P., Cousot, R.: Static determination of dynamic properties of programs. In: Proceedings of the Second International Symposium on Programming, Dunod, Paris, France, pp. 106–130 (1976)
21. Benque, D., Bourton, S., Cockerton, C., Cook, B., Fisher, J., Ishtiaq, S., Piterman, N., Taylor, A., Vardi, M.Y.: BMA: Visual tool for modeling and analyzing biological networks. In: Madhusudan, P., Seshia, S.A. (eds.) CAV 2012. LNCS, vol. 7358, pp. 686–692. Springer, Heidelberg (2012)
22. Taylor, A.S., Piterman, N., Ishtiaq, S., Fisher, J., Cook, B., Cockerton, C., Bourton, S., Benque, D.: At the interface of biology and computation. In: Proceedings of the SIGCHI Conference on Human Factors in Computing Systems, pp. 493–502. ACM (2013)
23. de Moura, L., Bjørner, N.: Z3: An Efficient SMT Solver. In: Ramakrishnan, C.R., Rehof, J. (eds.) TACAS 2008. LNCS, vol. 4963, pp. 337–340. Springer, Heidelberg (2008)
24. Beyer, A., Thomason, P., Li, X., Scott, J., Fisher, J.: Mechanistic insights into metabolic disturbance during type-2 diabetes and obesity using qualitative networks. T. Comp. Sys. Biology 12, 146–162 (2010)
25. Söderbom, F., Loomis, W.F.: Cell-cell signaling during Dictyostelium development. Trends in Microbiology 6, 402–406 (1998)

Invariant Verification of Nonlinear Hybrid Automata Networks of Cardiac Cells[*]

Zhenqi Huang[1], Chuchu Fan[1], Alexandru Mereacre[2],
Sayan Mitra[1], and Marta Kwiatkowska[2]

[1] Department of Electrical and Computer Engineering,
University of Illinois at Urbana-Champaign, USA
{zhuang25,cfan10,mitras}@illinois.edu
[2] Department of Computer Science,
University of Oxford, United Kingdom
{Marta.Kwiatkowska,Alexandru.Mereacre}@cs.ox.ac.uk

Abstract. Verification algorithms for networks of nonlinear hybrid automata (HA) can aid us understand and control biological processes such as cardiac arrhythmia, formation of memory, and genetic regulation. We present an algorithm for over-approximating reach sets of networks of nonlinear HA which can be used for sound and relatively complete invariant checking. First, it uses automatically computed input-to-state discrepancy functions for the individual automata modules in the network $\mathcal{A}$ for constructing a low-dimensional model $\mathcal{M}$. Simulations of both $\mathcal{A}$ and $\mathcal{M}$ are then used to compute the reach tubes for $\mathcal{A}$. These techniques enable us to handle a challenging verification problem involving a network of cardiac cells, where each cell has four continuous variables and 29 locations. Our prototype tool can check bounded-time invariants for networks with 5 cells (20 continuous variables, 29^5 locations) typically in less than 15 minutes for up to reasonable time horizons. From the computed reach tubes we can infer biologically relevant properties of the network from a set of initial states.

Keywords: Biological networks, hybrid systems, invariants, verification.

1 Introduction

Central to understanding and controlling behavior of complex biological networks are invariant properties. For example, synchronization of the action potentials of cardiac cells and neurons is responsible for normal functioning of the heart and for formation of memory [6, 16], and maintenance of synchrony is an invariant property. Real-time prediction of loss of synchrony can enable automatic deployment of counter-measures. For instance, embedded defibrillator devices are being designed to preempt possible cardiac arrest that arises

---

[*] The authors are supported by NSA SoS grant (W911NSF-13-0086), AFOSR YIP grant (FA9550-12-1-0336), NSF CAREER grant (CNS 10-54247), the ERC AdG VERIWARE, ERC PoC VERIPACE, and the Institute for the Future of Computing, Oxford Martin School.

A. Biere and R. Bloem (Eds.): CAV 2014, LNCS 8559, pp. 373–390, 2014.
© Springer International Publishing Switzerland 2014

from loss of synchrony. Offline invariant checks can aid in debugging pacemakers and brain-machine interfaces. Checking invariant properties for networks of dynamical systems is challenging. Analytical results exist only for modules with relatively simple dynamics and on special types of topologies such as scale-free and random graphs [7, 9, 38, 40, 43]. These approaches cannot be applied to modules with nonlinear and hybrid dynamics such as the models of cardiac cells in [11, 20]. Aside from the nonlinearities in the modules, the complete network model involves shared continuous variables between modules (ion-channels) which have limited support in analytical and verification approaches. In the absence of analytical approaches, one performs simulation experiments which are computationally inexpensive but fall short of providing guarantees and are of limited utility in studying invariants for sets of initial states or parameter values. For example, if we wanted to know if the voltage of an action potential stays within some range from a set of initial states, then a finite number of simulations cannot give us a provably correct answer.

In this paper, we present an algorithm for verifying bounded-time invariant properties of networks of deterministic nonlinear hybrid automata. The underlying principle is simulation-based verification which combines numerical simulations with formal analysis [5, 14, 15]. First, a simulation ψ is computed from a single initial state $\mathbf{v}$. This ψ is then bloated by *some factor* to over-approximate all executions from a neighborhood $B_{\mathbf{v}}$ of $\mathbf{v}$ of non-zero measure. By repeating this process for different $\mathbf{v}$'s, all behaviors from a set of initial states can be over-approximated and robust invariants can be checked. In [15], we used user-provided model annotations (*discrepancy functions*) to statically compute the bloating factor in a way that can make the over-approximations arbitrarily precise. The resulting algorithm enjoys scalability and relative completeness: if the system satisfies the invariant robustly, then the algorithm is guaranteed to terminate. The burden of finding discrepancy functions for large models is partly alleviated in [26] for nonlinear differential equations. That paper proposes *input-to-state (IS)* discrepancy functions for each module $\mathcal{A}_i$ of a larger system $\mathcal{A} = \mathcal{A}_1 \| \ldots \| \mathcal{A}_N$. These user-provided, albeit modular, annotations are used to construct a lower-dimensional nonlinear time-varying system whose trajectories give the necessary bloating factor for the trajectories of the system $\mathcal{A}$.

These previous results do not extend to hybrid systems with guards and resets, and their applicability is still limited by the annotation required from the user. One challenge is that individual simulations capture a particular sequence of locations. However, the states reached in a bloated version of the simulation may intersect with many other guards and visit a completely different sequence of locations. Our contributions address this and other technical hurdles, demonstrating a promising approach for invariant verification of nonlinear hybrid networks. (a) We present a new simulation-based verification algorithm for nonlinear hybrid networks that uses modular input-to-state (IS) discrepancy functions. Modular annotations and the simulation-based approach make it scalable. The algorithm is sound; it systematically discovers possible transitions and then generates new simulations for different location sequences. We identify general robustness conditions that yield relative-completeness. (b) We develop a set of techniques for automatically computing input-to-state discrepancy functions for a general class of nonlinear hybrid models. (c) The performance of our prototype implementation in checking bounded-time invariants of complex Simulink models of cardiac cell networks illustrate the promise of the approach [25]. For networks with 5 cells, each with 4 dimensions and 29 locations, and multi-affine dynamics (total of 20 continuous variables, 29^5 locations), invariants for up to reasonable time horizons are established typically in less than 15 minutes. In two minutes, it finds counter-examples of networks with 8 cells. All of this enables us to check biologically relevant properties for cardiac cells networks.

Section 2 provides background for hybrid automata, whereas Section 3 introduces IS discrepancy and techniques for computing them. Section 4 describes the main algorithm and Section 5 presents its applications in checking cardiac networks. Finally, Section 6 discusses related works and concludes the paper.

2   Hybrid Automata Modules and Networks

Hybrid Input/Output Automata. (HA) is a framework for specifying interacting modules that evolve discretely and continuously and share information over continuous variables and discrete transitions [31, 34, 35]. Please see the full version [25] for related definitions and notations.

For a variable v, its type, denoted by $type(v)$, is the set of values that it can take. For a set of variables V, a *valuation* **v** maps each $v \in V$ to a point in $type(v)$. Given a valuation **v** for V, the valuation of a particular variable $v' \in V$, denoted by $\mathbf{v}.v'$, is the restriction of **v** to v'; for a set $V \subseteq V$, $\mathbf{v}.V$ is the restriction of **v** to V. $Val(V)$ is the set of all valuations for V. A *trajectory* for V models continuous evolution of the values of the variables over a closed interval $[0, T]$ called the *domain*. A trajectory ξ is a map $\xi : [0, T] \to Val(V)$. Restriction of ξ to a subset of variables $X \subseteq V$ is denoted by $\xi \downarrow X$. For a trajectory ξ of $V \cup U$ with domain $[0, T]$, we define $\xi.\mathsf{fstate}$ as $(\xi \downarrow V)(0)$ and $\xi.\mathsf{lstate}$ as $(\xi \downarrow V)(T)$. A variable is *continuous* if all its trajectories are piece-wise continuous and it is *discrete* if its trajectories are piece-wise constant. A HA has a set of continuous variables X that evolve along trajectories (defined by differential equations with inputs U) and can be reset, and a set of discrete variables L that change with transitions.

Definition 1. *A Hybrid I/O Automaton (HA) A is a tuple (L, X, U, Θ, D, T) where (a) L is a set of discrete variables. $Val(L)$ is the set of locations. (b) X is a set of real-valued continuous variables. $V := X \cup L$ is the set of state variables; $Val(V)$ is the state space. (c) U is a set of real-valued input variables; $Val(U)$ is the input space. (d) $\Theta \subseteq Val(V)$ is a set of start states; (e) $D \subseteq Val(V) \times Val(V)$ is a set of discrete transitions. (f) T is the set of trajectories for $V \cup U$ that is closed under prefix, suffix, and concatenation [31]. Over any trajectory $\xi \in T$, L remains constant. For any state **v** and piece-wise continuous input trajectory η, there exists a state trajectory ξ such that $\xi.\mathsf{fstate} = \mathbf{v}$ and either (i) $\xi \downarrow U = \eta$, or (ii) $\xi \downarrow U$ matches a prefix of η with a transition enabled at $\xi.\mathsf{lstate}$.*

A transition $(\mathbf{v}, \mathbf{v}') \in \mathcal{D}$, for any two states $\mathbf{v}, \mathbf{v}'$, is written as $\mathbf{v} \to_{\mathcal{A}} \mathbf{v}'$ or as $\mathbf{v} \to \mathbf{v}'$ when $\mathcal{A}$ is clear from the context. The transitions of $\mathcal{A}$ are specified for pairs of locations in the guard-reset style. For each pair (ℓ, ℓ') of locations the guard $G_{\ell,\ell'} \subseteq Val(\mathcal{X})$ is the set of states from which a transition from location ℓ to ℓ' is enabled and the reset map is a continuous function $Val(\mathcal{X}) \to Val(\mathcal{X})$.

For location $\ell \in Val(\mathcal{L})$, the trajectories of $\mathcal{A}$ are defined by a *trajectory invariant* $I_\ell \subseteq Val(\mathcal{X})$ and a set of ordinary differential equations (ODEs) involving the variables in $\mathcal{X}$ and $\mathcal{U}$. The ODE is specified by a Lipschitz continuous function called *dynamic mapping* $f_\ell : Val(\mathcal{X}) \times Val(\mathcal{U}) \to Val(\mathcal{X})$. Given a input trajectory η of $\mathcal{U}$ and a state $\mathbf{v} \in Val(\mathcal{V})$, a state trajectory from $\mathbf{v}$ with η is a function $\xi_{\mathbf{v},\eta} : [0, T] \to Val(\mathcal{V})$ satisfying: (a) $\xi_{\mathbf{v},\eta}(0) = \mathbf{v}$, (b) for any $t \in [0, T]$, the time derivative of $\xi \downarrow \mathcal{X}$ at t satisfies the differential equation $\frac{d(\xi \downarrow \mathcal{X})(t)}{dt} = f_\ell((\xi \downarrow \mathcal{X})(t), \eta(t))$, and (c) $(\xi \downarrow \mathcal{X})(t) \in I_\ell$ and $(\xi \downarrow \mathcal{L})(t) = \ell$. As in the last two statements, we will drop the subscripts of a trajectory when the dependence on the initial state and the input is clear. Because of the invariant I_ℓ, in some location $\ell \in Val(\mathcal{L})$ all the trajectories might be of finite duration. Conditions (i) and (ii) in Definition 1 make the HA *input enabled*, that is, from any state $\mathcal{A}$ is able to consume any input η completely (i) or up to some time at which it reacts with a transition (ii).

A HA without inputs $(\mathcal{U} = \varnothing)$ is *closed*; otherwise, it is *open*. A HA with a single location and no transitions is called a *dynamical system*. We denote the components of HA $\mathcal{A}$ by $\mathcal{L}_{\mathcal{A}}, \mathcal{X}_{\mathcal{A}}, \mathcal{U}_{\mathcal{A}}, \Theta_{\mathcal{A}}, \mathcal{D}_{\mathcal{A}}, \to_{\mathcal{A}}$ and $\mathcal{T}_{\mathcal{A}}$, and for $\mathcal{A}_i$ its components are denoted by $\mathcal{L}_i, \mathcal{X}_i, \mathcal{U}_i, \Theta_i, \mathcal{D}_i, \to_i$ and $\mathcal{T}_i$.

Semantics. We assume that the discrete transitions are urgent and deterministic. That is, from any state $\mathbf{v} = (\mathbf{x}, \ell)$ at most one of following two things can happen: (a) a transition to a unique state $(\mathbf{x}', \ell')$, or (b) a trajectory $\xi_{\mathbf{v}}$ of non-zero duration. A bounded execution of $\mathcal{A}$ records the evolution of the variables along a particular run. A *bounded execution fragment* is a finite sequence of trajectories $\xi_{(0)}, \xi_{(1)}, \ldots$, such that, for each i, $\xi_{(i)} \in \mathcal{T}$ and $\xi_{(i)}.\mathsf{lstate} \to \xi_{(i+1)}.\mathsf{fstate}$. A *bounded execution* is an execution fragment with $\xi_{(0)}.\mathsf{fstate}$ in Θ. A state $\mathbf{v}$ is *reachable* if it is the last state of some execution. We denote the set of reachable states of $\mathcal{A}$ by $\mathsf{Reach}_{\mathcal{A}}$. The reachable states up to a bounded time horizon $T > 0$ are denoted by $\mathsf{Reach}_{\mathcal{A}}(T)$. The reachable states from a subset of initial states $\Theta' \subseteq \Theta$ up to T are denoted by $\mathsf{Reach}_{\mathcal{A}}(\Theta', T)$. A set $Inv \subseteq Val(\mathcal{V})$ is an *invariant* of a closed HA $\mathcal{A}$ if $\mathsf{Reach}_{\mathcal{A}} \subseteq Inv$. Checking invariants corresponds to verifying safety properties. Computing $\mathsf{Reach}_{\mathcal{A}}$ exactly is undecidable but for the simplest classes of hybrid automata [1, 23, 32, 44].

For relative completeness, we define robustness of HA. A HA $\mathcal{A}(c)$ is a *c-perturbation* of $\mathcal{A}$ if $\mathcal{A}(c)$ is obtained by perturbing the initial set and dynamical mappings of $\mathcal{A}$ by at most c. That is, $\mathcal{A}$ and $\mathcal{A}(c)$ are identical except that (i) $d(\Theta_{\mathcal{A}}, \Theta_{\mathcal{A}(c)}) \leq c$ where $d(\cdot, \cdot)$ is the Hausdorff distance and (ii) for every location ℓ and any continuous state $\mathbf{x} \in Val(\mathcal{X})$, the dynamical mappings of the two HA satisfy $|f_{\ell,\mathcal{A}}(\mathbf{x}) - f_{\ell,\mathcal{A}(c)}(\mathbf{x})| \leq c$. The *c-perturbed reach set* of $\mathcal{A}$, denoted by $c\text{-}\mathsf{Reach}_{\mathcal{A}}$, is the set of states reachable by some c-perturbation of $\mathcal{A}$. For a time bound $T > 0$, Inv is a *robust invariant* up to time T if there exists a positive constant $c > 0$ such that $c\text{-Reach}_{\mathcal{A}}(T) \subseteq Inv$. In this paper we will present semi-decision procedures for bounded-time robust invariant checking of networks of deterministic nonlinear HA.

Composition. Large and complex models can be created by *composing* smaller automata. The composition operation identifies ("plugs-in") the input variables of one automaton $\mathcal{A}_i$ with the state variables of another automaton[1]. A pair of HAs $\mathcal{A}_1$ and $\mathcal{A}_2$ are *compatible* if their state variables are disjoint $\mathcal{V}_1 \cap \mathcal{V}_2 = \varnothing$.

Definition 2. *Given a pair of compatible HAs $\mathcal{A}_1$ and $\mathcal{A}_2$ the composed automaton $\mathcal{A} = \mathcal{A}_1 \| \mathcal{A}_2$ is $\langle \mathcal{L}, \mathcal{X}, \mathcal{U}, \Theta, \mathcal{D}, \mathcal{T} \rangle$, where (a) $\mathcal{L} := \mathcal{L}_1 \cup \mathcal{L}_2$, (b) $\mathcal{X} := \mathcal{X}_1 \cup \mathcal{X}_2$, (c) $\Theta = \Theta_1 \times \Theta_2$, (d) $\mathcal{U} = \mathcal{U}_1 \cup \mathcal{U}_2 \setminus (\mathcal{V}_1 \cup \mathcal{V}_2)$, (e) $\mathcal{D}$: $\mathbf{v} \to \mathbf{v}'$ iff either $\mathbf{v}.\mathcal{V}_1 \to_1 \mathbf{v}'.\mathcal{V}_1$ and $\mathbf{v}.\mathcal{V}_2 = \mathbf{v}'.\mathcal{V}_2$, or $\mathbf{v}.\mathcal{V}_2 \to_2 \mathbf{v}'.\mathcal{V}_2$ and $\mathbf{v}.\mathcal{V}_1 = \mathbf{v}'.\mathcal{V}_1$, and (f) A trajectory ξ of $\mathcal{V} \cup \mathcal{U}$ is in $\mathcal{T}$ iff $\xi \downarrow (\mathcal{V}_i \cup \mathcal{U}_i) \in \mathcal{T}_i$ for each $i \in \{1,2\}$.*

Note that the composition of two or more HA will define a *network*. $\mathcal{A}$ satisfies the requirements for Definition 1 and can be constructed by syntactically combining the guards, resets, and ODEs of its components.

Example 1. In the 2-dimensional FitzHugh-Nagumo (FHN) cardiac cell network, the ith cell automaton $\mathcal{A}_i$ has a single location, two continuous variables $\mathcal{X} = \{x_{i1}, x_{i2}\}$ corresponding to fast and slow currents, and inputs (u_{i1}, u_{i2}), corresponding to diffusion from neighboring cells, and u_{i3}, a stimulus. The evolution is given by the ODEs (dynamic mapping): $\dot{x}_{i1} = (a - x_{i1})(x_{i1} - 1)x_{i1} - x_{i2} + u_{i3} + \frac{D}{h^2}(u_{i1} + u_{i2} - 2x_{i1})$, $\dot{x}_{i2} = \epsilon(\beta x_{i1} - \gamma x_{i2} - \delta)$, where $a, \beta, \delta, \gamma, \epsilon$ are parameters of the cell, the u_{i3} term models direct stimulus input, and the $\frac{D}{h^2}(.)$ term models the effect of the diffusion coupling with neighboring cells. In Figure 1, three FHN cells $\mathcal{A}_1, \mathcal{A}_2$ and $\mathcal{A}_3$ are interconnected in a ring and with a pulse generator. In each cycle, the pulse is activated for S_{on} time and stays off for S_{off} time. The composed system is defined by identifying input variables of one automaton with the state variables of another. For example, $u_{11} = x_{21}, u_{12} = x_{31}$ defines the part of the ring where $\mathcal{A}_1$ gets diffused current inputs from its neighbors and and $u_{13} = st$ connects the output of the pulse generator to $\mathcal{A}_1$.

3 Annotations for Modules in a Network

We proposed simulation-based robust invariant verification of dynamical and switched systems in [15]. The approach requires the designers to provide special annotations called *discrepancy functions* for each location of the automaton. The algorithm first computes a validated numerical simulation from an initial state, say $\mathbf{v}$, and then bloats the simulation using the discrepancy function to compute arbitrarily precise over-approximations of $\text{Reach}_{\mathcal{A}}(B_\delta(\mathbf{v}), T)$. Repeating this over a set of initial states $\mathbf{v}$ and with varying precision δ, one obtains a decision procedure for robust invariant checking. Towards our goal of verifying hybrid networks, in this section we present new techniques for computing discrepancy functions for such models.

---

[1] We do not allow HA to interact via transition synchronization as in [31, 35].

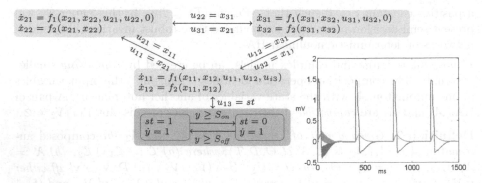

Fig. 1. Ring of 3 FHN-modules with a simple pulse generator. Reach set from a set of initial states projected on x_{11} and x_{12}.

3.1 IS Discrepancy and Approximations

First of all, we will use the definition of Input-to-State (IS) discrepancy function [26], which enables us to use annotations for individual modules in a dynamical system to then check invariants of the composed system. The IS discrepancy function for a location ℓ of $\mathcal{A}$ (or for a dynamical system) bounds the distance between two trajectories in location ℓ from different initial states, as a function of time and the inputs they receive.

Definition 3. *For a HA* $\mathcal{A} = (\mathcal{L}, \mathcal{X}, \mathcal{U}, \Theta, \mathcal{D}, \mathcal{T})$, *a continuous function* $V :$ $Val(\mathcal{X})^2 \to \mathbb{R}_{\geq 0}$ *is an* input-to-state discrepancy function *for a location* ℓ *if*

(a) $\exists$ *class-$\mathcal{K}$ functions (see [26])* $\underline{\alpha}, \overline{\alpha}$, *s.t.,* $\forall$ $\mathbf{x}, \mathbf{x}' \in Val(\mathcal{X})$, $\underline{\alpha}(|\mathbf{x} - \mathbf{x}'|) \leq$ $V(\mathbf{x}, \mathbf{x}') \leq \overline{\alpha}(|\mathbf{x} - \mathbf{x}'|)$, *and*
(b) $\exists \beta : \mathbb{R}_{\geq 0} \times \mathbb{R}_{\geq 0} \to \mathbb{R}_{\geq 0}$ *and* $\gamma \in \mathcal{K}$ *such that for any* $\mathbf{x}, \mathbf{x}'$, *any pair of input trajectories* $u, u' : \mathcal{U}$, *and any* $t \in \mathbb{R}_{\geq 0}$,

$$V(\xi_{\mathbf{x},\ell,u}(t), \xi_{\mathbf{x}',\ell,u'}(t)) \leq \beta(|\mathbf{x} - \mathbf{x}'|, t) + \int_0^t \gamma(|u(s) - u'(s)|)ds.$$

In addition, $\beta(\cdot, \cdot)$ *is of class-$\mathcal{K}$ in the first argument and* $\beta(\cdot, 0) = \overline{\alpha}(\cdot)$.

Here $\xi_{\mathbf{x},\ell,u}$ denotes the trajectory of the continuous variables $\mathcal{X}$ in location ℓ from state $\mathbf{x}$ and with the input trajectory u. The tuple $(\underline{\alpha}, \overline{\alpha}, \beta, \gamma)$ is called the *witness* of the discrepancy function V. The first condition merely bounds V in terms of the norm of its arguments. The more important second condition ensures that the distance between the trajectories is bounded as a function of β and γ, and can be reduced arbitrarily by making $\mathbf{x} \to \mathbf{x}'$ and $u \to u'$. IS discrepancy is related to integral input-to-state stability [2–4, 42]. However, for our verification algorithms, we do not require neighboring trajectories to converge over time. Using the IS discrepancy functions along with their witnesses, we construct a reduced order model M which can be employed to compute precise over-approximations of $\text{Reach}_{\mathcal{A}}(T)$. Given a dynamical system (HA with one location) $\mathcal{A} = \mathcal{A}_1 \| \mathcal{A}_2$ connected in a ring and IS discrepancy with witnesses for each of the modules, the IS approximation of $\mathcal{A}$ is a $(2+1)$-dimensional closed deterministic dynamical system M defined as follows.

Definition 4. *For a pair of nonnegative constants (δ_1, δ_2), the (δ_1, δ_2)-IS approximation of $\mathcal{A}$ is a closed dynamical system with three variables $\mathcal{X} = \{m_1, m_2, clk\}$ initialized to $\{\beta_1(\delta_1, 0), \beta_2(\delta_2, 0), 0\}$, and dynamics $\dot{\mathbf{x}} = f_M(\mathbf{x})$, where*

$$f_M(\mathbf{x}) = \begin{bmatrix} \dot{\beta}_1(\delta_1, \mathbf{x}(clk)) + \gamma_1 \circ \underline{\alpha}_2^{-1}(\mathbf{x}(m_2)) \\ \dot{\beta}_2(\delta_2, \mathbf{x}(clk)) + \gamma_2 \circ \underline{\alpha}_1^{-1}(\mathbf{x}(m_1)) \\ 1 \end{bmatrix}. \tag{1}$$

The variable clk tracks the real time, and both the initial state and the dynamics of M depend on the choice of the parameters δ_1 and δ_2. It can be shown that the valuations of m_i along μ (the trajectory of M) give an upperbound on the distance between any trajectories of $\mathcal{A}_i$ that start from initial states and are at most δ_i apart. The following theorem establishes that the reach set of $\mathcal{A}$ from a set of states can be precisely over-approximated by bloating an individual execution ξ of $\mathcal{A}$ by a factor that is entirely determined by (a) a pair $V = (V_1, V_2)$ of IS discrepancy functions of $\mathcal{A}_1$ and $\mathcal{A}_2$ along with their witnesses, and (b) the trajectory μ.

Theorem 1 (Theorems 5.4 and 5.7 from [26]). *Let $\xi_{\mathbf{v}}$ be a trajectory of $\mathcal{A}$. For any nonnegative pair $\delta = (\delta_1, \delta_2)$, and any time $T \geq 0$, suppose μ is the trajectory of the (δ_1, δ_2)-IS approximation M. Then $\mathsf{Reach}_{\mathcal{A}}(B_\delta(\mathbf{v}), T) \subseteq \bigcup_{t \in [0,T]} B^V_{\mu(t)}(\xi_{\mathbf{v}}(t))$. Further, for any $\epsilon > 0$ and $T > 0$, $\exists \, \delta_1, \delta_2 > 0$ such that, for the (δ_1, δ_2)-IS approximation M, $\bigcup_{t \in [0,T]} B^V_{\mu(t)}(\xi_{\mathbf{v}}(t)) \subseteq \epsilon\text{-}\mathsf{Reach}_{\mathcal{A}}(B_\delta(\mathbf{v}), T)$.*

The precision of the over-approximation can be improved by reducing the parameters δ_1 and δ_2, and thus creating a finer covering of the initial set $\Theta_{\mathcal{A}}$. The result is generalized to dynamical systems with N modules connected in general network topologies [26], where the IS approximation is $(N+1)$-dimensional.

For a hybrid system $\mathcal{A} = \mathcal{A}_1 \| \mathcal{A}_2$, instead of providing annotations for the total of $|Val(\mathcal{L}_1)| \times |Val(\mathcal{L}_2)|$ locations of $\mathcal{A}$, the user has to provide IS discrepancy functions for $|Val(\mathcal{L}_1)| + |Val(\mathcal{L}_2)|$ locations. From there, our algorithm automatically constructs $|Val(\mathcal{L}_1)| \times |Val(\mathcal{L}_2)|$ IS approximations corresponding to each location-pair of $\mathcal{A}$. For cardiac cell networks, where all the automata modules are identical, this means working with $|Val(\mathcal{L}_1)|$ IS discrepancy functions. The next proposition gives a technique for computing IS discrepancy functions.

Proposition 1. *For a dynamical system with linear input $\dot{\mathbf{x}} = f(\mathbf{x}) + B\mathbf{u}$, where B is a matrix, $V(\mathbf{x}_1, \mathbf{x}_2) = |\mathbf{x}_1 - \mathbf{x}_2|$ is an IS discrepancy function with*

$$V(\xi_1(t), \xi_2(t)) \leq e^{\lambda_{max} t} |\mathbf{x}_1 - \mathbf{x}_2| + \int_0^t M|B| |(v_1(\tau) - v_2(\tau))| d\tau,$$

where λ_{max} is the largest eigenvalue of the Jacobian matrix $J = \frac{1}{2}(\frac{\partial^T}{\partial \mathbf{x}} f(\mathbf{x}) + \frac{\partial}{\partial \mathbf{x}} f(\mathbf{x}) + I)$, $M = \sup_{s \in [0,t]} e^{\lambda_{max} s}$ is the supremum of an exponential function of

λ_{max}, and ξ_i is the state trajectory from $\mathbf{x}_i$ with input trajectory v_i. Specifically, for a linear time invariant system $\dot{\mathbf{x}} = A\mathbf{x} + B\mathbf{u}$, λ_{max} is the largest eigenvalue of the matrix A, and $M = \sup_{s\in[0,t]} |e^{As}|$.

For linear dynamical systems, we use the special case to obtain tight IS discrepancy functions by solving Linear Matrix Inequalities. The more general case establishes IS discrepancy functions for a larger class of non-linear systems for which the Jacobian matrix has bounded eigenvalues. For the nonlinear dynamic maps in this paper, computing the maximum eigenvalue of the Jacobian is solved using the MATLAB optimization toolbox or by a sum of squares solver [41].

4   Checking Bounded Invariants of HA Networks

First we define simulations for hybrid automata, and then we describe the verification algorithm that uses simulations and IS discrepancy functions.

4.1   Simulations of Dynamical Systems

For a closed dynamical system $\mathcal{A}$ with an initial state $\mathbf{v}$, validated ODE solvers [10, 12, 37] can compute a sequence of sets $R_0, \ldots, R_l \subseteq \mathit{Val}(\mathcal{X})$ such that the trajectory $\xi_{\mathbf{v}}$ of $\mathcal{A}$ is contained in R_k over the interval $[(k-1)\tau, k\tau]$, where τ is the simulation time-step. We formalize this as follows:

Definition 5. *Consider a deterministic closed HA $\mathcal{A}$, an initial state $\mathbf{v}$, an error bound $\epsilon > 0$, and time step $\tau > 0$. Let the location of $\mathbf{v}.\mathcal{L}$ be ℓ and $\xi_{\mathbf{v}}$ be the execution of $\mathcal{A}$ starting from $\mathbf{v}$. A $(\mathbf{v}, \epsilon, \tau)$-simulation fragment is a finite sequence $\rho = (R_0, t_0), \ldots, (R_l, t_l)$ where, for each $k \in \{0, \ldots, l\}$, (a) $0 < t_k - t_{k-1} \leq \tau$, (b) R_k is contained in the invariant I_ℓ except possibly the last R_l, (c) $dia(R_k) \leq \epsilon$, and (d) for any time $t \in [t_{k-1}, t_k]$, $\xi_{\mathbf{v}}(t).\mathcal{X} \in R_k$.*

For relative completeness of verification, we will require that for a desired error bound $\epsilon > 0$ the diameter of R_k can be made smaller than ϵ by reducing the step size τ. A simulation for a HA is a sequence of simulation fragments (for different locations) that captures all the transitions of at least one execution.

Definition 6. *Consider a HA $\mathcal{A}$, an initial state $\mathbf{v}$, an error bound $\epsilon > 0$, a time bound $T > 0$, a transition bound l, and a time step $\tau > 0$. Let $\xi_{\mathbf{v}}$ be the execution from $\mathbf{v}$ with $\xi_{\mathbf{v}}.dur \leq T$, where $\xi_{\mathbf{v}}.dur$ is the time duration of the trajectory $\xi_{\mathbf{v}}$, and with l transitions at times $\sigma_1, \ldots, \sigma_l \in \mathbb{R}_{\geq 0}$; let $\sigma_0 = 0$. A $(\mathbf{v}, \epsilon, \tau, T, l)$-simulation is a finite sequence $\psi = \rho_0, \ldots, \rho_l$ where (a) each $\rho_k = (R_{k(1)}, t_{k(1)}), \ldots, (R_{k(m_k)}, t_{k(m_k)})$ is a $(\xi(\sigma_k), \epsilon, \tau)$-simulation fragment with m_k samples, (b) $t_0 = 0$, $t_{l(m_l)-1} = T$, and for each $k > 0$, $t_{k(m_k)} \geq t_{(k+1)(1)}$, and (c) $\sigma_k \in [t_{(k+1)(1)}, t_{k(m_k)}]$.*

A $(\mathbf{v}, \epsilon, \tau, T, l)$-simulation ψ is a sequence of l simulation fragments where each fragment ρ_k has m_k elements with indices $k(1), \ldots, k(m_k)$. The kth transition on the actual execution $\xi_{\mathbf{v}}$ has to occur between the last sample period of ρ_{k-1} and the first sample interval of ρ_k (condition (c)). In addition, ρ_k is a $(\xi_\mathbf{v}(\sigma_k), \epsilon, \tau)$-simulation fragment, that is, it *contains* the trajectory of $\mathcal{A}$ starting from the post state $\xi_\mathbf{v}(\sigma_k)$ of the kth transition. In Algorithm 2, the subroutine *Simulate* computes a simulation of HA of the above type. The simulation ψ represents other executions that start near $\mathbf{v}$. Formally, we say an execution fragment ξ is *captured* by ψ if duration of ξ is at most T, ξ experiences exactly the same sequence of locations as recorded in some prefix of ψ, and its $k^{(th)}$ transition occurs in the intervals $[t_{k(m_k)}, t_{(k+1)(1)}]$.

4.2 Verification Algorithm

We sketch the key ideas that enable the checking of bounded-time invariants of closed networks of hybrid automata. The main inputs of *InvVerify* (Algorithm 1) are the specification of the composed automaton $\mathcal{A} = \mathcal{A}_1 \| \dots \| \mathcal{A}_N$, the open unsafe set $\mathbb{U}$, and the collection of discrepancy functions and witnesses *ISD* for every location of each subsystem. The variable $\mathcal{C}$ (line 2) is initialized to a collection of tuples $\{(\mathbf{v}_k, \delta, \epsilon, \tau)\}_{k \in |\mathcal{C}|}$, such that $\{\mathbf{v}_k\}$ is a δ-cover of Θ, that is, $\Theta \subseteq \cup_{k \in |\mathcal{C}|} B_\delta(\mathbf{v}_k)$, and (δ, ϵ, τ) are parameters. For each $(\mathbf{v}, \delta, \epsilon, \tau)$ in $\mathcal{C}$, the subroutine *ReachFromCover* (Algorithm 2) computes *flag* and a set S. The *flag* is set to SAFE if all executions from $B_\delta(\mathbf{v})$ are disjoint from $\mathbb{U}$ up to time T and in that case $\mathbf{v}$ is removed from $\mathcal{C}$. The *flag* is set to UNSAFE if at least one execution reaches $\mathbb{U}$, and in that case *InvVerify* returns UNSAFE and $\mathcal{R}$. Finally, if the *flag* is set to REFINE then $\mathbf{v}$ is replaced by a finer cover of $\Theta \cap B_\delta(\mathbf{v})$. In addition to having $\delta/2$-radius balls covering $B_\delta(\mathbf{v})$, the parameters ϵ and τ are also halved to compute more precise over-approximations. The sets S and $\mathcal{R}$ compute over-approximations of $\mathrm{Reach}_\mathcal{A}(B_\delta(\mathbf{v}), T)$ and $\mathrm{Reach}_\mathcal{A}(T)$, respectively. *ReachFromCover* checks safety with respect to $\mathbb{U}$ of the states reachable from $B_\delta(\mathbf{v})$ up to time T and with at most $n > 0$ transitions. First, it computes an over-approximation $(\mathcal{R})$ of $\mathrm{Reach}_\mathcal{A}(B_\delta(\mathbf{v}), T)$ with certain precision

---

Algorithm 1. *InvVerify*($\mathcal{A}$, *ISD*, $\mathbb{U}$, T, ϵ_0, δ_0, n_0): Verifies invariants of hybrid networks.

```
1  end R ← ∅; δ ← δ₀; ε ← ε₀; τ ← τ₀; n ← n₀;
2  C ← {(v, δ, ε, τ) | {v} is a δ-Cover(Θ)};
3  while C ≠ ∅ for each (v, δ, ε, τ) ∈ C do
4      (flag, S) ← ReachFromCover(A, v, δ, ε, τ, T, ISD, n);
5      switch flag do
6          case SAFE: C ← C\{(v, δ, ε, τ)}; R ← R ∪ S case UNSAFE: return
              (UNSAFE, R)  case REFINE:
7              C ← C\{(v, δ, ε, τ)}; δ ← δ/2; ε ← ε/2; τ ← τ/2; n ← 2n;
8              C ← C ∪ {(v, δ, ε, τ) | {v} is a δ−Cover(Θ ∩ Bδ(v))};
9          end
10     end
11 end
12 return (SAFE, R);
```

Algorithm 2. $ReachFromCover(\mathcal{A}, ISD, \mathbb{U}, \mathbf{v}, \delta, \epsilon, \tau, T, n)$: Over-approx $\mathsf{Reach}_{\mathcal{A}}(B_\delta(\mathbf{v}))$.

---

1 $\mathcal{R} \leftarrow \varnothing;\ \mathcal{C} \leftarrow \{(\mathbf{v}, 0)\};\ count \leftarrow 0;$
2 **while** $\mathcal{C} \neq \varnothing$ **for each** $(\mathbf{v}, t_0) \in \mathcal{C}$ **do**
3 $\quad$ $r \leftarrow \delta;\ \psi \leftarrow Simulate(\mathcal{A}, \mathbf{v}, T - t_0, \epsilon, \tau);\ count \leftarrow count + 1;$
4 $\quad$ **for** $k = 0 : l$, **where** $\psi = \rho_0, \rho_1, \dots, \rho_l$ **do**
5 $\quad\quad$ $\mid$ $(S_k, r) \leftarrow BloatWithISD(\rho_k, ISD, r, \epsilon, \tau, \mathcal{A});$
6 $\quad$ **end**
7 $\quad$ **if** *a transition* (ℓ, ℓ') *is enabled from* S_j *but is not captured by* ψ **then**
8 $\quad\quad$ $\mid$ $\mathcal{C} \leftarrow \mathcal{C} \cup \{(\mathbf{v}, t_0) \mid \{\mathbf{v}\}$ is the δ-$Cover(R_{\ell,\ell'}(S_k \cap G_{\ell,\ell'})),$
9 $\quad\quad$ $\mid$ $\quad\quad t_0$ is the first $time(\ell, \ell')$ is enabled$\};$
10 $\quad$ **if** *a transition is captured by* ψ *but is not enabled for a subset* $S'_k \subseteq S_k$ **then**
11 $\quad\quad$ $\mid$ $\mathcal{C} \leftarrow \mathcal{C} \cup \{(\mathbf{v}, t_0) \mid \{\mathbf{v}\}$ is the δ-$Cover(S'_k),$
12 $\quad\quad$ $\mid$ $\quad\quad t_0$ is the first time the transition is captured$\};$
13 $\quad$ **end**
14 $\quad$ **if** $(\cup_j s_j \cap \mathbb{U} = \varnothing) \wedge (count < n)$ **then** $\mathcal{R} \leftarrow \mathcal{R} \cup (\cup_j s_j);\ \mathcal{C} \leftarrow \mathcal{C} \backslash \{(\Theta, t_0)\}$
$\quad\quad$ **else if** $(\exists\ R_j \subseteq \mathbb{U}) \wedge (count = 1)$ **then return** $(\text{UNSAFE}, \mathcal{R})$ **else**
$\quad\quad$ **return** $(\text{REFINE}, \mathcal{R})$
15 **end**
16 **return** $(\text{SAFE}, \mathcal{R});$

(determined by the parameters $\delta, \epsilon,$ and τ). If this over-approximation is sufficient to prove/disprove safety with respect to $\mathbb{U}$ then it sets the *flag* to SAFE or UNSAFE, and otherwise it returns REFINE. If it detects that more than n transitions are possible within time T, then also it returns REFINE.

In computing $\mathcal{R}$ in *ReachFromCover*, the set $\mathcal{C}$ stores a set of state-time pairs that are yet to be processed. If $(\mathbf{v}, t_0) \in \mathcal{C}$ then $\mathsf{Reach}_{\mathcal{A}}(B_\delta(\mathbf{v}), T - t_0)$ is yet to be evaluated and added to $\mathcal{R}$. For each $(\mathbf{v}, t_0)$ in the cover $\mathcal{C}$, a $(\mathbf{v}, \epsilon, \tau, T, l)$-simulation $\psi = \rho_0, \dots \rho_l$ is computed. The variable $count$ tracks the number of new simulation branches initiated in a run of the algorithm. Let ξ be the actual execution starting from $\mathbf{v}$ and $G_{\ell, \ell'}$ be the guard from location ℓ to ℓ'. By Definition 6, each ρ_k of ψ is a simulation fragment. By Definition 4, the IS approximation is a (small) dynamical system, whose trajectory gives an upper bound of the distance between continuous trajectories of $\mathcal{A}$. The subroutine $BloatWithISD(\rho_k, ISD, r, \epsilon, \tau, \mathcal{A})$ (i) creates an IS Approximation M of $\mathcal{A}$ using the discrepancy functions in ISD that correspond to the location of ρ_k, (ii) generates a $(r, \epsilon, \tau, T, 0)$-simulation of M, say μ, (iii) bloats each set R_j in ρ_k with the valuation of $\mu(t_j)$ to obtain a set s_j, (iv) returns the sequence of sets $S_k = (s_{k(1)}, t_{k(1)}), \dots, (s_{k(m)}, t_{k(m)})$, and finally (v) applies the transition between ρ_k and ρ_{k+1} on the set $s_{k(m)}$ and returns r as the radius of image of the reset function. From Theorem 1, S_k contains all continuous trajectories of $\mathcal{A}$ that start from $B_r(R_{k(1)})$. It can be checked that $\cup_j s_j$ precisely over-approximates all the executions from $B_r(\mathbf{v})$ that are captured by ψ (Proposition 2-3).

To over-approximate the states reached via executions from $B_\delta(\mathbf{v})$ that are *not* captured by ψ, the algorithm generates new simulations (line 7-13) and adds up $count$. The algorithm transverses S_k and generates and checks two possible cases as described in line 7 and 10. Then the algorithm decides whether the computed over-approximation $\mathcal{R}$ is safe, unsafe, or needs further refinement.

4.3 Soundness and Relative Completeness

We will state the key propositions of the algorithms that are used for proving correctness. The details of the proofs are given in the technical report [25]. In what follows, all the program variables refer to their valuations at the pth iteration of the **while** loop of *ReachFromCover*, unless otherwise stated. That is, $(\mathbf{v}, t_0)$ is the time-state pair being explored in the pth iteration. Propositions 2 and 3 follow from straightforward inductive application of Theorem 1, the fact that ψ is a simulation from $\mathbf{v}$ with the properties stated in Definition 6, and the continuity of the reset functions for all location pairs.

Proposition 2. *Let ψ be a simulation from $\mathbf{v}^{(p)}$. For any execution fragment ξ starting from a state in $B_\delta(\mathbf{v}^{(p)})$, if the transition sequence of ξ is captured by ψ then, for any $t \in [0, T - t_0^{(p)}]$, $\xi(t) \in \cup_{j=1}^{l(m_l)} s_j$. Recall that $l(m_l)$ denotes the last index of ρ_l and thus the total number of elements in ψ.*

Proposition 3. *For the execution $\xi_{\mathbf{v}}$ from $\mathbf{v}$, and any $r > 0$, there exists sufficiently small δ, ϵ, τ, such that $\cup_{j=1}^{l(m_l)} s_j \subseteq \cup_{t \in [0, T-t_0]} B_r(\xi_{\mathbf{v}}(t))$.*

Using Proposition 2, we can prove the soundness of the algorithm. We show that every execution from Θ can be decomposed into execution segments that are captured by some simulation generated during the **while** loop of *ReachFromCover*.

Theorem 2 (Soundness). *If InvVerify returns SAFE then $\mathcal{A}$ is safe with respect to $\mathbb{U}$ up to T, and if it returns UNSAFE then $\mathcal{A}$ is unsafe.*

We establish termination of *InvVerify* under the following robustness assumption.

Assumption 1. *(i) $\mathcal{A}$ has an average dwell time [24]. That is, there exists $N' \geq 0$ and $\tau' > 0$ such that, for any execution fragment ξ of $\mathcal{A}$, the number of transitions occurring in ξ is upperbounded by $N' + \frac{\xi \cdot \text{dur}}{\tau'}$. (ii) One of the following conditions hold: (a) $\bar{\mathbb{U}}$ is a robust invariant of $\mathcal{A}$ up to time T. (b) There exists $c > 0$, such that all c-perturbations of $\mathcal{A}$ reach $\mathbb{U}$ with in T.*

Assumption 1(i) is standard for well-designed systems and can be automatically checked for certain model classes [36]. Part (ii) is a robustness condition with respect to the invariant $\bar{\mathbb{U}}$ (complement of $\mathbb{U}$) such that the satisfaction of the invariant remains unchanged under sufficiently small perturbations to the models. Since the over-approximation can be computed up to arbitrary precision (Proposition 3), *InvVerify* is guaranteed to terminate.

Theorem 3 (Relative completeness). *Under Assumption 1, InvVerify terminates.*

5 Checking Invariants for Cardiac Cell Networks

We present a challenging case study modeling a cardiac cell that involves non-linear HA networks. The purpose of the case study is to demonstrate the effectiveness of *InvVerify*. Our case study is the minimal ventricular (MV) model of Bueno-Orovio et al. [11] that generates action ptential (APs) on cardiac rings [17]. Unlike the FHN model of Example 1, the MV model can reproduce realistic and important AP phenomena, e.g. alternans [22], and yet is computationally more efficient than some of the other models in the literature. Using the techniques from Grosu et al. [19], we abstract the MV model into a network of multi-affine hybrid (MAH) automata (see Figure 2). On the resulting network we check a key invariant property.

5.1 The MAH Cardiac Cell Network Model

The MV model describes the flow of currents through a cell. The model is defined by four nonlinear PDEs representing the transmembrane potential $x_1(\boldsymbol{d}, t)$, the fast channel gate $x_2(\boldsymbol{d}, t)$, and two slow channel gates, $x_3(\boldsymbol{d}, t)$ and $x_4(\boldsymbol{d}, t)$. All of the four variables are time and position $\boldsymbol{d} := (d_x, d_y, d_z) \in \mathbb{R}^3$ dependent. For one dimensional tissue, i.e., $\boldsymbol{d} := d_x$, the evolution of transmembrane potential is given by:

$$\frac{\partial x_1(d_x, t)}{\partial t} = D \frac{\partial^2 x_1(d_x, t)}{\partial d_x^2} + e(x_1, t) - (J_{\mathrm{fi}} + J_{\mathrm{so}} + J_{\mathrm{si}}), \qquad (2)$$

where $D \in \mathbb{R}$ is the diffusion coefficient, $e(\boldsymbol{d}, t)$ is the external stimulus applied to the cell, J_{fi} is the fast inward current, J_{si} is the slow inward current and J_{so} is the slow outward current. The currents J_{fi}, J_{so} and J_{si} are described by Heaviside function. To define the propagation of the action potential on a cardiac ring of length L, we set the boundary conditions to: $x_i(0, t) = x_i(L, t)$ for all $i \in \{0, \ldots, 4\}$ and $t \in \mathbb{R}$.

MAH approximation. One alternative to solving these highly nonlinear PDEs is to discretize space and hybridize the dynamics. The result is the MAH model. Following the approach of [19] we first hybridize the dynamics and obtain a HA with 29 locations. The basic idea is to approximate the Heaviside function from J_{fi}, J_{so} and J_{si} with a sequence of ramp functions. Each location of the resulting HA contains a multi-affine ODE such as:

$$\dot{x}_1 = -0.935x_1 + 12.70x_2 - 8.0193x_1x_2 + 0.529x_3x_4 + 0.87 + st$$
$$\dot{x}_2 = -0.689x_2; \quad \dot{x}_3 = -0.0025x_3; \quad \dot{x}_4 = 0.0293x_1 - 0.0625x_4 + 0.0142,$$

where st is the time-varying stimulus input. Urgent transitions from each location ℓ_i to the next (and predecessor) location ℓ_{i+1}, $i \in [29]$, are enabled by the guards of the form $x_1 \geq \theta_i'$ and $x_1 < \theta_i$, where θ_i, θ_i' are the constants arising from ramp approximations of the Heaviside functions.

Next, we discretize the 2nd order derivative $D\frac{\partial^2 x_1(d_x,t)}{\partial d_x^2}$ from Eq. (2) with a discretization step of Δ using 2nd order central difference method and obtain $D\frac{x_1(d_x+\Delta,t)-2x_1(d_x,t)+x_1(d_x-\Delta,t)}{\Delta^2}$. Informally, Δ represents the spatial discretization and corresponds to the length of the cell in the ring. This 2nd order central difference term is added to the right hand side of the dynamic mapping for x_1 (in each location) to obtain the final MAH model of a single cardiac cell. Note that by using the central difference method the approximation error for the original MV model is of the order $\mathcal{O}(\Delta^2)$. To check invariants of a cardiac ring of length L, we connect all of the $\lfloor\frac{L}{\Delta}\rfloor$ HA into a network such that the input variables of every HA $\mathcal{A}_i$, $i \in \left[\lfloor\frac{L}{\Delta}\rfloor\right]$, are identified with the variable $x_{(i+1)1}$ of the successor $\mathcal{A}_{i+1}$ and the state variable $x_{(i-1)1}$ of $\mathcal{A}_{i-1}$ in the ring. We consider scenarios where one HA in the ring gets a sequence of stimuli from a pulse generator and for the remaining HA $st(t) := 0$.

5.2   Experimental Results

For understanding the effect of stimuli on cardiac tissue (cell networks) the key invariant properties of interest are of the form $x_1 \leq \theta_{max}$, where θ_{max} is a threshold voltage value. Other properties about timing of action potentials can be constructed using these building block invariants and additional timers. We implemented the algorithms of Section 4 in MATLAB programs that take as input Simulink/Stateflow models of FHM and MAH networks (see Figure 2). For

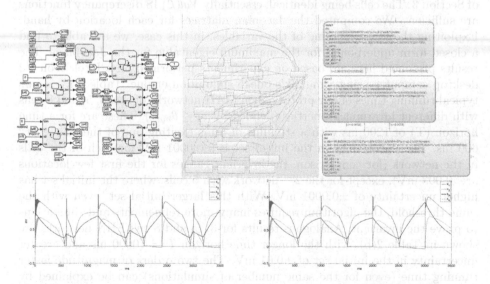

Fig. 2. Top left: top-level Simulink/Stateflow model for a ring of five MAH cells; the *Pacemaker* block stimulates one cell. Center: Stateflow model of a single MAH cell. Top right: dynamics and guards in 3 locations of a single cell. Bottom: reach set projected on x_{11} (AP) for stimulation period of 1000 msec (left) and 600 msec (right) with x-axis for time and y-axis for voltage.

Table 1. (a) Scaling with network size. N: number of cells in the ring network, θ_{max}: threshold voltage defining invariant, Sims: number of simulations, Refs: max. number of refinements, RT: running time in seconds. (b) Verification of FHM networks with time horizon T=1200 ms, initial set uncertainty ±0.01 mV. (c) Comparison of running time with S-taliro over 3 cell MAH networks for cases where both tools find counter-examples.

N	θ_{max}	Sims	Refs	RT(s)	$x_{i1} \leq \theta_{max}$
3	2	16	0	104.8	✓
3	1.65	16	0	103.8	✓
3	1.55	17	1	110.6	✓
3	1.5	NA	NA	9.0	✗
5	2	3	0	208.0	✓
5	1.65	5	1	281.6	✓
5	1.65	170	125	945.0	✓
5	1.5	NA	NA	63.4	✗
8	2	3	0	240.1	✓
8	1.65	73	9	2376.5	✓
8	1.5	NA	NA	119.7	✗

(a)

N	θ_{max}	Sims	Refs	RT	$x_{i1} \leq \theta_{max}$
3	1.5	1	0	1.5	✓
3	1.0	16	1	20.4	✓
5	1.5	8	2	9.2	✓
5	1.0	NA	NA	1.1	✗
8	1.5	1	0	1.8	✓
8	1.0	24	3	33.5	✓

(b)

T	S-taliro	Our tool
100	24.2	3.1
1000	27.4	9.3
10000	55.5	62.9

(c)

all the locations the IS-discrepancy functions are computed using the techniques of Section 3. The cells being identical, essentially $Val(\mathcal{L})$ IS discrepancy functions are sufficient. We computed the Jacobian matrices for each location by hand. Exploiting the loose coupling of the variables, in this case, we are able to find a closed form upperbound for the maximum eigenvalue for the Jacobians. The results presented here are based on experiments performed on a Intel Xeon V2 desktop computer using Simulink's ode45 simulation engine. Table 2(a) shows typical running times of our prototype on MAH networks of size 3, 5, and 8 cells with different invariant properties (defined by $x_1 \leq \theta_{max}$). These are for a time horizon (T) of 1200 ms with a stimulus of 5 ms exciting one of the cells every 600 ms. The uncertainty in the initial set is ±0.0001 mV for each of the cells in the network (for comparison, the invariant ranges for the first few locations are 0.003 mV), except for the 2nd network with 5 cells, where the initial set has higher uncertainty of ±0.0001 mV. With this larger initial set, even with the same threshold, the algorithm requires many more refinements and simulations to prove the invariant. Analogous results for 3, 5, and 8 cell FHN networks are shown in Table 2(b), with the longer time horizon $T = 10000$ ms and greater uncertainty in the initial set of ±0.01 mV. The two orders of magnitude faster running time (even for the same number of simulations) can be explained by the lower dimension (2) of FHN cells, and the absence of any transitions which spawn new branches in the execution of MAH -simulations. A comparable tool that can check for counter-examples in this class of HA models models is S-taliro [5]. We were able to find counter-examples using S-taliro for the 3 cell MAH networks with similar initial states (running times shown in Table 2(c)).

On average, for smaller time horizons (T) S-taliro found counter-examples faster, but for longer T (and appropriate initial sets) the running times were comparable to our prototype.

It is known that electrical alternans initiate and destabilize reentrant waves which my induce cardiac arrhythmia such as ventricular fibrillation [27]. The electrical alternans involve long-short beat-to-beat alternation of AP duration at fast pacing rates. In Figure 2 (bottom left) we plot the reach set from a set of initial states with pacing rate of 1000 msec and observe that the AP durations do not change, whereas at a pacing rate of 600 msec (bottom right) the AP durations alternate. The reach set approximations computed by our tool enable us to prove absence of alternans over bounded-time horizons and also to find initial states from which they may arise.

6 Related Work, Discussion and Conclusions

Networks of timed automata to model the propagation of APs in human heart are employed in the Virtual Heart Model [28–30, 39] and hybrid automata are used in [8,45]. In [18,33], the authors develop a model of the cardiac conduction system that addresses the stochastic behavior of the heart, validated via simulation. However, the hybrid behavior of the heart is not considered. Grosu et al. [21] carry out automated formal analysis of a realistic cardiac cell model. In [19] a method to learn and to detect the emergent behavior (i.e. the spiral formation) is proposed. Simulation-based analysis of general nonlinear HA has been investigated in [5], where a search for counter-examples is carried out using sampling and stochastic optimization. Our approach is designed to prove bounded-time invariants. Other promising tools include Breach [14] and *Flow** [13]; their application to cardiac cell networks will be an interesting direction to explore once support for these types of Simulink/Stateflow models is established.

In this paper, we present an algorithm to check robust bounded-time invariants for networks of nonlinear hybrid automata. We used automatically computed input-to-state discrepancy functions for individual locations of individual automata modules to over-approximate reachable states of the network. All of the developed techniques and the symmetry in the network of cells enabled us to check key invariants of networks of nonlinear cardiac cells, where each cell has four continuous variables and 29 locations. We will extend our algorithms to support richer classes of properties specified in metric or signal temporal logic. These results also suggest new strategies for pacemaker control algorithms, for example, for avoiding alternans and other undesirable behavior.

References

1. Alur, R., Courcoubetis, C., Halbwachs, N., Henzinger, T.A., Ho, P.-H., Nicollin, X., Olivero, A., Sifakis, J., Yovine, S.: The algorithmic analysis of hybrid systems. Theoretical Computer Science 138(1), 3–34 (1995)

2. Angeli, D.: Further results on incremental input-to-state stability. IEEE Transactions on Automatic Control 54(6), 1386–1391 (2009)
3. Angeli, D.: A lyapunov approach to incremental stability properties. IEEE Transactions on Automatic Control 47(3), 410–421 (2002)
4. Angeli, D., Sontag, E.D., Wang, Y.: A characterization of integral input-to-state stability. IEEE Transactions on Automatic Control 45(6), 1082–1097 (2000)
5. Annpureddy, Y., Liu, C., Fainekos, G., Sankaranarayanan, S.: S-TALiRo: A tool for temporal logic falsification for hybrid systems. In: Abdulla, P.A., Leino, K.R.M. (eds.) TACAS 2011. LNCS, vol. 6605, pp. 254–257. Springer, Heidelberg (2011)
6. Axmacher, N., Mormann, F., Fernández, G., Elger, C.E., Fell, J.: Memory formation by neuronal synchronization. Brain Research Reviews 52(1), 170–182 (2006)
7. Barrat, A., Barthelemy, M., Vespignani, A.: Dynamical processes on complex networks, vol. 1. Cambridge University Press, Cambridge (2008)
8. Bartocci, E., Corradini, F., Berardini, M.R.D., Entcheva, E., Smolka, S.A., Grosu, R.: Modeling and simulation of cardiac tissue using hybrid I/O automata. Theor. Comput. Sci. 410(33-34), 3149–3165 (2009)
9. Boccaletti, S., Latora, V., Moreno, Y., Chavez, M., Hwang, D.-U.: Complex networks: Structure and dynamics. Physics Reports 424(4), 175–308 (2006)
10. Bouissou, O., Martel, M.: Grklib: A guaranteed runge kutta library. In: 12th GAMM-IMACS International Symposium on Scientific Computing, Computer Arithmetic and Validated Numerics, SCAN 2006, p. 8. IEEE (2006)
11. Bueno-Orovio, A., Cherry, E.M., Fenton, F.H.: Minimal model for human ventricular action potentials in tissue. Journal of Theoretical Biology 253(3), 544–560 (2008)
12. CAPD. Computer assisted proofs in dynamics (2002)
13. Chen, X., Ábrahám, E., Sankaranarayanan, S.: Flow*: An analyzer for non-linear hybrid systems. In: Sharygina, N., Veith, H. (eds.) CAV 2013. LNCS, vol. 8044, pp. 258–263. Springer, Heidelberg (2013)
14. Donzé, A.: Breach, a toolbox for verification and parameter synthesis of hybrid systems. In: Touili, T., Cook, B., Jackson, P. (eds.) CAV 2010. LNCS, vol. 6174, pp. 167–170. Springer, Heidelberg (2010)
15. Duggirala, P.S., Mitra, S., Viswanathan, M.: Verification of annotated models from executions. In: EMSOFT (2013)
16. Fenton, F., Karma, A.: Vortex dynamics in three-dimensional continuous myocardium with fiber rotation: filament instability and fibrillation. Chaos: An Interdisciplinary Journal of Nonlinear Science 8(1), 20–47 (1998)
17. Garzón, A., Grigoriev, R.O., Fenton, F.H.: Model-based control of cardiac alternans on a ring. Physical Review E 80 (2009)
18. Greenhut, S., Jenkins, J., MacDonald, R.: A stochastic network model of the interaction between cardiac rhythm and artificial pacemaker. IEEE Transactions on Biomedical Engineering 40(9), 845–858 (1993)
19. Grosu, R., Batt, G., Fenton, F.H., Glimm, J., Le Guernic, C., Smolka, S.A., Bartocci, E.: From cardiac cells to genetic regulatory networks. In: Gopalakrishnan, G., Qadeer, S. (eds.) CAV 2011. LNCS, vol. 6806, pp. 396–411. Springer, Heidelberg (2011)
20. Grosu, R., Batt, G., Fenton, F.H., Glimm, J., Le Guernic, C., Smolka, S.A., Bartocci, E.: From cardiac cells to genetic regulatory networks. In: Gopalakrishnan, G., Qadeer, S. (eds.) CAV 2011. LNCS, vol. 6806, pp. 396–411. Springer, Heidelberg (2011)

21. Grosu, R., Smolka, S.A., Corradini, F., Wasilewska, A., Entcheva, E., Bartocci, E.: Learning and detecting emergent behavior in networks of cardiac myocytes. Commun. ACM 52(3), 97–105 (2009)
22. Guevara, M.R., Ward, G., Shrier, A., Glass, L.: Electrical alternans and period-doubling bifurcations. In: Computers in Cardiology, pp. 167–170 (1984)
23. Henzinger, T.A., Kopke, P.W., Puri, A., Varaiya, P.: What's decidable about hybrid automata? In. In: ACM Symposium on Theory of Computing, pp. 373–382 (1995)
24. Hespanha, J.P., Morse, A.: Stability of switched systems with average dwell-time. In: Proceedings of 38th IEEE Conference on Decision and Control, pp. 2655–2660 (1999)
25. Huang, Z., Fan, C., Mitra, S., Mereacre, A., Kwiatkowska, M.: Invariant verification of nonlinear hybrid automata networks of cardiac cells, Online supporting material: Models, code, and data (2014), https://wiki.cites.illinois.edu/wiki/display/MitraResearch/Complex+Networks+of+Nonlinear+Modules
26. Huang, Z., Mitra, S.: Proofs from simulations and modular annotations. In: In 17th International Conference on Hybrid Systems: Computation and Control. ACM Press, Berlin
27. Ideker, R.E., Rogers, J.M.: Human ventricular fibrillation: Wandering wavelets, mother rotors, or both? Circulation 114(6), 530–532 (2006)
28. Jee, E., Wang, S., Kim, J.-K., Lee, J., Sokolsky, O., Lee, I.: A safety-assured development approach for real-time software. In: RTCSA, pp. 133–142 (2010)
29. Jiang, Z., Pajic, M., Connolly, A., Dixit, S., Mangharam, R.: Real-Time Heart model for implantable cardiac device validation and verification. In: ECRTS, pp. 239–248. IEEE Computer Society (2010)
30. Jiang, Z., Pajic, M., Moarref, S., Alur, R., Mangharam, R.: Modeling and verification of a dual chamber implantable pacemaker. In: Flanagan, C., König, B. (eds.) TACAS 2012. LNCS, vol. 7214, pp. 188–203. Springer, Heidelberg (2012)
31. Kaynar, D.K., Lynch, N., Segala, R., Vaandrager, F.: The Theory of Timed I/O Automata. Synthesis Lectures on Computer Science. Morgan Claypool, Also available as Technical Report MIT-LCS-TR-917 (November 2005)
32. Lafferriere, G., Pappas, G.J., Yovine, S.: A new class of decidable hybrid systems. In: Vaandrager, F.W., van Schuppen, J.H. (eds.) HSCC 1999. LNCS, vol. 1569, pp. 137–151. Springer, Heidelberg (1999)
33. Lian, J., Krätschmer, H., Müssig, D.: Open source modeling of heart rhythm and cardiac pacing. The Open Pacing, Electrophysiology & Therapy Journal, 28–44 (2010)
34. Lynch, N., Segala, R., Vaandrager, F.: Hybrid I/O automata. Information and Computation 185(1), 105–157 (2003)
35. Mitra, S.: A Verification Framework for Hybrid Systems. PhD thesis. Massachusetts Institute of Technology, Cambridge, MA 02139 (September 2007)
36. Mitra, S., Liberzon, D., Lynch, N.: Verifying average dwell time of hybrid systems. ACM Trans. Embed. Comput. Syst. 8(1), 1–37 (2008)
37. Nedialkov, N.S., Jackson, K.R., Corliss, G.F.: Validated solutions of initial value problems for ordinary differential equations. Applied Mathematics and Computation 105(1), 21–68 (1999)
38. Olfati-Saber, R., Fax, J.A., Murray, R.M.: Consensus and cooperation in networked multi-agent systems. Proceedings of the IEEE 95(1), 215–233 (2007)

39. Pajic, M., Jiang, Z., Lee, I., Sokolsky, O., Mangharam, R.: From verification to implementation: A model translation tool and a pacemaker case study. In: IEEE Real-Time and Embedded Technology and Applications Symposium, pp. 173–184 (2012)
40. Romualdo Pastor-Satorras and Alessandro Vespignani. Epidemic dynamics and endemic states in complex networks. Physical Review E 63(6), 066117 (2001)
41. Prajna, S., Papachristodoulou, A., Parrilo, P.A.: Introducing sostools: A general purpose sum of squares programming solver. In: Proceedings of the 41st IEEE Conference on Decision and Control, 2002, vol. 1, pp. 741–746. IEEE (2002)
42. Sontag, E.D.: Comments on integral variants of iss. Systems & Control Letters 34(1-2), 93–100 (1998)
43. Strogatz, S.H.: Exploring complex networks. Nature 410(6825), 268–276 (2001)
44. Vladimerou, V., Prabhakar, P., Viswanathan, M., Dullerud, G.: Stormed hybrid systems. In: Aceto, L., Damgård, I., Goldberg, L.A., Halldórsson, M.M., Ingólfsdóttir, A., Walukiewicz, I. (eds.) ICALP 2008, Part II. LNCS, vol. 5126, pp. 136–147. Springer, Heidelberg (2008)
45. Ye, P., Entcheva, E., Grosu, R., Smolka, S.A.: Efficient Modeling of Excitable Cells Using Hybrid Automata. In: CMSB, pp. 216–227 (2005)

Diamonds Are a Girl's Best Friend:
Partial Order Reduction for Timed Automata
with Abstractions

Henri Hansen[1], Shang-Wei Lin[2], Yang Liu[3], Truong Khanh Nguyen[4], and Jun Sun[5]

[1] Tampere University of Technology, Department of Mathematics
henri.hansen@tut.fi
[2] Temasek Laboratories, National University of Singapore
[3] School of Computer Engineering, Nanyang Technological University
[4] National University of Singapore
[5] Singapore University of Technology and Design

Abstract. A major obstacle for using partial order reduction in the context of real time verification is that the presence of clocks and clock constraints breaks the usual *diamond structure* of otherwise independent transitions. This is especially true when information of the relative values of clocks is preserved in the form of diagonal constraints. However, when diagonal constraints are relaxed by a suitable abstraction, some diamond structure is re-introduced in the zone graph. In this article, we introduce a variant of the stubborn set method for reducing an abstracted zone graph. Our method works with all abstractions, but especially targets situations where one abstract execution can simulate several permutations of the corresponding concrete execution, even though it might not be able to simulate the permutations of the abstract execution. We define independence relations that capture this "hidden" diamond structure, and define stubborn sets using these relations. We provide a reference implementation for verifying timed language inclusion, to demonstrate the effectiveness of our method.

1 Introduction

State space methods for timed systems have to deal with not only *state explosion* but also *clock explosion*, i.e., complexity resulting from time constraints of the runs of the system. In a non-timed system, state explosion caused by concurrency and interleaving semantics can often be alleviated by commutativity based reductions, a.k.a. *partial order reductions*, that work by eliminating unnecessary interleaving of sequences.

Fig. 1 shows a simple example of how partial order reduction works. Two processes P_1 and P_2 can perform events a and b, respectively, as shown in Figs. 1 (a) and (b). The concurrent behaviors, ab and ba, of P_1 and P_2 constitute a diamond structure as shown in Fig. 1 (c). If the property checks for the reachability of state l_2m_2, it is sufficient to only explore the representative path ba marked in solid arrows.

The presence of clocks interferes with partial order reduction, because the relative order of events is preserved in time stamps. Consider a simple timed system of two concurrent events, a and b, and two clocks x_a and x_b, which record the time elapsed since the previous occurrence of the events. If both events occur, but a takes place before

A. Biere and R. Bloem (Eds.): CAV 2014, LNCS 8559, pp. 391–406, 2014.

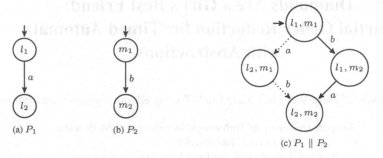

Fig. 1. Diamond Structure

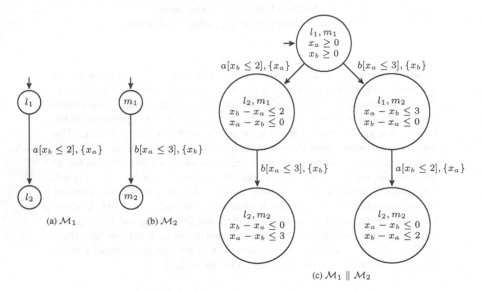

Fig. 2. Broken Diamond Structure

b, then the time constraint $x_a \geq x_b$ will hold, and if the order is reversed, then $x_b \geq x_a$ will hold. Fig. 2 shows the broken diamond structure that results from time constraints.

Abstraction in this article refers to relaxing of some constraints of a system so that we will lose the ability to distinguish between some configurations. We deal exclusively with time abstraction and safety in this article. When verifying safety properties, abstractions give over-approximations, so that all errors are preserved, and some new errors may be introduced. *Abstraction refinement* means that verification starts with a coarse over-approximation which is then refined until either the property is verified or a concrete counterexample is found.

The objectives of this article are the following. Firstly, we define novel relations called *weak and strong independence* for an abstract transition system. They guarantee that one order of executing two independent abstract events can simulate the other order. Strong independence is symmetric, but weak independence is not. Fig. 2 serves as an example. Observing the bottom left configuration, if we relax the constraint $x_b - x_a \leq 0$

and replace it with a constraint $x_b - x_a \leq n$ for any sufficiently large n, the resulting abstract configuration can simulate the configuration on the bottom right of the same figure. The independence relations preserve their validity when an abstraction is made coarser, which is summarized in Theorem 1.

Secondly, we modify the stubborn set method to make use of these relations and reduce an abstract state graph. Our reduction works so that if the original state graph contains a counterexample, then the reduced version of the abstract state graph contains one as well, and this is proven in Theorem 2. Due to the two theorems, our theory is general enough, so that it could be combined with any form of abstraction, as long as one can analyse the independence relations for some finer grained abstraction.

We chose to experiment with the approach in combination with an abstraction refinement loop. The abstraction in our implementation combines a simple family of abstractions that omit some diagonal constraints, with LU-simulation check. Even this rudimentary implementation provides excellent improvement in scalability.

Organization. In the following we discuss how our work relates to previous work in the literature. In Section 2, we define timed automata, timed languages, and the composition of a system from component automata, and their semantics over transition systems. Section 3 defines the stubborn set reduction for an abstract transition system, and explains a state exploration algorithm for checking non-emptiness under reduction. In Section 3.3, we discuss one possible implementation. Section 4 discusses some experiments, while the final section concludes.

Related Work. The seminal work on stubborn sets are [16] and [17]. In particular, [17] explores the use of stubborn sets in a synchronous model. Both deal with *strong* stubborn sets, although earlier work does identify weak sets as well. Dependency and reduction of the control structures for weak stubborn sets have been presented in [9], along with an algorithm for calculating stubborn sets. This article generalizes weak and strong (in)dependence to time constraints. Weak sets have the potential (at least in theory) to reduce more than strong sets.

The theory of timed automata is mostly from [1]. We use the original timed automata definition that does not include invariants. Invariants can be taken into account in our theory as additional guards for transition entering or leaving locations that have them, without compromising safety. Earlier work on partial order reduction for timed automata includes [4] and [12], which identify the problems related to commutativity. Both consider a concept of *local time*, where delays are either global or local to component automata, but provide no empirical evidence. The problematic nature of time zones is also discussed in [5], where a concept called *covering* is applied. Weak independence is a generalization of covering, and localized time can be viewed as an abstraction technique compatible with our method. *Event zones* that record the time elapsed between given events, have been used in [11] and [13] to implement Mazurkiewicz-trace-reduction, which is based on a symmetric concept of independence. Various abstraction techniques for zones exist [6,3,10], we combined our method with the latter two. The idea behind our timed abstraction refinement loop originates from [2].

An alternative approach to using commutativity is discussed in [14]. The method is a search where the zones resulting from different permutations of a set of events are merged. The exact relationship to our method is unknown to us, but we conjecture that the two methods can be combined to increase the effectiveness of both; we leave this for future work.

2 Preliminaries

Let Σ be a finite alphabet and $\mathbb{R}^+$ be the set of non-negative real numbers. A *timed word* over Σ is a finite sequence $w_t = (a_1, t_1)(a_2, t_2) \ldots (a_n, t_n) \in (\Sigma \times \mathbb{R}^+)^*$, such that the sequence $t_1 t_2 \ldots t_n$ of time-stamps is non-decreasing.

Let C be a set of clocks where a clock is a variable over non-negative real numbers $\mathbb{R}^+$. We assume that all clocks progress at the same rate. Let $\sim \in \{<, \leq, \geq, >\}$ and $\prec \in \{<, \leq\}$. An *atomic clock constraint* η is defined as $\eta = x_a \sim n \mid x_a - x_b \prec n$ for $x_a, x_b \in C$, and $n \in \mathbb{Z}$. A *clock constraint* ϕ is a conjunction of atomic clock constraints.

A clock constraint ϕ identifies a convex $|C|$-dimensional polyhedron $[\![\phi]\!] \subseteq (\mathbb{R}^+)^{|C|}$. An *atomic clock guard* is an inequality of the form $x_a \sim n$ for $x_a \in C$, $\sim \in \{<, \leq, >, \geq\}$, and $n \in \mathbb{N}$. A *clock guard* g is a conjunction of atomic clock guards. A clock guard g identifies a $|C|$-dimensional cuboid $[\![g]\!] \subseteq (\mathbb{R}^+)^{|C|}$. We use G_C to denote the set of clock guards over C, and $G_C^A \subseteq G_C$ to denote the set of atomic clock guards.

A *clock valuation* $\gamma : C \mapsto \mathbb{R}^+$ assigns a non-negative real number to a clock. For a clock valuation γ, *clock resetting* $c \subseteq C$, denoted by $\gamma[c \mapsto 0]$, is the clock valuation γ' such that $\gamma'(x) = 0$ for all $x \in c$ and $\gamma'(y) = \gamma(y)$ for all $y \in C \setminus c$. Given a constant $d \in \mathbb{R}^+$ and a clock valuation γ, we use $\gamma + d$ to denote the valuation such that $(\gamma + d)(x) = \gamma(x) + d$ for all $x \in C$. The set of clock valuations is denoted Γ_C.

Definition 1. *Let C be a set of clocks. A* timed automaton *(TA) over C is a tuple $T = (\Sigma, L, L^0, \delta, L^f)$, where Σ is a finite input alphabet, L is a finite set of locations, $L^0 \subseteq L$ is a set of initial locations, $L^f \subseteq L$ is a set of accepting locations, and $\delta : L \times \Sigma \times G_C \times 2^C \mapsto 2^L$ is a partial transition function.*

In a transition $\delta(l, a, g, c)$, l is the starting control location, a is the event, g is a guard and c is the set of reset clocks, while the result is a set of control locations. It is common to think of transitions as edges between two control locations that are decorated with a, g and c. For convenience, sometimes we write $l \xrightarrow{a[g], c} l'$ or even $l \xrightarrow{a} l'$ when $l' \in \delta(l, a, g, c)$ for some $l, l' \in L$, $a \in \Sigma$, $g \in G_C$, and $c \subseteq C$. When such l' exists, we write $l \xrightarrow{a}$. $l \xrightarrow{ab} l'$ means there is some $l^* \in L$ such that $l \xrightarrow{a} l^*$ and $l^* \xrightarrow{b} l'$. We generalise this to longer sequences in the natural way.

We write $\mathcal{R}(a)$ as the union of all c such that $\delta(l, a, g, c)$ is defined for some l and g, i.e., $\mathcal{R}(a)$ is the set of clocks that *could* be reset by executing a. Likewise $\mathcal{G}(a)$ is the set of clocks that appear in some g such that $\delta(l, a, g, c)$ is defined for some l and c.

Definition 2. *A run σ of a TA $M = (\Sigma, L, L^0, \delta, L^f)$ over a timed word $w_t = (a_1, t_1)(a_2, t_2) \cdots (a_n, t_n)$ is a finite sequence of the form*

$$(l_0, \gamma_0) \xrightarrow[t_1]{a_1} (l_1, \gamma_1) \xrightarrow[t_2]{a_2} (l_2, \gamma_2) \xrightarrow[t_3]{a_3} \cdots \xrightarrow[t_n]{a_n} (l_n, \gamma_n)$$

with $l_i \in L$ and $\gamma_i \in \Gamma_C$ for all $0 \leq i \leq n$, satisfying the following requirements:

- $l_0 \in L^0$ and $\gamma_0(x) = 0$ for all $x \in C$
- there is a transition $l_{i-1} \xrightarrow{a_i[g_i],c_i} l_i$ such that $(\gamma_{i-1} + t_i - t_{i-1}) \models g_i$ and $\gamma_i = (\gamma_{i-1} + t_i - t_{i-1})[c_i \mapsto 0]$ for all $1 \leq i \leq n$

A run σ is an accepting run if $l_n \in L^f$. A timed word w_t is *accepted* by M if M has an accepting run over w_t. The *timed language* accepted by M, denoted by $\mathcal{L}(M)$, is the set of all the timed words accepted by M.

We call the set $V = \{a \in \Sigma \mid \exists l \in L \setminus L^f : \exists l' \in L^f : l \xrightarrow{a} l' \vee l' \xrightarrow{a} l\}$ *visible* events. Visible events are the events whose occurrence may change the control location from accepting to non-accepting or vice versa. For future reference, V does not need to be exact, approximating with a larger set will be sufficient.

Given a set of timed automata $M_i = (\Sigma_i, L_i, L_i^0, \delta_i, L_i^f)$ for $i \in \{1, 2, \ldots, n\}$, their *parallel composition* is the timed automaton $M_1 \parallel \cdots \parallel M_n = (\Sigma, L, L^0, \delta, L^f)$ where $\Sigma = \bigcup_{1 \leq i \leq n} \Sigma_i$, $L = L_1 \times \cdots \times L_n$, $L^0 = (L_1^0, \ldots, L_n^0)$, $L^f = L_1^f \times \cdots \times L_n^f$, and the transition relation δ is defined as follows. Let $\Sigma(a) = \{i \mid a \in \Sigma_i\}$. Then $(l_1, \ldots, l_n) \xrightarrow{a[\bigwedge_{i \in \Sigma(a)} g_i], \bigcup_{i \in \Sigma(a)} c_i} (l'_1, \ldots l'_n)$, if (1) $l_i \xrightarrow{a[g_i],c_i} l'_i$, whenever $i \in \Sigma(a)$, and (2) $l_i = l'_i$, whenever $i \notin \Sigma(a)$.

If a clock constraint ϕ is satisfiable, there is a unique canonical clock constraint, denoted by $Can(\phi)$, among all the clock constraints identifying the polyhedron $[\![\phi]\!]$, obtained by closing ϕ under all consequences of pairs of conjuncts in ϕ. Let $C_0 = C \cup \{x_0\}$ where x_0 is the *dummy clock*. We assume $x_0 = 0$ at all times. $Can(\phi)$ can always be expressed as $\bigwedge_{x,y \in C_0} x - y \prec_{xy} n_{xy}$. A common canonical representation is the *difference bound matrix* or DBM. A DBM represents $Can(\phi)$ in the following way. Given a numbering $\{0, 1, \ldots, |C|\}$ for the set of clocks, we represent any satisfiable constraint as a matrix $D = \langle n_{ij}, \prec_{ij} \rangle$, where $i, j \in \{0, 1, \ldots, |C|\}$. The conjunct $x_i - x_j \prec_{ij} n_{ij}$ is represented by the entry $\langle n_{ij}, \prec_{ij} \rangle$. The index 0 corresponds to the dummy clock, so that a lower bound $x_i \prec n_{i0}$ is represented by $\langle n_{i0}, \prec \rangle$, and an upper bound $-x_i \prec n_{0i}$ is represented by $\langle n_{0i}, \prec \rangle$.

Given a clock constraint ϕ, we define the *reset* of a set of clocks c in ϕ, denoted by $\phi[c \mapsto 0]$, as $Can(\phi[c \mapsto 0])$. This set of constraints is obtained from $Can(\phi)$ by removing all conjunctions where some $x \in c$ is included, adding the conjunct $x = 0$, and closing w.r.t. the remaining conjuncts. We define the time elapsing of ϕ, denoted by $\phi \uparrow$, as $Can(\phi \uparrow)$ where $\phi \uparrow$ is obtained from $Can(\phi)$ by removing all upper bounds on clocks. For example, given a constraint $\phi : 0 \leq x \leq 3 \wedge 0 \leq y \leq 2$, its canonical form is $Can(\phi) : 0 \leq x \leq 3 \wedge 0 \leq y \leq 2 \wedge -3 \leq y - x \leq 2$, $\phi[\{x\} \mapsto 0] : x = 0 \wedge 0 \leq y \leq 2 \wedge 0 \leq y - x \leq 2$, and time elapsing $\phi \uparrow : 0 \leq x \wedge 0 \leq y \wedge -3 \leq y - x \leq 2$.

Given a precondition ϕ, and an event a with guard g_a and reset clocks c_a, we define the *strongest postcondition* of a as $sp(\phi, (a, g_a, c_a)) = ((\phi \wedge g_a)[c_a \mapsto 0]) \uparrow$. We define a *abstract postcondition* $POST_\alpha$ as a mapping that satisfies $sp(\phi, (a, g_a, c_a)) \subseteq POST_\alpha(\phi, (a, g, c))$. If $POST_{\alpha_1}$ and $POST_{\alpha_2}$ are two abstract postconditions such that for every a, g and c, $POST_{\alpha_1}(\phi, (a, g, c)) \subseteq POST_{\alpha_2}(\phi, (a, g, c))$, we write $\alpha_1 \sqsubseteq \alpha_2$, and we say that α_2 is a *coarser abstraction*.

Definition 3. *The semantics of a timed automaton* $M = (\Sigma, L, L_0, \delta, L^f)$ *is defined by an* abstract transition system $(S, S_0, \Longrightarrow_\alpha)$, *where* $S \subseteq L \times \mathcal{P}((\mathbb{R}^+)^{|C|})$, *and* $S_0 = \{(l_0, Z_0) \mid l_0 \in L_0\}$. Z_0 *is called the* initial zone. $"\Longrightarrow_\alpha" \subseteq S \times \Sigma \times S$ *is defined as follows:*

- $(l, Z) \xrightarrow{a}_\alpha (l', Z')$, *if and only if* $a \in \Sigma$ *and* $l' \in \delta(l, a, g, c)$ *for some* g *and* c, *and* $Z' = POST_\alpha(Z, (a, g, c)) \neq \emptyset$.

where $POST_\alpha(Z, (a, g, c))$ *is an abstract postcondition operation. When such* (l', Z') *exists, we write* $(l, Z) \xrightarrow{a}_\alpha$.

Given $(l, Z) \in S$, we write $en_\alpha((l, Z)) = \{a \mid \exists(l', Z') : (l, Z) \xrightarrow{a}_\alpha (l', Z')\}$, for the set of enabled events at state (l, Z). The abstraction is determined by the postcondition $POST_\alpha(Z, (a, g, c))$. We leave that open for now, as well as what Z_0 really is. We write $POST_\alpha(Z, a)$ and omit the guard g and the set of clocks c if they do not matter or are clear from the context. We abuse the notations to write $(l, Z) \xrightarrow{a}_{sp} (l', Z')$, when $Z' = sp(Z, (a, g, c))$ for some g, c and $l \xrightarrow{a} l'$, even if (l, Z) is not an actual state of the transition system we are discussing. When $Z \subseteq Z'$ we say that the state (l, Z') simulates the state (l, Z), and write $(l, Z) \prec (l, Z')$.

Definition 4. *Given an abstract transition system* $(S, S_0, \Longrightarrow_\alpha)$, *a sequence* $\langle (l_0, Z_0), a_1, (l_1, Z_1), \ldots, a_n, (l_n, Z_n) \rangle$ *such that* $(l_{i-1}, Z_{i-1}) \xrightarrow{a_i}_\alpha (l_i, Z_i)$ *and* $l_n \in L^f$ *is called a* counterexample *of the transition system.*

The following proposition is the basis of timed verification using transition systems, and it is a standard result [1].

Proposition 1. *If* $(S, S_0, \Longrightarrow_{sp})$ *is the transition system of the timed automaton* $M = (\Sigma, L, L_0, \delta, L^f)$ *under strongest postcondition, then* $\mathcal{L}(M) = \emptyset$ *if and only if the transition system does not have a counterexample.*

A corollary to Proposition 1 follows immediately from the assumption that $sp(Z, a) \subseteq POST_\alpha(Z, a)$: If an abstract transition system of M under α has no counterexamples, then $\mathcal{L}(M) = \emptyset$.

3   Reduction of Abstract Transition Systems

We define reduction functions for abstract transition systems without specifying the abstraction function. The reduction preserves the existence of counterexamples of the concrete system, of which the abstract system is an over-approximation; the existence of spurious counterexamples may not be preserved.

3.1   Stubborn Sets

Definition 5. *Given a timed automaton* $M = (\Sigma, L, L^0, \delta, L^f)$ *and its abstract transition system* $(S, S_0, \Longrightarrow_\alpha)$, *we define a* reduction function *as* $T : S \to 2^\Sigma$. *Given a reduction* T, *we define the* reduced abstract transition system $(S_T, S_0, \Longrightarrow_\alpha^T)$ *as the minimal transition system such that,*

- $S_0 \subseteq S_T$
- if $s \in S_T, a \in T(s)$, and $s \xrightarrow{a}_\alpha s'$, then $s' \in S_T$ and $s \xrightarrow{a}_\alpha^T s'$.

Definition 6. *Given a timed automaton $M = (\Sigma, L, L^0, \delta, L^f)$, $I^S \subseteq \Sigma \times \Sigma$ is a*

- strong structural independence relation *iffor all $(a, b) \in I^S$ and all locations $l, l' \in L$ such that $l \xrightarrow{a} \wedge l \xrightarrow{b}$ we have $l \xrightarrow{ab} l'$ if and only if $l \xrightarrow{ba} l'$, and*
- *a* weak structural independence relation *if for all $(a, b) \in I^S$ locations $l, l' \in L$, $l \xrightarrow{ba} l'$ implies $l \xrightarrow{ab} l'$.*

When checking whether an event a is enabled, we consider a to have a set of *structural guards*, all of which need to be satisfied before a is enabled.

Definition 7. *Given a timed automaton $M = (\Sigma, L, L^0, \delta, L^f)$, a* structural guard *is a mapping $g : L \to \{true, false\}$. We denote the set of structural guards by G^S. The relation $R^S \subseteq \Sigma \times G^S$ is called a* structural guard relation, *if and only if 1) $(a, g) \in R^S$ and $l \xrightarrow{a}$ imply $g(l) = true$, and 2) $l \xrightarrow{a}\!\!\!\!\!/\; implies \exists (a, g) \in R^S : g(l) = false$.*

In a parallel composition of automata $M_1 \parallel \cdots \parallel M_n$, fix an event a. This a is *structurally enabled* in a location $l = (l_1, \ldots, l_n)$, if and only if for every i such that $a \in \Sigma_i$, $l_i \xrightarrow{a}$ in M_i. These conditions (one for each such i) can serve as structural guards. We can denote them g_i^a, i.e., $g_i^a(l) \Leftrightarrow l_i \xrightarrow{a}$.

The guard relation can be under-approximated, as long as for every disabled action we can find at least one unsatisfied guard.

We say that the event b *structurally enables* the guard g, if there is some l and l' such that $l \xrightarrow{b} l'$ and $g(l') = true$ and $g(l) = false$. A relation $E^S \subseteq G^S \times \Sigma$ is called a *structural enabling relation* if $(g, b) \in E^S$ whenever b structurally enables g.

In the context of a parallel composition we can look at the locations of component M_i. Let l_i, l_i' be locations such that $l_i \xrightarrow{b} l_i'$ and $l_i' \xrightarrow{a}$, then we would have $(g_i, b) \in E^S$.

The safe direction of approximating enabling relations is over-approximation. For instance if g is a guard of a then (g, b) holds for at least all those events that can locally lead to a state where a is enabled, but possibly others.

In Fig. 2, for instance, a would have a structural guard g_1, and any event that moves control on $\mathcal{M}_1$ to l_1, would enable g_1. The events a and b are structurally independent, but the figure demonstrates that this is not sufficient for reducing timed automata, as a and b are dependent in terms of time: After the event a, we have the zone indicated by $\phi_a \Leftrightarrow x_b - x_a \leq 2 \wedge x_a - x_b \leq 0$. After the event b, we have $\phi_b \Leftrightarrow x_b - x_a \leq 0 \wedge x_a - x_b \leq 3$. If we have no reason to know in which order a and b took place, we could merge the two zones into $\phi = \phi_a \vee \phi_b \Leftrightarrow x_b - x_a \leq 2 \wedge x_a - x_b \leq 3$.

Ideally we would like to have an abstraction that exactly removes such information. To achieve a more general theory, we will define independence relations for events, with respect to a given abstraction. The question of abstraction is deliberately left open, as it is relevant only with respect to a particular implementation.

Definition 8. *Given a timed automaton $M = (\Sigma, L, L^0, \delta, L^f)$ and an abstract transition relation $\Longrightarrow_\alpha$. $I^T \subseteq \Sigma \times \Sigma$ is a*

- strong temporal independence relation *under* α , *if for all* $(a, b) \in I^T$, *all clock constraints* Z *and for all transitions* $\delta(l_a, a, g_a, c_a)$ *and* $\delta(l_b, b, g_b, c_b)$, $Z \models g_a$ *and* $Z \models g_b$ *together imply that*
  1. $sp(sp(Z, (a, g_a, c_a)), (b, g_b, c_b)) \quad \subseteq \quad POST_\alpha(POST_\alpha(Z, (b, g_b, c_b)),$
     $(a, g_a, c_a))$, *and*
  2. $sp(sp(Z, (b, g_b, c_b)), (a, g_a, c_a)) \quad \subseteq \quad POST_\alpha(POST_\alpha(Z, (a, g_a, c_a)),$
     $(b, g_b, c_b))$.
- weak temporal independence relation *under* α, *if for all* $(a, b) \in I^T$ *and all clock constraints* Z, $Z \models g_b$ *and* $sp(Z, (b, g_b, c_b)) \models g_a$ *imply that*

$$sp(sp(Z, (b, g_b, c_b)), (a, g_a, c_a)) \subseteq POST_\alpha(POST_\alpha(Z, (a, g_a, c_a)), (b, g_b, c_b))$$

Strong temporal independence says that in any configuration, a and b can be executed in either order, and the resulting configuration can simulate all executions of the transition system under sp-semantics. Weak temporal independence promises that if a could be executed after b in the concrete system, the abstract system can execute a first and then b, and still simulate all the executions that were possible in the concrete system. For instance, if the constraint $x_b - x_a \leq 0$ in location (l_2, m_2) of Fig. 2(c) is replaced by $x_b - x_a \leq \infty$ then a is weakly temporally independent of b. Unless $x_a - x_b$ is not similarly relaxed, the converse does not hold, i.e., b is not weakly independent of a.

Theorem 1. *Let* α_1 *and* α_2 *be abstractions, such that* $\alpha_1 \sqsubseteq \alpha_2$. *If* I^T *is a strong (weak) temporal independence relation under* α_1, *then* I^T *is a strong (weak) temporal independence relation under* α_2.

Events have clock guards G_C, and these need to be taken into account in the reduction. We make no assumptions about the guards other than when an event is disabled due to time constraints, it has at least one (atomic) guard that is false.

Definition 9. *A relation* $R^T \subseteq \Sigma \times G_C$ *is a* time guard relation *if 1)* $(b, g) \in R^T$ *and* $(l, Z) \overset{b}{\Longrightarrow}_{sp}$ *imply that* $Z \models g$, *and 2) if* $l \overset{b}{\to}$ *and* $(l, Z) \overset{b}{\not\Longrightarrow}_{sp}$ *then* $\exists g : (b, g) \in R^T \wedge Z \not\models g$. *We say that the event* $a \in \Sigma$ *is* time enabling *for a guard* g *under* α *if there exists* $(l, Z) \overset{a}{\Longrightarrow}_\alpha (l', Z')$ *such that* $Z \not\models g$ *and* $Z' \models g$. *A relation* $E^T \subseteq G_C \times \Sigma$, *is a* time enabling *relation under* α, *if* $(a, g) \in E^T$ *if* a *is time enabling for* g.

In Fig. 2, a has the guard $x_b \leq 2$. If control is locally at l_1, but $x_b > 2$, then this guard is false. b is enabling for $x_b \leq 2$, because it resets x_b.

As with structural guards, the conservative approximation for a guard relation is an under approximation as long as the relation is non-empty. The conservative approximation for enabling is an over approximation. This is reflected in the definition by the fact that the time guard relation is defined in terms of sp-semantics and the enabling relation is defined in terms of abstract semantics.

In the following, let $G = G^S \cup G_C$, the set of all structural and clock guards.

Definition 10. *A relation* $I_S \subseteq \Sigma \times \Sigma$ *is a* strong independence relation, *if there exist a strong structural independence relation* I^S *and a strong temporal independence relation* I^T *such that* $I_S = I^S \cap I^T$. *A weak independence relation* I_W *is defined analogously. A relation* $R \subseteq \Sigma \times G$ *is a* guard relation *if there exist structural and time* *guard relations* R^S *and* R^T *such that* $R = R^S \cup R^T$. *A relation* $E \subseteq G \times \Sigma$ *is an enabling relation, if there exist structural and time enabling relations* E^S *and* E^T *such that* $E = E^S \cup E^T$.

Definition 11. *Let* $(S, S_0, \Longrightarrow_\alpha)$ *be the abstract transition system for the timed automaton* $M = (\Sigma, L, S^0, \delta, L^f)$, *and let* I_S, I_W, E *and* R *be the strong and weak independence, enabling, and guard relations under* α, *respectively, and let* $(l, Z) \in S$, *and let* $G_{(l,Z)} = \{g \mid g \in G \land (l, Z) \not\models g\}$. *let* $U \subseteq \Sigma \cup G_{(l,Z)}$. *Then* U *is a* Stubborn *set at* (l, Z) *if the following conditions hold:*

1. $\forall a \in en(l, Z) \cap U : (\forall b \in \Sigma \setminus U : (a, b) \in I_S) \lor (\forall b \in \Sigma \setminus U : (a, b) \in I_W)$,
2. *Either* $en(l, Z) = \emptyset$ *or* $\exists a \in en(l, Z) \cap U : \forall b \in \Sigma \setminus U : (a, b) \in I_S$. *When this condition holds for* a, *then* a *is called a* key *event.*
3. $\forall a \in (\Sigma \setminus en(l, Z)) \cap U : \exists g \in G_{(l,Z)} : (g, a) \in R \land g \in U$.
4. $\forall g \in G_{(l,Z)} \cap U : \forall a : (a, g) \in E \Rightarrow a \in U$.

Intuitively, a stubborn set contains events, and for computational convenience, also guards. Condition 1 states that each enabled stubborn event is either weakly independent of all non-stubborn events or strongly independent of all non-stubborn events. Condition 2 states that unless the current configuration is a deadlock, a stubborn set contains an enabled *key event*, which is strongly independent of all non-stubborn events, and as a consequence, non-stubborn events can never disable a key event. Condition 3 states that if a stubborn event is disabled, it has a guard that is inside the set, preventing it from becoming enabled. Condition 4 states that a guard of the set cannot be enabled by a non-stubborn event. In other words, conditions 3 and 4 work to guarantee that non-stubborn events alone cannot enable disabled stubborn events.

Stubborn sets can be easily calculated, for instance, using the modified deletion algorithm presented in [8]. We do not reproduce any algorithm here, as there are numerous algorithms in the literature.

Definition 12. *Let* $M = (\Sigma, L, L^0, \delta, L^f)$ *be a timed automaton, let* $V \subseteq \Sigma$ *be the set of visible events, and let* $(S, S_0, \Longrightarrow_\alpha)$ *be the abstract transition system for* M. *The reduction function* $T : S \to 2^\Sigma$ *is a* Stubborn set reduction function *if*

1. $T(l, Z)$ *is a stubborn set at every* $(l, Z) \in S$.
2. *If* $a \in en_\alpha(l, Z)$, *then there exists a sequence* $(l_0, Z_0) \overset{b_1}{\Longrightarrow}_\alpha (l_1, Z_1) \overset{b_2}{\Longrightarrow}_\alpha \cdots \overset{b_k}{\Longrightarrow}_\alpha$ (l_k, Z_k) *such that* $(l_0, Z_0) = (l, Z)$, b_i *is a key event for* (l_{i-1}, Z_{i-1}), *and* $a \in T(l_k, Z_k)$.
3. *If* $V \cap T(l, Z) \cap en_\alpha(l, Z) \neq \emptyset$, *then* $V \subseteq T(l, Z)$.

The conditions say: 1) the reduction function must produce a stubborn set, 2) if an action is ignored in a given state, it will be executed in some future state that is reachable using key events, and 3) if one of the enabled events in the stubborn set is visible, then all visible events must be included in the stubborn set. We reduce the abstract transition system, but unlike the usual reductions, our version of stubborn sets does not guarantee that non-emptiness of the abstract transition system is preserved. Instead, we prove only that if the *original system* contains counterexamples, then the reduced abstract transition system contains one.

Theorem 2. *Let $M = (\Sigma, L, L^0, \delta, L^f)$ be a timed automaton, Let $(S, S_0, \Longrightarrow_\alpha)$ be the abstract transition system for M. If T is a stubborn set reduction function for $(S, S_0, \Longrightarrow_\alpha)$, and $\mathcal{L}(M)$ is not empty, then the reduced abstract transition system $(S_T, S_0, \Longrightarrow_\alpha^T)$ has a counterexample.*

Proof. We prove a slightly stronger result, i.e., that if an arbitrary abstract configuration could reach an accepting location under strongest postcondition semantics, then the reduced system will reach one under the abstract semantics.

Let $(l, Z) \in S_T$ be arbitrary. Let β be a sequence of events such that $(l, Z) \overset{\beta}{\Longrightarrow}_{sp} (l^0, Z^0)$ is a minimal length execution to an accepting location l^0 under strongest postcondition semantics, with $|\beta| = n$. We show that there exists a state $(l', Z') \in S_T$, a location $l^1 \in L^f$ $Z^1 \neq \emptyset$, and a sequence of events ρ such that $(l', Z') \overset{\rho}{\Longrightarrow}_{sp} (l^1, Z^1)$, and $|\rho| < n$, which proves the claim by induction.

Let $\beta = b_1 \cdots b_n$, and let us denote $(l, Z) = (l_0, Z_0)$ and $(l_0, Z_0) \overset{b_1 \cdots b_i}{\Longrightarrow}_{sp} (l_i, Z_i)$ for the ith state in the sequence. Due to the minimality of n, no intermediate l_i is accepting, other than $l_n = l^0$. This means, that $b_n \in V$, by definition, as it leads from a non-accepting to an accepting location. The proof branches to two cases based on whether $\exists i : 1 \leq i \leq n \wedge b_i \in T(l, Z)$ holds or not.

As "case A", let us assume $b_i \in T(l, Z)$ for some i. Let $1 \leq i \leq n$ be minimal such that $b_i \in T(l, Z)$. Firstly, we prove $b_i \in en_\alpha(l, Z)$: If b_i is disabled, then there is some, either time or structural guard, that makes b_i disabled at (l, Z), say g, by point 3 of the definition of stubborn sets, and $g \in T(l, Z)$. Then, point 4 would guarantee, that any event that can cause g to become enabled would be in $T(l, Z)$, meaning, none of the b_j with $1 \leq j < i$ could enable it, as they are not in $T(l, Z)$, leading to a contradiction. To prove that b_i is also enabled in all the intermediate states before its appearance in the accepting sequence, notice that if b_i is strongly independent of all the b_j with $j < i$, none of them can disable b_i. If b_i is weakly independent of all b_j with $j < i$, then none of them can enable b_i. If b_i were disabled in some intermediate state, this would lead to a contradiction. We call this case A0.

When $i = 1$, A0 suffices as such. When $i > 1$, b_i, by property 1 of stubborn sets, is independent of b_j for $1 \leq j < i$, either weakly or strongly. By assumption, $(l_{i-2}, Z_{i-2}) \overset{b_{i-1}b_i}{\Longrightarrow}_{sp} (l_i, Z_i)$ holds and independence guarantees that $(l_{i-2}, Z_{i-2}) \overset{b_i b_{i-1}}{\Longrightarrow}_\alpha (l_i, Z_i^*)$ where $Z_i \subseteq Z_i^*$, which then implies $(l_i, Z_i^*) \overset{b_{i+1} \cdots b_n}{\Longrightarrow}_{sp} (l^0, Z^*)$ so that $Z^0 \subseteq Z^*$. Doing the same step i times, we permute b_i to (l_0, Z_0), and we get $(l, Z) \overset{b_i b_1}{\Longrightarrow}_\alpha (l'_1, Z'_1)$, and $(l'_1, Z'_1) \overset{b_2 \cdots b_{i-1}}{\Longrightarrow}_{sp} (l_i, Z_i^{**}) \overset{b_{i+1} \cdots b_n}{\Longrightarrow}_{sp} (l^0, Z^{**})$ so that $Z^0 \subseteq Z^{**}$.

Let us mark the sequence $b_2 \cdots b_{i-1} b_{i+1} \cdots b_n$ with β'. Therefore, we have $(l, Z) \overset{b_i}{\Longrightarrow}_\alpha (l', Z')$ so that $(l', Z') \in S_T$, and we have $(l', Z') \overset{b_1}{\Longrightarrow}_\alpha (l'_1, Z'_1)$, with $(l'_1, Z'_1) \overset{\beta'}{\Longrightarrow}_{sp} (l^0, Z'^0)$. We again have a branch, but with three cases. A1) If $b_1 \in T(l', Z')$ the claim is proven, as $(l'_1, Z'_1) \in S_T$, and $|\beta'| < n$. A2) If $b_j \in T(l', Z')$, with a similar deduction as before, we can find b_j that is, again, weakly (or strongly) independent of the events that precede it in β', and commute it, like before, so that $(l', Z') \overset{b_j}{\Longrightarrow}_\alpha (l'', Z'')$ so that $(l'', Z'') \overset{b_1}{\Longrightarrow}_\alpha (l''_1, Z''_1)$ and $(l''_1, Z''_1) \overset{\beta''}{\Longrightarrow}_{sp} (l^0, Z''^0)$, thereby shortening the distance by one, but otherwise like before: one abstract step, and then an actual counterexample. A2) can only repeat itself until the accepting state is just one abstract step away, otherwise it reduces to A0 or A3; we call case A3) the situation when none of the b_is of β' are in $T(l', Z'')$.

We merge cases B and A3, because they are similar. Let $(l, Z) \overset{b_1}{\Longrightarrow}_x \overset{b_2 \cdots b_n}{\Longrightarrow}_{sp} (l^0, Z^0)$ so that x is either sp or α, and $b_i \notin T(l, Z)$, for $1 \le i \le n$. Note that $(l, Z) \overset{b_i}{\Longrightarrow}_{sp}$ implies that $(l, Z) \overset{b_i}{\Longrightarrow}_{\alpha}$, so that at the least $b_1 \in en_\alpha(l, Z)$ holds. We mark the intermediate states on this path with superscripts indicating the number of steps remaining to (l^0, Z^0), so that $(l, Z) = (l^n, Z^n)$.

Stubborn set reduction function property 2 guarantees the existence of sequence of key events $a_1, \ldots, a_k$ with $k \ge 0$, such that $(l, Z) = (l_0, Z_0)$ and $(l_0, Z_0) \overset{a_1 \cdots a_k}{\Longrightarrow}_\alpha (l_k, Z_k)$. These subscripts are not to be confused with the notation in the A-case. We mark the intermediate states (l_i, Z_i). On this path – which in its entirety is in S_T – there is a state (l_i, Z_i) for which one of b_js is in $T(l_i, Z_i)$. At the very least, (l_k, Z_k) is such a state, as per property 2 of stubborn set reduction functions.

Let us choose the minimum such i. We must then show that $(l_i, Z_i) \overset{b_1}{\Longrightarrow}_x \overset{b_2 \cdots b_n}{\Longrightarrow}_{sp} (l_i^0, Z_i^0)$, so that l_i^0 is an accepting location; once this is proven, again, the property reduces to one of the cases A0 to A2.

Suppose this property holds for (l_j, Z_j) with $j < i$. It then holds for $j = 0$, as assumed in this case. $(l_{i-1}, Z_{i-1}) \overset{a_i}{\Longrightarrow}_\alpha (l_i, Z_i)$ is a key event, and $(l_{i-1}, Z_{i-1}) \overset{b_1}{\Longrightarrow}_x (l_{i-1}^{n-1}, Z_{i-1}^{n-1}) \overset{b_2 \cdots b_n}{\Longrightarrow}_{sp} (l_{i-1}^0, Z_{i-1}^0)$. Because a_i is a key event, it is strongly independent of all b_i, which (almost) gives us the result, so that $x = \alpha$ at (l_i, Z_i).

To show that $l_i^0 \in L^f$, inductive hypothesis gives us $l_{i-1}^0 \in L^f$. Structural strong independence gives us $l_{i-1}^0 \overset{a_i}{\longrightarrow} l_i^0$, and if $l_i^0 \notin L^f$, then $a_i \in V$ must hold. Bearing in mind that $b_n \in V$, this would contradict either point 3 of stubborn set reduction function or the assumption that none of the b_i is in $T(l_j, Z_j)$ for $j < i$. $\square$

3.2 Ignoring Problem and Key Events

Property 2 of the stubborn set reduction function in Definition 12 is intended to solve the *ignoring problem* [16]. Previously suggested solutions for the ignoring problem include techniques based on strongly connected components [16] and complex conditions that deal with on-stack states [7].

The fact that key events and other events need to be considered separately further complicates the matter. One solution for this problem was given in [8], in the context of the Tarjan algorithm, but here we discuss implementation details for algorithms that do not need to detect strong components.

Let us re-iterate Property 2 from the point of view of a search algorithm that explores the reduced state space: given a state s, with $en(s)$ as the set of enabled events, and $T(s)$ as the set of stubborn events, property 2 says that for every $a \in en(s) \setminus T(s)$, there must be some state s^*, reachable from s using key events, so that $a \in T(s^*)$.

Consider a usual depth-first search, which maintains a stack of states Q (along with other necessary information). Let us assume the top state of the stack is currently s. We can store a bitset of *satisfied* events, denoted $sat(s)$ for every state in the stack.

$a \in sat(s)$ means that we know there is a sequence of key events from s to some state s' such that $a \in T(s')$. Obviously $sat(s) = T(s)$ when state s is initially put on the stack and $T(s)$ calculated.

When we are about to backtrack from s, we check that $en(s) \subseteq sat(s)$; if not, then more events need to be explored. In out test implementation we fully expand the state s, which satisfies the condition trivially, but extending the stubborn set so that at least one new key event gets added would also be correct and potentially result in more reduction.

On the other hand, when we backtrack from s to some state s', this means that $s' \xrightarrow{a} s$ for some $a \in T(s')$. If a is a key event, then all the events that were satisfied in s, are also satisfied in s', so we can set $sat(s') = sat(s') \cup sat(s)$; we say that s is a *key-successor* of s'.

This concept points to alternatives that work for searches other than depth-first search. In a state s, with $T(s)$ as the stubborn set, we propagate information *forward* to one of the key-successors of the current state. The events in $en(s) \setminus T(s)$ need to be satisfied by one key-successor. If in a given state s, the key-successors are all old states, one calculates a larger $T(s)$ until either $T(s) = en(s)$ or an unexplored key-successor is generated. We did not experiment with this solution, as dept-first search makes is easier to extract counterexamples. We leave exploring such solutions for future work.

3.3 Abstraction-Refinement and Independence

An *abstraction refinement* loop in general works by successively refining abstraction until non-emptiness has been decided by either finding a concrete counterexample or an empty abstract transition system. The loop starts with the loosest abstraction, which in our implementation means omitting diagonal timing constraints altogether. In every iteration, we calculate the dependency relations with respect to the current abstraction α.

The abstract transition system is then checked for counterexamples; because we need counterexamples, we used depth-first search in our implementation, with the ignoring conditions as described in the previous subsection.

If no counterexample is found, the system is correct, due to Proposition 1 and Theorems 1 and 2. If we find a counterexample, it is a guarded word that leads to an accepting location in the abstract transition system. We then try to simulate the word using strongest postcondition semantics. If a simulation leads to an accepting location, we have found an actual counterexample.

If the counterexample cannot be replicated, all simulations (the system may be non-deterministic) lead to non-accepting locations or end in empty zones before they end. In this case we tighten the abstraction by considering more timing constraints. The exact details depend on the family of abstractions used, and we will discuss only one example in this section.

The particular abstraction is merely an example. Any abstraction or family of abstractions will work as long as we can calculate independence relations that satisfy Definition 8. Also, any abstraction technique that makes each abstraction more coarse, can be combined with our method, due to Theorem 1.

The example implementation uses an abstraction which we call *pairwise dependence of clocks* (PDC), in combination with LU-simulation [3,10]. The abstraction is implemented by partitioning the clocks into dependency classes. The diagonal constraints between clocks of different classes are omitted. Let $D_\alpha \subseteq C \times C$ be an equivalence relation for clocks. When calculating the post-condition of an event, diagonal constraints of the form $x - y \prec n$ are only considered when $(x, y) \in D_\alpha$, otherwise n is considered to be ∞.

The $POST_\alpha$-operation with respect to D_α is defined as follows. Time zones in the abstract transition system are given by the canonical constraints where $Can_\alpha(Z)$ is of the form $\bigwedge_{(x,y) \in D_\alpha^0} x - y \prec_{xy} n_{xy}$, where $(x, y) \in D_\alpha^0$ if $(x, y) \in D_\alpha$ or if either a of b is the dummy clock x_0 which is always 0.

Any independence relation for the events must meet the criteria of Definition 8 under $POST_\alpha$ to be valid. We propose the following: Let $C(a) = \mathcal{R}(a) \cup \mathcal{G}(a)$, and define temporal dependency relations using the following checklist:

1. If there are clocks x, y such that $x \in \mathcal{R}(a)$ and $y \in \mathcal{R}(b)$ and $(x, y) \in D_\alpha$ then a and b are dependent (both weakly and strongly).
2. If for all clocks x, y: $x \in C(a)$ and $y \in C(b)$ implies that $(x, y) \notin D_\alpha$, then $(a, b) \in I_S^T$, and symmetrically for (b, a). Intuitively, if the events do not share any dependent clocks, they are strongly (and weakly) independent under D_α.
3. If for every $x \in C(a)$ and $y \in C(b)$ such that $(x, y) \in D_\alpha$, the guard of a contains no lower bounds for x, then a is weakly independent of b.
4. If also in the previous case the guard of b contains no lower bounds for y, then a is strongly independent of b.

Lemma 1. *The relations described above are valid temporal independence relations for the abstract transition system under PDC-abstraction.*

4   Experiments

We created an implementation[1] of our method in the PAT framework [15]. The main question to answer is whether and how much the method is able to reduce, and whether the benefits (in reduced states) outweight the cost (in overhead in calculating the sets). Our implementation was an iterative version of the deletion algorithm [8], with optimizations that aim at faster calculation.

We measured the performance of a direct verification of the zone graph, using LU-simulation alone (with BFS), LU simulation and abstraction refinement that uses our stubborn sets, and for comparison, LU- simulation with abstraction refinement but without reduction. Our implementation of abstraction was the PDC-abstraction explained in Section 3.3, and LU-simulation was calculated on top of that. Structural relations were analyzed by examining the control structure of component automata and using simple heuristics for shared variable access, such as write/write and read/write of a shared variable. The algorithm for state exploration for the two AR implementations was a depth-first search, due to the need for counterexamples.

For reference, we did the tests also with UPPAAL on the same models; the models may not produce exactly the same number of states, as it is possible that there are small

---

[1] See https://sites.google.com/site/shangweilin/timedpor for additional updates on performance.

Table 1. Verification results

model	PAT/BFS+LU		PAT/AR+LU+POR		PAT/AR+LU		UPPAAL BFS	
	$|S|$	time	$|S|$	time	$|S|$	time	$|S|$	time
CSMACD 5	2705	0,18	**1131**	0,17	2942	0,19	2156	**0.03**
CSMACD 6	12355	0,25	**3488**	0,21	11585	0,79	8976	**0.08**
CSMACD 7	54522	1	**10146**	0,7	44349	3	35739	**0.36**
CSMACD 8	234600	7	**28272**	2	164257	17	137678	**1**
CSMACD 9	991483	40	**76185**	7	592113	78	516751	**6**
CSMACD 10	4139285	232	**199804**	21	O/M		1899028	28
CSMACD 11	O/M		**512344**	62	O/M		6857723	117
FDDI 5	459	0,02	**41**	**0**	41	0,35	286	**0**
FDDI 10	10637	1	**81**	0,02	**81**	0,04	6043	0.19
FDDI 15	O/M		**121**	0,04	**121**	0,06	105990	34
FDDI 20	O/M		**161**	0,1	**161**	0,1	O/M	
Fischer 5	3277	0,04	**807**	0,07	5785	0,38	2958	**0.02**
Fischer 6	15229	0,19	**2570**	0,27	20470	1	12777	**0.08**
Fischer 7	69602	1	**8185**	1	115633	7	54372	**0.42**
Fischer 8	313421	6	**26104**	3	578311	47	229559	**2**
Fischer 9	1393599	37	**83339**	14	O/M		965466	**12**
Fischer 10	6131109	242	**266118**	56	O/M		4053445	62
Fischer 11	O/M		**849213**	220	O/M		17005200	315
Railways 5	34197	0,7	**1587**	0,16	19217	1	16726	**0.09**
Railways 6	465634	10	**9572**	0,96	230714	14	200821	1
Railways 7	7250443	302	**67069**	7	O/M		2811642	22

differences in the models, and also, because the optimizations of UPPAAL are different from our implementation. The idea is to give some indication of scalability issues.

Our experiment set consisted of some well-known safe examples, CSMA/CD networking, Fiber distributed data interface (FDDI), the famous Fischer protocol, and a railway controller protocol. We measured the total number of generated configurations and time in seconds. We ran the experiments on a PC with an Intel Core-i7, 3.4GHz and 8GB of RAM. Running times should be taken only to indicate order of magnitude and scalability, because during the tests computer load and similar factors cause substantial variation in running times.

The results of our experiments are given in Table 1. The best performances in terms of number of states generated and execution time are indicated with boldface characters. The results under reduction are given in the second column, and in all the cases, no other approach generated fewer states.

The effects of reduction on scalability mean that eventually it is superior to every other solution in our tests. Comparing execution times, we notice that our method slows state generation down by a significant factor. However, this is more than compensated by the effect on scalability of larger models. Another observation from the first and third columns is that the abstraction refinement implementation without partial order reduction also slows down state generation significantly; It is plausible that our implementation of the PDC-abstraction is far from optimal and the time of actually calculating the abstract successors dominates the execution times.

Some of the reduction in the number of states comes from abstraction itself, (in FDDI, all of it) but for instance, in the Fischer model PDC abstraction actually makes the state space bigger, but when reduction is used, the state space is greatly reduced. UPPAAL was chosen as a reference, as it can be viewed as the gold-standard for timed verification. It performs significantly better than PAT when reduction is not used. UP-PAAL also clearly has the advantage that it seems to generate states much faster. However, despite this handicap, our partial order reduction eventually beats even UPPAAL, not only in terms of states, but also in verification time, when the models get large enough.

5 Conclusion

We defined a variant of the stubborn set method for timed verification, which makes use of abstraction. The method uses dependence and independence defined in terms of concrete behaviors that the abstract system must preserve instead of directly defining them on the abstract zone graph. We believe the method overcomes a fundamental hurdle for commutativity based reduction in real time verification, that of clocks causing superfluous dependency. To the best of our knowledge, this is the first successful application of the "standard" partial order reduction methods on timed automata.

In our measurements, our method was able to provide outstanding reduction, but naturally, it can only reduce models that exhibit a high degree of concurrency and interleaving. The theory is general and works with any abstract semantics as long as sufficient conditions for weak and strong (temporal) independence can be extracted. Even the simple heuristics in our reference implementation turned out to be very efficient in reducing the number of states explored during verification of some models.

Acknowledgement. We would like to thank all the anonymous reviewers for helpful and insightful comments that have helped us improve this paper. This research was partly supported by project "IDD11100102" from SUTD, "Formal Verification on Cloud" project under Grant No: M4081155.020, and TRF project "Research and Development in the Formal Verification of System Design and Implementation"

References

1. Alur, R., Dill, D.L.: A theory of timed automata. Theoretical Computer Science 126(2), 183–235 (1994)
2. Alur, R., Itai, A., Kurshan, R.P., Yannakakis, M.: Timing verification by successive approximation. Inf. Comput. 118(1), 142–157 (1995)
3. Behrmann, G., Bouyer, P., Larsen, K., Pelanek, R.: Lower and upper bounds in zone-based abstractions of timed automata. International Journal on Software Tools for Technology Transfer (STTT) 8, 204–215 (2006)
4. Bengtsson, J., Jonsson, B., Lilius, J., Yi, W.: Partial order reductions for timed systems. In: Sangiorgi, D., de Simone, R. (eds.) CONCUR 1998. LNCS, vol. 1466, pp. 485–500. Springer, Heidelberg (1998)
5. Dams, D., Gerth, R., Knaack, B., Kuiper, R.: Partial-order reduction techniques for real-time model checking. Formal Aspects of Computing 10, 469–482 (1998)

6. Daws, C., Tripakis, S.: Model checking of real-time reachability properties using abstractions. In: Steffen, B. (ed.) TACAS 1998. LNCS, vol. 1384, pp. 313–329. Springer, Heidelberg (1998)
7. Evangelista, S., Pajault, C.: Solving the ignoring problem for partial order reduction. International Journal on Software Tools for Technology Transfer 12(2), 155–170 (2010)
8. Hansen, H., Kwiatkowska, M., Qu, H.: Partial order reduction for model checking markov decision processes under unconditional fairness. In: QEST 2011, pp. 203–212. IEEE CS Press (2011)
9. Hansen, H., Wang, X.: Compositional analysis for weak stubborn sets. In: Caillaud, K.H.B., Carmona, J. (eds.) Proceedings of ACSD 2011, pp. 36–43. IEEE CS Press (2011)
10. Herbreteau, F., Srivathsan, B., Walukiewicz, I.: Better Abstractions for Timed Automata. In: LICS, pp. 375–384 (2012)
11. Lugiez, D., Niebert, P., Zennou, S.: A partial order semantics approach to the clock explosion problem of timed automata. Theoretical Computer Science 345(1), 27–59 (2005)
12. Minea, M.: Partial order reduction for model checking of timed automata. In: Baeten, J.C.M., Mauw, S. (eds.) CONCUR 1999. LNCS, vol. 1664, pp. 431–446. Springer, Heidelberg (1999)
13. Niebert, P., Qu, H.: Adding invariants to event zone automata. In: Asarin, E., Bouyer, P. (eds.) FORMATS 2006. LNCS, vol. 4202, pp. 290–305. Springer, Heidelberg (2006)
14. Salah, R., Bozga, M., Maler, O.: On interleaving in timed automata. In: Baier, C., Hermanns, H. (eds.) CONCUR 2006. LNCS, vol. 4137, pp. 465–476. Springer, Heidelberg (2006)
15. Sun, J., Liu, Y., Dong, J.S., Pang, J.: PAT: Towards Flexible Verification under Fairness. In: Bouajjani, A., Maler, O. (eds.) CAV 2009. LNCS, vol. 5643, pp. 709–714. Springer, Heidelberg (2009)
16. Valmari, A.: A stubborn attack on state explosion. Formal Methods in System Design 1(1), 297–322 (1992)
17. Valmari, A.: Stubborn set methods for process algebras. In: Proceedings of the DIMACS Workshop on Partial Order Methods in Verification, POMIV 1996, pp. 213–231. AMS Press, Inc., New York (1997)

Reachability Analysis of Hybrid Systems Using Symbolic Orthogonal Projections*

Willem Hagemann

Carl von Ossietzky Universität Oldenburg,
Ammerländer Heerstraße 114–118, 26111 Oldenburg, Germany
willem.hagemann@informatik.uni-oldenburg.de

Abstract. This paper deals with reachability analysis of hybrid systems with continuous dynamics described by linear differential inclusions and arbitrary linear maps for discrete updates. The invariants, guards, and sets of reachable states are given as convex polyhedra. Our reachability algorithm is based on a novel representation class for convex polyhedra, the symbolic orthogonal projections (sops), on which various geometric operations, including convex hulls, Minkowski sums, linear maps, and intersections, can be performed efficiently and exactly. The capability to represent intersections of convex polyhedra exactly is superior to support function-based approaches like the LGG-algorithm (Le Guernic and Girard [21]).

Accompanied by some simple examples, we address the problem of the monotonic growth of the exact representation and propose a combination of our reachability algorithm with the LGG-algorithm. This results in an efficient method of better accuracy than the LGG-algorithm and its productive implementation in SpaceEx [13].

1 Introduction

Reachability analysis of hybrid systems has to deal with two problems: The first one is a systematic representation of the reachable states. Aside from nonconvex approaches like [4,5,22], the reachable states are usually represented as unions of convex sets, for which different representations, including polyhedra [7], template polyhedra [23], zonotopes [15,16], ellipsoids [19], and support functions [20], are used. The choice of the representation has a wide influence on the approximations of the underlying sets and on the efficiency of the operations required for the reachability analysis, e. g. zonotopes, ellipsoids, and support functions are challenging for intersections with guard sets [1,16]. The second problem is to tackle the dynamics of the system. Typical classes of admissible dynamics vary from constant derivatives [9,18], linear differential equations or inclusions [13,15,19] to nonlinear differential equations [23,6]. However, in order to approximate complexer dynamics, the classes should allow differential inclusions [2,3,12]. In turn,

---

* This work was partly supported by the German Research Council (DFG) as part of the Transregional Collaborative Research Center "Automatic Verification and Analysis of Complex Systems" (SFB/TR 14 AVACS, http://www.avacs.org/).

A. Biere and R. Bloem (Eds.): CAV 2014, LNCS 8559, pp. 407–423, 2014.
© Springer International Publishing Switzerland 2014

the choice of the admissible dynamics has an impact on the required operations for the post image computation. Hence, both problems are highly related.

In this paper we focus on the reachability analysis of hybrid systems with continuous dynamics described by linear differential inclusions and arbitrary linear maps for discrete updates. The invariants, guards, and sets of reachable states are given as convex polyhedra, where we assume that the polyhedra are given as intersections of half-spaces ($\mathcal{H}$-*representation*) and not as convex hulls of vertices and rays ($\mathcal{V}$-*representation*). Our reachability algorithm is based on a novel representation class for convex polyhedra, the symbolic orthogonal projections (sops), on which various geometric operations, including convex hulls, Minkowski sums, linear maps, and intersections, can be performed efficiently and exactly. The capability to represent intersections of convex polyhedra exactly is superior to support function-based approaches.

Due to space limitations we omit the proofs. The interested reader will find the proofs and some additional materials in [17].

2   Template Polyhedra and Support Functions

In their 2009 article [21], Le Guernic and Girard proposed an algorithm for reachability analysis of hybrid systems based on the usage of support functions. This reachability algorithm, we call it the LGG-algorithm for short, as been implemented in the verification tool box SPACEEX [13]. The efficiency of the LGG-algorithm is achieved by a clever combination of support functions and template polyhedra. We briefly restate their representations of convex sets.

Template polyhedra are $\mathcal{H}$-polyhedra $\mathbf{P}\,(A_{\mathrm{fix}}, \mathbf{a}) = \{\mathbf{x} \mid A_{\mathrm{fix}}\mathbf{x} \leq \mathbf{a}\}$ where the template matrix A_{fix} is fixed a priori. For a – not necessarily convex – set $\mathbf{S} \subseteq \mathbb{R}^d$ and a direction $\mathbf{n} \in \mathbb{R}^d$ the value of the *support function* is defined as $h_{\mathbf{S}}(\mathbf{n}) = \sup_{\mathbf{x} \in \mathbf{S}} \mathbf{n}^T\mathbf{x}$. For an $\mathcal{H}$-polyhedron $\mathbf{P}\,(A, \mathbf{a})$ the value of the support function is given by the linear program "maximize $\mathbf{n}^T\mathbf{x}$ subject to $A\mathbf{x} \leq \mathbf{a}$". Support functions behaves nicely under most geometric operations; in detail, for any two compact convex sets $\mathbf{P}$, $\mathbf{Q}$ in $\mathbb{R}^d$, and any $(d \times d)$-matrix M the following equations are easily computable:

$$h_{M(\mathbf{P})}(\mathbf{n}) = h_{\mathbf{P}}(M^T\mathbf{n}), \qquad\qquad \text{(linear map)}$$
$$h_{\mathbf{P}+\mathbf{Q}}(\mathbf{n}) = h_{\mathbf{P}}(\mathbf{n}) + h_{\mathbf{Q}}(\mathbf{n}), \qquad\qquad \text{(Minkowski sum)}$$
$$h_{\mathrm{conv}(\mathbf{P}\cup\mathbf{Q})} = \max(h_{\mathbf{P}}(\mathbf{n}), h_{\mathbf{Q}}(\mathbf{n})), \qquad \text{(closed convex hull)}$$

while the intersection is not easily computable

$$h_{\mathbf{P}\cap\mathbf{Q}}(\mathbf{n}) = \inf_{\mathbf{m}\in\mathbb{R}^d} h_{\mathbf{P}}(\mathbf{n} - \mathbf{m}) + h_{\mathbf{Q}}(\mathbf{m}).$$

Given the template matrix A_{fix} and the support function $h_{\mathbf{S}}$ of some set $\mathbf{S}$, one easily obtains a closed convex over-approximation $\mathbf{P}\,(A_{\mathrm{fix}}, \mathbf{a_S})$ of $\mathbf{S}$: The ith coefficient of the vector $\mathbf{a_S}$ is given by $h_{\mathbf{S}}(\mathbf{n}_i)$, where $\mathbf{n}_i^T$ is the ith row of the template matrix. We will use the notation $\mathbf{a_S} = \mathbf{h_S}(A_{\mathrm{fix}})$ for such a row-wise computation of the vector $\mathbf{a_S}$.

3   Symbolic Orthogonal Projections

We introduce a novel representation class for polyhedral sets which we call *symbolic orthogonal projections*, or *sops*, for short. Sops can be realized in any vector space $\mathbb{K}^d$ over an ordered field $\mathbb{K}$. Any sop $\mathbf{P} = \mathbf{P}(A, L, \mathbf{a}) \subseteq \mathbb{K}^d$, where A is an $(m \times d)$-matrix, L is an $(m \times k)$-matrix, and $\mathbf{a}$ is a column vector in $\mathbb{K}^m$, is the orthogonal projection of an $\mathcal{H}$-polyhedron $\mathbf{P}\left((A\ L), \mathbf{a}\right) \subseteq \mathbb{K}^{d+k}$ onto $\mathbb{K}^d$, where k is the number of columns in L, i.e.,

$$\mathbf{P} = \mathbf{P}(A, L, \mathbf{a}) = \left\{ \mathbf{x} \in \mathbb{K}^d \mid \exists \mathbf{z} \in \mathbb{K}^k,\ A\mathbf{x} + L\mathbf{z} \leq \mathbf{a} \right\}.$$

Obviously, the sop $\mathbf{P}(A, L, \mathbf{a})$ is empty if and only if $\mathbf{P}\left((A\ L), \mathbf{a}\right)$ is empty, and any $\mathcal{H}$-polyhedron $\mathbf{P} = \mathbf{P}(A, \mathbf{a}) \in \mathbb{K}^d$ may be represented by the sop $\mathbf{P}(A, \emptyset, \mathbf{a})$, where $\emptyset$ denotes an empty matrix. Furthermore, for any sop $\mathbf{P}(A, L, \mathbf{a})$ in $\mathbb{K}^d$ and any given direction $\mathbf{n} \in \mathbb{K}^d$ the optimal value of the linear program "maximize $\mathbf{n}^T \mathbf{x}$ subject to $A\mathbf{x} + L\mathbf{z} \leq \mathbf{a}$" provides the value of the support function $h_{\mathbf{P}}(\mathbf{n})$. Hence, sops can easily be over-approximated by template polyhedra.

As a rather technical notion, we call a sop $\mathbf{P}(A, L, \mathbf{a})$ *complete* if there exists some $\mathbf{u} \geq 0$ with $\mathbf{0} = A^T \mathbf{u}$, $\mathbf{0} = L^T \mathbf{u}$, and $1 = \mathbf{a}^T \mathbf{u}$. Any sop can be completed by adding the redundant row $(\mathbf{0}^T, \mathbf{0}^T, 1)$ to its representation $(A, L, \mathbf{a})$.[1]

Convex Hull, Minkowski Sum, and Intersection. We show that symbolic orthogonal projections allow to efficiently represent closed convex hulls, Minkowski sums, and intersections of polyhedra. All these operations are realized as block matrices over the original matrices. The zero matrix is denoted by O.

Proposition 1. *Let* $\mathbf{P}_1 = \mathbf{P}(A_1, L_1, \mathbf{a}_1)$ *and* $\mathbf{P}_2 = \mathbf{P}(A_2, L_2, \mathbf{a}_2)$ *be two non-empty sops in* $\mathbb{K}^d$. *Then the following equations hold:*

$$\mathrm{conv}(\mathbf{P}_1 \cup \mathbf{P}_2) = \mathbf{P}\left(\begin{pmatrix} A_1 \\ O \end{pmatrix}, \begin{pmatrix} A_1 & L_1 & O & \mathbf{a}_1 \\ -A_2 & O & L_2 & -\mathbf{a}_2 \end{pmatrix}, \begin{pmatrix} \mathbf{a}_1 \\ \mathbf{0} \end{pmatrix} \right),$$

if $\mathbf{P}_1$ *and* $\mathbf{P}_2$ *are complete;*

$$\mathbf{P}_1 + \mathbf{P}_2 = \mathbf{P}\left(\begin{pmatrix} A_1 \\ O \end{pmatrix}, \begin{pmatrix} A_1 & L_1 & O \\ -A_2 & O & L_2 \end{pmatrix}, \begin{pmatrix} \mathbf{a}_1 \\ \mathbf{a}_2 \end{pmatrix} \right);$$

$$\mathbf{P}_1 \cap \mathbf{P}_2 = \mathbf{P}\left(\begin{pmatrix} A_1 \\ A_2 \end{pmatrix}, \begin{pmatrix} L_1 & O \\ O & L_2 \end{pmatrix}, \begin{pmatrix} \mathbf{a}_1 \\ \mathbf{a}_2 \end{pmatrix} \right).$$

Linear Mappings. Any linear mapping ϕ is uniquely determined by its *transformation matrix* $M \in \mathbb{K}^{n \times m}$, i.e., $\phi(\mathbf{x}) = M\mathbf{x}$. We are interested in three types of linear mappings, where the $(n \times n)$-identity matrix is denoted by I_n: (i) *automorphisms*, having invertible transformation matrices; (ii) *orthogonal projections* proj_k, for $0 \leq k \leq d$, having $(k \times d)$-matrices of the form $(I_k\ O)$; and (iii) *elementary embeddings* embed_l, for $l \geq d$, having $(l \times d)$-matrices of the form $\begin{pmatrix} I_d \\ O \end{pmatrix}$.

---

[1] One can show that any sop $\mathbf{P}$ which represents a fully dimensional polytope in $\mathbb{K}^d$ with $d \geq 1$ is complete. For a geometric interpretation of completeness, see [17].

Proposition 2. *Every transformation matrix M can be written as the product $M = S^{-1}EPT^{-1}$, where S and T are invertible, E is the matrix of an elementary embedding, and P is the matrix of an orthogonal projection.*

Proposition 3. *Let $\mathbf{P}_1 = \mathbf{P}\left(A_1, L_1, \mathbf{a}_1\right)$ be a sop in $\mathbb{K}^d$, S an invertible $(d \times d)$-transformation matrix of the linear mapping ϕ, proj_k an orthogonal projection with $0 \leq k \leq d$, and embed_l an elementary embedding with $l \geq d$. Then*

$$\phi(\mathbf{P}_1) = \mathbf{P}\left(A_1 S^{-1}, L_1, \mathbf{a}_1\right),$$

$$\mathrm{embed}_l(\mathbf{P}_1) = \mathbf{P}\left(\begin{pmatrix} A_1 & O \\ O & I_{l-d} \\ O & -I_{l-d} \end{pmatrix}, \begin{pmatrix} L_1 \\ O \\ O \end{pmatrix}, \begin{pmatrix} \mathbf{a}_1 \\ \mathbf{0} \\ \mathbf{0} \end{pmatrix}\right),$$

$$\mathrm{proj}_k(\mathbf{P}_1) = \mathbf{P}\left(A, L, \mathbf{a}_1\right),$$

where $\begin{pmatrix} A & L \end{pmatrix} = \begin{pmatrix} A_1 & L_1 \end{pmatrix}$ and A has k columns.

Problem of Set Entailment. We should address an open issue: Up to now, there is – to the author's best knowledge – no efficient method to decide subset relations for polyhedra represented as support functions or sops, and it is questionable whether such efficient methods exists.

Overview. The adjacent table provides an overview on the hardness of performing linear transformations, Minkowski sums, closed convex hulls, intersections, and deciding subset relations on polyhedra in the respective representation. The tick indicates computability in (weakly) polynomial time and a minus-sign indicates that the enumeration problem is either NP-hard or its complexity is unknown, see [25].

Representation	$M(\cdot)$	$\cdot + \cdot$	conv $(\cdot \cup \cdot)$	$\cdot \cap \cdot$	$\cdot \subseteq \cdot$
$\mathcal{V}$-representation	✓	✓	✓	–	✓
$\mathcal{H}$-representation	✓[a]	–	–	✓	✓
support function	✓[b]	✓	✓	–	–
sop	✓	✓	✓	✓	–

[a]for automorphism, [b]for endomorphism

3.1 Beyond Template Polyhedra

Sops profit from the underlying $\mathcal{H}$-representation, i.e., we may solve linear programs to test for emptiness or to find relative interior points. Additionally, we may switch from the primal system of linear inequalities to its dual. In this section we shall make use of these techniques and present a method which allows to find the facet-defining half-space of a sop $\mathbf{P}$ in some given direction. This method is then extended to an interpolation method which improves existing over-approximations. The needed geometrical concepts are shortly introduced in the following. A comprehensive introduction can be found in [26]. For the theory of linear programming, see [24].

Let $\mathbf{P} = \mathbf{P}(A, \mathbf{a})$ be an $\mathcal{H}$-polyhedron. The points of $\mathbf{P}$ are those vectors $\mathbf{x}$ which satisfy the system $A\mathbf{x} \leq \mathbf{a}$. A point $\mathbf{x}$ of $\mathbf{P}$ is an *interior point* if there exists a ball $\mathbf{B}_\epsilon = \{\mathbf{x} \,|\, |\mathbf{x}| \leq \epsilon\}$ with $\epsilon > 0$ such that $\mathbf{x} + \mathbf{B}_\epsilon \subseteq \mathbf{P}$. Only full-dimensional polyhedra have interior points. However, any polyhedron $\mathbf{P} = \mathbf{P}(A, \mathbf{a})$ is full-dimensional relatively to its affine hull $\mathrm{aff}(\mathbf{P})$. Hence, we call a point $\mathbf{x}$ of $\mathbf{P}$ a *relative interior point* relatively to $\mathrm{aff}(\mathbf{P})$ if there exists a ball $\mathbf{B}_\epsilon$ with $\epsilon > 0$ such that $(\mathbf{x} + \mathbf{B}_\epsilon) \cap \mathrm{aff}(\mathbf{P}) \subseteq \mathbf{P}$. A *facet-defining* half-space $\mathbf{H}$ of $\mathbf{P}$ is a half-space $\mathbf{H} = \{\mathbf{x} \,|\, \mathbf{n}^T\mathbf{x} \leq b\}$, $\mathbf{P} \subseteq \mathbf{H}$, such that $\mathbf{P} \cap \{\mathbf{x} \,|\, \mathbf{n}^T\mathbf{x} = b\}$ has a relative interior point relatively to $\mathrm{aff}(\mathbf{P}) \cap \{\mathbf{x} \,|\, \mathbf{n}^T\mathbf{x} = b\}$.

The topological concept of a relative interior point can equivalently be defined on the system $A\mathbf{x} \leq \mathbf{a}$ of the polyhedron $\mathbf{P} = \mathbf{P}(A, \mathbf{a})$. Every solution $\mathbf{x}$ of the system of strict linear inequalities $A\mathbf{x} < \mathbf{a}$ is an interior point of $\mathbf{P}$. If $\mathbf{n}^T\mathbf{x} \leq b$ is an inequality of the system $A\mathbf{x} \leq \mathbf{a}$, and if all solutions $\mathbf{x}$ of the system $A\mathbf{x} \leq \mathbf{a}$ satisfy $\mathbf{n}^T\mathbf{x} = b$, then $\mathbf{n}^T\mathbf{x} = b$ is called an *implicit equality* of the system. For any set I of row indices of $A\mathbf{x} \leq \mathbf{a}$ we denote the corresponding subsystem by $A_I\mathbf{x} \leq \mathbf{a}_I$. The linear equalities representing the affine hull are linear combinations of the implicit equalities of the system $A\mathbf{x} \leq \mathbf{a}$ and vice versa. Let I be the set of indices of the implicit equalities in $A\mathbf{x} \leq \mathbf{a}$ and S be the set of the remaining indices. Each solution $\mathbf{x}$ of the system $A_I\mathbf{x} = \mathbf{a}_I$, $A_S\mathbf{x} < \mathbf{a}_S$ is a *relative interior point* of $\mathbf{P}$.

Relative interior points and implicit equalities can be found by means of linear programming: The optimal solution $(\mathbf{x}_0, \lambda_0)$ of the linear program "maximize λ subject to $A_I\mathbf{x} = \mathbf{a}_I$, $A_S + 1\lambda \leq \mathbf{a}_S$, $0 \leq \lambda \leq 1$" determines a relative interior point $\mathbf{x}_0$ if $\lambda_0 > 0$. For $\lambda_0 = 0$ one obtains sufficient hints to find further implicit equalities, see [14]. Let I be the set of indices of all implicit equalities of $\mathbf{P}$ and S the set of the remaining indices. The *facet-defining* inequalities of $\mathbf{P}$ are exactly those inequalities whose index j is in S and the linear program "maximize λ subject to $A_{I \cup \{j\}}\mathbf{x} = \mathbf{a}_{I \cup \{j\}}$, $A_{S \setminus \{j\}} + 1\lambda \leq \mathbf{a}_{S \setminus \{j\}}$, $0 \leq \lambda \leq 1$" has a positive optimal solution. The corresponding half-spaces to a facet-defining inequality are also facet-defining.

The orthogonal projection of a relative interior point is a relative interior point of the projected set. Let $\mathbf{P} = \mathbf{P}(A, L, \mathbf{a}) \subseteq \mathbb{K}^d$ be a sop, $\mathbf{z}$ be a relative interior point of $\mathbf{P}((A\ L), \mathbf{a})$, and $\mathbf{z}_d$ the vector of the first d coefficients of $\mathbf{z}$. Then $\mathbf{z}_d$ is a relative interior point of $\mathbf{P}$ and $\mathbf{P}' = \mathbf{P}(A, L, \mathbf{a} - (A\ L)\mathbf{z})$ is a sop representing the translated polyhedron $\mathbf{P}' = \mathbf{P} - \mathbf{z}_d$, which contains the origin $\mathbf{0}$ as a relative interior point.

Proposition 4 (Ray Shooting). *Let $\mathbf{P} = \mathbf{P}(A, L, \mathbf{a})$ be a nonempty and complete sop in $\mathbb{K}^d$ which contains the origin $\mathbf{0}$ as a relative interior point. Then the following linear program is feasible for any vector $\mathbf{r} \in \mathbb{K}^d$:*

$$\text{maximize } \mathbf{r}^T A^T \mathbf{u} \text{ subject to } L^T\mathbf{u} = 0, \ \mathbf{a}^T\mathbf{u} = 1, \ \mathbf{u} \geq 0,$$

and exactly one of the following statements holds:

1. *The linear program is unbounded and $\mathbf{r}$ is not in $\mathrm{aff}(\mathbf{P})$.*
2. *The optimal value equals zero and $\mathbf{P}$ is unbounded in direction $\mathbf{r}$.*
3. *The optimal value $\mathbf{r}^T A^T \mathbf{u}_0$ is positive and $\mathbf{P}$ is bounded in direction $\mathbf{r}$. Let $\lambda = \frac{1}{\mathbf{r}^T A^T \mathbf{u}_0}$, $\mathbf{n} = A^T\mathbf{u}_0$, and $\mathbf{H} = \mathbf{H}(\mathbf{n}, 1)$ be a half-space. Then $\lambda\mathbf{r}$ is a boundary point of $\mathbf{P}$ and $\mathbf{H}$ is a supporting half-space of $\mathbf{P}$ in $\lambda\mathbf{r}$.*

Hence, for any given ray $\mathbf{r}$ we find the maximal length $\lambda = \frac{1}{\mathbf{r}^T A^T \mathbf{u}_0}$ such that $\lambda \mathbf{r}$ is on the boundary of $\mathbf{P}$, and we obtain a supporting half-space of $\mathbf{P}$ in $\lambda \mathbf{r}$. If $\lambda \mathbf{r}$ is a relative interior point of a facet, – which is most likely the case if $\mathbf{r}$ was chosen randomly – then ray shooting returns a facet-defining half-space.[2]

A sop $\mathbf{P}$ and an over-approximating template polyhedron $\mathbf{P}'$ have, in general, none or only a few facet-defining half-spaces in common. Hence, we may use Proposition 4 to find facet-defining half-spaces of $\mathbf{P}$ and add them to $\mathbf{P}'$ yielding a better over-approximation $\mathbf{P}''$ of $\mathbf{P}$. We call $\mathbf{P}''$ an *interpolation* of $\mathbf{P}$ and $\mathbf{P}'$. Throughout this paper we use the following simple interpolation strategy: Initially, $\mathbf{P}''$ is set to the affine hull of $\mathbf{P}$. For an arbitrary inequality of $\mathbf{P}'$ we decide whether it is face-defining in $\mathbf{P}' \cap \mathbf{P}''$. If not, it is removed from $\mathbf{P}'$. Otherwise, we choose $\mathbf{r}$ as a relative interior point of the defined facet, and apply Proposition 4 on $\mathbf{P}$ and $\mathbf{r}$. The resulting half-space is then added to the representation of $\mathbf{P}''$. Now, we proceed with any inequality of $\mathbf{P}'$ until all inequalities of $\mathbf{P}'$ are removed.

More sophisticated interpolations are possible but not investigated here.

4   Reachability Analysis Using Sops

In this section we first give a short outline of the reachability analysis for linear hybrid systems. Then we discuss the usage of sops as a novel exact data structure for the reachability analysis. We will observe the monotonic growth of the assembled sops. While the assembly can be done efficiently, any evaluation of the assembled sops by means of linear programs gets increasingly harder. Finally, we analyze why the LGG-algorithm is that much faster and show how to combine both approaches to obtain a fast and improved reachability algorithm.

Hybrid Systems. A hybrid system $H = (\mathrm{Var}, \mathrm{Mod}, \mathrm{Init}, \mathrm{LDE}, \mathrm{Inv}, \mathrm{Trans})$ encodes the nondeterministic evolution of some initial states over time. A *state* of the hybrid system is uniquely determined by the pair $(\mathbf{x}, m)$ of a real-valued vector $\mathbf{x} \in \mathbb{R}^d$ and a mode m of the finite set Mod of *modes*. A *symbolic state* is a pair $(\mathbf{P}, m)$ of a polyhedron $\mathbf{P} \subseteq \mathbb{R}^d$ and a mode $m \in \mathrm{Mod}$. Each dimension of $\mathbb{R}^d$ is associated with a variable in Var. Init is a designated set of *initial states*. Each mode m is associated with a linear differential equation in LDE of the form $\dot{\mathbf{x}}(t) = A\mathbf{x}(t) + \mathbf{u}(t)$ describing the time derivative of the evolution of the continuous variables Var during the mode m. Here, A is a real-valued $(d \times d)$-matrix, and $\mathbf{u}(t) \in \mathbf{U} \subseteq \mathbb{R}^d$ is given as a bounded polyhedron which models the set of disturbances or admissible inputs of the continuous flow. The system may only remain in a mode m as long as the state $(\mathbf{x}, m)$ is inside the associated

---

[2] In any case, it is possible to test whether the resulting half-space $\mathbf{H}$ is face-defining: Let d be the dimension of the affine hull of the sop $\mathbf{P}$ and $\mathbf{H}_=$ be the bounding hyperplane of $\mathbf{H}$. Then $\mathbf{H}$ is a facet-defining half-space if and only if $\mathrm{aff}(\mathbf{P} \cap \mathbf{H}_=)$ has the dimension $d - 1$. In practice, one has to solve several linear programs which makes this test costly.

invariant $(\mathbf{I}, m) \in$ Inv, i.e., $\mathbf{x}$ is in the polyhedron $\mathbf{I} \subseteq \mathbb{R}^d$. Further, for each mode m there is a finite number of associated discrete transitions. A discrete transition $(\mathbf{G}, m, \mathrm{Asgn}, m') \in$ Trans is enabled if the state $(\mathbf{x}, m)$ satisfies the guard $(\mathbf{G}, m)$, i.e., $\mathbf{x}$ is in the polyhedron $\mathbf{G} \subseteq \mathbb{R}^d$. If a transition is enabled, the state $(\mathbf{x}, m)$ may jump to $(\mathbf{x}', m')$, where $\mathbf{x}'$ is in the image of $\mathbf{x}$ under the affine transformation Asgn.

For safety checks, we additionally use specialized transitions $(\mathbf{U}, m, \emptyset, \emptyset)$. Here, $(\mathbf{U}, m)$ represents designated states for which we want to decide whether the system can reach these states. As soon as such a reachability is established we may stop the reachability analysis and return an appropriate message.

Reachability Analysis of Linear Hybrid Systems. As in [13], we define the discrete post-operator $\mathrm{post}_d(\mathbf{P}, m)$ as the set of states which are reachable by a discrete transition of $(\mathbf{P}, m)$ and the continuous post-operator $\mathrm{post}_c(\mathbf{P}, m)$ as the set of states which are reachable from $(\mathbf{P}, m)$ by letting an arbitrary amount of time elapse. The set $\mathcal{R}$ of reachable states is then the fix-point of the sequence

$$\mathcal{R}_0 = \mathrm{post}_c(\mathrm{Init}), \quad \mathcal{R}_{k+1} = \mathcal{R}_k \cup \mathrm{post}_c(\mathrm{post}_d(\mathcal{R}_k)).$$

The fix-point computation needs an efficient method to decide set entailment. We already mentioned that for support functions and sops we do not have such an efficient method at hand. While this deficiency might be compensated by using template polyhedra, we restrict this paper to bounded model checking, i.e., we do not compute the actual fix-point, but compute a restricted sequence until a given time bound is exceeded.

The discrete post-operator simply comprises the individual application of the affine transformations to the symbolic states and can be done efficiently using sops. Hence, we dedicate our attention to the continuous post-operator.

Reachability Analysis of Linear Systems. For each symbolic state $(\mathbf{X}_0, m)$, the continuous post-operator boils down to a reachability analysis of a single linear system, as it can be found in [13,20]: Given some initial state set $\mathbf{X}_0 \subseteq \mathbb{R}^d$, we want to compute all reachable states $\mathcal{R}_{[0,t]}$ within the time interval $[0, t]$ under the linear differential equation

$$\dot{\mathbf{x}}(t) = A\mathbf{x}(t) + \mathbf{u}(t), \qquad \mathbf{x}(0) \in \mathbf{X}_0, \ \mathbf{u}(t) \in \mathbf{U}.$$

The computation of the reachable set $\mathcal{R}_{[0,t]}(\mathbf{X}_0)$ is done by a step-wise computation of flow segments $\mathcal{R}_{[k\delta,(k+1)\delta]}(\mathbf{X}_0)$ over a time interval of length δ:

$$\mathcal{R}_{[0,t]}(\mathbf{X}_0) = \bigcup_{k=0,\ldots,N} \mathcal{R}_{[k\delta,(k+1)\delta]}(\mathbf{X}_0).$$

The computation is based on two important ingredients:

- the *initial segment* $\mathcal{R}_{[0,\delta]}(\mathbf{X}_0)$ and a set which collects the influence of the bounded inputs $\mathcal{R}_\delta(\{\mathbf{0}\}) := \mathcal{R}_{[\delta,\delta]}(\{\mathbf{0}\})$;
- the *exact* recurrence relation for $k > 0$

$$\mathcal{R}_{[k\delta,(k+1)\delta]}(\mathbf{X}_0) = e^{\delta A}\mathcal{R}_{[(k-1)\delta,k\delta]}(\mathbf{X}_0) + \mathcal{R}_\delta(\{\mathbf{0}\}). \qquad (1)$$

In general, the sets in the first item are not convex. Hence, one has to compute convex over-approximations of these sets, which is called the *initial bloating* procedure. The recurrence relation (1) is then applied to the bloated sets resulting in an over-approximation of the reachable sets.

Initial Bloating. In this section we discuss how to compute convex over-approximations $\mathbf{R}_0$ of $\mathcal{R}_{[0,\delta]}(\mathbf{X}_0)$ and $\mathbf{V}$ of $\mathcal{R}_\delta(\{\mathbf{0}\})$. There are several ways to compute such over-approximations, varying from conservative over-approximation [15] to an accurate bloating of the convex hull clconv$(\mathbf{X}_0 \cup e^{\delta A}(\mathbf{X}_0))$ [8]. The novel method given below is inspired by the method proposed by Le Guernic [20], which has been slightly improved and implemented in SPACEEX [13]. Anyhow, we cannot apply that bloating method directly, since we are dealing with polyhedral sets only, while the method of Le Guernic involves piecewise quadratic functions to describe the support function of the bloated sets. Although we made no effort to give an precise comparison of both bloating methods, we expect the support functions based method to provide better results in general. However, since sops also have support functions, the following bloating procedure can also be applied to reachability analysis using support functions. A detailed comparison of both bloating methods is considered as future work.

We use the superposition principle to decompose $\mathcal{R}_{[0,\delta]}(\mathbf{X}_0)$ into the sum

$$\mathcal{R}_{[0,\delta]}(\mathbf{X}_0) = \underbrace{\bigcup_{t\in[0,\delta]} e^{tA}(\mathbf{X}_0)}_{} + \underbrace{\bigcup_{t\in[0,\delta]} \mathcal{R}_t(\{\mathbf{0}\})}_{}.$$

The first summand $\bigcup_{t\in[0,\delta]} e^{tA}(\mathbf{X}_0)$ is exactly the set of reachable states of the related autonomous system $\dot{\mathbf{x}} = A\mathbf{x}$ within the time interval $[0,\delta]$ and the latter summand $\mathcal{R}_{[0,\delta]}(\{\mathbf{0}\}) = \bigcup_{t\in[0,\delta]} \mathcal{R}_t(\{\mathbf{0}\})$ accounts for the accumulated influences of all admissible inputs. We over-approximate both summands separately and add them afterwards to obtain an over-approximation of the reachable states of the nonautonomous system.

For the following let $\square(\mathbf{X})$ be the symmetric interval hull of $\mathbf{X}$, that is, $\square(\mathbf{X}) = [-z_1, z_1] \times \cdots \times [-z_d, z_d]$ where $z_i = \max\left(\left|\inf_{\mathbf{x}\in\mathbf{X}} \mathbf{e}_i^T\mathbf{x}\right|, \left|\sup_{\mathbf{x}\in\mathbf{X}} \mathbf{e}_i^T\mathbf{x}\right|\right)$. Further, let $|\mathbf{x}|$ and $|A|$ be the vector and the matrix where all coefficients are replaced by their absolute values. Hence, for any vector $\mathbf{x}$ and any set $\mathbf{X}$ we have $\mathbf{x} \leq |\mathbf{x}|$ and, if $\mathbf{x} \in \mathbf{X}$, then $|\mathbf{x}| \in \square(\mathbf{X})$. We define the abbreviation $[\![e^{\delta A}\mathbf{X}]\!] = \square\left(e^{\delta|A|}(\square(\mathbf{X}))\right)$ and obtain the following over-approximation of $e^{tA}(\mathbf{X}_0)$.

Lemma 1. *For all $t \in [0,\delta]$ the set inclusion $e^{tA}(\mathbf{X}) \subseteq [\![e^{\delta A}\mathbf{X}]\!]$ holds.*

The next lemma is based on a Taylor approximation of mth order and an over-approximation of the Lagrange form of the remainder involving Lemma 1.

Lemma 2. *For any nonnegative integer* m *and any* $t \in [0, \delta]$ *the following set inclusions hold*

$$e^{tA}(\mathbf{X}_0) \subseteq \sum_{k=0}^{m} \frac{t^k}{k!} A^k(\mathbf{X}_0) + \frac{t^{m+1}}{(m+1)!} A^{m+1}([\![e^{\delta A}\mathbf{X}_0]\!]),$$

$$\mathcal{R}_t(\{\mathbf{0}\}) \subseteq \sum_{k=0}^{m} \frac{t^{k+1}}{(k+1)!} A^k(\mathbf{U}) + \frac{t^{m+2}}{(m+2)!} A^{(m+1)}([\![e^{\delta A}\mathbf{U}]\!]). \qquad (2)$$

For $t = \delta$, (2) already provides an over-approximation of $\mathcal{R}_\delta(\{\mathbf{0}\})$. We choose $m = 0$ and obtain the first-order approximation

$$\mathbf{V} = \delta A^k(\mathbf{U}) + \frac{t^2}{2} A([\![e^{\delta A}\mathbf{U}]\!]) \supseteq \mathcal{R}_\delta(\{\mathbf{0}\}).$$

We use the fact, that for any $\mathbf{x}$, $k \geq 0$, and $t \in [0, \delta]$ the term $\frac{t^k}{k!} A^k \mathbf{x}$ can be written as the convex combination $(1 - \lambda)\mathbf{0} + \lambda \frac{\delta^k}{k!} A^k \mathbf{x}$ with $\lambda = \frac{t^k}{\delta^k}$, and hence, as stipulated, $0 \leq \lambda \leq 1$. We introduce the notion $\lhd(\mathbf{X}) = \text{clconv}(\{\mathbf{0}\} \cup \mathbf{X})$ and obtain a first-order approximations of $\bigcup_{t \in [0,\delta]} e^{tA}(\mathbf{X}_0)$ and $\bigcup_{t \in [0,\delta]} \mathcal{R}_t(\{\mathbf{0}\})$.

Lemma 3. *The following set inclusions hold*

$$\bigcup_{t \in [0,\delta]} e^{tA}(\mathbf{X}_0) \subseteq \mathbf{X}_0 + \lhd(\delta A(\mathbf{X}_0)) + \lhd\left(\frac{\delta^2}{2} A^2([\![e^{\delta A}\mathbf{X}_0]\!])\right),$$

$$\bigcup_{t \in [0,\delta]} \mathcal{R}_t(\{\mathbf{0}\}) \subseteq \lhd(\delta\mathbf{U}) + \lhd\left(\frac{\delta^2}{2} A([\![e^{\delta A}\mathbf{U}]\!])\right).$$

The first inclusion in Lemma 3 provides an over-approximation of the reachable states in forward direction. We may also compute an over-approximation in backward direction starting from $e^{\delta A}(\mathbf{X}_0)$. Finally we obtain the proposition:

Proposition 5 (Over-Approximation of $\mathcal{R}_{[0,\delta]}(\mathbf{X}_0)$). *Let* $\mathbf{X}_1 = e^{\delta A}(\mathbf{X}_0)$. *Then the following set inclusion holds:*

$$\mathcal{R}_{[0,\delta]}(\mathbf{X}_0) \subseteq \left(\mathbf{X}_0 + \lhd(\delta A(\mathbf{X}_0)) + \lhd\left(\frac{\delta^2}{2} A^2([\![e^{\delta A}(\mathbf{X}_0)]\!])\right)\right)$$

$$\cap \left(\mathbf{X}_1 + \lhd(-\delta A(\mathbf{X}_1)) + \lhd\left(\frac{\delta^2}{2}(-A)^2([\![e^{-\delta A}(\mathbf{X}_1)]\!])\right)\right)$$

$$+ \lhd(\delta\mathbf{U}) + \lhd\left(\frac{\delta^2}{2} A([\![e^{\delta A}(\mathbf{U})]\!])\right) = \mathbf{R}_0.$$

4.1 A Reachability Algorithm for Linear Systems with Invariants

We compute the reachable states of a linear system according to Algorithm 1 [20,21]. The inputs of the algorithm are the first flow segment $\mathbf{R}_0$, the set $\mathbf{V}$ – both obtained by the initial bloating procedure –, the invariant $\mathbf{I}$, and the set

---

Algorithm 1. Reachability Algorithm for a Linear System (SOP)

Input: the matrix A of the linear differential equation, an invariant $\mathbf{I}$, the set $\mathcal{G}$ of guards, an over-approximation $\mathbf{R}_0 \subseteq \mathbf{I}$ of $\mathcal{R}_{[0,\delta]}(\mathbf{X}_0)$, an over-approximation $\mathbf{V}$ of $\mathcal{R}_\delta(\{\mathbf{0}\})$, and an integer $N = \lfloor \frac{t}{\delta} \rfloor$.

Output: A collection of the intersections of $\mathcal{R}_{[0,t]}(\mathbf{X}_0)$ and the guards in $\mathcal{G}$.

1. **for** $k \leftarrow 0, \ldots, N$ **do**
2.   **if** $\mathbf{R}_k = \emptyset$ **then break;**
3.   **for** each guard $\mathbf{G}_j \in \mathcal{G}$ **do**
4.   **if** $\mathbf{R}_k \cap \mathbf{G}_j \neq \emptyset$ **then** collect the intersection $\mathbf{R}_k \cap \mathbf{G}_j$;
5.   **end for;**
6. $\mathbf{R}_{k+1} \leftarrow (e^{\delta A}\mathbf{R}_k + \mathbf{V}) \cap \mathbf{I};$
7. **end for;**
8. **return** collected intersections with the guards;

$\mathcal{G} = \{\mathbf{G}_1, \ldots, \mathbf{G}_g\}$ of guards. The computation of the next flow segment in Line 6 is based on (1). Additionally, this computation fully respects the influences of the invariant. Hence, the sequence $(\mathbf{R}_k)$ of flow segments computed by the algorithm is exact provided $\mathbf{R}_0$, $\mathbf{V}$, and $e^{\delta A}$ are exact. In Lines 3-5 the intersections of the current flow segment with the guards are computed and collected. Yet, we did not specify how the actual collection is performed. There are several possibilities varying from returning each single intersection, which potentially leads to a multiplication of the symbolic state sets, to returning the convex hull of all intersections. We implemented a collection strategy where an individual convex hull is assembled of all intersections for each guard traversal.

The following observations were made on a implementation of Algorithm 1.

1. The algorithm provides a new degree of exactness. The only theoretical source of inexactness are the computation of the matrix exponential $e^{\delta A}$, the over-approximations due to the initial bloating procedure, and the over-approximations in the collection step (Line 4). In practice, we also have to care for numerical issues due to the usage of floats.

2. The main drawback of a pure sop-based approach is the monotonic growth of the representation matrices of the involved sops. While the assembly of huge sops (Line 6) can be done efficiently, the evaluation of such sops gets increasingly harder. Based on our experiences we assess the following parts of the reachability analysis in order of increasing influence on the growth of the sops:

   (a) The initial bloating procedure has the mildest influence on the growth, since it is only applied once for each symbolic state.

   (b) The intersection with the invariant can be efficiently combined with a redundancy removal to avoid unneeded growth.

   (c) While the implemented collection strategy keeps the number of symbolic states small, the representation matrices of such collections can be quite large. The size is highly dependent on the time step parameter δ.

   (d) The Minkowski sum in Line 6 has the highest influence: A nonempty set $\mathbf{V}$ leads to a linear growth of the representation matrices.

4.2 Le Guernic and Girard's Reachability Algorithm

Compared in run-time, our prototype of Algorithm 1 is clearly behind the reachability algorithm of Le Guernic and Girard [21]. Algorithm 2 restates their algorithm in our context. The algorithm is based on a clever combination of support functions and template polyhedra and profits from the weaker handling of the invariant. In fact, the influence of the invariant only accounts for the current flow segment and is not carried over to the next flow segment. This leads to an efficient computation of the next flow segment in Lines 7–9, where the invariant is completely ignored. The influences of the bounded input are accumulated in the sequence (s_k), and, instead of updating the state set $\mathbf{R}_0$, only an updated template matrix T_{k+1} is computed; based on the fact that the optimal values of the two linear programs "maximize $\mathbf{n}^T\mathbf{x}$ subject to $\mathbf{x} \in e^{k\delta A}(\mathbf{R}_0)$" and "maximize $(\mathbf{n}^T e^{k\delta A})\mathbf{x}$ subject to $\mathbf{x} \in \mathbf{R}_0$" agree. In every step the computation of the template polyhedra $\mathbf{P}(T_0, \mathbf{b}_{k+1})$, which over-approximate the flow segments $\mathbf{R}_{k+1}$, can be done in constant time[3]. The quality of the over-approximation highly depends on the template matrix T_0. In order to improve the handling of the invariant, the facet normals of the invariant should be added to the template directions [13].

Algorithm 2. Reachability Algorithm for a Linear System (LGG)

Input: A, I, $\mathcal{G}$, $\mathbf{R}_0$, $\mathbf{V}$, N as specified in Algorithm 1 and an additional template polyhedron $\mathbf{P}(T_0, \mathbf{b}_0)$ over-approximating $\mathbf{R}_0$.

Output: A collection of the intersections of $\mathcal{R}_{[0,t]}(\mathbf{X}_0)$ and the guards in $\mathcal{G}$.

 1. $s_0 \leftarrow \mathbf{0}$;
 2. **for** $k \leftarrow 0, \dots, N$ **do**
 3.   **if** $\mathbf{P}(T_0, \mathbf{b}_k) \cap I = \emptyset$ **then break;**
 4.   **for** each guard $\mathbf{G}_j \in \mathcal{G}$ **do**
 5.   **if** $\mathbf{P}(T_0, \mathbf{b}_k) \cap I \cap \mathbf{G}_j \neq \emptyset$ **then** collect the intersection $\mathbf{P}(T_0, \mathbf{b}_k) \cap I \cap \mathbf{G}_j$;
 6.   **end for;**
 7. $s_{k+1} \leftarrow s_k + \mathbf{h}_\mathbf{V}(T_k)$;
 8. $T_{k+1} \leftarrow T_k e^{\delta A}$;
 9. $\mathbf{b}_k \leftarrow \mathbf{h}_{\mathbf{R}_0}(T_{k+1}) + s_{k+1}$;
10. **end for;**
11. **return** collected intersections with the guards;

Combining Algorithm 1 and Algorithm 2. Algorithm 3 is a combination of Algorithm 1 and Algorithm 2. While it preserves the exactness of the sop-based algorithm, all involved linear programs have a constant number of variables and constraints (Lines 3, 5, and 12). Also the assembly of the sop in Line 10 and

---

[3] This is more a practical observation than a theoretical result. Although there exists an algorithm which solves *rational* linear programs of fixed dimension and m constraints in $\mathcal{O}(m)$ elementary arithmetic operations on numbers of polynomial size, the complexity of linear programs is usually given by a polynomial bound which also depends on the maximum bit size of the coefficients [24].

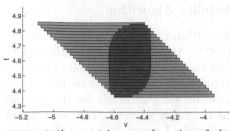

This figure shows the first intersection of a bouncing ball with the guard (the floor). For the model description see Sect. 5. We used the time step $\delta = 0.02$. The outer slices show the intersections computed by Algorithm 2 using a rectangular template matrix. Each inner slice shows a tight rectangular over-approximation of the sops computed by Algorithm 1. Their representation matrices reach a size of about 3500 rows and 2000 columns with 9000 nonzero coefficients. The convex hull of all intersections has a size of 82652 rows, 46999 columns and 283006 nonzero coefficients.

Fig. 1. Comparison of Algorithm 1 and 2

Line 12 can be done in constant time. Lines 10–13 are an equivalent replacement for the assignment $\mathbf{R}_{k+1} \leftarrow (e^{\delta A}\mathbf{R}_k + \mathbf{V}) \cap \mathbf{I}$ with an additional redundancy removal, see also Item 2b in Sect. 4.1.

Algorithm 3. Reachability Algorithm for a Linear System (SOP + LGG)

Input: A, I, $\mathcal{G}$, $\mathbf{R}_0$, $\mathbf{V}$, N as specified in Algorithm 1 and an additional template polyhedron $\mathbf{P}(T_0, \mathbf{b}_0)$ over-approximating $\mathbf{R}_0$.
Output: A collection of the intersections of $\mathcal{R}_{[0,t]}(\mathbf{X}_0)$ and the guards in $\mathcal{G}$.
1. $\mathbf{s}_0 \leftarrow \mathbf{0}$;
2. **for** $k \leftarrow 0, \ldots, N$ **do**
3.   **if** $\mathbf{P}(T_0, \mathbf{b}_k) \cap \mathbf{I} = \emptyset$ **then break**;
4.   **for** each guard $\mathbf{G}_j \in \mathcal{G}$ **do**
5.   **if** $\mathbf{P}(T_0, \mathbf{b}_k) \cap \mathbf{I} \cap \mathbf{G}_j \neq \emptyset$ **then** collect the intersection $\mathbf{R}_k \cap \mathbf{G}_j$;
6.   **end for**;
7. $\mathbf{s}_{k+1} \leftarrow \mathbf{s}_k + \mathbf{h}_{\mathbf{V}}(T_k)$;
8. $T_{k+1} \leftarrow T_k e^{\delta A}$;
9. $\mathbf{b}_{k+1} \leftarrow \mathbf{h}_{\mathbf{R}_0}(T_{k+1}) + \mathbf{s}_{k+1}$;
10. $\mathbf{R}_{k+1} \leftarrow e^{\delta A}\mathbf{R}_k + \mathbf{V}$;
11.   **for** each constraint $\mathbf{c}_i$ of $\mathbf{I}$ **do**
12.   **if** $\mathbf{c}_i$ is not redundant in $\mathbf{P}(T_0, \mathbf{b}_{k+1})$ **then** $\mathbf{R}_{k+1} \leftarrow \mathbf{R}_{k+1} \cap \mathbf{c}_i$;
13.   **end for**;
14. **end for**;
15. **return** collected intersections with the guards;

Fighting the Monotonic Growth by Interpolation. In practice, the step computation of Algorithm 3 is done in constant time. But the size of the sops still grows monotonically. While this growth can still be handled during the collection and the discrete updates, latest in the next continuous iteration, when the discrete post-image of a symbolic state is passed to Algorithm 3 again, the enormous size of the sop has an effect: All involved linear programs of Algorithm 3 have to be solved over systems of linear inequalities of enormous size.[4] To overcome this problem, we use the ray shooting based interpolation as described in Sect. 3.1. In every step, we have two representations of the current flow segment: the template polyhedron $\mathbf{P}(T_0, \mathbf{b}_k) \cap \mathbf{I}$ and the set $\mathbf{R}_k$ represented by a sop. Hence, we compute an interpolating $\mathcal{H}$-polyhedron $\mathbf{Q}$ with $\mathbf{R}_k \subseteq \mathbf{Q} \subseteq \mathbf{P}(T_0, \mathbf{b}_k) \cap \mathbf{I}$. This interpolating polyhedron is a tight over-approximation of $\mathbf{R}_k$ and is at least as good as the template polyhedron computed by the LGG-algorithm 2. Then we replace $\mathbf{R}_k$ by the interpolating polyhedron and still achieve results which are at least as good as the results we would achieve by the pure LGG-algorithm. In our prototype the interpolation and replacement of $\mathbf{R}_k$ is applied after `interpolate_after` step computations. The interpolation can be disabled by setting `interpolate_after` = 0.

We use a similar strategy to confine the growth of the collected intersections. Instead of building the convex hull of an arbitrary sequence, we apply the convex hull and the template hull on at most `max_conv_hull` consecutive elements of the sequence. Then we compute the interpolation between the template hull and the convex hull. The resulting interpolations form a new sequence for which we proceed as before. We iterate this process until only one element remains. Again, this interpolation strategy can be disabled. The resulting set is at least as good as the result one would achieve with template polyhedra only.

5 Experimental Results

We compare our prototypical implementations of Algorithm 3 and Algorithm 2 against the productive implementation of the LGG-algorithm in SPACEEX, where we used the SPACEEX Virtual Machine Server v0.9.8b for the comparison. The prototype, called SOAPBOX, is implemented in MATLAB and uses GUROBI OPTIMIZER 5.6[5] for the linear programming tasks. Furthermore, it has successfully been applied in a case study [10,11].

Bouncing Ball. For our benchmarks we have chosen a simple model of a bouncing ball. The dynamics of the model are given by $\dot{x} = v$, $\dot{v} = -1 \pm 0.05$, and $\dot{t} = 1$. The ball bounces as soon as it reaches the floor which is modeled by the invariant $x \geq 0$ and the transition $v \leftarrow -\frac{3}{4}v$, guarded by $x \leq 0$ and $v \leq 0$. The initial states are given by the interval hull of $10 \leq x \leq 10.2$, $0 \leq v \leq 0.2$, and $t = 0$.

Table 1 shows the run-times in seconds for different time steps δ and different numbers of iterations. Throughout all computations we used a rectangular template matrix, and the sop-specific configuration parameters were set as follows: `interpolate_after` = 20 and `max_conv_hull` = 4. Clearly, a C++-implementation of the LGG-algorithm, as it can be found in SPACEEX, outperforms our MATLAB-implementation. The run-times of our LGG-algorithm and

---

[4] Actually, the enormous size of the sops already effects the initial bloating procedure.
[5] http://www.gurobi.com

Table 1. Run-Time Comparison of Algorithm 3, Algorithm 2, and SPACEEx (SPX)

# It:	4			5			6		
δ	Alg. 3	Alg. 2	SPX	Alg. 3	Alg. 2	SPX	Alg. 3	Alg. 2	SPX
0.08	21.16	15.87	1.88	27.25	29.32	3.90	31.55	56.47	5.78
0.04	46.08	29.74	4.33	58.59	56.92	8.28	68.48	106.69	11.51
0.02	89.24	58.45	7.65	116.59	109.69	14.33	137.16	209.93	25.69
0.01	178.85	114.91	17.03	227.56	218.89	28.88	270.91	424.64	48.47

SPACEEx differ by a factor of 6.9 to 9.8. We have to bear in mind that SPACEEx additionally performs fix-point checks. Anyhow, the comparison with SPACEEx might give a hint what speed-up could be expected for a C++-implementation of our algorithms. We also should note that SPACEEx uses nonpolyhedral bloating.

More significant is a comparison of our prototypes of the LGG-algorithm 2 and the combined Algorithm 3, since they are embedded in the same overall reachability algorithm. For an increasing number of iterations, we observe that Algorithm 3 outperforms Algorithm 2 despite the computational overhead. Figure 2 shows the reachable positions x over the time t for 6 iterations. The left hand side diagram shows the reachable states computed by Algorithm 3 and the right hand side diagram shows the reachable states computed by the LGG-algorithm[6]. The reachable states computed by Algorithm 3 lie within the time interval $[0, 35]$, while the reachable states computed by the LGG-algorithm extend to nearly $t \in [0, 90]$ due to the poor handling of intersections and invariants. Hence, the LGG-algorithm has to perform much more flow-segment computations.

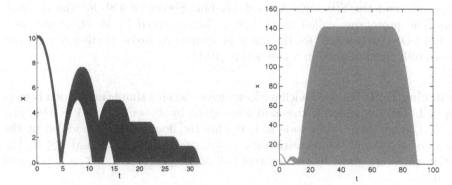

Fig. 2. Comparison of Algorithm 3 and SPACEEx

Approach Velocity Controller. In Fig. 3 we compare the reachable states computed by Algorithm 3 on the left and SPACEEx on the right. We used a rectangular template matrix and the parameters $\delta = 0.5$ and `interpolate_after` =

---

[6] The figure actually show the SPACEEx output. The output of Algorithm 2 looks quite the same, but we think it is more impressive to compare with SPACEEx here.

40. The underlying model is a single mode approach velocity controller (AVC). The AVC controls the velocity v of a following car in order to establish the desired distance d_{des} to the leading car which has the velocity v_a. The current distance of the cars can be read off the variable d. The dynamics are

$$\dot{d} = v_a - v, \qquad \dot{v} = 0.29(v_a - v) + 0.01(d - d_{des}), \qquad \dot{t} = 1,$$
$$-0.5 \le \dot{v}_a \le 0.5, \qquad 0 \le v_a \le 20. \tag{3}$$

The inequalities (3) restrict the allowed velocity of the leading car: While the differential inclusion allows some restricted change of the velocity, the invariant restricts the velocity to a bounded interval. Initially, both cars have a velocity of $20\frac{m}{s}$ and a distance of $450m$. By the invariant, the leader is not allowed to drive backward or exceed some maximal velocity. Clearly, one should expect that this behavior carries over to the following car, i. e., that the velocity of the follower is asymptotically bounded by some interval. A comparison of the right and the left figure shows that SPACEEX (right) is not able to establish any bound on the velocity of the follower while Algorithm 3 (left) shows the desired behavior.

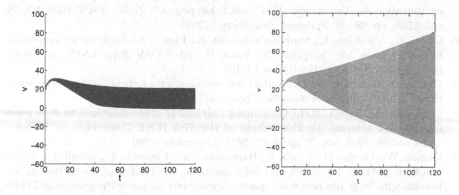

Fig. 3. Comparison of Algorithm 3 and SPACEEX

6   Conclusion

We introduced a novel representation class for polyhedra, the symbolic orthogonal projections (sops). Various geometric operations can efficiently be performed on this representation class. Together with linear programming, sops can be used to implement an reachability algorithm where all polyhedral operations are done exactly (Algorithm 1). Due to the monotonic growth of the representation size, this algorithm is not suitable for practical applications. After combining Algorithm 1 with the LGG-algorithm we achieve an efficient reachability algorithm (Algorithm 3). The applicability, accuracy, and efficiency of the resulting algorithm is demonstrated on some simple examples.

Acknowledgements. I would like to thank Uwe Waldmann for the useful discussion on this paper. Also, I am thankful for the anonymous reviewers for their constructive comments.

References

1. Althoff, M., Krogh, B.H.: Avoiding geometric intersection operations in reachability analysis of hybrid systems. In: Proceedings of the 15th ACM International Conference on Hybrid Systems: Computation and Control, HSCC 2012, pp. 45–54. ACM, New York (2012)
2. Asarin, E., Dang, T., Girard, A.: Reachability analysis of nonlinear systems using conservative approximation. In: Maler, O., Pnueli, A. (eds.) HSCC 2003. LNCS, vol. 2623, pp. 20–35. Springer, Heidelberg (2003)
3. Asarin, E., Dang, T., Girard, A.: Hybridization methods for the analysis of nonlinear systems. Acta Informatica 43(7), 451–476 (2007)
4. Asarin, E., Dang, T., Maler, O.: The d/dt tool for verification of hybrid systems. In: Brinksma, E., Larsen, K.G. (eds.) CAV 2002. LNCS, vol. 2404, pp. 365–370. Springer, Heidelberg (2002)
5. Bournez, O., Maler, O., Pnueli, A.: Orthogonal polyhedra: Representation and computation. In: Vaandrager, F.W., van Schuppen, J.H. (eds.) HSCC 1999. LNCS, vol. 1569, pp. 46–60. Springer, Heidelberg (1999)
6. Chen, X., Ábrahám, E., Sankaranarayanan, S.: Flow*: An analyzer for non-linear hybrid systems. In: Sharygina, N., Veith, H. (eds.) CAV 2013. LNCS, vol. 8044, pp. 258–263. Springer, Heidelberg (2013)
7. Chutinan, A., Krogh, B.: Computational techniques for hybrid system verification. IEEE Transactions on Automatic Control 48(1), 64–75 (2003)
8. Chutinan, A., Krogh, B.H.: Computing polyhedral approximations to flow pipes for dynamic systems. In: Proceedings of the 37th IEEE Conference on Decision and Control, 1998, vol. 2, pp. 2089–2094 (December 1998)
9. Damm, W., Dierks, H., Disch, S., Hagemann, W., Pigorsch, F., Scholl, C., Waldmann, U., Wirtz, B.: Exact and fully symbolic verification of linear hybrid automata with large discrete state spaces. Science of Computer Programming 77(10-11), 1122–1150 (2012), aVoCS 2009
10. Damm, W., Hagemann, W., Möhlmann, E., Rakow, A.: Component based design of hybrid systems: A case study on concurrency and coupling. Reports of SFB/TR 14 AVACS 95, SFB/TR 14 AVACS (2014), http://www.avacs.org, ISSN: 1860-9821
11. Damm, W., Möhlmann, E., Rakow, A.: Component based design of hybrid systems: A case study on concurrency and coupling. In: Proceedings of the 17th International Conference on Hybrid Systems: Computation and Control, HSCC 2014, pp. 145–150. ACM, New York (2014)
12. Dang, T., Maler, O., Testylier, R.: Accurate hybridization of nonlinear systems. In: Proceedings of the 13th ACM International Conference on Hybrid Systems: Computation and Control, HSCC 2010, pp. 11–20. ACM, New York (2010)
13. Frehse, G., et al.: SpaceEx: Scalable verification of hybrid systems. In: Gopalakrishnan, G., Qadeer, S. (eds.) CAV 2011. LNCS, vol. 6806, pp. 379–395. Springer, Heidelberg (2011)
14. Fukuda, K.: Lecture: Polyhedral computation, spring 2011 (2011), http://stat.ethz.ch/ifor/teaching/lectures/poly_comp_ss11/lecture_notes

15. Girard, A.: Reachability of uncertain linear systems using zonotopes. In: Morari, M., Thiele, L. (eds.) HSCC 2005. LNCS, vol. 3414, pp. 291–305. Springer, Heidelberg (2005)
16. Girard, A., Le Guernic, C.: Zonotope/hyperplane intersection for hybrid systems reachability analysis. In: Egerstedt, M., Mishra, B. (eds.) HSCC 2008. LNCS, vol. 4981, pp. 215–228. Springer, Heidelberg (2008)
17. Hagemann, W.: Reachability analysis of hybrid systems using symbolic orthogonal projections. Reports of SFB/TR 14 AVACS 98, SFB/TR 14 AVACS (2014), http://www.avacs.org, ISSN: 1860-9821
18. Henzinger, T.A., Ho, P.H., Wong-Toi, H.: Hytech: Amodel checker for hybrid systems. International Journal on Software Tools for Technology Transfer 1(1-2), 110–122 (1997)
19. Kurzhanski, A.B., Varaiya, P.: Ellipsoidal techniques for reachability analysis. In: Lynch, N.A., Krogh, B.H. (eds.) HSCC 2000. LNCS, vol. 1790, pp. 202–214. Springer, Heidelberg (2000)
20. Le Guernic, C.: Reachability analysis of hybrid systems with linear continuous dynamics. Ph.D. thesis, Université Grenoble 1 - Joseph Fourier (2009)
21. Le Guernic, C., Girard, A.: Reachability analysis of hybrid systems using support functions. In: Bouajjani, A., Maler, O. (eds.) CAV 2009. LNCS, vol. 5643, pp. 540–554. Springer, Heidelberg (2009)
22. Prabhakar, P., Viswanathan, M.: A dynamic algorithm for approximate flow computations. In: Proceedings of the 14th International Conference on Hybrid Systems: Computation and Control, HSCC 2011, pp. 133–142. ACM, New York (2011)
23. Sankaranarayanan, S., Dang, T., Ivančić, F.: Symbolic model checking of hybrid systems using template polyhedra. In: Ramakrishnan, C.R., Rehof, J. (eds.) TACAS 2008. LNCS, vol. 4963, pp. 188–202. Springer, Heidelberg (2008)
24. Schrijver, A.: Theory of Linear and Integer Programming. John Wiley & Sons, Chichester (1986)
25. Tiwary, H.R.: On the hardness of computing intersection, union and Minkowski sum of polytopes. Discrete & Computational Geometry 40(3), 469–479 (2008)
26. Ziegler, G.M.: Lectures on polytopes, vol. 152. Springer (1995)

Verifying LTL Properties of Hybrid Systems
with K-LIVENESS*

Alessandro Cimatti, Alberto Griggio, Sergio Mover, and Stefano Tonetta

Abstract. The verification of liveness properties is an important challenge in the design of real-time and hybrid systems.

In contrast to the verification of safety properties, for which there are several solutions available, there are really few tools that support liveness properties such as general LTL formulas for hybrid systems, even in the case of timed automata.

In the context of finite-state model checking, K-Liveness is a recently proposed algorithm that tackles the problem by proving that an accepting condition can be visited at most K times. K-Liveness has shown to be very efficient, thanks also to its tight integration with IC3, a very efficient technique for safety verification. Unfortunately, the approach is neither complete nor effective (even for simple properties) in the case of infinite-state systems with continuous time.

In this paper, we extend K-Liveness to deal with LTL for hybrid systems. On the theoretical side, we show how to extend the reduction from LTL to the reachability of an accepting condition in order to make the algorithm work with continuous time. In particular, we prove that the new reduction is complete for a class of rectangular hybrid automata, in the sense that the LTL property holds if and only if there exists K such that the accepting condition is visited at most K times. On the practical side, we present an efficient integration of K-Liveness in an SMT-version of IC3, and demonstrate its effectiveness on several benchmarks.

1 Introduction

Hybrid systems are an ideal modeling paradigm to represent embedded systems since they combine discrete behaviors, useful to model protocols and control components, with continuous behaviors, useful to model physical entities such as time, temperature, speed, etc. Hybrid systems are becoming increasingly interesting in order to apply formal methods to the design of safety-critical systems in different domains such as aerospace, railways, and automotive.

The verification of liveness properties on hybrid systems is very challenging because infinite paths must be considered. In particular, we focus on Linear-time Temporal Logic (LTL), which is suitable to represent many safety and liveness properties. The standard approach to verify if a model M satisfies an LTL property ϕ builds the automaton $M_{\neg\phi}$ equivalent to the negation of ϕ and check if the accepting state of the product $M \times M_{\neg\phi}$ can be visited infinitely often.

---

* This work was carried out within the D-MILS project, which is partially funded under the European Commission's Seventh Framework Programme (FP7).

A. Biere and R. Bloem (Eds.): CAV 2014, LNCS 8559, pp. 424–440, 2014.

In the context of finite-state model checking, many efficient algorithms reduce liveness properties to one or more safety properties. For example, K-LIVENESS is a recently proposed technique that proves that the accepting state is visited finitely many times by checking that it is visited at most K times for increasing values of K. The latter can be easily reduced to a reachability problem. K-Liveness has shown to be very efficient, thanks also to its tight integration with IC3, probably the current most effective technique for safety verification. Unfortunately, the approach is neither complete nor effective (even for simple properties) in the case of infinite-state systems with continuous time.

The main problem of techniques based on the reduction to safety is that they rely for soundness or completeness on the existence of a lasso-shape counterexample, but in the case of infinite-state systems such as hybrid systems, there may be infinite traces that do not correspond to any lasso-shape fair path. Moreover, the model may include Zeno paths where time converges, which must be excluded when checking the liveness properties. Techniques based on abstraction refinement can prove that a property holds, but in general the refinement is not guaranteed to converge.

In this paper, we provide a new method that, by forcing the progress of time beyond symbolic bounds, links the number of iterations of K-LIVENESS to the time elapsed in the counterexamples, rather than to the number of transitions. We prove that the reduction is complete for initialized Rectangular Hybrid Automata (RHA) with bounded non-determinism even in the presence of parameters. We implemented the techniques on top of HYCOMP [1], a tool for the verification of hybrid systems. The verification of reachability is based on an SMT version of IC3 that integrates predicate abstraction in an efficient way. An experimental evaluation demonstrates the efficiency of the approach on several benchmarks. To the best of our knowledge, this is the first effective tool that verifies general LTL properties on Hybrid Automata.

The paper is organized as follows: Section 2 presents some basic notations on RHA, LTL, and SMT-based techniques to verify hybrid systems; we also give a brief overview of IC3 and K-LIVENESS; in Section 3, we present the new approach to the LTL verification of hybrid systems; in Section 4, we overview the related work; in Section 5, we describe the implementation, the experimental evaluation, and we present the results; finally, in Section 6 we draw some conclusions and discuss future directions.

2 Background

2.1 Hybrid and Timed Automata

Hybrid systems have a discrete part, which ranges over the nodes of a graph, and a continuous part, which ranges over an Euclidian space $\mathbb{R}^n$. Although the approach presented in this paper can be applied to any hybrid system that can be encoded into a symbolic transition system, the theoretical results are restricted to the parametric version of *Rectangular Hybrid Automata* [2]. A Parametric Rectangular Hybrid Automaton (PRHA) is a tuple $H = \langle P, Q, Q_0, E, X, flow, init, inv, jump, guard, update \rangle$ where:

- P is a finite set of parameters,
- Q is the (possibly infinite) set of locations,
- $Q_0 \subseteq Q$ is the (possibly infinite) set of initial locations,

- $E \subseteq Q \times Q$ is the (possibly infinite) set of discrete transitions,
- X is the finite set of continuous variables,
- $flow : Q \to X \to \mathcal{R}$ is the flow function,
- $init : Q \to X \to \mathcal{R}(P)$ is the initial function,
- $inv : Q \to X \to \mathcal{R}(P)$ is the invariant function,
- $jump : E \to 2^X$ is the jump function,
- $guard : E \to X \to \mathcal{R}(P)$ is the guard function,
- $update : E \to X \to \mathcal{R}(P)$ is the update function,

where $\mathcal{R}$ is the set of (possibly unbounded) real intervals and $\mathcal{R}(P)$ represents the set of parametric intervals, whose endpoints are either a constant, or $\pm\infty$, or a parameter in P (e.g., $[0,0], (1,+\infty), (-\infty, p]$). We can see parametric intervals as function from an evaluation of the parameters to the intervals of $\mathbb{R}$. So, if c is an assignment to the parameters in P and $I \in \mathcal{R}(P)$, then $I(c)$ is a real interval.

A Rectangular Hybrid Automaton (RHA) is simply a PRHA with $P = \emptyset$. A (Parametric) Timed Automaton (TA) is an RHA (resp. PHRA) such that, for all $q \in Q$, for all $x \in X$, $flow(q)(x) = [1,1]$, $init(q)(x) = [0,0]$, and for all $e \in E$, for all $x \in X$, $update(e)(x) = [0,0]$. A (P)RHA H is *initialized* iff for every edge $\langle q, q' \rangle \in E$, for all $x \in X$, if $flow(q)(x) \neq flow(q')(x)$, then $x \in jump(\langle q, q' \rangle)$. H has bounded non-determinism iff for all $x \in X$, for all $q \in Q$, for all $e \in E$, $init(q)(x)$, $flow(q)(x)$, and $update(e)(x)$ are bounded.

As in [3], we use a variable $pc \notin X \cup P$ as a control variable that ranges over the set Q of locations (properly encoded in $\mathbb{R}$). Moreover, we use a variable $time$ to represent the elapsing time and let $V_H = \{time, pc\} \cup P \cup X$. A state is an assignment to V_H, i.e., a function $V_H \to \mathbb{R}$. We can see a state also as a tuple $\langle q, s, c, t \rangle$ where $q \in Q$, s is an assignment to X, c is an assignment to P, and t is an assignment to $time$. A path of a PRHA H is a sequence of states $\langle q_0, s_0, c_0, t_0 \rangle, \langle q_1, s_1, c_1, t_1 \rangle, \ldots$ such that:

- for all $i, j \geq 0$, $c_i = c_j = c$, for some c;
- $t_0 = 0$ and for all $i \geq 0$, $t_i \leq t_{i+1}$; let $\delta_i = t_{i+1} - t_i$;
- for all $i \geq 0$, if $\delta_i > 0$, then $q_{i-1} = q_i$ and, for all $x \in X$, $\frac{s_{i+1}(x) - s_i(x)}{\delta_i} \in flow(q_i)(x)$ (note that, in more general classes of hybrid automata, this would require a condition on all time points);
- $q_0 \in Q_0$ and, for all $x \in X$, $s_0(x) \in init(q_0)(x)(c)$;
- for all $i \geq 0$, if $\delta_i = 0$, then
  - $\langle q_i, q_{i+1} \rangle \in E$,
  - for all $x \notin jump(\langle q_i, q_{i+1} \rangle)$, $s_{i+1}(x) = s_i(x)$;
  - for all $x \in X$, $s_i(x) \in guard(\langle q_i, q_{i+1} \rangle)(x)(c)$;
  - for all $x \in jump(\langle q_i, q_{i+1} \rangle)$, $s_{i+1}(x) \in update(\langle q_i, q_{i+1} \rangle)(x)(c)$;
- for all $i \geq 0$, for all $x \in X$, $s_i(x) \in inv(q_i)(x)(c)$.

Given a sequence of states $\sigma = \sigma_0, \sigma_1, \ldots$, we denote with $\sigma[i]$ the $i + 1$-th state σ_i and with σ^i the suffix sequence starting from the $\sigma[i]$.

A path whose sequence $t_0, t_1, \ldots$ of time points does not diverge is called *Zeno path* (non-Zeno otherwise). A state s is *Zeno* or *time-locking* iff there is no non-Zeno path starting from s. A state s is reachable iff there exists a non-Zeno path σ such that $\sigma[i] = s$ for some $i \geq 0$.

2.2 LTL

We use Linear-time Temporal Logic (LTL) [4] to specify properties on a PRHA H. The atomic formulas *Atoms* are predicates over the variables V_H. Besides the Boolean connectives, LTL uses the temporal operators $\mathbf{X}$ ("next") and $\mathbf{U}$ ("until"). Formally,

- a predicate $a \in Atoms$ is an LTL formula,
- if ϕ_1 and ϕ_2 are LTL formulas, then $\neg\phi_1$, and $\phi_1 \wedge \phi_2$ are LTL formulas,
- if ϕ_1 and ϕ_2 are LTL formulas, then $\mathbf{X}\phi_1$ and $\phi_1\mathbf{U}\phi_2$ are LTL formulas.

We use the standard abbreviations: $\top := p \vee \neg p$, $\bot := p \wedge \neg p$, $\mathbf{F}\phi := \top\mathbf{U}\phi$, $\mathbf{G}\phi := \neg\mathbf{F}\neg\phi$, and $\phi_1\mathbf{R}\phi_2 := \neg(\neg\phi_1\mathbf{U}\neg\phi_2)$.

Given an LTL formula ϕ and a sequence σ of states of H, we define $\sigma \models \phi$, i.e., that the path σ satisfies the formula ϕ, as follows:

- $\sigma \models a$ iff $\sigma[0] \models a$ $- \sigma \models \phi \wedge \psi$ iff $\sigma \models \phi$ and $\sigma \models \psi$
- $\sigma \models \neg\phi$ iff $\sigma \not\models \phi$ $- \sigma \models \mathbf{X}\phi$ iff $\sigma^1 \models \phi$
- $\sigma \models \phi\mathbf{U}\psi$ iff for some $j \geq 0$, $\sigma^j \models \psi$ and for all $0 \leq k < j$, $\sigma^k \models \phi$.

Given a PRHA H and an LTL formula ϕ over V_H, we focus on the model checking problem of finding if, for all non-Zeno paths σ of H, $\sigma \models \phi$.

Note that, although the predicates can contain references to the *time* variable, the logic is interpreted over discrete sequences of states.

The problem is in general undecidable for PRHA and decidable for some fragments such as initialized RHA with bounded non-determinism [2].

2.3 Transition Systems

A *transition system* M is a tuple $M = \langle V, I, T \rangle$ where V is a set of (state) variables, $I(V)$ is a formula representing the initial states, and $T(V, V')$ is a formula representing the transitions. In this paper, we shall deal with *linear rational arithmetic* formulas, that is, Boolean combinations of propositional variables and linear inequalities over rational variables. A *state* of M is an assignment to the variables V. We denote with Σ_V the set of states. A [finite] *path* of M is an infinite sequence $s_0, s_1, \ldots$ [resp., finite sequence $s_0, s_1, \ldots, s_k$] of states such that $s_0 \models I$ and, for all $i \geq 0$ [resp., $0 \leq i < k$], $s_i, s'_{i+1} \models T$. Given two transitions systems $M_1 = \langle V_1, I_1, T_1 \rangle$ and $M_2 = \langle V_2, I_2, T_2 \rangle$, we denote with $M_1 \times M_2$ the synchronous product $\langle V_1 \cup V_2, I_1 \wedge I_2, T_1 \wedge T_2 \rangle$.

Given a Boolean combination ϕ of predicates, the invariant model checking problem, denoted with $M \models_{fin} \phi$, is the problem to check if, for all finite paths $s_0, s_1, \ldots, s_k$ of M, for all i, $0 \leq i \leq k$, $s_i \models \phi$.

Given a LTL formula ϕ, the LTL model checking problem, denoted with $M \models \phi$, is the problem to check if, for all (infinite) paths σ of M, $\sigma \models \phi$.

The automata-based approach [5] to LTL model checking is to build a transition system $M_{\neg\phi}$ with a fairness condition $f_{\neg\phi}$ such that $M \models \phi$ iff $M \times M_{\neg\phi} \models \mathbf{FG}\neg f_{\neg\phi}$. This reduces to finding a counterexample as a fair path, i.e., a path of the system that visits the fairness condition $f_{\neg\phi}$ infinitely many times. In case of finite-state systems, if the property fails there is always a counterexample in a lasso-shape, i.e., formed by a prefix and a loop.

2.4 SMT-Based Verification of Reachability for PRHA

Given a PRHA H, we encode H into a transition system M_H in order to apply SMT-based verification techniques for infinite-state systems. Such kind of encoding has been widely used in the literature (e.g., [6,7]). $M_H = \langle V_H, I_H, T_H \rangle$ is defined as follows:

- $I_H \stackrel{\text{def}}{=} (time = 0) \wedge \bigwedge_{q \in Q} \bigwedge_{x \in X} x \in init(q)(x) \wedge x \in inv(q)(x)$.

- $T_H \stackrel{\text{def}}{=} (\text{TIMED} \vee \text{UNTIMED}) \wedge \bigwedge_{q \in Q} inv(q)(X) \wedge inv(q)(X') \wedge \bigwedge_{p \in P} p' = p$, where

$\text{UNTIMED} \stackrel{\text{def}}{=} \quad \delta = 0 \wedge \bigwedge_{\langle q, q' \rangle \in E} (pc = q \wedge pc = q') \wedge \bigwedge_{x \in X} guard(q)(x) \wedge$

$\bigwedge_{x \notin jump(\langle q, q' \rangle)} x' = x \wedge \bigwedge_{x \in jump(\langle q, q' \rangle)} x' \in update(q)(x)$

$\text{TIMED} \stackrel{\text{def}}{=} \quad \delta > 0 \wedge pc' = pc \wedge \bigwedge_{q \in Q} \bigwedge_{x \in X} (pc = q \to (x' - x) \in \delta \cdot flow(q)(x))$

$\delta \stackrel{\text{def}}{=} time' - time$.

There is a one-to-one mapping between the states of H and those of M_H, and also between the paths of H and those of M_H. We say that a path of M_H is Zeno [non-Zeno] iff the sequence of assignments to $time$ does not diverge [resp., diverges].

Given a PRHA H, assuming that H does not have Zeno states, a state s is reachable in H iff $M_H \not\models_{fin} \neg s$ (where s is seen as a formula).

2.5 IC3 and K-LIVENESS

SAT-based algorithms take in input a propositional (with Boolean variables) transition system and a property, and try to solve the verification problem with a series of satisfiability queries. These algorithms can be naturally lifted to SMT in order to tackle the verification of infinite-state systems.

IC3 [8] is a SAT-based algorithm for the verification of invariant properties of transition systems. It builds an over-approximation of the reachable state space, using clauses obtained by generalization while disproving candidate counterexamples.

We recently presented in [9] a novel approach to lift IC3 to the SMT case, which is able to deal with infinite-state systems by means of a tight integration with *predicate abstraction* (PA) [10]. The approach leverages *Implicit Abstraction* (IA) [11], which allows to express abstract transitions without computing explicitly the abstract system, and is fully incremental with respect to the addition of new predicates.

In this paper, we focus on K-LIVENESS [12], an algorithm recently proposed to reduce liveness (and so also LTL verification) to a sequence of invariant checking. Differently from other reductions (such as [13]), it lifts naturally to infinite-state systems without requiring counterexamples to be in a lasso-shape form. K-LIVENESS uses a standard approach to reduce LTL verification for proving that a certain signal f is eventually never visited (**FG**$\neg f$). The key insight of K-LIVENESS is that, for finite-state systems, this is equivalent to find a K such that f is visited at most K times, which in turn can be reduced to invariant checking.

Given a transition system M, a Boolean combination of predicates ϕ, and a positive integer K, for every finite path σ of M, let $\sigma \models_{fin} \sharp(\phi) \leq K$ iff the size of the set $\{i \mid \sigma[i] \models \phi\}$ is less or equal to K. In [12], it is proved that, for finite-state systems, $M \models \mathbf{FG}\neg f$ iff there exists K such that $M \models_{fin} \sharp(f) \leq K$. The last check can be reduced to an invariant checking problem. K-LIVENESS is therefore a simple loop that increases K at every iteration and calls a subroutine SAFE to check the invariant.

In particular, the implementation in [12] uses IC3 as SAFE and exploits the incrementality of IC3 to solve the sequence of invariant problems in an efficient way.

3 SMT-Based Verification of LTL for PRHA

3.1 K-LIVENESS for Hybrid Automata

K-LIVENESS is not complete for infinite-state systems, because even if the property holds, the system may visit the fairness condition an unbounded number of times. Consider for example a system with an integer counter and a parameter p such that the counter is used to count the number of times the condition f is visited and once the counter reaches the value of p, the condition is no more visited. This system satisfies $\mathbf{FG} \neg f$ because for any value of p, f is visited at most p times. However, K-LIVENESS will obtain a counterexample to the safety property $\sharp(f) \leq K$ for every K, by setting p to K.

Similarly, K-LIVENESS does not work on the transition system representing a TA. In particular, a fair Zeno path forbids K-LIVENESS to prove the property: for every K, the fairness is visited more than K times, but in a finite amount of (real) time. Removing Zeno paths by adding an automaton to force progress is not sufficient for PTA and in general hybrid systems. In fact, in these systems a finite amount of time can be bounded by a parameter or a variable that is dynamically set. Therefore, in some cases, there is no K to bound the occurrences of the fairness, although there is no fair non-Zeno path.

In the following, we show how we make K-LIVENESS work on hybrid automata. The goal is to provide a method so that K-LIVENESS checks if there is a bound on the number of times the fairness is visited along a diverging sequence of time points. The essential point is to use a symbolic expression β based on the automaton structure to force a minimum distance between two fair time points. We use an additional transition system Z_β, with a condition f_Z, to reduce the problem of proving that $H \models \phi$ to proving that $M_H \times M_{\neg \phi} \times Z_\beta \models \mathbf{FG} \neg f_Z$. In Section 3.2, we prove that the two problems are equivalent for any positive β. In Section 3.3, we define β so that K-LIVENESS is not deemed to diverge and, on the contrary, must converge for some class of automata.

3.2 Linking the Fairness to Time Progress

In this section, we define the transition system Z_β that is later used to make K-LIVENESS converge. We first define a simpler version Z_B that works only for timed automata.

Consider the fair transition system $M = M_H \times M_{\neg \phi}$ resulting from the product of the encoding of an PRHA H and of the negation of the property ϕ. Let f be the fairness condition of M. We build a new transition system $Z_B(f, time)$ that filters the occurrences of f along a time sequence where $time$ values are distant more than B time units. $Z_B(f, time)$ is depicted in Figure 1. It has two locations (represented by a Boolean variable l) and a local real variable t_0. The initial condition is $l = 0$. The fairness condition f_Z is $l = 1$. The system moves or remains in $l = 0$ keeping t_0 unchanged. It moves or remains in $l = 1$ if f is true and $time \geq t_0 + B$ and sets t_0 to $time$.

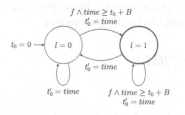

Fig. 1. Monitor $Z_B(f, time)$

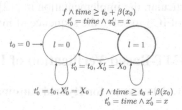

Fig. 2. Monitor $Z_\beta(f, time, X)$

We reduce the problem of checking whether ϕ holds in H to checking that the fairness condition f_Z cannot be true infinitely often in $M_H \times M_{\neg\phi} \times Z_B$, i.e. $M_H \times M_{\neg\phi} \times Z_B \models \mathbf{FG}\neg f_Z$.

Theorem 1. *If $B > 0$, $H \models \phi$ iff $M_H \times M_{\neg\phi} \times Z_B \models \mathbf{FG}\neg f_Z$.*

Proof. If there exists a non-Zeno path π of M_H that violates ϕ, then there exists a fair path π' of $M_{\neg\phi}$ so that $\pi \times \pi'$ is a fair non-Zeno path of $M \times M_{\neg\phi}$. We can build a matching path π_Z of Z_B. In fact, if the path $\pi_Z[i]$ is in $l = 0$, there are infinitely many $j \geq i$ such that $\pi'(j) \models f_{\neg\phi}$ and we can pick one moving to $l = 1$ with $time(j) > time(i) + B$ since π is non-Zeno.

If a path π of $M \times M_{\neg\phi} \times Z_B$ visits f_Z infinitely often, then for infinitely many points $i \geq 0$, $\pi^i \models f_{\neg\phi}$ and there exists $j \geq i$ such that $\pi^j \models f_{\neg\phi} \wedge time > t_0 + B$. Therefore the projection of π over M_H corresponds to a fair non-Zeno path of H violating ϕ. $\square$

We generalize the construction of Z_B considering as bound on time a function β over some continuous variables of the model. The new monitor is $Z_\beta(f, time, X)$ shown in Figure 2. It has a local variable x_0 for every variable x occurring in β. X_0 is the set of such variables. Now, when t_0 is set to $time$, we set also x_0 to x and this value is kept until moving to $l = 1$. The condition on time is now $time > t_0 + \beta(X_0)$. It is easy to see that we can still prove that if $\beta(X)$ is always positive, then $H \models \phi$ iff $M_H \times M_{\neg\phi} \times Z_\beta \models \mathbf{FG}\neg f_Z$.

We say that the reduction is *complete* for K-LIVENESS for a certain class $\mathcal{H}$ of automata iff for every $H \in \mathcal{H}$ there exists β_H such that $H \models \phi$ iff there exists K such that $M \times M_{\neg\phi} \times Z_{\beta_H} \models_{fin} \sharp(f_Z) \leq K$. Thus, if $H \models \phi$, and the reduction is complete, and the subroutine SAFE terminates at every call, then K-LIVENESS also terminates proving the property.

3.3 The K-ZENO Algorithm

The K-ZENO algorithm is a simple extension of K-LIVENESS which, given the problem $H \models \phi$, builds $M = M_H \times M_{\neg\phi} \times Z_\beta$ and calls K-LIVENESS with inputs M and f_Z. As K-LIVENESS, either K-ZENO proves that the property holds or diverges increasing K up to a certain bound. The crucial part is the choice of β, because the completeness of the reduction depends on β. Note that the reduction may be complete, but the completeness of K-ZENO still depends on the completeness of the SAFE algorithm.

As for TAs, we take as β the maximum among the constants of the model and 1. For example, consider the TA in figure 3 (it is actually a compact representation of the TA where $loc1$ is split into two locations corresponding to $b = \top$ and $b = \bot$). It represents an unbounded number of switches of b within 1 time unit. The model satisfies the property $\mathbf{FG}pc = loc2$. Taking $\beta = 1$, K-ZENO proves the property with $K = 1$. In fact, starting from the location $loc1$, after 1 time unit, the automaton cannot reach $loc1$ anymore. For PTAs, we consider as β the maximum among the parameters, the constants of the model and 1.

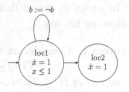

Fig. 3. Example of TA

We generalize the above idea to consider PRHA with bounded non-determinism. We also assume an endpoint of a flow interval is 0, it cannot be open (must me included in the interval). Guards and invariants of PRHA are conjunctions of inequalities of the form $x \bowtie B$ where $\bowtie \in \{\leq, \geq, <, >\}$. Hereafter, we refer to one of such inequalities as a *constraint* of the PRHA.

For every constraint g in the form $x \leq B$ or $x < B$ (guard or invariant) of HA, we consider the minimum positive lower bound r_g for the derivative of x, if exists. For example, if we have three locations with $\dot{x} \in [1, 2]$, $\dot{x} \in [0, 3]$, $\dot{x} \in [-1, 2]$, we take $r_g = 1$ (since 0 and -1 are not positive). We consider the minimum lower bound v_g for the non-deterministic reset of x. For example, if we have three transitions with resets $x' \in [1, 2]$, $x' \in [0, 3]$, $x' \in [-1, 2]$, we take $v_g = -1$. In case g is in the form $x \geq B$ or $x > B$, we define r_g and v_g similarly by considering the maximum negative upper bound of the derivative of x and the maximum upper bound of the reset of x. We define the bound $\beta_g(x_0)$ as follows: $\beta_g(x_0) = max((B - x_0)/r_g, (B - v_g)/r_g)$.

Finally, as β we take the maximum among the β_g for all g in the automaton H for which r_g exists and the constant 1. Note that this coincides with the β defined above for TA and Parametric TA, where r_g is always 1 and v_g is always 0 and x_0 is always non negative.

3.4 Completeness for Rectangular Hybrid Automata

In this section, we restrict the focus to PRHA that are initialized and have bounded non-determinism. Moreover, we restrict the LTL formula to have the atoms that predicate over pc only. In this settings, we prove that the reduction to K-LIVENESS defined in the previous section is complete.

Given a PRHA $H = \langle P, Q, Q_0, E, X, flow, init, inv, jump, guard, update \rangle$ and an LTL formula ϕ with transition system $M_{\neg\phi} = \langle V, I, T \rangle$ and fairness condition $f_{\neg\phi}$, we build a new PRHA $H_{\neg\phi} = \langle P, Q', Q_0', E', X, flow', init', inv', jump', guard', update' \rangle$ where:

- $Q' = \{q \times s \in Q \times \Sigma_V \mid q \in Q, s \models q\}$;
- $Q_0' = \{q \times s \in Q' \mid q \in Q_0, s \models I\}$;
- $E' = \{\langle q \times s, q' \times s' \rangle \in Q' \times Q' \mid \langle q, q' \rangle \in E, s, s' \models T\}$;
- for all $q \times s \in Q$, $flow'(q \times s) = flow(q)$, $init'(q \times s) = init(q)$, $inv'(q \times s) = inv(q)$; for all $\langle q \times s, q' \times s' \rangle \in E'$, $jump'(\langle q \times s, q' \times s' \rangle) = jump(\langle q, q' \rangle)$, $guard'(\langle q \times s, q' \times s' \rangle) = guard(\langle q, q' \rangle)$, $update'(\langle q \times s, q' \times s' \rangle) = update(\langle q, q' \rangle)$.

It is easy to see that $H \models \phi$ iff $H_{\neg\phi} \models \mathbf{FG}\neg f_{\neg\phi}$ iff $M_{H_{\neg\phi}} \times Z_\beta \models \mathbf{FG}\neg f_Z$.

In order to prove that the reduction to K-LIVENESS is complete, we prove the following lemma.

Lemma 1. *Consider an initialized with bounded non-determinism PRHA H. Suppose* $M_{H_{\neg\phi}} \times Z_\beta \models \mathbf{FG}\neg f_Z$. *Let* K_H *and* N_H *be respectively the number of edges and locations of* $H_{\neg\phi}$. *Then* $M_{H_{\neg\phi}} \times Z_\beta \models_{fin} \sharp(f_Z) \leq (K_C \cdot N_C) + 1$.

Proof. We prove the lemma by induction on K_H. Suppose $K_H = 0$, i.e., there is no edge. Therefore, there cannot be a reset of the variables and, therefore, the time spent along a path of $M_{H_{\neg\phi}} \times Z_\beta$ must be less than $\beta(X_0)$ where X_0 is the initial value of X. Thus, f_Z cannot be visited twice.

Suppose $K_H \geq 1$. First, note that, since $M_{H_{\neg\phi}} \times Z_\beta \models \mathbf{FG}\neg f_Z$, $M_{H_{\neg\phi}} \times Z_\beta$ cannot have fair non-Zeno paths. Therefore, for every fair path σ of $M_{H_{\neg\phi}}$, there must be a constraint (or more than one) of $H_{\neg\phi}$ that eventually blocks the transition to f_Z in Z_β. Suppose f_Z is visited at least once (although for a finite number of times). Then, there must exist an edge e of $H_{\neg\phi}$ that is eventually no more taken along σ. Therefore, σ, after a certain point t, will coincide with a path of $M_{H'}$ where $M_{H'}$ is the encoding of a PRHA H' obtained from $H_{\neg\phi}$ by removing e and setting as initial state the state reached by σ at point t. Therefore $M_{H'} \times Z_\beta \models \mathbf{FG}\neg f_Z$ and H' has $K_H - 1$ edges. Thus, by induction f_Z must be visited less or equal than $(K_H - 1) \cdot N_H + 1$ times.

Finally we have to show that the number of times f_Z is visited before t is less than or equal to N_H. Suppose by contradiction, f_Z is visited $N_H + 1$ times. Then, at least one fair location of $H_{\neg\phi}$ is repeated so that we have a fair loop in the graph of $H_{\neg\phi}$. Due to the definition of Z_β, for any constraint $\bar{g}$ in the form $\bar{x} \leq B$ (and similar for the other cases), if $\bar{x}$ has a positive derivative and is not reset, $\bar{g}$ must become false between two fair states. Thus, either $\bar{g}$ is not used along the loop or $\bar{x}$ is reset or the derivative may be non positive. Since H is initialized, if the lower bound of the derivative becomes non positive, $\bar{x}$ must be reset. Therefore, every variable involved in a constraint along the path must be reset or the derivative can remain non-positive never violating the constraint. This means that there would be an infinite fair non-Zeno loop, which contradicts the hypothesis. We conclude that the number of times f_Z can be visited along σ is less than $(K_H - 1) \cdot N_H + 1 + N_H = (K_H \cdot N_H) + 1$.   □

Theorem 2. *If* $H \models \phi$, *then there exists* K *such that* $M_H \times M_{\neg\phi} \times Z_\beta \models_{fin} \sharp(f_Z) \leq K$.

Proof. Since there exists a one-to-one mapping between the paths of $M_H \times M_{\neg\phi} \times Z_\beta$ and those of $M_{H_{\neg\phi}} \times Z_\beta$, by Lemma 1, $M_H \times M_{\neg\phi} \times Z_\beta \models_{fin} \sharp(f_Z) \leq (K_H \cdot N_H) + 1$ where K_H and N_H are respectively the edges and locations of $H_{\neg\phi}$.   □

If the hybrid automaton falls outside of the class of initialized PRHA with bounded non-determinism, K-ZENO is still sound, but no longer guaranteed to be complete. A simple counterexample is shown in Figure 4, in which the stopwatch variable x is not reset when its dynamic changes. The automaton satisfies the property ($\mathbf{FG}good$), because the invariant on x and the guard on y make sure that the total time spent in *bad* is at most 1

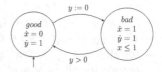

Fig. 4. Stopwatch automaton

time unit. However, K-ZENO cannot prove it with any K because time can pass indefinitely in *good*, while x is stopped. Therefore, it is always possible to visit *bad* and f_Z an unbounded number of times. Finally, note that K-ZENO is able to prove other properties such as for example that the stopwatch automaton satisfies the formula **GF** *good*.

4 Related Work

There are many works that focus on the verification of safety properties on hybrid systems [14,15,16,17,18,19], see [20] for a recent survey. We concentrate on the problem of liveness and deal with a semantics based on infinite paths.

The problem of checking time progress is well known and efficient solutions for TAs are based either on transforming the automaton in a strongly non-Zeno automaton [21], forcing the original TA to move to an additional (non-accepting) location in case of Zeno behavior, or on checking if from all reachable states, time can elapse from the 1 time unit [22]. In UPPAAL, this is achieved by taking the product of the model with a monitor automaton that changes state every c time units (where c is a "constant set to a good value w.r.t. the rest of the model") [23]. This approach is also used by DIVINE [24], an explicit-state model checker that is capable of verifying LTL properties over UPPAAL models. The monitors that we use in K-ZENO can be seen as a generalization of this approach. As discussed, using a constant is not enough for PTAs and (P)RHAs. Our method uses as bounds for time progress symbolic expressions over variables that change along a path.

A well-known reduction of liveness to safety is presented in [13]. The approach uses copies of the state variables to store the value of a state and search for a fair loop. In [25], the above technique is extended for different kinds of infinite-state systems such as pushdown systems and TAs, but each reduction is ad-hoc for the specific class of systems. A similar technique is also used in [26] for hybrid systems. The technique is not sound in general for infinite-state systems because there are simple cases where there are counterexamples but none of them has a lasso shape. So, it may be possible that the invariant holds in the reduced system but the original property does not hold. K-LIVENESS and K-ZENO are always sound: if the invariant holds for some K, then the original property is true.

Restricted to timed automata, apart from DIVINE, the UPPAAL model checker [27] does not support LTL, but a different fragment of temporal properties. However, this fragment of temporal logic does not consider infinite Zeno paths, but it is based on finite paths that possibly end in time-locks. A recent approach [28] considers LTL model checking for TAs. However, the authors explicitly assume to have TAs without Zeno paths. First, our approach differs since we allow Zeno paths in the model. Then, our technique is more general, since we handle hybrid automata with parameters.

With respect to hybrid systems, an interesting liveness property is stability, which requires that all the paths of the system eventually stay in a region. The work [29] reduces the verification of stability properties to compute a special kind of relations, called *snapshot sequences*, and to prove that these relations are well-founded. In principle, the same approach could be used to verify general LTL properties. However, the application of this technique to LTL properties seems not straightworward and we are not aware of a publicly-available implementation with which to compare. Stability is reduced to termination analysis also in [30], assuming non-Zeno hybrid automata (i.e. bounded switching speed). In contrast, we focus on LTL properties and we take into account Zeno paths. In [31] the authors consider the problem of LTL model checking for discrete-time robust hybrid systems. Instead, we consider continuous-time systems.

Another line of work [32,33,34] for timed and hybrid systems focuses only on the falsification problem (i.e. find a counterexample if the LTL property does not hold). For timed automata, the work in [32] extends SMT-based BMC to search for a lasso-shaped path in the region abstraction. The proposed encoding also removes Zeno paths and, due to its nature, it could be used to complement our technique in the TA case to find counterexamples. For hybrid systems, the approach presented in [33] falsifies an LTL property by a randomized search while the one in [34] falsifies an MTL property under robustness assumptions. Both approaches do not consider Zeno paths and are not able to prove that a property holds.

Using the technique of [35], LTL model checking of infinite-state systems (including hybrid automata) may be reduced to finding disjunctively well-founded transition invariants, whose discovery can then be attempted with a solver for recursive Horn-like clauses like HSF [36]. However, the current implementation of HSF does not handle strict inequalities with real variables (e.g. $A < B$ is converted into $A + 1 \leq B$), and thus it cannot be applied easily to real-time systems.

5   Experimental Evaluation

5.1   Implementation

We have implemented the K-ZENO algorithm on top of the SMT extension of IC3 described in [9]. Given a symbolic system M and an LTL property ϕ, we use HYCOMP [1] (an extension of the NUSMV model checker) to generate the transition system $M_{\neg\phi}$ and to compute the function β for the transition system $Z_\beta(f, time, X)$ of Figure 2. $Z_\beta(f, time, X)$ is then added automatically to the system. In order to count the number of violations of f_Z, we use a simple integer counter. We remark that, although the completeness results hold only for initialized PHRA with bounded non-determinism, our implementation supports a more general class of HAs with rectangular dynamics. However, it currently can only be used to *verify* LTL properties, and not to disprove them. If a property does not hold, our tool does not terminate. Similarly to the Boolean case [12], our implementation consists of relatively few (and simple) lines of code on top of IC3. Both the tool and the benchmarks used in the evaluation can be downloaded at http://es.fbk.eu/people/griggio/papers/cav14-kzeno.tar.bz2 for reproducing our results.

5.2   Benchmarks

We tried our approach on various kinds of benchmarks and properties.

Fischer family benchmarks. We considered 4 different versions of the Fischer mutual exclusion protocol: the TA version from the UPPAAL distribution (*Fischer*), a parametric version (*Fischer Param*), a hybrid one (*Fischer Hybrid*), and one that ensures that every request is eventually served (*Fischer Fair*). All the variants are scalable in the number of processes involved, except for *Fischer Fair* that only considers 2 processes.

Distributed Controller [37] models the interactions of n sensors with a preemptive scheduler and a controller. We scaled the benchmark increasing the number of sensors.

Nuclear Reactor [38] models the control of a nuclear reactor with n rods. The benchmark is scaled increasing the number of control rods in the reactor.

Navigation family benchmarks: the models are inspired by the benchmarks presented in [39]. The benchmark describes the movement of an object in an $n \times n$ grid of square cells. Independently from the initial position, the object will eventually reach and stay in a target region. We created two versions of the benchmark, depending on whether the initial position of the object is given (*NavigationInit*) or not (*NavigationFree*). The benchmark is scaled by increasing the number of cells in the grid.

Diesel Generator [32]: the benchmark is an *industrial* model of an emergency diesel generator intended for the use in a nuclear power plant. The benchmark has three different versions (*small, medium, large*).

Bridge: the benchmark is from the UPPAAL distribution and models the bridge and torch puzzle. We used the same LTL properties used in the distribution of DIVINE [24].

Counter: the benchmark consists of an automaton with two locations, *bad* and *good*, and $n + 1$ clocks, $x_0, x_1, \ldots, x_n$. The initial location *bad* has the invariant $x_0 \leq 1$ and a transition to *good*. *bad* has n self loops: each i-th self loop has guard $x_i \leq 1$ and reset x_{i-1}. The automaton is shown in Figure 5. On this model the LTL property ($\mathbf{FG}$ *good*) holds, since x_0 will eventually reach $x = 1$, forcing the transition to *good*. The example is interesting because the actual K needed to prove the property depends on the number of edges of the model, as shown in Lemma 1.

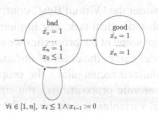

Fig. 5. *Counter* with $n + 1$ clocks

Note that the benchmarks fall in different classes: some of them are timed automata (*Fischer, Diesel Generator, Bridge, Counter*), some are parametrized timed automata (*Fischer Param, Fischer Fair*), some are initialized rectangular automata (*Fischer Hybrid, Nuclear Reactor*), while some have rectangular dynamics but are not initialized (*Distributed Controller, NavigationInit, NavigationFree*).

We manually generated several meaningful LTL properties for the benchmarks of the Fischer family, the *Distributed Controller* and the *Nuclear Reactor*. The properties match several common patterns for LTL like fairness ($\mathbf{GF}p$), strong fairness ($\mathbf{GF}p \rightarrow \mathbf{GF}q$), and "leads to" ($\mathbf{G}(p \rightarrow \mathbf{F}q)$). Moreover, in several cases we added additional fairness constraints to the common patterns to generate properties that hold in the model. For the *Bridge* and *Diesel Generator* benchmarks we used the properties already specified in the models. For the navigation benchmark we checked that eventually the object will stay forever in the "stability" region. Finally, we used the property ($\mathbf{FG}$ *good*) in the *Counter* benchmarks.

Table 1. Selected experimental results

Instance	Class	Property	# Bool vars	# Real vars	Trans size	k	Time
Fischer (8 processes)	T	$(\bigwedge_{i=1}^{17} \mathbf{GF}p_i) \to \mathbf{G}(\neg p_{18} \to \mathbf{F}p_{18})$	132	20	1286	3	6.37
Fischer Fair (2 processes)	P	$(p_1 \wedge \mathbf{GF}p_2) \to \mathbf{G}(p_3 \to \mathbf{F}p_4)$	38	12	622	4	76.14
Fischer Hybrid (10 procs)	R	$(\mathbf{GF}p_1 \wedge \mathbf{GF}p_2 \wedge \mathbf{FG}p_3) \to \mathbf{G}(p_4 \to \mathbf{F}p_5)$	106	64	8759	1	325.03
Dist Controller (3 sensors)	N	$(\mathbf{GF}p_1) \to (\mathbf{GF}p_2)$	58	27	1737	1	397.24
Nuclear Reactor (9 rods)	R	$\mathbf{G}(p_1 \to \mathbf{F}p_2)$	82	24	3258	1	530.40
NavigationInit (3x3)	N	$\mathbf{FG}(p_1 \vee p_2 \vee p_3 \vee p_4)$	16	8	808	2	4.37
NavigationInit (10x10)	N	$\mathbf{FG}(p_1 \vee p_2 \vee p_3 \vee p_4)$	22	8	4030	2	453.74
NavigationFree (3x3)	N	$\mathbf{FG}(p_1 \vee p_2 \vee p_3 \vee p_4)$	16	8	808	2	3.37
NavigationFree (9x9)	N	$\mathbf{FG}(p_1 \vee p_2 \vee p_3 \vee p_4)$	22	8	3461	2	872.07
Counter 10	T	$\mathbf{FG}p$	10	24	294	10	52.74
Diesel Gen (small)	T	$\mathbf{G}(p_1 \to \mathbf{F}(\neg p_2 \vee p_3))$	84	24	724	1	16.55
Diesel Gen (medium)	T	$\mathbf{G}(p_1 \to \mathbf{F}(\neg p_2 \vee p_3))$	140	30	1184	1	51.24
Diesel Gen (large)	T	$\mathbf{G}(p_1 \to \mathbf{F}(\neg p_2 \vee p_3 \vee p_4))$	264	62	2567	1	538.39

Classes: T: timed, P: parametric timed, R: rectangular, N: non-initialized rectangular.

5.3   Evaluation

Effectiveness. In order to evaluate the feasibility of our approach, we have run it on a total of 276 verification tasks, consisting of various LTL properties on the benchmark families described above. Our best configuration could solve 205 instances within the resource constraints (900 seconds of CPU time and 3Gb of memory). If instead we consider the "Virtual Best" configuration, obtained by picking the best configuration for each individual task, our implementation could solve 238 problems. We report details about some of the properties we could prove in Table 1. On each row, the table shows the model name, the class of instances it belongs to (timed, parametric, rectangular, non-initialized rectangular), the property proved (with variables p_i's used as placeholders for atomic propositions), the size of the symbolic encoding (number of Boolean and Real variables, and number of nodes in the formula DAG of the transition relation), the value of k reached by K-LIVENESS[1], and the total execution time. We remark that we are not aware of any other tool capable of verifying similar kinds of LTL properties on the full class of instances we support.

Heuristics and Implementation Choices. We analyze the performance impact of different heuristics and implementation choices along the following dimensions:

Invariant checking engine. We have two versions of SMT-based IC3, one based on approximated preimage computations with quantifier elimination (called IC3(QE) here), and one based on implicit predicate abstraction (IC3(IA)). Our recent results [9] indicate that IC3(IA) is generally superior to IC3(QE) on software verification benchmarks. However, the situation is less clear in the domain of timed and hybrid systems.

Incrementality. We compare our fully-incremental implementation of K-LIVENESS to a non-incremental one, in which IC3 is restarted from scratch every time the K-LIVENESS counter is incremented.

---

[1] On most of the instances the value of k reached by K-LIVENESS is small. The explanation is that, on real models, the number of constraints that must be violated inside a loop that contains $f_{\neg\phi}$ before time diverges is usually low. The benchmarks of the *Counter* family were created on purpose, to show that k can increase arbitrarily.

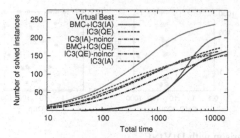

Configuration	# solved	Tot time
Virtual Best	238	10603
BMC+IC3(IA)	205	13525
IC3(QE)	173	12895
IC3(IA)-NOINCR	164	12476
BMC+IC3(QE)	164	16888
IC3(QE)-NOINCR	156	17643
IC3(IA)	154	8493

Fig. 6. Experimental comparison of various configuration options

Initial value of the K-LIVENESS *counter.* We consider the impact of starting the search with a right (or close to) value for the K-LIVENESS counter k, instead of always starting from zero, in IC3. For this, we use a simple heuristic that uses BMC to guess a value for the counter: we run BMC for a limited time (20 seconds in our experiments), increasing k every time a violation is detected. We then start IC3 with the k value found.

Overall, we considered six different configurations: IC3(IA) and IC3(QE) are the default, incremental versions of K-LIVENESS with IC3, using either approximate quantifier elimination or implicit abstraction; IC3(IA)-NOINCR and IC3(QE)-NOINCR are the non-incremental versions; BMC+IC3(IA) and BMC+IC3(QE) are the versions using a time-limited initial BMC run for computing an initial value for the K-LIVENESS counter k. The six configurations are compared in Fig. 6, showing the number of instances solved (y-axis) and the total execution time (x-axis). The figure also includes the "Virtual Best" configuration, constructed by taking the best result for each individual instance.

Fig. 6 shows that, differently from the case of software verification, the default version of IC3(QE) performs much better than IC3(IA). Although we currently do not have a clear explanation for this, our conjecture is that this is due to the "bad quality" of the predicates found by IC3(IA) in the process of disproving invariants when the value of k is too small. Since IC3(IA) never discards predicates, and it only tries to add the minimal amount of new predicates when performing refinements, it might simply get lost in computing clauses of poor quality due to the "bad" language of predicates found. This might also be the reason why IC3(IA)-NOINCR performs better than IC3(IA), despite the runtime cost of restarting the search from scratch every time k changes: when restarting, IC3(IA)-NOINCR can also throw away bad predicates. A similar argument can also be applied to BMC+IC3(IA): using BMC to skip the bad values of k allows IC3(IA) to find predicates that are more relevant/useful for proving the property with the good (or close to) value of k.

The situation for IC3(QE) is instead completely different. In this case, not only turning off incrementality significantly hurts performance, as we expected, but also using BMC is detrimental. This is consistent with the behavior observed in the finite-state case for the original K-LIVENESS implementation [12]. However, as the authors of [12], also in this case we do not have a clear explanation for this behavior.

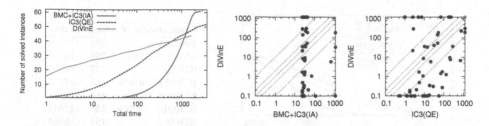

Fig. 7. Comparison with DIVINE

Comparison with Other Tools. We conclude our evaluation with a comparison of our implementation with alternative tools and techniques working on similar systems. As already remarked above, we are not aware of any tool that is able to handle arbitrary LTL properties on the class of systems that we support. Therefore, we concentrate our comparison only on Timed Automata, comparing with DIVINE [24]. We use a total of 64 instances from the *Fischer*, *Bridge* and *Counter* families. Unfortunately, we could not include the industrial *Diesel Generator* model, since it is modeled as a symbolic transition system, whereas DIVINE expects a network of timed automata (in UPPAAL format) as input. However, the *Diesel Generator* benchmark was reported to be very challenging for explicit-state approaches [32].

The results are shown in Fig. 7, where we compare DIVINE with our two best configurations, BMC+IC3(IA) and IC3(QE). We can see that DIVINE is very fast for simple instances, outperforming our tool by orders of magnitude. However, its performance degrades quickly as the size of the instances increases. In contrast, both BMC+IC3(IA) and IC3(QE) scale better to larger instances. This is particularly evident for BMC+IC3(IA): after having found a good initial value for the K-LIVENESS counter with BMC, IC3(IA) can solve almost all the instances in just a few seconds.

6 Conclusions and Future Work

We presented a new approach to the verification of liveness properties on hybrid systems, in particular of LTL properties, with SMT-based techniques. The approach relies on the K-LIVENESS idea of reducing the problem for finite-state systems to proving that an accepting condition can be visited at most K times. The new algorithm, K-ZENO, exploits the divergence of time to make the reduction succeed in proving properties on hybrid systems. We prove that the reduction is complete for a class of parametric rectangular hybrid automata. An extensive evaluation shows the effectiveness and scalability of the approach.

There are various directions for future work. Some of our objectives are to find optimizations for linear hybrid systems using relational abstraction [40], to apply the approach to LTL satisfiability in order to enable compositional contract-based reasoning [41], and to extend the idea to deal with continuous-time temporal logics and first-order theories different from reals.

References

1. HYCOMP: https://es.fbk.eu/tools/hycomp/
2. Henzinger, T., Kopke, P., Puri, A., Varaiya, P.: What's decidable about hybrid automata? In: STOC, pp. 373–382 (1995)
3. Alur, R., Courcoubetis, C., Henzinger, T.A., Ho, P.H.: Hybrid Automata: An Algorithmic Approach to the Specification and Verification of Hybrid Systems. In: Grossman, R.L., Ravn, A.P., Rischel, H., Nerode, A. (eds.) HS 1991 and HS 1992. LNCS, vol. 736, pp. 209–229. Springer, Heidelberg (1993)
4. Pnueli, A.: The Temporal Logic of Programs. In: FOCS, pp. 46–57 (1977)
5. Vardi, M.: An Automata-Theoretic Approach to Linear Temporal Logic. In: Banff Higher Order Workshop, pp. 238–266 (1995)
6. Audemard, G., Bozzano, M., Cimatti, A., Sebastiani, R.: Verifying industrial hybrid systems with mathsat. Electr. Notes Theor. Comput. Sci. 119(2), 17–32 (2005)
7. Cimatti, A., Mover, S., Tonetta, S.: Quantifier-free encoding of invariants for hybrid systems. Formal Methods in System Design, 1–24 (2013)
8. Bradley, A.R.: SAT-Based Model Checking without Unrolling. In: Jhala, R., Schmidt, D. (eds.) VMCAI 2011. LNCS, vol. 6538, pp. 70–87. Springer, Heidelberg (2011)
9. Cimatti, A., Griggio, A., Mover, S., Tonetta, S.: IC3 Modulo Theories via Implicit Predicate Abstraction. In: Ábrahám, E., Havelund, K. (eds.) TACAS 2014. LNCS, vol. 8413, pp. 46–61. Springer, Heidelberg (2014)
10. Graf, S., Saïdi, H.: Construction of Abstract State Graphs with PVS. In: Grumberg, O. (ed.) CAV 1997. LNCS, vol. 1254, pp. 72–83. Springer, Heidelberg (1997)
11. Tonetta, S.: Abstract Model Checking without Computing the Abstraction. In: Cavalcanti, A., Dams, D.R. (eds.) FM 2009. LNCS, vol. 5850, pp. 89–105. Springer, Heidelberg (2009)
12. Claessen, K., Sörensson, N.: A liveness checking algorithm that counts. In: Cabodi, G., Singh, S. (eds.) FMCAD, pp. 52–59. IEEE (2012)
13. Schuppan, V., Biere, A.: Efficient reduction of finite state model checking to reachability analysis. STTT 5(2-3), 185–204 (2004)
14. Henzinger, T.A., Ho, P., Wong-Toi, H.: HYTECH: A Model Checker for Hybrid Systems. STTT 1(1-2), 110–122 (1997)
15. Frehse, G., Le Guernic, C., Donzé, A., Cotton, S., Ray, R., Lebeltel, O., Ripado, R., Girard, A., Dang, T., Maler, O.: SpaceEx: Scalable Verification of Hybrid Systems. In: Gopalakrishnan, G., Qadeer, S. (eds.) CAV 2011. LNCS, vol. 6806, pp. 379–395. Springer, Heidelberg (2011)
16. Platzer, A.: Differential Dynamic Logic for Hybrid Systems. J. Autom. Reasoning 41(2), 143–189 (2008)
17. Alur, R., Dang, T., Ivancic, F.: Predicate abstraction for reachability analysis of hybrid systems. ACM Trans. Embedded Comput. Syst. 5(1), 152–199 (2006)
18. Clarke, E.M., Fehnker, A., Han, Z., Krogh, B.H., Ouaknine, J., Stursberg, O., Theobald, M.: Abstraction and counterexample-guided refinement in model checking of hybrid systems. Int. J. Found. Comput. Sci. 14(4), 583–604 (2003)
19. Prabhakar, P., Duggirala, P.S., Mitra, S., Viswanathan, M.: Hybrid automata-based cegar for rectangular hybrid systems. In: Giacobazzi, R., Berdine, J., Mastroeni, I. (eds.) VMCAI 2013. LNCS, vol. 7737, pp. 48–67. Springer, Heidelberg (2013)
20. Alur, R.: Formal verification of hybrid systems. In: EMSOFT, pp. 273–278 (2011)
21. Tripakis, S., Yovine, S., Bouajjani, A.: Checking timed büchi automata emptiness efficiently. Formal Methods in System Design 26(3), 267–292 (2005)
22. Tripakis, S.: Verifying Progress in Timed Systems. In: Katoen, J.-P. (ed.) ARTS 1999. LNCS, vol. 1601, pp. 299–314. Springer, Heidelberg (1999)

23. David, A., Larsen, K.: More features in UPPAAL
24. Barnat, J., et al.: DiVinE 3.0 - An Explicit-State Model Checker for Multithreaded C & C++ Programs. In: Sharygina, N., Veith, H. (eds.) CAV 2013. LNCS, vol. 8044, pp. 863–868. Springer, Heidelberg (2013)
25. Schuppan, V., Biere, A.: Liveness Checking as Safety Checking for Infinite State Spaces. Electr. Notes Theor. Comput. Sci. 149(1), 79–96 (2006)
26. Bresolin, D.: HyLTL: A temporal logic for model checking hybrid systems. In: HAS, pp. 73–84 (2013)
27. Larsen, K.G., Pettersson, P., Yi, W.: Uppaal in a nutshell. STTT 1(1-2), 134–152 (1997)
28. Laarman, A., Olesen, M.C., Dalsgaard, A.E., Larsen, K.G., van de Pol, J.: Multi-core Emptiness Checking of Timed Büchi Automata Using Inclusion Abstraction. In: Sharygina, N., Veith, H. (eds.) CAV 2013. LNCS, vol. 8044, pp. 968–983. Springer, Heidelberg (2013)
29. Podelski, A., Wagner, S.: Region stability proofs for hybrid systems. In: Raskin, J.-F., Thiagarajan, P.S. (eds.) FORMATS 2007. LNCS, vol. 4763, pp. 320–335. Springer, Heidelberg (2007)
30. Duggirala, P., Mitra, S.: Abstraction Refinement for Stability. In: ICCPS, pp. 22–31 (2011)
31. Damm, W., Pinto, G., Ratschan, S.: Guaranteed termination in the verification of ltl properties of non-linear robust discrete time hybrid systems. Int. J. Found. Comput. Sci. 18(1), 63–86 (2007)
32. Kindermann, R., Junttila, T., Niemelä, I.: Beyond lassos: Complete smt-based bounded model checking for timed automata. In: Giese, H., Rosu, G. (eds.) FMOODS/FORTE 2012. LNCS, vol. 7273, pp. 84–100. Springer, Heidelberg (2012)
33. Plaku, E., Kavraki, L.E., Vardi, M.Y.: Falsification of ltl safety properties in hybrid systems. STTT 15(4), 305–320 (2013)
34. Nghiem, T., Sankaranarayanan, S., Fainekos, G.E., Ivancic, F., Gupta, A., Pappas, G.J.: Monte-carlo techniques for falsification of temporal properties of non-linear hybrid systems. In: HSCC, pp. 211–220 (2010)
35. Podelski, A., Rybalchenko, A.: Transition Invariants. In: LICS, pp. 32–41. IEEE Computer Society (2004)
36. Grebenshchikov, S., Lopes, N.P., Popeea, C., Rybalchenko, A.: Synthesizing software verifiers from proof rules. In: Vitek, J., Lin, H., Tip, F. (eds.) PLDI, pp. 405–416 (2012)
37. Henzinger, T.A., Ho, P.-H.: Hytech: The cornell hybrid technology tool. In: Antsaklis, P., Kohn, W., Nerode, A., Sastry, S. (eds.) Hybrid Systems II. LNCS, vol. 999, pp. 265–293. Springer, Heidelberg (1995)
38. Wang, F.: Symbolic parametric safety analysis of linear hybrid systems with bdd-like datastructures. IEEE Trans. Software Eng. 31(1), 38–51 (2005)
39. Fehnker, A., Ivančić, F.: Benchmarks for hybrid systems verification. In: Alur, R., Pappas, G.J. (eds.) HSCC 2004. LNCS, vol. 2993, pp. 326–341. Springer, Heidelberg (2004)
40. Mover, S., Cimatti, A., Tiwari, A., Tonetta, S.: Time-aware relational abstractions for hybrid systems. In: EMSOFT, pp. 1–10 (2013)
41. Cimatti, A., Dorigatti, M., Tonetta, S.: OCRA: A tool for checking the refinement of temporal contracts. In: ASE, pp. 702–705 (2013)

Safraless Synthesis for Epistemic Temporal Specifications*

Rodica Bozianu[1], Cătălin Dima[1], and Emmanuel Filiot[2],[**]

[1] Université Paris Est, LACL (EA 4219), UPEC, 94010 Créteil Cedex, France
[2] Université Libre de Bruxelles, CP 212 - 1050 Bruxelles Belgium

Abstract. In this paper we address the synthesis problem for specifications given in linear temporal single-agent epistemic logic, KLTL (or KL_1), over single-agent systems having imperfect information of the environment state. [17] have shown that this problem is 2Exptime complete. However, their procedure relies on complex automata constructions that are notoriously resistant to efficient implementations as they use Safra-like determinization.

We propose a "Safraless" synthesis procedure for a large fragment of KLTL. The construction transforms first the synthesis problem into the problem of checking emptiness for universal co-Büchi tree automata using an information-set construction. Then we build a safety game that can be solved using an antichain-based symbolic technique exploiting the structure of the underlying automata. The technique is implemented and applied to a couple of case studies.

1 Introduction

The goal of system verification is to check that a system satisfies a given property. One of the major achievements in system verification is the theory of *model checking*, that uses automata-based techniques to check properties expressed in temporal logics, for systems modelled as transitions systems. The *synthesis* problem is more ambitious: given a specification of the system, the aim is to automatically synthesise a system that fulfils the constraints defined by the specification. Therefore, the constraints do not need to be checked a posteriori, and this allows the designer to focus on defining high-level specifications, rather than designing complex computational models of the systems.

Reactive systems are non-terminating systems that interact with some environment, e.g., hardware or software that control transportations systems, or medical devices. One of the main challenge of synthesis of reactive systems is to cope with the uncontrollable behaviour of the environment, which usually leads to computationally harder decision problems, compared to system verification. For instance, model-checking properties expressed in *linear time temporal logic* (LTL) is PSpace-c while LTL synthesis is 2Exptime-c [14]. Synthesis of reactive systems from temporal specifications has gain a lot of interest recently as several works have shown its practical feasibility [13,4,3,12,9]. These progresses were supported by Kupferman and Vardi's breakthrough in automata-based synthesis techniques [13]. More precisely, they have shown that the complex

---

* Work partially supported by the ANR research project "EQINOCS" no. ANR-11-BS02-0004.
** F.R.S.-FNRS research associate (chercheur qualifié).

A. Biere and R. Bloem (Eds.): CAV 2014, LNCS 8559, pp. 441–456, 2014.
© Springer International Publishing Switzerland 2014

Safra's determinization operation, used in the classical LTL synthesis algorithm [14], could be avoided by working directly with universal co-Büchi automata. Since then, several other "Safraless" procedures have been defined [13,16,10,9]. In [16,9], it is shown that LTL synthesis reduces to testing the emptiness of a universal co-Büchi tree automaton, that in turn can be reduced to solving a safety game. The structure of the safety games can be exploited to define a symbolic game solving algorithm based on compact antichain representations [9].

In these works, the system is assumed to have perfect information about the state of the environment. However in many practical scenarios, this assumption is not realistic since some environment information may be hidden to the system (e.g. private variables). Towards the (more realistic) synthesis of partially informed systems, imperfect information two-player games on graphs have been studied [15,7,2,8]. However, they consider explicit state transition systems rather than synthesis from temporal specifications. Moreover, the winning objectives that they consider cannot express fine properties about imperfect information, i.e., cannot speak about knowledge.

Epistemic Temporal Logics. [11] are logics formatted for reasoning about multi-agent situations. They are extensions of temporal logics with knowledge operators K_i for each agent. They have been successfully used for verification of various distributed systems in which the knowledge of the agents is essential for the correctness of the system specification.

Synthesis problem with temporal epistemic objectives. Vardi and van der Meyden [17] have considered epistemic temporal logics to define specifications that can, in addition to temporal properties, also express properties that refer to the imperfect information, and they studied the synthesis problem. They define the synthesis problem in a multi-agent setting, for specifications written in LTL extended with knowledge operators K_i for each agent (KLTL). In such models, transitions between states of the environment model depend on actions of the environment and the system. The system does not see which actions are played by the environment but get some observation on the states in which the environment can be (observations are subsets of states). An execution of the environment model, from the point of view of the system, is therefore an infinite sequence alternating between its own actions and observations.

The goal of the KLTL synthesis problem is to automatically generate a strategy for the system (if it exists) that tells it which action should be played, depending on finite histories, so that whatever the environment does, all the (concrete) infinite executions resulting from this strategy satisfy the KLTL formula. In [17], this problem was shown to be undecidable even for two agents against an environment. For a single agent, they show that the problem is **2Exptime-c**, by reduction to the emptiness of alternating Büchi automata. This theoretically elegant construction is however difficult to implement and optimize, as it relies on complex Safra-like automata operations (Muller-Schupp construction).

Contributions. In this paper, we follow the formalisation of [17] and, as our main contribution, define and implement a Safraless synthesis procedure for the positive fragment of KLTL (KLTL$^+$), i.e., KLTL formulas where the operator K does not occur under any negations. Our procedure relies on universal co-Büchi tree automata (UCT). More precisely, given a KLTL$^+$ formula φ and some environment model $\mathcal{M}_E$, we show how to construct a UCT $\mathcal{T}_\varphi$ whose language is exactly the set of strategies that realize φ in $\mathcal{M}_E$.

Despite the fact that our procedure has 2-ExpTime worst-case complexity, we have implemented it and shown its practical feasibility through a set of examples. In particular, based on ideas of [9], we reduce the problem of checking the emptiness of $\mathcal{T}_\varphi$ to solving a safety game whose state space can be ordered and compactly represented by antichains. Moreover, rather than using the reduction of [9] as a blackbox, we further optimize the antichain representations to improve their compactness. Our implementation is based on the tool Acacia [5] and, to the best of our knowledge, it is the first implementation of a synthesis procedure for epistemic temporal specifications. As an application, this implementation can be used to solve two-player games of imperfect information whose objectives are given as LTL formulas, or universal co-Büchi automata.

Organization of the paper. In Section 2, we define the KLTL synthesis problem. In Section 3, we define universal co-Büchi automata for infinite words and trees. In Section 4, we consider the particular case of LTL synthesis in an environment model with imperfect information. The construction explained in that section will be used in the generalization to KLTL$^+$ and moreover, it can be used to solve two-player imperfect information games with LTL (and more generally ω-regular) objectives. In Section 5, we define our Safraless procedure for KLTL$^+$, and show in Section 6 how to implement it with antichain-based symbolic techniques. Finally, we describe our implementation in Section 7. *Full proofs can be found in the full version of the paper[6] in which, for self-containdness, we also explain the reduction to safety games.*

2   KLTL Realizability and Synthesis

In this section, we define the realizability and synthesis problems for KLTL specifications, for one partially informed agent, called the *system*, against some environment.

Environment Model. We assume to have, as input of the problem, a model of the behaviour of the environment as a transition system. This transition system is defined over two disjoint sets of actions Σ_1 and Σ_2, for the system and the environment respectively. The transition relation from states to states is defined with respect to pairs of actions in $\Sigma_1 \times \Sigma_2$. Additionally, each state s of the environment model carries an interpretation $\tau_e(s)$ over a (finite) set of propositions $\mathcal{P}$. However, the system is not perfectly informed about the value of some propositions, i.e., some propositions are visible to the system, and some are not. Therefore, we partition the set $\mathcal{P}$ into two sets $\mathcal{P}_v$ (the visible propositions) and $\mathcal{P}_i$ (the invisible ones).

An *environment model* is a tuple $\mathcal{M}_E = (\mathcal{P}, \Sigma_1, \Sigma_2, S_e, S_0, \Delta_e, \tau_e)$ where

- $\mathcal{P}$ is a finite set of propositions, Σ_1 and Σ_2 are finite set of actions for the system and the environment resp.,
- S_e is a set of states, $S_0 \subseteq S_e$ a set of initial states,
- $\tau_e : S_e \to 2^{\mathcal{P}}$ is a labelling function,
- $\Delta_e \subseteq S_e \times \Sigma_1 \times \Sigma_2 \times S_e$ is a transition relation.

The model is assumed to be deadlock-free, i.e. from any state, there exists at least one outgoing transition. Moreover, the model is assumed to be complete for all actions of the system, i.e. for all states and all actions of the system, there exists an outgoing transition. The set of *executions* of $\mathcal{M}_E$, denoted by $\text{exec}(\mathcal{M}_E)$, is the set of infinite sequences of states $\rho = s_0 s_1 \cdots \in S_e^\omega$ such that $s_0 \in S_0$ and for all $i > 0$, $(s_i, a_1, a_2, s_{i+1}) \in \Delta_e$

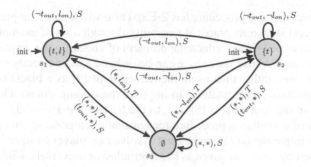

Fig. 1. Environment model $\mathcal{M}_E$ of Example 1

for some $(a_1, a_2) \in \Sigma_1 \times \Sigma_2$. Given a sequence of states $\rho = s_0 s_1 \ldots$ and a set $P \subseteq \mathcal{P}$, we denote by $\text{trace}_P(\rho)$ its projection over P, i.e. $\text{trace}_P(\rho) = (\tau_e(s_0) \cap P)(\tau_e(s_1) \cap P) \ldots$. The *visible trace* of ρ is defined by $\text{trace}_v(\rho) = \text{trace}_{\mathcal{P}_v}(\rho)$. The *language* of $\mathcal{M}_E$ with respect to P is defined as $\mathcal{L}_P(\mathcal{M}_E) = \{\text{trace}_P(\rho) \mid \rho \in \text{exec}(\mathcal{M}_E)\}$. The language of $\mathcal{M}_E$ is defined as $\mathcal{L}_{\mathcal{P}}(\mathcal{M}_E)$. The visible language of $\mathcal{M}_E$ is defined as $\mathcal{L}_{\mathcal{P}_v}(\mathcal{M}_E)$. Finally, given an infinite sequence of actions $a = a_1^0 a_2^0 \cdots \in (\Sigma_1.\Sigma_2)^\omega$ and an execution $\rho = s_0 s_1 \ldots$ of $\mathcal{M}_E$, we say that a is compatible with ρ if for all $i \geq 0$, $(s_i, a_1^i, a_2^i, s_{i+1}) \in \Delta_e$.

This formalization is very close to that of [17]. However in [17], partial observation is modeled as a partition of the state space. The two models are equivalent. In particular, we will see that partitioning the propositions into visible and invisible ones also induces a partition of the state space into observations.

Example 1. We illustrate the notion of environment model on the example of [17], that describes the behaviour of an environment against a system acting on a timed toggle switch with two positions (on,off) and a light. It is depicted in Fig. 1. The set $\mathcal{P} = \{t, l\}$ contains two propositions t (true iff the toggle is on) and l (true iff the light is on). Actions of the system are $\Sigma_1 = \{T, S\}$ for "toggle" and "skip" respectively. The system can change the position of the toggle only if it plays T, and S has no effect. Actions of the environment are $\Sigma_2 = \{(t_{out}, l_{on}) \mid t_{out}, l_{on} \in \{0, 1\}\}$. The boolean variables t_{out} and l_{on} indicate that the environment times out the toggle and that it switches on the light. The transition function is depicted on the figure as well as the labelling function $\tau_e : S_e \to 2^\mathcal{P}$. The star $*$ means "any action". The light can be on only if the toggle in on (state s_1), but it can be off even if the toggle is on (state s_2), in case it is broken. This parameter is uncontrollable by the system, and therefore it is controlled by the environment (action l_{on}). The timer is assumed to be unreliable and therefore the environment can timeout at any time (action t_{out}). The system sees only the light, i.e. $\mathcal{P}_v = \{l\}$ and $\mathcal{P}_i = \{t\}$. The goal of the system is to have a strategy such that he always knows the position of the toggle.

Observations. The partition of the set of propositions $\mathcal{P}$ into a set of visible propositions $\mathcal{P}_v$ and a set of invisible propositions $\mathcal{P}_i$ induces an indistinguishability relation over the states S_e. Two states are *indistinguishable*, denoted $s_1 \sim s_2$, if they have the same visible propositions, i.e. $\tau_e(s_1) \cap \mathcal{P}_v = \tau_e(s_2) \cap \mathcal{P}_v$. It is easy to see that $\sim$ is an equivalence relation over S_e. Each equivalence class of S_e induced by $\sim$ is called an *observation*. The equivalence class of a state $s \in S_e$ is denoted by $o(s)$ and the set of observations is denoted by $\mathcal{O}$. The relation $\sim$ is naturally extended to (finite or infinite) executions: $\rho_1 \sim \rho_2$ if $\text{trace}_v(\rho_1) = \text{trace}_v(\rho_2)$. Similarly, two executions $\rho = s_0 s_1 \ldots$ and $\rho' = s_0' s_1' \ldots$ are said to be indistinguishable *up to some position i* if $\text{trace}_v(s_0 \ldots s_i) = \text{trace}_v(s_0' \ldots s_i')$. This indistinguishability notion is also an equivalence relation over executions that we denote by $\sim_i$.

Coming back to Example 1, since the set of visible propositions is $\mathcal{P}_v = \{l\}$ and the set of invisible ones is $\mathcal{P}_i = \{t\}$, the states s_2 and s_3 are indistinguishable (in both s_2, s_3 the light is off) and therefore $\mathcal{O} = \{o_0, o_1\}$ with $o_0 = \{s_2, s_3\}$ and $o_1 = \{s_1\}$.

Given an infinite sequence $u = a_1 o_1 a_2 o_2 \cdots \in (\Sigma_1.\mathcal{O})^\omega$ of actions of Player 1, and observations, we associate with u the set of possible executions of $\mathcal{M}_E$ that are compatible with u. Formally, we define $\text{exec}(\mathcal{M}_E, u)$ the set of executions $\rho = s_0 s_1 \cdots \in \text{exec}(\mathcal{M}_E)$ such that for all $i \geq 1$, $o(s_i) = o_i$ and there exists an action b_i of the environment such that $(s_{i-1}, a_i, b_i, s_i) \in \Delta_e$. We also define the traces of u as the set of traces of all executions of $\mathcal{M}_E$ compatible with u, i.e. $\text{traces}(u) = \{\text{traces}(\rho) \mid \rho \in \text{exec}(\mathcal{M}_E, u)\}$.

Epistemic Linear Time Temporal Logic (KLTL). We now define the logic KLTL for one-agent (the system). The logic KLTL extends the logic LTL with an epistemic operator $K\phi$, modelling the property that the system knows that the formula ϕ holds. *KLTL formulae* are defined over the set of atomic propositions $\mathcal{P}$ by:

$$\varphi ::= p \mid \neg\varphi \mid \varphi \vee \varphi \mid \bigcirc\varphi \mid \varphi_1 \mathcal{U} \varphi_2 \mid K\varphi$$

in which $p \in \mathcal{P}$ and $\bigcirc$ and $\mathcal{U}$ are the "next" and "until" operators from linear temporal logic. Formulas of the type $K\varphi$ are read as "the system knows that φ holds". We define the macros $\Diamond$ (eventually) and $\square$ (always) as usual. LTL is the fragment of KLTL without the K operator.

The semantics of a KLTL formula φ is defined for an environment model $\mathcal{M}_E = (\mathcal{P}, \Sigma_1, \Sigma_2, S_e, S_0, \Delta_e, \tau_e)$, a set of executions $R \subseteq \text{exec}(\mathcal{M}_E)$, an execution $\rho = s_0 s_1 \cdots \in R$ and a position $i \geq 0$ in ρ. It is defined inductively:

- $R, \rho, i \models p$ if $p \in \tau_e(s_i)$,
- $R, \rho, i \models \neg\varphi$ if $R, \rho, i \not\models \varphi$,
- $R, \rho, i \models \varphi_1 \vee \varphi_2$ if $R, \rho, i \models \varphi_1$ or $R, \rho, i \models \varphi_2$,
- $R, \rho, i \models \bigcirc\varphi$ if $R, \rho, i+1 \models \varphi$,
- $R, \rho, i \models \varphi_1 \mathcal{U} \varphi_2$ if $\exists j \geq i$ s.t. $R, \rho, j \models \varphi_2$ and $\forall i \leq k < j$, $R, \rho, k \models \varphi_1$,
- $R, \rho, i \models K\varphi$ if for all $\rho' \in R$ s.t. $\rho \sim_i \rho'$, we have $R, \rho', i \models \varphi$.

In particular, the system knows φ at position i in the execution ρ, if all other executions in R whose prefix up to position i are indistinguishable from that of ρ, also satisfy φ. We write $R, \rho \models \varphi$ if $R, \rho, 0 \models \varphi$, and $R \models \varphi$ if $R, \rho \models \varphi$ for all executions $\rho \in R$. We also write $\mathcal{M}_E \models \varphi$ to mean $\text{exec}(\mathcal{M}_E) \models \varphi$. Note that $\mathcal{M}_E \models \varphi$ iff $\mathcal{M}_E \models K\varphi$.

Consider Example 1 and the set R of executions that eventually loop in s_1. Pick any ρ in R. Then $R, \rho, 0 \models \square K\Diamond(l)$. Indeed, take any position i in ρ and any other executions $\rho' \in R$ such that $\rho \sim_i \rho'$. Then since ρ' will eventually loop in s_1, it will satisfy $\Diamond(l)$. Therefore $R, \rho, i \models K\Diamond(l)$, for all $i \geq 0$.

KLTL Realizability and Synthesis. As presented in [9] for the perfect information setting, the realizability problem, given the environment model $\mathcal{M}_E$ and the KLTL formula φ, is best seen as a turn-based game between the system (Player 1) and the environment (Player 2). In the first round of the play, Player 1 picks some action $a_1^0 \in \Sigma_1$, then Player 2 picks some action in $a_2^0 \in \Sigma_2$ and solves the nondeterminism in Δ_e, and a new round starts. The two players play for an infinite duration and the outcome is an infinite sequence $w = a_1^0 a_2^0 a_1^1 a_2^1 \ldots$. The winning objective is given by some KLTL formula φ. Player 1 wins the play if for all executions ρ of $\mathcal{M}_E$ that are compatible with w, we have $\mathcal{M}_E, \rho \models \varphi$.

Player 1 plays according to *strategies* (called *protocols* in [17]). Since Player 1 has only partial information about the state of the environment, his strategies are based on the histories of his own actions and the observations he got from the environment. Formally, a strategy for Player 1 is a mapping $\lambda : (\Sigma_1 \mathcal{O})^* \to \Sigma_1$, where, as defined before, $\mathcal{O}$ denotes the set of observations of Player 1 over the states of $\mathcal{M}_E$. Fixing a strategy λ of Player 1 restricts the set of executions of the environment model $\mathcal{M}_E$. An execution $\rho = s_0 s_1 \cdots \in \text{exec}(\mathcal{M}_E)$ is said to be *compatible* with λ if there exists an infinite sequence of actions $a = a_1^0 a_2^0 \ldots \in (\Sigma_1.\Sigma_2)^\omega$, compatible with ρ, such that for all $i \geq 0$, $a_1^i = \lambda(a_1^0 o(s_0) a_1^1 o(s_1) \ldots a_1^{i-1} o(s_{i-1}))$. We denote by $\text{exec}(\mathcal{M}_E, \lambda)$ the set of executions of $\mathcal{M}_E$ compatible with λ.

Definition 1. *A KLTL formula φ is realizable in $\mathcal{M}_E$ if there exists a strategy λ for the system such that* $\text{exec}(\mathcal{M}_E, \lambda) \models \phi$.

Theorem 1 (R. van der Meyden and M. Vardi in [17]). *The KLTL realizability problem (for one agent) is* 2ExpTime-complete.

If a formula is realizable, the *synthesis* problem asks to generate a finite-memory strategy that realizes the formula. Such a strategy always exists if the specification is realizable [17]. Finite memory strategies can be represented by Moore machines that read observations and output actions of Player 1. We refer the reader to [9] for a formal definition of finite-memory strategies.

Considering again Example 1, the formula $\varphi = \Box(K(t) \lor K(\neg t))$ expresses the fact that the system knows at each step the position of the toggle. As argued in [17], this formula is realizable if the initial set of the environment is $\{s_1, s_2\}$ since both states are labelled with t. Then, a winning strategy of the system is to play first time T (it will lead to s_3) and then always play S in order to stay in that state. Following this strategy, in the first step the formula $K(t)$ is satisfied and then $K(\neg t)$ becomes true forever. However, the formula is not realizable if the set of initial states of the environment is $\{s_2, s_3\}$ since from the beginning the system doesn't know the value of the toggle.

3   Automata for Infinite Words and Trees

Automata on Infinite Words. An *infinite word automaton* over some (finite) alphabet Σ is a tuple $A = (\Sigma, Q, Q_0, \Delta, \alpha)$ where Σ is the finite input alphabet, Q is the finite set of states, $Q_0 \subseteq Q$ is the set of initial states, $\alpha \subseteq Q$ is the set of final states (accepting states) and $\Delta \subseteq Q \times \Sigma \times Q$ is the transition relation.

For all $q \in Q$ and all $\sigma \in \Sigma$, we let $\Delta(q, \sigma) = \{q' | (q, \sigma, q') \in \Delta\}$. We let $|A| = |Q| + |\Delta|$. We say that A is *deterministic* if $|Q_0| = 1$ and $\forall q \in Q, \forall \sigma \in \Sigma, |\Delta(q, \sigma)| \leq 1$. It is *complete* if $\forall q \in Q, \forall \sigma \in \Sigma, \Delta(q, \sigma) \neq \emptyset$. In this paper we assume, w.l.o.g., that the word automata are always complete.

A *run* of the automaton A on an infinite input word $w = w_0w_1w_2...$, is a sequence $r = q_0q_1q_2... \in Q^\omega$ such that $(q_i, w_i, q_{i+1}) \in \Delta$ for all $i \geq 0$ and $q_0 \in Q_0$. We denote by $Runs_A(w)$ the set of runs of A on w and by $Visit(r, q)$ the number of times the state q is visited along the run r(or ∞ if the path visit the state q infinitely often). Here, we consider two accepting conditions for infinite word automata and name the infinite word automata according to the accepting condition being used. Let $B \in \mathbb{N}$. A word $w \in \Sigma^\omega$ is accepted by A if (according to the accepting condition):

Universal Co-Büchi : $\forall r \in Runs_A(w), \forall q \in \alpha, \; Visit(r, q) < \infty$

Universal B-Co-Büchi : $\forall r \in Runs_A(w), \forall q \in \alpha, \; Visit(r, q) \leq B$

The set of words accepted by A with the universal co-Büchi (resp. B-co-Büchi) accepting condition is denoted by $\mathcal{L}_{uc}(A)$ (resp. $\mathcal{L}_{uc,B}(A)$). We say that A is a *universal co-Büchi word automaton* (UCW) if the first acceptance condition is used and that (A, B) is an *universal B-co-Büchi word automaton* (UBCW) if the second one is used.

Given an LTL formula φ, we can translate it into an equivalent universal co-Büchi word automaton A_φ. This can be done with a single exponential blow-up by first negating φ, then translating $\neg\varphi$ into an equivalent nondeterministic Büchi word automaton, and then dualize it into a universal co-Büchi word automaton [9,13].

Automata on Infinite Trees. Given a finite set D of directions, a $D-tree$ is a prefix-closed set $T \subseteq D^*$, i.e., if $x \cdot d \in T$, where $d \in D$, then $x \in T$. The elements of T are called *nodes* and the empty word ϵ is the *root* of T. For every $x \in T$, the nodes $x \cdot d$, for $d \in D$, are the *successors* of x. A node x is a *leaf* if it has no successor in T, i.e., $\forall d \in D, x \cdot d \notin T$. The tree T is *complete* if for all nodes, there are successors in all directions, formally, $\forall x \in T, \forall d \in D, x \cdot d \in T$. Finite and infinite branches π in a tree T are naturally defined, respectively, as finite and infinite paths in T starting from the root node. Given an alphabet Σ, a $\Sigma-labelled$ $D-tree$ is a pair $\langle T, \tau \rangle$ where T is a tree and $\tau : T \to \Sigma$ maps each node of T to a letter in Σ. We omit τ when it is clear from the context. Then, in a tree T, an infinite (resp. finite) branch π induces an infinite (resp. finite) sequence of labels and directions in $(\Sigma.D)^\omega$ (resp. $(\Sigma.D)^*\Sigma$). We denote this sequence by $\tau(\pi)$. For instance, for a set of system's actions Σ_1 and a set of observations $\mathcal{O}$, a strategy $\lambda : (\Sigma_1\mathcal{O})^* \to \Sigma_1$ of the system can be seen has a Σ_1-labelled $\mathcal{O}$-tree whose nodes are finite outcomes[1].

A *universal co-Büchi tree automaton* (UCT) is a tuple $\mathcal{T} = (\Sigma, Q, Q_0, D, \Delta, \alpha)$ where Σ is the finite alphabet, Q is a finite set of states, $Q_0 \subseteq Q$ is the set of initial states, D is the set of directions, $\Delta : Q \times \Sigma \times D \to 2^Q$ is the transition relation (assumed to be total) and α is the set of final states. If the tree automaton is in some state q at some node x labelled by some $\sigma \in \Sigma$, it will evaluate, for all $d \in D$, the subtree rooted at $x.d$ in parallel from all the states of $\Delta(q, \sigma, d)$. Let us define the notion of run formally. For all $q \in Q$ and $\sigma \in \Sigma$, we denote by $\Delta(q, \sigma) = \{(q_1, d_1), \ldots, (q_n, d_n)\}$ the *disjoint union* of all sets $\Delta(q, \sigma, d)$ for all $d \in D$. A *run* of $\mathcal{T}$ on an infinite $\Sigma-labelled$ $D-tree$ $\langle T, \tau \rangle$ is a $(Q \times D^*)-labelled$ $\mathbb{N}-tree$ $\langle T_r, \tau_r \rangle$ such that $\tau_r(\epsilon) \in Q_0 \times \{\epsilon\}$ and, for

---

[1] Technically, a strategy λ is defined also for histories that are not accessible by λ itself from the initial (empty) history ϵ. The tree represents only accessible histories but we can, in the rest of the paper, assume that strategies are only defined for their accessible histories. Formally, we assume that a strategy is a partial function whose domain H satisfies $\epsilon \in H$ and for all $h \in H$ and all $o \in \mathcal{O}, h.\lambda(h).o \in H$, and H is minimal (for inclusion) w.r.t. this property.

all $x \in T_r$ such that $\tau_r(x) = (q, v)$, if $\Delta(q, \tau(v)) = \{(q_1, d_1), \ldots, (q_n, d_n)\}$, we have $x \cdot i \in T_r$ and $\tau_r(x \cdot i) = (q_i, v \cdot d_i)$ for all $0 < i \leq n$, . Note that there is at most one run per input tree (up to tree isomorphism). A run $\langle T_r, \tau_r \rangle$ is *accepting* if for all infinite branches π of T_r, $\tau_r(\pi)$ visits a finite number of accepting states. The language of $\mathcal{T}$, denoted by $\mathcal{L}_{uc}(\mathcal{T})$, is the set of Σ-labelled D-trees such that there exists an accepting run on them. Similarly, we define universal B-co-Büchi tree automata by strengthening the acceptance conditions on all branches to the B-co-Büchi condition.

As noted in [9,16], testing the emptiness of a UCT automaton reduces to testing the emptiness of a universal B-co-Büchi accepting condition for a sufficiently large bound B, which in turn reduces to solving a safety game. Symbolic techniques, that are also exploited in this paper, have been used to solve the safety games[9].

4 LTL Synthesis under Imperfect Information

In this section, we first explain an automata-based procedure to decide realizability under imperfect information of LTL formulas against an environment model. This procedure will be extended in the next section to handle the K operator.

Take an environment model $\mathcal{M}_E = (\mathcal{P}, \Sigma_1, \Sigma_2, S_e, S_0, \Delta_e, \tau_e)$. Then, a complete Σ_1-labelled $\mathcal{O}$-tree $\langle T, \tau \rangle$ defines a strategy of the system. Any infinite branch π of $\langle T, \tau \rangle$ defines an infinite sequence of actions and observations of $\mathcal{M}_E$, which in turn corresponds to a set of possible traces in $\mathcal{M}_E$. We denote by traces(π) this set of traces, and it is formally defined by traces$(\pi) = $ traces$(\tau(\pi))$ (recall that the set of traces of a sequence of actions and observations has been defined in Section 2).

Given an LTL formula ψ, we construct a universal co-Büchi tree automaton $\mathcal{T} = (\Sigma_1, Q, Q_0, \mathcal{O}, \Delta, \alpha)$ that accepts all the strategies of Player 1 (the system) that realize ψ under the environment model $\mathcal{M}_E$. First, one converts ψ into an equivalent UCW $\mathcal{A} = (2^\mathcal{P}, Q^\mathcal{A}, Q_0^\mathcal{A}, \Delta^\mathcal{A}, \alpha^\mathcal{A})$. Then, as a direct consequence of the definition of KLTL realizability:

Proposition 1. *Given a complete Σ_1-labelled $\mathcal{O}$-trees $\langle T, \tau \rangle$, $\langle T, \tau \rangle$ defines a strategy that realizes ψ under $\mathcal{M}_E$ iff for all infinite branches π of $\langle T, \tau \rangle$ and all traces $\rho \in$ traces(π), $\rho \in L(\mathcal{A})$.*

We now show how to construct a universal tree automaton that checks the property mentioned in the previous proposition, for all branches of the trees. We use universal transitions to check, on every branch of the tree, that all the possible traces (possibly uncountably many) compatible with the sequence of actions in Σ_1 and observations in $\mathcal{O}$ defined by the branch satisfy ψ. Based on finite sequences of observations that the system has received, it can define its *knowledge* I of the possible states in which the environment can be, as a subset of states of S_e. Given an action $a_1 \in \Sigma_1$ of the system and some observation $o \in \mathcal{O}$, we denote by post$_a(I, o)$ the new knowledge that the system can infer from observation o, action a and its previous information I. Formally, post$_a(I, o) = \{s \in S_e \cap o \mid \exists a_2 \in \Sigma_2, \exists s' \in I$ s.t. $(s', a, a_2, s) \in \Delta_e\}$.

The states of the universal tree automaton $\mathcal{T}$ are pairs of states of $\mathcal{A}$ and knowledges, plus some extra state $(q_w, \varnothing)$, i.e. $Q = Q^\mathcal{A} \times 2^{S_e} \cup \{(q_w, \varnothing)\}$ where $(q_w, \varnothing)$ is added for completeness. The final states are defined as $\alpha = \alpha^\mathcal{A} \times 2^{S_e}$ and initial states as $Q_0 = Q_0^\mathcal{A} \times S_0$. To define the transition relation, let us consider a state $q \in Q^\mathcal{A}$, a knowledge set $I \subseteq S_e$, an action $a \in \Sigma_1$ and some observation $o \in \mathcal{O}$. We now define

$\Delta((q,I),a,o)$. It could be the case that there is no transition in $\mathcal{M}_E$ from a state of I to a state of o, i.e. $post_a(I,o) = \varnothing$. In that case, all the paths from the next o-node of the tree should be accepting. This situation is modelled by going to the extra state $(q_w, \varnothing)$, i.e. $\Delta((q,I),a,o) = (q_w, \varnothing)$.

Now suppose that $post_a(I,o)$ is non-empty. Since the automaton must check that all the traces of $\mathcal{M}_E$ that are compatible with actions of Σ_1 and observations are accepted by $\mathcal{A}$, intuitively, one would define $\Delta((q,I),a,o)$ as the set of states of the form $(q', post_a(I,o))$ for all states q' such that there exists $s \in I$ such that $(q, \tau_e(s), q') \in \Delta^{\mathcal{A}}$. However, it is not correct for several reasons. First, it could be that s has no successor in o for action a, and therefore one should not consider it because the traces up to state s die at the next step after getting observation o. Therefore, one should only consider states of I that have a successor in o. Second, it is not correct to associate the new knowledge $post_a(I,o)$ with q', because it could be that there exists a state $s' \in post_a(I,o)$ such that for all its predecessors s'' in I, there is no transition $(q, \tau_e(s''), q')$ in $\Delta^{\mathcal{A}}$, and therefore, one would also take into account sequences of interpretations of propositions that do not correspond to any trace of $\mathcal{M}_E$.

Taking into account these two remarks, we define, for all states q', the set $I_{q,q'} = \{s \in I \mid (q, \tau(s), q') \in \Delta^{\mathcal{A}}\}$. Then, $\Delta((q,I),a,o)$ is defined as the set

$$\Delta((q,I),a,o) = \{(q', post_a(I_{q,q'},o)) \mid \exists s \in I, (q, \tau(s), q') \in \Delta^{\mathcal{A}}\}$$

Note that, since $\bigcup_{q' \in Q^{\mathcal{A}}} post_a(I_{q,q'}, o) = post_a(I,o)$ and the automaton is universal, the system does not have better knowledge by restricting the knowledge sets.

Lemma 1. *The LTL formula ψ is realizable in $\mathcal{M}_E$ iff $\mathcal{L}(\mathcal{T}) \neq \varnothing$.*

Moreover, it is known that if a UCT has a non-empty language, then it accepts a tree that is the unfolding of a finite graph, or equivalently, that can be represented by a Moore machine. Therefore if ψ is realizable, it is realizable by a finite-memory strategy. In this paper we will also use the notation $\mathcal{T}_{\psi,X}$ for the UCT built for the LTL formula ψ where the executions of $\mathcal{M}_E$ start from the set $X \subseteq S_e$, i.e., $Q_0 = Q_0^{\mathcal{A}} \times X$.

5   Safraless Procedure for Positive KLTL Synthesis

In this section, we extend the construction of Section 4 to the positive fragment of KLTL. Positive formulas are defined by the following grammar:

$$\varphi ::= p \mid \neg p \mid \varphi \wedge \varphi \mid \varphi \vee \varphi \mid \bigcirc\varphi \mid \square\varphi \mid K\varphi \mid \varphi\mathcal{U}\varphi$$

Note that this fragment is equivalent to the fragment of KLTL in which all the knowledge operators K in formulas occur under an even number of negations. This is obtained by straightforwardly pushing the negations downwards the atoms. We denote this fragment of KLTL by KLTL$^+$.

Sketch of the Construction. Given a KLTL$^+$ formula φ and an environment model $\mathcal{M}_E = (\mathcal{P}, \Sigma_1, \Sigma_2, S_e, S_0, \Delta_e, \tau_e)$, we show how to construct a UCT $\mathcal{T}$ such that $\mathcal{L}(\mathcal{T}) \neq \varnothing$ iff φ is realizable in $\mathcal{M}_E$. The construction is compositional and follows, for the basic blocks, the construction of Section 4 for LTL formulas. The main idea is to replace subformulas of the form $K\gamma$ by fresh atomic propositions k_γ so that we get an LTL formula for which the realizability problem can be transformed into the emptiness of a UCT. The realizability of the subformulas $K\gamma$ that have been replaced by k_γ is checked by branching universally to a UCT for γ, constructed as in Section 4. Since transitions are universal, this will ensure that all the infinite branches of the tree from the current node where a new UCT has been triggered also satisfy γ. The UCTs we construct are defined over an extended alphabet that contains the new atomic propositions, but we show that we can safely project the final UCT on the alphabet Σ_1. The assumption on positivity of KLTL formulas implies that there is no subformulas of the form $\neg K\gamma$. The rewriting of subformulas by fresh atomic propositions cannot be done in any order. We now describe it formally.

We inductively define a sequence of formulas associated with φ as: $\varphi^0 = \varphi$ and, for all $i > 0$, φ^i is the formula φ^{i-1} in which the *innermost* subformulas $K\gamma$ are replaced by fresh atomic propositions k_γ. Let d be the smallest index such that φ^d is an LTL formula (in other words, d is the maximal nesting level of K operators). Let $\mathbb{K}$ denote the set of new atomic propositions, i.e., $\mathbb{K} = \bigcup_{i=0}^{d}\{k_\gamma \mid K\gamma \in \varphi^i\}$, and let $\mathcal{P}' = \mathcal{P} \cup \mathbb{K}$. Note that by definition of the formulas φ^i, for all atomic proposition k_γ occurring in φ^i, γ is an LTL formula over $\mathcal{P}'$. E.g. if $\varphi = p \to K(q \to Kr \vee Kz)$ and $\mathcal{P} = \{p, q, r, z\}$, then the sequence of formulas is: $\varphi^0 = \varphi$, $\varphi^1 = p \to K(q \to k_r \vee k_z)$, $\varphi^2 = p \to k_\gamma$ where $\gamma = q \to k_r \vee k_z$.

Then, we construct incrementally a chain of universal co-Büchi tree automata $\mathcal{T}^d, \ldots, \mathcal{T}^0$ such that $\mathcal{L}(\mathcal{T}^d) \supseteq \mathcal{L}(\mathcal{T}^{d-1}) \supseteq \cdots \supseteq \mathcal{L}(\mathcal{T}^0)$ and, the following invariant is satisfied: for all $i \in \{0, \ldots, d\}$, $\mathcal{T}^i$ accepts exactly the set of strategies that realize φ^i in $\mathcal{M}_E$. Intuitively, the automaton $\mathcal{T}^i$ is defined by adding new transitions in $\mathcal{T}^{i+1}$, such that for all atomic propositions k_γ occurring in φ^{i+1}, $\mathcal{T}^i$ will ensure that $K\gamma$ is indeed satisfied, by branching to a UCT checking γ whenever the atomic proposition k_γ is met. Since formulas φ^i are defined over the extended alphabet $\mathcal{P}' = \mathcal{P} \cup \mathbb{K}$ and $\mathcal{M}_E$ is defined over $\mathcal{P}$, we now make clear what we mean by realizability of a formula φ^i in $\mathcal{M}_E$. It uses the notion of *extended model executions* and *extended strategies*.

Extended Actions, Model Executions and Strategies. We extend the actions of the system to $\Sigma_1' = \Sigma_1 \times 2^{\mathbb{K}}$ (call e-actions). Informally, the system plays an e-action (a, K) if it considers formulas $K\gamma$ for all $k_\gamma \in K$ to be true. An *extended execution* (e-execution) of $\mathcal{M}_E$ is an infinite sequence $\rho = (s_0, K_0)\ldots \in (S_e \times 2^{\mathbb{K}})^\omega$ such that $s_0 s_1 \ldots \in \text{exec}(\mathcal{M}_E)$. We denote $s_0 s_1 \ldots$ by $\text{proj}_1(\rho)$ and $K_0 K_1 \ldots$ by $\text{proj}_2(\rho)$. The extended labelling function τ_e' is a function from $S_e \times 2^{\mathbb{K}}$ to $\mathcal{P}'$ defined by $\tau_e'(s, K) = \tau_e(s) \cup K$. The indistinguishability relation between extended executions is defined, for any two extended executions ρ_1, ρ_2, by $\rho_1 \sim \rho_2$ iff $\text{proj}_1(\rho_1) \sim \text{proj}_1(\rho_2)$ and $\text{proj}_2(\rho_1) = \text{proj}_2(\rho_2)$, i.e., the propositions in $\mathbb{K}$ are visible to the system. We define $\sim_i$ over extended executions similarly. Given the extended labelling functions and indistinguishability relation, the KLTL satisfiability notion $R, \rho, i \models \psi$ can be naturally defined for a set of e-execution R, $\rho \in R$ and ψ a KLTL formula over $\mathcal{P}' = \mathcal{P} \cup \mathbb{K}$.

An extended strategy is a strategy defined over e-actions, i.e. a function from $(\Sigma_1'\mathcal{O})^*$ to Σ_1'. For an infinite sequence $u = (a_0, K_0)o_0(a_1, K_1)o_1 \cdots \in (\Sigma_1'\mathcal{O})^\omega$, we define $\text{proj}_1(u)$ as $a_0 o_0 \ldots$. The sequence u defines a set of compatible e-executions $\text{exec}(\mathcal{M}_E, u)$ as follows: it is the set of e-executions $\rho = (s_0, K_0)(s_1, K_1)\ldots \in (S_e \times 2^{\mathbb{K}})^\omega$ such that $\text{proj}_1(\rho) \in \text{exec}(\mathcal{M}_E, \text{proj}_1(u))$. Similarly, we define for e-strategies λ' the set $\text{exec}(\mathcal{M}_E, \lambda')$ of e-executions compatible with λ'. A KLTL formula ψ

over $\mathcal{P}'$ is realizable in $\mathcal{M}_E$ if there exists an e-strategy λ' such that for all runs $\rho \in \text{exec}(\mathcal{M}_E, \lambda')$, we have $\text{exec}(\mathcal{M}_E, \lambda'), \rho, 0 \models \psi$.

Proposition 2. *There exists an e-strategy $\lambda' : (\Sigma_1' \mathcal{O})^* \to \Sigma_1'$ realizing φ^0 in $\mathcal{M}_E$ iff there exists a strategy $\lambda : (\Sigma_1 \mathcal{O})^* \to \Sigma_1$ realizing φ^0 in $\mathcal{M}_E$.*

Proof. Let see e-strategies and strategies as Σ_1'-labelled (resp. Σ_1-labelled) $\mathcal{O}$-trees. Given a tree representing λ', we project its labels on Σ_1 to get a tree representing λ. The strategy λ defined in this way realises φ^0, as φ^0 does not contain any occurrence of propositions in $\mathbb{K}$. Conversely, given a tree representing λ, we extend its labels with $\emptyset$ to get a tree representing λ'. It can be shown for the same reasons that λ' realizes φ^0.   □

Incremental Tree Automata Construction. The invariant mentioned before can now be stated more precisely: for all i, $\mathcal{T}^i$ accepts the e-strategies $\lambda' : (\Sigma_1' \mathcal{O}) \to \Sigma_1'$ that realise φ^i in $\mathcal{M}_E$. Therefore, the UCT $\mathcal{T}^i$ are labelled with e-actions Σ_1'. We now explain how they are constructed.

Since φ^d is an LTL formula, we follow the construction of Section 4 to build the UCT $\mathcal{T}^d$. Then, we construct $\mathcal{T}^i$ from $\mathcal{T}^{i+1}$, for $0 \le i < d$. The invariant tells us that $\mathcal{T}^{i+1}$ defines all the e-strategies that realize φ^{i+1} in $\mathcal{M}_E$. It is only an over-approximation of the set of e-strategies that realize φ^i in $\mathcal{M}_E$ (and *a fortiori* φ^0), since the subformulas of φ^i of the form $K\gamma$ correspond to atomic propositions k_γ in φ^{i+1}, and therefore $\mathcal{T}^{i+1}$ does not check that they are satisfied. Therefore to maintain the invariant, $\mathcal{T}^i$ is obtained from $\mathcal{T}^{i+1}$ such that whenever an action that contains some formula $k_\gamma \in sub(\varphi^{i+1})$ occurs on a transition of $\mathcal{T}^{i+1}$, we trigger (universally) a new transition to a UCT $\mathcal{T}_{\gamma,I}$, for the current information set I in $\mathcal{T}^{i+1}$, that will check that $K\gamma$ indeed holds. The assumption on positivity of KLTL formulas is necessary here as we do not have to check for formulas of the form $\neg K\gamma$, which could not be done without an involved "non Safraless" complementation step. Since γ is necessarily an LTL formula over $\mathcal{P}'$ by definition of the formula φ^{i+1}, we can apply the construction of Section 4 to build $\mathcal{T}_{\gamma,I}$.

Formally, from the incremental way of constructing the automata $\mathcal{T}^j$ for $j \ge i$, we know that $\mathcal{T}^{i+1}$ has a set of states Q_{i+1} where all states are of the form (q, I) where $I \subseteq S_e$ is some knowledge. In particular, it can be verified to be true for the state space of $\mathcal{T}^d$ by definition of the construction of Section 4. Let also Δ_{i+1} be the transition relation of $\mathcal{T}^{i+1}$. For all formulas γ such that k_γ occurs in φ^{i+1}, we let Q_γ be the set of states of $\mathcal{T}_{\gamma,I}$ and Δ_γ its set of transitions. Again from the construction of Section 4, we know that $Q_\gamma = Q \times 2^{S_e}$ where Q is the set of states of a UCW associated with γ (assumed to be disjoint from that of $\mathcal{T}^{i+1}$) and $Q_\gamma^0 = Q \times I$.

We define the set of states Q_i of $\mathcal{T}^i$ by $Q_{i+1} \cup \bigcup_{k_\gamma \in sub(\varphi^{i+1})} Q_\gamma$. Its set of transitions Δ_i is defined as follows. Assume w.l.o.g. that there is a unique initial state $q_0 \in Q$ in the UCW $\mathcal{A}_\gamma$. If $(q', I') \in \Delta_{i+1}((q, I), (a, K), o)$ where $I, I' \subseteq S_e$, $a \in \Sigma_1$, $K \subseteq \mathbb{K}$, $o \in \mathcal{O}$ and $k_\gamma \in K$ is such that $k\gamma$ occurs in φ^{i+1}, then we let $(q', I') \in \Delta_i((q, I), (a, K), o)$ and $\Delta_\gamma((q_0, I), (a, K), o) \subseteq \Delta_i((q, I), (a, K), o)$. The whole construction is given in [6], as well as the proof of its correctness. The invariant is satisfied:

Lemma 2. *For all $i \ge 0$, $\mathcal{L}(\mathcal{T}^i)$ accepts the set of e-strategies that realize φ^i in $\mathcal{M}_E$.*

From Lemma 2, we know that $\mathcal{L}(\mathcal{T}^0)$ accepts the set of e-strategies that realize $\varphi^0 = \varphi$ in $\mathcal{M}_E$. Then by Proposition 2 we get:

Corollary 1. *The* KLTL$^+$ *formula* φ *is realizable in* $\mathcal{M}_E$ *iff* $\mathcal{L}(\mathcal{T}^0) \neq \varnothing$.

We now let $\mathcal{T}_\varphi$ be the UCT obtained by projecting $\mathcal{T}^0$ on Σ_1. We have:

Theorem 2. *For any* KLTL$^+$ *formula* φ, *one can construct a UCT* $\mathcal{T}_\varphi$ *such that* $\mathcal{L}(\mathcal{T}_\varphi)$ *is the set of strategies that realize* φ *in* $\mathcal{M}_E$.

The number of states of $\mathcal{T}_\varphi$ is (in the worst-case) $2^{|S_e|}.(2^{|\varphi^d|} + \sum_{k_\gamma \in \mathbb{K}} 2^{|\gamma|})$, and since $|\varphi^d| + \sum_{\gamma \in \mathbb{K}} |\gamma|$ is bounded by $|\varphi|$, the number of states of $\mathcal{T}_\varphi$ is $O(2^{|S_e|+|\varphi|})$.

6   Antichain Algorithm

In the previous sections, we have shown how to reduce the problem of checking the realizability of a KLTL$^+$ formula φ to the emptiness of a UCT $\mathcal{T}_\varphi$ (Theorem 2). In this section, we describe an antichain symbolic algorithm to test the emptiness of $\mathcal{T}_\varphi$.

It is already known from [9] that checking emptiness of the language defined by a UCT $\mathcal{T}$ can be reduced to checking the emptiness of $\mathcal{L}_{uc,B}(\mathcal{T})$ for a sufficiently large bound B, which in turn can be reduced to solving a safety game. Clearly, for all $b \geq 0$, if $\mathcal{L}_{uc,b}(\mathcal{T}) \neq \emptyset$, then $\mathcal{L}_{uc}(\mathcal{T}) \neq \emptyset$. This has led to an incremental algorithm that starts with the bound 0, and the experiments have shown that in general, a small bound b is necessary to conclude for realizability of an LTL formula (transformed into the emptiness of a UCT). We also exploit this idea in our implementation and show that for the KLTL$^+$ specifications that we considered, this observation still holds: small bounds are enough.

In [9], it is shown that the safety games can be solve on-the-fly without constructing them explicitly, and that the fixpoint algorithm used to solve these safety games could be optimized by using some antichain representation of the sets constructed during the fixpoint computation. Rather than using the algorithm of [9] as a black box, we study the state space of the safety games constructed from the UCT $\mathcal{T}_\varphi$ and show that they are also equipped with a partial order that allows one to get more compact antichain representations. We briefly recall the reduction of [9], the full construction of the safety games is given in [6].

Given a bound $b \geq 0$ and a UCT $\mathcal{T}$, the idea is to construct a safety game $G(\mathcal{T}, b)$ such that Player 1 has a winning strategy in $G(\mathcal{T}, b)$ iff $\mathcal{L}_{uc,b}(\mathcal{T})$ is non-empty. The game $G(\mathcal{T}, b)$ is obtained by extending the classical automata subset construction with counters which count, up to b, the maximal number of times all the runs, up to the current point, have visited accepting states. If Q is the set of states of $\mathcal{T}$, the set of states of the safety game $G(\mathcal{T}, b)$ is all the functions $F : Q \to \{-1, 0, \ldots, b+1\}$. The value $F(q) = -1$ means that no run have reached q and $F(q) \in \{0, \ldots, b\}$ means that the maximal number of accepting states that has been visited by some run reaching q is $F(q)$. The safe states are all the functions F such that $F(q) \leq b$ for all $q \in Q$. The set of states can be partially ordered by the pairwise comparison between functions and it is shown that the sets of states manipulated by the fixpoint algorithm are downward closed for this order.

Consider now the UCT $\mathcal{T}_\varphi$ constructed from the KLTL$^+$ formula φ. Its state space is of the form $Q \times 2^{S_e}$ where S_e is the set of states of the environment, because the construction also takes into account the knowledge the system has from the environment. Given a bound b, the state space of the safety game $G(\mathcal{T}_\varphi, b)$ is therefore functions from $Q \times 2^{S_e}$ to $\{-1, \ldots, b+1\}$. However, we can reduce this state space thanks to the following result:

Proposition 3. *For all runs $\langle T_r, \tau \rangle$ of $\mathcal{T}_\varphi$ on some tree T, for all branches π, π' in T_r of the same length such that they follow the same sequence of observations, if $\tau(\pi) = (q, I)$ and $\tau(\pi') = (q, I')$, then $I = I'$.*

In other words, given the same sequence of observations, the tree automaton $\mathcal{T}_\varphi$ computes, for a given state q, the same knowledge.

Based on this proposition, it is clear that reachable states F of $G(\mathcal{T}_\varphi, b)$ satisfy, for all states $q \in Q$ and knowledges I, I', if $F(q, I) \neq -1$ and $F(q, I') \neq -1$ then $I = I'$. We can therefore define the state space of $G(\mathcal{T}_\varphi, b)$ as the set of pairs $(F, \overline{K})$ such that $F : Q \to \{-1, \ldots, b+1\}$ and $\overline{K} : Q \to 2^{S_e}$ associates with each state q a knowledge (we let $G(q) = \emptyset$ if $F(q) = -1$). This state space is naturally ordered by $(F_1, \overline{K}_1) \preceq (F_2, \overline{K}_2)$ if for all $q \in Q$, $F_1(q) \leq F_2(q)$ and $\overline{K}_1(q) \subseteq \overline{K}_2(q)$. We show that all the sets manipulated during the fixpoint computation used to solve the safety games are downward closed for this order and therefore can be represented by the antichain of their maximal elements. A detailed analysis of the size of the safety game shows that $G(\mathcal{T}_\phi, B)$ is doubly exponential in the size of φ, and therefore, since safety games can be solved in linear time, one gets a 2Exptime upper bound for KLTL$^+$ realizability. The technical details are given in [6].

7   Implementation and Case Studies

In this section we briefly present our prototype implementation Acacia-K for KLTL$^+$ synthesis [1], and provide some interesting examples on which we tested the tool, on a laptop equipped with an Intel Core i7 2.10Ghz CPU. Acacia-K extends the LTL synthesis tool Acacia+[5]. As Acacia+, the implementation is made in Python together with C for the low level operations that need efficiency.

As Acacia+, the tool is available in one version working on both Linux and MacOsX and can be executed using the command-line interface. As parameters, in addition to the files containing the KLTL$^+$ formula and the partition of the signals and actions, Acacia-K requires a file with the environment model. The output of the tool is a winning strategy, if the formula is realizable, given as a Moore machine described in Verilog and if this strategy is small, Acacia-K also outputs it as a picture.

In order to have a more efficient implementation, the construction of the automata for the LTL formulas γ is made on demand. That is, we construct the UCT $\mathcal{T}_\gamma$ incrementally by updating it as soon as it needs to be triggered from some state (q, I) which has not been constructed yet.

As said before, the synthesis problem is reduced to the problem of solving a safety game for some bound b on the number of visits to accepting states. The tool is incremental: it tests realizability for small values of b first and increments it as long as it cannot conclude for realizability. In practice, we have observed, as for classical LTL synthesis, that small bounds b are sufficient to conclude for realizability. However if the formula is not realizable, we have to iterate up to a large upper bound, which in practice is too large to give an efficient procedure for testing unrealizability. We leave as future work the implementation of an efficient procedure for testing unrealizability.

Taking now Example 1, the strategy provided by the tool is depicted in Figure 2. It asks to play first "toggle" and then keep on playing "skip" and, depending on the observation he gets, the system goes in a different state. The state 0 is for the start, the state 1 is the "error" state in which the system goes if he receives a wrong observation. That is, the environment gives an observation even if he cannot go in a state having that observation. Then, if the observation is correct, after playing the action "toggle" from the initial states $\{s_1, s_2\}$, the environment is forced to go in s_3 and by playing the action "skip", the system forces the environment to stay in s_3 and he will know that t is false. In the strategy, this situation corresponds to the state 2. For this example, Acacia-K constructed a UCT with 31 states and the total running time is 0.2s.

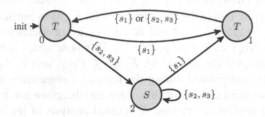

Fig. 2. Winning strategy synthesized by Acacia-K for Example 1

Example 2 (The 3-Coin Game). Another example that we tried is a game played using three coins which are arranged on a table with either *head* or *tail* up. The system doesn't see the coins, but knows at each time the number of tails and heads. Then, the game is infinitely played as follows. At the beginning the environment chooses an initial configuration and then at each round, the system chooses a coin and the environment has to flip that coin and inform the system about the new number of heads and tails. The objective of the system is to reach, at least once, the state in which all the coins have the *heads* up and to avoid all the time the state in which all the coins are *tails*. Depending on the initial number of tails up, the system may or may not have a winning strategy.

In order to model this, we considered an environment model whose states are labelled with atomic propositions c_1, c_2, c_3 for the three coins, which are not visible for the system, and two other variables b_1, b_0 which are visible and represent the bits encoding the number of *heads* in the configuration. The actions of the system are C_1, C_2, C_3 with which he chooses a coin and the environment has to flip the coin chosen by the system by playing only the action *done*. A picture of the environment is in [6].

Then, the specification is translated into the KLTL$^+$ formula $K\Diamond(c_1 \wedge c_2 \wedge c_3) \wedge \Box K(c_1 \vee c_2 \vee c_3)$. Then, assuming that the initial state of the environment has two *heads*, the synthesized strategy proposes to "check" the position of every coin by double flipping. If after one flip, the winning state is not reached, the system flips back the coin and at the third round he chooses another coin to check. A picture of the strategy can be found in [6]. For this example, Acacia-K constructs a UCT with 79 states, synthesises a strategy with 10 states, and the total running time is 3.9s.

Example 3 (n-Prisoners Enigma). Finally, the last example is about n prisoners in a prison, each one in his own cell and they cannot communicate. There is a special room with a light bulb and a switch and a policeman that, at each moment of time, sends only one prisoner in that room and gives him the possibility to turn on or off the light. The prisoners can only observe the light when they are in the special room. The guardians ensure that each prisoner is sent into the room an infinite number of times (fairness assumption). Before the game starts, the prisoners are allowed to communicate, and they know the initial state of the light. The goal of the prisoners is to learn whether all of them have visited the special room at least once – more specifically, whenever all prisoners have visited the room, one specially designated prisoner must know that fact.

Assume that the light is initially off. Then the winning strategy is that the special prisoner, say prisoner n, will count up to $n - 1$. For all $1 \leq j \leq n - 1$, the fairness assumption ensures that prisoner j will visit the room again and again until the game stops. The first time j visits the room and the light is off, he turns it on, otherwise he does nothing. Prisoner n will turn the light off next time he enters the room, and increment his counter by 1. When the counter reaches $n - 1$, prisoner n will be sure that all prisoners have visited the room at least once.

We have tried 3/4/5/6 prisoners versions (including the protagonist) of this problem, obtaining a one hour timeout for 6 agents. The statistics we obtained are the following:

Pris #	$\|\mathcal{M}_E\|$	$\|UCT\|$	$\|tb - UCT\|$	Aut constr (s)	$\|\mathcal{M}_\lambda\|$	Total time(s)
3	21	144	692	1.79s	12	1.87s
4	53	447	2203	1.98s	16	13.20s
5	129	1310	6514	199.06s	20	553.45s ($\simeq$ 9 min)
6	305	3633	18125	6081.69s	N/A	N/A

Again, Acacia-K generates strategies that are natural, the same that one would synthesize intuitively. For more details about this example see [6]. This fact is remarkable itself since, in synthesis, it is often a difficult task to generate small and natural strategies.

8 Conclusion

In this paper, we have defined a Safraless procedure for the synthesis of KLTL$^+$ specifications in environment with imperfect information. This problem is 2ExpTime-c but we have shown that our procedure, based on universal co-Büchi tree automata, can be implemented efficiently thanks to an antichain symbolic approach. We have implemented a prototype and run some preliminary experiments that prove the feasibility of our method. While the UCT constructed by the tool are not small (around 1300 states), our tool can handle them, although in theory, the safety games could be exponentially larger than the UCT. Moreover, our tool synthesises small strategies that correspond to the intuitive strategies we would expect, although it goes through a non-trivial automata construction. As a future work, we want to see if Acacia-K scales well on larger examples. We also want to extend the tool to handle the full KLTL logic in an efficient way. This paper is an encouraging (and necessary) step towards this objective. In a first attempt to generalize the specifications, we plan to consider assume-guarantees specifications $K\phi \to \psi$, where ϕ is an LTL formula and ψ a KLTL$^+$ formula.

References

1. Acacia-k, http://lacl.fr/rbozianu/Acacia-K/
2. Berwanger, D., Doyen, L.: On the power of imperfect informatio. In: Hariharan, R., Mukund, M., Vinay, V., R. Hariharan, M.M.a.V.V. (eds.) FSTTCS. LIPIcs, vol. 2, pp. 73–82. Schloss Dagstuhl - Leibniz-Zentrum fuer Informatik (2008)
3. Bloem, R., Cimatti, A., Greimel, K., Hofferek, G., Könighofer, R., Roveri, M., Schuppan, V., Seeber, R.: Ratsy a new requirements analysis tool with synthesis. In: Touili, T., Cook, B., Jackson, P. (eds.) CAV 2010. LNCS, vol. 6174, pp. 425–429. Springer, Heidelberg (2010)
4. Bloem, R., Jobstmann, B., Piterman, N., Pnueli, A., Sa'ar, Y.: Synthesis of reactive (1) designs. J. Comput. Syst. Sci. 78(3), 911–938 (2012)
5. Bohy, A., Bruyère, V., Filiot, E., Jin, N., Raskin, J.-F.: Acacia+, a tool for LTL synthesis. In: Madhusudan, P., Seshia, S.A. (eds.) CAV 2012. LNCS, vol. 7358, pp. 652–657. Springer, Heidelberg (2012)
6. Bozianu, R., Dima, C., Filiot, E.: Safraless synthesis for epistemic temporal specifications (2014), http://arxiv.org/abs/1405.0424
7. Chatterjee, K., Doyen, L., Filiot, E., Raskin, J.-F.: Doomsday equilibria for omega-regular games. In: McMillan, K.L., Rival, X. (eds.) VMCAI 2014. LNCS, vol. 8318, pp. 78–97. Springer, Heidelberg (2014)
8. Chatterjee, K., Doyen, L., Henzinger, T.A.: A survey of partial-observation stochastic parity games. Formal Methods in System Design 43(2), 268–284 (2013)
9. Filiot, E., Jin, N., Raskin, J.-F.: Antichains and compositional algorithms for LTL synthesis. Formal Methods in System Design 39(3), 261–296 (2011)
10. Di Giampaolo, B., Geeraerts, G., Raskin, J.-F., Sznajder, N.: Safraless procedures for timed specifications. In: Chatterjee, K., Henzinger, T.A. (eds.) FORMATS 2010. LNCS, vol. 6246, pp. 2–22. Springer, Heidelberg (2010)
11. Halpern, J.Y., Moses, Y.: Knowledge and common knowledge in a distributed environment. In: Kameda, T., Misra, J., Peters, J.G., Santoro, N. (eds.) PODC, pp. 50–61. ACM (1984)
12. Jobstmann, B., Bloem, R.: Optimizations for LTL synthesis. In: Formal Methods in Computer-Aided Design (FMCAD), pp. 117–124. IEEE Computer Society (2006)
13. Kupferman, O., Vardi, M.Y.: Safraless decision procedures. In: FOCS, pp. 531–542. IEEE Computer Society (2005)
14. Pnueli, A., Rosner, R.: On the synthesis of a reactive module. In: POPL, pp. 179–190. ACM Press (1989)
15. Raskin, J.-F., Chatterjee, K., Doyen, L., Henzinger, T.A.: Algorithms for omega-regular games with imperfect information. Logical Methods in Computer Science 3(3) (2007)
16. Schewe, S., Finkbeiner, B.: Bounded synthesis. In: Namjoshi, K.S., Yoneda, T., Higashino, T., Okamura, Y. (eds.) ATVA 2007. LNCS, vol. 4762, pp. 474–488. Springer, Heidelberg (2007)
17. van der Meyden, R., Vardi, M.Y.: Synthesis from knowledge-based specifications (Extended abstract). In: Sangiorgi, D., de Simone, R. (eds.) CONCUR 1998. LNCS, vol. 1466, pp. 34–49. Springer, Heidelberg (1998)

Minimizing Running Costs in Consumption Systems*

Tomáš Brázdil, David Klaška, Antonín Kučera, and Petr Novotný

Faculty of Informatics, Masaryk University, Brno, Czech Republic

Abstract. A standard approach to optimizing long-run running costs of discrete systems is based on minimizing the *mean-payoff*, i.e., the long-run average amount of resources ("energy") consumed per transition. However, this approach inherently assumes that the energy source has an unbounded capacity, which is not always realistic. For example, an autonomous robotic device has a battery of finite capacity that has to be recharged periodically, and the total amount of energy consumed between two successive charging cycles is bounded by the capacity. Hence, a controller minimizing the mean-payoff must obey this restriction. In this paper we study the controller synthesis problem for *consumption systems* with a finite battery capacity, where the task of the controller is to minimize the mean-payoff while preserving the functionality of the system encoded by a given linear-time property. We show that an optimal controller always exists, and it may either need only finite memory or require infinite memory (it is decidable in polynomial time which of the two cases holds). Further, we show how to compute an effective description of an optimal controller in polynomial time. Finally, we consider the limit values achievable by larger and larger battery capacity, show that these values are computable in polynomial time, and we also analyze the corresponding rate of convergence. To the best of our knowledge, these are the first results about optimizing the long-run running costs in systems with bounded energy stores.

1 Introduction

A standard tool for modelling and analyzing the long-run average running costs in discrete systems is *mean-payoff*, i.e., the average amount of resources (or "energy") consumed per transition. More precisely, a system is modeled as a finite directed graph C, where the set of states S corresponds to configurations, and transitions model the discrete computational steps. Each transition is labeled by a non-negative integer specifying the amount of energy consumed by a given transition. Then, to every run ϱ in C one can assign the associated *mean-payoff*, which is the limit of average energy consumption per transition computed for longer and longer prefixes of ϱ. A basic algorithmic task is to find a suitable *controller* for a given system which minimizes the mean-payoff. Recently, the problem has been generalized by requiring that the controller should also achieve a given *linear time property* φ, i.e., the run produced by a controller should satisfy φ while minimizing the mean-payoff (see, e.g., [15]). This is motivated by the fact that the system is usually required to achieve some functionality, and not just "run" with minimal average costs.

---

* The authors are supported by the Czech Science Foundation, grant No P202/10/1469.

A. Biere and R. Bloem (Eds.): CAV 2014, LNCS 8559, pp. 457–472, 2014.
© Springer International Publishing Switzerland 2014

Note that in the above approach, it is inherently assumed that all transitions are always enabled, i.e., the amount of energy consumed by a transition is always available. In this paper, we study the long-run average running costs in systems where the energy stores ("tanks" or "batteries") have a *finite* capacity $cap \in \mathbb{N}$. As before, the energy stored in the battery is consumed by performing transitions, but if the amount of energy currently stored in the battery is smaller than the amount of energy required by a given transition, then the transition is disabled. From time to time, the battery must be reloaded, which is possible only in certain situations (e.g., when visiting a petrol station). These restrictions are directly reflected in our model, where some states of C are declared as *reload states*, and the run produced by a controller must be *cap-bounded*, i.e., the total amount of energy consumed between two successive visits to reload states cannot exceed cap.

The main results of this paper can be summarized as follows. Let C be a system (with a given subset of reload states) and φ a linear-time property encoded as a nondeterministic Büchi automaton.

(A) We show that for a given capacity $cap \in \mathbb{N}$ and a given state s of C, there exists a controller μ *optimal* for s which produces a cap-bounded run satisfying φ while minimizing the mean payoff. Further, we prove that there is a dichotomy in the structural complexity of μ, i.e., one of the following possibilities holds:
- The controller μ can be constructed so that it has finitely many memory elements and can be compactly represented as a *counting controller* κ which is computable in time polynomial in the size of C and cap (all integer constants are encoded in *binary*).
- The controller μ *requires* infinite memory (i.e., every optimal controller has infinite memory) and there exists an optimal *advancing controller* π which admits a finite description computable in time polynomial in the size of C and cap.

Further, we show that it is decidable in polynomial time which of the two possibilities holds.

(B) For every state s of C, we consider its *limit value*, which is the *inf* of all mean-payoffs achievable by controllers for larger and larger battery capacity. We show that the limit value is computable in polynomial time. Further, we show that the problem whether the limit value is achievable by some *fixed* finite battery capacity is decidable in polynomial time. If it is the case, we give an explicit upper bound for cap; and if not, we give an upper bound for the difference between the limit value and the best mean-payoff achievable for a given capacity cap.

Technically, the most difficult part is (A), where we need to analyze the structure of optimal controllers and invent some tricks that allow for compact representation and computation of optimal controllers. Note that all constants are encoded in binary, and hence we cannot afford to construct any "unfoldings" of C where the current battery status (i.e., an integer between 0 and cap) is explicitly represented, because such an unfolding is exponentially larger than the problem instance. This is overcome by nontrivial insights into the structure of optimal controllers.

Previous and Related Work. A combination of mean-payoff and linear-time (parity) objectives has been first studied in [15] for 2-player games. It has been shown that optimal strategies exist in such games, but they may require infinite memory. Further, the values can be computed in time which is pseudo-polynomial in the size of the game and exponential in the number of priorities. Another closely related formalisms are *energy games* and *one-counter games*, where each transition can both increase and decrease the amount of energy, and the basic task of the controller is to avoid the situation when the battery is empty. Energy games with parity objectives have been considered in [11]. In these games, the controller also needs to satisfy a given parity condition apart of avoiding zero. Polynomial-time algorithms for certain subclasses of "pure" energy games (with zero avoidance objective only) have recently been designed in [14]. Energy games with capacity constraints were studied in [18]. Here it was shown, that deciding whether a given one-player energy game admits a run along which the accumulated reward stays between 0 and a given positive capacity is already an NP-hard problem. *One-counter Markov decision processes* and *one-counter stochastic games*, where the counter may change at most by one in each transition, have been studied in [6,5] for the objective of *zero reachability*, which is dual to zero avoidance. It has been shown that for one-counter MDPs (both maximizing and minimizing), the existence of a controller that reaches zero with probability one is in **P**. If such a controller exists, it is computable in polynomial time. For one-counter stochastic games, it was shown that the same problem is in **NP ∩ co-NP**. In [10], it was shown how to compute an ε-optimal controller minimizing the expected number of transitions needed to visit zero in one-counter MDPs. Another related model with only one counter are *energy Markov decision processes* [12], where the counter updates are arbitrary integers encoded in binary, and the controller aims at maximizing the probability of all runs that avoid visiting zero and satisfy a given parity condition. The main result of [12] says that the existence of a controller such that the probability of all runs satisfying the above condition is equal to one for a sufficiently large initial counter value is in **NP ∩ co-NP**. Yet another related model are *solvency games* [3], which can be seen as rather special one-counter Markov decision processes (with counter updates encoded in binary). The questions studied in [3] concern the structure of an optimal controller for maximizing the probability of all runs that avoid visiting negative values, which is closely related to zero avoidance.

There are also results about systems with more than one counter (resource). Examples include games over vector addition systems with states [8], *multiweighted energy games* [18,4], *generalized energy games* [13], *consumption games* [7], etc. We refer to [19] for a more detailed overview.

2 Preliminaries

The sets of all integers, positive integers, and non-negative integers are denoted by $\mathbb{Z}$, $\mathbb{N}$, and $\mathbb{N}_0$, respectively. Given a set A, we use $|A|$ to denote the cardinality of A. The encoding size of a given object B is denoted by $\|B\|$. In particular, all integer numbers are encoded in *binary*, unless otherwise stated.

A *labelled graph* is a tuple $G = (V, \rightarrow, L, \ell)$ where V is a non-empty finite set of vertices, $\rightarrow \subseteq V \times V$ is a set of *edges*, L is a non-empty finite set of *labels*, and ℓ is a function which to every edge assigns a label of L. We write $s \xrightarrow{a} t$ if $s \rightarrow t$ and a is the label of (s, t).

A *finite path* in G of *length* $n \in \mathbb{N}_0$ is a finite sequence $\alpha \equiv v_0 \ldots v_n$ of vertices such that $v_i \to v_{i+1}$ for all $0 \le i < n$. The length of α is denoted by $len(\alpha)$, and the label of $v_i \to v_{i+1}$ is denoted by a_i. An *infinite path* (or *run*) in G is an infinite sequence of vertices ϱ such that every finite prefix of ϱ is a finite path in G. Finite paths and runs in G are also written as sequences of the form $v_0 \overset{a_0}{\to} v_1 \overset{a_1}{\to} v_2 \overset{a_2}{\to} \cdots$. Given a finite or infinite path $\varrho \equiv v_0 v_1 \ldots$ and $i \in \mathbb{N}_0$, we use $\varrho(i)$ to denote the i-th vertex v_i of ϱ, and $\varrho_{\le i}$ to denote the prefix $v_0 \ldots v_i$ of ϱ of length i.

A finite path $\alpha \equiv v_0 \ldots v_n$ in G is a *cycle* if $n \ge 1$ and $v_0 = v_n$, and a *simple cycle* if it is a cycle and $v_i \ne v_j$ for all $0 \le i < j < n$. Given a finite path $\alpha \equiv v_0 \ldots v_n$ and a finite or infinite path $\varrho \equiv u_0 u_1 \ldots$ such that $v_n = u_0$, we use $\alpha \cdot \varrho$ to denote the *concatenation* of α and ϱ, i.e., the path $v_0 \ldots v_n u_1 u_2 \ldots$. Further, if α is a cycle, we denote by α^ω the infinite path $\alpha \cdot \alpha \cdot \alpha \cdots$.

In our next definition, we introduce consumption systems that have been informally described in Section 1. Recall that an optimal controller for a consumption system should minimize the mean-payoff of a *cap*-bounded run and satisfy a given linear-time property φ (encoded by a non-deterministic Büchi automaton $\mathcal{B}$). For technical convenience, we assume that $\mathcal{B}$ has already been multiplied with the considered consumption system (i.e., the synchronized product has already been constructed[1]). Technically, we declare some states in consumption systems as accepting and require that a *cap*-bounded run visits an accepting state infinitely often.

Definition 1. *A consumption system is a tuple* $C = (S, \to, c, R, F)$ *where S is a finite non-empty set of states,* $\to \subseteq S \times S$ *is a transition relation, c is a function assigning a non-negative integer* cost *to every transition, $R \subseteq S$ is a set of reload states, and $F \subseteq S$ a non-empty set of accepting states. We assume that $\to$ is total, i.e., for every $s \in S$ there is some $t \in S$ such that $s \to t$.*

The encoding size of C is denoted by $\|C\|$ (transition costs are encoded in binary). All notions defined for labelled graphs naturally extend to consumption systems.

The *total cost* of a given finite path $\alpha \equiv s_0 \overset{c_0}{\to} s_1 \overset{c_1}{\to} \cdots \overset{c_n}{\to} s_{n+1}$ is defined as $c(\alpha) = \sum_{i=0}^{n} c_i$, and the *mean cost* of α as $MC(\alpha) = c(\alpha)/(n+1)$. Further, we define the *end cost* of α as the total cost of the longest suffix $s_i \overset{c_i}{\to} \cdots \overset{c_n}{\to} s_{n+1}$ of α such that $s_{i+1}, \ldots, s_{n+1} \notin R$ (intuitively, the end cost of α is the total amount of resources consumed since the last reload, or since the start if no reload happened on α).

Let $cap \in \mathbb{N}$. We say that a finite or infinite path $\varrho \equiv s_0 \overset{c_0}{\to} s_1 \overset{c_1}{\to} s_2 \overset{c_2}{\to} \cdots$ is *cap-bounded* if the end cost of every finite prefix of ϱ is bounded by cap. Intuitively, this means that the total amount of resources consumed between two consecutive visits to reload states in ϱ is bounded by cap (we assume that initially the battery is loaded to a full capacity). Further, we say a run ϱ in C is *accepting* if $\varrho(i) \in F$ for infinitely many $i \in \mathbb{N}$. For every run ϱ in C we define

$$Val_C^{cap}(\varrho) = \begin{cases} \limsup_{i\to\infty} MC(\varrho_{\le i}) & \text{if } \varrho \text{ is } cap\text{-bounded and accepting;} \\ \infty & \text{otherwise.} \end{cases}$$

---

[1] It will become clear later that $\mathcal{B}$ being non-deterministic is not an obstacle here, since we work in a non-stochastic one-player setting.

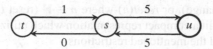

Fig. 1. An optimal controller may require memory of exponential size. Here $R = \{u\}$ and $F = S$.

The *cap-value* of a given state $s \in S$ is defined by

$$Val_C^{cap}(s) = \inf_{\varrho \in Run(s)} Val_C^{cap}(\varrho)$$

where $Run(s)$ is the set of all runs in C initiated in s. Intuitively, $Val_C^{cap}(s)$ is the minimal mean cost of a *cap*-bounded accepting run initiated in s. The *limit value* of s is defined by $Val_C(s) = \lim_{cap \to \infty} Val_C^{cap}(s)$.

Definition 2. *Let* $C = (S, \to, c, R, F)$ *be a consumption system. A controller for C is a tuple* $\mu = (M, \sigma_n, \sigma_u, m_0)$ *where M is a set of memory elements,* $\sigma_n : S \times M \to S$ *is a next function satisfying* $s \to \sigma_n(s, m)$ *for every* $(s, m) \in S \times M$, $\sigma_u : S \times M \to M$ *is an update function, and m_0 is an initial memory element. If M is finite, we say that μ is a finite-memory controller (FMC).*

For every finite path $\alpha = s_0 \ldots s_n$ in C, we use $\hat{\sigma}_u(\alpha)$ to denote the unique memory element "entered" by μ after reading α. Formally, $\hat{\sigma}_u(\alpha)$ is defined inductively by $\hat{\sigma}_u(s_0) = \sigma_u(s_0, m_0)$, and $\hat{\sigma}_u(s_0 \ldots s_{n+1}) = \sigma_u(s_{n+1}, \hat{\sigma}_u(s_0 \ldots s_n))$. Observe that for every $s_0 \in S$, the controller μ determines a unique run $run(\mu, s_0)$ defined as follows: the initial state of $run(\mu, s_0)$ is s_0, and if $s_0 \ldots s_n$ is a prefix of $run(\mu, s_0)$, then the next state is $\sigma_n(s_n, \hat{\sigma}_u(s_0 \ldots s_n))$. The size of a given FMC μ is denoted by $\|\mu\|$ (in particular, note that $\|\mu\| \geq |M|$).

Definition 3. *Let C be a consumption system, μ a controller for C, and cap $\in \mathbb{N}$. We say that μ is cap-optimal for a given state s of C if* $Val_C^{cap}(run(\mu, s)) = Val_C^{cap}(s)$.

As we shall see, a *cap*-optimal controller for s always exists, but it may require infinite memory. Further, even if there is a FMC for s, it may require exponentially many memory elements. To see this, consider the simple consumption system of Fig. 1. An optimal controller for s has to (repeatedly) perform $cap - 10$ visits to t and then one visit to the only reload state u, which requires $cap - 10$ memory elements (recall that cap is encoded in binary). Further examples of a non-trivial optimal behaviour can be found in the full version of this paper [9].

To overcome these difficulties, we introduce a special type of finite-memory controllers called *counting controllers*, and a special type of infinite memory controllers called *advancing controllers*.

Intuitively, memory elements of a counting controller are pairs of the form (r, d) where r ranges over a finite set *Mem* and d is a non-negative integer of a bounded size. The next and update functions depend only on r and the information whether d is zero or positive. The update function may change (r, d) to some (r', d') where d' is obtained from d by performing a *counter action*, i.e., an instruction of the form *dec* (decrement), *noc* (no change), or *reset(n)* where $n \in \mathbb{N}$ (reset the value to n). Hence, counting controllers admit a compact representation which utilizes the special structure of memory elements and the mentioned restrictions.

Definition 4. *Let $C = (S, \rightarrow, c, R, F)$ be a consumption system. A counting controller for C is a tuple $\kappa = (Mem, \sigma_n^+, \sigma_n^0, Act, \sigma_u^+, \sigma_u^0, r_0)$ where*

- *Mem is a finite set of basic memory elements,*
- *$\sigma_n^+, \sigma_n^0 : S \times Mem \rightarrow S$ are positive and zero next functions satisfying $s \rightarrow \sigma_n^+(s, r)$ and $s \rightarrow \sigma_n^0(s, r)$ for every $(s, r) \in S \times Mem$, respectively,*
- *Act is a finite set of counter actions (note that Act may contain instructions of the form reset(n) for different constants n);*
- *$\sigma_u^+ : S \times Mem \rightarrow Mem \times Act$ is a positive update function,*
- *$\sigma_u^0 : S \times Mem \rightarrow Mem \times (Act \setminus \{dec\})$ is a zero update function,*
- *$r_0 \in Mem$ is an initial basic memory element.*

The encoding size of a counting controller κ is denoted by $\|\kappa\|$, where all constants used in counter actions are encoded in binary.

The functionality of a counting controller $\kappa = (Mem, \sigma_n^+, \sigma_n^0, Act, \sigma_u^+, \sigma_u^0, r_0)$ is determined by its associated finite-memory controller $\mu_\kappa = (M, \sigma_n, \sigma_u, m_0)$ where

- $M = Mem \times \{0, \ldots, k_{max}\}$ where k_{max} is the largest n such that $reset(n) \in Act$ (or 0 if no such n exists);
- $\sigma_n(s, (r, d)) = \sigma_n^\odot(s, r)$, where $\odot$ is either $+$ or 0 depending on whether $d > 0$ or $d = 0$, respectively;
- $\sigma_u(s, (r, d)) = (r', d')$, where r' is the first component of $\sigma_u^\odot(s, r)$, and d' is either d, $d - 1$, or n, depending on whether the counter action in the second component of $\sigma_u^\odot(s, r)$ is *noc*, *dec*, or *reset(n)*, respectively (again, $\odot$ is either $+$ or 0 depending on whether $d > 0$ or $d = 0$);
- $m_0 = (r_0, 0)$.

Observe that $\|\kappa\|$ can be exponentially smaller than $\|\mu_\kappa\|$. Slightly abusing our notation, we write $run(\kappa, s_0)$ instead of $run(\mu_\kappa, s_0)$.

A counting controller κ can be seen as a program for a computational device with $O(\|Mem\|)$ control states and $\log(k_{max})$ bits of memory needed to represent the bounded counter. This device "implements" the functionality of μ_κ.

Definition 5. *Let $C = (S, \rightarrow, c, R, F)$ be a consumption system and $s \in S$. An advancing controller for C and s is a controller π for C such that $run(\pi, s)$ takes the form $\alpha \cdot \beta \cdot \gamma \cdot \beta^2 \cdot \gamma \cdot \beta^4 \cdots \gamma \cdot \beta^{2^i} \cdots$ where $\beta(0) \neq \beta(i)$ for all $0 < i < len(\beta)$.*

The encoding size of an advancing controller π, denoted by $\|\pi\|$, is given by the total encoding size of α, β, and γ. Typically, α and γ will be of polynomial length, but the length of β is sometimes exponential and in this case we use a counting controller to represent β compactly. Formally, we say that $\|\pi\|$ *is polynomial* in $\|C\|$ and $\|cap\|$ if α and γ are of polynomial length and there exists a counting controller $\kappa[\beta]$ such that $run(\kappa[\beta], \beta(0)) = \beta^\omega$ and $\|\kappa\|$ is polynomial in $\|C\|$ and $\|cap\|$.

An advancing controller π can be seen as a program for a computational device equipped with two unbounded counters (the first counter maintains the current i and the other counter is used to count from 2^i to zero; if the device cannot implement the '2^x' function directly, an auxiliary third counter may be needed). Also note that the device can use the program of $\kappa[\beta]$ as a subroutine to produce the finite path β (and hence also finite paths of the form β^{2^i}). Since $\beta(0) \neq \beta(i)$ for all $0 < i < len(\beta)$, the device simply simulates $\kappa[\beta]$ until revisiting $\beta(0)$.

3   The Results

In this section, we present the main results of our paper. Our first theorem concerns the existence and computability of values and optimal controllers in consumption systems.

Theorem 6. *Let C be a consumption system, $cap \in \mathbb{N}$, and s a state of C. Then $Val_C^{cap}(s)$ is computable in polynomial time (i.e., in time polynomial in $\|C\|$ and $\|cap\|$, where cap is encoded in binary). Further, there exists an optimal controller for s. The existence of an optimal finite memory controller for s is decidable in polynomial time. If there exists an optimal FMC for s, then there also exists an optimal counting controller for s computable in polynomial time. Otherwise, there exists an optimal advancing controller for s computable in polynomial time.*

Our second theorem concerns the limit values, achievability of limit values, and the rate of convergence to limit values.

Theorem 7. *Let C be a consumption system and s a state of C. Then $Val_C(s)$ can be computed in polynomial time (i.e., in time polynomial in $\|C\|$).*

Further, the problem whether $Val_C(s) = Val_C^{cap}(s)$ for some sufficiently large $cap \in \mathbb{N}$ is decidable in polynomial time. If the answer is positive, then $Val_C(s) = Val_C^{cap}(s)$ for every $cap \geq 3 \cdot |S| \cdot c_{max}$, where c_{max} is the maximal cost of a transition in C. Otherwise, for every $cap > 4 \cdot |S| \cdot c_{max}$ we have that $Val_C^{cap}(s) - Val_C(s) \leq (3 \cdot |S| \cdot c_{max})/(cap - 4 \cdot |S| \cdot c_{max})$.

The next subsections are devoted to the proofs of Theorems 6 and 7. Due to space constrains, some proofs and algorithms have been omitted. They can be found in [9].

3.1   A Proof of Theorem 6

For the rest of this section, we fix a consumption system $C = (S, \rightarrow, c, R, F)$, a capacity $cap \in \mathbb{N}$, and an initial state $s \in S$.

An *admissibility witness* for a state $q \in S$ is a cycle γ initiated in q such that γ contains an accepting state and there is a cap-bounded run initiated in s of the form $\alpha \cdot \gamma^\omega$. We say that $q \in S$ is *admissible* if there is at least one admissibility witness for q.

Observe that if γ is an admissibility witness for a reload state q, then γ can be freely "inserted" into any cap-bounded run of the form $\xi \cdot \delta$ where $\delta(0) = q$ so that the run $\xi \cdot \gamma \cdot \delta$ is again cap-bounded. Such simple observations about admissibility witnesses are frequently used in our proof of Theorem 6, which is obtained in several steps:

(1) We show how to compute all states $t \in S$ such that $Val_C^{cap}(t) = \infty$. Note that if $Val_C^{cap}(t) = \infty$, then *every* controller is optimal in t. Hence, if $Val_C^{cap}(s) = \infty$, we are done. Otherwise, we remove all states with infinite value from C together with their adjacent transitions.

(2) We compute and remove all states $t \in S$ that are not reachable from s via a *cap*-bounded finite path. This "cleaning" procedure simplifies our considerations and it can be performed in polynomial time.

(3) We show that $Val_C^{cap}(s) = 0$ iff C contains a *simple* cycle with zero total cost initiated in an admissible state (such a cycle is called a *zero-cost* cycle). Next, we show that if there is a zero-cost cycle β containing an accepting state, then there is an optimal FMC μ for s of *polynomial* size such that $run(\mu, s) = \alpha \cdot \beta^\omega$. Otherwise, *every* optimal controller for s has infinite memory, and we show how to compute finite paths α, γ of polynomial length such that the (*cap*-bounded) run $\varrho \equiv \alpha \cdot \beta \cdot \gamma \cdot \beta^2 \cdot \gamma \cdot \beta^4 \cdots \gamma \cdot \beta^{2^i} \cdots$ initiated in s satisfies $Val_C^{cap}(\varrho) = 0$. Thus, the finite paths α, β (which is a simple cycle), and γ represent an optimal advancing controller of polynomial size.

The existence of a zero-cost cycle (and the existence of a zero-cost cycle that contains an accepting state) is decidable in polynomial time. If a zero-cost cycle exists, we are done. Otherwise, we proceed to the next step.

(4) Now we assume that C does not contain a zero-cost cycle. We show that there exist

- a *cap*-bounded cycle β initiated in an admissible state such that β is *reload-short* (i.e., it contains at most $|R|$ occurrences of a reload state), $MC(\beta) \le MC(\delta)$ for every *cap*-bounded cycle δ initiated in an admissible state, and $\beta(0) \ne \beta(i)$ for all $0 < i < len(\beta)$;
- a reload-short *cap*-bounded cycle $\hat{\beta}$ containing an accepting state such that $MC(\hat{\beta}) \le MC(\hat{\delta})$ for every *cap*-bounded cycle $\hat{\delta}$ containing an accepting state.

We prove that $Val_C^{cap}(s) = MC(\beta)$. Further, we show the following:

- If $MC(\beta) = MC(\hat{\beta})$, then there exists an optimal FMC μ for s such that $run(\mu, s) = \alpha \cdot \hat{\beta}^\omega$, where α is a finite path of polynomial length. In general, $len(\hat{\beta})$ (and hence also $\|\mu\|$) is *exponential* in $\|C\|$ and $\|cap\|$. However, we show that there is always $\hat{\beta}$ of a special structure for which we can compute (in polynomial time) a *counting* controller $\kappa[\hat{\beta}]$ of *polynomial* size such that $run(\kappa[\hat{\beta}], \hat{\beta}(0)) = \hat{\beta}^\omega$. Since α can be computed in polynomial time, it follows that we can obtain, in polynomial time, a counting controller κ of polynomial size such that $run(\kappa, s) = run(\mu, s)$, i.e., κ is *cap*-optimal in s.
- If $MC(\beta) < MC(\hat{\beta})$, then *every cap*-optimal controller for s has infinite memory. Again, we show that there is always β of a special structure, for which we can efficiently compute finite paths α, γ of polynomial length and a counting controller $\kappa[\beta]$ of polynomial size such that $run(\kappa[\beta], \beta(0)) = \beta^\omega$ and the run $\varrho \equiv \alpha \cdot \beta \cdot \gamma \cdot \beta^2 \cdot \gamma \cdot \beta^4 \cdots \gamma \cdot \beta^{2^i} \cdots$ initiated in s satisfies $Val_C^{cap}(\varrho) = Val_C^{cap}(s)$. Thus, we obtain a *cap*-optimal advancing controller π for s of polynomial size.

We start with step (1).

Lemma 8. *Let $t \in S$. The problem whether $Val_C^{cap}(t) = \infty$ is decidable in polynomial time.*

The next lemma implements step (2).

Lemma 9. *Let $t \in S$. The existence of a cap-bounded path from s to t is decidable in polynomial time. Further, an example of a cap-bounded path from s to t (if it exists) of length at most $|S|^2$ is computable in polynomial time.*

We also need the following lemma which says that for every admissible state, there is an efficiently computable admissibility witness.

Lemma 10. *The problem whether a given* $q \in S$ *is admissible is decidable in polynomial time. Further, if* q *is admissible, then there are finite paths* α, γ *computable in polynomial time such that* $\alpha \cdot \gamma^\omega$ *is a cap-bounded run initiated in* s *and* γ *is an admissibility witness for* q *of length at most* $6 \cdot |S|^2$.

As we already indicated in the description of step (2), from now on we assume that all states of C have a finite value and are reachable from s via a *cap*-bounded finite path. Recall that a *zero-cost* cycle is a cycle in C initiated in an admissible state with zero total cost. Now we proceed to step (3).

Lemma 11. *We have that* $Val_C^{cap}(s) = 0$ *iff there exists a zero-cost cycle. Further, the following holds:*

1. *If there is a zero-cost cycle* β *containing an accepting state, then the run* $\varrho \equiv \alpha \cdot \beta^\omega$, *where* α *is any cap-bounded finite path from* s *to* $\beta(0)$, *satisfies* $Val_C^{cap}(\varrho) = Val_C^{cap}(s)$. *Hence, there is a FMC* μ *optimal for* s *where* $\|\mu\|$ *is polynomial in* $\|C\|$ *and* $\|cap\|$.
2. *If there is a zero-cost cycle* β *but no zero-cost cycle contains an accepting state, then every cap-optimal controller for* s *has infinite memory. Further, for a given zero-cost cycle* β *there exist finite paths* α *and* γ *computable in polynomial time such that the run* $\varrho \equiv \alpha \cdot \beta \cdot \gamma \cdot \beta^2 \cdots \gamma \cdot \beta^{2^i} \cdots$ *satisfies* $Val_C^{cap}(\varrho) = Val_C^{cap}(s)$. *Hence, there exists an advancing controller* π *optimal for* s *where* $\|\pi\|$ *is polynomial in* $\|C\|$ *and* $\|cap\|$.

In the next lemma we show how to decide the existence of a zero-cost cycle efficiently, and how to construct an example of a zero-cost cycle if it exists. The same is achieved for zero-cost cycles containing an accepting state. Thus, we finish step (3).

Lemma 12. *The existence of a zero-cost cycle is decidable in polynomial time, and an example of a zero-cost cycle* β *(if it exists) is computable in polynomial time. The same holds for zero-cost cycles containing an accepting state.*

It remains to complete step (4), which is the most technical part of our proof. From now on we assume that C does not contain any zero-cost cycles.

We say that a cycle β in C is *reload-short*, if β contains at most $|R|$ occurrences of a reload state. Further, we say that a cycle β is *T-visiting*, where $T \subseteq S$, if β is a *cap*-bounded reload-short cycle initiated in an admissible reload state such that β contains a state of T and $\beta(0) \neq \beta(i)$ for all $0 < i < len(\beta)$. We say that β is an *optimal T-visiting cycle* if $MC(\beta) \leq MC(\delta)$ for every T-visiting cycle δ. Note that every state of a T-visiting cycle β is admissible.

Lemma 13. *If* C *does not contain any zero-cost cycle, then it contains an optimal F-visiting cycle and an optimal S-visiting cycle.*

Proof. We give an explicit proof just for F-visiting cycles (the argument for S-visiting cycles is very similar). First, we show that there is at least one F-visiting cycle, and then we prove that every F-visiting cycle has a bounded length. Thus, the set of all F-visiting cycles is finite, which implies the existence of an optimal one.

Since $Val_C^{cap}(s) < \infty$, there is a cap-bounded accepting run ϱ initiated in s. Note that if ϱ contained only finitely many occurrences of reload states, it would have to contain zero-cost cycle, which contradicts our assumption. Hence, ϱ contains infinitely many occurrences of a reload state and infinitely many occurrences of an accepting state. Let ϱ' be a suffix of ϱ such that every state that appears in ϱ' appears infinitely often in ϱ' (hence, all states that appear in ϱ' are admissible). We say that a subpath $\varrho'(i) \ldots \varrho'(j)$ of ϱ' is *useless* if $\varrho'(i) = \varrho'(j) \in R$ and no accepting state is visited along this subpath. Let $\hat{\varrho}$ be a run obtained from ϱ' by removing all useless subpaths (observe that $\hat{\varrho}$ is still a cap-bounded accepting run). Then, there must be a subpath $\hat{\varrho}(i) \ldots \hat{\varrho}(j)$ of $\hat{\varrho}$ such that the length of this subpath is positive, $\hat{\varrho}(i) = \hat{\varrho}(j) \in R$, the subpath visits an accepting state, and no reload state is visited more than once along $\hat{\varrho}(i) \ldots \hat{\varrho}(j-1)$. Hence, this subpath is an F-visiting cycle.

Now let β be an F-visiting cycle. Then every state on β is admissible, which means that every simple cycle δ that is a subpath of β has positive cost, otherwise δ would be a zero-cost cycle. This implies that a maximal length of a subpath of β which does not contain any reload state is $(|S| + 1) \cdot (cap + 1)$ (because β is cap-bounded). From the reload-shortness of β we get that $len(\beta) \leq |R| \cdot (|S| + 1) \cdot (cap + 1)$.   □

We use MCF and MCS to denote the mean cost of an optimal F-visiting cycle and the mean cost of an optimal S-visiting cycle, respectively. Now we prove the following:

Lemma 14. *Suppose that C does not contain any zero-cost cycle. Then $Val_C^{cap}(s) = MCS \leq MCF$. Moreover, the following holds:*

1. *If $MCF = MCS$, then for every optimal F-visiting cycle β and every cap-bounded path α from s to $\beta(0)$ we have that the run $\varrho \equiv \alpha \cdot \beta^\omega$ satisfies $Val_C^{cap}(\varrho) = Val_C^{cap}(s)$. Hence, there exists an optimal FMC for s.*
2. *If $MCS < MCF$, then every cap-optimal controller for s has infinite memory. Further, for a given optimal S-visiting cycle β there exist finite paths α and γ computable in polynomial time such that the run $\varrho \equiv \alpha \cdot \beta \cdot \gamma \cdot \beta^2 \cdots \gamma \cdot \beta^{2^i} \cdots$ satisfies $Val_C^{cap}(\varrho) = Val_C^{cap}(s)$. Hence, there exists an optimal advancing controller for s.*

Proof. Clearly, $MCS \leq MCF$, because every F-visiting cycle is also S-visiting. Now we show that for every run ϱ we have $Val_C^{cap}(\varrho) \geq MCS$. This clearly holds for all non-accepting runs. Every accepting run ϱ must contain infinitely many occurrences of a reload state, otherwise it would contain a zero-cost cycle as a subpath, which contradicts our assumption. Let ϱ' be a suffix of ϱ initiated in a reload state such that every state which appears in ϱ' appears infinitely often in ϱ'. Then ϱ' takes the form $\beta_0 \cdot \beta_1 \cdot \beta_2 \cdots$, where for every $i \geq 0$, the subpath β_i is a cycle initiated in a reload state. Every β_i can be decomposed into reload-short cycles $\beta_{i,1}, \beta_{i,2}, \ldots, \beta_{i,i_m}$ that are initiated in reload states (here the decomposition is meant in a graph-theoretical sense, i.e., a transition appears b times on β_i if and only if $b = b_1 + \cdots + b_m$, where b_j is a number of occurrences of this transition on $\beta_{i,j}$). Each of these cycles is an S-visiting cycle (since every state on ϱ' is admissible) and clearly $MC(\varrho) = MC(\varrho') \geq \inf_{i \geq 1} MC(\beta_i) \geq \inf_{i \geq 0, 1 \leq j \leq i_m} MC(\beta_{i,j}) \geq MCS$.

Now let us consider the case when $MCF = MCS$, i.e., for every optimal F-visiting cycle β we have that $MC(\beta) = MCS$. If α is a cap-bounded path from s to $\beta(0)$, then we have that the run $\varrho \equiv \alpha \cdot \beta^\omega$ satisfies $Val_C^{cap}(\alpha \cdot \beta^\omega) = MCS = Val_C^{cap}(s)$, and hence there exists an optimal FMC for s.

If $MCS < MCF$, consider an optimal S-visiting cycle β. Since $\beta(0)$ is admissible, there is a cap-bounded run $\alpha \cdot \gamma^\omega$ initiated in s where γ is an admissibility witness for $\beta(0)$ and α and γ are computable in polynomial time (see Lemma 10). Further, the run $\varrho \equiv \alpha \cdot \beta \cdot \gamma \cdot \beta^2 \cdots \gamma \cdot \beta^{2^i} \cdots$ is accepting and cap-bounded, and one can easily show that $Val_C^{cap}(\varrho) = MC(\beta) = MCS = Val_C^{cap}(s)$. Hence, there exists an optimal advancing controller for s. It remains to show that there is no optimal finite memory controller for s. For every FMC μ we can write $run(\mu, s) \equiv \hat{\alpha} \cdot \hat{\beta}^\omega$, where $\hat{\beta}$ is a cycle on a reload state containing an accepting state. Further, $Val_C^{cap}(\mu) = MC(\hat{\beta})$. The cycle $\hat{\beta}$ can be decomposed, using the same technique as in the first paragraph of this proof, into *finitely many* reload-short cycles on reloading states, whose mean cost is at least MCS. At least one of these cycles is F-visiting. Since $MC(\hat{\beta})$ is a convex combination of the mean-costs of these cycles and $MCF > MCS$, we obtain $MC(\hat{\beta}) > MCS$. □

Note that Lemma 14 does not specify any bound on the length of β and in general, this length can be exponential. Now we show that an optimal F-visiting cycle and an optimal S-visiting cycle can be represented by a counting controller constructible in polynomial time. This is the technical core of our construction which completes the proof of Theorem 6.

Lemma 15. *Suppose that C does not contain any zero-cost cycle, and let T be either S or R. Then there exist a counting controller κ and a reload state r computable in polynomial time such that $run(\kappa, r) = \beta^\omega$ where β is an optimal T-visiting cycle.*

3.2 A Proof of Lemma 15

We start by refining the notion of an optimal T-visiting cycle and identifying those cycles that can be represented by counting controllers of polynomial size.

A *segment* of a path β is a finite subpath η of β such that the first and the last state of η are reload states and η does not contain any other occurrence of a reload state. Note that every reload-short cycle is composed of at most $|R|$ segments. Furthermore, we say that a finite path is *compact*, if it is a cap-bounded path of the form $\gamma \cdot \delta^k \cdot \gamma'$, where γ and γ' are finite paths satisfying $len(\gamma) + len(\gamma') \le 5|S|^3$, δ is either a cycle of length at most $|S|$ or a path of length 0 (i.e., a state), and $k \le cap$. A *compact segment* is a compact path that is also a segment.

Later we show that there is an optimal T-visiting cycle β such that every segment of β is a compact segment. Intuitively, such a cycle can be produced by a counting controller of polynomial size which has at most $|R|$ reset actions. However, this does not yet imply that such a counting controller can be efficiently constructed, because there are exponentially many possible compact segments. Hence, we need to show that we can restrict our attention to some set of compact segments of polynomial size.

We say that a compact segment $\gamma \cdot \delta^k \cdot \gamma'$ has a *characteristic* (r, q, t, m, n, b), where $r, t \in R$, $q \in S$, $m, n \in \mathbb{N}$ are such that $0 \le m \le 5|S|^3$ and $0 \le n \le |S|$, and $b \in \{0, 1\}$, if the following holds:

- $\gamma(0) = r$, $last(\gamma) = \gamma'(0) = q$, $last(\gamma') = t$, and $len(\gamma \cdot \gamma') = m$;
- $\delta(0) = q$, $len(\delta) = n$;
- we either have that $n = 0$ and $k = 1$, or $n > 0$ and then $c(\delta) > 0$ and k is the maximal number such that $\gamma \cdot \delta^k \cdot \gamma$ is a cap-bounded path;
- if $b = 1$, then $\gamma \cdot \gamma'$ contains a state of T;
- if δ contains a state of T, then $\gamma \cdot \gamma'$ also contains a state of T.

Note that for a given consumption system there are at most polynomially many distinct characteristics of compact segments. Also note that not all compact segments have a characteristic (because of the third and the fifth condition in the above definition), and conversely, some compact segments may have multiple characteristics (e.g., if a compact segment has a characteristic where $b = 1$, then it also has one where $b = 0$). Finally, note that for any compact segment $\gamma \cdot \delta^k \cdot \gamma'$ with a characteristic (r, q, t, m, n, b), the path $\gamma \cdot \gamma'$ is a compact segment with the characteristic $(r, q, t, m, 0, b)$.

A characteristic χ of a compact segment $\gamma \cdot \delta^k \cdot \gamma'$ imposes certain restrictions on the form of $\gamma \cdot \gamma'$ and δ. Such a compact segment is *optimal* for χ if $\gamma \cdot \gamma'$ and δ are paths of minimal cost among those that meet this restriction. Formally, a compact segment $\gamma \cdot \delta^k \cdot \gamma'$ with a characteristic $\chi = (r, q, t, m, n, b)$ is *optimal for* χ if

- $c(\gamma \cdot \gamma')$ is minimal among the costs of all segments with the characteristic $(r, q, t, m, 0, b)$, and
- $c(\delta)$ is minimal among the costs of all cycles of length n and positive cost, that are initiated in q, and that do not contain any reload state with a possible exception of q (if $n = 0$, we consider this condition to be satisfied trivially).

Lemma 16. *If there is at least one compact segment with a given characteristic χ, then there is also an optimal compact segment for χ. Moreover, all compact segments optimal for a given characteristic have the same total cost and length.*

Hence, to each of the polynomially many characteristics χ we can assign a segment optimal for χ and thus form a polynomial-sized candidate set of compact segments. The following lemma, which is perhaps the most intricate step in the proof of Lemma 15, shows that there is an optimal T-visiting cycle β such that every segment of β belongs to the aforementioned candidate set.

Lemma 17. *There is an optimal T-visiting cycle β whose every segment is a compact segment optimal for some characteristic.*

Given a characteristic χ, it is easy to compute a succinct representation of some compact segment optimal for χ, as the next lemma shows.

Lemma 18. *Given a characteristic χ, the problem whether the set of all compact segments with the characteristic χ is non-empty is decidable in polynomial time. Further, if the set is non-empty, then a tuple $(\gamma, \gamma', \delta, k)$ such that $\gamma \cdot \delta^k \cdot \gamma'$ is a compact segment optimal for χ is computable in polynomial time.*

For a given characteristic χ, we denote by $CTuple(\chi)$ the tuple $(\gamma, \gamma', \delta, k)$ returned for χ by the algorithm of Lemma 18 (if an optimal compact segment for χ does not exist, we put $CTuple(\chi) = \bot$), and by $CPath(\chi)$ the corresponding compact segment $\gamma \cdot \delta^k \cdot \gamma'$ (if $CTuple(\chi) = \bot$, we put $CPath(\chi) = \bot$). The next lemma is a simple corollary to Lemma 16 and Lemma 17.

Lemma 19. *There is an optimal T-visiting cycle β such that every segment of β is of the form $CPath(\chi)$ for some characteristic χ.*

Now we can easily prove the existence of a polynomial-sized counting controller representing some optimal T-visiting cycle β. According to Lemma 19, there is a sequence $\chi_0, \chi_1, \ldots, \chi_j$ of at most $|R|$ characteristics such that $\beta = CPath(\chi_0) \cdot CPath(\chi_1) \cdots CPath(\chi_j)$ is an optimal T-visiting cycle. To iterate the cycle β forever (starting in $\beta(0)$), a counting controller requires at most $|R| \cdot n$ basic memory elements, where n is the maximal number of basic memory elements needed to produce a compact segment $CPath(\chi_i)$, for $0 \le i \le j$. So, consider a compact segment $CPath(\chi_i) = \gamma \cdot \delta^k \cdot \gamma'$. Note that $k \le cap$ since $CPath(\chi_i)$ has a characteristic and thus $c(\delta) > 0$. To produce $CPath(\chi_i)$, the controller requires at most $5|S|^3$ basic memory elements to produce the prefix γ and the suffix γ' of $CPath(\chi_i)$, and at most $|S|$ basic memory elements to iterate the cycle δ (whose length is at most $|S|$) exactly k times. The latter task also requires counting down from $k \le cap$ to 0. Overall, the counting controller producing β^ω needs a polynomial number of basic memory elements, and requires at most $|R|$ reset actions parameterized by numbers of encoding size at most $\log(cap)$. To compute such a counting controller, it clearly suffices to compute the corresponding sequence of tuples $CTuple(\chi_0), \cdots, CTuple(\chi_j)$.

Now we can present the algorithm promised in Proposition 15. In the following, we use X to denote the set of all possible characteristics of compact segments in C, $X_{r,t}$ to denote the set of all characteristics of the form (r, q, t, m, n, b) for some q, m, n, b, and $X^1_{r,t}$ to denote the set of all characteristics in $X_{r,t}$ where the last component is equal to 1. The algorithm first computes the set $R' \subseteq R$ of all admissible reload states (see Lemma 10). Note that R' is non-empty because there exists at least one T-visiting cycle. The idea now is to compute, for every $\hat{q} \in R'$, a polynomial-sized labelled graph $G_{\hat{q}}$ such that cycles in this graph correspond to T-visiting cycles in C that are initiated in $\hat{q}$ and that can be decomposed into segments of the form $CPath(\chi)$. An optimal T-visiting cycle is then found via a suitable analysis of the constructed graphs.

Formally, for a given $\hat{q} \in R'$ we construct a labelled graph $G_{\hat{q}} = (V, \mapsto, L, \ell)$, where $L \subset \mathbb{N}_0^2$, and where:

- $V = (R' \cup \{CTuple(\chi) \mid \chi \in X\}) \times \{0, \ldots, |S|\}$.
- For every $0 \le i < |S|$, every pair of states $r, t \in R'$ such that $r \ne \hat{q}$, and every characteristic $\chi \in X_{r,t}$ there is an edge $((r, i), (CTuple(\chi), i))$ labelled by $(c(CPath(\chi)), len(CPath(\chi)))$ and an edge $((CTuple(\chi), i), (t, i+1))$ labelled by $(0, 0)$.
- For every state $t \in R'$ and every characteristic $\chi \in X^1_{\hat{q},t}$ there is an edge $((\hat{q}, 0), (CTuple(\chi), 0))$ labelled by $(c(CPath(\chi)), len(CPath(\chi)))$ and an edge $((CTuple(\chi), 0), (t, 1))$ labelled by $(0, 0)$.
- For every $1 \le i \le |S|$ there is an edge $((\hat{q}, i), (\hat{q}, 0))$ labelled by $(0, 0)$.
- There are no other edges.

The labelling function of $G_{\hat{q}}$ can be computed in polynomial time, because given a characteristic χ, we can compute $CTuple(\chi) = (\gamma, \gamma', \delta, k)$ using Lemma 18. Then, $len(CPath(\chi)) = len(\gamma) + len(\gamma') + k \cdot len(\delta)$, and similarly for $c(CPath(\chi))$. Note that every cycle in $G_{\hat{q}}$ contains the vertex $(\hat{q}, 0)$. Some of the constructed graphs $G_{\hat{q}}$ may not contain a cycle (the out-degree of $(\hat{q}, 0)$ may be equal to 0), but, as we shall see, at least one of them does.

The *ratio* of a cycle $\hat{\beta} = v_0 \stackrel{(c_0,d_0)}{\mapsto} v_1 \stackrel{(c_1,d_1)}{\mapsto} v_2 \cdots \stackrel{(c_{h-1},d_{h-1})}{\mapsto} v_h$ in $G_{\hat{q}}$ is the value $rat(\hat{\beta}) = (c_0 + c_1 + \cdots + c_{h-1})/(d_0 + d_1 + \cdots d_{h-1})$ (the denominator is positive due to the construction of $G_{\hat{q}}$). Now let $\hat{q} \in R'$ be arbitrary. Every cycle $\beta_{\hat{q}}$ in $G_{\hat{q}}$ (we can assume that it is initiated in $(\hat{q}, 0)$) uniquely determines a T-visiting cycle $\Psi(\beta_{\hat{q}})$ in C that is initiated in $\hat{q}$ and whose every segment has the form $CPath\chi$ for some χ. To see this, note that every second vertex on $\beta_{\hat{q}}$ is a 4-tuple of the form $CTuple(\chi)$ for some χ, so if $CTuple(\chi_0), CTuple(\chi_1), \ldots, CTuple(\chi_j)$ is the sequence of these 4-tuples in order in which they appear in $\beta_{\hat{q}}$, then we put $\Psi(\beta_{\hat{q}}) = CPath(\chi_0) \cdot CPath(\chi_1) \cdots CPath(\chi_j)$. Clearly $MC(\Psi(\beta_{\hat{q}})) = rat(\beta_{\hat{q}})$. Moreover, it is easy to see that Ψ is a bijection between the set of all cycles that appear in some $G_{\hat{q}}$ and the set of all T-visiting cycles in C whose segments are all of the form $CPath(\chi)$ for some χ (by Lemma 13, the latter of these sets – and thus both of them – must be non-empty). Thus, in order to find an optimal T-visiting cycle, the algorithm finds, for every $\hat{q} \in R'$, a simple cycle $\beta_{\hat{q}}$ of minimal ratio among all cycles in $G_{\hat{q}}$ (this is done using a polynomial-time algorithm for a well-studied problem of *minimum cycle ratio*, see, e.g., [16,17]), then simply picks $\hat{r} \in R'$ such that the ratio of $\beta_{\hat{r}}$ is minimal and computes $\Psi(\beta_{\hat{r}})$. The fact that $\Psi(\beta_{\hat{r}})$ is an optimal T-visiting cycle follows from the above observations and from Lemma 19.

3.3   Proof of Theorem 7

For the rest of this section we fix a consumption system $C = (S, \rightarrow, c, R, F)$ and an initial state $s \in S$. Intuitively, the controller can approach the limit value of s by interleaving a large number of iterations of some "cheap" cycle with visits to an accepting state. This motivates our definitions of *safe* and *strongly safe* cycles. Intuitively, a cycle is safe if, assuming unbounded battery capacity, the controller can interleave an arbitrary finite number of iterations of this cycle with visits to an accepting state. A cycle is strongly safe if the same behaviour is achievable for some finite (though possibly large) capacity.

Formally, we say that two states $q, t \in S$ are *inter-reachable* if there is a path from q to t and a path from t to q. We say that a cycle β of length at most $|S|$ and with $\beta(0)$ reachable from s is *safe*, if one of the following conditions holds:

– $c(\beta) = 0$ and β contains an accepting state,
– $\beta(0)$ is inter-reachable with a reload state and an accepting state,

A cycle β reachable from s with $len(\beta) \leq |S|$ is *strongly safe*, if one of the following holds:

– $c(\beta) = 0$ and β contains an accepting state,
– $c(\beta) = 0$ and $\beta(0)$ is inter-reachable with a reload state and an accepting state,
– β contains a reload state and $\beta(0)$ is inter-reachable with an accepting state.

The following lemma characterizes the limit value of s.

Lemma 20. *$Val_C(s)$ is finite iff there is a safe cycle, in which case $Val_C(s) = \min\{MC(\beta) \mid \beta$ is a safe cycle$\}$. Further, there is a finite $cap \in \mathbb{N}_0$ such that $Val_C^{cap}(s) = Val_C(s)$ iff either $Val_C(s) = \infty$, or there is a strongly safe cycle $\hat{\beta}$ such that $MC(\hat{\beta}) = Val_C(s)$. In such a case $Val_C^{cap}(s) = Val_C(s)$ for every $cap \geq 3 \cdot |S| \cdot c_{\max}$, where $c_{\max}$ is the maximal cost of a transition in C.*

So, in order to compute the limit value and to decide whether it can be achieved with some finite capacity, we need to compute a safe and a strongly safe cycle of minimal mean cost.

Lemma 21. *The existence of a safe (or strongly safe) cycle is decidable in polynomial time. Further, if a safe (or strongly safe) cycle exists, then there is a safe (or strongly safe) cycle β computable in polynomial time such that $MC(\beta) \le MC(\beta')$ for every safe (or strongly safe) cycle β'.*

Now we can prove the computation-related statements of Theorem 7.

To compute the limit value of s, we use the algorithm of Lemma 21 to obtain a safe cycle β of minimal mean cost. If no such cycle exists, we have $Val_C(s) = \infty$, otherwise $Val_C(s) = MC(\beta)$. To decide whether $Val_C(s)$ can be achieved with some finite capacity, we again use the algorithm of Lemma 21 to compute a strongly safe cycle $\hat{\beta}$ of minimal mean cost. If such a cycle exists and $MC(\hat{\beta}) = MC(\beta)$, then $Val_C(s)$ can be achieved with some finite capacity, otherwise not. The correctness of this approach follows from Lemma 20.

It remains to bound the rate of convergence to the limit value in case when no finite capacity suffices to realize it. This is achieved in the following lemma.

Lemma 22. *Let c_{max} be the maximal cost of a transition in C. For every $cap > 4 \cdot |S| \cdot c_{max}$ we have that*

$$Val_C^{cap}(s) - Val_C(s) \le \frac{3 \cdot |S| \cdot c_{max}}{cap - 4 \cdot |S| \cdot c_{max}}.$$

4 Future work

We have shown that an optimal controller for a given consumption system always exists and can be efficiently computed. We have also exactly classified the structural complexity of optimal controllers and analyzed the limit values achievable by larger and larger battery capacity.

The concept of *cap*-bounded mean-payoff is natural and generic, and we believe it deserves a deeper study. Since mean-payoff has been widely studied (and applied) in the context of Markov decision processes, a natural question is whether our results can be extended to MDPs. Some of our methods are surely applicable, but the question appears challenging.

References

1. Proceedings of FST&TCS 2010. Leibniz International Proceedings in Informatics, vol. 8. Schloss Dagstuhl–Leibniz-Zentrum für Informatik (2010)
2. Abramsky, S., Gavoille, C., Kirchner, C., Meyer auf der Heide, F., Spirakis, P.G. (eds.): ICALP 2010. LNCS, vol. 6199. Springer, Heidelberg (2010)
3. Berger, N., Kapur, N., Schulman, L.J., Vazirani, V.: Solvency Games. In: Proceedings of FST&TCS 2008. Leibniz International Proceedings in Informatics, vol. 2, pp. 61–72. Schloss Dagstuhl–Leibniz-Zentrum für Informatik (2008)

4. Bouyer, P., Fahrenberg, U., Larsen, K.G., Markey, N., Srba, J.: Infinite Runs in Weighted Timed Automata with Energy Constraints. In: Cassez, F., Jard, C. (eds.) FORMATS 2008. LNCS, vol. 5215, pp. 33–47. Springer, Heidelberg (2008)

5. Brázdil, T., Brožek, V., Etessami, K.: One-Counter Stochastic Games. In: Proceedings of FST&TCS 2010 [1], pp. 108–119 (2010)

6. Brázdil, T., Brožek, V., Etessami, K., Kučera, A., Wojtczak, D.: One-Counter Markov Decision Processes. In: Proceedings of SODA 2010, pp. 863–874. SIAM (2010)

7. Brázdil, T., Chatterjee, K., Kučera, A., Novotný, P.: Efficient Controller Synthesis for Consumption Games with Multiple Resource Types. In: Madhusudan, P., Seshia, S.A. (eds.) CAV 2012. LNCS, vol. 7358, pp. 23–38. Springer, Heidelberg (2012)

8. Brázdil, T., Jančar, P., Kučera, A.: Reachability Games on Extended Vector Addition Systems with States. In: Abramsky, S., Gavoille, C., Kirchner, C., Meyer auf der Heide, F., Spirakis, P.G. (eds.) ICALP 2010, Part II. LNCS, vol. 6199, pp. 478–489. Springer, Heidelberg (2010)

9. Brázdil, T., Klaška, D., Kučera, A., Novotný, P.: Minimizing Running Costs in Consumption Systems. Technical report, http://arxiv.org/abs/1402.4995

10. Brázdil, T., Kučera, A., Novotný, P., Wojtczak, D.: Minimizing Expected Termination Time in One-Counter Markov Decision Processes. In: Czumaj, A., Mehlhorn, K., Pitts, A., Wattenhofer, R. (eds.) ICALP 2012, Part II. LNCS, vol. 7392, pp. 141–152. Springer, Heidelberg (2012)

11. Chatterjee, K., Doyen, L.: Energy Parity Games. In: Abramsky, S., Gavoille, C., Kirchner, C., Meyer auf der Heide, F., Spirakis, P.G. (eds.) ICALP 2010, Part II. LNCS, vol. 6199, pp. 599–610. Springer, Heidelberg (2010)

12. Chatterjee, K., Doyen, L.: Energy and Mean-Payoff Parity Markov Decision Processes. In: Murlak, F., Sankowski, P. (eds.) MFCS 2011. LNCS, vol. 6907, pp. 206–218. Springer, Heidelberg (2011)

13. Chatterjee, K., Doyen, L., Henzinger, T., Raskin, J.-F.: Generalized Mean-payoff and Energy Games. In: Proceedings of FST&TCS 2010 [1], pp. 505–516 (2010)

14. Chatterjee, K., Henzinger, M., Krinninger, S., Nanongkai, D.: Polynomial-Time Algorithms for Energy Games with Special Weight Structures. In: Epstein, L., Ferragina, P. (eds.) ESA 2012. LNCS, vol. 7501, pp. 301–312. Springer, Heidelberg (2012)

15. Chatterjee, K., Henzinger, T., Jurdziński, M.: Mean-Payoff Parity Games. In: Proceedings of LICS 2005, pp. 178–187. IEEE Computer Society Press (2005)

16. Dantzig, B., Blattner, W., Rao, M.R.: Finding a cycle in a graph with minimum cost to times ratio with applications to a ship routing problem. In: Rosenstiehl, P. (ed.) Theory of Graphs, pp. 77–84. Gordon and Breach (1967)

17. Dasdan, A., Irani, S.S., Gupta, R.K.: Efficient algorithms for optimum cycle mean and optimum cost to time ratio problems. In: Proceedings of 36th Design Automation Conference,1999, pp. 37–42 (1999)

18. Fahrenberg, U., Juhl, L., Larsen, K.G., Srba, J.: Energy Games in Multiweighted Automata. In: Cerone, A., Pihlajasaari, P. (eds.) ICTAC 2011. LNCS, vol. 6916, pp. 95–115. Springer, Heidelberg (2011)

19. Kučera, A.: Playing Games with Counter Automata. In: Finkel, A., Leroux, J., Potapov, I. (eds.) RP 2012. LNCS, vol. 7550, pp. 29–41. Springer, Heidelberg (2012)

CEGAR for Qualitative Analysis
of Probabilistic Systems[*,**]

Krishnendu Chatterjee, Martin Chmelík, and Przemysław Daca

IST Austria

Abstract. We consider Markov decision processes (MDPs) which are a standard
model for probabilistic systems. We focus on qualitative properties for MDPs that
can express that desired behaviors of the system arise almost-surely (with probability 1) or with positive probability. We introduce a new simulation relation to
capture the refinement relation of MDPs with respect to qualitative properties, and
present discrete graph theoretic algorithms with quadratic complexity to compute
the simulation relation. We present an automated technique for assume-guarantee
style reasoning for compositional analysis of MDPs with qualitative properties by
giving a counterexample guided abstraction-refinement approach to compute our
new simulation relation. We have implemented our algorithms and show that the
compositional analysis leads to significant improvements.

1 Introduction

Markov decision processes. *Markov decision processes (MDPs)* are standard models for analysis of probabilistic systems that exhibit both probabilistic and non-
deterministic behavior [46,39]. In verification of probabilistic systems, MDPs have been
adopted as models for concurrent probabilistic systems [32], probabilistic systems operating in open environments [60], under-specified probabilistic systems [9], and applied
in diverse domains [6,52] such as analysis of randomized communication and security
protocols, stochastic distributed systems, biological systems, etc.

Compositional Analysis and CEGAR. One of the key challenges in analysis of probabilistic systems (as in the case of non-probabilistic systems) is the *state explosion*
problem [29], as the size of concurrent systems grows exponentially in the number of
components. One key technique to combat the state explosion problem is the *assume-
guarantee* style composition reasoning [58], where the analysis problem is decomposed
into components and the results for components are used to reason about the whole system, instead of verifying the whole system directly. For a system with two components,
the compositional reasoning can be captured as the following simple rule: consider a
system with two components G_1 and G_2, and a specification G' to be satisfied by the
system; if A is an abstraction of G_2 (i.e., G_2 refines A) and G_1 in composition with A

---

[*] The research was partly supported by Austrian Science Fund (FWF) Grant No P 23499- N23,
FWF NFN Grant No S11407-N23 and S11402-N23 (RiSE), ERC Start grant (279307: Graph
Games), Microsoft faculty fellows award, the ERC Advanced Grant QUAREM (Quantitative
Reactive Modeling).

[**] Full version [15]: Link http://arxiv.org/abs/1405.0835

A. Biere and R. Bloem (Eds.): CAV 2014, LNCS 8559, pp. 473–490, 2014.
© Springer International Publishing Switzerland 2014

satisfies G', then the composite systems of G_1 and G_2 also satisfies G'. Intuitively, A is an assumption on G_1's environment that can be ensured by G_2. This simple, yet elegant asymmetric rule is very effective in practice, specially with a *counterexample guided abstraction-refinement* (CEGAR) loop [30]. There are many symmetric [56] as well as circular compositional reasoning [35,56,53] rules; however the simple asymmetric rule is most effective in practice and extensively studied, mostly for non-probabilistic systems [56,38,12,44].

Compositional Analysis for Probabilistic Systems. There are many works that have studied the abstraction-refinement and compositional analysis for probabilistic systems [11,45,51,37]. Our work is most closely related to and inspired by [50] where a CEGAR approach was presented for analysis of MDPs (or labeled probabilistic transition systems); and the refinement relation was captured by *strong simulation* that captures the logical relation induced by safe-pCTL [41,4,9].

Qualitative Analysis and Its Importance. In this work we consider the fragment of pCTL* [41,4,9] that is relevant for *qualitative analysis*, and refer to this fragment as QCTL*. The qualitative analysis for probabilistic systems refers to *almost-sure* (resp. *positive*) properties that are satisfied with probability 1 (resp. positive probability). The qualitative analysis for probabilistic systems is an important problem in verification that is of interest independent of the quantitative analysis problem. There are many applications where we need to know whether the correct behavior arises with probability 1. For instance, when analyzing a randomized embedded scheduler, we are interested in whether every thread progresses with probability 1 [17]. Even in settings where it suffices to satisfy certain specifications with probability $\lambda < 1$, the correct choice of λ is a challenging problem, due to the simplifications introduced during modeling. For example, in the analysis of randomized distributed algorithms it is quite common to require correctness with probability 1 (see, e.g., [59,62]). Furthermore, in contrast to quantitative analysis, qualitative analysis is robust to numerical perturbations and modeling errors in the transition probabilities. The qualitative analysis problem has been extensively studied for many probabilistic models, such as for MDPs [24,25,26], perfect-information stochastic games [27,13], concurrent stochastic games [36,18], partial-observation MDPs [5,28,16,20], and partial-observation stochastic games [22,8,19,21,55,23].

Our Contributions. In this work we focus on the compositional reasoning of probabilistic systems with respect to qualitative properties, and our main contribution is a CEGAR approach for qualitative analysis of probabilistic systems. The details of our contributions are as follows:

1. To establish the logical relation induced by QCTL* we consider the logic ATL* for two-player games and the two-player game interpretation of an MDP where the probabilistic choices are resolved by an adversary. In case of non-probabilistic systems and games there are two classical notions for refinement, namely, *simulation* [54] and *alternating-simulation* [1]. We first show that the logical relation induced by QCTL* is *finer* than the intersection of simulation and alternating simulation. We then introduce a new notion of simulation, namely, *combined simulation*, and show that it captures the logical relation induced by QCTL*.

2. We show that our new notion of simulation, which captures the logic relation of QCTL*, can be computed using discrete graph theoretic algorithms in quadratic time. In contrast, the current best known algorithm for strong simulation is polynomial of degree seven and requires numerical algorithms. The other advantage of our approach is that it can be applied uniformly both to qualitative analysis of probabilistic systems as well as analysis of two-player games (that are standard models for open non-probabilistic systems).
3. We present a CEGAR approach for the computation of combined simulation, and the counterexample analysis and abstraction refinement is achieved using the ideas of [43] proposed for abstraction-refinement for games.
4. We have implemented our approach both for qualitative analysis of MDPs as well as games, and experimented on a number of well-known examples of MDPs and games. Our experimental results show that our method achieves significantly better performance as compared to the non-compositional verification as well as compositional analysis of MDPs with strong simulation.

Related Works. Compositional and assume-guarantee style reasoning has been extensively studied mostly in the context of non-probabilistic systems [56,38,12,44]. Game-based abstraction refinement has been studied in the context of probabilistic systems [51]. The CEGAR approach has been adapted to probabilistic systems for reachability [45] and safe-pCTL [11] under non-compositional abstraction refinement. The work of [50] considers CEGAR for compositional analysis of probabilistic system with strong simulation. An abstraction-refinement algorithm for a class of quantitative properties was studied in [33,34] and also implemented [49]. Our logical characterization of the simulation relation is similar in spirit to [31], which shows how a fragment of the modal μ-calculus can be used to efficiently decide behavioral preorders between components. Our work focuses on CEGAR for compositional analysis of probabilistic systems for qualitative analysis: we characterize the required simulation relation; present a CEGAR approach for the computation of the simulation relation; and show the effectiveness of our approach both for qualitative analysis of MDPs and games.

2 Game Graphs and Alternating-Time Temporal Logics

Notations. Let AP denote a non-empty finite set of atomic propositions. Given a finite set S we will denote by S^* (respectively S^ω) the set of finite (resp. infinite) sequences of elements from S, and let $S^+ = S^* \setminus \{\epsilon\}$, where ϵ is the empty string.

2.1 Two-player Games

Two-player Games. A *two-player* game is a tuple $G = (S, A, \text{Av}, \delta, \mathcal{L}, s_0)$, where
- S is a finite set of states and $s_0 \in S$ is an initial state; and A is a finite set of actions.
- $\text{Av} : S \to 2^A \setminus \emptyset$ is an *action-available* function that assigns to every state $s \in S$ the set $\text{Av}(s)$ of actions available in s.
- $\delta : S \times A \to 2^S \setminus \emptyset$ is a non-deterministic *transition* function that given a state $s \in S$ and an action $a \in \text{Av}(s)$ gives the set $\delta(s, a)$ of successors of s given action a.
- $\mathcal{L} : S \to 2^{\text{AP}}$ is a *labeling* function that labels the states $s \in S$ with the set $\mathcal{L}(s)$ of atomic propositions true at s.

Alternating Games. A two-player game G is *alternating* if in every state either Player 1 or Player 2 can make choices. Formally, for all $s \in S$ we have either (i) $|\mathsf{Av}(s)| = 1$ (then we refer to s as a Player-2 state); or (ii) for all $a \in \mathsf{Av}(s)$ we have $|\delta(s,a)| = 1$ (then we refer to s as a Player-1 state). For technical convenience we consider that in the case of alternating games, there is an atomic proposition turn $\in$ AP such that for Player-1 states s we have turn $\in \mathcal{L}(s)$, and for Player 2 states s' we have turn $\notin \mathcal{L}(s')$.

Plays. A two-player game is played for infinitely many rounds as follows: the game starts at the initial state, and in every round Player 1 chooses an available action from the current state and then Player 2 chooses a successor state, and the game proceeds to the successor state for the next round. Formally, a *play* in a two-player game is an infinite sequence $\omega = s_0 a_0 s_1 a_1 s_2 a_2 \cdots$ of states and actions such that for all $i \geq 0$ we have that $a_i \in \mathsf{Av}(s_i)$ and $s_{i+1} \in \delta(s_i, a_i)$. We denote by Ω the set of all plays.

Strategies. Strategies are recipes that describe how to extend finite prefixes of plays. Formally, a *strategy* for Player 1 is a function $\sigma : (S \times A)^* \times S \to A$, that given a finite history $w \cdot s \in (S \times A)^* \times S$ of the game gives an action from $\mathsf{Av}(s)$ to be played next. We write Σ for the set of all Player-1 strategies. A strategy for Player 2 is a function $\theta : (S \times A)^+ \to S$, that given a finite history $w \cdot s \cdot a$ of a play selects a successor state from the set $\delta(s, a)$. We write Θ for the set of all Player-2 strategies. *Memoryless* strategies are independent of the history, but depend only on the current state for Player 1 (resp. the current state and action for Player 2) and hence can be represented as functions $S \to A$ for Player 1 (resp. as $S \times A \to S$ for Player 2).

Outcomes. Given a strategy σ for Player 1 and θ for Player 2 the *outcome* is a unique play, denoted as $\mathsf{Plays}(s, \sigma, \theta) = s_0 a_0 s_1 a_1 \cdots$, which is defined as follows: (i) $s_0 = s$; and (ii) for all $i \geq 0$ we have $a_i = \sigma(s_0 a_0 \ldots s_i)$ and $s_{i+1} = \theta(s_0 a_0 \ldots s_i a_i)$. Given a state $s \in S$ we denote by $\mathsf{Plays}(s, \sigma)$ (resp. $\mathsf{Plays}(s, \theta)$) the set of possible plays given σ (resp. θ), i.e., $\bigcup_{\theta' \in \Theta} \mathsf{Plays}(s, \sigma, \theta')$ (resp. $\bigcup_{\sigma' \in \Sigma} \mathsf{Plays}(s, \sigma', \theta)$).

Parallel Composition of Two-Player Games. Given games $G = (S, A, \mathsf{Av}, \delta, \mathcal{L}, s_0)$ and $G' = (S', A, \mathsf{Av}', \delta', \mathcal{L}', s_0')$ the *parallel composition* of the games $G \parallel G' = (\overline{S}, A, \overline{\mathsf{Av}}, \overline{\delta}, \overline{\mathcal{L}}, \overline{s}_0)$ is defined as follows: (1) The states of the composition are $\overline{S} = S \times S'$. (2) The set of actions is A. (3) For all (s, s') we have $\overline{\mathsf{Av}}((s, s')) = \mathsf{Av}(s) \cap \mathsf{Av}'(s')$. (4) The transition function for a state $(s, s') \in \overline{S}$ and an action $a \in \overline{\mathsf{Av}}((s, s'))$ is defined as $\overline{\delta}((s, s'), a) = \{(t, t') \mid t \in \delta(s, a) \wedge t' \in \delta'(s', a)\}$. (5) The labeling function $\overline{\mathcal{L}}((s, s'))$ is defined as $\mathcal{L}(s) \cup \mathcal{L}'(s')$. (6) The initial state is $\overline{s}_0 = (s_0, s_0')$.

Remark 1. For simplicity we assume that the set of actions in both components is identical, and for every pair of states the intersection of their available actions is non-empty. Parallel composition can be extended to cases where the sets of actions are different [2].

2.2 Alternating-time Temporal Logic

We consider the Alternating-time Temporal Logic (ATL*) [3] as a logic to specify properties for two-player games.

Syntax. The syntax of the logic is given in positive normal form by defining the set of *path formulas* (φ) and *state formulas* (ψ) according to the following grammar:

$$\text{state formulas:} \quad \psi ::= q \mid \neg q \mid \psi \vee \psi \mid \psi \wedge \psi \mid \mathsf{PQ}(\varphi)$$
$$\text{path formulas:} \quad \varphi ::= \psi \mid \varphi \vee \varphi \mid \varphi \wedge \varphi \mid \bigcirc \varphi \mid \varphi \mathcal{U} \varphi \mid \varphi \mathcal{W} \varphi;$$

where $q \in$ AP is an atomic proposition and PQ is a path quantifier. The operators $\bigcirc$ (next), $\mathcal{U}$ (until), and $\mathcal{W}$ (weak until) are the temporal operators. We will use true as a shorthand for $q \vee \neg q$ and false for $q \wedge \neg q$ for some $q \in$ AP. The path quantifiers PQ are as follows: ATL* path quantifiers: $\langle\!\langle 1 \rangle\!\rangle$, $\langle\!\langle 2 \rangle\!\rangle$, $\langle\!\langle 1, 2 \rangle\!\rangle$, and $\langle\!\langle \emptyset \rangle\!\rangle$.

Semantics. Given a play $\omega = s_0 a_0 s_1 a_1 \cdots$ we denote by $\omega[i]$ the suffix starting at the i-th state element of the play ω, i.e., $\omega[i] = s_i a_i s_{i+1} a_{i+1} \cdots$. The semantics of path formulas is defined inductively in a standard way. Given a path formula φ, we denote by $[\![\varphi]\!]_G$ the set of plays ω such that $\omega \models \varphi$. We omit the G lower script when the game is clear from context. The semantics of state formulas for ATL* is defined as follows (the semantics for Boolean formulas is omitted):

$$s \models \langle\!\langle 1 \rangle\!\rangle(\varphi) \qquad \text{iff } \exists \sigma \in \Sigma, \forall \theta \in \Theta : \text{Plays}(s, \sigma, \theta) \in [\![\varphi]\!]$$
$$s \models \langle\!\langle 2 \rangle\!\rangle(\varphi) \qquad \text{iff } \exists \theta \in \Theta, \forall \sigma \in \Sigma : \text{Plays}(s, \sigma, \theta) \in [\![\varphi]\!]$$
$$s \models \langle\!\langle 1, 2 \rangle\!\rangle(\varphi) \qquad \text{iff } \exists \sigma \in \Sigma, \exists \theta \in \Theta : \text{Plays}(s, \sigma, \theta) \in [\![\varphi]\!]$$
$$s \models \langle\!\langle \emptyset \rangle\!\rangle(\varphi) \qquad \text{iff } \forall \sigma \in \Sigma, \forall \theta \in \Theta : \text{Plays}(s, \sigma, \theta) \in [\![\varphi]\!];$$

where $s \in S$. Given an ATL* state formula ψ and a two-player game G, we denote by $[\![\psi]\!]_G = \{s \in S \mid s \models \psi\}$ the set of states that satisfy the formula ψ. We omit the G lower script when the game is clear from context.

Logic Fragments. We define several fragments of the logic ATL*:

- *Restricted temporal operator use.* An important fragment of ATL* is ATL where every temporal operator is immediately preceded by a path quantifier.
- *Restricting path quantifiers.* We also consider fragments of ATL* (resp. ATL) where the path quantifiers are restricted. We consider (i) 1-fragment (denoted 1-ATL*) where only $\langle\!\langle 1 \rangle\!\rangle$ path quantifier is used; (ii) the $(1, 2)$-fragment (denoted $(1, 2)$-ATL*) where only $\langle\!\langle 1, 2 \rangle\!\rangle$ path quantifier is used; and (iii) the combined fragment (denoted C-ATL*) where both $\langle\!\langle 1 \rangle\!\rangle$ and $\langle\!\langle 1, 2 \rangle\!\rangle$ path quantifiers are used. We use a similar notation for the respective fragments of ATL formulas.

Logical Characterization of States. Given two games G and G', and a logic fragment $\mathcal{F}$ of ATL*, we consider the following relations on the state space induced by the logic fragment $\mathcal{F}$: $\preccurlyeq_\mathcal{F} (G, G') = \{(s, s') \in S \times S' \mid \forall \psi \in \mathcal{F} : \text{if } s \models \psi \text{ then } s' \models \psi\}$; and when the games are clear from context we simply write $\preccurlyeq_\mathcal{F}$ for $\preccurlyeq_\mathcal{F} (G, G')$. We will use the following notations for the relation induced by the logic fragments we consider: (i) $\preccurlyeq_1^*$ (resp. $\preccurlyeq_1$) for the relation induced by the 1-ATL* (resp. 1-ATL) fragment; (ii) $\preccurlyeq_{1,2}^*$ (resp. $\preccurlyeq_{1,2}$) for the relation induced by the $(1, 2)$-ATL* (resp. $(1, 2)$-ATL) fragment; and (iii) $\preccurlyeq_C^*$ (resp. $\preccurlyeq_C$) for the relation induced by the C-ATL* (resp. C-ATL) fragment. Given G and G' we can also consider G'' which is the disjoint union of the two games, and consider the relations on G''; and hence we will often consider a single game as input for the relations.

3   Combined Simulation Relation Computation

In this section we first recall the notion of simulation [54] and alternating simulation [1]; and then present a new notion of *combined simulation*.

Simulation. Given two-player games $G = (S, A, \text{Av}, \delta, \mathcal{L}, s_0)$ and $G' = (S', A', \text{Av}', \delta', \mathcal{L}', s_0')$, a relation $\mathcal{S} \subseteq S \times S'$ is a *simulation* from G to G' if for all $(s, s') \in \mathcal{S}$ the following conditions hold:

1. *Proposition match:* The atomic propositions match, i.e., $\mathcal{L}(s) = \mathcal{L}'(s')$.
2. *Step-wise simulation condition:* For all actions $a \in \mathsf{Av}(s)$ and states $t \in \delta(s, a)$ there exists an action $a' \in \mathsf{Av}'(s')$ and a state $t' \in \delta(s', a')$ such that $(t, t') \in \mathcal{S}$.

We denote by $\mathcal{S}_{\max}^{G,G'}$ the largest simulation relation between the two games (we write $\mathcal{S}_{\max}$ instead of $\mathcal{S}_{\max}^{G,G'}$ when G and G' are clear from the context). We write $G \sim_S G'$ when $(s_0, s_0') \in \mathcal{S}_{\max}$. The largest simulation relation characterizes the logic relation of $(1, 2)$-ATL and $(1, 2)$-ATL*: the $(1, 2)$-ATL fragment interprets a game as a transition system and the formulas coincide with existential CTL, and hence the logic characterization follows from the classical results on simulation and CTL [54,2].

Proposition 1. *For all games G and G' we have $\mathcal{S}_{\max} = \preccurlyeq_{1,2}^* = \preccurlyeq_{1,2}$.*

Alternating Simulation. Given two games $G = (S, A, \mathsf{Av}, \delta, \mathcal{L}, s_0)$ and $G' = (S', A', \mathsf{Av}', \delta', \mathcal{L}', s_0')$, a relation $\mathcal{A} \subseteq S \times S'$ is an *alternating simulation* from G to G' if for all $(s, s') \in \mathcal{A}$ the following conditions hold:

1. *Proposition match:* The atomic propositions match, i.e., $\mathcal{L}(s) = \mathcal{L}'(s')$.
2. *Step-wise alternating-simulation condition:* For all actions $a \in \mathsf{Av}(s)$ there exists an action $a' \in \mathsf{Av}'(s')$ such that for all states $t' \in \delta'(s', a')$ there exists a state $t \in \delta(s, a)$ such that $(t, t') \in \mathcal{A}$.

We denote by $\mathcal{A}_{\max}^{G,G'}$ the largest alternating-simulation relation between the two games (we write $\mathcal{A}_{\max}$ instead of $\mathcal{A}_{\max}^{G,G'}$ when G and G' are clear from the context). We write $G \sim_A G'$ when $(s_0, s_0') \in \mathcal{A}_{\max}$. The largest alternating-simulation relation characterizes the logic relation of 1-ATL and 1-ATL* [1].

Proposition 2. *For all games G and G' we have $\mathcal{A}_{\max} = \preccurlyeq_1^* = \preccurlyeq_1$.*

Combined Simulation. We present a new notion of combined simulation that extends both simulation and alternating simulation, and we show how the combined simulation characterizes the logic relation induced by C-ATL* and C-ATL. Intuitively, the requirements on the combined-simulation relation combine the requirements imposed by alternating simulation and simulation in a step-wise fashion. Given two-player games $G = (S, A, \mathsf{Av}, \delta, \mathcal{L}, s_0)$ and $G' = (S', A', \mathsf{Av}', \delta', \mathcal{L}', s_0')$, a relation $\mathcal{C} \subseteq S \times S$ is a *combined simulation* from G to G' if for all $(s, s') \in \mathcal{C}$ the following conditions hold:

1. *Proposition match:* The atomic propositions match, i.e., $\mathcal{L}(s) = \mathcal{L}'(s')$.
2. *Step-wise simulation condition:* For all actions $a \in \mathsf{Av}(s)$ and states $t \in \delta(s, a)$ there exists an action $a' \in \mathsf{Av}'(s')$ and a state $t' \in \delta(s', a')$ such that $(t, t') \in \mathcal{C}$.
3. *Step-wise alternating-simulation condition:* For all actions $a \in \mathsf{Av}(s)$ there exists an action $a' \in \mathsf{Av}'(s')$ such that for all states $t' \in \delta'(s', a')$ there exists a state $t \in \delta(s, a)$ such that $(t, t') \in \mathcal{C}$.

We denote by $\mathcal{C}_{\max}^{G,G'}$ the largest combined-simulation relation between the two games (and write $\mathcal{C}_{\max}$ when G and G' are clear from the context). We also write $G \sim_C G'$ when $(s_0, s_0') \in \mathcal{C}_{\max}$. We first illustrate with an example that the logic relation $\preccurlyeq_C$ induced by C-ATL is finer than the intersection of simulation and alternating-simulation relation; then present a game theoretic characterization of $\mathcal{C}_{\max}$; and finally show that $\mathcal{C}_{\max}$ gives the relations $\preccurlyeq_C^*$ and $\preccurlyeq_C$.

Example 1. Consider the games G and G' shown in Figure 1. White nodes are labeled by an atomic proposition p and gray nodes by q. The largest simulation and alternating-simulation relations between G and G' are: $\mathcal{S}_{\max} = \{(s_0, t_0), (s_1, t_1)\}, \mathcal{A}_{\max} = $

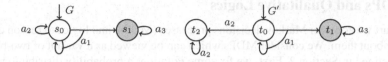

Fig. 1. Games G, G' such that $G \sim_S G'$ and $G \sim_A G'$, but $G \not\sim_C G'$

$\{(s_0, t_0), (s_0, t_2), (s_1, t_1)\}$. However, consider the formula $\psi = \langle\!\langle 1 \rangle\!\rangle (\bigcirc (p \wedge \langle\!\langle 1, 2 \rangle\!\rangle (\bigcirc q)))$. We have that $s_0 \models \psi$, but $t_0 \not\models \psi$. It follows that $(s_0, t_0) \notin \preccurlyeq_C$. □

Combined-Simulation Games. The simulation and the alternating-simulation relation can be obtained by solving two-player safety games [42,1,14]. We now define a two-player game G^C for the combined-simulation relation characterization. The game is played on the synchronized product of the two input games. Given a state (s, s'), first Player 2 decides whether to check for the step-wise simulation condition or the step-wise alternating-simulation condition.

1. The step-wise simulation condition is checked by playing a two-step game. Intuitively, first Player 2 chooses an action $a \in Av(s)$ and a successor $t \in \delta(s, a)$ and challenges Player 1 to match, and Player 1 responds with an action $a' \in Av'(s')$ and a state $t' \in \delta'(s', a')$.
2. The step-wise alternating-simulation condition is checked by playing a four-step game. Intuitively, first Player 2 chooses an action a from $Av(s)$ and Player 1 responds with an action $a' \in Av'(s')$ (in the first two-steps); then Player 2 chooses a successor $t' \in \delta'(s', a')$ and Player 1 responds by choosing a successor $t \in \delta(s, a)$.

After checking the step-wise conditions, the game proceeds from the state (t, t'). Intuitively, Player 2's goal is to reach a state (s, s') where the labeling of the original games do not match; states that satisfy this condition are labeled by atomic proposition p.

In the combined simulation game we refer to Player 1 as the *proponent* (trying to establish the combined simulation) and Player 2 as the *adversary* (trying to violate the combined simulation).

Shorthand for Safety Objectives. We will use the following shorthand for *safety* objectives: $\square \varphi \equiv \varphi \, \mathcal{W} \, \text{false}$.

Theorem 1. *For all games G and G' we have $C_{max} = [\![\langle\!\langle 1 \rangle\!\rangle (\square \neg p)]\!]_{G^C} \cap (S \times S')$.*

We establish the relation between combined simulation and C-ATL*.

Theorem 2. *For all games G and G' we have $C_{max} = \preccurlyeq_C^* = \preccurlyeq_C$.*

Remark 2. Theorem 2 also holds for alternating games. Note that in most cases the action set is constant and the state space of the games are huge. Then the combined simulation game construction is quadratic, and solving safety games on them can be achieved in linear time using discrete graph theoretic algorithms [47,7].

Theorem 3. *Given two-player games G and G', the C_{max}, $\preccurlyeq_C^*$, and $\preccurlyeq_C$ relations can be computed in quadratic time using discrete graph theoretic algorithms.*

4   MDPs and Qualitative Logics

In this part we consider Markov decisions processes (MDPs) and logics to reason quali-
tatively about them. We consider MDPs which can be viewed as a variant of two-player
games defined in Section 2. First, we fix some notation: a probability distribution f on
a finite set X is a function $f : X \to [0, 1]$ such that $\sum_{x \in X} f(x) = 1$, and we denote
by $\mathcal{D}(X)$ the set of all probability distributions on X. For $f \in \mathcal{D}(X)$ we denote by
$\mathrm{Supp}(f) = \{x \in X \mid f(x) > 0\}$ the *support of* f.

4.1   Markov Decision Processes

MDPs. A *Markov decision process* (MDP) is a tuple $G = (S, (S_1, S_P), A, \mathsf{Av}, \delta_1,$
$\delta_P, \mathcal{L}, s_0)$; where (i) S is a finite set of states with a partition of S into Player-1 states
S_1 and probabilistic states S_P; (ii) A is a finite set of actions; (iii) $\mathsf{Av} : S_1 \to 2^A \setminus \emptyset$ is
an action-available function that assigns to every Player-1 state the non-empty set $\mathsf{Av}(s)$
of actions available in s; (iv) $\delta_1 : S_1 \times A \to S$ is a deterministic transition function
that given a Player-1 state and an action gives the next state; (v) $\delta_P : S_P \to \mathcal{D}(S)$
is a probabilistic transition function that given a probabilistic state gives a probability
distribution over the successor states (i.e., $\delta_P(s)(s')$ is the transition probability from s
to s'); (vi) the function $\mathcal{L}$ is the proposition labeling function as for two-player games;
and (vii) s_0 is the initial state. Strategies for Player 1 are defined as for games.

Interpretations. We interpret an MDP in two distinct ways: (i) as a $1\frac{1}{2}$-player game
and (ii) as an alternating two-player game. In the $1\frac{1}{2}$-player setting in a state $s \in S_1$,
Player 1 chooses an action $a \in \mathsf{Av}(s)$ and the MDP moves to a unique successor s'. In
probabilistic states $s_p \in S_P$ the successor is chosen according to the probability distribution $\delta_P(s_p)$. In the alternating two-player interpretation, we regard the probabilistic
states as Player-2 states, i.e., in a state $s_p \in S_P$, Player 2 chooses a successor state
s' from the support of the probability distribution $\delta_P(s)$. Given an MDP G we denote
by $\widehat{G}$ its two-player interpretation, and $\widehat{G}$ is an alternating game. The $1\frac{1}{2}$-player interpretation is the classical definition of MDPs. We will use the two-player interpretation
to relate logical characterizations of MDPs and logical characterization of two-player
games with fragments of ATL^*.

$1\frac{1}{2}$**-Player Interpretation.** Once a strategy $\sigma \in \Sigma$ for Player 1 is fixed, the outcome of
the MDP is a random walk for which the probabilities of *events* are uniquely defined,
where an *event* $\Phi \subseteq \Omega$ is a measurable set of plays [40]. For a state $s \in S$ and an event
$\Phi \subseteq \Omega$, we write $\mathrm{Pr}_s^\sigma(\Phi)$ for the probability that a play belongs to Φ if the game starts
from the state s and Player 1 follows the strategy σ.

4.2   Qualitative Logics for MDPs

We consider the qualitative fragment of pCTL^* [41,4,9] and refer to the logic as *qualitative pCTL** (denoted as QCTL^*) as it can express qualitative properties of MDPs.

Syntax and Semantics. The syntax of the logic is given in positive normal form and is
similar to the syntax of ATL^*. It has the same state and path formulas as ATL^* with the
exception of path quantifiers. The logic QCTL^* comes with two path quantifiers (PQ),
namely $\langle \mathrm{Almost} \rangle$ and $\langle \mathrm{Positive} \rangle$ (instead of $\langle\!\langle 1 \rangle\!\rangle$, $\langle\!\langle 2 \rangle\!\rangle$, $\langle\!\langle 1, 2 \rangle\!\rangle$, and $\langle\!\langle \emptyset \rangle\!\rangle$). The semantics
of the logic QCTL^* is the same for the fragment shared with ATL^*, therefore we
only give semantics for the new path quantifiers. Given a path formula φ, we denote

by $[\![\varphi]\!]_G$ the set of plays ω such that $\omega \models \varphi$. For a state s and a path formula φ we have: $s \models \langle\text{Almost}\rangle(\varphi)$ (resp. $s \models \langle\text{Positive}\rangle(\varphi)$) iff $\exists \sigma \in \Sigma : \Pr_s^\sigma([\![\varphi]\!]) = 1$ (resp. $\Pr_s^\sigma([\![\varphi]\!]) > 0$). As before, we denote by QCTL the fragment of QCTL* where every temporal operator is immediately preceded by a path quantifier, and for a state formula ψ the set $[\![\psi]\!]_G$ denotes the set of states in G that satisfy the formula ψ.

Logical Relation Induced by QCTL and QCTL*. Given two MDPs G and G', the logical relation induced by QCTL*, denoted as $\preccurlyeq_Q^*$, (resp. by QCTL, denoted as $\preccurlyeq_Q$), is defined as: $\preccurlyeq_Q^* = \{(s, s') \in S \times S' \mid \forall \psi \in \text{QCTL}^* : \text{ if } s \models \psi \text{ then } s' \models \psi\}$ (resp. $\forall \psi \in \text{QCTL}$).

4.3 Characterization of Qualitative Simulation for MDPs

In this section we establish the equivalence of the $\preccurlyeq_Q^*$ relation on MDPs with the $\preccurlyeq_C^*$ relation on the two-player interpretation of MDPs, i.e., we prove that for all MDPs G and G' we have $\preccurlyeq_Q^* (G, G') = \preccurlyeq_C (\widehat{G}, \widehat{G}')$, where $\widehat{G}$ (resp. $\widehat{G}'$) is the two-player interpretation of the MDP G (resp. G'). In the first step we show how to translate some of the QCTL formulas into C-ATL formulas. We only need to translate the path quantifiers due to the similarity of path formulas in the logics.

Lemma 1. *For all atomic propositions q, r and for all MDPs, we have:*
(i) $[\![\langle\text{Almost}\rangle(\bigcirc q)]\!] = [\![\langle\langle 1\rangle\rangle(\bigcirc q)]\!]$; *(ii) $[\![\langle\text{Almost}\rangle(q\mathcal{W}r)]\!] = [\![\langle\langle 1\rangle\rangle(q\mathcal{W}r)]\!]$;*
(iii) $[\![\langle\text{Positive}\rangle(\bigcirc q)]\!] = [\![\langle\langle 1,2\rangle\rangle(\bigcirc q)]\!]$; *(iv) $[\![\langle\text{Positive}\rangle(q\mathcal{U}r)]\!] = [\![\langle\langle 1,2\rangle\rangle(q\mathcal{U}r)]\!]$;*
(v) $[\![\langle\text{Positive}\rangle(q\mathcal{W}r)]\!] = [\![\langle\langle 1,2\rangle\rangle(q\mathcal{U}r)]\!] \cup [\![\langle\langle 1,2\rangle\rangle(q\mathcal{U}(\langle\langle 1\rangle\rangle(q\mathcal{W}\text{false})))]\!]$.

To complete the translation of temporal operators we also express the QCTL formula $[\![\langle\text{Almost}\rangle(q\mathcal{U}r)]\!]$ in terms of C-ATL* [15]. We establish the following result.

Theorem 4. *For all MDPs G and G' we have $\preccurlyeq_Q = \preccurlyeq_C$; and $\preccurlyeq_Q^* = \preccurlyeq_Q$. The relation $\preccurlyeq_Q^*$ can be computed in quadratic time using discrete graph theoretic algorithms.*

5 CEGAR for Combined Simulation

In this section we present a CEGAR approach for computing combined simulation.

5.1 Simulation Abstraction and Alternating-Simulation Abstraction

Abstraction. An *abstraction* of a game consists of a partition of the game graph such that in each partition the atomic proposition labeling match for all states. Given an abstraction of a game, the abstract game can be defined by collapsing states of each partition and redefining the action-available and transition functions. The redefinition of the action-available and transition functions can either increase or decrease the power of the players. If we increase the power of Player 1 and decrease the power of Player 2, then the abstract game will be in alternating simulation with the original game, and if we increase the power of both players, then the abstract game will simulate the original game. We now formally define the partitions, and the two abstractions.

Partitions for Abstraction. A *partition* of a game $G = (S, A, \text{Av}, \delta, \mathcal{L}, s_0)$ is an equivalence relation $\Pi = \{\pi_1, \pi_2, \ldots, \pi_k\}$ on S such that: (i) for all $1 \leq i \leq k$ we have $\pi_i \subseteq S$ and for all $s, s' \in \pi_i$ we have $\mathcal{L}(s) = \mathcal{L}(s')$ (labeling match); (ii) $\bigcup_{1 \leq i \leq k} \pi_i = S$ (covers the state space); and (iii) for all $1 \leq i, j \leq k$, such that $i \neq j$

we have $\pi_i \cap \pi_j = \emptyset$ (disjoint). Note that in alternating games Player 1 and Player 2 states are distinguished by proposition turn, so they belong to different partitions.

Simulation Abstraction. Given a two-player game $G = (S, A, \mathsf{Av}, \delta, \mathcal{L}, s_0)$ and a partition Π of G, we define the *simulation abstraction of* G as a two-player game $Abs_S^\Pi(G) = (\overline{S}, A, \overline{\mathsf{Av}}, \overline{\delta}, \overline{\mathcal{L}}, \overline{s}_0)$, where: (i) $\overline{S} = \Pi$: the partitions in Π are the states of the abstract game. (ii) For all $\pi_i \in \Pi$ we have $\overline{\mathsf{Av}}(\pi_i) = \bigcup_{s \in \pi_i} \mathsf{Av}(s)$: the set of available actions is the union of the actions available to the states in the partition, and this gives more power to Player 1. (iii) For all $\pi_i \in \Pi$ and $a \in \overline{\mathsf{Av}}(\pi_i)$ we have $\overline{\delta}(\pi_i, a) = \{\pi_j \mid \exists s \in \pi_i : (a \in \mathsf{Av}(s) \wedge \exists s' \in \pi_j : s' \in \delta(s, a))\}$: there is a transition from a partition π_i given an action a to a partition π_j if some state $s \in \pi_i$ can make an a-transition to some state in $s' \in \pi_j$. This gives more power to Player 2. (iv) For all $\pi_i \in \Pi$ we have $\overline{\mathcal{L}}(\pi_i) = \mathcal{L}(s)$ for some $s \in \pi_i$: the abstract labeling is well-defined, since all states in a partition are labeled by the same atomic propositions. (v) $\overline{s}_0$ is the partition in Π that contains state s_0.

Alternating-Simulation Abstraction. Given a two-player game $G = (S, A, \mathsf{Av}, \delta, \mathcal{L}, s_0)$ and a partition Π of G, we define the *alternating-simulation abstraction of* G as a two-player game $Abs_A^\Pi(G) = (\widetilde{S}, A, \widetilde{\mathsf{Av}}, \widetilde{\delta}, \widetilde{\mathcal{L}}, \widetilde{s}_0)$, where: (i) $\widetilde{S} = \Pi$; (ii) for all $\pi_i \in \Pi$ we have $\widetilde{\mathsf{Av}}(\pi_i) = \bigcup_{s \in \pi_i} \mathsf{Av}(s)$; (iii) for all $\pi_i \in \Pi$ we have $\widetilde{\mathcal{L}}(\pi_i) = \mathcal{L}(s)$ for some $s \in \pi_i$; (iv) $\widetilde{s}_0$ is the partition in Π that contains state s_0 (as in the case of simulation abstraction). (v) For all $\pi_i \in \Pi$ and $a \in \widetilde{\mathsf{Av}}(\pi_i)$ we have $\widetilde{\delta}(\pi_i, a) = \{\pi_j \mid \forall s \in \pi_i : (a \in \mathsf{Av}(s) \wedge \exists s' \in \pi_j : s' \in \delta(s, a))\}$: there is a transition from a partition π_i given an action a to a partition π_j if all states $s \in \pi_i$ can make an a-transition to some state in $s' \in \pi_j$. This gives less power to Player 2. For technical convenience we assume $\widetilde{\delta}(\pi_i, a)$ is non-empty.

The following proposition states that (alternating-)simulation abstraction of a game G is in (alternating-)simulation with G.

Proposition 3. *For all partitions Π of a two-player game G we have: (1) $G \sim_A Abs_A^\Pi(G)$; and (2) $G \sim_S Abs_S^\Pi(G)$.*

5.2 Sound Assume-Guarantee Rule

We now present the sound assume-guarantee rule for the combined-simulation problem. To achieve this we first need an extension of the notion of combined-simulation game.

Modified Combined-Simulation Games. Consider games $G^{\mathsf{Alt}} = (S, A, \delta^{\mathsf{Alt}}, \mathsf{Av}^{\mathsf{Alt}}, \mathcal{L}, s_0)$, $G^{\mathsf{Sim}} = (S, A, \delta^{\mathsf{Sim}}, \mathsf{Av}^{\mathsf{Sim}}, \mathcal{L}, s_0)$ and $G' = (S', A, \delta', \mathsf{Av}', \mathcal{L}', s_0')$. The *modified simulation game* $G^{\mathcal{M}} = (S^{\mathcal{M}}, A^{\mathcal{M}}, \mathsf{Av}^{\mathcal{M}}, \delta^{\mathcal{M}}, \mathcal{L}^{\mathcal{M}}, s_0^{\mathcal{M}})$ is defined exactly like the combined simulation game given G^{Alt} and G', with the exception that the step-wise simulation gadget is defined using the transitions of G^{Sim} instead of G^{Alt}. We write $(G^{\mathsf{Alt}} \otimes G^{\mathsf{Sim}}) \sim_{\mathcal{M}} G'$ if and only if $(s_0, s_0') \in [\![\langle\!\langle 1 \rangle\!\rangle(\Box \neg p)]\!]_{G^{\mathcal{M}}}$.

Proposition 4. *Let $G, G', G^{\mathsf{Alt}}, G^{\mathsf{Sim}}$ be games such that $G \sim_A G^{\mathsf{Alt}}$ and $G \sim_S G^{\mathsf{Sim}}$. Then $(G^{\mathsf{Alt}} \otimes G^{\mathsf{Sim}}) \sim_{\mathcal{M}} G'$ implies $G \sim_C G'$.*

The key proof idea for the above proposition is as follows: if $G \sim_A G^{\mathsf{Alt}}$ and $G \sim_S G^{\mathsf{Sim}}$, then in the modified combined-simulation game $G^{\mathcal{M}}$ the adversary is stronger than in the combined-simulation game $G^{\mathcal{C}}$. Hence winning in $G^{\mathcal{M}}$ for the proponent implies winning in $G^{\mathcal{C}}$ and gives the desired result of the proposition.

Sound Assume-Guarantee Method. Given two games G_1 and G_2, checking whether their parallel composition $G_1 \parallel G_2$ is in combined simulation with a game G' can be done explicitly by constructing the synchronized product. The composition, however, may be much larger than the components and thus make the method ineffective in practical cases. We present an alternative method that proves combined simulation in a compositional manner, by abstracting G_2 with some partition Π and then composing it with G_1. The sound assume-guarantee rule follows from Propositions 3 and 4.

Proposition 5 (Sound assume-guarantee rule). *Given games G_1, G_2, G', and a partition Π of G_2, let $A = G_1 \parallel Abs_{\mathcal{A}}^{\Pi}(G_2)$ and $S = G_1 \parallel Abs_{\mathcal{S}}^{\Pi}(G_2)$. If $(A \otimes S) \sim_{\mathcal{M}} G'$, then $(G_1 \parallel G_2) \sim_{\mathcal{C}} G'$, i.e.,*

$$\frac{A = G_1 \parallel Abs_{\mathcal{A}}^{\Pi}(G_2); \quad S = G_1 \parallel Abs_{\mathcal{S}}^{\Pi}(G_2); \quad (A \otimes S) \sim_{\mathcal{M}} G'}{(G_1 \parallel G_2) \sim_{\mathcal{C}} G'} \quad (1)$$

If the partition Π is coarse, then the abstractions in the assume-guarantee rule can be smaller than G_2 and also their composition with G_1. As a consequence, combined simulation can be proved faster as compared to explicitly computing the composition. In Section 5.4 we describe how to effectively compute the partitions Π and refine them using CEGAR approach.

5.3 Counter-examples Analysis

If the premise $(A \otimes S) \sim_{\mathcal{M}} G'$ of the assume-guarantee rule (1) is not satisfied, then the adversary (Player 2) has a memoryless winning strategy in $G^{\mathcal{M}}$, and the memoryless strategy is the *counter-example*. To use the sound assume-guarantee rule (1) in a CEGAR loop, we need analysis of counter-examples.

Representation of counter-examples. A counter-example is a memoryless winning strategy for Player 2 in $G^{\mathcal{M}}$. Note that in $G^{\mathcal{M}}$ Player 2 has a reachability objective, and thus a winning strategy ensures that the target set is always reached from the starting state, and hence no cycle can be formed without reaching the target state once the memoryless winning strategy is fixed. Hence we represent counter-examples as directed-acyclic graphs (DAG), where the leafs are the target states and every non-leaf state has a single successor chosen by the strategy of Player 2 and has all available actions for Player 1.

Abstract, concrete, and spurious counter-examples. Given two-player games G_1 and G_2, let $G = (G_1 \parallel G_2)$ be the parallel composition. Given G and G', let $G^{\mathcal{C}}$ be the combined-simulation game of G and G'. The abstract game $G^{\mathcal{M}}$ is the modified combined-simulation game of $(A \otimes S)$ and G', where $A = G_1 \parallel Abs_{\mathcal{A}}^{\Pi}(G_2)$ and $S = G_1 \parallel Abs_{\mathcal{S}}^{\Pi}(G_2)$. We refer to a counter-example θ_{abs} in $G^{\mathcal{M}}$ as *abstract*, and to a counter-example θ_{con} in $G^{\mathcal{C}}$ as *concrete*. An abstract counter-example is *feasible* if we can substitute partitions in A and S with states of G_2 to obtain a concrete counter-example. An abstract counter-example is *spurious* if it is not feasible.

Concretization of counter-examples. We follow the approach of [43] to check the feasibility of a counter-example by finding a *concretization* function Conc from states in

$G^{\mathcal{M}}$ to a set of states in G_2 that witness a concrete strategy from the abstract strategy. A state in $G^{\mathcal{M}}$ has a component which is a partition for G_2, and the concretization constructs a subset of the partition. Intuitively, for a state $\bar{s}$ of $G^{\mathcal{M}}$ in the counter-example DAG, the concretization represents the subset of states of G_2 in the partition where a concrete winning strategy exists using the strategy represented by the DAG below the state $\bar{s}$. Informally, the witness concrete strategy is constructed inductively, going bottom-up in the DAG as follows: (i) the leaves already represents winning states and hence their concretization is the entire partition; (ii) for non-leaf states in the DAG of the abstract counter-example, the concretization represents the set of states of G_2 of the partition which lead to a successor state that belongs to the concretization of the successor in the DAG. An abstract counter-example is feasible, if the concretization of the root of the DAG contains the initial state of G_2.

5.4 CEGAR

The counter-example analysis presented in the previous section allows us to automatically refine abstractions using the CEGAR paradigm [30]. The algorithm takes games G_1, G_2, G' as arguments and answers whether $(G_1 \parallel G_2) \sim_C G'$ holds. Initially, the algorithms computes the coarsest partition Π of G_2. Then, it executes the CEGAR loop: in every iteration the algorithm constructs A (resp. S) as the parallel composition of G_1 and the alternating-simulation abstraction (resp. simulation abstraction) of G_2. Let $G^{\mathcal{M}}$ be the modified combined-simulation game of $(\mathsf{A} \otimes \mathsf{S})$ and G'. If Player 1 has a winning strategy in $G^{\mathcal{M}}$ then the algorithm returns YES; otherwise it finds an abstract counter-example Cex in $G^{\mathcal{M}}$. In case Cex is feasible, then it corresponds to a concrete counter-example, and the algorithm returns NO. If Cex is spurious a refinement procedure is called that uses the concretization of Cex to return a partition Π' finer than Π.

Refinement Procedure. Given a partition Π and a spurious counter-example Cex together with its concretization function Conc we describe how to compute the refined partition Π'. Consider a partition $\pi \in \Pi$ and let $\overline{S}_\pi = \{\bar{s}_1, \bar{s}_2, \ldots, \bar{s}_m\}$ denote the states of the abstract counter-example Cex that contain π as its component. Every state $\bar{s}_i$ splits π into at most two sets $\mathsf{Conc}(\bar{s}_i)$ and $\pi \setminus \mathsf{Conc}(\bar{s}_i)$, and let this partition be denoted as T_i. We define a partition $\mathcal{P}_\pi$ as the largest equivalence relation on π that is finer than any equivalence relation T_i for all $1 \le i \le m$. Formally, $\mathcal{P}_\pi = \{\bar{\pi}_1, \bar{\pi}_2, \ldots, \bar{\pi}_k\}$ is a partition of π such that for all $1 \le j \le k$ and $1 \le i \le m$ we have $\bar{\pi}_j \subseteq \mathsf{Conc}(\bar{s}_i)$ or $\bar{\pi}_j \subseteq \pi \setminus \mathsf{Conc}(\bar{s}_i)$. The new partition Π' is then defined as the union over $\mathcal{P}_\pi$ for all $\pi \in \Pi$.

Proposition 6. *Given a partition Π and a spurious counter-example* Cex, *the partition Π' obtained as refinement of Π is finer than Π.*

Since we consider finite games, the refinement procedure only executes for finitely many steps and hence the CEGAR loop eventually terminates.

6 Experimental Results

We implemented our CEGAR approach for combined simulation in Java, and experimented with our tool on a number of MDPs and two-player games examples. We use PRISM [52] model checker to specify the examples and generate input files for our tool.

Observable actions. To be compatible with the existing benchmarks (e.g. [50]) in our tool actions are observable instead of atomic propositions. Our algorithms are easily adapted to this setting. We also allow the user to specify silent actions for components, which are not required to be matched by the specification G'.

Improved (modified) combined-simulation game. We leverage the fact that MDPs are interpreted as alternating games to simplify the (modified) combined-simulation game. When comparing two Player-1 states, the last two steps in the alternating-simulation gadget can be omitted, since the players have unique successors given the actions chosen in the first two steps. Similarly, for two probabilistic states, the first two steps in the alternating-simulation gadget can be skipped.

Improved partition refinement procedure. In the implementation we adopt the approach of [43] for refinement. Given a state $\bar{s}$ of the abstract counter-example with partition π as its component, the equivalence relation may split the set $\pi \setminus \mathsf{Conc}(\bar{s})$ into multiple equivalence classes. Intuitively, this ensures that similar-shaped spurious counter-examples do not reappear in the following iterations. This approach is more efficient than the naive one, and also implemented in our tool.

MDP Examples. We used our tool on all the MDP examples from [50]:
- CS_1 *and* CS_n model a Client-Server protocol with mutual exclusion with probabilistic failures in one or all of the n clients, respectively.
- MER is an arbiter module of NASAs software for Mars Exploration Rovers which grants shared resources for several users.
- SN models a network of sensors that communicate via a bounded buffer with probabilistic behavior in the components.

In addition, we also considered two other classical MDP examples:
- LE is based on a PRISM case study [52] that models the *Leader election protocol* [48], where n agents on a ring randomly pick a number from a pool of K numbers. The agent with the highest number becomes the leader. In case there are multiple agents with the same highest number the election proceed to the next round. The specification requires that two leaders cannot be elected at the same time. The MDP is parametrized by the number of agents and the size of the pool.
- PETP is based on a Peterson's algorithm [57] for mutual exclusion of n threads, where the execution order is controlled by a randomized scheduler. The specification requires that two threads cannot access the critical section at the same time. We extend Peterson's algorithm by giving the threads a non-deterministic choice to restart before entering the critical section. The restart operation succeeds with probability $\frac{1}{2}$ and with probability $\frac{1}{2}$ the thread enters the critical section.

Details of experimental results. Table 1 shows the results for MDP examples we obtained using our assume-guarantee algorithm and the monolithic approach (where the composition is computed explicitly). We also compared our results with the tool presented in [50] that implements both assume-guarantee and monolithic approaches for *strong simulation* [61]. All the results were obtained on a Ubuntu-13.04 64-bit machine running on an Intel Core i5-2540M CPU of 2.60GHz. We imposed a 4.3GB upper bound on Java heap memory and one hour time limit. For MER(6) and PETP(5) PRISM cannot parse the input file (probably it runs out of memory).

Table 1. Results for MDPs examples: AGCS stands for our assume-guarantee combined simulation; AGSS stands for assume-guarantee with strong simulation; MONCS stands for our monolithic combined simulation; and MONSS stands for monolithic strong simulation. The number I denotes the number of CEGAR iterations and $|\Pi|$ the size of the abstraction in the last CEGAR iteration. TO and MO stand for a time-out and memory-out, respectively, and Error means an error occurred during execution. The memory consumption is measured using the `time` command.

Ex.	$|G_1|$	$|G_2|$	$|G'|$	AGCS Time	Mem	I	$|\Pi|$	AGSS Time	Mem	I	$|\Pi|$	MONCS Time	Mem	MONSS Time	Mem
$CS_1(5)$	36	405	16	1.13s	112MB	49	85	6.11s	213MB	32	33	**0.04s**	**34MB**	0.18s	95MB
$CS_1(6)$	49	1215	19	2.52s	220MB	65	123	11.41s	243MB	40	41	**0.04s**	**51MB**	0.31s	99MB
$CS_1(7)$	64	3645	22	5.41s	408MB	84	156	31.16s	867MB	56	57	**0.05s**	**82MB**	0.77s	113MB
$CS_n(3)$	125	16	54	0.65s	102MB	9	24	33.43s	258MB	11	12	**0.09s**	**35MB**	11.29s	115MB
$CS_n(4)$	625	25	189	6.22s	495MB	15	42	TO	-	-	-	**0.4s**	**106MB**	1349.6s	577MB
$CS_n(5)$	3k	36	648	117.06s	2818MB	24	60	TO	-	-	-	**2.56s**	**345MB**	TO	-
MER(3)	278	1728	11	**1.42s**	**143MB**	8	14	2.74s	189MB	6	7	1.96s	228MB	128.1s	548MB
MER(4)	465	21k	14	**4.63s**	**464MB**	13	22	10.81s	870MB	10	11	11.02s	1204MB	TO	-
MER(5)	700	250k	17	**29.23s**	**1603MB**	20	32	67s	2879MB	15	16	-	MO	MO	-
SN(1)	43	32	18	0.13s	38MB	3	6	0.28s	88MB	2	3	**0.04s**	**29MB**	3.51s	135MB
SN(2)	796	32	54	0.9s	117MB	3	6	66.09s	258MB	2	3	**0.38s**	**103MB**	3580.83s	1022MB
SN(3)	7k	32	162	4.99s	**408MB**	3	6	TO	-	-	-	4.99s	612MB	TO	-
SN(4)	52k	32	486	**34.09s**	**2448MB**	3	6	TO	-	-	-	44.47s	3409MB	TO	-
LE(3,4)	2	652	256	**0.24s**	**70MB**	6	14	1.63s	223MB	6	7	0.38s	103MB	TO	-
LE(3,5)	2	1280	500	**0.31s**	**87MB**	6	14	Error	-	-	-	1.77s	253MB	Error	-
LE(4,4)	3	3160	1280	**0.61s**	**106MB**	6	16	TO	-	-	-	9.34s	1067MB	TO	-
LE(5,5)	4	18k	12k	3.37s	**364MB**	6	18	TO	-	-	-	-	MO	TO	-
LE(6,4)	5	27k	20k	6.37s	**743MB**	6	20	TO	-	-	-	-	MO	TO	-
LE(6,5)	5	107k	78k	23.72s	**2192MB**	6	20	TO	-	-	-	-	MO	TO	-
PETP(2)	68	3	3	0.04s	31MB	0	2	0.04s	87MB	0	1	0.04s	**30MB**	0.04s	90MB
PETP(3)	4	1730	4	**0.19s**	**65MB**	6	8	0.29s	153MB	3	4	0.24s	72MB	1.07s	170MB
PETP(4)	5	54k	5	**1.58s**	**325MB**	8	10	3.12s	727MB	4	5	7.04s	960MB	31.52s	1741MB

Summary of results. For all examples, other than the Client-Server protocol, the assume-guarantee method scales better than the monolithic reasoning; and in all examples our qualitative analysis scales better than the strong simulation approach.

Two-player Games Examples. We also experimented with our tool on several examples of games, where one of the players controls the choices of the system and the other player represents the environment.

- EC is based on [10] and models an error-correcting device that sends and receives data blocks over a communication channel. Notation $EC(n, k, d)$ means that a data block consists of n bits and it encodes k bits of data; value d is the minimum Hamming distance between two distinct blocks. In the first component Player 2 chooses a message to be sent over the channel and is allowed to flip some bits in the block. The second component restricts the number of bits that Player 2 can flip. The specification requires that every message is correctly decoded.
- PETG is the Peterson's algorithm [57] example for MDPs, with the following differences: (a) the system may choose to restart instead of entering the critical section; (b) instead of a randomized scheduler we consider an adversarial scheduler. As before, the specification requires mutual exclusion.
- VIR1 models a virus that attacks a computer system with n nodes (based on case study from PRISM [52]). Player 1 represents the virus and is trying to infect as

Table 2. Results for two-player games examples

Ex.	$|G_1|$	$|G_2|$	$|G'|$	AGCS		I	$|\Pi|$	MONCS		AGAS		I	$|\Pi|$	MONAS	
				Time	Mem			Time	Mem	Time	Mem			Time	Mem
EC(32, 6, 16)	71k	193	129	3.55s	446MB	1	7	**1.15s**	281MB	2.34s	391MB	0	2	1.03s	**251MB**
EC(64, 7, 16)	549k	385	257	70.5s	3704MB	1	131	9.07s	1725MB	16.79s	1812MB	0	2	**4.83s**	**1467MB**
EC(64, 8, 16)	1.1m	769	513	-	MO	-	-	-	MO	**52.63s**	**3619MB**	0	2	-	MO
EC(64, 8, 32)	1.1m	1025	513	-	MO	-	-	-	MO	**54.08s**	**3665MB**	0	2	-	MO
PETG(2)	3	52	3	0.08s	35MB	4	6	0.03s	30MB	0.07s	35MB	4	6	0.03s	**29MB**
PETG(3)	4	1514	4	**0.2s**	63MB	6	8	0.25s	74MB	0.22s	**62MB**	6	8	0.21s	64MB
PETG(4)	5	49k	5	1.75s	316MB	8	10	8.16s	1080MB	**1.6s**	**311MB**	8	10	6.94s	939MB
VIR1(12)	14	4097	1	0.91s	159MB	15	30	1.69s	255MB	**0.35s**	**114MB**	2	4	1.53s	215MB
VIR1(13)	15	8193	1	1.47s	197MB	16	32	4.36s	601MB	**0.6s**	**178MB**	2	4	2.8s	402MB
VIR1(14)	16	16k	1	3.09s	326MB	17	34	8.22s	992MB	**0.75s**	**241MB**	2	4	6.49s	816MB
VIR1(15)	17	32k	1	4.47s	643MB	18	36	15.13s	2047MB	**1.05s**	**490MB**	2	4	9.67s	1361MB
VIR1(16)	18	65k	1	8.65s	1015MB	19	38	41.28s	3785MB	**1.37s**	**839MB**	2	4	23.71s	2591MB
VIR1(17)	19	131k	1	18.68s	1803MB	20	40	-	MO	**2.12s**	**1653MB**	2	4	62.24s	4309MB
VIR1(18)	20	262k	1	38.68s	3079MB	21	42	-	MO	**3.35s**	**2878MB**	2	4	-	MO
VIR2(12)	13	4096	1	1.02s	151MB	19	34	0.81	154MB	0.68s	**122MB**	9	14	**0.57s**	133MB
VIR2(13)	14	8192	1	1.48s	190MB	20	36	1.13s	216MB	1.01s	**183MB**	9	14	1.01s	208MB
VIR2(14)	15	16k	1	2.9s	315MB	21	38	2.33s	389MB	1.94s	**311MB**	9	14	2.09s	388MB
VIR2(15)	16	32k	1	5s	631MB	22	40	6.29s	964MB	2.12s	**489MB**	9	14	4.69s	757MB
VIR2(16)	17	65k	1	9.82s	949MB	23	42	7.55s	1468MB	3.96s	**897MB**	9	14	6.09s	1315MB
VIR2(17)	18	131k	1	23.33s	1815MB	24	44	23.54s	3012MB	8.16s	**1676MB**	9	14	15.36s	2542MB
VIR2(18)	19	262k	1	45.89s	3049MB	25	46	55.28s	4288MB	20.3s	**2875MB**	9	14	28.79s	3755MB

many nodes of the network as possible. Player 2 represents the system and may recover an infected node to an uninfected state. The specification requires that the virus has a strategy to avoid being completely erased, i.e., maintain at least one infected node in the network. VIR2 is a modified version of VIR1 with two special critical nodes in the network. Whenever both of the nodes are infected, the virus can overtake the system. The specification is as for VIR1, i.e., the virus can play such that at least one node in the network remains infected, but it additionally requires that even if the system cooperates with the virus, the system is designed in a way that the special nodes will never be infected at the same time.

The results for two-player game examples are shown in Table 2. Along with AGCS and MONCS for assume-guarantee and monolithic combined simulation, we also consider AGAS and MONAS for assume-guarantee and monolithic alternating simulation, as for properties in 1-ATL it suffices to consider only alternating simulation. For all the examples, the assume-guarantee algorithms scale better than the monolithic ones. Combined simulation is finer than alternating simulation and therefore combined simulation may require more CEGAR iterations.

Concluding Remarks. In this work we considered compositional analysis of MDPs for qualitative properties and presented a CEGAR approach. Our algorithms are discrete graph theoretic algorithms. An interesting direction of future work would be to consider symbolic approaches to the problem.

Acknowledgements. We thank Anvesh Komuravelli for sharing his implementation.

References

1. Alur, R., Henzinger, T., Kupferman, O., Vardi, M.: Alternating refinement relations. In: Sangiorgi, D., de Simone, R. (eds.) CONCUR 1998. LNCS, vol. 1466, pp. 163–178. Springer, Heidelberg (1998)
2. Alur, R., Henzinger, T.A.: Computer-aided verification (2004) (unpublished), http://www.cis.upenn.edu/cis673/
3. Alur, R., Henzinger, T.A., Kupferman, O.: Alternating-time temporal logic. J. ACM 49(5), 672–713 (2002)
4. Aziz, A., Singhal, V., Balarin, F., Brayton, R., Sangiovanni-Vincentelli, A.: It usually works: The temporal logic of stochastic systems. In: Wolper, P. (ed.) CAV 1995. LNCS, vol. 939, pp. 155–165. Springer, Heidelberg (1995)
5. Baier, C., Bertrand, N., Größer, M.: On decision problems for probabilistic büchi automata. In: Amadio, R.M. (ed.) FOSSACS 2008. LNCS, vol. 4962, pp. 287–301. Springer, Heidelberg (2008)
6. Baier, C., Katoen, J.-P.: Principles of model checking. MIT Press (2008)
7. Beeri, C.: On the membership problem for functional and multivalued dependencies in relational databases. ACM Trans. on Database Systems 5, 241–259 (1980)
8. Bertrand, N., Genest, B., Gimbert, H.: Qualitative determinacy and decidability of stochastic games with signals. In: Proc. of LICS, pp. 319–328. IEEE Computer Society (2009)
9. Bianco, A., de Alfaro, L.: Model checking of probabalistic and nondeterministic systems. In: Thiagarajan, P.S. (ed.) FSTTCS 1995. LNCS, vol. 1026, pp. 499–513. Springer, Heidelberg (1995)
10. Cerný, P., Chmelik, M., Henzinger, T.A., Radhakrishna, A.: Interface simulation distances. In: GandALF, EPTCS 96, pp. 29–42 (2012)
11. Chadha, R., Viswanathan, M.: A counterexample-guided abstraction-refinement framework for Markov decision processes. ACM Trans. Comput. Log. 12, 1 (2010)
12. Chaki, S., Clarke, E.M., Sinha, N., Thati, P.: Automated assume-guarantee reasoning for simulation conformance. In: Etessami, K., Rajamani, S.K. (eds.) CAV 2005. LNCS, vol. 3576, pp. 534–547. Springer, Heidelberg (2005)
13. Chatterjee, K.: Stochastic ω-Regular Games. PhD thesis, UC Berkeley (2007)
14. Chatterjee, K., Chaubal, S., Kamath, P.: Faster algorithms for alternating refinement relations. In: CSL. LIPIcs, vol. 16, pp. 167–182. Schloss Dagstuhl (2012)
15. Chatterjee, K., Chmelík, M., Daca, P.: CEGAR for qualitative analysis of probabilistic systems. CoRR, abs/1405.0835 (2014)
16. Chatterjee, K., Chmelik, M., Tracol, M.: What is decidable about partially observable Markov decision processes with omega-regular objectives. In: Proceedings of CSL 2013: Computer Science Logic (2013)
17. Chatterjee, K., de Alfaro, L., Faella, M., Majumdar, R., Raman, V.: Code-aware resource management. Formal Methods in System Design 42(2), 146–174 (2013)
18. Chatterjee, K., de Alfaro, L., Henzinger, T.A.: Qualitative concurrent parity games. ACM Trans. Comput. Log. 12(4), 28 (2011)
19. Chatterjee, K., Doyen, L.: Partial-observation stochastic games: How to win when belief fails. In: Proceedings of LICS 2012: Logic in Computer Science, pp. 175–184. IEEE Computer Society Press (2012)
20. Chatterjee, K., Doyen, L., Henzinger, T.A.: Qualitative analysis of partially-observable markov decision processes. In: Hliněný, P., Kučera, A. (eds.) MFCS 2010. LNCS, vol. 6281, pp. 258–269. Springer, Heidelberg (2010)
21. Chatterjee, K., Doyen, L., Henzinger, T.A.: A survey of partial-observation stochastic parity games. Formal Methods in System Design 43(2), 268–284 (2013)

22. Chatterjee, K., Doyen, L., Henzinger, T.A., Raskin, J.-F.: Algorithms for omega-regular games with imperfect information'. In: Ésik, Z. (ed.) CSL 2006. LNCS, vol. 4207, pp. 287–302. Springer, Heidelberg (2006)

23. Chatterjee, K., Doyen, L., Nain, S., Vardi, M.Y.: The complexity of partial-observation stochastic parity games with finite-memory strategies. In: Muscholl, A. (ed.) FOSSACS 2014. LNCS, vol. 8412, pp. 242–257. Springer, Heidelberg (2014)

24. Chatterjee, K., Henzinger, M.: Faster and dynamic algorithms for maximal end-component decomposition and related graph problems in probabilistic verification. In: SODA, pp. 1318–1336 (2011)

25. Chatterjee, K., Henzinger, M.: An $O(n^2)$ time algorithm for alternating Büchi games. In: SODA, pp. 1386–1399 (2012)

26. Chatterjee, K., Henzinger, M., Joglekar, M., Shah, N.: Symbolic algorithms for qualitative analysis of Markov decision processes with Büchi objectives. Formal Methods in System Design 42(3), 301–327 (2013)

27. Chatterjee, K., Jurdziński, M., Henzinger, T.A.: Simple stochastic parity games. In: Baaz, M., Makowsky, J.A. (eds.) CSL 2003. LNCS, vol. 2803, pp. 100–113. Springer, Heidelberg (2003)

28. Chatterjee, K., Tracol, M.: Decidable problems for probabilistic automata on infinite words. In: LICS, pp. 185–194 (2012)

29. Clarke, E., Grumberg, O., Peled, D.: Model Checking. MIT Press (1999)

30. Clarke, E.M., Grumberg, O., Jha, S., Lu, Y., Veith, H.: Counterexample-guided abstraction refinement. In: Emerson, E.A., Sistla, A.P. (eds.) CAV 2000. LNCS, vol. 1855, pp. 154–169. Springer, Heidelberg (2000)

31. Cleaveland, R., Steffen, B.: Computing behavioural relations, logically. In: Leach Albert, J., Monien, B., Rodríguez-Artalejo, M. (eds.) ICALP 1991. LNCS, vol. 510, pp. 127–138. Springer, Heidelberg (1991)

32. Courcoubetis, C., Yannakakis, M.: The complexity of probabilistic verification. J. ACM 42(4), 857–907 (1995)

33. D'Argenio, P.R., Jeannet, B., Jensen, H.E., Larsen, K.G.: Reachability analysis of probabilistic systems by successive refinements. In: de Luca, L., Gilmore, S. (eds.) PAPM-PROBMIV 2001. LNCS, vol. 2165, pp. 39–56. Springer, Heidelberg (2001)

34. D'Argenio, P.R.: Reduction and refinement strategies for probabilistic analysis. In: Hermanns, H., Segala, R. (eds.) PAPM-PROBMIV 2002. LNCS, vol. 2399, pp. 57–76. Springer, Heidelberg (2002)

35. de Alfaro, L., Henzinger, T.A., Jhala, R.: Compositional methods for probabilistic systems. In: Larsen, K.G., Nielsen, M. (eds.) CONCUR 2001. LNCS, vol. 2154, pp. 351–365. Springer, Heidelberg (2001)

36. de Alfaro, L., Henzinger, T.A., Kupferman, O.: Concurrent reachability games. In: FOCS, pp. 564–575 (1998)

37. Etessami, K., Kwiatkowska, M.Z., Vardi, M.Y., Yannakakis, M.: Multi-objective model checking of Markov decision processes. Logical Methods in Computer Science 4(4) (2008)

38. Feng, L., Kwiatkowska, M.Z., Parker, D.: Automated learning of probabilistic assumptions for compositional reasoning. In: Giannakopoulou, D., Orejas, F. (eds.) FASE 2011. LNCS, vol. 6603, pp. 2–17. Springer, Heidelberg (2011)

39. Filar, J., Vrieze, K.: Competitive Markov Decision Processes. Springer (1997)

40. Grädel, E., Thomas, W., Wilke, T. (eds.): Automata, logics, and infinite games: A guide to current research. LNCS, vol. 2500. Springer, Heidelberg (2002)

41. Hansson, H., Jonsson, B.: A logic for reasoning about time and reliability. Formal Asp. Comput. 6(5), 512–535 (1994)

42. Henzinger, M.R., Henzinger, T.A., Kopke, P.W.: Computing simulations on finite and infinite graphs. In: FOCS, pp. 453–462 (1995)
43. Henzinger, T.A., Jhala, R., Majumdar, R.: Counterexample-guided control. In: Baeten, J.C.M., Lenstra, J.K., Parrow, J., Woeginger, G.J. (eds.) ICALP 2003. LNCS, vol. 2719, pp. 886–902. Springer, Heidelberg (2003)
44. Henzinger, T.A., Jhala, R., Majumdar, R., Qadeer, S.: Thread-modular abstraction refinement. In: Hunt Jr., W.A., Somenzi, F. (eds.) CAV 2003. LNCS, vol. 2725, pp. 262–274. Springer, Heidelberg (2003)
45. Hermanns, H., Wachter, B., Zhang, L.: Probabilistic CEGAR. In: Gupta, A., Malik, S. (eds.) CAV 2008. LNCS, vol. 5123, pp. 162–175. Springer, Heidelberg (2008)
46. Howard, R.A.: Dynamic Programming and Markov Processes. MIT Press (1960)
47. Immerman, N.: Number of quantifiers is better than number of tape cells. Journal of Computer and System Sciences 22, 384–406 (1981)
48. Itai, A., Rodeh, M.: Symmetry breaking in distributed networks. Information and Computation 88(1) (1990)
49. Jeannet, B., dArgenio, P., Larsen., K.: Rapture: A tool for verifying Markov decision processes. Tools Day 2, 149 (2002)
50. Komuravelli, A., Păsăreanu, C.S., Clarke, E.M.: Assume-guarantee abstraction refinement for probabilistic systems. In: Madhusudan, P., Seshia, S.A. (eds.) CAV 2012. LNCS, vol. 7358, pp. 310–326. Springer, Heidelberg (2012)
51. Kwiatkowska, M.Z., Norman, G., Parker, D.: Game-based abstraction for Markov decision processes. In: QEST, pp. 157–166 (2006)
52. Kwiatkowska, M.Z., Norman, G., Parker, D.: Prism 4.0: Verification of probabilistic real-time systems. In: Gopalakrishnan, G., Qadeer, S. (eds.) CAV 2011. LNCS, vol. 6806, pp. 585–591. Springer, Heidelberg (2011)
53. Kwiatkowska, M.Z., Norman, G., Parker, D., Qu, H.: Assume-guarantee verification for probabilistic systems. In: Esparza, J., Majumdar, R. (eds.) TACAS 2010. LNCS, vol. 6015, pp. 23–37. Springer, Heidelberg (2010)
54. Milner, R.: An algebraic definition of simulation between programs. IJCAI, 481–489 (1971)
55. Nain, S., Vardi, M.Y.: Solving partial-information stochastic parity games. In: LICS, pp. 341–348 (2013)
56. Pasareanu, C.S., Giannakopoulou, D., Bobaru, M.G., Cobleigh, J.M., Barringer, H.: Learning to divide and conquer: applying the l* algorithm to automate assume-guarantee reasoning. Formal Methods in System Design 32(3), 175–205 (2008)
57. Peterson, G.L.: Myths about the mutual exclusion problem. Information Processing Letters 12(3), 115–116 (1981)
58. Pnueli, A.: In: transition from global to modular temporal reasoning about programs. In: Logics and Models of Concurrent Systems, NATO Advanced Summer Institutes F-13, pp. 123–144. Springer (1985)
59. Pogosyants, A., Segala, R., Lynch, N.: Verification of the randomized consensus algorithm of Aspnes and Herlihy: a case study. Distributed Computing 13(3), 155–186 (2000)
60. Segala, R.: Modeling and Verification of Randomized Distributed Real-Time Systems. PhD thesis, MIT Press, Technical Report MIT/LCS/TR-676 (1995)
61. Segala, R., Lynch, N.A.: Probabilistic simulations for probabilistic processes. Nord. J. Comput. 2(2), 250–273 (1995)
62. Stoelinga, M.: Fun with FireWire: Experiments with verifying the IEEE1394 root contention protocol. In: Formal Aspects of Computing (2002)

Optimal Guard Synthesis for Memory Safety

Thomas Dillig[1], Isil Dillig[1], and Swarat Chaudhuri[2]

[1] UT Austin
[2] Rice University

Abstract. This paper presents a new synthesis-based approach for writing low-level memory-safe code. Given a partial program with missing guards, our algorithm synthesizes concrete predicates to plug in for the missing guards such that all buffer accesses in the program are memory safe. Furthermore, guards synthesized by our technique are the simplest and weakest among guards that guarantee memory safety, relative to the inferred loop invariants. Our approach is fully automatic and does not require any hints from the user. We have implemented our algorithm in a prototype synthesis tool for C programs, and we show that the proposed approach is able to successfully synthesize guards that closely match hand-written programmer code in a set of real-world C programs.

1 Introduction

Memory safety errors are a perennial source of crashes and vulnerabilities in programs written in unsafe languages, and even expert programmers often write erroneous code that accesses out-of-bounds buffers or invalid memory. Over the past few decades, there has been much research on helping programmers write memory safe code. Broadly speaking, existing approaches fall into two categories:

Dynamic instrumentation. Many approaches, such as those employed in memory managed languages like Java and C#, add run-time checks to guarantee the safety of each memory access. While such approaches prevent memory corruption and associated security vulnerabilities, they do not prevent run-time failures and often add significant performance overhead.

Static verification. Much recent research has focused on statically guaranteeing memory safety of programs written in unsafe languages [1–5]. While these techniques can uncover all potential memory safety errors, the errors identified by the verifier may be hard to understand, debug, and fix.

In this paper, we propose a new approach based on *program synthesis* to the design of memory-safe low-level code. Concretely, suppose that a programmer wishes to write a region of code R implementing a given functionality, but R can access out-of-bounds memory under certain assumptions about program inputs or previously taken branches. In our approach, the programmer embeds R within the scope of an unknown *guard* predicate whose sole purpose is to ensure the memory safety of R. This is done using a syntax of the form:

```
if(??) {R}  else { /* handle error */ }
```

A. Biere and R. Bloem (Eds.): CAV 2014, LNCS 8559, pp. 491–507, 2014.
© Springer International Publishing Switzerland 2014

where the unknown guard is indicated by **??**. Our approach uses a new *guard synthesis* algorithm to compute a predicate P over program variables such that, when **??** is replaced by P, all memory accesses within R are provably memory-safe.

Unlike dynamic approaches, our method does not require run-time instrumentation to track allocation sizes or pointer offsets, thereby avoiding the associated performance overhead. Instead, we statically infer a single guard that guarantees the safety of *all* memory accesses within a code block. Furthermore, our approach goes beyond static verification: It not only guarantees memory safety, but also helps the programmer write safe-by-construction code. The programmer is only asked to tell us *which* code snippets must be protected by a guard, rather than the tedious, low-level details of *how* to protect them.

Our synthesis algorithm is based on the principle of *logical abduction*. Abduction is the problem of finding missing hypotheses in a logical inference task. In more detail, suppose we have a premise P and a desired conclusion C for an inference (P and C will be typically generated as constraints from a program) such that $P \not\models C$. Given P and C, abduction infers a simplest and most general explanation E such that $P \wedge E \models C$ and $P \wedge E \not\models$ false.

Previous work has shown how to use abduction for program verification, by framing unknown invariants as missing hypotheses in a logical inference problem [5–7]. While adapting abduction to synthesis is a nontrivial technical challenge, the end result is an algorithm with several appealing properties:

Optimality of Synthesis. Our algorithm gives a guarantee of *optimal synthesis* — i.e., the synthesized guards are optimal according to a quantitative criterion among all guards that guarantee memory safety. Optimality has been argued to be an important criterion in program synthesis. For instance, Alur et al. [8] argue that "Ideally, [in synthesis] we would like to associate a cost with each [synthesized] expression, and consider the problem of optimal synthesis which requires the synthesis tool to return the expression with the least cost among the correct ones. A natural cost metric is the size of the expression." However, few existing approaches to software synthesis take on such an optimality goal.

The notion of costs used in this paper is two-dimensional: one dimension quantifies expression complexity (we use the number of variables as a proxy for complexity), and the other quantifies generality (weaker guards have lower costs). The guards we synthesize are *Pareto-optimal* with respect to this notion of costs — i.e., there is no solution that is weaker as well as less complex.

Automation. Unlike most recent approaches to program synthesis [9–11], our algorithm can synthesize expressions without the aid of user-specified structural hints. In particular, the programmer does not need to provide expression templates with unknown coefficients to be inferred.

Practicality. Our algorithm incorporates precise reasoning about array bounds and low-level pointer arithmetic, which are necessary ingredients for synthesizing guards to guarantee memory safety. Furthermore, as shown in our experimental evaluation, the proposed synthesis algorithm can successfully synthesize guards required for memory safety in real C applications and produces guards that closely match hand-written code.

```
1.   int main(int argc, char** argv) {
2.     char *command = NULL;
3.     if (argc <= 1)  {
4.         error (0, 0, _("too few arguments"));
5.         usage (EXIT_FAIL);
6.     }
7.     argv++; argc--;
8.     while ((optc = getopt(argc, argv, ...)) != -1) {
9.       switch(optc) {
10.        case 'c':
11.            command =  optarg; break;
12.        ...
13.        }
14.     }
15.   if (??)  usage (EXIT_CANCELED);
16.     timeout = parse (argv[optind++]);
17.     files = argv + optind;
18.     if (!target_dir) {
19.       if (! (mkdir_and_install ? install_in_parents(files[0], files[1])
20                                 : install_in_file(files[0], files[1])))
21.        ...
22.     }
23.   }
```

Fig. 1. Motivating example

2   Motivating Example and Overview

We now present an overview of our approach using a motivating example. Consider the code snippet shown in Figure 1, which is based on the Unix coreutils. This program parses command line arguments with the help of a clib function called getopt. Specifically, lines 8-14 process the optional command line arguments while the code after line 16 performs the program's required functionality. Here, variable optind used at lines 16-17 is initialized by getopt to be the index of the next element to be processed in argv. Looking at lines 16-23, the programmer expects the user to pass some required arguments and accesses them at lines 16, 19, and 20. However, since the user may have forgotten to pass the required arguments, the programmer must explicitly check whether the memory accesses at lines 16,19,20 are safe in order to prevent potentially disastrous buffer overflow or underflow errors. If her assumptions are not met, the programmer wishes to terminate the program by calling the exit function called usage. However, coming up with the correct condition under which to terminate the program is tricky even on the small code snippet shown here: The programmer has performed pointer arithmetic on argv at line 7, and the variable files is an alias of argv at offset optind which has previously been modified at line 16.

Using our technique, the programmer can use the ?? predicate at line 15 to indicate the unknown check required for ensuring memory safety of the remainder of the program. Our technique then automatically synthesizes the guard (argc

- `optind) > 2` as a sufficient condition for the safety of all buffer accesses in lines 16-23. Since the check inferred by our technique is correct-by-construction, the remainder of the program is guaranteed to be memory safe.

Algorithm Overview. Our algorithm proceeds in two phases, consisting of constraint generation and solving. During constraint generation, we represent the unknown guards using placeholder formulas χ and then generate verification conditions over these unknown χ's. The constraint solving phase, which employs an iterative abduction-based algorithm, infers a concrete predicate for each χ that makes all generated VCs valid. In addition to guaranteeing Pareto-optimality, this approach does not require the user to specify templates describing the shape of the unknown guards. Furthermore, since the abduced solutions imply the validity of the VCs, we do not need to externally validate the correctness of the synthesized program using a separate verifier or model checker.

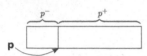

Fig. 2. Auxiliary variables

The constraint generation phase consists of two key ingredients: First, to reason about out-of-bounds memory accesses, we introduce ghost variables that track allocation sizes and pointer offsets. Specifically, for each pointer p, a variable p^- indicates the offset of p in the block of memory it points to, and p^+ tracks the size of p relative to p^-. This is shown in Figure 2. These ghost variables enable reasoning about pointer arithmetic in a precise way and allow us to generate symbolic verification conditions for memory safety.

The second key ingredient of constraint generation is a dual forwards and backwards static analysis that simultaneously computes strongest postconditions and weakest preconditions. For each unknown guard to be synthesized, the forwards analysis computes a formula ϕ representing facts that are known at this program point, while the backwards analysis provides a weakest precondition ψ for the safety of the code protected by this unknown guard. Now, given a statement S involving an unknown guard and the two formulas ϕ and ψ, our technique generates the VC $(\phi \wedge \chi(\boldsymbol{v})) \rightarrow \psi$ where χ is a predicate representing the unknown guard and $\boldsymbol{v}$ represents all program variables in scope at this program point. Here, formulas ϕ and ψ may also contain other unknowns.

In the constraint solving phase, we use an iterative, worklist-based algorithm that employs abduction to solve for the unknown χ predicates. Given a set of constraints C of the form $(F_1(\chi_1, \ldots \chi_{i-1}) \wedge \chi_i) \rightarrow F_2(\chi_{i+1}, \ldots \chi_n)$ where $F(\boldsymbol{\chi})$ denotes a formula over unknowns $\boldsymbol{\chi}$, we show how to infer a solution for each χ_i such that all constraints in C become valid. Our algorithm guarantees the Pareto-optimality of the solution relative to the inferred loop invariants. That is, assuming a fixed set of loop invariants, if we pick any unknown guard and try to improve it according to our cost metric, then the resulting set of guards is no longer a solution to our synthesis problem.

Example Redux. We now go back to the code example from Figure 1 to illustrate our approach. Initially, we assume that `argv` points to the beginning of an allocated block of size `argc`; hence, our analysis starts with the fact:

$$\mathrm{argv}^+ = \mathrm{argc} \wedge \mathrm{argv}^- = 0 \tag{1}$$

Next, we perform forward reasoning to compute the strongest postcondition of (1) right before line 20. Here, the forward analysis yields the condition:

$$\phi : \ \text{argc} > 0 \wedge \text{argv}^+ = \text{argc} \wedge \text{argv}^- = 1 \wedge \text{optind} \geq 0 \tag{2}$$

The first part of the conjunct ($\text{argc} > 0$) comes from the condition at line 3: Since **usage** is an exit function, we know $\text{argc} > 1$ at line 6, which implies $\text{argc} > 0$ after line 7. The second part ($\text{argv}^+ = \text{argc}$) states that the size of **argv** is still **argc**; this is because **argc** is decremented while **argv** is incremented at line 7. According to the third conjunct ($\text{argv}^- = 1$), **argv** points to the second element in the original argument array due to the pointer increment at line 7. Finally, the last conjunct ($\text{optind} \geq 0$) is a postcondition established by the call to **getopt**.

Next, we focus on the backwards analysis. To guarantee the safety of the buffer access **files[1]** at line 19, we need $1 < \text{files}^+$ and $1 \geq -\text{files}^-$ to ensure there are no buffer overflows and underflows respectively. Using similar reasoning for the accesses **files[0]** and **argv[optind++]**, our analysis generates the following necessary condition for the safety of the code after line 15:

$$\psi : \ \begin{aligned} &\text{optind} < \text{argv}^+ \wedge \text{optind} \geq -\text{argv}^- \wedge \\ &\text{target\_dir} = 0 \rightarrow (1 < \text{argv}^+ - \text{optind} - 1) \wedge \\ &\text{target\_dir} = 0 \rightarrow 0 \geq -\text{argv}^- - \text{optind} - 1) \end{aligned} \tag{3}$$

Observe that files^- and files^+ do not appear in this formula because the backwards analysis relates the size and offset of **files** to those of **argv** when computing the weakest precondition of **files = argv + optind** at line 17. Now, to synthesize the unknown guard at line 15, we generate the following constraint:

$$(\phi \wedge \chi(v)) \rightarrow \psi \tag{4}$$

where ϕ and ψ come from Equations 2 and 3, χ is the unknown guard, and v represents program variables in scope at line 15. Note that, since $\text{argv}^-, \text{argv}^+$ etc. are ghost variables, they are not allowed to appear in our solution for χ.

Now, inferring a formula to plug in for χ that makes Equation 4 valid is a logical abduction problem. By using abduction to solve for χ, we obtain the solution **argc - optind > 2**. Observe that there are other guards that also guarantee memory safety in this example, such as:

(S1) $\text{argc} > \text{optind} \wedge (\text{target\_dir} = 0 \rightarrow \text{argc} - \text{optind} > 2)$, or
(S2) $\text{argc} = 4 \wedge \text{optind} = 1$

However, both of these solutions are undesirable because (S1) is overly complicated, while (S2) is not sufficiently general.

3   Language and Preliminaries

We describe our techniques using the small imperative language given in Figure 3. Here, a program takes inputs v and consists of one or more statements. We

$$\text{Program P} \quad := \lambda v.\ S$$
$$\text{Guard } G \quad := ??_i \mid C$$
$$\text{Statement S} \quad := \text{skip} \mid v := E \mid S_1; S_2 \mid [p] := \text{alloc}(E) \mid [p_1] := [p_2] \oplus E$$
$$\mid \text{access}([p], E) \mid \text{if}(G) \text{ then } S_1 \text{ else } S_2;$$
$$\mid \text{while}(C) \text{ do } S \mid \text{while}(C \wedge ??_i) \text{ do } S$$
$$\text{Conditional } C := E_1 \text{ comp } E_2 \ (\text{comp} \in \{<, >, =\}) \mid C_1 \wedge C_2 \mid C_1 \vee C_2 \mid \neg C$$
$$\text{Expression } E \ := \text{int} \mid v \mid E_1 + E_2 \mid E_1 - E_2 \mid E_1 \cdot E_2$$

Fig. 3. Language used for the formal development

syntactically differentiate between scalar variables v and pointers $[p]$, which are always written inside brackets. Statements include skip, scalar assignments ($v := E$), sequencing, memory allocations ($[p] = \text{alloc}(E)$), and pointer arithmetic ($[p_1] = [p_2] \oplus E$) which makes p_1 point to offset E in the memory block pointed to by $[p_2]$. The statement access($[p], E$) accesses the E'th offset of $[p]$. Since our main concern is to guarantee the safety of memory accesses, we use the access statement to model both array reads and writes. In particular, access($[p], E$) fails if E is not a valid offset in the memory region pointed to by E. We say that an access is *safe* if it can never fail in any execution; otherwise, it is *unsafe*. A program P is *memory-safe* if all accesses in P are safe.

In this language, unknown predicates $??_i$ occur either as tests in if statements or as continuation conditions of while loops. We say a guard G_1 is an *ancestor* of guard G_2 if G_2 is nested inside G_1; conversely, we say G_2 is a *descendant* of G_1. We call a program *complete* if it does not contain any unknown guards. Given a program P and a mapping σ from unknown guards to concrete predicates, we write $P[\sigma]$ to denote the program obtained by substituting each $??_i$ with $\sigma(??_i)$.

Definition 1. *Mapping σ is a solution to the guard synthesis problem defined by program P iff (i) $P[\sigma]$ is a complete and memory-safe program, and (ii) $\forall v \in \text{dom}(\sigma).\ \sigma(v) \not\Rightarrow \text{false}$.*

According to the second condition, a valid solution cannot instantiate any unknown predicate with false. Hence, the synthesis problem is unsolvable if we cannot guarantee memory safety without creating dead code.

Definition 2. *Given solutions σ and σ' to the synthesis problem, we say that σ refines σ', written $\sigma' \preceq \sigma$, if for some unknown $\chi \in \text{dom}(\sigma)$, we have either (i) $\sigma'(\chi) \Rightarrow \sigma(\chi)$ and $\sigma(\chi) \not\Rightarrow \sigma'(\chi)$, or (ii) $|\text{vars}(\sigma(\chi))| < |\text{vars}(\sigma'(\chi))|$.*

In other words, solution σ refines σ' if it improves some guard either in terms of generality or simplicity.

Definition 3. *Solution σ is a Pareto-optimal solution to the synthesis problem if for all other solutions σ', we have $\sigma' \preceq \sigma$.*

Intuitively, this means that, if we take solution σ and try to improve any guard in σ according to our cost metric, then the resulting mapping is no longer a solution. In the rest of the paper, we use the word "optimality" to mean Pareto-optimality in the above sense.

$$(1) \quad \frac{}{\phi, \psi \vdash \mathrm{skip} : \phi, \psi, \emptyset}$$

$$(2) \quad \frac{\phi' = \exists v'.(v = E[v'/v] \wedge \phi[v'/v])}{\phi, \psi \vdash v := E : \phi', \psi[E/v], \emptyset}$$

$$(3) \quad \frac{\phi, \psi_1 \vdash S_1 : \phi_1, \psi_2, \mathcal{C}_1 \quad \phi_1, \psi \vdash S_2 : \phi_2, \psi_1, \mathcal{C}_2}{\phi, \psi \vdash S_1; S_2 : \phi_2, \psi_2, \mathcal{C}_1 \cup \mathcal{C}_2}$$

$$(4) \quad \frac{\phi, \psi \vdash p^- := 0; p^+ := E : \phi', \psi', \emptyset}{\phi, \psi \vdash [p] := \mathrm{alloc}(E) : \phi', \psi', \emptyset}$$

$$(5) \quad \frac{\phi, \psi \vdash (p_1^- := p_2^- + E) : \phi_1, \psi_1, \emptyset \quad \phi_1, \psi_1 \vdash (p_1^+ := p_2^+ - E) : \phi_2, \psi_2, \emptyset}{\phi, \psi \vdash [p_1] := [p_2] \oplus E : \phi_2, \psi_2, \emptyset}$$

$$(6) \quad \frac{\varphi_{\mathrm{safe}} = (E \geq -p^- \wedge E < p^+)}{\phi, \psi \vdash \mathrm{access}([p], E) : \phi \wedge \varphi_{\mathrm{safe}}, \psi \wedge \varphi_{\mathrm{safe}}, \emptyset}$$

$$(7a) \quad \frac{\begin{array}{c} \phi \wedge C, \psi \vdash S_1 : \phi_1, \psi_1, \mathcal{C}_1 \quad \phi \wedge \neg C, \psi \vdash S_2 : \phi_2, \psi_2, \mathcal{C}_2 \\ \psi' = (C \rightarrow \psi_1) \vee (\neg C \rightarrow \psi_2) \end{array}}{\phi, \psi \vdash \mathrm{if}(C) \text{ then } S_1 \text{ else } S_2 : \phi_1 \vee \phi_2, \psi', \mathcal{C}_1 \cup \mathcal{C}_2}$$

$$(7b) \quad \frac{\begin{array}{c} \phi \wedge \chi_i(v), \mathrm{true} \vdash S_1 : \_, \varphi, \mathcal{C}_1 \\ \mathrm{VC} = (\phi \wedge \chi_i(v) \rightarrow \varphi) \\ \phi \wedge \chi_i(v), \psi \vdash \widetilde{S_1} : \phi_1, \psi_1, \_ \\ \phi \wedge \neg\chi_i(v), \psi \vdash S_2 : \phi_2, \psi_2, \mathcal{C}_2 \\ \psi' = (\chi_i(v) \rightarrow \psi_1) \wedge (\neg\chi_i(v) \rightarrow \psi_2) \end{array}}{\phi, \psi \vdash \mathrm{if}(??_i) \text{ then } S_1 \text{ else } S_2 : \phi_1 \vee \phi_2, \psi', \mathrm{VC} \cup \mathcal{C}_1 \cup \mathcal{C}_2}$$

$$(8a) \quad \frac{I \wedge C, I \vdash S : \_, I', \mathcal{C} \quad I \wedge C \Rightarrow I'}{\phi, \psi \vdash \mathrm{while}(C) \text{ do } S : I \wedge \neg C, I, \mathcal{C}}$$

$$(8b) \quad \frac{\begin{array}{c} \_, I \vdash \widetilde{S} : \_, I', \_ \quad I \wedge C \Rightarrow I' \\ I \wedge C \wedge \chi_i(v), \mathrm{true} \vdash S : \_, \psi, \mathcal{C} \\ \mathrm{VC} = (I \wedge C \wedge \chi_i(v) \rightarrow \psi) \end{array}}{\phi, \psi \vdash \mathrm{while}(C \wedge ??_i) \text{ do } S : I \wedge \neg(C \wedge \chi_i(v)), I, \mathcal{C} \cup \mathrm{VC}}$$

$$(9) \quad \frac{\mathrm{true}, \mathrm{true} \vdash S : \phi, \psi, \mathcal{C}}{\vdash \lambda v.S : \phi, \psi, \psi \cup \mathcal{C}}$$

Fig. 4. Inference Rules for Constraint Generation

4 Constraint Generation

The constraint generation phase is shown in Figure 4 as inference rules of the form $\phi, \psi \vdash S : \phi', \psi', \mathcal{C}$ where S is a statement, ϕ, ψ, ϕ', ψ' are formulas, and $\mathcal{C}$ is a set of constraints. The meaning of this judgment is that, if all constraints in $\mathcal{C}$ are valid, then $\{\phi\}S\{\phi'\}$ and $\{\psi'\}S\{\psi\}$ are valid Hoare triples. We call the computation of postcondition ϕ' from ϕ the *forward analysis* and the computation of precondition ψ' from ψ the *backward analysis*. The constraints $\mathcal{C}$ track assumptions about unknown predicates that must hold to ensure memory safety.

Since some of the rules in Figure 4 describe standard pre- and post-condition computation, we only explain some of these rules. Rule (4) for memory allocation $[p] = \text{alloc}(E)$ uses ghost variables p^- and p^+. Since $[p]$ points to the beginning of a memory block of size E, the allocation has the effect of assigning p^- to 0 and p^+ to E. Hence, ϕ' and ψ' are obtained by computing the strongest postcondition of ϕ and weakest precondition of ψ with respect to the statement $p^- := 0; p^+ := E$.

Rule (5) for pointer arithmetic computes the effect of this statement on p_1^- and p_1^+. Since $[p_2]$ points to offset p_2^- in memory block M, $[p_1]$ points to offset $p_2^- + E$ within M. Hence, we obtain ϕ_1 as $\text{sp}(p_1^- := p_2^- + E, \phi)$ and ψ_1 as $\text{wp}(p_1^- := p_2^- + E, \psi)$. Similarly, $\phi_2 = \text{sp}(p_1^+ := p_2^+ - E, \phi_1)$ and $\psi_2 = \text{wp}(p_1^+ := p_2^+ - E, \psi_1)$.

Rule (6) describes memory accesses. To guarantee that ψ holds after the memory access, expression E must evaluate to a valid offset in the memory block pointed to by $[p]$. Using ghost variables p^- and p^+, we can express this as $\varphi_{\text{safe}} \equiv E < p^+ \wedge E \geq -p^-$ Hence, the weakest precondition of ψ with respect to the access statement is $\psi \wedge \varphi_{\text{safe}}$.

Constraint generation for conditionals with unknown guards is given in Rule (7b). The first line of this rule computes a weakest sufficient condition for ensuring memory safety of statement S_1. Here, we compute the precondition of S_1 with respect to true rather than ψ because the unknown guard is only required to guarantee the safety of S_1 rather than the remainder of the entire program. Thus, the formula φ computed here represents the weakest sufficient condition for ensuring memory safety of S_1. When we analyze S_1, observe that the forward analysis propagates $\phi \wedge \chi_i(v)$ as the precondition of S_1; hence, statement preconditions computed by the forward analysis may refer to unknown predicates χ_i. The constraints $\mathcal{C}_1$ obtained in this rule describe the restrictions that must be satisfied by the unknown guards nested inside S_1.

The second line in rule (7b) generates a constraint (VC) on the unknown predicate χ_i. Specifically, VC stipulates that the conjunction of the unknown guard χ_i and the precondition ϕ should be strong enough to imply the safety of memory accesses within S_1. Note that the generated VC may contain multiple unknown predicates since both ϕ and φ may refer to other χ_j's.

The third line in rule (7b) uses the notation $\widetilde{S}$, which denotes statement S with each access($[p], E$) statement within S replaced by skip. Here, we analyze statement S_1 a second time but with two important differences from our previous analysis. First, since we consider $\widetilde{S_1}$, we ignore any memory accesses within S_1. Second, we compute the weakest precondition of $\widetilde{S_1}$ with respect to ψ rather than true because we need to ensure the safety of memory accesses that come after S_1. However, we ignore all memory accesses within S_1 because the synthesized guard already ensures the safety of these accesses. Also, observe that this rule discards constraints generated when analyzing $\widetilde{S_1}$, which is sound because any constraints generated while analyzing $\widetilde{S_1}$ are trivially valid.

Another important point to note about rule (7b) is that the backwards analysis propagates the constraint $(\chi_i(\boldsymbol{v}) \to \psi_1) \wedge (\neg\chi_i(\boldsymbol{v}) \to \psi_2)$ as the weakest precondition for the if statement. Hence, statement postconditions computed by the backwards analysis may also refer to unknown predicates.

Example 1. Consider the following code example:

1. $[p] := \mathrm{alloc}(n);\quad [q] := \mathrm{alloc}(n);\quad [p] := [p] \oplus 1;$
2. $\mathrm{if}(??_1)$ then
3. $\qquad n := n + 1;\quad \mathrm{access}([p], 3);$
4. $\qquad \mathrm{if}(??_2)$ then $\mathrm{access}([q], n - 2)$ else skip
5. else skip

In the forward direction, our analysis computes the following precondition ϕ for the if statement at line 2: $\phi : p^- = 1 \wedge p^+ = n - 1 \wedge q^- = 0 \wedge q^+ = n$. Before the assignment at line 3, the forwards analysis computes the precondition $\chi_1(n) \wedge p^- = 1 \wedge p^+ = n-1 \wedge q^- = 0 \wedge q^+ = n$ where χ_1 denotes unknown guard $??_1$ and n is the only scalar variable in scope at this point. For the if statement at line 4, we have the following precondition:

$$\exists n'. \, (\chi_1(n') \,\wedge n = n' + 1 \,\wedge p^- = 1 \wedge\, p^+ = n' - 1$$
$$\wedge \, q^- = 0 \wedge q^+ = n' \wedge p^+ > 3 \wedge p^- \geq -3)$$

Note that, since there is an assignment to n at line 3, the variable n inside the unknown predicate $\chi_1(n)$ gets substituted by n'.

Now, in the backwards direction, the precondition for the then branch of the second if statement is $(n - 2) < q^+ \wedge (n - 2) \geq -q^-$. Hence, when analyzing the if statement at line 4, we generate the following VC:

$$\mathrm{VC}_2 : \begin{array}{l}(\chi_2(n) \wedge \exists n'. \, (\chi_1(n') \,\wedge n = n' + 1 \,\wedge p^- = 1 \wedge\, p^+ = n' - 1 \wedge\, q^- = 0 \\ \wedge \, q^+ = n' \,\wedge\, p^+ > 3 \wedge p^- \geq -3)) \to ((n - 2) < q^+ \wedge (n - 2) \geq -q^-)\end{array}$$

where χ_2 represents $??_2$ and the right-hand-side of the implication is the safety precondition for the then branch. For the if statement at line 2, the backwards analysis computes the precondition for the then branch as $\varphi : 3 < p^+ \wedge 3 \geq -p^-$. Using φ and formula ϕ obtained through the forward analysis, we generate the following VC for the if statement at line 2:

$$\mathrm{VC}_1 : (\chi_1(n) \wedge p^- = 1 \wedge p^+ = n - 1 \wedge q^- = 0 \wedge q^+ = n) \to (3 < p^+ \wedge 3 \geq -p^-)$$

Hence, our algorithm generates the constraints $\mathrm{VC}_1 \cup \mathrm{VC}_2$.

Continuing with the inference rules in Figure 4, rules (8b) and (8a) describe the analysis of while loops with and without unknown safety guards respectively. Rule (8a) gives the standard Hoare rule for while loops, asserting that I is an inductive loop invariant. Since the automatic inference of loop invariants is an orthogonal problem, this paper assumes that loop invariants are provided by an oracle, and our implementation uses standard abstract interpretation based techniques for loop invariant generation.

In rule (8b), our goal is to infer an additional guard as part of the loop continuation condition such that all memory accesses within the loop body are safe. As in rule (8a), the first line of rule (8b) asserts that I is inductive. However, an important difference is that we check the inductiveness of I with respect to $\tilde{S}$ rather than S because I is not required to be strong enough to prove the safety of memory accesses inside the loop body. In fact, if I was strong enough to prove memory safety, this would mean the additional unknown guard is unnecessary.

The last two lines of rule (8b) compute the safety precondition ψ for the loop body (i.e., $\psi = \mathrm{wp}(\mathrm{true}, S)$) and generate the constraint VC : $I \wedge C \wedge \chi_i(\boldsymbol{v}) \to \psi$. In other words, together with continuation condition C and known loop invariant I, unknown predicate χ_i should imply the memory safety of the loop body.

Example 2. Consider the following code snippet:

> 1. $[p] = \mathrm{alloc}(n); \ i = 0;$
> 2. while(true $\wedge$??$_1$) do
> 3. $\mathrm{access}([p], 1); \ [p] = [p] \oplus 1; \ i = i + 1;$

Assume we have the loop invariant $I : \ p^- + p^+ = n \ \wedge \ i \geq 0 \ \wedge i = p^-$. The safety precondition ψ for the loop body is $1 < p^+ \wedge 1 \geq -p^-$. Hence, rule (8b) from Figure 4 generates the following verification condition:

$$(\chi_1(i, n) \ \wedge \ p^- + p^+ = n \ \wedge \ i \geq 0 \ \wedge \ i = p^-) \to (1 < p^+ \wedge 1 \geq -p^-)$$

The last rule in Figure 4 generates constraints for the entire program. Since we add the program's weakest precondition to $\mathcal{C}$, *the synthesis problem has a solution only if all accesses that are not protected by unknown guards are safe.*

5   Constraint Solving

The rules described in Section 4 generate constraints of the form:

$$\mathcal{C}_i : \ (F_1(\chi_1, \ldots \chi_{i-1}) \wedge \chi_i(\boldsymbol{v})) \to F_2(\chi_{i+1}, \ldots \chi_n) \tag{5}$$

where F_1 and F_2 are arbitrary formulas containing program variables and unknowns. In each constraint, there is exactly one key unknown χ_i that does not appear inside boolean connectives or quantifiers. Hence, we refer to $\mathcal{C}_i$ as the constraint associated with χ_i (or the χ_i-constraint). Also, the only unknowns appearing on the right hand side of an implication (i.e., inside F_2) in a χ_i-constraint represent unknown guards that are syntactically nested inside χ_i. Hence, we refer to $\chi_{i+1}, \ldots \chi_n$ as the *descendants* of $\mathcal{C}_i$, denoted $\mathrm{DESCENDS}(\mathcal{C}_i)$. In contrast, the unknowns that appear inside F_1 are either ancestors of χ_i or appear in the code before χ_i. We say that $\mathcal{C}_i$ *sequentially depends* on χ_j if χ_j appears inside F_1 and is not an ancestor of χ_i. We write $\mathrm{SEQDEP}(\mathcal{C}_i)$ to denote the set of χ_j-constraints such that $\mathcal{C}_i$ is sequentially dependent on χ_j.

Example 3. Consider the following code snippet:

> 1. $[a] := \mathrm{alloc}(x);$
> 2. if(??$_1$) then $\mathrm{access}([a], 1)$ else skip
> 3. if(??$_2$) then
> 4.   if(??$_3$) then $\mathrm{access}([a], x - 3); [b] := \mathrm{alloc}(4);$ else $[b] := \mathrm{alloc}(2);$
> 5. $\mathrm{access}([b], 3);$
> 6. else skip

Let χ_1, χ_2, χ_3 denote the unknowns $??_1$, $??_2$, and $??_3$, and let $\mathcal{C}_i$ denote each χ_i constraint. Here, we have:

$\mathcal{C}_1 : (a^- = 0 \wedge a^+ = x \wedge \chi_1(x)) \rightarrow (1 < a^+ \wedge 1 \geq -a^-)$

$\mathcal{C}_2 : (a^- = 0 \wedge a^+ = x \wedge \chi_1(x) \wedge \chi_2(x)) \rightarrow ((\chi_3(x) \rightarrow 3 < 4) \wedge (\neg\chi_3(x) \rightarrow 3 < 2))$

$\mathcal{C}_3 : (a^- = 0 \wedge a^+ = x \wedge \chi_1(x) \wedge \chi_2(x) \wedge \chi_3(x)) \rightarrow (x - 3 < a^+ \wedge x - 3 \geq -a^-)$

Therefore, $\text{DESCENDS}(\mathcal{C}_1) = \emptyset$, $\text{DESCENDS}(\mathcal{C}_2) = \{\mathcal{C}_3\}$, and $\text{DESCENDS}(\mathcal{C}_3) = \emptyset$. Also, $\text{SEQDEPS}(\mathcal{C}_1) = \emptyset$, $\text{SEQDEPS}(\mathcal{C}_2) = \{\mathcal{C}_1\}$, $\text{SEQDEPS}(\mathcal{C}_3) = \{\mathcal{C}_1\}$.

Our constraint solving algorithm is given in Figure 5. A key underlying insight is that we only solve a constraint $\mathcal{C}_i$ when all sequential dependencies of $\mathcal{C}_i$ are resolved. The intuition is that if χ_i sequentially depends on χ_j, χ_j will appear in a χ_i-constraint, but not the other way around. Hence, by fixing the solution for χ_j before processing χ_i, we cannot break the optimality of the solution for χ_j.

The SOLVE algorithm shown in Figure 5 takes as input constraints C and returns a mapping S from each unknown χ to a concrete predicate or $\emptyset$ if no solution exists. Initially, we add all constraints C to worklist W and initialize RESOLVED to $\emptyset$. In each iteration of the SOLVE loop, we dequeue constraints Δ that have their sequential dependencies resolved (line (3)) and substitute any resolved unknowns in Δ with the solution given by S, yielding a new set Δ' (line 4). Hence, a χ_i-constraint in Δ' does not contain any unknowns that χ_i sequentially depends on. Now, to solve Δ', we first obtain a sound, but not necessarily optimal, solution using the function SOLVEINIT. In particular, although the solutions returned by SOLVEINIT may be stronger than necessary, we iteratively weaken this initial solution using WEAKEN until we obtain an optimal solution.

The procedure SOLVEINIT processes constraints C top-down, starting with the outermost guard χ_i. In each iteration, we pick an unsolved constraint $\mathcal{C}_i$ that has only one unknown on the left-hand side of the implication (line 13). However, since we don't yet have a solution for the unknowns $\mathcal{V}$ on the right-hand side, we strengthen $\mathcal{C}_i$ to Φ by universally quantifying $\mathcal{V}$ (line 16).[1] Observe that the universal quantification of $\mathcal{V}$ has the same effect as treating any unknown guard inside χ_i as a non-deterministic choice. The resulting constraint Φ is of the form $(\chi_i(\boldsymbol{v}) \wedge \phi_1) \rightarrow \phi_2$ where ϕ_1 and ϕ_2 do not contain any unknowns; hence, we can solve for unknown χ_i using standard logical abduction. In the algorithm of Figure 5, this is done by calling an abduction procedure called ABDUCE (line 17). We do not describe the ABDUCE procedure in this paper and refer the interested reader to [12] for a description of an abduction algorithm which computes a logically weakest solution containing a fewest number of variables. Now, given solution γ for χ_i, we add it to our solution set S and eliminate unknown χ_i from other constraints in C using the SUBSTITUTE procedure.

Because of the universal quantification of the unknowns on the right-hand side, the solution S_0 returned by SOLVEINIT may be stronger than necessary. Hence, procedure WEAKEN iteratively weakens the initial solution until we obtain an optimal solution. In contrast to SOLVEINIT, WEAKEN processes the constraints

---

[1] Recall that $\forall\chi_j.\Phi \equiv \Phi[\text{true}/\chi_j] \wedge \Phi[\text{false}/\chi_j]$.

procedure SOLVE($\mathcal{C}$):
   input: set of constraints $\mathcal{C}$
   output: mapping S from each χ_i to γ or $\emptyset$ if no solution exists

(1) RESOLVED := $\emptyset$; S:= $\emptyset$; W := $\mathcal{C}$
(2) while($W \neq \emptyset$)
(3) $\Delta := \{\mathcal{C}_i \mid \mathcal{C}_i \in W \wedge$ SEQDEP($\mathcal{C}_i$) $\subseteq$ RESOLVED $\}$
(4) $W := W - G$
(5) $\Delta' :=$ SUBSTITUTE(Δ, S)
(6) $S_0 :=$ SOLVEINIT(Δ')
(7) $S :=$ WEAKEN(Δ', S_0, S, RESOLVED)
(8)   if($S = \emptyset$) return $\emptyset$
(9)   RESOLVED := RESOLVED $\uplus \Delta$
(10) return S;

procedure SOLVEINIT($\mathcal{C}$):
(11) $S := \emptyset$
(12) while($\mathcal{C} \neq \emptyset$)
(13)   let $\mathcal{C}_i \in \mathcal{C}$ with one unknown χ on LHS
(14) $\mathcal{C} := \mathcal{C} - \mathcal{C}_i$
(15) $\mathcal{V} :=$ unknowns of $\mathcal{C}_i$ on RHS
(16) $\Phi := \forall \mathcal{V}.\mathcal{C}_i$
(17) $\gamma :=$ ABDUCE(Φ)
(18) $S := S \uplus [\chi \mapsto \gamma]$
(19) $\mathcal{C} :=$ SUBSTITUTE($\mathcal{C}, S$)
(20) return S

procedure WEAKEN(Δ, S, S_0, RESOLVED)
(21) DONE := $\{\Delta_i \mid \Delta_i \in \Delta \wedge$ DESCENDS(Δ_i) $= \emptyset\}$
(22) RESOLVED := RESOLVED $\uplus$ DONE
(23) $S := S \uplus \{[\chi_i \mapsto \gamma_i] \mid \mathcal{C}_i \in$ DONE $\wedge S_0(\chi_i) = \gamma_i\}$
(24) $\Delta := \Delta -$ DONE; $S_0 := S_0 -$ DONE
(25) while($\Delta \neq \emptyset$)
(26)   let CUR $\in \Delta$ s/t DESCENDS(CUR) $\subseteq$ RESOLVED
(27)   let $\chi =$ UNKNOWN(CUR)
(28) $\Delta := \Delta -$ CUR; $S_0 := S_0 - \chi$
(29) $\theta :=$ CUR $\uplus \{\mathcal{C}_i \mid \mathcal{C}_i \in$ RESOLVED $\wedge \chi \in$ UNKNOWNS($\mathcal{C}_i$) $\}$
(30) $\theta' :=$ SUBSTITUTE($S \uplus S_0$)
(31) $\gamma :=$ ABDUCE(θ')
(32)   if UNSAT(γ) return $\emptyset$
(33) $S := S \uplus [\chi \mapsto \gamma]$
(34)   RESOLVED := RESOLVED $\uplus$ CUR
(35) return S

Fig. 5. The constraint solving algorithm

bottom-up, starting with the innermost guard first. Specifically, the solution computed by SOLVEINIT for the innermost guard χ_i cannot be further weakened, as it is not possible to obtain a weaker solution for χ_i by plugging in weaker solutions for the unknowns appearing on the left-hand side of a χ_i-constraint.

Hence, we add all constraints with no descendants in Δ to RESOLVED and update S with the corresponding solutions given by S_0 (lines 21-23).

The while loop in lines 25-34 iterates over the constraints bottom-up and, in each iteration, picks a χ-constraint CUR all of whose descendants have been resolved (line 26). Now, the solution given by S_0 for χ could be stronger than necessary; thus, we would like to weaken it using the new optimal solutions for χ's descendants. However, since χ will appear on the left-hand side of a constraint $\mathcal{C}_i$ associated with a descendant χ_i of χ, we need to take care not to invalidate the solution for χ_i as we weaken χ. Hence, at line 29, we collect in set θ all resolved constraints in which χ appears. The idea here is that, when we abduce a new solution for χ, we will simultaneously solve all constraints in θ so that we preserve existing solutions for χ's descendants. Now, to solve for χ using abduction, we first eliminate all unknowns in θ except for χ. For this purpose, we substitute all resolved unknowns in θ with their solution given by S (line 30). However, observe that there may also be unknowns in θ that have not yet been resolved; these unknowns correspond to ancestors of χ, which only appear (unnegated) on the outerlevel conjunction of the left-hand side of the constraints in θ. Hence, to eliminate the unresolved unknowns, we will use the initial solution given by S_0 (also line 30). Observe that we can do this without undermining optimality because we will later only further weaken the solutions given by S_0, which cannot cause us to further weaken the solution for χ.

After performing the substitution at line 30, the set of constraints θ' only contains one unknown χ, which we can now solve using standard abduction (line 31).[2] If the resulting solution γ is false, this means our synthesis problem does not have a solution. Otherwise, we add the mapping $\chi \mapsto \gamma$ to our solution set and continue until all constraints in θ have been processed.

Let us call a solution S to the synthesis problem *optimal relative to a set of loop invariants* if, among the set of solutions that any algorithm can generate using these loop invariants, S is optimal. We have:

Theorem 1. *Consider program P such that $\vdash P : \phi, \psi, \mathcal{C}$ according to Figure 4, and let S be the result of SOLVE($\mathcal{C}$). If $S \neq \emptyset$, then $P[S]$ is memory safe. Furthermore, S is an optimal solution to the synthesis problem defined by P relative to the loop invariants used during constraint generation.*

Example 4. Consider the constraints VC_1 and VC_2 from Example 1. Here, neither VC_1 nor VC_2 have sequential dependencies, and since VC_1 contains only one unknown, we first solve for χ_1 in SOLVEINIT, for which abduction yields the solution $n > 4$. Next, we plug this solution into VC_2 (renaming n to n'), which yields the following constraint in Prenex Normal Form:

$$\forall n'.(n' > 4 \ \wedge \ \chi_2(n) \ \wedge \ n = n' + 1 \ \wedge p^- = 1 \wedge \ p^+ = n' - 1 \wedge q^- = 0 \wedge q^+ = n'$$
$$\wedge \ p^+ > 3 \wedge p^- \geq -3) \rightarrow (n - 2) < q^+ \wedge (n - 2) \geq -q^-)$$

---

[2] Observe that we can simultenously solve all constraints in θ using abduction because a pair of constraints of the form $\chi \wedge \phi_1 \Rightarrow \phi_2$ and $\chi \wedge \psi_1 \Rightarrow \psi_2$ (where the ϕ's and ψ's are unknown free) can be rewritten as $(\chi \wedge \phi_1 \wedge \psi_1) \Rightarrow (\phi_2 \wedge \psi_2)$, which corresponds to a standard abduction problem.

Program	Lines	# holes	Time (s)	Memory	Synthesis successful?	Bug?
Coreutils hostname	160	1	0.15	10 MB	Yes	No
Coreutils tee	223	1	0.84	10 MB	Yes	Yes
Coreutils runcon	265	2	0.81	12 MB	Yes	No
Coreutils chroot	279	2	0.53	23 MB	Yes	No
Coreutils remove	710	2	1.38	66MB	Yes	No
Coreutils nl	758	3	2.07	80 MB	Yes	No
SSH - sshconnect	810	3	1.43	81 MB	Yes	No
Coreutils mv	929	4	2.03	42 MB	Yes	No
SSH - do_authentication	1,904	4	3.92	86 MB	Yes	Yes
SSH - ssh_session	2,260	5	4.35	81 MB	Yes	No

Fig. 6. Experimental benchmarks and results

Since VC_2 has only one unknown left, we solve it using ABDUCE and obtain $\chi_2(n)$ = true. Next, we attempt to weaken the solution for χ_1 in WEAKEN, but since χ_2 does not appear on the right hand side of VC_1, we cannot further weaken the solution for χ_1. Hence, we obtain the solution $[\chi_1 \mapsto n > 4, \chi_2 \mapsto \text{true}]$.

Example 5. Consider constraints C_1, C_2, and C_3 from Example 3. Since C_1 does not have sequential dependencies, we first solve C_1 and obtain the solution $\chi_1 = (x > 1)$. In the next iteration, both C_2 and C_3 have their sequential dependencies resolved; hence we plug in $x > 1$ for χ_1 in C_2 and C_3. In SOLVEINIT, we first solve C_2 since it now contains only one unknown (χ_2) on the left hand side. When we universally quantify χ_3 on the right hand side, ABDUCE yields the solution $\chi_2 = \text{false}$. In the next iteration of SOLVEINIT, we obtain the solution *true* for χ_3. Observe that our initial solution for χ_2 is stronger than necessary; hence we will weaken it. In the procedure WEAKEN, we simultaneously solve constraints C_2 and C_3, using existing solutions for χ_1 and χ_3. ABDUCE now yields $\chi_2 = x > 2$. Hence, the final solution is $[\chi_1 = x > 1, \ \chi_2 = x > 2, \ \chi_3 = \text{true}]$.

Example 6. For the constraint generated in Example 2, the SOLVE procedure computes the solution $\chi_1(i, n) = i < n - 1$.

6   Implementation and Evaluation

We implemented a prototype tool for synthesizing safety guards for C programs. Our tool is based on the SAIL infrastructure [13] and uses the Mistral SMT solver [12] for solving abduction problems in linear integer arithmetic.

We evaluated our tool on ten benchmark programs written in C. As shown in Figure 6, all of our benchmarks are taken either from the Unix coreutils, which implements basic command line utilities for Unix [14], or OpenSSH, which provides encrypted communication sessions based on the SSH protocol [15]. For each benchmark program, we manually removed 1-5 safety guards from the source code and then used our algorithm to infer these missing guards. [3] In total, we used our tool to synthesize 27 different safety guards.

---

[3] The URL http://www.cs.utexas.edu/~tdillig/cav14-benchmarks.tar.gz contains all benchmarks, where each missing guard is indicated with _SYN.

The results of our experimental evaluation are shown in Figure 6. Our tool was able to successfully synthesize all of the missing guards present in these benchmarks. For 23 of these 27 missing guards, our tool inferred the *exact same predicate* that the programmer had originally written, and for 4 out of the 27 missing guards, it inferred a syntactically different but semantically equivalent condition (e.g., our tool synthesized the guard $x \neq 0$ when the programmer had originally written $x > 0$ but x is already known to be non-negative). In two applications (Coreutils tee and SSH do_authentication), the guards synthesized by our tool did not match the guards in the original program. However, upon further inspection, we found that both of these programs were in fact buggy. For example, in Coreutils tee, the program could indeed access the `argv` array out-of-bounds. We believe that the existence of such bugs in even extremely well-tested applications is evidence that writing memory safe code is hard and that many programmers can benefit from our guard synthesis technique.

As shown in Figure 6, the running time of our algorithm ranges from 0.15 seconds to 4.35 seconds with an average memory consumption of 49 MB. We believe these results suggest that our approach can be integrated into the development process, helping programmers write safe-by-construction low level code.

7 Related Work

Program Synthesis. The last few years have seen a flurry of activity in constraint-based software synthesis [9, 10, 16, 17]. As the first abduction-based approach to synthesis, our work is algorithmically very different from prior methods in this area. A concrete benefit is that, unlike prior constraint-based approaches to synthesis [10, 11, 18, 19], our method does not require a template for the expressions being synthesized. A second benefit is that we can show the synthesized expressions to be optimal relative to loop invariants.

There are a few approaches to synthesis that consider optimality as an objective [20–23]. However, in these papers, optimality is defined with respect to an explicit quantitative aspect of program executions, for example execution time. In contrast, in the current work, the cost metric is on the guards that we synthesize; we want to infer guards that are as simple and as general as possible.

Program Analysis for Memory Safety. Memory safety is a core concern in low-level programming, and there is a huge literature on program analysis techniques to guarantee memory safety [3, 24–33]. While many of these techniques can statically detect memory safety errors, they do not help the programmer write safe-by-construction code. Furthermore, unlike dynamic approaches to memory safety [27, 28, 32, 33], our technique guarantees the absence of runtime failures and does not require additional runtime book-keeping.

Abduction-based Verification. Many memory safety verifiers based on separation logic use abductive (or bi-abductive) reasoning for performing modular heap reasoning [5, 34, 35]. In these approaches, abductive reasoning is used to infer missing preconditions of procedures. A more algorithmic form of abduction for first-order theories is considered in [12]. The abduction algorithm described in [12] computes a maximally simple and general solution and is used as a key building block in the constraint solving phase of our synthesis algorithm. This form of SMT-based abduction has also been used for loop invariant generation [6, 7] and for error explanation and diagnosis [36]. The contribution of the present paper is to show how abduction can be used in program synthesis.

References

1. Berdine, J., Cook, B., Ishtiaq, S.: sLAYER: Memory safety for systems-level code. In: Gopalakrishnan, G., Qadeer, S. (eds.) CAV 2011. LNCS, vol. 6806, pp. 178–183. Springer, Heidelberg (2011)
2. Beyer, D., Henzinger, T.A., Jhala, R., Majumdar, R.: Checking memory safety with blast. In: Cerioli, M. (ed.) FASE 2005. LNCS, vol. 3442, pp. 2–18. Springer, Heidelberg (2005)
3. Chatterjee, S., Lahiri, S.K., Qadeer, S., Rakamarić, Z.: A reachability predicate for analyzing low-level software. In: Grumberg, O., Huth, M. (eds.) TACAS 2007. LNCS, vol. 4424, pp. 19–33. Springer, Heidelberg (2007)
4. Dillig, I., Dillig, T., Aiken, A.: Fluid updates: Beyond strong vs. Weak updates. In: Gordon, A.D. (ed.) ESOP 2010. LNCS, vol. 6012, pp. 246–266. Springer, Heidelberg (2010)
5. Calcagno, C., Distefano, D., O'Hearn, P., Yang, H.: Compositional shape analysis by means of bi-abduction. In: POPL, pp. 289–300 (2009)
6. Dillig, I., Dillig, T., Li, B., McMillan, K.: Inductive invariant generation via abductive inference. In: OOPSLA, pp. 443–456. ACM (2013)
7. Li, B., Dillig, I., Dillig, T., McMillan, K., Sagiv, M.: Synthesis of circular compositional program proofs via abduction. In: Piterman, N., Smolka, S.A. (eds.) TACAS 2013. LNCS, vol. 7795, pp. 370–384. Springer, Heidelberg (2013)
8. Alur, R., Bodik, R., Juniwal, G., Martin, M.M., Raghothaman, M., Seshia, S., Singh, R., Solar-Lezama, A., Torlak, E., Udupa, A.: Syntax-guided synthesis. In: FMCAD (2013)
9. Solar-Lezama, A.: The sketching approach to program synthesis. In: Hu, Z. (ed.) APLAS 2009. LNCS, vol. 5904, pp. 4–13. Springer, Heidelberg (2009)
10. Srivastava, S., Gulwani, S., Foster, J.S.: Template-based program verification and program synthesis. STTT 15(5-6), 497–518 (2013)
11. Srivastava, S., Gulwani, S., Chaudhuri, S., Foster, J.: Path-based inductive synthesis for program inversion. In: PLDI, pp. 492–503 (2011)
12. Dillig, I., Dillig, T.: EXPLAIN: A tool for performing abductive inference. In: Sharygina, N., Veith, H. (eds.) CAV 2013. LNCS, vol. 8044, pp. 684–689. Springer, Heidelberg (2013)
13. Dillig, I., Dillig, T., Aiken, A.: SAIL: Static Analysis Intermediate Language. Stanford University Technical Report
14. Unix coreutils, http://www.gnu.org/software/coreutils/:
15. Openssh 5.3p1, http://www.openssh.com/:
16. Vechev, M., Yahav, E., Yorsh, G.: Abstraction-guided synthesis of synchronization. In: POPL, pp. 327–338 (2010)
17. Seshia, S.: Sciduction: combining induction, deduction, and structure for verification and synthesis. In: DAC, pp. 356–365 (2012)
18. Srivastava, S., Gulwani, S., Foster, J.: From program verification to program synthesis. In: POPL, pp. 313–326 (2010)

19. Beyene, T., Chaudhuri, S., Popeea, C., Rybalchenko, A.: A constraint-based approach to solving games on infinite graphs. In: POPL (2014)
20. Bloem, R., Chatterjee, K., Henzinger, T.A., Jobstmann, B.: Better quality in synthesis through quantitative objectives. In: Bouajjani, A., Maler, O. (eds.) CAV 2009. LNCS, vol. 5643, pp. 140–156. Springer, Heidelberg (2009)
21. Jha, S., Seshia, S., Tiwari, A.: Synthesis of optimal switching logic for hybrid systems. In: 2011 Proceedings of the International Conference on Embedded Software (EMSOFT), pp. 107–116 (2011)
22. Chaudhuri, S., Solar-Lezama, A.: Smooth interpretation. In: PLDI (2010)
23. Chaudhuri, S., Clochard, M., Solar-Lezama, A.: Bridging boolean and quantitative synthesis using smoothed proof search. In: POPL (2014)
24. Younan, Y., Joosen, W., Piessens, F.: Runtime countermeasures for code injection attacks against c and c++ programs. ACM Comput. Surv. 44(3), 17 (2012)
25. Dhurjati, D., Kowshik, S., Adve, V., Lattner, C.: Memory safety without runtime checks or garbage collection. In: LCTES 2003, pp. 69–80 (2003)
26. Balakrishnan, G., Reps, T.: Analyzing memory accesses in x86 executables. In: Duesterwald, E. (ed.) CC 2004. LNCS, vol. 2985, pp. 5–23. Springer, Heidelberg (2004)
27. Condit, J., Harren, M., Anderson, Z., Gay, D.M., Necula, G.C.: Dependent types for low-level programming. In: De Nicola, R. (ed.) ESOP 2007. LNCS, vol. 4421, pp. 520–535. Springer, Heidelberg (2007)
28. Beyer, D., Henzinger, T.A., Jhala, R., Majumdar, R.: Checking memory safety with blast. In: Cerioli, M. (ed.) FASE 2005. LNCS, vol. 3442, pp. 2–18. Springer, Heidelberg (2005)
29. Yang, H., Lee, O., Berdine, J., Calcagno, C., Cook, B., Distefano, D., O'Hearn, P.W.: Scalable shape analysis for systems code. In: Gupta, A., Malik, S. (eds.) CAV 2008. LNCS, vol. 5123, pp. 385–398. Springer, Heidelberg (2008)
30. Berdine, J., Cook, B., Ishtiaq, S.: sLAYER: Memory safety for systems-level code. In: Gopalakrishnan, G., Qadeer, S. (eds.) CAV 2011. LNCS, vol. 6806, pp. 178–183. Springer, Heidelberg (2011)
31. Wagner, D., Foster, J.S., Brewer, E.A., Aiken, A.: A first step towards automated detection of buffer overrun vulnerabilities. In: Network and Distributed System Security Symposium, pp. 3–17 (2000)
32. Necula, G.C., McPeak, S., Weimer, W.: CCured: type-safe retrofitting of legacy code. In: POPL, pp. 128–139 (2002)
33. Jim, T., Morrisett, J.G., Grossman, D., Hicks, M.W., Cheney, J., Wang, Y.: Cyclone: A safe dialect of c. In: USENIX Annual Technical Conference, General Track, pp. 275–288 (2002)
34. Distefano, D., Filipović, I.: Memory leaks detection in java by bi-abductive inference. In: Rosenblum, D.S., Taentzer, G. (eds.) FASE 2010. LNCS, vol. 6013, pp. 278–292. Springer, Heidelberg (2010)
35. Botinčan, M., Distefano, D., Dodds, M., Grigore, R., Parkinson, M.J.: corestar: The core of jstar. In. In: Boogie. Citeseer (2011)
36. Dillig, I., Dillig, T., Aiken, A.: Automated error diagnosis using abductive inference. In: PLDI, pp. 181–192. ACM

Don't Sit on the Fence[*]

A Static Analysis Approach to Automatic Fence Insertion

Jade Alglave[1], Daniel Kroening[2], Vincent Nimal[2], and Daniel Poetzl[2]

[1] University College London
[2] University of Oxford

Abstract. Modern architectures rely on memory fences to prevent undesired weakenings of memory consistency. As the fences' semantics may be subtle, the automation of their placement is highly desirable. But precise methods for restoring consistency do not scale to deployed systems code. We choose to trade some precision for genuine scalability: our technique is suitable for large code bases. We implement it in our new **musketeer** tool, and detail experiments on more than 350 executables of packages found in Debian Linux 7.1, e.g. **memcached** (about 10000 LoC).

1 Introduction

Concurrent programs are hard to design and implement, especially when running on multiprocessor architectures. Multiprocessors implement *weak memory models*, which feature e.g. *instruction reordering*, *store buffering* (both appearing on x86), or *store atomicity relaxation* (a particularity of Power and ARM). Hence, multiprocessors allow more behaviours than Lamport's *Sequential Consistency* (SC) [20], a theoretical model where the execution of a program corresponds to an interleaving of the different threads. This has a dramatic effect on programmers, most of whom learned to program with SC.

Fortunately, architectures provide special *fence* (or *barrier*) instructions to prevent certain behaviours. Yet both the questions of *where* and *how* to insert fences are contentious, as fences are architecture-specific and expensive.

Attempts at automatically placing fences include Visual Studio 2013, which offers an option to guarantee acquire/release semantics (we study the performance impact of this policy in Sec. 2). The C++11 standard provides an elaborate API for inter-thread communication, giving the programmer some control over which fences are used, and where. But the use of such APIs might be a hard task, even for expert programmers. For example, Norris and Demsky reported a bug found in a published C11 implementation of a work-stealing queue [27].

We address here the question of how to *synthesise* fences, i.e. automatically place them in a program to enforce robustness/stability [9,5] (which implies SC). This should lighten the programmer's burden. The fence synthesis tool needs to be based on a precise model of weak memory. In verification, models commonly adopt an *operational* style, where an execution is an interleaving of transitions accessing the memory (as in SC). To address weaker architectures, the models are augmented with buffers and

---

[*] Supported by SRC/2269.002, EPSRC/H017585/1 and ERC/280053.

A. Biere and R. Bloem (Eds.): CAV 2014, LNCS 8559, pp. 508–524, 2014.
© Springer International Publishing Switzerland 2014

queues that implement the features of the hardware. Similarly, a good fraction of the fence synthesis methods, e.g. [23,18,19,24,3,10] (see also Fig. 2), rely on operational models to describe executions of programs.

Challenges. Thus, methods using operational models inherit the limitations of methods based on interleavings, *e.g.* the *"severely limited scalability"*, as [24] puts it. Indeed, none of them scale to programs with more than a few hundred lines of code, due to the very large number of executions a program can have. Another impediment to scalability is that these methods establish if there is a need for fences by exploring the executions of a program one by one.

Finally, considering models à la Power makes the problem significantly more difficult. Intel x86 offers only one fence (mfence), but Power offers a variety of synchronisation: fences (e.g. sync and lwsync), or dependencies (address, data or control). This diversity makes the optimisation more subtle: one cannot simply minimise the number of fences, but rather has to consider the costs of the different synchronisation mechanisms; it might be cheaper to use one full fence than four dependencies.

Our approach. We tackle these challenges with a static approach. Our choice of model almost mandates this approach: we rely on the axiomatic semantics of [6]. We feel that an axiomatic semantics is an invitation to build abstract objects that embrace all the executions of a program.

Previous works, e.g. [30,5,9,10], show that weak memory behaviours boil down to the presence of certain cycles, called *critical cycles*, in the executions of the program. A critical cycle essentially represents a minimal violation of SC, and thus indicates where to place fences to restore SC. We detect these cycles statically, by exploring an over-approximation of the executions of the program.

Contributions. Our method is sound for a wide range of architectures, including x86-TSO, Power and ARM; and scales for large code bases, such as memcached (about 10000 LoC). We implemented it in our new musketeer tool. Our method is the most precise of the static analysis methods (see Sec. 2). To do this comparison, we implemented all these methods in our tool; for example, the pensieve policy [32] was designed for Java only, and we now provide it for x86-TSO, Power and ARM. Thus, our tool musketeer gives a comparison point for the field.

Outline. We discuss the performance impact of fences in Sec. 2, and survey related work in Sec. 3. We recall our weak memory semantics in Sec. 4. We detail how we detect critical cycles in Sec. 5, and how we place fences in Sec. 6. In Sec. 7, we compare existing tools and our new tool musketeer. We provide the sources, benchmarks and experimental reports online at http://www.cprover.org/wmm/musketeer.

2 Motivation

Before optimising the placement of fences, we investigated whether naive approaches to fence insertion indeed have a negative performance impact. To that end, we measured the overhead of different fencing methods on a stack and a queue from the liblfds

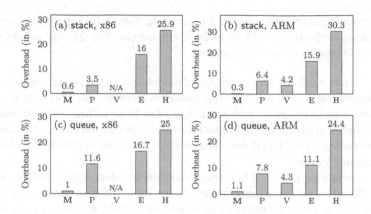

Fig. 1. Overheads for the different fencing strategies

lock-free data structure package (http://liblfds.org). For each data structure, we built a harness (consisting of 4 threads) that concurrently invokes its operations. We built several versions of the above two programs:

- (M) with fences inserted by our tool musketeer;
- (P) with fences following the *delay set analysis* of the pensieve compiler [32], i.e. a static over-approximation of Shasha and Snir's eponymous (dynamic) analysis [30] (see also the discussion of Lee and Padua's work [22] in Sec. 3);
- (V) with fences following the *Visual Studio* policy, i.e. guaranteeing acquire/release semantics (in the C11 sense [2]), but not SC, for reads and writes of volatile variables (see http://msdn.microsoft.com/en-us/library/vstudio/jj635841.aspx, accessed 04-11-2013). On x86, no fences are necessary as the model is sufficiently strong already; hence, we only provide data for ARM;
- (E) with fences after each access to a shared variable;
- (H) with an mfence (x86) or a dmb (ARM) after every assembly instruction that writes (x86) or reads or writes (ARM) *static global* or *heap data*.

We emphasise that these experiments required us to implement (P), (E) and (V) ourselves, so that they would handle the architectures that we considered. This means in particular that our tool provides the pensieve policy (P) for TSO, Power and ARM, whereas the original pensieve targeted Java only.

We ran all versions 100 times, on an x86-64 Intel Core i5-3570 with 4 cores (3.40 GHz) and 4 GB of RAM, and on an ARMv7 (32-bit) Samsung Exynos 4412 with 4 cores (1.6 GHz) and 2 GB of RAM.

For each program version, Fig. 1 shows the mean overhead w.r.t. the unfenced program. We give the overhead in *user time* (as given by Linux time), i.e. the time spent by the program in user mode on the CPU. We refer the reader to our study of the statistical significance of these experiments (using confidence intervals) in the full version of this paper [8]. Amongst the approaches that guarantee SC (i.e. all but V), the best results were achieved with our tool musketeer.

3   Related Work

The work of Shasha and Snir [30] is a foundation for the field of fence synthesis. Most of the work cited below inherits their notions of *delay* and *critical cycle*. A delay is a pair of instructions in a thread that can be reordered by the underlying architecture. A critical cycle essentially represents a minimal violation of SC. Fig. 2 classifies the methods mentioned in this section

authors	tool	model style	objective
Abdulla et al. [3]	memorax	operational	reachability
Alglave et al. [6]	offence	axiomatic	SC
Bouajjani et al. [10]	trencher	operational	SC
Fang et al. [15]	pensieve	axiomatic	SC
Kuperstein et al. [18]	fender	operational	reachability
Kuperstein et al. [19]	blender	operational	reachability
Linden et al. [23]	remmex	operational	reachability
Liu et al. [24]	dfence	operational	specification
Sura et al. [32]	pensieve	axiomatic	SC

Fig. 2. Fence synthesis tools

w.r.t. their style of model (operational or axiomatic). We report our experimental comparison of these tools in Sec. 7. Below, we detail fence synthesis methods per style. We write TSO for Total Store Order, implemented in Sparc TSO [31] and Intel x86 [28]. We write PSO for Partial Store Order and RMO for Relaxed Memory Order, two other Sparc architectures. We write Power for IBM Power [1].

Operational models. Linden and Wolper [23] explore all executions (using what they call *automata acceleration*) to simulate the reorderings occuring under TSO and PSO. Abdulla et al. [3] couple predicate abstraction for TSO with a counterexample-guided strategy. They check if an error state is reachable; if so, they calculate what they call the *maximal permissive* sets of fences that forbid this error state. Their method guarantees that the fences they find are *necessary*, i.e., removing a fence from the set would make the error state reachable again.

Kuperstein et al. [18] explore all executions for TSO, PSO and a subset of RMO, and along the way build constraints encoding reorderings leading to error states. The fences can be derived from the set of constraints at the error states. The same authors [19] improve this exploration under TSO and PSO using an abstract interpretation they call *partial coherence abstraction*, relaxing the order in the write buffers after a certain bound, thus reducing the state space to explore. Liu et al. [24] offer a *dynamic synthesis* approach for TSO and PSO, enumerating the possible sets of fences to prevent an execution picked dynamically from reaching an error state.

Bouajjani et al. [10] build on an operational model of TSO. They look for *minimum violations* (viz. critical cycles) by enumerating *attackers* (viz. delays). Like us, they use linear programming. However, they first enumerate all the solutions, then encode them as an ILP, and finally ask the solver to pick the least expensive one. Our method directly encodes the whole decision problem as an ILP. The solver thus both constructs the solution (avoiding the exponential-size ILP problem) and ensures its optimality.

All the approaches above focus on TSO and its siblings PSO and RMO, whereas we also handle the significantly weaker Power, including quite subtle barriers (e.g. lwsync) compared to the simpler mfence of x86.

Axiomatic models. Krishnamurthy et al. [17] apply Shasha and Snir's method to *single program multiple data* systems. Their abstraction is similar to ours, except that they do not handle pointers.

Lee and Padua [22] propose an algorithm based on Shasha and Snir's work. They use dominators in graphs to determine which fences are redundant. This approach was later implemented by Fang et al. [15] in pensieve, a compiler for Java. Sura et al. later implemented a more precise approach in pensieve [32] (see (P) in Sec. 2). They pair the cycle detection with an analysis to detect synchronisation that could prevent cycles.

Alglave and Maranget [6] revisit Shasha and Snir for contemporary memory models and insert fences following a refinement of [22]. Their offence tool handles snippets of assembly code only, where the memory locations need to be explicitly given.

Others. We cite the work of Vafeiadis and Zappa Nardelli [35], who present an optimisation of the certified CompCert-TSO compiler to remove redundant fences on TSO. Marino et al. [25] experiment with an SC-preserving compiler, showing overheads of no more than 34 %. Nevertheless, they emphasise that *"the overheads, however small, might be unacceptable for certain applications"*.

4   Axiomatic Memory Model

Weak memory can occur as follows: a thread sends a write to a store buffer, then a cache, and finally to memory. While the write transits through buffers and caches, a read can occur before the value is available to all threads in memory.

mp	
T_0	T_1
$(a)\, \mathrm{x} \leftarrow 1$	$(c)\, \mathrm{r1} \leftarrow \mathrm{y}$
$(b)\, \mathrm{y} \leftarrow 1$	$(d)\, \mathrm{r2} \leftarrow \mathrm{x}$
Final state? r1=1 $\wedge$ r2=0	

To describe such situations, we use the framework of [6], embracing in particular SC, Sun TSO (i.e. the x86 model [28]), and a fragment of Power. The core of this framework consists of *relations* over *memory events*.

We illustrate this framework using a *litmus test* (Fig. 3). The top shows a multi-threaded program.

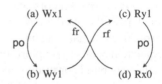

Fig. 3. Message Passing (**mp**)

The shared variables x and y are assumed to be initialised to zero. A store instruction (e.g. $\mathrm{x} \leftarrow 1$ on T_0) gives rise to a write event $((a)\mathrm{Wx1})$, and a load instruction (e.g. $\mathrm{r1} \leftarrow \mathrm{y}$ on T_1) to a read event $((c)\mathrm{Ry1})$. The bottom of Fig. 3 shows one particular execution of the program (also called *event graph*), corresponding to the final state r1=1 and r2=0.

In the framework of [6], an execution that is not possible on SC has a cyclic event graph (as the one shown in Fig. 3). A weaker architecture may *relax* some of the relations contributing to a cycle. If the removal of the relaxed edges from the event graph makes it acyclic, the architecture allows the execution. For example, Power relaxes the program order po (amongst other things), thereby making the graph in Fig. 3 acyclic. Hence, the given execution is allowed on Power.

Formalisation. An *event* is a memory read or a write to memory, composed of a unique identifier, a direction (R for read or W for write), a memory address, and a value. We represent each instruction by the events it issues. In Fig. 3, we associate the store instruction $x \leftarrow 1$ in thread T_0 with the event $(a)\mathrm{W}x1$.

A set of events $\mathbb{E}$ and their program order po form an *event structure* $E \triangleq (\mathbb{E}, \text{po})$. The program order po is a per-thread total order over $\mathbb{E}$. We write dp (with dp $\subseteq$ po) for the relation that models *dependencies* between instructions. For instance, there is a *data dependency* between a load and a store when the value written by the store was computed from the value obtained by the load.

We represent the *communication* between threads via an *execution witness* $X \triangleq$ (co, rf), which consists of two relations over the events. First, the *coherence* co is a per-address total order on write events which models the *memory coherence* widely assumed by modern architectures. It links a write w to any write w' to the same address that hits the memory after w. Second, the *read-from* relation rf links a write w to a read r such that r reads the value written by w. Finally, we derive the *from-read* relation fr from co and rf. A read r is in fr with a write w if the write w' from which r reads hits the memory before w. Formally, we have: $(r, w) \in \text{fr} \triangleq \exists w'.(w', r) \in \text{rf} \land (w', w) \in \text{co}$.

In Fig. 3, the specified outcome corresponds to the execution below if each location initially holds 0. If r1=1 in the end, the read (c) on T_1 took its value from the write (b) on T_0, hence $(b, c) \in \text{rf}$. If r2=0 in the end, the read (d) took its value from the initial state, thus before the write (a) on T_0, hence $(d, a) \in \text{fr}$. In the following, we write rfe (resp. coe, fre) for the *external read-from* (resp. coherence, from-read), i.e. when the source and target belong to different threads.

	SC	x86	Power
poWR	yes	mfence	sync
poWW	yes	yes	sync, lwsync
poRW	yes	yes	sync, lwsync, dp
poRR	yes	yes	sync, lwsync, dp, branch;isync

Fig. 4. ppo and fences per architecture

Relaxed or safe. When a thread can read from its own store buffer [4] (the typical TSO/x86 scenario), we relax the internal read-from, that is, rf where source and target belong to the same thread. When two threads T_0 and T_1 can communicate privately via a cache (a case of *write atomicity* relaxation [4]), we relax the external read-from rfe, and call the corresponding write *non-atomic*. This is the main particularity of Power and ARM, and cannot happen on TSO/x86. Some program-order pairs may be relaxed (e.g. write-read pairs on x86, and all but dp ones on Power), i.e. only a subset of po is guaranteed to occur in order. This subset constitutes the *preserved program order*, ppo. When a relation must not be relaxed on a given architecture, we call it *safe*.

Fig. 4 summarises ppo per architecture. The columns are architectures, e.g. x86, and the lines are relations, e.g. poWR. We write e.g. poWR for the program order between a write and a read. We write "yes" when the relation is in the ppo of the architecture: e.g. poWR is in the ppo of SC. When we write something else, typically the name of a fence, e.g. mfence, the relation is not in the ppo of the architecture (e.g. poWR is not in the ppo of x86), and the fence can restore the ordering: e.g. mfence maintains write-read pairs in program order.

Following [6], the relation fence (with fence $\subseteq$ po) induced by a fence is *non-cumulative* when it only orders certain pairs of events surrounding the fence. The relation fence is *cumulative* when it additionally makes writes atomic, e.g. by flushing caches. In our model, this amounts to making sequences of external read-from and fences (rfe; fence or fence; rfe) safe, even though rfe alone would not be safe. In Fig. 3, placing a cumulative fence between the two writes on T_0 will not only prevent their reordering, but also enforce an ordering between the write (a) on T_0 and the read (c) on T_1, which reads from T_0.

Architectures. An *architecture* A determines the set safe$_A$ of relations safe on A. Following [6], we always consider the coherence co, the from-read relation fr and the fences to be safe. SC relaxes nothing, i.e. rf and po are safe. TSO authorises the reordering of write-read pairs and store buffering but nothing else.

Critical cycles. Following [30,5], for an architecture A, a *delay* is a po or rf edge that is not safe (i.e. is relaxed) on A. An execution (E, X) is valid on A yet not on SC iff it contains critical cycles [5]. Formally, a *critical cycle* w.r.t. A is a cycle in po $\cup$ com, where com $\triangleq$ co $\cup$ rf $\cup$ fr is the *communication relation*, which has the following characteristics (the last two ensure the minimality of the critical cycles): (1) the cycle contains at least one delay for A; (2) per thread, (i) there are at most two accesses a and b, and (ii) they access distinct memory locations; and (3) for a memory location ℓ, there are at most three accesses to ℓ along the cycle, which belong to distinct threads.

Fig. 3 shows a critical cycle w.r.t. Power. The po edge on T_0, the po edge on T_1, and the rf edge between T_0 and T_1, are all unsafe on Power. On the other hand, the cycle in Fig. 3 does not contain a delay w.r.t. TSO, and is thus not a critical cycle on TSO.

To forbid executions containing critical cycles, one can insert fences into the program to prevent delays. To prevent a po delay, a fence can be inserted between the two accesses forming the delay, following Fig. 4. To prevent an rf delay, a cumulative fence must be used (see Sec. 6 for details). For the example in Fig. 3, for Power, we need to place a cumulative fence between the two writes on T_0, preventing both the po and the adjacent rf edge from being relaxed, and use a dependency or fence to prevent the po edge on T_1 from being relaxed.

5 Static Detection of Critical Cycles

We want to synthesise fences to prevent weak behaviours and thus restore SC. We explained in Sec. 4 that we should place fences along the critical cycles of the program executions. To find the critical cycles, we look for cycles in an over-approximation of all the executions of the program. We hence avoid enumeration of all traces, which would hinder scalability, and get all the critical cycles of all program executions at once. Thus we can find all fences preventing the critical cycles corresponding to two executions in one step, instead of examining the two executions separately.

To analyse a C program, e.g. on the left-hand side of Fig. 5, we convert it to a *goto-program* (right-hand side of Fig. 5), the internal representation of the CProver framework; we refer to http://www.cprover.org/goto-cc for details. The pointer analysis we use is a standard concurrent points-to analysis that we have shown to be sound for our weak memory models in earlier work [7]. A full explanation of how we handle pointers is available in [8]. The C program in Fig. 5 features two threads which can interfere. The first thread writes the argument "input" to x, then randomly writes 1 to y or reads z, and then writes 1 to x. The second thread successively reads y, z and x. In the corresponding goto-program, the **if-else** structure has been transformed into a guard with

```
void thread_1(int input)       void thread_2()
{                              {
    int r1;                        int r2, r3, r4;
    x = input;                     r2 = y;
    if (rand()%                    r3 = z;
        y = 1;                     r4 = x;
    else                       }
        r1 = z;
    x = 1;
}
```

```
thread_1                   thread_2
    int r1;                    int r2, r3, r4;
    x = input;                 r2 = y;
    _Bool tmp;                 r3 = z;
    tmp = rand();              r4 = x;
    [! tmp%                end_function
    y = 1;
    goto 2;
1:  r1 = z;
2:  x = 1;
end_function
```

Fig. 5. A C program (left) and its goto-program (right)

the condition of the **if** followed by a goto construct. From the goto-program, we then compute an *abstract event graph* (**aeg**), shown in Fig. 6(a). The events a, b_1, b_2 and c (resp. d, e and f) correspond to thread$_1$ (resp. thread$_2$) in Fig. 5. We only consider accesses to shared variables, and ignore the local variables. We finally explore the **aeg** to find the potential critical cycles.

An **aeg** represents all the executions of a program (in the sense of Sec. 4). Fig. 6(b) and (c) give two executions associated with the **aeg** shown in Fig. 6(a). For readability, the transitive **po** edges have been omitted (e.g. between the two events d' and f'). The concrete events that occur in an execution are shown in bold. In an **aeg**, the events do not have concrete values, whereas in an execution they do. Also, an **aeg** merely indicates that two accesses to the same variable could form a data race (see the competing pairs (**cmp**) relation in Fig. 6(a), which is a symmetric relation), whereas an execution has oriented relations (e.g. indicating the write that a read takes its value from, see e.g. the **rf** arrow in Fig. 6(b) and (c)). The execution in Fig. 6(b) has a critical cycle (with respect to e.g. Power) between the events a', b'_2, d', and f'. The execution in Fig. 6(c) does not have a critical cycle.

Full details of the construction of the **aeg**s from goto-programs, including a semantics of goto-programs in terms of abstract events, are available in the full version of this paper [8]. Function calls are inlined for better precision. Currently, the implementation does not handle recursion.

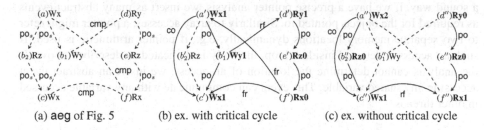

(a) **aeg** of Fig. 5   (b) ex. with critical cycle   (c) ex. without critical cycle

Fig. 6. The **aeg** of Fig. 5 and two executions corresponding to it

Loops and arrays. We explain how to deal with loops statically. If we build our **aeg** directly following the **cfg**, with a **po**$_s$ back-edge connecting the end of the body to its entry, we already handle most of the cases. Recall from Sec. 4 that in a critical cycle

(2.i) there are two events per thread, and (2.ii) two events on the same thread target two different locations. Let us analyse the cases.

The first case is an iteration i of this loop on which a critical cycle connects two events (a_i) and (b_i). The critical cycle will be trivially captured by its static counterpart that abstracts in particular these events with abstract events (a) and (b).

Now, for a given execution, if a critical cycle connects the event (a_i) of an iteration i to the event (b_j) of a later iteration j (i.e., $i \leq j$), then these events are abstracted respectively by (a) and (b) in the aeg. As we do not evaluate the expressions, we abstracted the loop guard and any local variable that would vary across the iterations. Thus, all the iterations can be statically captured by one abstract representation of the body of the loop. Then, thanks to the po_s back-edge and the transitivity of our cycle search, any critical cycle involving (a_i) and (b_j) is abstracted by a static critical cycle relating (a) and (b), even though (b) might be before (a) in the body of the loop.

The only case that is not handled by this approach is when (a_i) and (b_j) are abstracted by the same abstract event, say (c). As the variables addressed by the events on the same thread of a cycle need to be different, this case can only occur when (a_i) and (b_j) are accessing an array or a pointer whose index or offset depends on the iteration. We do not evaluate these offsets or indices, which implies that two accesses to two distinct array positions might be abstracted by the same abstract event (c).

In order to detect such critical cycles, we copy the body of the loop and do not add a po_s back-edge. Hence, a static critical cycle will connect (c) in the first instance of the body and (c) in the second instance of the body to abstract the critical cycle involving (a_i) and (b_j). The back-edge is no longer necessary, as the abstract events reachable through this back-edge are replicated in the second body. Thus, all the previous cases are also covered.

We have implemented the duplication of the loop bodies only for loops that contain accesses to arrays. In case of nested loops, we ensure that we duplicate each of the sub-bodies only once in order to avoid an exponential explosion. This approach is again sufficient owing to the maximum of two events per thread in a critical cycle and the transitivity of po.

Pointers. We explain how to deal with the varying imprecision of pointer analyses in a sound way. If we have a precise pointer analysis, we insert as many abstract events as required for the objects pointed to. Similarly to array accesses, a pointer might refer to two separate memory locations dynamically, e.g., if pointer arithmetic is used. If such an access is detected inside a loop, the body is replicated as described above. If the analysis cannot determine the location of an access, we insert an abstract event accessing any shared variable. This event can communicate with any variable accessed in other threads.

Cycle detection. Once we have the aeg, we enumerate (using Tarjan's algorithm [34]) its potential critical cycles by searching for cycles that contain at least one edge that is a delay, as defined in Sec. 4.

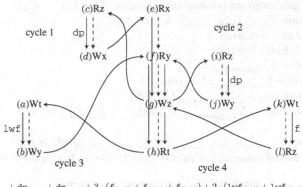

$$\mathbf{min}\quad \mathrm{dp}_{(e,g)} + \mathrm{dp}_{(f,h)} + \mathrm{dp}_{(f,g)} + 3 \cdot (\mathrm{f}_{(e,f)} + \mathrm{f}_{(f,g)} + \mathrm{f}_{(g,h)}) + 2 \cdot (\mathrm{lwf}_{(e,f)} + \mathrm{lwf}_{(f,g)} + \mathrm{lwf}_{(g,h)})$$

$\mathbf{s.t.}$ cycle 1, delay (e,g): $\mathrm{dp}_{(e,g)} + \mathrm{f}_{(e,f)} + \mathrm{f}_{(f,g)} + \mathrm{lwf}_{(e,f)} + \mathrm{lwf}_{(f,g)} \geq 1$

cycle 2, delay (f,g): $\mathrm{dp}_{(f,g)} + \mathrm{f}_{(f,g)} + \mathrm{lwf}_{(f,g)} \geq 1$

cycle 3, delay (f,h): $\mathrm{dp}_{(f,h)} + \mathrm{f}_{(f,g)} + \mathrm{f}_{(g,h)} + \mathrm{lwf}_{(f,g)} + \mathrm{lwf}_{(g,h)} \geq 1$

cycle 4, delay (g,h): $\mathrm{f}_{(g,h)} \geq 1$

Fig. 7. Example of resolution with **between**

6   Synthesis

In Fig. 7, we have an **aeg** with five threads: $\{a, b\}$, $\{c, d\}$, $\{e, f, g, h\}$, $\{i, j\}$ and $\{k, l\}$. Each node is an abstract event computed as in the previous section. The dashed edges represent the po_s between abstract events in the same thread. The full lines represent the edges involved in a cycle. Thus the **aeg** of Fig. 7 has four potential critical cycles. We derive the set of constraints in a process we define later in this section. We now have a set of cycles to forbid by placing fences. Moreover, we want to optimise the placement of the fences.

Challenges. If there is only one type of fence (as in TSO, which only features **mfence**), optimising only consists of placing a minimal amount of fences to forbid as many cycles as possible. For example, placing a full fence **sync** between f and g in Fig. 7 might forbid cycles 1, 2 and 3 under Power, whereas placing it somewhere else might forbid at best two amongst them.

Since we handle several types of fences for a given architecture (e.g. dependencies, **lwsync** and **sync** on Power), we can also assign some cost to each of them. For example, following the folklore, a dependency is less costly than an **lwsync**, which is itself less costly than a **sync**. Given these costs, one might want to minimise their sum along different executions: to forbid cycles 1, 2 and 3 in Fig. 7, a single **lwsync** between f and g can be cheaper at runtime than three dependencies respectively between e and g, f and g, and f and h. However, if we had only cycles 1 and 2, the dependencies would be cheaper. We see that we have to optimise both the placement and the type of fences at the same time.

We model our problem as an *integer linear program* (**ILP**) (see Fig. 8), which we explain in this section. Solving our **ILP** gives us a set of fences to insert to forbid the cycles. This set of fences is optimal in that it minimises the cost function. More

Input: aeg ($\mathbb{E}_s$,po$_s$,cmp) and potential critical cycles $C = \{C_1, ..., C_n\}$
Problem: minimise $\sum_{(l,t)\in\text{potential-places}(C)} t_l \times \text{cost(t)}$
Constraints: for all $d \in \text{delays}(C)$
(* for TSO, PSO, RMO, Power *)
  if $d \in$ poWR then $\sum_{e\in\text{between}(d)} f_e \geq 1$
  if $d \in$ poWW then $\sum_{e\in\text{between}(d)} f_e + \text{lwf}_e \geq 1$
  if $d \in$ poRW then $\text{dp}_d + \sum_{e\in\text{between}(d)} f_e + \text{lwf}_e \geq 1$
  if $d \in$ poRR then $\text{dp}_d + \sum_{e\in\text{between}(d)} f_e + \text{lwf}_e + \sum_{e\in\text{ctrl}(d)} \text{cf}_e \geq 1$
(* for Power *)
  if $d \in$ cmp then $\sum_{e\in\text{cumul}(d)} f_e + \sum_{e\in\text{cumul}(d)\cap\neg\text{poWR}\cap\neg\text{poRW}} \text{lwf}_e \geq 1$
Output: the set actual-places(C) of pairs (l, t) s.t. t_l is set to 1 in the ILP solution

Fig. 8. ILP for inferring fence placements

precisely, the constraints are the cycles to forbid, each variable represents a fence to insert, and the cost function sums the cost of all fences.

6.1 Cost Function of the ILP

We handle several types of fences: full (f), lightweight (lwf), control fences (cf), and dependencies (dp). On Power, the full fence is sync, the lightweight one lwsync. We write $\mathbb{T}$ for the set $\{\text{dp}, \text{f}, \text{cf}, \text{lwf}\}$. We assume that each type of fence has an *a priori* cost (e.g. a dependency is cheaper than a full fence), regardless of its location in the code. We write cost(t) for t $\in \mathbb{T}$ for this cost.

We take as input the aeg of our program and the potential critical cycles to fence. We define two sets of pairs (l, t) where l is a po$_s$ edge of the aeg and t a type of fence. We introduce an ILP variable t_l (in $\{0, 1\}$) for each pair (l, t).

The set potential-places is the set of such pairs that can be inserted into the program to forbid the cycles. The set actual-places is the set of such pairs that have been set to 1 by our ILP. We output this set, as it represents the locations in the code in need of a fence and the type of fence to insert for each of them. We also output the total cost of all these insertions, i.e. $\sum_{(l,t)\in\text{potential-places}(C)} t_l \times \text{cost(t)}$. The solver should minimise this sum whilst satisfying the constraints.

6.2 Constraints in the ILP

We want to forbid all the cycles in the set that we are given after filtering, as explained in the preamble of this section. This requires placing an appropriate fence on each delay for each cycle in this set. Different delay pairs might need different fences, depending e.g. on the directions (write or read) of their extremities. Essentially, we follow the table in Fig. 4. For example, a write-read pair needs a full fence (e.g. mfence on x86, or sync on Power). A read-read pair can use anything amongst dependencies and fences. Our constraints ensure that we use the right type of fence for each delay pair.

Inequalities as constraints. We first assume that all the program order delays are in po$_s$ and we ignore Power and ARM special features (dependencies, control fences and communication delays). This case deals with relatively strong models, ranging from TSO to RMO. We relax these assumptions below.

In this setting, potential-places(C) is the set of all the po_s delays of the cycles in C. We ensure that every delay pair for every execution is fenced, by placing a fence on the static po_s edge for this pair, and this for each cycle given as input. Thus, we need at least one constraint per static delay pair d in each cycle.

If d is of the form poWR, as (g, h) in Fig. 7 (cycle 4), only a full fence can fix it (cf. Fig. 4), thus we impose $\mathsf{f}_d \geq 1$. If d is of the form poRR, as (f, h) in Fig. 7 (cycle 3), we can choose any type of fence, i.e. $\mathsf{dp}_d + \mathsf{cf}_d + \mathsf{lwf}_d + \mathsf{f}_d \geq 1$.

Our constraints cannot be equalities because it is not certain that the resulting system would be satisfiable. To see this, suppose our constraints were equalities, and consider Fig. 7 limited to cycles 2, 3 and 4. Using only full fences, lightweight fences, and dependencies (i.e. ignoring control fences for now), we would generate the constraints **(i)** $\mathsf{lwf}_{(f,g)} + \mathsf{f}_{(f,g)} = 1$ for the delay (f, g) in cycle 2, **(ii)** $\mathsf{dp}_{(f,h)} + \mathsf{lwf}_{(f,h)} + \mathsf{f}_{(f,h)} + \mathsf{lwf}_{(g,h)} + \mathsf{f}_{(g,h)} = 1$ for the delay (f, h) in cycle 3, and **(iii)** $\mathsf{f}_{(g,h)} = 1$ for the delay (g, h) in cycle 4.

Preventing the delay (g, h) in cycle 4 requires a full fence, thus $\mathsf{f}_{(g,h)} = 1$. By the constraint **(ii)**, and since $\mathsf{f}_{(g,h)} = 1$, we derive $\mathsf{f}_{(f,g)} = 0$ and $\mathsf{lwf}_{(f,g)} = 0$. But these two equalities are not possible given the constraint **(i)**. By using inequalities, we allow several fences to live on the same edge. In fact, the constraints only ensure the soundness; the optimality is fully determined by the cost function to minimise.

Delays. are in fact in po_s^+, not always in po_s: in Fig. 7, the delay (e, g) in cycle 1 does not belong to po_s but to po_s^+. Thus given a po_s^+ delay (x, y), we consider all the po_s pairs which appear between x and y, i.e.: between$(x, y) \triangleq \{(e_1, e_2) \in \mathsf{po}_s \mid (x, e_1) \in \mathsf{po}_s^* \wedge (e_2, y) \in \mathsf{po}_s^*\}$. For example in Fig. 7, we have between$(e, g) = \{(e, f), (f, g)\}$. Thus, ignoring the use of dependencies and control fences for now, for the delay (e, g) in Fig. 7, we will not impose $\mathsf{f}_{(e,g)} + \mathsf{lwf}_{(e,g)} \geq 1$ but rather $\mathsf{f}_{(e,f)} + \mathsf{lwf}_{(e,f)} + \mathsf{f}_{(f,g)} + \mathsf{lwf}_{(f,g)} \geq 1$. Indeed, a full fence or a lightweight fence in (e, f) or (f, g) will prevent the delay in (e, g).

Dependencies. need more care, as they cannot necessarily be placed anywhere between e and g (in the formal sense of between(e, g)): $\mathsf{dp}_{(e,f)}$ or $\mathsf{dp}_{(f,g)}$ would not fix the delay (e, g), but simply maintain the pairs (e, f) or (f, g), leaving the pair (e, g) free to be reordered. Thus if we choose to synchronise (e, g) using dependencies, we actually need a dependency from e to g: $\mathsf{dp}_{(e,g)}$. Dependencies only apply to pairs that start with a read; thus for each such pair (see the poRW and poRR cases in Fig. 8), we add a variable for the dependency: (e, g) will be fixed with the constraint $\mathsf{dp}_{(e,g)} + \mathsf{f}_{(e,f)} + \mathsf{lwf}_{(e,f)} + \mathsf{f}_{(f,g)} + \mathsf{lwf}_{(f,g)} \geq 1$.

Control fences. placed after a conditional branch (e.g. bne on Power) prevent speculative reads after this branch (see Fig. 4). Thus, when building the aeg, we built a set poC for each branch, which gathers all the pairs of abstract events such that the first one is the last event before a branch, and the second is the first event after that branch. We can place a control fence before the second component of each such pair, if the second component is a read. Thus, we add cf_e as a possible variable to the constraint for read-read pairs (see poRR case in Fig. 8, where $ctrl(d) = between(d) \cap poC$).

Cumulativity. For architectures like Power, where stores are non-atomic, we need to look for program order pairs that are connected to an external read-from (e.g. (c, d) in Fig. 3 has an rf connected to it via event c). In such cases, we need to use a *cumulative fence*, e.g. lwsync or sync, and not, for example, a dependency.

The locations to consider in such cases are: before (in po_s) the write w of the rfe, or after (in po_s) the read r of the rfe, i.e. $cumul(w, r) = \{(e_1, e_2) \mid (e_1, e_2) \in po_s \land ((e_2, w) \in po_s^* \lor (r, e_1) \in po_s^*)\}$. In Fig. 7 (cycle 2), (g, i) over-approximates an rfe edge, and the edges where we can insert fences are in $cumul(g, i) = \{(f, g), (i, j)\}$.

We need a cumulative fence as soon as there is a potential rfe, even if the adjacent po_s pairs do not form a delay. For example in Fig. 3, suppose there is a dependency between the reads on T_1, and a fence maintaining write-write pairs on T_0. In that case we need to place a cumulative fence to fix the rfe, even if the two po_s pairs are themselves fixed. Thus, we quantify over all po_s pairs when we need to place cumulative fences. As only f and lwf are cumulative, we have $\text{potential-places}(C) \triangleq \{(l, t) \mid (t \in \{dp\} \land l \in delays(C)) \lor (t \in \mathbb{T} \setminus \{dp\} \land l \in \bigcup_{d \in delays(C)} between(d)) \lor (t \in \{f, lwf\} \land l \in po_s(C))\}$.

Comparison with trencher. We illustrate the difference between trencher [10] and our approach using Fig. 9. There are three cycles that share the edge (a, b). They differ in the path taken between nodes c and g. Suppose that the user has inserted a full fence between a and b. To forbid the three cycles, we need to fence the thread on the right.

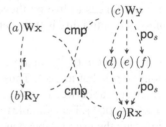

Fig. 9. Cycles sharing the edge (a, b)

The trencher algorithm first calculates which pairs can be reordered: in our example, these are (c, g) via d, (c, g) via e and (c, g) via f. It then determines at which locations a fence could be placed. In our example, there are 6 options: (c, d), (d, g), (c, e), (e, g), (c, f), and (f, g). The encoding thus uses 6 variables for the fence locations. The algorithm then gathers all the *irreducible* sets of locations to be fenced to forbid the delay between c and g, where "irreducible" means that removing any of the fences would prevent this set from fully fixing the delay. As all the paths that connect c and g have to be covered, trencher needs to collect all the combinations of one fence per path. There are 2 locations per path, leading to 2^3 sets. Consequently, as stated in [10], trencher needs to construct an exponential number of sets.

Each set is encoded in the ILP with one variable. For this example, trencher thus uses $6 + 8$ variables. It also generates one constraint per delay (here, 1) to force the solver to pick a set, and 8 constraints to enforce that all the location variables are set to 1 if the set containing these locations is picked.

By contrast, musketeer only needs 6 variables: the possible locations for fences. We detect three cycles, and generate only three constraints to fix the delay. Thus, on a parametric version of the example, trencher's ILP grows exponentially whereas musketeer's is linear-sized.

	CLASSIC					FAST					
	Dek	Pet	Lam	Szy	Par	Cil	CL	Fif	Lif	Anc	Har
LoC	50	37	72	54	96	97	111	150	152	188	179
dfence	–	–	–	–	–	7.8 3	6.2 3	~ 0	~ 0	~ 0	~ 0
memorax	0.4 2	1.4 2	79.1 4	–	–	–	–	–	–	–	–
musketeer	**0.0 5**	**0.0 3**	**0.0 8**	**0.0 8**	**0.0 3**	**0.0 3**	**0.0 1**	**0.1 1**	**0.0 1**	**0.1 1**	**0.6 4**
offence	0.0 2	0.0 2	0.0 8	0.0 8	–	–	–	–	–	–	–
pensieve	0.0 16	0.0 6	0.0 24	0.0 22	0.0 7	0.0 14	0.0 8	0.1 33	0.0 29	0.0 44	0.1 72
remmex	0.5 2	0.5 2	2.0 4	1.8 5	–	–	–	–	–	–	–
trencher	1.6 2	1.3 2	1.7 4	–	0.5 1	8.6 3	–	–	–	–	–

Fig. 10. All tools on the CLASSIC and FAST series for TSO

7   Implementation and Experiments

We implemented our new method, in addition to all the methods described in Sec. 2, in our tool musketeer, using glpk (http://www.gnu.org/software/glpk) as the ILP solver. We compare these methods to the existing tools listed in Sec. 3.

Our tool analyses C programs. dfence also handles C code, but requires some high-level specification for each program, which was not available to us. memorax works on a process-based language that is specific to the tool. offence works on a subset of assembler for x86, ARM and Power. pensieve originally handled Java, but we did not have access to it and have therefore re-implemented the method. remmex handles Promela-like programs. trencher analyses transition systems. Most of the tools come with some of the benchmarks in their own languages; not all benchmarks were however available for each tool. We have re-implemented some of the benchmarks for offence.

We now detail our experiments. CLASSIC and FAST gather examples from the literature and related work. The DEBIAN benchmarks are packages of Debian Linux 7.1. CLASSIC and FAST were run on a x86-64 Intel Core2 Quad Q9550 machine with 4 cores (2.83 GHz) and 4 GB of RAM. DEBIAN was run on a x86-64 Intel Core i5-3570 machine with 4 cores (3.40 GHz) and 4 GB of RAM.

CLASSIC consists of Dekker's mutex (Dek) [14]; Peterson's mutex (Pet) [29]; Lamport's fast mutex (Lam) [21]; Szymanski's mutex (Szy) [33]; and Parker's bug (Par) [13]. We ran all tools in this series for TSO (the model common to all). For each example, Fig. 10 gives the number of fences inserted, and the time (in sec) needed. When an example is not available in the input language of a tool, we write "–". The first four tools place fences to enforce stability/robustness [5,9]; the last three to satisfy a given safety property. We used memorax with the option -o1, to compute one *maximal permissive* set and not all. For remmex on Szymanski, we give the number of fences found by default (which may be non-optimal). Its "maximal permissive" option lowers the number to 2, at the cost of a slow enumeration. As expected, musketeer is less precise than most tools, but outperforms all of them.

FAST gathers Cil, Cilk 5 Work Stealing Queue (WSQ) [16]; CL, Chase-Lev WSQ [11]; Fif, Michael et al.'s FIFO WSQ [26]; Lif, Michael et al.'s LIFO WSQ [26]; Anc, Michael et al.'s Anchor WSQ [26]; Har, Harris' set [12]. For each example and tool, Fig. 10

	LoC	nodes	TSO		Power	
			fences	time	fences	time
memcached	9944	694	3	13.9s	70	89.9s
lingot	2894	183	0	5.3s	5	5.3s
weborf	2097	73	0	0.7s	0	0.7s
timemachine	1336	129	2	0.8s	16	0.8s
see	2626	171	0	1.4s	0	1.5s
blktrace	1567	615	0	6.5s	–	timeout
ptunnel	1249	1867	2	95.0s	–	timeout
proxsmtpd	2024	10	0	0.1s	0	0.1s
ghostess	2684	1106	0	25.9s	0	25.9s
dnshistory	1516	1466	1	29.4s	9	64.9s

Fig. 11. musketeer on selected benchmarks in DEBIAN series for TSO and Power

gives the number of fences inserted (under TSO) and the time needed to do so. For dfence, we used the setting of [24]: the tool has up to 20 attempts to find fences. We were unable to apply dfence on some of the FAST examples: we thus reproduce the number of fences given in [24], and write $\sim$ for the time. We applied musketeer to this series, for all architectures. The fencing times for TSO and Power are almost identical, except for the largest example, namely Har ($0.1\,s$ vs $0.6\,s$).

DEBIAN gathers 374 executables. These are a subset of the goto-programs that have been built from packages of Debian Linux 7.1 by Michael Tautschnig. A small excerpt of our results is given in Fig. 11. The full data set, including a comparison with the methods from Sec. 2, is provided at http://www.cprover.org/wmm/musketeer. For each program, we give the lines of code and number of nodes in the aeg. We used musketeer on these programs to demonstrate its scalability and its ability to handle deployed code. Most programs already contain fences or operations that imply them, such as compare-and-swaps or locks. Our tool musketeer takes these fences into account and infers a set of additional fences sufficient to guarantee SC. The largest program we handle is memcached ($\sim$ 10000 LoC). Our tool needs $13.9\,s$ to place fences for TSO, and $89.9\,s$ for Power. A more meaningful measure for the hardness of an instance is the number of nodes in the aeg. For example, ptunnel has 1867 nodes and 1249 LoC. The fencing takes $95.0\,s$ for TSO, but times out for Power due to the number of cycles.

8   Conclusion

We introduced a novel method for deriving a set of fences, which we implemented in a new tool called musketeer. We compared it to existing tools and observed that it outperforms them. We demonstrated on our DEBIAN series that musketeer can handle deployed code, with a large potential for scalability.

Acknowledgements. We thank Michael Tautschnig for the Debian binaries, Mohamed Faouzi Atig, Egor Derevenetc, Carsten Fuhs, Alexander Linden, Roland Meyer, Tyler Sorensen, Martin Vechev, Eran Yahav and our reviewers for their feedback. We thank Alexander Linden and Martin Vechev again for giving us access to their tools.

References

1. Power ISA Version 2.06 (2009)
2. Information technology – Programming languages – C. In: BS ISO/IEC 9899:2011 (2011)
3. Abdulla, P.A., Atig, M.F., Chen, Y.-F., Leonardsson, C., Rezine, A.: MEMORAX, a precise and sound tool for automatic fence insertion under TSO. In: Piterman, N., Smolka, S.A. (eds.) TACAS 2013 (ETAPS 2013). LNCS, vol. 7795, pp. 530–536. Springer, Heidelberg (2013)
4. Adve, S.V., Gharachorloo, K.: Shared memory consistency models: A tutorial. IEEE Computer 29(12), 66–76 (1995)
5. Alglave, J., Maranget, L.: Stability in weak memory models. In: Gopalakrishnan, G., Qadeer, S. (eds.) CAV 2011. LNCS, vol. 6806, pp. 50–66. Springer, Heidelberg (2011)
6. Alglave, J., Maranget, L., Sarkar, S., Sewell, P.: Fences in weak memory models. In: Touili, T., Cook, B., Jackson, P. (eds.) CAV 2010. LNCS, vol. 6174, pp. 258–272. Springer, Heidelberg (2010)
7. Alglave, J., Kroening, D., Lugton, J., Nimal, V., Tautschnig, M.: Soundness of data flow analyses for weak memory models. In: Yang, H. (ed.) APLAS 2011. LNCS, vol. 7078, pp. 272–288. Springer, Heidelberg (2011)
8. Alglave, J., Kroening, D., Nimal, V., Poetzl, D.: Don't sit on the fence: A static analysis approach to automatic fence insertion. CoRR abs/1312.1411 (2013)
9. Bouajjani, A., Meyer, R., Möhlmann, E.: Deciding robustness against total store ordering. In: Aceto, L., Henzinger, M., Sgall, J. (eds.) ICALP 2011, Part II. LNCS, vol. 6756, pp. 428–440. Springer, Heidelberg (2011)
10. Bouajjani, A., Derevenetc, E., Meyer, R.: Checking and enforcing robustness against TSO. In: Felleisen, M., Gardner, P. (eds.) ESOP 2013. LNCS, vol. 7792, pp. 533–553. Springer, Heidelberg (2013)
11. Chase, D., Lev, Y.: Dynamic circular work-stealing deque. In: SPAA, pp. 21–28. ACM (2005)
12. Detlefs, D.L., Flood, C.H., Garthwaite, A.T., Martin, P.A., Shavit, N.N., Steele Jr., G.L.: Even better DCAS-based concurrent deques. In: Herlihy, M.P. (ed.) DISC 2000. LNCS, vol. 1914, pp. 59–73. Springer, Heidelberg (2000)
13. Dice, D.: (November 2009), https://blogs.oracle.com/dave/entry/a_race_in_locksupport_park
14. Dijkstra, E.W.: Solution of a problem in concurrent programming control. Commun. ACM 8(9), 569 (1965)
15. Fang, X., Lee, J., Midkiff, S.P.: Automatic fence insertion for shared memory multiprocessing. In: International Conference on Supercomputing (ICS), pp. 285–294. ACM (2003)
16. Frigo, M., Leiserson, C.E., Randall, K.H.: The implementation of the Cilk-5 multithreaded language. In: PLDI, pp. 212–223. ACM (1998)
17. Krishnamurthy, A., Yelick, K.A.: Analyses and optimizations for shared address space programs. J. Par. Dist. Comp. 38(2) (1996)
18. Kuperstein, M., Vechev, M.T., Yahav, E.: Automatic inference of memory fences. In: Formal Methods in Computer-Aided Design (FMCAD), pp. 111–119. IEEE (2010)
19. Kuperstein, M., Vechev, M.T., Yahav, E.: Partial-coherence abstractions for relaxed memory models. In: PLDI, pp. 187–198 (2011)
20. Lamport, L.: How to Make a Correct Multiprocess Program Execute Correctly on a Multiprocessor. IEEE Trans. Comput. 46(7) (1979)
21. Lamport, L.: A fast mutual exclusion algorithm. ACM Trans. Comput. Syst. 5(1) (1987)
22. Lee, J., Padua, D.A.: Hiding relaxed memory consistency with a compiler. IEEE Transactions on Computers 50, 824–833 (2001)

23. Linden, A., Wolper, P.: A verification-based approach to memory fence insertion in PSO memory systems. In: Piterman, N., Smolka, S.A. (eds.) TACAS 2013 (ETAPS 2013). LNCS, vol. 7795, pp. 339–353. Springer, Heidelberg (2013)
24. Liu, F., Nedev, N., Prisadnikov, N., Vechev, M.T., Yahav, E.: Dynamic synthesis for relaxed memory models. In: PLDI, pp. 429–440. ACM (2012)
25. Marino, D., Singh, A., Millstein, T.D., Musuvathi, M., Narayanasamy, S.: A case for an SC-preserving compiler. In: PLDI, pp. 199–210. ACM (2011)
26. Michael, M.M., Vechev, M.T., Saraswat, V.A.: Idempotent work stealing. In: Principles and Practice of Parallel Programming (PPOPP), pp. 45–54. ACM (2009)
27. Norris, B., Demsky, B.: CDSchecker: checking concurrent data structures written with C/C++ atomics. In: Object Oriented Programming Systems Languages & Applications (OOPSLA), pp. 131–150 (2013)
28. Owens, S., Sarkar, S., Sewell, P.: A better x86 memory model: x86-TSO. In: Berghofer, S., Nipkow, T., Urban, C., Wenzel, M. (eds.) TPHOLs 2009. LNCS, vol. 5674, pp. 391–407. Springer, Heidelberg (2009)
29. Peterson, G.L.: Myths about the mutual exclusion problem. Inf. Process. Lett. 12(3), 115–116 (1981)
30. Shasha, D., Snir, M.: Efficient and correct execution of parallel programs that share memory. TOPLAS 10 (2), 282–312 (1988)
31. Sparc Architecture Manual Version 9 (1994)
32. Sura, Z., Fang, X., Wong, C.-L., Midkiff, S.P., Lee, J., Padua, D.A.: Compiler techniques for high performance sequentially consistent Java programs. In: PPOPP, pp. 2–13. ACM (2005)
33. Szymanski, B.K.: A simple solution to Lamport's concurrent programming problem with linear wait. In: ICS, pp. 621–626 (1988)
34. Tarjan, R.: Enumeration of the elementary circuits of a directed graph. SIAM J. Comput. 2(3), 211–216 (1973)
35. Vafeiadis, V., Zappa Nardelli, F.: Verifying fence elimination optimisations. In: Yahav, E. (ed.) Static Analysis. LNCS, vol. 6887, pp. 146–162. Springer, Heidelberg (2011)

MCMAS-SLK: A Model Checker for the Verification of Strategy Logic Specifications

Petr Čermák[1], Alessio Lomuscio[1], Fabio Mogavero[2], and Aniello Murano[2]

[1] Imperial College London, UK
[2] Università degli Studi di Napoli Federico II, Italy

1 Introduction

Model checking has come of age. A number of techniques are increasingly used in industrial setting to verify hardware and software systems, both against models and concrete implementations. While it is generally accepted that obstacles still remain, notably handling infinite state systems efficiently, much of current work involves refining and improving existing techniques such as predicate abstraction.

At scientific level a major avenue of work remains the development of verification techniques against rich and expressive specification languages. Over the years there has been a natural progression from checking reachability only to a large number of techniques (BDDs, BMC, abstraction, etc.) catering for LTL [28], CTL [10], and CTL* [12]. More recently, ATL and ATL* [3] were introduced to analyse systems in which some components, or *agents*, can enforce temporal properties on the system. The paths so identified correspond to infinite games between a coalition and its complement. ATL is well explored theoretically and at least two toolkits now support it [4,19,20].

It has however been observed that ATL* suffers from a number of limitations when one tries to apply it to multi-agent system reasoning and games [1,2,5,15, 17,21,31]. One of these is the lack of support for binding strategies explicitly to various agents or to the same agent in different contexts. To overcome this and other difficulties, *Strategy Logic* (SL) [27], as well as some useful variants of it [8,24–26], has been put forward. Key game-theoretic properties such as *Nash equilibria*, not expressible in ATL*, can be captured in SL.

In this paper we describe the model checker MCMAS-SLK. The tool supports the verification of systems against specifications expressed in a variant of SL that includes epistemic modalities. The synthesis of agents' strategies to satisfy a given parametric specification, as well as basic counterexample generation, are also supported. MCMAS-SLK, released as open-source, implements novel labelling algorithms for SL, encoded on BDDs, and reuses existing algorithms for the verification of epistemic specifications [29].

2 Epistemic Strategy Logic

Underlying Framework. Differently from other treatments of SL, originally defined on concurrent game structures, we here define the logic on *interpreted*

A. Biere and R. Bloem (Eds.): CAV 2014, LNCS 8559, pp. 525–532, 2014.

systems [14]. Doing so enables us to integrate the logic with epistemic concepts. Each agent is modelled in terms of its local states (given as a set of variables), a set of actions, a protocol specifying what actions may be performed at a given local state, and a local evolution function returning a target local state given a local state and a joint action for all the agents in the system. Interpreted systems are attractive for their modularity; they naturally express systems with incomplete information, and are amenable to verification [16, 19].

Syntax. SL has been introduced as a powerful formalism to reason about various equilibria concepts in non-zero sum games and sophisticated cooperation concepts in multi-agent systems [8, 27]. These are not expressible in previously explored logics including those in the ATL* hierarchy. We here put forward an epistemic extension of SL by adding a family of knowledge operators [14].

Formulas in epistemic strategy logic, or strategy logic with knowledge (SLK), are built by the following grammar over atomic propositions $p \in \text{AP}$, variables $x \in \text{Vr}$, and agents $a \in \text{Ag}$ ($A \subseteq \text{Ag}$ denotes a set of agents):

$$\varphi ::= p \mid \neg\varphi \mid \varphi \wedge \varphi \mid X\varphi \mid \varphi U\varphi \mid \langle\!\langle x \rangle\!\rangle \varphi \mid (a, x)\varphi \mid K_a\varphi \mid D_A\varphi \mid C_A\varphi.$$

SLK extends LTL [28] by means of an *existential strategy quantifier* $\langle\!\langle x \rangle\!\rangle$ and *agent binding* (a, x). It also includes the epistemic operators K_a, D_A, and C_A for individual, distributed, and common knowledge, respectively [14]. Intuitively, $\langle\!\langle x \rangle\!\rangle \varphi$ is read as *"there exists a strategy x such that φ holds"*, whereas $(a, x)\varphi$ stands for *"bind agent a to the strategy associated with the variable x in φ"*. The epistemic formula $K_a\varphi$ stands for *"agent a knows that φ"*; $D_A\varphi$ encodes *"the group A has distributed knowledge of φ"*; while $C_A\varphi$ represents *"the group A has common knowledge of φ"*. Similarly to first-order languages, we use free(φ) to represent the *free agents and variables* in a formula φ. Formally, free(φ) $\subseteq$ Ag $\cup$ Vr contains *(i)* all agents having no binding after the occurrence of a temporal operator and *(ii)* all variables having a binding but no quantification. For simplicity, we here consider only formulas where the epistemic modalities are applied to sentences, *i.e.*, formulas without free agents or variables. Lifting this restriction is not problematic. To establish the truth of a formula, the set of strategies over which a variable can range needs to be determined. For this purpose we use the set sharing(φ, x) containing all agents bound to a variable x within a formula φ.

Semantics. The concepts of *path*, *play*, *strategy*, and *assignment* (for agents and variables) can be defined on interpreted systems similarly to the way they are defined on concurrent game structures. We refer to [23, 27] for a detailed presentation. Intuitively, a strategy identifies paths in the model on which a formula needs to be verified. Various variants of interpreted systems have been studied. We here adopt the memoryless version where the agents' local states do not necessarily include the local history of the run. Consequently, strategies are also memoryless. Note that this markedly differs from the previous perfect recall semantics of SL, which is defined on memoryful strategies. We consider this setting because memoryful semantics with incomplete information leads to an undecidable model checking problem [11].

Given an interpreted system $\mathcal{I}$ having G as a set of global states, a state $g \in G$, and an assignment χ defined on free(φ), we write $\mathcal{I}, \chi, g \models \varphi$ to indicate that the SLK formula φ holds at g in $\mathcal{I}$ under χ. The semantics of SLK formulas is inductively defined by using the usual LTL interpretation for the atomic propositions, the Boolean connectives $\neg$ and $\wedge$, as well as the temporal operators X and U. The epistemic modalities are interpreted as standard by relying on notions of equality on the underlying sets of local states [14]. The inductive cases for strategy quantification $\langle\!\langle x \rangle\!\rangle$ and agent binding (a, x) are given as follows. $\mathcal{I}, \chi, g \models \langle\!\langle x \rangle\!\rangle \varphi$ iff there is a memoryless strategy f for the agents in sharing(φ, x) such that $\mathcal{I}, \chi[x \mapsto f], g \models \varphi$ where $\chi[x \mapsto f]$ is the assignment equal to χ except for the variable x, for which it assumes the value f. $\mathcal{I}, \chi, g \models (x, a)\varphi$ iff $\mathcal{I}, \chi[a \mapsto \chi(x)], g \models \varphi$, where $\chi[a \mapsto \chi(x)]$ denotes the assignment χ in which agent a is bound to the strategy $\chi(x)$.

Model Checking and Strategy Synthesis. Given an interpreted system $\mathcal{I}$, an initial global state g_0, an SLK specification φ, and an assignment χ defined on free(φ), the *model checking problem* concerns determining whether $\mathcal{I}, \chi, g_0 \models \varphi$. Given an interpreted system $\mathcal{I}$, an initial global state g_0, and an SLK specification φ, the *strategy synthesis problem* involves finding an assignment χ such that $\mathcal{I}, \chi, g_0 \models \varphi$.

The model checking problem for systems with memoryless strategies and imperfect information against ATL and ATL* specifications is in PSPACE [7]. The algorithm can be adapted to show that the same result applies to SLK. It follows that SLK specifications do not generate a harder model checking problem even though they are more expressive.

3 The Model Checker MCMAS-SLK

State Labelling Algorithm. The model checking algorithm for SLK extends the corresponding ones for temporal logic in two ways. Firstly, it takes as input not only a formula, but also a binding which assigns agents to variables. Secondly, it does not merely return sets of states, but sets of pairs $\langle g, \chi \rangle$ consisting of a state g and an assignment of variables to strategies χ. A pair $\langle g, \chi \rangle \in$ Ext is called an *extended state*; intuitively, χ represents a strategy assignment under which the formula holds at state g.

Given an SLK formula φ and a binding $b \in$ Bnd $\triangleq$ Ag $\to$ Vr, the model checking algorithm Sat: SLK $\times$ Bnd $\to 2^{\text{Ext}}$, returning a set of extended states, is defined as follows, where $a \in$ Ag is an agent, A $\subseteq$ Ag a set of agents, and $x \in$ Vr a variable:

- Sat$(p, b) \triangleq \{\langle g, \chi \rangle : g \in h(p) \wedge \chi \in \text{Asg}\}$, with $p \in$ AP;
- Sat$(\neg \varphi, b) \triangleq$ neg(Sat(φ, b));
- Sat$(\varphi_1 \wedge \varphi_2, b) \triangleq$ Sat$(\varphi_1, b) \cap$ Sat(φ_2, b);
- Sat$((a, x)\varphi, b) \triangleq$ Sat$(\varphi, b[a \mapsto x])$;
- Sat$(\langle\!\langle x \rangle\!\rangle \varphi, b) \triangleq \{\langle g, \chi \rangle : \exists f \in \text{Str}_{\text{sharing}(\varphi, x)} \cdot \langle g, \chi[x \mapsto f] \rangle \in$ Sat$(\varphi, b)\}$;
- Sat$(X\varphi, b) \triangleq$ pre(Sat$(\varphi, b), b$);

- $\mathsf{Sat}(\varphi_1 \mathsf{U}\varphi_2, b) \triangleq \mathrm{lfp}_X[\mathsf{Sat}(\varphi_2, b) \cup (\mathsf{Sat}(\varphi_1, b) \cap \mathsf{pre}(X, b))]$;
- $\mathsf{Sat}(\mathsf{K}_a\varphi, b) \triangleq \mathsf{neg}(\{\langle g, \chi \rangle : \exists \langle g', \chi' \rangle \in \mathsf{Sat}(\neg\varphi, \varnothing).g' \sim_a g\})$;
- $\mathsf{Sat}(\mathsf{D}_A\varphi, b) \triangleq \mathsf{neg}(\{\langle g, \chi \rangle : \exists \langle g', \chi' \rangle \in \mathsf{Sat}(\neg\varphi, \varnothing).g' \sim_A^D g\})$;
- $\mathsf{Sat}(\mathsf{C}_A\varphi, b) \triangleq \mathsf{neg}(\{\langle g, \chi \rangle : \exists \langle g', \chi' \rangle \in \mathsf{Sat}(\neg\varphi, \varnothing).g' \sim_A^C g\})$.

Above we use $h(p)$ to denote the set of global states where atom p is true; $\mathsf{pre}(C, b)$ is the set of extended states that temporally precede C subject to a binding b; $\mathsf{neg}(C)$ stands for the set of extended states $\langle g, \chi \rangle$ such that for each extended state $\langle g, \chi' \rangle \in C$, there is some variable $x \in \mathsf{dom}(\chi) \cap \mathsf{dom}(\chi')$, such that the strategies $\chi(x)$ and $\chi'(x)$ disagree on the action to be carried out in some global state $g' \in \mathsf{dom}(\chi(x)) \cap \mathsf{dom}(\chi'(x))$ (*i.e.*, $\chi(x)(g') \neq \chi'(x)(g')$); $\mathsf{Str}_{\mathsf{sharing}(\varphi,x)}$ is the set of strategies shared by the agents bound to the variable x in the formula φ; finally, $\sim_a$, $\sim_A^D$, and $\sim_A^C$ represent the individual, distributed, and common epistemic accessibility relations for agent a and agents A defined on the respective notions of equality of agents' local states. The set of global states of an interpreted system $\mathcal{I}$ satisfying a given formula $\varphi \in \mathrm{SLK}$ is calculated from the algorithm above by computing $\|\varphi\|_{\mathcal{I}} \triangleq \{g \in G : \langle g, \varnothing \rangle \in \mathsf{Sat}(\varphi, \varnothing)\}$.

BDD Translation. Given an interpreted system $\mathcal{I}$ and an SLK formula φ, we now summarise the steps required to implement the labelling algorithm above using OBDDs [6]. We represent global states and joint actions as Boolean vectors $\overline{v}$ and $\overline{w}$, respectively [29]. Similarly, an assignment χ is represented as a Boolean vector $\overline{u}$ with $K = \sum_{x \in \mathrm{Vr}} \sum_{S \in G/\sim_{\mathsf{sharing}(\varphi,x)}^C} \left\lceil \log_2 \left| \bigcap_{g \in S} \bigcap_{a \in \mathsf{sharing}(\varphi,x)} P_a(l_a(g)) \right| \right\rceil$ Boolean variables. Intuitively, for each variable $x \in \mathrm{Vr}$ and set of shared local states $S \in G/\sim_{\mathsf{sharing}(\varphi,x)}^C$, we store which action should be carried out. An extended state $\langle g, \chi \rangle \in \mathrm{Ext}$ is then represented as a conjunction of the variables in $\overline{v}_g$ and $\overline{u}_\chi$.

Given a binding $b \in \mathrm{Bnd}$, we encode the protocol $P(\overline{v}, \overline{w})$, the evolution function $t(\overline{v}, \overline{w}, \overline{v'})$, and the strategy restrictions $S^b(\overline{v}, \overline{w}, \overline{u})$, as in [20]. The temporal transition is encoded as $R_t^b(\overline{v}, \overline{v'}, \overline{u}) = \bigvee_{\overline{w} \in Act} t(\overline{v}, \overline{w}, \overline{v'}) \wedge P(\overline{v}, \overline{w}) \wedge S^b(\overline{v}, \overline{w}, \overline{u})$. Observe that we quantify over actions, encoded as $\overline{w}$, as in [20], but we store the variable assignment in the extra parameter $\overline{u}$. Quantification over the variable assignment is performed when a strategy quantifier is encountered.

Given this, the algorithm $\mathsf{Sat}(\cdot, \cdot)$ is translated into operations on BDDs representing the encoded sets of extended states.

Implementation and Usage. The model checker MCMAS-SLK [22] contains an implementation of the procedure described previously. To do this, we took MCMAS as baseline [19]. MCMAS is an open-source model checker for the verification of multi-agent systems against ATL and epistemic operators. We used MCMAS to parse input and used some of its existing libraries for handling counter-examples, which were extended to handle SLK modalities.

MCMAS-SLK takes as input a system description given in the form of an ISPL file [19] providing the agents in the system, their possible local states, their protocols, and their evolution functions. Upon providing SLK specifications, the checker calculates the set of reachable extended states, encoded as OBDDs, and computes the results by means of the labelling algorithm described previously. If

the formula is not satisfied, a counterexample is provided in the form of strategies
for the universally quantified variables.

4   Experimental Results and Conclusions

Evaluation. To evaluate the proposed approach, we present the experimental
results obtained on the dining cryptographers protocol [9,19] and a variant of the
cake-cutting problem [13]. The experiments were run on an Intel Core i7-2600
CPU 3.40GHz machine with 8GB RAM running Linux kernel version 3.8.0-34-
generic. Table 1 reports the results obtained when verifying the dining cryptog-
raphers protocol against the specifications $\phi_{CTLK} \triangleq AG\psi$ and $\phi_{SLK} \triangleq \wp G\psi$, with
$[\![x]\!]\varphi \triangleq \neg\langle\langle x\rangle\rangle\neg\varphi$, where:

$$\psi \triangleq (\text{odd}\wedge\neg\text{paid}_1) \to (K_{c_1}(\text{paid}_2 \vee\cdots\vee \text{paid}_n)) \wedge (\neg K_{c_1}\text{paid}_2 \wedge\cdots\wedge \neg K_{c_1}\text{paid}_n)$$

$$\wp \triangleq [\![x_1]\!]\cdots[\![x_n]\!][\![x_{\text{env}}]\!](c_1,x_1)\cdots(c_n,x_n)(\text{Environment},x_{\text{env}})$$

Table 1. Verification results for the dining cryptographers protocol

n crypts	possible states	reachable states	reachability (s)	CTLK (s)	SLK (s)
10	3.80×10^{14}	45056	4.41	0.30	2.11
11	9.13×10^{15}	98304	1.79	0.04	5.51
12	2.19×10^{17}	212992	2.43	0.02	11.78
13	5.26×10^{18}	458752	2.17	0.11	32.41
14	1.26×10^{20}	983040	2.08	0.09	85.29
15	3.03×10^{21}	2.10×10^6	22.67	0.33	171.61
16	7.27×10^{22}	4.46×10^6	7.13	0.09	451.41
17	1.74×10^{24}	9.44×10^6	9.77	0.13	768.34

ϕ_{CTLK} is the usual epistemic specification for the protocol [19,30] and ϕ_{SLK} is
its natural extension where strategies are quantified. The results show that the
checker can verify reasonably large state spaces. The performance depends on
the number of Boolean variables required to represent the extended states. In
the case of SLK specifications, the number of Boolean variables is proportional
to the number of strategies (here equal to the number of agents). The last two
columns of Table 1 show that the tool's performance drops considerably faster
when verifying SLK formulas compared to CTLK ones. This is because CTLK
requires no strategy assignments and extended states collapse to plain states. In
contrast, the performance for CTLK is dominated by the computation of the
reachable state space.

   We now evaluate MCMAS-SLK with respect to strategy synthesis and specifications expressing Nash equilibria. Specifically, we consider a variation of the
model for the classic cake-cutting problem [13] in which a set of n *agents* take
turns to slice a cake of size d and the *environment* responds by trying to ensure the cake is divided fairly. We assume that at each even round the agents
concurrently choose how to divide the cake; at each odd round the environment

decides how to cut the cake and how to assign each of the pieces to a subset of the agents. Therefore, the problem of cutting a cake of size d between n agents is suitably divided into several simpler problems in which pieces of size $d' < d$ have to be split between $n' < n$ agents. The multi-player game terminates once each agent receives a slice.

The model uses as atomic propositions pairs $\langle i, c \rangle \in [1, n] \times [1, d]$ indicating that agent i gets a piece of cake of size c. The existence of a protocol for the cake-cutting problem is given by the following SL specification φ:

$$\varphi \triangleq \langle\langle x \rangle\rangle (\varphi_F \wedge \varphi_S), \text{where}$$

- $\varphi_F \triangleq [[y_1]] \dots [[y_n]] (\psi_{NE} \to \psi_E)$ ensures that the protocol x is fair, *i.e.*, all Nash equilibria $(y_1, \dots, y_n)$ of the agents guarantee equity of the splitting;
- $\varphi_S \triangleq \langle\langle y_1 \rangle\rangle \dots \langle\langle y_n \rangle\rangle \psi_{NE}$ ensures that the protocol has a solution, *i.e.*, there is at least one Nash equilibrium;
- $\psi_{NE} \triangleq \bigwedge_{i=1}^{n} (\bigwedge_{v=1}^{d} (\langle\langle z \rangle\rangle \flat_i p_i(v)) \to (\bigvee_{c=v}^{d} \flat p_i(c)))$ ensures that if agent i has a strategy z allowing him to get from the environment a slice of size v once the strategies of the other agents are fixed, he is already able to obtain a slice of size $c \geq v$ by means of his original strategy y_i (this can be ensured by taking $\flat \triangleq (\text{Environment}, x)(1, y_1) \dots (n, y_n)$, $\flat_i \triangleq (\text{Environment}, x)(1, y_1) \cdots (i, z) \cdots (n, y_n)$, and $p_i(c) \triangleq F \langle i, c \rangle$);
- $\psi_E \triangleq \flat \bigwedge_{i=1}^{n} p_i(\lfloor d/n \rfloor)$ ensures that each agent i is able to obtain a piece of size $\lfloor d/n \rfloor$ ($\flat$ and p_i are the same as in the item above).

We were able to verify the formula φ defined above on a system with $n = 2$ agents and a cake of size $d = 2$. Moreover, we automatically synthesised a strategy x for the environment (see [22] for more details). We were not able to verify larger examples; for example with $n = 2, d = 3$, there are 29 reachable states; the encoding required 105 Boolean variables (most of them represent the assignments in the sets of extended states), and the intermediate BDDs were found to be in the order of 10^9 nodes. This should not be surprising given the theoretical difficulty of the cake-cutting problem. Moreover, we are synthesising the entire protocol and not just the agents' optimal behaviour.

Conclusions. In this paper we presented MCMAS-SLK, a novel symbolic model checker for the verification of systems against specifications given in SLK. A notable feature of the approach is that it allows for the automatic verification of sophisticated game concepts such as various forms of equilibria, including Nash equilibria. Since MCMAS-SLK also supports epistemic modalities, this further enables us to express specifications concerning individual and group knowledge of cooperation properties; these are commonly employed when reasoning about multi-agent systems. Other tools supporting epistemic or plain ATL specifications exist [4, 16, 18, 19]. In our experiments we found that the performance of MCMAS-SLK on the ATL and CTLK fragments was comparable to that of MCMAS, one of the leading checkers for multi-agent systems. This is because we adopted an approach in which the colouring with strategies is specification-dependent and is only performed after the set of reachable states is computed.

As described, a further notable feature of MCMAS-SLK is the ability to synthesise behaviours for multi-player games, thereby going beyond the classical setting of two-player games.

We found that the main impediment to better performance of the tool is the size of the BDDs required to encode sets of extended states. Future efforts will be devoted to mitigate this problem as well as to support other fragments of SL.

Acknowledgements. This research was partly funded by the EPSRC (grant EP/I00520X), the Regione Campania (Embedded System Cup project B25B09090 100007), the EU (FP7 project 600958-SHERPA), and the MIUR (ORCHESTRA project). Aniello Murano acknowledges support from the Department of Computing at Imperial College London for his research visit in July 2013.

References

1. Ågotnes, T., Goranko, V., Jamroga, W.: Alternating-Time Temporal Logics with Irrevocable Strategies. In: Theoretical Aspects of Rationality and Knowledge 2007, pp. 15–24 (2007)
2. Ågotnes, T., Walther, D.: A Logic of Strategic Ability Under Bounded Memory. JLLI 18(1), 55–77 (2009)
3. Alur, R., Henzinger, T.A., Kupferman, O.: Alternating-Time Temporal Logic. Journal of the ACM 49(5), 672–713 (2002)
4. Alur, R., Henzinger, T.A., Mang, F.Y.C., Qadeer, S., Rajamani, S.K., Tasiran, S.: MOCHA: Modularity in Model Checking.. In: Vardi, M.Y. (ed.) CAV 1998. LNCS, vol. 1427, pp. 521–525. Springer, Heidelberg (1998)
5. Brihaye, T., Da Costa, A., Laroussinie, F., Markey, N.: ATL with strategy contexts and bounded memory. In: Artemov, S., Nerode, A. (eds.) LFCS 2009. LNCS, vol. 5407, pp. 92–106. Springer, Heidelberg (2008)
6. Bryant, R.E.: Graph-Based Algorithms for Boolean Function Manipulation. Transactions on Computers 35(8), 677–691 (1986)
7. Bulling, N., Dix, J., Jamroga, W.: Model Checking Logics of Strategic Ability: Complexity. In: Specification and Verification of Multi-Agent Systems, pp. 125–159. Springer (2010)
8. Chatterjee, K., Henzinger, T.A., Piterman, N.: Strategy Logic. Information and Computation 208(6), 677–693 (2010)
9. Chaum, D.: The Dining Cryptographers Problem: Unconditional Sender and Recipient Untraceability. Journal of Cryptology 1, 65–75 (1988)
10. Clarke, E.M., Emerson, E.A.: Design and Synthesis of Synchronization Skeletons Using Branching-Time Temporal Logic. In: Kozen, D. (ed.) Logic of Programs 1981. LNCS, vol. 131, pp. 52–71. Springer, Heidelberg (1982)
11. Dima, C., Tiplea, F.L.: Model-checking ATL under Imperfect Information and Perfect Recall Semantics is Undecidable. Technical report, arXiv (2011)
12. Emerson, E.A., Halpern, J.Y.: "Sometimes" and "Not Never" Revisited: On Branching Versus Linear Time. Journal of the ACM 33(1), 151–178 (1986)
13. Even, S., Paz, A.: A Note on Cake Cutting. Discrete Applied Mathematics 7, 285–296 (1984)
14. Fagin, R., Halpern, J.Y., Moses, Y., Vardi, M.Y.: Reasoning about Knowledge. MIT Press (1995)

15. Finkbeiner, B., Schewe, S.: Coordination logic. In: Dawar, A., Veith, H. (eds.) CSL 2010. LNCS, vol. 6247, pp. 305–319. Springer, Heidelberg (2010)
16. Gammie, P., van der Meyden, R.: MCK: Model Checking the Logic of Knowledge. In: Alur, R., Peled, D.A. (eds.) CAV 2004. LNCS, vol. 3114, pp. 479–483. Springer, Heidelberg (2004)
17. Jamroga, W., Murano, A.: On Module Checking and Strategies. In: Autonomous Agents and MultiAgent Systems 2014, pp. 701–708. International Foundation for Autonomous Agents and Multiagent Systems (2014)
18. Kacprzak, M., Nabialek, W., Niewiadomski, A., Penczek, W., Pólrola, A., Szreter, M., Wozna, B., Zbrzezny, A.: VerICS 2007 - a Model Checker for Knowledge and Real-Time. Fundamenta Informaticae 85(1-4), 313–328 (2008)
19. Lomuscio, A., Qu, H., Raimondi, F.: MCMAS: A Model Checker for the Verification of Multi-Agent Systems. In: Bouajjani, A., Maler, O. (eds.) CAV 2009. LNCS, vol. 5643, pp. 682–688. Springer, Heidelberg (2009)
20. Lomuscio, A., Raimondi, F.: Model Checking Knowledge, Strategies, and Games in Multi-Agent Systems. In: Autonomous Agents and MultiAgent Systems 2006, pp. 161–168. International Foundation for Autonomous Agents and Multiagent Systems (2006)
21. Lopes, A.D.C., Laroussinie, F., Markey, N.: ATL with Strategy Contexts: Expressiveness and Model Checking. In: Foundations of Software Technology and Theoretical Computer Science 2010. LIPIcs, vol. 8, pp. 120–132. Leibniz-Zentrum fuer Informatik (2010)
22. MCMAS-SLK - A Model Checker for the Verification of Strategy Logic Specifications, http://vas.doc.ic.ac.uk/software/tools/
23. Mogavero, F., Murano, A., Perelli, G., Vardi, M.Y.: Reasoning About Strategies: On the Model-Checking Problem. Technical report, arXiv (2011)
24. Mogavero, F., Murano, A., Perelli, G., Vardi, M.Y.: What Makes ATL* Decidable? A Decidable Fragment of Strategy Logic. In: Koutny, M., Ulidowski, I. (eds.) CONCUR 2012. LNCS, vol. 7454, pp. 193–208. Springer, Heidelberg (2012)
25. Mogavero, F., Murano, A., Sauro, L.: On the Boundary of Behavioral Strategies. In: Logic in Computer Science 2013, pp. 263–272. IEEE Computer Society (2013)
26. Mogavero, F., Murano, A., Sauro, L.: Strategy Games: A Renewed Framework. In: Autonomous Agents and MultiAgent Systems 2014, pp. 869–876. International Foundation for Autonomous Agents and Multiagent Systems (2014)
27. Mogavero, F., Murano, A., Vardi, M.Y.: Reasoning About Strategies. In: Foundations of Software Technology and Theoretical Computer Science 2010. LIPIcs, vol. 8, pp. 133–144. Leibniz-Zentrum fuer Informatik (2010)
28. Pnueli, A.: The Temporal Logic of Programs. In: Foundation of Computer Science 1977, pp. 46–57. IEEE Computer Society (1977)
29. Raimondi, F., Lomuscio, A.: Automatic Verification of Multi-Agent Systems by Model Checking via Ordered Binary Decision Diagrams. Journal of Applied Logic 5(2), 235–251 (2007)
30. van der Meyden, R., Su, K.: Symbolic Model Checking the Knowledge of the Dining Cryptographers. In: Computer Security Foundations Workshop 2004, pp. 280–291. IEEE Computer Society (2004)
31. Walther, D., van der Hoek, W., Wooldridge, M.: Alternating-Time Temporal Logic with Explicit Strategies. In: Theoretical Aspects of Rationality and Knowledge 2007, pp. 269–278 (2007)

Solving Games without Controllable Predecessor

Nina Narodytska[1,2], Alexander Legg[1], Fahiem Bacchus[2],
Leonid Ryzhyk[1,2], and Adam Walker[1]

[1] NICTA* and UNSW, Sydney, Australia
[2] University of Toronto, Canada

Abstract. Two-player games are a useful formalism for the synthesis of reactive systems. The traditional approach to solving such games iteratively computes the set of winning states for one of the players. This requires keeping track of all discovered winning states and can lead to space explosion even when using efficient symbolic representations. We propose a new method for solving reachability games. Our method works by exploring a subset of the possible concrete runs of the game and proving that these runs can be generalised into a winning strategy on behalf of one of the players. We use counterexample-guided backtracking search to identify a subset of runs that are sufficient to consider to solve the game. We evaluate our algorithm on several families of benchmarks derived from real-world device driver synthesis problems.

1 Introduction

Two-player games are a useful formalism for the synthesis of reactive systems, with applications in software [15] and hardware design [4], industrial automation [7], etc. We consider finite-state *reachability games*, where player 1 (the controller) must force the game into a *goal region* given any valid behaviour of player 2 (the environment).

The most successful method for solving two-player games is based on the *controllable predecessor* (*Cpre*) operator [14], which, given a target set of states, computes the set from which the controller can force the game into the target set in one round. *Cpre* is applied iteratively, until a fixed point is reached. The downside of this method is that it keeps track of all discovered winning states, which can lead to a space explosion even when using efficient symbolic representation such as BDDs or DNFs.

We propose a new method for solving reachability games. Our method works by exploring a subset of the concrete runs of the game and proving that these runs can be generalised into a winning strategy on behalf of one of the players. In contrast to the *Cpre*-based approach, as well as other existing synthesis methods, it does not represent, in either symbolic or explicit form, the set of states visited by the winning strategy. Instead, it uses counterexample-guided backtracking search to identify a small subset of runs that are sufficient to solve the game.

We evaluate our algorithm on several benchmarks derived from driver synthesis problems. We find that it outperforms a highly optimised BDD-based solver on the subset of benchmarks that do not admit a compact representaion of the winning set, thus demonstrating the potential of the new approach.

* NICTA is funded by the Australian Government through the Department of Communications and the Australian Research Council through the ICT Centre of Excellence Program.

A. Biere and R. Bloem (Eds.): CAV 2014, LNCS 8559, pp. 533–540, 2014.
© Springer International Publishing Switzerland 2014

2   Related Work

Our algorithm is inspired by the RAReQS QBF solver [10]. RAReQS treats a QBF formula in the prenex normal form as a game between the universal and the existential player. It uses counterexample-guided backtracking search to efficiently expand quantifier blocks. We build on the ideas of RAReQS, to construct a domain-specific solver for reachability games that takes advantage of the structure of such games.

One alternative to the $Cpre$-based method encodes the game as a quantified boolean formula (QBF), where controller and environment moves are encoded as alternating existential and universal quantifiers [2]. More recently several SAT-based synthesis methods have been proposed [13,5]. Similarly to $Cpre$-based techniques, they incrementally compute the set of winning (or losing) states, in the DNF form, and refine it using a SAT solver. Sabharwal et al. [16] explore the duality of games and QBF formulas and propose a hybrid CNF/DNF-based encoding of games that helps speed up QBF solving. The bounded synthesis method [11] aims to synthesise a controller implementation with a bounded number of states. In the present work, we impose a bound on the number of rounds in the game, which is necessary to encode it into SAT.

Our method uses counterexample-guided abstraction refinement to identify potentially winning moves of the game. Several abstraction refinement algorithms for games have been proposed in the literature [9,1]. Our algorithm is complementary to these techniques and can be combined with them.

The idea of solving games by generalising a winning run into a complete strategy has been explored in explicit-state synthesis [6]. In contrast to these methods, we use a SAT solver to compute and generalise winning runs symbolically. This enables us to solve games with very large state spaces, which is not possible using explicit search, even when performing it on the fly.

3   Background

Games and Strategies. A reachability game $G = \langle S, L_c, L_u, I, O, \delta \rangle$ consists of a set of states S, controllable actions L_c, uncontrollable actions L_u, initial state $I \in S$, a set $O \in 2^S$ of goal states, and a transition function $\delta : (S, L_c, L_u) \to S$. The game proceeds in a sequence of rounds, starting from an initial state. In each round, the controller picks an action $c \in L_c$. The environment responds by picking an action $u \in L_u$, and the game transitions to a new state $\delta(s, c, u)$.

A *controller strategy* $\pi : S \to L_c$ associates with every state a controllable action to play in this state. Given a bound n on the number of rounds, π is a *winning* strategy in state s at round $i \leq n$ if any sequence $(s_i, u_i, s_{i+1}, u_{i+1}, ..., s_n)$, such that $s_i = s$ and $s_{k+1} = \delta(s_k, \pi(s_k), u)$, visits the goal set: $\exists j \in [i, n].s_j \in O$. A state-round pair $\langle s, i \rangle$ is winning if there exists a winning strategy in s at round i. A state-round-action tuple $\langle s, i, c \rangle$ is winning if there does *not* exist a spoiling strategy for s and c at round i.

In this paper we are concerned with the problem of *solving the game*, i.e., checking whether the initial state I is winning at round 0 for the given bound n. Note that bounding the number of rounds to reach the goal is a conservative restriction: any winning strategy in the bounded game is winning in the unbounded game. If, on the other hand, a winning strategy for a bound n cannot be found, n can be relaxed.

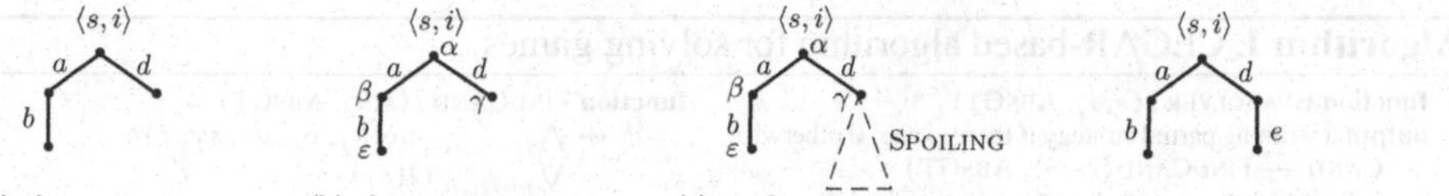

(a) abstract game tree   (b) abstract game tree   (c) spoiling strategy   (d) refined abstract game tree
                               with partial strategy   in leaf (d)

Fig. 1. Abstract game tree

Symbolic Games. In this paper we deal with *symbolic games* defined over three sets of boolean variables X, Y_c, and Y_u. Each state $s \in S$ represents a valuation of variables X, each action $c \in L_c$ ($u \in L_u$) represents a valuation of variables Y_c (Y_u). The transition relation δ of the game is given as a boolean formula $\Delta(X, Y_c, Y_u, X')$ over state, action, and next-state variables.

4   Abstract Game Trees

Our algorithm constructs a series of abstractions of the input game. An abstraction restricts actions available to one of the players. Specifically, we consider abstractions represented as trees of actions, referred to as *abstract game trees*. Together with a state-round pair $\langle s, i \rangle$, an abstract game tree defines an *abstract game* played from this state. Figure 1a shows an example abstract game. In the abstract game, the environment player is required to pick actions from the tree, starting from the root node. After reaching a leaf, it continues playing unrestricted. The tree in Figure 1a restricts the initial environment action to the set $\{a, d\}$. After choosing action d, the environment reaches a leaf of the tree and continues playing unrestricted. Alternatively, after choosing a, the environment is required to play action b in the next round.

Nodes of an abstract game tree are uniquely identified by the list of edge labels along the path from the root to the node. We identify an abstract game tree with the set of its nodes. For example, the tree in Figure 1a can be written as $\{(), (d), (a), (a, b)\}$. We denote $leaves(T)$ the subset of leaf nodes of a tree T.

A *partial strategy Strat* : $T \to L_c$ assigns a controllable action to be played in each node of the abstract game tree. Figure 1b shows an example partial strategy. The controller starts by choosing action α. If the environment plays a, the controller responds with β in the next round, and so on. Given a partial strategy $Strat$, we can map each leaf l of the abstract game tree to $\langle s', i' \rangle = outcome(\langle s, i \rangle, Strat, l)$ obtained by playing all controllable and uncontrollable actions on the path from the root to the leaf.

5   The Algorithm

Figure 2 and Algorithm 1 illustrate our algorithm, called EVASOLVER. The algorithm takes a concrete game G as an implicit argument. In addition, it takes a state-round pair $\langle s, i \rangle$ and an abstract game tree ABSGT and returns a winning partial strategy for it, if one exists. The initial invocation of the algorithm takes the initial state $\langle I, 0 \rangle$ and an empty abstract game tree $\emptyset$. The empty game tree does not constrain opponent moves, hence solving such an abstraction is equivalent to solving the original concrete

---

Algorithm 1. CEGAR-based algorithm for solving games

function EVASOLVER ($\langle s, i \rangle$, ABSGT)
  output a winning partial strategy if there is one; $\emptyset$ otherwise
  CAND $\leftarrow$ FINDCAND($\langle s, i \rangle$, ABSGT)
  // FINDCAND *returns a precise solution for* $i = n - 1$
  if $i = n - 1$ return CAND
  ABSGT' $\leftarrow$ ABSGT
  loop
    if CAND $= \emptyset$ return $\emptyset$
    COUNTEREX $\leftarrow$ VERIFY($\langle s, i \rangle$, ABSGT, CAND)
    if COUNTEREX $= NULL$ return CAND
    else
      ABSGT' $\leftarrow$ REFINE(ABSGT', COUNTEREX)
      CAND $\leftarrow$ EVASOLVER ($\langle s, i \rangle$, ABSGT')
  end loop
end function

function REFINE(ABSGT, $\langle l,$ SPOILING$\rangle$)
  let $l = (e_i, \ldots, e_r)$
  return ABSGT $\cup \{(e_i, \ldots, e_r),$ SPOILING$((()))\}$
end function

function FINDCAND ($\langle s, i \rangle$, ABSGT)
  $\phi \leftarrow \bigwedge_{j=i\ldots n-1} \delta(s_j, c_j, u_j, s_{j+1}) \wedge$
         $\bigvee_{j=i\ldots n} O(s_j)$
  for $l \in leaves($ABSGT$)$ do
    // e_j *are environment actions along the path from*
    // *the root to* l *in* ABSGT
    let $l = (e_i, \ldots, e_r)$
    $p \leftarrow \bigwedge_{m=i\ldots r} u_m = e_m$
    $\phi_l \leftarrow rename(\phi, l) \wedge (s_i = s) \wedge p$
  $sol \leftarrow SAT(\bigwedge_{l \in leaves(\text{ABSGT})} \phi_l)$
  if $sol = unsat$ return $\emptyset$
  return $\{(v, c) | v \in nodes($ABSGT$), c = sol \mid_{c_v}\}$
end function

function VERIFY($\langle s, i \rangle$, ABSGT, CAND)
  for $l \in leaves(\langle s, i \rangle$, ABSGT$)$ do
    $\langle s', i' \rangle = outcome(\langle s, i \rangle$, ABSGT, $l)$
    SPOILING $\leftarrow \overline{\text{EVASOLVER}}(\langle s', i' \rangle, \emptyset)$
    if SPOILING $\neq \emptyset$ return $\langle l,$ SPOILING$\rangle$
  return $NULL$ // *no spoiling strategy found*
end function

---

game. The algorithm is organised as a counterexample-guided abstraction refinement (CEGAR) loop. The first step of the algorithm uses the FINDCAND function, described in detail below, to come up with a candidate partial strategy for ABSGT. If it fails to find a strategy, this means that no winning partial strategy exists for ABSGT. If, on the other hand, a candidate partial strategy is found, we need to verify if it is indeed winning for ABSGT.

The VERIFY procedure searches for a *spoiling* counterexample strategy in each leaf of the candidate partial strategy by calling the *dual solver* $\overline{\text{EVASOLVER}}$. The dual solver solves a *safety* game on behalf of the environment player, where the environment must stay away from the

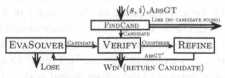

Fig. 2. CEGAR loop of Algorithm 1

goal for a bounded number of steps. Figure 1c shows a spoiling strategy discovered in one of the leaves of the abstract game tree. The dual algorithm is analogous to the primary solver. We do not present its pseudocode due to limited space. If the dual solver can find no spoiling strategy at any of the leaves, then the candidate partial strategy is a winning one. Otherwise, the REFINE function extracts the first move of the spoiling strategy (i.e., the move that the strategy plays in the root node () of the abstract game tree constructed by the dual solver) and uses it to refine the abstract game by adding a new edge labelled with this move to the leaf (Figure 1d).

We solve the refined game by recursively invoking EVASOLVER on it. If no partial winning strategy is found for the refined game then there is also no partial winning strategy for the original abstract game, and the algorithm returns a failure. Otherwise, the partial strategy for the refined game is *projected* on the original abstract game by removing the leaves introduced by refinements. The resulting partial strategy becomes a candidate strategy to be verified at the next iteration of the loop.

The loop terminates, in the worst case, after refining the game with all possible environment actions. However, to achieve good performance, the algorithm must be able to solve the game using a small number of refinements. The FINDCAND procedure plays the key role in achieving this. We use the following criterion to find potentially winning candidates efficiently: we search for a partial strategy such that after playing the strategy from the root to any of the leaves of the abstract game tree, we can choose a sequence of follow-up moves for both players taking the game into the goal region. Effectively, we try to win the game under the assumption that the players cooperate to reach the goal rather than competing with each other. If such an optimistic partial strategy does not exist, then we cannot win the abstract game. On the other hand, if we do find such a strategy, it is likely to either be a winning one or to produce a useful counterexample that will speed up the search for a winning strategy. This is based on the observation that in industrial synthesis problems the environment typically represents a hardware or software system designed to allow efficient control. Environment actions model responses to control signals, which require appropriate reaction from the controller, but are not aimed to deliberately counteract the controller. Unlike in truly competitive games like chess, a straightforward path to the goal is likely to be a good first approximation of a correct winning strategy.

We find a candidate partial strategy that satisfies the above criterion using a SAT solver, as shown by the FINDCAND function. We unroll the transition relation δ into a formula ϕ that encodes a winning run of the game starting from the ith round. For each leaf l of the abstract game tree with the path from the root to the leaf labelled with environment actions $(e_i, \ldots, e_r)$, we construct a formula ϕ_l describing a winning run through the leaf. The formula consists of three conjuncts. The first conjunct $rename(\phi, l)$ renames variables in ϕ so that the resulting formulas for leaves sharing a common edge of the abstract game tree share the corresponding action and state variables, while using separate copies of all other variables. The second and third conjuncts fix initial state and environment actions along the path from the root to the leaf. We invoke a SAT solver to find assignments to state and action variables simultaneously satisfying all leaf formulas ϕ_l. If this formula is unsatisfiable, then state $\langle s, i \rangle$ is losing and the algorithm returns $\emptyset$; otherwise, it constructs a spoiling strategy by extracting values of controllable moves in nodes of the abstract game tree from the solution returned by the SAT solver.

Correctness of EVASOLVER follows from the following properties of the algorithm: (1) the counterexample-guided search strategy is complete, i.e., it is guaranteed to find a winning strategy, if one exists, possibly after exploring all possible runs of the game, and (2) our SAT encoding of the game is sound, i.e., if the SAT formula generated by FINDCAND is unsatisfiable then there does not exist a winning strategy from state $\langle s, i \rangle$.

Memoising Losing States. Our implementation of EVASOLVER uses an important optimisation. Whenever the SAT solver invocation in FINDCAND returns $unsat$, we obtain a proof that s is a losing state for the controller. We generalise this fact by extracting a minimal unsatisfiable core from the SAT solver and projecting it on state variables x. This gives us a cube of states losing for the controller. We modify the winning run formula ϕ to exclude this cube from a winning run. This guarantees that candidate partial strategies generated by the algorithm avoid previously discovered losing states.

6   Evaluation

We evaluate our algorithm on four families of benchmarks derived from driver synthesis problems. These benchmarks model the data path of four I/O devices in the abstracted form. In particular, we model the transmit buffer of an Ethernet adapter, the send queue of a UART serial controller, the command queue of an SPI Flash controller, and the IDE hard disk DMA descriptor list. Models are parameterised by the size of the corresponding data structure. Specifications are written in a simple input language based on the NuSMV syntax [8]. The transition relation of the game is given in the form of variable update functions $x := f(X, Y_c, Y_u)$, one for each state variable $x \in X$.

We compare our solver against two existing approaches to solving games. First, we encode input specifications as QBF instances and solve them using two state-of-the-art QBF solvers: RAReQS [10] and depqbf [12], having first run them through the bloqqer [3] preprocessor. Second, we solve our benchmarks using the Termite [17] BDD-based solver that uses dynamic variable reordering, variable grouping, transition relation partitioning, and other optimisations.

Our experiments, summarised in Figure 3, show that off-the-shelf QBF solvers are not well-suited for solving games. Although our algorithm is inspired by RAReQS, we achieve much better performance, since our solver takes into account the structure of the game, rather than treating it as a generic QBF problem.

All four benchmarks have very large sets of winning states. Nevertheless, in the UART and IDE benchmarks, Termite is able to represent winning states compactly with only a few thousand BDD nodes. It scales well and outperforms EVASOLVER on these benchmarks. However, in the two other benchmarks, Termite does not find a compact BDD-based representation of the winning set. EVASOLVER outperforms Termite on these benchmarks as it does not try to enumerate all winning states.

Detailed performance analysis shows that abstract game trees generated in our benchmarks had average branching factors in the range between 1.03 and 1.2, with the maximal depth of the trees ranging from 3 to 58. This confirms the the key premise behind the design of EVASOLVER, namely, solving real-world synthesis problems requires considering only a small number of opponent moves in every state of the game.

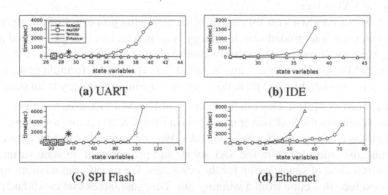

(a) UART   (b) IDE

(c) SPI Flash   (d) Ethernet

Fig. 3. Performance of different solvers on four parameterised benchmarks. The X-axis shows the number of state vars in the game (determined by the benchmark parameter).

7 Conclusion

We presented a method for solving reachability games without constructing the game's winning set, and demonstrated that this method can be more efficient than conventional approaches. Our ongoing work concentrates on further performance improvements as well as on applying the new technique to a broader class of omega-regular games.

Our ongoing work focuses on further improving the performance of EVASOLVER via optimised CNF encodings of abstract games, stronger memoisation techniques, and additional domain-specific heuristics for computing candidate strategies.

References

1. de Alfaro, L., Roy, P.: Solving games via three-valued abstraction refinement. In: Caires, L., Vasconcelos, V.T. (eds.) CONCUR 2007. LNCS, vol. 4703, pp. 74–89. Springer, Heidelberg (2007)
2. Alur, R., Madhusudan, P., Nam, W.: Symbolic computational techniques for solving games. STTT 7(2), 118–128 (2005)
3. Biere, A., Lonsing, F., Seidl, M.: Blocked clause elimination for QBF. In: Bjørner, N., Sofronie-Stokkermans, V. (eds.) CADE 2011. LNCS, vol. 6803, pp. 101–115. Springer, Heidelberg (2011)
4. Bloem, R., Galler, S., Jobstmann, B., Piterman, N., Pnueli, A., Weiglhofer, M.: Specify, compile, run: Hardware from PSL. ENTCS 190(4), 3–16 (2007)
5. Bloem, R., Könighofer, R., Seidl, M.: SAT-based synthesis methods for safety specs. CoRR abs/1311.3530 (2013)
6. Cassez, F.: Efficient on-the-fly algorithms for partially observable timed games. In: Raskin, J.-F., Thiagarajan, P.S. (eds.) FORMATS 2007. LNCS, vol. 4763, pp. 5–24. Springer, Heidelberg (2007)
7. Cassez, F., Jessen, J.J., Larsen, K.G., Raskin, J.F., Reynier, P.A.: Automatic synthesis of robust and optimal controllers - an industrial case study. In: HSCC, San Francisco, CA, USA, pp. 90–104 (April 2009)
8. Cavada, R., Cimatti, A., Jochim, C.A., Keighren, G., Olivetti, E., Pistore, M., Roveri, M., River, A.T.: NuSMV 2.5 user manual
9. Henzinger, T.A., Jhala, R., Majumdar, R.: Counterexample-guided control. In: Baeten, J.C.M., Lenstra, J.K., Parrow, J., Woeginger, G.J. (eds.) ICALP 2003. LNCS, vol. 2719, pp. 886–902. Springer, Heidelberg (2003)
10. Janota, M., Klieber, W., Marques-Silva, J., Clarke, E.: Solving QBF with counterexample guided refinement. In: Cimatti, A., Sebastiani, R. (eds.) SAT 2012. LNCS, vol. 7317, pp. 114–128. Springer, Heidelberg (2012)
11. Kupferman, O., Lustig, Y., Vardi, M.Y., Yannakakis, M.: Temporal synthesis for bounded systems and environments. In: STACS, pp. 615–626 (March 2011)
12. Lonsing, F., Biere, A.: Integrating dependency schemes in search-based QBF solvers. In: Strichman, O., Szeider, S. (eds.) SAT 2010. LNCS, vol. 6175, pp. 158–171. Springer, Heidelberg (2010)
13. Morgenstern, A., Gesell, M., Schneider, K.: Solving games using incremental induction. In: IFM, Turku, Finland, pp. 177–191 (June 2013)

14. Piterman, N., Pnueli, A., Sa'ar, Y.: Synthesis of Reactive(1) designs. In: Emerson, E.A., Namjoshi, K.S. (eds.) VMCAI 2006. LNCS, vol. 3855, pp. 364–380. Springer, Heidelberg (2006)
15. Ryzhyk, L., Chubb, P., Kuz, I., Le Sueur, E., Heiser, G.: Automatic device driver synthesis with Termite. In: Proceedings of the 22nd ACM Symposium on Operating Systems Principles, Big Sky, MT, USA (October 2009)
16. Sabharwal, A., Ansótegui, C., Gomes, C.P., Hart, J.W., Selman, B.: QBF modeling: Exploiting player symmetry for simplicity and efficiency. In: Biere, A., Gomes, C.P. (eds.) SAT 2006. LNCS, vol. 4121, pp. 382–395. Springer, Heidelberg (2006)
17. Walker, A., Ryzhyk, L.: Predicate abstraction for reactive synthesis. Technical Report

G4LTL-ST: Automatic Generation of PLC Programs

Chih-Hong Cheng[1], Chung-Hao Huang[2], Harald Ruess[3], and Stefan Stattelmann[1]

[1] ABB Corporate Research, Ladenburg, Germany
[2] Department of Electrical Engineering, National Taiwan University, Taipei, Taiwan
[3] fortiss - An-Institut Technische Universität München, München, Germany

Abstract. G4LTL-ST automatically synthesizes control code for industrial Programmable Logic Controls (PLC) from timed behavioral specifications of input-output signals. These specifications are expressed in a linear temporal logic (LTL) extended with non-linear arithmetic constraints and timing constraints on signals. G4LTL-ST generates code in IEC 61131-3-compatible *Structured Text*, which is compiled into executable code for a large number of industrial field-level devices. The synthesis algorithm of G4LTL-ST implements pseudo-Boolean abstraction of data constraints and the compilation of timing constraints into LTL, together with a counterstrategy-guided abstraction-refinement synthesis loop. Since temporal logic specifications are notoriously difficult to use in practice, G4LTL-ST supports engineers in specifying realizable control problems by suggesting suitable restrictions on the behavior of the control environment from failed synthesis attempts.

Keywords: industrial automation, synthesis, theory combination, assumption generation.

1 Overview

Programmable Logic Controllers (PLC) are ubiquitous in the manufacturing and processing industries for realizing real-time controls with stringent dependability and safety requirements. A PLC is designed to read digital and analog inputs from various sensors and other PLCs, execute a user-defined program, and write the resulting digital and analog output values to various output elements including hydraulic and pneumatic actuators or indication lamps. The time it takes to complete such a scan cycle typically ranges in the milliseconds.

The languages defined in the IEC 61131-3 norm are the industry standard for programming PLCs [1]. Programming in these rather low-level languages can be very inefficient, and yields inflexible controls which are difficult to maintain and arduous to port. Moreover, industry is increasingly moving towards more flexible and modular production systems, where the control software is required to adapt to frequent specification changes [2].

With this motivation in mind, we developed the synthesis engine G4LTL-ST for generating IEC 61131-3-compatible Structured Text programs from behavioral specifications. Specifications of industrial control problems are expressed in a suitable extension of linear temporal logic (LTL) [14]. The well-known LTL operators **G**, **F**, **U**, and **X** denote "always", "eventually", "(strong) until", and "next"s relations over linear execution traces. In addition to vanilla LTL, specifications in G4LTL-ST may also include

A. Biere and R. Bloem (Eds.): CAV 2014, LNCS 8559, pp. 541–549, 2014.

1   Input: $x, y \in [0, 4] \cap \mathbb{R}$, err $\in \mathbb{B}$,   Output: grant1, grant2, light $\in \mathbb{B}$,   Period: 50ms
2
3        $\mathbf{G}(x + y > 3 \rightarrow \mathbf{X}\,\text{grant1})$
4        $\mathbf{G}(x^2 + y^2 < \frac{7}{2} \rightarrow \mathbf{X}\,\text{grant2})$
5        $\mathbf{G}(\neg(\text{grant1} \wedge \text{grant2}))$
6        $\mathbf{G}(\text{err} \rightarrow 10\text{sec}(\text{light}))$
7        $\mathbf{G}((\mathbf{G}\neg\text{err}) \rightarrow (\mathbf{FG}\neg\text{light}))$

Fig. 1. Linear temporal logic specification with arithmetic constraints and a timer

- non-linear arithmetic constraints for specifying non-linear constraints on real-valued inputs;
- timing constraints based on timer constructs specified in IEC 61131-3.

A timing constraint of the form 10sec(light), for example, specifies that the light signal is on for 10 seconds. Moreover, the semantics of temporal specifications in G4LTL-ST is slightly different from the standard semantics as used in model checking, since the execution model of PLCs is based on the concept of *Mealy machines*. Initial values for output signals are therefore undefined, and the synthesis engine of G4LTL-ST assumes that the environment of the controller makes the first move by setting the inputs.

Consider, for example, the PLC specification in Figure 1 with a specified scan cycle time of 50ms (line 1). The input variables x, y, err store bounded input and sensor values, and output values are available at the end of each scan cycle at grant1, grant2, and light (line 1). According to the specification in line 6, the output light must be on for at least 10 seconds whenever an error occurs, that is, input signal err is raised. Line 7 requires that if err no longer appears, then eventually the light signal is always off. The transition-style LTL specifications 3 and 4 in Figure 1 require setting grant1 (resp. grant2) to true in the next cycle whenever the condition $x + y > 3$ (resp. $x^2 + y^2 < \frac{7}{2}$) holds. Finally, grant1 and grant2 are supposed to be mutually exclusive (line 5).

The synthesis engine of G4LTL-ST builds on top of traditional LTL synthesis techniques [13,9,15,4] which view the synthesis problem as a game between the (sensor) environment and the controller. The moves of the environment in these games are determined by setting the input variables, and the controller reacts by setting output variables accordingly. The controller wins if the resulting input-output traces satisfy the given specification. Notably, arithmetic constraints and timers are viewed as theories and thus abstracted into a pseudo-Boolean LTL formula. This enables G4LTL-ST to utilize CEGAR-like [8,12,10] techniques for successively constraining the capabilities of the control environment.

Since specifications in linear temporal logic are often notoriously difficult to use in practice, G4LTL-ST diagnoses unrealizable specifications and suggests additional *assumptions* for making the controller synthesis problem realizable. The key hypothesis underlying this approach is that this kind of feedback is more useful for the engineer compared to, say, counter strategies. The assumption generation of G4LTL-ST uses built-in templates and heuristics for estimating the importance and for ordering the generated assumptions accordingly.

Synthesis of control software, in particular, has been recognized as a key *Industrie 4.0* technology for realizing flexible and modular controls (see, for example, [3],

Table 1. Real-time specification patterns and their encodings

Real-time specification pattern	Encoding in LTL
Whenever a, then b for t seconds	$G\,(a \to (t1.start \wedge b \wedge X(b\,U\,t1.expire)))$
Whenever a continues for more than t seconds, then b	$(a \leftrightarrow t1.start) \wedge G(\neg(a \wedge X\,a) \leftrightarrow X\,t1.start)$ $\wedge\,G(t1.expire \to b)$
Whenever a, then b, until c for more than t seconds	$G(a \leftrightarrow t1.start) \wedge G(\neg(c \wedge X\,c) \leftrightarrow X\,t1.start)$ $\wedge\,G\,(a \to (b \wedge X((b\,U\,t1.expire)) \vee G\neg t1.expire))$

RE-2 on page 44). The synthesis engine G4LTL-ST is planned to be an integral part of a complete development tool chain towards meeting these challenges. G4LTL-ST is written in Java and is available (under the GPLv3 open source license) at

http://www.sourceforge.net/projects/g4ltl/files/beta

In the following we provide an overview of the main features of G4LTL-ST including Pseudo-Boolean abstractions of timing constraints, the abstraction-refinement synthesis loop underlying G4LTL-ST and its implementation, and, finally, the template-based generation for suggesting new constraints of the behavior of the environment for making the control synthesis problem realizable. These features of G4LTL-ST are usually only illustrated by means of examples, but the initiated reader should be able to fill in missing technical details.

2   Timing Abstractions

The timing constraint in Figure 1 with its 10 seconds time-out may be encoded in LTL by associating each discrete step with a 50ms time delay. Notice, however, that up to 200 consecutive X operators are needed for encoding this simple example.

Instead we propose a more efficient translation, based on standard IEC 61131-3 timing constructs, for realizing timing specifications. Consider, for example, the timed specification $G\,(err \to 10sec(light))$. In a first step, fresh variables t1.start and t1.expire are introduced, where t1 is a *timer variable* of type TON in IEC 61131-3. The additional output variable t1.start starts the timer t1, and the additional input variable t1.expire receives a time-out signal from t1 ten seconds after this timer has been started. Now, the timing specification $G\,(err \to 10sec(light))$ is rewritten as an LTL specification for a function block in the context of a timer.

$$G\,(t1.start \to X\,F\,t1.expire) \to G\,(err \to (t1.start \wedge light \wedge X(light\,U\,t1.expire))$$

The antecedent formula ensures that the expire signal is eventually provided by the timing block of the environment. Since no provision is being made that there is a time-out exactly after 10 seconds, however, the precise expected behavior of the time-out environment is over-approximated.

It is straightforward to generate PLC code using timing function blocks from winning strategies of the controller (see below for the automatically generated code). Whenever t1.start is set to true the instruction t1(IN:=0, PT:=TIME#10s) is generated for starting the timer t1. Instructions that set t1.start to false is ignored based on the underlying semantics of timers. Finally, time-out signals t1.expire are simply replaced with the variable t1.Q of the IEC 61131-3 timing construct.

```
FUNCTION_BLOCK FB_G4LTL
VAR_INPUT       error: BOOL;        END_VAR
VAR_OUTPUT      light: BOOL;        END_VAR
VAR             cstate : INT := 0;  t1: TON;    END_VAR
VAR CONST       T1_VALUE  : TIME := TIME#10s;    END_VAR

CASE cstate OF
    0: IF ((error = TRUE) AND  (TRUE)) THEN cstate := 12; light := TRUE; t1(IN:=0, PT:=T1_VALUE);
        ELSIF ((error = FALSE) AND  (TRUE)) THEN cstate := 6; light := FALSE;
        END_IF;
   43: IF ((error = TRUE) AND  (TRUE)) THEN cstate := 12; light := TRUE; t1(IN:=0, PT:=T1_VALUE);
        ELSIF ((error = FALSE) AND  (TRUE)) THEN cstate := 43; light := FALSE;
        END_IF;
    6: IF ((error = TRUE) AND  (TRUE)) THEN cstate := 12; light := TRUE; t1(IN:=0, PT:=T1_VALUE);
        ELSIF ((error = FALSE) AND  (TRUE)) THEN cstate := 6; light := FALSE;
        END_IF;
  396: IF ((error = TRUE) AND  (TRUE)) THEN cstate := 12; light := TRUE; t1(IN:=0, PT:=T1_VALUE);
        ELSIF ((error = FALSE) AND  (t1.Q = FALSE)) THEN cstate := 396; light := TRUE;
        ELSIF ((error = FALSE) AND  (t1.Q = TRUE)) THEN cstate := 43; light := FALSE;
        END_IF;
   81: IF ((error = TRUE) AND  ( TRUE )) THEN cstate := 12; light := TRUE; t1(IN:=0, PT:=T1_VALUE);
        ELSIF ((error = FALSE) AND  (t1.Q = FALSE)) THEN cstate := 396; light := TRUE;
        ELSIF ((error = FALSE) AND  (t1.Q = TRUE)) THEN cstate := 43; light := FALSE;
        END_IF;
   12: IF ((error = TRUE) AND  (TRUE)) THEN cstate := 12; light := TRUE; t1(IN:=0, PT:=T1_VALUE);
        ELSIF ((error = FALSE) AND  (t1.Q = FALSE)) THEN cstate := 81; light := TRUE;
        ELSIF ((error = FALSE) AND  (t1.Q = TRUE)) THEN cstate := 6; light := FALSE;
        END_IF;
END_CASE;
END_FUNCTION_BLOCK
```

In Table 1 we describe some frequently encountered specification patterns and their translations using IEC 61131-3-like timing constructs. Each of these patterns requires the introduction of a fresh timer variable t1 together with the assumption $\mathbf{G}\,($t1.start $\rightarrow$ $\mathbf{X}\,\mathbf{F}\,$t1.expire$)$ on the environment providing time-outs. These specification patterns, however, are not part of the G4LTL-ST input language, since there is no special support in the synthesis engine for these language constructs, and G4LTL-ST is intended to be used in integrated development frameworks, which usually come with their own specification languages.

3   Abstraction-Refinement Synthesis Loop

The input to the synthesis engine of G4LTL-ST are LTL formulas with non-linear arithmetic constraints with bounded real (or rational) variables, and the workflow of this engine is depicted in Figure 2. Notice, however, that the abstraction-refinement loop in Figure 2 is more general in that it works for any decidable theory Th.

In a preliminary step Abstract simply replaces arithmetic constraints on the inputs with fresh Boolean input variables. The resulting specification therefore is (like the timer abstraction in Section 2) an over-approximation of the behavior of the environment. In our running example in Figure 1 (ignoring line 6, 7), Abstract creates two fresh Boolean variables, say req1 and req2, for the two input constraints $x + y > 3$ and $x^2 + y^2 < \frac{7}{2}$ to obtain the pseudo-Boolean specification

$$\mathbf{G}(\text{req1} \rightarrow \mathbf{X}\,\text{grant1}) \wedge \mathbf{G}(\text{req2} \rightarrow \mathbf{X}\,\text{grant2}) \wedge \mathbf{G}(\neg(\text{grant1} \wedge \text{grant2})) \quad (1)$$

Clearly, this pseudo-Boolean specification with input variables req1 and req2 over-approximates the behavior of the environment, since it does not account for inter-relationships of the arithmetic input constraints.

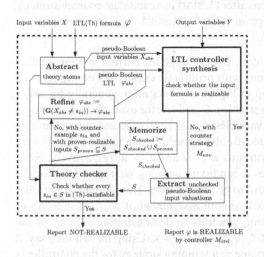

Fig. 2. Abstraction-refinement synthesis loop

In the next step, LTL controller synthesis checks whether or not the pseudo-Boolean LTL formula generated by Abstract is realizable. If the engine is able to realize a winning strategy for the control, say M_{ctrl}, then a controller is synthesized from this strategy. Otherwise, a candidate counter-strategy, say M_{env}, for defeating the controller's purpose is generated.

The pseudo-Boolean specification (1), for example, is unrealizable. A candidate counter-strategy for the environment is given by only using the input (true, true), since, in violation of the mutual exclusion condition (1), the controller is forced to subsequently set both grant1 and grant2 .

The Extract module extracts candidate counter-strategies with fewer pseudo-Boolean input valuations (via a greedy-based method) whose validity are not proven at the theory level. Consequently, the Extract module generates a candidate counter-strategy that only uses (req1, req2) = (true, true) and the input valuations $S = \{(true, true)\}$ are passed to the Theory Checker.

A candidate counter-strategy is a genuine counter-strategy only if all pseudo-Boolean input patterns are satisfiable at the theory level; in these cases the environment wins and Theory Checker reports the un-realizability of the control problem. In our running example, however, the input (true, true) is not satisfiable at the theory level, since the conjunction of the input constraints $x + y > 3$ and $x^2 + y^2 < \frac{7}{2}$ is unsatisfiable for $x, y \in [0, 4]$. G4LTL-ST uses the JBernstein [5] verification engine for discharging quantifier-free verification conditions involving non-linear real arithmetic. In order to avoid repeated processing at the theory level, all satisfiable inputs are memorized.

Unsatisfiable input combinations s_{in} are excluded by Refine. In our running example, the formula $G(\neg(req1 \wedge req2))$ is added as a new assumption on the environment, since the input pair (true, true) has been shown to be unsatisfiable.

$$G(\neg(req1 \wedge req2)) \rightarrow (1) \tag{2}$$

In this way, Refine successively refines the over-approximation of the behavior of the environment. Running the LTL synthesis engine on the refined specification 2 yields a controller: if one of req1 ($x + y > 3$) and req2 ($x^2 + y^2 < \frac{7}{2}$) holds, the controller may grant the corresponding client in the next round, since req1 and req2 do not hold simultaneously.

Refinement of Timer Environments. The refinement of over-approximations of environmental behavior also works for the abstracted timer environments. Recall from Section 2 that the initial abstraction is given by $\mathbf{G}$ (t1.start $\rightarrow$ $\mathbf{X}\,\mathbf{F}$ t1.expire). Assuming, for example, that t1.expire appears two iterations after t1.start in a candidate counter-strategy, one might strengthen this initial assumption with $\mathbf{G}$ (t1.start $\rightarrow$ (($\mathbf{X}$¬t1.expire) $\wedge$ ($\mathbf{XX}$¬t1.expire) $\wedge$ ($\mathbf{XXX}\,\mathbf{F}$ t1.expire))).

Constraints over input and output variables. Even though the current implementation of G4LTL-ST is restricted to specifications with arithmetic constraints on inputs only, the abstraction-refinement synthesis loop in Figure 2 works more generally for arithmetic constraints over input and output variables. Consider, for example, the specification $\mathbf{G}(x > y \rightarrow \mathbf{X}(z > x))$ with input variables $x, y \in [1, 2] \cap \mathbb{R}$ and output variable $z \in [0, 5] \cap \mathbb{R}$. Abstraction yields a pseudo-Boolean specification $\mathbf{G}(\text{in} \rightarrow \mathbf{X}\text{out})$ with in, out fresh input variables for the constraints $x > y$ and $z > x$, respectively. Now, pseudo-Boolean LTL synthesis generates a candidate winning strategy M_{ctrl} for the controller, which simply sets the output out to be always true. The candidate controller M_{ctrl} is realizable if every pseudo-Boolean output assignment of M_{ctrl} is indeed satisfiable on the theory level. This condition amounts to demonstrating validity of the quantified formula $(\forall x \in [1, 2] \cap \mathbb{R}) (\exists z \in [0, 5] \cap \mathbb{R}) z > x$. Using the witness, say, 3 for the existentially quantified output variable z, a winning strategy for the controller is to always set the output z to 3, and the control synthesis problem therefore is realizable.

Otherwise, the candidate controller strategy is not realizable at the theory level, and, for pseudo-Boolean outputs, refinement due to un-realizability of the control synthesis problem is achieved by adding new constraints as *guarantees* to the pseudo-Boolean specification. For example the constraint $\mathbf{G}(\neg(\text{grant1} \wedge \text{grant2}))$ is added to the pseudo-Boolean specification, if pseudo-Boolean outputs grant1 and grant2 are mutually exclusive at the theory level.

In this way, the abstraction-refinement synthesis loop in Figure 2 may handle arbitrary theory constraints on input and output variables as long as corresponding verification conditions in a first-order theory with one quantifier-alternation can be decided. The implementation of G4LTL-ST could easily be extended in this direction by using, for examples the verification procedure for the exists-forall fragment of non-linear arithmetic as described in [7]. So far we have not yet encountered the need for this extensions, since the PLC case studies currently available to us are restricted to Boolean outputs.

4   Assumption Generation

An unrealizable control synthesis problem can often be made realizable by restricting the capabilities of the input environment in a suitable way. In our case studies from the manufacturing domain, for example, suitable restrictions on the arrival rate of workpieces were often helpful. G4LTL-ST supports the generation of these assumptions from a set of given templates. For example, instantiations of the template $\mathbf{G}(?a \rightarrow (\mathbf{X}(\neg?a\,\mathbf{U}\,?b)))$, where ?a and ?b are meta-variables for inputs, disallows successive arrivals of an input signal ?a. For a pre-specified set of templates, G4LTL-ST performs a heuristic match of the meta-variables with input variables by analyzing possible ways of the environment to defeat the control specification.

Table 2. Experimental result based on the predefined unroll depth (3) of **G4LTL-ST**. Execution time annotated with "(comp)" denotes that the value is reported by the compositional synthesis engine.

# Example (synthesis)	Timer(T)/ Data(d)	lines of spec	Synthesis Time	Lines of ST
Ex1	T, D	9	1.598s (comp)	110
Ex2	T	13	0.691s	148
Ex3	T	9	0.303s	80
Ex4	T	13	21s	1374
Ex5	T	11	0.678s (comp)	210
Ex6	-	7	0.446s	41
Ex7	D	8	17s	43
Ex8	T	8	0.397s (comp)	653
Ex9	abstract D,T	3 + model ($<$ 200 loc)	1.55s	550
Ex10	abstract D,T	3 + model ($<$ 200 loc)	3.344s	229
Ex11	abstract D,T	3 + model ($<$ 200 loc)	0.075s	105

# Example (Assump. gen)	# Learned Assump.	Time of Learning
Ex1	1	0.127s
Ex2	1	0.452s
Ex3	1	3.486s
Ex4	4	22s (DFS)
Ex5	1	2.107s
Ex6	1	1.046s
Ex7	1	0.154
Ex8	1	2.877
Ex9	1	8.318

The underlying LTL synthesis engine performs bounded unroll [15] of the negated property to safety games. Therefore, whenever the controller can not win the safety game, there exists an environment strategy which can be expanded as a finite tree, whose leaves are matched with the risk states of the game. Then, the following three steps are performed successively:

- *Extract* a longest path from the source to the leaf. Intuitively, this path represents a scenario where the controller endeavors to resist losing the game (without intentionally losing the game). For example, assume for such a longest path, that the environment uses $(a)(\neg a)(\neg a)(\neg a)$ to win the safety game.
- *Generalize* the longest path. Select from the set of templates one candidate which can *fit* the path in terms of generalization. For example, the path above may be generalized as **FG**$\neg$a. For every such template, the current implementation of **G4LTL-ST** defines a unique generalization function.
- *Resynthesize* the controller based on the newly introduced template. For example, given ϕ as the original specification, the new specification will be $(\neg\textbf{FG}\neg a) \rightarrow \phi$, which is equivalent to $(\textbf{GF}a) \rightarrow \phi$. Therefore, the path is generalized as an assumption stating that a should appear infinitely often.

If this process fails to synthesize a controller, then new assumptions are added to further constrain the environment behavior. When the number of total assumptions reaches a pre-defined threshold but no controller is generated, the engine stops and reports its inability to decide the given controller synthesis problem.

5   Outlook

The synthesis engine of **G4LTL-ST** has been evaluated on a number of simple automation examples extracted both from public sources and from ABB internal projects[1]. This synthesized function block can readily be passed to industry-standard PLC development tools for connecting function blocks with concrete field device signals inside the main program to demonstrate desired behavior. The evaluation results in Table 2 demonstrate that, despite the underlying complexity of the LTL synthesis, **G4LTL-ST** can still

---

[1] Due to space limits, short descriptions of the case studies have been moved to the extended version [6].

provide a practical alternative to the prevailing low-level encodings of PLC programs, whose block size are (commonly) within 1000 LOC. This is due to the fact that many modules are decomposed to only process a small amount of I/Os. For small sized I/Os, the abstraction of timers and data in G4LTL-ST together with counter-strategy-based lazy refinement are particularly effective in fighting the state explosion problem, since unnecessary unrolling (for timing) and bit-blasting (for data) are avoided. Data analysis is also effective when no precise (or imprecise) environment model is provided, as is commonly the case in industrial automation scenarios.

Mechanisms such as assumption generation are essential for the wide-spread deployment of G4LTL-ST in industry, since they provide feedback to the designer in the language of the problem domain. Extensive field tests, however, are needed for calibrating assumption generation in practice. Moreover, a targeted front-end language for high-level temporal specification of typical control problems for (networks of) PLCs needs to be developed [11].

References

1. International Electrotechnical Commission IEC 61131-3 Ed. 3.0: Programmable Controllers – Part 3: Programming languages. International Electrotechnical Commission, Geneva, Switzerland (2013)
2. Recommendations for implementing the strategic initiative - INDUSTRIE 4.0. German National Academy of Science and Engineering (AcaTech) (April 2013)
3. Die Deutsche Normungs-Roadmap - INDUSTRIE 4.0. DKE German Commission for Electrical, Electronic & Information Technologies (December 2013)
4. Bohy, A., Bruyère, V., Filiot, E., Jin, N., Raskin, J.-F.: Acacia+, a tool for LTL synthesis. In: Madhusudan, P., Seshia, S.A. (eds.) CAV 2012. LNCS, vol. 7358, pp. 652–657. Springer, Heidelberg (2012)
5. Cheng, C.-H., Ruess, H., Shankar, N.: JBernstein - a validity checker for generalized polynomial constraints. In: Sharygina, N., Veith, H. (eds.) CAV 2013. LNCS, vol. 8044, pp. 656–661. Springer, Heidelberg (2013)
6. Cheng, C.-H., Huang, C.-H., Ruess, H., Stattlemann, S.: G4LTL-ST: Automated Generation of PLC Programs (full version). arXiv:1405.2409 (2014)
7. Cheng, C.-H., Shankar, N., Ruess, H., Bensalem, S.: EFSMT: A Logical Framework for Cyber-Physical Systems. arXiv:1306.3456 (2013)
8. Clarke, E., Grumberg, O., Jha, S., Lu, Y., Veith, H.: Counterexample-guided abstraction refinement. In: Emerson, E.A., Sistla, A.P. (eds.) CAV 2000. LNCS, vol. 1855, pp. 154–169. Springer, Heidelberg (2000)
9. Jobstmann, B., Bloem, R.: Optimizations for LTL synthesis. In: FMCAD, pp. 117–124. IEEE (2006)
10. Henzinger, T.A., Jhala, R., Majumdar, R.: Counterexample-Guided Control. In: Baeten, J.C.M., Lenstra, J.K., Parrow, J., Woeginger, G.J. (eds.) ICALP 2003. LNCS, vol. 2719, pp. 886–902. Springer, Heidelberg (2003)
11. Ljungkrantz, O., Akesson, K., Fabian, M., Yuan, C.: Formal Specification and Verification of Industrial Control Logic Components. IEEE Tran. on Automation Science and Engineering 7(3), 538–548 (2010)

12. Nieuwenhuis, R., Oliveras, A., Tinelli, C.: Abstract DPLL and abstract DPLL modulo theories. In: Baader, F., Voronkov, A. (eds.) LPAR 2004. LNCS (LNAI), vol. 3452, pp. 36–50. Springer, Heidelberg (2005)
13. Pnueli, A., Rosner, R.: On the synthesis of a reactive module. In: POPL, pp. 179–190. ACM (1989)
14. Pnueli, A.: The temporal logic of programs. In: FOCS, pp. 46–57. IEEE (1977)
15. Schewe, S., Finkbeiner, B.: Bounded synthesis. In: Namjoshi, K.S., Yoneda, T., Higashino, T., Okamura, Y. (eds.) ATVA 2007. LNCS, vol. 4762, pp. 474–488. Springer, Heidelberg (2007)

Automatic Atomicity Verification for Clients of Concurrent Data Structures

Mohsen Lesani, Todd Millstein, and Jens Palsberg

University of California, Los Angeles
{lesani,todd,palsberg}@cs.ucla.edu

Abstract. Mainstream programming languages offer libraries of concurrent data structures. Each method call on a concurrent data structure appears to take effect atomically. However, clients of such data structures often require stronger guarantees. For instance, a histogram class that is implemented using a concurrent map may require a method to atomically increment a histogram bar, but its implementation requires multiple calls to the map and hence is not atomic by default. Indeed, prior work has shown that atomicity errors in clients of concurrent data structures occur frequently in production code.

We present an automatic and modular verification technique for clients of concurrent data structures. We define a novel sufficient condition for atomicity of clients called condensability. We present a tool called Snowflake that generates proof obligations for condensability of Java client methods and discharges them using an off-the-shelf SMT solver. We applied Snowflake to an existing suite of client methods from several open-source applications. It successfully verified 76.9% of the atomic methods without any change and verified the rest of them with small code refactoring and/or annotations.

1 Introduction

Many modern programming languages provide libraries of *concurrent data structures* (e.g., the `java.util.concurrent` package and Intel Threading Building Blocks library) that are widely used. A concurrent data structure is an object that satisfies the well-known correctness criterion called *linearizability* [19]. At a high level, this property ensures that the operations of the data structure can be invoked concurrently from multiple threads while still appearing to execute atomically and behaving according to the sequential specification of the data structure. The linearizability guarantee relieves the programmer from complex reasoning about possible interference among data-structure methods and removes the need to add explicit synchronization.

While the linearizability guarantee is very useful, it only pertains to an *individual* operation on the data structure. In practice, clients of a concurrent data structure may require stronger guarantees. For example, consider the `AtomicMap` class in Figure 1, which is a subset of Java's `ConcurrentHashMap` class and provides atomic methods for getting, putting and removing elements, as well as

A. Biere and R. Bloem (Eds.): CAV 2014, LNCS 8559, pp. 550–567, 2014.
© Springer International Publishing Switzerland 2014

```
1  class AtomicMap<K, V> { // data structure
2    V get(K k) { /*..*/ }
3    void put(K k, V v) { /*..*/ }
4    V remove(K k) { /*..*/ }
5    V putIfAbsent(K k, V v) { /*..*/ }
6    boolean replace(K k, V ov, V nv) { /*..*/ }
7  }
```

```
1  class AtomicHistogram<K> { // client
2    private AtomicMap<K, Integer> m;
3
4    V get(K k) {
5      return m.get(k);
6    }
7
8    Integer inc(K key) {
9      while (true) {
10       Integer i = m.get(key);
11       if (i == null) {
12         Integer r = m.putIfAbsent(key, 1); ⊛
13         if (r == null)
14           return 1;
15       } else {
16         Integer ni = i + 1;
17         boolean b = m.replace(key, i, ni); ⊛
18         if (b)
19           return ni;
20  } } } }
```

Fig. 1. The classes AtomicMap and AtomicHistogram

conditional versions of put: putIfAbsent only performs the put if the given key is currently unmapped, and replace only performs the put if the given key is currently mapped to a given value. As Figure 1 shows, a programmer may use the AtomicMap class to implement the client AtomicHistogram class, which supports the method inc to increment one bar of the histogram. The figure shows a correct implementation of atomic increment [30], which is subtle and error prone. For example, a naive implementation of this client method, which simply gets the current value and puts back an incremented value, is not atomic and can easily violate the sequential specification in the presence of multiple threads. In this paper, we present an automatic and modular technique for verification of the atomicity of clients of concurrent data structures, such as our histogram class.

Prior work on automatic atomicity verification leverages Lipton's notion of *moverness* [23]. Moverness can be applied to verify conflict-serializability of transactions [4] and atomicity of both data-structure and client methods [14, 15, 35].

The main idea is to prove that individual operations in a method M can commute with operations from other threads, in such a way that M's operations can be always "moved" to be contiguous in any execution. Moverness has been successfully applied to automatically check atomicity of concurrent code that uses locks for synchronization [14, 15] and was later extended to support non-blocking synchronization by paired load-link (LL) and store-conditional (SC) instructions [35]. Unfortunately, the ABA problem [27] makes moverness too strong a requirement to prove atomicity of non-blocking algorithms that employ compare-and-swap (CAS) [35]. Similarly, as we will show in the next section, the ABA problem makes the moverness requirement too strong to prove the atomicity of the increment method in Figure 1.

Instead, we define and check a novel sufficient condition for atomicity called *condensability*. Our approach handles client classes that use a single concurrent data structure in their implementation. Consider a client method M that uses an atomic object o. Intuitively, a call to M in a concurrent execution e is condensable if there is a method call m on o in M's execution such that (a) either m does not modify the state of o or it is the only method call in M's execution that does so; and (b) the sequential execution of the entire method M at the place of m in e results in the same final state of o as m and the same return value as the original execution of M. A client object is condensable if every execution of every method of it is condensable. The notion of condensability is similar in spirit to the idea of moverness, but instead of moving individual operations in a method, condensability allows relocating the entire method at once. Condensability targets a common class of clients that access a single concurrent data structure and provides a modular verification technique for atomicity of this class of clients. Specifically, condensability can be separately checked for each method, so changes to one method do not affect the condensability of other methods. In Section 3, we formalize condensability and prove that condensability implies atomicity.

We demonstrate the applicability of condensability with an automatic checking tool for Java called Snowflake. The tool takes as input a client class C along with a sequential specification for each of the methods in the concurrent data structure that C employs. As we will show later, such specifications are typically quite simple and are obtainable from documentation of the data structures. For each method in C, Snowflake generates a set of proof obligations that are sufficient for condensability and provides them to the Z3 SMT solver [8]. If the proof obligations are discharged, the method is verified to be atomic.

We applied Snowflake to a suite of open-source benchmarks that was used to evaluate prior work by others [30]. Snowflake succeeds in verifying atomicity of 76.9% of the atomic methods and rejecting all non-atomic methods in the benchmark suite. In addition, Snowflake can verify the remaining 23.1% of the atomic methods after some manual code refactoring.

Related Work. Shacham et al. [30] provide a tool called Colt for finding atomicity bugs in client methods of concurrent data structures by heuristically executing such code with interference from other threads. They reported many bugs in a variety of real-world applications. Tools like Colt identify actual executions with atomicity bugs and as such have no false positives, but they cannot prove the absence of such errors.

In later work, Shacham and colleagues have explored conditions on client methods that allow for exhaustive testing for interference, thereby supporting atomicity verification. Shacham [29] shows that a *data-independent* client method, whose control flow does not depend on the specific data values used, need only be tested using a bounded number of data values in order to cover all possible atomicity violations. Zomer et al. [37] show that an *encapsulated* client method, whose only shared state is the underlying data structure, need only be tested using two threads and one occurrence of the client method. They also provide a condition called *composition closure* on the underlying data structure that allows each client method to be tested separately for interference. Our work requires client methods to be encapsulated and to support additional restrictions but does not restrict the data structure itself; indeed maps are not composition closed. Our restrictions allow us to verify atomicity via a few simple and modular condensability conditions on each method.

Work on atomicity refinement provides sound rules for extending the scope of atomic blocks [12, 20]. Some refinement rules, such as Jonsson's *absorption rule* [20], are similar in spirit to our requirements for condensability. However, the refinement rules must be applied step by step in order to eventually produce a single atomic block, while condensability directly compares an interleaved execution to a sequential version.

Others have ensured atomicity for clients of linearizable data structures by automatically inserting additional synchronization [5, 16, 18]. Such approaches provide strong atomicity guarantees by construction but incur synchronization overheads that our approach avoids.

In addition to prior work on atomicity, condensability is closely related to the notion of *linearization points* in linearizability proofs, which are points where each method can be seen to atomically satisfy its sequential specification. Linearizability is a strong property that combines atomicity with functional correctness. Therefore, most prior works on linearizability either do not support complete automation [9, 10, 22, 26, 28, 31] or search for linearizability bugs in a bounded number of threads [6, 7, 24, 33, 34, 36]. Notable exceptions are techniques based on abstract interpretation [2, 3, 11, 32] and observer automata [1]. The first approach [2, 3, 11, 32] instruments each linearization point with the surrounding method's specification and relies on abstract interpretation of the instrumented class to check that the implementation and specification methods always return the same value in the context of the most general client. The second approach [1] instruments each method to generate an *abstract event* whenever a linearization point is passed, captures the specification as an observer automata on the abstract events, and checks the safety of the cross-product of the program and the observer. These approaches are more general than ours and can verify low-level concurrent data structures, but they require explicit reasoning about all possible interactions among the methods of the data structure. Condensability imposes

$$((v, m) = m.get(k)) \Rightarrow (v = m(k) \wedge m' = m)$$

$$(m' = m.put(k, v)') \Rightarrow (m' = m[k \mapsto v])$$

$$(m', v') = m.putIfAbsent(k, v) \Rightarrow \\ v' = m(k) \wedge \\ ((m(k) = null) \wedge (m' = m[k \mapsto v])) \vee \\ (\neg(m(k) = null) \wedge (m = m'))$$

Fig. 2. Axioms for get, put and putIfAbsent methods

stronger requirements but in turn enables separate verification of methods of a client class. Finally, a modular set of sufficient conditions for linearizability has been proposed specifically for concurrent queues [17].

2 Example

We now illustrate our approach for automatically verifying atomicity for clients of concurrent data structures through the AtomicHistogram example in Figure 1. Our approach verifies the atomicity of each method in the class in isolation; we will illustrate how it works on the inc method.

Specifications. We assume that AtomicMap is atomic and that we are given specifications for its methods. Figure 2 depicts the axioms characterizing the behavior of the get, put and putIfAbsent methods of a map. The specifications are first-order logic assertions with equality and uninterpreted functions. We model each method as returning a pair of a return value (when the return type is not void) and a new map, and we model the abstract map state as a function from each key in the map to its value and from each key not in the map to null. We use $m[k \mapsto v]$ to denote the state that maps the key k to the value v and otherwise agrees with the map state m. The axiom for the putIfAbsent method states that the mapping of the input key k is updated to the input value v if the previous mapping of k is null, and otherwise the map state remains unchanged. The return value of putIfAbsent is always the old mapping for the key k.

Purity. To show that the inc method in AtomicHistogram is atomic, we will show that every possible execution of the method is condensable. Due to the while loop there are an unbounded number of execution paths. We address this challenge by leveraging the notion of *purity* from past work on atomicity [13, 35]. At a high level, a loop is pure if only the last iteration of the loop has externally observable effects. If a loop is pure then only the last iteration needs to be considered when reasoning about atomicity, thereby reducing verification of atomicity to loop-free programs. Our approach requires and checks that each loop in a method is pure.

The loop in inc in Figure 1 is pure: each loop iteration attempts to write to the map (via either putIfAbsent or replace) and only continues to iterate if the write fails to happen (putIfAbsent returns a non-null value or replace returns

```
1 // First path
2 Integer i = m.get(key);
3 assume (i == null);
4 Integer r = m.putIfAbsent(key, 1); ⊛
5 assume (r == null);
6 return 1;
```

```
1 // Second path
2 Integer i = m.get(key);
3 assume (!(i == null));
4 Integer ni = i + 1;
5 Boolean b = m.replace(key, i, ni); ⊛
6 assume (b);
7 return ni;
```

Fig. 3. The two loop-free paths of `inc`

false). Given the specifications for the map operations shown above, it is easy to automatically verify the purity of this loop. Since the loop is pure, henceforth we need only consider the two loop-free execution paths shown in Figure 3. We use an `assume` statement to record the choices made at each conditional.

Condensability. Consider the first path shown in Figure 3. Unfortunately, moverness cannot prove the atomicity of the path. Though both of the calls to `get` and `putIfAbsent` indicate that the key is not in the map, other threads can add and then remove the key between `get` and `putIfAbsent`, causing an ABA problem [27]. Using moverness would require that either `get` be a *right mover*, commuting with any subsequent operation from another thread, or that `putIfAbsent` be a *left mover*, commuting with any preceding operation from another thread. However the `get` call does not commute with a subsequent operation from another thread that `put`s the same key into the map. Similarly the `putIfAbsent` call does not commute with a preceding operation from another thread that removes the same key from the map. Although the path is atomic, the moverness requirement is too strong to prove it.

Instead, given an interleaved execution of the client method, condensability identifies a method call on the base atomic object called the *condensation point* and attempts to prove that the interleaved execution of the client method can be replaced by a sequential execution of the client method at the condensation point, which we call the *condensed execution*. We heuristically identify the condensation point as a method call that mutates the state of the underlying concurrent data structure. If the heuristic fails, the static analysis can be repeated for each method call in the path. The heuristically identified condensation points are marked with ⊛ in the paths of Figure 3.

Consider an arbitrary execution X of a concurrent program on a histogram h that includes the first path of the `inc` method. We assume the methods of m are atomic but make no other atomicity assumptions. Since m is atomic, there is some execution S of the program such that S is *equivalent* to X for m (i.e. the execution S contains the same method calls and return values on m as X) and

S is *sequential* for m (i.e. each method call on m in S is immediately followed by its associated return). Therefore, the portion of S that includes the execution of the first path has the following form:

```
1 // m0
2 Integer i = m.get(key);
3 // m1
4 // Interleaving (other method calls on m)
5 // m2
6 Integer r = m.putIfAbsent(key, 1); ⊛
7 // m3
```

Here, the states m0 and m1 denote the pre-state and post-state of the method call m.get(key), and m2 and m3 denote the pre-state and post-state of the method call m.putIfAbsent(key, 1) for m in S. While S is sequential for the map m, it is not necessarily sequential for the histogram h due to the interleaving of other method calls from other threads between the calls to get and putIfAbsent.

To prove the condensability of this execution of inc, we must prove the following conditions:

1. None of the method calls other than the condensation method call mutate the state of m.
2. Consider a *condensed* execution of inc from the condensation point, that is, a sequential execution of inc starting from the state m2 for the map m.

   ```
   1 // m2
   2 Integer result = h.inc(key);
   3 // m3'
   ```

   2.1. The state of the map after the condensed execution should be the same as the post-state of the condensation method call.
   2.2. The two calls to inc should have the same return value.

The first condition above requires us to prove that m0 = m1, which is easily discharged given our earlier specification for get. The second condition requires us to reason about the execution path taken by the condensed execution of inc which in general can differ from the path taken in the original execution. Since in the original execution, the call to putIfAbsent from state m2 returns null, it is easily seen using the specifications for get and putIfAbsent that the condensed execution of inc will look as follows:

```
1 // m2
2 Integer i' = m.get(key);
3 // m2
4 Integer r' = m.putIfAbsent(key, 1);
5 // m3'
6 return 1;
```

Specifically, the call to get will return null, so the "then" branch at line 11 in inc will be executed. Therefore putIfAbsent is called from the same state m2 as in the original execution, so the (assumed) determinism of putIfAbsent implies that m3 = m3', discharging condition 2.1. Finally, condition 2.2 is trivial in this case, since both executions of inc end with the statement return 1.

A similar analysis can be done to show that the second path in Figure 3 is also condensable, and hence that inc is condensable. Note that this analysis is completely *modular*: the condensability of inc can be proven without having to explicitly enumerate the possible interactions with the other methods in the histogram class, or even to know the full set of such methods.

If each method in the histogram is condensable, then we say that the histogram itself is condensable. In the next section we formalize the notion of condensability and show that condensability implies atomicity.

3   Atomicity and Condensability

In this section, we first present some preliminary definitions and formalize the standard notion of atomicity. Then we define condensability and state our main theorem, that condensability implies atomicity.

3.1   Executions and Atomicity

Method Calls and Events. Let l, o, n, T, and v denote a label, an object, a method name, a thread and a value. Let $inv(l \triangleright o.n_T(v))$ denote an invocation event of a method call labeled l by thread T that calls the method n on the object o with the argument v. Let $ret(l \triangleright v)$ denote a response event of the method call labeled l that returns v.

Operations on event sequences. Let E and E' be event sequences. For a thread T, we use $E|T$ to denote the subsequence of all events of T in E. For an object o, we use $E|o$ to denote the subsequence of all events of o in E.

Executions. An *execution* X is a sequence of events where each invocation event has a unique label and every thread T is well-formed in X (i.e. $X|T$ is an alternating sequence of invocations and responses, with each pair of an invocation and response having the same label). We say label l is in X and write $l \in X$ if there is an invocation event with label l in X. Let $Labels(X)$ denote the set of labels in X. The functions iEv and rEv on $Labels(X)$ map a label to the invocation and the response events associated with the label.

An execution X is *equivalent* to an execution X' if one is a permutation of the other one; that is, only the events are reordered but the components of the events (including the argument and return values) are preserved.

Real-time relations. For an execution X, we define the real-time relations $\prec_X$, and $\preceq_X$ on $Labels(X)$ as follows: $l_1 \prec_X l_2$ if and only if $rEv(l_1)$ precedes $iEv(l_2)$ in X, and $l_1 \preceq_X l_2$ if and only if $l_1 \prec_X l_2 \vee l_1 = l_2$.

An execution X is sequential iff $\forall l, l' \in X : l \preceq_X l' \vee l' \preceq_X l$.

Definition 1 (Atomicity). *An execution X of a program p is* atomic *for an object o if and only if there exists an execution S of p (called the* justifying *execution of X for o) such that*

- $S|o$ is sequential,
- $S|o$ is equivalent to $X|o$, and
- $S|o$ is real-time-preserving i.e. $\prec_{X|o} \subseteq \prec_{S|o}$.[1]

An object o is atomic iff every execution of every program is atomic for o.

Atomicity considers sequential executions on the object as justifying executions. On the other hand, linearizability requires the justifying execution to be a member of a pre-defined sequential specification for the object. In other words, an atomic object is linearizable with respect to its sequential executions.

3.2   Condensability

Now we can define condensable objects and state our condensability theorem.

A method call on an object o is an *accessor* if it does not change the state of o, and otherwise the method is a *mutator*. For example, a call to `putIfAbsent` is a mutator if it returns `null` and is an accessor otherwise. We say that an object c *composes* object o if the only shared object in the implementation of c is o; any other object accessed by methods of c is either local or thread-local.

The following definition formalizes the notion of condensability that we informally described in the previous section.

Definition 2 (Condensable). *Consider an object c that composes an atomic object o. A method m of c is condensable if and only if for every execution X and justifying execution S of X for o, and for every execution e of m in S, there exists a method call $\mathcal{P}(e)$ on o in e such that*

1. *All the method calls on o in e other than $\mathcal{P}(e)$ are accessors.*
2. *Let s be the sequential execution of m with the same arguments as in e and the same pre-state for o as $\mathcal{P}(e)$ in S,*
   2.1. *s results in the same post-state for o as $\mathcal{P}(e)$ in S, and*
   2.2. *s results in the same return value as e.*

The method call $\mathcal{P}(e)$ is called the condensation point and the execution s is called the condensed execution. An object is condensable if and only if all of its methods are condensable.

Note that the condensed execution s of m may take a different path from the original execution e.

A notable property of the above definition is that the condensability of a method is independent of that of other methods. This independence supports modular verification of condensability for each method of an object.

The following theorem states our main result.

Theorem 1 (Condensability). *Every condensable object is atomic.*

---

[1] Real-time-preservation is often implicitly assumed.

Please see the technical report [21] for the proof. Let us intuitively explain why the condensability conditions are sufficient for atomicity. Consider an arbitrary execution X of a program on c. As o is atomic, there is a justifying execution S of X for the atomicity of o. Our goal is to produce a justifying execution S' for the atomicity of c. The idea is to construct the execution S' from S as follows: every execution of a method call on c is removed from S and replaced by its condensed execution at its condensation point.

By construction, no two method calls on c interleave in S'; thus, $S'|c$ is sequential. To prove that S' is real-time-preserving for c, we need to show that if a method call m_1 on c with execution e_1 is before a method call m_2 on c with execution e_2 in X, then m_1 is before m_2 in S'. As e_1 is before e_2 in X, $\mathcal{P}(e_1)$ is before $\mathcal{P}(e_2)$ in X. We have that S is real-time-preserving for o thus, as $\mathcal{P}(e_1)$ is before $\mathcal{P}(e_2)$ in X, we have that $\mathcal{P}(e_1)$ is before $\mathcal{P}(e_2)$ in S as well. Thus, by the construction of S', m_1 is before m_2 in S'.

Therefore, it remains to show that S' is an execution of the program that is equivalent to X. Consider two consecutive condensed executions s_1 and s_2 in S' that replace two condensation methods calls m_1 and m_2 in S. To prove that S' is an execution of the program, we should show that the state of o in the post-state of s_1 is equal to the state of o that is assumed in the pre-state of s_2. This fact is derived from the following three equalities. First, by condition 2.1 above the state of o in the post-state of s_1 is equal to the state of o in the post-state of m_1. Second, since there is no condensation method call between m_1 and m_2 and by condition 1 all the other method calls on o are accessors, the state of o in the post-state of m_1 is equal to the the state of o in the pre-state of m_2. Third, by construction the state of o in the pre-state of s_2 is equal to the state of o in the pre-state of m_2. Finally, to complete the proof that S' is equivalent to S we leverage condition 2.2 above, which requires each call in S' to have the same return value as its counterpart in X.

4   Checking Condensability

In this section, we show how condensability of a loop-free client method can be represented as constraints and automatically checked. We assume that all method calls in the client method are on the underlying atomic data structure. We will relax this assumption in the next section.

Consider a loop-free client method with the input parameter p. Let o be the underlying atomic data structure. Let $\overline{P}$ be the set of paths of the method. Let P_i denote the ith path. Let $|P|$ denote the size of P. Let us denote a path with the triple $(b, \overline{m}, r)$ where b is the conjunction of the branch conditions of the path, $\overline{m}$ is the sequence of method calls $y = o.n(x)$ of the path and r is the returned variable of the path. In the sequence of method calls $\overline{m}$, let m_k denote the kth method call. Let $|\overline{m}|$ denote the size of $\overline{m}$. See the technical report [21] for how we compute the paths.

Assumptions:

Let $P_i = (b, \overline{m}, r)$:

1. $\quad b$

Forall $k: 0 \leq k < |\overline{m}|$

Let $m_k = (y = o.n(x))$:

2. $\quad (o_{2*k+1}, y) = o_{2*k}.n(x)$

Forall $j: 0 \leq j < |P|$

Let $P_j = (b^j, \overline{m^j}, r^j)$:

3. $\quad p^j = p \wedge$

4. $\quad o_0^j = o_{2*l}$

Forall $k: 0 \leq k < |\overline{m^j}|$

Let $m_k = (y = o.n(x))$:

5. $\quad (o_{k+1}^j, y^j) = o_k^j.n(x^j)$

6. $\quad b^j \Rightarrow$

$post = o_{\overline{|m^j|}}^j \wedge$

$ret = r^j$

Obligations:

Let $P_i = (b, \overline{m}, r)$:

Forall $k: 0 \leq k < |\overline{m}|, k \neq l$

7. $\quad o_{2*k} = o_{2*k+1} \wedge$

8. $\quad post = o_{2*l+1} \wedge$

9. $\quad ret = r$

p : Input parameter

x, y, r, ret : Variable

$o, post$: Object state variable

b : Condition

Fig. 4. Checking Condensability of the ith path at its lth method call

We check the condensability of each path separately. Let us focus on the ith path $P_i = (b, \overline{m}, r)$. The condensation point of a path is one of its method calls. Let us consider the condensability of the ith path at its lth method call. We want to generate assumptions and obligations that verify that for every execution X and justifying execution S of X for o, for every execution of the ith path in S, the method call m_l is the condensation point. We consider an arbitrary execution X and an arbitrary justifying execution S of X for o. We assume that the ith path is executed in S. The set of assumptions and obligations to check the condensability of the ith path at the lth method call is depicted in Figure 4. We describe each of them in turn.

To indicate that the ith path is executed in S, we assert the branch conditions of the path (line 1) and assert that each method call on the path is executed (line 2). The assertion $(o_2, y) = o_1.n(x)$ denotes a method call n on o with pre-state o_1 and argument x that results in post-state o_2 and return value y. The pre-state and post-state variables of the kth method are o_{2*k} and o_{2*k+1} respectively. Note that due to arbitrary interleaving with other threads, the method calls of the path are not necessarily adjacent in S. Therefore, the post-state variable o_{2*k+1} of the kth method call is different from the pre-state variable $o_{2*(k+1)}$ of the $(k+1)$th method call in the path.

Next, we represent the condensed execution s of the client method at the condensation point. The condensed execution could take any of the possible paths through the client method, so we must consider all of them. The states and variables of each path are superscripted with the index of the path, so that they do not conflict with one another. Consider one such path P_j. First we assert that the input parameter to the condensed execution is equal to the input value of the original method execution (line 3). Next we assert that the pre-state of the condensed execution o_0^j is equal to the pre-state of the condensation point o_{2*l} (recall that the condensation point is the lth method call in the original path) (line 4). Finally the method calls of the condensed execution are asserted (line 5). Note that since the condensed execution s is sequential, the post-state of each method call is the same as the pre-state of the subsequent method call.

Next, we identify which path is actually taken by the condensed execution. Specifically, the path taken is the unique path whose branch conditions are satisfied. Therefore, line 6 has the effect of equating *post* to the post-state of the condensed execution and *ret* to the return value of the condensed execution.

Finally, we present the proof obligations for condensability of the ith path. All the method calls in the ith path other than the condensation point must be accessors i.e., their pre and post-states must be equal (line 7). The post-state of the condensed execution path *post* must be equal to the post-state of the condensation method call o_{2*l+1} in the ith path (line 8). The return value of the condensed execution *ret* must equal the return value of the ith path (line 9).

As an example, we present the constraints that each line of Figure 4 generates for the first path of the inc method in Figure 3. Line 1 generates $i = null \land r = null$. Line 2 generates $(m_1, i) = get(m_0, key)$ and $(m_3, r) = putIfAbsent(m_2, key, 1)$. For the first path of the inc method, line 3 generates $key^0 = key$, line 4 generates $m_0^0 = m_2$, line 5 generates $(m_1^0, i^0) = get(m_0^0, key^0)$ and $(m_2^0, r^0) = putIfAbsent(m_1^0, key^0, 1)$, and line 6 generates $(i^0 = null \land r^0 = null) \Rightarrow (post = m_2^0 \land ret = r^0)$. Similar constraints are generated for the second path. The proof obligations are as follows: Line 7 generates $m_0 = m_1$. Lines 8 and 9 generate $post = m_3$ and $ret = r$.

Note that in Figure 4, the universal quantification can be expanded. Therefore, the assumptions and proof obligations are quantifier free formulas that an SMT solver can discharge automatically.

5   Snowflake

Now we present our tool called Snowflake that automatically verifies condensability of Java methods.

User Input. The user must provide Snowflake with the client method to check along with the axioms that characterize the methods of the data structure used by the client method. The user also specifies the variable/field in the client code that holds the underlying data structure object with the `BaseObject` Java annotation. Finally, Snowflake supports optional annotations to declare that a certain method call in the client method is *functional*, meaning that the call is side-effect-free and that its return value is solely a function of the states of the given receiver object and arguments. A variation on this annotation declares a method call to be *argument-functional*, which is identical except that the method's return value does not depend on the receiver object's state. These annotations allow Snowflake to verify condensability modularly, without having to recursively analyze calls to auxiliary methods in the given client method.

We presented the axioms for the `get`, `put`, and `putIfAbsent` methods of the atomic map in Figure 2. The documentation of current data structures typically presents a pseudocode specification for the *conditional* atomic methods in terms of the more basic methods. For example, the sequential specification of `putIfAbsent` in terms of `get` and `put` methods is depicted in Figure 5. The axiom of `putIfAbsent` in Figure 2 can be derived from its sequential specifications in Figure 5 along with the axioms of the `get` and `put` methods in Figure 2. Our tool has embedded axioms for common methods of Java concurrent map and set data structures and can be extended to support other collection types. We present the full set of axioms in the technical report [21].

```
1  V putIfAbsent(K k, V v) {
2    atomic {
3      V v1 = get(k);
4      if (v1 == null)
5        put(k, v);
6      return v1;
7    }
8  }
```

Fig. 5. The specification of `putIfAbsent` in terms of `get` and `put`

Paths and Purity. As the first step, Snowflake computes the set of paths of the client method. We adopt the terminology of paths from [13] and [35]. A path of a loop is *exceptional* if it is executed as the last iteration of the loop. An exceptional loop path ends in a break or return statement or by the condition of the loop evaluating to false. A path of a loop is *normal* if it is not exceptional. Informally, a loop is pure if its normal paths have no side effects. We conservatively determine a loop to be pure if for every method call $y = o.n(x)$ in a normal path of the loop:

- If o is a shared variable, then the method call is an accessor.
- The variable y is a local variable.
- For all paths in the control flow graph from the end of this normal path to the return of the method call, the next access to y, if any, overwrites it.

For example, the method calls in the normal paths of the `inc` method of Figure 1 satisfy these conditions.

An *exceptional variant* of a method is a copy of the method where each pure loop of the method is replaced by one of its exceptional paths. The exceptional variant of an object is the copy of the object where each method is replaced by all of its exceptional variants. The following theorem is a restatement of Theorem 5.2 from [35]:

Theorem 2. *If the exceptional variant of an object is atomic, then the object is atomic.*

The theorem reduces verification of atomicity for methods with pure loops to loop-free methods.

Given a client method, Snowflake computes the normal paths of the loops and the exceptional variants of the method. It then converts each path to its static single assignment (SSA) form. It first checks the purity of the normal paths using the conditions described above. If the purity of a normal path cannot be verified, the client method is rejected.

We check the condensability of each exceptional variant using the method described in Section 4. We use the following heuristics to guess the condensation point of a path. If there is a call to a method that can mutate the data structure's state in the path, the condensation point is the last such method; otherwise, it is the first method on the data structure in the path. As mentioned before, if the heuristic fails, we can iterate our approach with a different method call as the condensation point.

Now, let us relax the assumption that all the method calls in a path are on the atomic data structure. If there is a method call that is not on the atomic data structure and is not annotated as functional, the client method is rejected because we cannot modularly ensure atomicity. Otherwise, we treat each functional method as an uninterpreted function. Specifically, a functional method call $y = o.n(x)$ is translated to the assertion $y = n(o, x)$. Therefore, as long as the ith path and the condensed execution call such a method with equal arguments, we can prove that they will have equal results. Mathematical operations are treated similarly but we additionally assert axioms such as commutativity and associativity.

Snowflake represents all of the assertions and obligations, along with axioms for the atomic data structure in the SMT2 format and invokes the Z3 SMT solver to check their validity. A method is considered condensable if this process succeeds for each of the method's exceptional variants. An object is considered condensable if each of its methods is found to be condensable.

6 Results

Benchmarks and Platform. We adopt the benchmark suite available from Colt [30]. This benchmark suite is a collection 112 client methods from 51 real-world applications such as Apache Tomcat, Cassandra, and MyFaces Trinidad. We call this collection the Colt suite. It consists of 26 atomic and 86 non-atomic methods.

Snowflake is written in Java, compiled and executed with JDK version 1.7.0.07 and uses Polyglot [25] version 2.5.1 and Z3 version 4.3.2 [8]. The source code of Snowflake is available [21].

Results. Snowflake is sound, so it correctly rejects all 86 non-atomic benchmarks in the Colt suite. Figure 6 shows the result of applying Snowflake to the 26 atomic benchmarks of Colt suite. The pie chart partitions these benchmarks into three groups. Twenty of the benchmarks (76.9%) are proven atomic without any change. The other six benchmarks are rejected as non-atomic by Snowflake.

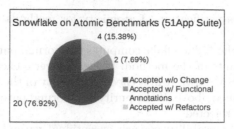

Fig. 6. Evaluation of Snowflake

However, with small modifications they can also be proven to be atomic: two of them simply require the addition of functional annotations on some methods, and the other four benchmarks require some code refactoring. For example, we refactored a block of code that initializes a new object to a method call and annotated the method call as functional. Snowflake verified each of the 26 atomic benchmarks in an average time of 1.45 seconds with a minimum of 1.16 seconds and a maximum of 2.66 seconds. We present a list of benchmarks and the run times of our tool in the accompanying web page [21].

A comparison with Colt is instructive. Since Snowflake is a verification tool, if it accepts a method, it is atomic, but if it rejects the method, it may still be atomic. On the other hand, since Colt is a bug-finding tool, if it rejects a method, it is non-atomic, so it does not find any atomicity errors in the 26 atomic benchmarks of Colt suite. However Colt may not reject non-atomic benchmarks and indeed Colt is not able to find atomicity errors in four of the non-atomic benchmarks. Each of these benchmarks first atomically gets the current value or puts a value for a key and then performs a separate operation on the value. Although each operation is atomic, they are not atomic together.

7 Conclusion

We introduced condensability as a modular verification technique for atomicity of clients of concurrent data structures. We defined the notion of condensability and proved that it implies atomicity. Condensability of an object can be separately checked for each method of the object. We showed how condensability of a method can be represented as constraints and automatically checked. We presented our tool, Snowflake, that automatically verifies condensability and applied it to real-world client methods. In future work, we are interested to generalize our approach to support impure loops as well as multiple writes to the data structure.

Acknowledgements. Thanks to Madan Musuvathi and Erez Petrank for initial discussions on this topic, and to Lorenzo Gomez for contributions to the Snowflake tool.

References

1. Abdulla, P.A., Haziza, F., Holík, L., Jonsson, B., Rezine, A.: An integrated specification and verification technique for highly concurrent data structures. In: Piterman, N., Smolka, S.A. (eds.) TACAS 2013. LNCS, vol. 7795, pp. 324–338. Springer, Heidelberg (2013)
2. Amit, D., Rinetzky, N., Reps, T., Sagiv, M., Yahav, E.: Comparison under abstraction for verifying linearizability. In: Damm, W., Hermanns, H. (eds.) CAV 2007. LNCS, vol. 4590, pp. 477–490. Springer, Heidelberg (2007)
3. Berdine, J., Lev-Ami, T., Manevich, R., Ramalingam, G., Sagiv, M.: Thread quantification for concurrent shape analysis. In: Gupta, A., Malik, S. (eds.) CAV 2008. LNCS, vol. 5123, pp. 399–413. Springer, Heidelberg (2008)
4. Bernstein, P.A., Hadzilacos, V., Goodman, N.: Concurrency control and recovery in database systems, vol. 370. Addison-wesley, New York (1987)
5. Bronson, N.G., Casper, J., Chafi, H., Olukotun, K.: Transactional predication: High-performance concurrent sets and maps for stm. In: Proceedings of the 29th ACM SIGACT-SIGOPS Symposium on Principles of Distributed Computing, PODC 2010, pp. 6–15. ACM, New York (2010)
6. Burckhardt, S., Dern, C., Musuvathi, M., Tan, R.: Line-up: A complete and automatic linearizability checker. In: Proceedings of the 2010 ACM SIGPLAN Conference on Programming Language Design and Implementation, PLDI 2010, pp. 330–340. ACM, New York (2010)
7. Burckhardt, S., Gotsman, A., Musuvathi, M., Yang, H.: Concurrent library correctness on the tso memory model. In: Seidl, H. (ed.) ESOP 2012. LNCS, vol. 7211, pp. 87–107. Springer, Heidelberg (2012)
8. de Moura, L., Bjørner, N.S.: Z3: An efficient smt solver. In: Ramakrishnan, C.R., Rehof, J. (eds.) TACAS 2008. LNCS, vol. 4963, pp. 337–340. Springer, Heidelberg (2008)
9. Derrick, J., Schellhorn, G., Wehrheim, H.: Verifying linearisability with potential linearisation points. In: Butler, M., Schulte, W. (eds.) FM 2011. LNCS, vol. 6664, pp. 323–337. Springer, Heidelberg (2011)
10. Doherty, S., Groves, L., Luchangco, V., Moir, M.: Formal verification of a practical lock-free queue algorithm. In: de Frutos-Escrig, D., Núñez, M. (eds.) FORTE 2004. LNCS, vol. 3235, pp. 97–114. Springer, Heidelberg (2004)
11. Drăgoi, C., Gupta, A., Henzinger, T.A.: Automatic linearizability proofs of concurrent objects with cooperating updates. In: Sharygina, N., Veith, H. (eds.) CAV 2013. LNCS, vol. 8044, pp. 174–190. Springer, Heidelberg (2013)
12. Elmas, T., Qadeer, S., Tasiran, S.: A calculus of atomic actions. In: Proceedings of the 36th Annual ACM SIGPLAN-SIGACT Symposium on Principles of Programming Languages, POPL 2009, pp. 2–15. ACM, New York (2009)
13. Flanagan, C., Freund, S.N., Qadeer, S.: Exploiting purity for atomicity. IEEE Trans. Software Eng. 31(4), 275–291 (2005)
14. Flanagan, C., Qadeer, S.: A type and effect system for atomicity. In: Proceedings of the ACM SIGPLAN 2003 Conference on Programming Language Design and Implementation, PLDI 2003, pp. 338–349. ACM, New York (2003)
15. Flanagan, C., Qadeer, S.: Types for atomicity. In: Proceedings of the 2003 ACM SIGPLAN International Workshop on Types in Languages Design and Implementation, TLDI 2003, pp. 1–12. ACM, New York (2003)
16. Golan-Gueta, G., Ramalingam, G., Sagiv, M., Yahav, E.: Concurrent libraries with foresight. In: Proceedings of the 34th ACM SIGPLAN Conference on Programming

Language Design and Implementation, PLDI 2013, pp. 263–274. ACM, New York (2013)

17. Henzinger, T.A., Sezgin, A., Vafeiadis, V.: Aspect-oriented linearizability proofs. In: D'Argenio, P.R., Melgratti, H. (eds.) CONCUR 2013 – Concurrency Theory. LNCS, vol. 8052, pp. 242–256. Springer, Heidelberg (2013)

18. Herlihy, M., Koskinen, E.: Transactional boosting: A methodology for highly-concurrent transactional objects. In: Proceedings of the 13th ACM SIGPLAN Symposium on Principles and Practice of Parallel Programming, PPoPP 2008, pp. 207–216. ACM, New York (2008)

19. Herlihy, M.P., Wing, J.M.: Linearizability: A correctness condition for concurrent objects. ACM Trans. Program. Lang. Syst. 12(3), 463–492 (1990)

20. Jonsson, B.: Using refinement calculus techniques to prove linearizability. Formal Aspects of Computing 24(4-6), 537–554 (2012)

21. Lesani, M., Millstein, T., Palsberg, J.: Automatic atomicity verification for clients of concurrent data structures, the companion, http://www.cs.ucla.edu/~lesani/companion/cav14, http://fmdb.cs.ucla.edu/tech_reports/default.lasso

22. Liang, H., Feng, X.: Modular verification of linearizability with non-fixed linearization points. In: Proceedings of the 34th ACM SIGPLAN Conference on Programming Language Design and Implementation, PLDI 2013, pp. 459–470. ACM, New York (2013)

23. Lipton, R.J.: Reduction: A method of proving properties of parallel programs. Commun. ACM 18(12), 717–721 (1975)

24. Liu, Y., Chen, W., Liu, Y.A., Sun, J.: Model checking linearizability via refinement. In: Cavalcanti, A., Dams, D.R. (eds.) FM 2009. LNCS, vol. 5850, pp. 321–337. Springer, Heidelberg (2009)

25. Nystrom, N., Clarkson, M.R., Myers, A.C.: Polyglot: An extensible compiler framework for java. In: Hedin, G. (ed.) CC 2003. LNCS, vol. 2622, pp. 138–152. Springer, Heidelberg (2003)

26. O'Hearn, P.W., Rinetzky, N., Vechev, M.T., Yahav, E., Yorsh, G.: Verifying linearizability with hindsight. In: Proceedings of the 29th ACM SIGACT-SIGOPS Symposium on Principles of Distributed Computing, PODC 2010, pp. 85–94. ACM, New York (2010)

27. International Business Machines Corporation. Product Publications. IBM System/370 Extended Architecture: Principles of Operation. IBM Corporation (1983)

28. Schellhorn, G., Wehrheim, H., Derrick, J.: How to prove algorithms linearisable. In: Madhusudan, P., Seshia, S.A. (eds.) CAV 2012. LNCS, vol. 7358, pp. 243–259. Springer, Heidelberg (2012)

29. Shacham, O.: Verifying Atomicity of Composed Concurrent Operations. PhD thesis, Tel Aviv University (2012)

30. Shacham, O., Bronson, N., Aiken, A., Sagiv, M., Vechev, M., Yahav, E.: Testing atomicity of composed concurrent operations. In: Proceedings of the 2011 ACM International Conference on Object Oriented Programming Systems Languages and Applications, OOPSLA 2011, pp. 51–64. ACM, New York (2011)

31. Vafeiadis, V.: Modular fine-grained concurrency verification. Technical Report UCAM-CL-TR-726, University of Cambridge, Computer Laboratory (July 2008)

32. Vafeiadis, V.: Automatically proving linearizability. In: Touili, T., Cook, B., Jackson, P. (eds.) CAV 2010. LNCS, vol. 6174, pp. 450–464. Springer, Heidelberg (2010)

33. Černý, P., Radhakrishna, A., Zufferey, D., Chaudhuri, S., Alur, R.: Model checking of linearizability of concurrent list implementations. In: Touili, T., Cook, B., Jackson, P. (eds.) CAV 2010. LNCS, vol. 6174, pp. 465–479. Springer, Heidelberg (2010)
34. Vechev, M., Yahav, E.: Deriving linearizable fine-grained concurrent objects. In: Proceedings of the 2008 ACM SIGPLAN Conference on Programming Language Design and Implementation, PLDI 2008, pp. 125–135. ACM, New York (2008)
35. Wang, L., Stoller, S.D.: Static analysis of atomicity for programs with non-blocking synchronization. In: Proceedings of the Tenth ACM SIGPLAN Symposium on Principles and Practice of Parallel Programming, PPoPP 2005, pp. 61–71. ACM, New York (2005)
36. Zhang, S.J.: Scalable automatic linearizability checking. In: Proceedings of the 33rd International Conference on Software Engineering, ICSE 2011, pp. 1185–1187. ACM, New York (2011)
37. Zomer, O., Golan-Gueta, G., Ramalingam, G., Sagiv, M.: Checking linearizability of encapsulated extended operations. In: Shao, Z. (ed.) ESOP 2014 (ETAPS). LNCS, vol. 8410, pp. 311–330. Springer, Heidelberg (2014)

Regression-Free Synthesis for Concurrency*

Pavol Černý[1], Thomas A. Henzinger[2], Arjun Radhakrishna[2],
Leonid Ryzhyk[3,4], and Thorsten Tarrach[2]

[1] University of Colorado Boulder
[2] IST Austria
[3] University of Toronto
[4] NICTA, Sydney, Australia*

Abstract. While fixing concurrency bugs, program repair algorithms may introduce new concurrency bugs. We present an algorithm that avoids such regressions. The solution space is given by a set of program transformations we consider in for repair process. These include reordering of instructions within a thread and inserting atomic sections. The new algorithm learns a constraint on the space of candidate solutions, from both positive examples (error-free traces) and counterexamples (error traces). From each counterexample, the algorithm learns a constraint necessary to remove the errors. From each positive examples, it learns a constraint that is necessary in order to prevent the repair from turning the trace into an error trace. We implemented the algorithm and evaluated it on simplified Linux device drivers with known bugs.

1   Introduction

The goal of program synthesis is to simplify the programming task by letting the programmer specify (parts of) her intent declaratively. *Program repair* is the instance of synthesis where we are given both a program and a specification. The specification classifies the execution of the program into *good traces* and *bad traces*. The synthesis task is to automatically modify the program so that the bad traces are removed, while (many of) the good traces are preserved.

In *program repair for concurrency*, we assume that all errors are caused by concurrent execution. We formalize this assumption into a requirement that all preemption-free traces are good. The program may contain concurrency errors that are triggered by more aggressive, preemptive scheduling. Such errors are notoriously difficult to detect and, in extreme cases, may only show up after years of operation of the system. Program repair for concurrency allows the programmer to focus on the preemption-free correctness, while putting the intricate task of proofing the code for concurrency to the synthesis tool.

---

* This research was funded in part by the European Research Council (ERC) under grant agreement 267989 (QUAREM), by the Austrian Science Fund (FWF) project S11402-N23 (RiSE), and by a gift from Intel Corporation. NICTA is funded by the Australian Government through the Department of Communications and the Australian Research Council through the ICT Centre of Excellence Program.

A. Biere and R. Bloem (Eds.): CAV 2014, LNCS 8559, pp. 568–584, 2014.

Program Repair for Concurrency. The specification is provided by assertions placed by the programmer in the code. A trace, which runs without any assertion failure, is called "good", and conversely a trace with an assertion failure is "bad". We assume that the good traces specify the intent of the programmer. A trace is complete if every thread finishes its execution. A trace of a multi-threaded program is preemption-free if a thread is de-scheduled only at preemption-points, i.e., when a thread tries to execute a blocking operation, such as obtaining a lock.

Given a multithreaded program in which all complete preemption-free traces are good, the program repair for concurrency problem is to find a program for which the following two conditions hold: (a) all bad traces of the original program are removed; and (b) all the complete preemption-free traces are preserved. We further extend this problem statement by saying that if not all preemption-free traces are good, but all complete sequential traces are good, then we need to find a program such that (a) holds, and all complete sequential traces are preserved.

Regression-free Algorithms. Let us consider a trace-based algorithm for program repair, that is, an iterative algorithm that in each iteration is given a trace (good or bad) of the program-under-repair, and produces a new program based on the traces seen. We say that such an algorithm is *regression-free* if after every iteration, we have that: first, all bad traces examined so far are removed, and second, all good traces examined so far are not turned into bad traces of the new program. (Of course, to make this definition precise, we will need to define a correspondence between traces of the original program and the new program.)

Program Transformations. In order to remove bad traces, we apply the following program transformations: (1) reordering of adjacent instructions $i_1; i_2$ within a thread if the instructions are sequentially independent (i.e., if $i_1; i_2$ is sequentially equivalent to $i_2; i_1$), and (2) inserting atomic sections. The reordering of instructions is given priority as it may result in a better performance than the insertion of atomic sections. Furthermore, the reordering of instructions removes a surprisingly large number of concurrency bugs that occur in practice; according to a study of how programmers fix concurrency bugs in Linux device drivers [4], reordering of instructions is the most commonly used.

Our Algorithm. Our algorithm learns constraints on the space of candidate solutions from both good traces and bad traces. We explain the constraint learning using as an example the program transformation (1), which reorders instructions within threads. From a bad trace, we learn reordering constraints that eliminate the counterexample using the algorithm of [4]. While eliminating the counterexample, such reorderings may transform a (not necessarily preemption-free) good trace into a bad trace — this would constitute a regression. In order to avoid regressions, our algorithm learns also from good traces. Intuitively, from a good trace π, we want to learn all the ways in which π can be transformed by reordering without turning it into an error trace— this is expressed as a program constraint. The program constraint is (a) sound, if all programs satisfying the constraint are regression-free; and (b) complete, if all programs violating the constraint have regressions. However, as learning a sound and complete constraint is computationally expensive, given a good trace π we learn a sound constraint that only guarantees that π is not transformed into a bad trace. We generate the constraint using data-flow analysis on the instructions in π. The main idea of the analysis is that in good traces, the data-flow into passing assertions is protected by synchronization mechanisms (such as locks) and data-flow into conditionals along the trace. This protection may fail if we reorder instructions. We thus find a constraint that prevents such bad reorderings.

Summarizing, as the algorithm progresses and sees a set of bad traces and a set of good traces, it learns constraints that encode the ways in which the program can be transformed in order to eliminate the bad traces without turning the good traces into bad traces of the resulting program.

CEGIS vs PACES. A popular recent approach to synthesis is counterexample-guided inductive synthesis (CEGIS) [17]. Our algorithm can be viewed as an instance of CEGIS with the important feature that we learn from positive examples. We dub this approach PACES, for *Positive- and Counter-Examples in Synthesis*. The input to the CEGIS algorithm is a specification φ (possibly in multiple pieces – say, as a temporal formula and a language of possible solutions [3]). In the basic CEGIS loop, the synthesizer proposes a candidate solution S, which is then checked against φ. If it is correct, the CEGIS loop terminates; if not, a counterexample is provided and the synthesizer uses it to improve S. In practice, the CEGIS loop often faces performance issues, in particular, it can suffer from regressions: new candidate solutions may introduce errors that were not present in previous candidate solutions. We address this issue by *making use of positive examples* (good traces) in addition to counterexamples (bad traces). The good traces are used to learn constraints that ensure that these good traces are preserved in the candidate solution programs proposed by the CEGIS loop. The PACES approach applies in many program synthesis contexts, but in this paper, we focus on program repair for concurrency.

Related Work. The closest related work is by von Essen and Jobstmann [7], which continues the work on program repair [11,9,12]. In [7], the goal is to repair reactive systems (given as automata) according to an LTL specification, with a guarantee that good traces do not disappear as a result of the repair. Their algorithm is based on the classic synthesis algorithm which translates the LTL specification to an automaton. In contrast, we focus on the repair of concurrent programs, and our algorithm uses positive examples and counterexamples.

There are several recent algorithms for inserting synchronization by locks, fences, atomic sections, and other synchronization primitives ([18,5,6,16]). Deshmukh et al. [6] is the only one of these which uses information about the correct parts of the program in bug fixing – a proof of sequential correctness is used to identify positions for locks in a concurrent library that is sequentially correct. CFix (Jin et al. [10]) can detect and fix concurrency bugs using specific bug detection patterns and a fixing strategy for each pattern of bug. Our approach relies on a general-purpose model checker and does not use any patterns.

Our algorithm for fixing bad traces starts by generalizing counterexample traces. In verification (as opposed to synthesis), concurrent trace generalization

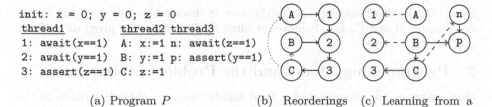

```
init: x = 0; y = 0; z = 0
thread1          thread2 thread3
1: await(x==1)   A: x:=1 n: await(z==1)
2: await(y==1)   B: y:=1 p: assert(y==1)
3: assert(z==1)  C: z:=1
```

(a) Program P (b) Reorderings   (c) Learning from a
                       from bad traces   good trace

Fig. 1. Program analysis with good and bad traces

was used by Sinha et al. [14,15]; and by Alglave et al. [2] for detecting errors due to weak memory models. Generalizations of good traces was previously used by Farzan et al. [8], who create an inductive data-flow graph (iDFG) to represent a proof of program correctness. They do not attempt to use iDFGs in synthesis.

We use the model checker CBMC [1] to generate both good and bad traces. Sen introduced concurrent directed random testing [13], which can be used to obtain good or bad traces much faster than a model checker. For a 30k LOC program their tool needs only about 2 seconds. We could use this tool to initially obtain good and bad traces faster, thus increasing the scalability of our tool.

Illustrative Example. We motivate our approach on the program P in Figure 1a. There is a bug witnessed by the following trace: $\pi_1 = A \to B \to 1 \to 2 \to 3$ (the assertion at line 3 fails). Let us attempt to fix the bug using the algorithm from [4]. The algorithm discovers possible fixes by first generalizing the trace into a partial order (Figure 1b, without the dotted edges) representing the happens-before relations necessary for the bug to occur, and second, trying to create a cycle in the partial order to eliminate the generalized counterexample. It finds three possible ways to do this: swapping B and C, or moving C before A, or moving A after C, indicated by the dotted edges in Figure 1b. Assume that we continue with swapping B and C to obtain program P_1 where the first thread is $A; C; B$. Program P_1 contains an error trace $\pi_2 = A \to C \to n \to p$ (the assertion at line p fails). This bug was not in the original program, but was introduced by our fix. We refer to this type of bug as a regression.

In order to prevent regressions, the algorithm learns from good traces. Consider the following good trace $\pi_3 = A \to B \to C \to 1 \to 2 \to n \to 3 \to p$. The algorithm analyses the trace, and produces the graph in Figure 1c. Here, the thick red edges indicate the reads-from relation for **assert** commands, and the dashed blue edges indicate the reads-from relation for **await** commands. Intuitively, the algorithm now analyses why the assertion at line p holds in the given trace. This assertion reads the value written in line B (indicated by the thick red edge). The algorithm finds a path from B to p composed entirely from intra-thread sequential edges ($B \to C$ and $n \to p$) and dashed blue edges ($C \to n$). This path guarantees that this trace cannot be changed by different scheduler choices into a path where p reads from elsewhere and fails. From the good trace π_2 we thus find that there could be a regression unless B precedes C and n precedes p. Having learned this constraint, the synthesizer can find a better way to fix π_1. Of the three options described above, it chooses the only way which does not reorder B and C, i.e., it moves A after C. This fixes the program without regressions.

2   Programming Model and the Problem Statement

Our programs are composed of a fixed number (say n) threads written in the CWHILE language (Figure 2). Each statement has a unique program location and each thread has unique initial and final program locations. Further, we assume that execution does not stop on assertion failure, but instead, a variable *err* is set to 1. The `await` construct is a blocking assume, i.e., execution of `await(cond)` stops till `cond` holds. For example, a lock construct can be modelled as `atomic { await(lock_var == 0); lock_var := 1 }`. Note that `await` is the only blocking operation in CWHILE – hence, we call the `await` operations *preemption-points*.

```
iexp ::= iexp + iexp | iexp / iexp | iexp * iexp | var | constant
bexp ::= iexp >= iexp | iexp == iexp | bexp && bexp | !bexp
stmt ::= variable := iexp | variable := bexp | stmt; stmt | assume(bexp)
         | if (*) stmt else stmt | while (*) stmt | atomic { stmt }
         | assert(bexp) | await(bexp)
thrd ::= stmt                              prog  ::= thrd | prog‖thrd
```

Fig. 2. Syntax of programming language

Semantics. The *program-state* S of a program P is given by $(\mathcal{D}, (l^1, \ldots, l^n))$ where $\mathcal{D}$ is a valuation of variables, and each l^t is a thread t program location. Execution of the thread t statement at location l^t is represented as Sl^tS' where $S = (\mathcal{D}, (\ldots, l^t, \ldots))$ and $S' = (\mathcal{D}', (\ldots, l^{t'}, \ldots))$, and $l^{t'}$ and $\mathcal{D}'$ are the program location and variable valuation after executing the statement from $\mathcal{D}$. A *trace* π of P is a sequence $S_0 l_0 \ldots S_m$ where (a) $S_0 = (\mathcal{D}, (l_i^1, \ldots, l_i^n))$ where each l_i^t is the initial location of thread t; and (b) each $S_i l_i S_{i+1}$ is a thread t transition for some t. Trace π is *complete* if $S_m = (\mathcal{D}_m, (l_f^1, \ldots, l_f^k))$, where each l_f^t is the final location of thread t. We say $S_i l_i \ldots S_n$ is *equal modulo error-flag* to $S_i' l_i \ldots S_n'$ if each S_k and S_k' differ only in the valuation of the variable *err*.

Trace π is *preemption-free* if every context-switch occurs either at a preemption-point (`await` statement) or at the end of a thread's execution, i.e., if where $S_i l_i S_{i+1}$ and $S_{i+1} l_{i+1} S_{i+2}$ are transitions of different threads (say threads t and t'), either the next thread t instruction after l_i is an `await`, or the thread t is in the final location in S_{i+1}. Similarly, we call a trace *sequential* if every context-switch happens at the end of a thread's execution.

A trace $\pi = S_0 l_0 \ldots S_m$ is *bad* if the error variable *err* has values 0 and 1 in S_0 and S_m, respectively; otherwise, π is *good* trace. We assume that the bugs present in the input programs are *data-independent* – if $\pi = S_0 l_0 S_1 \ldots S_n$ is bad, so is every trace $\pi' = S_0' l_0' S_1' \ldots S_n'$ where $l_i = l_i'$ for all $0 \le i < n$.

Program Transformations and Program Constraints. We consider two kinds of transformations for fixing bugs:

- A *reordering transformation* $\theta = l_1 \rightsquigarrow l_2$ transforms P to P' if location l_1 immediately precedes l_2 in P and l_2 immediately precedes l_1 in P'. We only consider cases where the sequential semantics are preserved, i.e., if (a) l_1 and l_2 are from the same basic block; and (b) $l_1; l_2$ is equivalent to $l_2; l_1$.
- An *atomic section transformation* $\theta = [l_1; l_2]$ transforms P to P' if neighbouring locations l_1 and l_2 are in an atomic section in P', but not in P.

We write $P \xrightarrow{\theta_1 \dots \theta_k} P'$ if applying each of θ_i in order transforms P to P'. We say transformation θ *acts across preemption-points* if either $\theta = l_1 \rightsquigarrow l_2$ and one of l_1 or l_2 is a preemption-point; or if $\theta = [l_1; l_2]$ and l_2 is a preemption-point.

Given a program P, we define *program constraints* to represent sets of programs that can be obtained through applying program transformations on P.
- *Atomicity constraint*: Program $P' \models [l_i; l_j]$ if l_i and l_j are in an atomic block.
- *Ordering constraint*: Program $P' \models l_i \leq l_j$ if l_i and l_j are from the same basic block and either l_i occurs before l_j, or P' satisfies $[l_i; l_j]$.

If $P' \models \Phi$, we say that P' *satisfies* Φ. Further, we define conjunction of Φ_1 and Φ_2 by letting $P' \models \Phi_1 \wedge \Phi_2 \Leftrightarrow (P' \models \Phi_1 \wedge P' \models \Phi_2)$.

Trace Transformations and Regressions. A trace $\pi = S_0 l_0 \dots S_m$ *transforms* into a trace $\pi' = S'_0 l'_0 \dots S'_m$ by *switching* if: (a) $S_0 l_0 \dots S_n = S'_0 l'_0 \dots S'_n$ and the suffixes $S_{n+2} l_{n+2} \dots S_m$ and $S'_{n+2} l'_{n+2} \dots S'_m$ are equal modulo error-flag; and (b) $l_n = l'_{n+1} \wedge l_{n+1} = l'_n$. We label switching transformations as a:
- *Free transformation* if l_n and l_{n+1} are from different threads. We write $\pi' \in f(\pi)$ if a sequence of free transformations takes π to π'.
- *Reordering transformation* $\theta = l^\sharp \rightsquigarrow l^\flat$ *acting on* π if $l_n = l^\sharp$ and $l_{n+1} = l^\flat$. We have $\pi' \in \theta(\pi)$ if repeated applications of θ transformations acting on π give π'. Similarly, $\pi' \in \theta^f(\pi)$ if repeated applications of θ and free transformations acting on π give π'.

Similarly, π' is obtained by *atomicity transformation* $\theta = [l_1, l_2]$ *acting on a trace* π if $\pi' \in f(\pi)$, and there are no context-switches between l_1 and l_2 in π'.

Trace analysis graphs. We use trace analysis graphs to characterize data-flow and scheduling in a trace. First, given a trace $\pi = S_0 l_0 \dots$, we define the function *depends* to recursively find the data-flow edges into the l_i. Formally, $depends(i) = \cup_v \{(last(i,v), i)\} \cup depends(last(i,v))$ where v ranges over variables read by l_i, and $last(i,v)$ returns j if l_i reads the value of v written by l_j and $last(i,v) = \bot$ if no such j exists. As the base case, we define $depends(\bot) = \emptyset$.

Now, a *trace analysis graph* for trace $\pi = S_0 l_0 \dots S_n$ is a multi-graph $G(\pi) = \langle V, \rightarrow \rangle$, where $V = \{\bot\} \cup \{i | 0 \leq i \leq n\}$ are the positions in the trace along with $\bot$ (representing the initial state) and $\rightarrow$ contains the following types of edges.
1. *Intra-thread order* (*IntraThreadOrder*): We have $x \rightarrow y$ if either $x < y$, and l_x and l_y are from the same thread, or if $x = \bot$.
2. *Data-flow into conditionals* (*DFConds*): We have $\bigcup_{a \in conds} depends(a) \subseteq \rightarrow$ where $x \in conds$ iff l_x is an assume or an await statement.
3. *Data-flow into assertions* (*DFAsserts*): We have $\bigcup_{a \in asserts} depends(a) \subseteq \rightarrow$ where $x \in asserts$ iff l_x is an assert statement.

4. *Non-free order* (*NonFreeOrder*): We have $x \to y$ if l_x and l_y write two different values to the same variable. Intuitively, the non-free orders prevent switching transformations that switch l_x and l_y.

Regressions. Suppose $P \xrightarrow{\theta_1,\dots,\theta_k} P'$. We say $\theta_1, \dots, \theta_k$ introduces a *regression* with respect to a good trace $\pi = S_0 l_0 \dots S_m$ of P if there exists a trace $\pi' = S'_0 l'_0 \dots S'_m \in \theta_k^f \circ \dots \circ \theta_1^f(\pi)$ such that: (a) π' is a bad trace of P'; (b) π does not freely transform into any bad trace of P; and (c) for every data-flow into conditionals edge $x \to y$ (say l_y reads the variables $\mathcal{V}$ from l_x) in $G(\pi)$, the edge $p(x) \to p(y)$ is a data-flow into conditionals edge in $G(\pi')$ (where $l'_{p(y)}$ reads the same variables $\mathcal{V}$ from $l'_{p(x)}$). Here, $p(i)$ is the position in π' of instruction at position i in π after the sequence of switching transformations that take π to π'. We say $\theta_1 \dots \theta_k$ introduces a regression with respect to a set T_G of good traces if it introduces a regression with respect to at least one trace $\pi \in T_G$.

Intuitively, a program-transformation induces a regression if it allows a good trace π to become a bad trace π' due to the program transformations. Further, we require that π and π' have the conditionals enabled in the same way, i.e., the `assume` and `await` statements read from the same locations.

Remark 1. The above definition of regression attempts to capture the intuition that a good trace transforms into a "similar" bad trace. The notion of similar asks that the traces have the same data-flow into conditionals – this condition can be relaxed to obtain more general notions of regression. However, this makes trace analysis and finding regression-free fixes much harder (See Example 3).

Example 1. In Figure 1, the trace $\pi = A; B; C; n; p$ transforms under $B \leftrightsquigarrow C$ to $\pi' = A; C; B; n; p$, which freely transforms to $\pi'' = A; C; n; p; B$. Hence, $B \leftrightsquigarrow C$ introduces a regression with respect to π as π does not freely transform into a bad trace, and π' is bad while the `await` in n still reads from C.

The Regression-free Program-Repair Problem. Intuitively, the program-repair problem asks for a correct program P' that is a transformation of P. Further, P' should preserve all sequential behaviour of P; and if all preemption-free behaviour of P is good, we require that P' preserves it.

Program repair problem. The input is a program P where all complete sequential traces are good. The result is a sequence of program transformations $\theta_1 \dots \theta_n$ and P', such that (a) $P \xrightarrow{\theta_1 \dots \theta_n} P'$; (b) P' has no bad traces; (c) for each complete sequential trace π of P, there exists a complete sequential trace π' of P' such that $\pi' \in \theta_1 \circ \theta_2 \dots \circ \theta_n(\pi)$; and (d) if all complete preemption-free traces of P are good, then for each such trace π, there exists a complete preemption-free trace π' of P' such that $\pi' \in \theta_1 \circ \theta_2 \dots \circ \theta_n(\pi)$. We call the conditions (c) and (d) the *preservation of sequential and correct preemption-free behaviour.*

Regression-free error fix. Our approach to the above problem is through repeated regression-free error fixing. Formally, the regression-free error fix problem takes a set of good traces T_G, a program P and a bad trace π as input, and produces transformations $\theta_1, \ldots, \theta_k$ and P' such that $P \xrightarrow{\theta_1 \ldots \theta_k} P'$, $\pi' \in \theta_k^f \circ \ldots \circ \theta_1^f(\pi)$ is a trace in P', and $\theta_1, \ldots, \theta_k$ does not introduce a *regression* with respect to T_G.

3   Good and Bad Traces

Our approach to program-repair is through learning regression preventing constraints from good traces and error eliminating constraints from bad traces.

3.1   Learning from Good Traces

Given a trace π of P, a program constraint Φ is a *sound regression preventing constraint* for π if every sequence of program transformations $\theta_1, \ldots, \theta_k$, such that $P \xrightarrow{\theta_1 \ldots \theta_k} P'$ and $P' \models \Phi$, does not introduce a regression with respect to π. Further, if every $\theta_1 \ldots \theta_k$, such that $P \xrightarrow{\theta_1 \ldots \theta_k} P'$ and $P' \not\models \Phi$, introduces a regression with respect to π, then Φ is a *complete regression preventing constraint*.

Example 2. Let the program P be $\{1 : \mathtt{x} := 1; 2 : \mathtt{y} := 1\} \| \{A : \mathtt{await}(\mathtt{y} = 1);$ $B : \mathtt{assert}(\mathtt{x} = 1)\}$. In Figure 3a, the constraint $\Phi^* = (1 < 2 \wedge A < B)$ is a sound and complete regression-preventing constraint for the trace $1 \to 2 \to A \to B$.

Lemma 1. *For a program P and a good trace π, the sound and complete regression-preventing constraint Φ^* is computable in exponential time in $|\pi|$.*

Intuitively, the proof relies on an algorithm that iteratively applies all possible free and program transformations in different combinations (there are a finite, though exponential, number of these) to π. It then records the constraints satisfied by programs obtained by transformations that do not introduce regressions.

The sound and complete constraints are usually large and impractical to compute. Instead, we present an algorithm to compute sound regression-preventing constraints. The main issue here is non-locality, i.e., statements that are not close to the assertion may influence the regression-preventing constraint.

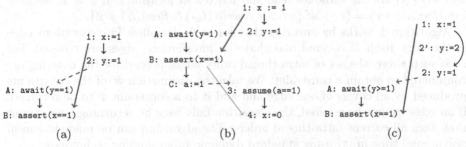

Fig. 3. Sample Good Traces for Regression-preventing constraints

Example 3. The trace in Figures 3b is a simple extension of Figure 3a. However, the constraint $(1 \le 2 \wedge A \le B)$ (from Example 2) does not prevent regressions for Figure 3b. An additional constraint $B \le C \wedge 3 \le 4$ is needed as reordering these statements can lead to the assertion failing by reading the value of x "too late", i.e., from the statement 4 (trace: $1 \to 2 \to A \to C \to 3 \to 4 \to B$).

Figure 3c clarifies our definition of regression, which requires that the data-flow edges into assumptions and awaits need to be preserved. The await can be activated by both 2 and 2'; in the trace we analyse it is activated by 2. Moving 2' before 1 could activate the await "too early" and the assertion would fail (trace: $2' \to A \to B$). However, it is not possible to learn this purely with data-flow analysis – for example, if statement 2' was y := -1, then this would not lead to a bad trace. Hence, we exclude such cases from our definition of regressions by requiring that the await reads A reads from the same location.

Learning Sound Regression-Preventing Constraints. The sound regression-preventing constraint learned by our algorithm for a trace ensures that the data-flow into an assertion is preserved. This is achieved through two steps: suppose an assertion at location l_a reads from a write at location l_w. First, the constraint ensures that l_w always happens before l_a. Second, the constraint ensures that no other writes interfere with the above read-write relationship.

For ensuring happens-before relationships, we use the notion of a *cover*. Intuitively, given a trace π of P where location l_x happens before location l_y, we learn a Φ that ensures that if $P' \models \Phi$, then each trace π' of P' obtained as free and program transformations acting on π satisfies the happens-before relationship between l_x and l_y. Formally, given a trace π of program P, we call a path $x_1 \to x_2 \to \ldots \to x_n$ in the trace analysis graph a *cover* of edge $x \to y$ if $x = x_1 \wedge y = x_n$ and each of $x_i \to x_{i+1}$ is either a intra-thread order edge, or a data-flow into conditionals edge, or a non-free order edge.

Given a trace $\pi = S_0 l_0 S_1 l_1 \ldots S_n$, where statement at position r (i.e., l_r) reads a set of variables (say $\mathcal{V}$) written by a statement at position w (i.e., l_w), the the non-interference edges define a sufficient set of happens-before relations to ensure that no other statements can interfere with the read-write pair, i.e., that every other write to $\mathcal{V}$ either happens before w or after r. Formally, we have that $interfere(w \to r) = \{r \to w' \mid w' > r \wedge write(l_{w'}) \cap write(l_w) \cap Read(l_r) \neq \emptyset\} \cup \{w' \to w \mid w' < w \wedge write(l_{w'}) \cap write(l_w) \cap Read(l_r) \neq \emptyset\}$ where $Read(l)$ and $write(l)$ are the variables read and written at location l. If $w = \bot$, we have $interfere(w \to r) = \{r \to w' \mid w' > r \wedge write(l_{w'}) \cap Read(l_r) \neq \emptyset\}$.

Algorithm 1 works by ensuring that for each data-flow into assertions edge e, the edge itself is covered and that the interference edges are covered. For each such cover, the set of intra-thread order edges needed for the covering are conjuncted to obtain a constraint. We take the disjunction Φ' of the constraints produced by all covers of one edge and add it to a constraint Φ to be returned. If an edge cannot be covered, the algorithm falls back by returning a constraint that fixes all current intra-thread orders. The algorithm can be made to run in polynomial time in $|\pi|$ using standard dynamic programming techniques.

Algorithm 1. Algorithm *LearnGoodUnder*

Require: A good trace π
Ensure: Regression-preventing constraint Φ
1. $\Phi \leftarrow true; G \leftarrow G(\pi)$
2. **for all** $e \in \left(DFAsserts(G) \cup \bigcup_{f \in DFAsserts(G)} interfere(f) \right)$ **do**
3.   **if** e is not covered **then return** $\bigwedge \{ l_x \leq l_y \mid x \rightarrow y$ is a intra-thread order edge$\}$
4. $\Phi' \leftarrow$ **false**
5.   **for all** $x_1 \rightarrow x_2 \rightarrow \ldots \rightarrow x_n$ cover of e **do**
6. $\Phi' \leftarrow \Phi' \vee \bigwedge \{ l_{x_i} \leq l_{x_{i+1}} \mid x_i \rightarrow x_{i+1}$ is a intra-thread order edge and $x_i \neq \bot$
                  l_{x_i} and $l_{x_{i+1}}$ are from the same execution of a basic block in $\pi \}$
7. $\Phi \leftarrow \Phi \wedge \Phi'$
8. **return** Φ

Theorem 1. *Given a trace π, Algorithm 1 returns a constraint Φ that is a sound regression-preventing constraint for π and runs in polynomial time in $|\pi|$.*

Proof (Outline). The fallback case (line 3) is trivially sound. Let us assume towards contradiction that there is a bad trace $\pi' = S_0' l_0' S_1' l_1' \ldots S_n'$ of $P' \models \Phi$, that is obtained by transformation of $\pi = S_0 l_0 S_1 l_1 \ldots S_n$. For each $0 \leq i < n$, let $p(i)$ be such that the instruction at position i in π is at position $p(i)$ in π' after the sequence of switching transformations taking π to π'.

If for every data-flow into assertion edge in $x \rightarrow y$ in $G(\pi)$, we have that $p(x) \rightarrow p(y)$ is a corresponding data-flow into assertion edge in $G(\pi')$, then it can be easily shown that π' is also good (each corresponding edge in π' reads the same values as in π). Now, suppose $x \rightarrow y$ is the first (with minimal x) such edge in π that does not hold in π'. We will show in two steps that $p(x)$ happens before $p(y)$ in π', and that $p(y)$ reads from $p(x)$ which will lead to a contradiction.

For the first step, we know that there exists a cover of $x \rightarrow y$ in π. For now, assume there is exactly one cover – the other case is similar. For each edge $a \rightarrow b$ in this cover, no switching transformation can switch the order of l_a and l_b:
- If $a \rightarrow b$ is a data-flow into conditionals edge, as π' has to preserve all *DFConds* edges (definition of regression), $p(a)$ happens before $p(b)$ in π'.
- If $a \rightarrow b$ is a non-free order edge, no switching transformation can reorder a and b as that would change variables values (by definition of non-free edges).
- If $a \rightarrow b$ is a intra-thread order edge, we have that $P' \models \Phi$ and $\Phi \implies a \leq b$, and hence, no switching transformation would change the order of a and b.
Hence, we have that all the happens before relations given by the cover are all preserved by π' and hence, $p(a)$ happens before $p(a)$ in π'. The fact that $p(y)$ reads from $p(x)$ follows from a similar argument with the *interfere*$(x \rightarrow y)$ edges showing that every interfering write either happens before $p(x)$ or after $p(y)$. $\square$

3.2   Eliminating Bad Traces

Given a bad trace π of P, a program constraint Φ is a *error eliminating constraint* if for all transformations $\theta_1, \ldots, \theta_k$ and P' such that $P \xrightarrow{\theta_1 \ldots \theta_k} P'$ and $P' \models \Phi$,

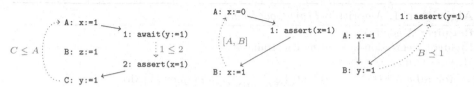

Fig. 4. Eliminating bad traces

each bad trace π' in $\theta_k^f \circ \ldots \circ \theta_1^f(\pi)$ is not a trace of P'. In [4], we presented an algorithm to fix bad traces using reordering and atomic sections. The main idea behind the algorithm is as follows. Given a bad trace π, we (a) first, generalize the trace into a partial order trace; and (b) then, compute a program constraint that violates some essential part of the ordering necessary for the bug.

More precisely, the procedure builds a trace elimination graph which contain edges corresponding to the orderings necessary for the bug to occur, as well as the edges corresponding program constraints. Fixes are found by finding cycles in this graph – the conjunction of the program constraints in a cycle form an error elimination constraint. Intuitively, the program constraints in the cycle will enforce a happens-before conflicting with the orderings necessary for the bug.

Example 4. Consider the program in Figure 4(left) and the trace elimination graph for the trace $A; B; 1; 2; C$. The orderings A happens-before 1 and 2 happens-before C are necessary for the error to happen. The cycle $C \to A \to 1 \to 2 \to C$ is the elimination cycle. The corresponding error eliminating constraint is $C \leq A \wedge 1 \leq 2$, and one possible fix is to move C ahead of A. For the bad trace $A; 1; B$ in Figure 4(center), the elimination cycle is $A \to 1 \to B \to A$ giving us the constraint $[A; B]$ and an atomic section around $A; B$ as the fix.

The FixBad algorithm. The *FixBad* algorithm takes as input a program P, a constraint Φ and a bad trace π. It outputs a program constraint Φ', sequence of program transformations $\theta_1, \ldots, \theta_k$, and a new program P', such that $P \xrightarrow{\theta_1 \ldots \theta_k} P'$. The algorithm guarantees that (a) Φ' is an error eliminating constraint; (b) $P' \models \Phi \wedge P' \models \Phi'$; and (c) if there is no preemption-free trace π' of P such that π freely transforms to π' (i.e., $\pi' \in f(\pi)$), then none of the transformations $\theta \in \{\theta_1, \ldots, \theta_k\}$ acts across preemption-points. The fact that $\theta_1 \ldots \theta_k$ and P' can be chosen to satisfy (c) is a consequence of the algorithm described in [4].

Fixes Using Wait/Notify Statements. Some programs cannot be fixed by statement reordering or atomic section insertion. These programs are in general outside our definition of the program repair problem as they have bad sequential traces. However, they can be fixed by the insertion of wait/notify statements. One such example is depicted in Figure 4(right) where the trace $1; A; B$ causes an assertion failure. A possible fix is to add a `wait` statement before 1 and a corresponding `notify` statement after B. The algorithm *FixBad* can be modified to insert such wait-notify statements by also considering constraints of the form $X \preceq Y$ to represent that X is scheduled before Y – the corresponding program transfomation is to add a wait statement before Y and a notify statement after X. In Figure 4(right), the edge $B \to 1$ represents such a constraint $B \preceq 1$ – the elimination cycle $1 \to B \to 1$ corresponds to the above described fix.

4   The Program-Repair Algorithm

Algorithm 2 is a program-repair procedure to fix concurrency bugs while avoiding regressions. The algorithm maintains the current program P, and a constraint Φ that restricts possible reorderings. In each iteration, the algorithm tests if P is correct and if so returns P. If not it picks a trace π in P (line 4). If the trace is good it learns the regression-preventing constraint Φ for π and the trace π is added to the set of good traces T_G (T_G is required only for the correctness proof). If π is bad it calls $FixBad$ to generate a new program that excludes π while respecting Φ, and Φ is strengthened by conjunction with the error elimination constraint Φ' produced by $FixBad$. The algorithm terminates with a valid solution for all choices of P' in line 8 as the constraint Φ is strengthened in each $FixBad$ iteration. Eventually, the strongest program-constraint will restrict the possible program P' to one with large enough atomic sections such that it will have only preemption-free or sequential traces.

Theorem 2 (Soundness). *Given a program P, Algorithm 2 returns a program P' with no bad traces that preserves the sequential and correct preemption-free behaviour of P. Further, each iteration of the* **while** *loop where a bad trace π is chosen performs a regression-free error fix with respect to the good traces T_G.*

The extension of the $FixBad$ algorithm to wait/notify fixes in Algorithm 2 may lead to P' not preserving the good preemption-free and sequential behaviours of P. However, in this case, the input P violates the pre-conditions of the algorithm.

Theorem 3 (Fair Termination). *Assuming that a bad trace will eventually be chosen in line 4 if one exists in P, Algorithm 2 terminates for any instantiation of FixBad.*

Algorithm 2. Program-Repair Algorithm for Concurrency

Require: A concurrent program P, all sequential traces are good
Ensure: Program P^* such that P^* has no bad traces

1. $\Phi \leftarrow true; T_G \leftarrow \emptyset$
2. **while true do**
3.   **if** $Verify(P) = $ **true then return** P
4.   Choose π from P (non-deterministic)
5.   **if** π is non-erroneous **then**
6. $\Phi \leftarrow \Phi \wedge LearnGood(\pi); T_G \leftarrow T_G \cup \{\pi\}$
7.   **else**
8. $([\theta_1, \ldots, \theta_k], P, \Phi') \leftarrow FixBad(P, \Phi, \pi); \quad \Phi \leftarrow \Phi \wedge \Phi'$
9. $T_G \leftarrow \bigcup_{\pi_g \in T_G} \{\pi_g' | \pi_g' \in \theta_k \circ \ldots \circ \theta_1(\pi^g) \wedge \pi_g' \in P\}$

A Generic Program-Repair Algorithm. We now explain how our program-repair algorithm relates to generic synthesis procedures based on *counter-example guided inductive synthesis* (CEGIS) [17]. In the CEGIS approach, the input is a *partial-program* $\mathcal{P}$, i.e., a non-deterministic program and the goal is to specialize $\mathcal{P}$ to a program P so that all behaviours of P satisfy a specification. In our case, the partial-program would non-deterministically choose between various reorderings and atomics sections. Let $\mathcal{C}$ be the set of choices (e.g., statement orderings) available in $\mathcal{P}$. For a given $\mathbf{c} \in \mathcal{C}$, let $\mathbb{P}(\mathcal{P}, \mathbf{c}, \mathbf{i})$ be the predicate that program obtained by specializing $\mathcal{P}$ with $\mathbf{c}$ behaves correctly on the input $\mathbf{i}$.

The CEGIS algorithm maintains a set $\mathcal{E}$ of inputs called experiments. In each iteration, it finds $\mathbf{c}^* \in \mathcal{C}$ such that the $\forall \mathbf{i} \in \mathcal{E} : \mathbb{P}(\mathcal{P}, \mathbf{c}^*, \mathbf{i})$. Then, it attempts to find an input $\mathbf{i}^*$ such that $\mathbb{P}(\mathbf{c}^*, \mathbf{i}^*)$ does not hold. If there is no such input, then $\mathbf{c}^*$ is the correct specialization. Otherwise, $\mathbf{i}^*$ is added to $\mathcal{E}$. This procedure is illustrated in Figure 5(left). Alternatively, CEGIS can be rewritten in terms of constraints on $\mathcal{C}$. For each input $\mathbf{i}$, we associate the constraint $\phi_{\mathbf{i}}$ where $\phi_{\mathbf{i}}(\mathbf{c}) \Leftrightarrow \mathbb{P}(\mathcal{P}, \mathbf{c}, \mathbf{i})$. Now, instead of $\mathcal{E}$, the algorithm maintains the constraint $\Phi = \bigwedge_{\mathbf{i} \in \mathcal{E}} \phi_{\mathbf{i}}$. Every iteration, the algorithm picks a $\mathbf{c}$ such that $\mathbf{c} \models \Phi$; tries to find an input $\mathbf{i}^*$ such that $\neg \mathbb{P}(\mathcal{P}, \mathbf{c}, \mathbf{i})$ holds, and then strengthens Φ by $\phi_{\mathbf{i}^*}$.

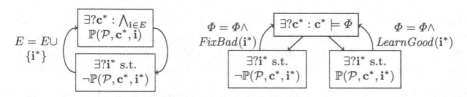

Fig. 5. The CEGIS and PACES spectrum

This procedure is exactly the else branch (i.e., *FixBad* procedure) of an iteration in Algorithm 2 where $\mathbf{i}^*$ and $\phi_{\mathbf{i}^*}$ correspond to π and $FixBad(\pi)$. Intuitively, the initial variable values in π and the scheduler choices are the inputs to our concurrent programs. This suggests that the then branch in Algorithm 2 could also be incorporated into the standard CEGIS approach. This extension (dubbed PACES for *Positive and Counter-Examples in Synthesis*) to the CEGIS approach is shown in Figure 5(right). Here, the algorithm in each iteration may choose to find an input for which the program is correct and use the constraints arising from it. We discuss the advantages and disadvantages of this approach below.

Constraints vs. Inputs. A major advantage of using constraints instead of sample inputs is the possibility of using over- and under-approximations. As seen in Section 3.1, it is sometimes easier to work with approximations of constraints due to simplicity of representation at the cost of potentially missing good solutions. Another advantage is that the sample inputs may have no simple representations in some domains. The scheduler decisions are one such example – the scheduler choices for one program are hard to translate into the scheduler choices for another. For example, the original CEGIS for concurrency work [16] uses ad-hoc trace projection to translate the scheduler choices between programs.

Positive-examples and Counter-examples vs. Counter-examples. In standard program-repair tasks, although the faulty program and the search space $\mathcal{C}$ may be large, the solution program is usually "near" the original program, i.e., the fix is small. Further, we do not want to change the given program unnecessarily. In this case, the use of positive examples and over-approximations of learned constraints can be used to narrow down the search space quickly. Another possible advantage comes in the case where the search space for synthesis is structured (for example, in modular synthesis). In this case, we can use the correct behaviour displayed by a candidate solution to fix parts of the search space.

5 Implementation and Experiments

We implemented Algorithm 2 in our tool ConRepair The tool consists of 3300 lines of Scala code and is available at https://github.com/thorstent/ConRepair. Model checker CBMC [1] is used for generating both good and bad traces, and on an average more than 95% of the total execution time is spent in CBMC. Model checking is far from optimal to obtain good traces, and we expect that techniques from [13] can be used to generate good traces much faster. Our tool can operate in two modes: In "mixed" mode it first analyses good traces and then proceeds to fixing the program. The baseline "badOnly" mode skips the analysis of good traces (corresponds to the algorithm in [4]).

In practice the analysis of bad traces usually generates a large number of potential reorderings that could fix the bug. Our original algorithm from [4] (badOnly ce1) prefers reorderings over atomic sections, but in examples where an atomic section is the only fix, this algorithm has poor performance. To address this we implemented a heuristic (ce2) that places atomic sections before having tried all possible reorderings, but this can result in solutions having unnecessary atomic sections.

The fall back case in Algorithm 1 severely limits further fixes – it forces further fixes involving the same instructions to be atomic sections. Hence, in our implementation, we omit this step and prefer an unsound algorithm (i.e., not necessarily regression-free) that can fix more programs with reorderings. While the implemented algorithm is unsound, our experiments show that even without the fallback, in our examples, there is no regression except for one artificial example (ex-regr.c) constructed precisely for that purpose.

Benchmarks. We evaluate our tool on a set of examples that model real bugs found and fixed in Linux device drivers by their developers. To this end, we explored a history of bug fixes in the drivers subtree of the Linux kernel and identified concurrency bugs. We further focused our attention on a subset of particularly subtle bugs involving more than two racing threads and/or a mix of different synchronization mechanisms, e.g., lock-based and lock-free synchronization. Approximately 20% of concurrency bugs that we considered satisfy this criterion. Such bugs are particularly tricky to fix either manually or automatically, as new races or deadlocks can be easily introduced while eliminating them. Hence, these bugs are most likely to benefit from good trace analysis.

Table 5 shows our experimental results: the iterations and the wall-clock time needed to find a valid fix for our mixed algorithm and the two heuristics of the badOnly algorithm. For the mixed algorithm the time is split into the time needed to generate and analyse good traces (first number) and the time needed for the fixing afterwards.

Table 1. Results in iterations and time needed

File	LOC	mixed	badOnly ce1	badOnly ce2
ex1.c	60	1	2	2
ex2.c	37	2	5	6
ex3.c	35	1	2	2
ex4.c	60	1	2	2
ex5.c	43	1	8	3
ex-regr.c	30	2	2	2
paper1.c	28	1	3	3^a
dv1394.c	81	1 (13+4s)	51 (60s)	5^a (9s)
iwl3945.c	66	1(3+2s)	2(2s)	2(2s)
lc-rc.c	40	10 (2+7s)	179 (122s)	203 (134s)
rtl8169.c	405	7 (10+45m)	>100 (>6h)	8 (54m)
usb-serial.c	410	4 (56+20m)	6 (38m)	6 (38m)

Detailed analysis. The artificial examples ex1.c to ex5.c are used for testing and take only a few seconds; example paper1.c is the one in Figure 1a. Example ex-regr.c was constructed to show unsoundness of the implementation. Example usb-serial.c models the USB-to-serial adapter driver. Here, from the good traces the tool learns that two statements should not be reordered as it will trigger another bug. This prompts them to be reordered above a third statement together, while the badOnly analysis would first move one, find a new bug, and then fix that by moving the other statement. Thus, the good trace analysis saves us two rounds of bug fixing and reduces bug fixing time by 18 minutes.

The rtl8169.c example models the Realtek 8169 driver containing 5 concurrency bugs. One of the reorderings that the tool considers introduces a new bug; further, after doing the reordering, the atomic section is the only valid fix. The good trace analysis discover that the reordering would lead to a new bug, and thus does the algorithm does not use it. But, without good traces, the tool uses the faultly reordering and then ce1 takes a very long time to search through all possible reorderings and then discover that an atomic section is required. The situation is improved when using heuristic ce2 as it interrupts the search early. However, the same heuristic has an adverse effect in the dv1394.c example: by interrupting the search early, it prevents the algorithm from finding a correct reordering and inserts an unnecessary atomic section. The dv1394.c example also benefits from good traces in a different way than the other examples. Instead of preventing regressions, they are used to obtain *hints* as to what reorderings would provide coverage for a specific data-flow into assertion edge. Then, if a bad trace is encountered and can be fixed by the hinted reordering, the hinted reordering is preferred over all other possible ones. Without hints the dv1394.c example would require 5 iterations. Though hints are not part of our theory they are a simple and logical extension.

Example `lc-rc.c` models a bug in an ultra-wide band driver that requires two reorderings to fix. Though there is initially no deadlock, one may easily be introduced when reordering statements. Here, the good-trace analysis identifies a dependency between two `await` statements and learns not to reorder statements to prevent a deadlock. Without good traces, a large number of candidate solutions that cause a regression are generated.

6   Conclusion

We have developed a regression-free algorithm for fixing errors that are due to concurrent execution of the program. The contributions include the problem setup (the definitions of program repair for concurrency, and the regression-free algorithm), the PACES approach that extends the CEGIS loop with learning from positive examples, and the analysis of positive examples using data flow to assertions and to synchronization constructs.

There are several possible directions for future work. One interesting direction is to examine the possibility of extending the definition of regressions (see Remark 1 and Example 3) – this requires going beyond data-flow analysis for learning regression-preventing constraints. Another possible extension is to remove the assumption that the errors are data-independent. A more pragmatic goal would be to develop a practical version of the tool for device-driver synthesis starting from the current prototype.

Acknowledgements. We would like to thank Daniel Kroening and Michael Tautschnig for their prompt help with all our questions about CBMC. We would also like to thank Roderick Bloem, Bettina Könighofer and Roopsha Samanta for fruitful discussions regarding repair of concurrent programs.

References

1. CBMC, http://www.cprover.org/cbmc/
2. Alglave, J., Kroening, D., Tautschnig, M.: Partial Orders for Efficient Bounded Model Checking of Concurrent Software. In: Sharygina, N., Veith, H. (eds.) CAV 2013. LNCS, vol. 8044, pp. 141–157. Springer, Heidelberg (2013)
3. Alur, R., Bodík, R., Juniwal, G., Martin, M., Raghothaman, M., Seshia, S., Singh, R., Solar-Lezama, A., Torlak, E., Udupa, A.: Syntax-guided synthesis. In: FMCAD, pp. 1–17 (2013)
4. Černý, P., Henzinger, T.A., Radhakrishna, A., Ryzhyk, L., Tarrach, T.: Efficient synthesis for concurrency by semantics-preserving transformations. In: Sharygina, N., Veith, H. (eds.) CAV 2013. LNCS, vol. 8044, pp. 951–967. Springer, Heidelberg (2013)
5. Cherem, S., Chilimbi, T., Gulwani, S.: Inferring locks for atomic sections. In: PLDI 2008 (2008)
6. Deshmukh, J., Ramalingam, G., Ranganath, V.P., Vaswani, K.: Logical Concurrency Control from Sequential Proofs. In: LMCS (2010)

7. von Essen, C., Jobstmann, B.: Program repair without regret. In: Sharygina, N., Veith, H. (eds.) CAV 2013. LNCS, vol. 8044, pp. 896–911. Springer, Heidelberg (2013)
8. Farzan, A., Kincaid, Z., Podelski, A.: Inductive data flow graphs. In: POPL, pp. 129–142 (2013)
9. Griesmayer, A., Bloem, R., Cook, B.: Repair of boolean programs with an application to C. In: Ball, T., Jones, R.B. (eds.) CAV 2006. LNCS, vol. 4144, pp. 358–371. Springer, Heidelberg (2006)
10. Jin, G., Zhang, W., Deng, D., Liblit, B., Lu, S.: Automated Concurrency-Bug Fixing. In: OSDI 2012 (2012)
11. Jobstmann, B., Griesmayer, A., Bloem, R.: Program repair as a game. In: Etessami, K., Rajamani, S.K. (eds.) CAV 2005. LNCS, vol. 3576, pp. 226–238. Springer, Heidelberg (2005)
12. Samanta, R., Deshmukh, J., Emerson, A.: Automatic generation of local repairs for boolean programs. In: FMCAD, pp. 1–10 (2008)
13. Sen, K.: Race Directed Random Testing of Concurrent Programs. In: PLDI 2008 (2008)
14. Sinha, N., Wang, C.: On Interference Abstractions. In: POPL 2011 (2011)
15. Sinha, N., Wang, C.: Staged concurrent program analysis. In: FSE 2010 (2010)
16. Solar-Lezama, A., Jones, C., Bodík, R.: Sketching concurrent data structures. In: PLDI, pp. 136–148 (2008)
17. Solar-Lezama, A., Tancau, L., Bodík, R., Seshia, S.A., Saraswat, V.A.: Combinatorial sketching for finite programs. In: ASPLOS 2006 (2006)
18. Vechev, M., Yahav, E., Yorsh, G.: Abstraction-guided synthesis of synchronization. In: POPL 2010 (2010)

Bounded Model Checking of Multi-threaded C Programs via Lazy Sequentialization

Omar Inverso[1], Ermenegildo Tomasco[1], Bernd Fischer[2],
Salvatore La Torre[3], and Gennaro Parlato[1]

[1] Electronics and Computer Science, University of Southampton, UK
[2] Division of Computer Science, Stellenbosch University, South Africa
[3] Università degli Studi di Salerno, Italy

Abstract. Bounded model checking (BMC) has successfully been used
for many practical program verification problems, but concurrency still
poses a challenge. Here we describe a new approach to BMC of sequentially consistent C programs using POSIX threads. Our approach first
translates a multi-threaded C program into a nondeterministic sequential C program that preserves reachability for all round-robin schedules
with a given bound on the number of rounds. It then re-uses existing
high-performance BMC tools as backends for the sequential verification
problem. Our translation is carefully designed to introduce very small
memory overheads and very few sources of nondeterminism, so that it
produces tight SAT/SMT formulae, and is thus very effective in practice:
our prototype won the concurrency category of SV-COMP14. It solved
all verification tasks successfully and was 30x faster than the best tool
with native concurrency handling.

1 Introduction

Bounded model checking (BMC) has successfully been used to verify sequential
software and to discover subtle errors in applications [11]. However, attempts to
apply BMC directly to the analysis of multi-threaded programs (e.g., [18]) face
problems as the number of possible interleavings grows exponentially with the
number of threads and statements. Context-bounded analysis (CBA) methods
[42,35,48] limit the number of context switches they explore and so fit well into
the general BMC framework. They are empirically justified by work that has
shown that errors manifest themselves within few context switches [44].

In this paper, we develop and evaluate a new technique for context-bounded
BMC of multi-threaded C programs. It is based on *sequentialization*, an idea
proposed by Qadeer and Wu [49] to reuse without any changes verification tools
that were originally developed for sequential programs. Sequentializations can
be implemented as a code-to-code translation of the input program into a corresponding nondeterministic sequential program. However, such translations alter
the original program structure by injecting control code that represents an overhead for the backend. Therefore, the design of well-performing tools under this
approach requires careful attention to the details of the translation.

A. Biere and R. Bloem (Eds.): CAV 2014, LNCS 8559, pp. 585–602, 2014.
© Springer International Publishing Switzerland 2014

The first sequentialization for an arbitrary but bounded number of context switches was given by Lal and Reps [42] (LR). Its basic idea is to simulate in the sequential program all round-robin schedules of the threads in the concurrent program, in such a way that (*i*) each thread is run to completion, and (*ii*) each simulated round works on its own copy of the shared global memory. The initial values of all memory copies are nondeterministically guessed in the beginning (*eager* exploration), while the context switch points are guessed during the simulation of each thread. At the end a checker prunes away all infeasible runs where the initial values guessed for one round do not match the values computed at the end of the previous round. This requires a second set of memory copies. LR thus uses a large number of extra variables; the number of assignments involved in handling these variables, the high degree of nondeterminism, and the late pruning of infeasible runs can all cause performance problems for the backend tool. Moreover, due to the eager exploration, LR cannot rely on error checks built into the backend and also requires specific techniques to handle programs with heap-allocated memory [40].

Since the set of states reachable by a concurrent program can be much smaller than the whole state space explored by LR, *lazy* techniques that explore only the reachable states can be much more efficient. The first lazy sequentialization schema was given by La Torre, Madhusudan, and Parlato [35] (LMP). It also uses several copies of the shared memory, but in contrast to LR these copies are always computed and not guessed. However, since the local state of a thread is not stored on context switches, the values of the thread-local variables must be recomputed from scratch when a thread is resumed. This recomputation poses no problem for tools that compute function summaries [35,36] since they can re-use the summaries from previous rounds. However, it is a serious drawback for applying LMP in connection with BMC because it leads to exponentially growing formula sizes [29]. It is thus an open question whether it is possible to design an effective lazy sequentialization for BMC-based backends.

In this paper, we answer this question and design a new, surprisingly simple but effective lazy sequentialization schema that aggressively exploits the structure of bounded programs and works well with BMC-based backends. The resulting sequentialized program simulates all bounded executions of the original program for a bounded number of rounds. It is composed of a main driver and an individual function for each thread, where function calls and loops of the input program are inlined and unrolled, respectively [17]. In each round, the main driver calls each such thread simulation function; however, their execution does not repeat all the steps done in the previous rounds but instead jumps (in multiple hops) back to the stored program location where the previous round has finished. We keep the values of the thread-local variables between the different function activations (by turning them into `static` variables), which avoids their recomputation and thus the exponentially growing formula sizes observed by Ghafari et al. [29]. The size of the formulas is instead proportional to the product of the size of the original program, the number of threads and the number of rounds. The translation is carefully designed to introduce very small memory overheads and very few sources of nondeterminism, so that it produces simple formulas, and is thus very effective in practice. In contrast to LR, only reachable states of the input program are explored, and thus the translation requires no built-in error checks nor any special dynamic memory allocation handling, but can rely on the backend for these.

We have implemented this sequentialization in a prototype tool Lazy-CSeq that handles (i) the main parts of the POSIX thread API [31], such as dynamic thread creation and deletion, and synchronization via thread join, locks, and condition variables; (ii) the full C language with all its peculiarities such as different data types, dynamic memory allocation, and low-level programming features such as pointer arithmetics. Lazy-CSeq implements both bounding and sequentialization as source-to-source translations. The resulting sequential C program can be given to any existing verification tool for sequential C programs. We have tested Lazy-CSeq with BLITZ [16], CBMC [4], ESBMC [19], and LLBMC [24].

We have evaluated our approach and tool over the SV-COMP benchmark suite [9]. Lazy-CSeq [30] won the concurrency category of SV-COMP14, where it significantly outperformed both Threader [46], the previous winner in the concurrency category [8], and CBMC v4.5 [4], a mature BMC tool with recently added native concurrency support. The results thus justify the general sequentialization approach, and in contrast to the findings by Ghafari et al. [29], also demonstrate that a lazy translation can be more suitable for use in BMC than the more commonly applied LR translation [42,22], as Lazy-CSeq also outperforms by orders of magnitude our own LR-based CSeq tool [25].

2   Bounded Multi-threaded C Programs

pthread_t: type of thread identifiers

pthread_create(&t,&f,&arg):
    creates a thread with unique identifier t,
    by calling function f with argument arg

pthread_join(t):
    suspends current thread until t terminates

pthread_mutex_t: type of mutex variables

pthread_mutex_init(&m): creates an unlocked mutex m

pthread_mutex_lock(&m): blocks until m is unlocked,
    then acquires and locks it

pthread_mutex_unlock(&m):
    unlocks m if called by the owning thread,
    returns an error otherwise

pthread_mutex_destroy(&m): frees m

Fig. 1. Example Pthreads routines

Multi-threaded C programs with Pthreads. Pthreads is a POSIX standard [31] for threads that defines a set of C functions, types and constants. In the following, we will refer to C programs that use the Pthreads API simply as multi-threaded C programs. In Fig. 1 we show the part of the API we use in our running example, in particular thread creation and join, and mutex primitives for thread synchronization; for simplicity, we omit the attribute and status arguments that various routines use. We also handle condition variables but omit them here. During the execution of a multi-threaded C program, we can assume that only one thread is *active* at any given time. Initially, only the **main** thread is active; new threads can be spawned from any thread by a call to **pthread_create**. Once created, a thread is added to the pool of inactive threads. At a *context switch* the current thread is suspended and becomes inactive, and one of the inactive threads is resumed and becomes the new active thread. When a thread is resumed its execution continues either from the point where it was suspended or, if it becomes active for the first time, from the beginning.

All threads share the same address space: they can write to or read from global (*shared*) variables of the program to communicate with each other. Since threads can allocate memory dynamically using `malloc`, different threads can simultaneously access and alter shared dynamic data structures. We assume the *sequential consistency* memory model: when a shared variable is updated its new valuation is immediately visible to all the other threads [43]. We further assume that each statement is atomic. This is not guaranteed in general, but we can always rewrite each statement in a way that it involves only one operation on a shared variable by possibly using fresh temporary local variables, so that different interleavings always yield the same result as the original program with atomic executions. We say a statement is *visible* if its execution involves either a read or a write operation of a shared variable, and *invisible* otherwise.

```
pthread_mutex_t m; int c=0;
void P(void *b) {
  int tmp=(*b);
  pthread_mutex_lock(&m);
  if(c>0)
    c++;
  else {
    c=0;
    while(tmp>0) {
      c++; tmp--;
    }
  }
  pthread_mutex_unlock(&m);
}
void C() {
  assume(c>0);
  c--;
  assert(c>=0);
}
int main(void) {
  int x=1,y=5;
  pthread_t p0,p1,c0,c1;
  pthread_mutex_init(&m);
  pthread_create(&p0,P,&x);
  pthread_create(&p1,P,&y);
  pthread_create(&c0,C,0);
  pthread_create(&c1,C,0);
  return 0;
}
```

Fig. 2. Running Example

Running example. We use a producer/consumer system (see Fig. 2) as running example to illustrate our approach. It has two shared variables, a mutex m and an integer c that stores the number of items that have been produced but not yet consumed. The `main` function initializes the mutex and spawns two threads executing P (*producer*) and two threads executing C (*consumer*). Each producer acquires m, increments c, and terminates by releasing m. Each consumer first checks whether there are still elements not yet consumed; if so (i.e., the `assume`-statement on $c > 0$ holds), it decrements c, checks the assertion $c \geq 0$ and terminates. Otherwise it terminates immediately.

Note that the mutex ensures that at any point of the computation at most one producer is operating. However, the assertion can still be violated since there are two consumer threads, whose behaviors can be freely interleaved: with $c = 1$, both consumers can pass the assumption, so that both decrement c and one of them will write the value -1 back to c, and thus violate the assertion.

Bounded multi-threaded programs. Given a program, an assertion, and a depth bound, BMC translates the program into a formula that is satisfiable if and only if the assertion has a counterexample of the given depth or less. The resulting formula thus gives a static view of the bounded computations of the program. Since BMC only explores bounded computations, we can simplify the program before translating it; in particular, we can replace or *unwind* loops and function calls by appropriately guarded repeated copies of the corresponding loop and

```
bool active[T]={1,0,0,0,0};
int cs,ct,pc[T],size[T]={5,8,8,2,2};
#define G(L) assume(cs>=L);
#define J(A,B) if(pc[ct]>A||A>=cs) goto B;
pthread_mutex_t m; int c=0;
void P0(void *b) {
0:J(0,1) static int tmp=(*b);
1:J(1,2) pthread_mutex_lock(&m);
2:J(2,3) if(c>0)
3:J(3,4)    c++;
         else { G(4)
4:J(4,5)    c=0;
         if(!(tmp>0)) goto _l1;
5:J(5,6)    c++; tmp--;
         if(!(tmp>0)) goto _l1;
6:J(6,7)    c++; tmp--;
         assume(!(tmp>0));
         _l1: G(7);
         } G(7)
7:J(7,8) pthread_mutex_unlock(&m);
         goto _P0; _P0: G(8)
8:       return;
}
void P1(void *b) {...}
void C0() {
0:J(0,1) assume(c>0);
1:J(1,2) c--;
         assert(c>=0);
         goto _C0; _C0: G(2)
2:       return;
}
void C1() {...}
int main0() {
         static int x=1,y=5;
         static pthread_t p0,p1,c0,c1;
0:J(0,1) pthread_mutex_init(&m);
1:J(1,2) pthread_create(&p0,P0,&x,1);
1:J(2,3) pthread_create(&p1,P1,&y,2);
2:J(3,4) pthread_create(&c0,C0,0,3);
3:J(4,5) pthread_create(&c1,C1,0,4);
         goto _main; _main: G(4)
5:       return 0;
}
int main() {...see Fig. 4...}
```

Fig. 3. Translation of running example with unwinding bound of 2

function bodies to yield a *bounded program*. Unwinding has one important property that is exploited by our approach: in the resulting bounded program, all jumps are forwards, and each statement is executed at most once in a run.

We implement unwinding with a few modifications for multi-threaded C programs. We do not unwind calls to any Pthreads routines and convert the program's main function into a thread. We also create and unwind a fresh copy of each function that appears as an argument in a call to pthread_create in the unwound program; these copies will be used to simulate the threads. If the original program can spawn multiple threads with the same start function we thus get multiple copies of that function. We assume the second argument of pthread_create is statically determined. We denote any programs with this structure as *bounded multi-threaded C programs*.

Fig. 3 shows the transformation result for the producer/consumer example (cf. Fig. 2), obtained using an unwind bound of 2. The black parts are the unwound original program, while the light gray parts are the instrumentation added by the sequentialization proper, as described in Section 3. Note that we get two separate unwound copies of each of the functions P and C, since the original program spawns two producer and two consumer threads.

3 Lazy Sequentialization for Bounded Programs

We now describe our code-to-code translation from a bounded multi-threaded program P (which can for example be obtained by the unwinding process sketched in the previous section) to a sequential program P_K^{seq} that simulates all round-robin executions with $K > 0$ rounds of P.

P consists by definition of $n + 1$ functions $f_0, \ldots, f_n$ (where f_0 denotes the unwound main function) and contains n calls to pthread_create, which create (at most) n threads with the start functions $f_1, \ldots, f_n$. Each start function is associated with at most one thread, so that we can identify threads and functions. For round-robin executions, we fix an arbitrary schedule ρ by permuting $f_0, \ldots, f_n$; in each round we execute an arbitrary number of statements from each thread $\rho_0, \ldots, \rho_n$. For any fixed ρ our translation then guarantees that P fails an assertion in K rounds if and only if P_K^{seq} fails the same assertion. The translation thus preserves not only bounded reachability, but allows us to perform on the bounded multi-threaded program all analyses that are supported by the sequential backend tool.

P_K^{seq} is composed of a new function $\texttt{main}$ and a thread simulation function f_i^{seq} for each thread f_i in P. The new $\texttt{main}$ of P_K^{seq} calls, in the order given by ρ, the functions f_i^{seq} for K complete rounds. For each thread it maintains the label at which the context switch was simulated in the previous round and where the computation must thus resume in the current round. Each f_i^{seq} is essentially f_i with few lines of additional control code and with labels to denote the relevant context switch points in the original code. When executed, each f_i^{seq} jumps (in multiple hops) to the saved position in the code and then restarts its execution until the label of the next context switch is reached. We make the local variables persistent (i.e., of storage class $\texttt{static}$) such that we do not need to re-compute them when resuming suspended executions.

We describe our translation in a top-down fashion. We also convey a correctness proof and provide implementation details as we go along. We start by describing the (global) auxiliary variables used in the translation. Then, we give the details of the function $\texttt{main}$ of P_K^{seq}, and illustrate how to construct each f_i^{seq} from f_i. Finally, we discuss how the Pthreads routines are simulated.

Auxiliary Data Structures. While simulating P, the sequentialized program P_K^{seq} maintains the data structures below; here T is a symbolic constant denoting the maximal number of threads in the program, i.e., $n + 1$.

- $\texttt{bool active[T]}$; tracks whether a thread is active, i.e., has been created but not yet terminated. Initially, only $\texttt{active[0]}$ is $\texttt{true}$ since f_0^{seq} simulates the $\texttt{main}$ function of P.
- $\texttt{void* arg[T]}$; stores the argument used for thread creation.
- $\texttt{int size[T]}$; stores the largest label used as jump target in the thread simulation functions f_i^{seq}.
- $\texttt{int pc[T]}$; stores the label of the last context switch point for each thread simulation function.
- $\texttt{int ct}$; tracks the index of the thread currently under simulation.
- $\texttt{int cs}$; contains the label at which the next context switch will happen.

Note that the thread simulation functions f_i^{seq} read but do not write any of the data structures. T and $\texttt{size[]}$ are computed by the unwinding phase and remain unchanged during the simulation. $\texttt{arg[]}$ is set by (the simulation of) $\texttt{pthread\_create}$ and remains unchanged once it is set. $\texttt{active[]}$ is set by $\texttt{pthread\_create}$ and unset by $\texttt{pthread\_exit}$. $\texttt{pc[]}$, $\texttt{ct}$, and $\texttt{cs}$ are updated by the driver.

Main Driver. Fig. 4 shows the new function `main` in P_K^{seq}, which drives the simulation. Each iteration of the loop simulates one entire round of a computation of P. The simulation of each thread f_{ct} invokes the corresponding simulation function f_{ct}^{seq} with the argument `arg[ct]` that was originally used to create the thread. The order in which the functions are called corresponds to the round-robin schedule ρ, here $0, \ldots, n$. For each active thread the driver thus executes the following steps: (i) nondeterministically guess the label for next context switch and store it in `cs`, (ii) check that the value is appropriate, (iii) simulate the thread from `pc[ct]` through to `cs`, and (iv) store `cs` in `pc[ct]`, since in the next round the computation must restart from this label.

```
void main(void) {
  for(r=1; r<=K; r++) {
    ct=0;
    // only active threads
    if(active[ct]) {
      // next context switch
      cs=pc[ct]+nondet_uint();
      // appropriate value?
      assume(cs<=size[ct]);
      // thread simulation
      fseq_0(arg[ct]);
      // store context switch
      pc[ct]=cs;
    }
    .........
    ct=n;
    if(active[ct]) {
      .........
}}}
```

Fig. 4. P_K^{seq} : `main()`

The choice of an appropriate value for `cs` is simplified by the structure of P, more precisely, by the fact that the control flow always moves forward because all jumps are forward. We can thus pick any value for `cs` that is between the value stored in `pc[ct]` (corresponding to the case that the thread will not make any progress, hence skips the round) and the largest label in f_{ct}^{seq} that is added in the translation (which corresponds to the last possible context switch point in the code of the corresponding thread f_{ct}). We stress that this guess is the only source of nondeterminism introduced by our translation.

Thread Translation. Each function f_i representing a thread in P is converted into a corresponding function f_i^{seq} in P_K^{seq} that is obtained as follows.

Turning local variables into static variables. Each thread f_i in P is simulated in P_K^{seq} by repeated calls to f_i^{seq}; each invocation executes a fragment of the code according to the context switch points that are guessed nondeterministically in the `main` function. Since each thread simulation function is only called once in each round, we can persist the thread-local variables between consecutive invocations (by turning them into `static` variables), and so avoid the inefficient recomputation of their values. However, uninitialized local variables may contain undefined values, while static variables are initialized to 0 by default. Thus, after the declaration of these variables we assign them with a nondeterministic value. For instance, `int tmp;` is turned into `static int tmp=nondet_int();`. This directly applies to all primitive C types. For arrays and structured types, we just do this at the level of the components.

Positioning and returning from a thread. When a function f_i^{seq} is called for the first time (i.e., in the first round), it starts its execution from the beginning. In the subsequent calls, it must skip over the statements already executed in previous calls, in order to resume the simulation from the context switch point. When the control reaches the label guessed for the context switch, it must return without executing any further statements. Different solutions exist to implement this using `goto` statements and distinct labels associated with every meaningful context switch point in the code. We tried to use a multiplexer at the top of the thread's body, implemented with a `switch` and a series of `goto` statements, to jump over the statements already executed, directly to the starting label. We injected additional code at the context switch label to return immediately when the thread is pre-empted. However, this schema has performed poorly in our experiments, possibly because it introduces complex control flow branching.

In contrast, the schema we present here, although at first perhaps counter-intuitive, scales well when used together with BMC backends. We use `goto` statements in a way that avoids complex branching in the control flow. We use consecutive natural numbers as labels, starting with 0 for the first statement in each function, and label the other statements with numbers increasing in program order (see Fig. 3). To reduce the nondeterminism, we insert the labels (which are only used to simulate the context switches) only at the first statement, the last statement, and every visible statement. Note that this suffices, as we are only interested in assertion violations and in general properties involving only the shared memory and the local state of one thread.

Together with each label i (except for the last one) we also inject a conditional goto of the form `if( pc[ct]>`i` || `i` >=cs ) goto `$i+1$`;` in front of the statement. Note that the fragment $i+1$ is evaluated at translation time, and thus simplifies to an integer literal that also occurs as label. When the thread simulation function tries to execute statements before the context switch of the previous round, or after the guessed context switch, the condition becomes true, and the control jumps to the next label without executing actual statements of the thread. This achieves the positioning of the control at the program counter corresponding to `pc[ct]` with potentially multiple hops, and similarly when the guessed context switch label is reached, the fall-through to the last statement of the thread (which is by assumption always a `return`). Note that, whenever the control is between these two labels, the injected code is immaterial, and the statements of f_{ct}^{seq} in this part of the code are executed as in the original thread. We use a macro J to package up the injected control code (see Fig. 3).

As an example, consider the program in Fig. 3, and assume that P0 is called (i.e., `ct`=1) with `pc[1]`=2 and `cs`=6. At label 0, the condition of the injected `if` statement holds, thus the `goto` statement is executed and the control jumps to label 1. Again, the condition is true, and then the control jumps to label 2. Now, the condition fails, thus the underlying code is executed, up to label 5. At label 6, the condition of the injected `if`-statement holds again, thus the control jumps to label 7, and then to label 8, thus reaching the `return` statement without executing any other code of the producer thread.

Handling branching statements. Eager schemas such as LR need to prune away guesses for the shared variables that lead to infeasible computations. A similar issue arises in our schema for the guesses of context switches. We remark that this is the only source of nondeterminism introduced by our translation.

Consider for example the `if-then-else` in P0, as shown in Fig. 3, and assume that `pc[0]`=2 and `cs`=3, i.e., in this round the sequentialized program is assumed to simulate (feasible) control flows between labels 2 and 3. However, if $c \leq 0$, then the program jumps from label 2 directly to label 4 in the `else`-branch; if we ignore the G(4) macro, the condition in the if statement inserted by J(4,5) would be tested, and since it would hold, the control flow would slide through to label 8, and return to the main driver, which would then set pc[0] to 3. In the next round, the computation would then duly resume from this label—which should be unreachable! Similar problems may occur when the context switch label is in the body of the else-branch, and with goto statements.

Note that assigning pc in the called function rather than in the main driver would fix this problem. However, this would require to inject at each possible context-switch point an assignment to pc guarded by a nondeterministic choice. This has performed poorly in our experiments. The main reason for this is that the control code is spread "all over" and thus even small increments of its complexity may significantly increase the complexity of the formulas computed by the backend tools. We therefore simply prune away simulations that would store unreachable labels in pc. For this, we use a simple guard of the form assume(cs>=j);, where j is the next inserted label in the code. We insert such guards at all control flow locations that are target of an explicit or implicit jump, i.e., right at the beginning of each else block, right after the if statement, and right after any label in the actual code of the simulated thread. Again, we package this up in a macro called G (see Fig. 3).

This solution prunes away all spurious control flows. Consider first the case of goto statements. We assume without loss of generality that the statement's execution is feasible in the multi-threaded program and that the target's label l is in the code after the planned context switch point. But then the inserted G assumption fails, and the simulation is correctly aborted. The argument for if statements is more involved but follows the same lines. First consider that the planned context switch is the then branch. If the simulation takes the control flow into the else branch, then the guard fails because the first label in this branch is guaranteed to be greater than any label in the then branch, and the simulation is aborted. In the symmetric scenario, the guard after the if statement will do the job because cs is guaranteed to be smaller than the next label used as argument in the G. Note that the J macro at the last context switch point in the else branch (in the example J(6,7)) jumps over this guard so that it never prunes feasible control flows.

We stress that though the guess of context-switch point is done eagerly and thus we need to prune away infeasible guesses, the simulation of the input program is still done lazily. In fact, even when we halt a simulation at a guard, all the statements of the input program executed until that point correspond to a prefix of a feasible computation of the input program.

Simulation of Pthreads Routines. For each Pthreads routine we provide a verification stub, i.e., a simple standard C function that replaces the original implementation for verification purposes. Fig. 5 shows the stubs for the routines used in this paper. Variables of type pthread_t are simply mapped to integers, which serve as unique thread identifiers; all other relevant information is stored in the auxiliary data structures, as described in Sect. 3.

```
typedef pthread_t int;
int pthread_create(pthread_t *t,
        void *(*f)(void*), void *arg, int id)
  { active[id] = ACTIVE;
    arg[id]=arg;
    *t=id;
    return 0; }
int pthread_join(pthread_t t)
  { assume(pc[t]==size[t]); }
int pthread_exit(void *value_ptr)
  { return 0; }
typedef pthread_mutex_t int;
int pthread_mutex_init(pthread_mutex_t *m)
  { *m=FREE; }
int pthread_mutex_destroy(pthread_mutex_t *m)
  { *m=DESTROY; }
int pthread_mutex_lock(pthread_mutex_t *m)
  { assert(*m!=DESTROY);
    assume(*m==FREE); *m=t; }
int pthread_mutex_unlock(pthread_mutex_t *m)
  { assert(*m==t); *m=FREE; }
```

Fig. 5. Pthreads verification stubs

In `pthread_create` we simply set the thread's `active` flag and store the argument to be passed to the thread simulation function. Note that we do not need to store the thread start function, as the `main` driver calls all thread simulation functions explicitly, and that the `pthread_create` stub uses an additional integer argument `id` that serves as thread identifier and is copied into the `pthread_t` argument `t`. The `id` values are added to the `pthread_create` calls by the unwinding phase, corresponding to the order in which the calls occur in the unwound program.

In a real Pthreads implementation a thread invoking `pthread_join(t)` should be blocked until `t` is terminated. In the simulation a thread is terminated if it has reached the thread's last label, which corresponds to a `return` but there is no notion of blocking and unblocking. Instead, the stub for `pthread_join` uses an `assume` statement with the condition `pc[t]==size[t]` (which checks that the argument thread `t` has reached its last label) to prune away any simulation that corresponds to a blocking join. We can then see that this pruning does not change the reachability of error states. Assume that the joining thread `t` terminates after the invocation of `pthread_join(t)`. The invoking thread should be unblocked then but the simulation has already been pruned. However, this execution can be captured by another simulation in which a context switch is simulated right before the execution of the `pthread_join`, and the invoking thread is scheduled to run only after the thread `t` is terminated, hence avoiding the pruning as above.

For mutexes we need to know whether they are free or already destroyed, or which thread holds them otherwise. We thus map the type `pthread_mutex_t` to integers, and define two constants `FREE` and `DESTROY` that have values different from any possible thread index. When we initialize or destroy a mutex we assign it the appropriate constant. If we want to lock a variable we assert that it is not destroyed and then check whether it is free before we assign to it the index of the thread that has invoked `pthread_mutex_lock`. Similarly to the case of `pthread_join` we block the simulation if the lock is held by another thread. If a thread executes `pthread_mutex_unlock`, we first assert that the lock is held by the invoking thread and then set it to `FREE`.

4   Implementation and Evaluation

Implementation. We have implemented the sequentialization described in the previous sections in the prototype tool Lazy-CSeq. It takes as input a multi-threaded C program p.c and two parameters r and u representing the round and unwind bounds, respectively, and produces the sequentialized program _cs_p.c. This is an un-threaded but nondeterministic bounded C program that can be processed by any analysis tool for sequential C (note not just BMC tools).

Lazy-CSeq can also be used as a wrapper around existing sequential verification backends. If the optional parameter b to specify the backend is given, it calls the tool to check for the reachability (within the given bounds) of the ERROR label in the original program. If the label is reachable, Lazy-CSeq returns in a separate file a counterexample trace (in the backend format) as witness to the error. The current version of Lazy-CSeq supports as backends the bounded model-checkers BLITZ, CBMC, LLBMC and ESBMC. However, since the implemented schema is very generic, the instrumentation for the different backends differs only in a few lines and other backends can be integrated easily.

Lazy-CSeq is implemented in Python on top of pycparser [7]. It consists of three main phases, where the input program is first parsed into an abstract syntax tree (AST) then transformed by repeatedly visiting the AST, and finally un-parsed into C program text. The transformation phase is implemented as a chain of several modules, each taking the program at some step in the overall translation process, and producing the program for next step. The modules can be grouped according to the following main phases of the translation, (*i*) preprocessing: merge, introduce workarounds to avoid known backend corner-cases, perform light input program simplifications; (*ii*) program bounding: perform function and loop unwinding, and thread duplication; (*iii*) instrumentation: insert code for simulation of the pthread API, concurrency simulation, and finalize the backend specific instrumentation.

Evaluation. We have evaluated our sequentialization approach with Lazy-CSeq on the benchmark set from the concurrency category of the SV-COMP14 [9] software verification competition. This set consists of 76 concurrent C files using the Pthread library, with a total size of about 4,500 lines of code. 20 of the files contain a reachable error location. We chose this benchmark set because it is widely used and all tools (but Corral) we compare against have been trained on this set for the competition.

We ran the experiments on an otherwise idle PC with a Xeon W3520 2.6GHz processor and 12GB of memory, running Linux with a 64-bit kernel (3.0.6). We set a 10GB memory limit and a 750s timeout for each benchmark.

The experiments are split into two parts. The first part concerns only the unsafe programs, where we investigate the effectiveness of several tools at finding errors. The second part concerns the safe programs, where we estimate whether limiting the round bounds to small values allows a more extensive exploration of programs in terms of increased values of loop unwinding bounds. The tools used in the experiments are BLITZ [16] (4.0), CBMC [4] (4.5 and 4.7), Corral [41], CSeq [25] (0.5) ESBMC [19] (1.22), LLBMC [24] (2013.1), and Threader [46].

Unsafe instances. The evaluation on unsafe instances is, again, split into two parts. We first evaluated the performance of Lazy-CSeq with the different sequential backend tools; the results are shown on the left of Table 1. Note that

Table 1. Bug-hunting performance (unsafe instances); $-^1$: timeout (750s); $-^2$: internal error; $-^3$: manual translation not done; $-^4$: test case rejected; $-^5$: unknown failure

	unwind	round	Sequentialized version					Concurrent version					
			BLITZ 4.0	CBMC 4.5	CBMC 4.7	ESBMC 1.22	LLBMC 2013.1	CBMC 4.5	CBMC 4.7	Corral	CSeq 0.5	ESBMC 1.22	Threader
27_boop_simple_v	2	2	0.3	0.3	0.3	0.8	0.4	$-^5$	0.4	1.9	1.0	$-^1$	117.6
28_buggy_simple_loop1	2	1	0.2	0.2	0.2	0.3	0.3	$-^5$	0.3	0.8	0.2	624.7	0.3
32_pthread5_vs	2	2	0.4	0.2	0.3	0.2	0.2	$-^5$	0.8	2.2	$-^2$	$-^1$	$-^1$
40_barrier_v	4	1	0.2	0.3	0.2	0.3	0.3	$-^5$	0.6	0.8	$-^2$	$-^2$	0.7
49_bigshot_p	1	2	0.3	0.4	0.3	0.3	0.6	0.4	0.3	$-^3$	$-^4$	1.7	$-^2$
50_bigshot_s	1	2	0.3	0.4	0.3	0.3	0.6	$-^5$	0.5	$-^3$	$-^4$	4.0	$-^2$
53_fib_bench	5	5	36.6	1.1	1.0	15.2	2.1	0.7	1.8	5.8	6.3	31.1	6.9
55_fib_bench_longer	6	6	155.5	4.1	1.5	402.1	3.1	1.6	3.2	14.4	7.2	150.9	10.4
57_fib_bench_longest	11	11	$-^1$	425.7	214.0	$-^1$	$-^1$	645.9	75.2	$-^1$	$-^2$	$-^1$	54.3
61_lazy01	1	1	0.3	0.2	0.2	0.2	0.4	0.6	0.5	1.3	0.7	398.6	7.1
63_qrcu	1	2	1.4	0.6	0.8	0.7	$-^5$	0.6	0.7	5.8	$-^5$	$-^1$	$-^1$
65_queue	2	2	1.6	8.4	8.8	1.1	$-^1$	18.8	20.9	$-^3$	128.7	$-^1$	$-^2$
67_read_write_lock	1	2	0.5	0.3	0.3	0.4	$-^5$	0.4	0.4	1.8	2.6	$-^1$	38.4
69_reorder_2	2	1	0.3	0.6	0.6	$-^2$	1.3	1.0	0.7	1.3	$-^2$	$-^1$	2.4
70_reorder_5	4	1	0.4	0.8	0.9	$-^2$	3.3	2.1	0.7	1.9	$-^2$	$-^1$	3.5
72_sigma	16	1	1.4	7.6	7.8	$-^2$	73.0	$-^1$	219.1	$-^3$	$-^4$	$-^1$	$-^2$
73_singleton	1	3	0.7	0.6	0.5	0.5	$-^5$	$-^5$	1.6	$-^3$	$-^4$	$-^1$	$-^2$
75_stack	2	1	0.2	0.3	0.3	0.3	1.0	3.2	0.8	2.1	2.1	$-^1$	151.9
77_stateful01	1	1	0.2	0.2	0.2	0.3	0.5	0.7	0.7	2.0	0.7	$-^1$	0.9
82_twostage_3	2	1	0.3	0.7	0.8	$-^2$	8.0	9.1	4.9	3.6	$-^4$	$-^1$	$-^1$

only the backend run-times are given. The additional Lazy-CSeq pre-processing time, which is the same for every backend, is about one second for each file with our current Python prototype implementation. This could easily and substantially be reduced with a more efficient implementation. The results show that the tools were able to process most of the files generated by Lazy-CSeq's generic pre-processing, and found most of the errors. This is in marked contrast to our experience with CSeq, where the integration of a new backend required a substantial development effort, due to the nature of the LR schema. They also show that the different backends generally perform relatively uniformly, except for few cases where the performance gap is noticeably wide, probably due to a different handling of subtle corner-cases in the input from the backends. Both observations gives us further confidence that our approach is general and not bound to a specific verification backend tool.

We then compared the bug-hunting performances of Lazy-CSeq and several tools with different native concurrency handling approaches. CBMC and ESBMC are both BMC tools; CBMC uses partial orders to handle concurrency symbolically while ESBMC explicitly explores the different schedules [18]. CSeq is based on eager sequentialization, implementing a variant of LR, and uses CBMC as sequential backend. Corral uses a dynamic unwinding of function calls and loops, and implements abstractions on variables with the aim of discovering bugs faster. Threader, the winner in the Concurrency category of the SV-COMP13 competition, is based on predicate abstraction. For each tool (except Threader) we adjusted, for each file, all parameters to the minimum needed to spot the error. The results, given on the right of Table 1, show that Lazy-CSeq is highly competitive. Of the "native" tools only CBMC is able to find all errors, but only with the most recent bug-fix version. All other tools time out, crash, or produce wrong results for several files. This shows how difficult it is to integrate concurrency handling into a verification tool—in contrast to the conceptual and practical simplicity of our approach. Moreover, for simple problems (with verification times around one second), Lazy-CSeq performs comparably with the fastest competitor. On the more demanding instances, Lazy-CSeq is almost always the fastest, except for the Fibonacci tests (53, 55 and 57) that are specifically crafted to force particularly twisted interleavings. In most cases (again except for the Fibonacci tests), Lazy-CSeq successfully finds the errors in all test cases using only three rounds, confirming that few context switches are sufficient to find bugs.

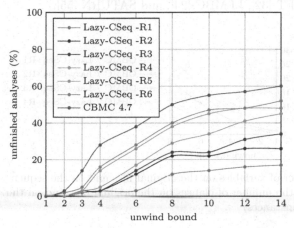

Safe instances. The evaluation on safe instances consisted in comparing Lazy-CSeq using CBMC v4.7 as backend with the best tool with native concurrency handling. We ran nine sets of experiments for CBMC, with unwinding bound to 1, 2, 3, 4, 6, 8, 10, 12, and 14, respectively. Notice that CBMC considers all possible interleavings. For Lazy-CSeq, we ran six repetitions of the sets, with a bound on the number of rounds from one to six, for each of the above unwinding values, respectively.

Fig. 6. Evaluation of safe benchmarks for increasing loop unwind bounds

As shown in Fig. 6, we observe that CBMC starts performing worse than Lazy-CSeq, in terms of number of instances on which the analysis is completed, as we increase the loop unwinding bound. Overall, with the settings from the SV-COMP, Lazy-CSeq, is about 30x faster than CBMC for safe instances. This points out how the introduction of an extra parameter for BMC, i.e., the bound on the number of rounds, can offer a different, alternative coverage of the state-space. In fact, it allows larger loop unwindings, and therefore a deeper exploration of loops, than feasible with other methods.

5 Related Work

We already discussed the main sequentialization approaches [49,42,35] in the introduction. The lazy schema LMP was empirically shown to be more effective than LR in analyzing multithreaded Boolean programs [35,34]. This work has

been extended to parametrized programs [36,37] and used to prove correctness
of abstractions of several Linux device drivers. Other sequentializations cope
with the problem of handling thread creation [22,12] and use different bounding
parameters [39,38,53]. Ghafari et al. [29] observed that LMP is inefficient with
BMC backends. LR has been implemented in CSeq for Pthreads C programs
with bounded thread creation [25,26], and in STORM that also handles dynamic
memory allocation [40]. Poirot [47,22] and Corral [41] are successors of STORM.
Rek implements a sequentialization targeted to real-time systems [15]. None of
the tools specifically targets BMC backends, though.

Biere *et al.* [11] introduced BMC to capitalize on the capacity of modern
SAT/SMT solvers; see [10,21] for a survey on BMC. The idea of loop unwinding
in BMC of software was inspired by Currie *et al.* [20]. Several industrial-strength
BMC tools have been implemented for the C language, including CBMC [17],
ESBMC [18], EXE [14], F-SOFT [32], LLMBC [24], and SATURN [55].

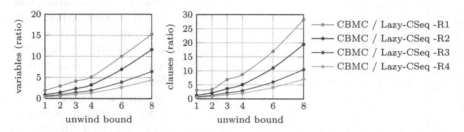

Fig. 7. Ratio between the number of variables on the original files and on the sequentialized files (left), and between the number of clauses on the original files and on the
sequentialized files (right) (safe instances)

Several approaches [50,28,52,51,4] encode program executions as partial orders,
in which each thread is an SSA program and operations on the shared memory are
constrained by a global conjunct modeling the memory model. In [4] the authors
argued that the formula size of their encodings on the considered benchmarks
(among which are 36 from SV-COMP14) is smaller than those of [50,28,52,51]. In
our work, we have empirically evaluated the formula size of our encoding against
CBMC (see Fig. 7). The main result is that our approach yields smaller formulas
already for small unwind bounds, even for four rounds; with increasing unwind
bounds (e.g., $n = 8$), CBMC's formulas contain 5x to 15x more variables and 5x
to 25x more clauses, depending on the number of rounds.

6   Conclusions

We have presented a novel lazy sequentialization schema for bounded multi-
threaded C programs that has been carefully designed to take advantage of BMC
tools developed for sequential programs. We have implemented our approach in
the prototype tool Lazy-CSeq as a code-to-code translation. Lazy-CSeq can also
be used as a stand-alone model checker that currently supports four different

BMC tools as backends. We validated our approach experimentally on the SV-COMP14 [9] concurrency benchmarks suite. The results show that:

- Lazy-CSeq can detect all the errors in the unsafe files, and is competitive with or even outperforms state-of-the art BMC tools that natively handle concurrency;
- it allows a more extensive analysis of safe programs with a higher number of loop unwindings by imposing small bounds on the number of rounds;
- it is generic in the sense that works well with different backends.

Laziness allows us to avoid handling all spurious errors that can occur in an eager exploration. Thus, we can inherit from the backend tool all checks for sequential C programs such as array-bounds-check, division-by-zero, pointer-checks, overflow-checks, reachability of error labels and assertion failures, etc.

A core feature of our code-to-code translation that significantly impacts its effectiveness is that it just injects light-weight, non-invasive control code into the input program. The control code is composed of few lines of guarded goto statements and, within the added function main, also very few assignments. It does not use the program variables and it is clearly separated from the program code. This is in sharp contrast with the existing sequentializations (LR, LMP and the like, which can handle also unbounded programs) where multiple copies of the shared variables are used and assigned in the control code.

As consequence, we get three general benefits that set our work apart from previous approaches, and that simplify the development of full-fledged, robust model-checking tools based on sequentialization. First, the translation only needs to handle concurrency—all other features of the programming language remain opaque, and the backend tool can take care of them. This is in contrast to, for example, LR where dynamic allocation of the memory is handled by using maps [40]. Second, the original motivation for sequentializations was to reuse for concurrent programs the technology built for sequential program verification, and in principle, a sequentialization could work as a generic concurrency preprocessor for such tools. However, previous implementations needed specific tuning and optimizations for the different tools (see [25]). In contrast, Lazy-CSeq works well with different backends (currently BLITZ, CBMC, ESBMC, and LLBMC), and the only required tuning was to comply with the actual program syntax supported by them. Finally, the clean separation between control code and program code makes it simple to generate a counter-example starting from the one generated by the backend tool.

Future work. We see two main future directions. One is to investigate optimizations to improve the performance of our approach. Partial order reduction techniques combined with symbolic model checking can improve the performance [54], and the approach of [33] for SAT-based analysis fits well in our sequentialisation schema. Also, a tuning of the backends on the class of programs generated in our translations could boost performance. It is well known that static code optimizations such as constant propagation are essential for performance gain in BMC. The other direction is to extend our approach to weak memory models implemented in modern architectures (see for example [5,3]), and to other communication primitives such as MPI [27].

Lazy-CSeq homepage:
http://users.ecs.soton.ac.uk/gp4/cseq/cseq.html.

References

1. 2013 28th IEEE/ACM International Conference on Automated Software Engineering, ASE 2013, Silicon Valley, CA, USA, November 11-15. IEEE (2013)
2. Ábrahám, E., Havelund, K. (eds.): TACAS 2014 (ETAPS). LNCS, vol. 8413. Springer, Heidelberg (2014)
3. Alglave, J., Kroening, D., Nimal, V., Tautschnig, M.: Software Verification for Weak Memory via Program Transformation. In: Felleisen, M., Gardner, P. (eds.) ESOP 2013. LNCS, vol. 7792, pp. 512–532. Springer, Heidelberg (2013)
4. Alglave, J., Kroening, D., Tautschnig, M.: Partial Orders for Efficient Bounded Model Checking of Concurrent Software. In: Sharygina, N., Veith, H. (eds.) CAV 2013. LNCS, vol. 8044, pp. 141–157. Springer, Heidelberg (2013)
5. Atig, M.F., Bouajjani, A., Parlato, G.: Getting Rid of Store-Buffers in TSO Analysis. In: Gopalakrishnan, G., Qadeer, S. (eds.) CAV 2011. LNCS, vol. 6806, pp. 99–115. Springer, Heidelberg (2011)
6. Ball, T., Sagiv, M. (eds.): Proceedings of the 38th ACM SIGPLAN-SIGACT Symposium on Principles of Programming Languages, POPL 2011, Austin, TX, USA, January 26-28. ACM (2011)
7. Bendersky, E.: http://code.google.com/p/pycparser/
8. Beyer, D.: Second Competition on Software Verification - (Summary of SV-COMP 2013). In: Piterman, Smolka (eds.) [45], pp. 594–609
9. Beyer, D.: Status report on software verification - (competition summary sv-comp 2014). In: Ábrahám, Havelund (eds.) [2], pp. 373–388
10. Biere, A.: Bounded Model Checking. In: Biere, A., Heule, M., van Maaren, H., Walsh, T. (eds.) Handbook of Satisfiability. Frontiers in Artificial Intelligence and Applications, vol. 185, pp. 457–481. IOS Press (2009)
11. Biere, A., Cimatti, A., Clarke, E., Zhu, Y.: Symbolic model checking without bDDs. In: Cleaveland, W.R. (ed.) TACAS 1999. LNCS, vol. 1579, pp. 193–207. Springer, Heidelberg (1999)
12. Bouajjani, A., Emmi, M., Parlato, G.: On Sequentializing Concurrent Programs. In: Yahav, E. (ed.) Static Analysis. LNCS, vol. 6887, pp. 129–145. Springer, Heidelberg (2011)
13. Bouajjani, A., Maler, O. (eds.): CAV 2009. LNCS, vol. 5643. Springer, Heidelberg (2009)
14. Cadar, C., Ganesh, V., Pawlowski, P.M., Dill, D.L., Engler, D.R.: EXE: Automatically Generating Inputs of Death. In: Juels, A., Wright, R.N., di Vimercati, S.D.C. (eds.) ACM Conference on Computer and Communications Security, pp. 322–335. ACM (2006)
15. Chaki, S., Gurfinkel, A., Strichman, O.: Time-bounded Analysis of Real-time Systems. In: Bjesse, P., Slobodová, A. (eds.) FMCAD, pp. 72–80. FMCAD Inc. (2011)
16. Cho, C.Y., D'Silva, V., Song, D.: BLITZ: Compositional Bounded Model Checking for Real-world Programs. In: ASE [1], pp. 136–146
17. Clarke, E., Kroning, D., Lerda, F.: A Tool for Checking ANSI-C Programs. In: Jensen, K., Podelski, A. (eds.) TACAS 2004. LNCS, vol. 2988, pp. 168–176. Springer, Heidelberg (2004)

18. Cordeiro, L., Fischer, B.: Verifying Multi-threaded Software using SMT-based Context-bounded Model Checking. In: Taylor, R.N., Gall, H., Medvidovic, N. (eds.) ICSE, pp. 331–340. ACM (2011)
19. Cordeiro, L., Fischer, B., Marques-Silva, J.: SMT-Based Bounded Model Checking for Embedded ANSI-C Software. IEEE Trans. Software Eng. 38(4), 957–974 (2012)
20. Currie, D.W., Hu, A.J., Rajan, S.P.: Automatic Formal Verification of DSP software. In: DAC, pp. 130–135 (2000)
21. D'Silva, V., Kroening, D., Weissenbacher, G.: A Survey of Automated Techniques for Formal Software Verification. IEEE Trans. on CAD of Integrated Circuits and Systems 27(7), 1165–1178 (2008)
22. Emmi, M., Qadeer, S., Rakamaric, Z.: Delay-bounded Scheduling. In: Ball, Sagiv (eds.) [6], pp. 411–422
23. Etessami, K., Rajamani, S.K. (eds.): CAV 2005. LNCS, vol. 3576. Springer, Heidelberg (2005)
24. Falke, S., Merz, F., Sinz, C.: The Bounded Model Checker LLBMC. In: ASE [1], pp. 706–709
25. Fischer, B., Inverso, O., Parlato, G.: CSeq: A Concurrency Pre-processor for Sequential C Verification Tools. In: ASE [1], pp. 710–713
26. Fischer, B., Inverso, O., Parlato, G.: CSeq: A Sequentialization Tool for C - (Competition Contribution). In: Piterman, Smolka (eds.) [45], pp. 616–618
27. Forum, M.P.I.: MPI: A Message-Passing Interface Standard Version 3.0, 09, Chapter author for Collective Communication, Process Topologies, and One Sided Communications (2012)
28. Ganai, M.K., Gupta, A.: Efficient Modeling of Concurrent Systems in BMC. In: Havelund, K., Majumdar, R. (eds.) SPIN 2008. LNCS, vol. 5156, pp. 114–133. Springer, Heidelberg (2008)
29. Ghafari, N., Hu, A.J., Rakamarić, Z.: Context-Bounded Translations for Concurrent Software: An Empirical Evaluation. In: van de Pol, J., Weber, M. (eds.) SPIN 2010. LNCS, vol. 6349, pp. 227–244. Springer, Heidelberg (2010)
30. Inverso, O., Tomasco, E., Fischer, B., La Torre, S., Parlato, G.: Lazy-CSeq: A Lazy Sequentialization Tool for C - (Competition Contribution). In: Ábrahám, Havelund (eds.) [2], pp. 398–401
31. ISO/IEC. Information technology—Portable Operating System Interface (POSIX) Base Specifications, Issue 7, ISO/IEC/IEEE 9945:2009 (2009)
32. Ivancic, F., Yang, Z., Ganai, M.K., Gupta, A., Shlyakhter, I., Ashar, P.: F-Soft: Software Verification Platform. In: Etessami, Rajamani (eds.) [23], pp. 301–306
33. Kahlon, V., Gupta, A., Sinha, N.: Symbolic Model Checking of Concurrent Programs Using Partial Orders and On-the-Fly Transactions. In: Ball, T., Jones, R.B. (eds.) CAV 2006. LNCS, vol. 4144, pp. 286–299. Springer, Heidelberg (2006)
34. La Torre, S., Madhusudan, P., Parlato, G.: Analyzing Recursive Programs Using a Fixed-point Calculus. In: Hind, M., Diwan, A. (eds.) PLDI, pp. 211–222. ACM (2009)
35. La Torre, S., Madhusudan, P., Parlato, G.: Reducing Context-Bounded Concurrent Reachability to Sequential Reachability. In: Bouajjani, Maler (eds.) [13], pp. 477–492
36. La Torre, S., Madhusudan, P., Parlato, G.: Model-Checking Parameterized Concurrent Programs Using Linear Interfaces. In: Touili, T., Cook, B., Jackson, P. (eds.) CAV 2010. LNCS, vol. 6174, pp. 629–644. Springer, Heidelberg (2010)
37. La Torre, S., Madhusudan, P., Parlato, G.: Sequentializing Parameterized Programs. In: Bauer, S.S., Raclet, J.-B. (eds.) FIT. EPTCS, vol. 87, pp. 34–47 (2012)

38. La Torre, S., Napoli, M., Parlato, G.: Scope-Bounded Pushdown Languages. In: Shur, A., Volkov, M. (eds.) DLT. LNCS. Springer (2014)
39. La Torre, S., Parlato, G.: Scope-bounded Multistack Pushdown Systems: Fixed-Point, Sequentialization, and Tree-Width. In: D'Souza, D., Kavitha, T., Radhakrishnan, J. (eds.) FSTTCS. LIPIcs, vol. 18, pp. 173–184. Schloss Dagstuhl - Leibniz-Zentrum fuer Informatik (2012)
40. Lahiri, S.K., Qadeer, S., Rakamaric, Z.: Static and Precise Detection of Concurrency Errors in Systems Code Using SMT Solvers. In: Bouajjani, Maler (eds.) [13], pp. 509–524
41. Lal, A., Qadeer, S., Lahiri, S.K.: A Solver for Reachability Modulo Theories. In: Madhusudan, P., Seshia, S.A. (eds.) CAV 2012. LNCS, vol. 7358, pp. 427–443. Springer, Heidelberg (2012)
42. Lal, A., Reps, T.W.: Reducing Concurrent Analysis Under a Context Bound to Sequential Analysis. Formal Methods in System Design 35(1), 73–97 (2009)
43. Lamport, L.: A New Approach to Proving the Correctness of Multiprocess Programs. ACM Trans. Program. Lang. Syst. 1(1), 84–97 (1979)
44. Musuvathi, M., Qadeer, S.: Iterative Context Bounding for Systematic Testing of Multithreaded Programs. In: Ferrante, J., McKinley, K.S. (eds.) PLDI, pp. 446–455. ACM (2007)
45. Piterman, N., Smolka, S.A. (eds.): TACAS 2013 (ETAPS 2013). LNCS, vol. 7795. Springer, Heidelberg (2013)
46. Popeea, C., Rybalchenko, A.: Threader: A Verifier for Multi-threaded Programs - (Competition Contribution). In: Piterman, Smolka (eds.) [45], pp. 633–636
47. Qadeer, S.: Poirot - A Concurrency Sleuth. In: Qin, S., Qiu, Z. (eds.) ICFEM 2011. LNCS, vol. 6991, pp. 15–15. Springer, Heidelberg (2011)
48. Qadeer, S., Rehof, J.: Context-Bounded Model Checking of Concurrent Software. In: Halbwachs, N., Zuck, L.D. (eds.) TACAS 2005. LNCS, vol. 3440, pp. 93–107. Springer, Heidelberg (2005)
49. Qadeer, S., Wu, D.: KISS: Keep It Simple and Sequential. In: Pugh, W., Chambers, C. (eds.) PLDI, pp. 14–24. ACM (2004)
50. Rabinovitz, I., Grumberg, O.: Bounded Model Checking of Concurrent Programs. In: Etessami, Rajamani (eds.) [23], pp. 82–97
51. Sinha, N., Wang, C.: Staged Concurrent Program Analysis. In: Roman, G.-C., Sullivan, K.J. (eds.) SIGSOFT FSE, pp. 47–56. ACM (2010)
52. Sinha, N., Wang, C.: On Interference Abstractions. In: Ball, Sagiv (eds.) [6], pp. 423–434
53. Tomasco, E., Inverso, O., Fischer, B., La Torre, S., Parlato, G.: MU-CSeq: Sequentialization of C Programs by Shared Memory Unwindings - (Competition Contribution). In: Ábrahám, Havelund (eds.) [2], pp. 402–404
54. Wang, C., Chaudhuri, S., Gupta, A., Yang, Y.: Symbolic Pruning of Concurrent Program Executions. In: van Vliet, H., Issarny, V. (eds.) ESEC/SIGSOFT FSE, pp. 23–32. ACM (2009)
55. Xie, Y., Aiken, A.: Saturn: A SAT-Based Tool for Bug Detection. In: Etessami, Rajamani (eds.) [23], pp. 139–143

An SMT-Based Approach
to Coverability Analysis

Javier Esparza[1], Ruslán Ledesma-Garza[1], Rupak Majumdar[2],
Philipp Meyer[1], and Filip Niksic[2]

[1] Technische Universität München
[2] Max Planck Institute for Software Systems (MPI-SWS)

Abstract. Model checkers based on Petri net coverability have been
used successfully in recent years to verify safety properties of concurrent
shared-memory or asynchronous message-passing software. We revisit a
constraint approach to coverability based on classical Petri net analysis
techniques. We show how to utilize an SMT solver to implement the
constraint approach, and additionally, to generate an inductive invariant from a safety proof. We empirically evaluate our procedure on a
large set of existing Petri net benchmarks. Even though our technique is
incomplete, it can quickly discharge most of the safe instances. Additionally, the inductive invariants computed are usually orders of magnitude
smaller than those produced by existing solvers.

1 Introduction

In recent years many papers have proposed and developed techniques for the
verification of concurrent software [10,6,1,11,4]. In particular, model checkers
based on Petri net coverability have been successfully applied. Petri nets are a
simple and natural automata-like model for concurrent systems, and can model
certain programs with an unbounded number of threads or thread creation. In a
nutshell, the places of the net correspond to program locations, and the number
of tokens in a place models the number of threads that are currently at that
location. This point was first observed in [9], and later revisited in [3] and, more
implicitly, in [10,6].

The problem whether at least one thread can reach a given program location
(modelling some kind of error), naturally reduces to the *coverability problem* for
Petri nets: given a net N and a marking M, decide whether some reachable
marking of N *covers* M, i.e., puts at least as many tokens as M on each place.
While the decidability and EXPSPACE-completeness of the coverability problem
were settled long ago [12,17], new algorithmic ideas have been developed in recent
years [8,7,21,11,13]. The techniques are based on forward or backward state-space
exploration, which is accelerated in a number of ways in order to cope with the
possibly infinite number of states.

In this paper we revisit an approach to the coverability problem based on
classical Petri net analysis techniques: the marking equation and traps [16,18].
The marking equation is a system of linear constraints that can be easily derived

A. Biere and R. Bloem (Eds.): CAV 2014, LNCS 8559, pp. 603–619, 2014.
© Springer International Publishing Switzerland 2014

from the net, and whose set of solutions overapproximates the set of reachable markings. This system can be supplemented with linear constraints specifying a set of unsafe markings, and solved using standard linear or integer programming. If the constraints are infeasible, then all reachable markings are safe. If not, then one can try different aproaches. In [5] a solution of the constraints is used to derive an additional constraint in the shape of a *trap*: a set of places that, loosely speaking, once marked cannot be "emptied"; the process can be iterated. More recently, in [22], Wimmel and Wolf propose to use the solution to guide a state space exploration searching for an unsafe marking; if the search fails, then information gathered during it is used to construct an additional constraint.

Constraint-based techniques, while known for a while, have always suffered from the absence of efficient decision procedures for linear arithmetic together with Boolean satisfiability. Profiting from recent advances in SMT-solving technology, we reimplement the technique of [5] on top of the Z3 SMT solver [2], and apply it to a large collection of benchmarks.

The technique is theoretically incomplete, i.e., the set of linear constraints derived from the marking equation and traps may be feasible even if all reachable markings are safe. Our first and surprising finding is that, despite this fact, the technique is powerful enough to prove safety of 96 out of a total of 115 safe benchmarks gathered from current research papers in concurrent software verification. In contrast, three different state-of-the-art tools for coverability proved only 61, 51, or 33 of these 115 cases! Moreover, and possibly due to the characteristics of the application domain, even the simplest version of the technique —based on the marking equation— is successful in 84 cases.

As a second contribution, and inspired by work on interpolation, we show that a dual version of the classical set of constraints, equivalent in expressive power, can be used not only to check safety, but to produce an inductive invariant. While some existing solvers based on state-space exploration can also produce such invariants, we show that inductive invariants obtained through our technique are usually orders of magnitude smaller. Additionally, while we can use the SMT solver iteratively to minimize the invariant, the tool almost always provides a minimal one at the first attempt.

Related Work. Our starting point was the work of Esparza and Melzer on extending the marking equation with trap conditions to gain a stronger method for proving safety of Petri nets [5]. We combined the constraint-based approach there with modern SMT solvers. Their focus on (integer) linear programming tools of the time enforced some limitations. First, while traps are naturally encoded using Boolean variables, [5] encoded traps and the marking equation together into a set of linear constraints. This encoding came at a practical cost: the encoding required (roughly) $n \times m$ constraints for a Petri net with n places and m transitions, whereas the natural Boolean encoding requires m constraints. Moreover, (I)LP solvers were not effective in searching large Boolean state spaces; our use of modern SAT techniques alleviates this problem. Second, (I)LP solvers used by [5] did not handle strict inequalities. Hence, the authors used additional tricks, such as posing the problem that includes a strict inequality as a minimization

procedure PROCESS 1		procedure PROCESS 2	
	begin		**begin**
	$bit_1 := false$		$bit_2 := false$
	while *true* **do**		**while** *true* **do**
p_1:	$bit_1 := true$	q_1:	$bit_2 := true$
p_2:	**while** bit_2 **do skip od**	q_2:	**if** bit_1 **then**
p_3:	(∗ critical section ∗)	q_3:	$bit_2 := false$
	$bit_1 := false$	q_4:	**while** bit_1 **do skip od**
	od		**goto** q_1
	end		**fi**
		q_5:	(∗ critical section ∗)
			$bit_2 := false$
			od
			end

Fig. 1. Lamport's 1-bit algorithm for mutual exclusion [14]

problem, with the goal of minimizing the involved expression, and testing if the minimal value equaled zero. Unfortunately, this trick led to numerical instabilities. All of these concerns vanish by using an SMT solver.

The marking equation is also the starting point of [22], but the strategies of this approach and ours are orthogonal: while we use the solutions of the marking equation to derive new constraints, [22] uses them to guide state space explorations that search for unsafe markings; new constraints are generated only if the searches fail.

In contrast to other recent techniques for coverability [7,11,13], our technique and the one of [22] are incomplete. However, in [22] Wimmel and Wolf obtain very good results for business process benchmarks, and in this paper we empirically demonstrate that our technique is effective for safe software verification benchmarks, often beating well-optimized state exploration approaches.

Our technique theoretically applies not only to coverability but also to *reachability*. It will be interesting to see whether the techniques can effectively verify reachability questions, e.g., arising from liveness verification [6].

2 Preliminaries

A *Petri net* is a tuple (P, T, F, m_0), where P is a set of *places*, T is a (disjoint) set of *transitions*, $F : (P \times T) \cup (T \times P) \to \{0, 1\}$ is the *flow function*, and $m_0 : P \to \mathbb{N}$ is the initial marking. For $x \in P \cup T$, the *pre-set* is $^\bullet x = \{y \in P \cup T \mid F(y, x) = 1\}$ and the *post-set* is $x^\bullet = \{y \in P \cup T \mid F(x, y) = 1\}$. We extend the pre- and post-set to a subset of $P \cup T$ as the union of the pre- and post-sets of its elements.

A *marking* of a Petri net is a function $m : P \to \mathbb{N}$, which describes the number of tokens $m(p)$ in each place $p \in P$. Assuming an enumeration $p_1, \ldots, p_n$ of P, we often identify m and the vector $(m(p_1), \ldots, m(p_n))$. For a subset $P' \subseteq P$ of places, we write $m(P') = \sum_{p \in P'} m(p)$.

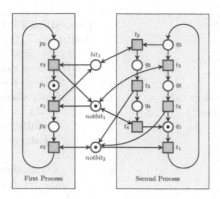

Fig. 2. Petri net for Lamport's 1-bit algorithm

A transition $t \in T$ is *enabled at* m iff for all $p \in {}^{\bullet}t$, we have $m(p) \geq F(p,t)$. A transition t enabled at m may *fire*, yielding a new marking m' (denoted $m \xrightarrow{t} m'$), where $m'(p) = m(p) + F(t,p) - F(p,t)$. A sequence of transitions, $\sigma = t_1 t_2 \dots t_r$ is an *occurrence sequence* of N iff there exist markings $m_1, \dots, m_r$ such that $m_0 \xrightarrow{t_1} m_1 \xrightarrow{t_2} m_2 \dots \xrightarrow{t_r} m_r$. The marking m_r is said to be *reachable* from m_0 by the occurrence of σ (denoted $m_0 \xrightarrow{\sigma} m_r$).

A *property* φ is a linear arithmetic constraint over the free variables P. The property φ holds on a marking m iff $m \models \varphi$. A Petri net N satisfies a property φ (denoted by $N \models \varphi$) iff for all reachable markings $m_0 \xrightarrow{\sigma} m$, we have $m \models \varphi$. A property φ is an *invariant* of N if it holds for every reachable marking. A property is inductive if whenever $m \models \varphi$ and $m \xrightarrow{t} m'$ for some $t \in T$ and marking m', we have $m' \models \varphi$.

Petri nets are represented graphically as follows: places and transitions are represented as circles and boxes, respectively. For $x, y \in P \cup T$, there is an arc leading from x to y iff $F(x,y) = 1$. As an example, consider Lamport's 1-bit algorithm for mutual exclusion [14], shown in Fig. 1. Fig. 2 shows a Petri net model for the code. The two grey blocks model the control flow of the two processes. For instance, the token in place p_1 models the current position of process 1 at program location p_1. The three places in the middle of the diagram model the current values of the variables. For instance, a token in place $notbit_1$ indicates that the variable bit_1 is currently set to *false*. The mutual exclusion property, which states that the two processes cannot be in the critical section at the same time, corresponds to the property that places p_3 and q_5 cannot both have a token at the same time.

3   Marking Equation

We now recall a well-known method, which we call SAFETY, that provides a sufficient condition for a given Petri net N to satisfy a property φ by reducing the problem to checking satisfiability of a linear arithmetic formula. We illustrate the method on Lamport's 1-bit algorithm for mutual exclusion.

Before going into details, we state several conventions. For a Petri net $N = (P, T, F, m_0)$, we introduce a vector of $|P|$ variables M, and a vector of $|T|$ variables X. The vectors M and X will be used to represent the current marking and the number of occurrences of transitions in the occurrence sequence leading to the current marking, respectively. If a place or a transition is given a specific name, we use the same name for its associated variable. Given a place p, the intended meaning of a constraint like $p \geq 3$ is "at the current marking place p must have at least 3 tokens." Given a transition t, the intended meaning of a constraint like $t \leq 2$ is "in the occurrence sequence leading to the current marking, transition t must fire at most twice."

The key idea of the SAFETY method lies in the *marking equation*:

$$M = m_0 + CX \,,$$

where the incidence matrix C is a $|P| \times |T|$ matrix given by

$$C(p, t) = F(t, p) - F(p, t) \,.$$

For each place p, the marking equation contains a constraint that formulates a simple token conservation law: the number of tokens in p at the current marking is equal to the initial number of tokens $m_0(p)$, plus the number of tokens added by the input transitions of p, minus the number of tokens removed by the output transitions. So, for instance, in Lamport's algorithm the constraint for place $notbit_1$ is:

$$notbit_1 = 1 + s_3 + t_5 + t_4 - s_1 - t_4 - t_5 = 1 + s_3 - s_1 \,.$$

We equip the marking equation with the non-negativity conditions, modeling that the number of tokens in a place, or the number of occurrences of a transition in an occurrence sequence cannot become negative. All together, we get the following set of *marking constraints*:

$$\mathcal{C}(P, T, F, m_0) :: \begin{cases} M = m_0 + CX & \text{marking equation} \\ M \geq 0 & \text{non-negativity conditions for places} \\ X \geq 0 & \text{non-negativity conditions for transitions} \end{cases}$$

Method SAFETY for checking that a property φ is invariant for a Petri net $N = (P, T, F, m_0)$ consists of checking for satisfiability of the constraints

$$\mathcal{C}(P, T, F, m_0) \wedge \neg \varphi(M) \,. \tag{1}$$

If the constraints are unsatisfiable, then no reachable marking violates φ. To see that this is true, consider the converse: If there exists an occurrence sequence $m_0 \overset{\sigma}{\to} m$ leading to a marking m that violates the property, then we can construct a valuation of the variables that assigns $m(p)$ to $M(p)$ for each place

p, and the number of occurrences of t in σ to $X(t)$ for each transition t. This valuation then satisfies the constraints.

The method does not work in the other direction: If the constraints (1) are satisfiable, we cannot conclude that the property φ is violated.

As an example, consider the Lamport's algorithm. SAFETY successfully proves the property "if process 1 is at location p_3, then $bit_1 = true$" by showing that $\mathcal{C}(P, T, F, m_0) \wedge p_3 \geq 1 \wedge bit_1 \neq 1$ is unsatisfiable. However, if we apply it to the mutual exclusion property, i.e., check for satisfiability of $\mathcal{C}(P, T, F, m_0) \wedge p_3 \geq 1 \wedge q_5 \geq 1$, we obtain a solution, but we cannot conclude that the mutual exclusion property does not hold.

Note that the marking constraints (1) are interpreted over integer variables. As usual in program analysis, one can solve the constraints over rationals to get an approximation of the method. Solving the constraints over rationals will become useful in Section 5.

4   Refining Marking Equations with Traps

Esparza and Melzer [5] strengthened SAFETY with additional *trap constraints*. A *trap* of a Petri net $N = (P, T, F, m_0)$ is a subset of places $Q \subseteq P$ satisfying the following condition for every transition $t \in T$: if t is an output transition of at least one place of Q, then it is also an input transition of at least one place of Q. Equivalently, Q is a trap if its set of output transitions is included in its set of input transitions, i.e., if $Q^\bullet \subseteq {}^\bullet Q$. Here we present a variant of Esparza's and Melzer's method that encodes traps using Boolean constraints. We call the new method SAFETYBYREFINEMENT.

The method SAFETYBYREFINEMENT is based on the following observation about traps. If Q is a trap and a marking m marks Q, i.e., $m(p) > 0$ for some $p \in Q$, then for each occurrence sequence σ and marking m' such that $m \xrightarrow{\sigma} m'$, we also have $m'(p') > 0$ for some $p' \in Q$. Indeed, by the trap property any transition removing tokens from places of Q also adds at least one token to some place of Q. So, while $m'(Q)$ can be smaller than $m(Q)$, it can never become 0. In particular, if a trap Q satisfies $m_0(Q) > 0$, then every reachable marking m satisfies $m(Q) > 0$ as well.

Since the above property must hold for any trap, we can restrict the constraints from method SAFETY as follows. First, we add an additional vector B of $|P|$ Boolean variables. These variables are used to encode traps: for $p \in P$, $B(p)$ is true if and only if place p is part of the trap. The following constraint specifies that B encodes a trap:

$$trap(B) ::= \bigwedge_{t \in T} \left[\bigvee_{p \in {}^\bullet t} B(p) \implies \bigvee_{p \in t^\bullet} B(p) \right].$$

Next, we define a predicate $mark(m, B)$ that specifies marking m marks a trap:

$$mark(m, B) ::= \bigvee_{p \in P} B(p) \wedge (m(p) > 0).$$

Finally, we conjoin the following constraint to the constraints (1):

$$\forall B : trap(B) \land mark(m_0, B) \implies mark(M, B).\qquad(2)$$

This constraint conceptually enumerates over all subsets of places, and ensures that if the subset forms a trap, and this trap is marked by the initial marking, then it is also marked by the current marking. Thus, markings violating the trap constraint are eliminated.

While the above constraint provides a refinement of the SAFETY method, it requires the SMT solver to reason with universally quantified variables. Instead of directly using universal quantifiers, we use a counterexample-guided heuristic [5,20] of adding trap constraints one-at-a-time in the following way.

If the set of constraints constructed so far (for instance, the set given by the method SAFETY) is feasible, the SMT solver delivers a model that assigns values to each place, corresponding to a potentially reachable marking m. We search for a trap P_m that violates the trap condition (2) for this specific model m. If we find such a trap, then we know that m is unreachable, and we can add the constraint $\sum_{p \in P_m} M(p) \geq 1$ to exclude all markings that violate this specific trap condition.

The search for P_m is a pure Boolean satisfiability question. We ask for an assignment to

$$trap(B) \land mark(m_0, B) \land \neg mark(m, B)\qquad(3)$$

Notice that for a fixed marking m, the predicate $mark(m, B)$ simplifies to a Boolean predicate. Given a satisfying assignment b for this formula, we add the constraint

$$\sum_{\substack{p \in P \\ b(p) = true}} M(p) \geq 1\qquad(4)$$

to the current set of constraints to rule out solutions that do not satisfy this trap constraint. We iteratively add such constraints until either the constraints are unsatisfiable or the Boolean constraints (3) are unsatisfiable (i.e., no traps are found to invalidate the current solution).

This yields the method SAFETYBYREFINEMENT. It is still not complete [5]: one can find nets and unreachable markings that mark all traps of the net.

Let us apply the algorithm SAFETYBYREFINEMENT to Lamport's algorithm and the mutual exclusion property. Recall that the markings violating the property are those satisfying $p_3 \geq 1$ and $q_5 \geq 1$. SAFETY yields a satisfying assignment with $p_3 = bit_1 = q_5 = 1$, and $p = 0$ for all other places p, which corresponds to a potentially reachable marking m. We search for a trap marked at m_0 but not at m. To simplify the notation, we simply write p instead of $B(p)$. The constraints derived from the trap property are:

$$p_1 \lor notbit_1 \implies p_2 \lor bit_1 \qquad q_1 \lor notbit_2 \implies q_2$$
$$p_2 \lor notbit_2 \implies p_3 \lor notbit_2 \qquad q_2 \lor bit_1 \implies q_3 \lor bit_1$$
$$p_3 \lor bit_1 \implies p_1 \lor notbit_1 \qquad q_3 \implies q_4 \lor notbit_2$$
$$q_4 \lor notbit_1 \implies q_1 \lor notbit_1$$
$$q_2 \lor notbit_1 \implies q_5 \lor notbit_1$$
$$q_5 \implies q_1 \lor notbit_2$$

and the following constraints model that at least one of the places initially marked belongs to the trap, but none of the places marked at the satisfying assigment do:

$$p_1 \lor q_1 \lor notbit_1 \lor notbit_2 \qquad \neg p_3 \land \neg q_5 \land \neg bit_1$$

For this set of constraints we find the satisfying assignment that sets p_2, $notbit_1$, $notbit_2$, q_2, q_3 to *true* and all other variables to *false*. So this set of places is an initially marked trap, and so every reachable marking should put at least one token in it. Hence we can add the refinement constraint to marking constraints (1):

$$p_2 + q_2 + q_3 + notbit_1 + notbit_2 \geq 1 \,.$$

On running the SMT solver again, we find the constraints are unsatisfiable, proving that the mutual exclusion property holds.

5   Constructing Invariants from Constraints

We now show that one can compute inductive invariants from the method SAFE-TYBYREFINEMENT. That is, given a Petri net $N = (P, T, F, m_0)$ and a property φ, if SAFETYBYREFINEMENT (over the rationals) can prove N satisfies φ, then in fact we can construct a linear inductive invariant that contains m_0 and does not intersect $\neg \varphi$. We call the new method INVARIANTBYREFINEMENT.

The key observation is to use a constraint system dual to the constraint system for SAFETYBYREFINEMENT. We assume φ is a co-linear property, i.e., the negation $\neg \varphi$ is represented as the constraints:

$$\neg \varphi \; :: \; AM \geq b$$

where A is a $k \times |P|$ matrix, and b is a $k \times 1$ vector, for some $k \geq 1$. Furthermore, we assume that there are $l \geq 0$ trap constraints (4), which are collected in matrix form $DM \geq 1$, for an $l \times |P|$ matrix D, and an $l \times 1$ vector of ones, denoted simply by 1. Consider the following primal system $\mathcal{S}$:

$$\mathcal{C}(P, T, F, m_0) \qquad \text{marking constraints}$$
$$AM \geq b \qquad \text{negation of property } \varphi$$
$$DM \geq 1 \qquad \text{trap constraints}$$

By transforming $\mathcal{S}$ into a suitable form and applying Farkas' Lemma [19], we get the following theorem.

Theorem 1. *The primal system $\mathcal{S}$ is unsatisfiable over the rational numbers if and only if the following dual system $\mathcal{S}'$ is satisfiable over the rational numbers.*

$$
\begin{array}{ll}
\lambda C \leq 0 & \text{inductivity constraint} \\
\lambda m_0 < Y_1 b + Y_2 1 & \text{safety constraint} \\
\lambda \geq Y_1 A + Y_2 D & \text{property constraint} \\
Y_1, Y_2 \geq 0 & \text{non-negativity constraint}
\end{array}
$$

Here λ, Y_1 and Y_2 are vectors of variables of size $1 \times |P|$, $1 \times k$ and $1 \times l$, respectively.

If the primal system $\mathcal{S}$ is unsatisfiable, we can take λ from a solution to $\mathcal{S}'$ and construct an inductive invariant:

$$I(M) ::= DM \geq 1 \wedge \lambda M \leq \lambda m_0.$$

In order to show that $I(M)$ is an invariant, recall that for every reachable marking m there is a solution to $m = m_0 + CX$, with $X \geq 0$. Multiplying by λ and taking into account that λ is a solution to $\mathcal{S}'$, we get

$$\lambda m = \lambda m_0 + \lambda CX \leq \lambda m_0.$$

Furthermore, every reachable marking satisfies the trap constraints $DM \geq 1$. On the other hand, a marking m that violates the property φ does not satisfy $I(M)$, for it either does not satisfy $DM \geq 1$, or both $Am \geq b$ and $Dm \geq 1$ hold. But in the latter case we have

$$\lambda m \geq (Y_1 A + Y_2 D)m = Y_1 Am + Y_2 Dm \geq Y_1 b + Y_2 1 > \lambda m_0.$$

In order to show that $I(M)$ is inductive, we have to show that if $I(m)$ holds for some marking m (reachable or not), and $m \xrightarrow{t} m'$ for some transition t, then $I(m')$ holds as well. Indeed, in this case we have $m' = m + Ce_t$, where e_t is the unit vector with 1 in the t-th component and 0 elsewhere. Hence

$$\lambda m' = \lambda(m + Ce_t) = \lambda m + \lambda Ce_t \leq \lambda m \leq \lambda m_0,$$

and furthermore, as m satisfies the trap constraints, m' also satisfies them.

So far, we have assumed that property φ is a co-linear property. However, it is easy to extend the method to the case when $\varphi = \varphi_1 \wedge \ldots \wedge \varphi_r$, and each φ_i is a co-linear property. In that case, for each φ_i we invoke INVARIANTBYREFINEMENT to obtain an inductive invariant I_i. One can easily verify that $I_1 \wedge \ldots \wedge I_r$ is an inductive invariant with respect to φ.

Minimizing invariants. Note that the system $\mathcal{S}'$ from Theorem 1 may in general have many solutions, and each solution yields an inductive invariant. Solutions where λ has fewer non-zero components yield shorter inductive invariants $I(M)$, assuming terms in $I(M)$ with coefficient zero are left out. We can force the

Inductivity constraints

$$
\begin{array}{lll}
- p_1 + p_2 \quad\quad + bit_1 - notbit_1 \le 0 & - q_1 + q_2 \quad\quad\quad\quad\quad\quad - notbit_2 \le 0 \\
\quad\quad - p_2 + p_3 \quad\quad\quad\quad\quad\quad \le 0 & \quad\quad - q_2 + q_3 \quad\quad\quad\quad\quad\quad \le 0 \\
p_1 \quad\quad - p_3 - bit_1 + notbit_1 \le 0 & \quad\quad\quad\quad - q_3 + q_4 \quad\quad + notbit_2 \le 0 \\
& q_1 \quad\quad\quad\quad\quad - q_4 \quad\quad\quad\quad\quad\quad \le 0 \\
& \quad\quad - q_2 \quad\quad\quad\quad + q_5 \quad\quad\quad\quad \le 0 \\
& q_1 \quad\quad\quad\quad\quad\quad\quad - q_5 + notbit_2 \le 0
\end{array}
$$

Safety constraint

$$
p_1 + q_1 + notbit_1 + notbit_2 < target_1 + target_2 + trap_1
$$

Property constraints

$$
\begin{array}{lllll}
p_1 \ge 0 & q_1 \ge 0 & q_4 \ge 0 & bit_1 \ge 0 \\
p_2 \ge trap_1 & q_2 \ge trap_1 & q_5 \ge target_2 & notbit_1 \ge trap_1 \\
p_3 \ge target_1 & q_3 \ge trap_1 & & notbit_2 \ge trap_1
\end{array}
$$

Non-negativity constraints

$$
target_1, target_2, trap_1 \ge 0
$$

Fig. 3. System of constraints S' for Lamport's algorithm and the mutual exclusion property. Here, $\lambda = (p_1\ p_2\ p_3\ q_1\ q_2\ q_3\ q_4\ q_5\ bit_1\ notbit_1\ notbit_2)$, $Y_1 = (target_1\ target_2)$ and $Y_2 = (trap_1)$.

number of non-zero components to be at most K by introducing a vector of $|P|$ variables Z, adding for each $p \in P$ constraints

$$
\begin{aligned}
\lambda(p) > 0 &\implies Z(p) = 1 \\
\lambda(p) = 0 &\implies Z(p) = 0
\end{aligned}
$$

and adding a constraint $\sum_{p \in P} Z(p) \le K$. By varying K, we can find a solution with the smallest number of non-zero components in λ.

Example. Consider again Lamport's algorithm and the mutual exclusion property. Recall that the negation of the property for this example is $p_3 \ge 1 \wedge q_5 \ge 1$, and the trap constraint is $p_2 + q_2 + q_3 + notbit_1 + notbit_2 \ge 1$. Fig. 3 shows the system of constraints S' for this example. A possible satisfying assignment sets q_1, q_4, and bit_1 to 0, p_2, p_3, and $target_1$ to 2, and all other variables to 1. The corresponding inductive invariant is:

$$
\begin{aligned}
I(M) ::= &\ (p_2 + q_2 + q_3 + notbit_1 + notbit_2 \ge 1) \wedge \\
&\ (p_1 + 2p_2 + 2p_3 + notbit_1 + notbit_2 + q_2 + q_3 + q_5 \le 3).
\end{aligned}
$$

If we add constraints that bound the number of non-zero components in λ to 7, the SMT solver finds a new solution, setting p_2, p_3, $notbit_1$, $notbit_2$, q_2, q_3,

$target_1$, $target_2$, and $trap_1$ to 1, and all other variables to 0. The corresponding inductive invariant for this solution is

$$I'(M) ::= (p_2 + q_2 + notbit_1 + notbit_2 + q_3 \geq 1) \land$$
$$(p_2 + p_3 + notbit_1 + notbit_2 + q_2 + q_3 + q_5 \leq 2).$$

6   Experimental Evaluation

We implemented our algorithms in a tool called *Petrinizer*. Petrinizer is implemented as a script on top of the Z3 SMT solver [2]. It takes as input coverability problem instances encoded in the MIST input format[1], and it runs one of the selected methods. We implemented all possible combinations of methods: with and without trap refinement, with rational and integer arithmetic, with and without invariant construction, with and without invariant minimization.

Our evaluation had two main goals. First, as the underlying methods are incomplete, we wanted to measure their success rate on standard benchmark sets. As a subgoal, we wanted to investigate the usefulness and necessity of traps, the benefit of using integer arithmetic over rational arithmetic, and the sizes of the constructed invariants. The second goal was to measure Petrinizer's performance and to compare it with state-of-the-art tools: IIC [13], BFC[2] [11], and MIST[3].

Benchmarks. For the inputs used in the experiments, we collected coverability problem instances originating from various sources. The collection contains 178 examples, out of which 115 are safe, and is organized into five example suites. The first suite is a collection of Petri net examples from the MIST toolkit. This suite contains a mixture of 29 examples, both safe and unsafe. It contains both real-world and artificially created examples. The second suite consists of 46 Petri nets that were used in the evaluation of BFC [11]. They originate from the analysis of concurrent C programs, and they are mostly unsafe. The third and the fourth suites come from the provenance analysis of messages in a medical system and a bug-tracking system [15]. The medical suite contains 12 safe examples, and the bug-tracking suite contains 41 examples, all safe except for one. The fifth suite contains 50 examples that come from the analysis of Erlang programs [4]. We generated them ourselves using an Erlang verification tool called Soter [4], from the example programs found on Soter's website[4]. Out of 50 examples in this suite, 38 are safe. This suite also contains the largest example in the collection, with 66,950 places and 213,635 transitions. For our evaluation, only the 115 safe instances are interesting.

---

[1] https://github.com/pierreganty/mist

[2] The most recent version of BFC at the time of writing the paper was 2.0. However, we noticed it sometimes reports inconsistent results, so we used version 1.0 instead. The tool can be obtained at http://www.cprover.org/bfc/.

[3] MIST consists of several methods, most of them based on EEC [8]. We used the abstraction refinement method that tries to minimize the number of places in the Petri net [7].

[4] http://mjolnir.cs.ox.ac.uk/soter/

Table 1. Safe examples that were successfully proved safe. Symbols $\mathbb{Q}$ and $\mathbb{Z}$ denote rational and integer numbers.

Suite	Safety/$\mathbb{Q}$	Safety/$\mathbb{Z}$	Ref./$\mathbb{Q}$	Ref./$\mathbb{Z}$	IIC	BFC	MIST	Total
MIST	14	14	20	20	**23**	21	19	23
BFC	2	2	2	2	2	2	**2**	2
Medical	4	4	4	4	9	**12**	10	12
Bug-tracking	32	32	32	32	0	0	0	40
Erlang	32	32	36	**38**	17	26	2	38
Total	84	84	94	96	51	61	33	115

Rate of success on safe examples. As shown in Table 1, even with the weakest of the methods —safety based on marking equation over rationals— Petrinizer is able to prove safety for 84 out of 115 examples. Switching to integer arithmetic does not help: the number of examples proved safe remains 84. Using refinement via traps, Petrinizer proves safety for 94 examples. Switching to integer arithmetic in this case helps: Another two examples are proved safe, totaling 96 out of 115 examples. In contrast to these numbers, the most successful existing tool turned out to be BFC, proving safety for only 61 examples. Even though the methods these tools implement are theoretically complete, the tools themselves are limited by the time and space they can use.

Looking at the results accross different suites, we see that Petrinizer performed poorest on the medical suite, proving safety for only 4 out of 12 examples. On the other hand, on the bug-tracking suite, which was completely intractable for other tools, it proved safety for 32 out of 40 examples. Furthermore, using traps and integer arithmetic, Petrinizer successfuly proved safety for all safe Erlang examples. We find this result particularly surprising, as the original verification problems for these examples seem non-trivial.

Invariant sizes. We measure the size of inductive invariants produced by Petrinizer without minimization. We took the number of atomic (non-zero) terms appearing in an invariant's linear expressions as a measure of its size. When we relate sizes of invariants to number of places in the corresponding Petri net (top left graph in Fig. 4), we see that invariants are usually very succinct. As an example, the largest invariant had 814 atomic terms, and the corresponding Petri net, coming from the Erlang suite, had 4,763 places. For the largest Petri net, with 66,950 places, the constructed invariant had 339 atomic terms.

The added benefit of minimization is negligible: there are only four examples where the invariant was reduced, and the reduction was about 2-3%. Thus, invariant minimization does not pay off for these examples.

We also compared sizes of constructed invariants with sizes of invariants produced by IIC [13]. IIC's invariants are expressed as CNF formulas over atoms of the form $x < a$, for a variable x and a constant a. As a measure of size for these formulas, we took the number of atoms they contain. As the bottom left graph in Fig. 4 shows, when compared to IIC's invariants, Petrinizer's invariants are never larger, and are often orders of magnitude smaller.

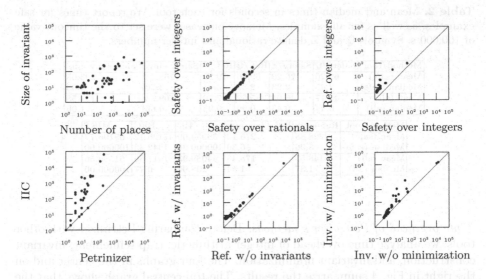

Fig. 4. Graph on the top left shows a relation of sizes of constructed invariants to the number of places in the corresponding Petri nets. Graph on the bottom left shows comparison in size of invariants produced by Petrinizer and IIC. Axes represent size on a logarithmic scale. Each dot represents one example. The four graphs in the center and on the right show time overhead of integer arithmetic, trap refinement, invariant construction and invariant minimization. Axes represent time in seconds on a logarithmic scale. Each dot represents execution time on one example. The graph on the top right only shows examples for which at least one trap appeared in the refinement. Similarly, the bottom center and bottom right graphs only show safe examples.

Performance. To ensure accuracy and fairness, all experiments were performed on identical machines, equipped with Intel Xeon 2.66 GHz CPUs and 48 GB of memory, running Linux 3.2.48.1 in 64-bit mode. Execution time was limited to 100,000 seconds (27 hours, 46 minutes and 40 seconds), and memory to 2 GB.

Due to dissimilarities between the compared tools, selecting a fair measure of time was non-trivial. On the one hand, as Petrinizer communicates with Z3 via temporary files, it spends a considerable amount of time doing I/O operations. On the other hand, as BFC performs both a forward and a backward search, it naturally splits the work into two threads, and runs them in parallel on two CPU cores. In both cases, the actual elapsed time does not quite correspond to the amount of computational effort we wanted to measure. Therefore, for the measure of time we selected the *user time*, as reported by the *time* utility on Linux. User time measures the total CPU time spent executing the process and its children. In the case of Petrinizer, it excludes the I/O overhead, and in the case of BFC, it includes total CPU time spent on both CPU cores.

We report mean and median times measured for each tool in Table 2.

Table 2. Mean and median times in seconds for each tool. We report times for safe examples, as well as for all examples. Memory-out cases were set to the timeout value of 100,000 s. Symbols $\mathbb{Q}$ and $\mathbb{Z}$ denote rational and integer numbers.

Method/tool	Safety/$\mathbb{Q}$	Safety/$\mathbb{Z}$	Ref./$\mathbb{Q}$	Ref./$\mathbb{Z}$	Safety+inv.	Safety+inv.min.
Mean (safe)	69.26	70.20	69.36	72.20	168.46	203.05
Median (safe)	2.45	2.23	2.35	3.81	3.70	4.03
Mean (all)	45.17	46.04	45.52	47.70	109.23	131.58
Median (all)	0.44	0.43	0.90	0.93	0.66	1.00

Method/tool	Ref.+inv.	Ref.+inv.min.	IIC	BFC	MIST
Mean (safe)	228.88	275.12	56954.09	47126.12	69196.77
Median (safe)	5.96	6.30	100000.00	1642.43	100000.00
Mean (all)	148.57	178.45	44089.93	31017.80	61586.56
Median (all)	1.37	1.94	138.00	0.77	100000.00

Time overhead of Petrinizer's methods. Before comparing Petrinizer with other tools, we analyze time overhead of integer arithmetic, trap refinement, invariant construction, and invariant minimization. The four graphs in the center and on the right in Fig. 4 summarize the results. The top central graph shows that the difference in performance between integer and rational arithmetic is negligible.

The top right graph in Fig. 4 shows that traps incur a significant overhead. This is not too surprising as, each time a trap is found, the main system has to be updated with a new trap constraint and solved again. Thus the actual overhead depends on the number of traps that appear during the refinement. In the experiments, there were 32 examples for refinement with integer arithmetic where traps appeared at least once. The maximal number of traps in a single example was 9. In the examples where traps appear once, we see a slowdown of 2-3×. In the extreme cases with 9 traps we see slowdowns of 10-16×.

In the case of invariant construction, as shown on the bottom central graph in Fig. 4, the overhead is more uniform and predictable. The reason is that constructing the invariant involves solving the dual form of the main system as many times as there are disjuncts in the property violation constraint. In most cases, the property violation constraint has one disjunct. A single example with many disjuncts, having 8989 of them, appears on the graph as an outlier.

In the case of invariant minimization, as the bottom right graph in Fig. 4 shows, time overhead is quite severe. The underlying data contains examples of slowdowns of up to 30×.

Comparison with other tools. The six graphs in Fig. 5 show the comparison of execution times for Petrinizer vs. IIC, BFC, and MIST. In the comparison, we used the refinement methods, both with and without invariant construction. In general, we observe that other tools outperform Petrinizer on small examples, an effect that can be explained by the overhead of starting script interpreters and Z3. However, on large examples Petrinizer consistently outperforms other tools. Not only does it finish in all cases within the given time and memory constraints, it even finishes in under 100 seconds in all but two cases. The two cases are the large example from the Erlang suite, with 66,950 places and 213,635 transitions

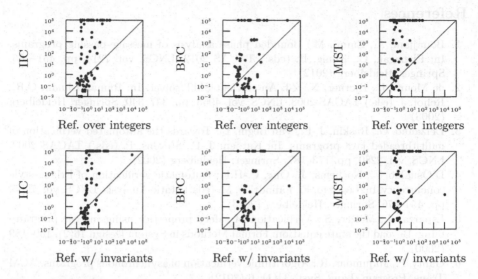

Ref. over integers   Ref. over integers   Ref. over integers

Ref. w/ invariants   Ref. w/ invariants   Ref. w/ invariants

Fig. 5. Comparison of execution time for Petrinizer vs. IIC, BFC and MIST. Graphs in the top row show comparison in the case without invariant construction, and graphs in the bottom row show comparison in the case with invariant construction. Axes represent time in seconds on a logarithmic scale. Each dot represents execution time on one example.

and, in the case of invariant construction, the example from the MIST suite, with 8989 disjuncts in the property violation constraint.

Conclusions. Marking equations and traps are classical techniques in Petri net theory, but have fallen out of favor in recent times in comparison with state-space traversal techniques in combination with abstractions or symbolic representations. Our experiments demonstrate that, when combined with the power of a modern SMT solver, these techniques can be surprisingly effective in finding proofs of correctness (inductive invariants) of common benchmark examples arising out of software verification.

Our results also suggest incorporating these techniques into existing tools as a cheap preprocessing step. A finer integration with these tools is conceivable, where a satisfying assignment to a system of constraints is used to guide the more sophisticated search, similar to [22].

Acknowledgements. We thank Emanuele D'Osualdo for help with the Soter tool. Ledesma-Garza was supported by the Collaborative Research Center 1480 "Program and Model Analysis" funded by the German Research Council.

References

1. Bouajjani, A., Emmi, M.: Bounded phase analysis of message-passing programs. In: Flanagan, C., König, B. (eds.) TACAS 2012. LNCS, vol. 7214, pp. 451–465. Springer, Heidelberg (2012)
2. de Moura, L., Bjørner, N.: Z3: An efficient SMT solver. In: Ramakrishnan, C.R., Rehof, J. (eds.) TACAS 2008. LNCS, vol. 4963, pp. 337–340. Springer, Heidelberg (2008)
3. Delzanno, G., Raskin, J.-F., Van Begin, L.: Towards the automated verification of multithreaded java programs. In: Katoen, J.-P., Stevens, P. (eds.) TACAS 2002. LNCS, vol. 2280, pp. 173–187. Springer, Heidelberg (2002)
4. D'Osualdo, E., Kochems, J., Ong, C.-H.L.: Automatic verification of Erlang-style concurrency. In: Logozzo, F., Fähndrich, M. (eds.) Static Analysis. LNCS, vol. 7935, pp. 454–476. Springer, Heidelberg (2013)
5. Esparza, J., Melzer, S.: Verification of safety properties using integer programming: Beyond the state equation. Formal Methods in System Design 16(2), 159–189 (2000)
6. Ganty, P., Majumdar, R.: Algorithmic verification of asynchronous programs. ACM Trans. Program. Lang. Syst. 34(1), 6 (2012)
7. Ganty, P., Raskin, J.-F., Van Begin, L.: From many places to few: Automatic abstraction refinement for Petri nets. Fundam. Inform. 88(3), 275–305 (2008)
8. Geeraerts, G., Raskin, J.-F., Begin, L.V.: Expand, enlarge and check: New algorithms for the coverability problem of WSTS. J. Comput. Syst. Sci. 72(1), 180–203 (2006)
9. German, S.M., Sistla, A.P.: Reasoning about systems with many processes. Journal of the ACM (JACM) 39(3), 675–735 (1992)
10. Kaiser, A., Kroening, D., Wahl, T.: Dynamic cutoff detection in parameterized concurrent programs. In: Touili, T., Cook, B., Jackson, P. (eds.) CAV 2010. LNCS, vol. 6174, pp. 645–659. Springer, Heidelberg (2010)
11. Kaiser, A., Kroening, D., Wahl, T.: Efficient coverability analysis by proof minimization. In: Koutny, M., Ulidowski, I. (eds.) CONCUR 2012. LNCS, vol. 7454, pp. 500–515. Springer, Heidelberg (2012)
12. Karp, R., Miller, R.: Parallel program schemata. J. Comput. Syst. Sci. 3(2), 147–195 (1969)
13. Kloos, J., Majumdar, R., Niksic, F., Piskac, R.: Incremental, inductive coverability. In: Sharygina, N., Veith, H. (eds.) CAV 2013. LNCS, vol. 8044, pp. 158–173. Springer, Heidelberg (2013)
14. Lamport, L.: The mutual exclusion problem: Part II—statement and solutions. J. ACM 33(2), 327–348 (1986)
15. Majumdar, R., Meyer, R., Wang, Z.: Static provenance verification for message passing programs. In: Logozzo, F., Fähndrich, M. (eds.) SAS 2013. LNCS, vol. 7935, pp. 366–387. Springer, Heidelberg (2013)
16. Murata, T.: Petri nets: Properties, analysis and applications. Proceedings of the IEEE 77(4), 541–580 (1989)
17. Rackoff, C.: The covering and boundedness problems for vector addition systems. Theor. Comput. Sci. 6, 223–231 (1978)
18. Reisig, W.: Understanding Petri Nets - Modeling Techniques, Analysis Methods, Case Studies. Springer (2013)

19. Schrijver, A.: Theory of Linear and Integer Programming. John Wiley & Sons Ltd. (1986)
20. Solar-Lezama, A., Tancau, L., Bodík, R., Seshia, S., Saraswat, V.: Combinatorial sketching for finite programs. In: ASPLOS, pp. 404–415. ACM (2006)
21. Valmari, A., Hansen, H.: Old and new algorithms for minimal coverability sets. In: Haddad, S., Pomello, L. (eds.) PETRI NETS 2012. LNCS, vol. 7347, pp. 208–227. Springer, Heidelberg (2012)
22. Wimmel, H., Wolf, K.: Applying CEGAR to the Petri net state equation. Logical Methods in Computer Science 8(3) (2012)

LEAP: A Tool for the Parametrized Verification of Concurrent Datatypes*

Alejandro Sánchez[1] and César Sánchez[1,2]

[1] IMDEA Software Institute, Madrid, Spain
[2] Institute for Information Security, CSIC, Spain

Abstract. This tool paper describes LEAP, a tool for the verification of concurrent datatypes and parametrized systems composed by an unbounded number of threads that manipulate infinite data[1].
LEAP receives as input a concurrent program description and a specification and automatically generates a finite set of verification conditions which are then discharged to specialized decision procedures. The validity of all discharged verification conditions implies that the program executed by any number of threads satisfies the specification. Currently, LEAP includes not only decision procedures for integers and Booleans, but it also implements specific theories for heap memory layouts such as linked-lists and skiplists.

1 Introduction

The target application motivating the development of LEAP is the verification of concurrent datatypes [16]. Concurrent datatypes are designed to exploit the parallelism of multiprocessor architectures by employing very weak forms of synchronization, like lock-freedom and fine-grain locking, allowing multiple threads to concurrently access the underlying data. The formal verification of these concurrent programs is a very challenging task, particularly considering that they manipulate complex data structures capable of storing unbounded data, and are executed by an unbounded number of threads.

The problem of verifying parametrized finite state systems has received a lot of attention in recent years. In general, the problem is undecidable [3]. There are two general ways to overcome this limitation: (*i*) algorithmic approaches, which are necessarily incomplete; and (*ii*) deductive proof methods. Typically, algorithmic methods—in order to regain decidability—are restricted to finite state processes [8,9,14] and finite state shared data. LEAP follows an alternative approach, by extending temporal deductive methods like Manna-Pnueli [20] with specialized proof rules for parametrized systems, thus sacrificing full automation to handle complex concurrency and data manipulation. Our target with LEAP is wide applicability, while improving automation is an important secondary goal.

---

* This work was funded in part by Spanish MINECO Project "TIN2012-39391-C04-01 STRONGSOFT"
[1] LEAP is under development at the IMDEA Software Institute. All examples and code can be downloaded from http://software.imdea.org/leap

A. Biere and R. Bloem (Eds.): CAV 2014, LNCS 8559, pp. 620–627, 2014.
© Springer International Publishing Switzerland 2014

Most algorithmic approaches to parametrized verification abstract both control and data altogether [1,2,21] reducing the safety to a (non)reachability problem in a decidable domain. In these approaches, data manipulation and control flow are handled altogether, and the verification is limited to simple theories such as Booleans and linear arithmetic. LEAP, on the other hand, separates the two concerns: (*i*) the concurrent interaction between threads; and (*ii*) the data being manipulated. The first concern is tackled with specialized deductive parametrized proof rules, which, starting from a parametrized system and a temporal specification, generate a finite number of verification conditions (VCs). The second aspect is delegated to decision procedures (DP) specifically designed for each datatype, which can prove the validity of VCs automatically. Our proof rules are designed to generate *quantifier free* VCs, for which it is much easier to design decidable theories and obtain automatic decision procedures.

There exists a wide range of tools for verifying concurrent systems. Smallfoot [4] is an automatic verifier that uses concurrent separation logic for verifying sequential and concurrent programs. Smallfoot depends on built-in rules for the datatypes, which are typically recursive definitions in separation logic. Unlike LEAP, Smallfoot cannot handle programs without strict separation (like shared readers) or algorithms that do not follow the unrolling that is explicit in the recursive definitions. TLA+ [7] is able to verify temporal properties of concurrent systems with the aid of theorem provers and SMT solvers, but TLA+ does not support decision procedures for data in the heap. Similarly, HAVOC [11] is capable of verifying C programs relying on Boogie as intermediate language and Z3 as backend. Neither Frama-C [12] nor Jahob [17] handle parametrized verification, which is necessary to verify concurrent datatypes (for any number of threads). The closest system to LEAP is STeP [19], but STeP only handled temporal proofs for simple datatypes. Unlike LEAP, none of these tools can reason about parametrized systems.

Chalice [18] is an experimental language that explores specification and verification of concurrency in programs with dynamic thread creation, and locks. VeriCool [28] uses dynamic framing (as Chalice does) to tackle the verification of concurrent programs using Z3 as backend. However, none of these tools implement specialized DPs for complex theories of datatypes. VCC [10] is an industrial-strength verification environment for low-level concurrent system code written in C. Despite being powerful, in comparison to LEAP it requires a great amount of program annotation.

So far, the current version of LEAP only handles safety properties, but support for liveness properties is ongoing work.

2 Formal Verification Using LEAP

Fig. 1 shows the structure of LEAP. LEAP receives as input a program and a specification. Fig. 2 presents an example of a procedure for inserting an element into a concurrent lock-coupling single-linked list. The input language is a C-like language with support for assignments—including pointers—, conditionals,

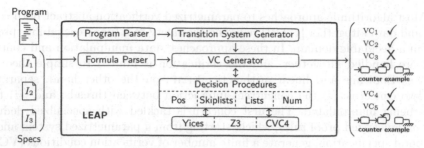

Fig. 1. Scheme of LEAP

loops and non-recursive function calls. Program lines can be assigned a label to refer to them later in a specification (e.g., connect labels line 15 in Fig. 2). In a specification both program lines and labels can be used to refer to an specific section of the program. The input language also supports atomic sections and ghost code. Ghost code is written between $ and, is added only for verification purposes, and it is removed during compilation. Fig. 2 declares a global ghost variable region for keeping track of address of nodes belonging to the list, which is updated at line 15 when a new node is connected added to the list. LEAP requires only small annotations of extra ghost. A specification consists of quantifier-free parametrized formulas describing

```
global
    addr head, tail
    ghost addrSet region
procedure insert (e:elem)
    addr prev, curr, aux
begin
1:  prev := head;
2:  prev->lock;
3:  curr := prev->next;
4:  curr->lock;
5:  while curr->data < e do
6:      aux := prev;
7:      prev := curr;
8:      aux->unlock;
9:      curr := curr->next;
10:     curr->lock;
11: end while
12: if curr != null /\ curr->data > e then
13:     aux := malloc(e,null,#);
14:     aux->next := curr;
    :connect
15:     prev->next := aux
            $region := region Union {aux};$
16: end if
17: prev->unlock;
18: curr->unlock;
19: return
    end procedure
```

Fig. 2. Example of input program

the property to be verified. Consider the following specification, parametrized by thread id i:

```
vars: tid i
specification [aux_ready] :
  @connect(i). ->
    (rd(heap, prev(i)).data < e /\ rd(heap, curr(i)).data > e /\
     rd(heap, aux(i)).data = e /\
     rd(heap, prev(i)).next = curr(i) /\ rd(heap, aux(i)).next = curr(i))
```

This formula describes conditions that every thread i satisfy during insertion and that guarantee the preservation of the list shape when connecting the node pointed by aux to the list. In particular, aux_ready states that: (1) the node pointed by prev (resp. curr) stores a value lower (resp. higher) than e, (2) the node pointed by aux stores value e, and (3) the field next of the nodes pointed by prev and aux points to curr. We now give a brief description of how LEAP generates the VCs starting from the program and the specifications received as input.

Verification Condition Generation. Given an input program P, LEAP internally creates an implicit representation of a parametrized transition system $S[M] = P_1 \| P_2 \| \ldots \| P_M$, where each P_j is an instance of program P. For example, if we consider the program from Fig. 2, $S[1]$ is the instance of $S[M]$ consisting of in a single thread running `insert` in isolation, and $S[2]$ is the instance of $S[M]$ consisting of two threads running `insert` concurrently. LEAP solves the uniform verification problem showing that all instances of the parametrized system satisfy the safety property by using specialized proof rules [25] which generate a finite number of VCs.

Each VC describes a small-step in the execution. All VCs generated by LEAP are quantifier free as long as the specification is quantifier free. We use the theory of arrays [5] to encode the local variables of a system with an arbitrary number of threads, but the dependencies with arrays are eliminated by symmetry. VCs are discharged to specialized DPs which automatically decide their validity. If all VCs are proved valid, then the specification is verified to be an invariant of the parametrized program. If a VC is not valid, then the DP generates a counter-model corresponding to an offending small-step of the system that leads to a violation of the specification. This is typically a very small heap snippet that the programmer can use to either identify a bug or instrument the program with intermediate invariants. Consider property `is_list` which states the list shape property, including that the ghost variable `region` stores the set of addresses of all nodes belonging to the list. Property `aux_ready` is not enough to prove `is_list` invariant. Fig. 3 shows a counter example returned by the decision procedure. The output can be used by the user as hint to strengthen `aux_ready`, in this case, indicating that `prev` must belong to `region` before executing line 15 of `insert`.

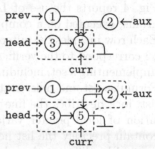

Fig. 3. A counter-example for `is_list` when executing line 15 (up shows before, down shows after). Dashed box represents `region`.

Decision Procedures. LEAP implements specialized decision procedures including some theories of heap memory layouts and locks [23, 24, 27] whose decidability is based on finite model theorems. Our implementation transforms each VC into queries to the corresponding DP. The decision procedures are implemented on top of off-the-shelf SMT solvers [13, 15]. LEAP currently includes decision procedures for Presburger arithmetic with finite sets and minimum, lock-based concurrent single-linked lists [23], concurrent skiplists of bounded height [24] and skiplists of arbitrary height [27]. The modular design of LEAP makes it straightforward to implement extensions for new program statements, theories and DPs.

Proof Graphs and Tactics. Proofs in LEAP are structured as *proof graphs*, which describes the inter-dependency between invariants. Proof graphs improve the efficiency of proof development and proof checking, by establishing the necessary support for proving consecution (see [20] and optionally specifying tactics and heuristics. Current implemented tactics include the use of simpler DPs with some symbols uninterpreted, lazy instantiation of supporting invariants, and applications of typical first-order tactics like equality propagation and removal of irrelevant literals. Tactics are very useful when performed prior to the discharge of a VC to the SMT solver, as bound sizes of candidate models are reduced. For instance, the proof graph for is_list includes:

```
=> is_list [15:aux_ready] { pruning : split-goal | | | simplify-pc}
```

indicating that in order to prove consecution for is_list at line 15, aux_ready is a useful support. The annotation pruning establishes a tighter domain bound calculation for the list DP. The graph also lists tactics split-goal and simplify-pc. In proof creation, these tactics can be explored automatically in parallel dumping the fastest option to the proof graph file for efficient proof checking.

3 Empirical Evaluation

Fig. 4 reports the use of LEAP to verify some concurrent and sequential programs, executed on a computer with a 2.8 GHz processor and 8GB of memory. Each row includes the outcome of the verification of a single invariant. Rows 1 to 12 correspond to the verification of a concurrent lock-coupling single-linked lists implementing a set, including both shape preservation and functional properties. Formulas list and order state that the shape is that of an ordered single-linked list, lock describes the fine-grain lock ownership, next captures the relative position of local pointer variables, region constraints the region of the heap to contain precisely the list nodes and disj encodes the separation of new cells allocated by different threads. Functional properties include funSchLinear: search returns whether the element is present at the linearization point; funSchInsert and funSchRemove: a search is successful precisely when the element was inserted and not removed after; funRemove, funInsert and funSearch describe a scenario in which a thread manipulates different elements than all other threads: an element is found if and only if it is in the list, an element is not present after removal, and an element is present after insertion. Rows 13 to 16, and 17 to 20 describe the verification of two sequential implementation of a skiplist. The first implementation limits the maximum height to 3 levels, and the second considers an implementation in which the height can grow beyond any bound, using a more sophisticated DP. Rows 21 to 23 correspond to a parametrized ticket based mutual exclusion protocol. This protocol is infinite state using integers as tickets. Lines 24 to 26 correspond to a similar protocol that uses sets of integers.

The first four columns show (1) the formula's index (i.e., the number of threads parametrizing the formula), (2) the number of VCs discharged, (3) the number of such VCs proved by program location reasoning, and (4) by using a specialized DP. In all cases, all VCs are automatically verified. The next two columns report the total running time of discharging and proving all VCs (5) without using any tactic and (6) with tactics enabled. The next columns present the slowest (7) and average (8) running time to solve VCs, and the final column

		formula		#solved vc		Brute	Heurist.	DP time		LEAP
		idx	#vc	pos	dp	time	time	slowest	average	time
1	list	0	61	38	23	∞	18.67	11.90	0.30	0.20
2	order	1	121	62	59	998.35	1.12	0.03	0.01	0.47
3	lock	1	121	76	45	778.15	0.47	0.02	0.01	0.18
4	next	1	121	60	61	∞	2.11	0.61	0.01	0.59
5	region	1	121	95	26	∞	22.58	18.17	0.18	0.23
6	disj	2	181	177	4	121.74	0.19	0.01	0.01	0.12
7	funSchLinear	1	121	97	24	∞	6.29	3.04	0.05	0.08
8	funSchInsert	1	121	93	28	∞	4.15	1.91	0.03	0.08
9	funSchRemove	1	121	93	28	∞	5.40	2.60	0.04	0.10
10	funSearch	1	208	198	10	∞	3.54	1.57	0.01	0.34
11	funInsert	1	208	200	8	∞	0.50	0.01	0.01	0.22
12	funRemove	1	208	200	8	∞	1.41	0.95	0.01	0.24
13	skiplist$_3$	0	154	92	62	∞	1221.97	776.45	15.27	0.45
14	region$_3$	0	124	97	27	∞	27.50	17.36	0.34	0.58
15	next$_3$	0	84	65	19	∞	0.67	0.09	0.01	0.20
16	order$_3$	0	84	59	25	∞	9.66	7.80	0.10	1.31
17	skiplist	0	560	532	28	∞	19.79	5.40	0.24	0.15
18	region	0	1583	1527	56	∞	44.28	22.66	0.54	1.35
19	next	0	1899	1869	30	∞	3.19	0.32	0.02	1.59
20	order	0	2531	2474	57	∞	11.19	2.35	0.84	6.75
21	mutex	2	28	26	2	0.32	0.01	0.01	0.01	0.01
22	minticket	1	19	18	1	0.04	0.01	0.01	0.01	0.01
23	notsame	2	28	26	2	0.13	0.03	0.01	0.01	0.01
24	mutexS	2	28	26	2	0.44	0.04	0.01	0.01	0.01
25	minticketS	1	19	18	1	0.31	0.01	0.01	0.01	0.01
26	notsameS	2	28	26	2	0.14	0.02	0.01	0.01	0.01

Fig. 4. Verification running times (in secs.). ∞ represents a timeout of 30 minutes.

includes the analysis time without considering the running time of decision procedures. Our results indicate that LEAP can verify sophisticated concurrent programs and protocols with relatively small human intervention. Required annotation for our examples was around 15% of the source code (roughly 1 invariant—containing 6 primitive predicates each—every 7 lines). The time employed by LEAP to analyze the program and generate all VCs is a negligible part of the total running time, which suggests that research in DP design and implementation is the crucial bottleneck for scalability. Also, in practice, tactics are important for efficiency to handle non-trivial systems.

4 Future Work

We are considering the use of CIL/Frama-C as a front-end for C. Extending LEAP with support for liveness properties is ongoing work. Our approach consists of specializing generalized verification diagrams [6] and transition invariants [22] for parametrized systems. The development of new theories and decision procedures for new datatypes such as hash-maps and lock-free lists is currently under development. We are also exploring the possibility of increasing automation by automatically generating intermediate specifications. Our approaches include (1) how to apply effectively weakest precondition propagation for parametrized systems, and (2) extending our previous work on abstract interpretation-based invariant generation for parametrized systems [26] to handle complex heap layouts.

References

1. Abdulla, P.A., Bouajjani, A., Jonsson, B., Nilsson, M.: Handling global conditions in parametrized system verification. In: Halbwachs, N., Peled, D. (eds.) CAV 1999. LNCS, vol. 1633, pp. 134–145. Springer, Heidelberg (1999)
2. Abdulla, P.A., Delzanno, G., Rezine, A.: Approximated parameterized verif. of infinite-state processes with global conditions. FMSD 34(2), 126–156 (2009)
3. Apt, K.R., Kozen, D.C.: Limits for automatic verification of finite-state concurrent systems. Information Processing Letters 22(6), 307–309 (1986)
4. Berdine, J., Calcagno, C., O'Hearn, P.W.: Smallfoot: Modular automatic assertion checking with separation logic. In: de Boer, F.S., Bonsangue, M.M., Graf, S., de Roever, W.-P. (eds.) FMCO 2005. LNCS, vol. 4111, pp. 115–137. Springer, Heidelberg (2006)
5. Bradley, A.R., Manna, Z., Sipma, H.B.: What's decidable about arrays? In: Emerson, E.A., Namjoshi, K.S. (eds.) VMCAI 2006. LNCS, vol. 3855, pp. 427–442. Springer, Heidelberg (2006)
6. Browne, I.A., Manna, Z., Sipma, H.B.: Generalized verification diagrams. In: Thiagarajan, P.S. (ed.) FSTTCS 1995. LNCS, vol. 1026, pp. 484–498. Springer, Heidelberg (1995)
7. Chaudhuri, K., Doligez, D., Lamport, L., Merz, S.: The TLA $^+$ proof system: Building a heterogeneous verification platform. In: Cavalcanti, A., Deharbe, D., Gaudel, M.-C., Woodcock, J. (eds.) ICTAC 2010. LNCS, vol. 6255, p. 44. Springer, Heidelberg (2010)
8. Clarke, E.M., Grumberg, O.: Avoiding the state explosion problem in temporal logic model checking. In: Proc. of PODC 1987, pp. 294–303. ACM (1987)
9. Clarke, E.M., Grumberg, O., Browne, M.C.: Reasoning about networks with many identical finite-state procs. In: Proc. of PODC 1986, pp. 240–248. ACM (1986)
10. Cohen, E., Dahlweid, M., Hillebrand, M., Leinenbach, D., Moskal, M., Santen, T., Schulte, W., Tobies, S.: VCC: A practical system for verifying concurrent C. In: Berghofer, S., Nipkow, T., Urban, C., Wenzel, M. (eds.) TPHOLs 2009. LNCS, vol. 5674, pp. 23–42. Springer, Heidelberg (2009)
11. Condit, J., Hackett, B., Lahiri, S.K., Qadeer, S.: Unifying type checking and property checking for low-level code. In: Proc. of POPL 2009, pp. 302–314. ACM Press (2009)
12. Cuoq, P., Kirchner, F., Kosmatov, N., Prevosto, V., Signoles, J., Yakobowski, B.: Frama-C – a software analysis perspective. In: Eleftherakis, G., Hinchey, M., Holcombe, M. (eds.) SEFM 2012. LNCS, vol. 7504, pp. 233–247. Springer, Heidelberg (2012)
13. de Moura, L., Bjørner, N.: Z3: An efficient SMT solver. In: Ramakrishnan, C.R., Rehof, J. (eds.) TACAS 2008. LNCS, vol. 4963, pp. 337–340. Springer, Heidelberg (2008)
14. Emerson, E.A., Kahlon, V.: Reducing model checking of the many to the few. In: McAllester, D. (ed.) CADE-17. LNCS (LNAI), vol. 1831, pp. 236–254. Springer, Heidelberg (2000)
15. Ganzinger, H., Hagen, G., Nieuwenhuis, R., Oliveras, A., Tinelli, C.: DPLL(T): Fast decision procedures. In: Alur, R., Peled, D.A. (eds.) CAV 2004. LNCS, vol. 3114, pp. 175–188. Springer, Heidelberg (2004)
16. Herlihy, M., Shavit, N.: The Art of Multiprocessor Programming. Morgan-Kaufmann (2008)
17. Kuncak, V., Rinard, M.C.: An overview of the Jahob analysis system: Project goals and current status. In: Proc. of IPDPS 2006. IEEE Computer Society Press (2006)
18. Leino, K.R.M.: Verifying concurrent programs with Chalice. In: Barthe, G., Hermenegildo, M. (eds.) VMCAI 2010. LNCS, vol. 5944, p. 2. Springer, Heidelberg (2010)

19. Manna, Z., Anuchitanukul, A., Bjørner, N., Browne, A., Chang, E., Colón, M., de Alfaro, L., Devarajan, H., Sipma, H., Uribe, T.: STeP: The stanford temporal prover. Technical Report STAN-CS-TR-94-1518, Computer Science Department, Stanford University (July 1994)
20. Manna, Z., Pnueli, A.: Temporal Verification of Reactive Systems. Springer (1995)
21. Bozzano, M., Delzanno, G.: Beyond parameterized verification. In: Katoen, J.-P., Stevens, P. (eds.) TACAS 2002. LNCS, vol. 2280, pp. 221–235. Springer, Heidelberg (2002)
22. Podelsky, A., Rybalchenko, A.: Transition invariants. In: Proc. of LICS 2004, pp. 32–41. IEEE Computer Society Press (2004)
23. Sánchez, A., Sánchez, C.: Decision procedure for the temporal verification of concurrent lists. In: Dong, J.S., Zhu, H. (eds.) ICFEM 2010. LNCS, vol. 6447, pp. 74–89. Springer, Heidelberg (2010)
24. Sánchez, A., Sánchez, C.: A theory of skiplists with applications to the verification of concurrent datatypes. In: Bobaru, M., Havelund, K., Holzmann, G.J., Joshi, R. (eds.) NFM 2011. LNCS, vol. 6617, pp. 343–358. Springer, Heidelberg (2011)
25. Sánchez, A., Sánchez, C.: Parametrized invariance for infinite state processes. CoRR, abs/1312.4043 (2013)
26. Sanchez, A., Sankaranarayanan, S., Sánchez, C., Chang, B.-Y.E.: Invariant generation for parametrized systems using self-reflection. In: Miné, A., Schmidt, D. (eds.) SAS 2012. LNCS, vol. 7460, pp. 146–163. Springer, Heidelberg (2012)
27. Sánchez, C., Sánchez, A.: A decidable theory of skiplists of unbounded size and arbitrary height. CoRR, abs/1301.4372 (2013)
28. Smans, J., Jacobs, B., Piessens, F.: Vericool: An automatic verifier for a concurrent object-oriented language. In: Barthe, G., de Boer, F.S. (eds.) FMOODS 2008. LNCS, vol. 5051, pp. 220–239. Springer, Heidelberg (2008)

Monadic Decomposition

Margus Veanes[1], Nikolaj Bjørner[1], Lev Nachmanson[1], and Sergey Bereg[2]

[1] Microsoft Research
{margus,nbjorner,levnach}@microsoft.com
[2] The University of Texas at Dallas
besp@utdallas.edu

Abstract. Monadic predicates play a prominent role in many decidable cases, including decision procedures for symbolic automata. We are here interested in *discovering* whether a formula can be rewritten into a Boolean combination of monadic predicates. Our setting is quantifier-free formulas over a decidable background theory, such as arithmetic and we here develop a semi-decision procedure for extracting a monadic decomposition of a formula when it exists.

1 Introduction

Classical decidability results of fragments of logic [7] are based on careful systematic study of restricted cases either by limiting allowed symbols of the language, limiting the syntax of the formulas, fixing the background theory, or by using combinations of such restrictions. Many decidable classes of problems, such as monadic first-order logic or the Löwenheim class [29], the Löb-Gurevich class [28], monadic second-order logic with one successor (S1S) [8], and monadic second-order logic with two successors (S2S) [35] impose at some level restrictions to *monadic* or unary predicates to achieve decidability.

Here we propose and study an orthogonal problem of *whether* and *how* we can transform a formula that uses multiple free variables into a *simpler* equivalent formula, but where the formula is *not* a priori syntactically or semantically restricted to any fixed fragment of logic. *Simpler* in this context means that we have eliminated all theory specific dependencies between the variables and have transformed the formula into an equivalent Boolean combination of predicates that are "essentially" unary. We call the problem *monadic decomposition*:

> Given an effective representation of a nonempty binary relation R, decide if R equals a **finite** union $\bigcup_{0 \leq i < k} R_i$ of k Cartesian products $R_i = A_i \times B_i$, and if so, construct such $\bar{R}_i$ effectively.

The fundamental assumption that we are making here is:

> We have a Boolean closed class of formulas Ψ and a **solver** for Ψ.

More precisely, we assume a background structure $\mathfrak{U}$ with an r.e. (recursively enumerable) universe $\mathcal{U}$ (so all elements $a \in \mathcal{U}$ can be named; we write a also for a term denoting a) and an r.e. set Ψ of formulas such that:

A. Biere and R. Bloem (Eds.): CAV 2014, LNCS 8559, pp. 628–645, 2014.

1. If $a \in \mathcal{U}$, x is a variable and $\varphi \in \Psi$ then $\varphi[x/a] \in \Psi$,
2. If $\psi, \varphi \in \Psi$ then $\psi \wedge \varphi, \psi \vee \varphi, \neg\varphi \in \Psi$.
3. Satisfiability of $\varphi(\bar{x}) \in \Psi$ (i.e., $\mathfrak{U} \models \exists \bar{x}\varphi(\bar{x})$) is decidable by the solver.

When $\varphi(\bar{x})$ is satisfiable it follows that we can also effectively generate a *witness* $\bar{a}$ such that $\varphi(\bar{a})$ holds, because $\mathcal{U}$ is r.e.. *Effectiveness* means that the solver uses a finite number of steps for deciding satisfiability and for finding a witness. An *effective representation* of a relation is given by a formula from Ψ. The above formulation is very natural from the standpoint of modern logical inference engines, because Ψ embodies the basic properties supported by any state-of-the-art *satisfiability modulo theories* (SMT) solver [12]. One observation that we can immediately make about Ψ is that it is (without loss of generality) closed under formation of tuples, i.e., we can always group variables together and view the group as a single variable. We can also note certain properties that Ψ *cannot* express. For example, Ψ cannot represent formulas $\varphi_L(x)$ that are at least as expressive as deterministic context free languages L. Otherwise construct φ_L such that $w \in L$ iff $\varphi_L(w)$ holds; then $\varphi_L(x) \wedge \varphi_{L'}(x)$ is satisfiable if and only if $L \cap L' \neq \emptyset$, but that is an undecidable problem [22].

A formula $\varphi(x, y) \in \Psi$ denotes the relation $R = \{(a, b) \in \mathcal{U} \times \mathcal{U} \mid \mathfrak{U} \models \varphi(a, b)\}$. The main two questions that we are interested in are: 1) deciding if R is monadic; 2) constructing a monadic decomposition of R if R is monadic. The key insight is that we can define the following *equivalence* relation over $A = \{a \mid \exists b\, R(a, b)\}$,

$$x \sim x' \stackrel{\text{def}}{=} \forall y\, y'((R(x, y) \wedge R(x', y')) \Rightarrow (R(x', y) \wedge R(x, y')))$$

Moreover, we can *decide* if $a \sim a'$ because $a \nsim a'$ has the equivalent form $\exists y\, y'\, \psi(y, y')$ for some $\psi(y, y') \subset \Psi$. This gives us a systematic way of how to subdivide A into equivalence classes $A_\sim$, namely by using the solver for Ψ to enumerate enough witnesses that cover $A_\sim$. The main technical lemma is that there are finitely many such witnesses if and only if R is monadic. The question of *deciding* if R is monadic is not completely settled here. We show that the problem is decidable for integer linear arithmetic and real algebraic polynomial arithmetic but the general case is an open problem.

As the main strength of this approach we see its *simplicity* combined with its *generality*. For monadic decomposition to work, there are no assumptions on Ψ other than the ones listed above. The technique works in all theories where a *solver* is available, such as *linear arithmetic, bit-vectors, arrays, uninterpreted function symbols, algebraic data types, algebraic reals*, as well as combinations thereof. The technique provides a general simplification principle, tantamount to a semantic normal form. It can be used in many different contexts where it is useful to simplify formulas by eliminating variable dependencies, such as *program analysis, optimization, theorem proving*, and *compiler optimization*. It also provides a new way how to investigate new decidability results.

Rest of the paper: § 2 describes the motivation. In § 3 and § 4 the problem is defined formally, we prove the main decomposition Theorem 1, correctness of the main algorithm, Theorem 2, and we prove some decidable cases, Theorems 3 and 4. § 5 provides some evaluation. § 6 is related work. § 7 concludes.

$$\lambda x.(0 \leq x \leq 7F_{16})/[x]$$
$$\lambda x.(7F_{16} < x \leq 7FF_{16})/[6 \cdot x_{\langle 10,6 \rangle}, \; 2 \cdot x_{\langle 5,0 \rangle}]$$
$$\lambda x.(7FF_{16} < x \leq FFFF_{16} \wedge \neg Surrogate(x))/[14 \cdot x_{\langle 15,12 \rangle}, 2 \cdot x_{\langle 11,6 \rangle}, \; 2 \cdot x_{\langle 5,0 \rangle}]$$
$$\lambda x.(FFFF_{16} < x \leq 10FFFF_{16})/[30 \cdot x_{\langle 20,18 \rangle}, 2 \cdot x_{\langle 17,12 \rangle}, 2 \cdot x_{\langle 11,6 \rangle}, \; 2 \cdot x_{\langle 5,0 \rangle}]$$

Fig. 1. SFT *EncUTF8*: UTF8 encoder for valid Unicode code points; $x_{\langle h,l \rangle}$ extracts bits from h to l from x, e.g., $8_{\langle 3,2 \rangle} = 2$; *Surrogate* $\overset{\text{def}}{=} \lambda x.\text{D800}_{16} \leq x \leq \text{DFFF}_{16}$, surrogates are not valid code points; $x \cdot y$ denotes bit-append, e.g., $6 \cdot x_{\langle 10,6 \rangle} = \text{CO}_{16} + x_{\langle 10,6 \rangle}$.

2 Motivation

We start by describing the concrete application that originally lead us to investigate monadic decomposition. We then list other potential applications.

Symbolic Automata and Transducers. In the context of web security, it is important to understand and analyze various properties of *sanitizers* [38]. Sanitizers are special purpose string encoders that escape or remove potentially dangerous strings in order to prevent *cross site scripting* (XSS) attacks. *Bek* is a programming language that is specifically designed for this purpose [20] and builds on the theory and algorithms of *Symbolic Finite Transducers* or *SFTs* [44]. Monadic decomposition is a useful technique for enabling many analyses involving SFTs. One such case is to decide if the range of an SFT is regular and, if so, to construct the corresponding symbolic automaton or SFA. Unlike in the classical case [32,45], a *range automaton* of an SFT is not always regular but accepted by an *Extended* SFA or *ESFA* (SFA with bounded lookahead over the input) and intersection emptiness of ESFAs is undecidable [9]. Transforming an ESFA into and SFA, when possible, requires monadic decomposition.

Figure 1 illustrates an SFT *EncUTF8* that performs UTF8 encoding that is also used by some sanitizers [1] as the first encoding step. The input to *EncUTF8* is a sequence of Unicode code points, that are integers ranging from 0 to $10FFFF_{16}$, and the output is a sequence of bytes. Each of the four transitions of *EncUTF8* corresponds to the number of bytes needed in the encoding of the code point.[1] For example $EncUTF8([1F60A_{16}]) = [F0_{16}, 9F_{16}, 98_{16}, 8A_{16}]$, where $1F60A_{16}$ is the code point of the ☺ emoticon [40].

For example, the second rule of *EncUTF8* becomes the following transition of the range ESFA and has lookahead 2, i.e., it reads 2 bytes at a time

$$q \xrightarrow{\lambda(y,z).\exists x(7F_{16}<x\leq 7FF_{16} \wedge y=(6\cdot x_{\langle 10,6 \rangle}) \wedge z=(2\cdot x_{\langle 5,0 \rangle}))} q$$

The existential quantifier over x can be eliminated automatically by using any known quantifier elimination technique for integer linear arithmetic [31].

---

[1] The corresponding encoder in [10, Figure 3] uses 5 states and 11 transitions because there the input is assumed to be UTF16 encoded.

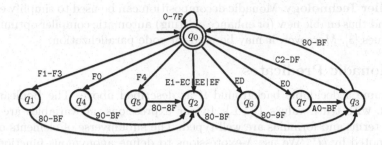

Fig. 2. Minimal symbolic automaton that recognizes valid UTF8 encoded strings

For ease of presentation we use the fact that $x = y_{\langle 4,0\rangle} \cdot z_{\langle 5,0\rangle}$. This gives us the equivalent transition $q \xrightarrow{\lambda(y,z).7\text{F}_{16} < (y_{\langle 4,0\rangle} \cdot z_{\langle 5,0\rangle}) \leq 7\text{FF}_{16} \wedge y=6\cdot y_{\langle 4,0\rangle} \wedge z=2\cdot z_{\langle 5,0\rangle}} q$. Next, *monadic decomposition* of the guard yields the following equivalent transition, $q \xrightarrow{\lambda(y,z).y_{\langle 5,1\rangle} \neq 0 \wedge y_{\langle 5,5\rangle}=0 \wedge y=6\cdot y_{\langle 4,0\rangle} \wedge z=2\cdot z_{\langle 5,0\rangle}} q$ that, after simplification, is equivalent to the following two transition path $q \xrightarrow{\lambda y.\text{C2}_{16} \leq y \leq \text{DF}_{16}} q_3 \xrightarrow{\lambda z.80_{16} \leq z \leq \text{BF}_{16}} q$ where q_3 is a new state. The ESFA rules with lookahead 3 and 4 are a bit more challenging and yield monadic decompositions with higher widths. After further *minimization* [11] of the resulting SFA we obtain the SFA in Figure 2 that accepts the range of *EncUTF8*.

Program Analysis. Monadic decomposition can be used to break down dependencies between program variables and thus simplify various symbolic techniques that are used in the context of modern program analysis [30]. The use of an SMT solver as a black box is particularly well suited in this context because it allows seamless combination of different theories for different data types.

Program Synthesis. The range SFA construction of *EncUTF8* illustrates another potential usage. We can *automatically* invert *EncUTF8* into a *UTF8 decoder DecUTF8* in a way that guarantees the correctness criterion that for all valid input sequences s, $DecUTF8(EncUTF8(s)) = s$, by using the SFA in Figure 2 as the control-flow graph of the corresponding transducer and by inverting the individual rules of the encoder.

Linear Optimization. A new SMT based optimization algorithm SYMBA is described in [27] that uses linear real arithmetic objective functions and an SMT solver as a black box. Monadic decomposition is a potential simplification technique of objective functions in this context [4].

Theorem Proving. In the context of automated first-order resolution based theorem proving modulo theories, *Skolemization* may benefit from monadic decomposition by enabling simpler Skolem functions [26]. The use of SMT solvers in this context comes into play when the classical resolution technique is extended to work modulo background theories [24,25].

Compiler Technology. Monadic decomposition can be used to simplify expressions and thus enable new (or enhance existing) automatic compiler optimization techniques [3]. Moreover, it may be used for code parallelization.

3   Monadic Predicates

We assume a decidable background $\mathfrak{U}$ as described above. The Boolean type is BOOL with truth values $\{\top, \bot\}$. In our expressions, all variables are typed and all terms and formulas are well-typed. The subuniverse of elements of type τ is denoted by $\mathcal{U}^\tau$. We use λ-expressions to define anonymous functions and relations, given $\varphi(\bar{x}) \in \Psi$ where all the free variables of $\varphi(\bar{x})$ are among $\bar{x} = (x_1, \ldots, x_n)$, we write $\lambda\bar{x}.\varphi(\bar{x})$ or simply φ, when the arity n and types of x_i are clear from the context, for the corresponding predicate and $[\![\varphi]\!]$ for the n-ary relation defined by φ.

Let R be an n-ary relation for some $n \geq 2$ and of type $\prod_{i=1}^n \tau_i$.[2] R is *Cartesian* if there exist sets $U_i \subseteq \mathcal{U}^{\tau_i}$, for $1 \leq i \leq n$, such that $R = \prod_{i=1}^n U_i$. R is *monadic* if there exists finite $k > 0$ and Cartesian R_i, for $1 \leq i \leq k$, s.t. $R = \bigcup_{i=1}^k R_i$; $\{R_i\}_{i=1}^k$ is called a *monadic decomposition of R of width k*. R is *k-monadic* if R has a monadic decomposition of width k. The *(monadic) width* of R is the smallest k such that R is k-*monadic*. Note that R has width 1 iff it is Cartesian.

Example 1. Let φ be the predicate $\lambda(x,y).(x + (y \mod 2)) > 5$, where x and y have integer type. Then $R = [\![\varphi]\!]$ is the corresponding binary relation over integers. R is not Cartesian but it is 2-monadic because $R = ([\![\lambda x.x > 5]\!] \times [\![\lambda y.\top]\!]) \cup ([\![\lambda x.x > 4]\!] \times [\![\lambda y.odd(y)]\!])$.   ⊠

We lift the notions to predicates. A *unary* formula is a formula with at most one free variable. An *explicitly monadic* formula is some Boolean combination of unary formulas. Observe that the difference between monadic and explicitly monadic, is that the first notion is semantic (depends on $\mathfrak{U}$) while the second is syntactic (independent of $\mathfrak{U}$).

4   Monadic Decomposition

We are interested in the following two problems: 1) Deciding if a predicate φ is monadic; 2) Given a monadic predicate φ, effectively constructing a monadic decomposition of φ. We restrict our attention to *binary* predicates. The decomposition can be reduced recursively to the binary case and applied to n-ary predicates with $n > 2$, such as the range predicates arising from the third and fourth rules of *EncUTF8* in Figure 1.

4.1   Deciding If a Predicate Is Monadic

Consider any term $f(x)$ in the background theory denoting a function over integers. Let $\varphi_f(x,y)$ be the formula $f(x) \doteq y$.[3] Then $\varphi_f(x,y)$ is monadic iff there

---

[2] Type $\prod_{i=1}^2 \tau_i$ is also denoted $\tau_1 \times \tau_2$.
[3] We assume that formal equality $\doteq$ is allowed.

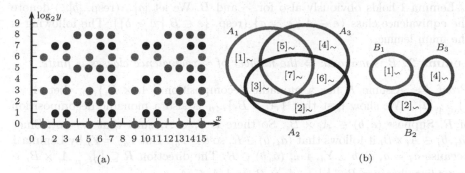

(a)   (b)

Fig. 3. Let $R^k(x,y) \stackrel{\text{def}}{=} y{>}0 \wedge y\&(y{-}1){=}0 \wedge x\&(y \bmod (2^k-1)){\neq}0$ over $\mathbb{N}$, & is bit-wise-AND; a) *Geometrical view of R^3:* (x,y) is marked iff $R^3(x,y)$ holds; if two Y-cuts Y_m and Y_n are identical then $m \sim n$, e.g., $1 \sim 9$; if two X-cuts X_m and X_n are identical then $m \smile n$, e.g., $2^2 \smile 2^5$; b) *Venn Diagram view of R^3:* $R^3 = \bigcup_{i=1}^{3} A_i \times B_i$.

exists k such that $\varphi_f(x,y)$ is equivalent to $\bigvee_{i<k} \alpha_i(x) \wedge \beta_i(y)$. Since there can only be one y for a given x (because f is a function) it follows that $\|[\beta_i]\| = 1$ for all $i < k$. So φ_f is monadic iff f is bounded (finite-valued). While boundedness of f is an undecidable problem in general by using Rice's Theorem [37], we cannot use this argument because we cannot even encode context free languages in Ψ, so much less arbitrary recursive languages. We show in Section 4.4 that the question is decidable for some cases, but the general case is an open problem.

4.2   Decomposition Procedure

In the following, we provide a brute force semidecision procedure for monadic decomposition. While the procedure is complete for monadic predicates, in the nonmonadic case it will not terminate. The input is a binary predicate $\varphi \in \Psi$. Let $R = [\![\varphi]\!] \subseteq A \times B$, where we assume that $R \neq \emptyset$ and

$$A \stackrel{\text{def}}{=} \{a \mid \exists b\, R(a,b)\}, \quad B \stackrel{\text{def}}{=} \{b \mid \exists a\, R(a,b)\}.$$

Define the relations:

$$x \sim x' \stackrel{\text{def}}{=} \forall y\, y'((\varphi(x,y) \wedge \varphi(x',y')) \Rightarrow (\varphi(x',y) \wedge \varphi(x,y')))$$
$$y \smile y' \stackrel{\text{def}}{=} \forall x\, x'((\varphi(x,y) \wedge \varphi(x',y')) \Rightarrow (\varphi(x',y) \wedge \varphi(x,y')))$$

For $a \in A$, define the *Y-cut of R by a* as the set $Y_a = \{b \mid R(a,b)\}$. Similarly, for $b \in B$, define the *X-cut of R by b* as the set $X_b = \{a \mid R(a,b)\}$. The idea of cuts can be illustrated geometrically. See Figure 3(a). The following properties are used below.

Lemma 1. *Let R and A be given as above. 1) For all $a, a' \in A$: $a \sim a'$ if and only if $Y_a = Y_{a'}$. 2) The relation $\sim$ is an equivalence relation over A.*

Lemma 1 holds obviously also for $\frown$ and B. We let $[a]_\sim$ (resp. $[b]_\frown$) denote the equivalence class $\{e \in A \mid e \sim a\}$ (resp. $\{e \in B \mid e \frown b\}$). The following is the main lemma.

Lemma 2. *R is monadic $\Leftrightarrow$ the number of $\sim$-equivalence classes is finite.*

Proof. $\Rightarrow$: Assume R has a monadic decomposition $\{A_i \times B_i\}_{i<n}$. Let $\tilde{A}_i = \bigcup_{a \in A_i} [a]_\sim$. We show first that $\{\tilde{A}_i \times B_i\}_{i<n}$ is also a monadic decomposition of R. Suppose $(a, b) \in \tilde{A}_i \times B_i$. So there is $a_i \in A_i$ such that $a \sim a_i$. Since $(a_i, b) \in A_i \times B_i$ it follows that $(a_i, b) \in R$, so $b \in Y_{a_i}$. But $Y_{a_i} = Y_a$ by Lemma 1 because $a_i \sim a$, so $b \in Y_a$, i.e., $(a, b) \in R$. The direction $R \subseteq \bigcup_{i<n} \tilde{A}_i \times B_i$ is immediate because $R \subseteq \bigcup_{i<n} A_i \times B_i$ and $A_i \subseteq \tilde{A}_i$.

Next, we normalize $\{\tilde{A}_i \times B_i\}_{i<n}$ into a form $\{A'_i \times B'_i\}_{i<m}$ where each A'_i ends up being exactly one $\sim$-equivalence class of A. For all $I \subseteq \{i \mid 0 \le i < n\}$ let M_I be the *minterm* $(\bigcap_{i \in I} \tilde{A}_i) \setminus (\bigcup_{j \notin I} \tilde{A}_j)$. By using standard Boolean laws, each $\tilde{A}_i$ is a finite union of disjoint nonempty minterms. Apply the following equivalence preserving transformations to the monadic decomposition $\{\tilde{A}_i \times B_i\}_{i<n}$ until no more transformations can be made:

- replace $(M_I \cup M) \times B_i$ by $(M_I \times B_i) \cup (M \times B_i)$,
- replace $(M_I \times B_i) \cup (M_I \times B_j)$ by $M_I \times (B_i \cup B_j)$.

Let the resulting decomposition be $\{A'_i \times B'_i\}_{i<m}$, where, for all $a \in A$ and $b \in B$, we have $(a, b) \in R$ iff there exists exactly one i such that $(a, b) \in A'_i \times B'_i$. In other words, for all $a \in A$, Y_a is the set B'_i such that $a \in A'_i$. It follows that $a \sim a'$ for all $a, a' \in A'_i$.

Thus, the number of $\sim$-equivalence classes is bounded by $2^n - 1$ where n is the monadic width of R, because the number m of different (nonempty) minterms M_I is, due to the powerset construction, at most $2^n - 1$.

$\Leftarrow$: Assume that the number of $\sim$-equivalence classes is finite. Let $A = \bigcup_{i=0}^{n-1} A_i$ where $A_i = [a_i]_\sim$. Let $B_i = Y_{a_i}$ for $0 \le i < n$. Thus if $(a, b) \in A_i \times B_i$ then $a \sim a_i$ and $b \in Y_{a_i}$, i.e., $Y_a = Y_{a_i}$ and $b \in Y_{a_i}$. So $b \in Y_a$, i.e., $(a, b) \in R$. Conversely, if $(a, b) \in R$ then $b \in Y_a$. But $Y_a = Y_{a_i} = B_i$, for some $i < n$, where $a \in A_i$ and $b \in B_i$. Thus, $\{A_i \times B_i\}_{i<n}$ is a monadic decomposition of R.   ⊠

Next, we provide a simple iterative procedure to compute a *witness set* W_A that covers $A_\sim$. We use the negated form of $\sim$:

$$x \not\sim x' \Leftrightarrow \exists y\, y'(\varphi(x, y) \wedge \varphi(x', y') \wedge (\neg\varphi(x', y) \vee \neg\varphi(x, y')))$$

So, for all $a, a' \in A$, $a \not\sim a'$ means that a and a' must participate in distinct Cartesian components of a monadic decomposition of φ, i.e., if $\{R_i\}_{i<k}$ is a monadic decomposition of R, then there exist $b, b' \in B$ and $i \ne j$ such that $(a, b) \in R_i \setminus R_j$ and $(a', b') \in R_j \setminus R_i$.

Computation of W_A : Let $(a_0, b_0) \in [\![\varphi]\!]$ and let $W_A = \{a_0\}$. Repeat:
1. Let $\psi(x)$ be the formula $\bigwedge_{a \in W_A} x \not\sim a$.
2. If there exists a such that $\psi(a)$ holds then $W_A := W_A \cup \{a\}$ else terminate.

Observe that satisfiability checking of ψ in the above procedure as well as generating the witness a is decidable because we can transform ψ to prenex normal form as an $\exists$-formula and treat all the existential variables as free variables. In other words, the resulting formula is in Ψ. When ψ becomes unsatisfiable then any further element from A must be $\sim$-equivalent to one of the elements already in W_A, while all elements in W_A belong to distinct $\sim$-equivalence classes. Therefore, if φ is monadic then the process terminates by Lemma 2, and upon termination W_A is a finite collection of witnesses that divides A into a set $A_\sim$ of $\sim$-equivalence classes $[a]_\sim$ for $a \in W_A$. For example, if φ is Cartesian then ψ is unsatisfiable initially, because then $A_\sim = \{[a_0]_\sim\}$.

Computation of *witness set* W_B is analogous to computation of W_A. Observe that $|W_B|, |W_A| < 2^n$ where n is the monadic width of φ, which follows from the proof of Lemma 2. We also have that $n \le |W_B|, |W_A|$.

Example 2. Consider the relation $R = R^3$ in Figure 3. The width of R is 3. We have $A_\sim = \{[a]_\sim \mid 1 \le a \le 7\}$ where $[a]_\sim = \{n \mid n_{\langle 2,0 \rangle} = a\}$ and $B_\sim = \{[2^0]_\sim, [2^1]_\sim, [2^2]_\sim\}$ were $[2^m]_\sim = \{2^n \mid n \bmod 3 = m\}$. Figure 3(b) illustrates the equivalence classes as nonempty regions of a Venn Diagram view of R. $\boxtimes$

Lemma 3. *If R is monadic then, for all $\mathbf{a} \in A_\sim$ and $\mathbf{b} \in B_\sim$, we can effectively construct $\alpha_\mathbf{a}, \beta_\mathbf{b} \in \Psi$ such that $[\![\alpha_\mathbf{a}]\!] = \mathbf{a}$ and $[\![\beta_\mathbf{b}]\!] = \mathbf{b}$.*

Proof. By using Lemma 2 let W_A be constructed as above, so $A_\sim = \{[a]_\sim \mid a \in W_A\}$. Similarly to W_A, construct a finite W_B s.t. $B_\sim = \{[b]_\sim \mid b \in W_B\}$. Let

$$(\text{for } b \in W_B) \quad \beta_b(y) \overset{\text{def}}{=} \beta_{[b]_\sim}(y) \overset{\text{def}}{=} (\bigwedge_{a \subset W_A \cap X_b} \varphi(a, y)) \wedge (\bigwedge_{a \in W_A \setminus X_b} \neg\varphi(a, y))$$

$$(\text{for } a \in W_A) \quad \alpha_a(x) \overset{\text{def}}{=} \alpha_{[a]_\sim}(x) \overset{\text{def}}{=} (\bigwedge_{b \in W_B \cap Y_a} \varphi(x, b)) \wedge (\bigwedge_{b \in W_B \setminus Y_a} \neg\varphi(x, b))$$

Observe that α_a is well-defined because for all $a' \in [a]_\sim$ we have that $Y_a = Y_{a'}$. Similarly for β_b. One can show that $[\![\beta_b]\!] = [b]_\sim$ and $[\![\alpha_a]\!] = [a]_\sim$. Fix $a \in W_A$ and consider the definition of α_a. Suppose $W_B \cap Y_a = \{b_1, b_2\}$ and $W_B \setminus Y_a = \{b_3, b_4\}$. Then $[a]_\sim \subseteq X_{b_1} \cap X_{b_2}$ and $[a]_\sim \subseteq (X_{b_3} \cup X_{b_4})^c$. So $[a]_\sim \subseteq [\![\alpha_a]\!]$. For the direction $[\![\alpha_a]\!] \subseteq [a]_\sim$ take $a' \in [\![\alpha_a]\!]$. Suppose, by way of contradiction that, $a \not\sim a'$ and thus $Y_{a'} \ne Y_a$. Then there exists $b \in W_B \setminus Y_a$ such that $a' \in X_b$. But, by definition of α_a, $X_b \cap [\![\alpha_a]\!] = \emptyset$, which contradicts that $a' \in X_b$ and $a' \in [\![\alpha_a]\!]$. $\boxtimes$

Lemma 3 is essentially a quantifier elimination property that allows us to eliminate the $\forall$ quantifier from the definition of $\lambda x.x \sim a$ (resp. $\lambda y.y \sim b$) by stating that it is enough to consider the elements in W_B (resp. W_A). We can now prove the following result. It gives us a brute force method for monadic decomposition.

Theorem 1. *If $\varphi(x, y)$ is monadic then*
a) $\varphi(x, y)$ is equivalent to $\lambda(x, y). \bigvee_{a \in W_A}(\alpha_a(x) \wedge \varphi(a, y))$.
b) $\varphi(x, y)$ is equivalent to $\lambda(x, y). \bigvee_{b \in W_B}(\beta_b(y) \wedge \varphi(x, b))$.
c) $\varphi(x, y)$ is equivalent to $\lambda(x, y). \bigvee_{a \in W_A, b \in W_B, (a,b) \in [\![\varphi]\!]}(\alpha_a(x) \wedge \beta_b(y))$.

Proof. We prove (a). The other cases are similar. By Lemma 3 we have $[\![\alpha_a]\!] = [a]_\sim$. By construction of W_A we have that, for all $a \in W_A$ we have $[a]_\sim \times Y_a \subseteq [\![\varphi]\!]$ where $[a]_\sim \times Y_a = [\![\lambda(x,y).\alpha_a(x) \wedge \varphi(a,y)]\!]$. In the other direction, if $(a,b) \in [\![\varphi]\!]$ then $a \in [\![\alpha_a]\!]$ and $b \in Y_a$. In other words, $(a,b) \in [\![\lambda(x,y).\alpha_a(x) \wedge \varphi(a,y)]\!]$.   ⊠

Theorem 1 does not guarantee smallest monadic width. Example 3 shows that the monadic width may be strictly smaller than $\min(|W_B|, |W_A|)$.

Example 3. Take $R = \{(1,1),(2,2),(3,3),(4,4),(5,1),(5,2),(3,5),(4,5)\}$ where $A = B = \{1,2,3,4,5\}$. Then $|W_A| = 5$ and $|W_B| = 5$ but R has width 4: $R = (\{1,5\} \times \{1\}) \cup (\{2,5\} \times \{2\}) \cup (\{3\} \times \{3,5\}) \cup (\{4\} \times \{4,5\})$.   ⊠

Example 4. Let $\phi(x,y) := (0 \leq x \leq 1 \wedge 0 \leq y \leq 1 \wedge x + y < 2)$. The example illustrates a case where ϕ is satisfied by a finite model of the form:

We get the following predicates by using Lemma 3 and simplifications.

$$\alpha_a(x) \overset{\text{def}}{=} x \doteq a, \quad \alpha_{a'}(x) \overset{\text{def}}{=} x \doteq a', \quad \beta_b(y) \overset{\text{def}}{=} y \doteq b, \quad \beta_{b'}(y) \overset{\text{def}}{=} y \doteq b'$$

where $a = 0, a' = 1, b = 0, b' = 1$. Monadic decomposition of ϕ reconstructs the formula $\alpha_a(x) \wedge \beta_b(y) \vee \alpha_a(x) \wedge \beta_{b'}(y) \vee \alpha_{a'}(x) \wedge \beta_b(y)$ by using Theorem 1(c). Case $\alpha_{a'}(x) \wedge \beta_{b'}(y)$ is not included because $\phi(1,1)$ is false.   ⊠

4.3   Another Decomposition Algorithm

If implemented directly, Theorem 1 suggests creating a decomposition which is in a disjunctive normal form (DNF) with respect to the unary sub-formulas. Instead of creating what amounts to a DNF, we can use case analysis on $\varphi(a,y) \wedge \varphi(x,b)$ for all $([a]_\sim, [b]_\frown) \in A_\sim \times B_\frown$. The output may be any explicitly monadic formula, not necessarily in DNF. Moreover, Theorem 1 suggests full exploration of W_A and W_B. We show how to avoid this by using lifted versions of the definitions of $\sim$ and $\frown$. We lift the definitions of $\sim$ (resp. $\frown$) to all elements of the type of x (resp. y). We define $a_1 \sim a_2 \overset{\text{def}}{=} Y_{a_1} = Y_{a_2}$ and $b_1 \frown b_2 \overset{\text{def}}{=} X_{b_1} = X_{b_2}$. This is consistent with the earlier definition (due to Lemma 1) and is simpler to work with because the equivalence classes cover the full universe (of the given type) and are identical for φ and $\neg\varphi$. For example, consider the equivalence classes $\mathbb{N}_\sim$ in Figure 3. Then $[0]_\sim = \mathbb{N} \setminus (A_1 \cup A_2 \cup A_3)$. Thus

$$x \not\sim x' \Leftrightarrow \exists z(\neg(\varphi(x,z) \Leftrightarrow \varphi(x',z))), \quad y \not\frown y' \Leftrightarrow \exists z(\neg(\varphi(z,y) \Leftrightarrow \varphi(z,y'))).$$

We introduce a procedure named ***mondec*** that given a monadic predicate $\varphi(x,y)$ produces an equivalent explicitly monadic predicate ***mondec***(φ); it uses a recursive procedure **δ**. The argument π of **δ** below is the path condition and ν is the

the accumulated side condition; the purpose of ν is to ensure *new* combinations from $A_\sim \times B_\backsim$. Here A (resp. B) is the set of all values of the type of x (resp. y). We write $(\psi \,?\, \phi_t : \phi_f)$ for $((\psi \wedge \phi_t) \vee (\neg\psi \wedge \phi_f))$.

$\boldsymbol{mondec}(\varphi) \stackrel{\text{def}}{=} \boldsymbol{\delta}(\top, \top)$,   where

$$\boldsymbol{\delta}(\nu, \pi) \stackrel{\text{def}}{=} \begin{cases} \bot, & \text{if } \boldsymbol{unsat}(\pi \wedge \varphi); \\ \top, & \text{else if } \boldsymbol{unsat}(\pi \wedge \neg\varphi); \\ (\psi_b^a \,?\, \boldsymbol{\delta}(\nu \wedge \nu_b^a, \pi \wedge \psi_b^a) : \boldsymbol{\delta}(\nu \wedge \nu_b^a, \pi \wedge \neg\psi_b^a)), \text{else let } (a, b) \models \nu, \end{cases}$$

$$\nu_b^a \stackrel{\text{def}}{=} a \not\sim x \vee b \not\backsim b,$$
$$\psi_b^a \stackrel{\text{def}}{=} \varphi(a, y) \wedge \varphi(x, b).$$

Theorem 2. *If φ is monadic then $\boldsymbol{mondec}(\varphi)$ is defined and $\boldsymbol{mondec}(\varphi)$ is an explicitly monadic predicate that is equivalent to φ.*

Proof. Assume φ is monadic. Assume also that φ is satisfiable or else it is trivially equivalent to the explicitly monadic predicate $\bot$. Let A and B be as above. By using Lemma 2, $A_\sim$ and $B_\backsim$ are finite. Observe that the argument ν of $\boldsymbol{\delta}$ remains of the form that all existential quantifiers occur *positively* in it, so the selection of $(a, b) \models \nu$ in $\boldsymbol{\delta}$ is decidable (using the solver for Ψ).

The procedure $\boldsymbol{mondec}$ creates an if-then-else expression that can be thought of as a binary tree whose leaves are either $\top$ or $\bot$ and whose nodes are formulas ψ_b^a for some $a \in A$ and $b \in B$. The formula $\boldsymbol{mondec}(\varphi)$ is explicitly monadic because each ψ_b^a is explicitly monadic.

First, we show that $\boldsymbol{mondec}(\varphi)$ is well-defined (terminates) by showing that there are finitely many nodes. A new node ψ_b^a is created only when there exists $a \in A$ and $b \in B$ such that $(a, b) \models \nu$. In the subsequent recursive calls, any node that is equivalent to ψ_b^a is eliminated by the constraint ν_b^a. Termination follows because $A_\sim$ and $B_\backsim$ are finite and $\psi_b^a \Leftrightarrow \psi_{b'}^{a'}$ iff $a \sim a'$ and $b \backsim b'$.

Next, we show that ν must be satisfiable if both $\pi \wedge \varphi$ and $\pi \wedge \neg\varphi$ are satisfiable. Let $(a, b) \models \pi \wedge \varphi$ and $(a', b') \models \pi \wedge \neg\varphi$. We know that it is possible to strengthen π to π_1 so that π_1 is equivalent to $\alpha_a(x) \wedge \beta_b(y)$ and currently this is not the case because $a \not\sim a'$ or $b \not\backsim b'$. Moreover, and without loss of generality, π_1 is of the form $\pi \wedge \psi$ where ψ is a conjunction of predicates ψ_d^c or $\neg\psi_d^c$ for some $c \in A$ and $d \in B$. We have, by definition of $\boldsymbol{\delta}$, that π has the form

$$\bigwedge_{i=1}^{m} \psi_{b_i}^{a_i} \wedge \bigwedge_{i=m+1}^{n} \neg\psi_{b_i}^{a_i}$$

for some $n \geq m \geq 0$ and $n \geq 1$, and that $\neg\nu$ is equivalent to $\bigvee_{i=1}^{n} a_i \sim x \wedge b_i \backsim y$. Thus, any use of a predicate ψ_d^c such that $(c, d) \models \neg\nu$ is useless because it makes ψ_d^c equivalent to some $\psi_{b_i}^{a_i}$ for some i, $1 \leq i \leq n$, and so $\pi \wedge \psi_d^c$ or $\pi \wedge \neg\psi_d^c$ is either equivalent to π or to $\bot$. Therefore, ν must be satisfiable or else π_1 cannot be constructed.

To show that $\boldsymbol{mondec}(\varphi) \Leftrightarrow \varphi$ is immediate from the definition of $\boldsymbol{\delta}$. First, consider a branch π in $\boldsymbol{mondec}(\varphi)$ ending in $\top$. We know that π implies φ as a condition for $\top$. The case $\neg\boldsymbol{mondec}(\varphi) \Rightarrow \neg\varphi$ is symmetrical by considering branches π in $\boldsymbol{mondec}(\varphi)$ ending in $\bot$.   ⊠

To illustrate **mondec**, take $\varphi(x, y)$ to be the predicate R^3 in Figure 3. Consider the result of **mondec**(φ) that starts with $(4,4) \models \varphi$ so the root is ψ_4^4. In the depiction of **mondec**(φ) in Figure 4, the left subtree of a node is the true case and right subtree of a node is the false case. For example, $\neg\psi_4^4 \wedge \psi_2^3 \wedge \psi_2^2$ is a branch that implies φ, this branch covers the case $A_2 \times B_2$ in Figure 3(b).

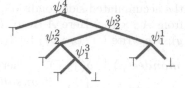

Fig. 4. mondec(R^3)

4.4 Two Decidable Cases

We show decidability of monadic decomposition in two cases. We leave decidabilty of monadicity for other theories and tight complexity bounds as open problems.

Consider first integer linear arithmetic. It clearly meets the requirements of $\mathfrak{U}$. Take a linear arithmetic formula $\varphi(x, y)$. Let the predicate $\sim$ be defined as above, let '$x \in A$' stand for the formula $\exists y \varphi(x, y)$. Construct the following quantified formula: $IsMonadic(\varphi) \stackrel{\text{def}}{=} \exists \hat{x}(\forall x(x \in A \Rightarrow \exists x'(|x'| < \hat{x} \wedge x \sim x')))$

Theorem 3. *Monadic decomposition is decidable for integer linear arithmetic.*

Proof. Let $\varphi(x, y)$ be a formula in integer linear arithmetic. We show that φ is monadic $\Leftrightarrow IsMonadic(\varphi)$ is true in Presburger arithmetic. Decidability follows by [34]. Proof of $\Rightarrow$: Assume φ is monadic. Then $A_\sim$ is finite by Lemma 2. Let $\hat{a} = \max\{\min(abs(C)) \mid C \in A_\sim\} + 1$. Then, for all $a \in A$, a belongs to some C in $A_\sim$, and so there is $a' \in C$ such that $|a'| = \min(abs(C))$ and so $|a'| < \hat{a}$ and $a \sim a'$. Proof of $\Leftarrow$: Assume $IsMonadic(\varphi)$ holds. Choose a witness $\hat{a}$ for $\hat{x}$ and consider the classes $\mathcal{A} = \{[a]_\sim \mid 0 \leq |a| < \hat{a}\}$. It follows that $\mathcal{A} = A_\sim$ is finite, so φ is monadic by Lemma 2.   ☒

The formula $IsMonadic(\varphi)$ has the quantifier prefix $\exists\forall\exists\forall$ in Prenex normal form when φ is quantifier free. So there are *three* quantifier alternations in $IsMonadic(\varphi)$. This implies an upper bound on time complexity $2^{2^{cn^7}}$ for some constant c and size n of φ for deciding if φ is monadic [36]. This is one exponent lower than the upper bound $2^{2^{2^{cn}}}$ known for the full Presburger arithmetic [14]. Moreover, the structure of the formula is quite specific and may justify the design of a special purpose algorithm. Likewise, but for a different reason:

Theorem 4. *Monadic decomposition is decidable for real algebraic arithmetic with addition and multiplication.*

Proof (Sketch). The atomic subformulas of φ are of the form $p(x, y) \geq 0$, where $p(x, y)$ is in general a multi-variate polynomial. Thus, for every value b, $\varphi(x, b)$ is a uni-variate polynomial, and the sign of such polynomials induce a finite set of intervals that partition the reals. Without loss of generality consider the case for an a, b and ϵ, such that for all b' where $\epsilon \geq b' > b$ we have $\varphi(a, b)$ but $\neg\varphi(a, b')$. Then φ contains an atomic formula $p(x, y) \geq 0$ whose truth value changes over

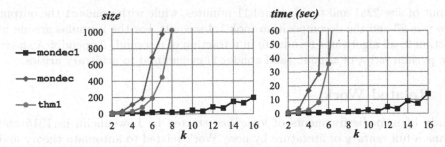

Fig. 5. Comparison of monadic decomposition algorithms

b, b'. Monadicity of φ fails if it is determined by signs of polynomials $p(x, y)$ that depend on both x and y (recall that polynomials are continuous and differentiable). Thus, we can limit the search for a monadic decomposition up to the maximal number of regions induced by the polynomials in φ. This (potentially very large) number is bounded by the polynomial degrees and number of atomic subformulas.   ☒

5   Experiments

We present here a set of micro benchmarks using the sample predicate R^k from Figure 3 by letting k range from 2 to 16; k also happens to be the monadic width of R^k. The worst case scenario of the size of a monadic decomposition of R^k, according to Theorem 1(c), is $O(k2^k)$ because $|A_\sim| = 2^k$ and $|B_\sim| = k$ (including the classes $[0]_\sim$ and $[0]_\smile$). We compare three algorithms, implemented as z3 python scripts, that are indicated in Figure 5 by thm1, mondec, and mondec1. The output is in all cases an explicitly monadic formula in form of an if-then-else expression, its *size* is the number of ψ_b^a nodes in it, e.g., the size of the expression in Figure 4 is 5.[4] Algorithm thm1 is based on Theorem 1 but avoids explicit DNF construction. Algorithm mondec1 is a variant of mondec; its python script is shown in Appendix A. The only difference compared to mondec is that mondec1 uses the following heuristic for selecting a witness $(a, b) \models \nu$:

$$(a, b) \models \text{if } \mathbf{sat}(\nu \wedge \varphi \wedge \pi) \text{ then } \nu \wedge \varphi \wedge \pi \text{ else if } \mathbf{sat}(\nu \wedge \varphi) \text{ then } \nu \wedge \varphi \text{ else } \nu$$

that amounts to changing a single line of code in the python script. In other words, for selecting new (a, b) first try to do so in the context of φ and π. The most interesting aspect about this experiment is that it shows that different heuristics can influence the performance characteristics of monadic decomposition by an exponential factor. The above heuristic reduces the size of the decomposition exponentially in this experiment, while constructing nodes in mondec based solely on ν provides worse performance than exhaustive search of W_A and W_B, as in thm1. For example, the time to decompose R^9 with mondec gave an

---

[4] The experiments were carried out on a laptop with a 2GHz CPU.

ouput of size 2281 and took around 11 minutes, while with `mondec1` the output size was 23 and the decomposition took 1.4 seconds. For the formulas arising in Section 2, all algorithms terminate in a fraction of a second. Appendix A shows the python script of `mondec` (and `mondec1`) generalized to arbitrary arities.

6   Related Work

Study of monadic fragments of logic was started by Löwenheim in 1915 and spans a full *century* of literature by now. Work related to automata theory and its relation to monadic fragments of logic is, likewise, a very thoroughly studied topic [39]. Despite this, there is renewed interest in this topic, but with a new angle. From our perspective, this is due to many advances in *automated logical inference engines*. The angle is, how to make use of such advances in a modular way in the context of automata theoretic problems. This makes questions like the one posed in this paper relevant in many different potential application areas. Monadic decomposition can also be used to study new decidable fragments of logics; revisiting techniques in [13,18,6] could be relevant in this context.

Monadic Fragments. Unary relations play a key role in many decision problems and decidable logics. *Monadic first-order logic*, or the Löwenheim class [29], is the classical example of a decidable fragment of first-order logic where all symbols are unary relation symbols. The Löb-Gurevich class [28], is the extension of the Löwenheim class where also unary function symbols are allowed. Both classes are decidable by having the *finite model property* [7]. *Monadic second-order logic* allows quantification over unary predicates. Among one of the most celebrated and applied decidability results are those of the monadic second-order theory *S1S* with one successor relation by Büchi [8] and decidability of the monadic second-order theory *S2S* of the binary tree with two successor relations by Rabin [35]. The ability to apply Rabin's theorem and automata based techniques to establish decidability results of a logic is often described as the logic having the *tree model property*. *Modal logics* do not have the finite model property but they do have the tree model property. Vardi attributes [41] their decidability to this. Grädel discusses this topic further in [17] and its relation to the *guarded fragment* [5]. Unlike in modal logics, simple extensions of the guarded fragment cause undecidability [16], one exception is the *monadic* guarded fragment with two variables and equivalence relations that does have the tree model property [15]. The theorems of Büchi and Rabin have also been revisited and extended by Gurevich through game based techniques [18]. Another technique discussed in [18] is the use of the *Feferman-Vaught* generalized products [13] as a model-theoretic method for establishing decidability results in the context of monadic second-order logic.

Symbolic Automata. Remarkably, the Feferman-Vaught theorem is revisited in [6] where it is shown that a special version of it is closely related to the theory of $\mathfrak{M}$-*automata* where $\mathfrak{M}$ is a first-order structure. Although $\mathfrak{M}$-automata are defined as *multi-tape* automata, by using tuples, they correspond precisely to SFAs. Independently, a variant of SFAs was originally introduced in the context of natural language processing, where they are called *predicate-augmented finite state recognizers* [33]. Symbolic finite transducers were introduced in [44], a different notion of symbolic transducers is also studied in [33]. The extension from SFTs to ESFTs is introduced in [10]. Equivalence of ESFTs, properties of ESFAs, and the notion of Cartesian ESFTs are studied in [9]. The monadic decomposition problem first surfaced in the context of trying to lift algorithms for symbolic automata *without lookahead* to symbolic automata *with lookahead*. In classical automata theory this problem does not exist because lookahead can be eliminated by introducing more states since the alphabet is finite. Most other SFA algorithms can, in theory, be lifted to finite alphabets. For example, closure under complement [6, Proposition 2.6] is shown by reduction to NFA determinization through *minterm* construction by considering the Boolean combinations of all guards of the $\mathfrak{M}$-automaton as the finite alphabet of the NFA. Practically this approach does not scale, it suffers from an exponential blowup of the number of transitions, even before the actual NFA determinization algorithm starts.

Applications. For many analysis tasks, some of which are discussed in Secion 2, monadic decomposition plays a key role in enabling the use of SFA and SFT algorithms in the context of symbolic automata and transducers. Other SFA algorithms, such as difference and complement, are discussed in [43] in the context of SMT solvers, and more algorithms are discussed in [21] in the more specialized context of string analysis. A symbolic automata toolkit is described in [42]. SFT algorithms, in particular equivalence checking, are studied in [44] and their use for web security is discussed in [20]. A new minimization algorithm of SFAs was recently presented in [11], showing that the new algorithm can enable some analysis scenarios involving monadic second-order logic that did not scale with earlier techniques; the reduction itself from monadic second-order formulas to SFAs is essentially the classical one [39] and the performance is compared to Mona [19,23].

7   Conclusion

We introduced the problem of monadic decomposition of predicates in decidable theories. Theorem 1 provided an effective means to computing a monadic decomposition and we described an implementation with correctness proof, Theorem 2, that avoids expanding solutions directly into DNF; it leverages a Shannon decomposition. We left the general case of *decidability* of monadic decomposition as an open problem. Deciding if a predicate is monadic in a specific background theory is another interesting open problem. While we show that the problem is decidable for integer linear arithmetic and polynomial real algebraic arithmetic, we have not investigated concrete algorithms for these cases.

Acknowledgements. We thank the anonymous reviewers for their constructive feedback that greatly helped to improve the paper.

A   Monadic Decomposition in Python

Below is a self-contained python script `mondec` that computes a monadic decomposition of a predicate R with given variables. It uses z3.

```
from z3 import *

def nu_ab(R, x, y, a, b):
    x_ = [ Const("x_%d" %i,x[i].sort()) for i in range(len(x))]
    y_ = [ Const("y_%d" %i,y[i].sort()) for i in range(len(y))]
    return Or(Exists(y_,R(x+y_)!=R(a+y_)),Exists(x_,R(x_+y)!=R(x_+b)))

def isUnsat(fml):
    s = Solver(); s.add(fml); return unsat == s.check()

def lastSat(s, m, fmls):
    if len(fmls) == 0: return m
    s.push(); s.add(fmls[0])
    if s.check() == sat: m = lastSat(s, s.model(), fmls[1:])
    s.pop(); return m

def mondec(R, variables):
    phi = R(variables);
    if len(variables)==1: return phi
    m = len(variables)/2
    x,y = variables[0:m],variables[m:]
    def d(nu, pi):
        if isUnsat(And(pi, phi)): return BoolVal(False)
        if isUnsat(And(pi, Not(phi))): return BoolVal(True)
        fmls = [BoolVal(True)]
        if FLAG: fmls = [BoolVal(True), phi, pi] #---- use the heuristic from Section 5
        m = lastSat(nu, None, fmls)              #---- try to extend nu with fmls
        assert(m != None)                        #---- nu must be consistent
        a,b = [ m.evaluate(z,True) for z in x ],[ m.evaluate(z,True) for z in y ]
        psi_ab = And(R(a+y), R(x+b))
        phi_a, phi_b = mondec(lambda z: R(a+z),y), mondec(lambda z: R(z+b),x)
        nu.push()
        nu.add(nu_ab(R, x, y, a, b))             #---- extend nu to exlude case: x~a and y~b
        t, f = d(nu, And(pi, psi_ab)), d(nu, And(pi, Not(psi_ab)))
        nu.pop()
        return If(And(phi_a, phi_b), t, f)
    return d(Solver(),BoolVal(True))             #---- nu is initially a fresh z3 solver

def test_mondec(k):                              #---- decompose R^k from Figure 3
    R = lambda v:And(v[1]>0,(v[1]&(v[1]-1))==0,(v[0]&(v[1]%((1<<k)-1)))!=0)
    bvs = BitVecSort(2*k)                        #---- use 2k-bit bitvectors
    x,y = Const("x",bvs),Const("y",bvs)
    res = mondec(R,[x,y])
    assert(isUnsat(res != R([x,y])))             #---- check correctness of decomposition
    print "mondec1(", R([x,y]), ") ="; print res
FLAG = True                                      #---- run as mondec1
test_mondec(2)                                   #---- decompose R^2
```

Running it produces the following decomposition of R^2 where R^k is defined in Figure 3. The output corresponds to the expression $(\psi_2^2 ? \top : (\psi_1^5 ? \top : \bot))$ where ψ_b^a is the formula $R^2(a,y) \wedge R^2(x,b)$. The script can be run online using Z3Py [2].

```
mondec1( And(y > 0, y & y - 1 == 0, x & y%3 != 0) ) =
If(And(And(y > 0, y & y - 1 == 0, 2 & y%3 != 0),
       And(2 > 0, 2 & 2 - 1 == 0, x & 2%3 != 0)),
   True,
   If(And(And(y > 0, y & y - 1 == 0, 5 & y%3 != 0),
          And(1 > 0, 1 & 1 - 1 == 0, x & 1%3 != 0)),
      True,
      False))
```

References

1. URL Encode and Decode Tool, http://www.url-encode-decode.com
2. Z3 Python, http://rise4fun.com/Z3Py
3. Aho, A.V., Lam, M.S., Sethi, R., Ullman, J.D.: Compilers: Principles, Techniques, and Tools, 2nd edn. Addison-Wesley (2006)
4. Albarghouthi, A., Gurfinkel, A.: Personal communication (January 2014)
5. Andréka, H., Németi, I., van Benthem, J.: Modal languages and bounded fragments of predicate logic. Journal of Philosophical Logic 27, 217–274 (1998)
6. Bés, A.: An application of the Feferman-Vaught theorem to automata and logics for words over an infinite alphabet. Logical Methods in Computer Science 4, 1–23 (2008)
7. Börger, E., Grädel, E., Gurevich, Y.: The Classical Decision Problem. Springer (1997)
8. Büchi, J.R.: On a decision method in restricted second order arithmetic. In: Nagel, E., Suppes, P., Tarski, A. (eds.) Logic, Methodology and Philosophy of Science (Proc. 1960 Internat. Congr.), pp. 1–11. Stanford Univ. Press (1962)
9. D'Antoni, L., Veanes, M.: Equivalence of extended symbolic finite transducers. In: Sharygina, N., Veith, H. (eds.) CAV 2013. LNCS, vol. 8044, pp. 624–639. Springer, Heidelberg (2013)
10. D'Antoni, L., Veanes, M.: Static analysis of string encoders and decoders. In: Giacobazzi, R., Berdine, J., Mastroeni, I. (eds.) VMCAI 2013. LNCS, vol. 7737, pp. 209–228. Springer, Heidelberg (2013)
11. D'Antoni, L., Veanes, M.: Minimization of symbolic automata. In: POPL 2014, pp. 541–553. ACM (2014)
12. De Moura, L., Bjørner, N.: Satisfiability modulo theories: introduction and applications. Commun. ACM 54(9), 69–77 (2011)
13. Feferman, S., Vaught, R.L.: The first-order properties of algebraic systems. Fundamenta Mathematicae 47, 57–103 (1959)
14. Fischer, M.J., Rabin, M.O.: Super-exponential complexity of Presburger arithmetic. In: SIAMAMS: Complexity of Computation: Proceedings of a Symposium in Applied Mathematics of the American Mathematical Society and the Society for Industrial and Applied Mathematics, pp. 27–41 (1974)
15. Ganzinger, H., Meyer, C., Veanes, M.: The two-variable guarded fragment with transitive relations. In: LICS 1999, pp. 24–34. IEEE (1999)
16. Grädel, E.: On the restraining power of guards. Journal of Symbolic Logic 64, 1719–1742 (1998)
17. Grädel, E.: Why are modal logics so robustly decidable? Bulletin EATCS 68, 90–103 (1999)
18. Gurevich, Y.: Monadic second-order theories. In: Barwise, J., Feferman, S. (eds.) Model-Theoretical Logics, ch. XIII, pp. 479–506. Springer (1985)
19. Henriksen, J.G., Jensen, J., Jørgensen, M., Klarlund, N., Paige, B., Rauhe, T., Sandholm, A.: Mona: Monadic second-order logic in practice. In: Brinksma, E., Steffen, B., Cleaveland, W.R., Larsen, K.G., Margaria, T. (eds.) TACAS 1995. LNCS, vol. 1019, pp. 89–110. Springer, Heidelberg (1995)
20. Hooimeijer, P., Livshits, B., Molnar, D., Saxena, P., Veanes, M.: Fast and precise sanitizer analysis with Bek. In: Proceedings of the USENIX Security Symposium (August 2011)
21. Hooimeijer, P., Veanes, M.: An evaluation of automata algorithms for string analysis. In: Jhala, R., Schmidt, D. (eds.) VMCAI 2011. LNCS, vol. 6538, pp. 248–262. Springer, Heidelberg (2011)

22. Hopcroft, J.E., Ullman, J.D.: Introduction to Automata Theory, Languages, and Computation. Addison Wesley (1979)
23. Klarlund, N., Møller, A., Schwartzbach, M.I.: MONA implementation secrets. International Journal of Foundations of Computer Science 13(4), 571–586 (2002)
24. Korovin, K.: Instantiation-based automated reasoning: From theory to practice. In: Schmidt, R.A. (ed.) CADE-22. LNCS (LNAI), vol. 5663, pp. 163–166. Springer, Heidelberg (2009)
25. Korovin, K.: Inst-gen – A modular approach to instantiation-based automated reasoning. In: Voronkov, A., Weidenbach, C. (eds.) Ganzinger Festschrift. LNCS, vol. 7797, pp. 239–270. Springer, Heidelberg (2013)
26. Korovin, K.: Personal communication (December 2013)
27. Li, Y., Albarghouthi, A., Kincaid, Z., Gurfinkel, A., Chechik, M.: Symbolic optimization with SMT solvers. In: POPL 2014, pp. 607–618. ACM (2014)
28. Löb, M.: Decidability of the monadic predicate calculus with unary function symbols. Journal of Symbolic Logic 32, 563 (1967)
29. Löwenheim, L.: Über Möglichkeiten im Relativkalkül. Math. Annalen 76, 447–470 (1915)
30. Nielson, F., Nielson, H.R., Hankin, C.: Principles of Program Analysis. Springer (2010)
31. Nipkow, T.: Linear quantifier elimination. In: Armando, A., Baumgartner, P., Dowek, G. (eds.) IJCAR 2008. LNCS (LNAI), vol. 5195, pp. 18–33. Springer, Heidelberg (2008)
32. Nivat, M.: Transductions des langages de Chomsky. Annales de l'institut Fourier 18(1), 339–455 (1968)
33. Noord, G.V., Gerdemann, D.: Finite state transducers with predicates and identities. Grammars 4, 263–286 (2001)
34. Presburger, M.: Über die Vollständigkeit eines gewissen Systems der Arithmetik ganzer Zahlen, in welchem die Addition als einzige Operation hervortritt. In: In Comptes Rendus du I congrés de Mathématiciens des Pays Slaves, Warsaw, Poland, pp. 92–101 (1929)
35. Rabin, M.O.: Decidability of second-order theories and automata on infinite trees. Trans. Amer. Math. Soc. 141, 1–35 (1969)
36. Reddy, C.R., Loveland, D.W.: Presburger arithmetic with bounded quantifier alternation. In: Proceedings of the Tenth Annual ACM Symposium on Theory of Computing, STOC 1978, pp. 320–325. ACM, New York (1978)
37. Rice, H.G.: Classes of recursively enumerable sets and their decision problems. Trans. Amer. Math. Soc. 74, 358–366 (1953)
38. Saxena, P., Molnar, D., Livshits, B.: Scriptgard: Preventing script injection attacks in legacy web applications with automatic sanitization. Technical Report MSR-TR-2010-128, Microsoft Research (August 2010)
39. Thomas, W.: Languages, automata, and logic. In: Handbook of Formal Languages, vol. 3, pp. 389–455. Springer (1996)
40. The Unicode Consortium. The Unicode Standard 6.3, Emoticons, http://unicode.org/charts/PDF/U1F600.pdf
41. Vardi, M.Y.: Why is modal logic so robustly decidable? In: Immerman, N., Kolaitis, P.G. (eds.) Descriptive Complexity and Finite Models. DIMACS Series in Discrete Mathematics and Theoretical Computer Science, vol. 31, pp. 149–184. American Mathematical Society (1996)
42. Veanes, M., Bjørner, N.: Symbolic automata: The toolkit. In: Flanagan, C., König, B. (eds.) TACAS 2012. LNCS, vol. 7214, pp. 472–477. Springer, Heidelberg (2012)

43. Veanes, M., Bjørner, N., de Moura, L.: Symbolic automata constraint solving. In: Fermüller, C.G., Voronkov, A. (eds.) LPAR-17. LNCS, vol. 6397, pp. 640–654. Springer, Heidelberg (2010)
44. Veanes, M., Hooimeijer, P., Livshits, B., Molnar, D., Bjørner, N.: Symbolic finite state transducers: Algorithms and applications. In: POPL 2012, pp. 137–150 (2012)
45. Yu, S.: Regular languages. In: Rozenberg, G., Salomaa, A. (eds.) Handbook of Formal Languages, vol. 1, pp. 41–110. Springer (1997)

A DPLL(T) Theory Solver for a Theory of Strings and Regular Expressions*

Tianyi Liang[1], Andrew Reynolds[1], Cesare Tinelli[1],
Clark Barrett[2], and Morgan Deters[2]

[1] Department of Computer Science, The University of Iowa
[2] Department of Computer Science, New York University

Abstract. An increasing number of applications in verification and security rely on or could benefit from automatic solvers that can check the satisfiability of constraints over a rich set of data types that includes character strings. Unfortunately, most string solvers today are standalone tools that can reason only about (some fragment) of the theory of strings and regular expressions, sometimes with strong restrictions on the expressiveness of their input language. These solvers are based on reductions to satisfiability problems over other data types, such as bit vectors, or to automata decision problems. We present a set of algebraic techniques for solving constraints over the theory of unbounded strings natively, without reduction to other problems. These techniques can be used to integrate string reasoning into general, multi-theory SMT solvers based on the DPLL(T) architecture. We have implemented them in our SMT solver CVC4 to expand its already large set of built-in theories to a theory of strings with concatenation, length, and membership in regular languages. Our initial experimental results show that, in addition, over pure string problems, CVC4 is highly competitive with specialized string solvers with a comparable input language.

1 Introduction

In the last few years a number of techniques originally developed for verification purposes have been adapted to support software security analyses as well. These techniques have benefited from the rise of powerful specialized reasoning engines such as SMT solvers. Security analyses are frequently required to reason about string values. One reason is that program inputs, especially in web-based applications, are often provided as strings which are then processed using operations such as matching against regular expressions, concatenation, and substring extraction or replacement. In general, both safety and security analyses could benefit from solvers that can check the satisfiability of constraints over a rich set of data types that includes character strings. Despite their power and success as back-end reasoning engines, however, general multi-theory SMT solvers so far have provided minimal or no native support for reasoning over strings.

A major difficulty is that any reasonably comprehensive theory of character strings is undecidable [3]. However, several more restricted, but still quite useful, theories of strings do have a decidable satisfiability problem. These include any theories of fixed-length strings, which are trivially decidable for having a finite domain, but also some

---

* This work was partially funded by NSF grants #1228765 and #1228768.

A. Biere and R. Bloem (Eds.): CAV 2014, LNCS 8559, pp. 646–662, 2014.

fragments over unbounded strings (e.g., word equations [14]). Recent research has focused on identifying decidable fragments suitable for program analysis and, more crucially, on developing efficient solvers for them. Unfortunately, most string solvers today are standalone tools that can reason only about (some fragment of) the theory of strings and regular expressions, sometimes with strong restrictions on the expressiveness of their input language such as, for instance, the imposition of exact length bounds on all string variables. These solvers are based on reductions to satisfiability problems over other data types, such as bit vectors, or to decision problems over automata.

Contribution and Significance. We present an alternative approach, based on algebraic techniques for solving (quantifier-free) constraints natively over a theory of unbounded strings with length and regular language membership. Our techniques can be used to construct solvers that can be integrated into general, multi-theory SMT solvers based on the DPLL(T) architecture [16]. We have implemented these techniques in our SMT solver CVC4. As as result and to our knowledge, CVC4 is the first solver able to reason about a language of mixed constraints that includes strings together with integers, reals, arrays, and algebraic datatypes. Our experimental results show that, in addition, over pure string problems CVC4 has superior performance and reliability over specialized string solvers that can reason about the same fragment of the theory of strings.

We describe our approach here abstractly in terms of derivation rules. After discussing related work, we define in Section 2 the theory of strings and regular expressions we work with, and present a calculus for this theory. Our string solver is essentially a specific a proof strategy for this calculus. In Section 3, we present an experimental evaluation of our implementation in CVC4 against other tools specializing in string constraints. We conclude in Section 4 mentioning several areas of future work.

1.1 Related Work

A popular approach for solving string constraints, especially if they involve regular expressions, is to encode them into automata problems. For example, Hooimeijer and Weimer [9] present an automata-based solver, DPRLE, for matching problems of the form $e \subseteq r$ where, in essence, r is a regular expression over a given alphabet and e is a concatenation of alphabet symbols and string variables. The solver has been used to check programs against SQL injection vulnerabilities. This approach was improved in later work by generating automata lazily from the input problem without requiring *a priori* length bounds [10]. A comprehensive set of algorithms and data structures for performing fast automata operations to support constraint solving over strings is described by Hooimeijer and Veanes [8]. Generally speaking, there are two sorts of automata-based approaches: one where each transition in the automaton represents a single character (e.g., [5, 23]), and one where each transition represents a set of characters (e.g., [10, 21, 22]). Most tools based on these approaches provide very limited support for reasoning about constraints mixing strings and other data types. Also, automata refinement is typically the main bottleneck, although it is still very useful in solving membership constraints. Further discussion can be found in [7, 12].

A different class of solvers is based on reducing string constraints to constraints in other theories. A successful representative of this approach is the Hampi solver [11], used in a variety of static analysis systems. Hampi works only with string constraints over fixed-size string variables. It extends the constraint language to membership in fixed-size context-free languages but considers only problems over one string variable. Input problems are reduced first to bit-vector problems and then to SAT. An alternative approach, developed to support Pex [20], a white-box test generation tool, targets path feasibility problems for programs using the .NET string library [3]. There, string constraints over a large set of string operators, but no language membership predicates, are abstracted to linear integer arithmetic constraints and then sent to an SMT solver. Each satisfying solution, if any, induces a fixed-length version of the original string problem which is then solved using finite domain constraint satisfaction techniques. The Kaluza solver [19] extends Hampi's input language to multiple variables and string concatenation by following an approach similar to one used in Pex, except that it simply feeds fixed-length versions of the input problem to Hampi.

The Java String Analyzer (JSA) [4] works with Java string constraints. It first translates them to a flow graph and then analyzes the graph by converting it into a context-free grammar. That grammar is approximated to a regular one which is then encoded as a multi-level automaton. PASS [12] combines ideas from automata and SMT. Similarly to JSA, it handles almost all Java string operations, regular expressions, and string-number conversions. However, it represents strings as arrays with symbolic length. This leads to the generation of several quantified constraints over such arrays, which are then solved with the aid of a specialized quantifier instantiation procedure.

The work most closely related to ours is Z3-STR [24], a recent string solver developed as an extension of the Z3 SMT solver through Z3's user plug-in interface. It considers unbounded strings with concatenation, substring, replace and length functions and accepts equational constraints over strings as well as linear integer arithmetic constraints. Its main idea is to have Z3 treat string function and predicate symbols as uninterpreted but monitor the inferences of Z3's equality solver and generate and pass to Z3 selected string theory lemmas as needed. Roughly speaking, these lemmas are used to force the identification of equivalent string terms (e.g., the lemma $s \cdot \epsilon \approx s$ where $\cdot$ is concatenation and ϵ is the empty string), or the dis-identification of terms that Z3 has wrongly guessed to be equal (e.g., $\text{len}(t) > 0 \Rightarrow s \not\approx s \cdot t$). The approach is refutationally incomplete because it does not always generate enough axioms to recognize an unsatisfiable problem. At a very high level, our approach is similar, and similarly incomplete, except that it uses a different and more comprehensive set of rules to generate suitable axioms, and so is able to recognize more unsatisfiable cases. Another big difference is that we have devised it with the goal of implementing it in an internal, fully integrated theory solver for CVC4, as opposed to an external plug-in, which allows us to leverage several features of the DPLL(T) architecture.

1.2 Formal Preliminaries

We work in the context of many-sorted first-order logic with equality. We assume the reader is familiar with the notions of many-sorted signature, term, literal, formula, free variable, interpretation, and satisfiability of a formula in an interpretation (see, e.g., [2] for more details). A *theory* is a pair $T = (\Sigma, \mathbf{I})$ where Σ is a signature and $\mathbf{I}$ is a class of Σ-interpretations, the *models* of T, that is closed under variable reassignment (i.e., every Σ-interpretation that differs from one in $\mathbf{I}$ only in how it interprets the variables is also in $\mathbf{I}$). If $\mathcal{I}$ is an interpretation and t is a term, we denote by $\mathcal{I}(t)$ the value of t in $\mathcal{I}$. A Σ-formula φ is *satisfiable* (resp., *unsatisfiable*) *in* T if it is satisfied by some (resp., no) interpretation in $\mathbf{I}$. A set Γ of formulas *entails in* T a Σ-formula φ, written $\Gamma \models_T \varphi$, if every interpretation in $\mathbf{I}$ that satisfies all formulas in Γ satisfies φ as well. The set Γ is *satisfiable in* T if $\Gamma \not\models_T \bot$ where $\bot$ is the universally false atom. We will write $\Gamma \models \varphi$ to denote that Γ entails φ in the class of all Σ-interpretations. We will use $\approx$ as the (infix) logical symbol for equality—which has type $\sigma \times \sigma$ for all sorts σ in Σ and is always interpreted as the identity relation. We write $s \not\approx t$ as an abbreviation of $\neg\, s \approx t$. If e is a term or a formula, we denote by $\mathcal{V}(e)$ the set of e's free variables, extending the notation to tuples and sets of terms/formulas as expected.

2   A Theory of Strings and Regular Language Membership

We consider a theory T_{SLRp} of strings with length and positive regular language membership constraints over a signature Σ_{SLRp} with three sorts, Str, Int, and Lan, and an infinite set of variables of each sort. The interpretations of T_{SLRp} differ only on the variables. They all interpret Int as the set of integer numbers, Str as the language $\mathcal{A}^*$ of all words over some fixed finite alphabet $\mathcal{A}$ of *characters*, and Lan as the power set of $\mathcal{A}^*$. The signature includes the following predicate and function symbols: the usual symbols of linear integer arithmetic, interpreted as expected; a constant symbol, or *string constant*, for each word of $\mathcal{A}^*$, interpreted as that word; a variadic function symbol con : Str $\times \ldots \times$ Str $\rightarrow$ Str, interpreted as word concatenation; a function symbol len : Str $\rightarrow$ Int, interpreted as the word length function; a function symbol set : Str $\rightarrow$ Lan, interpreted as the function mapping each word $w \in \mathcal{A}^*$ to the language $\{w\}$; a function symbol star : Lan $\rightarrow$ Lan, interpreted as the Kleene closure operator; an infix predicate symbol in : Str $\times$ Lan, interpreted as the set membership predicate; a suitable set of additional function symbols corresponding to regular expression operators such as language concatenation, conjunction, disjunction, and so on.

We call: *string term* any term of sort Str or of the form (len s); *arithmetic term* any term of sort Int all of whose occurrences of len are applied to a variable; *regular expression* any term of sort Lan (possibly with variables). A string term is *atomic* if it is a variable or a string constant. A *string constraint* is a (dis)equality $(\neg)s \approx t$ with s and t string terms. What algebraists call *word equations* are, in our terminology, positive string constraints $s \approx t$ with s and t of sort Str. An *arithmetic constraint* is a (dis)equality $(\neg)s \approx t$ or an inequality $s > t$ where s and t are arithmetic terms. Note that if x and y are string variables, len x is both a string and an arithmetic term and $(\neg)$len $x \approx$ len y is both a string and an arithmetic constraint. A *(positive) RL constraint* is a literal of the form $(s$ in $r)$ where s is a string term and r is a regular expression. A T_{SLRp}-*constraint* is a string, arithmetic or RL constraint. We will denote entailment in T_{SLRp} ($\models_{\mathsf{SLRp}}$) more simply as $\models_{\mathsf{SLRp}}$.

2.1   The Satisfiability Problem in T_{SLRp}

We are interested in checking the satisfiability in T_{SLRp} of finite sets of T_{SLRp}-constraints. We are not aware of any results on the decidability of this problem. In fact, the decidability of a strict sublanguage of the above, just word equations with length constraints, is classified as an open question by other authors (e.g., [6]). Some other sublanguages do have a decidable satisfiability problem. For instance, the satisfiability of word equations was proven decidable by Makanin [14] and then given a PSPACE algorithm by Plandowski [17]; that algorithm, however, is highly impractical.

In this work we focus on practical solvers for T_{SLRp} that, although incomplete and non-terminating in general, can be used to solve efficiently string constraints arising from verification and security applications. In addition to efficiency, we also strive for correctness. We want a solver that is both *refutation sound*: any problem the solver classifies as unsatisfiable is indeed so; and *solution sound*: any variable assignment that the solver claims to be a solution of the input constraints does indeed satisfy them.

Our solver is based on the modular combination of an off-the-shelf solver for linear integer arithmetic and a novel solver for string and RL constraints, which we will call just string solver, for brevity. The string solver is in turn obtained as a modular extension of a congruence-closure-based solver for EUF, the theory of equality with uninterpreted functions. The extension is obtained by means of theory-specific derivation rules that assert additional string constraints and RL constraints to the congruence closure module (which treats all functions symbols as uninterpreted). The combination between the string solver and the arithmetic solver is achieved, Nelson-Oppen style, by exchanging equalities over shared terms, which however are not variables, as in traditional combination procedures [15], but terms of the form $(\mathsf{len}\, x)$ where x is a variable.[1]

In the following, we describe the essence of our combined solver for T_{SLRp} abstractly and declaratively, as a tableaux-style calculus. Because of the computational complexity of solving even just word equations, this calculus is non-deterministic and allows many possible proof strategies. Our solver can be understood then as a specific proof procedure for the calculus. In our description below we focus only on the derivation rules that deal with string and arithmetic constraints. This is both because of space constraints and because currently our treatment of RL constraints is fairly naive—and so not very interesting. In particular, the Kleene star operator is processed by unrolling: $(s\ \mathsf{in}\ \mathsf{star}\ r)$ is reduced to $s = \epsilon$ or to $s \approx \mathsf{con}(x, y) \wedge (x\ \mathsf{in}\ r) \wedge (y\ \mathsf{in}\ \mathsf{star}\ r)$ where x and y are fresh variables, which makes the solver non-terminating in general over such constraints. A more sophisticated treatment of RL constraints is in the works and will be presented in a later paper.

2.2 A Calculus for T_{SLRp}

Let S be a set of string constraints and let $\mathcal{T}(S)$ be the set of all terms (and subterms) occurring in S. The *congruence closure* of S is the set

$$\mathcal{C}(S) = \{s \approx t \mid s, t \in \mathcal{T}(S),\ S \models s \approx t\} \cup \{l_1 \not\approx l_2 \mid l_1, l_2\ \text{distinct string const.}\} \cup$$
$$\{s \not\approx t \mid s, t \in \mathcal{T}(S),\ s' \not\approx t' \in S,\ S \models s \approx s' \wedge t \approx t'\ \text{for some}\ s', t'\}$$

The set $\mathcal{C}(S)$ induces an equivalence relation $\mathbf{E}_S$ over $\mathcal{T}(S)$ where two terms s, t are equivalent iff $s \approx t \in \mathcal{C}(S)$ (or, equivalently, iff $S \models s \approx t$). For all $t \in \mathcal{T}(S)$, we denote its equivalence class in $\mathbf{E}_S$ by $[t]_S$ or just $[t]$ when S is clear or not important.

---

[1] This difference is not substantial if the arithmetic solver treats $(\mathsf{len}\, x)$ like an integer variable.

$$\mathsf{con}(s, \mathsf{con}(t), u) \to \mathsf{con}(s, t, u) \qquad \mathsf{con}(s, c_1 \cdots c_i, c_{i+1} \cdots c_n, u) \to \mathsf{con}(s, c_1 \cdots c_n, u)$$
$$\mathsf{con}(s, \epsilon, u) \to \mathsf{con}(s, u) \qquad \mathsf{len}(\mathsf{con}(s_1, \ldots, s_n)) \to \mathsf{len}\, s_1 + \cdots + \mathsf{len}\, s_n$$
$$\mathsf{con}(s) \to s \qquad \mathsf{len}(c_1 \cdots c_n) \to n$$
$$\mathsf{con}() \to \epsilon$$

Fig. 1. Normalization rewrite rules for terms

We will denote characters (i.e., elements of the alphabet $\mathcal{A}$) by the letter c and string constants by l or the juxtaposition $c_1 \cdots c_n$ of their individual characters, with $c_1 \cdots c_n$ denoting the empty string ϵ when $n = 0$. We will use x, y, z to denote string variables and s, t, u, v, w to denote terms in general.

We will consider term tuples $(s_1, \ldots, s_n)$, with $n \geq 0$, and denote them by letters in bold font, with comma denoting tuple concatenation. For example, if $s = (s_1, s_2)$ and $t = (t_1, t_2, t_3)$ we will write (s, t) to denote the tuple $(s_1, s_2, t_1, t_2, t_3)$. Similarly, if u is a term, (s, u, t) denotes the tuple $(s_1, s_2, u, t_1, t_2, t_3)$.

Configurations. Our calculus operates over *configurations* consisting of the distinguished configuration unsat and of tuples of the form $\langle \mathsf{S}, \mathsf{A}, \mathsf{R}, \mathsf{F}, \mathsf{N}, \mathsf{C}, \mathsf{B} \rangle$ where

- $\mathsf{S}, \mathsf{A}, \mathsf{R}$ are respectively a set of string, arithmetic, and RL constraints;
- F is a set of pairs $s \mapsto a$ where $s \in \mathcal{T}(\mathsf{S})$ and a is a tuple of atomic string terms;
- N is a set of pairs $e \mapsto a$ where e is an equivalence class of $\mathbf{E}_\mathsf{S}$, the equivalence relation induced by the constraints in S, and a is a tuple of atomic string terms;
- C is a set of terms of sort Str;
- B is a set of *buckets* where each bucket is a set of equivalence classes of $\mathbf{E}_\mathsf{S}$.

Informally, the sets $\mathsf{S}, \mathsf{A}, \mathsf{R}$ initially store the input problem and grow with additional constraints derived by the calculus; N stores a normal form for each equivalence class in $\mathbf{E}_\mathsf{S}$; F maps selected input terms to an intermediate form, which we call a *flat form*, used to compute the normal forms in N; C stores terms whose flat form should not be computed, to prevent loops in the computation of their equivalence class' normal form; B eventually becomes a partition of $\mathbf{E}_\mathsf{S}$ used to generate a satisfying assignment that assigns string constants of different lengths to variables in different buckets, and different string constants of the *same* length to different variables in the same bucket.

Derivation Trees. The calculus is defined by the derivation rules described below. A *derivation tree* for the calculus is a tree where each node is a configuration and each non-root node is obtained by applying one of the derivation rules to its parent node. We call the root of a derivation tree an *initial* configuration. A branch of a derivation tree is *closed* if it ends with unsat. A derivation tree is *closed* if all of its branches are closed.

Initial configurations encode a satisfiability problem by storing it in the components S, A and R. By standard transformations, one can convert any finite set of T_{SLRp}-constraints into an equisatisfiable set $S \cup A \cup R$ where S is a set of string constraints, A is a set of arithmetic constraints, and R is a set of RL constraints. We consider only initial configurations where the other components are empty. For convenience, we assume that the S component of the initial configuration contains an equation $x \approx t$ for each non-variable term $t \in \mathcal{T}(\mathsf{S})$, where x is a variable of the same sort as t.[2] We also assume

---

[2] Such equations can always be added as needed using fresh variables.

$$\text{A-Prop} \; \frac{S \models \operatorname{len} x \approx \operatorname{len} y}{A := A, \operatorname{len} x \approx \operatorname{len} y} \qquad \text{S-Prop} \; \frac{A \models_{\mathsf{LIA}} \operatorname{len} x \approx \operatorname{len} y}{S := S, \operatorname{len} x \approx \operatorname{len} y}$$

$$\text{Len} \; \frac{x \approx t \in \mathcal{C}(S) \quad x \in \mathcal{V}(S)}{A := A, \operatorname{len} x \approx (\operatorname{len} t)\!\downarrow} \qquad \text{Len-Split} \; \frac{x \in \mathcal{V}(S \cup A) \quad x : \mathsf{Str}}{S := S, x \approx \epsilon \quad \| \quad A := A, \operatorname{len} x > 0}$$

$$\text{A-Conflict} \; \frac{A \models_{\mathsf{LIA}} \bot}{\text{unsat}} \qquad \text{R-Star} \; \frac{s \text{ in } \operatorname{star}(\operatorname{set} t) \in R \quad s \not\approx \epsilon \in \mathcal{C}(S)}{S := S, s \approx \operatorname{con}(t, z) \quad R := R, z \text{ in } \operatorname{star}(\operatorname{set} t)}$$

Fig. 2. Rules for theory combination, arithmetic and RL constraints. The letter z denotes a fresh Skolem variable

that all terms in the initial configuration are reduced with respect to the rewrite rules in Figure 1, which can be shown to be terminating and confluent modulo the axioms of arithmetic.

We say that a configuration is *derivable* if it occurs in a derivation tree whose initial configuration satisfies the restrictions above.

We denote by $t\!\downarrow$ the normal form of a term t with respect to the rewrite rules in Figure 1. It is not difficult to see that if t is of sort Str, then $t\!\downarrow$ is either an atomic string term or has the form $\operatorname{con}(a_1, \ldots, a_n)$ where $n > 1$ and $a_1, \ldots, a_n$ are atomic; if t is of integer sort, then $t\!\downarrow$ is an arithmetic term. In a similar vein, we consider *normalized* tuples $a\!\downarrow$ of atomic terms obtained from an atomic term tuple a by dropping its empty string components and replacing adjacent string constants by the constant corresponding to their concatenation. For example, $(x, \epsilon, c_1, c_2 c_3, y)\!\downarrow = (x, c_1 c_2 c_3, y)$.

Invariant 1 We are interested in proof procedures that maintain these invariants on the derivable configurations of the form $\langle S, A, R, F, N, C, B \rangle$:

1. All terms are reduced with respect to the rewrite system in Figure 1.
2. F is a partial map from $\mathcal{T}(S)$ to normalized tuples of atomic terms.
3. N is a partial map from $\mathbf{E}_S$ to normalized tuples of atomic terms.
4. For all terms s where $[s] \mapsto (a_1, \ldots, a_n) \in N$ or $s \mapsto (a_1, \ldots, a_n) \in F$, we have $S \models_{\mathsf{SLRp}} s \approx \operatorname{con}(a_1, \ldots, a_n)$ and $S \models a_i \not\approx \epsilon$ for $i = 1, \ldots, n$.
5. For all $B_1, B_2 \in B$, $[s] \in B_1$ and $[t] \in B_2$, $S \models \operatorname{len} s \approx \operatorname{len} t$ iff $B_1 = B_2$.
6. C contains only reduced terms of the form $\operatorname{con}(a)$.

We denote by $\mathcal{D}(N)$ the *domain* of the partial map N, i.e., the set $\{e \mid e \mapsto a \in N \text{ for some } a\}$. For all $e \in \mathcal{D}(N)$, we will write $N\,e$ to denote the (unique) tuple associated to e by N. We will use a similar notation for F.

Derivation Rules. The rules of the calculus are provided in Figures 2 through 6 in *guarded assignment form*. A derivation rule applies to a configuration K if all of the rule's premises hold for K. A rule's conclusion describes how each component of K is changed, if at all. We write S, t as an abbreviation for $S \cup \{t\}$. Rules with two conclusions, separated by the symbol $\|$, are non-deterministic branching rules.

In the rules of the calculus, we treat a string constant l in a tuple of terms indifferently as term or a tuple $l_1, \ldots, l_n$ of string constants whose concatenation equals l. For example, a tuple $(x, c_1 c_2 c_3, y)$ with the three-character constant $c_1 c_2 c_3$ will be seen

$$\text{S-Cycle} \; \frac{t = \mathrm{con}(t_1, \ldots, t_i, \ldots, t_n) \quad t \in \mathcal{T}(\mathsf{S}) \setminus \mathsf{C}}{\mathsf{S} := \mathsf{S}, t \approx t_i \quad \mathsf{C} := (\mathsf{C}, t) \setminus \{t_i\}}$$

$$\text{Reset} \; \frac{}{\mathsf{F} := \emptyset \quad \mathsf{N} := \emptyset \quad \mathsf{B} := \emptyset}$$

$$\text{S-Split} \; \frac{x, y \in \mathcal{V}(\mathsf{S}) \quad x \approx y, \; x \not\approx y \notin \mathcal{C}(\mathsf{S})}{\mathsf{S} := \mathsf{S}, x \approx y \;\;\|\;\; \mathsf{S} := \mathsf{S}, x \not\approx y}$$

$$\text{S-Conflict} \; \frac{s \approx t \in \mathcal{C}(\mathsf{S}) \quad s \not\approx t \in \mathcal{C}(\mathsf{S})}{\mathsf{unsat}}$$

$$\text{L-Split} \; \frac{x, y \in \mathcal{V}(\mathsf{S}) \quad x, y : \mathsf{Str} \quad \mathsf{S} \not\models \mathrm{len}\, x \approx \mathrm{len}\, y \quad \mathsf{S} \not\models \mathrm{len}\, x \not\approx \mathrm{len}\, y}{\mathsf{S} := \mathsf{S}, \mathrm{len}\, x \approx \mathrm{len}\, y \;\;\|\;\; \mathsf{S} := \mathsf{S}, \mathrm{len}\, x \not\approx \mathrm{len}\, y}$$

Fig. 3. Basic string derivation rules

also as the tuple $(x, c_1, c_2 c_3, y)$, $(x, c_1 c_2, c_3, y)$, or (x, c_1, c_2, c_3, y). All equalities and disequalities in the rules are treated modulo symmetry of $\approx$. We assume the availability of a procedure for checking entailment in the theory of linear integer arithmetic ($\models_{\mathsf{LIA}}$) and one for computing congruence closures and checking entailment in EUF ($\models$).

The first four rules in Figure 2 describe the interaction between arithmetic reasoning and string reasoning, achieved via the propagation of entailed constraints in the shared language. R-Star is the only rule for handling RL constraints that we provide here. We chose it because the constraints matching its premise can be generated, by rule F-Loop in Figure 5, even if the initial configuration contains no RL constraints. The basic rules for string constraints are shown in Figure 3. The functionality and rationale of the last three should be straightforward. Reset is meant to be applied after the set S changes since in that case normal and flat forms may need updating. S-Cycle identifies a concatenation of terms with one them when the remaining ones are all equivalent to ϵ.

The bulk of the work is done by the rules in Figures 4 and 5. Those in Figure 4 compute an equivalent flat form (consisting of a sequence of atomic terms) for all non-variable terms that are not in the set C. Flat forms are used in turn to compute normal forms as follows. When all terms of an equivalence class e except for variables and terms in C have the same flat form, that form is chosen by N-Form1 as the normal form of e. When an equivalence class e consists only of variables and terms in C, one of them is chosen by N-Form2 as the normal form of e. The first two rules of Figure 5 use flat forms to add to S new equations entailed by S in the theory of strings. F-Loop is used to recognize and break certain occurrences of reasoning *loops* that lead to infinite paths in a derivation tree (see [13] for more details).

The rules in Figure 6 are used to put equivalence classes of terms of sort Str into buckets based on the expected length of the value they will be given eventually by a satisfying assignment. The main idea is that different equivalence classes go into different buckets (using D-Base) unless they have the same length. In the latter case, they go into the same bucket only if we can tell they cannot have the same value (using D-Add). D-Split is used to reduce the problem to one of the two previous cases. The goal is that, on saturation, each bucket B can be assigned a unique length n_B, and each equivalence class in B can evaluate to a unique string constant of that length. Card makes sure that n_B is big enough to have enough string constants of length n_B.

$$F\text{-Form1} \quad \frac{t = \mathsf{con}(t_1, \ldots, t_n) \quad t \in \mathcal{T}(\mathsf{S}) \setminus (\mathcal{D}(\mathsf{F}) \cup \mathsf{C})}{\mathsf{N}\,[t_1] = s_1 \quad \cdots \quad \mathsf{N}\,[t_n] = s_n}{\mathsf{F} := \mathsf{F}, t \mapsto (s_1, \ldots, s_n)\!\downarrow}$$

$$F\text{-Form2} \quad \frac{l \in \mathcal{T}(\mathsf{S}) \setminus \mathcal{D}(\mathsf{F})}{\mathsf{F} := \mathsf{F}, l \mapsto (l)}$$

$$N\text{-Form1} \quad \frac{[x] \notin \mathcal{D}(\mathsf{N}) \quad s \in [x] \setminus (\mathsf{C} \cup \mathcal{V}(\mathsf{S}))}{\mathsf{F}\,t = \mathsf{F}\,s \ \text{for all } t \in [x] \setminus (\mathsf{C} \cup \mathcal{V}(\mathsf{S}))}{\mathsf{N} := \mathsf{N}, [x] \mapsto \mathsf{F}\,s}$$

$$N\text{-Form2} \quad \frac{[x] \notin \mathcal{D}(\mathsf{N}) \quad [x] \subseteq \mathsf{C} \cup \mathcal{V}(\mathsf{S})}{\mathsf{N} := \mathsf{N}, [x] \mapsto (x)}$$

Fig. 4. Normalization derivation rules. The letter l denotes a string constant.

$$F\text{-Unify} \quad \frac{\mathsf{F}\,s = (\boldsymbol{w}, u, \boldsymbol{u}_1) \quad \mathsf{F}\,t = (\boldsymbol{w}, v, \boldsymbol{v}_1) \quad s \approx t \in \mathcal{C}(\mathsf{S}) \quad \mathsf{S} \models \mathsf{len}\,u \approx \mathsf{len}\,v}{\mathsf{S} := \mathsf{S}, u \approx v}$$

$$F\text{-Split} \quad \frac{\mathsf{F}\,s = (\boldsymbol{w}, u, \boldsymbol{u}_1) \quad \mathsf{F}\,t = (\boldsymbol{w}, v, \boldsymbol{v}_1) \quad s \approx t \in \mathcal{C}(\mathsf{S}) \quad \mathsf{S} \models \mathsf{len}\,u \not\approx \mathsf{len}\,v}{u \notin \mathcal{V}(\boldsymbol{v}_1) \quad v \notin \mathcal{V}(\boldsymbol{u}_1)}{\mathsf{S} := \mathsf{S}, u \approx \mathsf{con}(v, z) \quad \| \quad \mathsf{S} := \mathsf{S}, v \approx \mathsf{con}(u, z)}$$

$$F\text{-Loop} \quad \frac{\mathsf{F}\,s = (\boldsymbol{w}, x, \boldsymbol{u}_1) \quad \mathsf{F}\,t = (\boldsymbol{w}, v, \boldsymbol{v}_1, x, \boldsymbol{v}_2) \quad s \approx t \in \mathcal{C}(\mathsf{S}) \quad x \notin \mathcal{V}((v, \boldsymbol{v}_1))}{\mathsf{S} := \mathsf{S}, x \approx \mathsf{con}(z_2, z), \mathsf{con}(v, \boldsymbol{v}_1) \approx \mathsf{con}(z_2, z_1), \mathsf{con}(\boldsymbol{u}_1) \approx \mathsf{con}(z_1, z_2, \boldsymbol{v}_2)}{\mathsf{R} := \mathsf{R}, z \ \mathsf{in}\ \mathsf{star}(\mathsf{set}\ \mathsf{con}(z_1, z_2)) \quad \mathsf{C} := \mathsf{C}, t}$$

Fig. 5. Equality reduction rules. The letters z, z_1, z_2 denote fresh Skolem variables.

Correctness. We now formalize the main correctness properties of our calculus. For space constraints we must refer the interested reader to a longer version of this paper [13] for their proof. Since our solver can be seen as a specific proof procedure, it immediately inherits those properties. This means in particular that when our solver terminates with a sat or unsat answer, that answer is correct. We describe here only the more restricted case of input problems with no RL constraints, as those constraints are not the focus of this work. Also, we consider only derivation trees satisfying Invariant 1.

Proposition 1 (Refutation Soundness). *For all closed derivation trees with initial configuration $\langle S_0, A_0, \emptyset, \emptyset, \emptyset, \emptyset, \emptyset \rangle$, the set $S_0 \cup A_0$ is unsatisfiable in T_{SLRP}.*

A derivable configuration $\langle \mathsf{S}, \mathsf{A}, \mathsf{R}, \mathsf{F}, \mathsf{N}, \mathsf{C}, \mathsf{B} \rangle$ is *saturated* if (i) N is a total map over $\mathbf{E_S}$, (ii) B is a partition of $\mathbf{E_S}$, and (iii) any derivation rule that applies to it except for Reset leaves the configuration unchanged modulo renaming of Skolem variables.

Proposition 2 (Solution Soundness). *If a derivation tree with root $\langle S_0, A_0, \emptyset, \emptyset, \emptyset, \emptyset, \emptyset \rangle$ contains a saturated configuration then $S_0 \cup A_0$ is satisfiable in T_{SLRP}.*

The proof of Proposition 2 is constructive since it shows how to build systematically from a saturated configuration a satisfying assignment for the (string and arithmetic) variables in the input problem $S_0 \cup A_0$. Our implementation follows that construction.

Proof Procedure. A possible proof procedure, a highly simplified version of the one we have implemented, is defined by the repeated application of the calculus rules according to the six steps below. When applying a branching rule the procedure tries the

$$\text{D-Base} \quad \frac{s \in \mathcal{T}(\mathsf{S}) \quad s : \mathsf{Str}}{\mathsf{B} := \mathsf{B}, \{[s]\}} \quad \text{Card} \quad \frac{B \in \mathsf{B} \quad |B| > 1}{\mathsf{A} := \mathsf{A}, len_B > \lfloor \log_{|\mathcal{A}|}(|B| - 1) \rfloor}$$

$$\text{D-Add} \quad \frac{\begin{array}{c} s \in \mathcal{T}(\mathsf{S}) \quad s : \mathsf{Str} \quad B = B', B \quad S \models \mathsf{len}\, s \approx len_B \quad [s] \notin B \\ \text{for all } e \in B \text{ there are } \boldsymbol{w}, u, \boldsymbol{u}_1, v, \boldsymbol{v}_1 \text{ such that} \\ (\mathsf{N}\,[s] = (\boldsymbol{w}, u, \boldsymbol{u}_1), \ \mathsf{N}\, e = (\boldsymbol{w}, v, \boldsymbol{v}_1), \ S \models \mathsf{len}\, u \approx \mathsf{len}\, v, \ u \not\approx v \in \mathcal{C}(\mathsf{S})) \end{array}}{\mathsf{B} := B', (B \cup \{[s]\})}$$

$$\text{D-Split} \quad \frac{\begin{array}{c} s \in \mathcal{T}(\mathsf{S}) \quad s : \mathsf{Str} \quad B = B', B \quad S \models \mathsf{len}\, s \approx len_B \quad [s] \notin B \quad e \in B \\ \mathsf{N}\,[s] = (\boldsymbol{w}, u, \boldsymbol{u}_1) \quad \mathsf{N}\, e = (\boldsymbol{w}, v, \boldsymbol{v}_1) \quad S \models \mathsf{len}\, u \not\approx \mathsf{len}\, v \end{array}}{\mathsf{S} := \mathsf{S}, u \approx \mathsf{con}(z_1, z_2), \mathsf{len}\, z_1 \approx \mathsf{len}\, v \quad \| \quad \mathsf{S} := \mathsf{S}, v \approx \mathsf{con}(z_1, z_2), \mathsf{len}\, z_1 \approx \mathsf{len}\, u}$$

Fig. 6. Disequality reduction rules. Letters z_1, z_2 denote fresh Skolem variables. For each bucket $B \in \mathsf{B}$, len_B denotes a unique term $(\mathsf{len}\, x)$ where $[x] \in B$. $\lfloor \_ \rfloor$ denotes the cardinality operator.

left-branch configuration first. It interrupts a step and restarts with Step 0 as soon as a constraint is added to S. The procedure keeps cycling through the steps until it derives a saturated configuration or the unsat one. In the latter case, it continues with another configuration in the derivation tree, if any.

Step 0: Reset: Apply Reset to reset buckets, and flat and normal forms.

Step 1: Check for conflicts, propagate: Apply S-Conflict or A-Conflict if the configuration is unsatisfiable due to the current string or arithmetic constraints; otherwise, propagate entailed equalities between S and A using S-Prop and A-Prop.

Step 2: Add length constraints: Apply Len and then Len-Split to completion.

Step 3: Compute Normal Forms for Equivalence Classes. Apply S-Cycle to completion and then the rules in Figure 4 to completion. If this does not produce a total map N, there must be some $s \approx t \in \mathcal{C}(\mathsf{S})$ such that F s and F t have respectively the form $(\boldsymbol{w}, u, \boldsymbol{u}_1)$ and $(\boldsymbol{w}, v, \boldsymbol{v}_1)$ with u and v distinct terms. Let x, y be variables with $x \in [u]$ and $y \in [v]$. If S entails neither $\mathsf{len}\, x \approx \mathsf{len}\, y$ nor $\mathsf{len}\, x \approx \mathsf{len}\, y$, apply L-Split to them; otherwise, apply any applicable rules from Figure 5, giving preference to F-Unify.

Step 4: Partition equivalence classes into buckets. First apply D-Base and D-Add to completion. If this does not make B a partition of E_S, there must be an equivalence class $[x]$ contained in no bucket but such that $S \models \mathsf{len}\, x \approx len_B$ for some bucket B (otherwise D-Base would apply). If there is a $[y] \in B$ such that $x \not\approx y \notin \mathcal{C}(\mathsf{S})$, split on $x \approx y$ and $x \not\approx y$ using S-Split. Otherwise, let $[y] \in B$ such that $x \not\approx y \in \mathcal{C}(\mathsf{S})$. It must be that N $[x]$ and N $[y]$ share a prefix followed by two distinct terms u and v. Let x_u, x_v be variables with $x_u \in [u]$ and $x_v \in [v]$. If $S \models \mathsf{len}\, x_u \not\approx \mathsf{len}\, x_v$, apply the rule D-Split to u and v. If $S \models \mathsf{len}\, x_u \approx \mathsf{len}\, x_v$, since it is also the case that neither $x_u \approx x_v$ nor $x_u \not\approx x_v$ is in $\mathcal{C}(\mathsf{S})$, apply S-Split to x_u and x_v. If S entails neither $\mathsf{len}\, x_u \approx \mathsf{len}\, x_v$ nor $\mathsf{len}\, x_u \not\approx \mathsf{len}\, x_v$, split on them using L-Split.

Step 5: Add length constraint for cardinality. Apply Card to completion.

One can show that all derivation trees generated with this proof procedure satisfy Invariant 1. We illustrate the procedure's workings with a couple of examples.

Example 1. Suppose we start with $A = \emptyset$ and $S = \{\text{len}\, x \approx \text{len}\, y,\, x \not\approx \epsilon,\, z \not\approx \epsilon,\, \text{con}(x, l_1, z) \approx \text{con}(y, l_2, z)\}$ where l_1, l_2 are distinct constants of the same length. After checking for conflicts, the procedure applies Len and Len-Split to completion. All resulting derivation tree branches except one can be closed with S-Conflict. In the leaf of the non-closed branch every string variable is in a disequality with ϵ. In that configuration, the string equivalence classes are $\{x\}$, $\{y\}$, $\{z\}$, $\{l_1\}$, $\{l_2\}$, $\{\epsilon\}$, and $\{\text{con}(x, l_1, z), \text{con}(y, l_2, z)\}$. The normal form for the first three classes is computed with N-Form2; the normal form for the other three with F-Form2 and N-Form1. For the last equivalence class, the procedure uses F-Form1 to construct the flat forms $F\,\text{con}(x, l_1, z) = (x, l_1, z)$ and $F\,\text{con}(y, l_2, z) = (y, l_2, z)$, and F-Unify to add the equality $x \approx y$ to S. The procedure then restarts but now with the string equivalence classes $\{x, y\}$, $\{z\}$, $\{l_1\}$, $\{l_2\}$, $\{\epsilon\}$, and $\{\text{con}(x, l_1, z), \text{con}(y, l_2, z)\}$. After similar steps as before, the terms in the last equivalence class get the flat form (x, l_1, z) and (x, l_2, z) respectively (assuming x is chosen as the representative term for $\{x, y\}$). Using F-Unify, the procedure adds the equality $l_1 \approx l_2$ to S and then derives unsat with S-Conflict. This closes the derivation tree, showing that the input constraints are unsatisfiable.   □

Example 2. Suppose now the input constraints are $A = \emptyset$ and $S = \{\text{len}\, x \approx \text{len}\, y,\, x \not\approx \epsilon,\, z \not\approx \epsilon,\, \text{con}(x, l_1, z) \not\approx \text{con}(y, l_2, z)\}$ with l_1, l_2 as in Example 1. After similar steps as in that example, the procedure can derive a configuration where the string equivalence classes are $\{x\}$, $\{y\}$, $\{z\}$, $\{l_1\}$, $\{l_2\}$, $\{\epsilon\}$, $\{\text{con}(x, l_1, z)\}$, and $\{\text{con}(y, l_2, z)\}$. After computing normal forms for these classes, it attempts to construct a partition B of them into buckets. However, notice that if it adds $\{[x]\}$, say, to B using D-Base, then neither D-Base (since $S \models \text{len}\, x \approx \text{len}\, y$) nor D-Add (since $x \not\approx y \notin \mathcal{C}(S)$) is applicable to $[y]$. So it applies S-Split to x and y. In the branch where $x \approx y$, the proof procedure subsequently restarts, and computes normal forms as before. At that point it succeeds in making B a partition of the string equivalence classes, by placing $[\text{con}(x, l_1, z)]$ and $[\text{con}(y, l_2, z)]$ into the same bucket using D-Add, which applies because their corresponding normal forms are (x, l_1, z) and (x, l_2, z) respectively. Any further rule applications lead to branches with a saturated configuration, each of which indicates that the input constraints are satisfiable.   □

Implementation in DPLL(T). Theory solvers based on the calculus we have described can be integrated into the DPLL(T) framework used by modern SMT solvers, which combines a SAT solver with multiple specialized *theory solvers* for conjunctions of constraints in a certain theory. These SMT solvers maintain an evolving set F of quantifier-free clauses and a set M of literals representing a (partial) Boolean assignment for F. Periodically, a theory solver is asked whether M is satisfiable in its theory.

In terms of our calculus, we assume that the literals of an assignment M are partitioned into string constraints (corresponding to the set S), arithmetic constraints (the set A) and RL constraints (the set R). These sets are subsequently given to three independent solvers, which we will call the string solver, the arithmetic solver, and the RL solver, respectively. The rules A-Prop and S-Prop model the standard mechanism for Nelson-Oppen theory combination, where entailed equalities are communicated between these solvers. The satisfiability check performed by the arithmetic solver is modeled by the rule A-Conflict. Note that there is no additional requirement on the arithmetic solver, and thus a standard DPLL(T) theory solver for linear integer arithmetic can be

used. The behavior of the RL solver is described by the rule R-Star and others we have
omitted here. The remaining rules model the behavior of the string solver.

The case splitting done by the string solver (with rules S-Split and L-Split) is achieved
by means of the *splitting on demand* paradigm [1], in which a solver may add theory
lemmas to F consisting of clauses possibly with literals not occurring in M. The case
splitting in rules F-Split and D-Split can be implemented by adding a lemma of the form
$\psi \Rightarrow (l_1 \vee l_2)$ to F, where l_1 and l_2 are new literals. For instance, in the case of F-Split,
we add the lemma $\psi \Rightarrow (u \approx \mathsf{con}(v, z) \vee v \approx \mathsf{con}(u, z))$, where ψ is a conjunction of
literals in M entailing $s \approx t \wedge s \approx \mathsf{F} s \wedge t \approx \mathsf{F} t \wedge \mathsf{len}\, u \not\approx \mathsf{len}\, v$ in the overall theory.

The rules Len, Len-Split, and Card involve adding constraints to A. This is done by
the string solver by adding lemmas to F containing arithmetic constraints. For instance,
if $x \approx \mathsf{con}(y, z) \in \mathcal{C}(\mathsf{S})$, the solver may add a lemma of the form $\psi \Rightarrow \mathsf{len}\, x \approx$
$\mathsf{len}\, y + \mathsf{len}\, z$ to F, where ψ is a conjunction of literals from M entailing $x \approx \mathsf{con}(y, z)$,
after which the conclusion of this lemma is added to M (and hence to A).

In DPLL(*T*), when a theory solver determines that M is unsatisfiable (in the solver's
theory) it generates a *conflict clause*, the negation of an unsatisfiable subset of M. The
string solver maintains a compact representation of $\mathcal{C}(\mathsf{S})$ at all times. To construct conflict clauses it also maintains an *explanation* $\psi_{s,t}$ for each equality $s \approx t$ it adds to S by
applying S-Cycle, F-Unify or standard congruence closure rules. The explanation $\psi_{s,t}$
is a conjunction of string constraints in M such that $\psi_{s,t} \models_{\mathsf{SLRp}} s \approx t$. For F-Unify,
the string solver maintains an explanation ψ for the flat form of each term $t \in \mathcal{D}(\mathsf{F})$
where $\psi \models_{\mathsf{SLRp}} t \approx \mathsf{con}(\mathsf{F}\, t)$. When a configuration is determined to be unsatisfiable
by S-Conflict, that is, when $s \approx t, s \not\approx t \in \mathcal{C}(\mathsf{S})$ for some s, t, it replaces the occurrence
of $s \approx t$ with its corresponding explanation ψ, and then replaces the equalities in ψ
with their corresponding explanation, and so on, until ψ contains only equalities from
M. Then it reports as a conflict clause (the clause form of) $\psi \rightarrow s \approx t$.

All other rules (such as those that modify N, F and B) model the internal behavior of
the string solver.

3 Experimental Results

We have implemented a theory solver based on the calculus and proof procedure described in the previous section within the latest version of our SMT solver CVC4. The
string alphabet $\mathcal{A}$ for this implementation is the set of all 256 ASCII characters. To
evaluate our solver we did an experimental comparison with two of the string solvers
mentioned in Section 1.1: Z3-STR (version 20140120) and Kaluza (latest version from
its website). These solvers, which have been widely used in security analysis, were
chosen because they are publicly available and have an input language that largely intersects with that of our solver. All results in this section were collected on a 2.53 GHz
Intel Xeon E5540 with 8 MB cache and 12 GB main memory.[3]

Modulo superficial differences in the concrete input syntax, all three tools accept
as input a set of T_{SLRp} constraints and report on its satisfiability with a sat, unsat or
unknown answer. In the first case, CVC4 and Z3-STR can also provide a *solution*, i.e., a

---

[3] Detailed results and binaries can be found at
http://cvc4.cs.nyu.edu/papers/CAV2014-strings/.

Table 1. Comparative results

Result	CVC4		Z3-str		Kaluza		Kaluza-orig	
	✗	✓	✗	✓	✗	✓	✗	✓
unsat	11,625	317	11,769	7,154	13,435	27,450	805	
sat	33,271	1,583	31,372	n/a	25,468	n/a	3	
unknown	0		0		3		0	
timeout	2,388		2,123		84		84	
error	0		120		1,140		18,942	

satisfying assignment for the variables in the input set. Kaluza can do that for at most one *query variable* which must be specified before-hand in the input file.

An initial series of regression tests on all three tools revealed several usability and correctness issues with Kaluza and a few with Z3-STR. In Kaluza, they were caused by bugs in its top level script which communicates with different tools, e.g. the solvers Yices and Hampi, via the file system. They range from failure to clean up temporary files to an incorrect use of the Unix grep tool to extract information from the output of those tools. Since Kaluza is not in active development anymore, we made an earnest, best effort attempt to fix these bugs ourselves. However, there seem to be more serious flaws in Kaluza's interface or algorithm. Specifically, often Kaluza incorrectly reports unsat for problems that are satisfiable only if some of their input variables are assigned the empty string. Moreover, in several cases, Kaluza's sat/unsat answer for the same input problem changes depending on the query variable chosen. Because of this arbitrariness, in our experiments we removed all query variables in Kaluza's input.

We found that in several cases Z3-STR returns *spurious solutions*, assignments to the input variables that do not in fact satisfy the input problem. Also, it classifies some satisfiable problems as unsat. Prompted by our inquiries, the Z3-STR developers have produced a new version of Z3-STR that fixes the spurious solutions problem. Unfortunately, that version was not ready in time for us to redo the experiments. As for Z3-STR's unsoundness, it looks like it is caused by an internal restriction that, for efficiency but without loss of generality, limits the possible values of "free" string variables to a fixed finite set of string constants. The authors define a variable as free in an input problem if its values are completely unconstrained by the problem. For instance, in the constraint set $\{x \approx con(y, z)\}$ variables y and z would be free according to this definition, while x would not. It appears that the criterion used by Z3-STR to recognize free variables sometimes misclassifies a variable as free when in fact it is not, causing the system to miss solutions that are outside the finite domain imposed on free variables.

In contrast, on our full set of benchmarks, we did not find any evidence of erroneous behavior in CVC4 when compared with the other two solvers. Every solution produced by CVC4 was *confirmed* by both CVC4 and Z3-STR by adding the solution as a set of constraints to the input problem and checking that the strengthened problem was satisfiable. Furthermore, no unsat answers from CVC4 were contradicted by a confirmed solution from Z3-STR.

Comparative Evaluation. For our evaluation we selected 47,284 benchmark problems from a set of about 50K benchmarks generated by Kudzu, a symbolic execution framework for Javascript, and available on the Kaluza website [18]. The discarded problems either had syntax errors or included a macro function (CapturedBrack) whose meaning is not fully documented. We translated those benchmarks into CVC4's extension of the SMT-LIB 2 format to the language of T_{SLRp}[4] and into the Z3-STR format. Some benchmarks contain regular membership constraints (s in r), which Z3-STR does not support. However, in all of these constraints the regular language denoted by r is finite and small, so we were able to translate them into equivalent string constraints.

We ran CVC4, Z3-STR and two versions of Kaluza, the original one and the one with our debugged main script, on each benchmark with a 20-second CPU time limit. The results are summarized in Table 1. There, the column Kaluza-orig refers to the original version of Kaluza while the error line counts the total number of runtime errors. The results for Z3-STR and the two versions of Kaluza are separated in two columns: the $\times$ column contains the number of provably incorrect answers while the $\checkmark$ column contains the rest. By *provably incorrect* here we mean an unsat answer for a problem that has a verified solution or a sat answer but with a spurious solution. Note that the figures for the two versions of Kaluza are unfairly skewed in their favor because neither version returns solutions, which means that their sat answers are unverifiable unless one of the other solvers produces a solution for the same problem. For a more detailed discussion, we look at the benchmark problem set broken down by the CVC4 results. For brevity we discuss only our amended version of Kaluza below.

None of the 11,625 unsat answers provided by CVC4 were provably incorrect. Z3-STR also answered sat on 11,568 of them and returned an error for the remaining 57; Kaluza agreed on 11,394 and returned an error for the rest. All of CVC4's 33,271 sat answers were corroborated by a confirmed solution. Z3-STR agreed on 31,616 of those problems although it returned a spurious solution for 244 of them. Also, it incorrectly found 317 problems unsatisfiable and produced an error on 29 problems, timing out on the remaining 1,304. Kaluza agreed on 25,468 problems (unverifiable because of the absence of solutions), erroneously classified 7,154 as unsatisfiable, reported unknown for 3, produced an error for 562, and timed out on 84.

CVC4 timed out on 2,388 problems, but produced no errors and no unknown answers. For the problems that CVC4 timed out on, Z3-STR classified 201 as unsatisfiable, returned an error for 34 and produced solutions for the remaining 1,339, all of which were spurious. Kaluza classified 2,041 as unsatisfiable and returned an error on the rest.

These results provide strong evidence that CVC4's string solver is sound. They also provide evidence that unsat answers from Z3-STR and Kaluza for problems on which CVC4 times out cannot be trusted. They also show that CVC4's string solver answers sat more often than both Z3-STR and Kaluza, providing a correct solution in each case. Thus, it is overall the best tool for both satisfiable and unsatisfiable problems.

Moving to run time performance, a comparison with Kaluza is not very meaningful because of its high unreliability and the unverifiability of its sat answers. In principle,

---

[4] The SMT-LIB 2 standard does not include a theory of strings yet although there are plans to do so. CVC4's extension is documented at http://cvc4.cs.nyu.edu/wiki/Strings

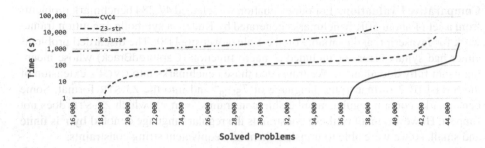

Fig. 7. Runtime comparison of CVC4, Z3-STR and the amended Kaluza. Times are in seconds

the same could be said of Z3-STR due to its refutation unsoundness.[5] However, an analysis of our detailed results shows that CVC4 has nonetheless better runtime performance overall. This can be easily seen from the cactus plot in Figure 7, which shows for each of the three systems how many non-provably incorrect benchmarks it cumulatively solves within a certain amount of time.

4　Conclusion and Further Work

We have presented a new approach for solving quantifier-free constraints over a theory of unbounded strings with length and regular language membership. Our approach integrates a specialized theory solver for such constraints within the DPLL(T) framework. We have given experimental evidence that our implementation in the SMT solver CVC4 is highly competitive with existing tools.

In our ongoing work, we plan to extend the scope of our string solver to support a richer language of string constraints that occur often in practice, especially in security applications. In preliminary implementation work in CVC4, we have found that commonly used predicates (such as the predicate contains for string containment) can be handled in an efficient manner by extending the calculus mentioned in this paper. We are also working on a more sophisticated approach for dealing with RL constraints, using a separate dedicated solver that is similarly integrated into the DPLL(T) framework.

At the theoretical level, we would like to devise a proof strategy that is solution-complete, that is, guaranteed to eventually produce a solution for every satisfiable input. Note that a fair proof strategy can be trivially obtained by incrementally setting an upper bound on the total length of all strings in a problem solution. The challenge is to devise a more efficient fair strategy than that one. Additionally, we would like to identify fragments where our calculus is terminating, and thus refutation complete.

Acknowledgments. We would like to thank Nestan Tsiskaridze for her insightful comments, and the developers of Z3-STR for their technical support in using their tool and several clarifications on it.

---

[5] Z3-STR could be faster and time out less often simply because it unduly prunes search space.

References

[1] Barrett, C., Nieuwenhuis, R., Oliveras, A., Tinelli, C.: Splitting on demand in SAT modulo theories. In: Hermann, M., Voronkov, A. (eds.) LPAR 2006. LNCS (LNAI), vol. 4246, pp. 512–526. Springer, Heidelberg (2006)

[2] Barrett, C., Sebastiani, R., Seshia, S., Tinelli, C.: Satisfiability modulo theories. In: Biere, A., Heule, M.J.H., van Maaren, H., Walsh, T. (eds.) Handbook of Satisfiability, vol. 185, ch. 26, pp. 825–885. IOS Press (February 2009)

[3] Bjørner, N., Tillmann, N., Voronkov, A.: Path feasibility analysis for string-manipulating programs. In: Kowalewski, S., Philippou, A. (eds.) TACAS 2009. LNCS, vol. 5505, pp. 307–321. Springer, Heidelberg (2009)

[4] Christensen, A.S., Møller, A., Schwartzbach, M.I.: Precise analysis of string expressions. In: Cousot, R. (ed.) SAS 2003. LNCS, vol. 2694, pp. 1–18. Springer, Heidelberg (2003)

[5] Fu, X., Li, C.: A string constraint solver for detecting web application vulnerability. In: Proceedings of the 22nd International Conference on Software Engineering and Knowledge Engineering, SEKE 2010, Knowledge Systems Institute Graduate School (2010)

[6] Ganesh, V., Minnes, M., Solar-Lezama, A., Rinard, M.: Word equations with length constraints: What's decidable? In: Biere, A., Nahir, A., Vos, T. (eds.) HVC. LNCS, vol. 7857, pp. 209–226. Springer, Heidelberg (2013)

[7] Ghosh, I., Shafiei, N., Li, G., Chiang, W.-F.: JST: An automatic test generation tool for industrial Java applications with strings. In: Proceedings of the 2013 International Conference on Software Engineering, ICSE 2013, pp. 992–1001. IEEE Press (2013)

[8] Hooimeijer, P., Veanes, M.: An evaluation of automata algorithms for string analysis. In: Jhala, R., Schmidt, D. (eds.) VMCAI 2011. LNCS, vol. 6538, pp. 248–262. Springer, Heidelberg (2011)

[9] Hooimeijer, P., Weimer, W.: A decision procedure for subset constraints over regular languages. In: Proceedings of the 2009 ACM SIGPLAN Conference on Programming Language Design and Implementation, pp. 188–198. ACM (2009)

[10] Hooimeijer, P., Weimer, W.: Solving string constraints lazily. In: Proceedings of the IEEE/ACM International Conference on Automated Software Engineering, pp. 377–386. ACM (2010)

[11] Kiezun, A., Ganesh, V., Guo, P.J., Hooimeijer, P., Ernst, M.D.: HAMPI: a solver for string constraints. In: Proceedings of the Eighteenth International Symposium on Software Testing and Analysis, pp. 105–116. ACM (2009)

[12] Li, G., Ghosh, I.: PASS: String solving with parameterized array and interval automaton. In: Bertacco, V., Legay, A. (eds.) HVC 2013. LNCS, vol. 8244, pp. 15–31. Springer, Heidelberg (2013)

[13] Liang, T., Reynolds, A., Tinelli, C., Barrett, C., Deters, M.: A DPLL(T) theory solver for a theory of strings and regular expressions. Technical report, Department of Computer Science, The University of Iowa (2014),
http://cvc4.cs.nyu.edu/papers/CAV2014-strings/

[14] Makanin, G.S.: The problem of solvability of equations in a free semigroup. English transl. in Math USSR Sbornik 32, 147–236 (1977)

[15] Nelson, G., Oppen, D.C.: Simplification by cooperating decision procedures. ACM Trans. on Programming Languages and Systems 1(2), 245–257 (1979)

[16] Nieuwenhuis, R., Oliveras, A., Tinelli, C.: Solving SAT and SAT Modulo Theories: from an abstract Davis-Putnam-Logemann-Loveland Procedure to DPLL(T). Journal of the ACM 53(6), 937–977 (2006)

[17] Plandowski, W.: Satisfiability of word equations with constants is in PSPACE. Journal of the ACM 51(3), 483–496 (2004)

[18] Saxena, P., Akhawe, D.: Kaluza web site (2010),
     http://webblaze.cs.berkeley.edu/2010/kaluza/
[19] Saxena, P., Akhawe, D., Hanna, S., Mao, F., McCamant, S., Song, D.: A symbolic execution
     framework for JavaScript. In: Proceedings of the 2010 IEEE Symposium on Security and
     Privacy, pp. 513–528. IEEE Computer Society (2010)
[20] Tillmann, N., de Halleux, J.: Pex–white box test generation for. NET. In: Beckert, B.,
     Hähnle, R. (eds.) TAP 2008. LNCS, vol. 4966, pp. 134–153. Springer, Heidelberg (2008)
[21] Veanes, M.: Applications of symbolic finite automata. In: Konstantinidis, S. (ed.) CIAA
     2013. LNCS, vol. 7982, pp. 16–23. Springer, Heidelberg (2013)
[22] Veanes, M., Bjørner, N., de Moura, L.: Symbolic automata constraint solving. In: Fermüller,
     C.G., Voronkov, A. (eds.) LPAR-17. LNCS, vol. 6397, pp. 640–654. Springer, Heidelberg
     (2010)
[23] Yu, F., Alkhalaf, M., Bultan, T.: STRANGER: An automata-based string analysis tool for
     PHP. In: Esparza, J., Majumdar, R. (eds.) TACAS 2010. LNCS, vol. 6015, pp. 154–157.
     Springer, Heidelberg (2010)
[24] Zheng, Y., Zhang, X., Ganesh, V.: Z3-str: A z3-based string solver for web application
     analysis. In: Proceedings of the 2013 9th Joint Meeting on Foundations of Software Engi-
     neering, ESEC/FSE 2013. ESEC/FSE 2013, pp. 114–124. ACM (2013)

Bit-Vector Rewriting
with Automatic Rule Generation

Alexander Nadel

Intel Corporation, P.O. Box 1659, Haifa 31015, Israel
alexander.nadel@intel.com

Abstract. Rewriting is essential for efficient bit-vector SMT solving. The rewriting algorithm commonly used by modern SMT solvers iteratively applies a set of ad hoc rewriting rules hard-coded into the solver to simplify the given formula at the preprocessing stage. This paper proposes an automatic approach to rewriting. The solver starts each invocation with an empty set of rewriting rules. The set is extended by applying at run-time an automatic SAT-based algorithm for new rewriting rule generation. The set of rules differs from instance to instance. We implemented our approach in the framework of an algorithm for equivalence and constant propagation, called 0-saturation, which we extended from purely propositional reasoning to bit-vector reasoning. Our approach results in a substantial performance improvement in a state-of-the-art SMT solver over various SMT-LIB families.

1 Introduction

Bit-vector reasoning is applied in a variety of domains [10,8,13,21,15,18,14]. Modern bit-vector solvers, such as Boolector [6] and Mathsat [7], employ *rewriting* [11,1,9] at the preprocessing stage. Rewriting applies a set of rewriting rules until fixed point to simplify the formula. For example, the statement $x = \mathtt{bvule}(0, z)$ (where $\mathtt{bvule}$ stands for unsigned-less-than-equal) can be rewritten to $x = true$, while $x = \mathtt{bvadd}(y, -y)$ (where $\mathtt{bvadd}$ stands for addition) can be rewritten to $x = 0$. Normally, the rewriting rules are designed manually by the developers of each solver and are embedded into the solver's code offline (that is, during solver development time). The same set of rules is used irrespective of the input instance. Rewriting is applied to simplify the directed acyclic graph (DAG) representing the formula. The number of rewriting rules can reach into the hundreds. For example, citing [9], "in MathSAT, close to 300 rewrite rules have been defined".

We propose an alternative approach to rewriting. Table 1 summarizes the differences between our approach and the standard method. In our approach, the solver starts with an empty set of rules. It then attempts to generate a rule on the fly at run-time whenever it identifies a situation where a rewriting rule is likely to be applied. For example, when one of the operands of an operation belongs to a set of pre-defined constants, such as 0, as in $x = \mathtt{bvule}(0, z)$, the solver checks whether the result can be rewritten to a pre-defined constant. To that end, it uses incremental SAT solver invocations over a new CNF instance

A. Biere and R. Bloem (Eds.): CAV 2014, LNCS 8559, pp. 663–679, 2014.
© Springer International Publishing Switzerland 2014

comprising the formula under consideration ($x = $ bvule$(0, z)$ in our case), bit-blasted to CNF. In our case, the algorithm will learn that $x = $ bvule$(0, z)$ can be rewritten to $x = true$. The process of trying to generate a rule is also triggered when two operands are related by a simple function, such as unary minus, as in $x = $ bvadd$(y, -y)$. Hence, the algorithm will realize that $x = $ bvadd$(y, -y)$ can be rewritten to $x = 0$. Whenever a new rule is generated, it is immediately applied and also stored in a hash table of rules, which is reused as long as the solver is alive. Hence the set of rules is instance-specific.

Our algorithm is implemented in the framework of 0-saturation [19,12,17], a process of constant and equivalence propagation, initially proposed in the context of propositional reasoning. We extended 0-saturation to handle bit-vector reasoning. The added value of 0-saturation over DAG rewriting is that 0-saturation enables propagating equivalences implied by user-given assertions.

We implemented our algorithm in Intel's SMT solver Hazel on top of an existing preprocessor. Section 4 shows that using our approach pays off experimetally. It improves the performance of Hazel on 20 out of 23 tested SMT-LIB [4] families. New Hazel outperforms the leading SMT solvers Boolector and Mathsat on most of the tested families. Moreover, there are 10 families on which new Hazel outperforms base Hazel, Boolector and Mathsat significantly: it either solves more instances or is at least 2x faster. The overhead of generating the rules at run-time rather than offline is negligible in practice.

The most relevant previous work is [20], where an offline instance-generic *automatic* generator of rewriting rules for bit-vector reasoning is proposed. Unfortunately, it does not work in practice [20]. The algorithm was halted after generating approximately 120,000 rules, and the generated rules could not simplify real-world problems. In contrast, our approach explores a narrower rule space and, being instance-specific, restricts it further by exploring only rules relevant to the input problem. [20] successfully applies a *semi-automatic* algorithm. First the algorithm automatically generates rule candidates for a specific width range from a rule space restricted to equivalences. Then, based on unspecified criteria, a human manually chooses which of those rules to embed into the solver. One problem that might have prevented full automation of this algorithm is that the set of candidates is width-specific, hence manual effort is required to choose width-independent rules only. Our approach avoids this problem since, being instance-specific, it knows the widths of the operations it needs to generate rules for. Offline instance-generic automatic rule generation is also applied for peephole super-optimization [2,3] and symbolic binary execution [18].

In what follows, Section 2 provides preliminaries and describes 0-saturation. Section 3 introduces bit-vector 0-saturation with automatic rule generation. Section 4 provides experimental results. We conclude in Section 5.

Table 1. Comparing Our Approach to Rewriting to the Standard Method

	Standard Method	Our Approach
When are the rules created?	Offline (solver development time)	Run-time
How are the rules generated?	Manually	Automatically
Where are the rules stored?	Hard-coded	Hash table
Are the rules instance-specific?	No	Yes
Rewriting framework	DAG-based rewriting	0-Saturation

2 Preliminaries and 0-Saturation

We start with some basic notions. A *bit* is a Boolean variable, which can be interpreted as 0 or 1. A *bit-vector* v of width n is a sequence of n bits, where the right-most bit is the least significant bit. The set of all bit-vectors of width n is denoted by $\mathcal{BV}_n$. A *constant* is a bit-vector whose every bit is substituted by 0 or 1. The set of all constants for width n is denoted by $\mathcal{BC}_n$. We do not define a separate Boolean type `Bool` for propositional variables, but use $\mathcal{BV}_1$ to formally represent propositional variables (unlike in the SMT-LIB 2.0 language [5]).

We denote bitwise negation by $\sim$. Generalizing propositional logic, we let a bit-vector *literal* be a bit-vector variable v or its bitwise negation $\sim v$. We denote the set of bit-vector literals of width n by $\mathcal{BL}_n$. Next we define a binary operation and a triplet. Our definition of a triplet is a strict generalization of the definition of a propositional triplet [19,12,17].

Definition 1 (Binary Operation; Binary Operation Width; Predicate/ Non-Predicate Binary Operation). *A binary operation o is a function that maps any two constants in $\mathcal{BC}_n$ to a constant in $\mathcal{BC}_m$, where $w(o) = n$ is the operation width. Each binary operation belongs to one of the following categories:*

1. *A predicate operation has $m = 1$ and $w(o) > 1$.*
2. *A non-predicate operation has $m = w(o)$.*

Definition 2 (Triplet; Triplet Member/Width/Type; Predicate/Non-Predicate Triplet). *A triplet is an application of a binary operation o: $x = o(y, z)$, where $y, z \in \mathcal{BL}_n \cup \mathcal{BC}_n$, $x \in \mathcal{BL}_m \cup \mathcal{BC}_m$, $w(t) = w(o) = n$ is the triplet width, and x, y, z are triplet members. The pair $\{o, w(o)\}$ constitutes the triplet type. A triplet is predicate/non-predicate iff o is predicate/non-predicate, respectively.*

For example, given $y, z \in \mathcal{BV}_{n>1}$, $x = $ `bvule`(y, z) is a predicate triplet, while $x = $ `bvadd`(y, z) is a non-predicate triplet. We define a binding as follows:

Definition 3 (Binding). *A binding $x = y$ for $x, y \in \mathcal{BL}_n \cup \mathcal{BC}_n$ stands for the equality between x and y.*

Next we review the *0-saturation* algorithm [19,12,17], initially presented as a way to simplify a propositional formula by constant and equivalence propagation. Our paper generalizes 0-saturation to handle bit-vectors. We provide a generic framework for the algorithm that fits both the propositional and the bit-vector cases.

Consider the 0-saturation algorithm in Alg. 1. Given a set of triplets T and a set of bindings B, 0-saturation carries out *in-place* rewriting of T to a set of triplets equisatisfiable to $T \wedge B$, but potentially having fewer triplets and variables than T, since the algorithm may render triplets tautological and replace variables by the representatives of their respective equivalence classes (see below). The algorithm classifies the triplets into three categories by associating one of the following statuses with each triplet:

1. *unknown*: The triplet must be evaluated by the main loop of the algorithm (lines 5 to 7). Initially all the triplets are unknown (see line 2).
2. *tautological*: The triplet is a tautology. Once a triplet becomes tautological, its status will never change. Tautological triplets are essentially removed from T.
3. *active*: No further information can be learned from the triplet at this stage. An active triplet becomes unknown if and when one of its members is changed.

The algorithm divides the set of variables and constants into separate equivalence classes, where one literal of each variable appears in the equivalence classes. Each equivalence class has one and only one *representative*. Initially each class contains one constant or one variable serving as the representative (see line 3). For example, for the propositional case, assuming that both constants 0 and 1 appear, the initial equivalence classes would look as follows: $[\underline{0}], [\underline{1}], [\underline{v_1}], [\underline{v_2}], \ldots, [\underline{v_n}]$ (representatives are underlined). Line 4 *merges* each binding $\{p = q\} \in B$, that is, it merges the equivalence classes of p and q by applying the function MERGE.

Consider the function MERGE at line 10. If a literal or a constant is merged with its negation or if two different constants are merged, a contradiction exception is thrown. Otherwise, MERGE negates all the members of the equivalence classes of p and/or q, if p and/or q appear negated in their respective equivalence classes; then, it merges the equivalence classes of p and q. The new representative can be picked in an arbitrary manner, except that a constant must always be a representative. Line 14 forces the algorithm to reevaluate each triplet containing the former representative q or its negation by changing the status of such triplets to unknown. Finally, line 15 replaces all the occurences of the former representative q or its negation $\sim q$ with the new representative p or its negation $\sim p$, respectively.

The main loop of the algorithm (line 5) tries to rewrite the formula by applying the function PROPAGATE over unknown triplets. PROPAGATE may change the status of t and other triplets. The main loop operates until no more unknown triplets exist or until MERGE discovers a contradiction. We assume that a contradiction in MERGE is handled through the exception mechanism.

The function PROPAGATE (line 16) comprises the heart of the algorithm. It tries, if possible, to apply rewriting rules in order to infer and merge new bindings and render the triplet under evaluation tautological. We discuss the core rewriting algorithm at length in Section 3.

3   Bit-Vector 0-Saturation with Automatic Rule Generation

This section introduces our algorithm for automatic rule generation in the context of bit-vector 0-saturation. Section 3.1 provides the algorithm's high-level scheme, while Section 3.2 refines and formalizes the algorithm.

In order to look for rewriting rules systematically, it is necessary to define all the possible conditions that may trigger a rule and all the possible conclusions

---

Algorithm 1. 0-Saturation Algorithm

1: **function** 0-SATURATION(Triplets S, Bindings B)
2:     For each $t \in S$, set $stt(t) := unknown$
3:     Initialize equivalence classes to hold one variable and one constant each
4:     For each $\{p = q\} \in B$, MERGE(p, q)
5:     **while** There exists $t \in S$, such that $stt(t) = unknown$ **do**
6:         $t := t \in S$, such that $stt(t) = unknown$
7:         $stt(t) := $ PROPAGATE(t)

8: **function** NEGATEEQCLASSIFREQUIRED(Literal or constant r)
9:     **if** (r is negated in its eq. class) **then** Negate all the members of r's eq. class

10: **function** MERGE(Literal or constant p, Literal or constant q)
11:     **if** ($p = \sim q$) or (($p \neq q$) and p and q are constants) **then throw** contradiction
12:     NEGATEEQCLASSIFREQUIRED(p); NEGATEEQCLASSIFREQUIRED(q)
13:     Merge   the   eq.   classes $[\underline{p}, v_1^p, \ldots, v_k^p]$ and $[\underline{q}, v_1^q, \ldots, v_l^q]$ into
        $[\underline{p}, v_1^p, \ldots, v_k^p, q, v_1^q, \ldots, v_l^q]$ ▷ See text for the way to pick the new representative
14:     For any triplet t containing q or $\sim q$, s.t. $stt(t) = active$, set $stt(t) := unknown$
15:     Replace q and $\sim q$ by p and $\sim p$, respectively, in any triplet containing q or $\sim q$

16: **function** PROPAGATE(Triplet t)
17:     **if** A rewriting rule is applicable for t **then**
18:         Use MERGE to merge new bindings resulting from applying the rule
19:         **if** t becomes a tautology after applying the rule **return** *tautological*
20:     **return** *active*

---

that a rule may imply. One can then learn the actual rules implied by the logic under consideration.

For the propositional case, an exhaustive list of rewriting rules for 0-saturation of the following form per a Boolean operation is provided in [17]: a rule is triggered when one of the members of a triplet t is either the constant 0 or 1 or is equivalent up to negation to another member. The rule implies either a contradiction or one or two new bindings of t members or their negations to the constants or to other t members. Whenever a rule is triggered, t becomes tautological. For example, one of the rewriting rules listed in [17] would infer the binding $\sim x = y$ from the triplet $\sim x = \text{and}(y, y)$ (where **and** stands for the Boolean and), rendering the triplet tautological. In [17] the rules are hard-coded into the solver, and no formal procedure for generating the rules is provided.

3.1 Automatic Rule Generation: High-Level Algorithm

In our approach to bit-vector 0-saturation, a rule may be triggered when, given a triplet $x = o(y, z)$, one of its members x, y, z is a pre-defined *rewriting constant* and/or when one member constitutes a pre-defined *rewriting function* of another member (rewriting constants and functions will be defined shortly). Usually, applying a rewriting rule binds triplet members to rewriting constants or to rewriting functions of other members.

Next we define a successor, a predecessor and a neighbor. The two equations in the following definition result from substituting x by $\sim x$ and $-x$, respectively, in the definition of unary minus $-x = \sim x + 1$.

Definition 4 (Successor; Predecessor; Neighbor). *The* successor *of* $x \in \mathcal{BL}_n \cup \mathcal{BC}_n$ *is* $x + 1 = -\sim x$; *the* predecessor *of* x *is* $x - 1 = \sim -x$. x's *successor or predecessor is* x's *neighbor.*

The following definitions capture the notion of rewriting constants, rewriting functions, rewriting identities, and rewriting values:

Definition 5 (Rewriting Constant). *The set of* Rewriting Constants $\mathcal{RC}$ *comprises the following constants defined for every type* $\mathcal{BC}_w$:

1. $0 = \underbrace{0 \ldots 0}_{w}$

2. $-1 = \underbrace{1 \ldots 1}_{w}$

3. $1 = \underbrace{0 \ldots 0}_{w-1} 1$

4. $2 = \underbrace{0 \ldots 0}_{w-2} 10$ *for* $w \geq 2$; $2 = 0$ *for* $w = 1$.

5. $-2 = \underbrace{1 \ldots 1}_{w-1} 0$

Definition 6 (Rewriting Function). *Given a bit-vector formula e, the set of* Rewriting Functions $\mathcal{RF}_e$ *comprises the following parametrized set of functions:*

1. $f_1(e) = e$
2. $f_2(e) = e - 1 = \sim -e$
3. $f_3(e) = e - 2 = \sim -\sim -e$
4. $f_4(c) = e + 1 = -\sim e$
5. $f_5(e) = e + 2 = -\sim -\sim e$
6. $f_6(e) = -e$
7. $f_7(e) = -e - 1 = \sim e$
8. $f_8(e) = -e - 2 = \sim -\sim e$
9. $f_9(e) = -e + 1 = -\sim -e$
10. $f_{10}(e) = -e + 2 = -\sim -\sim -e$

Definition 7 (Rewriting Identity; x-identity; y-identity; z-identity). *The set of* rewriting identities $I = \{i_x, i_y, i_z\}$ *comprises the x-identity* i_x, *the y-identity* i_y, *and the z-identity* i_z.

The rewriting identities i_x, i_y, and i_z are used to represent situations where, given a triplet $x = o(y, z)$, x, y, and z, respectively, are neither rewriting constants nor rewriting functions of another triplet member.

Definition 8 (Rewriting Value; Trivial Rewriting Value). *Let* $x = o(y, z)$ *be a triplet. The set* $I \cup \mathcal{RC} \cup \mathcal{RF}_x \cup \mathcal{RF}_y \cup \mathcal{RF}_z$ *comprises all the* rewriting values. *The rewriting value is* trivial *if and only if it is a rewriting identity.*

If one or more triplet members is a non-trivial rewriting value (that is, it is either a rewriting constant or a rewriting function of another triplet member), a rewriting rule may be triggered. Triplet members may be bound to non-trivial rewriting values as a result of applying a rule. We picked the rewriting values bearing the following reasons in mind:

1. The constants 0, -1 and 1 are essential to be able to generate a variety of rules for multiple operations. For example, both $x = \text{bvadd}(y, 0)$ and $x = \text{bvmul}(y, 1)$ (where bvmul stands for multiplication) can be rewritten to $x = y$, while $x = \text{bvule}(y, -1)$ can be rewritten to $x = -1$.
2. Bitwise negation is essential for rewriting bitwise operations. For example, $-1 = \text{bvand}(y, \sim y)$ is a contradiction (where bvand stands for bitwise and). In addition, having bitwise negation and the constants $-1, 0$ ensures that our procedure covers the propositional case.
3. Unary minus is essential for rewriting arithmetic operations. For example, $x = \text{bvadd}(y, -y)$ can be rewritten to $x = 0$.
4. Capturing the neighbors of a literal and the neighbors of its unary minus is useful for rewriting a variety of operations. For example, $x = \text{bvadd}(y, -y-1)$ can be rewritten to $x = -1$. We have chosen to look at neighbors up to depth 2 in order to attempt to create rules to capture sequences of successors and predecessors. To that end, we have also included the constants 2 and -2.
5. Our algorithm can check whether triplet members are rewriting values instantaneously by holding a pointer to each literal's negation and unary minus, since all our rewriting values can be expressed using constants, bitwise negation and unary minus only.

Next we define the notions of a premise and a skeleton, where the expression $g^{e_1 \mapsto e_2}$ stands for g, where each instance of e_1 is *substituted* by e_2.

Definition 9 (Premise). *Given a formula F, a triplet $t \equiv x = o(y, z)$, the ordered set $\{\sigma_x, \sigma_y, \sigma_z\}$, where $\sigma_x \in \{i_x\} \cup \mathcal{RC} \cup \mathcal{RF}_y \cup \mathcal{RF}_z$, $\sigma_y \in \{i_y\} \cup \mathcal{RC} \cup \mathcal{RF}_x \cup \mathcal{RF}_z$, and $\sigma_z \in \{i_z\} \cup \mathcal{RC} \cup \mathcal{RF}_x \cup \mathcal{RF}_y$, is a premise if the following conditions hold*

1. *$F \implies x = \sigma_x^{i_x \mapsto x} \land y = \sigma_y^{i_y \mapsto y} \land z = \sigma_z^{i_z \mapsto z}$*
2. *One of the values $\{\sigma_x, \sigma_y, \sigma_z\}$ is non-trivial.*

Definition 10 (Skeleton; Skeleton Member). *Given a triplet $t \equiv x = o(y, z)$ and a premise $\{\sigma_x, \sigma_y, \sigma_z\}$, the formula $S \equiv \sigma_x^{i_x \mapsto x} = o(\sigma_y^{i_y \mapsto y}, \sigma_z^{i_z \mapsto z})$ is a skeleton and $\left\{\sigma_x^{i_x \mapsto x}, \sigma_y^{i_y \mapsto y}, \sigma_z^{i_z \mapsto z}\right\}$ are skeleton members.*

In the definitions above, we assume that F is the current formula (that is, a set of triplets, and, possibly, bindings), maintained by the 0-saturation algorithm. If F implies that at least one of the members of a given triplet $t \equiv x = o(y, z)$ is a non-trivial rewriting value, a premise is well-defined. For example, given the triplet $x = \text{bvadd}(y, 1)$ and assuming $x = y + 1$, the sets

$\{i_x, i_y, 1\}$, $\{y + 1, i_y, i_z\}$, and $\{y + 1, i_y, 1\}$ are all premises. Premise definition will be refined in Section 3.2.

A skeleton is used to isolate an application of the triplet's operation, given a premise, irrespectively of irrelevant triplet members. In our example, $x = \mathtt{bvadd}(y, 1)$ is the skeleton given the premise $\{i_x, i_y, 1\}$; $y + 1 = \mathtt{bvadd}(y, z)$ is the skeleton given the premise $\{y + 1, i_y, i_z\}$; and $y + 1 = \mathtt{bvadd}(y, 1)$ is the skeleton given the premise $\{y + 1, i_y, 1\}$.

Let us move now to a high-level sketch of our algorithm.

1. When the SMT solver starts, it applies 0-saturation as part of preprocessing. The solver maintains a hash table of rewriting rules for each triplet type that had at least one rule generated for it. The hash tables map each rule's premise to the rule's *conclusion*, which can either be a contradiction, a set of bindings of triplet members to rewriting values, or empty (meaning that no action can be carried out under the current premise). The conclusion also defines whether the triplet becomes a tautology after application of the rule.

2. Whenever an unknown triplet t is evaluated by the propagation algorithm PROPAGATE (line 16), the solver first checks whether both y and z are constants of any kind (not necessarily rewriting constants). If they are, it merges x with the constant $o(y, z)$, marks the triplet tautological, and exits. Otherwise, it carries out *premise detection*, that is, it checks whether the current formula implies any premise, given t.[1] If a premise is not detected, no further information can be learned from the triplet and the algorithm renders it active.

3. If a premise is detected, the solver checks if a rule with the corresponding premise appears in the hash table. If it does, the solver *applies* the rule in the following sense. If the conclusion is empty, the solver renders the triplet active (storing empty conclusions prevents regeneration of the same empty conclusion over and over again). If the conclusion is a contradiction, a contradiction exception is thrown. If the conclusion is a set of bindings, the solver binds triplet members to their corresponding values. The solver may also mark the triplet tautological, if required by the conclusion.

4. If a premise is detected, but no corresponding rule is found in the hash table, the solver enters the *conclusion generation* stage. It bit-blasts the skeleton, corresponding to the triplet and the premise, to a fresh SAT instance. Then, the solver checks for a contradiction in the instance and for all the possible new bindings between the skeleton members and non-trivial rewriting constants or rewriting functions of other skeleton members using incremental SAT invocations. If there is no contradiction and no bindings can be learned, the conclusion is empty. The newly generated conclusion is either a contradiction, an empty set, or a set of bindings. In the latter case, the conclusion also specifies whether the triplet becomes tautological (more details are provided in Section 3.2). In the end, the conclusion is inserted into the hash table, and the new rule is applied as described in the previous step.

---

[1] Let us assume for now that an arbitrary premise is picked whenever more than one premise exists. Section 3.2 discusses premise redundancy and premise subsumption.

We distinguish between tautological and non-tautological conclusions, since, unlike in propositional case, in bit-vector 0-saturation, it is possible to conceive of an operation and a rule, where applying the rule would not make the corresponding triplet a tautology. For example, one could design an operation such that when x becomes 0, y must also become 0, but while z's range is reduced, z is still neither fixed nor a don't care. We did not find such operations in the current SMT-LIB language, but our algorithm takes into consideration their possible existence.

Note that we restrict ourselves to rewriting rules of a certain pre-defined format, which is most relevant to 0-saturation. It is possible to extend our procedure, e.g., by rewriting triplets to triplets of a different type or by considering more than one triplet at once for rewriting. We leave the exploration of such possibilities to future work.

Our procedure can be applied in a straightforward manner given a bit-vector formula in the SMT-LIB 2.0 language [5], since the vast majority of that language's operations are binary, and hence can be represented as triplets. However, some of the operations, such as unary minus, are unary, while ite (if-then-else) has 3 operators. In principle our procedure can easily be extended to accomodate non-binary operators. However, in our current implementation we use simple hard-coded rules for unary operators and ite.

3.2 Refining and Formalizing the Algorithm

This section refines the algorithm described in the previous section, bearing the following three main goals in mind:

1. *Eliminating premise redundancy* mainly by disallowing syntactically different but semantically identical premises so as to prevent the algorithm from generating essentially the same rule multiple times. For example, only the first of the two sets $\{y, i_y, i_z\}$, $\{i_x, x, i_z\}$ will qualify as a premise by our refined definition, given the triplet $v = \mathtt{bvadd}(v, z)$.
2. *Generating stronger conclusions* by binding triplet members to rewriting constants rather than to rewriting functions, whenever possible. For example, given the triplet $x = \mathtt{bvand}(y, z)$ and the premise $\{-1, i_y, i_z\}$, binding both y and z to -1 is likely to simplify the instance more substantially than just binding y to z.
3. *Generating weaker premises* by disqualifying rules whose premise would be subsumed by another rule with the same conclusion. For example, if for some triplet t the same conclusion is implied by both $p = \{i_x, -z + 2, i_z\}$ and $p' = \{-1, -z + 2, i_z\}$, then p is the desirable premise for the new rule, since it leaves more opportunities for applying the rule by not restricting x.

We refine the notion of rewriting values by defining the notions of x-value, y-value, and z-value, the rewriting values for x, y, and z, respectively.

Definition 11 (x-value). *Given a triplet $x = o(y, z)$, the rewriting value σ_x is an x-value if it belongs to the set $V_x \cup \{i_x\}$, where V_x is defined as follows:*

1. $V_x := \{0, -1\}$ *if o is a predicate operation*
2. $V_x := \mathcal{RC} \cup \mathcal{RF}_y \cup \mathcal{RF}_z$ *if o is a non-predicate operation and $w > 1$*
3. $V_x := \{0, -1, y, \sim y, z, \sim z\}$ *if o is a non-predicate operation and $w = 1$*

For a predicate operation, a non-trivial x-value can only be one of the constants $\{0, -1\}$. For non-predicate operations, a non-trivial x-value can belong to the set $\mathcal{RC} \cup \mathcal{RF}_y \cup \mathcal{RF}_z$ as expected, except in cases where the width is 1, and the set is refined to eliminate redundancies.

Definition 12 (y-value). *Given a triplet $x = o(y, z)$, the rewriting value σ_y is a y-value if it belongs to the set $V_y = \mathcal{RC} \cup \mathcal{RF}_z \cup \{i_y\}$.*

Definition 13 (z-value). *Given a triplet $x = o(y, z)$, the rewriting value σ_z is a z-value if it belongs to the set $V_z = \mathcal{RC} \cup \{i_z\}$.*

A y-value or a z-value may not belong to $\mathcal{RF}_x$ to eliminate redundancy. This is because any expression of the form $y = f(x) \in \mathcal{RF}_x$ or $z = f(x) \in \mathcal{RF}_x$ can be represented as $x = f^{-1}(y) \in \mathcal{RF}_y$ or $x = f^{-1}(z) \in \mathcal{RF}_z$, respectively. For the same reason, a z-value may not belong to $\mathcal{RF}_y$ (hence, a non-trivial z-value may only be a rewriting constant). Note that the set $\mathcal{RF}_x$ is redundant and is used no more. Now we can formulate a refined notion of a premise.

Definition 14 (Premise (Refined)). *Given a formula F, a triplet t, the ordered set $\{\sigma_x, \sigma_y, \sigma_z\}$, where $\sigma_x \in V_x$, $\sigma_y \in V_y$, $\sigma_z \in V_z$, is a premise if $F \implies x = \sigma_x^{i_x \mapsto x} \wedge y = \sigma_y^{i_y \mapsto y} \wedge z = \sigma_z^{i_z \mapsto z}$ and one of the following conditions hold:*

1. *One and only one of the values $\{\sigma_x, \sigma_y, \sigma_z\}$ is non-trivial, or*
2. *$\sigma_x \in \mathcal{RC}$ and $\sigma_y \in \mathcal{RC} \cup \mathcal{RF}_z$ and $\sigma_z = i_z$, or*
3. *$\sigma_x \in \mathcal{RF}_y$ and $\sigma_y = i_y$ and $\sigma_z \in \mathcal{RC}$, or*
4. *$\sigma_x \in \mathcal{RF}_z$ and $\sigma_y \in \mathcal{RC}$ and $\sigma_z = i_z$, or*
5. *$\sigma_x \in \mathcal{RF}_y$ and $\sigma_y \in \mathcal{RF}_z$ and $\sigma_z = i_z$*

Our refined definition of a premise is aimed towards eliminating redundancy. In particular, the case where both y and z are constants is *not* part of the definition, since it is covered by the higher-level algorithm, which simply binds x to the constant $o(y, z)$. We also skip all the cases where some triplet member v is a constant and there is another triplet member u, such that $u = f(v)$ (for example, $\{y + 1, 1, i_z\}$ is thus skipped). This is because such cases are mostly covered by the case where both v, u are constants ($\{2, 1, i_z\}$ in our case), while cases which are not covered by our rewriting constant set are simply skipped (e.g., $\{y + 2, 2, i_z\}$ would be covered by $\{4, 2, i_z\}$, but 4 is not a rewriting constant). In addition, we skip the case where both x and y are functions of z, since it is mostly covered by the case where x is a function of y and y is a function of z.

Next we define a total order between values, which is essential for generating stronger conclusions, and formalize the notion of a conclusion.

Definition 15 (Order over Values). *The following order relation induces a total order between any two values in $I \cup \mathcal{RF}_y \cup \mathcal{RF}_z \cup \mathcal{RC}$: $I < \mathcal{RF}_y \cup \mathcal{RF}_z < \mathcal{RC}$.*

Definition 16 (Conclusion; Contradictory/Empty/Partial/Tautological /Interesting Conclusion). *Given a triplet t and a premise $\{\sigma_x, \sigma_y, \sigma_z\}$, c is a conclusion if the following conditions hold. Let $S \equiv \sigma_x^{i_x \mapsto x} = o(\sigma_y^{i_y \mapsto y}, \sigma_z^{i_z \mapsto z})$ be the skeleton.*

1. *If $S \implies \bot$, then $c \equiv \bot$, in which case the conclusion is* contradictory.
2. *If $S \not\implies \bot$, then $c \equiv \{\rho_x, \rho_y, \rho_z, taut \in \{false, true\}\}$, where $\rho_x \in V_x$, $\rho_y \in V_y$, $\rho_z \in V_z$, and the following equations hold:*
   (a) *ρ_z is the maximal value, such that $S \implies \sigma_z^{i_z \mapsto z} = \rho_z^{i_z \mapsto z}$*
   (b) *ρ_y is the maximal value, such that $S \implies \sigma_y^{i_y \mapsto y} = \rho_y^{i_y \mapsto y}$*
   (c) *ρ_x is the maximal value, such that $S \implies \sigma_x^{i_x \mapsto x} = \rho_x^{i_x \mapsto x}$, where the order is refined in the following two cases: if $\sigma_x \in \mathcal{RF}_y$, then $I < \mathcal{RF}_y < \mathcal{RF}_z < \mathcal{RC}$; if $\sigma_x \in \mathcal{RF}_z$, then $I < \mathcal{RF}_z < \mathcal{RF}_y < \mathcal{RC}$*
   (d) *$taut = true$ iff $\sigma_x^{i_x \mapsto x} = \rho_x^{i_x \mapsto x} \wedge \sigma_y^{i_y \mapsto y} = \rho_y^{i_y \mapsto y} \wedge \sigma_z^{i_z \mapsto z} = \rho_z^{i_z \mapsto z} \implies S$*

If the conclusion is $\{\sigma_x, \sigma_y, \sigma_z, false\}$, it is empty. *The conclusion is* interesting *if it is not empty. An interesting conclusion with $taut = false$ or $taut = true$ is* partial *or* tautological, *respectively.*

A conclusion can be characterized as follows:

1. If the skeleton is contradictory, then the conclusion must be contradictory.
2. A conclusion always exists, since setting each value in the conclusion to the corresponding value in the premise comprises the empty conclusion, if no other conclusion is available.
3. Any non-empty conclusion (if available) is preferred to the empty conclusion.
4. Rewriting constants are always preferred to rewriting functions.
5. A non-contradictory conclusion is tautologial iff binding its values to the premise values implies the skeleton.

Finally, we formally define a rule aiming towards generating rules with weaker premises as we discussed.

Definition 17 (Rule;   Contradictory/Empty/Partial/Tautological/ Interesting Rule). *Given a triplet t, a premise $p = \{\sigma_x, \sigma_y, \sigma_z\}$, and a conclusion c, $r \equiv p \implies c$ is a rule if there exists no premise $p' = \{\sigma'_x, \sigma'_y, \sigma'_z\}$ that subsumes p, where p' subsumes p iff:*

1. *c is a conclusion, given p', and*
2. *$\sigma'_x \in \{\sigma_x, i_x\}$ and $\sigma'_y \in \{\sigma_y, i_y\}$ and $\sigma'_z \in \{\sigma_z, i_z\}$, and*
3. *$(\sigma'_x = i_x$ and $\sigma_x \neq i_x)$ or $(\sigma'_y = i_y$ and $\sigma_y \neq i_y)$ or $(\sigma'_z = i_z$ and $\sigma_z \neq i_z)$*

The rule is contradictory/empty/partial/tautological/interesting *if c is contradictory/empty/partial/tautological/interesting, respectively.*

We are now ready to present our algorithm for bit-vector 0-saturation with automatic rule generation. Consider Alg. 2. The main function PROPAGATEBV is designed so as to be inserted into Alg. 1 in place of PROPAGATE. PROPA-GATEBV receives a triplet t. It may apply empty rewriting rules and/or zero or one interesting rules for the triplet. It returns the status, that is, either *unknown*, *active*, or *tautological*. The status is active if no rules or only empty rules could be applied; it is tautological if a tautological rule was applied, and it is unknown if a partial rule was applied. The function may also throw a contradiction exception. Any expression of the form "**if** c **then** s_1 & s_2" in the pseudo-code of Alg. 2 means that if c holds, the algorithm applies s_1 and then immediately applies s_2.

First, the algorithm enters the premise detection stage to check whether the triplet has a premise. The structure and the order of premise detection (lines 3 to 14) ensure that any generated rule will be correct w.r.t both premise subsumption as dictated by Def. 17 and premise redundancy as dictated by Def. 14. PROPAGATEBV triggers the process of conclusion generation by invoking the function GETC for any identified premise. GETC returns active for an empty conclusion, tautological for a tautological conclusion, and unknown for a partial conclusion. We will describe GETC later.

When an empty rule is returned by GETC, PROPAGATEBV will continue looking for other rules. PROPAGATEBV returns immediately if it finds a non-empty rule. Consider a situation where different non-empty rules may be applied for a given triplet. For example, both the rules $\{i_x, -1, i_z\} \implies \{-1, -1, -1, \text{true}\}$ and $\{i_x, i_y, -1\} \implies \{-1, -1, -1, \text{true}\}$ are applicable for rewriting the triplet $x = \text{bvor}(-1, -1)$ (where bvor stands for bitwise or). Our algorithm will generate one of the rules and exit. It might seem at first that if the generated rule is partial, while there exists at least one tautological rule for the same triplet, exiting is undesirable, since the opportunity to render the triplet tautological might be missed. However, if a partial rule is applied, PROPAGATEBV returns unknown, thus PROPAGATEBV will be invoked again over the same triplet, hence one of the tautological rules will eventually be applied.

Let us consider the function GETC. It maintains a hash table for every triplet type with a non-empty set of rules. Each hash table entry contains a rule: its premise is mapped to its conclusion. GETC starts by looking for a conclusion for the given triplet in the corresponding hash table. If it is found, the algorithm acts based on the conclusion type. Namely, it returns active for an empty conclusion and throws a contradiction for a contradicting conclusion. For other conclusions, it merges the resulting bindings and returns tautological for a tautological conclusion and unknown for a partial conclusion.

If no rule is found in the hash table (line 28), GETC generates one. To generate a rule, GETC bit-blasts the skeleton to a new SAT solver instance Q. If Q is unsatisfiable, a contradictory rule is generated, otherwise the function generates a conclusion by invoking the auxiliary function CL to find maximal values for the conclusion. If the conclusion is interesting, the function checks whether the rule is tautological with another new SAT solver instance. The function then inserts the rule into the corresponding hash table and triggers the same behavior as if the newly generated rule was found in the hash table.

Algorithm 2. Rewriting for Bit-Vector 0-saturation

1: **function** PROPAGATEBV(Triplet $t \equiv x = o(y, z)$)
2:     $r := active$
3:     **if** Both y and z are constants **then** MERGE($x, o(y, z)$) & **return** *tautological*
4:     **if** $z \in \mathcal{RC}$ **then** $r :=$ GETC(t, i_x, i_y, z) & **if** $r \neq active$ **return** r
5:     **if** $y \in \mathcal{RC}$ **then** $r :=$ GETC(t, i_x, y, i_z) & **if** $r \neq active$ **return** r
6:     **if** $x \in \mathcal{RC}$ **then** $r :=$ GETC(t, x, i_y, i_z) & **if** $r \neq active$ **return** r
7:     **if** $x \in \mathcal{RF}_y$ **then** $r :=$ GETC(t, x, i_y, i_z) & **if** $r \neq active$ **return** r
8:     **if** $x \in \mathcal{RF}_z$ **then** $r :=$ GETC(t, x, i_y, i_z) & **if** $r \neq active$ **return** r
9:     **if** $y \in \mathcal{RF}_z$ **then** $r :=$ GETC(t, i_x, y, i_z) & **if** $r \neq active$ **return** r
10:    **if** $x, y \in \mathcal{RC}$ **then** $r :=$ GETC(t, x, y, i_z) & **if** $r \neq active$ **return** r
11:    **if** $x \in \mathcal{RC}$ and $y \in \mathcal{RF}_z$ **then** $r :=$ GETC(t, x, y, i_z) & **if** $r \neq active$ **return** r
12:    **if** $x \in \mathcal{RF}_y$ and $z \in \mathcal{RC}$ **then** $r :=$ GETC(t, x, i_y, z) & **if** $r \neq active$ **return** r
13:    **if** $x \in \mathcal{RF}_z$ and $y \in \mathcal{RC}$ **then** $r :=$ GETC(t, x, y, i_z) & **if** $r \neq active$ **return** r
14:    **if** $x \in \mathcal{RF}_y$ and $y \in \mathcal{RF}_z$ **then** $r :=$ GETC(t, x, y, i_z)
15:    **return** r

16: **function** CL(SAT Instance Q; $\sigma \in \{\sigma_x, \sigma_y, \sigma_z\}$)
17:    **return** a maximal ρ, such that $Q \wedge (\sigma \neq \rho)$ is UNSAT, where ρ must be
     x-value/y-value/z-value iff σ is $\sigma_x/\sigma_y/\sigma_z$, respectively

18: **function** GETC(Triplet $t \equiv x = o(y, z)$ of type $= \{o, w\}$; Premise $p = \{\sigma_x, \sigma_y, \sigma_z\}$)
19:    **if** rules [type] [p] exists **then**
20:       $c :=$ rules [type] [p]
21:       **if** c is empty **then return** *active*
22:       **if** c is contradictory **then throw** contradiction
23:       c must be of the form $\{\rho_x, \rho_y, \rho_z, \text{taut}\}$
24:       **if** $\rho_x \neq \sigma_x$ **then** MERGE($x, \rho_x^{i_x \mapsto x}$)
25:       **if** $\rho_y \neq \sigma_y$ **then** MERGE($y, \rho_y^{i_y \mapsto y}$)
26:       **if** $\rho_z \neq \sigma_z$ **then** MERGE($z, \rho_z^{i_z \mapsto z}$)
27:       **if** taut = true **then return** *tautological* **else return** *unknown*
28:    **else**
29:       Bit-blast the skeleton $\sigma_x^{i_x \mapsto x} = o(\sigma_y^{i_y \mapsto y}, \sigma_z^{i_z \mapsto z})$ to a new SAT instance Q
30:       **if** Q is unsatisfiable **then**
31:          rules [type] [p] $:= \bot$
32:       **else**
33:          $\rho_x :=$ CL(Q, σ_x); $\rho_y :=$ CL(Q, σ_y); $\rho_z :=$ CL(Q, σ_z)
34:          **if** $\rho_x \neq \sigma_x$ or $\rho_y \neq \sigma_y$ or $\rho_z \neq \sigma_z$ **then**
35:             Bit-blast $\sigma_x^{i_x \mapsto x} = \rho_x^{i_x \mapsto x} \wedge \sigma_y^{i_y \mapsto y} = \rho_y^{i_y \mapsto y} \wedge \sigma_z^{i_z \mapsto z} = \rho_z^{i_z \mapsto z} \wedge (\sigma_x^{i_x \mapsto x} \neq$
        $o(\sigma_y^{i_y \mapsto y}, \sigma_z^{i_z \mapsto z}))$ to a new SAT instance R
36:             **if** R is unsatisfiable **then** taut := true **else** taut := false
37:             rules [type] [p] $:= \{\rho_x, \rho_y, \rho_z, \text{taut}\}$
38:          **else**
39:             rules [type] [p] $:= \{\sigma_x, \sigma_y, \sigma_z, \text{false}\}$
40:          Go to line 20

---

4   Experimental Results

We implemented our new algorithm in Intel's eager bit-vector solver Hazel, which operates by invoking bit-vector preprocessing, followed by bit-blasting to CNF and SAT solving. Both base and new Hazel use the standard manual offline instance-generic DAG-based rewriting, where the novel automatic rewriting in new Hazel is applied after the manual rewriting (switching off manual rewriting in Hazel is impossible). We compared the performance of the new version of Hazel to base Hazel and the latest publicly available versions of the state-of-the-art SMT solvers Boolector [6] (version 1.6.0) and Mathsat [7] (version 5.2.10; SMT'11 competition configuration). We also gathered some statistics.

The benchmark families we used belong to the QF_BV category of SMT-LIB [5]. Since this category contains tens of thousands of benchmarks, we could not use all of them. We decided to pick all 23 families of the ASP sub-category, since, while these families are difficult and versatile, they contain a tractable number of benchmarks. In our analysis we skipped about 12% of the benchmarks that could not be solved by any of the four solvers within the time-out of 20 minutes. We used machines running Intel® Xeon® processors with 3Ghz CPU frequency and having 32Gb of memory. Detailed experimental results are available at [16].

Consider Table 2, which presents the results. Each row corresponds to one family. Column 1 contains the family name, abbreviated to the first three letters (except for GraphColouring and GraphPartitioning, which are represented as GC and GP, respectively). Column 2 contains the number of instances. Each pair of neighboring columns of the subsequent eight columns provides the overall run-time in seconds (where the time-out value was added to the run-time for unsolved instances) and the number of unsolved instances for the solver listed in the column heading. The best performance is highlighted.

Compare the performance of the new version of Hazel over the 23 families to that of the other solvers. New Hazel outperforms base Hazel on 20 families (that is, new Hazel either solves more instances or the same number of instances in less time on 20 families). New Hazel outperforms Mathsat on 21 families and Boolector on 14 families. Moreover, there are 10 families on which new Hazel significantly outperforms all the other solvers: it either solves more instances or is at least 2x faster. These results testify clearly that our approach can considerably boost the performance of modern SMT solvers.

The final seven columns of Table 2 contain statistics. Column 11 shows the average 0-saturation run-time, including automatic rule generation, as a percent of the overall run-time of new Hazel. One can see that the run-time of 0-saturation is negligible. Columns 12 and 13 demonstrate the impact of 0-saturation on the size of the CNF by showing the average percent of CNF clauses and variables, respectively, in new Hazel as compared to base Hazel (for example, f in Column 12 means that if base Hazel generated c clauses, then new Hazel generated $f/100 * c$ CNF clauses). Note that for the vast majority of families 0-saturation significantly reduces the number of CNF clauses and variables. One notable exception is the Wei family, where the number of CNF clauses is slightly greater when 0-saturation is applied. This can happen because 0-saturation may need to *create* variables, if required by the rule's conclusion (e.g., new neighbors may be created). Although 0-saturation did not reduce the number of clauses in the Wei case, it did simplify the CNF instances considerably, as the performance speed-up attests. Columns 14 and 15 provide the *average* number of interesting rules generated and applied, respectively, by new Hazel, while columns 16 and 17 provide the same data for the non-interesting rules. One can see that 0-saturation creates only few rules, but applies them very often, sometimes up to hundreds of thousands of times.

Finally, we report that our algorithm did not generate any contradictory or partial rules in our experiments.

Table 2. Performance Comparison and Statistics

Fam	#	Boolector Time	Un	Mathsat Time	Un	Base Hazel Time	Un	New Hazel Time	Un	0-sat %Tm	CNF Red %Cls	%Var	Intr Rules #	Applied	Non-I Rules #	Applied
Dis	4	3582	2	2523	2	4800	4	**515**	0	0.7	49	25	7	1707424	10	915729
Sol	23	5825	1	24802	18	27600	23	**2200**	1	0.5	56	52	8	48037	10	15890
Lab	10	12000	10	12000	10	10342	8	**6996**	0	0.1	67	48	12	1070897	15	209523
Edg	29	30693	23	32391	24	25073	19	**5345**	0	0.2	61	56	3	322700	11	85153
Wei	29	5550	2	20228	10	25625	16	**2591**	0	0.1	101	100	6	6390	5	2940
Sud	8	7213	6	7213	6	5918	4	**3229**	0	0.4	63	67	6	156591	10	122519
GC	12	**2771**	1	5674	4	4952	4	3362	1	0.8	71	44	2	16077	9	8496
GP	7	1418	0	2939	2	2514	1	**205**	0	0.6	74	72	3	29798	13	6234
Fas	17	3869	0	6487	3	4272	2	**1152**	0	2.7	81	57	2	125189	5	4445
Ham	29	**271**	0	4036	3	3678	3	2694	1	0.7	81	71	5	10700	10	7134
Sok	29	872	0	15700	8	2662	0	**833**	0	0.7	23	20	11	45167	16	14044
Hie	12	1165	0	267	0	123	0	**56**	0	1.2	65	63	2	45234	9	26376
15P	15	477	0	2654	0	359	0	**168**	0	1.8	35	25	8	146586	11	18110
Han	15	1345	0	1584	0	200	0	**101**	0	1.9	63	48	10	136458	11	44241
Gen	29	1226	0	506	0	352	0	**220**	0	2.6	89	82	3	29794	12	11944
Cha	8	117	0	60	0	18	0	**12**	0	4.7	67	29	2	105654	9	35987
Kni	3	**67**	0	1347	1	1798	1	1280	1	0.3	70	65	9	17734	12	9014
Blo	29	**1023**	0	30521	22	16213	5	11737	5	0.0	67	61	2	13208	9	6037
Sch	29	**1053**	0	8061	4	6938	3	6643	3	2.7	65	23	8	61756	11	32450
Wir	19	**6330**	0	16511	12	8712	5	8567	5	0.6	85	63	9	172717	15	60664
Tra	29	**6449**	0	33339	26	34800	29	34800	29	0.0	73	80	6	20007	12	9811
Con	21	**294**	0	612	0	382	0	499	0	0.7	87	62	2	6538	4	651
Maz	29	**879**	0	2610	0	2518	0	3543	1	0.9	92	53	6.5	10009	3	1995

5 Conclusion

We have proposed a new preprocessing algorithm for bit-vector SMT solving: bit-vector 0-saturation with automatic rewriting rule generation. Applying our algorithm in Intel's SMT solver Hazel resulted in a substantial performance improvement over 23 ASP families from SMT-LIB. New Hazel outperforms the base version of Hazel on 20 families; it outperforms Mathsat on 21 families and Boolector on 14 families. Moreover, there are 10 families on which new Hazel outperforms base Hazel, Boolector, and Mathsat significantly: it either solves more instances or is at least 2x faster. Our approach can be improved further by extending it to generate more types of rewriting rules automatically.

References

1. Babic, D.: Exploiting structure for scalable software verification. Dissertation, The University of British Columbia (2008)
2. Bansal, S.: Peephole Superoptimization. Dissertation, Stanford University (2008)
3. Bansal, S., Aiken, A.: Automatic generation of peephole superoptimizers. In: Shen, J.P., Martonosi, M. (eds.) ASPLOS, pp. 394–403. ACM (2006)
4. Barrett, C., Stump, A., Tinelli, C.: The Satisfiability Modulo Theories Library, SMT-LIB (2010), http://www.SMT-LIB.org
5. Barrett, C., Stump, A., Tinelli, C.: The SMT-LIB Standard: Version 2.0. In: Gupta, A., Kroening, D. (eds.) Proceedings of the 8th International Workshop on Satisfiability Modulo Theories, Edinburgh, UK (2010)
6. Brummayer, R., Biere, A.: Boolector: An efficient SMT solver for bit-vectors and arrays. In: Kowalewski, S., Philippou, A. (eds.) TACAS 2009. LNCS, vol. 5505, pp. 174–177. Springer, Heidelberg (2009)
7. Cimatti, A., Griggio, A., Schaafsma, B.J., Sebastiani, R.: The mathSAT5 SMT solver. In: Piterman, N., Smolka, S.A. (eds.) TACAS 2013 (ETAPS 2013). LNCS, vol. 7795, pp. 93–107. Springer, Heidelberg (2013)
8. Falke, S., Merz, F., Sinz, C.: LLBMC: Improved bounded model checking of C programs using LLVM. In: Piterman, N., Smolka, S.A. (eds.) TACAS 2013. LNCS, vol. 7795, pp. 623–626. Springer, Heidelberg (2013)
9. Franzén, A.: Efficient Solving of the Satisfiability Modulo Bit-Vectors Problem and Some Extensions to SMT. Dissertation, University of Trento (2010)
10. Franzén, A., Cimatti, A., Nadel, A., Sebastiani, R., Shalev, J.: Applying SMT in symbolic execution of microcode. In: Formal Methods in Computer-Aided Design (FMCAD), pp. 121–128. IEEE (2010)
11. Ganesh, V., Berezin, S., Dill, D.L.: A Decision Procedure for Fixed-Width Bit-Vectors. Technical report, Computer Science Department, Stanford University (April 2005)
12. Harrison, J.: Stålmarck's algorithm as a HOL derived rule. In: von Wright, J., Harrison, J., Grundy, J. (eds.) TPHOLs 1996. LNCS, vol. 1125, pp. 221–234. Springer, Heidelberg (1996)
13. Katelman, M., Meseguer, J.: vlogsl: A strategy language for simulation-based verification of hardware. In: Barner, S., Harris, I., Kroening, D., Raz, O. (eds.) HVC 2010. LNCS, vol. 6504, pp. 129–145. Springer, Heidelberg (2010)
14. Marić, F., Janičić, P.: URBiVA: Uniform reduction to bit-vector arithmetic. In: Giesl, J., Hähnle, R. (eds.) IJCAR 2010. LNCS, vol. 6173, pp. 346–352. Springer, Heidelberg (2010)
15. Michel, R., Hubaux, A., Ganesh, V., Heymans, P.: An SMT-based approach to automated configuration. In: SMT Workshop 2012 10th International Workshop on Satisfiability Modulo Theories SMT-COMP 2012, p. 107 (2012)
16. Nadel, A.: Detailed experimental results for bit-vector rewriting with automatic rule generation, https://drive.google.com/file/d/0B0zXW5t7in-fcOdmdXNVUWttVXc/edit?usp=sharing
17. Nordström, J.: Stålmarck's method versus resolution: A comparative theoretical study. Master's thesis, Stockholm University, Stockholm, Sweden (2001)
18. Romano, A., Engler, D.: Expression reduction from programs in a symbolic binary executor. In: Bartocci, E., Ramakrishnan, C.R. (eds.) SPIN 2013. LNCS, vol. 7976, pp. 301–319. Springer, Heidelberg (2013)

19. Sheeran, M., Stålmarck, G.: A Tutorial on Stålmarck's Proof Procedure for Propositional Logic. In: Gopalakrishnan, G.C., Windley, P. (eds.) FMCAD 1998. LNCS, vol. 1522, pp. 82–99. Springer, Heidelberg (1998)
20. Trevor, A.H.: A constraint solver and its application to machine code test generation. Dissertation, Dept. of Computing and Information Systems, The University of Melbourne (2012)
21. Wille, R., Große, D., Haedicke, F., Drechsler, R.: SMT-based stimuli generation in the SystemC verification library. In: Borrione, D. (ed.) Advances in Design Methods from Modeling Languages for Embedded Systems and SoC's. LNEE, vol. 63, pp. 227–244. Springer, Heidelberg (2010)

A Tale of Two Solvers:
Eager and Lazy Approaches to Bit-Vectors*

Liana Hadarean[1], Kshitij Bansal[1], Dejan Jovanović[3],
Clark Barrett[1], and Cesare Tinelli[2]

[1] New York University
[2] The University of Iowa
[3] SRI International

Abstract. The standard method for deciding bit-vector constraints is via eager reduction to propositional logic. This is usually done after first applying powerful rewrite techniques. While often efficient in practice, this method does not scale on problems for which top-level rewrites cannot reduce the problem size sufficiently. A lazy solver can target such problems by doing many satisfiability checks, each of which only reasons about a small subset of the problem. In addition, the lazy approach enables a wide range of optimization techniques that are not available to the eager approach. In this paper we describe the architecture and features of our lazy solver (**LBV**). We provide a comparative analysis of the eager and lazy approaches, and show how they are complementary in terms of the types of problems they can efficiently solve. For this reason, we propose a portfolio approach that runs a lazy and eager solver in parallel. Our empirical evaluation shows that the lazy solver can solve problems none of the eager solvers can and that the portfolio solver outperforms other solvers both in terms of total number of problems solved and the time taken to solve them.

1 Introduction

Many software and hardware verification tasks require precise modeling of computer arithmetic and bit-level operations. The verification conditions coming from such applications can be expressed as satisfiability problems in the theory of fixed-width bit-vectors (T_{bv}). The standard technique for deciding the satisfiability in T_{bv} of a quantifier-free formula, vividly called *bit-blasting*, reduces the problem to a Boolean satisfiability (SAT) one, by replacing word-level operators with their bit-level circuit equivalents. Current state-of-the-art decision procedures for T_{bv} build on bit-blasting by applying powerful rewriting simplifications to the input formula before the final bit-blasting step. While often efficient in practice, this *eager* approach has several limitations: (i) the entire formula must be bit-blasted and solved at once, which may be difficult if the problem is too large; (ii) word-level structure and information can only be leveraged during preprocessing, not during solving; (iii) the complexity of the problem is a function of the bit-width; and (iv) eager solvers do not fit cleanly into theory combination frameworks.

* Work supported in part by the Semiconductor Research Corporation (SRC), tasks 1850.001 and 1850.002, and the National Science Foundation (grants 0644299, 1049495, and 1228768).

A. Biere and R. Bloem (Eds.): CAV 2014, LNCS 8559, pp. 680–695, 2014.
© Springer International Publishing Switzerland 2014

A *lazy* solver can address these limitations, explicitly targeting problems that are difficult for eager solvers and thus providing a complementary approach. The lazy approach for bit-vectors was first proposed in [8, 16]. In this paper, we revisit this approach, extending and improving it in several ways. Our lazy solver integrates algebraic, word-level reasoning with bit-blasting. Designed for easy plug-and-play combination with solvers for other theories, the procedure integrates an on-line lazy T_{bv} solver (LBV) into the DPLL(T) framework [20], separating theory-specific reasoning from the search over the Boolean structure of the input problem. This separation offers benefits orthogonal to those provided by eager bit-vector solvers but also poses interesting trade-offs. On one hand, it has the potential of incurring additional overhead and losing important connections between subproblems; on the other hand, depending on the Boolean structure of the problem, it often allows the T_{bv} solver to reason about much smaller problems at a time. We use a specialized decision heuristic to reduce the size of these sub-problems even further by considering only literals relevant to the current search context.

Our approach is particularly useful on problems whose subproblems fall into one of the efficiently decidable fragment of the bit-vector theory (e.g., the core theory of concatenation and extraction [11], the theory of bit-vector inequalities, or fragments decidable using equational reasoning). To target such problems, our LBV solver is built as the combination of several algebraic solvers specialized for some of these fragments together with a complete bit-blasting solver. The bit-blasting solver uses a dedicated SAT solver SAT_{bb}, distinct from the DPLL(T) Boolean engine driving the main search (SAT_{main}). The separation of the two SAT engines fits cleanly into the DPLL(T) framework and allows the solvers to be tuned independently.

Experiments (described in Section 6) confirm our claim that the lazy approach is complementary to the eager approach, as the lazy solver efficiently solves problems that are either impossible or very difficult for eager solvers. At the same time, it is not realistic to expect the lazy solver to do well on problems that are easy for eager solvers (and indeed it is often slower on these problems). For this reason we propose a portfolio approach that runs an eager solver and a lazy solver in parallel. Additional experiments show that our portfolio solver outperforms eager solvers both in terms of the number of problems solved and the time taken to solve them.

The rest of the paper is organized as follows. Section 2 frames our contributions in terms of related work. Sections 3 and 4 provide technical preliminaries and a brief overview of the DPLL(T) framework. Section 5 describes the components of our lazy solver LBV including some optimizations enabled by the lazy framework. We present an experimental evaluation of the solver followed by an in-depth analysis in Section 6. Finally, we conclude with future work in Section 7.

2   Related Work

The predominant approach to solving bit-vector constraints is via reduction to SAT. Boolector, a specialized solver for bit-vectors and arrays, and the winner of the 2012 SMT-COMP for QF_BV logic, employs preprocessing before encoding the bit-vector formula into the AIG format [7]. Z3, a DPLL(T)-style SMT solver, applies bit-blasting to all bit-vector operators, but has specialized equality reasoning [13]. STP2 does simplifications and solving for linear modular arithmetic, and then uses an eager encoding into CNF for bit-vector reasoning as well as an abstraction refinement loop for array axiom instantiation [18].

Some solvers encode the problem into a different domain such as (linear and non-linear) modular arithmetic [1]. These solvers are efficient at dealing with large data-paths and arithmetic operations. However some constructs, such as bit-wise operations, cannot be encoded and have to be bit-blasted away, while others, such as selection and concatenation, are very expensive for arithmetic solvers. Yet another approach [6, 11], based on word-level reasoning, uses Shostak-style canonizers and solvers to compute a canonical form for bit-vector expressions. However, it is limited to a restricted set of operators: concatenation, extraction and linear equations over bit-vectors.

The framework for a lazy bit-vector solver was first introduced by Bruttomesso et al. [8]. They describe an implementation of a DPLL(T)-style lazy layered solver for T_{bv} in the SMT solver MathSAT [10]. Their approach lazily encodes the problem into linear integer constraints and uses word-level inference rules during solving. Later work by Franzen [16] moves from encoding the problem into linear integer arithmetic to bit-blasting the formula to the main SAT solver instead.

Our work explores significant new ideas within this lazy framework, with the following contributions: (i) a dedicated SAT solver for T_{bv} that supports bit-blasting-based propagation with lazy explanations; (ii) specialized T_{bv} sub-solvers that reason about fragments of T_{bv}; (iii) inprocessing techniques to reduce the size of the bit-blasted formula when possible; and (iv) decision heuristics to minimize the number of literals sent to the bit-vector solver by the main SAT engine.

These new features greatly improve performance: our solver solves 450 more problems in roughly one third of the time compared to the only other lazy bit-vector solver. This brings the lazy framework from a niche player to a serious contender.

3   Formal Preliminaries

We assume familiarity with standard notions from many-sorted first-order logic. A *signature* Σ is a non-empty set of sort symbols together with a set of function symbols and a set of predicate symbols, each equipped with their respective arity and sorts. We call 0-arity function symbols *constants*.

A *constraint* is a conjunction of literals. We are concerned with the *constraint satisfiability* problem for a theory T with signature Σ_T, which consists of deciding whether a Σ_T-constraint is *T-satisfiable*, that is, satisfiable in a model of T. We will use $\models$ to denote propositional satisfiability and $vars(F)$ for the set of variables of a propositional formula F.

A bit-vector is a finite vector over the set $\{0, 1\}$ of binary digits. We consider the theory T_{bv} of bit-vectors with signature $\Sigma_{bv} = \Sigma_{eq} \cup \Sigma_{con} \cup \Sigma_{ineq} \cup \Sigma_{ari} \cup \Sigma_{bool} \cup \Sigma_{shift}$, consisting of infinitely many sort symbols $[n]$ with $n > 0$, and the function and predicate symbols listed in Table 1 together with their type (given after the symbol ::). Each sort $[n]$ denotes the set of bit-vectors of width n.

Table 1. T_{bv} signature Σ_{bv}

Σ_{eq}	sorts	$[n]$ $n > 0$		constants	$0, 1$	$:: [1]$
	equal	$\_ = \_ :: [n] \times [n]$			$\ldots$	
Σ_{con}	concat	$\_ \circ \_ :: [m] \times [n] \to [m+n]$		extract	$\_[i:j] :: [m] \to [i-j+1]$	
Σ_{ineq}	less	$\_ < \_ :: [n] \times [n]$		less-eq	$\_ \leq \_ :: [n] \times [n]$	
Σ_{ari}	plus	$\_ + \_ :: [n] \times [n] \to [n]$		neg	$- \_ :: [n] \to [n]$	
	times	$\_ \times \_ :: [n] \times [n] \to [n]$		div	$\_ / \_ :: [n] \times [n] \to [n]$	
	rem	$\_ \% \_ :: [n] \times [n] \to [n]$				
Σ_{bool}	and	$\_ \& \_ :: [n] \times [n] \to [n]$		or	$\_ \mid \_ :: [n] \times [n] \to [n]$	
	not	$\sim \_ :: [n] \to [n]$		xor	$\_ \oplus \_ :: [n] \times [n] \to [n]$	
Σ_{shift}	left shift	$\_ << \_ :: [n] \times [n] \to [n]$		right shift	$\_ >> \_ :: [n] \times [n] \to [n]$	

We will write $t_{[n]}$ for some fixed n to denote that t is a Σ_{bv}-term of sort $[n]$. Note that except for the constants, the function and predicate symbols in Table 1 are overloaded; for example, $+$ stands for any of the symbols in the infinite family $\{ + :: [n], [n] \to [n] \}_{n>0}$. For simplicity, we restrict our attention to a subset of the bit-vector operators described in the SMT-LIB v2.0 standard [4]; the missing ones can easily be expressed in terms of those given here.

The T_{bv}-satisfiability of conjunctions of equalities between terms over the *core* sub-signature $\Sigma_{eq} \cup \Sigma_{con}$ is decidable in polynomial time [9, 11]. However, adding almost any of the additional operators, or allowing for arbitrary Boolean structure, makes the T_{bv}-satisfiability problem NP-hard [6].

4 The DPLL(T) Framework

State-of-the-art SMT solvers efficiently decide the satisfiability of quantifier-free first-order formulas with respect to a background theory T by using the DPLL(T) framework [20]. The framework extends the Davis-Putnam-Logemann-Loveland (DPLL) decision procedure for SAT to handle reasoning in a theory T by relying on a *theory solver* (T-solver): a decision procedure for the T-satisfiability of Σ_T-constraints. Algorithm 1 gives a simplified algorithmic view of the DPLL(T) framework with a generalized theory interface. The algorithm takes as input a T-formula ψ and returns *sat* if ψ is T-satisfiable and *unsat* otherwise. Variable C stores the set of working clauses and A the current truth assignment for C as a sequence of T-literals. We use [] for the empty assignment and ; for the concatenation of two assignments. Initially, A is empty and C is simply the set of clauses obtained by converting ψ to Conjunctive Normal Form (CNF). We say that a pair $\langle A, C \rangle$ is *inconsistent* if the assignment A falsifies some clause in C; it is *consistent* otherwise. An assignment A *propositionally satisfies* ψ if ψ is satisfied by every full assignment extending A.

In Algorithm 1, the SAT and theory solver work together to augment A and C via SatSolve and TheoryCheck, respectively. The input to SatSolve is an assignment and a set of clauses $\langle A, C \rangle$. The return value is a new pair $\langle A', C' \rangle$ derived from the

---

Algorithm 1. DPLL(T)

Input: ψ input formula
A $\leftarrow$ [];
C $\leftarrow$ toCNF (ψ) ;
while true do
    $\langle$A, C$\rangle$ $\leftarrow$ SatSolve (A, C) ;
    if $\perp$ $\in$ C **then**
        $\lfloor$ **return** *unsat*;
    final $\leftarrow$ Satisfies (A, ψ) ;
    $\langle$P, L$\rangle$ $\leftarrow$ TheoryCheck(A, final) ;
    if L = $\emptyset$ **and** final **then**
        $\lfloor$ **return** *sat*;
    $\langle$A, C$\rangle$ $\leftarrow$ $\langle$A; P, C $\cup$ L$\rangle$

---

input one such that either $\langle A', C' \rangle$ is consistent or $\perp \in C'$.[1] If the input pair $\langle A, C \rangle$ is consistent, SatSolve can extend A with *implied literals*, deduced by Boolean Constraint Propagation (BCP), or with one *decision literal*, chosen non-deterministically from the currently unassigned ones. On the other hand, suppose that $\langle A, C \rangle$ is inconsistent. If A contains no decision literals, then the search is complete (no satisfying assignment can be found) and SatSolve indicates this by extending C with the empty clause $\perp$. Otherwise, it resolves the conflict in $\langle A, C \rangle$ by doing CDCL-style conflict analysis [19], popping literals from A until $\langle A, C \rangle$ becomes consistent, and then adding at least one new implied literal.

The function Satisfies checks whether A propositionally satisfies the input formula ψ, setting final to true if so, and to false otherwise. An efficient implementation of Satisfies is described in Section 5.2.

The function TheoryCheck implements a T-solver and returns a sequence P of propagations and a set L of theory lemmas that are used to update $\langle A, C \rangle$ as follows:

1. If TheoryCheck finds A to be T-unsatisfiable it identifies a T-unsatisfiable subset $\{l_1, \ldots, l_n\}$ of literals in A and returns $\langle [], \{\neg l_1 \vee \cdots \vee \neg l_n\} \rangle$. Adding this clause to C forces SatSolve to backtrack and search for a different assignment.
2. If A is T-satisfiable, TheoryCheck computes a (possibly empty) sequence P of *theory-propagated* literals (unassigned literals in C that are T-entailed by A), returning $\langle P, \emptyset \rangle$. P is added to A, which helps guide the SAT search in the right direction by avoiding unnecessary decisions.
3. TheoryCheck may not be able to efficiently determine the T-satisfiability of A as this may require reasoning by cases. TheoryCheck can request case splits by returning a set L of clauses encoding a T-valid formula. This effectively delegates the case splitting to the main Boolean engine.[2]

---

[1] SatSolve, which encapsulates the SAT solver, also manages the mapping between atoms and their propositional abstractions and vice versa.

[2] For Satisfies to work correctly, it is then necessary to update the current formula ψ to $\psi \wedge \bigwedge_{\varphi \in L} \varphi$.

We say a call to TheoryCheck is *final* when the parameter final is set to true. Final calls to TheoryCheck must either ensure that A is T-satisfiable, or return one or more theory lemmas.

Two important aspects of theory solvers are not captured here. The first is that actual implementations of TheoryCheck are stateful: they store a copy of the assignment A internally and are instructed to push and pop literals from it as A is modified by the main loop. In practice, it is crucial that the theory solver be able to backtrack efficiently when A is shrunk, and reason incrementally when it is extended. The second aspect is that a theory solver must be able to provide an *explanation* for each theory-propagated literal p. This is a clause of the form $\neg l_1 \vee \cdots \vee \neg l_n \vee l$ for some subset $\{l_1, \ldots, l_n\}$ of A, explaining why the literal was entailed. Explanations are needed by SatSolve during its conflict analysis. It is important for efficiency that the theory solver be able to compute explanations lazily, only as needed by SatSolve.

5   A Lazy Bit-Vector Solver

We now proceed to give the details of our lazy bit-vector solver LBV, designed to fulfill the requirements of the TheoryCheck interface described above.

5.1   Subsolvers

The LBV solver consists of four sub-solvers: the equality solver LBV$_{eq}$, the core solver LBV$_{core}$, the inequality solver LBV$_{ineq}$ and the bit-blasting solver LBV$_{bb}$. Each sub-solver is incremental and provides the theory solver functionalities described in Section 4. The architecture of LBV was designed to be modular and extensible: all the bit vector reasoning is confined within the solver, and it is easy to enhance it by adding more sub-solvers.

Algorithm 2. LBVCheck

Input: $\langle$A, final $\rangle$
$\langle P_{eq}, L_{eq}, \text{complete} \rangle \leftarrow \text{LBVCheck}_{eq}$ (A, final) ;
if complete **then**
  $\llcorner$ **return** $\langle P_{eq}, L_{eq} \rangle$;
$\langle P_{ineq}, L_{ineq}, \text{complete} \rangle \leftarrow \text{LBVCheck}_{ineq}$ (A; P_{eq}, final) ;
if complete **then**
  $\llcorner$ **return** $\langle P_{eq}; P_{ineq}, L_{eq} \cup L_{ineq} \rangle$;
$\langle P_{bb}, L_{bb} \rangle \leftarrow \text{LBVCheck}_{bb}$ (A; P_{eq}; P_{ineq}, final) ;
return $\langle P_{eq}; P_{ineq}; P_{bb}, L_{eq} \cup L_{ineq} \cup L_{bb} \rangle$

Algorithm 2 shows the implementation of LBVCheck, the TheoryCheck from Algorithm 1 corresponding to the LBV solver. LBVCheck calls the subsolvers in increasing order of computational cost. For each $i \in \{\text{eq}, \text{ineq}, \text{bb}\}$, LBVCheck$_i$ returns a sequence

P_i of literals, a set L_i of clauses, and a Boolean value indicating whether the solver is complete or not. A solver i is *complete* if LBVCheck$_i$ detects an inconsistency or if it determines that A is consistent (which it can only do if all the literals in A fall into the sub-solver's fragment of T_{bv}). If none of the solvers detect an inconsistency, LBVCheck returns the collection of all the propagated literals and lemmas generated by the individual sub-solvers.

The sub-solvers process all literals in A. However, except for LBV$_{bb}$, they reason on an abstraction of the literals. In particular, LBV$_{eq}$ treats all function and predicate symbols other than $=$ as uninterpreted, while LBV$_{ineq}$ (as well as LBV$_{core}$) treats as fresh variables any terms or predicates whose top symbol does not belong to its signature.

Equality Solver. The equality solver LBV$_{eq}$, corresponding to LBVCheck$_{eq}$, uses a variant of well-known polynomial-time congruence-closure (CC) algorithms [14] to decide the satisfiability of constraints in Σ_{eq}. Standard CC algorithms assume that sorts have an unbounded cardinality. This makes them incomplete for reasoning about equality and disequality constraints in T_{bv}. For example, the formula $x_{[1]} \neq y_{[1]} \wedge x_{[1]} \neq z_{[1]} \wedge y_{[1]} \neq z_{[1]}$ is not satisfiable: there are only two distinct bit-vectors of width 1.

We handle the finite cardinality of the bit-vector sorts by trying to build a satisfying valuation for all the terms in a given Σ_{eq}-constraint. In final calls to check, once the CC algorithm is done and has not detected any inconsistency, LBV$_{eq}$ attempts to assign a distinct constant value to each congruence class $c_{[n]}^0, \ldots, c_{[n]}^k$ for each sort $[n]$ in the input problem. If this is not possible (because $k > 2^n$), it returns a lemma of the form:

$$\bigvee_{0 \leq i < j \leq 2^n} r_{[n]}^i = r_{[n]}^j$$

where r_i is a representative for class $c_{[n]}^i$, stating that at least two of the first $2^n + 1$ congruence classes must be merged.

This process continues until either the splits lead to an inconsistency or the sub-solver finds a satisfying valuation. The cardinality lemmas are currently generated only if the congruence classes consist just of bit-vector constants and variables (otherwise the solver reports that it is incomplete).

Core Solver. The core solver is based on the slicing algorithms presented in [9, 11]. It decides conjunctions of equalities over $\Sigma_{eq} \cup \Sigma_{con}$ in polynomial time, by reducing the problem to just equality reasoning. The key idea of the algorithm is expressing each variable as a concatenation of disjoint slices. The coarsest such decomposition that guarantees that none of the slices overlap given the input set of equalities, is called the *coarsest base*. In our experience, the core solver is most efficient on problems involving only core theory terms, and thus it is heuristically turned on for such instances.

Inequality Solver. The inequality solver LBV$_{ineq}$ can decide the satisfiability of $(\Sigma_{eq} \cup \Sigma_{ineq})$-constraints by using an incremental special-purpose algorithm.[3] LBV$_{ineq}$ only

---

[3] This problem is a special case of modular difference logic that can be reduced to integer difference logic, as there is no wrap-around behavior due to overflows.

needs to reason about $<$ and $\leq$ since equality can be expressed in terms of $\leq$, and disequalities can be reasoned about by requesting a splitting lemma. For the rest of this section we assume all inequalities are unsigned (the signed case is analogous). We will use $\lhd$ to denote either $<$ or $\leq$, and $\lhd^*$ for the transitive closure of $\lhd$. A *valuation* M is a mapping from bit-vector variables $v_{[n]}$ to constant values in $[n]$. For convenience, we extend M to map constants to themselves, and to map other bit-vector terms and formulas to the constants obtained by mapping their sub-expressions and simplifying. A valuation M *satisfies* a bit-vector constraint ϕ if $M(\phi) = true$.

Definition 1. Let I be a conjunction of inequality constraints over variables and constants of the same sort $[n]$. A valuation M is the *least model* of I if M satisfies I and for all valuations M' satisfying I and all terms t in I, $M(t) \leq M'(t)$.

It can be shown that every such satisfiable constraint I has a least model. Given I, $\mathsf{LBV}_{\mathsf{ineq}}$ builds the least model by incrementally processing the inequalities. We will use $\mathcal{I}$ to refer to the already processed inequalities, and define the starting model M as:

$$M(t_{[n]}) := \begin{cases} t_{[n]} & \text{if } t_{[n]} \text{ is a constant,} \\ 0_{[n]} & \text{otherwise} \end{cases}$$

where $0_{[n]}$ is the binary representation of 0 in n bits. We maintain the invariant that M is the least model of $\mathcal{I}$. Given a new inequality $a \lhd b$, we want to extend M to a least model of $\mathcal{I} \cup \{a \lhd b\}$, or discover that the problem is unsatisfiable. If $M(a) \lhd M(b)$ already holds, we are done. Otherwise, the least model property guarantees that terms a and b have the least possible values. Therefore, to satisfy $a \lhd b$ we must increase b's value, if possible, to match that of a. The update cannot violate previously satisfied inequalities of the form $\{t_1 \lhd t_2 \mid t_2 \lhd^* b\}$. The only terms whose values may need to be updated further are terms t such that $b \lhd^* t$. We reach a conflict when: (i) we try to update the model value of a constant, (ii) increasing the model value leads to an overflow or (iii) we detect an inequality cycle. The algorithm can be efficiently implemented using a priority queue that prioritizes updating the value of terms with lower model values.

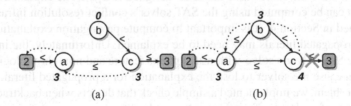

(a)   (b)

Fig. 1. The nodes are bit-vector terms; gray nodes are constants and white ones variables. Each node has an associated constant, its M value. The continuous edges represent inequalities. The dotted edges are *reason* edges: they point to the node that forced the last update to the current node's value.

Example 1. Consider the following set of inequalities over bit-vector terms of bit-width 8 where, for brevity, we use decimal numerals to denote bit-vector constants: $\mathcal{I} = \{2 < a, a \leq c, b < c, c \leq 3\}$. Figure 1a shows the least satisfying model for $\mathcal{I}$. To process the new inequality $a \leq b$, we add the corresponding inequality edge, and update the value of b to $M(a)$. This in turn requires increasing the value of c to $M(b) + 1$. We identify a conflict while revisiting $c \leq 3$: 3 is a constant and $M(c) \leq 3$ does not hold (Figure 1b). Because c has the lowest possible value, $\mathcal{I}$ must be unsatisfiable. We build the following conflict by including $c \leq 3$ and traversing back along the constraints that force the value of c to be 4: $\{2 < a, a \leq b, b < c, c \leq 3\}$.

Bit-Blasting Solver. Finally, the bit-blasting solver $\mathsf{LBV_{bb}}$ can decide the satisfiability of bit-vector constraints over the entire Σ_{bv} signature. At its heart is a second SAT solver $\mathsf{SAT_{bb}}$ distinct from the DPLL(T) Boolean engine. Our implementation uses the open source MiniSAT solver [15]. We instrumented MiniSAT to efficiently implement the main requirements on a T-solver: incrementality, conflict detection and propagation of entailed literals.

Incrementality. Most SAT solvers do not have full support for incremental solving.[4] Incrementality can be simulated through a feature known as *solve with assumptions* [15]: given a fixed set C of input clauses, the SAT solver can check their satisfiability with respect to the assumption that some of the variables appearing in C are assigned to be true or false. We exploit this feature by creating a *marker variable* a_{BB} for each atom a in the formula being checked. When a appears in an assertion, instead of bit-blasting a, we bit-blast $a_{BB} \Leftrightarrow a$. We can then call solve with assumptions with the set of literals $A_{BB} := \{a_{BB} \mid a \in \mathsf{A}\} \cup \{\neg a_{BB} \mid \neg a \in \mathsf{A}\}$.

Conflict Generation. If A is unsatisfiable, we use $\mathsf{SAT_{bb}}$ to determine an inconsistent subset of A_{BB} via resolution and return the corresponding subset of A as a conflict.

Propagation. On a non-final call to $\mathsf{LBVCheck_{bb}}$, we want to be able to determine whether any theory literals can be propagated without doing a full SAT check. To do this, we again use solve with assumptions but only allow the SAT solver to do Boolean Constraint Propagation (BCP), stopping it before any decisions are made. If BCP succeeds in deducing the value of a marker variable a_{BB}, the corresponding atom a can be propagated to have the same value that BCP assigned to a_{BB}. The explanation for the propagation can be computed using the SAT solver's conflict resolution infrastructure. As mentioned in Section 4, it is important to compute propagation explanations lazily as not all propagated literals may need to be explained. Unfortunately, the interaction between the SAT solver's solve-with-assumptions feature and non-chronological backtracking can cause the solver to lose the explanation for a propagated literal. To overcome this problem, we implemented a simple check that detects when backtracking can lead to the loss of explanations, and in such cases backtrack to a more conservative level instead. Algorithm 3 shows the implementation of $\mathsf{LBVCheck_{bb}}$. BvSatBCP implements the call to $\mathsf{SAT_{bb}}$ limited to BCP, while BvSatSolve is a normal full call to $\mathsf{SAT_{bb}}$.

---

[4] More input clauses can be added during solving, but the main challenge of removing problem clauses remains.

Algorithm 3. LBVCheck$_{bb}$

Input: $\langle$A, final $\rangle$
$\langle$P, L$\rangle \leftarrow$ BvSatBCP(A) ;
if final **and** L = $\emptyset$ **then**
   $\lfloor$ L $\leftarrow$ BvSatSolve(A) ;
return $\langle$P, L$\rangle$;

5.2 Lazy Techniques

The lazy DPLL(T) framework enables several techniques that are difficult or impossible to use with eager solvers. In this section we discuss two of these techniques: applying word-level rewrites during solving (*inprocessing*) and reducing the problem size by only reasoning about atoms relevant in the current search context (*relevancy-based decision heuristics*).

Inprocessing Techniques. Before engaging in potentially expensive SAT reasoning, LBV$_{bb}$ relies on the inprocessing module to check if the problem can be solved or significantly simplified by word-level simplification techniques. This is done by a process, described in Algorithm 4, that has the flavor of Gaussian elimination. It works by iterating over a worklist of theory literals W while maintaining a substitution map σ.

Initially, W is initialized to the set of literals A assigned to true in the current search context. For each worklist assertion $w \in W$, we first apply the substitution map, and then rewrite it using word-level simplification techniques (Simplify). The SolveEq procedure then attempts to solve the updated assertion w to obtain a new substitution. Alternatively, it can also learn new equalities entailed by w and add these to the working list.[5] The working list W and the substitution map σ are updated with this new information, and the process is repeated to a fixpoint.[6]

If any of the assertions in W reduces to *false*, we have a conflict. If there are no such obvious inconsistencies we can run the LBVCheck$_{bb}$ routine on the simplified set of assertions W. We do this heuristically, if the problem has been reduced enough in terms of the circuit size. We found checking the simplified assertions when they are less than 50% of the size of the original assertions to be a good heuristic.

Relevancy-Aware Decision Heuristics. The idea of *relevancy* is best understood with a simple example. Let $\psi = \neg a \wedge (b \vee \varphi)$ with assignment A = $[\neg a; b]$. Note that A propositionally satisfies ψ regardless of how many unassigned literals are in φ. The literals in φ are *irrelevant*.

The DPLL(T) framework makes it easy to add a decision heuristic that avoids splitting on irrelevant literals. In particular, we can (i) detect when an assignment A becomes propositionally satisfying and *stop early* in order to reduce the number of literals

---

[5] In our implementation, we solve xor equations and slice equations between concatenation expressions to get new equalities.

[6] The data-structures are enhanced with extra book-keeping information to keep track of explanations. We omit these details for simplicity.

Algorithm 4. IN-PROCESSING

Input: A
$\langle W, \sigma \rangle \leftarrow \langle A, [] \rangle$;
changed $\leftarrow$ **true**;
while changed **do**
    changed $\leftarrow$ **false**;
    for w $\in$ W **do**
        w $\leftarrow$ Simplify($\sigma(w)$) ;
        $\langle W', \sigma' \rangle \leftarrow$ SolveEq(w);
        if W' $\neq \emptyset$ *or* $\sigma \neq []$ **then**
            changed $\leftarrow$ **true** ;
        $\langle W, \sigma \rangle \leftarrow \langle W \cup W', \sigma; \sigma' \rangle$;

if false $\in$ W **then**
    return Conflict;
return BvSatSolve(W);

---

sent to theory solvers and (*ii*) employ *decision heuristics* that allow the SAT solver to decide only on literals relevant in the current search context. We use circuit-based techniques of maintaining *justification frontiers* [2, 17] to track which literals are relevant in each context.[7] The call to Satisfies in Algorithm 1 examines the Boolean structure of ψ and determines whether the current assignment A is sufficient to propositionally satisfy it. It does so by incrementally computing the *justification frontier* as the assignment A changes.

This heuristic, which we also call the *justification* heuristic, has a significant performance impact on bit-vector benchmarks, as shown in Section 6.

6 Experimental Results

In this section we present a comparative experimental evaluation of the eager and lazy approaches[8]. To this end we implemented both the lazy theory solver LBV as well as an eager theory solver within the SMT solver CVC4. After applying the same preprocessing steps as the lazy solver, the eager solver uses standard bit-blasting techniques to assert the formula to its MiniSAT backend. To gauge the complementarity of the two approaches we used CVC4's portfolio infrastructure which allows us to run the two solvers in different parallel threads. In this setup, CVC4 waits for the first thread that finishes with an answer and then kills the other, thus getting the best performance between the two theory solvers each time (modulo memory usage).

All experiments were performed on AMD Opteron 250 2.4GHz machines with a time limit of 5 minutes and memory limit of 3GB. We evaluate our solvers' performance on a large selection of SMT-LIB v2.0 benchmarks from the QF_BV logic [5]. Because of time constraints, we could not include all 31K QF_BV benchmarks from

---

[7] A different technique to reduce the number of literals sent to theory solvers is proposed in [12].

[8] Source code and binaries at http://cvc4.cs.nyu.edu/papers/CAV2014-bitvectors/

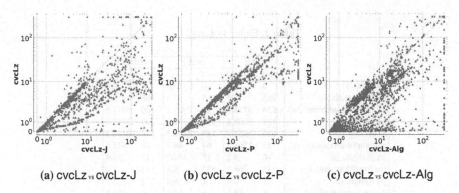

(a) cvcLz vs cvcLz-J   (b) cvcLz vs cvcLz-P   (c) cvcLz vs cvcLz-Alg

Fig. 2. Impact of various features of the lazy solver. All plots are on a logarithmic scale.

SMT-LIB v2.0. Instead, we selected 3786 of them by focusing on examples coming from verification applications: we excluded the answer-set programming asp family as well as the check2 and crafted families that contain toy examples. To prevent very large families such as sage (26K) and spear (1694) from dominating the results, we used a randomized process to select a representative fraction of the benchmarks from them. Because many of the sage problems are very easy, we considered only benchmarks that take more than 10 seconds to solve. From the spear family we included all small sub-families, and randomly selected a fraction of the largest subfamily. For brevity, we merge here the four families with a brummayerbiere prefix into brummayerbiere*, uclid and uclid-contrib-smtcomp09 into uclid*, and stp and stp-samples into stp*.

We use cvcE to refer to the implementation of the eager solver in CVC4, cvcLz for the lazy LBV solver and cvcPll for the parallel solver. The letters preceeded by a minus sign represent which feature of cvcLz has been *turned off*: J for the justification heuristic, P for LBV_{bb} propagation, Alg for all of the algebraic sub-solvers (LBV_{eq}, LBV_{core}, LBV_{ineq}) plus the word-level in-processing techniques.

The scatter plots in Figure 2 compare the runtime performance of the full featured lazy solver with a version without one of the features above. Figure 2a shows the impact of the justification heuristic. While overall the justification heuristic improves performance, it has a negative impact on benchmarks in the mcm family. These problems consist of conjunctions of large disjunctions. On such problems the justification heuristic forces SAT_{main} to choose a naive pattern of decisions by always initially deciding on the first disjunct of each conjunct. Figure 2b shows that LBV_{bb} propagation is essential to solving difficult benchmarks, although it adds some overhead to the easier ones. Figure 2c shows the impact of all the word-level techniques enabled by the lazy approach. The plot shows a relatively small overhead when these techniques do not help, but dramatic improvements when they do apply.

Table 2 compares the performance of cvcE, cvcLz and that of the only other bit-vector solver that supports lazy bit-blasting: mathsatL (smtcomp2012 version with lazy solving enabled). The eager solver cvcE performs better on families that involve bit-level manipulations, such as the brummayerebiere* families. The lazy solver cvcLz excels on families calypto, tacas07, lfsr, core and simple_processors that benefit from algebraic reasoning. Furthermore, cvcLz solves 6 problems that none of the other solvers

Table 2. Eager vs Lazy

set	cvcE		cvcLz		mathsatL	
	solved	time (s)	solved	time (s)	solved	time (s)
vs (VS3,11)	**0**	**0.0**	0	0.0	0	0.0
be (bench-ab,285)	285	57.5	285	2.4	**285**	**2.4**
br (brummayerbiere*,206)	**138**	**3732.3**	112	2923.2	100	3937.5
co (core,672)	132	3208.4	**672**	**596.4**	509	22345.5
lf (lfsr,240)	186	9451.9	**240**	**2286.3**	177	12412.2
si (simple-processor,64)	33	1566.4	**64**	**48.7**	18	845.6
ca (calypto,23)	10	9.2	**15**	**100.7**	11	233.4
dw (dwp-formulas,332)	332	68.2	**332**	**5.5**	332	5.9
ga (galois,4)	1	0.4	**1**	**0.4**	1	2.5
gu (gulwani-pldi08,6)	**6**	**49.1**	6	63.9	6	73.8
mc (mcm,185)	**64**	**3937.7**	13	392.9	2	278.9
pi (pipe,1)	**0**	**0.0**	0	0.0	0	0.0
ru (rubik,7)	5	157.9	2	110.6	**6**	**313.4**
sa (sage,189)	188	205.0	188	174.9	**189**	**51.2**
sp (spear,680)	**675**	**24057.0**	648	9347.0	478	14579.5
st (stp*,427)	424	170.3	424	108.6	**425**	**70.5**
ta (tacas07,5)	3	19.3	5	294.4	**5**	**136.8**
uc (uclid*,423)	414	2651.5	420	3148.9	**420**	**1132.5**
uu (uum,8)	**2**	**33.9**	1	1.5	1	0.3
wi (wienand-cav2008,18)	**14**	**32.2**	14	34.7	14	37.5
	2912	49408.4	**3442**	**19641.2**	2979	56459.6
us (unique-solve)	4		6		0	

Table 3. Comparison with other solvers

set	cvcPll		yices2		stp2		z3		boolector		sonolar		mathsat	
	solved	time (s)	solved	time (s)	solved	time (s)	solved	time (s)	solved	time (s)	solved	time (s)	solved	time (s)
vs (11)	0	0.0	0	0.0	1	270.3	**3**	**341.7**	2	258.7	0	0.0	0	0.0
be (285)	285	39.1	**285**	**0.0**	285	0.2	285	8.5	285	3.0	285	0.1	285	2.5
br (206)	137	3024.0	113	1718.1	143	3188.5	115	4005.1	**155**	**4060.8**	125	1858.9	123	3741.9
co (672)	**672**	**726.6**	326	5717.9	191	3126.4	672	798.4	656	32176.8	266	2796.8	587	21791.1
lf (240)	**240**	**2481.3**	181	8394.7	196	8896.3	232	12183.3	213	15939.2	219	3385.1	139	7644.1
si (64)	**64**	**57.8**	35	824.3	54	1911.1	60	1134.6	60	2377.2	37	1038.4	25	1283.3
ca (23)	**15**	**349.1**	9	6.1	11	3.5	11	50.8	9	45.0	9	20.4	11	56.2
dw (332)	332	47.4	**332**	**0.0**	332	0.9	332	10.0	332	0.0	332	0.2	332	4.2
ga (4)	1	0.5	1	0.1	**1**	**0.1**	1	0.2	1	0.3	1	0.1	1	0.6
gu (6)	6	44.8	**6**	**25.5**	6	26.7	6	31.2	6	42.1	6	39.3	6	56.5
mc (185)	63	6152.2	54	5308.3	44	3616.9	55	4302.8	45	3452.2	50	3592.0	42	3429.4
pi (1)	**0**	**0.0**	0	0.0	0	0.0	0	0.0	0	0.0	0	0.0	0	0.0
ru (7)	5	142.7	5	99.5	7	323.4	6	148.2	7	343.5	**7**	**190.1**	6	342.8
sa (189)	188	215.5	**189**	**9.9**	189	35.2	189	49.5	189	706.9	189	39.9	189	49.1
sp (680)	677	11028.4	**680**	**400.5**	679	1756.6	675	7546.6	676	5360.9	677	6910.1	676	13175.0
st (427)	424	168.0	**425**	**5.1**	425	41.9	425	58.8	425	22.9	425	46.7	425	47.1
ta (5)	5	249.8	3	1.5	5	348.4	3	7.2	5	465.6	5	410.4	**5**	**54.9**
uc (423)	419	3315.6	416	58.6	422	902.0	421	1856.4	422	1368.0	**423**	**1207.7**	423	1226.6
uu (8)	2	605.9	2	30.4	2	29.1	**2**	**11.1**	2	11.5	2	17.7	2	64.5
wi (18)	14	30.8	14	68.6	14	64.6	14	41.4	**14**	**23.3**	9	36.1	14	36.6
	3549	**28679.7**	3076	22669.3	3007	24542.1	3507	32585.9	3504	66658.1	3067	21590.1	3291	53006.6
us	*		3		1		2		10		0		1	

we considered could solve in the given time limit. The unique-solve row at the bottom of Table 2 and Table 3 shows this figure for all other solvers.

Finally, in Table 3 we compare cvcPII with other state-of-the-art bit-vector solvers: yices (2.1.1), stp2 (r1673), z3 (r0e74362), boolector (1.6), sonolar (smtcomp2012) and mathsat (smtcomp2012 with eager solver). For the parallel solver cvcPII we report wall clock time. The portfolio solver cvcPII solves the largest number of problems. We attribute this increase in performance to the complementary nature of the two approaches. To illustrate that the lazy cvcLz approach complements eager solvers, we also simulated running cvcLz in parallel with two of the most efficent eager bit-vector solvers: boolector and z3. We did this by chosing the best result from either solver for each problem. Even for these solvers, cvcLz greatly improves on their performance: the combined boolector+cvc4L solves 57 more problems in a quarter of the original boolector total time and z3+cvcL solves 42 more problems in just over half the total time.

Discussion. We now provide a more detailed analysis of the tradeoffs between the two approaches, based on our experimental results.

The eager solver cvcE is particularly efficient on hardware equivalence checking benchmarks that verify the equivalence of a bit-level implementation to its word-level specification. In such cases the correctness of the proof often depends on bit-level properties that benefit from efficient propositional analysis more than the kind of algebraic reasoning done in the lazy solver. This is especially obvious in the difference in the performance of cvcE and cvcLz on the brummayerbiere* family, as can be seen in Table 2.

Maintaining the word-level structure during the computation in LBV requires establishing a common language between SAT_{main}, the SAT solver driving the main $DPLL(T)$ search, and SAT_{bb}. In our approach, this language consists of the T_{bv}-atoms and represents a frontier that partitions the problem between the two solvers. LBV conflicts can be seen as interpolants between the part of the problem describing the control flow (the Boolean abstraction) and the datapath. Restricting the conflict language to T_{bv}-atoms limits the granularity of the conflicts: we cannot express bit-level conflicts. In some cases this can prove inefficient. Consider the following example.

Example 2. The following assertions are unsatisfiable. All paths through the disjunction force the last bit of the x_i variables to be $0_{[1]}$. Therefore their disjunction must also have the least significant bit equal to $0_{[i]}$ which makes the equality false.

$$\bigvee_{i=0}^{n} x_i = y \circ 1_{[1]} \wedge \bigwedge_{i=0}^{n} (x_i = t_i \circ 0_{[1]} \vee x_i = s_i \circ 0_{[1]})$$

In Example 2, an eager solver may potentially learn that the last bit of x_i has to be 0. The lazy solver on the other hand, will have to try all possible paths through the disjunction and learn a conflict for each one of them.

For problems with expensive arithmetic operators, the benefits of maintaining the word-level structure outweigh this limitation. While eager solvers have sophisticated rewrite techniques, such techniques are usually only applicable at the top level. Equivalence checking problems between higher level designs can require proving the equivalence of results obtained by taking different control-flow paths. These can be encoded as large *ite* (if-then-else) term trees with a similar structure, as in the following example.

Example 3. The formula below is unsatisfiable. The conditions on all paths through the *ite* trees force the leaves to be equal.

$$ite(x_0 = y_0, x_0 * (ite(x_1 = y_1, 2 * x_1, 2)), 2) \neq$$
$$2 * ite(x_0 = y_0, y_0 * (ite(x_1 = y_1, y_1, 1)), 1)$$

Collecting the assertions down any *ite* path in the example, and applying simple equality substitutions renders each such path trivially unsatisfiable. No multiplication reasoning is required. However, bitblasting this expression results in a difficult SAT problem as the large circuits required to model the products obscure the trivial inconsistency. The calypto, lfsr and simple_processors (Table 2) exhibit this type of structure. On these families, our LBV in-processing module can often simplify each call to TheoryCheck to false or a significantly simpler circuit. Other verification problems, such as checking the correctness of sorting algorithms, rely on the arithmetic properties of a total order. The equality, core and inequality subsolvers can decide such problems, often without any bit-level reasoning at all.

7   Future Work

For future work, we plan to both improve the performance of the lazy solver and investigate heuristics for automatically selecting between the eager and lazy solvers. In Section 6 we gave some intuition for which of the two approaches is best suited for which problem structure. It would be interesting to see if it is possible to statically determine which solver is likely to perform better.

The lazy solver can be improved by adding more sub-theory solvers, such as a subsolver complete for some fragment of modular arithmetic. The inprocessing module currently only handles equality reasoning, xor solving and slicing. Although it is already remarkably efficient, the SolveEq routine could be generalized to other types of equation solving.

Another way to improve the performance of the lazy solver is to minimize the conflicts obtained from the bit-blasting subsolver. The conflicts returned by that subsolver with assumptions infrastructure are not guaranteed to be minimal. Indeed, in our experience they are often non-minimal, in some cases larger than minimal ones by a factor of 10. The challenge here is to minimize the conflict in an efficiently since satisfiability queries in T_{bv} are potentially very expensive.

One way to expand the scope of the lazy bit-vector solver, and overcome some of its limitation, would be to increase the kind of conflicts it can return. Currently, the solver can only return conflicts in terms of bit-vector atoms. It would be interesting to experiment with expanding this vocabulary dynamically, by adding conflicts that refer to individual bits of the terms. This could potentially be supported by using the *splitting on demand* framework [3].

References

1. Babić, D., Musuvathi, M.: Modular arithmetic decision procedure. Microsoft Research Redmond, Tech. Rep. TR-2005-114 (2005)
2. Barrett, C., Donham, J.: Combining SAT methods with non-clausal decision heuristics. Electronic Notes in Theoretical Computer Science 125(3), 3–12 (2005)
3. Barrett, C.W., Nieuwenhuis, R., Oliveras, A., Tinelli, C.: Splitting on demand in SAT modulo theories. In: Hermann, M., Voronkov, A. (eds.) LPAR 2006. LNCS (LNAI), vol. 4246, pp. 512–526. Springer, Heidelberg (2006)
4. Barrett, C., Stump, A., Tinelli, C.: The smt-lib standard: Version 2.0. In: SMT, vol. 13 (2010)
5. Barrett, C., Stump, A., Tinelli, C.: The Satisfiability Modulo Theories Library, SMT-LIB (2010), http://www.SMT-LIB.org
6. Barrett, C.W., Dill, D.L., Levitt, J.R.: A decision procedure for bit-vector arithmetic. In: DAC, pp. 522–527 (1998)
7. Brummayer, R., Biere, A.: Boolector: An efficient SMT solver for bit-vectors and arrays. In: Kowalewski, S., Philippou, A. (eds.) TACAS 2009. LNCS, vol. 5505, pp. 174–177. Springer, Heidelberg (2009)
8. Bruttomesso, R., Cimatti, A., Franzén, A., Griggio, A., Hanna, Z., Nadel, A., Palti, A., Sebastiani, R.: A lazy and layered SMT BV solver for hard industrial verification problems. In: Damm, W., Hermanns, H. (eds.) CAV 2007. LNCS, vol. 4590, pp. 547–560. Springer, Heidelberg (2007)
9. Bruttomesso, R., Sharygina, N.: A scalable decision procedure for fixed-width bit-vectors. In: ICCAD 2009, pp. 13–20 (2009)
10. Cimatti, A., Griggio, A., Schaafsma, B.J., Sebastiani, R.: The mathSAT5 SMT solver. In: Piterman, N., Smolka, S.A. (eds.) TACAS 2013 (ETAPS 2013). LNCS, vol. 7795, pp. 93–107. Springer, Heidelberg (2013)
11. Cyrluk, D., Möller, O., Rueß, H.: An efficient decision procedure for the theory of fixed-sized bit-vectors. In: Grumberg, O. (ed.) CAV 1997. LNCS, vol. 1254, pp. 60–71. Springer, Heidelberg (1997)
12. de Moura, L., Bjørner, N.: Relevancy propagation. Technical Report MSR-TR-2007-140, Microsoft Research (2007)
13. de Moura, L., Bjørner, N.S.: Z3: An efficient SMT solver. In: Ramakrishnan, C.R., Rehof, J. (eds.) TACAS 2008. LNCS, vol. 4963, pp. 337–340. Springer, Heidelberg (2008)
14. Detlefs, D., Nelson, G., Saxe, J.B.: Simplify: a theorem prover for program checking. JACM 52(3), 365–473 (2005)
15. Eén, N., Sörensson, N.: An extensible SAT-solver. In: Giunchiglia, E., Tacchella, A. (eds.) SAT 2003. LNCS, vol. 2919, pp. 502–518. Springer, Heidelberg (2004)
16. Franzén, A.: Efficient Solving of the Satisfiability Modulo Bit-Vectors Problem and Some Extensions to SMT. PhD thesis, University of Trento (2010)
17. Fujiwara, H., Member, S., Shimono, T., Member, S.: On the acceleration of test generation algorithms. IEEE Transactions on Computers 32, 1137–1144 (1983)
18. Ganesh, V., Dill, D.L.: A decision procedure for bit-vectors and arrays. In: Damm, W., Hermanns, H. (eds.) CAV 2007. LNCS, vol. 4590, pp. 519–531. Springer, Heidelberg (2007)
19. Marques-Silva, J., Lynce, I., Malik, S.: Conflict-driven clause learning SAT solvers. In: Biere, A., Heule, M.J.H., van Maaren, H., Walsh, T. (eds.) Handbook of Satisfiability. Frontiers in Artificial Intelligence and Applications, vol. 185, ch. 4, pp. 131–153. IOS Press (February 2009)
20. Nieuwenhuis, R., Oliveras, A., Tinelli, C.: Solving SAT and SAT modulo theories: From an abstract DPLL procedure to DPLL(T). JACM 53(6), 937–977 (2006)

AVATAR: The Architecture
for First-Order Theorem Provers

Andrei Voronkov

University of Manchester, Manchester, UK

Abstract. This paper describes a new architecture for first-order resolution and superposition theorem provers called AVATAR (Advanced Vampire Architecture for Theories and Resolution). Its original motivation comes from a problem well-studied in the past — dealing with problems having clauses containing propositional variables and other clauses that can be split into components with disjoint sets of variables. Such clauses are common for problems coming from applications, for example in program verification and program analysis, where many ground literals occur in the problems and even more are generated during the proof-search.

This problem was previously studied by adding various versions of splitting. The addition of splitting resulted in some improvements in performance of theorem provers. However, even with various versions of splitting, the performance of superposition theorem provers is nowhere near SMT solvers on variable-free problems or SAT solvers on propositional problems.

This paper describes a new architecture for superposition theorem provers, where a superposition theorem prover is tightly integrated with a SAT or an SMT solver. Its implementation in our theorem prover Vampire resulted in drastic improvements over all previous implementations of splitting. Over four hundred TPTP problems previously unsolvable by any modern prover, including Vampire itself, have been proved, most of them with short runtimes. Nearly all problems solved with one of 481 variants of splitting previously implemented in Vampire can also be solved with AVATAR.

We also believe that AVATAR is an important step towards efficient reasoning with both quantifiers and theories, which is one of the key areas in modern applications of theorem provers in program analysis and verification.

Definitions of *Avatar* (from various dictionaries):

(Hindu Mythology) the descent of a deity to the earth in an incarnate form or some manifest shape; the incarnation of a god

(Science Fiction) a hybrid creature, composed of human and alien DNA and remotely controlled by the mind of a genetically matched human being

(Automated Reasoning) a first-order theorem prover, which embodies a SAT solver controlling the prover's behaviour

---

1 Introduction

The work described in this paper started with an attempt to make further improvement in dealing with problems having clauses containing propositional variables and other clauses that can be split into components with disjoint sets of variables. The problem

A. Biere and R. Bloem (Eds.): CAV 2014, LNCS 8559, pp. 696–710, 2014.

of dealing with such clauses started with splitting with backtracking, implemented in Spass [20] and splitting without backtracking [12] implemented in Vampire [9]. A very extensive investigation of various ways of organising splitting in a theorem prover was undertaken in [7], where both kinds of splitting were augmented with various options, including the use of BDDs and SAT solvers. Though the use of splitting results in the improvement of theorem provers performance, the methods used in them cannot compete with the methods used in SAT solvers on propositional problems or methods used in SMT solvers on ground problems with equality.

In first-order theorem proving, theorem provers based on variants of resolution and superposition calculi (in the sequel simply called *superposition provers*) are predominant. This is confirmed by the results of the last CASC competitions[1], see [19] for a description of CASC. The top three theorem provers Vampire [9], E-MaLeS and E [17] are resolution and superposition-based, while the fourth one iProver [8] implements both an instance-based calculus and resolution with superposition.

Superposition theorem provers use *saturation algorithms*. They deal with a search space consisting of clauses. Inferences performed by saturation algoritms are of three different kinds:

1. *Generating inferences* derive news clause from clauses in the search space. These new clauses can then be immediately simplified and/or deleted by other kinds of inference. Examples of generating inferences are binary resolution and superposition.
2. *Simplifying inferences* replace a clause by another clause that is simpler in some strict sense. Examples of simplifying inferences are demodulation (rewriting by ordered unit equalities) and subsumption resolution (binary resolution inference whose conclusion subsumes one of the premises).
3. *Deletion inferences* delete clauses from the search space. Examples of deletion inferences are subsumption and tautology deletion.

On hard problems the search space of superposition provers is often growing rapidly, and simplifications and deletions consume considerable time. Performance of such provers degrades especially fast when they generate many clauses having more than one literal (*multi-literal clauses* for short) and heavy clauses (clauses of large sizes). There are several reasons for this degradation of performance:

1. The complexity of algorithms implementing inference rules depends on the size of clauses. For example, subsumption and subsumption resolution are known to be NP-complete and algorithms implementing them are exponential in the number of literals in clauses.
2. Storing heavy clauses requires more memory. Moreover, every literal in a clause (and sometimes every term occurring in such a literal) are normally added to one or more indexes. Index maintenance requires considerable space and time and operations on these indexes slow down significantly when the indexes become large.
3. Generating inferences applied to heavy clauses usually generate heavy clauses. Generating inferences applied to clauses with many literals usually generate clauses with many literals. For example, resolution applied to two clauses containing n_1 and n_2 literals typically gives a clause with $n_1 + n_2 - 2$ literals.

---

[1] http://www.cs.miami.edu/~tptp/CASC/24/

To deal with multi-literal and heavy clauses, one can simply start discarding them after some time, thus losing completeness as in [14]. Alternatively, one can use *splitting*. There are two kinds of splitting described in the literature: splitting with backtracking (originally introduced in SPASS [20]) or splitting without backtracking (originally introduced in Vampire [13]).

In this paper we introduce a new way of splitting clauses, driven by a SAT or an SMT solver. This results in a new architecture for first-order theorem proving, which we call AVATAR. We show that the use of AVATAR instead of standard architectures results in a considerable improvement in the performance of theorem provers. Hundreds of problems unsolvable by any prover for years were solved when AVATAR was implemented in Vampire. Moreover, we believe that AVATAR is a significant step towards major improvements in one of the main problems in modern first-order theorem proving: reasoning with both quantifiers and theories.

2 Preliminaries

We assume that the reader is familiar with SAT solving and has some knowledge of first-order theorem provers. A deeper knowledge of superposition theorem proving, as well as SMT solving, is useful, but not necessary, since we give some background material on saturation algorithms implemented in superposition theorem provers.

Recall that a *(first-order) clause* is a disjunction $L_1 \vee \ldots \vee L_n$ of *literals*, where a literal is an atomic formula or a negation of an atomic formula. A literal or clause is *ground* if it contains no occurrences of variables. In the context of splitting we sometimes consider a clause as a set of its literals. In other words, we assume that clauses do not contain multiple occurrences of the same literal and clauses equal up to permutation of literals are considered equal. We assume that all predicates and functions in first-order logic are uninterpreted and that the language may contain (but not necessarily contains) the equality predicate, denoted by $=$. The empty clause is denoted by $\square$.

Unlike SMT solving, clauses containing variables are considered implicitly universally quantified. Suppose that C is a clause with variables $x_1, \ldots, x_k$. Then $\forall C$ will denote the formula $(\forall x_1) \ldots (\forall x_k)C$, also called the *universal closure* of C. In first-order theorem proving the semantics of a clause is its universal closure, so a set of clauses $C_1, \ldots, C_n$ is satisfiable if and only if so is the set of formulas $\forall C_1, \ldots, \forall C_n$. Any clause obtained by applying a substitution to a clause C is called an *instance* of C. If this instance is also a ground clause, it is called a *ground instance* of C. Satisfiability of a set of clauses in first-order predicate logic (in the SMT terminology it is the logic of equality and uninterpreted predicates and functions) is characterised by the Herbrand theorem: a set S of clauses is unsatisfiable if and only if some finite set of ground instances of clauses in S in unsatisfiable.

Our next aim is to explain splitting. In very simple terms, splitting is based on the following idea. Suppose that S is a set of (first-order) clauses and $C_1 \vee C_2$ a clause such that the variables of C_1 and C_2 are disjoint. Then $\forall (C_1 \vee C_2)$ is equivalent to $(\forall C_1) \vee (\forall C_2)$, which implies that the set $S \cup \{C_1 \vee C_2\}$ is unsatisfiable if and only if both $S \cup \{C_1\}$ and $S \cup \{C_2\}$ are unsatisfiable.

Let $C_1, \ldots, C_n$ be clauses such that $n \geq 2$ and all the C_i's have pairwise disjoint sets of variables. Then we say that the clause $D \stackrel{\text{def}}{=} C_1 \vee \ldots \vee C_n$ is *splittable* into *components* $C_1, \ldots, C_n$. We will also say that the set $C_1, \ldots, C_n$ is a *splitting* of D. For example, every ground multi-literal clause is splittable. There may be more than one way to split a clause, however there is always a unique splitting such that each component C_i is non-splittable; we call this splitting *maximal*. It is easy to see that a maximal splitting has the largest number of components and every splitting with the largest number of components is the maximal one. There is a simple algorithm for finding the maximal splitting of a clause [12], which is, essentially, the union-find algorithm.

In the sequel, when we speak about a splitting of a clause we will only consider maximal splittings and only deal with components that are non-splittable. We will denote arbitrary clauses by D and components by C, maybe with indexes.

Splittable clauses appear especially often when theorem provers are used for software verification and static analysis. Problems used in these applications usually have a large number of ground clauses (coming from program analysis) and a small number of non-ground clauses (for example, axiomatisations of memory or objects).

3 Saturation Algorithms

In this section we briefly discuss *saturation algorithms with redundancy elimination* used in superposition theorem provers. Essentially, a saturation algorithm works with a set of clauses S (the current search space) and uses a collection of generating, simplifying and deletion inferences. The theoretical basis of saturation algorithms is the notion of *redundancy* given e.g., in [1]: a clause D is redundant if D is a logical consequence of clauses in the search space, which are strictly smaller than D w.r.t. a simplification ordering $\succ$ on clauses. Both simplifying and deletion inferences in saturation algorithms are designed in such a way that they only remove redundant clauses.

There is more than one saturation algorithm. For illustration we will use the *Otter saturation algorithm* [9], though AVATAR works equally well with other saturation algorithms. For an overview of saturation algorithms we refer to [15,9].

A simplified description of the Otter saturation algorithm is shown in Figure 1. The algorithms maintains three sets of clauses:

1. *active*: the set of clauses selected for generating inferences. The algorithm is designed in such a way that all generating inferences among active clauses are applied.
2. *passive*: clauses that are waiting to be activated. The Otter saturation algorithm uses passive clauses for simplifying and deletion inferences.
3. *unprocessed*: clauses that have been generated recently. Unprocessed clauses are waiting in a queue for a *retention test*, which normally includes simplification and deletion inferences applied to these clauses. If a clause C passes the retention test, this clause (or a clause obtained by simplifying C) is added to passive clauses, otherwise it is discarded.

At every step, the algorithm either processes a clause *new*, picked from unprocessed clauses, or performs generating inferences with the so-called *given clause*, which is the clause most recently added to *active*.

```
input: init: set of clauses;
var active, passive, unprocessed: set of clauses;
var given, new: clause;
active := ∅;
unprocessed := init;
loop
   while unprocessed ≠ ∅
      new := pop(unprocessed);
      if new = □ then return unsatisfiable;
      if retained(new) then                              (* retention test *)
         simplify new by clauses in active ∪ passive ;   (* forward simplification *)
         if new = □ then return unsatisfiable;
         if retained(new) then                           (* another retention test *)
            delete and simplify clauses in active and    (* backward simplification *)
                                passive using new;
            move the simplified clauses to unprocessed;
            add new to passive
   if passive = ∅ then return satisfiable or unknown
   given := select(passive);                             (* clause selection *)
   move given from passive to active;
   unprocessed := forward_infer(given, active);          (* forward generating inferences *)
   add backward_infer(given, active) to unprocessed;
                                                          (* backward generating inferences *)
```

Fig. 1. Otter Saturation Algorithm

All operations performed by the saturation algorithm that may take considerable time to execute, are normally implemented using *term indexing*, that is, building a special purpose index data structure that makes the operation faster. For example, all theorem provers with built-in equality reasoning have an index for forward demodulation (rewriting by ordered unit equalities from $active \cup passive$).

4   AVATAR

In this section we describe AVATAR and how it handles splitting. AVATAR consists of two components: a resolution (or resolution and superposition) theorem prover FO and a SAT solver SAT. Later we will consider how an SMT solver can be used in place of SAT. The SAT solver stores propositional clauses, which considered clause components as propositional literals. To consider them as propositional literals, we will use a mapping [·] from components to propositional literals. This mapping satisfies the following properties:

1. $[C]$ is a positive literal if and only if C is either a non-ground component or a positive ground literal;
2. For a negative ground component $\neg C$ we have $[\neg C] = \neg[C]$.
3. $[C_1] = [C_2]$ if and only if C_1 is equal to C_2 up to variable renaming and symmetry of equality.

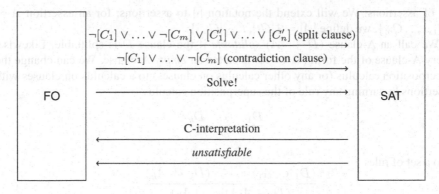

Fig. 2. Cooperation between the components of AVATAR

To implement this mapping, Vampire uses a *component index*, which maps every component C that is either positive or non-ground, into $[C]$. For every such component C passed to this index, if C is equal to an already stored component C' up to variable renaming and symmetry of equality, the index returns $[C']$, otherwise it introduces a new propositional variable $[C]$ and stores the association between C and $[C]$. We call a C-interpretation, or a *component interpretation* any set of propositional variables of the form $[C]$ or their negations, which does not contain both a variable and its negation. The definition of a truth of a propositional variable literal in a C-interpretation is standard. If, for a component C, neither $[C]$, not $\neg[C]$ belongs to the interpretation, $[C]$ is considered undefined, that is, neither true nor false.

During the proof search, FO and SAT exchange information. The information exchange is described in Figure 2.

In a nutshell, AVATAR works as follows. The superposition prover FO works as usual, using a saturation algorithm. The difference is in the treatment of splittable clauses. If there is a splittable clause $C_1 \vee \ldots \vee C_n$ with components $C_1, \ldots, C_n$, which passed the retention test, it is not added to *passive*. Instead, $[C_1] \vee \ldots \vee [C_n]$ it is passed to the SAT solver. The SAT solver adds the new clause to existing clauses and checks all clauses for satisfiability. If it is unsatisfiable, we are done. Otherwise, it computes a C-interpretation I, which is a model of all clauses stored in it. For each literal in the interpretation, if this literal has a form $[C]$ for some component C, the component C is passed to FO where it is used as an *assertion*. The exception are literals of the form $\neg[C]$, where C is a non-ground component, since such a literal does not correspond to any component.

To explain the cooperation in more detail, we should modify the superposition calculus to deal with these assertions. The description is similar, but not the same as in splitting with backtracking.

An *assertion* is a finite set of components. A *clause with assertions*, or simply an *A-clause* is a pair, consisting of a clause D and an assertion A. Such a clause with assertions will be denoted by $(D \leftarrow A)$, or simply D when the assertion A is empty. We will denote assertions by A and A-clauses as F. An A-clause $(D \leftarrow C_1, \ldots, C_m)$ is logically equivalent to $\forall D \vee \neg \forall C_1 \vee \ldots \vee \neg \forall C_m$ (or, equivalently, to $\forall C_1 \wedge \ldots \wedge \forall C_m \rightarrow \forall D$). A standard clause D can be considered as an A-clause with the empty set of assertions. We will extend the notation $[\cdot]$ to assertions: for an assertion $A = \{C_1, \ldots, C_m\}$, we define $[A] = \{[C_1], \ldots, [C_m]\}$.

We call an A-clause $(D \leftarrow A)$ *splittable* if the clause D is splittable. Likewise, every A-clause of the form $(\square \leftarrow A)$ is called an *empty* A-clause. We can change the superposition calculus (or any other calculus on clauses) to a calculus on clauses with assertions by turning any rule of the superposition calculus

$$\frac{D_1 \quad \cdots \quad D_k}{D}$$

into a set of rules

$$\frac{(D_1 \leftarrow A_1) \quad \cdots \quad (D_k \leftarrow A_k)}{(D \leftarrow A_1 \cup \ldots \cup A_k)} \;,$$

where $A_1, \ldots, A_k$ are assertions. Later we will explain how the addition of assertions affects simplification and deletion rules.

AVATAR uses A-clauses instead of ordinary clauses. At each time moment, the components used in assertions are those that are computed by the SAT solver as its last model. Since this model changes over time, clauses with assertions can be added and deleted.

We are now ready to describe the AVATAR algorithm. It is defined as a sequence of steps performed by the superposition prover FO and the SAT solver SAT. These steps are interleaved. Each step performed by the superposition prover is followed by a step by the SAT solver and vice versa. After each step performed by FO, some information is passed from it to SAT, as shown in Figure 2. Likewise, after each step performed by SAT, some information is passed from it to FO. These steps are described in detail in the next two sections.

5   The SAT Algorithm

We start with the SAT algorithm since it is simpler that the algorithm employed by FO. Essentially, the SAT solver is behaving like a standard incremental SAT solver. It receives, from time to time, new propositional clauses from FO and checks, upon a "solve" request, satisfiability of the clauses it stores. If they are satisfiable, it passes back to FO a C-interpretation satisfying all the propositional clauses. Otherwise, it returns *unsatisfiable*.

6   The FO Algorithm

In a nutshell, the FO algorithm behaves like a standard saturation algorithm. The main differences are that it operates on A-clauses and that splittable clauses are not stored. Instead, for each splittable or empty A-clause $(C_1 \vee \ldots \vee C_n \leftarrow C'_1, \ldots, C'_m)$, FO passes the propositional clause $[C_1] \vee \ldots \vee [C_n] \vee \neg[C'_1] \vee \ldots \vee \neg[C'_m]$ to SAT.

In reality, the FO algorithm is more sophisticated than standard saturation algorithms because of the way it treats simplified and deleted A-clauses. To illustrate the problem, consider an example. Suppose that we have two clauses D, D' such that D subsumes D'. If D and D' occur in the search space of a standard saturation algorithm, D' will be treated as redundant and can be deleted. In AVATAR, we deal with A-clauses. Suppose that A-clauses $(D \leftarrow A)$ and $(D' \leftarrow A')$ occur in the current search space and D subsumes D'. If $A \subseteq A'$, then $(D' \leftarrow A')$ can still be considered as redundant and deleted. If not, we can only delete it temporarily, since the model computed by the SAT solver can change and make a literal in $[A]$ false, while all the literals in $[A']$ remain true. In this case $(D \leftarrow A)$ will later be removed from the search space and, to preserve completeness, $(D' \leftarrow A')$ must then be undeleted.

For this reason we introduce a special storage for A-clauses that can be temporarily deleted and then undeleted. This storage will be denoted in the saturation algorithm as *locked*. Elements of *locked* are pairs (F, λ), where F is an A-clause and λ a set of C-literals. If $(F, \lambda) \in$ *locked*, we will informally call λ a *lock* of F. The same A-clause F can occur in *locked* with different locks.

We say that a C-interpretation I *unlocks* a pair $((C \leftarrow A), \lambda)$ if

1. all C-literals in $[A]$ are true in I;
2. at least one C-literal in λ is either false or undefined in A.

When a pair (F, λ) is added to *locked*, all of the literals in λ are true in the current model *int* computed by the SAT solver (this follows from a general invariant of the AVATAR algorithm: for every A-clause $(D \leftarrow A)$ in the search space, each literal in $[A]$ is true in this model). If one of the literals in λ later becomes false or undefined, the A-clause F must be unlocked by removing it from *locked* and adding it to the set of unprocessed clauses.

The FO algorithm is shown on Figure 3. Its parts that are specific to AVATAR are marked by ✓. Simplifications will be explained separately.

The AVATAR algorithm maintains, in addition to the sets *active*, *passive*, and *unprocessed*, the following collections.

- A C-interpretation *int* returned by the SAT solver. This interpretation makes the assertions of all stored clauses, apart from locked ones, true. We store this interpretation to maintain locking and unlocking operations. To check which clauses should be locked or unlocked, we compute, at each step, the difference between the current and the previous values of *int*.
- The set of A-clauses *sat_queue* waiting to be passed to the SAT solver. We store A-clauses in *sat_queue* instead of passing them immediately to the SAT solver because changes in the model found by the SAT solver can induce considerable changes in A-clauses and other data structures used by the saturation algorithm, so recomputing this model too often may result in the overall degradation of performance. The only exception is made when an empty A-clause is derived. In this case we recompute the interpretation immediately, since the new model *int* will make the given clause (and potentially many other stored clauses) locked or even deleted.
- The set *locked* of locked A-clauses with locks. A-clauses in this set are temporarily deleted, since for some components C in their assertions, $[C]$ can be false or undefined in the current C-interpretation *int*. However, they can be unlocked later.

input: *init*: set of clauses;
var *active, passive, unprocessed*: sets of A-clauses, initially empty;
var *given, new*: A-clauses;
√**var** *sat_queue*: set of A-clauses, initially empty;
√**var** *locked*: set of pairs (A-clause,lock), initially empty;
√**var** *int*: C-interpretation, initially empty;
  forall $D \in init$
√ **if** D is splittable or empty
√   **then** move it to *sat_queue*
    else move it to *unprocessed*
loop   (* *main loop* *)
√ **if** *sat_queue* $\neq \varnothing$ **then**
√   **forall** A-clauses $(C_1 \vee \ldots \vee C_n \leftarrow C'_1, \ldots, C'_m) \in sat\_queue$
√   pass the clause $[C_1] \vee \ldots \vee [C_n] \vee \neg[C'_1] \vee \ldots \vee \neg[C'_m]$ to **SAT**
√   *sat_queue* : =$\varnothing$;
√   send the request "solve" to **SAT**;
√   **if** SAT returns *unsatisfiable*, **then return** *unsatisfiable*;
√   *int* := the the C-interpretation returned by **SAT**
√   **forall** pairs $((C \leftarrow A), \lambda) \in locked$ unlocked by *int*
√   remove this pair from *locked* and add $(C \leftarrow A)$ it to *unprocessed*;
√   **forall** A-clauses $(C \leftarrow A)$ in the set *active, passive* or *unprocessed* such that $[A] \not\subseteq int$
√   remove $(C \leftarrow A)$ from this set and add $((C \leftarrow A), \varnothing)$ to *locked*;
√   **forall** components $[C] \in int$ such that $(C \leftarrow C) \notin active \cup passive \cup unprocessed$
      add $(C \leftarrow C)$ to *unprocessed*
    forall *new* $\in unprocessed$
√   **if** *new* is splittable or empty
√   **then** add *new* to *sat_queue*
      else if *retained*(*new*)   (* *retention test* *)
√   **then** simplify *new* by clauses in *active* $\cup$ *passive* ;   (* *forward simplification* *)
√   **if** *new* was added to *unprocessed*
√   (* *backward simplification* *)
              then simplify clauses in *active* $\cup$ *passive* by *new*
√ **if** *sat_queue* is non-empty, then start the main loop again;
  if *passive* $= \varnothing$ **then return** *satisfiable* or *unknown*;
  given := *select*(*passive*);   (* *clause selection* *)
  move *given* from *passive* to *active*;
  unprocessed :=*forward_infer*(*given, active*);   (* *forward generating inferences* *)
  add *backward_infer*(*given, active*) to *unprocessed*; (* *backward generating inferences* *)

Fig. 3. The FO Algorithm

7 Simplifications

We already gave a hint as to how simplifications are performed, when we discussed the use of locking and treatment of subsumed clauses.

Consider now simplification rules. All simplification rules in Vampire and other superposition provers have the following form:

if *new* is unconditionally deleted by A-clauses in *active* ∪ *passive*
    then do nothing
else if *new* is conditionally deleted by A-clauses in *active* ∪ *passive* with a lock λ
    then add (new, λ) to *locked*
else if *new* is unconditionally simplified by A-clauses in *active* ∪ *passive* into *new'*
    then add *new'* to *unprocessed*
else if *new* is conditionally simplified by A-clauses in *active* ∪ *passive* into *new'*
    with a lock λ
    then add *new'* to *unprocessed* ;
        add (new, λ) to *locked*

Fig. 4. Forward Simplification

$$\frac{D_1 \quad \cdots \quad D_m}{D} . \tag{1}$$

This means that D is a logical consequence of $D_1, \ldots, D_m$ and addition of D to the search space makes D_m redundant. There are three commonly used simplification rules: subsumption, subsumption resolution, and demodulation (rewriting by unit equalities). A inference on A-clauses corresponding to (1) is

$$\frac{(D_1 \leftarrow A_1) \quad \cdots \quad (D_m \leftarrow A_m)}{(D \leftarrow A)} ,$$

where $A = A_1 \cup \ldots \cup A_m$. If $A = A_m$, then $(D_m \leftarrow A_m)$ can be safely deleted. Otherwise, consider the assertion $A' = A - A_m$. At the moment this inference is performed, all literals in $[A]$ are true in the current C-interpretation *int*. However, there may be a moment in the future, when $[A_m]$ is still true, while some literals in $[A']$ false. In that case $(D_m \leftarrow A_m)$ must be put back in the search space. Thus, we lock $(D_m \leftarrow A_m)$ with the lock A'. Any change to *int*, which makes a C-literal in $[A']$ false will trigger unlocking of this A-clause.

To define simplifications formally, we introduce new notions. Suppose that a clause C can be simplified into a clause C' using clauses $C_1, \ldots, C_m$. Consider A-clauses $(C \leftarrow A)$ and $F_i = (C_i \leftarrow A_i)$ for $i = 1, \ldots, m$. Define $A' = A_1 \cup \ldots \cup A_m$. If $A' \subseteq A$, then we say that $(C \leftarrow A)$ is *unconditionally simplified by* $F_1, \ldots, F_m$ *into* $(C \leftarrow A)$. If $A' \nsubseteq A$, then we say that $(C \leftarrow A)$ is *conditionally simplified by* $F_1, \ldots, F_m$ *into* $(C \leftarrow A \cup A')$ *with the lock* $A' - A$. In a similar way we can define notions $(C \leftarrow A)$ *is unconditionally deleted by* $F_1, \ldots, F_m$ and $(C \leftarrow A)$ *is conditionally deleted by* $F_1, \ldots, F_m$ *with the lock* $A' - A$.

Forward simplification in AVATAR is shown in Figure 4. Backward simplification is similar and not included in this paper.

To avoid excessive locking and unlocking, it is desirable to have a SAT solver, which tries to return a model similar to the previously returned one. To this end, one can use the following simple rule: if a new A-clause passed to the SAT solver contains a C-literal $[C]$ undefined in the previous C-interpretation, we satisfy this clause by making $[C]$ true. Such A-clauses are common and appear when a new component is found. Using this rule also helps the SAT solver, since it does not have to be run at all when all recently added A-clauses have this property.

When all literals in a new A-clause passed to the SAT solver are false in the current C-interpretation int, this interpretation must change. For example, this always happens when we derive an empty A-clause ($\Box \leftarrow A$). *Phase saving* in SAT solvers introduced in [10] assigns to a propositional variable a value that was most recently assigned to it. Although we did not make experiments with various strategies in a SAT solver, phase saving seems to be useful for achieving a "small model difference" effect. We also use a data structure allowing one to find locked and unlocked clauses upon changes in the SAT solver model in time linear in the size of the number of found clauses plus the number of variables that changed their values.

8 Term Indexing

When we discuss the use of splitting in superposition theorem provers, it is very important to understand how the use of splitting affects other components of such provers. The efficiency and power of modern superposition theorem provers comes from two techniques: *redundancy elimination* (see [1] for the theory and [14] for the implementation aspects) and *term indexing* [18].

Even when simplifications are used, the search space can quickly grow to hundreds of thousands of clauses. To perform inferences on such a large search space efficiently, theorem provers maintain several indexes storing information about terms and clauses. These indexes make it easier to find candidates for inferences. In some cases inferences can be performed only by using the relevant index, without retrieving clauses used for these inferences. The number of different indexes in theorem provers varies and can be as many as about 10. Frequent insertions and deletions in an index can affect performance of a theorem prover. A typical example is when a theorem prover generates an equality $a = b$ between two constants and uses it to rewrite a into b. For nearly all indexing techniques used in the superposition theorem provers, every term and clause containing a must be removed from all indexes and a new term containing b inserted in them again. Doing this single simplification step on an indexed set with 100,000 clauses can take a very long time.

In AVATAR, clauses can be locked and then unlocked. This happens often when the number of clauses stored by the SAT solver grows and it recomputes its C-model int. Frequent deletions of a clause from all indexes it is stored in, followed by its insertion in these indexes, can be very expensive. There is an alternative to deleting locked clauses and information about them from indexes. If an A-clause is deleted or simplified conditionally, we do not remove it from indexes at all. Instead, we change index retrieval operations. For each successful retrieval operation we check if the result is a locked clause. If it is locked, we ignore the retrieved clause and the corresponding inference. This alternative is not yet implemented in Vampire and requires further experiments.

9   Experiments

For our experiments we reproduced the experiments from [7], where various versions of splitting were considered. In fact, AVATAR and some decisions made in it (such as treatment of locked literals in indexes and addition of negations of ground components) are due to what we learned from experiments [7]. We will not show all results from [7] but only consider the most relevant part, where we compare the performance of different versions of splitting. Note that such comparisons are very hard for the following reasons:

1. One cannot simply compare AVATAR to, say, splitting with backtracking, since the latter can be used with different options, giving very different results.
2. In general, a value of a strategy (a collection of parameter-value pairs) is hard to understand. Some strategies perform very well on the average but cannot solve problems unsolvable by other strategies. Modern theorem provers treat hard problems with a cocktail of strategies. For example, Vampire has a CASC mode [9] doing exactly that. A collection of strategies, each of which is bad on the average, can easily outperform a collection of strategies, each of which is good on the average. On the other hand, having too many strategies is not good, since running all of them may consume a considerable time, so strategies that solve many problems are useful as part of a collection: indeed, theorem provers are normally used with short time limits, so that one cannot afford running too many strategies on a problem.

New strategies are most useful if they solve many new problems, and especially with short running times. In this case they can be used to create more powerful cocktails than those used before.

Our experiments have shown that AVATAR shows outstanding results both in terms of its average performance and in the number of problems that it can solve and that were previously unsolvable by any existing prover.

For benchmarking we used unsatisfiable TPTP problems having non-unit clauses and rating greater than 0.2 and less than 1. Essentially, the rating is the percentage of existing provers that cannot solve a problem. For example, rating greater than 0.2 means that less than 80% of existing theorem provers can solve the problem. Likewise, rating 1 means that the problem cannot be solved by the existing provers. However, the rating evaluation uses a single mode of every prover, so it is possible that the same prover can solve a problem of rating 1 using a different mode. For this reason, we also added problems of rating 1 that are solvable by some version of Vampire. We excluded very large problems since for them it was preprocessing, but not other options, that affects results the most. This resulted in selecting 6892 TPTP problems for our experiments.

To conduct our experiments, we took a Vampire strategy that is believed to be nearly the best in the overall number of solved problems, and generated the 481 variations of this strategy obtained by setting the splitting parameters to all possible values described in [7]. In addition, we used a single run of this strategy using AVATAR.

Only 5,273 (about 77% of all problems) were solved by at least one splitting strategy. The results are summarised in Table 1. They show that AVATAR is very robust, resulting in a considerable increase of the number of solved problems over the best strategies using other versions of splitting.

Table 1. Problems solved by each setting of the splitting strategy

splitting	strategies	worst	average	best
off	25	3833	3869	3880
backtracking	64	2538	3889	4381
non-backtracking	416	2489	3595	4126
AVATAR	1	4716	4716	4716

The second series of experiments was run on our cluster of 45 servers. Each server has 16G RAM and 4 cores. We used 3 cores on each server since we observed that using all 4 often results in the operating system putting two instances of Vampire on the same core. This results in 135 instances on Vampire running in parallel. The experiments were run for over 6 months in 2012–2013. The aim of this series of experiments was to solve as many TPTP problems overall as possible; and its results were used to configure Vampire for the last CASC competition CASC-24. Eventually, Vampire with AVATAR was able to solve 421 problems unsolvable by Vampire without AVATAR and by any other prover. To get the results of other provers, we used the file ProblemAndSolutionStatistics shipped with TPTP, which records results on every TPTP problem by nearly all theorem provers in the recent history. On the contrary, Vampire using splitting with and without backtracking was able to solve only 17 problems unsolvable by any strategy using AVATAR. Solving over 400 previously unsolvable problems is a remarkable result since such all these problems are very hard. In the past, the implementation of various novelties in Vampire would normally result in solving from a few to about 30 previously unsolvable problems.

The experimental results were so successful that all previously implemented code for handling splitting was completely removed from the latest versions of Vampire, resulting in considerable simplifications in its code and better maintainability.

10   Using an SMT Solver or Other Theory Solvers

Another interesting feature of AVATAR is that for a combination of first-order logic with theories one can use any theory solver instead of a SAT solver. In particular, for problems with equality one can use an SMT solver for logic with equality and uninterpreted functions. Non-ground components are then treated in the SMT solver as before, as propositional variables. Ground components can be used by the SMT solver as theory literals. We added to Vampire a very simple SMT solver for logic with equality and uninterpreted functions. This addition allowed us to solve some TPTP problems previously unsolved by any prover, including Vampire using AVATAR and a SAT solver.

The SAT and the SMT solvers implemented in Vampire are very simple and much weaker than best SAT and SMT solvers. It will be interesting to see how the use of better SAT and SMT solvers affects the performance of AVATAR.

There is an interesting option that can be used for logic with equality and maybe other theories. Instead of passing back to FO a propositional model, an SMT solver can pass some canonical representation of the congruence relation computed by it. Also, the SMT solver can use ground (and maybe also non-ground) unit equalities produced by the superposition prover. We leave these extensions as future work.

11   Related Work

The author believes that proving theorems with both quantifiers and theories is the main problem in modern first-order theorem proving. In particular, it is crucial for applications of theorem provers in program analysis and also in interactive theorem provers. AVATAR offers an architecture different from those proposed in first-order theorem provers able to handle theories, including SPASS+T [2,11], Z3 [5], CVC4 [3], Princess [16] and Beagle [4].

This paper was motivated by our analysis of the results [7], which contains an extensive discussion of splitting in superposition theorem provers. In particular, it uses splitting in various forms and SAT solvers, but not in the way discussed in this paper. Earlier work on splitting includes [20] and [13].

Paper [6] describes a calculus DPLL(Γ) using a superposition prover together with a SAT or an SMT solver (Z3) in a way similar to AVATAR. Ground literals decided and implied by the SAT solver were used as hypotheses to first-order clauses. Our approach is different in several aspects:

1. We use arbitrary components, while DPLL(Γ) uses only ground literals;
2. We consider the SAT solver as a black box producing models, while in DPLL(Γ) the SAT solver and the superposition prover architectures and calculi are mutually dependent. The backjump rule and locking (disabling) first-order clauses in DPLL(Γ) essentially uses decision levels of the SAT solvers. The use of decision levels makes DPLL(Γ) is very similar to splitting with backtracking, though with some improvements due to the use of a SAT solver.

Also, [6] discuss very different benchmarks, where theory reasoning and E-matching are often required to solve problems.

12   Conclusion

We described a new architecture AVATAR for first-order theorem provers. In this architecture, splitting in a theorem prover is driven by a SAT (or an SMT) solver. When the input problem is ground, AVATAR is as efficient as a SAT solver (or an SMT solver for logic with equality). On non-ground problems, an implementation of AVATAR in Vampire outperforms the previous versions of Vampire by a very large margin. In particular, using AVATAR allowed us to solve 421 TPTP problems previously unsolvable by any first-order theorem prover.

We believe that AVATAR will become a standard architecture for future first-order theorem provers and can be especially successful in reasoning with both quantifiers and theories. It turned out to be effective in passing information from a first-order theorem prover to a SAT or an SMT solver. Nonetheless, AVATAR does not solve the reverse problem: passing information from an SMT solver to the first-order prover, which is currently done by other approaches, such as E-matching.

Acknowledgments. We thank Krystof Hoder, who implemented the first version of AVATAR, Giles Reger, Laura Kovács and Martin Suda for discussions and reading preliminary versions of this paper.

References

1. Bachmair, L., Ganzinger, H.: Resolution theorem proving. In: Robinson, A., Voronkov, A. (eds.) Handbook of Automated Reasoning. ch. 2, vol. I, pp. 19–99. Elsevier Science (2001)
2. Bachmair, L., Ganzinger, H., Waldmann, U.: Refutational theorem proving for hierarchic first-order theories. Appl. Algebra Eng. Commun. Comput. 5, 193–212 (1994)
3. Barrett, C., Conway, C.L., Deters, M., Hadarean, L., Jovanović, D., King, T., Reynolds, A., Tinelli, C.: CVC4. In: Gopalakrishnan, G., Qadeer, S. (eds.) CAV 2011. LNCS, vol. 6806, pp. 171–177. Springer, Heidelberg (2011)
4. Baumgartner, P., Waldmann, U.: Hierarchic Superposition with Weak Abstraction. In: Bonacina, M.P. (ed.) CADE 2013. LNCS, vol. 7898, pp. 39–57. Springer, Heidelberg (2013)
5. de Moura, L., Bjørner, N.S.: Z3: An Efficient SMT Solver. In: Ramakrishnan, C.R., Rehof, J. (eds.) TACAS 2008. LNCS, vol. 4963, pp. 337–340. Springer, Heidelberg (2008)
6. de Moura, L., Bjørner, N.S.: Engineering DPLL(T) + saturation. In: Armando, A., Baumgartner, P., Dowek, G. (eds.) IJCAR 2008. LNCS (LNAI), vol. 5195, pp. 475–490. Springer, Heidelberg (2008)
7. Hoder, K., Voronkov, A.: The 481 ways to split a clause and deal with propositional variables. In: Bonacina, M.P. (ed.) CADE 2013. LNCS, vol. 7898, pp. 450–464. Springer, Heidelberg (2013)
8. Korovin, K.: iProver—an instantiation-based theorem prover for first-order logic (system description). In: Armando, A., Baumgartner, P., Dowek, G. (eds.) IJCAR 2008. LNCS (LNAI), vol. 5195, pp. 292–298. Springer, Heidelberg (2008)
9. Kovács, L., Voronkov, A.: First-order theorem proving and vampire. In: Sharygina, N., Veith, H. (eds.) CAV 2013. LNCS, vol. 8044, pp. 1–35. Springer, Heidelberg (2013)
10. Pipatsrisawat, K., Darwiche, A.: A lightweight component caching scheme for satisfiability solvers. In: Marques-Silva, J., Sakallah, K.A. (eds.) SAT 2007. LNCS, vol. 4501, pp. 294–299. Springer, Heidelberg (2007)
11. Prevosto, V., Waldmann, U.: SPASS+T. In: Proc. of ESCoR, pp. 18–33 (2006)
12. Riazanov, A., Voronkov, A.: Splitting without backtracking. In: Nebel, B. (ed.) 17th International Joint Conference on Artificial Intelligence, IJCAI 2001, vol. 1, pp. 611–617 (2001)
13. Riazanov, A., Voronkov, A.: The design and implementation of Vampire. AI Commun. 15(2,3), 91–110 (2002)
14. Riazanov, A., Voronkov, A.: Limited resource strategy in resolution theorem proving. Journal of Symbolic Computations 36(1-2), 101–115 (2003)
15. Riazanov, A., Voronkov, A.: Limited resource strategy in resolution theorem proving. Journal of Symbolic Computations 36(1-2), 101–115 (2003)
16. Rümmer, P.: E-Matching with Free Variables. In: Bjørner, N., Voronkov, A. (eds.) LPAR-18. LNCS, vol. 7180, pp. 359–374. Springer, Heidelberg (2012)
17. Schulz, S.: E – a brainiac theorem prover. Journal of AI Communications 15(2-3), 111–126 (2002)
18. Sekar, R., Ramakrishnan, I.V., Voronkov, A.: Term indexing. In: Robinson, A., Voronkov, A. (eds.) Handbook of Automated Reasoning. ch. 26, vol. II, pp. 1853–1964. Elsevier Science (2001)
19. Sutcliffe, G.: TPTP, TSTP, CASC, etc. In: Diekert, V., Volkov, M.V., Voronkov, A. (eds.) CSR 2007. LNCS, vol. 4649, pp. 6–22. Springer, Heidelberg (2007)
20. Weidenbach, C.: Combining superposition, sorts and splitting. In: Robinson, A., Voronkov, A. (eds.) Handbook of Automated Reasoning. ch. 27, vol. II, pp. 1965–2013. Elsevier Science (2001)

Automating Separation Logic with Trees and Data

Ruzica Piskac[1], Thomas Wies[2,*], and Damien Zufferey[3,**]

1 Yale University
2 New York University
3 MIT CSAIL

Abstract. Separation logic (SL) is a widely used formalism for verifying heap manipulating programs. Existing SL solvers focus on decidable fragments for list-like structures. More complex data structures such as trees are typically unsupported in implementations, or handled by incomplete heuristics. While complete decision procedures for reasoning about trees have been proposed, these procedures suffer from high complexity, or make global assumptions about the heap that contradict the separation logic philosophy of local reasoning. In this paper, we present a fragment of classical first-order logic for local reasoning about tree-like data structures. The logic is decidable in NP and the decision procedure allows for combinations with other decidable first-order theories for reasoning about data. Such extensions are essential for proving functional correctness properties. We have implemented our decision procedure and, building on earlier work on translating SL proof obligations into classical logic, integrated it into an SL-based verification tool. We successfully used the tool to verify functional correctness of tree-based data structure implementations.

1 Introduction

Separation logic (SL) [30] has proved useful for building scalable verification tools for heap-manipulating programs that put no or very little annotation burden on the user [2,5,6,12,15,40]. The high degree of automation of these tools relies on solvers for checking entailments between SL assertions. Typically, the focus is on decidable fragments such as separation logic of linked lists [4] for which entailment can be checked efficiently [10, 31]. Although there exist expressive decidable SL fragments that support complex data structures such as trees [18], these fragments have very high complexity. Therefore, reasoning about tree data structures is mostly unsupported in actual implementations, or handled by incomplete heuristics [29, 35]. This raises the question whether a practical and complete entailment procedure for SL of trees can be realized.

Contributions. In this paper, we give a positive answer to this question. Our solution builds on our earlier work on reducing entailment checking in separation logic to satisfiability checking in classical first-order logic [32]. Our main technical contribution therefore lies in the identification of a fragment of first-order logic that (1) supports reasoning about mutable tree data structures; (2) is sufficiently expressive to serve as

---

* Supported in part by NSF grant CCS-1320583.
** Supported by DARPA (Grant FA8650-11-C-7192).

A. Biere and R. Bloem (Eds.): CAV 2014, LNCS 8559, pp. 711–728, 2014.

a target of our SL reduction; and (3) is decidable in NP. We call this logic GRIT (for Graph Reachability and Inverted Trees). The decision procedure for GRIT exploits locality of an axiomatic encoding of the logic's underlying theory and reduces satisfiability of GRIT formulas to satisfiability in effectively propositional logic (EPR). The latter is automated using an SMT solver. One advantage of this approach is that it allows for combinations with other decidable first-order theories. We therefore study several decidable extensions of our basic logic that utilize such combinations to support reasoning about data values stored in trees (e.g., sortedness constraints).

We have implemented our decision procedure on top of the SMT solver Z3 [11] and integrated it into our SL-based verification tool GRASShopper [33]. We successfully used the tool to automatically verify memory safety and consistency properties of tree-based data structures such as skew heaps and binary search trees. We have further used the tool to verify functional correctness of a tree-based set data structure and a union-find data structure. Proving such strong functional correctness properties often requires user-provided hints in the form of intermediate lemmas. However, GRASShopper can verify them completely automatically.

Related Work. The decision procedure for the target logic of our SL reduction draws ideas from the efficient SMT-based techniques for reasoning about reachability in function graphs [19, 23, 36, 38]. These techniques can be generalized to logics of trees [39] by viewing trees as inverted lists [3]. We make three important improvements over [39]. First, our logic does not make the global assumption that the entire heap forms a forest. This is important because such global assumptions contradict the philosophy of separation logic, where assertions express properties of heap regions rather than the entire heap. In particular, such assumptions preclude the encoding of the frame rule, which is crucial for enabling compositional program verification using separation logic. Second, we greatly simplify the decision procedure presented in [39]. This simplification turns a decision procedure that is mostly of theoretical interest into a procedure that is efficiently implementable. Finally, we consider extensions for reasoning about data.

Most other known decidable logics for reasoning about trees rely on monadic second-order logic (MSOL) [22, 37]. However, the high complexity of MSOL over trees limits its usefulness in verification. There exist some other expressive logics that support reachability in trees with lower complexity [8, 13, 17, 41]. All these logics are still at least in EXPTIME, and their decision procedures are given in terms of automata-theoretic techniques, tableaux procedures, or small model properties. These can be difficult to combine efficiently with SMT solvers. One exception is the STRAND logic [26], which combines MSOL over trees with a data logic. There exists an implementation of a decision procedure for a decidable fragment of STRAND, which integrates MONA and an SMT solver. While the complexity of this procedure is at least double exponential, it has shown to be practically efficient [27]. However, similar to the logic in [39], STRAND makes global assumptions about the structure of the heap and is therefore inappropriate for an encoding of separation logic. Another orthogonal logic for reasoning about heap structures and data is described in [7]. This logic is incomparable to GRIT because it supports nested list structures but not trees, while GRIT supports trees but no nested structures.

Other tools that have been used for proving functional correctness of linked data structure implementations include Bedrock [9], Dafny [24], Jahob [42], HIP/SLEEK

```
1   struct Node { var d: int; var l, r: Node; ghost var p: Node; }
2
3   procedure extract_max(rt, ghost pr: Node, implicit ghost C: set[int]) returns (nrt, max: Node)
4     requires bst(rt, pr, C) * rt ≠ null;
5     ensures bst(nrt, pr, C \ {max.d}) * acc(max);
6     ensures max.r = null ∧ max.p = null ∧ max.d ∈ C ∧ (∀z ∈ (C \ {max.d})). z < max.d);
7   {
8     var c, m: Node;
9     if (rt.r != null) {
10      c, m := extract_max(rt.r, rt);
11      rt.r := c;
12      return rt, m;
13    } else {
14      c := rt.l; rt.p := null;
15      if (c != null) c.p := pr;
16      return c, rt;
17  } }
```

Fig. 1. Extracting the node with the maximal value from a sorted binary search tree

[29], and VeriFast [21]. While these tools can handle more programs and properties than GRASShopper supports, they also require more user guidance, either in the form of annotated ghost state or lemmas for discharging intermediate proof obligations.

Static shape analysis tools such as Forester [2] can automatically infer data structure invariants, e.g., that a specific reference points to a sorted tree. However, they only infer restricted properties about data stored in the heap and can usually not verify full functional correctness of data structure implementations.

2   Motivating Example and Overview

We motivate our approach through an example of a procedure that extracts the node storing the maximal value from a sorted binary search tree. The procedure and its specification are shown in Figure 1.

Specification. The extract_max procedure takes as argument the root of a binary search tree. The tree represents a set of integer values C, which is declared as an additional ghost parameter of the procedure. The precondition of the procedure, denoted by the **requires** clause, is an SL assertion that relates the two parameters using the inductive predicate bst(rt,pr,C). This predicate describes a heap region that forms a sorted binary search tree with root rt, parent node pr, and that stores the set of values C. We call the heap nodes in the region that are described by an SL assertion the *footprint* of the assertion. Note that the contract of extract_max provides the implicit guarantee that the procedure does not modify any allocated heap nodes that are outside of the footprint of its precondition.

The predicate bst is defined as follows:

$$\mathsf{bst}(x, y, C) \equiv x = \mathsf{null} \wedge C = \varnothing \vee (\exists DE.\, \mathsf{acc}(x) * \mathsf{bst}(x.\mathsf{l}, x, D) * \mathsf{bst}(x.\mathsf{r}, x, E) *$$
$$x.\mathsf{p} = y * C = \{x.\mathsf{d}\} \cup D \cup E * \forall u \in D.\, u < x.\mathsf{d} * \forall u \in E.\, u > x.\mathsf{d})$$

The atomic predicate acc(x) in the definition of bst represents a heap region that consists of the single heap node x. That is, acc(x) means that x is in the footprint of the predicate.

Such SL assertions are combined to assertions describing larger heap regions using *spatial conjunction*, denoted by '*'. Spatial conjunction asserts that the composed heap regions are disjoint in memory. Hence, bst describes an actual tree and not a DAG. Note that atomic assertions such as x = null only express constraints on values but describe empty heap regions.

The procedure extract_max returns a pair of nodes (nrt, max) where nrt is the new root of the remaining tree, and max the node that has been removed. The postcondition, denoted by the ensures clauses, states that the procedure indeed yields the modified tree with the maximal node max properly removed.

One important detail in the contract of extract_max is the keyword implicit in the declaration of the ghost variable C. This annotation means that C is existentially quantified across the procedure contract. That is, we do not need to explicitly provide the actual value of C at call sites to extract_max, such as the recursive call on line 10. Instead, the verifier will automatically infer the existence of the actual value and use it when assuming the postcondition. This is in contrast to most other automated verification systems, which do not support implicit ghost parameters. However, to make our approach for reasoning about trees work, we do require the program to be annotated with ghost parent pointers. These must be updated along with the forward pointers that span the trees. We argue in the companion report [34] that in many cases these annotations with ghost parent pointers can be inferred automatically using simple heuristics.

Verification. The actual verification of extract_max involves a sequence of transformations that progressively make the semantics of separation logic explicit until we obtain a program in which all contracts are expressed in GRIT. The logic is closed under verification condition (VC) generation, and the generated VCs are then discharged using the decision procedure that we present in Sec. 5. The transformation includes the translation of SL assertions into first-order logic, the encoding of the semantics of SL Hoare triples by making the footprints of procedure contracts explicit, the insertion of checks for memory safety and absence of memory leaks, etc. The details of these transformations are described in our previous work [32, 33]. In the following, we only provide an abridged summary.

GRIT. The GRIT logic can express properties of sets of heap nodes using set operations and certain forms of set comprehensions. The logic further provides predicates that describe the structure of the heap. For example, the GRIT predicate $\text{Tree}(S, x, y, l, r, p)$ expresses that the heap region described by the set S forms a tree with root x, parent node y, left pointer field l, right pointer field r, and parent pointer field p. Another important predicate is the *reachability predicate* $\text{R}(f, x, y)$, which expresses that x can reach y by following the pointer field f in the heap. The logic also provides special constructs for expressing updates of pointer fields and frame conditions of procedure calls. Specifically, the *frame predicate* $\text{Frame}(S, F, f, f')$ expresses that the values of the pointer fields f and f' agree on the heap nodes in the set $S \backslash F$.

Reduction to GRIT. We next explain how we reduce the problem of checking verification conditions with SL assertions to checking satisfiability of GRIT formulas. To this end, consider the path of extract_max that goes through the "then" branch of the conditional on line 9 to the return point on line 12. Our goal is to check that the postcondition

$$S = S_1 \cup S_2 \wedge S_1 = \{x. \, \mathsf{R}(\mathsf{p}, x, \mathsf{rt})\} \wedge S_2 = \varnothing \wedge \qquad \text{footprint of precondition}$$
$$\mathsf{Tree}(S_1, \mathsf{rt}, \mathsf{pr}, \mathsf{l}, \mathsf{r}, \mathsf{p}) \wedge \mathsf{rt} \neq \mathsf{null} \wedge S_1 \cap S_2 = \varnothing \wedge \qquad \text{precondition}$$
$$\mathsf{rt.r} \neq \mathsf{null} \wedge \qquad \text{line 9}$$
$$F = F_1 \cup F_2 \wedge F_1 = \{x. \, \mathsf{R}(\mathsf{p}, x, \mathsf{rt.r})\} \wedge F_2 = \varnothing \wedge \qquad \text{initial footprint of rec. call}$$
$$F = F_1' \cup F_2' \wedge F_1' = \{x. \, \mathsf{R}(\mathsf{p}_1, x, \mathsf{c})\} \wedge F_2' = \{\mathsf{m}\} \wedge \qquad \text{final footprint of rec. call}$$
$$\mathsf{Tree}(F_1, \mathsf{c}, \mathsf{rt}, \mathsf{l}_1, \mathsf{r}_1, \mathsf{p}_1) \wedge \mathsf{m.r}_1 = \mathsf{m.p}_1 = \mathsf{null} \wedge F_1' \cap F_2' = \varnothing \wedge \qquad \text{postcondition of rec. call}$$
$$\mathsf{Frame}(S, F, \mathsf{l}, \mathsf{l}_1) \wedge \mathsf{Frame}(S, F, \mathsf{r}, \mathsf{r}_1) \wedge \mathsf{Frame}(S, F, \mathsf{p}, \mathsf{p}_1) \wedge \qquad \text{frame condition of rec. call}$$
$$\mathsf{r}_2 = \mathsf{write}(\mathsf{r}_1, \mathsf{rt}, \mathsf{c}) \wedge \qquad \text{line 11}$$
$$\mathsf{nrt} = \mathsf{rt} \wedge \mathsf{max} = \mathsf{m} \wedge \qquad \text{line 12}$$
$$S' = S_1' \cup S_2' \wedge S_1' = \{x. \, \mathsf{R}(\mathsf{p}_2, x, \mathsf{nrt})\} \wedge S_2' = \{\mathsf{max}\} \wedge \qquad \text{footprint of postcondition}$$
$$\neg (\mathsf{Tree}(S_1', \mathsf{nrt}, \mathsf{pr}, \mathsf{l}_1, \mathsf{r}_2, \mathsf{p}_2) \wedge \mathsf{max.p}_2 = \mathsf{null} \wedge \mathsf{max.r}_2 = \mathsf{null} \wedge \qquad \text{negated postcondition}$$
$$S_1' \cap S_2' = \varnothing \wedge S' = S)$$

Fig. 2. Verification condition for a path of extract_max with simplified pre and postconditions

of extract_max holds after this path has been executed, assuming the precondition holds initially. For exposition purposes, we consider the simplified precondition tree(rt,pr) $*$ rt $\neq$ null and the simplified postcondition

$$\mathsf{tree}(\mathsf{nrt}, \mathsf{pr}) * \mathsf{acc}(\mathsf{max}) * (\mathsf{max.r} = \mathsf{null} \wedge \mathsf{max.p} = \mathsf{null})$$

That is, we abstract from the data values by defining the predicate tree as follows:

$$\mathsf{tree}(x, y) \equiv x = \mathsf{null} \vee \mathsf{acc}(x) * \mathsf{tree}(x.\mathsf{l}, x) * \mathsf{tree}(x.\mathsf{r}, x) * x.\mathsf{p} = y$$

The VC that is obtained from the simplified contract of extract_max and the considered path reduces to the GRIT formula shown in Fig. 2. This formula is unsatisfiable and thus the obtained VC is valid. We next explain this GRIT formula in more detail.

Translation of SL Assertions. The reduction to GRIT translates each SL assertion into a conjunction of two GRIT formulas: one formula that describes the footprint of the SL assertion, and another formula that describes the structure of the heap region captured by the assertion. The generation of the footprint formula proceeds recursively on the structure of the SL assertion, introducing auxiliary set variables to represent the footprints of all spatial conjuncts. These auxiliary set variables are implicitly existentially quantified, capturing the semantics of spatial conjunction. For example, in Fig. 2, the footprint of the precondition is described by the set S, which is itself the disjoint union of the sets S_1 and S_2. Here, S_1 represents the actual footprint of the tree rooted in rt. The variable S_1 is defined as the set of all nodes that can reach rt via the parent field p. S_2 is the footprint of the SL assertion rt $\neq$ null. Note that the defining formula for the footprint S' of the negated postcondition is pulled over the negation. Yet, we do not introduce universal quantifiers for the set variables S_1' and S_2' in the negated postcondition. The dualization of the universal quantifiers for the auxiliary set variables is possible because these variables are uniquely defined by the translated SL assertions. We refer the reader to the companion tech report [34] for the details of how to translate SL assertions with tree predicates to GRIT.

Implicit Frame Inference. The recursive call to extract_max on line 10 is handled by assuming the translated postcondition of the call and the defining formula of the footprint F of the call's precondition. The latter is used to express the call's frame condition using the predicate Frame. Note that the actual frame $S \backslash F$, i.e., the set of heap nodes that are not touched by the recursive call, is automatically inferred by the decision procedure of GRIT from the defining formulas of the footprint sets S and F.

3   Graph Reachability and Stratified Sets

Our reduction of separation logic to first-order logic decomposes SL assertions into constraints on the shape of the heap and constraints on the footprint sets. The crux in this translation is the handling of inductive predicates such as bst and tree. To avoid the need for reasoning about induction, both the shape constraints and the footprint sets are expressed in terms of reachability over pointer fields in the heap. To support such an encoding, we define a first-order logic of *graph reachability and stratified sets* (GRASS). This logic can express structural properties of mutable finite graphs as well as sets of nodes in these graphs. The general GRASS logic is undecidable. The logic GRIT, which we formally introduce in the next section, then imposes syntactic restrictions on GRASS that will ensure decidability while being sufficiently expressive to serve as a target for our reduction of separation logic over trees.

We follow standard notation and conventions for syntax and semantics of many-sorted first-order logic with equality. The signature of the GRASS logic is $\Sigma_{GS} = (S_{GS}, \Omega_{GS}, \Pi_{GS})$ where $S_{GS} = \{\text{node}, \text{field}, \text{set}\}$ is the set of sorts. The set of function symbols Ω_{GS} consists of the symbols null : node, read : field × node → node, write : field × node × node → field, and a countable infinite set of constant symbols for each sort in S_{GS}. The constant symbol null is a dedicated constant symbol of sort node that we use to represent null pointers. The set of predicate symbols Π_{GS} consists of the symbols B : field × node × node × node and $\in$: node × set. The GRASS logic then comprises all first-order formulas over the signature Σ_{GS}.

We define the semantics of GRASS formulas with respect to a theory $\mathcal{T}_{GS}$ of first-order structures over Σ_{GS}. A structure $\mathcal{A}$ is in $\mathcal{T}_{GS}$ iff the following conditions are satisfied. First, $\mathcal{A}$ interprets the sort node by a finite set node$^{\mathcal{A}}$. The interpretation of the remaining sorts and symbols, with the exception of constant symbols, is then uniquely determined by the interpretation of node$^{\mathcal{A}}$ as follows. First, the sort field is interpreted by the set of all functions in node$^{\mathcal{A}} \to$ node$^{\mathcal{A}}$, and the sort set by the set of all subsets of node$^{\mathcal{A}}$. We consider the elements of node$^{\mathcal{A}}$ to represent nodes in a heap graph and the elements of field$^{\mathcal{A}}$ pointer fields. The function symbols read and write represent field look-up and field update. They must satisfy the following properties

$$\forall u \in \text{node}^{\mathcal{A}}, f \in \text{field}^{\mathcal{A}}. \ \text{read}^{\mathcal{A}}(f, u) = (\text{if } u = \text{null}^{\mathcal{A}} \text{ then } u \text{ else } f(u)) \quad \text{and}$$

$$\forall u, v \in \text{node}^{\mathcal{A}}, f \in \text{field}^{\mathcal{A}}. \ \text{write}^{\mathcal{A}}(f, u, v) = \lambda w \in \text{node}^{\mathcal{A}}. \text{ if } w = u \text{ then } v \text{ else } f_{\mathcal{A}}(w)$$

The *between predicate* $B(f, x, y, z)$ denotes that x reaches z via an f-path that must go though y. To formally define the semantics of B, we note that for a binary relation r over a set X (respectively, a unary function $r : X \to X$), we denote by r^* the reflexive transitive closure of r. Furthermore, for $f \in \text{field}^{\mathcal{A}}$ we define $f_{\mathcal{A}} = \lambda u \in \text{node}^{\mathcal{A}}. \text{read}^{\mathcal{A}}(f, u)$. Then for all $u, v, w \in \text{node}^{\mathcal{A}}$ and $f \in \text{field}^{\mathcal{A}}$ we require

$$B^{\mathcal{A}}(f, u, v, w) \Leftrightarrow (u, w) \in f_{\mathcal{A}}^* \wedge (u, v) \in \{(u_1, f_{\mathcal{A}}(u_1)) \mid u_1 \in \text{node}^{\mathcal{A}} \wedge u_1 \neq w\}^*$$

x : node variable, t : node constant, S : set constant,   Fld $\in \{P, L, R\}$, $f \in$ Fld
$T ::= x \mid t \mid \text{null} \mid \text{read}(f, T)$ $\qquad\qquad\qquad\qquad\qquad$ $T_{\text{Fld}} ::= f \mid \text{write}(T_{\text{Fld}}, T, T)$
$A ::= T = T \mid T_{\text{Fld}} = T_{\text{Fld}} \mid \text{B}(T_P, T, T, T) \mid T \in S$ $\qquad$ $R ::= A \mid \neg R \mid R \wedge R$
$F_\forall ::= \forall x.R$ where the variables x do not occur below read or write in R
$F ::= A \mid F_\forall \mid \text{Tree}(S, T, T_L, T_R, T_P) \mid \text{Frame}(S, S, T_{\text{Fld}}, T_{\text{Fld}}) \mid \neg F \mid F \wedge F$

Fig. 3. Logic of graph reachability and inverted trees (GRIT)

The second conjunct states that u reaches v without going through w. Finally, the interpretation of the set membership relation $\in$ in $\mathcal{A}$ is as expected. We define the reachability predicate $\text{R}(f, x, y)$ as a short-hand for $\text{B}(f, x, y, y)$.

4 The GRIT Logic

We now introduce the logic of graph reachability and inverted trees (GRIT). In our formal treatment, we restrict ourselves to the case of binary trees. However, the logic and decision procedure can be easily generalized to trees of arbitrary bounded rank. We do not discuss the case of unranked trees. Surprisingly, the treatment of unranked trees is much simpler than the bounded case.

Syntax. Figure 3 defines the syntax of GRIT formulas. A GRIT formula F is a Boolean combination of atomic formulas A, restricted quantified formulas $F_\forall$, tree predicates $\text{Tree}(S, t, l, r, p)$, and frame predicates $\text{Frame}(A, S, f, f')$. The atomic formulas A form a subset of the atomic formulas of GRASS. Namely, we partition the constant symbols of sort field into three disjoint sets: a set of parent fields P, a set of left successor fields L, and a set of right successor fields R. Equalities between terms of sort field are then restricted to terms that are built from field constants in the same partition. To ensure decidability of the logic, we do not allow quantification over formulas that contain terms in which node variables appear below the function symbols read and write, as in $\text{read}(p, x)$. Also, we restrict the reachability predicate B to parent fields. This restriction yields a much simpler and more practical decision procedure compared to the logic proposed in [39]. We assume that all GRIT formulas are closed.

Syntactic Short-Hands. Throughout the remainder of the paper, we will use syntactic short-hands for disjunction, implication, bi-implication, and existential quantification in GRIT formulas. Further note that we can express standard set operations such as union and intersection using restricted quantified GRIT formulas and fresh auxiliary set constants. For example, the formula $t \notin S \cup T$ stands for the GRIT formula

$$\neg(t \in S_1) \wedge \forall x. x \in S_1 \Leftrightarrow x \in S \vee x \in T$$

where S_1 is a fresh set constant. Set equality, subset inclusion, and set comprehensions can be expressed similarly. To ease the notation, we will use the expected syntactic short-hands for such encodings. Finally, we write $t.f$ to mean $\text{read}(f, t)$.

Semantics. GRIT formulas are interpreted in the models of the theory $\mathcal{T}_{GS}$, which we have defined in the previous section. Thus, we only need to provide the semantics of the predicates Tree and Frame. We define the semantics of these predicates in terms of formulas in our general graph reachability logic with stratified sets. The defining formulas are chosen in such a way that we obtain a simple and efficient decision procedure by first expanding the predicates with their defining formulas and then applying quantifier instantiation techniques. In the following, let $\mathcal{A}$ be a structure in $\mathcal{T}_{GS}$.

As we have seen in Sec. 2, the tree predicate is crucial for the translation of SL tree predicates such as tree. A tree predicate Tree(S, t, l, r, p) holds true in $\mathcal{A}$ if $\mathcal{A}$ contains a tree with footprint S, root t, spanned by the given fields l, r, and p. Our formal definition of Tree, which we provide below, uses the reachability predicates to give a noninductive definition of trees. Formally, $\mathcal{A}$ satisfies Tree(S, t, l, r, p) iff the following formula holds in $\mathcal{A}$:

$$t = \text{null} \wedge S = \varnothing \ \vee \tag{1}$$

$$\forall x, y.\, x \in S \wedge y \in S \wedge \mathsf{R}(p, x, y) \wedge \mathsf{R}(p, y, x) \Rightarrow x = y \ \wedge \tag{2}$$

$$\forall x.\, x \in S \Rightarrow x.l = \text{null} \vee \mathsf{R}(p, x.l, x) \ \wedge \tag{3}$$

$$\forall x, y.\, x \in S \wedge \mathsf{B}(p, x.l, y, x) \Rightarrow y = x.l \vee y = x \ \wedge \tag{4}$$

$$\forall x.\, x \in S \Rightarrow x.r = \text{null} \vee \mathsf{R}(p, x.r, x) \ \wedge \tag{5}$$

$$\forall x, y.\, x \in S \wedge \mathsf{B}(p, x.r, y, x) \Rightarrow y = x.r \vee y = x \ \wedge \tag{6}$$

$$\forall x, y.\, y \in S \wedge \mathsf{R}(p, x, y) \Rightarrow x = y \vee \mathsf{B}(p, x, y.l, y) \vee \mathsf{B}(p, x, y.r, y) \ \wedge \tag{7}$$

$$\forall x.\, x \in S \wedge x.l = x.r \Rightarrow x.l = \text{null} \ \wedge \tag{8}$$

$$\forall x.\, x \in S \Rightarrow x.l \neq x \wedge x.r \neq x \ \wedge \tag{9}$$

$$\forall x.\, x \in S \Leftrightarrow \mathsf{R}(p, x, t) \tag{10}$$

The first disjunct (1) defines the structure of an empty tree and the second disjunct the structure of nonempty trees. We explain the conjuncts (2)-(10) in the second disjunct in more detail. The conjunct (2) ensures that the set S does not contain nontrivial p cycles. The conjuncts (3)-(7) express that on S the field p is the inverse of l and r. Specifically, (3) and (4) together are equivalent to the formula $\forall x.x \in S \Rightarrow x.l = \text{null} \vee x.l.p = x$. Using reachability constraints to express this property rather than field reads yields a simpler and more efficient decision procedure. Conjunct (8) expresses that fields l and r must not point to the same nodes on S, unless they both point to null. Conjunct (9) expresses that l and r do not have self-loops on S. Finally, conjunct (10) defines the footprint S as the set of all nodes that can reach t via the parent field.

The frame predicate Frame(A, S, f, f') expresses that the fields f and f' coincide when they are restricted to the nodes in the set $A \backslash S$. In our formal definition of the frame predicate, we distinguish between parent fields and successor fields. For successor fields $f, f' \in L$ (respectively R), we define Frame(A, S, f, f') by the GRASS formula

$$\forall x.x \in A \backslash S \Rightarrow x.f = x.f' \tag{11}$$

For parent fields $p, p' \in P$, it is not sufficient if the frame predicate states that the fields p and p' coincide on the set $A \backslash S$. Instead, we also need to ensure that all information contained in the reachability predicate B for the two fields is consistent on this set. For parent fields p, p', we therefore define Frame(A, S, p, p') by the formula

$$\forall x, y, z.x \in A \backslash S \Rightarrow (\mathsf{B}(p, x, y, z) \Leftrightarrow \mathsf{B}(p', x, y, z)) \tag{12}$$

Note that the formula (12) is stronger than formula (11). In fact, we are only allowed to use formula (12) for the encoding of the frame rule if we make sure that the set S is parent-closed. That is, for all nodes t, t', if $t \in S$ and $R(p, t', t)$, then $t' \in S$. This holds in particular if S is the footprint of an SL tree predicate whose parent field is p. There exists a more general treatment of the frame predicate that preserves reachability information and does not make assumptions about the set S. The details can be found in [20, 33]. Since the footprints of tree manipulating programs are typically defined by tree predicates and hence parent-closed, we stick to the simpler definition given by formula (12).

5 Decision Procedure for GRIT

We next describe the decision procedure for the satisfiability problem of GRIT. In the following, let F be a GRIT formula. The decision procedure works in two phases: the first phase reduces F to an equisatisfiable GRASS formula F'. The second phase reduces F' to an equisatisfiable formula in effectively propositional logic (EPR), which is then checked using an EPR decision procedure. The EPR fragment, also known as the Bernays-Schönfinkel class, consists of formula of the form $\exists x \forall y \varphi(x, y)$ where φ is quantifier-free and does not contain function symbols. Satisfiability of EPR formulas can be decided in NEXPTIME and reduces to NP, if the number of universally quantified variables is bounded [25].

The first phase of the reduction involves the following sequence of steps:

1. Substitute all occurrences of the predicates Tree and Frame in F by their defining formulas given in Sec. 4. The resulting formula is a GRASS formula F_1.
2. Convert F_1 into negation normal form, yielding F_2.
3. Replace every literal of the form $\neg(f = f')$ in F_2, where f and f' are terms of sort field, by the formula $\exists x. \neg(\text{read}(f, x) = \text{read}(f', x))$. The resulting formula is F_3.
4. Skolemize F_3, yielding F'.

Clearly, each of these transformation steps produces an equisatisfiable formula with respect to the theory $\mathcal{T}_{GS}$. Note that the Skolemization step only introduces fresh Skolem constants of sort node.

Next, conjoin F' with the theory axioms defining the predicate B and the functions read and write for the theory $\mathcal{T}_{GS}$. The axiom defining the predicate B are obtained from the inference rules in the decision procedure proposed in [23]. The axioms defining the functions read and write are McCarthy's well-known read over write axioms for arrays [28][1]. We denote the resulting formula by G.

All the remaining quantifiers in G are universal quantifiers. The final step of the reduction is to instantiate all those universally quantified variables in G that appear below function symbols. The resulting formula is then in EPR (modulo function symbols appearing in ground terms, which can be eliminated using Ackermann reduction). The quantifier instantiation step exploits the careful design of the defining formulas of the tree and frame predicates, as well as the restrictions on the quantified formulas that are

---

[1] The complete list of all axioms can be found in the companion tech report [34].

allowed to appear in the input formula F. These restrictions guarantee that the resulting quantified constraints can be viewed as a so-called Ψ-local theory extension [16]. That is, it is sufficient to instantiate the variables below function symbols in G with a finite set of ground terms T that we can compute from G. Suppose that $G[T]$ is the resulting EPR formula. The completeness argument for the reduction to EPR works by proving that each model $\mathcal{A}$ of $G[T]$ can be embedded into some structure in $\mathcal{T}_{GS}$ that satisfies F'. Specifically, we need to be able to construct actual binary trees in those regions of $\mathcal{A}$ that have been constrained by tree predicates. This construction must preserve the cardinality of model $\mathcal{A}$ for the resulting structure to satisfy F' and hence F.

To this end, let T_G be the set of all ground terms appearing in G, and let P_F be the set of all positive ground literals appearing in F. To ensure that each tree region $\mathsf{Tree}(S, t, l, r, p) \in P_F$ contains sufficiently many nodes to construct a binary tree, we use the idea from [39] to introduce an auxiliary function fca that denotes the first common ancestor of two nodes with respect to the parent field p and footprint set S. We define this function using the following axioms:

$$\forall x, y.\ \mathsf{R}(p, x, t) \wedge \mathsf{R}(p, y, t) \Rightarrow \mathsf{R}(p, x, fca(p, x, y))$$
$$\forall x, y.\ \mathsf{R}(p, x, t) \wedge \mathsf{R}(p, y, t) \Rightarrow \mathsf{R}(p, y, fca(p, x, y))$$
$$\forall x, y, z.\ \mathsf{R}(p, x, t) \wedge \mathsf{R}(p, y, t) \wedge \mathsf{R}(p, x, z) \wedge \mathsf{R}(p, y, z) \Rightarrow \mathsf{R}(p, fca(p, x, y), z)$$
$$\forall x, y, z, w.\ \mathsf{R}(p, w, t) \wedge fca(p, x, y) = w \wedge fca(p, x, z) = w \wedge fca(p, y, z) = w \Rightarrow$$
$$x = y \vee x = z \vee y = z \vee w = \mathsf{null}$$

For each atom $\mathsf{Tree}(S, t, l, r, p) \in P_F$, conjoin these axioms with G to obtain G_1.

Next, we define the set of ground terms T, which we use for the instantiation, as the least set of ground terms that satisfies the following properties:

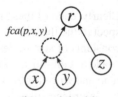

(a) spurious model

- $T_G \subseteq T$
- if $t.l \in T$ and $\mathsf{Tree}(S, c, l, r, p) \in P_F$ then $t.r \in T$
- if $t.r \in T$ and $\mathsf{Tree}(S, c, l, r, p) \in P_F$ then $t.l \in T$
- if $t.f \in T$ and $f = f' \in P_F$ then $t.f' \in T$
- if $t.f \in T$ and $\mathsf{Frame}(A, S, f, f') \in P_F$ then $t.f' \in T$
- if $t.f \in T$ and $\mathsf{Frame}(A, S, f', f) \in P_F$ then $t.f' \in T$
- if $t.\mathsf{write}(f, u, v) \in T$ then $t.f \in T$
- if $t.f \in T$ and $\mathsf{write}(f, u, v) \in T$ then $t.\mathsf{write}(f, u, v) \in T$
- if $\mathsf{write}(f, u, v) \in T$ then $u.\mathsf{write}(f, u, v) \in T$
- if $t \in T$, $t' \in T$, $\mathsf{Tree}(S, c, l, r, p) \in P_F$, and neither t nor t' contain fca then $fca(p, t, t') \in T$

$fca(p,x,y)$

(b) model with $fca(p, x, y)$

Fig. 4. Role of the fca

It is easy to see that T is polynomial in the size of T_G.

Let A be a universally quantified first-order formula. We denote by $A[T]$ the conjunction of all instances I of A that satisfy the following properties: I is obtained from A by instantiating all quantified variables of A that appear below function symbols with terms of matching sort in T. Moreover, all ground terms appearing in I are already in T. For example, if A is of the form $\forall x.\ A_1(f(x))$ and $t \in T$ then $A_1(f(t))$ is in $A[T]$ only if $f(t) \in T$. Now, let $G_1[T]$ be the formula that is obtained by substituting all universally quantified subformulas A in G_1 by $A[T]$.

By construction, the formula $G_1[T]$ is satisfiable if the input formula F is satisfiable modulo the theory $\mathcal{T}_{GS}$. Hence, our decision procedure is sound. To prove completeness, let $\mathcal{A}$ be a model of $G_1[T]$. Define the partial structure $\mathcal{A}|_T$ by restricting the interpretation of the sort node in $\mathcal{A}$ to the set $\{ t^{\mathcal{A}} \mid t \in T \}$. Let $\mathsf{PMod}(G_1[T])$ be the set of all such partial structures for $G_1[T]$. Then the following lemma implies the completeness of our decision procedure.

Lemma 1. *Let* $\mathcal{A}_T \in \mathsf{PMod}(G_1[T])$. *Then* $\mathcal{A}_T$ *can be completed to a structure* $\mathcal{A} \in$ $\mathcal{T}_{GS}$ *that satisfies G.*

The crucial observation in the proof of Lemma 1 is that the addition of fca ensures that in the partial models $\mathcal{A}_T$, for every tree node t, there are at most two other nodes which can reach t directly via the parent field, i.e., without visiting any other nodes. Hence, these two nodes can be chosen as the direct left and right successors of t in the model completion. We explain the importance of the first common ancestor terms for the completeness of the decision procedure through an example.

Example 1. Consider the following unsatisfiable formula:

$$\mathsf{Tree}(S,t,l,r,p) \wedge S = \{x,y,z,t\} \wedge S = \{w.\, \mathsf{R}(p,w,t)\} \wedge \neg\mathsf{R}(p,x,y) \wedge$$
$$\neg\mathsf{R}(p,x,z) \wedge \neg\mathsf{R}(p,y,x) \wedge \neg\mathsf{R}(p,y,z) \wedge \neg\mathsf{R}(p,z,x) \wedge \neg\mathsf{R}(p,z,y)$$

The formula is unsatisfiable because the nodes x, y, z and t cannot be arranged in a binary tree without adding auxiliary nodes to the tree (which violates the definition of S) or making at least two of x, y, z mutually reachable via p. Without the first common ancestor, the reduced formula produced by the decision procedure would admit the model shown in Fig. 4 (a). This happens because the original formula does not contain any l or r terms to trigger the instantiation of the quantifiers in the defining formula of Tree. However, with the additional fca terms and axioms, the instantiated formula implies that the tree must contain at least one additional node, as indicated in Fig. 4 (b). This yields the contradiction.

By construction, $G_1[T]$ is an EPR formula whose size is polynomial in the input formula F. It thus follows that the satisfiability problem for the quantifier-bounded fragments of GRIT is in NP. Since NP-hardness is immediate we obtain the following complexity result.

Theorem 1. *The satisfiability problem for the quantifier-bounded fragments of GRIT is NP complete.*

6   Extensions

In this section, we discuss several extensions of GRIT to support reasoning about trees and data. Such extensions are needed, for instance, to prove that a binary search tree is sorted. In general, it is possible to extend the logic with additional axioms about data as long as they preserve the locality properties that underpin the axiomatization of GRIT. We present extensions with data that we used in our experimental evaluation and we provide some general principles how to design such extensions. The extensions that we discuss preserve the decidability and complexity of GRIT.

To support reasoning about data, we extend the signature of GRIT with an additional sort data for data values, fields from node to data, and sets with data elements. The read and write functions are extended as expected. In the following, we let d range over data fields. In our implementation, we interpret the data sort in the theory of linear integer arithmetic. However, we can combine GRIT with any decidable quantifier-free first-order theory that is signature disjoint from GRIT and stably-infinite to interpret the data sort. The extensions that we discuss build on such quantifier-free combinations.

We consider three categories of extensions with data: monadic predicates on node, binary predicates on node, and projections of node sets to data sets.

Monadic Predicates. Properties such as upper and lower bounds on the values contained in a tree are expressible using monadic predicates. Such formulas have the following form: $\forall x.\ x \in S \to Q(x.d)$ where Q is a predicate over data and S a node set. One example of such a predicate is the ensures clause on line 6 in Fig. 1.

Monadic predicates also form Ψ-local theory extensions. To support such extensions, the set T of ground terms for the quantifier instantiation must additionally satisfy:

- if $d \in T$ and $t \in T$ then $t.d \in T$

For each ground node term $t \in T$, we add a ground term that reads t's data. The completeness of this instantiation follows from results about axioms satisfying stratified sort restrictions [1].

Binary Predicates. To define a sorted tree or a heap, we need to relate the data of a node to the data of its children. The following properties are examples of binary predicates:

- heap property: $\forall x, y \in S.\ R(p, x, y) \Rightarrow x.d \leqslant y.d$
- sorted tree (left subtree): $\forall x, y \in S.\ B(p, x, y.l, y) \Rightarrow x.d < y.d$

Here, we assume that S is the footprint of a tree. To ensure completeness of the decision procedure for such predicates, we first check that the relation on nodes is transitive. Without transitivity, the property cannot be generalized from direct successors in a tree to an entire path in that tree, and Lemma 1 does not hold anymore. Transitivity prevents us from expressing properties that require counting, but still allows ordering relations.

The case of the heap property is simple since it satisfies a stratified sort restriction. It does not require any additional treatment beyond the addition of data ground terms as in the case of monadic predicates. On the other hand, the sortedness property is more interesting because the variable y appears in a read term. Thus, instantiating the axiom can potentially generate new terms. However, our decision procedure performs only local instantiation. To obtain completeness we need to ensure that we have sufficiently many left and right successor terms. Therefore, the set T of ground terms must additionally satisfy:

- if $fca(p, t_1, t_2) \in T$ and $\mathsf{Tree}(S, c, l, r, p) \in P_F$ then $fca(p, t_1, t_2).l \in T$ and $fca(p, t_1, t_2).r \in T$.

Note that the axioms for the first common ancestor and the defining formula of Tree together imply that the following holds for all nodes x and y in a partial model:

$$fca(p, fca(p, x, y).l, fca(p, x, y).r) = fca(p, x, y)$$

The additional terms ensure that all nodes in a tree are assigned to the left, respectively, right subtrees of the first common ancestor nodes, enforcing sortedness across the tree.

Set Projection. Lastly, we consider a way of referring to the content of a data structure. This class of extensions enables reasoning about functional correctness properties. In common cases such as implementations of sets, the content is obtained by projecting the footprint onto a data field. For instance, given the footprint S of a data structure, the content C can be defined as $C = \{v \mid \exists x \in S. \ v = x.d\}$.

This definition does not directly fit into our logic, due to the existential quantifier inside the set comprehension. We replace this quantifier by a Skolem function which we call *witness*. The *witness* function maps an element c of C back to a node in S that stores c. The values not in C are mapped to null. *witness* is axiomatized as follows:

$$\forall x. x \in S \Rightarrow x.d \in C$$
$$\forall v. v \in C \Rightarrow witness(d, v, C) \in S \wedge v = witness(d, v, C).d$$
$$\forall v. v \notin C \Rightarrow witness(d, v, C) = \text{null}$$

The witness function maps the data values back to nodes. Therefore, it does not respect the stratification restriction used to prove the Ψ-locality of the monadic extensions. For completeness, the set of terms T needs to additionally satisfy:

- if $d \in T_{\text{data}}$ and $v, C \in T$ then $witness(d, v, C), witness(d, v, C).d \in T$

The axioms are local since *witness* is the inverse of d. Hence, reading the data of a witness gives a value which is already in the set of ground terms.

The set implementations which we used in our experiments do not store duplicate elements and *witness* becomes the one-to-one inverse of the data field. In such cases, we strengthen the above axioms with $\forall x. \ x \in S \Rightarrow x = witness(d, x.d, C)$.

Limitations. As mention earlier, there is no precise characterization of the limit of extensions that preserve the locality properties on which our decision procedure is built. However, not all extensions are local. For example, the following relation between a parent and child node does not generalize to reachability: $\forall x, y \in S. \ x.p = y \Rightarrow x.d = y.d + 1$. Therefore, the height of a tree cannot be expressed.

7   Implementation and Evaluation

Implementation. We have extended our tool GRASShopper with the decision procedure for tree data structures storing integer values. The tool is implemented in OCaml and available under a BSD license. The source code distribution including all benchmarks can be downloaded from the project web page [14]. GRASShopper takes as input an annotated C-like program and generates verification conditions which are checked using Z3 [11]. Annotations include procedure contracts and loop invariants expressed in a mixed specification language that supports both SL and GRASS assertions. The tool automatically adds checks to ensure that there are no memory safety violations such as accesses to unallocated memory, memory leaks, double frees, etc.

Currently, all annotations with ghost parent pointers must be manually provided. We plan to extend GRASShopper to automatically infer these annotations. For example, each modification of a forward successor field induces a matching modification of the parent field. Furthermore, a procedure that takes the root of a tree as parameter must be augmented with an additional ghost parameter for the parent of the root. The companion report [34] contains more information on how to automate these steps.

To handle dynamic memory allocation we require that the parent of all unallocated nodes points to null and that all nodes eventually reach null via parents. These restrictions are not harmful because outside of trees we can choose the parents arbitrarily.

The translation of SL tree predicates into GRIT is currently hard-coded into the implementation of the tool. The first-order specifications of common properties and features such as sortedness and content sets are provided as predefined building blocks. Using these building blocks, adding support for a new data structure requires about 10 lines of code. We plan to implement a heuristic translation of SL tree predicates to GRIT. The tool already provides such a heuristic for list data structures. GRASShopper also incorporates optimizations and sparser term generation. For instance, we do not currently generate the fca terms. This source of incompleteness proved irrelevant in our examples. In every example, the data structure is traversed along the left and right successor nodes which ensures that sufficiently many ground terms are already present.

Evaluation. We have used GRASShopper to verify complex properties of various data structure implementations. The results of our experiments are summarized in Table 1. For each procedure, the table lists the number of lines of code, lines of specification, lines of ghost annotations, the number of generated verification conditions, and the total running time of the tool. All examples in the table have been successfully verified. The number of lines of code does not include specifications or ghost state. The specifications include contracts and loop invariants. The ghost annotations include annotations that are needed to express the specification (e.g., implicit ghost parameter), or proof automation (e.g., updates of ghost fields). We now describe our experiments in more detail.

First, we used GRASShopper to prove functional correctness of set data structures that store integer values. We considered implementations based on binary search trees and sorted lists. The experiments with lists show that the extension we present for GRIT are applicable across different data structure types. We further verified a union-find data structure. We looked at the data structure from two different perspectives. One perspective views them as shared lists, the other as unranked inverted forests. Each perspective allows us to prove different properties of the implementation. Using the tree view, we proved functional correctness, e.g., that the union operation indeed merges the equivalence classes associated with two given pointers into the data structure. The list view allows us to reason about single paths from a node n in the data structure to the root node of the tree that n belongs to (i.e., the representative of that equivalence class). Using the list view, we proved the correctness of path compaction in the find operation.

We have also considered other tree data structures for which we have proved the preservation of structural invariants under the data structure operation but not full functional correctness of these operations. In particular, we have proved that skew heap operations respect the heap property, i.e., that the data value of a child node is not greater than its parent's value. Skew heaps are typically used to implement priority queues. At

Table 1. Verified data structures

Data structure	Procedure	#L. Code	#L. Spec	#L. Ghost	# VCs	time in s
set as binary tree functional correctness	contains	17	3	3	9	3
	destroy	8	2	2	7	1
	extract_max	14	5	3	9	20
	insert	24	2	3	15	61
	remove	33	2	11	35	117
	rotate_left	8	3	4	11	15
	rotate_right	8	3	4	11	14
	traverse	7	2	3	5	9
set as sorted list functional correctness	contains	15	7	6	4	1
	delete	26	7	6	8	12
	difference	20	3	1	15	13
	insert	25	7	6	8	69
	traverse	12	7	6	2	0.1
	union	20	3	1	15	15
union-find (tree-view) functional correctness	find	12	2	1	4	0.2
	union	10	3	1	4	0.3
	create	11	3	0	3	0.1
union-find (list-view) path compaction	find	12	3	1	4	0.1
	union	9	7	1	4	3
	create	10	1	0	3	0.1
skew heap shape, heap property	insert	17	2	2	7	0.3
	union	11	2	4	12	35
	extract_max	9	2	1	11	6

the moment, we cannot prove functional correctness of this data structure because our tool does not yet support reasoning about the theories that are needed for specifying the priority queue operations (e.g., multisets or sequences).

8   Conclusions

We have presented a new approach for automated verification of programs that manipulate heap-allocated data structures. The approach is based on a decidable fragment of first-order logic that supports reasoning about mutable finite graphs and can express that certain subgraphs form trees. The logic makes no global assumptions about the structure of its graph models such as that the entire graph is a forest. This allows us to use the logic for automated reasoning about separation logic of trees. Furthermore, we have studied extensions of our graph logic for reasoning about data stored in heap structures. We used these extensions to automatically verify complex properties (including full functional correctness) of tree data structures such as binary search trees, skew heaps, and union-find. In the future, we will investigate how to extend our techniques to reason about nested data structures that combine trees, lists, and arrays.

References

1. Abadi, A., Rabinovich, A., Sagiv, M.: Decidable fragments of many-sorted logic. In: Dershowitz, N., Voronkov, A. (eds.) LPAR 2007. LNCS (LNAI), vol. 4790, pp. 17–31. Springer, Heidelberg (2007)
2. Abdulla, P.A., Holík, L., Jonsson, B., Lengál, O., Trinh, C.Q., Vojnar, T.: Verification of heap manipulating programs with ordered data by extended forest automata. In: Van Hung, D., Ogawa, M. (eds.) ATVA 2013. LNCS, vol. 8172, pp. 224–239. Springer, Heidelberg (2013)
3. Balaban, I., Pnueli, A., Zuck, L.D.: Shape analysis of single-parent heaps. In: Cook, B., Podelski, A. (eds.) VMCAI 2007. LNCS, vol. 4349, pp. 91–105. Springer, Heidelberg (2007)
4. Berdine, J., Calcagno, C., O'Hearn, P.W.: A decidable fragment of separation logic. In: Lodaya, K., Mahajan, M. (eds.) FSTTCS 2004. LNCS, vol. 3328, pp. 97–109. Springer, Heidelberg (2004)
5. Berdine, J., Calcagno, C., O'Hearn, P.W.: Smallfoot: Modular automatic assertion checking with separation logic. In: de Boer, F.S., Bonsangue, M.M., Graf, S., de Roever, W.-P. (eds.) FMCO 2005. LNCS, vol. 4111, pp. 115–137. Springer, Heidelberg (2006)
6. Berdine, J., Cook, B., Ishtiaq, S.: SLAyer: Memory Safety for Systems-Level Code. In: Gopalakrishnan, G., Qadeer, S. (eds.) CAV 2011. LNCS, vol. 6806, pp. 178–183. Springer, Heidelberg (2011)
7. Bouajjani, A., Drăgoi, C., Enea, C., Sighireanu, M.: A logic-based framework for reasoning about composite data structures. In: Bravetti, M., Zavattaro, G. (eds.) CONCUR 2009. LNCS, vol. 5710, pp. 178–195. Springer, Heidelberg (2009)
8. Calvanese, D., di Giacomo, G., Nardi, D., Lenzerini, M.: Reasoning in expressive description logics. In: Handbook of Automated Reasoning. Elsevier (2001)
9. Chlipala, A.: The bedrock structured programming system: Combining generative metaprogramming and hoare logic in an extensible program verifier. In: ICFP, pp. 391–402. ACM (2013)
10. Cook, B., Haase, C., Ouaknine, J., Parkinson, M., Worrell, J.: Tractable reasoning in a fragment of separation logic. In: Katoen, J.-P., König, B. (eds.) CONCUR 2011. LNCS, vol. 6901, pp. 235–249. Springer, Heidelberg (2011)
11. de Moura, L., Bjørner, N.S.: Z3: An efficient SMT solver. In: Ramakrishnan, C.R., Rehof, J. (eds.) TACAS 2008. LNCS, vol. 4963, pp. 337–340. Springer, Heidelberg (2008)
12. Dudka, K., Peringer, P., Vojnar, T.: Predator: A practical tool for checking manipulation of dynamic data structures using separation logic. In: Gopalakrishnan, G., Qadeer, S. (eds.) CAV 2011. LNCS, vol. 6806, pp. 372–378. Springer, Heidelberg (2011)
13. Genevès, P., Layaïda, N., Schmitt, A.: Efficient static analysis of XML paths and types. In: ACM PLDI (2007)
14. GRASShopper tool web page, http://cs.nyu.edu/wies/software/grasshopper (accessed: May 2014)
15. Haase, C., Ishtiaq, S., Ouaknine, J., Parkinson, M.J.: Seloger: A tool for graph-based reasoning in separation logic. In: Sharygina, N., Veith, H. (eds.) CAV 2013. LNCS, vol. 8044, pp. 790–795. Springer, Heidelberg (2013)
16. Ihlemann, C., Jacobs, S., Sofronie-Stokkermans, V.: On local reasoning in verification. In: Ramakrishnan, C.R., Rehof, J. (eds.) TACAS 2008. LNCS, vol. 4963, pp. 265–281. Springer, Heidelberg (2008)
17. Immerman, N., Rabinovich, A., Reps, T., Sagiv, M., Yorsh, G.: The boundary between decidability and undecidability for transitive-closure logics. In: Marcinkowski, J., Tarlecki, A. (eds.) CSL 2004. LNCS, vol. 3210, pp. 160–174. Springer, Heidelberg (2004)
18. Iosif, R., Rogalewicz, A., Simacek, J.: The tree width of separation logic with recursive definitions. In: Bonacina, M.P. (ed.) CADE 2013. LNCS, vol. 7898, pp. 21–38. Springer, Heidelberg (2013)

19. Itzhaky, S., Banerjee, A., Immerman, N., Nanevski, A., Sagiv, M.: Effectively-propositional reasoning about reachability in linked data structures. In: Sharygina, N., Veith, H. (eds.) CAV 2013. LNCS, vol. 8044, pp. 756–772. Springer, Heidelberg (2013)
20. Itzhaky, S., Lahav, O., Banerjee, A., Immerman, N., Nanevski, A., Sagiv, M.: Modular reasoning on unique heap paths via effectively propositional formulas. In: POPL (2014)
21. Jacobs, B., Smans, J., Philippaerts, P., Vogels, F., Penninckx, W., Piessens, F.: VeriFast: A Powerful, Sound, Predictable, Fast Verifier for C and Java. In: Bobaru, M., Havelund, K., Holzmann, G.J., Joshi, R. (eds.) NFM 2011. LNCS, vol. 6617, pp. 41–55. Springer, Heidelberg (2011)
22. Klarlund, N., Møller, A.: MONA Version 1.4 User Manual. BRICS Notes Series NS-01-1, Department of Computer Science, University of Aarhus (January 2001)
23. Lahiri, S.K., Qadeer, S.: Back to the future: Revisiting precise program verification using SMT solvers. In: POPL, pp. 171–182 (2008)
24. Leino, K.R.M.: Developing verified programs with dafny. In: ICSE, pp. 1488–1490. ACM (2013)
25. Lewis, H.R.: Complexity results for classes of quantificational formulas. J. Comput. Syst. Sci. 21(3), 317–353 (1980)
26. Madhusudan, P., Parlato, G., Qiu, X.: Decidable logics combining heap structures and data. In: POPL, pp. 611–622. ACM (2011)
27. Madhusudan, P., Qiu, X.: Efficient Decision Procedures for Heaps Using STRAND. In: Yahav, E. (ed.) Static Analysis. LNCS, vol. 6887, pp. 43–59. Springer, Heidelberg (2011)
28. McCarthy, J.: Towards a mathematical science of computation. In: IFIP Congress, pp. 21–28 (1962)
29. Nguyen, H.H., David, C., Qin, S.C., Chin, W.-N.: Automated verification of shape and size properties via separation logic. In: Cook, B., Podelski, A. (eds.) VMCAI 2007. LNCS, vol. 4349, pp. 251–266. Springer, Heidelberg (2007)
30. O'Hearn, P., Reynolds, J., Yang, H.: Local reasoning about programs that alter data structures. In: Fribourg, L. (ed.) CSL 2001. LNCS, vol. 2142, pp. 1–19. Springer, Heidelberg (2001)
31. Pérez, J.A.N., Rybalchenko, A.: Separation logic + superposition calculus = heap theorem prover. In: PLDI, pp. 556–566. ACM (2011)
32. Piskac, R., Wies, T., Zufferey, D.: Automating Separation Logic Using SMT. In: Sharygina, N., Veith, H. (eds.) CAV 2013. LNCS, vol. 8044, pp. 773–789. Springer, Heidelberg (2013)
33. Piskac, R., Wies, T., Zufferey, D.: GRASShopper: Complete Heap Verification with Mixed Specifications. In: Ábrahám, E., Havelund, K. (eds.) TACAS 2014. LNCS, vol. 8413, pp. 124–139. Springer, Heidelberg (2014)
34. Piskac, R., Wies, T., Zufferey, D.: On automating separation logic with trees and data. Technical Report NYU Technical Report TR2014-963, NYU (2014)
35. Qiu, X., Garg, P., Stefanescu, A., Madhusudan, P.: Natural proofs for structure, data, and separation. In: PLDI, pp. 231–242 (2013)
36. Rakamarić, Z., Bingham, J.D., Hu, A.J.: An inference-rule-based decision procedure for verification of heap-manipulating programs with mutable data and cyclic data structures. In: Cook, B., Podelski, A. (eds.) VMCAI 2007. LNCS, vol. 4349, pp. 106–121. Springer, Heidelberg (2007)
37. Thatcher, J.W., Wright, J.B.: Generalized finite automata theory with an application to a decision problem of second-order logic. Mathematical Systems Theory 2(1), 57–81 (1968)
38. Totla, N., Wies, T.: Complete instantiation-based interpolation. In: POPL. ACM (2013)
39. Wies, T., Muñiz, M., Kuncak, V.: An efficient decision procedure for imperative tree data structures. In: Bjørner, N., Sofronie-Stokkermans, V. (eds.) CADE 2011. LNCS, vol. 6803, pp. 476–491. Springer, Heidelberg (2011)

40. Yang, H., Lee, O., Berdine, J., Calcagno, C., Cook, B., Distefano, D., O'Hearn, P.W.: Scalable shape analysis for systems code. In: Gupta, A., Malik, S. (eds.) CAV 2008. LNCS, vol. 5123, pp. 385–398. Springer, Heidelberg (2008)
41. Yorsh, G., Rabinovich, A.M., Sagiv, M., Meyer, A., Bouajjani, A.: A logic of reachable patterns in linked data-structures. J. Log. Algebr. Program. (2007)
42. Zee, K., Kuncak, V., Rinard, M.C.: Full functional verification of linked data structures. In: PLDI, pp. 349–361. ACM (2008)

A Nonlinear Real Arithmetic Fragment*

Ashish Tiwari and Patrick Lincoln

SRI International, Menlo Park, CA
`firstname.lastname@sri.com`

Abstract. We present a new procedure for testing satisfiability (over the reals) of a conjunction of polynomial equations. There are three possible return values for our procedure: it either returns *a model* for the input formula, or it says that the input is *unsatisfiable*, or it fails because the applicability condition for the procedure, called the eigen-condition, is violated. For the class of constraints where the eigen-condition holds, our procedure is a *decision procedure*. We describe satisfiability-preserving transformations that can potentially convert problems into a form where eigen-condition holds. We experimentally evaluate the procedure and discuss applicability.

1 Introduction

Satisfiability problems in nonlinear real arithmetic arise in several applications, including formal verification and synthesis of software programs, control systems, and cyber-physical systems. In this paper, we consider the problem of checking satisfiability of a *conjunction of multilinear polynomial equations* over the reals.

There has been significant progress recently on solving nonlinear real arithmetic constraints [12,13,9,10,16,4,1,7]. Our main interest is identifying efficiently decidable nonlinear arithmetic fragments that arise in formal verification and synthesis, and developing procedures for those fragments that easily integrate with and complement existing techniques in SMT [8]. We present here a procedure that is tailored for a subclass of nonlinear problems that have *finitely-many* (maybe zero) models over an algebraically closed field (complex numbers). Our procedure can be viewed as inspired by SAT solvers: we search for a model by finding the finitely-many values a variable can potentially take in any model, and then nondeterministically guessing the right value. Whereas in SAT, each variable is known *a priori* to take one of two values, in our setting, we have to do some work to determine if there is a variable that takes only finitely-many values. We describe the procedure and report preliminary experimental results.

Why restrict to conjunction of equations? Consider a simple loop that computes the product of two input natural numbers x_0, y_0:

$$s := 0; \ y := y_0 \ ; \ \text{while} \ (y > 0) \ \{ \ s := s + x_0; \ y := y-1 \ \}$$

---

* Supported in part by DARPA under contract FA8750-12-C-0284 and by the NSF grant SHF:CSR-1017483. Any opinions, findings, and conclusions or recommendations expressed in this material are those of the authors and do not necessarily reflect the views of the funding agencies.

A. Biere and R. Bloem (Eds.): CAV 2014, LNCS 8559, pp. 729–736, 2014.
© Springer International Publishing Switzerland 2014

Suppose we want to find a loop invariant of the form $s = ax_0y_0 + bx_0y$ (we could pick a general degree 2 polynomial over x_0, y_0, y here, but just to keep expressions small we picked a restricted template here). We want to know if

$$\exists a, b \forall s, x_0, y_0, y, s_1, y_1 : s = ax_0y_0 + bx_0y \wedge s_1 = s + x_0 \wedge y_1 = y - 1 \Rightarrow s_1 = ax_0y_0 + bx_0y_1$$

We can answer the above by checking if the right-hand side polynomial can be written as a sum of (multiples of) the polynomials on the left. Again picking just the minimal template for the multipliers for ease of presentation, we get

$$\exists a, b, u, v, w : \forall s, x_0, y_0, y, s_1, y_1 :$$
$$s_1 - ax_0y_0 - bx_0y_1 = u(s - ax_0y_0 - bx_0y) + v(s_1 - s - x_0) + wx_0(y_1 - y + 1)$$

Equating the coefficients of the monomials over the $\forall$ variables, we get

$$\exists a, b, u, v, w : 1 = v \wedge -a = -ua \wedge -b = w \wedge 0 = u - v \wedge 0 = -ub - w \wedge 0 = -v + w$$

which is a *conjunction of polynomial equations*; see also [15,23,21,27,11,22,25].

A Running Example. We illustrate the main idea in the new procedure for satisfiability testing of nonlinear equations using a small example. Consider the conjunction of the following three equations:

$$x_1x_2 - x_1x_3 = -2x_2 \qquad x_1x_2 = x_3 \qquad x_2x_3 = 1$$

The first two equations can be written in matrix notation as

$$\begin{pmatrix} x_2 - x_3 \\ x_2 \end{pmatrix} x_1 = \begin{pmatrix} -2x_2 \\ x_3 \end{pmatrix}$$

Here, it is possible to write the right-hand side vector, $(-2x_2; x_3)$, as a linear combination of the vector, $(x_2 - x_3; x_2)$, on the left-hand side. Doing so, we get

$$\begin{pmatrix} x_2 - x_3 \\ x_2 \end{pmatrix} x_1 = \begin{pmatrix} 0 & -2 \\ -1 & 1 \end{pmatrix} \begin{pmatrix} x_2 - x_3 \\ x_2 \end{pmatrix}$$

This constraint can be true iff either x_1 is an eigenvalue of the 2×2 matrix or the vector $(x_2 - x_3; x_2)$ is identically zero. The two eigenvalues of the matrix are -1 and 2.

Let us branch on the three cases. In the first branch, $x_1 = -1$. The original three equations simplify to $x_2 + x_3 = 0$, $x_2x_3 = 1$. Recursively applying the same analysis, we find that these two equations can be written as

$$\begin{pmatrix} 1 \\ x_3 \end{pmatrix} x_2 = \begin{pmatrix} -x_3 \\ 1 \end{pmatrix} = \begin{pmatrix} 0 & -1 \\ 1 & 0 \end{pmatrix} \begin{pmatrix} 1 \\ x_3 \end{pmatrix}$$

Hence, the value of x_2 should be an eigenvalue of the matrix $(0, -1; 1, 0)$ or the vector $(1; x_3)$ should be identically zero. There are no real eigenvalues of this matrix and the vector $(1; x_3)$ can never be equal to 0. Hence, we get a contradiction in each subcase, and we backtrack.

In the second branch, $x_1 = 2$. The original three equations simplify to $2x_2 = x_3$, $x_2 x_3 = 1$. Again, we rewrite the two equations in matrix notation as

$$\begin{pmatrix} 2 \\ x_3 \end{pmatrix} x_2 = \begin{pmatrix} x_3 \\ 1 \end{pmatrix} = \begin{pmatrix} 0 & 1 \\ 0.5 & 0 \end{pmatrix} \begin{pmatrix} 2 \\ x_3 \end{pmatrix}$$

Hence, the value of x_2 should be an eigenvalue of the matrix $(0, 1; 0.5, 0)$ or the vector $(2; x_3)$ should be identically zero. The matrix has two real eigenvalues, namely $\pm\sqrt{2}/2$. If we pick $x_2 = \sqrt{2}/2$ and continue, we find a value $\sqrt{2}$ for x_3 and thus get a model for the original three constraints.

2 Search-Based Procedure

In this section, we formally describe our satisfiability checking procedure for nonlinear equations.

We first fix some notation. Let X be a finite set of variables. Elements of X are denoted by x, y with possible subscripts. We use $\mathbb{Q}$, $\mathbb{R}$ and $\mathbb{C}$ to denote the set of rationals, (algebraic) reals and complex numbers respectively, and we use c, d with subscripts to denote elements of these sets. The set of polynomials over X with coefficients in $\mathbb{R}$ is denoted by $\mathbb{R}[X]$, and its elements are denoted by p, q with possible subscripts. Let us assume that we can represent and compute over algebraic numbers. Our description of the procedure will represent and compute using constants in $\mathbb{R}$, but all these constants will be algebraic.

A (partial) model M is simply a set of assignments $x \mapsto c$ where x is a variable and c is an algebraic real number from $\mathbb{R}$. Each variable x occurs at most once in M.

The input to our procedure is a set $S := \{p_1 = 0, \ldots, p_n = 0\}$ of polynomial equations where every $p_i \in \mathbb{Q}[X]$. The output is either a model M binding every variable occurring in an input polynomial to a constant, or a string "Unsatisfiable" or a string "Condition Failed".

We describe our search procedure using inference rules that operate over the state (S', M') consisting of the set S' of equations, and partial model M'. The initial state is $(S, \emptyset)$, where S is the input equations. The procedure works by applying one of the inference rules in Figure 1. The Split inference rule makes a *non-deterministic* guess. Starting from the initial state, if we are able to reach a state $(\emptyset, M)$ using the inference rules, then we output the model M (Rule Success). If every derivation starting from $(M, \emptyset)$ (irrespective of the guesses) reaches a contradiction $\perp$, then we output the string "Unsatisfiable". In all other cases, we output the string "Condition Failed".

Among the inference rules in Figure 1, the rules Fail, Delete, and Success are self explanatory. The rule Unit_Prop checks to see if there is an equation of the form $x = c$ in S, and if so, it adds it to the model M and replaces x by c in S (the result is denoted by $S[x \mapsto c]$). We assume expressions are normalized to polynomial forms with leading coefficient 1.

The rule Split first checks if the set S satisfies the eigen-condition.

Split:	$$\dfrac{(S \cup \{Av = xv\}, M)}{(S \cup \{x = \lambda_1\}, M) \mid \ldots \mid (S \cup \{x = \lambda_k\}, M) \mid (S \cup \{v = 0\}, M)}$$ where $\lambda_1, \ldots, \lambda_k$ are all the real eigenvalues of A.

Unit_Prop:	$\dfrac{(S \cup \{x = c\}, M)}{(S[x \mapsto c], M \cup \{x \mapsto c\})}$	Success:	$\dfrac{(\emptyset, M)}{\text{output model } M}$
Delete:	$\dfrac{(S \cup \{0 = 0\}, M)}{(S, M)}$	Fail:	$\dfrac{(S \cup \{1 = 0\}, M)}{\perp}$

Fig. 1. Inference rules describing the satisfiability checking procedure

Definition 1 (eigen-condition). *A set S satisfies the eigen-condition if there exists a variable x such that some subset $S_1 \subseteq S$ of k equations can written in the form $xv = Av$ for some $(k \times 1)$-vector v of polynomials in $\mathbb{R}[X - \{x\}]$ and some constant $(k \times k)$-matrix A in $\mathbb{R}^{(k \times k)}$.*

If the set S satisfies the eigen-condition and A, x, v are the corresponding witnesses, then the inference rule Split non-deterministically picks either a *real* eigenvalue of A as the value of x, or sets v to 0. Note that if A has no real eigenvalues, then setting v to 0 is the only option.

The eigen-condition can be efficiently tested using a greatest fixpoint procedure: we start with a set $T = \{p_i x = q_i \mid p_i, q_i \in \mathbb{R}[X - \{x\}], i = 1, 2, \ldots\}$ containing all polynomials in S that are linear in x. In each iteration, we remove one element, say $p_i x = q_i$, from T if q_i is not in the linear subspace spanned by all the p_j's (i.e., if q_i can not be written as a linear combination of p_j's) in the monomial basis. If the fixpoint is nonempty, the eigen-condition holds for S. If the fixpoint is empty for all choices of x, the eigen-condition is violated for S.

The monomial basis of polynomials and eigenvalues of matrices have been used for discovering (formal power series) invariants for nonlinear (hybrid) systems [17,20]. Our work uses similar ideas, but to more generally find models for nonlinear polynomial equations.

Theorem 1 (Soundness). *Let $S := \{p_1 = 0, \ldots, p_n = 0\}$ be a set of polynomial equations where each $p_i \in \mathbb{Q}[X]$. Starting from the state $(S, \emptyset)$, if there is a derivation that reaches $(\emptyset, M)$, then M is a model for S in the theory $\mathbb{R}$ of reals. Starting from $(S, \emptyset)$, if every derivation reaches the state $\perp$, then S is unsatisfiable in the theory $\mathbb{R}$ of reals.*

The procedure can fail on certain inputs. We provide some examples below where the procedure fails. These examples will motivate some "pre-processing" steps that will make the procedure "fail" less often, and also lead to a characterization of the class of problems for which the procedure will not fail.

Example 1. Consider the set $S_{\text{quad}} = \{x^2 + 2x + 2 = 0\}$, the set $S_{\text{gb}} = \{x = 2y, x = 3y\}$, and the set $S_{\text{inf}} = \{x = y\}$. None of these sets satisfy the eigen-condition. None of the inference rules is applicable on the state $(S, \emptyset)$, where S is one of the above sets, and hence, our procedure "fails" on each of them.

A polynomial is called *multilinear* if every variable has degree at most one in every monomial in that polynomial. Note that $x^2 + 2x + 2$ is not multilinear, whereas $xy + 2x + 2$ is multilinear.

3   Transformations: Toward Completeness

In this section, we describe satisfiability-preserving transformations, and also characterize the class of problems where our procedure will not fail.

The first transformation, called *multilinear transformation*, turns a non-multilinear polynomial equations (such as $x^2 + 2x + 2 = 0$) into a multilinear equations by introducing new *clone* variables. Instead of defining it formally, we just illustrate it on the example S_{quad}. The multilinear transformation transforms S_{quad} into the *equi-satisfiable* set $S'_{\text{quad}} = \{x = x_{\text{clone}}, xx_{\text{clone}} + 2x + 2 = 0\}$. The set S'_{quad}, which can be written as $(1; x_{\text{clone}} + 2)x = (-2, 1; -2, 0)(1; x_{\text{clone}} + 2)$, satisfies the eigen-condition and our procedure can detect that it is unsatisfiable. Note that if p is a polynomial over a single variable, then the multilinear transformation transforms $p = 0$ into a equation set $xv = Av$ such that p is the characteristic polynomial of A.

The second transformation, called *Gröbner basis (GB) transformation*, applies the inference rules for computing Gröbner basis [3,2] to the polynomials in S. If these GB computation rules are exhaustively applied, then $\{p_1 = 0, \ldots, p_n = 0\}$ is replaced by the equi-satisfiable $\{q_1 = 0, \ldots, q_k = 0\}$ where $\{q_1, \ldots, q_k\}$ is a Gröbner basis of $\{p_1, \ldots, p_n\}$. Again, we just illustrate the GB transformation by an example. Using the GB transformation, the set S_{gb} is transformed into the set $S'_{\text{gb}} = \{x = 2y, y = 0\}$, which can be deduced to be satisfiable by our procedure using two applications of the Unit_Prop inference rule.

Finally, consider the third example, $S_{\text{inf}} = \{x = y\}$, on which our procedure fails. If our procedure does not fail on a set S, then it implies that the set S has *finitely many* (maybe zero) models. The set $S_{\text{inf}} = \{x = y\}$ has infinitely-many models, and hence our procedure necessarily fails on it; moreover, any simple "model count preserving" transformation will not help.

Theorem 2 (Completeness). *Let S be the class of polynomial equation sets that have finitely-many (maybe zero) models over the complex numbers. If $S \in \mathcal{S}$, then the the procedure that uses the inference rules in Figure 1 along with the inference rules for computing multilinear transformations and Gröbner bases, will never fail on S.*

Proof (Sketch). If S is unsatisfiable over the complex numbers, then by Hilbert's Nullstellensatz, the Gröbner basis of S will be $\{1 = 0\}$, which will be detected as "unsatisfiable" by the Fail rule. Note that we only need the GB rules and the Fail rule in this case. If S is satisfiable and has finitely many models over the complex numbers, let $c_1, \ldots, c_m$ be all the (complex) values that some specific variable, say x, takes in all the models. Consider the polynomial $p := (x - c_1)(x - c_2) \cdots (x - c_m)$ in $\mathbb{C}[x]$. Since S contains polynomials in $\mathbb{Q}[X]$, the polynomial p is in $\mathbb{R}[x]$. If we compute GB using a purely lexicographic ordering where

x has the least precedence, then p^k will belong to the GB (for some $k > 0$, by Hilbert's Nullstellensatz). Using the multilinear transformation, the single variable equation, $p^k = 0$, can be transformed into a set of equations where eigen-condition holds and the real values among $c_1, \ldots, c_m$ can be computed using the Split rule. The argument is then recursively applied to prove completeness.   □

The completeness result suggests that we can improve applicability of rules in Figure 1 by *lazily* applying GB transformation steps. Our model searching procedure complements the GB procedure that detects unsatisfiability (over complex numbers). In analogy to SAT solving, GB procedure is similar to a resolution-based procedure, whereas our procedure is similar to the DPLL algorithm [6].

4 Experiments

Boolean SAT problems can be encoded as nonlinear real arithmetic problems: for e.g., the clause $\neg x \lor y \lor z$ can be encoded as $x(1 - y)(1 - z) = 0$. These nonlinear problems satisfy the eigen-condition and our base procedure never fails on them. It performs DPLL-style search for a model on these examples. In fact, optimizations that have been developed for SAT (conflict-driven clause learning) can be adapted and incorporated into our nonlinear procedure.

Our procedure also works well on problems coming from template-based verification and synthesis [23,15] (see some nonlinear benchmark examples in [14]) and hybrid systems [21,27,11,22,25]. In fact, using a preliminary (and rather naive) implementation of our procedure (in Python, using floats and not using algebraic numbers) with some heuristics for handling cases where eigen-condition fails, we were able to solve all the nonlinear examples in [14] in time competitive with Z3 [13,18] (and faster than Z3 on a couple of problems). On the nonlinear encodings of SAT benchmarks, we are competitive with Z3's nonlinear solver on small problems, but much worse when problem size is larger – this is perhaps because our implementation does not learn from conflicts.

All nonlinear benchmarks and the tool itself can be obtained from http://www.csl.sri.com/users/tiwari/softwares/nl_eigen_solver.

5 Conclusion

We presented a backtracking-based search procedure for checking satisfiability of polynomial equations over the reals, which is complete for a subclass of non-linear problems that have finitely-many (maybe zero) models over the complex numbers. Our procedure can be viewed as a generalization of DPLL-style SAT solving to nonlinear arithmetic. Preliminary results indicate it is effective on a wide range of (exists-forall) nonlinear real arithmetic problems that arise during analysis and synthesis of programs and cyber-physical systems. General non-linear satisfiability problems, as well as $\exists\forall$ nonlinear problems [5], can both be turned into a conjunction of polynomial *equations* using the Positivstellen-satz [24,19,26], and our procedure can then be used to solve these problems.

References

1. Akbarpour, B., Paulson, L.C.: Metitarski: An automatic theorem prover for real-valued special functions. J. Autom. Reasoning 44(3), 175–205 (2010)
2. Bachmair, L., Ganzinger, H.: Buchberger's algorithm: A constraint-based completion procedure. In: Jouannaud, J.-P. (ed.) CCL 1994. LNCS, vol. 845, pp. 285–301. Springer, Heidelberg (1994)
3. Buchberger, B.: A critical-pair completion algorithm for finitely generated ideals in rings. In: Börger, E., Hasenjaeger, G., Rödding, D. (eds.) Rekursive Kombinatorik 1983. LNCS, vol. 171, pp. 137–161. Springer, Heidelberg (1983)
4. Cheng, C.-H., Ruess, H., Shankar, N.: Jbernstein: A validity checker for generalized polynomial constraints. In: Sharygina, N., Veith, H. (eds.) CAV 2013. LNCS, vol. 8044, pp. 656–661. Springer, Heidelberg (2013)
5. Cheng, C.-H., Shankar, N., Ruess, H., Bensalem, S.: Efsmt: A logical framework for cyber-physical systems. CoRR, abs/1306.3456 (2013)
6. Davis, M., Logemann, G., Loveland, D.: A machine program for theorem-proving. CACM 5(7), 394–397 (1962)
7. Fränzle, M., Herde, C., Teige, T., Ratschan, S., Schubert, T.: Efficient solving of large non-linear arithmetic constraint systems with complex boolean structure. JSAT 1(3-4), 209–236 (2007)
8. Ganzinger, H., Hagen, G., Nieuwenhuis, R., Oliveras, A., Tinelli, C.: DPLL(T): Fast decision procedures. In: Alur, R., Peled, D.A. (eds.) CAV 2004. LNCS, vol. 3114, pp. 175–188. Springer, Heidelberg (2004)
9. Gao, S., Avigad, J., Clarke, E.M.: δ-complete decision procedures for satisfiability over the reals. In: Gramlich, B., Miller, D., Sattler, U. (eds.) IJCAR 2012. LNCS, vol. 7364, pp. 286–300. Springer, Heidelberg (2012)
10. Gao, S., Kong, S., Clarke, E.M.: dReal: An SMT solver for nonlinear theories over the reals. In: Bonacina, M.P. (ed.) CADE 2013. LNCS, vol. 7898, pp. 208–214. Springer, Heidelberg (2013)
11. Gulwani, S., Tiwari, A.: Constraint-based approach for analysis of hybrid systems. In: Gupta, A., Malik, S. (eds.) CAV 2008. LNCS, vol. 5123, pp. 190–203. Springer, Heidelberg (2008)
12. Iwane, H., Yanami, H., Anai, H.: An effective implementation of a symbolic-numeric cylindrical algebraic decomposition for optimization problems. In: Proc. Intl. Workshop on Symb. Numeric Comp., SNC, pp. 168–177. ACM (2011)
13. Jovanović, D., de Moura, L.: Solving non-linear arithmetic. In: Gramlich, B., Miller, D., Sattler, U. (eds.) IJCAR 2012. LNCS, vol. 7364, pp. 339–354. Springer, Heidelberg (2012)
14. Leike, J.: Software and benchmarks for synthesis for polynomial lasso programs (2014), http://www.csl.sri.com/~tiwari/softwares/synthesis_for_polynomial_lasso_programs_source.zip
15. Leike, J., Tiwari, A.: Synthesis for polynomial lasso programs. In: McMillan, K.L., Rival, X. (eds.) VMCAI 2014. LNCS, vol. 8318, pp. 434–452. Springer, Heidelberg (2014)
16. Loup, U., Scheibler, K., Corzilius, F., Ábrahám, E., Becker, B.: A symbiosis of interval constraint propagation and cylindrical algebraic decomposition. In: Bonacina, M.P. (ed.) CADE 2013. LNCS, vol. 7898, pp. 193–207. Springer, Heidelberg (2013)
17. Matringe, N., Moura, A.V., Rebiha, R.: Generating invariants for non-linear hybrid systems by linear algebraic methods. In: Cousot, R., Martel, M. (eds.) SAS 2010. LNCS, vol. 6337, pp. 373–389. Springer, Heidelberg (2010)

18. Microsoft Research. Z3: An efficient SMT solver, `http://research.microsoft.com/projects/z3/`
19. Parrilo, P.A.: Semidefinite programming relaxations for semialgebraic problems. Mathematical Programming Ser. B 96(2), 293–320 (2003)
20. Rebiha, R., Matringe, N., Moura, A.V.: Transcendental inductive invariants generation for non-linear differential and hybrid systems. In: Proc. Hybrid Syst.: Comp. and Cntrl., HSCC, pp. 25–34. ACM (2012)
21. Sankaranarayanan, S., Sipma, H.B., Manna, Z.: Constructing invariants for hybrid systems. In: Alur, R., Pappas, G.J. (eds.) HSCC 2004. LNCS, vol. 2993, pp. 539–554. Springer, Heidelberg (2004)
22. Sankaranarayanan, S., Sipma, H.B., Manna, Z.: Constructing invariants for hybrid systems. Formal Methods in System Design 32(1), 25–55 (2008)
23. Srivastava, S., Gulwani, S., Foster, J.S.: Template-based program verification and program synthesis. STTT 15(5-6), 497–518 (2013)
24. Stengle, G.: A Nullstellensatz and a Positivstellensatz in semialgebraic geometry. Math. Ann. 207 (1974)
25. Sturm, T., Tiwari, A.: Verification and synthesis using real quantifier elimination. In: Proc. Intl. Symp. on Symb. and Alg. Comp., ISSAC, pp. 329–336. ACM (2011)
26. Tiwari, A.: An algebraic approach for the unsatisfiability of nonlinear constraints. In: Ong, L. (ed.) CSL 2005. LNCS, vol. 3634, pp. 248–262. Springer, Heidelberg (2005)
27. Tiwari, A., Khanna, G.: Nonlinear Systems: Approximating reach sets. In: Alur, R., Pappas, G.J. (eds.) HSCC 2004. LNCS, vol. 2993, pp. 600–614. Springer, Heidelberg (2004)

Yices 2.2*

Bruno Dutertre

Computer Science Laboratory, SRI International,
333 Ravenswood Avenue, Menlo Park, CA 94025, USA
bruno@csl.sri.com

Abstract. Yices is an SMT solver developed by SRI International. The first version of Yices was released in 2006 and has been continuously updated since then. In 2007, we started a complete re-implementation of the solver to improve performance and increase modularity and flexibility. We describe the latest release of Yices, namely, Yices 2.2. We present the tool's architecture and discuss the algorithms it implements, and we describe recent developments such as support for the SMT-LIB 2.0 notation and various performance improvements.

1 Introduction

SRI International has a long history in developing formal verification tools. Shostak developed his decision procedures and combination method while at SRI in the 1980s [1]. Since then, SRI has continuously extended and supported decision procedures as part the PVS theorem prover [2, 3]. Methods for combining Boolean satisfiability solvers and decision procedures were also pioneered at SRI in the ICS solver [4]. In 2006, we released Yices 1, an efficient SMT solver that was the state of the art. Yices 1 introduced an innovative Simplex-based decision procedure designed to efficiently integrate with a SAT solver [5], included a congruence-closure algorithm inspired by Simplify's E-graph [6], and used an approach for theory combination based on the Nelson-Oppen method [7] complemented with lazy generation of interface equalities (an optimization of the method proposed by Bozzano et al. [8]). These main ingredients and others introduced by Yices 1 are now common in general-purpose SMT solvers such as Z3, CVC, MathSAT, VeriT, and SMTInterpol [9–13].

Although Yices 1 remains a decent SMT solver to this day, it has some limitations:

- Yices 1 relies on a complex type system that includes predicate subtypes as in PVS. This logic is very expressive but it has a major drawback: type-correctness is undecidable in general. This is very confusing for users and leads to many problems as the behavior of Yices 1 on specifications that are not type correct is chaotic.
- Yices 1 was designed to be used mostly via a textual interface (i.e., by reading specifications from files), but many applications require close interaction with an SMT solver via a programmable interface. Yices 1 can be used as a library but its

---

* This work was supported in part by DARPA under contract FA8750-12-C-0284 and by the NSF Grant SHF:CSR-1017483. Any opinions, findings, and conclusions or recommendations expressed in this material are those of the author and do not necessarily reflect the views of the funding agencies.

A. Biere and R. Bloem (Eds.): CAV 2014, LNCS 8559, pp. 737–744, 2014.
© Springer International Publishing Switzerland 2014

API is cumbersome and incomplete, which makes it difficult to integrate Yices 1 in other software.
- Yices 1 has poor performance on certain classes of problems, most notably problems that involve bitvectors.

To address these issues, we started a complete re-implementation of Yices in 2007. Prototypes of the resulting new Yices 2 solver entered the SMT Competition in 2008 and in 2009. We then released a full-featured version of Yices 2 in May 2012, with a few updates for bug fixes since then. This paper describes our latest SMT solver— Yices 2.2—the first solver in the Yices family to support the SMT-LIB 2.0 notation.

2 Logic

The Yices 2 logic is the Yices 1 logic without the most complex type constructs. Primitive types include the arithmetic types int and real, bitvectors, and Boolean. One can extend this set by declaring new *uninterpreted* and *scalar* types. An uninterpreted type denotes a nonempty collection of object with no cardinality constraint. A scalar type denotes a nonempty finite collection of objects. In addition to these atomic types, Yices 2 provides constructors for function and tuple types. Yices 2 uses a simple form of subtyping: int is a subtype of real, and the subtyping relation extends in a natural way to tuple and function types. Details are given in the Yices 2 manual [14].

Yices 2 supports the usual Boolean and arithmetic operators, and all the bitvector operators defined in the SMT-LIB 1.2 and SMT-LIB 2.0 specifications [15, 16]. It also includes operations on tuples, and an update operation that applies to any function type. If f is a function, then the term (update f $t_1 \ldots t_n$ v) is the function that maps $(t_1, \ldots, t_n)$ to v and is equal to f at all other points. This generalizes the SMT-LIB store operation to arbitrary function types.

In summary, the Yices 2 logic is broadly similar to the array, arithmetic, and bitvector logics defined in SMT-LIB 2.0, with extensions to support tuples and scalar types, and with a more general function-update operation. Yices 2's subtyping mechanism allows arithmetic terms of integer and real types to be mixed arbitrarily (whereas Int and Real are disjoint types in SMT-LIB 2.0).

3 System Architecture

Figure 1 shows the core architecture of the Yices 2 library. The software is decomposed into three main modules for manipulating terms and types, contexts, and models, which are the main data types available in the Yices API. Additional components include the front ends that process specifications in different input languages, but these components are not part of the library.

Internally, Yices 2 maintains a global database of terms and types. The API provides a large number of functions for constructing terms and types, for pretty printing, and so forth. Unlike Yices 1, Yices 2 provides a complete API: all term and type constructors defined in the Yices 2 language are present in the API. We have paid special attention

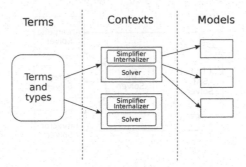

Fig. 1. Toplevel Architecture

to memory consumption by using compact data structures for terms and types, and by employing hash-consing to maximize sharing of subterms.

The second main module implements operations on *contexts*. A context is a central data structure that stores assertions to be checked for satisfiability. The API includes operations for creating and configuring contexts, adding and removing assertions, and for checking satisfiability of the asserted formulas. Internally, a context includes a solver and a module to simplify assertions and convert them into the internal form used by the solver. Contexts are highly flexible and can be configured to support a specific class of formulas, to apply different preprocessing and simplification procedures, and to use a specific solver or combination of solvers.

If the set of assertions in a context is satisfiable, then one can build a *model* of the formulas. Such a model maps uninterpreted symbols present in the assertions to concrete values such as rational or bitvector constants. A model is a separate object that can be queried and examined independently of the context from which it was built. Once a model is created from a context, it is not affected by further operations on this context. The model can remain in existence after the context is deleted.

A particular focus is to make Yices 2 easy to use as a library and enable flexible operations on multiple contexts and models while using a shared set of terms. Efficient operation on multiple contexts is crucial to applications related to software or control synthesis, such as exists/forall SMT solving [17–19].

4   Solvers

Yices includes a Boolean satisfiability solver and theory solvers for four main theories: uninterpreted functions with equalities, linear arithmetic, bitvectors, and arrays. These solvers can be combined as illustrated in Figure 2. It is also possible to select different solvers or combinations depending on the problem. For example, a specialized solver can be built by attaching the arithmetic solver directly to the SAT solver. The API provides functions to select the right solver combination when a context is created.

The SAT solver uses the CDCL approach. It is similar in performance and implementation to solvers such as Minisat 1.4 [20] or Picosat [21], with extensions to communicate

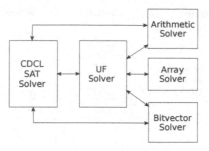

Fig. 2. Solver Architecture

with the theory solvers. For example, theory solvers can dynamically create literals and add clauses during the CDCL search, and can assign literals via theory propagation.

The solver for uninterpreted functions (UF) implements a congruence closure algorithm. The implementation is inspired by Simplify [6] with support for explanations [22], and a heuristic for *dynamic Ackermannization* [23, 24]. This UF solver supports Boolean terms. This enables the UF solver to store equalities as binary terms of the form $(\text{eq } t\ u)$ and efficiently perform propagation by congruence closure. A simple example is the following propagation

$$(\text{eq } t\ u) = \texttt{false} \ \wedge \ t = v \ \wedge \ u = w \ \Rightarrow \ (\text{eq } w\ v) = \texttt{false},$$

effectively deducing that $w \neq v$ follows from $t \neq u$ by congruence. This idea was introduced by the first Yices 2 prototype in 2008 and has since been adopted by other solvers.

The main arithmetic solver implements a decision procedure based on Simplex [5]. Yices also includes two specialized solvers for the *difference-logic fragments* of linear arithmetic. These two solvers rely on a variant of the Floyd-Warshall algorithm. One deals with integer difference logic and the other with real difference logic.

The bitvector solver is based on the "bit-blasting" approach. It applies various simplifications to bitvector constraints, then convert them to a pure Boolean SAT problem that is handled by the CDCL solver. In problems that combine uninterpreted functions and bitvectors or arrays and bitvectors, the bitvector solver dynamically adds constraints in the SAT solver as it receives equalities from the UF solver.

The array solver relies on instantiating the classic array axioms:

$$((\text{update } f\ i\ v)\ i) = v \tag{1}$$

$$((\text{update } f\ i\ v)\ j) = (f\ j) \ \text{ if } i \neq j \tag{2}$$

The solver eagerly generates instances of axiom (1) for every `update` term. On the other hand, it uses a lazy strategy for generating instances of axiom (2). After the UF and other theory solvers have built a consistent model (as explained below), the array solver searches for instances of axiom (2) that are false in this model. It adds these instances to the clause database, which triggers search for a different model.

5 Recent Developments

Yices 2.1 was released in August 2012. Since then, we have implemented new features, most notably a front end for SMT-LIB 2.0. Yices 2.2 supports most of the SMT-LIB 2.0 specification, except proof generation and construction of unsat cores.

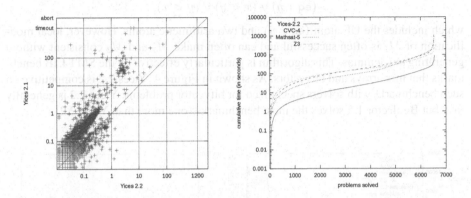

Fig. 3. Yices-2.2 on QF_UF Benchmarks

We have also added new preprocessing procedures, such as, the symmetry-breaking algorithm of Déharbe et al. [25]. Figure 3 shows the resulting performance improvement on the QF_UF benchmarks of SMT-LIB. The left part is a "scatter plot" comparing Yices-2.2 and Yices-2.1. Every point above the diagonal is a benchmark that Yices-2.2 solves faster than Yices 2.1. Yices-2.2 solves all benchmarks, whereas Yices-2.1 has two timeouts. The right part of the figure compares Yices-2.2 with other solvers[1] on the same benchmarks. All solvers in this graph use symmetry breaking, but Yices-2.2 is significantly faster. This data was collected on Linux machines (Ubuntu 12.04) with a timeout of 20 min. and a memory limit of 6 GB.

Another recent development is a new theory-combination method. In Yices, theory combination always involves UF on one side and another theory T (arithmetic or bitvector) on the other. Given two sets of formulas Γ_1 and Γ_2, such that Γ_1 is satisfiable in UF and Γ_2 is satisfiable in T, the goal is to ensure that $\Gamma_1 \cup \Gamma_2$ is satisfiable in the combined theory. For this purpose, Yices 2.2 uses a model-based approach [24]. Given a model M_1 of Γ_1 (computed by the UF solver) and a model M_2 of Γ_2, we must ensure that M_1 and M_2 agree on equalities between variables that occur in $\Gamma_1 \cap \Gamma_2$. By construction, the UF solver propagates all implied equalities to the bitvector and arithmetic solvers. The only conflicts between M_1 and M_2 are then pairs of shared variables (x, y) such that

$$M_2 \models x = y \quad \text{but} \quad M_1 \models x \neq y.$$

To fix this conflict, Yices 2.2 attempts to modify M_1 locally by merging the congruence classes of x and y while keeping M_2 unchanged. This merging is applied if it does not

---

[1] All experiments mentioned in this paper used solvers that entered the main track of SMT-COMP 2012, plus Z3 version 4.2.

conflict with existing disequalities in the UF solver, and if it does imply an equality $u = v$ where u and v are shared variables that have distinct values in M_2 (i.e., merging of x and y would cause more variables to become equal in theory T). If the conflict cannot be solved, Yices 2.2 generates an *interface lemma* that forces backtracking and search for different models. For example, in linear arithmetic, an interface lemma has the form

$$(\text{eq } x \, y) \vee (x < y) \vee (y < x),$$

which includes the UF atom $(\text{eq } x \, y)$ and two arithmetic atoms. However, local modification of M_1 is often successful and can often make M_1 and M_2 consistent without generating any lemmas. This algorithm is particularly effective on the SMT-LIB benchmarks that mix arrays and bitvectors. As shown in Figure 4, Yices 2.2 is competitive on such benchmarks with solvers specialized for bitvector problems. Yices 2.2 is generally fast, but Boolector 1.5 solves the most benchmarks (one more than Yices 2.2).

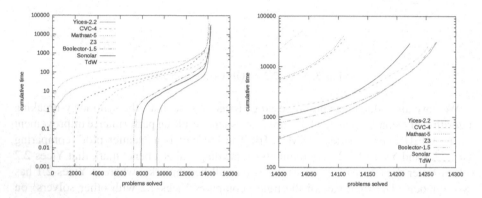

Fig. 4. Yices-2.2. vs. other Solvers on QF_AUFBV Problems

6 Conclusion

Yices 2 is a complete re-implementation of the Yices 1 solver. It is designed to be modular and extensible, to be efficient on a large class of problems, and to provide a rich API to enable advanced applications of SMT solving such as exists/forall SMT. Yices 2 now supports both versions of the SMT-LIB notation in addition to its own input language. Yices 2.2 is distributed at `http://yices.csl.sri.com`. Precompiled binaries are available for common operating systems such as Linux, Windows, Mac OS X and FreeBSD. Yices 2.2 is free for research and other non-commercial use.

References

1. Shostak, R.E.: Deciding Combinations of Theories. In: Loveland, D.W. (ed.) CADE 1982. LNCS, vol. 138, pp. 209–222. Springer, Heidelberg (1982)
2. Owre, S., Rushby, J.M., Shankar, N.: PVS: A Prototype Verification System. In: Kapur, D. (ed.) CADE 1992. LNCS (LNAI), vol. 607, pp. 748–752. Springer, Heidelberg (1992)

3. Owre, S., Rushby, J., Shankar, N., von Henke, F.: Formal Verification of Fault-Tolerant Architectures: Prolegomena to the Design of PVS. IEEE Transactions on Software Engineering 21(2), 107–125 (1995)
4. de Moura, L., Owre, S., Rueß, H., Rushby, J., Shankar, N.: The ICS Decision Procedures for Embedded Deduction. In: Basin, D., Rusinowitch, M. (eds.) IJCAR 2004. LNCS (LNAI), vol. 3097, pp. 218–222. Springer, Heidelberg (2004)
5. Dutertre, B., de Moura, L.: A fast linear-arithmetic solver for DPLL(T). In: Ball, T., Jones, R.B. (eds.) CAV 2006. LNCS, vol. 4144, pp. 81–94. Springer, Heidelberg (2006)
6. Detlefs, D., Nelson, G., Saxe, J.B.: Simplify: A Theorem Prover for Program Checking. Journal of the ACM 52(3), 365–473 (2005)
7. Nelson, G., Oppen, D.: Simplification by cooperating decision procedures. ACM Transactions on Programming Languages and Systems 1(2), 245–257 (1979)
8. Bozzano, M., Bruttomesso, R., Cimatti, A., Junttila, T.A., Ranise, S., van Rossum, P., Sebastiani, R.: Efficient Satisfiability Modulo Theories via Delayed Theory Combination. In: Etessami, K., Rajamani, S.K. (eds.) CAV 2005. LNCS, vol. 3576, pp. 335–349. Springer, Heidelberg (2005)
9. de Moura, L., Bjørner, N.S.: Z3: An Efficient SMT Solver. In: Ramakrishnan, C.R., Rehof, J. (eds.) TACAS 2008. LNCS, vol. 4963, pp. 337–340. Springer, Heidelberg (2008)
10. Barrett, C., Conway, C.L., Deters, M., Hadarean, L., Jovanović, D., King, T., Reynolds, A., Tinelli, C.: CVC4. In: Gopalakrishnan, G., Qadeer, S. (eds.) CAV 2011. LNCS, vol. 6806, pp. 171–177. Springer, Heidelberg (2011)
11. Cimatti, A., Griggio, A., Schaafsma, B.J., Sebastiani, R.: The MathSAT5 SMT Solver. In: Piterman, N., Smolka, S.A. (eds.) TACAS 2013. LNCS, vol. 7795, pp. 93–107. Springer, Heidelberg (2013)
12. Bouton, T., de Oliveira, D.C.B., Déharbe, D., Fontaine, P.: veriT: An Open, Trustable, and Efficient SMT Solver. In: Schmidt, R.A. (ed.) CADE 2009. LNCS (LNAI), vol. 5663, pp. 151–156. Springer, Heidelberg (2009)
13. Christ, J., Hoenicke, J., Nutz, A.: SMTInterpol: An Interpolating SMT Solver. In: Donaldson, A., Parker, D. (eds.) SPIN 2012. LNCS, vol. 7385, pp. 248–254. Springer, Heidelberg (2012)
14. Dutertre, B.: Yices 2 Manual. Technical report, Computer Science Laboratory, SRI International, Included in the Yices 2 distribution (2014)
15. Ranise, S., Tinelli, C.: The SMT-LIB Standard: Version 1.2. Technical report, SMT-LIB Initiative (2006), http://www.smtlib.org
16. Barrett, C., Sump, A., Tinelli, C.: The SMT-LIB Standard: Version 2.0. Technical report, SMT-LIB Initiative (2012), http://www.smtlib.org
17. Jha, S., Gulwani, S., Seshia, S.A., Tiwari, A.: Oracle-Guided Component-Based Program Synthesis. In: Kramer, J., Bishop, J., Devanbu, P.T., Uchitel, S. (eds.) Proceedings of the 32nd ACM/IEEE International Conference on Software Engineering (ICSE), pp. 215–224. ACM (2010)
18. Taly, A., Gulwani, S., Tiwari, A.: Synthesizing Switching Logic using Constraint Solving. In: Jones, N.D., Müller-Olm, M. (eds.) VMCAI 2009. LNCS, vol. 5403, pp. 305–319. Springer, Heidelberg (2009)
19. Cheng, C.H., Shankar, N., Rueß, H., Bensalem, S.: EFSMT: A Logical Framework for Cyber-Physical Systems. arXiv:1306:3456b2 (June 2014), http://www6.in.tum.de/~chengch/efsmt/
20. Eén, N., Sörensson, N.: An Extensible SAT Solver. In: Giunchiglia, E., Tacchella, A. (eds.) SAT 2003. LNCS, vol. 2919, pp. 502–518. Springer, Heidelberg (2004)
21. Biere, A.: PicoSAT Essentials. Journal on Satisfiability, Boolean Modelling, and Computation (JSAT) 4, 75–97 (2008)
22. Nieuwenhuis, R., Oliveras, A.: Fast Congruence Closure and Extensions. Information and Computation 205(4), 557–580 (2007)

23. Dutertre, B., de Moura, L.: The Yices SMT Solver (2006), http://yices.csl.sri.com/tool-paper.pdf
24. de Moura, L., Bjørner, N.: Model-Based Theory Combination. Electronic Notes on Theoretical Computer Science 198(2), 37–49 (2008)
25. Déharbe, D., Fontaine, P., Merz, S., Woltzenlogel Paleo, B.: Exploiting Symmetry in SMT Problems. In: Bjørner, N., Sofronie-Stokkermans, V. (eds.) CADE 2011. LNCS, vol. 6803, pp. 222–236. Springer, Heidelberg (2011)

A Simple and Scalable Static Analysis for Bound Analysis and Amortized Complexity Analysis*

Moritz Sinn, Florian Zuleger, and Helmut Veith

Vienna University of Technology
{sinn,zuleger,veith}@forsyte.at

Abstract. We present the first scalable *bound analysis* that achieves *amortized complexity analysis*. In contrast to earlier work, our bound analysis is not based on general purpose reasoners such as abstract interpreters, software model checkers or computer algebra tools. Rather, we derive bounds directly from abstract program models, which we obtain from programs by comparatively simple invariant generation and symbolic execution techniques. As a result, we obtain an analysis that is more predictable and more scalable than earlier approaches. We demonstrate by a thorough experimental evaluation that our analysis is fast and at the same time able to compute bounds for challenging loops in a large real-world benchmark. Technically, our approach is based on lossy vector addition systems (VASS). Our bound analysis first computes a lexicographic ranking function that proves the termination of a VASS, and then derives a bound from this ranking function. Our methodology achieves amortized analysis based on a new insight how lexicographic ranking functions can be used for bound analysis.

1 Introduction

Automatic methods for computing bounds on the resource consumption of programs are an active area of research [22,19,7,20,28,8,5,21,6]. We present the first scalable *bound analysis* for imperative programs that achieves *amortized complexity analysis*. Our techniques can be applied for deriving upper bounds on how often loops can be iterated as well as on how often a single or several control locations can be visited in terms of the program input.

The majority of earlier work on bound analysis has focused on mathematically intriguing frameworks for bound analysis. These analyses commonly employ general purpose reasoners such as abstract interpreters, software model checkers or computer algebra tools and therefore rely on elaborate heuristics to work in practice. In this paper we take an orthogonal approach that complements previous research. We propose a bound analysis based on a simple abstract program model, namely *lossy vector addition systems with states*. We present a static analysis with four well-defined analysis phases that are executed one after each other: program abstraction, control-flow abstraction, generation of a lexicographic ranking function and bound computation.

* Supported by the Austrian National Research Network S11403-N23 (RiSE) of the Austrian Science Fund (FWF) and by the Vienna Science and Technology Fund (WWTF) through grants PROSEED and ICT12-059.

A. Biere and R. Bloem (Eds.): CAV 2014, LNCS 8559, pp. 745–761, 2014.
© Springer International Publishing Switzerland 2014

A main contribution of this paper is a thorough experimental evaluation. We compare our approach against recent bounds analysis tools [7,5,6,12], and show that our approach is faster and at the same time achieves better results. Additionally, we demonstrate the scalability of our approach by a comparison against our earlier tool [28], which to the best of our knowledge represents the only tool evaluated on a large publicly available benchmark of C programs. We show that our new approach achieves better results while increasing the performance by an order of magnitude. Moreover, we discuss on this benchmark how our tool achieves amortized complexity analysis in real-world code.

Our technical key contribution is a new insight how lexicographic ranking functions can be used for bound analysis. Earlier approaches such as [7] simply count the number of elements in the image of the lexicographic ranking function in order to determine an upper bound on the possible program steps. The same idea implicitly underlies the bound analyses [15,19,16,20,28,6,12]. However, this reasoning misses arithmetic dependencies between the components of the lexicographic ranking function (see Section 2). In contrast, our analysis calculates how much a lexicographic ranking function component is increased when another component is decreased. This enables amortized analysis.

Related Work. An interesting line of research studies the *amortized analysis* of first-order functional programs (e.g. [22,21]) formulated as type rules over a template potential function with unknown coefficients; these coefficients are then found by linear programming. It is not clear how to transfer this approach to an imperative setting. Promising first steps for the amortized analysis of imperative programs are reported in [8]. Quantifier elimination is applied for simplifying a constraint system over template cost functions. Since quantifier elimination is expensive, the technique does not yet scale to larger programs.

Lexicographic ranking functions in automated termination analysis have been pioneered by Bradley et al. (see [10] and follow-up papers) who employ an elaborate constraint solving technique. A recent paper experimentally compares termination analysis by lexicographic ranking and transition invariants [13] implemented on top of a software model checker. [7] iteratively constructs a lexicographic ranking function by solving linear constraint systems. [11] is a hybrid of the approaches [13] and [7]. [10], [13] and [11] compute a lexicographic ranking function for a *single* control location (i.e., one loop header) at a time, while the application of bound analysis requires to find a common lexicographic ranking function for *all* control locations. [7] computes such a ranking function, but is limited to fairly small programs. Our approach complements the cited approaches as it represents a simple and scalable construction of a lexicographic ranking function for all control locations.

Bound Analysis. The COSTA project (e.g. [5,6]) studies the extraction of cost recurrence relations from Java bytecode programs and proposes new methods for solving them with the help of computer algebra systems. [15] proposes to extend the polyhedra abstract domain with max- and non-linear expressions. [19] introduces multiple counters and exploits their dependencies such that upper bounds have to be computed only for restricted program parts. [16] proposes an abstract

```
        void main(uint n) {
          int a = n, b = 0;
l1:       while (a > 0) {
            a--; b++;
l2:         while (b > 0) {
              b--;
l3:           for (int i = n-1; i > 0; i--)
              if (a > 0 && ?) {
l4:             a--; b++;
          } } } }
```

$$begin$$
$$\downarrow \begin{array}{c} a = n \\ b = 0 \\ i = 0 \end{array}$$

$$end \xleftarrow{Id} l_1$$

$$Id \left(\downarrow \tau_1 \equiv \begin{array}{c} a' \leq a - 1 \\ b' \leq b + 1 \\ i' \leq i \end{array} \right.$$

$$l_2$$

$$Id \left(\downarrow \tau_2 \equiv \begin{array}{c} a' \leq a \\ b' \leq b - 1 \\ i' \leq i + (n - 1) \end{array} \right.$$

$$l_3$$

$$\tau_4 \equiv \begin{array}{c} a' \leq a - 1 \\ b' \leq b + 1 \\ i' \leq i - 1 \end{array} \left(\downarrow Id \right) \tau_3 \equiv \begin{array}{c} a' \leq a \\ b' \leq b \\ i' \leq i - 1 \end{array}$$

$$l_4$$

Fig. 1. Our running example, '?' denotes non-determinism (arising from a condition not modeled in the analysis). On the right we state the lossy VASS obtained by abstraction, Id denotes $a' \leq a$, $b' \leq b$, $i' \leq i$.

interpretation-guided program transformation that separates the different loop phases such that bounds can be computed for each phase in isolation. [20] employs proof-rules for bound computation combined with disjunctive abstract domains for summarizing inner loops. [28] proposes a bound analysis based on the size-change abstract domain. [17,12] discuss how to alternate between bound analysis and invariant analysis for the mutual benefit of the computed bounds and invariants.

2   Motivation and Overview

The example presented in Figure 1 (encountered during our experiments) is challenging for an automated bound analysis: (C1) There are loops whose loop counter is modified by an inner loop: the innermost loop modifies the counter variables a and b of the two outer loops. Thus, the inner loop *cannot be ignored* (i.e., cannot be sliced away) during the analysis of the two outer loops. (C2) The middle loop with loop counter b requires a *path-sensitive* analysis to establish the linear loop bound n: it is not enough to consider how often the innermost loop can be executed (at most n^2 times) but rather how often the if-branch of the innermost loop (on which b is actually incremented) can be executed (at most n times). (C3) Current bound analysis techniques cannot model *increments* and instead approximate increments by *resets*, e.g., approximate the increment of b by an assignment to a value between 0 and n (using the fact that n is an upper bound of b)! Because of this overapproximation no bound analysis from the literature is able to compute the linear loop bound n for the middle loop. We now illustrate the main steps of our analysis:

1. Program Abstraction: First, our analysis abstracts the program to the VASS depicted in Figure 1. We introduce VASSs in Section 3. In this paper we are using *parameterized* VASSs, where we allow increments that are symbolic but constant throughout the program (such as $n - 1$). We extract lossy VASSs from C programs using simple invariant generation and symbolic execution techniques (described in Section 7).

2. Control Flow Abstraction: We propose a new abstraction for bound analysis, which we call *control flow abstraction* (CA) (described in Section 4). CA abstracts the VASS from Figure 1 into a transition system with four transitions:
$\rho_1 \equiv a' \leq a - 1 \wedge b' \leq b + 1 \wedge i' \leq i,$ $\rho_2 \equiv a' \leq a \wedge b' \leq b - 1 \wedge i' \leq i + (n - 1),$
$\rho_3 \equiv a' \leq a \wedge b' \leq b \wedge i' \leq i - 1,$ $\rho_4 \equiv a' \leq a - 1 \wedge b' \leq b + 1 \wedge i' \leq i - 1.$
CA effectively merges loops at different control locations into a single loop creating one transition for every cyclic path of every loop (without unwinding inner loops). This significantly simplifies the design of the later analysis phases.

3. Ranking Function Generation: Our ranking function generation (Algorithm 2 stated in Section 5) finds an *order* on the transitions resulting from CA such that there is a variable for every transition, which decreases on that transition and does not increase on the transitions that are lower in the order. This results in the lexicographic ranking function $l = \langle a, a, b, i \rangle$ for the transitions $\rho_1, \rho_4, \rho_2, \rho_3$ in that order. Our soundness theorem (Theorem 1) guarantees that l proves the termination of Figure 1.

4. Bound Analysis: Our bound analysis (Algorithm 3 stated in Section 6) computes a bound for every transition ρ by adding for every other transition τ how often τ increases the variable of ρ and by how much. In this way, our bound analysis computes the bound n for ρ_2, because ρ_2 can be incremented by ρ_1 and ρ_4, but this can only happen n times, due to the initial value n of a. Further, our bound analysis computes the bound $n * (n - 1)$ for ρ_3 from the fact that only ρ_2 can increase the counter i by $n - 1$ and that ρ_2 has the already computed transition-bound n. Our soundness result (Theorem 2) guarantees that the bound n obtained for ρ_2 is indeed a bound on how often the middle loop of Figure 1 can be executed.

Our bound analysis solves the challenges (C1)-(C3): CA allows us to analyze all loops at once (C1) creating one transition for every loop path (C2). The abstract model of lossy VASS is precise enough to model counter increments, which is a key requirement for achieving amortized complexity analysis (C3).

2.1   Amortized Complexity Analysis

In his influential paper [27] Tarjan introduces amortized complexity analysis using the example of a stack, which supports two operations *push* (which puts an element on the stack) and *popMany* (which removes several elements from the stack). He assumes that the cost of *push* is 1 and the cost of *popMany* is the number of removed elements. We use his example (see Figure 2) to discuss how our bound analysis achieves amortized analysis: Our analysis first abstracts the program to a VASS and then applies CA. This results in the three transitions $\rho_1 \equiv i' = i - 1 \wedge n' = n + 1, \rho_2 \equiv i' = i - 1 \wedge n' = n, \rho_3 \equiv i' = i \wedge n' = n - 1$ (the first two transitions come from the outer loop, the last transition from the inner loop). Algorithm 2 then computes the lexicographic ranking function $\langle i, i, n \rangle$ for the transitions ρ_1, ρ_2, ρ_3 in that order. Our bound analysis (Algorithm 3) then computes the joint bound m for the transitions ρ_1 and ρ_2. Our bound analysis further computes the bound m for transition ρ_3 from the fact that only ρ_1 can

```
    void main(int m) {
        int i=m, n = 0;    //stack = emptyStack();
l₁:     while (i > 0) {
            i--;
            if (?) //push
                n++;           //stack.push(element);
            else   //popMany
l₂:             while (n > 0 && ?)
                    n--;       //element = stack.pop();
} }
```

Fig. 2. Model of Tarjan's stack example [27] for amortized complexity analysis

increase the counter n by 1 and that ρ_1 has the already computed bound m. Adding these two bounds gives the amortized complexity bound $2m$ for Figure 2. We highlight that our analysis has actually used the variable n of transition ρ_3 as a *potential function* (see [27] for a definition)! A lexicographic ranking function $\langle x_1, \ldots, x_n \rangle$ can be seen as a *multidimensional potential function*. Consider, for example, the ranking function $\langle a, a, b, i \rangle$ for the transitions $\rho_1, \rho_4, \rho_2, \rho_3$ of Figure 1. The potential of ρ_3 can be increased by ρ_2 whose potential in turn can be increased by ρ_1 and ρ_4.

3   Lossy VASSs and Basic Definitions

In this section we define lossy VASSs (introduced in [9]) and state definitions that we need later on. We will often drop the 'lossy' in front of 'VASS' because we do not introduce non-lossy VASSs and there is no danger of confusion. In this paper, we will use VASSs as *minimal program model* for bound analysis of sequential programs without procedures. We leave the extension to concurrent and recursive programs for future work.

Definition 1 (Lossy Vector Addition System with States (VASS)). *We fix some finite set of variables $Var = \{x_1, \ldots, x_n\}$. A lossy vector addition system with states (VASS) is a tuple $P = (L, E)$, where L is a finite set of locations, and $E \subseteq L \times \mathbb{Z}^n \times L$ is a finite set of transitions. We write $l_1 \xrightarrow{d} l_2$ to denote an edge (l_1, d, l_2) for some vector $d \in \mathbb{Z}^n$. We often specify the vector $d \in \mathbb{Z}^n$ by predicates $x_i' \leq x_i + d_i$ with $d_i \in \mathbb{Z}$.*

A path of P is a sequence $l_0 \xrightarrow{d_0} l_1 \xrightarrow{d_1} \cdots$ with $l_i \xrightarrow{d_i} l_{i+1} \in E$ for all i. A path is cyclic, if it has the same start- and end-location. A path is simple, if it does not visit a location twice except for start- and end-location. We write $\pi = \pi_1 \cdot \pi_2$ for the concatenation of two paths π_1 and π_2, where the end-location of π_1 is the start-location of π_2. We say π' is a subpath of a path π, if there are paths π_1 and π_2 with $\pi = \pi_1 \cdot \pi' \cdot \pi_2$.

The set of valuations of Var is the set $V_{Var} = Var \to \mathbb{N}$ of mappings from Var to the natural numbers. A trace of P is a sequence $(l_0, \sigma_0) \xrightarrow{d_0} (l_1, \sigma_1) \xrightarrow{d_1} \cdots$

such that $l_0 \xrightarrow{d_0} l_1 \xrightarrow{d_1} \cdots$ *is path of* P, $\sigma_i \in V_{Var}$ *and* $\sigma_{i+1}(x_j) \leq \sigma_i(x_j) + d_i$ *for all* i *and* $1 \leq j \leq n$. P *is* terminating, *if there is no infinite trace of* P.

Values of VASS variables are always non-negative. We describe how to obtain VASSs from programs by abstraction in Section 7. The non-negativity of VASS values has two important consequences: (1) Transitions in VASSs contain implicit guards: for example a transition $x' \leq x + c$ can only be taken if $x + c \geq 0$. (2) VASS transitions can be used to model variable increments as well as variable resets: we replace the assignment $x := k$, where $k \in \mathbb{Z}$, by the VASS transition $x' \leq x + k$ during program abstraction (we point out that lossiness is essential for abstracting assignments). This only increases the set of possible program traces and thus provides a conservative abstraction.

Parameterized VASSs. In our implementation we use a slight generalization of lossy VASSs. We allow the increment n in a transition predicate $x' \leq x + n$ to be symbolic but constant; in particular, we require that n does not belong to the set of variables *Var*. Our bound algorithm works equally well with symbolic increments under the condition that we know the sign of n. We call these extended systems *parameterized VASSs*. See Figure 1 for an example.

In the following we introduce some standard terminology that allows us to precisely speak about loops and related notions.

Definition 2 (Reducible Graph, Loop Header, Natural Loop, Loop-nest Tree, e.g. [4]). *Let* $G = (V, E)$ *be a directed graph with a unique entry point such that all nodes are reachable from the entry point. A node* a *dominates a node* b, *if every path from entry to* b *includes* a. *An edge* $l_1 \rightarrow l_2$ *is a* back edge, *if* l_2 *dominates* l_1. G *is* reducible, *if* G *becomes acyclic after removing all back edges. A node is a* loop header, *if it is the target of a back edge. The* (natural) loop *of a loop header* h *in a reducible graph is the maximal set of nodes* L *such that for all* $x \in L$ *(1)* h *dominates* x *and (2) there is a back edge from some node* n *to* h *such that there is a path from* x *to node* n *that does not contain* h.

In the rest of this paper we restrict ourselves to VASSs and programs whose control flow graph is reducible. This choice is justified by the fact that irreducible control flow is *very rare* in practice (e.g. see the study in [26]). For analyzing irreducible programs we propose to use program transformations that make the program reducible; we do not elaborate this idea further due to lack of space.

Next, we define a special case of path, which corresponds to the notion of bound used in this paper (defined below).

Definition 3 (Loop-path). *A* loop-path π *is a simple cyclic path, which starts and ends at some loop header* l, *and visits only locations inside the natural loop of* l.

Example: $l_2 \xrightarrow{\tau_2} l_3 \xrightarrow{Id} l_2$ is a loop-path for the VASS in Figure 1. However, $l_2 \xrightarrow{Id} l_1 \xrightarrow{\tau_1} l_2$ is not a loop-path because it does not stay inside the natural loop of l_2. $l_2 \xrightarrow{\tau_2} l_3 \xrightarrow{Id} l_4 \xrightarrow{\tau_4} l_3 \xrightarrow{Id} l_2$ is not a loop-path, because it is not simple (l_3 is visited twice).

Procedure: CA(P)
Input: a reducible VASS P
Output: a transition system $\mathcal{T}$
$\mathcal{T} := \emptyset;$
foreach *loop header l in P* **do**
  foreach *loop-path $\pi = l \xrightarrow{d_1} l_1 \cdots l_{n-1} \xrightarrow{d_n} l$* **do**
    $\mathcal{T} := \mathcal{T} \cup \{d_1 + \cdots + d_n\};$
return $\mathcal{T};$

Algorithm 1. CA creates a *transition system* from a given VASS

Definition 4 (Instance of a loop-path). *Let* $\pi = l_1 \xrightarrow{d_1} l_2 \xrightarrow{d_2} \cdots l_{n-1} \xrightarrow{d_{n-1}}$
l_1 *be a loop-path. A path ν is an* instance of π *iff ν is of the form* $l_1 \xrightarrow{d_1} l_2 * l_2 \xrightarrow{d_2}$
$l_3 * l_3 \cdots l_{n-1} * l_{n-1} \xrightarrow{d_{n-1}} l_n = l_1$, *where $l_i * l_i$ denotes any (possibly empty) path*
starting and ending at location l_i which does not contain l_1. A path p contains
an instance ν of π iff ν is a subpath of p. Let be ν be an instance of π contained
in p; a transition t on p belongs to ν, *if t is on ν and $t = l_i \xrightarrow{d_i} l_{i+1}$ for some i.*

We note the following facts about instances: Every transition in a path belongs
to *at most one* instance of a loop-path. Every transition in a given cyclic path
belongs to *exactly one* instance of a loop-path.

Example: There are four instances of loop-paths in the path $\pi = l_1 \xrightarrow{\tau_1} l_2 \xrightarrow{\tau_2}$
$l_3 \xrightarrow{Id} l_4 \xrightarrow{\tau_3} l_3 \xrightarrow{Id} l_2 \xrightarrow{\tau_2} l_3 \xrightarrow{Id} l_2 \xrightarrow{Id} l_1$ of the VASS in Figure 1: $l_1 \xrightarrow{\tau_1} l_2 \xrightarrow{Id} l_1$,
$l_2 \xrightarrow{\tau_2} l_3 \xrightarrow{Id} l_2$ (twice) and $l_3 \xrightarrow{Id} l_4 \xrightarrow{\tau_3} l_3$.

Definition 5 (Path-bound). *A* path-bound *for a loop-path π is an expression*
b over Var such that for every trace $(l_0, \sigma_0) \xrightarrow{d_0} \cdots$ of P the path $l_0 \xrightarrow{d_0} \cdots$
contains at most $b(\sigma_0)$ instances of π.

Path-bounds have various applications in bound and complexity analysis: the
computational complexity of a program can be obtained by adding the bounds of
the loop-paths of all loops; a *loop bound* can be obtained by adding the bounds
of all loop-paths of a given loop; the number of *visits* to a *single control location*
l can be obtained by adding the bounds of the loop-paths that include l (our
notion of a path-bound can be seen as a path-sensitive generalization of the
notion of a "reachability-bound" [20]); similarly one can obtain a bound on the
number of *visits* to a *set of control locations*. More generally, one can obtain
resource bounds for a given *cost model* by multiplying the bound on the number
of visits to a control location with the *cost* for visiting this location.

4   Control Flow Abstraction

Control flow abstraction (CA), stated in Algorithm 1, is based on two main
ideas: (1) Given a program P, CA results into one transition for every loop-path

---

Procedure: Ranking($\mathcal{T}$)
Input: a transition system $\mathcal{T}$
Output: a lexicographic ranking function l, which has one component for every
        transition $\rho \in \mathcal{T}$
$\mathcal{S} := \mathcal{T}$;
$l :=$ "lexicographic ranking function with no components";
while *there is a transition $\rho \in \mathcal{S}$ and a variable x such that $\rho \models x' < x$ and for
all $\rho' \in \mathcal{S}$ we have $\rho' \models x' \leq x$* **do**
  $\quad \lfloor \quad \mathcal{S} := \mathcal{S} \setminus \rho$;
  $\quad \lfloor \quad l := l.append(x)$;
if $\mathcal{S} = \emptyset$ **then return** l **else return** "Transitions $\mathcal{S}$ maybe non-terminating"

Algorithm 2. Ranking computes a lexicographic ranking function

π for all loop   headers l of P. This enables a path-sensitive analysis, which
ensures high precision during ranking function generation and bound analysis.
(2) The control structure is abstracted: effectively, all loops are merged into a
single loop. This allows to compute a common lexicographic ranking function for
all loops later on. CA maps VASSs to *transition systems*. Transition systems are
not meant to be executed; their sole purpose is to be used for ranking function
generation and bound analysis.

Definition 6 (Transition System). *A transition system is a set of vectors
$d \in \mathbb{Z}^n$. We often specify a transition $d \in \mathbb{Z}^n$ by predicates $x_i' \leq x_i + d_i$, where
$d_i \in \mathbb{Z}$. We also write $d \models x_i' \leq x_i$ (resp. $d \models x_i' < x_i$) for $d_i \leq 0$ (resp. $d_i < 0$).*

Loop-Path Contraction. Algorithm 1 creates one transition for every loop-path $\pi =
l \xrightarrow{d_1} l_1 \cdots l_{n-1} \xrightarrow{d_n} l$. The transition $d_1 + \cdots + d_n$ represents the accumulated effect
of all variable increments along the path. The key idea of loop-path contraction is
to *ignore any inner loop* on π. We will incorporate the effects of the inner loops only
later on during the ranking function generation and bound analysis phase.

CA Represents Our Choice of Precision in the Analysis: CA facilitates a high
degree of disjunctiveness in the analysis, where we keep one disjunct for every
loop-path. By encapsulating the level of precision in a single analysis phase, we
achieve a modular analysis (only during CA we need to deal with the control
structure of the VASS). This simplifies the design of the later termination and
bound analysis and also allows us to easily adjust the analysis precision if the
number of paths is prohibitively high (see the discussion on *path merging* in [25]).

5   Ranking Function Generation

In this section we introduce our algorithm for ranking function generation: Algorithm 2 reads in a transition system obtained from CA and returns a lexicographic
ranking function that provides a witness for termination. The key idea of the algorithm is to incrementally construct a lexicographic ranking function from local

ranking functions. We call a variable x a *local ranking function* for a transition ρ, if $\rho \models x' < x$. A tuple $l = \langle y_1, y_2, \cdots, y_k \rangle \in Var^k$ is a *lexicographic ranking function* for a transition system $\mathcal{T}$ iff for each $\rho \in \mathcal{T}$ there is a ranking function component y_i that is a local ranking function for ρ and $\rho \models y'_j \leq y_j$ for all $j < i$. Algorithm 2 maintains a candidate lexicographic ranking function l and a set of transitions $\mathcal{S}$ for which no ranking function component has been added to l. In each step the algorithm checks if there is a transition ρ in $\mathcal{S}$ and a variable x such that (1) x is a local ranking function for ρ and (2) no remaining transition increases the value of x, i.e., the condition $\forall \rho' \in \mathcal{S}.\rho' \models x' \leq x$ is satisfied. If (1) and (2) are satisfied, ρ is removed from the set of remaining transitions $\mathcal{S}$ and x is added as the component for ρ in the lexicographic ranking function l. Conditions (1) and (2) ensure that the transition ρ cannot be taken infinitely often if only transitions from $\mathcal{S}$ are taken. The algorithm stops, if no further transition can be removed. If $\mathcal{S}$ is empty, the lexicographic ranking function l is returned. Otherwise it is reported that the remaining transitions $\mathcal{S}$ might lead to non-terminating executions.

Next we state the correctness of the combined application of Algorithm 1 and Algorithm 2. The proof can be found in [25].

Theorem 1. *If Algorithm 2 returns a lexicographic ranking function l for the transition system $\mathcal{T}$ obtained from Algorithm 1 then VASS P is terminating.*

Reasons for Failure. There are two reasons why our ranking function generation algorithm may fail: (1) There is a transition ρ without a *local ranking function*, i.e., there is no variable x with $\rho \models x' < x$. Such a transition ρ will never be removed from $\mathcal{S}$. (2) There is a *cyclic dependency* between local ranking functions, i.e., for every transition $\rho \in \mathcal{S}$ there is a local ranking function x but the condition "$\rho' \models x' \leq x$ for all $\rho' \in \mathcal{S}$" is never satisfied. We found cyclic dependencies to be very rare in practice (only 4 instances); we provide a discussion of the failures encountered in our experiments in [25].

Non-determinism. We note that in presence of transitions with more than one local ranking function, the result of Algorithm 2 may depend on the choice for x. However, it is straight-forward to extend Algorithm 2 to generate all possible lexicographic ranking functions.

6 Bound Computation

In this section we introduce our bound algorithm: Algorithm 3 computes a bound b for a transition ρ of the transition system $\mathcal{T}$. The main idea of Algorithm 3 is to rely only on the components of the lexicographic ranking function l for bound computation. Let x be the component of ρ in l. We recall that the termination algorithm has already established that x is a local ranking function for ρ and therefore we have $\rho \models x > x'$. Thus ρ can be executed at most $\texttt{InitialValue}(x)$ often unless x is increased by other transitions: Algorithm 3 initializes $b := \texttt{InitialValue}(x)$ and then checks for every other transition ρ' if it increases x,

---

Procedure: Bound(ρ)
Input: a transition ρ
Output: a bound for transition ρ
Global: transition system $\mathcal{T}$, lexicographic ranking function l
$x :=$ ranking function component of ρ in l;
$b :=$ InitialValue(x);
foreach *transition* $\rho' \in \mathcal{T}$ *with* $\rho' \not\models x' \leq x$ **do**
 Let $k \in \mathbb{N}$ s.t. $x' \leq x + k$ in ρ';
 $b := b + $ Bound(ρ') $\cdot k$;
Let $k \in \mathbb{N}$ s.t. $x' \leq x - k$ in ρ;
return $b = b/k$;

Algorithm 3. Bound returns a bound for transition ρ

i.e., $\rho' \not\models x' \leq x$. For every such transition ρ' Algorithm 3 recursively computes a bound, multiplies this bound by the height of the increase k and adds the result to b. Finally, we divide b by the decrease k of x on transition ρ.

Termination. Algorithm 3 terminates because the recursive calls cannot create a cycle. This is because Algorithm 3 uses only the components of l for establishing bounds and the existence of the lexicographic ranking function l precludes cyclic dependencies.

Soundness. Our soundness result (Theorem 2, for a proof see [25]) rests on the assumption that the CFG of P is an SCC whose unique entry point is also its unique exit point. We can always ensure this condition by a program transformation that encloses P in a dummy while-loop while($y > 0$)$\{P;y\text{--};\}$, where y is a fresh variable with InitialValue(y) $= 1$. We point out that this program transformation enable us to compute path-bounds in terms of the program inputs for CFGs with multiple SCCs (e.g., a program with two successive loops).

Theorem 2. *Let b be a bound computed by Algorithm 3 for a transition ρ obtained from a loop-path π during CA. Then b is a path-bound for π.*

Greedy Bound Computation. The bound computed by Algorithm 3 depends on the lexicographic ranking function l. Clearly, it is possible to run the algorithm for multiple lexicographic ranking functions and choose the minimum over the generated bounds. However, we found the greedy approach to work well in practice and did not see a need for implementing the enumeration strategy.

Complexity of the Algorithm / Size of Bound Expressions. For ordinary VASS, the complexity of Algorithm 3 is polynomial in the size of the input with a small exponent (depending on the exact definition of the complexity parameters). Unfortunately, this statement does not hold for *parameterized* VASSs, for which bound expressions can be exponentially big: We consider n transitions $\rho_1, \ldots, \rho_n$

with the local ranking functions $x_1, \ldots, x_n$ and the lexicographic ranking function $\langle x_1, \ldots, x_n \rangle$. We assume that transition ρ_i increments x_j by some constant c_{ij} for $i < j$. Then, Algorithm 3 computes the bound stated in the following formula, which is exponentially big for symbolic coefficients c_{ij}:

$$b(\rho_n) = \sum_{k \in [0,n-1]} \prod_{i_1 < \cdots < i_k \in [1,n-1]} \texttt{InitialValue}(x_{i_1}) c_{i_1 i_2} \cdots c_{i_k n}$$

However, in practical examples the variable dependencies are *sparse*, i.e., most coefficients c_{ij} are zero (confirmed by our experiments). We highlight that Algorithm 3 exploits this sparsity as it does not compute the bound using the explicit formula stated above but rather computes the bound for the current transition ρ using only the bounds of the transitions that actually increase the counter of ρ (i.e., $c_{ij} > 0$). We note that in our experiments the computed bounds are small and the running time of Algorithm 3 is basically linear in the number of transitions. We conclude that in practice one should make use of the fine-grained precision offered by the possibly exponentially-sized bound expressions.

Preprocessing: Merging Transitions. Before the bound computation our analysis applies the following rule until no more transitions can be merged: Let ρ_1 and ρ_2 be two transitions with the same local ranking function x in l such that $x' \leq x + k \in \rho_1$ and $x' \leq x + k \in \rho_2$ for some k (i.e., both transitions decrement x by the same amount). We replace ρ_1 and ρ_2 by the transition $\rho = \{y' \leq y + \max\{k_1, k_2\} \mid y' \leq y + k_1 \in \rho_1 \wedge y' \leq y + k_2 \in \rho_2\}$. It is not difficult to see that merging transitions is sound and always improves the bound computed by Algorithm 3 (we do not give a formal proof here for lack of space).

Example: We have obtained the *loop bound* of the middle loop in Figure 1 from the path-bound n of its single transition ρ_2 (see Section 2). We have obtained $2m$ as the *amortized complexity* of Figure 2 by adding the path-bounds of its transitions ρ_1, ρ_2, ρ_3 applying merging to ρ_1 and ρ_2 (see Section 2.1).

7 Program Abstraction

In this section we describe how to abstract programs to VASSs.

Definition 7 (Program). *Let Σ be a set of* states. *The set of transition relations $\Gamma = 2^{\Sigma \times \Sigma}$ is the set of relations over Σ. A program is a tuple $P = (L, E)$, where L is a finite set of* locations, *and $E \subseteq L \times \Gamma \times L$ is a finite set of transitions. We write $l_1 \xrightarrow{\rho} l_2$ to denote a transition (l_1, ρ, l_2). We assume the set of reachable states $Reach(l)$ is defined for every location $l \in L$ in the standard way. Let $e_1, e_2 \in \Sigma \to \mathbb{Z}$ be integer-valued expressions over the states, and let $c \in \mathbb{Z}$ be some integer. We say $e_1 \geq 0$ is invariant for l, if $e_1(s) \geq 0$ holds for all $s \in Reach(l)$. We say $e_2' \leq e_1 + c$ is invariant for $l_1 \xrightarrow{\rho} l_2$, if $e_2(s_2) \leq e_1(s_1) + c$ holds for all $(s_1, s_2) \in \rho$ with $s_1 \in Reach(l_1)$. We say e_1 is a* norm, *if $e_1 \geq 0$ is invariant for every location l.*

Definition 8 (Abstraction of a Program). *A VASS $V = (L, E')$ with variables Var is an* abstraction *of a program $P = (L, E)$ iff (1) every $x \in$ Var is a* norm *and (2) for each transition $l_1 \xrightarrow{\rho} l_2 \in E$ there is a transition $l_1 \xrightarrow{d} l_2 \in E'$ such that every $x' \leq x + c \in d$ is invariant for $l_1 \xrightarrow{\rho} l_2$.*

The above definition suggests a three-step methodology for abstracting programs: (1) Guess a set of norms $N \subseteq \Sigma \to \mathbb{Z}$. (2) For every $x \in N$ show that $x \geq 0$ is invariant at all locations l. If this is not the case, discard the norm x. (3) For every $x \in N$ and every transition $l_1 \xrightarrow{\rho} l_2$ find a constant expression c such that $x' \leq x + c$ is invariant for $l_1 \xrightarrow{\rho} l_2$. Next, we describe how we implement this methodology.

7.1   Abstracting Programs to VASSs: Our Implementation

Guessing Norms. The key idea of Algorithm 2 is to find a local ranking function for every transition. We recall that a transition is obtained from a loop-path during CA. For this reason, our main heuristic is to consider expressions as norms that are local ranking functions for at least one loop-path of the program under analysis. Our implementation iterates over all loop-paths $\pi = l \xrightarrow{\rho_1} l_1 \xrightarrow{\rho_2} \cdots l_{n-1} \xrightarrow{\rho_n} l$: Let $\mathtt{rel}(\pi) = \rho_1 \circ \cdots \circ \rho_n$ be the transition relation obtained by contracting all transition relations along π. We implement the computation of $\mathtt{rel}(\pi)$ by *symbolic backward execution*, which returns a set of *guards* $e \geq 0$ (we note that guards are normalized, e.g., $n \geq i$ is transformed into $n - i \geq 0$) and *updates* $x' = e$, where e is some expression over the program variables and x' denotes the value of x after executing π. A *local ranking function* is an expression r such that (a) $r \geq 0$ is a guard of $\mathtt{rel}(\pi)$ and (b) $\delta_r = r - r' > 0$, where r' denotes the expression r where every variables x is replaced by expression e according to the update $x' = e$ of $\mathtt{rel}(\pi)$. For every local ranking function r our implementation adds the expression $\max\{r + \delta_r, 0\}$ to the set of norms N. Clearly, all norms $x = \max\{r + \delta_r, 0\} \in N$ satisfy the invariant $x \geq 0$.

Abstracting Transitions. In our implementation we derive a transition predicate $x' \leq x + c$ for a given norm $x = \max\{e, 0\} \in N$ and transition $l_1 \xrightarrow{\rho} l_2$ as follows: We obtain the expression e' from e by replacing variables with their updates according to ρ. The expression e' either constitutes an *increment*, i.e., $e' = e + k_1$, or a *reset*, i.e., $e' = k_2$, for some expression k_i. For now, assume k_i is constant. We proceed by a case distinction: If $e' = e + k_1$ and $e + k_1 \geq 0$ is invariant for $l_1 \xrightarrow{\rho} l_2$, then our implementation derives the transition predicate $x' \leq x + k_1$. This derivation is sound, because of the invariant $e + k_1 \geq 0$. (We motivate this derivation rule as follows: assume $r \geq 0$ and $\delta_r = r - r'$ hold on ρ, we have $e' = e + (-\delta_r) \geq 0$ for $e = r + \delta_r$.) Otherwise, our implementation derives the transition predicate $x' \leq x + \max\{k_i, 0\}$. This derivation is sound because of properties of maxima. If k_i is not constant, we first search for an invariant $k_i \leq u$ with u constant, and then proceed as above (replacing k_i with u). We implement invariant analysis by symbolic backward execution (see [25]).

	Bounded	1	$logn$	n	$nlogn$	n^2	n^3	$n^{>3}$	EXP	Time w/o Time-outs	# Time-outs
Loopus	383	131	0	151	0	81	16	4	0	437s	5
KoAT	321	121	0	142	0	54	0	3	0	682s	282
PUBS	279	116	5	129	5	15	4	0	6	1000s	58
Rank	84	56	0	19	0	8	1	0	0	173s	6

Fig. 3. Analysis results for the benchmark from [12]

Non-linear Local Ranking Functions. In our experiments we only found few loops that do not have a linear local ranking function. However, these loops almost always involve the iterated division or multiplication of a loop counter by a constant such as in the transition relation $\rho \equiv x > 1 \wedge x' = x/2$. For such loops we can introduce the logarithm of x as a norm, i.e., $y = \log x$, and then try to establish $y > 0$ from the condition $x > 1$ and derive the transition relation by $y' \leq y - 1$ from the update $x' = x/2$.

Data Structures. Previous approaches [18,24] have described how to abstract programs with data structures to integer programs by making use of appropriate norms such as the length of a list or the number of elements in a tree. In our implementation we follow these approaches using a light-weight abstraction based on optimistic aliasing assumptions.

8 Experiments

We implemented the discussed approach as an intraprocedural analysis (we use function inlining) based on the LLVM [23] compiler framework. Our tool Loopus computes loop bounds (depending on a command-line parameter, see [1]) either in terms of (1) the inputs to the SCC to which the loop belongs, or (2) the function inputs (this is implemented by enclosing the function body in a dummy loop as described in Section 6). At the same time Loopus also computes the asymptotic complexity of the considered SCC. We use the Z3 SMT solver [14] for removing unsatisfiable paths during the analysis. Given a loop condition of form $a \neq 0$ Loopus heuristically decides to either assume $a > 0$ or $a < 0$ as loop-invariant; this assumption is reported to the user. Similarly, Loopus assumes $x > 0$ when an update of a loop counter of the form $x = x * 2$ or $x = x/2$ is detected. The task of validating these assumptions is orthogonal to our approach and can be performed by standard tools for invariant generation. Loopus and more details on our experimental evaluation are available at [1].

8.1 Comparison to Tools from the Literature

We compare Loopus against the tools KoAT [12], PUBS [5,6] and Rank [7]. For the comparison we use the benchmark [2], which consists of small example programs from the bound analysis literature and the benchmark suite which was used to evaluate T2 [11]. Since Loopus expects C code but KoAT expects a transition system as input, we needed to obtain C programs for comparison,

	Analyzed	Outer Dep.	Inner Dep.	Paths > 1	Non-Trivial
Loops	4210	255	305	1276	1475
Bounded	3205[3060]	120 [112]	148 [129]	744 [695]	831 [812]
/ Overall	76% [73%]	47% [44%]	49% [42%]	58%[54%]	56% [55%]
SCCs	2833	181	193	902	937
Bounded	2289	70	95	542	564
/ Overall	81%	39%	50%	60%	60%

Fig. 4. Loop and SCC Statistic of our current implementation for the cBench Benchmark, the results obtained with the implementation of [28] are given in square brackets

see [25] for details. Figure 3 states the results for the different tools (the results for KoAT, PUBS and Rank were taken from [12]). Columns 2 to 9 state the number of programs that were found to have the given complexity by the respective tool. The table shows that Loopus can compute bounds for more loops than the other tools. Moreover one can see significant differences in analysis time, which are due to time-outs (the table shows the analysis time without time-outs and the number of time-outs separately; the time-out is set to 60s for all tools). The detailed comparison available at [1] shows that there are 84 loops for which Loopus computes an asymptotically more precise bound than any of the 3 other tools, compared to 66 loops for which one of the 3 other tools computed an asymptotically more precise bound than Loopus .

8.2   Evaluation on Real-World Code

We evaluated Loopus on the program and compiler optimization benchmark *Collective Benchmark* [3](cBench), which contains a total of 1027 different C files (after removing code duplicates) with 211.892 lines of code.

Data Structures. For expressing bounds of loops iterating over arrays or recursive data structures Loopus introduces shadow variables representing appropriate norms such as the length of a list or the size of an array. Loopus makes the following optimistic assumptions which are reported to the user: Pointers do not alias, a recursive data structure is acyclic if a loop iterates over it, a loop iterating over an array of characters is assumed to be terminating if an inequality check on the string termination character '\0' is found.[1] We made these assumptions in order to find interesting examples, a manual check on a sample of around 100 loops in the benchmark found the assumptions to be valid with respect to termination. The task of validating an assumption is orthogonal to our approach and can be performed by standard tools for shape analysis.

Results. In Figure 4, we give our results on different loop classes. We recall that our bound analysis is based on an *explicitly* computed termination proof. We do not list the results of our termination analysis separately, because a bound was computed for 98% of all loops for which termination was proven.

---

[1] This assumption is necessary since the type system of C does not distinguish between an array of characters and a string.

Details on the reasons for failure of our termination analysis and bound analysis, which occurred during the experiments, are given in [25]. In column *Analyzed* we state the results over all loops in the benchmark. We summarize the results over all loop categories except *Analyzed* in the column *Non-Trivial*.

Challenging Loop Classes. The loop-class '*Outer Dependent*' captures all outer loops whose termination behavior is affected by the executions of an inner loop. (E.g., in Figure 1 termination of loop l_1 depends on loop l_3, while in Figure 2 termination of loop l_1 does *not* depend on loop l_2.) We define an inner loop to be in the set of '*Inner Dependent*' loops if it has a loop counter that is *not* reset before entering the loop. (E.g., in Figure 1 loop counter i of loop l_3 is always reset to $n - 1$ before entering the loop, while loop counter b of loop l_2 is never reset.) The loop-class '*Paths > 1*' contains all loops which have more than 1 path left after program slicing (see [25]). The categories for the SCCs are the same as for the loops: we define an SCC to be in a certain category if it contains at least one loop which is in that category. Success ratios of around 50% in the difficult categories demonstrate that our method is able to handle non-trivial termination and complexity behavior of real world programs.

Amortization. For 107 loops out of the 305 loops in the class '*Inner Dependent*', the bound that our tool computed was amortized in the sense that it is asymptotically smaller than one would expect from the loop-nesting depth of the loop. In 12 cases the amortization was caused by incrementing a counter of the inner loop in the outer loop as in Figures 1 and 2. The 12 loops are available at [1]. *For these loops a precise bound cannot be computed by any other tool (as discussed in the beginning of Section 2).*

Performance. The results were obtained on a Linux machine with a 3.2 Ghz dual core processor and 8 GB Ram. 92 loops of the 4302 loops in our benchmark are located in 44 SCCs with an irreducible control flow. We thus analyzed 4210 loops. The total runtime of our tool on the benchmark (more than 200.000 LoC) did not exceed 20 minutes. The time-out limit of maximal 420 seconds computation time per SCC was not reached. There were only 27 out of 2833 SCCs (174 out of 4210 loops) on which the analysis spent more than 10 seconds.

Experimental Comparison. For the purpose of a realistic comparison, we ran the tool of [28] on the same machine with an equal time out limit of 420 second. The results are given in square brackets in Figure 4. Note the significant increase in the number of loops bounded in each of the challenging categories. The execution of the tool [28] took an order of magnitude longer (nearly 13 hours) and we got 78 time-outs. The main reason for the drastic performance increase is our new reasoning on inner loops: The approach of [28] handles inner loops by inserting the transitive hull of an inner loop on a given path of the outer loop. This can blow up the number of paths exponentially. We avoid this exponential blow-up thanks to CA: CA allows us to analyze inner and outer loops at the same time and thus eliminates the need for transitive hull computation.

Acknowledgements. We thank Fabian Souczek and Thomas Pani for help with the experiments.

References

1. http://forsyte.at/static/people/sinn/loopus/
2. http://aprove.informatik.rwth-aachen.de/eval/IntegerComplexity
3. http://ctuning.org/wiki/index.php/CTools:CBench
4. Aho, A.V., Sethi, R., Ullman, J.D.: Compilers: Principles, Techniques, and Tools. Addison-Wesley (1986)
5. Albert, E., Arenas, P., Genaim, S., Puebla, G., Zanardini, D.: Cost analysis of object-oriented bytecode programs. Theor. Comput. Sci. 413(1), 142–159 (2012)
6. Albert, E., Genaim, S., Masud, A.N.: On the inference of resource usage upper and lower bounds. ACM Trans. Comput. Log. 14(3), 22 (2013)
7. Alias, C., Darte, A., Feautrier, P., Gonnord, L.: Multi-dimensional rankings, program termination, and complexity bounds of flowchart programs. In: Cousot, R., Martel, M. (eds.) SAS 2010. LNCS, vol. 6337, pp. 117–133. Springer, Heidelberg (2010)
8. Alonso-Blas, D.E., Genaim, S.: On the limits of the classical approach to cost analysis. In: Miné, A., Schmidt, D. (eds.) SAS 2012. LNCS, vol. 7460, pp. 405–421. Springer, Heidelberg (2012)
9. Bouajjani, A., Mayr, R.: Model checking lossy vector addition systems. In: Meinel, C., Tison, S. (eds.) STACS 1999. LNCS, vol. 1563, pp. 323–333. Springer, Heidelberg (1999)
10. Bradley, A.R., Manna, Z., Sipma, H.B.: Linear ranking with reachability. In: Etessami, K., Rajamani, S.K. (eds.) CAV 2005. LNCS, vol. 3576, pp. 491–504. Springer, Heidelberg (2005)
11. Brockschmidt, M., Cook, B., Fuhs, C.: Better termination proving through cooperation. In: Sharygina, N., Veith, H. (eds.) CAV 2013. LNCS, vol. 8044, pp. 413–429. Springer, Heidelberg (2013)
12. Brockschmidt, M., Emmes, F., Falke, S., Fuhs, C., Giesl, J.: Alternating runtime and size complexity analysis of integer programs. In: Ábrahám, E., Havelund, K. (eds.) TACAS 2014. LNCS, vol. 8413, pp. 140–155. Springer, Heidelberg (2014)
13. Cook, B., See, A., Zuleger, F.: Ramsey vs. lexicographic termination proving. In: Piterman, N., Smolka, S.A. (eds.) TACAS 2013. LNCS, vol. 7795, pp. 47–61. Springer, Heidelberg (2013)
14. de Moura, L., Bjørner, N.: Z3: An efficient smt solver. In: Ramakrishnan, C.R., Rehof, J. (eds.) TACAS 2008. LNCS, vol. 4963, pp. 337–340. Springer, Heidelberg (2008)
15. Gulavani, B.S., Gulwani, S.: A numerical abstract domain based on expression abstraction and max operator with application in timing analysis. In: Gupta, A., Malik, S. (eds.) CAV 2008. LNCS, vol. 5123, pp. 370–384. Springer, Heidelberg (2008)
16. Gulwani, S., Jain, S., Koskinen, E.: Control-flow refinement and progress invariants for bound analysis. In: PLDI, pp. 375–385 (2009)
17. Gulwani, S., Juvekar, S.: Bound analysis using backward symbolic execution. Technical Report MSR-TR-2004-95. Microsoft Research (2009)
18. Gulwani, S., Lev-Ami, T., Sagiv, M.: A combination framework for tracking partition sizes. In: POPL, pp. 239–251 (2009)

19. Gulwani, S., Mehra, K.K., Chilimbi, T.M.: Speed: precise and efficient static estimation of program computational complexity. In: POPL, pp. 127–139 (2009)
20. Gulwani, S., Zuleger, F.: The reachability-bound problem. In: PLDI, pp. 292–304 (2010)
21. Hoffmann, J., Aehlig, K., Hofmann, M.: Multivariate amortized resource analysis. ACM Trans. Program. Lang. Syst. 34(3), 14 (2012)
22. Hofmann, M., Jost, S.: Static prediction of heap space usage for first-order functional programs. In: POPL, pp. 185–197 (2003)
23. Lattner, C., Adve, V.S.: Llvm: A compilation framework for lifelong program analysis & transformation. In: CGO, pp. 75–88 (2004)
24. Magill, S., Tsai, M.-H., Lee, P., Tsay, Y.-K.: Automatic numeric abstractions for heap-manipulating programs. In: POPL, pp. 211–222 (2010)
25. Sinn, M., Zuleger, F., Veith, H.: A simple and scalable static analysis for bound analysis and amortized complexity analysis. CoRR, abs/1401.5842 (2014)
26. Stanier, J., Watson, D.: A study of irreducibility in c programs. Softw. Pract. Exper. 42(1), 117–130 (2012)
27. Tarjan, R.E.: Amortized computational complexity. SIAM Journal on Algebraic Discrete Methods 6(2), 306–318 (1985)
28. Zuleger, F., Gulwani, S., Sinn, M., Veith, H.: Bound analysis of imperative programs with the size-change abstraction. In: Yahav, E. (ed.) SAS 2011. LNCS, vol. 6887, pp. 280–297. Springer, Heidelberg (2011)

Symbolic Resource Bound Inference
for Functional Programs

Ravichandhran Madhavan and Viktor Kuncak

EPFL
{ravi.kandhadai,viktor.kuncak}@epfl.ch

Abstract. We present an approach for inferring symbolic resource bounds for purely functional programs consisting of recursive functions, algebraic data types and nonlinear arithmetic operations. In our approach, the developer specifies the desired shape of the bound as a program expression containing numerical holes which we refer to as *templates*. For e.g, time $\leq a * \mathsf{height}(\mathsf{tree}) + b$ where a, b are unknowns, is a template that specifies a bound on the execution time. We present a scalable algorithm for computing tight bounds for sequential and parallel execution times by solving for the unknowns in the template. We empirically evaluate our approach on several benchmarks that manipulate complex data structures such as binomial heap, lefitist heap, red-black tree and AVL tree. Our implementation is able to infer hard, nonlinear symbolic time bounds for our benchmarks that are beyond the capability of the existing approaches.

1 Introduction

This paper presents a new algorithm and a publicly available tool for inferring resource bounds of functional programs.[1] We focus on functional languages because they eliminate by construction low-level memory errors and allow the developer to focus on functional correctness and performance properties. Our tool is designed to automate reasoning about such high-level properties. We expect this research direction to be relevant both for improving the reliability of functional programming infrastructure used in many enterprises (e.g. LinkedIn, Twitter, several banks), as well as for reasoning about software and hardware systems within interactive theorem provers [17], [21], [29], [12], [19], which often model stateful and distributed systems using functional descriptions.

The analysis we present in this paper aims to discover invariants (e.g. function postconditions) that establish program correctness as well as bounds on parallel and sequential program execution time. Such invariants often contain invocations of user-defined recursive functions specific to the program being verified, such as size or height functions on a tree structure. We therefore need a verification technique that can prove invariants that are expressed in terms of user-defined

---

[1] To download the tool please see http://lara.epfl.ch/w/software

A. Biere and R. Bloem (Eds.): CAV 2014, LNCS 8559, pp. 762–778, 2014.

functions. To the best of our knowledge, our tool is the first available system that can establish such complex resource bounds with this degree of automation.

Our tool can show, for example, that a function converting a propositional formula into negation-normal form takes no more than $44 \cdot \text{size}(f) - 20$ operations, where $\text{size}(f)$ is the number of nodes in the formula f. The tool also proves that the depth of the computation graph (time in an infinitely parallel implementation) is bounded by $5 \cdot h(f) - 2$, where $h(f) \geq 1$ is the height of the formula tree. As another example, it shows that deleting from an AVL tree requires the number of operations given by $145 \cdot h(t) + 19$, where $h(t) \geq 0$ is the height of the tree t, whereas the depth of the computation graph is $51 \cdot h(t) + 4$.

Our tool takes as input the program, as well as the desired shapes of invariants, which we call *templates*. The goal of the analysis becomes finding coefficients in the templates. The coefficients in practice tend to be sufficiently large that simply trying out small values does not scale. We therefore turn to one of the most useful techniques for finding unknown coefficients in invariants: Farkas' lemma. This method converts a $\exists\forall$ problem on linear constraints into a purely existential problem over non-linear constraints.

The challenge that we address is developing a practical technique that makes such expensive non-linear reasoning work on programs and templates that contain invocations of user-defined recursive functions, that use algebraic data types (such as trees and lists), and that have complex control flow with many disjunctions.

We present a publicly available tool that handles these difficulties through an incremental and counterexample-driven algorithm that soundly encodes algebraic data types and recursive functions and that fully leverages the ability of an SMT solver to handle disjunctions efficiently. We show that our technique is effective for the problem of discovering highly application-specific inductive resource bounds in functional programs.

2 Background and Enabling Techniques

We first present key existing technology on which our tool builds.

2.1 Instrumenting Programs to Track Resource Bounds

Our approach decouples the semantics of resources such as execution time from their static analysis. We start with the exact instrumentation of programs with resource bounds, without approximating e.g. conditionals or recursive invocations. To illustrate our approach, consider a simple Scala [22] program shown in Fig. 1, which appends a list l2 to the reverse of l1. We use this program as our running example. The recursive function size counts the length of its list argument; it is user-defined and omitted for brevity.

Fig. 2 illustrates the instrumentation for tracking execution time on this example. For every expression e in the program the resource consumed by e is computed as a function of the resources consumed by its sub-expressions.

```
def revRec(l1:List, l2:List) : List =          def revRec(l1:List,l2:List):(List,Int) =
(l1 match {                                     (l1 match {
  case Nil() ⇒ l2                                 case Nil() ⇒ (l2, 1)
  case Cons(x,xs) ⇒                               case Cons(x,xs) ⇒
    revRec(xs, Cons(x, l2))                         val (e, t) = revRec(xs, Cons(x,l2))
})                                                  (e, 5 + t) })
ensuring(res ⇒ time ≤ a∗size(l1) + b))          ensuring(res ⇒ res._2 ≤ a∗size(l1) + b))
```

Fig. 1. Appending $l2$ to the reverse of $l1$ **Fig. 2.** After time instrumentation

For instance, the *execution time* of an expression (such as $e_1 * e_2$) is *the sum* of the execution times of its arguments (e_1 and e_2) plus the time taken by the operation (here, $*$) performed by the expression (in this case, 1). We expose the resource usage of a procedure to its callers by augmenting the return value of the procedure with its resource usage. The resource consumption of a function call is determined as the sum of the resources consumed by the called function (which is exposed through its augmented return value) plus the cost of invoking the function. The cost of primitive operations, such as $+$, variable access, etc., are parametrized by a cost model which is, by default, 1 for all primitive operations.

Another resource that we consider in this paper is *depth*, which is a measure of parallelism in an expression. *Depth* [6] is the longest chain of dependencies between the operations of an expression. The *depth* and *work* (the sequential execution time) of programs have been used by the previous works to accurately estimate the parallel running times on a given parallel system [6]. Fig. 3 and Fig. 4 illustrate the instrumentation our tool perform to compute the *depth* of a procedure that traverses a tree. We compute the *depth* of an expression

```
                                          def traverse(t: Tree):(Tree,Int)= (t match{
                                            case Leaf() ⇒ f(t)
def traverse(t: Tree) = (t match {          case Node(l,v,r) ⇒
  case Leaf() ⇒ f(t)                          val (el, dl) = traverse(l)
  case Node(l,v,r) ⇒                           val (er, dr) = traverse(r)
    traverse(l) + traverse(r) + f(t)          val (e, d) = f(t)
)                                             (el+er+e, max(max(dl,dr)+1,d)+5)) })
ensuring(res ⇒ depth ≤ a∗height(t) + b)    ensuring(res ⇒ res._2 ≤ a∗height(t) + b)
```

Fig. 3. A tree traversal procedure   **Fig. 4.** After *depth* instrumentation

similarly to its execution time, but instead of adding the resource usages of the sub-expressions, we compute their maximum.

Every inductive invariant for the instrumented procedure obtained by solving for the unknowns a, b is a valid bound for the resource consumed by the original procedure. Moreover, the strongest invariant is also the strongest bound on the resource. Notice that the instrumentation increases the program sizes, introduces tuples and, in the case of *depth* instrumentation, creates numerous max operations.

2.2 Solving Numerical Parametric Formulas

Our approach requires deciding validity of formulas of the form $\exists \mathbf{a}.\forall \mathbf{x}.\neg \phi$, where $\mathbf{a}$ is a vector of variables. The formulas have a single quantifier alternation. We thus need to find values for $\mathbf{a}$ that will make ϕ unsatisfiable. We refer to ϕ as a *parametric formula* whose parameters are the variables $\mathbf{a}$. When the formula ϕ consists only of *linear inequalities*, finding values for the parameters $\mathbf{a}$ can be converted to that of satisfying a quantifier-free nonlinear constraint (Farkas' constraint) using a known reduction, sketched below.

A conjunction of linear inequalities is unsatisfiable if one can derive a contradiction $1 \leq 0$ by multiplying the inequalities by non-negative values, subtracting the smaller terms by non-negative values and adding the coefficients in the inequalities. E.g, $ax+by+c \leq 0 \wedge x-1 \leq 0$ is unsatisfiable if there exist non-negative real numbers $\lambda_0, \lambda_1, \lambda_2$ such that $\lambda_1 \cdot (ax + by + c) + \lambda_2 \cdot (x - 1) - \lambda_0 \leq 0$ reduces to $1 \leq 0$. Hence, the coefficients of x and y should become 0 and the constant term should become 1. This yields a nonlinear constraint $\lambda_1 a + \lambda_2 = 0 \wedge \lambda_1 b = 0 \wedge \lambda_1 c - \lambda_2 - \lambda_0 = 1 \wedge \lambda_0 \geq 0 \wedge \lambda_1 \geq 0 \wedge \lambda_2 \geq 0$. The values of a and b in every model for this nonlinear constraint will make the inequalities unsatisfiable.

This approach has been used by previous works [7,9,15] to infer linear invariants for numerical programs. There are two important points to note about this approach: (a) In the presence of real valued variables, handling strict inequalities in the parametric formula requires an extension based on *Motzkin's transposition theorem* as discussed in [24]. (b) This approach is complete for linear real formulas by Farkas' Lemma, but not for linear integer formulas. However, the incompleteness did not manifest in any of our experiments. Similar observation has also been documented in the previous works such as [15].

2.3 Successive Function Approximation by Unfolding

To construct verification conditions (VCs) in the presence of algebraic data-types (ADTs) and recursive functions we use the approach employed in the Leon verifier [5,28]. The approach constructs VCs incrementally wherein each increment makes the VC more precise by unrolling the function calls that have not been unrolled in the earlier increments (referred to as VC refinement). The functions in the VCs at any given step are treated as uninterpreted functions. Hence, every VC created is a sufficient but not necessary condition for the postcondition to be inductive. The postcondition is inductive if any of the generated VCs are valid. The refinement of VCs continues forever until the postcondition is proven. In our implementation, we enforce termination by bounding the number of times a recursive function call is unrolled (fixed as 2 in our experiments).

We explain the VC generation and refinement on the revRec function shown in Fig. 2. The initial VC that we create for revRec is shown below

$$\forall l1, l2, res, x, xs, e, t, r, f1, f2, \text{size}, \text{revRec}. \neg\phi$$

$$\phi \equiv ((l1 = Nil() \wedge res = (l2, 1)) \vee (l1 = Cons(x, xs) \wedge res = (e, 5 + t) \wedge (e, t) =$$
$$\text{revRec}(xs, Cons(x, l2))) \wedge f2 > ar + b \wedge r = \text{size}(l1) \wedge res = (f1, f2) \tag{1}$$

The function symbols in the VC are universally quantified as they are treated as uninterpreted functions. The combined algorithm presented in the next section solves for the parameters a, b so that the VC holds for any definition of size and revRec. If the formula (1) has no solution, it then refines the VC by unrolling the calls to size and revRec. For instance, unrolling $r = \text{size}(l1)$ in the above formula will conjoin the predicate with the formula $(l1 = Nil() \wedge r = 0) \vee (l1 = Cons(x1, xs1) \wedge r = 1 + r2 \wedge r2 = \text{size}(xs1))$ that corresponds to the body of size. The subsequent refinements will unroll the call $r2 = \text{size}(xs1)$ and so on. Note that, whereas unfolding is the key mechanism in Leon [5, 28], here it is used in a new combination, with the inference of numerical parameters.

3   Invariant Inference Algorithm

We next present core techniques of our algorithm for inferring resource bounds. The algorithm introduces new techniques and combines the existing techniques to overcome their individual weaknesses.

3.1   Solving Formulas with Algebraic Data Types and Recursion

We first describe our approach for solving parametric formulas that are similar to constraint (1) with ADTs, uninterpreted functions, linear and nonlinear arithmetic operations.

Eliminating Uninterpreted Functions and ADT Constructors from Parametric Disjuncts. Let d be a parametric formula with parameters param defined over a set of variables X and uninterpreted function symbols X_f. We reduce this to a formula d' that does not have any uninterpreted functions and ADT constructors using the axioms of uninterpreted functions and ADTs as described below. We convert d to negation normal form and normalize the resulting formula so that every atomic predicate (atom) referring to uninterpreted functions or ADTs is of the form $r = f(v_1, v_2, \ldots, v_n)$ or $r = cons(v_1, v_2, \ldots, v_n)$ where f is a function symbol, $cons$ is the constructor of an ADT and $r, v_1, \ldots, v_n$ are variables. We refer to this process as *purification*. Let F and T be the set of function atoms and ADT atoms in the purified formula.

$$\text{let } \delta_1 = \bigwedge \{ (\bigwedge_{i=1}^{n} v_i = u_i) \Rightarrow (r = r') \mid r = f(v_1, \ldots, v_n),$$
$$r' = f(u_1, \ldots, u_n) \in F \}$$

$$\text{let } \delta_2 = \bigwedge \{ (\bigwedge_{i=1}^{n} v_i = u_i) \Leftrightarrow (r = r') \mid r = cons(v_1, \ldots, v_n),$$
$$r' = cons(u_1, \ldots, u_n) \in T \}$$

$$\text{let } \delta = (purify(d) \setminus (F \cup T)) \wedge \delta_1 \wedge \delta_2$$

where $\delta \setminus (F \cup T)$ is a formula obtained by substituting with true every atomic predicate in F or T. Notice that the above elimination procedure uses only the fact that the ADT constructors are *injective*. Due to this the completeness of our approach may not be immediately obvious. In section 3.2 we formalize the completeness property of our approach.

Applying the above reduction to the disjunct d_{ex} of Constraint (1) along which $l = Nil()$, results in a constraint of the form sketched below. We consider tuples also as ADTs.

$$purify(d_{ex}) = \begin{cases} (l1 = Nil() \wedge res = (l2, 1) \wedge f2 > ar + b \\ \wedge r = \mathsf{size}(n1) \wedge res = (f1, f2) \end{cases}$$

$$\delta_{ex} = (f2 > ar + b \wedge ((l2 = f1 \wedge f2 = 1) \Leftrightarrow res = res)) \qquad (2)$$

The formula δ obtained by eliminating uninterpreted function symbols and ADTs typically has several disjunctions. In fact, if there are n function symbols and ADT constructors in d then d' could potentially have $O(n^2)$ disjunctions and $O(2^{n^2})$ disjuncts. Our approach described in the next subsection solves the parametric formulas incrementally based on counter-examples.

3.2   Incrementally Solving Parametric Formulas

Figure 5 presents our algorithm for solving an alternating satisfiability problem. Given a parametric formula, the goal is to find an assignment ι for params such that replacing params according to ι results in unsatisfiable formula. We explain our algorithm using the example presented in the earlier section. Consider the VC given by constraint (1). Initially, we start with some arbitrary assignment ι for the parameters a and b (line 5 of the algorithm). Say $\iota(a) = \iota(b) = 0$ initially. Next, we instantiate (1) by replacing a and b by 0 (line 8), which results in the non-parametric constraint: $\phi_{ex} : ((l1 = Nil() \wedge res = (l2, 1)) \vee (l1 = Cons(x, xs) \wedge res = (e, 5 + t) \wedge (e, t) = \mathsf{revRec}(xs, Cons(x, l2)) \wedge f2 > 0 \wedge r = \mathsf{size}(l1) \wedge res = (f1, f2)$.

If the constraint becomes unsatisfiable because of the instantiation then we have found a solution. Otherwise, we construct a model σ for the instantiated formula as shown in line 11. For the constraint ϕ_{ex} shown above, $l1 \mapsto Nil(), l2 \mapsto Nil(), res \mapsto (Nil(), 1), r \mapsto -1$ and size $\mapsto \lambda x.(x = Nil() \rightarrow -1 \mid 0)$ is a model. In the next step, we combine the models ι and σ and construct σ'. Note that ι is an assignment for parameters and σ is an assignment for universally quantified variables. Using the model σ' we choose a disjunct of the parametric formula (1) that is satisfied by σ'. For our example, the disjunct chosen will be $d_{ex} : l1 = Nil() \wedge res = (l2, 1) \wedge f2 > ar + b \wedge r = \mathsf{size}(l1) \wedge res = (f1, f2)$. This operation of choosing a disjunct satisfying a given model can be performed efficiently in time linear in the size of the formula without explicitly constructing a disjunctive normal form.

The function elimFunctions invoked at line 14 eliminates the function symbols and ADT constructors from the disjunct d using the approach described in section 3.1. Applying elimFunctions on d_{ex} results in the formula δ_{ex} given by (2).

```
1   input : A parametric linear formula φ with parameters 'params'
2   output : Assignments for params such that φ(params) is unsatisfiable
3   or ∅ if no such assignment exists
4   def solveUNSAT(params, φ) {
5     construct an arbitrary initial mapping ι : params ↦ ℝ
6     var C = true
7     while(true) {
8       let φ_inst be obtained from φ by replacing every t ∈ params by ι(t)
9       if (φ_inst is unsatisfiable) return ι
10      else {
11        choose σ such that σ ⊨ φ_inst
12        let σ' be ι ⊎ σ
13        choose a disjunct d of φ such that σ' ⊨ d
14        let δ be elimFunctions(d)
15        choose a disjunct d' of δ such that σ' ⊨ d'
16        let d_num be elim(d')
17        let C_d be unsatConstraints(d_num)
18        C = C ∧ C_d
19        if (C is unsatisfiable) return ∅
20        else {
21          choose m such that m ⊨ C
22          let ι be the projection of m onto params }}}}
```

Fig. 5. A procedure for finding parameters for a formula to make it unsatisfiable. unsatConstraints generates nonlinear constraints for unsatisfiability of a disjunct as illustrated in section 2.2.

We choose a disjunct d' of δ that satisfies the model σ'. For our example, the disjunct of δ_{ex} that will be chosen is $d'_{ex} : l2 = f1 \wedge f2 = 1 \wedge res = res \wedge f2 > ar + b$.

Eliminating Non-numerical Predicates from a Disjunct (elim). We now describe the operation elim at line 16. Let d' be the parametric disjunct chosen in the previous step. d' is a conjunction of atomic predicates (atoms). Let d_t denote the atoms that consist of variables of ADT type or boolean type. Let d_n denote the atoms that do not contain any parameters and only contain variables of numerical type. Let d_p denote the remaining atoms that has parameters and numerical variables.

For the example disjunct d'_{ex}, d_t is $l2 = f1$, d_n is $f2 = 1$ and d_p is $f2 > ar + b$. The disjunct d_t can be dropped as d_t cannot be falsified by any instantiation of the parameters. This is because d_p and d_t will have no common variables. The remaining disjunct $d_n \wedge d_p$ is completely numerical. However, we simplify $d_n \wedge d_p$ further as explained below. We construct a simplified formula d'_n by eliminating variables in d_n that do not appear in d_p by applying the quantifier elimination rules of Presburger arithmetic on d_n [23]. In particular, we apply the one-point rule that uses equalities to eliminate variables and the rule that eliminates relations over variables for which only upper or lower bounds exist. $d_n \wedge d_p$ is unsatisfiable *iff* $d'_n \wedge d_p$ is unsatisfiable.

Typically, d_n has several variables that do not appear in d_p. This elimination helps reduce the sizes of the disjuncts and in turn the sizes of the nonlinear constraints generated from the disjunct. Our experiments indicate that the sizes of the disjuncts are reduced by 70% or more.

We construct nonlinear Farkas' constraints (line 17) for falsifying the disjunct d_{num}, obtained after elimination phase, as described in section 2.2. We conjoin the nonlinear constraint with previously generated constraints, if any (lines 17,18). A satisfying assignment to the new constraint will falsify every disjunct explored thus far. We consider the satisfying assignment as the next candidate model ι for the parameters and repeat the above process.

If the nonlinear constraint C is unsatisfiable at any given step then we conclude that there exists no solution that would make ϕ unsatisfiable. In this case, we refine the VC by unrolling the functions calls as explained in section 2.3 and reapply the algorithm solveUNSAT on the refined VC.

Correctness, Completeness and Termination of solveUNSAT

Let $\mathcal{F}$ denote parametric linear formulas belonging to the theory of real arithmetic, uninterpreted functions and ADTs, in which parameters are real valued and appear only as coefficients of variables.

Theorem 1. *Let $\phi \in \mathcal{F}$ be a linear parametric formula with parameters params.*

1. *The procedure solveUNSAT is correct for $\mathcal{F}$. That is, if $\iota \neq \emptyset$ then ι is an assignment for parameters that will make ϕ unsatisfiable.*
2. *The procedure solveUNSAT is complete for $\mathcal{F}$. That is, if $\iota = \emptyset$ then there does not exist an assignment for params that will make ϕ unsatisfiable.*
3. *The procedure solveUNSAT terminates.*

The correctness of procedure solveUNSAT is obvious as the procedure returns a model ι iff ι makes the formula ϕ unsatisfiable. The algorithm terminates since, in every iteration of the solveUNSAT algorithm, at least one satisfiable disjunct of elimFunctions(d) is made unsatisfiable, where d is a disjunct of ϕ. The number of disjuncts that can be falsified by the solveUNSAT procedure is bounded by $O(2^{n^2})$, where n is the number of atoms in ϕ. Note that, in practice, our tool explores a very small fraction of the disjuncts (see section 4). The proof of completeness of the procedure is detailed in [20]. An important property that ensures completeness is that the operation elimFunctions is applied only on a satisfiable disjunct d. This guarantees that the predicates in d involving ADT variables do not have any inconsistencies. Since the parameters can only influence the values of numerical variables, axioms that check for inconsistencies among the ADT predicates can be omitted.

Theorem 1 implies that the procedure we described in the previous sections for solving parametric VCs, in the presence of recursive functions, ADTs and arithmetic operations, that iteratively unrolls the recursive functions in the VC and applies the solveUNSAT procedure in each iteration is complete when the recursive functions are *sufficiently surjective* [27, 28] and when the arithmetic operations in the VCs are parametric linear operations over reals.

3.3 Solving Nonlinear Parametric Formulas

Nonlinearity is common in resource bounds. In this section, we discuss our approach for handling nonlinear parametric formulas like $\phi_{ex} : wz < xy \land x < w - 1 \land y < z - 1 \land ax + b \leq 0 \land ay + b \leq 0$ where a, b are parameters. Our approach is based on axiomatizing the nonlinearity operations. We handle multiplication by using axioms such as $\forall x, y. \; xy = (x-1)y+y, \forall x, y. \; xy = x(y-1)+x$ and monotonicity properties like $(x \geq 0 \land y \geq 0 \land w \geq x \land z \geq y) \Rightarrow xy \leq wz$. Similarly, we axiomatize exponential functions of the form C^x, where C is a constant. For example, we use the axiom $\forall x. \; 2^x = 2 \cdot 2^{x-1}$ together with the monotonicity axiom for modelling 2^x. The axioms are incorporated into the verification conditions by recursive instantiation as explained below.

Axioms such as $xy = (x-1)y+y$ that are recursively defined are instantiated similar to unrolling a recursive function during VC refinements. For example, in each VC refinement, for every atomic predicate $r = xy$ that occurs in the VC, we add a new predicate $r = (x - 1)y + y$ if it does not exist. We instantiate a binary axiom, such as monotonicity, on every pair of terms in the VC on which it is applicable. For instance, if $r = f(x)$, $r' = f(x')$ are two atoms in the VC and if f has a monotonicity axiom, then we conjoin the predicate $(x \leq x' \Rightarrow r \leq r') \land (x' \leq x \Rightarrow r' \leq r)$ to the VC. This approach can be extended to N-ary axioms. If the axioms define a *Local Theory Extension* [16] (like monotonicity) then the instantiation described above is complete.

Consider the example formula ϕ_{ex} shown above. Instantiating the multiplication axioms a few times will produce the following formula (simplified for brevity): $wz < xy \land xy = (x - 1)(y - 1) + x + y - 1 \land ((x \geq 0 \land y \geq 0 \land x \leq w \land y \leq z) \rightarrow xy \leq wz) \land x < w - 1 \land y < z - 1 \land ax + b \leq 0 \land ay + b \leq 0$. This formula can be solved without interpreting multiplication. $a = -1, b = 0$ is a solution for the parameters.

3.4 Finding Strongest Bounds

For computing strongest bounds, we assume that every parameter in the template appears as a coefficient of some expression. We approximate the rate of growth of an expression in the template by counting the number of function invocations (including nonlinear operations) performed by the expression. We order the parameters in the descending order of the estimated rate of growth of the associated expression, breaking ties arbitrarily. Let this order be $\sqsubseteq$. For instance, given a template res$\leq$a$*$f(g(x,f(y)))$+$c$*$g(x)$+$a$*$x $+$b, we order the parameters as $a \sqsubseteq c \sqsubseteq b$. We define an order $\leq^*$ on $Params \mapsto \mathbb{R}$ by extending $\leq$ lexicographically with respect to the ordering $\sqsubseteq$. We find a *locally* minimum solution ι_{min} for the parameters with respect to $\leq^*$ as explained below.

Let ι be the solution found by the solveUNSAT procedure. ι is obtained by solving a set of nonlinear constraints C. We compute a minimum satisfying assignment ι_{min} for C with respect to the total order $\leq^*$ by performing a *binary search* on the solution space of C starting with the initial upper bound given by ι. We stop the binary search when, for each parameter p, the difference between the values of p in the upper and lower bounds we found is ≤ 1. We need to bound the difference between the upper and lower bounds since the parameters in our case are reals. ι_{min} may not falsify ϕ although ι does. This is because C only encodes the constraints for falsifying the disjuncts of ϕ explored until some iteration. We use ι_{min} as the next candidate model and continue the iterations of the solveUNSAT algorithm.

In general, the inferred bounds are not guaranteed to be the strongest as the verification conditions we generate are sufficient but not necessary conditions. However, it would be the strongest solution if the functions in the program are *sufficiently surjective* [27, 28], if there are no nonlinear operations and there is no loss of completeness due to applying Farkas' Lemma on integer formulas. Our system also supports finding a concrete counter-example, if one exists, for the values smaller than those that are inferred.

3.5   Inference of Auxiliary Templates

We implemented a simple strategy for inferring invariant templates automatically for some functions. For every function f for which a template has not been provided, we assume a default template that is a linear combination of integer valued arguments and return values of f. For instance, for a function size(l) we assume a template a*res+b$\leq$0 (where, res is the return value of size). This enables us to infer and use correctness invariants like size(l)$\geq$0 automatically.

3.6   Analysis Strategies

Inter-Procedural Analysis. We solve the resource bound templates for the functions modularly in a bottom-up fashion. We solve the resource bound templates of the callees independent of the callers, minimize the solution to find strong bounds and use the bounds while analysing the callers. The auxiliary templates that we infer automatically are solved in the context of the callers in order to find context-specific invariants.

Targeted Unrolling. Recall that we unroll the functions in a VC if the VC is not solvable by solveUNSAT (i.e, when the condition at line 19 is true). As an optimization we make the unrolling process more demand-driven by unrolling only those functions encountered in the disjuncts explored by the solveUNSAT procedure. This avoids unrolling of functions along disjuncts that are already unsatisfiable in the VC.

Prioritizing Disjunct Exploration. Typically, the VCs we generate have a large number of disjuncts some of which are easier to reduce to false compared to others. We bias the implementation to pick the easier disjuncts by using timeouts on the nonlinear constraints solving process. Whenever we timeout while solving a nonlinear constraint, we block the disjunct that produced the nonlinear constraint in the VC so that it is not chosen again. In our experiments, we used a timeout of 20s. This strategy, though conceptually simple, made the analysis converge faster on many benchmarks.

4 Empirical Evaluation

We have implemented our algorithm on top of the Leon verifier for Scala [5], building on the release from the GitHub repository. We evaluate our tool on a set of benchmarks shown in Fig. 6 written in a purely functional subset of Scala programming language. The experiments were performed on a machine with 8 core, 3.5 GHz, intel i7 processor, having 16GB RAM, running Ubuntu operating system. For solving the SMT constraints generated by tool we use the Z3 solver of [10], version 4.3. The Benchmarks used in the evaluation comprises of approximately 1.5K lines of functional Scala code with 130 functions and 80 templates. All templates for execution bounds specified in the benchmarks were precise bounds. Fig. 6 shows the lines of codes loc, number of procedures P and a sample template for running time bound that was specified, for the benchmarks.

Benchmark	loc	P	Sample template used in benchmark
List Operations (*list*)	60	8	a*(size(l)*size(l))+b
Binary search tree (*bst*)	91	8	
addAll			a*(lsize(l)*(height(t)+lsize(l)))+b*lsize(l)+c
removeAll			a*(lsize(l)*height(t))+b*lsize(l)+c
Doubly ended queue (*deq*)	86	14	a*qsize(q)+b
Prop. logic transforms (*prop*)	63	5	a*size(formula)+b
Binary Trie (*trie*)	119	6	a*inpsize(inp)+c
qsort, isort, mergesort (*sort*)	123	12	a*(size(l)*size(l))+b
Loop transformations (*loop*)	102	10	a*size(program)+b
Concatenate variations (*cvar*)	40	5	
strategy 1			a*((n*m)*m)+c*(n*m)+d*n+e*m+f
strategy 2			a*(n*m)+b*n+c*m+d
Leftist heap (*lheap*)	81	10	
merge			a*rheight(h1)+b*rheight(h2)+c
removeMax			a*leftRightheight(h) + b
Redblack tree (*rbt*)	109	11	a*blackheight(t)+b
AVL tree (*avl*)	190	15	a*height(t)+b
Binomial heap (*bheap*)	204	12	
merge			a*treenum(h1)+b*treenum(h2)+c
deleteMin			a*treenum(h1)+b*minchildren(h2)+c
Speed benchmarks(*speed*)	107	8	a*((k+1)*(len(sb1)+len(sb2)))+b*size(str1)+c
Fold operations (*fold*)	88	7	
listfold, treefold			a*(k*k)+b, a*size(t)+b

Fig. 6. Benchmarks used in the evaluation comprising of approx. 1.5K lines of scala code, 130 functions and 80 templates. P denotes the number of procedures.

The benchmark *list* implements a set of list manipulation operations like *append, reverse, remove, find* and *distinct*–that removes duplicates. *bst* implements a binary search tree with operations like *insert, remove, find, addall* and *removeall*. The function lsize(l) (used in the templates) is the size of the list of elements to be inserted/removed from the tree. *deq* is an amortized, doubly-ended queue with *enqueue, dequeue, pop* and *concat* operations. *prop* is a set of propositional logic transformations like converting a formula to negation normal form and simplifying a formula. *lheap* is a leftist heap data-structure implementation with *merge, insert* and *removemax* operations. This benchmark also specified a logarithmic bound on the *right height*: $2^{\mathsf{rheight}(\mathsf{h})} \leq \mathsf{a} * \mathsf{heapSize}(\mathsf{h}) + \mathsf{b}$ which was solved by the tool. The function leftRightheight (used in the template) computes the right height of the left child of a heap.

trie is a binary prefix tree with operations: *insert*–that inserts a sequence of input bits into the tree, *find, create* –that creates a new tree from an input sequence and *delete*–that deletes a sequence of input bits from the tree. The benchmark *cvars* compares two different strategies for sequence concatenation. One strategy exhibits cubic behavior on a sequence of concatenation operations (templates shown in Fig. 6) and the other exhibits a quadratic behavior. *rbt* is an implementation of red-black tree with *insert* and *find* operations. This benchmark also specified a logarithmic bound on the black height: $2^{\mathsf{blackheight}(\mathsf{h})} \leq \mathsf{a} * \mathsf{treeSize}(\mathsf{h}) + \mathsf{b}$ which was solved by the tool.

avl is an implementation of AVL tree with *insert, delete* and *find* operations. *bheap* implements a binomial heap with *merge, insert* and *deletemin* operations. The functions treenum and minchildren (used in templates), compute the number of trees in a binomial heap and the number of children of the tree containing the minimum element, respectively. *speed* is a functional translation of the code snippets presented in figures 1,2, 9 of [14], and the code snippets on which it was mentioned that the tool failed (Page 138 in [14]). The benchmark *fold* is a collection of fold operations over trees and lists. These were mainly included for evaluation of *depth* bounds.

Fig. 7 shows the results of running our tool on the benchmarks. The column *bound* shows the time bound inferred by the tool for the sample template shown in Fig. 6. This may provide some insights into the constants that were inferred. The bounds inferred are inductive. Though the constants inferred could potentially be rationals, in many cases, the SMT solver returned integer values. In case a value returned by the solver for a parameter is rational, we heuristically check if the ceil of the value also yields an inductive bound. This heuristic allowed us to compute integer values for almost all templates.

The column *time* shows the total time taken for analysing a benchmark. In parentheses we show the time the tool spent in minimizing the bounds after finding a valid initial bound. The subsequent columns provide more insights into the algorithm. The column *VC size* shows the average size of the VCs generated by the benchmarks averaged over all refinements. The tool performed 11 to 42 VC refinements on the benchmarks. The column *disj.* shows the total number of disjuncts falsified by the tool and the column *NL size* shows the average size of the nonlinear constraints solved in each iteration of the solveUNSAT procedure.

Our tool was able to solve 78 out of 80 templates. Two templates were not solvable because of the incompleteness in the handling of nonlinearity. The results also show that our tool was able to keep the average size of the generated nonlinear constraints small in each iteration in spite of the large VC sizes, which

	Sample bound inferred time$\leq$	time (min.time)	avg.VC size	disj.	NL size
list	9*(size(l)*size(l))+2	17.7s (8.7s)	1539.7	108	59.9
bst	8*(lsize(l)*(height(t)+lsize(l))) +2*lsize(l)+1 29*(lsize(l)*height(t))+7*lsize(l)+1	31s (14.2s)	637.4	79	84
deq	9*qsize(q)+26	17.3s (8.6s)	405.7	80	27.9
prop	52*size(formula)−20	19.5s (1.2s)	1398.5	59	38.1
trie	42*inpsize(inp)+3	3.3s (0.5s)	356.8	54	23.5
sort †	8*(size(l)*size(l))+2	6.8s (1.6s)	274.9	85	29.6
loop	16*size(program)−10	10.6s (4.9s)	1133.8	44	52.4
cvar	5*((n*m)*m)−(n*m)+0*n+8*m+2 9*(n*m)+8*m+0*n+2	25.2s (14.7s)	1423.2	61	49.4
lheap	22*rheight(h1)+22*rheight(h2)+1 44*leftRightheight(h)+5	166.7s (144s)	1970.5s	152	106.4
rbt	178*blackheight(t)+96	124.5s (18.8s)	3881.2	149	132.6
avl	145*height(t)+19	412.1s (259.1s)	1731.8	216	114
bheap	31*treenum(h1)+38*treenum(h2)+1 70*treenum(h1)+31*minchildren(h2)+22	469.1s (427.1s)	2835.5	136	157.2
speed	39*((k+1)*(len(sb1)+len(sb2))) +18*size(str1)+34	28.6s (6.4s)	1084.9	111	85.8
fold	12*(k*k)+2 12*size(t)+1	8.5s (0.8s)	331.8	44	23

Fig. 7. Results of running our tool on the benchmarks. † the tool failed on 2 templates in the *sort* benchmark.

is very important since even the state-of-the-art nonlinear constraint solvers do not scale well to large nonlinear constraints.

Fig. 8 shows the results of applying our tool to solve templates for *depth* bounds for our benchmarks. All the templates used were precise. The tool was able to solve all 80 templates provided in the benchmarks. In Fig. 8, the benchmarks which have asymptotically smaller *depth* compared to their execution time (*work*) are starred. Notice that the constants involved in the depth bounds are much smaller for every benchmark compared to its work, even if the depth is not asymptotically smaller than work. Notice that the tool is able to establish that the depth of *mergesort* is linear in the size of its input; the depth of negation normal form transformation is proportional to the nesting depth of its input formula and also that the depth of fold operations on trees is linear in the height of the tree.

Comparison with CEGIS. We compared our tool with *Counter Example Guided Inductive Synthesis*(CEGIS) [26] which, to our knowledge, is the only existing approach that can be used to find values for parameters that would falsify a parametric formula containing ADTs, uninterpreted functions and nonlinear operations. CEGIS is an iterative algorithm that, given a parametric formula ϕ with parameters param and variables X, makes progress by finding a solution for param that rules out at least one assignment for X that was feasible in the

	Inferred depth bound: depth$\leq$	*time*
list	5*(size(l)*size(l))+1	9.7s
bst	4*(lsize(l)*(height(t)+lsize(l)))+2*lsize(l)+1	335.8s
	4*(lsize(l)*height(t))+4*lsize(l)+1	
deq	3*qsize(q)+13	106.4s
prop*	5*nestingDepth(formula)−2	31.4s
trie	8*inpsize(inp)+1	4.1s
msort*	45*size(l)+1	20.2s
qsort	7*(size(l)*size(l))+5*size(l)+1	164.5s
isort	5*(size(l)*size(l))+1	3s
loop	7*size(program)−3	404s
cvar	3*((n*m)*m)−$\frac{1}{8}$*(n*m)+n+5*m+1	270.8s
	3*(n*m)+3*n+4*m+1	
lheap	7*rheight(h1)+7*rheight(h1)+1	42s
	14*leftRightheight(h)+3	
rbt	22*height(t)+19	115.3s
avl	51*height(t)+4	185.3s
bheap	7*treenum(h1)+7*treenum(h2)+2	232.5s
	22*treenum(h1)+7*minchildren(h2)+16	
speed	6*((k+1)*(len(sb1)+len(sb2)))+5*size(str1)+6	41.8s
fold*	6*k+1	3.1s
	5*height(tree)+1	

Fig. 8. Results of inferring bounds on *depths* of benchmarks

earlier iterations. In contrast to our approach which is guaranteed to terminate, CEGIS may diverge if the possible values for X is infinite. We actually implemented CEGIS and evaluated it on our benchmarks. CEGIS diverges even on the simplest of our benchmarks. It follows an infinite ascending chain along which the parameter corresponding to the constant term of the template increases indefinitely. We also evaluated CEGIS by bounding the values of the parameters to be ≤ 200. In this case, CEGIS worked on 5 small benchmarks (viz. *list*, *bst*, *deq*, *trie* and *fold*) but timed out on the rest after 30min. For the benchmarks on which it worked, it was 2.5 times to 64 times slower than our approach.

5 Related Work

We are not aware of any existing approach that can handle the class of templates and programs that our approach handled in the experimental evaluation.

Template-Based Invariant Inference. The work of [8] is possibly closest to ours because it performs template-based analysis of imperative programs for finding heap bounds and handles program paths incrementally using the idea of path invariants from [4]. [8] infers only linear bounds. It handles data-structures using a separate shape analysis that tracks the heap sizes. Our approach is for functional programs. We handle a wide range of recursive functions over

ADTs and are not restricted to size. We integrate the handling of ADTs into the template solving process, which allows us to solve precise templates. We support nonlinearity and are capable of computing strongest bounds. We are able to handle complex data-structure implementations such as Binomial Heap. [3] presents an approach for handling uninterpreted functions in templates. We handle disjunctions that arise because of axiomatizing uninterpreted functions efficiently through our incremental algorithm that is driven by counter-examples and are able to scale to VCs with hundreds of uninterpreted functions. Our approach also supports algebraic data types and handles sophisticated templates that involve user-defined functions. The idea of using Farkas' lemma to solve linear templates of numerical programs goes back at least to the work of [7] and has been generalized in different directions by [25], [9], [15]. [9] and [25] present systematic approaches for solving nonlinear templates for numerical programs. Our approach is currently based on light-weight axiomatization of nonlinear operations which is targeted towards practical efficiency. It remains to be seen if we can integrate more complete non-linear reasoning into our approach without sacrificing scalability.

Symbolic Resource Bounds Analyses. [14] (SPEED) presents a technique for inferring symbolic bounds on loops of C programs that is based on instrumenting programs with counters, inferring linear invariants on counters and combining the linear invariants to establish a loop bound. This approach is orthogonal to ours where we attempt to find solutions to user-defined templates. In our benchmarks, we included a few code snippets on which it was mentioned that their tool did not work. Our approach was able to handle them when the templates were provided manually. Our approach is also extensible to other resource bounds such as *depth*. The COSTA system of [1] can solve recurrence equations and infer nonlinear time bounds, however, it does not appear to support algebraic data types nor user-defined functions within resource bounds.

Other Related Works. Counterexample-guided refinement ideas are ubiquitous in verification, as well as in software synthesis, where they are used in counterexample-guided inductive synthesis (CEGIS) algorithms by [26], [13], and [18]. One important difference in approaches such as ours is that an infinite family of counterexamples is eliminated at once. Our experimental results of comparison with CEGIS in section 4 indicates that these approaches may suffer from similar divergence issues particularly for the resource bound inference problem. Recent work [2] provides a general framework and system for inferring invariants, which can also handle $\exists \forall$ problems of the form we are considering. The comparison of two approaches requires further work because our target are contracts with function invocations whereas [2] targets temporal logic formulas. The underlying HSF tool [11] has been shown applicable to a wide range of analysis problems. HSF could simplify the building of a resource analyzer such as ours, though it does not support algebraic data types and resource bound computation out of the box.

References

1. Albert, E., Arenas, P., Genaim, S., Puebla, G., Zanardini, D.: Cost analysis of object-oriented bytecode programs. Theor. Comput. Sci. 413(1), 142–159 (2012)
2. Beyene, T.A., Popeea, C., Rybalchenko, A.: Solving existentially quantified horn clauses. In: Sharygina, N., Veith, H. (eds.) CAV 2013. LNCS, vol. 8044, pp. 869–882. Springer, Heidelberg (2013)
3. Beyer, D., Henzinger, T.A., Majumdar, R., Rybalchenko, A.: Invariant synthesis for combined theories. In: Cook, B., Podelski, A. (eds.) VMCAI 2007. LNCS, vol. 4349, pp. 378–394. Springer, Heidelberg (2007)
4. Beyer, D., Henzinger, T.A., Majumdar, R., Rybalchenko, A.: Path invariants. In: PLDI (2007)
5. Blanc, R.W., Kneuss, E., Kuncak, V., Suter, P.: An overview of the Leon verification system. In: Scala Workshop (2013)
6. Blelloch, G.E., Maggs, B.M.: Parallel algorithms. Communications of the ACM 39, 85–97 (1996)
7. Colón, M.A., Sankaranarayanan, S., Sipma, H.B.: Linear invariant generation using non-linear constraint solving. In: Hunt Jr., W.A., Somenzi, F. (eds.) CAV 2003. LNCS, vol. 2725, pp. 420–432. Springer, Heidelberg (2003)
8. Cook, B., Gupta, A., Magill, S., Rybalchenko, A., Simsa, J., Singh, S., Vafeiadis, V.: Finding heap-bounds for hardware synthesis. In: FMCAD (2009)
9. Cousot, P.: Proving program invariance and termination by parametric abstraction, lagrangian relaxation and semidefinite programming. In: Cousot, R. (ed.) VMCAI 2005. LNCS, vol. 3385, pp. 1–24. Springer, Heidelberg (2005)
10. de Moura, L., Bjørner, N.S.: Z3: An efficient smt solver. In: Ramakrishnan, C.R., Rehof, J. (eds.) TACAS 2008. LNCS, vol. 4963, pp. 337–340. Springer, Heidelberg (2008)
11. Grebenshchikov, S., Lopes, N.P., Popeea, C., Rybalchenko, A.: Synthesizing software verifiers from proof rules. In: PLDI (2012)
12. Guerraoui, R., Kuncak, V., Losa, G.: Speculative linearizability. In: PLDI (2012)
13. Gulwani, S., Jha, S., Tiwari, A., Venkatesan, R.: Synthesis of loop-free programs. In: PLDI (2011)
14. Gulwani, S., Mehra, K.K., Chilimbi, T.M.: Speed: Precise and efficient static estimation of program computational complexity. In: POPL (2009)
15. Gulwani, S., Srivastava, S., Venkatesan, R.: Program analysis as constraint solving. In: PLDI (2008)
16. Jacobs, S., Kuncak, V.: Towards complete reasoning about axiomatic specifications. In: Jhala, R., Schmidt, D. (eds.) VMCAI 2011. LNCS, vol. 6538, pp. 278–293. Springer, Heidelberg (2011)
17. Kaufmann, M., Manolios, P., Moore, J.S. (eds.): Computer-Aided Reasoning: ACL2 Case Studies. Kluwer Academic Publishers (2000)
18. Kneuss, E., Kuraj, I., Kuncak, V., Suter, P.: Synthesis modulo recursive functions. In: OOPSLA (2013)
19. Leroy, X.: Formal verification of a realistic compiler. Commun. ACM 52(7), 107–115 (2009)
20. Madhavan, R., Kuncak, V.: Symbolic resource bound inference. Technical Report EPFL-REPORT-190578, EPFL (2014), http://infoscience.epfl.ch/record/190578
21. Makarios, T.J.M.: The independence of Tarski's Euclidean axiom. Archive of Formal Proofs, Formal proof development (October 2012), http://afp.sf.net/entries/Tarskis_Geometry.shtml,

22. Odersky, M., Spoon, L., Venners, B.: Programming in Scala: A comprehensive step-by-step guide. Artima Press (2008)
23. Oppen, D.C.: Elementary bounds for presburger arithmetic. In: Proceedings of the Fifth Annual ACM Symposium on Theory of Computing (1973)
24. Rybalchenko, A., Sofronie-Stokkermans, V.: Constraint solving for interpolation. In: Cook, B., Podelski, A. (eds.) VMCAI 2007. LNCS, vol. 4349, pp. 346–362. Springer, Heidelberg (2007)
25. Sankaranarayanan, S., Sipma, H.B., Manna, Z.: Non-linear loop invariant generation using gröbner bases. In: POPL (2004)
26. Solar-Lezama, A., Tancau, L., Bodík, R., Seshia, S.A., Saraswat, V.A.: Combinatorial sketching for finite programs. In: ASPLOS (2006)
27. Suter, P., Dotta, M., Kuncak, V.: Decision procedures for algebraic data types with abstractions. In: POPL (2010)
28. Suter, P., Köksal, A.S., Kuncak, V.: Satisfiability modulo recursive programs. In: Yahav, E. (ed.) SAS 2011. LNCS, vol. 6887, pp. 298–315. Springer, Heidelberg (2011)
29. Yu, L.: A formal model of IEEE floating point arithmetic. Archive of Formal Proofs, Formal proof development (July 2013), http://afp.sf.net/entries/IEEE_Floating_Point.shtml

Proving Non-termination Using Max-SMT

Daniel Larraz[1], Kaustubh Nimkar[2], Albert Oliveras[1],
Enric Rodríguez-Carbonell[1], and Albert Rubio[1]

[1] Universitat Politècnica de Catalunya, Barcelona
[2] University College London

Abstract. We show how Max-SMT-based invariant generation can be exploited for proving non-termination of programs. The construction of the proof of non-termination is guided by the generation of *quasi-invariants* – properties such that if they hold at a location during execution once, then they will continue to hold at that location from then onwards. The check that quasi-invariants can indeed be reached is then performed separately. Our technique considers strongly connected subgraphs of a program's control flow graph for analysis and thus produces more generic witnesses of non-termination than existing methods. Moreover, it can handle programs with unbounded non-determinism and is more likely to converge than previous approaches.

1 Introduction

While the problem of proving program termination has now been extensively studied [1–22], relatively less work has been done on proving non-termination of programs.

In this paper we present a new method for proving non-termination of sequential non-deterministic programs that leverages Max-SMT-based invariant generation [23, 24]. Our method analyses each *Strongly Connected SubGraph (SCSG)* of a program's control flow graph and, by means of Max-SMT solving, tries to find a formula at every node of the SCSG that satisfies certain properties. First, the formula has to be a *quasi-invariant*, i.e, it must satisfy the consecution condition of inductive invariants, but not necessarily the initiation condition. Hence, if it holds at the node during execution once, then it continues to hold from then onwards. Second, the formula has to be *edge-closing*, meaning that it forbids taking any of the outgoing edges from that node that exit the SCSG. Now, once we have computed an edge-closing quasi-invariant for every node of the SCSG, if a state is reached that satisfies one of them, then program execution will remain within the SCSG from then onwards. The existence of such a state is tested with an off-the-shelf reachability checker. If it succeeds, we have proved non-termination of the original program, and the edge-closing quasi-invariants of the SCSG and the trace given by the reachability checker form the witness of non-termination.

Our approach differs from previous methods in two major ways. First, edge-closing quasi-invariants are more generic properties than non-termination witnesses produced by other provers, and thus are likely to carry more information and be more useful in bug finding. Second, our non-termination witnesses include SCSGs, which are larger structures than, e.g., *lassos*. Note that the number of SCSGs present in any CFG is finite, while the number of lassos is infinite. Because of these differences, our method

A. Biere and R. Bloem (Eds.): CAV 2014, LNCS 8559, pp. 779–796, 2014.
© Springer International Publishing Switzerland 2014

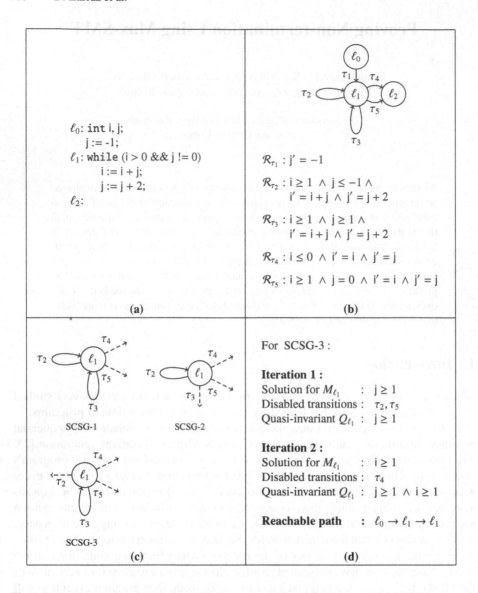

Fig. 1. Example program (a) together with its corresponding CFG (b), non-trivial SCSGs (c) and non-termination analysis (d)

is more likely to converge. Moreover, lasso-based methods can only handle periodic non-termination, while our approach can deal with aperiodic non-termination too.

Our technique is based on constraint solving for invariant generation [25] and is goal-directed. Before discussing it formally, we describe it with a simple example. Consider the program in Fig. 1(a). The CFG for this program is shown in Fig. 1(b). The edges of the CFG represent the transitions between the locations. For every transition τ, we denote the formula of its transition relation by $\mathcal{R}_\tau(i, j, i', j')$. The unprimed variables represent the values of the variables before the transition, and the primed ones represent the values after the transition. By $\mathcal{R}_\tau(i, j)$ we denote the *conditional part of* τ, which only involves the pre-variables. Fig. 1(c) shows all non-trivial (i.e. with at least one edge) SCSGs present in the CFG. For every SCSG, the dashed edges are those that exit the SCSG and hence are not part of it. Note that SCSG-1 is a maximal strongly connected subgraph, and thus is a strongly connected component of the CFG. Notice also that τ_3 is an additional exit edge for SCSG-2, and similarly τ_2 is an exit edge for SCSG-3. The non-termination of this example comes from SCSG-3.

Our approach considers every SCSG of the graph one by one. In every iteration of our method, we try to find a formula at every node of the SCSG under consideration. This formula is originally represented as a template with unknown coefficients. We then form a system of constraints involving the template coefficients in the Max-SMT framework. In a Max-SMT problem, some of the constraints are *hard*, meaning that any solution to the system of constraints must satisfy them, and others are *soft*, which may or may not be satisfied. Soft constraints carry a weight, and the goal of the Max-SMT solver is to find a solution for the hard constraints such that the sum of the weights for the soft constraints violated by the solution is minimized. In our method, essentially the hard constraints encode that the formula should obey the consecution condition, and every soft constraint encodes that the formula will disable an exit edge. A solution to this system of constraints assigns values to template coefficients, thus giving us the required formula at every node.

Consider the analysis of SCSG-3 (refer to Fig. 1(d)). Note that there is a single node ℓ_1 and a single transition τ_3 in SCSG-3. We denote by $E = \{\tau_2, \tau_4, \tau_5\}$ the set of exit edges for SCSG-3. By $Q_{\ell_1}(i, j)$ we denote the quasi-invariant at node ℓ_1. Initially $Q_{\ell_1}(i, j) \triangleq \texttt{true}$. In the first iteration, for node ℓ_1 we assign a template $M_{\ell_1}(i, j) : a.i + b.j \leq c$.

We then form the Max-SMT problem consisting of the following system of hard and soft constraints:

(**Consecution**) $\forall\, i, j, i', j'.\ M_{\ell_1}(i, j) \,\wedge\, Q_{\ell_1}(i, j) \,\wedge\, \mathcal{R}_{\tau_3}(i, j, i', j') \rightarrow M_{\ell_1}(i', j')$

(**Edge-Closing**) For all $\tau \in E$: $\forall\, i, j.\ M_{\ell_1}(i, j) \,\wedge\, Q_{\ell_1}(i, j) \rightarrow \neg \mathcal{R}_\tau(i, j)$

The consecution constraint is hard, while the edge-closing constraints are soft (with weight, say, 1). The edge-closing constraint for $\tau \in E$ encodes that, from any state satisfying $M_{\ell_1}(i, j) \wedge Q_{\ell_1}(i, j)$, the transition τ is disabled and cannot be executed.

In the first iteration, a solution for M_{ℓ_1} gives us the formula $j \geq 1$. This formula satisfies the edge-closing constraints for τ_2 and τ_5. We conjoin this formula to Q_{ℓ_1}, updating it to $Q_{\ell_1}(i, j) \triangleq j \geq 1$. We also update $E = \{\tau_4\}$ by removing τ_2 and τ_5, as these edges are now disabled.

In the second iteration, we again consider the same template $M_{\ell_1}(i, j)$ and try to solve the Max-SMT problem above with updated $Q_{\ell_1}(i, j)$ and E. This time we get a solution that gives us the formula $i \geq 1$, which satisfies the edge-closing constraint for τ_4. We again update $Q_{\ell_1}(i, j) \triangleq j \geq 1 \,\wedge\, i \geq 1$ by conjoining the new formula. We update $E = \emptyset$ by removing the disabled edge τ_4. Now all exit edges have been disabled, and thus the quasi-invariant $Q_{\ell_1}(i, j)$ is edge-closing.

In the final step of our method, we use a reachability checker to determine if any state satisfying $Q_{\ell_1}(i, j)$ at location ℓ_1 is reachable. This test succeeds, and a path $\ell_0 \rightarrow$

$\ell_1 \to \ell_1$ is obtained. Notice that the path goes through the loop once before we reach the required state. At this point, we have proved non-termination of the original program.

2 Preliminaries

2.1 SMT and Max-SMT

Let $\mathcal{P}$ be a finite set of *propositional variables*. If $p \in \mathcal{P}$, then p and $\neg p$ are *literals*. The *negation* of a literal l, written $\neg l$, denotes $\neg p$ if l is p, and p if l is $\neg p$. A *clause* is a disjunction of literals. A *propositional formula* is a conjunction of clauses. The problem of *propositional satisfiability* (abbreviated as SAT) consists in, given a formula, determining whether or not it is *satisfiable*, i.e., if it has a *model*: an assignment of Boolean values to variables that satisfies the formula.

An extension of SAT is the *satisfiability modulo theories (SMT)* problem [26]: to decide the satisfiability of a given quantifier-free first-order formula with respect to a background theory. In this setting, a model (which we may also refer to as a *solution*) is an assignment of values from the theory to variables that satisfies the formula. Here we will consider the theories of *linear real/integer arithmetic (LRA/LIA)*, where literals are linear inequalities over real and integer variables respectively, and the more general theories of *non-linear real/integer arithmetic (NRA/NIA)*, where literals are polynomial inequalities over real and integer variables, respectively.

Another generalization of SAT is the *Max-SAT* problem [26]: it consists in, given a *weighted* formula where each clause has a weight (a positive number or infinity), finding the assignment such that the cost, i.e., the sum of the weights of the falsified clauses, is minimized. Clauses with infinite weight are called *hard*, while the rest are called *soft*. Equivalently, the problem can be seen as finding the model of the hard clauses such that the sum of the weights of the falsified soft clauses is minimized.

Finally, the problem of *Max-SMT* [27] merges Max-SAT and SMT, and is defined from SMT analogously to how Max-SAT is derived from SAT. Namely, the *Max-SMT* problem consists in, given a weighted formula, to find an assignment that minimizes the sum of the weights of the falsified clauses in the background theory.

2.2 Transition Systems

Our technique is applicable to sequential non-deterministic programs with integer variables and commands whose transition relations can be expressed in linear (integer) arithmetic. By $\bar{v}$ we represent the tuple of program variables. For the sake of presentation, we assume that the non-determinism of programs can come only from non-deterministic assignments of the form $i := \texttt{nondet}()$, where $i \in \bar{v}$ is a program variable. Note that, however, this assumption still allows one to encode other kinds of non-determinism. For instance, any non-deterministic branching of the form **if**(*){} **else**{} can be cast into this framework by introducing a new program variable $k \in \bar{v}$ and rewriting into the form $k := \texttt{nondet}()$; **if**($k \geq 0$){} **else**{}.

We model programs with *transition systems*. A transition system $\mathcal{S} = (\bar{v}, \bar{u}, \mathcal{L}, \Theta, \mathcal{T})$ consists of a tuple of *program variables* $\bar{v}$, a tuple of *non-deterministic variables* $\bar{u}$, a set of *locations* $\mathcal{L}$, a map Θ from locations to formulas characterizing the initial values of the variables, and a set of *transitions* $\mathcal{T}$. Each transition $\tau \in \mathcal{T}$ is a triple $(\ell, \ell', \mathcal{R})$, where $\ell, \ell' \in \mathcal{L}$ are the *pre* and *post* locations respectively, and $\mathcal{R}$ is the *transition relation*: a formula over the non-deterministic variables $\bar{u}$, the program variables $\bar{v}$ and their primed versions $\bar{v}'$, which represent the values of the variables after the transition. The transition relation of a non-deterministic assignment of the form i := nondet(), where i $\in \bar{v}$, is represented by the formula i' = u_1, where $u_1 \in \bar{u}$ is a fresh non-deterministic variable. Note that u_1 is not a program variable, i.e., $u_1 \notin \bar{v}$, and is added only to model the non-deterministic assignment. Thus, without loss of generality on the kind of non-deterministic programs we can model, we will assume that every non-deterministic variable appears in at most one transition relation. A transition that includes a non-deterministic variable in its transition relation is called *non-deterministic* (abbreviated as nondet).

In what follows we will assume that transition relations are described as conjunctions of linear inequalities over program variables and non-deterministic variables. Given a transition relation $\mathcal{R} = \mathcal{R}(\bar{v}, \bar{u}, \bar{v}')$, we will use $\mathcal{R}(\bar{v})$ to denote the *conditional part of* $\mathcal{R}$, i.e., the conjunction of linear inequalities in $\mathcal{R}$ containing only variables in $\bar{v}$. For a transition system modeling real programs, the following conditions are true:

$$\text{For } \tau = (\ell, \ell', \mathcal{R}) \in \mathcal{T} : \forall \bar{v}, \bar{u} \, \exists \bar{v}'. \, \mathcal{R}(\bar{v}) \rightarrow \mathcal{R}(\bar{v}, \bar{u}, \bar{v}'). \tag{1}$$

$$\text{For } \ell \in \mathcal{L} : \bigvee_{(\ell,\ell',\mathcal{R})} \mathcal{R}(\bar{v}) \triangleq \text{true}. \tag{2}$$

$$\text{For } \tau_1 = (\ell, \ell_1, \mathcal{R}_1), \tau_2 = (\ell, \ell_2, \mathcal{R}_2) \in \mathcal{T}, \tau_1 \neq \tau_2 : \mathcal{R}_1(\bar{v}) \wedge \mathcal{R}_2(\bar{v}) \triangleq \text{false}. \tag{3}$$

Condition (1) guarantees that next values for the program variables always exist if the conditional part of the transition holds. Condition (2) expresses that, for any location, at least one of the outgoing transitions from that location can always be executed. Finally, condition (3) says that any two different transitions from the same location are mutually exclusive, i.e., conditional branching is always deterministic.

Example 1. Let us consider the program shown in Figure 2. Note how the two non-deterministic assignments have been replaced in the CFG by assignments to fresh non-deterministic variables u_1 and u_2. Condition (2) is trivially satisfied for ℓ_0 and ℓ_2, since the conditional part of their outgoing transition relations is empty. Regarding ℓ_1, clearly the formula x $\geq$ y $\vee$ x $<$ y is a tautology. Condition (3) is also easy to check: the conditional parts of $\mathcal{R}_{\tau_2}, \mathcal{R}_{\tau_3}$ and $\mathcal{R}_{\tau_4}$ are pairwise unsatisfiable. Finally, condition (1) trivially holds since the primed parts of the transition relations consist of equalities whose left-hand side is always a different variable. □

A *state* is an assignment of a value to each of the variables in $\bar{v}$ and $\bar{u}$. A *configuration* is a pair (ℓ, σ) consisting of a location $\ell \in \mathcal{L}$ and a state σ. For any pair of configurations (ℓ, σ) and (ℓ', σ'), if there is a transition $\tau = (\ell, \ell', \mathcal{R}) \in \mathcal{T}$ such that $(\sigma, \sigma') \models \mathcal{R}$, we write $(\ell, \sigma) \xrightarrow{\tau} (\ell', \sigma')$. A *computation* is a sequence of configurations (ℓ_0, σ_0), (ℓ_1, σ_1), ... such that $\sigma_0 \models \Theta(\ell_0)$, and for each pair of consecutive configurations there exists $\tau_i \in \mathcal{T}$ satisfying $(\ell_i, \sigma_i) \xrightarrow{\tau_i} (\ell_{i+1}, \sigma_{i+1})$. A configuration (ℓ, σ) is *reachable* if there exists a computation ending at (ℓ, σ). A transition system is *terminating* if all its

| ℓ_0: int x, y;
 ℓ_1: while $(x \geq y)$
       if $(x \geq 0)$
          x := nondet();
          y := y + 1;
       else
          y := nondet();
 ℓ_2: | τ_2

 $\ell_0 \xrightarrow{\tau_1} \ell_1 \xrightarrow{\tau_4} \ell_2$

 τ_3 | $\mathcal{R}_{\tau_1} : x' = x \wedge y' = y$

 $\mathcal{R}_{\tau_2} : x \geq y \wedge x \geq 0 \wedge$
         $x' = u_1 \wedge y' = y + 1$

 $\mathcal{R}_{\tau_3} : x \geq y \wedge x < 0 \wedge$
         $x' = x \wedge y' = u_2$

 $\mathcal{R}_{\tau_4} : x < y \wedge x' = x \wedge$
         $y' = y$ |

Fig. 2. Program involving non-deterministic assignments, together with its CFG

computations are finite, and *non-terminating* otherwise. The goal of this paper is, given a transition system, to prove that it is non-terminating.

3   Quasi-invariants and Non-termination

Here we will introduce the core concept of this work, that of a *quasi-invariant*: a property such that, if it is satisfied at a location during execution once, then it continues to hold at that location from then onwards. The importance of this notion resides in the fact that it is a key ingredient in our witnesses of non-termination: if each location of an SCSG can be mapped to a quasi-invariant that is *edge-closing*, i.e., that forbids executing any of the outgoing transitions that leave the SCSG, and the SCSG can be reached at a configuration satisfying the corresponding quasi-invariant, then the program is non-terminating (if nondet transitions are present, additional properties are required, as will be seen below). A constructive proof of this claim is given at the end of this section.

First of all, let us define basic notation. For a strongly connected subgraph (SCSG) C of a program's CFG, we denote by $\mathcal{L}^C$ the set of locations of C, and by $\mathcal{T}^C$ the set of edges of C. We define $\mathcal{E}^C \overset{def}{=} \{\tau = (\ell, \ell', \mathcal{R}) \mid \ell \in \mathcal{L}^C, \tau \notin \mathcal{T}^C\}$ to be the set of exit edges of C.

Consider a map Q that assigns a formula $Q_\ell(\overline{v})$ to each of the locations $\ell \in \mathcal{L}^C$. Consider also a map $\mathcal{U}$ that assigns a formula $U_\tau(\overline{v}, \overline{u})$ to each transition $\tau \in \mathcal{T}^C$, which represents the *restriction* that the non-deterministic variables must obey.[1] The map Q is a *quasi-invariant map* on C with restriction $\mathcal{U}$ if:

(Consecution)

For $\tau = (\ell, \ell', \mathcal{R}) \in \mathcal{T}^C : \forall \overline{v}, \overline{u}, \overline{v}'.\ Q_\ell(\overline{v}) \wedge \mathcal{R}(\overline{v}, \overline{u}, \overline{v}') \wedge U_\tau(\overline{v}, \overline{u}) \rightarrow Q_{\ell'}(\overline{v}')$ (4)

Condition (4) says that, whenever a state at $\ell \in \mathcal{L}^C$ satisfying Q_ℓ is reached and a transition from ℓ to ℓ' can be executed, then the resulting state satisfies $Q_{\ell'}$. This condition corresponds to the consecution condition for inductive invariants. Since inductive

---

[1] For the sake of presentation, we assume that U_τ is defined for all transitions, whether they are deterministic or not. In the former case, by convention U_τ is true.

invariants are additionally required to satisfy initiation conditions [25], we refer to properties satisfying condition (4) as quasi-invariants, hence the name for Q.

Example 2. In order to explain the roles of Q and $\mathcal{U}$, consider the program in Figure 2. It is easy to see that if $x \geq y$ were a quasi-invariant at ℓ_1, the program would be non-terminating (provided ℓ_1 is reachable with a state such that $x \geq y$). However, due to the non-deterministic assignments, the property is not a quasi-invariant. On the other hand, if we add the restrictions $U_{\tau_2} := u_1 \geq x + 1$ and $U_{\tau_3} := u_2 \leq y$, which constrain the non-deterministic choices in the assignments, the quasi-invariant holds and non-termination is proved. □

Additionally, our method also needs that Q and $\mathcal{U}$ are *reachable* and *unblocking*:

$$\textbf{(Reachability)} \ \exists \ \ell \in \mathcal{L}^C. \ \exists \ \sigma \ s.t. \ (\ell, \sigma) \text{ is reachable and } \sigma \models Q_\ell(\overline{v}) \qquad (5)$$

$$\textbf{(Unblocking)} \ \text{For } \tau = (\ell, \ell', \mathcal{R}) \in \mathcal{T}^C : \forall \overline{v} \exists \overline{u}. \ Q_\ell(\overline{v}) \wedge \mathcal{R}(\overline{v}) \rightarrow U_\tau(\overline{v}, \overline{u}) \qquad (6)$$

Condition (5) says that there exists a computation reaching a configuration (ℓ, σ) such that σ satisfies the quasi-invariant at location ℓ.

As for condition (6), consider a state σ at some $\ell \in \mathcal{L}^C$ satisfying $Q_\ell(\overline{v})$. This condition says that, for any transition $\tau = (\ell, \ell', \mathcal{R}) \in \mathcal{T}^C$ from ℓ, if σ satisfies the conditional part $\mathcal{R}(\overline{v})$, then we can always make a choice for the non-deterministic assignment that obeys the restriction $U_\tau(\overline{v}, \overline{u})$.

The last property we require from quasi-invariants is that they are edge-closing. Formally, the quasi-invariant map Q on C is *edge-closing* if it satisfies all of the following constraints:

$$\textbf{(Edge-Closing)} \ \text{For } \tau = (\ell, \ell', \mathcal{R}) \in \mathcal{E}^C : \forall \overline{v}. \ Q_\ell(\overline{v}) \rightarrow \neg \mathcal{R}(\overline{v}) \qquad (7)$$

Condition (7) says that, from any state at $\ell \in \mathcal{L}^C$ that satisfies $Q_\ell(\overline{v})$, all the exit transitions are disabled and cannot be executed.

The following is the main result of this section:

Theorem 1. *Q, $\mathcal{U}$ that satisfy (4), (5), (6) and (7) for a certain SCSG C of a CFG P imply non-termination of P.*

In order to prove Theorem 1, we need the following lemma:

Lemma 1. *Let us assume that Q, $\mathcal{U}$ satisfy (4), (6) and (7) for a certain SCSG C. Let (ℓ, σ) be a configuration such that $\ell \in \mathcal{L}^C$ and $\sigma \models Q_\ell(\overline{v})$. Then there exists a configuration (ℓ', σ') such that $\ell' \in \mathcal{L}^C$, $\sigma' \models Q_{\ell'}(\overline{v})$ and $(\ell, \sigma) \xrightarrow{\tau} (\ell', \sigma')$ for a certain $\tau \in \mathcal{T}^C$.*

Proof. By condition (2) (which is implicitly assumed to hold), there is a transition τ of the form $(\ell, \ell', \mathcal{R})$ for a certain $\ell' \in \mathcal{L}$ such that $\sigma \models \mathcal{R}(\overline{v})$. Now, by virtue of condition (7), since $\sigma \models Q_\ell(\overline{v})$ we have that $\tau \in \mathcal{T}^C$. Thus, $\ell' \in \mathcal{L}^C$. Moreover, thanks to condition (6) and $\sigma \models Q_\ell(\overline{v})$ and $\sigma \models \mathcal{R}(\overline{v})$, we deduce that there exist values v for the non-deterministic variables $\overline{u}$ such that $(\sigma, v) \models U_\tau(\overline{v}, \overline{u})$. Further, by condition (1) (which is again implicitly assumed), we have that there exists a state σ' such that $(\sigma, v, \sigma') \models$

PROVE-NT (SCSG C, CFG P)
   For $\ell \in \mathcal{L}^C$, set $Q_\ell(\bar{v}) \leftarrow$ true
   For $\tau \in \mathcal{T}^C$, set $U_\tau(\bar{v}, \bar{u}) \leftarrow$ true
   $E^C \leftarrow \mathcal{E}^C$
   while $E^C \neq \emptyset$ **do**
     At $\ell \in \mathcal{L}^C$, assign a template $M_\ell(\bar{v})$
     At $\tau \in \mathcal{T}^C$, assign a template $N_\ell(\bar{v}, \bar{u})$
     Solve Max-SMT problem with
        hard constraints (8), (9), (10) and soft constraints (11)
     if no model for hard clauses is found **then return** Unknown, $\perp$ **fi**
     For $\ell \in \mathcal{L}^C$, let $\widehat{M_\ell}(\bar{v})$ = Solution for $M_\ell(\bar{v})$
     For $\tau \in \mathcal{T}^C$, let $\widehat{N_\tau}(\bar{v}, \bar{u})$ = Solution for $N_\tau(\bar{v}, \bar{u})$
     For $\ell \in \mathcal{L}^C$, set $Q_\ell(\bar{v}) \leftarrow Q_\ell(\bar{v}) \wedge \widehat{M_\ell}(\bar{v})$
     For $\tau \in \mathcal{T}^C$ set $U_\tau(\bar{v}, \bar{u}) \leftarrow U_\tau(\bar{v}, \bar{u}) \wedge \widehat{N_\tau}(\bar{v}, \bar{u})$
     Remove from E^C disabled edges
   done
   for all $\ell \in \mathcal{L}^C$ **do**
     if Reachable (ℓ, σ) in P s.t. $\sigma \models Q_\ell(\bar{v})$ **then**
       let π = reachable path to (ℓ, σ)
       return Non-Terminating, $(Q, \mathcal{U}, \pi)$
     fi
   done
   return Unknown, $\perp$

Fig. 3. Procedure PROVE-NT for proving non-termination of a program P by analyzing SCSG C

$\mathcal{R}(\bar{v}, \bar{u}, \bar{v}')$. All in all, by condition (4) and the fact that $\sigma \models Q_\ell(\bar{v})$ and $(\sigma, v, \sigma') \models \mathcal{R}(\bar{v}, \bar{u}, \bar{v}')$ and $(\sigma, v) \models U_\tau(\bar{v}, \bar{u})$, we get that $\sigma' \models Q_{\ell'}(\bar{v}')$, or equivalently by renaming variables, $\sigma' \models Q_{\ell'}(\bar{v})$. So (ℓ', σ') satisfies the required properties.   □

Now we are ready to prove Theorem 1:

Proof (of Theorem 1). We will construct an infinite computation, which will serve as a witness of non-termination. Thanks to condition (5), we know that there exist a location $\ell \in \mathcal{L}^C$ and a state σ such that (ℓ, σ) is reachable and $\sigma \models Q_\ell(\bar{v})$. As (ℓ, σ) is reachable, there is a computation π whose last configuration is (ℓ, σ). Now, since $Q, \mathcal{U}$ satisfy (4), (6) and (7) for C, and $\ell \in \mathcal{L}^C$ and $\sigma \models Q_\ell(\bar{v})$, we can apply Lemma 1 to inductively extend π to an infinite computation of P.   □

4   Computing Proofs of Non-termination

In this section we explain how proofs of non-termination are effectively computed. As outlined in Section 1, first of all we exhaustively enumerate the SCSGs of the CFG. For each SCSG C, our non-termination proving procedure PROVE-NT, which will be described below, is called. By means of Max-SMT solving, this procedure iteratively computes an unblocking quasi-invariant map Q and a restriction map $\mathcal{U}$ for C. If the construction is successful and eventually edge-closedness can be achieved, and moreover the quasi-invariants of C can be reached, then the synthesized Q, $\mathcal{U}$ satisfy the properties of Theorem 1, and therefore the program is guaranteed not to terminate.

In a nutshell, the enumeration of SCSGs considers a strongly connected component (SCC) of the CFG at a time, and then generates all the SCSGs included in that SCC. More precisely, first of all the SCCs are considered according to a topological ordering in the CFG. Then, once an SCC S is fixed, the SCSGs included in S are heuristically enumerated starting from S itself (since taking a strictly smaller subgraph would imply discarding some transitions a priori arbitrarily), then simple cycles in S (as they are easier to deal with), and then the rest of SCSGs included in S.

Then, once the SCSG C is fixed, our non-termination proving procedure PROVE-NT (Fig. 3) is called. The procedure takes as input an SCSG C of the program's CFG, and the CFG itself. For every location $\ell \in \mathcal{L}^C$, we initially assign a quasi-invariant $Q_\ell(\overline{v}) \triangleq$ true. Similarly, for every transition $\tau \in \mathcal{T}^C$, we initially assign a restriction $U_\tau(\overline{v}, \overline{u}) \triangleq$ true. The set E^C keeps track of the exit edges of C that have not been discarded yet, and hence at the beginning we have $E^C = \mathcal{E}^C$. Then we iterate in a loop in order to strengthen the quasi-invariants and restrictions till $E^C = \emptyset$, that is, all the exit edges of C are disabled.

In every iteration we assign a template $M_\ell(\overline{v}) \equiv m_{\ell,0} + \sum_{v \in \overline{v}} m_{\ell,v} \cdot v \leq 0$ to each $\ell \in \mathcal{L}^C$. We also assign a template $N_\tau(\overline{v}, \overline{u}) \equiv n_{\tau,0} + \sum_{v \in \overline{v}} n_{\tau,v} \cdot v + \sum_{u \in \overline{u}} n_{\tau,u} \cdot u \leq 0$ to each $\tau \in \mathcal{T}^C$.[2] Then we form the Max-SMT problem with the following constraints:[3]

- For $\tau = (\ell, \ell', \mathcal{R}) \in \mathcal{T}^C$:

$$\forall \overline{v}, \overline{u}, \overline{v}'. \; Q_\ell(\overline{v}) \wedge M_\ell(\overline{v}) \wedge \mathcal{R}(\overline{v}, \overline{u}, \overline{v}') \wedge U_\tau(\overline{v}, \overline{u}) \wedge N_\tau(\overline{v}, \overline{u}) \rightarrow M_{\ell'}(\overline{v}') \qquad (8)$$

- For $\ell \in \mathcal{L}^C$: $\exists \overline{v}. \; Q_\ell(\overline{v}) \wedge M_\ell(\overline{v}) \wedge \bigvee_{\tau = (\ell, \ell', \mathcal{R}) \in \mathcal{T}^C} \mathcal{R}(\overline{v}) \qquad (9)$

- For $\tau = (\ell, \ell', \mathcal{R}) \in \mathcal{T}^C$:

$$\forall \overline{v} \exists \overline{u}. \; Q_\ell(\overline{v}) \wedge M_\ell(\overline{v}) \wedge \mathcal{R}(\overline{v}) \rightarrow U_\tau(\overline{v}, \overline{u}) \wedge N_\tau(\overline{v}, \overline{u}) \qquad (10)$$

- For $\tau = (\ell, \ell', \mathcal{R}) \in \mathcal{E}^C$: $\forall \overline{v}. \; Q_\ell(\overline{v}) \wedge M_\ell(\overline{v}) \rightarrow \neg \mathcal{R}(\overline{v}) \qquad (11)$

The constraints (8), (9) and (10) are hard, while the constraints (11) are soft.

The Max-SMT solver finds a solution $\widehat{M_\ell(\overline{v})}$ for every $M_\ell(\overline{v})$ for $\ell \in \mathcal{L}^C$ and a solution $\widehat{N_\tau(\overline{v}, \overline{u})}$ for every $N_\ell(\overline{v}, \overline{u})$ for $\tau \in \mathcal{T}^C$. The solution satisfies the hard constraints and as many soft constraints as possible. In other words, it is the best solution for hard constraints that disables the maximum number of transitions. We then update $Q_\ell(\overline{v})$ for every $\ell \in \mathcal{L}^C$ by strengthening it with $\widehat{M_\ell(\overline{v})}$, and update $U_\tau(\overline{v}, \overline{u})$ for every $\tau \in \mathcal{T}^C$ by strengthening it with $\widehat{N_\tau(\overline{v}, \overline{u})}$. We then remove all the disabled transitions from E^C and continue the iterations of the loop with updated Q, $\mathcal{U}$ and E^C. Note that, even if none of the exit edges is disabled in an iteration (i.e. no soft constraint is met), the quasi-invariants found in that iteration may be helpful for disabling exit edges later.

When all exit transitions are disabled, we exit the loop with the unblocking edge-closing quasi-invariant map Q and the restriction map $\mathcal{U}$.

---

[2] Actually templates $N_\tau(\overline{v}, \overline{u})$ are only introduced for nondet transitions. To simplify the presentation, we assume that for other transitions, $N_\tau(\overline{v}, \overline{u})$ is true.

[3] For clarity, leftmost existential quantifiers over the unknowns of the templates are implicit.

Finally, we check whether there exists a reachable configuration (ℓ, σ) such that $\ell \in \mathcal{L}^C$ and $\sigma \models Q_\ell(\overline{v})$ with an off-the-shelf reachability checker. If this test succeeds, we report non-termination along with $Q, \mathcal{U}$ and the path π reaching (ℓ, σ) as a witness of non-termination.

The next theorem formally states that PROVE-NT proves non-termination:

Theorem 2. *If procedure* PROVE-NT *terminates on input SCSG C and CFG P with Non-Terminating, $(Q, \mathcal{U}, \pi)$, then program P is non-terminating, and $(Q, \mathcal{U}, \pi)$ allow building an infinite computation of P.*

Proof. Let us prove that, if PROVE-NT terminates with Non-Terminating, then the conditions of Theorem 1, i.e., conditions (4), (5), (6) and (7) are met.

First of all, let us prove by induction on the number of iterations of the **while** loop that conditions (4) and (6) are satisfied, and also that for $\tau = (\ell, \ell', \mathcal{R}) \in \mathcal{E}^C - E^C$,

$$\forall \overline{v}. \; Q_\ell(\overline{v}) \to \neg\mathcal{R}(\overline{v}).$$

Before the loop is executed, for all locations $\ell \in \mathcal{L}^C$ we have that $Q_\ell(\overline{v}) \triangleq \mathtt{true}$ and for all $\tau \in \mathcal{T}^C$ we have that $U_\tau(\overline{v}, \overline{u}) \triangleq \mathtt{true}$. Conditions (4) and (6) are trivially met. The other remaining condition holds since initially $E^C = \mathcal{E}^C$.

Now let us see that each iteration of the loop preserves the three conditions. Regarding (4), by induction hypothesis we have that for $\tau = (\ell, \ell', \mathcal{R}) \in \mathcal{T}^C$,

$$\forall \overline{v}, \overline{u}, \overline{v}'. \; Q_\ell(\overline{v}) \wedge \mathcal{R}(\overline{v}, \overline{u}, \overline{v}') \wedge U_\tau(\overline{v}, \overline{u}) \to Q_{\ell'}(\overline{v}').$$

Moreover, the solution computed by the Max-SMT solver satisfies constraint (8), i.e., has the property that for $\tau = (\ell, \ell', \mathcal{R}) \in \mathcal{T}^C$,

$$\forall \overline{v}, \overline{u}, \overline{v}'. \; Q_\ell(\overline{v}) \wedge \widehat{M_\ell}(\overline{v}) \wedge \mathcal{R}(\overline{v}, \overline{u}, \overline{v}') \wedge U_\tau(\overline{v}, \overline{u}) \wedge \widehat{N_\tau}(\overline{v}, \overline{u}) \to \widehat{M_{\ell'}}(\overline{v}').$$

Altogether, we have that for $\tau = (\ell, \ell', \mathcal{R}) \in \mathcal{T}^C$,

$$\forall \overline{v}, \overline{u}, \overline{v}'.(Q_\ell(\overline{v}) \wedge \widehat{M_\ell}(\overline{v})) \wedge \mathcal{R}(\overline{v}, \overline{u}, \overline{v}') \wedge (U_\tau(\overline{v}, \overline{u}) \wedge \widehat{N_\tau}(\overline{v}, \overline{u})) \to (Q_{\ell'}(\overline{v}') \wedge \widehat{M_{\ell'}}(\overline{v}')).$$

Hence condition (4) is preserved.

As for condition (6), the solution computed by the Max-SMT solver satisfies constraint (10), i.e., has the property that for $\tau = (\ell, \ell', \mathcal{R}) \in \mathcal{T}^C$,

$$\forall \overline{v} \exists \overline{u}. \; (Q_\ell(\overline{v}) \wedge \widehat{M_\ell}(\overline{v})) \wedge \mathcal{R}(\overline{v}) \to (U_\tau(\overline{v}, \overline{u}) \wedge \widehat{N_\tau}(\overline{v}, \overline{u})).$$

Thus, condition (6) is preserved.

Regarding the last property, note that the transitions $\tau = (\ell, \ell', \mathcal{R}) \in E^C$ that satisfy the soft constraints (11), i.e., such that

$$\forall \overline{v}. \; (Q_\ell(\overline{v}) \wedge \widehat{M_\ell}(\overline{v})) \to \neg\mathcal{R}(\overline{v})$$

are those removed from E^C. Therefore, this preserves the property that for $\tau = (\ell, \ell', \mathcal{R}) \in \mathcal{E}^C - E^C$,

$$\forall \overline{v}. \; Q_\ell(\overline{v}) \to \neg\mathcal{R}(\overline{v}).$$

Now, if the **while** loop terminates, it must be the case that $E^C = \emptyset$. Thus, on exit of the loop, condition (7) is fulfilled.

Finally, if Non-Terminating is returned, then there is a location $\ell \in \mathcal{L}^C$ and a state satisfying $\sigma \models Q_\ell(\overline{v})$ such that configuration (ℓ, σ) is reachable. That is, condition (5) is satisfied.

Hence, all conditions of Theorem 1 are fulfilled. Therefore, P does not terminate. Moreover, the proof of Theorem 1 gives a constructive way of building an infinite computation by means of Q, $\mathcal{U}$ and π. ☐

Note that constraint (9):

$$\text{For } \ell \in \mathcal{L}^C : \exists \overline{v}. \ Q_\ell(\overline{v}) \wedge M_\ell(\overline{v}) \wedge \bigvee_{\tau = (\ell, \ell', \mathcal{R}) \in \mathcal{T}^C} \mathcal{R}(\overline{v})$$

is not actually used in the proof of Theorem 2, and thus is not needed for the correctness of the approach. Its purpose is rather to help PROVE-NT to avoid getting into dead-ends unnecessarily. Namely, without (9) it could be the case that for some location $\ell \in \mathcal{L}^C$, we computed a quasi-invariant that forbids all transitions $\tau \in \mathcal{T}^C$ from ℓ. Since PROVE-NT only strengthens quasi-invariants and does not backtrack, if this situation were reached the procedure would probably not succeed in proving non-termination.

Now let us describe how constraints are effectively solved. First of all, constraints (8), (9), and (11) are universally quantified over integer variables. Following the same ideas of constraint-based linear invariant generation [25], these constraints are soundly transformed into an existentially quantified formula in NRA by abstracting program and non-deterministic variables and considering them as reals, and then applying Farkas' Lemma [28]. As regards constraint (10), the alternation of quantifiers in

$$\forall \overline{v} \exists \overline{u}. \ Q_\ell(\overline{v}) \wedge M_\ell(\overline{v}) \wedge \mathcal{R}(\overline{v}) \rightarrow U_\tau(\overline{v}, \overline{u}) \wedge N_\tau(\overline{v}, \overline{u})$$

is dealt with by introducing a template $P_{u,\tau}(\overline{v}) \equiv p_{u,\tau,0} + \sum_{v \in \overline{v}} p_{u,\tau,v} \cdot v$ for each $u \in \overline{u}$ and skolemizing. This yields[4] the formula

$$\forall \overline{v}. \ Q_\ell(\overline{v}) \wedge M_\ell(\overline{v}) \wedge \mathcal{R}(\overline{v}) \rightarrow U_\tau(\overline{v}, P_{\overline{u},\tau}(\overline{v})) \wedge N_\tau(\overline{v}, P_{\overline{u},\tau}(\overline{v})),$$

which implies constraint (10), and to which the above transformation into NRA can be applied. Note that, since the Skolem function is not symbolic but an explicit linear function of the program variables, potentially one might lose solutions.

Finally, once a weighted formula in NRA containing hard and soft clauses is obtained, (some of the) existentially quantified variables are forced to take integer values, and the resulting problem is handled by a Max-SMT(NIA) solver [27, 29]. In particular, the unknowns of the templates $P_{u,\tau}(\overline{v})$ introduced for skolemizing non-deterministic variables are imposed to be integers. Since program variables have integer type, this guarantees that only integer values are assigned in the non-deterministic assignments of the infinite computation that proves non-termination.

There are some other issues about our implementation of the procedure that are worth mentioning. Regarding how the weights of the soft clauses are determined, we follow a

---

[4] Again, existential quantifiers over template unknowns are implicit.

heuristic aimed at discarding "difficult" transitions in $\mathcal{E}^C$ as soon as possible. Namely, the edge-closing constraint (11) of transition $\tau = (\ell, \ell', \mathcal{R}) \in \mathcal{E}^C$ is given a weight which is inversely proportional to the number of literals in $\mathcal{R}(\overline{v})$. Thus, transitions with few literals in their conditional part are associated with large weights, and therefore the Max-SMT solver prefers to discard them over others. The rationale is that for these transitions there may be more states that satisfy the conditional part, and hence they may be more difficult to rule out. Altogether, it is convenient to get rid of them before quasi-invariants become too constrained.

Finally, as regards condition (3), our implementation can actually handle transition systems for which this condition does not hold. This may be interesting in situations where, e.g., non-determinism is present in conditional statements, and one does not want to introduce additional variables and locations as was done in Section 2.2 for presentation purposes. The only implication of overriding condition (3) is that, in this case, the properties that must be discarded in soft clauses of condition (11) are not the transitions leaving the SCSG under consideration, but rather the negation of the transitions staying within the SCSG.

5 Experiments

In this section we evaluate the performance of a prototype implementation of the techniques proposed here in our termination analyzer CppInv, available at www.lsi.upc.edu/~albert/cppinv-CAV.tar.gz together with all of the benchmarks. This tool admits code written in (a subset of) C++ as well as in the language of T2 [20]. The system analyses programs with integer variables, linear expressions and function calls, as well as array accesses to some extent. As a reachability checker we use CPA [30].

Altogether, we compare CppInv with the following tools:

- T2 [20] version CAV'13 (henceforth, T2-CAV), which implements an algorithm that tightly integrates invariant generation and termination analysis [19].
- T2 [20] version TACAS'14 (henceforth, T2-TACAS), which reduces the problem of proving non-termination to the search of an under-approximation of the program guided by a safety prover [31].
- JULIA [32], which implements a technique described by Payet and Spoto [33] that reduces non-termination to constraint logic programming.
- APROVE [11] with the Java Bytecode front-end, which uses the SMT-based non-termination analysis proposed in [34].
- A reimplementation of TNT [35] by the authors of [31] that uses Z3 [36] as an SMT back-end.

Unfortunately, because of the unavailability of some of the tools (T2-TACAS, T2-CAV, TNT) or the fact that they do not admit a common input language (JULIA, APROVE), it was not possible to run all these systems on the same benchmarks on the same computer. For this reason, for each of the tables below we consider a different family of benchmarks taken from the literature and provide the results of executing our tool (on a 3.40 GHz Intel Core i7 with 16 GB of RAM) together with the data of competing systems reported in the respective publications. Note that the results of third-party systems in those publications may have some inaccuracies, due to, e.g., the conversion of benchmarks in different formats. However, in those cases the distances between the tools seem to be significant enough to draw conclusions on their relative performance.

Table 1 shows comparative results on benchmarks taken from [31]. In that paper, the tools T2-TACAS, APROVE, JULIA and TNT are considered. The time limit is set to 60 seconds both in that work as well as in the executions of CPPINV. The benchmarks are classified according to three categories: (a) all the examples in the benchmark suite known to be non-terminating previously to [31]; (b) all the examples in the benchmark suite known to be terminating previously to [31]; and (c) the rest of instances. Rows of the table correspond to non-termination provers. Columns are associated to each of these three categories of problems. Each column is split into three subcolumns reporting the number on "non-terminating" answers, the number of timed outs, and the number of other answers (which includes "terminating" and "unknown" answers), respectively. Even with the consideration that experiments were conducted on different machines, the results in columns (a) and (c) of Table 1 show the power of the proposed approach on these examples. As for column (b), we found out that instance 430.t2 was wrongly classified as terminating. Our witness of non-termination has been manually verified.

Table 1. Experiments with benchmarks from [31]

	(a)			(b)			(c)		
	Nonterm	TO	Other	Nonterm	TO	Other	Nonterm	TO	Other
CPPINV	70	6	5	1	16	237	113	35	9
T2-TACAS	51	0	30	0	45	209	82	3	72
APROVE	0	61	20	0	142	112	0	139	18
JULIA	3	8	70	0	40	214	0	91	66
TNT	19	3	59	0	48	206	32	12	113

Table 2 (a), which follows a similar format to Table 1, compares CPPINV, T2-CAV and APROVE on benchmarks from [19] (all with a time limit of 300 seconds). Note that, in the results reported in [19], due to a wrong abstraction in the presence of division, T2 was giving two wrong non-termination answers (namely, for the instances rlft3.t2 and rlft3.c.i.rlft3.pl.t2.fixed.t2, for which the termination proofs produced by CPPINV[24] have been checked by hand). For this reason we have discarded those two programs from the benchmark suite. In this case, the performance of our tool is slightly worse than that of T2-CAV. However, it has to be taken into account that T2-CAV was exploiting the cooperation between the termination and the non-termination provers, while we still do not apply this kind of optimizations.

In Table 2 (b), CPPINV is compared with the results of JULIA and APROVE from [34] on Java programs coming from [37]. CPPINV was run on C++ versions of these benchmarks, which admitted a direct translation from Java. The time limit was set to 60 seconds. Columns represent respectively the number of terminating instances (YES), non-terminating instances (NO), instances for which the construction of the proof failed before the time limit (MAYBE), and timeouts (TO). For these instances APROVE gets slightly better results than CPPINV. However, it should be taken into account that four programs of this set of benchmarks include non-linear expressions, which we cannot handle. Moreover, when compared on third-party benchmarks (see Tables 1 and 2 (a)), our results are better.

Finally, Table 2 (c) shows the results of running our tool on programs from the on-line programming learning environment Jutge.org [38] (see www.jutge.org), which is currently being used in several programming courses in the Universitat Politècnica de Catalunya. As a paradigmatic example in which it is easy to write wrong non-terminating code, we have considered the exercise **Binary Search**. The programs in this benchmark suite can be considered challenging since, having been written by students, their structure is often more complicated than necessary. In this case the time limit was 60 seconds. As can be seen from the results, for a ratio of 89% of the cases, CppInv is able to provably determine in less than one minute if the program is terminating or not.

Table 2. Experiments with benchmarks from [19] (a), from [37] (b) and from Jutge.org (c)

(a)

	Nonterm	TO	Other
CppInv	167	39	243
T2-CAV	172	14	263
AProVE	0	51	398

(b)

	YES	NO	MAYBE	TO
CppInv	1	44	9	1
AProVE	1	51	0	3
Julia	1	0	54	0

(c)

	YES	NO	MAYBE	TO
Binary search	2745	484	22	391

All in all, the experimental results show that our technique, although it is general and is not tuned to particular problems, is competitive with the state of the art and performs reasonably and uniformly well on a wide variety of benchmarks.

6 Related Work

Several systems have been developed in recent years for proving non-termination. One of these is, e.g., the tool TNT [35], which proceeds in two phases. The first phase exhaustively generates candidate lassos. The second one checks each lasso for possible non-termination by seeking a *recurrent set* of states, i.e., a set of states that is visited infinitely often along the infinite path that results from unrolling the lasso. This is carried out by means of constraint solving, as in our approach. But while there is an infinite number of lassos in a program, our SCSGs can be finitely enumerated. Further, we can handle unbounded non-determinism, whereas TNT is limited to deterministic programs.

Other methods for proving non-termination that use an off-the-shelf reachability checker like our technique have also been proposed [39, 31]. In [39], the reachability checker is used on instrumented code for inferring weakest preconditions, which give the most general characterization of the inputs under which the original program is non-terminating. While in [39] non-determinism can be dealt with in a very restricted manner, the method in [31] can deal with unbounded non-determinism as we do. In the case of [31], the reachability checker is iteratively called to eliminate every terminating path through a loop by restricting the state space, and thus may diverge on many loops. Our method does not suffer from this kind of drawbacks.

Some other approaches exploit theorem-proving techniques. For instance, the tool INVEL [37] analyzes non-termination of Java programs using a combination of theorem proving and invariant generation. INVEL is only applicable to deterministic programs. Another tool for proving non-termination of Java programs is APROVE [11], which uses SMT solving as an underlying reasoning engine. The main drawback of their method is that it is required that either recurrent sets are singletons (after program slicing) or loop conditions themselves are invariants. Our technique does not have such restrictions.

Finally, the tool TREX [40] integrates existing non-termination proving approaches within a TERMINATOR-like [41] iterative procedure. Unlike TREX, which is aimed at sequential code, Atig et al. [42] focus on concurrent programs: they describe a non-termination proving technique for multi-threaded programs, via a reduction to non-termination reasoning for sequential programs. Our work should complement both of these approaches, since we provide significant advantages over the underlying non-termination proving tools that were previously used.

7 Conclusions and Future Work

In this paper we have presented a novel Max-SMT-based technique for proving that programs do not terminate. The key notion of the approach is that of a *quasi-invariant*, which is a property such that if it holds at a location during execution once, then it continues to hold at that location from then onwards. The method considers an SCSG of the control flow graph at a time, and thanks to Max-SMT solving generates a quasi-invariant for each location. Weights of soft constraints guide the solver towards quasi-invariants that are also *edge-closing*, i.e., that forbid any transition exiting the SCSG. If an SCSG with edge-closing quasi-invariants is reachable, then the program is non-terminating. This last check is performed with an off-the-shelf reachability checker. We have reported experiments with encouraging results that show that a prototypical implementation of the proposed approach has comparable and often better efficacy than state-of-the-art non-termination provers.

As regards future research, a pending improvement is to couple the reachability checker with the quasi-invariant generator, so that the invariants synthesized by the former in unsuccessful attempts are reused by the latter when producing quasi-invariants. Another line for future work is to combine our termination [24] and non-termination techniques. Following a similar approach to [19], if the termination analyzer fails, it can communicate to the non-termination tool the transitions that were proved not to belong to any infinite computation. Conversely, when a failed non-termination analysis ends with an unsuccessful reachability check, one can pass the computed invariants to the termination system, as done in [40]. Finally, we also plan to extend our programming model to handle more general programs (procedure calls, non-linearities, etc.).

Acknowledgments. We thank the Jutge.org team for providing us with benchmarks.

References

1. Francez, N., Grumberg, O., Katz, S., Pnueli, A.: Proving Termination of Prolog Programs. In: Parikh, R. (ed.) Logic of Programs 1985. LNCS, vol. 193, pp. 89–105. Springer, Heidelberg (1985)
2. Dams, D., Gerth, R., Grumberg, O.: A heuristic for the automatic generation of ranking functions. In: Workshop on Advances in Verification, pp. 1–8 (2000)
3. Colón, M. A., Sipma, H. B.: Practical methods for proving program termination. In: Brinksma, E., Larsen, K.G. (eds.) CAV 2002. LNCS, vol. 2404, pp. 442–454. Springer, Heidelberg (2002)
4. Podelski, A., Rybalchenko, A.: A complete method for the synthesis of linear ranking functions. In: Steffen, B., Levi, G. (eds.) VMCAI 2004. LNCS, vol. 2937, pp. 239–251. Springer, Heidelberg (2004)
5. Bradley, A.R., Manna, Z., Sipma, H.B.: Termination of polynomial programs. In: Cousot, R. (ed.) VMCAI 2005. LNCS, vol. 3385, pp. 113–129. Springer, Heidelberg (2005)
6. Bradley, A.R., Manna, Z., Sipma, H.B.: The polyranking principle. In: Caires, L., Italiano, G.F., Monteiro, L., Palamidessi, C., Yung, M. (eds.) ICALP 2005. LNCS, vol. 3580, pp. 1349–1361. Springer, Heidelberg (2005)
7. Bradley, A.R., Manna, Z., Sipma, H.B.: Linear ranking with reachability. In: Etessami, K., Rajamani, S.K. (eds.) CAV 2005. LNCS, vol. 3576, pp. 491–504. Springer, Heidelberg (2005)
8. Bradley, A.R., Manna, Z., Sipma, H.B.: Termination analysis of integer linear loops. In: Abadi, M., de Alfaro, L. (eds.) CONCUR 2005. LNCS, vol. 3653, pp. 488–502. Springer, Heidelberg (2005)
9. Cousot, P.: Proving program invariance and termination by parametric abstraction, lagrangian relaxation and semidefinite programming. In: Cousot, R. (ed.) VMCAI 2005. LNCS, vol. 3385, pp. 1–24. Springer, Heidelberg (2005)
10. Cook, B., Podelski, A., Rybalchenko, A.: Termination proofs for systems code. In: Proc. PLDI 2006, pp. 415–426. ACM Press (2006)
11. Giesl, J., Schneider-Kamp, P., Thiemann, R.: AProVE 1.2: Automatic termination proofs in the dependency pair framework. In: Furbach, U., Shankar, N. (eds.) IJCAR 2006. LNCS (LNAI), vol. 4130, pp. 281–286. Springer, Heidelberg (2006)
12. Podelski, A., Rybalchenko, A.: ARMC: The logical choice for software model checking with abstraction refinement. In: Hanus, M. (ed.) PADL 2007. LNCS, vol. 4354, pp. 245–259. Springer, Heidelberg (2007)
13. Babic, D., Hu, A.J., Rakamaric, Z., Cook, B.: Proving termination by divergence. In: SEFM, pp. 93–102. IEEE Computer Society (2007)
14. Cook, B., Gulwani, S., Lev-Ami, T., Rybalchenko, A., Sagiv, M.: Proving conditional termination. In: Gupta, A., Malik, S. (eds.) CAV 2008. LNCS, vol. 5123, pp. 328–340. Springer, Heidelberg (2008)
15. Cook, B., Podelski, A., Rybalchenko, A.: Summarization for termination: No return! Formal Methods in System Design 35(3), 369–387 (2009)
16. Otto, C., Brockschmidt, M., Essen, C.V., Giesl, J.: Automated termination analysis of Java Bytecode by term rewriting. In: Proc. RTA 2010. LIPIcs, vol. 6, pp. 259–276. Schloss Dagstuhl - Leibniz-Zentrum fuer Informatik, Edinburgh (2010)
17. Kroening, D., Sharygina, N., Tsitovich, A., Wintersteiger, C.M.: Termination analysis with compositional transition invariants. In: Touili, T., Cook, B., Jackson, P. (eds.) CAV 2010. LNCS, vol. 6174, pp. 89–103. Springer, Heidelberg (2010)
18. Tsitovich, A., Sharygina, N., Wintersteiger, C.M., Kroening, D.: Loop summarization and termination analysis. In: Abdulla, P.A., Leino, K.R.M. (eds.) TACAS 2011. LNCS, vol. 6605, pp. 81–95. Springer, Heidelberg (2011)

19. Brockschmidt, M., Cook, B., Fuhs, C.: Better termination proving through cooperation. In: Sharygina, N., Veith, H. (eds.) CAV 2013. LNCS, vol. 8044, pp. 413–429. Springer, Heidelberg (2013)
20. Cook, B., See, A., Zuleger, F.: Ramsey vs. lexicographic termination proving. In: Piterman, N., Smolka, S.A. (eds.) TACAS 2013. LNCS, vol. 7795, pp. 47–61. Springer, Heidelberg (2013)
21. Babic, D., Cook, B., Hu, A.J., Rakamaric, Z.: Proving termination of nonlinear command sequences. Formal Asp. Comput. 25(3), 389–403 (2013)
22. Cook, B., Kroening, D., Rümmer, P., Wintersteiger, C.M.: Ranking function synthesis for bit-vector relations. Formal Methods in System Design 43(1), 93–120 (2013)
23. Larraz, D., Rodríguez-Carbonell, E., Rubio, A.: Smt-based array invariant generation. In: Giacobazzi, R., Berdine, J., Mastroeni, I. (eds.) VMCAI 2013. LNCS, vol. 7737, pp. 169–188. Springer, Heidelberg (2013)
24. Larraz, D., Oliveras, A., Rodríguez-Carbonell, E., Rubio, A.: Proving Termination of Imperative Programs Using Max-SMT. In: Proc. FMCAD 2013 (2013)
25. Colón, M.A., Sankaranarayanan, S., Sipma, H.B.: Linear invariant generation using nonlinear constraint solving. In: Hunt Jr., W.A., Somenzi, F. (eds.) CAV 2003. LNCS, vol. 2725, pp. 420–432. Springer, Heidelberg (2003)
26. Biere, A., Heule, M.J.H., van Maaren, H., Walsh, T. (eds.): Handbook of Satisfiability. Frontiers in Artificial Intelligence and Applications, vol. 185. IOS Press (February 2009)
27. Nieuwenhuis, R., Oliveras, A.: On SAT Modulo Theories and Optimization Problems. In: Biere, A., Gomes, C.P. (eds.) SAT 2006. LNCS, vol. 4121, pp. 156–169. Springer, Heidelberg (2006)
28. Schrijver, A.: Theory of Linear and Integer Programming. Wiley (June 1998)
29. Larraz, D., Oliveras, A., Rodríguez-Carbonell, E., Rubio, A.: Minimal-Model-Guided Approaches to Solving Polynomial Constraints and Extensions (submitted, 2014)
30. Beyer, D., Keremoglu, M.E.: CPAchecker: A Tool for Configurable Software Verification. In: Gopalakrishnan, G., Qadeer, S. (eds.) CAV 2011. LNCS, vol. 6806, pp. 184–190. Springer, Heidelberg (2011)
31. Chen, H.-Y., Cook, B., Fuhs, C., Nimkar, K., O'Hearn, P.: Proving nontermination via safety. In: Ábrahám, E., Havelund, K. (eds.) TACAS 2014. LNCS, vol. 8413, pp. 156–171. Springer, Heidelberg (2014)
32. Spoto, F., Mesnard, F., Payet, É.: A termination analyzer for Java bytecode based on path-length. ACM TOPLAS 32(3) (2010)
33. Payet, É., Spoto, F.: Experiments with Non-Termination Analysis for Java Bytecode. Electr. Notes Theor. Comput. Sci. 253(5), 83–96 (2009)
34. Brockschmidt, M., Ströder, T., Otto, C., Giesl, J.: Automated detection of non-termination and NullPointerExceptions for Java Bytecode. In: Beckert, B., Damiani, F., Gurov, D. (eds.) FoVeOOS 2011. LNCS, vol. 7421, pp. 123–141. Springer, Heidelberg (2012)
35. Gupta, A., Henzinger, T.A., Majumdar, R., Rybalchenko, A., Xu, R.G.: Proving nontermination. In: Necula, G.C., Wadler, P. (eds.) Proc. POPL 2008, pp. 147–158. ACM Press (2008)
36. de Moura, L., Bjørner, N.S.: Z3: An efficient SMT solver. In: Ramakrishnan, C.R., Rehof, J. (eds.) TACAS 2008. LNCS, vol. 4963, pp. 337–340. Springer, Heidelberg (2008)
37. Velroyen, H., Rümmer, P.: Non-termination checking for imperative programs. In: Beckert, B., Hähnle, R. (eds.) TAP 2008. LNCS, vol. 4966, pp. 154–170. Springer, Heidelberg (2008)
38. Petit, J., Giménez, O., Roura, S.: Jutge.org: An educational programming judge. In: King, L.A.S., Musicant, D.R., Camp, T., Tymann, P.T. (eds.) SIGCSE, pp. 445–450. ACM (2012)
39. Gulwani, S., Srivastava, S., Venkatesan, R.: Program analysis as constraint solving. In: Gupta, R., Amarasinghe, S.P. (eds.) Proc. PLDI 2008, pp. 281–292. ACM Press (2008)

40. Harris, W.R., Lal, A., Nori, A.V., Rajamani, S.K.: Alternation for termination. In: Cousot, R., Martel, M. (eds.) SAS 2010. LNCS, vol. 6337, pp. 304–319. Springer, Heidelberg (2010)
41. Cook, B., Podelski, A., Rybalchenko, A.: Terminator: Beyond safety. In: Ball, T., Jones, R.B. (eds.) CAV 2006. LNCS, vol. 4144, pp. 415–418. Springer, Heidelberg (2006)
42. Atig, M.F., Bouajjani, A., Emmi, M., Lal, A.: Detecting fair non-termination in multi-threaded programs. In: Madhusudan, P., Seshia, S.A. (eds.) CAV 2012. LNCS, vol. 7358, pp. 210–226. Springer, Heidelberg (2012)

Termination Analysis
by Learning Terminating Programs*

Matthias Heizmann, Jochen Hoenicke, and Andreas Podelski

University of Freiburg, Germany

Abstract. We present a novel approach to termination analysis. In a first step, the analysis uses a program as a black-box which exhibits only a finite set of sample traces. Each sample trace is infinite but can be represented by a finite lasso. The analysis can "learn" a program from a termination proof for the lasso, a program that is terminating by construction. In a second step, the analysis checks that the set of sample traces is representative in a sense that we can make formal. An experimental evaluation indicates that the approach is a potentially useful addition to the portfolio of existing approaches to termination analysis.

1 Introduction

Termination analysis is an active research topic, and a wide range of methods and tools exist [12,14,23,27,29,36,39]. Each method provides its own twist to address the same issue: in the presence of loops with branching or nesting, the termination argument has to account for all possible interleavings between the different paths through the loop.

If the program is *lasso-shaped* (a stem followed by a single loop without branching), the control flow is trivial; there is only one path. Consequently, the termination argument can be very simple. Many procedures are specialized to lasso-shaped programs and derive a simple termination argument rather efficiently [4,5,7,11,24,31,33]. The relevance of lasso-shaped programs stems from their use as the representation of an infinite trace through the control flow graph of a program with arbitrary nesting.

We present a new method that analyzes termination of a general program $\mathcal{P}$ but has to find termination arguments only for lasso-shaped programs. In our method we see the program $\mathcal{P}$ as a blackbox from which we can obtain sample traces. We transform a sample trace π_i into a lasso-shaped program and use existing methods to compute a termination argument for this lasso-shaped program. Afterwards we construct a "larger" program $\mathcal{P}_i$ (which may have branching and nested loops) for which the same termination argument is applicable. We call this construction *learning*, because we learned the terminating program $\mathcal{P}_i$ from a sample trace π_i. Our algorithm continues iteratively until we learned a set of

---

* This work is supported by the German Research Council (DFG) as part of the Transregional Collaborative Research Center "Automatic Verification and Analysis of Complex Systems" (SFB/TR14 AVACS).

A. Biere and R. Bloem (Eds.): CAV 2014, LNCS 8559, pp. 797–813, 2014.

programs $\mathcal{P}_1, \dots, \mathcal{P}_n$ that forms a decomposition of the original program $\mathcal{P}$. This decomposition can be seen as a program of the form $\mathsf{choose}(\mathcal{P}_1, \dots, \mathcal{P}_n)$, i.e., a nondeterministic choice of programs $\mathcal{P}_1, \dots, \mathcal{P}_n$, that is semantically equivalent to the original program $\mathcal{P}$.

Our technical contribution is this method, which does not only extend the existing portfolio of termination analyses but also provides a new functionality: the decomposition of a program $\mathcal{P}$ into modules $\mathcal{P}_1, \dots, \mathcal{P}_n$. This decomposition is not guided by the syntax of the program, this decomposition exploits a novel notion of modularity where a module is defined by a certain termination argument. This novel notion of modularity is the conceptual contribution of our paper.

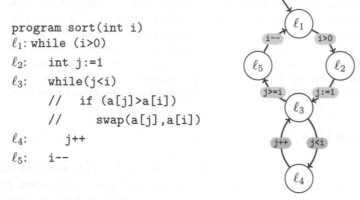

```
program sort(int i)
ℓ₁: while (i>0)
ℓ₂:    int j:=1
ℓ₃:    while(j<i)
       //  if (a[j]>a[i])
       //     swap(a[j],a[i])
ℓ₄:       j++
ℓ₅:    i--
```

Let us explain our algorithm informally using the program $\mathcal{P}^{\mathsf{sort}}$ depicted above which is an implementation of bubblesort. Termination of $\mathcal{P}^{\mathsf{sort}}$ can be shown, e.g., by using the quadratic ranking function $f(\mathtt{i},\mathtt{j}) = \mathtt{i}^2 - \mathtt{j}$, or the lexicographic ranking function $f(\mathtt{i},\mathtt{j}) = (\mathtt{i}, \mathtt{i} - \mathtt{j})$. Intuitively, neither of the two ranking functions is a simple termination argument.

Now, let us pick some ω-trace from $\mathcal{P}^{\mathsf{sort}}$. We take the trace that first enters the outer while loop and then takes the inner while loop infinitely often. We denote this trace using the ω-regular expression OUTER.INNER$^\omega$. We see that this trace is terminating. Its termination can be shown using the linear ranking function $f(\mathtt{i},\mathtt{j}) = \mathtt{i} - \mathtt{j}$. Moreover, we see that this ranking function is not only applicable to this trace, this ranking function is applicable to all traces that eventually always take the inner loop.

$$(\text{INNER} + \text{OUTER})^*.\text{INNER}^\omega \tag{1}$$

Now, let us pick another ω-trace from $\mathcal{P}^{\mathsf{sort}}$. This time we take the trace that always takes the outer while loop. We see that this trace is terminating. Its termination can be shown using the linear ranking function $f(\mathtt{i},\mathtt{j}) = \mathtt{i}$. Moreover, we see that this ranking function is not only applicable to this trace, this ranking function is applicable to all traces that take the outer while loop infinitely often.

$$(\text{INNER}^*.\text{OUTER})^\omega \tag{2}$$

Finally, we consider the set of all ω-trace of the program $\mathcal{P}^{\text{sort}}$

$$(\text{OUTER} + \text{INNER})^\omega,$$

check that each trace has the form (1) or has the form (2), and conclude that $\mathcal{P}^{\text{sort}}$ is terminating.

If we are to automate the reasoning from the example above, a number of questions arise.

(A) How does one effectively represent a set of traces that share a common reason for termination, like the sets (1) and (2) above? The answer is given in Section 2 where we define a *module*, which is a program whose traces adhere to a certain fairness constraint.

(B) What is a termination argument whose applicability to a whole set of traces can be checked effectively? The answer is given in Section 3 where we present a Floyd-Hoare style annotation for termination proofs.

(C) How can we learn a set of terminating traces (represented as a program with a fairness constraint) from a single terminating sample trace? The answer is given in Section 4 where we construct a terminating module from a given termination proof.

(D) How can we check that a set of modules $\mathcal{P}_1, \ldots, \mathcal{P}_n$ covers the behavior of the original program $\mathcal{P}$ and can we always decompose $\mathcal{P}$ into a set of modules $\mathcal{P}_1, \ldots, \mathcal{P}_n$? One facet of the question is the theoretical completeness, which is answered in Section 5. The other facet is the practical feasibility, which is analyzed via an experimental evaluation in Section 6.

2   Fair Module

Preliminaries. The key concept in our formal exposition is the notion of an ω-*trace*, which is an infinite sequence of program statements $\pi = \mathit{st}_1 \mathit{st}_2 \ldots$. We assume that the statements are taken from a given finite set of program statements Σ. If we consider Σ as an alphabet and each statement as a letter, then an ω-*trace* is an infinite word over this alphabet. In order to stress the usage of statements as letters of an alphabet, we sometimes frame each statement/letter. For example, we can write the alphabet of our running example $\mathcal{P}^{\text{sort}}$ as $\Sigma_{sort} = \{\boxed{\text{i>0}}, \boxed{\text{j:=1}}, \boxed{\text{j<i}}, \boxed{\text{j++}}, \boxed{\text{j>=i}}, \boxed{\text{i--}}\}$ and $\pi = \boxed{\text{j<i}}\,\boxed{\text{j:=1}}.(\boxed{\text{j:=1}}\,\boxed{\text{j++}}\,\boxed{\text{j:=1}})^\omega$ is an ω-trace.

The definition of an ω-trace as an arbitrary (infinite) sequence means that the notion is independent of the programming language semantics, which we even have not introduced yet. We will do so now. A *valuation* ν is a function that maps the program variables $\vec{v}$ to values. We use the term *valuation* instead of *state* to stress that this is independent from the program counter (and independent from control flow). We call a set of valuations a *predicate* and use the letter I to denote predicates. The letter I is used reminiscent to *invariant*, because we will use predicates to represent invariants at locations. We assume that each statement st comes with a binary relation over the set of valuations (the set of its precondition/postcondition pairs). We say that the Hoare triple $\{I\}\mathit{st}\{I'\}$ is valid, if the binary relation for st holds between precondition I and postcondition I'. We use the interleaved sequences of valuations and statements $\nu_0 \xrightarrow{\mathit{st}_1} \ldots \xrightarrow{\mathit{st}_n} \nu_n$ as a shorthand to denote that each pair of valuations (ν_i, ν_{i+1}) is contained in the transition relation of the statement st_{i+1}.

An ω-trace may not correspond to any possible execution for one out of two reasons. First, there may be a finite prefix that does not have any possible execution, like e.g., the prefix `x<0` `x:=1` `x<0` of the ω-trace $(\,$`x<0` `x:=1`$\,)^\omega$. Secondly, there may be no starting valuation ν_0 for any infinite execution, although every finite prefix is executable which holds e.g., for the ω-trace $(\,$`x>=0` `x++`$\,)^\omega$. In both cases we call such an ω-trace *terminating*.

The notion of an ω-trace is also independent of a program (a trace may not correspond to a path in the program's control flow graph). We introduce a program as a control flow graph whose edges are labeled with statements. Formally, a *program* is a graph $\mathcal{P} = \langle \mathsf{Loc}, \delta, \ell_{\mathsf{init}} \rangle$ with a finite set Loc of nodes called *locations*, a set δ of edges labeled with statements, i.e., $\delta \subseteq \mathsf{Loc} \times \Sigma \times \mathsf{Loc}$ and an initial node called the initial location ℓ_{init}. We call the program $\mathcal{P}$ *terminating* if each of its ω-traces is terminating.

Module: Program with Fairness Contraint. In our method we will decompose a program into *modules* such that each module represents traces that share a common reason for termination. We now formalize our notion of a module.

Definition 1 (module). *A module is a program together with a fairness constraint given by a distinguished location ℓ_{fin}, i.e.,*

$$\mathcal{P} = \langle \mathsf{Loc}, \delta, \ell_{\mathsf{init}}, \ell_{\mathsf{fin}} \rangle$$

where the set of location can be partitioned into two disjoint sets, Loc_U, and Loc_V, such that

- *the initial location is contained in Loc_U,*
- *the final location is contained in Loc_V, and*
- *no location in Loc_V has a successor in Loc_U, i.e.,*

$$(\ell, \mathit{st}, \ell') \in \delta \quad implies \quad \ell \in \mathsf{Loc}_U \ \ or \ \ \ell' \in \mathsf{Loc}_V$$

A fair ω-trace of a module $\mathcal{P}$ is an ω-trace that labels a fair path in the graph of $\mathcal{P}$, which is a path that visits the distinguished location ℓ_{fin} infinitely often. We call the module $\mathcal{P}$ terminating if each of its fair ω-traces is terminating.

A *non-fair* ω-trace of a terminating module (i.e., an ω-trace that labels a path in its control flow graph without satisfying the fairness constraint) can be non-terminating.

For the reader who is familiar with the concept of Büchi automata, a module is reminiscent of a Büchi automaton with exactly one final state. A Büchi automaton of this form recognizes an ω-regular language of the form $U.V^\omega$, where U and V are regular languages over the alphabet of statements $U, V \subseteq \Sigma^*$.

Example 1. Let us consider again our running example $\mathcal{P}^{\mathrm{sort}}$. The sets that we gave informally by the ω-regular expressions (1) and (2) can be represented as modules. The module $\mathcal{P}_1^{\mathrm{sort}}$ depicted on the left represents all traces that eventually only take the inner while loop. The module $\mathcal{P}_2^{\mathrm{sort}}$ depicted

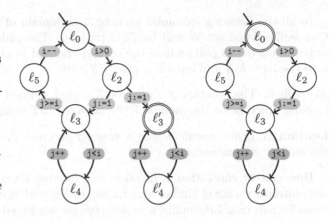

on the right represents all traces that take the outer while loop infinitely often.

In this example, the decomposition of the program into modules is defined by the nestings structure of while loops. In Section 5 we present an algorithm that finds a decomposition automatically but does not rely on any information about the structure of the while loops in the program.

3 Certified Module

In this section we present a termination argument for modules that consists of two parts: a ranking function and an annotation of the module's locations.

First, we extend the usual notion of a ranking function to our definition of a module. The crux in the following definition lies in the fact that we do not require that the value of the ranking function has to decrease after a fixed number of steps. We only require that the value of the ranking function has to decrease every time the final location ℓ_{fin} is visited. As a consequence our ranking function is a termination argument that is applicable to each fair ω-trace, but does not have to take non-fair ω-traces into account.

Definition 2 (ranking function for a module). *Given a module* $\mathcal{P}$, *we call a function* f *from valuations into a well-ordered set* $(\mathbb{W}, \prec)$ *a ranking function for* $\mathcal{P}$ *if for each finite path*

$$\ell_0 \xrightarrow{\mathit{st}_1} \cdots \xrightarrow{\mathit{st}_k} \ell_k \xrightarrow{\mathit{st}_{k+1}} \cdots \xrightarrow{\mathit{st}_n} \ell_n$$

that starts in the initial location (i.e., $\ell_0 = \ell_{\mathrm{init}}$*) and visits the final location in the k-th step and in the n-th step (i.e.,* $\ell_k = \ell_n = \ell_{\mathrm{fin}}$*) and for each sequence of valuations* $\nu_0, \ldots, \nu_n$ *such that the pair* (ν_i, ν_{i+1}) *is in the transition relation of the statement* st_i, *i.e.,*

$$\nu_0 \xrightarrow{\mathit{st}_1} \cdots \xrightarrow{\mathit{st}_k} \nu_k \xrightarrow{\mathit{st}_{k+1}} \cdots \xrightarrow{\mathit{st}_n} \nu_n$$

the value of the ranking function decreases whenever ℓ_{fin} *is visited, i.e.,*

$$f(\nu_n) \prec f(\nu_k).$$

In all the following examples we take $\mathbb{Z}$ as domain of the program variables. Our well-ordered set $\mathbb{W}$ will be $(\mathbb{Z} \cup \{\infty\}, \prec)$. The ordering $\prec$ is the natural order restricted to pairs where the second operand is greater than or equal to zero (i.e., $a \prec b$ if and only if $a < b \wedge b \geq 0$).

Example 2. The function $f : \mathsf{dom} \rightarrow \mathbb{Z} \cup \{\infty\}$ defined as $f(i,j) = i - j$ is a ranking function for the module $\mathcal{P}_1^{\mathsf{sort}}$ depicted in Example 1.

Lemma 1. *If the module $\mathcal{P}$ has a ranking function f, then each fair trace of the module is terminating.*[1]

How can we check that a function is a ranking function for a module? We next introduce a novel kind of annotation, called *rank certificate* that serves as a proof for this task. Informally, a *rank certificate* is a Floyd-Hoare annotation that ensures that the value of the ranking function has decreased whenever the final location ℓ_{fin} was visited. Therefore, we introduce an auxiliary variable oldrnk that represents the value of the ranking function at the previous visit of ℓ_{fin}. Initially, the auxiliary variable oldrnk has the value ∞ which is a value strictly greater than all other values from our well-ordered $\mathbb{W}$.

Definition 3 (certified module). *Given a module $\mathcal{P} = \langle \mathsf{Loc}, \delta, \ell_{\mathsf{init}}, \{\ell_{\mathsf{fin}}\} \rangle$ and a function f from valuations into a well-ordered set $(\mathbb{W}, \prec)$, we call a mapping $\mathcal{I}$ from locations to predicates a* rank certificate *for the function f and the module $\mathcal{P}$ if the following properties hold.*

- *The initial location ℓ_{init} is mapped to the predicate where the auxiliary variable oldrnk has the value ∞, i. e.,*

$$\mathcal{I}(\ell_{\mathsf{init}}) \Leftrightarrow \mathsf{oldrnk} = \infty.$$

- *The accepting state is mapped to a predicate in which the value of the ranking function f over the program variables is smaller than the value of the variable oldrnk, i. e.,*

$$\mathcal{I}(\ell_{\mathsf{fin}}) \Rightarrow \big(f(\vec{v}) \prec \mathsf{oldrnk}\big).$$

- *The outgoing edges of non-accepting locations correspond to valid Hoare triples, i.e.,*

$$\{\, \mathcal{I}(\ell) \,\} \; \mathit{st} \; \{\, \mathcal{I}(\ell') \,\} \text{ is valid for } (\ell, \mathit{st}, \ell') \in \delta, \ell \neq \ell_{\mathsf{fin}}$$

and outgoing edges of the final location correspond to valid Hoare triples if we insert an additional assignment statement that assigns the value of the ranking function to the auxiliary variable oldrnk, i.e.,

$$\{\, \mathcal{I}(\ell) \,\} \; \boxed{\mathsf{oldrnk} := f(\vec{v})} \,; \mathit{st} \; \{\, \mathcal{I}(\ell') \,\} \text{ is valid for } (\ell_{\mathsf{fin}}, \mathit{st}, \ell') \in \delta$$

We call the triple $(\mathcal{P}, f, \mathcal{I})$ a certified module.

---

[1] An extended version of this paper that also contains the correctness proofs is available online.

Example 3. The figure on the right depicts a certified module $(\mathcal{P}_1^{\mathtt{sort}}, f, \mathcal{I})$ where f is the ranking function $f(i, j) = i - j$ and $\mathcal{I}$ is the mapping of locations to predicates indicated by writing the predicate beneath the location.

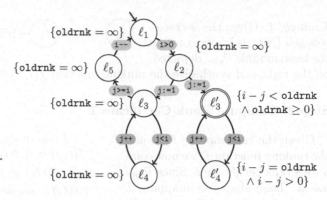

Theorem 1 (soundness). *Each fair ω-trace of a certified module $(\mathcal{P}, f, \mathcal{I})$ is terminating.*

4 Learning a Terminating Program

In this section we present a method for the construction of a certified module $(\mathcal{P}, f, \mathcal{I})$. The crux of this method is that we do not construct a termination argument (a ranking function f together with a rank certificate $\mathcal{I}$) for the resulting module $\mathcal{P}$. Instead, we construct vice versa the resulting module $\mathcal{P}$ as the largest module for which a given termination argument (a ranking function f together with a rank certificate $\mathcal{I}$) is applicable. We obtain this termination proof from a single ω-trace. We call this method learning, because we learn a terminating program (given as a certified module) from a single sample trace.

The input to our method is a terminating ω-trace $\mathit{st}_1 \ldots \mathit{st}_{k-1}(\mathit{st}_k \ldots \mathit{st}_n)^\omega$ that is ultimately periodic. We call an ultimately periodic trace a *lasso*. We call the prefix $\mathit{st}_1 \ldots \mathit{st}_{k-1}$ the *stem* of the lasso and we call the periodic part $\mathit{st}_k \ldots \mathit{st}_n$ the *loop* of the lasso. For better legibility we use u (resp. v) to denote the stem (resp. loop) of the lasso. We construct a certified module $(\mathcal{P}, f, \mathcal{I})$ in the following three steps.

Step 1. Synthesize Ranking Function f

First, we construct a module $\mathcal{P}_{uv^\omega}$ that has only one single ω-trace, namely the lasso uv^ω. We call $\mathcal{P}_{uv^\omega}$ the *lasso module* of uv^ω and construct $\mathcal{P}_{uv^\omega} = \langle \mathsf{Loc}, \delta, \ell_{\mathsf{init}}, \{\ell_{\mathsf{fin}}\}\rangle$ formally as the module that has one location for each statement (i.e., $\mathsf{Loc} = \{\ell_0, \ldots, \ell_{n-1}\}$), where ℓ_0 is the initial location, ℓ_k is the final location and the transition graph resembles the shape of a lasso, i.e., $\delta = \{(\ell_i, \mathit{st}_i, \ell_{i+1}) \mid i = 1, \ldots n - 2\} \cup \{(\ell_{n-1}, \mathit{st}_n, \ell_k)\}$.

The lasso module $\mathcal{P}_{uv^\omega}$ can be seen as a program that consists of a single while loop. This allows us to use existing methods [4,5,7,11,24,31,33] to synthesize a ranking function for $\mathcal{P}_{uv^\omega}$.

Example 4. Given the ω-trace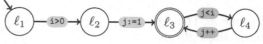
`i>0` `j:=1` (`j<i` `j++`)$^{\omega}$, we construct
the lasso module $\mathcal{P}_{uv^{\omega}}$ depicted
on the right and synthesize the ranking function $f(i,j) = i - j$ for this module.

Step 2. Compute Rank Certificate $\mathcal{I}$

Given the lasso module $\mathcal{P}_{uv^{\omega}}$ and
the ranking function f, we now com-
pute a rank certificate $\mathcal{I}$. Since $\mathcal{P}_{uv^{\omega}}$
has a "lasso shape" a mapping $\mathcal{I}$
from the locations of $\mathcal{P}_{uv^{\omega}}$ to predicates is a rank certificate if and only
if the Hoare triples and the implication shown on the right are valid.

$\{\,true\,\}$ `oldrnk:=∞` $\{\,\mathcal{I}(\ell_1)\,\}$
$\{\,\mathcal{I}(\ell_i)\,\}$ st_i $\{\,\mathcal{I}(\ell_{i+1})\,\}$ for $1 \leq i < k$
$\mathcal{I}(\ell_k) \Rightarrow f(\vec{v}) < $ `oldrnk`
$\{\,\mathcal{I}(\ell_k)\,\}$ `oldrnk:=`$f(\vec{v})$ st_k $\{\,\mathcal{I}(\ell_{k+1})\,\}$
$\{\,\mathcal{I}(\ell_i)\,\}$ st_{i+1} $\{\,\mathcal{I}(\ell_{i+1})\,\}$ for $k < i < n$
$\{\,\mathcal{I}(\ell_n)\,\}$ st_n $\{\,\mathcal{I}(\ell_k)\,\}$

```
program rankDecrease()

           oldrnk := ∞
   ℓ₁ :  𝑠𝑡₁
    ⋮    ⋮
  ℓₖ₋₁ : 𝑠𝑡ₖ₋₁
   ℓₖ :  while (true)
              assert(f(v⃗) < oldrnk)
              oldrnk := f(v⃗)
              𝑠𝑡ₖ
  ℓₖ₊₁ :        𝑠𝑡ₖ₊₁
    ⋮    ⋮
   ℓₙ :        𝑠𝑡ₙ
```

The predicates $\mathcal{I}(\ell_i)$ for which these implications are valid, can be obtained by
proving partial correctness of the program
`rankDecrease`$_{uvf}$ depicted on the left. The
program `rankDecrease`$_{uvf}$ first assigns the
value ∞ (which is strictly larger than any
other element in the well-ordered set $\mathbb{W}$) to
the variable `oldrnk`. Afterwards the state-
ments $\mathit{st}_1 \ldots \mathit{st}_{k-1}$ are executed and the program `rankDecrease`$_{uvf}$ enters a nonter-
minating `while` loop. We use an `assert`
statement to state the correctness specification of the program `rankDecrease`$_{uvf}$.
The program is correct if at the beginning
of the `while` loop the inequality $f(\vec{v}) < $ `oldrnk` holds. After this assert statement, the current value of the function f is assigned to the variable `oldrnk` and
then the statements $\mathit{st}_k \ldots \mathit{st}_n$ are executed.

A Floyd-Hoare annotation $\mathcal{I}(\ell_1), \ldots, \mathcal{I}(\ell_n)$ that shows partial correctness of
the program `rankDecrease`$_{uvf}$ is also a rank certificate for our ranking function
f and our lasso module $\mathcal{P}_{uv^{\omega}}$. This Floyd-Hoare annotation can be computed by
static analysis [15].

Example 5. Continuing
Example 4 we con-
struct the program
`rankDecrease`$_{uvf}$ for
$\mathcal{P}_{uv^{\omega}}$ and compute
the rank certificate

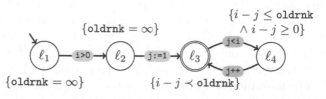

depicted in the figure on the right. The rank certificate $\mathcal{I}$ is represented by the
predicates denoted beneath the locations.

An Alternative Variant of Step 2. Some methods for the synthesis of a ranking function [7,24] also provide a *supporting invariant*. This is a predicate I such that

- I is invariant under executions of the loop $st_1 \ldots st_{k-1}$,
- I is an overapproximation of the reachable valuations after executing the stem $st_k \ldots st_n$,
- and each execution of the loop starting in a valuation contained I decreases the ranking function f.

If we have a supporting invariant I for the ranking function f, we do not have to construct and analyze the program $\mathtt{rankDecrease}_{uvf}$. Alternatively, we can set the predicate $\mathcal{I}(\ell_k)$ to

$$I \;\wedge\; f(\vec{v}) < \mathtt{oldrnk} \;\wedge\; \mathtt{oldrnk} \geq 0$$

and obtain the remaining predicates $\mathcal{I}(\ell_0), \ldots, \mathcal{I}(\ell_{k-1})$, and $\mathcal{I}(\ell_{k+1}), \ldots, \mathcal{I}(\ell_n)$ as strongest postconditions by using an interpolating theorem prover.

Step 3. Construct Module $\mathcal{P}$

We extend the lasso module $\mathcal{P}_{uv^\omega}$ to a module $\mathcal{P}$ that also has the ranking function f and that also has the rank certificate $\mathcal{I}$. Therefore we modify $\mathcal{P}_{uv^\omega}$ according to the following two rules.

Modification Rule 1: Merge Locations. If the predicates mapped to the locations ℓ_i and ℓ_j coincide (i.e., $\mathcal{I}(\ell_i) = \mathcal{I}(\ell_j)$) then we may merge both locations.

Modification Rule 2: Add Transitions. Let st be some program statement and let ℓ_i, and ℓ_j be locations. If $\ell_i \neq \ell_j$ and the Hoare triple $\{\, \ell_i \,\}\ st\ \{\, \ell_j \,\}$ is valid, we may add the transition (ℓ_i, st, ℓ_j). If $\ell_i = \ell_j$ and the Hoare triple $\{\, \ell_i \,\}$ $\boxed{\mathtt{oldrnk} := f(\vec{v})}$ $;st\ \{\, \ell_j \,\}$ is valid, we may add the transition (ℓ_i, st, ℓ_j).

If we apply these modifications to a certified module we obtain again a certified module. Every strategy for applying these modfications gives rise to an algorithm that is an instance of our method.

Example 6. Continuing Example 4 we merge locations ℓ_1 and ℓ_2. Afterwards we add for each program statement that occurs in $\mathcal{P}^{\mathtt{sort}}$ a selfloop at ℓ_1 and

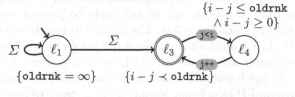

a transition between ℓ_1 and ℓ_3. We obtain the certified module $\mathcal{P}_{\mathtt{ext}}$ depicted on the right. The set of fair ω-traces of this module is given by the ω-regular expression $\Sigma^*.(\boxed{\mathtt{j<i}}\,\boxed{\mathtt{j++}})^\omega$. If we take the intersection of the program $\mathcal{P}^{\mathtt{sort}}$ and the module $\mathcal{P}_{\mathtt{ext}}$ we obtain the module $\mathcal{P}_1^{\mathtt{sort}}$ from Example 1. In our algorithm (Section 5), we do not need to construct modues such as $\mathcal{P}_1^{\mathtt{sort}}$ explicitly (we only use their implicit representation through $\mathcal{P}_{\mathtt{ext}}$).

5   Overall Algorithm

Until now, we have formalized (and automated) one part of our method, which is to construct a terminating module from a given sample trace. We still need to formalize (and automate) how to check that a set of modules covers all behaviours of the program. We will say that the program $\mathcal{P}$ has a decomposition into the modules $\mathcal{P}_1, \ldots, \mathcal{P}_n$ if the set of ω-traces of the program $\mathcal{P}$ is the union of the set of fair ω-traces of the modules $\mathcal{P}_1, \ldots, \mathcal{P}_n$.

We can automate the check that indeed all cases are covered by reducing it to the inclusion between Büchi automata. Both a program and a module are special cases of Büchi automata (where the set of states is the set of program locations and the set of final states contains all program locations respectively the final location ℓ_{fin} only). By definition, the ω-traces of the program $\mathcal{P}$ are exactly the infinite words accepted by the Büchi automaton $\mathcal{P}$ (and form the language $\mathcal{L}(\mathcal{P})$ recognized by $\mathcal{P}$), and the fair ω-traces of the module $\mathcal{P}_i$ are exactly the infinite words accepted by the Büchi automaton $\mathcal{P}_i$ (and form the language $\mathcal{L}(\mathcal{P}_i)$ recognized by $\mathcal{P}_i$), for $i = 1, \ldots, n$. The inclusion

$$\mathcal{L}(\mathcal{P}) \subseteq \mathcal{L}(\mathcal{P}_1) \cup \cdots \cup \mathcal{L}(\mathcal{P}_n)$$

can be checked by a model checker such as [26] or by a tool for manipulating Büchi automata such as [38].

We will use Büchi automata also in order to prove that decomposing a program into certified modules is in principle a complete method for termination analysis.

Theorem 2 (completeness). *If a program $\mathcal{P}$ is terminating then it can be decomposed into a finite set of certified modules, i.e., there are certified modules*

$$(\mathcal{P}_1, f_1, \mathcal{I}_1), \ldots, (\mathcal{P}_n, f_n, \mathcal{I}_n)$$

such that the following equality holds.

$$\mathcal{L}(\mathcal{P}) = \mathcal{L}(\mathcal{P}_1) \cup \cdots \cup \mathcal{L}(\mathcal{P}_n)$$

Overall Algorithm. Having reduced the check that a set of modules is a decomposition of a program, we are ready to present our algorithm for termination analysis, depicted below. The algorithm iteratively constructs certified modules $(\mathcal{P}_i, f_i, \mathcal{I}_i)$ until all ω-traces of the program are known to be terminating or we encounter an ω-trace for which we cannot find a termination argument.

At the beginning of each iteration (line 2) we check if there is an ω-trace of the program $\mathcal{P}$ that is not already a fair ω-trace of one of the modules $\mathcal{P}_1, \ldots, \mathcal{P}_{n-1}$ (for which termination has already been proven). As mentioned above, we reduce this check to language inclusion of Büchi automata. Therefore we know that whenever there exists a counterexample to language inclusion there exists also a lasso-shaped counterexample. We take such a lasso-shaped ω-trace uv^ω and construct a program (called lasso module) whose only ω-trace is uv^ω (see Step 1 in Section 4). Next, we analyze termination of the lasso module $\mathcal{P}_{uv^\omega}$. If

```
input  : program 𝒫
output: certified modules (𝒫₁, f₁, ℐ₁), . . . , (𝒫ₙ, fₙ, ℐₙ)
1  for n = 0, 1, 2, . . . do
2  │  if ℒ(𝒫) ⊈ ℒ(𝒫₁) ∪ · · · ∪ ℒ(𝒫ₙ₋₁) then
3  │  │  take ω-trace u.vω that is counterexample to inclusion;
4  │  │  construct lasso module 𝒫uvω;
5  │  │  fₙ := synthesizeRankingFunction(𝒫uvω);
6  │  │  if fₙ = no ranking function found then
7  │  │  │  return "unable to decide termination of 𝒫"
8  │  │  end
9  │  │  ℐₙ := computeRankCertificate(fₙ, 𝒫uvω);
10 │  │  𝒫ₙ := extendCertifiedModule(𝒫uvω, fₙ, ℐₙ);
11 │  else
12 │  │  return "𝒫 is terminating,"
   │  │         "found decomposition (𝒫₁, f₁, ℐ₁), . . . , (𝒫ₙ, fₙ, ℐₙ)"
13 │  end
14 end
```

Algorithm 1. Decomposition of a program 𝒫 into certified modules

we cannot find a ranking function f_n for $\mathcal{P}_{uv^\omega}$ our algorithm is unable to decide termination of $\mathcal{P}$ and returns. Otherwise we take a ranking function f_n and construct a rank certificate $\mathcal{I}_n$ for f_n and $\mathcal{P}_{uv^\omega}$ (see Step 2 in Section 4). Afterwards we use the rank certificate to construct the module $\mathcal{P}_n$. Termination of each fair ω-trace of $\mathcal{P}_n$ can be shown using the ranking function f_n and the rank certificate $\mathcal{I}_n$, i.e., $(\mathcal{P}_n, f_n, \mathcal{I}_n)$ is a certified module (see Step 3 in Section 4). If we were not able to find a counterexample to inclusion in line 2, the program $\mathcal{P}$ is already decomposed into certified modules. We have proven termination and return the certified modules $(\mathcal{P}_1, f_1, \mathcal{I}_1), \ldots, (\mathcal{P}_n, f_n, \mathcal{I}_n)$.

Our approach lends itself to a variation of the above algorithm where one uses an exit condition different from the inclusion check in line 2. In that case, the algorithm returns the modules $\mathcal{P}_1, \ldots, \mathcal{P}_{n-1}$ constructed so far and, in addition, a "remainder program" $\mathcal{P}_{rem}$ which is constructed via the language-theoretic difference of Büchi automata.

$$\mathcal{P}_{rem} := \mathcal{P} \backslash (\mathcal{P}_1 \cup \cdots \cup \mathcal{P}_{n-1})$$

This is interesting in a variety of contexts, e.g., when we found an ω-trace that is nonterminating, or when we found an ω-trace whose termination analysis failed, or simply in case of a timeout. The remainder program can then be analyzed manually, or it can be used as a runtime monitor, etc.

6   Evaluation

It is unlikely that one approach outperforms all others on all kinds of programs, either in effectiveness (how many termination problems can be solved?) or in efficiency (... in what time?). In this paper, we have presented the base algorithm of a new approach to termination analysis. To explore optimizations and possibilities of integration with other approaches must remain a topic of future work.

The question is whether our approach is a potentially useful addition to the portfolio of existing approaches. Therefore, the goal of the present experimental evaluation must be restricted to showing that the approach has a practical potential *in principle*, regarding effectiveness and regarding efficiency. This is not obvious since there are at least two "mission-critical" questions, namely:

- Will the algorithm just learn one terminating program $\mathcal{P}_1, \mathcal{P}_2, \ldots$ after the other, going through an infinite (or just unrealistically high) number of sample traces $\pi_1, \pi_2, \ldots$?
- Will the check of inclusion between Büchi automata (which is notoriously difficult and still an object of ongoing work [8,37]) be a 'bad' bottleneck?

We put the evaluation into the context of a previous, very thorough evaluation[2] in [9] that contained 260 terminating programs. Out of the 260 programs, our tool can handle 236 programs. This, we believe, indicates the potential effectiveness of our approach. In comparison regarding effectiveness, COOPERATING-T2, the "winner" of the evaluation in [9] (a highly optimized tool which integrates several approaches) can handle 14 programs that our tool cannot handle, but our tool can handle 5 programs that COOPERATING-T2 cannot handle (namely a.10.c.t2.c, eric.t2.c, sas2.t2.c, spiral.t2.c and sumit.t2.c). This confirms our point that no single approach provides a "silver bullet" and that it is desirable to have a large portfolio of approaches.

We implemented the algorithm presented in Section 5 in the tool ULTIMATE BÜCHIAUTOMIZER that analyzes termination of C programs. The input programs and the modules are represented by Büchi automata. In order to support (possibly recursive) functions, we use Büchi automata over nested words [1] (we do not introduce the formalism in order to avoid the notational overhead) and implemented an automata library for these automata. We do not check the inclusion

$$\mathcal{L}(\mathcal{P}) \subseteq \mathcal{L}(\mathcal{P}_1) \cup \cdots \cup \mathcal{L}(\mathcal{P}_n)$$

directly. Instead, we complement the modules and check the emptiness of their intersection with the program

$$\mathcal{L}(\mathcal{P}) \cap \mathcal{L}(\overline{\mathcal{P}_1}) \cup \cdots \cup \mathcal{L}(\overline{\mathcal{P}_n})$$

which allow us to reuse intermediate results in further iterations. For complementing our Büchi automata we extended[41] the rank-based approach [18] to (Büchi) nested word automata. The sample ω-traces whose termination we analyze are obtained as counterexamples of an emptiness check that is implemented in our automata library. This emptiness check is purely automata theoric, does not exploit any information about the program, but prefers short counterexamples. We use the tool LASSORANKER [24,31] to synthesize ranking functions

[2] http://verify.rwth-aachen.de/brockschmidt/Cooperating-T2/

and supporting invariants for lassos. The Floyd-Hoare annotation is obtained via interpolation (alternative variant of Step 2 in Section 4). For interprocedural ω-traces we resort to *nested interpolants*[25]. As interpolating theorem prover we use SMTInterpol [10]. While constructing the modules, we apply Modification rule 1 (merge locations) always and we apply Modification rule 2 (add transitions) lazily in the following sense. Only if the automata library queries the existence of a transition in the module, we check whether this transition can be added by applying Modification rule 2. Our tool is available as a command line version for download as well as via a web interface at the following URL.

http://ultimate.informatik.uni-freiburg.de/BuchiAutomizer/

The following table shows the results for a subset of the benchmarks from [9] where our tool run on a computer with an Intel Core i5-3340M CPU with 2.70GHz. Our tool and as well as LASSORANKER the SMT solver, and the automata library are written in Java. The maximum heap size of the Java virtual machine was set to 4GB (-Xmx4G).

For each example we list the lines of code of this example, the overall runtime that our tool needed and the time that our tool spend for analyzing lassos, constructing modules, and checking language inclusion of Büchi automata. Furthermore, we list the number of certified modules that had a trivial ranking function (e.g., $f(x) = 0$), the number of certified modules that had a non-trivial ranking function, and the number of states of the largest module that was constructed.

filename	program size	overall runtime	lasso analysis time	module constr. time	Büchi inclusion time	modules trivial rf	modules non-trivial rf	module size (maximum)
a.10.c.t2.c	183	9s	2.8s	0.7s	2.1s	2	9	5
bf20.t2.c	156	6s	0.7s	0.9s	1.9s	6	7	9
bubbleSort.t2.c	109	5s	0.7s	0.3s	1.2s	5	5	5
consts1.t2.c	40	2s	0.3s	0.1s	0.2s	2	1	5
edn.t2.c	294	119s	18.8s	7.7s	89.0s	141	15	58
eric.t2.c	53	10s	1.1s	1.7s	5.0s	4	6	14
firewire.t2.c	178	28s	3.6s	1.3s	19.0s	12	7	8
mc91.t2.c	47	12s	1.2s	0.6s	4.3s	4	10	8
p-43-terminate.t2.c	727	124s	2.1s	4.2s	110.6s	6	18	5
reverse.t2.c	1351	14s	3.1s	1.2s	2.9s	2	3	12
s3-work.t2.c	3229	28s	2.1s	4.1s	11.5s	6	12	22
sas2.t2.c	192	12s	1.3s	3.0s	5.5s	12	6	17
spiral.c	65	38s	0.9s	1.3s	32.7s	8	12	14
sumit.t2.c	83	4s	1.0s	0.2s	0.7s	4	2	4
traverse_twice.t2.c	1428	12s	1.7s	1.4s	3.2s	2	4	18
ud.t2.c	279	32s	2.1s	3.8s	22.1s	30	25	32

More results[3] of our tool can be found at the SV-COMP 2014 [6] where our tool participated in the demonstration category on termination.

---

[3] http://sv-comp.sosy-lab.org/2014/results/

Discussion. A reader who is familiar with Büchi automata may wonder why it is feasible to complement Büchi automata of these sizes. The answer lies in the flexibility that our definition of a module allows. We tuned the construction of modules in a way that the "amount of nondeterminism" is kept low. However, it is still part of our future work to find a class of Büchi automata that can be easily complemented but does not hinder the module from accepting many traces.

7   Related Work

Our method is related to control flow refinement [22]. There, a multi-path loop is transformed into a semantically equivalent code fragment with simpler loops. For example, following the algebraic decomposition rule

$$(a + b)^* = (b^*ab^*)^+ + b^*$$

the loop with the choice of two paths a and b is transformed into the nondeterministic choice of two loops, one where a appears and one where it does not.

We extend control flow refinement by adding fairness constraints [40] and our reasoning is based on ω-regular languages. In our running example (if we read a as the outer and b as the inner loop) we decomposed the ω-regular expression describing the nested loops as follows

$$(a + b)^\omega = (a + b)^*b^\omega + (b^*a)^\omega.$$

We do not enforce the use of a fixed set of algebraic decomposition rules. Instead, we propose an algorithm that builds a decomposition on demand from simple termination arguments. Thus, we partition a set of traces only when it is necessary and, *by construction*, we produce only modules that are guaranteed to have a simple termination argument.

There are many other termination analyses, e. g., [3,14,16,19,20,21,39]. Most related are the termination analyses based on transition invariants and termination analyses based on size-change termination.

Termination analyses based on transition invariants [9,12,13,23,27,29,34,35] combine different, independently obtained ranking functions to a termination argument. Using transition invariants it is sufficient to cover finite repetitions of the loop. In our running example, one could cover the loop by

$$(a + b)^+ = b^+ + (b^*ab^*)^+$$

using the same simple ranking functions as our method for each case. Covering only finite traces is sound, as it can be shown that

$$(a + b)^\omega = (a + b)^* \, b^\omega + (a + b)^* \, (b^*ab^*)^\omega$$

using Ramsey's Theorem. In our approach, instead of having to introduce $(a+b)^*$, we can get a more precise characterization of the code before the infinite loop;

also, we can base our case-distinction on which path was taken *before* the loop was reached. Furthermore, we get smaller expressions. Compare the expression

$$(a + b)^*(b^*ab^*)^\omega$$

with our expression $(b^*a)^\omega$. Although they describe exactly the same traces, our expression is simpler and therefore leads to a simpler termination proof. Redefining the loop entry point or unfolding the loops are intrinsic techniques in our approach (as opposed to add-on heuristics). If for the program $(ab)^\omega$, it is simpler to prove the correctness of the loop $(baba)$, we use the fact that

$$(ab)^\omega = a(baba)^\omega.$$

The idea of size-change termination [4,17,28] is to track the value of (auxiliary) variables and show the absence of infinite executions by showing that one value would be decreased infinitely often in a well-ordered domain. The (auxiliary) variables can be seen as a predefined set of mutually independent termination arguments.

In contrast with the above approaches, a termination argument in our setting is a *stand alone* module (its validity is checked for the corresponding fair ω-traces, independently from all other program traces). In contrast, a component of a lexicographic ranking function, a disjunct of a transition invariant, or a size-change variable makes sense only as part of a global termination argument (whose validity has to be checked for the global program).

Finally, we use "learning" as a metaphor rather than as a technical term, in contrast with the work in [30] which uses machine learning for termination analysis.

8 Conclusion and Future Work

We have presented a algorithm for termination analysis that transforms a program into a nondeterministic choice of programs. Our transformation is not guided by the syntactic structure of the program, but by its semantics. Instead of decomposing the program into modules and analyzing termination of the modules, we construct modules that we learned from sample traces and that are terminating by construction.

The general idea of such a transformation is the same as for *trace refinement* [32]: move disjunction over abstract values to the disjunction over sets of traces. The formalization of the shared idea and the exploration of its theoretical and practical consequences for program analyses is a topic of future work.

References

1. Alur, R., Madhusudan, P.: Adding nesting structure to words. J. ACM 56(3) (2009)
2. Apt, K.R., de Boer, F.S., Olderog, E.-R.: Verification of Sequential and Concurrent Programs, 3rd edn. Texts in Computer Science, p. 502. Springer (2009) ISBN 978-1-84882-744-8

3. Babic, D., Hu, A.J., Rakamaric, Z., Cook, B.: Proving termination by divergence. In: SEFM, pp. 93–102 (2007)
4. Ben-Amram, A.M.: Size-change termination, monotonicity constraints and ranking functions. In: Bouajjani, A., Maler, O. (eds.) CAV 2009. LNCS, vol. 5643, pp. 109–123. Springer, Heidelberg (2009)
5. Ben-Amram, A.M., Genaim, S.: On the linear ranking problem for integer linear-constraint loops. In: POPL, pp. 51–62 (2013)
6. Beyer, D.: Status report on software verification - (competition summary sv-comp 2014). In: Ábrahám, E., Havelund, K. (eds.) TACAS 2014. LNCS, vol. 8413, pp. 373–388. Springer, Heidelberg (2014)
7. Bradley, A.R., Manna, Z., Sipma, H.B.: Linear ranking with reachability. In: Etessami, K., Rajamani, S.K. (eds.) CAV 2005. LNCS, vol. 3576, pp. 491–504. Springer, Heidelberg (2005)
8. Breuers, S., Löding, C., Olschewski, J.: Improved ramsey-based büchi complementation. In: Birkedal, L. (ed.) FOSSACS 2012. LNCS, vol. 7213, pp. 150–164. Springer, Heidelberg (2012)
9. Brockschmidt, M., Cook, B., Fuhs, C.: Better termination proving through cooperation. In: Sharygina, N., Veith, H. (eds.) CAV 2013. LNCS, vol. 8044, pp. 413–429. Springer, Heidelberg (2013)
10. Christ, J., Hoenicke, J., Nutz, A.: Smtinterpol: An interpolating smt solver. In: Donaldson, A., Parker, D. (eds.) SPIN 2012. LNCS, vol. 7385, pp. 248–254. Springer, Heidelberg (2012)
11. Cook, B., Kroening, D., Rümmer, P., Wintersteiger, C.M.: Ranking function synthesis for bit-vector relations. In: Esparza, J., Majumdar, R. (eds.) TACAS 2010. LNCS, vol. 6015, pp. 236–250. Springer, Heidelberg (2010)
12. Cook, B., Podelski, A., Rybalchenko, A.: Termination proofs for systems code. In: PLDI, pp. 415–426 (2006)
13. Cook, B., Podelski, A., Rybalchenko, A.: Proving program termination. Commun. ACM 54(5), 88–98 (2011)
14. Cook, B., See, A., Zuleger, F.: Ramsey vs. lexicographic termination proving. In: Piterman, N., Smolka, S.A. (eds.) TACAS 2013. LNCS, vol. 7795, pp. 47–61. Springer, Heidelberg (2013)
15. Cousot, P., Cousot, R.: Abstract interpretation: A unified lattice model for static analysis of programs by construction or approximation of fixpoints. In: POPL, pp. 238–252 (1977)
16. Cousot, P., Cousot, R.: An abstract interpretation framework for termination. In: POPL, pp. 245–258 (2012)
17. Fogarty, S., Vardi, M.Y.: Büchi complementation and size-change termination. Logical Methods in Computer Science 8(1) (2012)
18. Friedgut, E., Kupferman, O., Vardi, M.Y.: Büchi complementation made tighter. In: Wang, F. (ed.) ATVA 2004. LNCS, vol. 3299, pp. 64–78. Springer, Heidelberg (2004)
19. Ganty, P., Genaim, S.: Proving termination starting from the end. In: Sharygina, N., Veith, H. (eds.) CAV 2013. LNCS, vol. 8044, pp. 397–412. Springer, Heidelberg (2013)
20. Giesl, J., Thiemann, R., Schneider-Kamp, P., Falke, S.: Automated termination proofs with aProVE. In: van Oostrom, V. (ed.) RTA 2004. LNCS, vol. 3091, pp. 210–220. Springer, Heidelberg (2004)
21. Grebenshchikov, S., Lopes, N.P., Popeea, C., Rybalchenko, A.: Synthesizing software verifiers from proof rules. In: PLDI, pp. 405–416 (2012)

22. Gulwani, S., Jain, S., Koskinen, E.: Control-flow refinement and progress invariants for bound analysis. In: PLDI, pp. 375–385 (2009)
23. Harris, W.R., Lal, A., Nori, A.V., Rajamani, S.K.: Alternation for termination. In: Cousot, R., Martel, M. (eds.) SAS 2010. LNCS, vol. 6337, pp. 304–319. Springer, Heidelberg (2010)
24. Heizmann, M., Hoenicke, J., Leike, J., Podelski, A.: Linear ranking for linear lasso programs. In: Van Hung, D., Ogawa, M. (eds.) ATVA 2013. LNCS, vol. 8172, pp. 365–380. Springer, Heidelberg (2013)
25. Heizmann, M., Hoenicke, J., Podelski, A.: Nested interpolants. In: POPL, pp. 471–482 (2010)
26. Holzmann, G.J.: The model checker spin. IEEE Trans. Software Eng. 23(5), 279–295 (1997)
27. Kroening, D., Sharygina, N., Tsitovich, A., Wintersteiger, C.M.: Termination analysis with compositional transition invariants. In: Touili, T., Cook, B., Jackson, P. (eds.) CAV 2010. LNCS, vol. 6174, pp. 89–103. Springer, Heidelberg (2010)
28. Lee, C.S., Jones, N.D., Ben-Amram, A.M.: The size-change principle for program termination. In: POPL, pp. 81–92 (2001)
29. Lee, W., Wang, B.-Y., Yi, K.: Termination analysis with algorithmic learning. In: Madhusudan, P., Seshia, S.A. (eds.) CAV 2012. LNCS, vol. 7358, pp. 88–104. Springer, Heidelberg (2012)
30. Lee, W., Wang, B.-Y., Yi, K.: Termination analysis with algorithmic learning. In: Madhusudan, P., Seshia, S.A. (eds.) CAV 2012. LNCS, vol. 7358, pp. 88–104. Springer, Heidelberg (2012)
31. Leike, J., Heizmann, M.: Ranking templates for linear loops. In: Ábrahám, E., Havelund, K. (eds.) TACAS 2014. LNCS, vol. 8413, pp. 172–186. Springer, Heidelberg (2014)
32. Mauborgne, L., Rival, X.: Trace partitioning in abstract interpretation based static analyzers. In: Sagiv, M. (ed.) ESOP 2005. LNCS, vol. 3444, pp. 5–20. Springer, Heidelberg (2005)
33. Podelski, A., Rybalchenko, A.: A complete method for the synthesis of linear ranking functions. In: Steffen, B., Levi, G. (eds.) VMCAI 2004. LNCS, vol. 2937, pp. 239–251. Springer, Heidelberg (2004)
34. Podelski, A., Rybalchenko, A.: Transition invariants. In: LICS, pp. 32–41 (2004)
35. Podelski, A., Rybalchenko, A.: Transition predicate abstraction and fair termination. In: POPL, pp. 132–144 (2005)
36. Popeea, C., Rybalchenko, A.: Compositional termination proofs for multi-threaded programs. In: Flanagan, C., König, B. (eds.) TACAS 2012. LNCS, vol. 7214, pp. 237–251. Springer, Heidelberg (2012)
37. Tsai, M.-H., Fogarty, S., Vardi, M.Y., Tsay, Y.-K.: State of Büchi complementation. In: Domaratzki, M., Salomaa, K. (eds.) CIAA 2010. LNCS, vol. 6482, pp. 261–271. Springer, Heidelberg (2011)
38. Tsai, M.-H., Tsay, Y.-K., Hwang, Y.-S.: Goal for games, omega-automata, and logics. In: Sharygina, N., Veith, H. (eds.) CAV 2013. LNCS, vol. 8044, pp. 883–889. Springer, Heidelberg (2013)
39. Urban, C., Miné, A.: An abstract domain to infer ordinal-valued ranking functions. In: Shao, Z. (ed.) ESOP 2014. LNCS, vol. 8410, pp. 412–431. Springer, Heidelberg (2014)
40. Vardi, M.Y.: Verification of concurrent programs: The automata-theoretic framework. Ann. Pure Appl. Logic 51(1-2), 79–98 (1991)
41. Wu, X.: Three operations on Büchi nested word automata for program verification. Master's thesis. University of Freiburg, Germany (2011)

Causal Termination
of Multi-threaded Programs*

Andrey Kupriyanov and Bernd Finkbeiner

Universität des Saarlandes, Saarbrücken, Germany

Abstract. We present a new model checking procedure for the termination analysis of multi-threaded programs. Current termination provers scale badly in the number of threads; our new approach easily handles 100 threads on multi-threaded benchmarks like Producer-Consumer. In our procedure, we characterize the existence of non-terminating executions as Mazurkiewicz-style concurrent traces and apply causality-based transformation rules to refine them until a contradiction can be shown. The termination proof is organized into a tableau, where the case splits represent a novel type of modular reasoning according to different causal explanations of a hypothetical error. We report on experimental results obtained with a tool implementation of the new procedure, called *Arctor*, on previously intractable multi-threaded benchmarks.

1 Introduction

One of the most exciting recent advances in computer-aided verification is the extension of CEGAR-based model checking to liveness properties. Counterexample-guided abstraction refinement (CEGAR) [5] has been very successful in the verification of safety properties, where model checkers like *Magic* [4], *ARMC* [23], and *SLAB* [10] can handle even complex multi-threaded programs. For quite some time, the common belief was that CEGAR is limited to safety — until a new generation of CEGAR-based model checkers, notably the termination checkers *Terminator* [6] and *T2* [2,8], proved capable of verifying the termination of difficult recursive functions, such as McCarthy's 91 function [16], as well as of reasonably complicated industrial software, such as device drivers. Unlike the model checkers for safety, however, the termination provers have been targeted to sequential programs only, and experiments show that they indeed scale badly for multi-threaded programs.

In this paper, we present *Arctor* (*A*bstraction *R*efinement of *C*oncurrent *T*emporal *Or*derings), the first termination checker that scales to a large number of concurrent threads. On typical multi-threaded programs such as the Producer-Consumer benchmark shown in Fig. 1, where the CEGAR-based tools and, likewise, termination provers based on classic techniques for term rewrite systems,

---

* This work was partly supported by the German Research Council (DFG) as part of the Transregional Collaborative Research Center "Automatic Verification and Analysis of Complex Systems" (SFB/TR 14 AVACS, www.avacs.org).

A. Biere and R. Bloem (Eds.): CAV 2014, LNCS 8559, pp. 814–830, 2014.

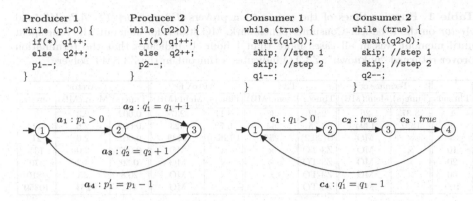

Fig. 1. The *Producer-Consumer* benchmark, shown here for 2 producers and 2 consumers (*Top*: pseudocode; *Bottom*: control flow graphs with labeled transitions for Producer 1 and Consumer 1). The producer threads draw tasks from individual pools and distribute them to nondeterministically chosen queues, each served by a dedicated consumer thread; two steps are needed to process a task. The integer variables p_1 and p_2 model the number of tasks left in the pools of Producers 1 and 2, the integer variables q_1 and q_2 model the number of tasks in the queues of Consumers 1 and 2.

such as *AProVE* [3,13], can handle no more than two threads, Arctor proves termination for 100 threads in less than three minutes. Table 1 shows the experimental data for the Producer-Consumer benchmark, the full experimental evaluation is presented in Section 7.

The CEGAR-based termination provers *Terminator* and *T2* build on the *Ramsey*-based approach, introduced by Podelski and Rybalchenko [21], which searches for a termination argument in the form of a *disjunction* of wellfounded relations. If the transitive closure of the transition relation is contained in the union of these relations, we call the disjunction a *transition invariant*; Ramsey's theorem then implies that the transition relation is wellfounded as well. The approach is attractive, because it is quite easy to find individual relations: one can look at the available program statements and take any decreasing transitions as hints for new relations. In the Producer-Consumer example, the termination can be proved with the disjunction of the relations $p_1' < p_1$, $p_2' < p_2$, $q_1' < q_1$, and $q_2' < q_2$. The bottleneck of this approach is the containment check: with an increasing number of relations it becomes very expensive to check the inclusion of the transitive closure of the program transition relation in the transition invariant.

Similar to the Ramsey-based approach, Arctor works with multiple wellfounded relations that are individually quite simple and therefore easy to discover. The key difference is that we avoid disjunctive combinations, which would require us to analyze the transitive closure of the transition relation, and instead combine the relations only either *conjunctively* or based on a *case-split* analysis. Intuitively, our proof in the Producer-Consumer example makes a case distinction based on which thread might run forever. The case that Producer 1 runs

Table 1. Running times of the termination provers *Terminator, T2, AProVE,* and *Arctor* on the Producer-Consumer benchmark. MO stands for memout; the time spent until memout was in all cases more than 1 hour. U indicates that the termination prover returned "unknown"; Z3-TO indicates a timeout in the Z3 SMT solver.

	Terminator		T2		AProVE		Arctor		
Threads	Time(s)	Mem.(MB)	Time(s)	Mem.(MB)	Time(s)	Mem.(MB)	Time(s)	Mem.(MB)	Vertices
1	3.37	26	2.42	38	3.17	237	0.002	2.3	6
2	1397	1394	3.25	44	6.79	523	0.002	2.6	11
3	×	MO	U(29.2)	253	U(26.6)	1439	0.002	2.6	21
10	×	MO	Z3-TO	×	×	MO	0.027	3.0	135
20	×	MO	Z3-TO	×	×	MO	0.30	4.2	470
60	×	MO	Z3-TO	×	×	MO	20.8	35	3810
100	×	MO	Z3-TO	×	×	MO	172	231	10350

forever is ruled out by the ranking function p_1. Analogously, Producer 2 cannot run forever because of the ranking function p_2. To rule out that one of the consumers, say Consumer 1, runs forever, we introduce the ranking function q_1, which allows an infinite execution of the while loop in Consumer 1 *only if* the while loop of Producer 1 or the while loop of Producer 2 also run forever, which we have already ruled out with the ranking functions p_1 and p_2. We discuss this example in more detail in Section 3; the informal reasoning should already make clear, however, that the case split has significantly simplified the proof: not only is the termination argument for the individual cases simpler than a direct argument for the full program, the cases also support each other in the sense that the termination argument from one case can be used to discharge the other cases.

Our termination checking algorithm is an extension of the *causality*-based proof technique for safety properties from our previous work [15]. To prove a safety property, we build a *tableau* of Mazurkiewicz-style *concurrent traces*, which capture causal dependencies in the system. The root of the tableau is labeled by a default initial trace, which expresses, by way of contradiction, the assumption that there exists a computation from the initial to the error configuration of the system. We then unwind the tableau by following proof rules that capture, step by step, more dependencies; for example, the *necessary action* rule uses Craig interpolation to find necessary intermediate transitions. We terminate as soon as all branches are found to be contradictory.

In Arctor, we show termination with a similar proof by contradiction that is also guided by the search for an erroneous computation. The difference to the safety case is that, instead of assuming the existence of a computation that leads to an error configuration, we start by assuming the existence of a non-terminating execution, and then pursue the causal consequences that follow from this assumption. In this way, we build a tableau of potentially non-terminating traces. The discovery of a ranking function for the currently considered trace may either close the branch, if the rank decreases along all transitions, or result in one or more new traces, if the rank remains equal or increases along some transitions: in this case, we conclude that the existence of an execution for the current trace implies the existence of an execution for some other trace, in which at least one of these transitions occurs infinitely often.

Related Work. In addition to the approaches discussed above, there is a substantial body of techniques for automated termination proofs, in particular for term rewrite systems. Many of these techniques, including simplification orders, dependency pairs, and the size-change principle, are implemented in APrOVE [3,13]. Arctor is the first termination checker that is capable of handling multi-threaded programs with a substantial number of threads. Arctor is based on three key innovations: a novel notion of modular reasoning, a novel composition of ranking functions, and a novel tableau construction based on causality. In the following we point to related work in each of these areas. *Modular reasoning.* The case split in Arctor is a new type of modularity, where the verification task is split according to different causal explanations of a hypothetical error. Other termination provers apply different types of modular reasoning, such as the traditional split according to threads [7], or a split according to ranking functions, by eliminating, after each discovery of a new ranking function, those computations from the program that can now be classified as terminating [12,2]. *Composition of ranking functions.* Similar to the lexicographic combination of ranking functions, constructed for example by T2 [2,8], Arctor combines ranking functions within a branch of the tableau conjunctively. The key difference is that Arctor only imposes a partial order, not a linear order, on the individual ranking functions: the same ranking function may be combined independently with multiple other ranking functions from further splits or previously discharged cases. *Causality-based tableaux.* Concurrent traces and the causality-based tableaux are related to other partial-order methods, such as partial order reduction [14], Mazurkiewicz traces [19], and Petri net theory [24]. As explained above, the tableau construction in Arctor is based on our previous work on the causality-based verification of safety properties [15].

2   Concurrent Traces

We begin by introducing *concurrent traces*, which are the basic objects that our verification algorithm constructs and transforms. Concurrent traces capture the dependencies in a transition system.

2.1   Transition Systems

We consider concurrent systems described in some first-order assertion language. For a set of variables $\mathcal{V}$, we denote by $\Phi(\mathcal{V})$ the set of first-order formulas over $\mathcal{V}$. For each variable $x \in \mathcal{V}$ we define a primed variable $x' \in \mathcal{V}'$, which denotes the value of x in the next state. We call formulas from the sets $\Phi(\mathcal{V})$ and $\Phi(\mathcal{V} \cup \mathcal{V}')$ *state predicates* and *transition predicates*, respectively.

A *transition system* is a tuple $\mathcal{S} = \langle \mathcal{V}, T, init \rangle$ where $\mathcal{V}$ is a finite set of system variables; $T \subseteq \Phi(\mathcal{V} \cup \mathcal{V}')$ is a finite set of system transitions; $init \in \Phi(\mathcal{V})$ is a state predicate, characterizing the initial system states. A *fair* transition system is enriched with two sets of *just* and *compassionate* transitions $J, C \subseteq T$. The requirement is that a just (compassionate) transition that is continuously (infinitely often) enabled, should be infinitely often taken.

A *state* of S is a valuation of system variables $\mathcal{V}$. We call an alternating sequence of states and transitions $s_0, t_1, s_1, t_2, \ldots$ a *run* of S, if $init(s_0)$ holds, and for all $i \geq 1$, $t_i(s_{i-1}, s_i)$ holds. We say that S is *terminating* if there does not exist an infinite run; otherwise S is *non-terminating*. We denote the set of runs by $\mathcal{L}(S)$, and the set of non-terminating runs by $\mathcal{L}_n(S) \subseteq \mathcal{L}(S)$.

Transition systems are well suited for the representation of multi-threaded programs with interleaving semantics: the set of transitions of the system consists of all the transitions of the individual threads.

2.2 Finite Concurrent Traces

Finite concurrent traces were introduced in our previous work on causality-based proofs of safety properties [15].

A *finite concurrent trace* is a labeled, directed, acyclic graph $A = \langle N, E, \nu, \eta \rangle$, where $\langle N, E \rangle$ is a graph with nodes N, called *actions*, and edges E; $\nu : N \to \Phi(V \cup V')$, $\eta : E \to \Phi(V \cup V')$ are labelings of nodes and edges with transition predicates. The source and target functions $s, t : E \to N$ map each edge to its first and second component, respectively. We denote the set of finite concurrent traces by $\mathbb{A}$.

A concurrent trace describes a set of system runs. For a particular concurrent trace its actions specify which transitions should necessarily occur in a run, while its edges represent the (partial) ordering between such transitions and constrain the transitions that occur in-between.

Trace Language. For a transition system $S = \langle \mathcal{V}, T, init \rangle$, the *language* of a concurrent trace $A = \langle N, E, \nu, \eta \rangle$ is defined as a set $\mathcal{L}(A)$ of finite system runs such that for each run $s_0, t_1, s_1, t_2, \ldots, t_n, s_n \in \mathcal{L}(A)$ there exists an injective mapping $\sigma : N \to \{t_1, \ldots, t_n\}$ such that:

1. for each action $a \in N$ and $t_i = \sigma(a)$ the formula $\nu(a)(s_{i-1}, s_i)$ holds.
2. for each edge $e = (a_1, a_2) \in E$, and $t_i = \sigma(a_1)$, $t_j = \sigma(a_2)$, we have that
   a) $i < j$, and b) for all $i < k < j$, the formula $\eta(e)(s_{k-1}, s_k)$ holds.

We call a concurrent trace $A = \langle N, E, \nu, \eta \rangle$ *contradictory* if any of its actions is labeled with an unsatisfiable predicate, i.e. if there exists $n \in N$ such that $\nu(n)$ implies $\bot$. Obviously, the language of such a trace is empty.

Given two concurrent traces $A = \langle N, E, \nu, \eta \rangle$ and $A' = \langle N', E', \nu', \eta' \rangle$, a *trace morphism* $f : A \to A'$ is a pair $f = \langle f_N : N \to N', f_E : E \to E' \rangle$ of injective mappings for nodes and edges of one trace to those of another, preserving sources and targets: $f_N \circ t = t' \circ f_E$, and $f_N \circ s = s' \circ f_E$.

Trace Inclusion. For any two concurrent traces $A = \langle N, E, \nu, \eta \rangle$ and $A' = \langle N', E', \nu', \eta' \rangle$ we define the *trace inclusion* relation $\subseteq$ as follows: $A \subseteq A'$ iff there exists a trace morphism $\lambda = \langle \lambda_N : N' \to N, \lambda_E : E' \to E \rangle$ such that for all $n' \in N' . \nu(\lambda_N(n')) \implies \nu'(n')$, and for all $e' \in E' . \eta(\lambda_E(e')) \implies \eta'(e')$.

We write $A \subseteq_\lambda A'$ if trace inclusion holds for a particular trace morphism λ.

Proposition 1 ([15]). *For $A, A' \in \mathbb{A}$, if $A \subseteq A'$ then $\mathcal{L}(A) \subseteq \mathcal{L}(A')$.*

2.3 Infinite Concurrent Traces

In order to reason about potentially non-terminating computations, we need infinite traces. We define an *infinite concurrent trace* as a tuple $I = \langle A_s, A_c, \phi_s, \phi_c \rangle$ where A_s, A_c are two finite concurrent traces, which we call the *stem* and the *cycle*, and ϕ_s, ϕ_c are two transition predicates. They define the set of infinite system runs in the following way: the stem should occur once in the beginning of the run, while the cycle should occur infinitely often after the stem. Transition predicates ϕ_s and ϕ_c restrict the transitions that are allowed to appear in the stem and cycle part of the run, respectively. We denote the set of infinite concurrent traces by $\mathbb{I}$, and in the following call them simply (concurrent) traces.

Trace Language. For a transition system $\mathcal{S} = \langle \mathcal{V}, T, init \rangle$, the *language* of an infinite concurrent trace $I = \langle A_s, A_c, \phi_s, \phi_c \rangle$ is defined as a set $\mathcal{L}(I)$ of infinite system runs such that for each run $s_0, t_1, s_1, t_2, \ldots \in \mathcal{L}(I)$ there exists an infinite sequence of indices $i_1, i_2, \ldots$ such that:

1. $s_0, t_1, \ldots t_{i_1}, s_{i_1} \in \mathcal{L}(A_s)$, and for all $0 < j \leq i_1$ the formula $\phi_s(s_{j-1}, s_j)$ holds.
2. for all $k \geq 2$ it holds that $s_{i_{k-1}}, t_{i_{k-1}+1}, \ldots t_{i_k}, s_{i_k} \in \mathcal{L}(A_c)$, and for all $i_{k-1} < j \leq i_k$ the formula $\phi_c(s_{j-1}, s_j)$ holds.

Trace Inclusion. We lift the trace inclusion relation to infinite concurrent traces. For any two infinite concurrent traces $I = \langle A_s, A_c, \phi_s, \phi_c \rangle$ and $I' = \langle A'_s, A'_c, \phi'_s, \phi'_c \rangle$ we define the *trace inclusion* relation $\subseteq$ as follows: $I \subseteq I'$ iff there exists a pair of trace morphisms $\lambda = \langle \lambda_s, \lambda_c \rangle$, where $\lambda_s : A'_s \to A_s$ and $\lambda_c : A'_c \to A_c$, written also $\lambda : I' \to I$, such that $A_s \subseteq_{\lambda_s} A'_s$, $A_c \subseteq_{\lambda_c} A'_c$, $\phi_s \implies \phi'_s$, and $\phi_c \implies \phi'_c$. For a particular pair of trace morphisms λ we write also $I \subseteq_\lambda I'$.

Proposition 2. *For $I, I' \in \mathbb{I}$, if $I \subseteq I'$ then $\mathcal{L}(I) \subseteq \mathcal{L}(I')$.*

Graphical Notation. We show action identities in circles, and labeling formulas in squares. We omit any of these parts when it is not important or would create clutter in the current context. The cycle part of the trace is depicted in round brackets, superscripted with ω. The predicate ϕ_c is shown under the edge, connecting opening and closing brackets.

3 Motivating Example

In the introduction, we gave an informal sketch of the termination proof for the Producer-Consumer benchmark from Fig. 1. Using the concept of concurrent traces from the previous section, we can now explain the termination argument more formally.

Our analysis starts with the assumption (by way of contradiction) that there exists some infinite run. The assumption is expressed as the concurrent trace at Position 1 in Fig. 2: infinitely often some transition should occur. The transition is so far unknown, and therefore characterized by the predicate $\top$. Our argument proceeds by instantiating this unknown action with the transitions of the

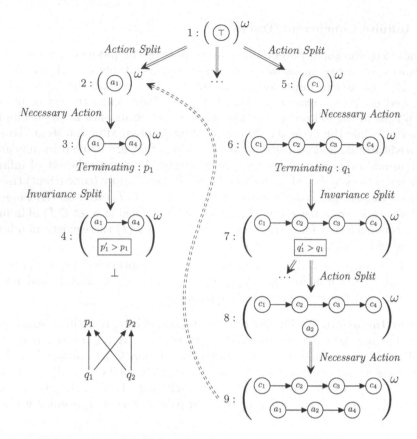

Fig. 2. Termination proof for the Producer-Consumer example. *Bottom left*: partially ordered ranking function discovered in the analysis.

transition system, resulting in one new trace per transition. The *Action Split* proof rule represents a case distinction, and we will need to discharge all cases.

For example, transition a_1 of Producer 1, gives us the trace shown in Position 2. A consequence of the decision that a_1 occurs infinitely often is that a_4 must also occur infinitely often: after the execution of a_1, the program counter of producer 1 equals 2, and the precondition for the execution of a_1 is that it is equal to 1. The only transition, that can achieve that goal, is a_4 (here we oversimplify to make the presentation clearer; in the algorithm we derive the necessity of action a_4 by an interpolation-based local safety analysis). The requirement that both a_1 and a_4 occur infinitely often is expressed as the trace in Position 3, obtained from the trace in Position 1 by the *Necessary Action* proof rule. The edge between a_1 and a_4 specifies an ordering between the two transitions; between them, there may be an arbitrary number of other transitions. The trace in Position 3 is terminating: p_1 is decreased infinitely often and is bounded from below; it is therefore a ranking function. The only remaining situation in which an infinite run might exist is if some transition increases p_1, i.e., that satisfies the predicate

$p'_1 > p_1$, is executed infinitely often. This situation is expressed by the trace in Position 4, obtained by the application of the *Invariance Split* proof rule. Since there is no transition in the program transition relation that satisfies $p'_1 > p_1$, we arrive at a contradiction.

Let us explore another instantiation of the unknown action in the trace at Position 1, this time with transition c_1 of Consumer 1: we obtain the trace of Position 5. Again, exploring causal consequences, local safety analysis gives us that actions c_2, c_3, and c_4 should also occur infinitely often in the trace: we insert them, and get the trace at Position 6. Termination analysis for that trace gives us the ranking function q_1: it is bounded from below by action c_1 and decreased by action c_4. Again, we conclude that the action increasing q_1 should occur infinitely often, and introduce it in the trace of Position 7. Next, we try all possible instantiations of the action characterized by the predicate $q'_1 > q_1$: there are two transitions that satisfy the predicate, namely a_2 and b_2. We explore the instantiation with a_2 in the trace at Position 8; for b_2, the reasoning proceeds similarly. The local safety analysis allows us to conclude that, besides a_2, transitions a_1 and a_4 should occur infinitely often (Position 9). At this point, we realize that the trace at Position 9 contains as a subgraph the trace at Position 2, namely the transition a_1. We can conclude, without repeating the analysis done at Positions 2–4, that there is no infinite run corresponding to the trace at Position 9.

We call the graph of traces corresponding to this analysis the *causal trace tableau*. The tableau for the Producer-Consumer benchmark is (partially) shown in Fig. 2. The analysis can also be understood as the construction of a partially-ordered composition of ranking functions; the final ranking for the Producer-Consumer example is shown at the bottom left of Fig. 2.

We study causal trace tableaux in more detail in the following Section 4. The proof rules driving the analysis are presented in Section 5.

4   Causal Trace Tableaux

We prove termination by constructing a graph labeled by concurrent traces. We call such graphs *causal trace tableaux*.

4.1   Initial Abstraction

At the root of the tableau, we start with a single infinite concurrent trace, containing two actions: the initial action i in the stem part, marked with $init'$, and the infinitely repeating action w in the cycle part, marked with $\top$. The marking ensures that all possible non-terminating system traces are preserved.

Initial Abstraction. For a transition system $\mathcal{S} = \langle V, T, init \rangle$ we define $InitialAbstraction(\mathcal{S})$ as an infinite concurrent trace $I = \langle A_s, A_c, \phi_s, \phi_c \rangle$, where
- $A_s = \langle N_s, E_s, \nu_s, \eta_s \rangle$, and $N = \{i\}$, $E = \emptyset$, $\nu = \{(i, init')\}$, $\eta = \emptyset$.
- $A_c = \langle N_c, E_c, \nu_c, \eta_c \rangle$, and $N = \{w\}$, $E = \emptyset$, $\nu = \{(w, \top)\}$, $\eta = \emptyset$.
- $\phi_s = \phi_c = \top$.

Proposition 3. $\mathcal{L}_n(\mathcal{S}) \subseteq \mathcal{L}(InitialAbstraction(\mathcal{S}))$.

4.2 Causal Transitions

The children of a node in the tableau are labeled with traces that refine the trace of the parent node. We call the rules that construct the children traces from the parent trace *causal transitions*. Technically, causal transitions are special graph morphisms, as described below.

We follow [9,11] and use the so-called *single-pushout (SPO)* and *double-pushout (DPO)* approaches to describe graph transformations. All graph transformations that we use are non-erasing and lie at the intersection of both approaches.

Trace Productions. A *finite trace production* $p : (L \xrightarrow{r} R)$ is a trace morphism $r : L \to R$, where $L, R \in \mathbb{A}$ are finite concurrent traces. The traces L and R are called the *left-hand side* and the *right-hand side* of p, respectively. A given production $p : (L \xrightarrow{r} R)$ can be applied to a trace A if there is an occurrence of L in A, i.e. a trace morphism $\lambda : L \to A$, called a *match*. The resulting trace A' can be obtained from A by adding all elements of R with no pre-image in L.

An *infinite trace production* $p : (L \xrightarrow{r} R)$ where $L, R \in \mathbb{I}$ are infinite concurrent traces and $r = \langle r_s, r_c \rangle$ is a pair of trace morphisms, describes a transformation of trace L into trace R as a composition of two finite trace productions. In the following we denote the set of infinite trace productions by Π, and call them simply trace productions. We denote the result of the application of a trace production p to a trace I under a pair of morphisms $\lambda = \langle \lambda_s, \lambda_c \rangle$ by $p^\lambda(I)$.

Causal Transitions. For the purpose of system analysis we use special trace productions; we call them *causal transitions*. For a given transition system $\mathcal{S}$, a *causal transition* $\tau : \{\tau_1, \dots, \tau_n\}$ is a set of trace productions $\tau_i : (L \xrightarrow{r_i} R_i)$, where all productions share the same left-hand side L; we will denote L by $\tau_\lhd$, and call transition *premise*. We say that a causal transition τ is *sound* if the condition below holds:

$$\forall I \in \mathbb{I} . \ I \subseteq_\lambda \tau_\lhd \implies \mathcal{L}(I) \subseteq \bigcup_{\tau_i \in \tau} \mathcal{L}\big(\tau_i^\lambda(I)\big)$$

4.3 Causal Trace Tableaux

Causal Trace Tableau. For a transition system $\mathcal{S}$, we define a *(causal) trace tableau* as a tuple $\Upsilon = \langle V, F, \gamma, \delta, \leadsto, \lambda \rangle$, where:

- (V, F) is a directed forest with vertices V and edges F. Vertices are partitioned into internal vertices and leaves: $V = V_N \uplus V_L$, $V_N = \{v \in V \mid \exists (v, v') \in F\}$, $V_L = \{v \in V \mid \nexists (v, v') \in F\}$.
- $\gamma : V \to \mathbb{I}$ is a labeling of vertices with concurrent traces.
- $\delta : F \to \Pi$ is a labeling of edges with trace productions. We require that for all edges with the same source v, the labeling productions have the same left-hand side. Thus, we have an induced labeling of internal vertices $v \in V_N$ with causal transitions: $\delta(v) = \{\delta((v, v')) \mid (v, v') \in F\}$.
- $\leadsto : V_L \nrightarrow V_N$ is a partial *covering* function; for $(v, v') \in \leadsto$ we call v a *covered* vertex, and v' a *covering* vertex.
- λ is a labeling of internal or covered vertices with trace morphisms: $\forall v \in V_N . \ \lambda(v) : \delta(v)_\lhd \to \gamma(v)$; for all $(v, v') \in \leadsto$. $\lambda(v) : \gamma(v') \to \gamma(v)$.

We call a trace tableau $\Upsilon = \langle V, F, \gamma, \delta, \rightsquigarrow, \lambda \rangle$ *complete* if all its leaf vertices are either contradictory or covered. A trace tableau is said to be *correct* if:

1. $\exists v \in V$. $InitialAbstraction(\mathcal{S}) \subseteq \gamma(v)$.
2. for all $v \in V_N$ we have that a) $\delta(v)$ is sound, b) $\gamma(v) \subseteq_{\lambda(v)} \delta(v)_{\lhd}$, and c) for
   all $(v, v') \in F$ it holds that $\delta((v, v'))^{\lambda(v)}(\gamma(v)) \subseteq \gamma(v')$.
3. for all $(v, v') \in \rightsquigarrow$ we have $\gamma(v) \subseteq_{\lambda(v)} \gamma(v')$ and $(v', v) \notin (F \cup \rightsquigarrow)^*$.

A trace tableau is a forest, which can be seen as an unwinding of the system causality relation from some set of initial vertices. The label $\gamma(v)$ of the vertex v represents all possible infinite runs for that vertex. The first correctness condition requires that a tableau contains all non-terminating system runs. The second one guarantees the applicability of the causal transition $\delta(v)$ of a vertex v to its label $\gamma(v)$ and the full exploration of the causal transition consequences, thus preserving the set of system runs. Indeed, we have:

$$\gamma(v) \subseteq_{\lambda(v)} \delta(v)_{\lhd} \implies \mathcal{L}(\gamma(v)) \subseteq \bigcup_{(v,v')\in F} \mathcal{L}(\delta((v,v'))^{\lambda(v)}(\gamma(v))) \subseteq \bigcup_{(v,v')\in F} \mathcal{L}(\gamma(v'))$$

The last correctness condition ensures that we can apply at the covered vertex all the causal transitions in the subtree originating from the covering vertex; additionally, it guarantees that the resulting tableau is acyclic.

5   Proof Rules for Termination

We now present the causal transitions needed for proving termination. We omit the proof rules for safety properties presented in [15], which can be applied to the stem part of a concurrent trace without any changes. The infinity-specific causal transitions are illustrated in Fig. 3; some have so called *application conditions*, showed to the right of the causal transition name.

Basic Rules. These are the most important causal transitions, sufficient for the approach completeness in the case of an unconditionally terminating system.

Action Split, given some action a in the cycle part of a trace, and a transition predicate ψ, considers two alternatives: either a satisfies ψ or $\neg\psi$ infinitely often.

Invariance Split makes a case distinction about the program behavior at infinity: for a predicate ϕ either all the actions in the cycle part satisfy it, or a violating action should happen infinitely often. We exploit the rule when we introduce new actions based on the ranking function: in that case the first branch is terminating, and we may consider only the second one. But, in general, the rule is useful without the *a priori* knowledge of a ranking function: it considers two cases, where each one is easier to reason about individually.

Local Safety Rules. The rules in this category make the approach efficient for the case we cannot find a perfect ranking function in one step.

Necessary Action is applied when there are two ordered actions a and b in the cycle part of a concurrent trace, and a transition predicate ϕ, such that the label of a implies ϕ, and the label of b implies $\neg\phi'$, i.e. there is a contradiction between these actions (b "ends" in the region $\neg\phi$, while a "starts" in the region ϕ). Given

Basic Rules

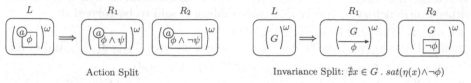

Action Split   Invariance Split: $\nexists x \in G . sat(\eta(x) \wedge \neg\phi)$

Local Safety Rules

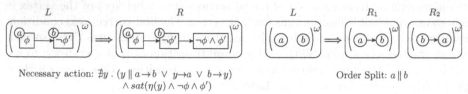

Necessary action: $\nexists y . (y \parallel a \rightarrow b \vee y \rightarrow a \vee b \rightarrow y)$
$\wedge sat(\eta(y) \wedge \neg\phi \wedge \phi')$

Order Split: $a \parallel b$

Unrolling Rules

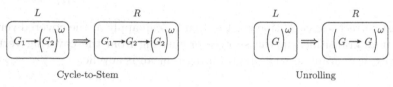

Cycle-to-Stem   Unrolling

Fairness Rules

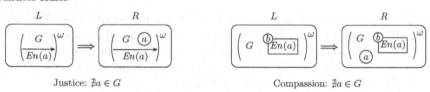

Justice: $\nexists a \in G$ Compassion: $\nexists a \in G$

Fig. 3. Proof rules for termination. Action identities are arbitrary, and used to show the context preserved by the application of a causal transition. G stands for the rest of the trace besides the depicted parts.

the repetitive character of the trace, we have that a should follow b again; the causal transition introduces a new "bridging" action x in between. Actions a and b can be the same single action, where the precondition contradicts the postcondition. The predicate ϕ may be obtained by Craig interpolation between the labels of b and a. The application condition for this causal transition ensures that there is no other action y in the trace already that could play the role of x.

Order Split considers alternative interleavings of two previously concurrent events. Either one or another ordering should happen infinitely often.

Unrolling rules use the infinite repetition of the cycle part of a trace.

Cycle-to-Stem causal transition allows us to shift the cycle part G_2 into the stem part G_1, thus going from the reasoning at infinity to the safety reasoning. This rule is need for the completeness of conditional termination.

Unrolling exploits the infinite repetition: we can unroll the complete graph G of the cycle part, and the unrolled version should still repeat infinitely often.

Fairness rules allow for the direct account of two well-known concurrent phenomena: weak and strong fairness (or justice and compassion) [17,18].

Justice causal transition allows to introduce a just transition a in the cycle part of a trace in case it is continuously enabled and never taken.

Compassion causal transition states that a compassionate transition a which is infinitely often enabled should be also infinitely often taken.

Proposition 4. *The defined above causal transitions are sound.*

The following lemma is applied in the combination with the *invariance split* causal transition: in case a ranking function can be found for the cycle part of a concurrent trace, it allows to discard the left branch of the result.

Lemma 1. *Assume that a set S is well-ordered by a relation $\preceq$. If, for an infinite sequence $s_1, s_2, \ldots$ of elements from S, for an infinite number of pairs (s_i, s_{i+1}) it holds that $s_i \succ s_{i+1}$, then there exists an infinite number of pairs (s_j, s_{j+1}) such that $s_j \prec s_{j+1}$.*

6   The Termination Analysis Algorithm

Our termination analysis algorithm (see Algorithm 1) operates on the causal trace tableau defined above. We start with the single vertex in the tableau, labeled with *InitialAbstraction*($\mathcal{S}$). At each iteration of the algorithm main loop we select some vertex v from the queue Q of unexplored tableau leaves, and analyze only the cycle part of its label. First, we try to cover v by some other vertex v': this can be done if the trace of v is included in the trace of v' (thus, all causal transitions at v' subtree can be repeated). Moreover, we require that the covering does not create any loops, and the resulting tableau is acyclic.

If the covering attempt was unsuccessful, we unroll and linearize the cyclic part of the v's label. The unrolling is necessary in order to detect possible conflicts between iterations of the cycle. If the linear trace L is unconcretizable - we apply the local safety refinement to the cyclic trace: this includes such causal transitions as *order split* and *necessary action*. The refinement procedure is essentially the same as in [15], so we do not repeat it here. After the refinement step, we put the newly created children of v into the queue and proceed.

On the contrary, if the unrolled cycle is concretizable, we check it for termination; any ranking function synthesis algorithm such as [1,22] can be used for that purpose. If we have found a ranking function for the cycle - we apply the *invariance split* causal transition and Lemma 1. As a result, we introduce into the cycle all possible system transitions able to "repair" it: preserve its infinite repetition despite the existence of a ranking function.

Algorithm 1. Causality-based Termination Analysis

Input : Transition system $\mathcal{S} = \langle \mathcal{V}, T, init \rangle$
Output: **terminating/termination unknown**
Data: Termination tableau $\Upsilon = \langle V, F, \gamma, \delta, \rightsquigarrow, \lambda \rangle$, queue $Q \subseteq V_L$,
     Safety tableau $\Upsilon_s = \langle V_s, F_s, \gamma_s, \delta_s, \rightsquigarrow_s, \lambda_s \rangle$, queue $Q_s \subseteq V_{Ls}$
begin
  set $V \longleftarrow \{v_0\}$, $\gamma(v_0) \longleftarrow InitialAbstraction(\mathcal{S})$, $Q \longleftarrow \{v_0\}$
  set all of $\{F, \delta, \rightsquigarrow, \lambda, V_s, F_s, \gamma_s, \delta_s, \rightsquigarrow_s, \lambda_s\} \longleftarrow \emptyset$
  while Q *not empty* **do**
    take some v from Q
    if $\exists\, v' \in V_N$ *and* $\lambda' : \gamma(v') \rightarrow \gamma(v)$.
      $\gamma(v) \subseteq_{\lambda'} \gamma(v')$ *and* v *is not reachable from* v' *by* $F \cup \rightsquigarrow$ **then**
      add (v, v') to $\rightsquigarrow$
      set $\lambda(v) \longleftarrow \lambda'$
    else
      set $L \longleftarrow Linearize(Unroll(\gamma(v)))$
      if $Unconcretizable(L)$ **then**
        $\mid$ $LocalSafetyRefine(v, L)$
      else if $Terminating(L)$ **then**
        $\mid$ $InvarianceSplit(v, L)$
      else
        $\mid$ put $CycleToStem(v)$ into V_s and Q_s
      put children of v into Q
  return $SafetyAnalysis(\Upsilon_s, Q_s)$

Finally, if the cycle is both concretizable and no ranking function can be found for it, the termination part of our algorithm gives up and transfers the analyzed trace to the safety part of the algorithm. For that purpose we concatenate the stem and the cycle into the finite concurrent trace, and put the resulting vertex into the safety tableau for processing. Thus, the safety tableau is the forest that originates from the vertices of the termination tableau for which no termination argument can be found. We apply the method of [15] to analyze it. If all the leaves of the safety tableau are found to be unreachable, we mark the corresponding leaves of the termination tableau as contradictory, and report the program as terminating; otherwise we report a possibly non-terminating execution. The following theorems show that the proposed approach is sound and relatively complete for the program termination analysis.

Theorem 1 (Soundness). *If there exists a correct and complete causal trace tableau for a transition system $\mathcal{S}$, then $\mathcal{S}$ is terminating.*

Theorem 2 (Relative Completeness). *If a transition system $\mathcal{S}$ is terminating, then a correct and complete causal trace tableau for $\mathcal{S}$ can be constructed, provided that all necessary first-order formulas are given.*

As the termination problem is, in general, undecidable, our approach has its limitations. In particular, it heavily depends on the power of termination proving

Table 2. Detailed experimental evaluation for the set of multi-threaded benchmarks. MO stands for memout; the time spent until memout was in all cases more than 1 hour. U indicates that the termination prover returned "unknown"; Z3-TO indicates a timeout in the Z3 SMT solver.

Benchmark	Terminator		T2		APROVE		Arctor		
	Time(s)	Mem.(MB)	Time(s)	Mem.(MB)	Time(s)	Mem.(MB)	Time(s)	Mem.(MB)	Vertices
Chain 2	0.65	20	0.52	20	1.58	131	0.002	2.0	3
Chain 4	1.45	25	0.54	22	2.13	153	0.002	2.2	7
Chain 6	24.4	57	0.58	24	2.58	171	0.002	2.5	11
Chain 8	×	MO	0.63	26	3.48	210	0.002	2.5	15
Chain 20	×	MO	2.36	55	16.5	941	0.007	2.5	39
Chain 40	×	MO	40.5	288	536	1237	0.023	2.8	79
Chain 60	×	MO	Z3-TO	×	×	MO	0.063	3.0	119
Chain 100	×	MO	Z3-TO	×	×	MO	0.320	3.9	199
Phase 1	×	MO	U(4.53)	48	1.60	132	0.002	2.4	7
Phase 2	×	MO	U(4.53)	48	2.16	144	0.002	2.4	7
Phase 3	×	MO	U(30.6)	301	3.83	199	0.002	2.5	16
Phase 8	×	MO	×	MO	47.0	1506	0.003	2.6	61
Phase 10	×	MO	×	MO	×	MO	0.012	2.7	79
Phase 20	×	MO	×	MO	×	MO	0.061	3.3	169
Phase 60	×	MO	×	MO	×	MO	1.18	4.2	529
Phase 100	×	MO	×	MO	×	MO	7.38	6.1	889
Semaphore 1	3.05	26	2.81	46	3.22	230	0.002	2.6	8
Semaphore 2	622	691	U(20.7)	219	U(6.52)	465	0.002	2.6	16
Semaphore 3	×	MO	U(15.8)	239	U(10.42)	1138	0.003	2.6	24
Semaphore 10	×	MO	U(83.5)	470	U(246)	1287	0.023	2.8	80
Semaphore 20	×	MO	×	MO	×	MO	0.073	3.3	160
Semaphore 60	×	MO	×	MO	×	MO	0.58	4.0	480
Semaphore 100	×	MO	×	MO	×	MO	1.59	5.1	800

techniques for simple loops such as [1,22], and on the methods for reachability analysis. For the latter we apply our previous work [15], which is limited to theories, supporting Craig interpolation.

7 Experimental Evaluation

We have implemented the termination analysis algorithm in a model checker called *Arctor*[1]. The implementation consists of approximately 1500 lines of Haskell code and can currently handle multi-threaded programs with arbitrary control flow, finite data variables, and unbounded counters.

Table 2 shows experimental results obtained with the termination provers Terminator, T2, APROVE, and Arctor on the benchmarks described below, except for the results on the Producer-Consumer benchmark, which were discussed already in the introduction (see Table 1). All experiments were performed on an Intel Core i7 CPU running at 2.7 GHz.

Producer-Consumer. The *Producer-Consumer* benchmark from the introduction (see Fig. 1) is a simplified model of the *Map-Reduce* architecture from distributed processing: producers model the mapping step for separate data sources, consumers model the reducing step for different types of input

---

[1] available at http://www.react.uni-saarland.de/tools/arctor/

data. The natural requirement for such an architecture is that the distributed processing terminates for any finite amount of input data.

Chain. The *Chain* benchmark consists of a chain of n threads, where each thread decreases its own counter x_i, but the next thread in the chain can counteract, and increase the counter of the previous thread. Only the last thread in the chain terminates unconditionally.

Phase. The *Phase* benchmark is similar to the Chain benchmark, except that now each thread can either increase or decrease its counter x_i. Each such *phase change* is, however, guarded by the next thread in the chain, which limits the number of times the phase change can occur.

Semaphore. The *Semaphore* benchmark represents a model of a concurrent system where access to a critical resource is guarded by semaphores. We verify *individual accessibility* for a particular thread (i.e., the system without the thread should terminate) under the assumption of a *fair scheduler*. Since other tools do not support fairness, we have eliminated the fairness assumption for all tools including Arctor using the transformation from [20], which enriches each `wait` statement with a decreasing and bounded counter.

Arctor verifies all benchmarks efficiently, requiring little time and memory to handle even 100 threads. We have also tried out our approach on more complicated examples (available from the tool homepage), which represent models of publicly available industrial programs. These include parallel executions of GNU `make`, parallel computations in CUDA programs for GPUs, and Google's implementation of the Map-Reduce architecture for its *App Engine* platform. While other tools are not able to handle even two concurrent threads in these programs, Arctor verifies programs with dozens of threads within several minutes.

8 Conclusion

We have presented a new model checking procedure for the termination analysis of multi-threaded programs. The procedure has been implemented in *Arctor*, the first termination prover that scales to a large number of concurrent threads. Our approach is based on three key innovations: a novel notion of modular reasoning, a novel composition of ranking functions, and a novel tableau construction based on causality. With respect to the modular reasoning, the case split in Arctor is a new, and very effective, type of modularity, where the verification task is split according to different causal explanations of a hypothetical error. With respect to the composition of ranking functions, Arctor combines ranking functions within a branch of the tableau conjunctively, similar to the lexicographic combination in T2, but Arctor only imposes a partial order, not a linear order, on the individual ranking functions: the same ranking function may be combined independently with multiple other ranking functions from further splits or previously discharged cases. Finally, Arctor explores causal dependencies in a tableau of Mazurkiewicz-style concurrent traces in order to systematically discover case splits and ranking functions.

References

1. Bradley, A.R., Manna, Z., Sipma, H.B.: Linear ranking with reachability. In: Etessami, K., Rajamani, S.K. (eds.) CAV 2005. LNCS, vol. 3576, pp. 491–504. Springer, Heidelberg (2005)
2. Brockschmidt, M., Cook, B., Fuhs, C.: Better termination proving through cooperation. In: Sharygina, N., Veith, H. (eds.) CAV 2013. LNCS, vol. 8044, pp. 413–429. Springer, Heidelberg (2013)
3. Brockschmidt, M., Emmes, F., Falke, S., Fuhs, C., Giesl, J.: Alternating runtime and size complexity analysis of integer programs. In: Ábrahám, E., Havelund, K. (eds.) TACAS 2014. LNCS, vol. 8413, pp. 140–155. Springer, Heidelberg (2014)
4. Chaki, S., Clarke, E., Groce, A., Ouaknine, J., Strichman, O., Yorav, K.: Efficient verification of sequential and concurrent c programs. Formal Methods in System Design 25(2-3), 129–166 (2004)
5. Clarke, E., Grumberg, O., Jha, S., Lu, Y., Veith, H.: Counterexample-guided abstraction refinement. In: Emerson, E.A., Sistla, A.P. (eds.) CAV 2000. LNCS, vol. 1855, pp. 154–169. Springer, Heidelberg (2000)
6. Cook, B., Podelski, A., Rybalchenko, A.: Termination proofs for systems code. SIGPLAN Not. 41(6), 415–426 (2006)
7. Cook, B., Podelski, A., Rybalchenko, A.: Proving thread termination. ACM SIGPLAN Notices 42(6), 320 (2007)
8. Cook, B., See, A., Zuleger, F.: Ramsey vs. lexicographic termination proving. In: Piterman, N., Smolka, S.A. (eds.) TACAS 2013. LNCS, vol. 7795, pp. 47–61. Springer, Heidelberg (2013)
9. Corradini, A., Montanari, U., Rossi, F., Ehrig, H., Heckel, R., Löwe, M.: Algebraic approaches to graph transformation - part i: Basic concepts and double pushout approach. In: Rozenberg [25], pp. 163–246
10. Dräger, K., Kupriyanov, A., Finkbeiner, B., Wehrheim, H.: Slab: A certifying model checker for infinite-state concurrent systems. In: Esparza, J., Majumdar, R. (eds.) TACAS 2010. LNCS, vol. 6015, pp. 271–274. Springer, Heidelberg (2010)
11. Ehrig, H., Heckel, R., Korff, M., Löwe, M., Ribeiro, L., Wagner, A., Corradini, A.: Algebraic approaches to graph transformation - part ii: Single pushout approach and comparison with double pushout approach. In: Rozenberg [25], pp. 247–312
12. Ganty, P., Genaim, S.: Proving Termination Starting from the End. Computer Aided Verification (10), 397–412 (2013)
13. Giesl, J., Thiemann, R., Schneider-Kamp, P., Falke, S.: Automated termination proofs with aProVE. In: van Oostrom, V. (ed.) RTA 2004. LNCS, vol. 3091, pp. 210–220. Springer, Heidelberg (2004)
14. Godefroid, P. (ed.): Partial-Order Methods for the Verification of Concurrent Systems. LNCS, vol. 1032. Springer-Verlag Inc., New York (1996)
15. Kupriyanov, A., Finkbeiner, B.: Causality-based verification of multi-threaded programs. In: D'Argenio, P.R., Melgratti, H. (eds.) CONCUR 2013. LNCS, vol. 8052, pp. 257–272. Springer, Heidelberg (2013)
16. Manna, Z.: Introduction to Mathematical Theory of Computation. McGraw-Hill, Inc., New York (1974)
17. Manna, Z., Pnueli, A.: Temporal verification of reactive systems - safety. Springer (1995)
18. Manna, Z., Pnueli, A.: Temporal verification of reactive systems: Response. In: Manna, Z., Peled, D.A. (eds.) Pnueli Festschrift. LNCS, vol. 6200, pp. 279–361. Springer, Heidelberg (2010)

19. Mazurkiewicz, A.: Concurrent program schemes and their interpretations. Technical Report DAIMI PB 78. Aarhus University (1977)
20. Olderog, E.-R., Apt, K.R.: Fairness in parallel programs: The transformational approach. ACM Trans. Program. Lang. Syst. 10(3), 420–455 (1988)
21. Podelski, A., Rybalchenko, A.: Transition invariants. In: Proceedings of the 19th Annual IEEE Symposium on Logic in Computer Science, pp. 32–41 (July 2004)
22. Podelski, A., Rybalchenko, A.: A complete method for the synthesis of linear ranking functions. In: Steffen, B., Levi, G. (eds.) VMCAI 2004. LNCS, vol. 2937, pp. 239–251. Springer, Heidelberg (2004)
23. Podelski, A., Rybalchenko, A.: ARMC: The logical choice for software model checking with abstraction refinement. In: Hanus, M. (ed.) PADL 2007. LNCS, vol. 4354, pp. 245–259. Springer, Heidelberg (2007)
24. Reisig, W.: Petri Nets – An Introduction. Springer (1985)
25. Rozenberg, G.: Handbook of Graph Grammars and Computing by Graph Transformations. Foundations, vol. 1. World Scientific (1997)

Counterexample to Induction-Guided Abstraction-Refinement (CTIGAR)

Johannes Birgmeier[1,*], Aaron R. Bradley[2,**], and Georg Weissenbacher[1,*]

[1] Vienna University of Technology
[2] Mentor Graphics

Abstract. Typical CEGAR-based verification methods refine the abstract domain based on full counterexample traces. The finite state model checking algorithm IC3 introduced the concept of discovering, generalizing from, and thereby eliminating individual state counterexamples to induction (CTIs). This focus on individual states suggests a simpler abstraction-refinement scheme in which refinements are performed relative to single steps of the transition relation, thus reducing the expense of refinement and eliminating the need for full traces. Interestingly, this change in refinement focus leads to a natural spectrum of refinement options, including when to refine and which type of concrete single-step query to refine relative to. Experiments validate that CTI-focused abstraction refinement, or CTIGAR, is competitive with existing CEGAR-based tools.

1 Introduction

IC3 [10,9] constructs an inductive proof of an invariance property by reacting to individual states. These states, called counterexamples to induction (CTIs), arise as counterexample models to one-step consecution queries: a CTI is not yet known to be unreachable and has at least one successor that either is or can lead to an error state. In focusing on states and single steps of the transition relation, IC3 differs from the k-induction [23] and interpolation [35,36] extensions of BMC [7], which fundamentally rely on unrolling the transition relation. IC3's practical value is now widely appreciated.

This paper suggests a similar refocusing from sequences to single steps of the transition relation when performing predicate abstraction-refinement-based analysis of infinite state systems. The new method is referred to as CTIGAR,

* Supported by the Austrian National Research Network S11403-N23 (RiSE) of the Austrian Science Fund (FWF) and by the Vienna Science and Technology Fund (WWTF) through grants PROSEED, ICT12-059, and VRG11-005.

** This material is based upon work supported in part by the National Science Foundation under grants No. 0952617 and No. 1219067 and by the Semiconductor Research Corporation under contract GRC 1859. Any opinions, findings, and conclusions or recommendations expressed in this material are those of the authors and do not necessarily reflect the views of the National Science Foundation.

A. Biere and R. Bloem (Eds.): CAV 2014, LNCS 8559, pp. 831–848, 2014.
© Springer International Publishing Switzerland 2014

for counterexample to induction-guided abstraction-refinement, to contrast with CEGAR's focus on counterexample traces [18,19].

Injecting predicate abstraction into IC3 is straightforward: an abstract CTI is a conjunction of the predicates that are satisfied by the corresponding concrete CTI. This straightforward and inexpensive abstraction contrasts with previous adaptations of IC3 to infinite state analysis that put excessive effort into computing non-trivial underapproximations of preimages [16,31]. Because IC3's inductive generalization procedure typically expands the (abstract) CTI cube well beyond a preimage, there is little point in making such an effort.[1]

In CEGAR, failure to concretize an abstract counterexample trace of arbitrary length is the trigger for domain refinement. In CTIGAR, there are two triggering situations for domain refinement, both over single-step queries: for lifting or for consecution. This focus on single-step queries rather than traces contrasts with a recent attempt at combining CEGAR with IC3 [17].

Lifting [15] a full state to a partial assignment is an important generalization mechanism in state-of-the-art IC3 implementations. The partial assignment describes similar states that also step into the same target as the original full state. With a concrete CTI, the one-step lifting query must succeed [15]; however, with an abstract CTI, it can fail. A failure is one possible point for refinement.

Consecution relative to frame F_i, which over-approximates the set of states reachable in at most i steps, for CTI s checks whether any s-state is reachable from an F_i-state other than an s-state. It can happen that an abstract CTI $\hat{s}$ fails consecution while its corresponding concrete CTI s passes consecution. This situation is another possible point for refinement.

In both scenarios, one can eagerly address the failure or lazily ignore it and continue. Lazy operation allows the introduction of spurious transitions into the partially constructed traces. The corresponding CTIs are marked as having allowed such transitions and can be revisited later if necessary. Morever, in both cases, addressing a failure requires only looking at a one-step concrete query, not an arbitrarily long unwinding of the transition relation. When the underlying theory admits interpolation, an interpolant derived from the concrete query enriches the domain sufficiently so that the refined abstract CTI passes its query.

Overall, then, the characteristics of CTIGAR are as follows:

1. *straightforward abstraction*: an abstract CTI is derived from a concrete CTI by evaluating the available predicates over the (possibly partial) assignment of the concrete CTI;
2. *intermediate refinement triggers*: refinement is suggested either when lifting an abstract CTI fails or when consecution against an abstract CTI fails but against the corresponding concrete CTI succeeds;

---

[1] Abstract CTIs constitute underapproximate preimages whenever the abstract domain is sufficiently precise (Section 3.1), which can be enforced. Our experiments in Section 4, however, show that abstract CTIs that are not underapproximate preimages can be eliminated without costly refinement in many cases. In fact, the best experimental configurations do not enforce preimages.

3. *lazy or eager modes*: a suggested refinement can be addressed immediately (eager), ignored in hopes that the overall analysis succeeds or until the discovery of a counterexample trace (lazy), or delayed until an intermediate trigger, such as encountering a threshold number of suggested refinements;

4. *simple refinement*: refinement considers one step of the transition relation rather than an arbitrarily long unwinding;

5. *explicit concrete states*: the concrete CTIs that are derived from SMT models can be useful for some types of predicate synthesis; see Section 4.1.

CTIGAR otherwise operates identically to finite state IC3, except that an SMT solver is used in place of a SAT solver, and atoms are predicates.

This paper is organized as follows. In Section 2, basic concepts and IC3 are recalled. Section 3 presents CTIGAR; Section 4 evaluates CTIGAR empirically. Finally, Section 5 discusses CTIGAR in a broader context.

2 Preliminaries

2.1 Formulas and Transition Relations

The term *formula* refers to either a propositional logic formula or a formula in first-order logic.

Propositional Formulas. A propositional formula is defined as usual over a set X of propositional atoms, the logical constants $\top$ and $\bot$ (denoting true and false, respectively), and the standard logical connectives $\land$, $\lor$, $\rightarrow$, and $\neg$ (denoting conjunction, disjunction, implication, and negation, respectively). A *literal* is an atom $x \in X$ or its negation $\neg x$. A *clause* C is a set of literals interpreted as a disjunction. A *cube* is the negation of a clause.

First-Order Logic. The logical connectives from propositional logic carry over into first-order logic. First-order terms are constructed as usual over a set of variables V, functions, and constant symbols. An atom in first-order logic is a predicate symbol applied to a tuple of terms.

Semantics and Satisfiability. A *model* of a formula consists of a non-empty domain and an interpretation that assigns a denotation to the predicate, function, and constant symbols. A formula is *satisfiable* if there is some model under which it is true, and unsatisfiable otherwise. A formula F implies another formula G, denoted $F \Rightarrow G$, if every model of F is a model of G. Given a conjunction, an *unsatisfiable core* is a subset of the conjuncts that is unsatisfiable.

Theories. A first-order *theory* is defined by a *signature*, which is a fixed set of function and predicate symbols, and a set of *axioms* restricting the models under consideration to those that satisfy the axioms. Symbols that do not occur in the axioms are called uninterpreted and interpreted otherwise. *Quantifier free linear arithmetic (QFLIA/QFLRA)* is the theory for the first order language over the functions $+$, $-$, the predicates $<$ and $=$, and the constants $0, 1, \ldots$ interpreted over either the integers $\mathbb{Z}$ or the rational numbers $\mathbb{Q}$.

Transition Systems. Let X be a fixed set of uninterpreted symbols representing the state variables or registers (in either propositional or first-order logic). A state s is an interpretation mapping X to elements of the domain. The symbolic representation of the state s is a cube that is true under s but false in all other states. Depending on the context, s may denote a state or its symbolic counterpart. A formula represents the set of states in which it evaluates to true. $I(X)$ and $P(X)$ are used to represent the initial and the safe states of a transition system, respectively. Given X, let X' be a corresponding set of primed symbols, and let A' be the formula obtained by replacing the symbols X in a formula A with the corresponding symbols in X'. Z is a set of symbols used to encode primary inputs (which may be introduced to "determinize" a non-deterministic choice). A transition relation $T : (X \cup Z) \times X'$ associates states s to their successor states t' under an input assignment z.

A formula S (representing a set of states) satisfies *consecution* if $S \wedge T \Rightarrow S'$. S satisfies consecution *relative to* a formula G if $G \wedge S \wedge T \Rightarrow S'$. A formula S satisfies *initiation* if $I \Rightarrow S$, i.e., if the corresponding set of states contains all initial states.

2.2 IC3 for Finite State Transition Systems

IC3 maintains a growing sequence of *frames* $F_0(X), \dots, F_k(X)$ satisfying the four invariants to the right. Each frame F_i over-approximates the states reachable from I in i or fewer steps (due to invariants 1, 2, and 4).

$$I \Leftrightarrow F_0 \tag{1}$$
$$\forall 0 \leq i < k \, . \, F_i \Rightarrow F_{i+1} \tag{2}$$
$$\forall 0 \leq i \leq k \, . \, F_i \Rightarrow P \tag{3}$$
$$\forall 0 \leq i < k \, . \, F_i \wedge T \Rightarrow F'_{i+1} \tag{4}$$

IC3 aims at finding either a counterexample to safety or an inductive invariant F_i such that $F_i \Leftrightarrow F_{i+1}$ for some level $0 \leq i < k$. Until this goal is reached, the algorithm alternates between two phases:

- If no bad state is reachable from the *frontier* F_k (i.e., $F_k \wedge T \Rightarrow P$), then k is increased, and the new frontier is initialized to P. Furthermore, consecution is checked for each clause in each frame, and passing clauses are pushed forward. Otherwise, IC3 adds a $\neg P$-predecessor s as *proof obligation* $\langle s, k-1 \rangle$.
- IC3 processes a queue of proof obligations $\langle s, i \rangle$, attempting to prove that the state s that is backwards reachable from $\neg P$ is unreachable from F_i. This attempt succeeds if IC3 finds a clause $c \subseteq \neg s$ satisfying consecution relative to F_i (i.e., $F_i \wedge c \wedge T \Rightarrow c'$), in which case the frames $F_1, \dots, F_{i+1}$ are strengthened by adding c.[2] Otherwise, the failed consecution query reveals a predecessor t of s. If $i = 0$ and $t \wedge I$ is satisfiable, then t provides the initial state of a counterexample. Otherwise, a new proof obligation $\langle t, i-1 \rangle$ is added.

For a more detailed introduction to IC3, the reader is referred to [10,11]. Proof obligations are the focus of the extension of IC3 to infinite state transition systems, presented in the next section.

---

[2] To initiate forward propagation and in anticipation that s will be rediscovered at a higher level, $\langle s, i+1 \rangle$ is added as a proof obligation unless $i = k$.

3   CTIGAR

CTIGAR is the natural abstraction-refinement extension of IC3 to infinite state systems. Not only does much of the algorithmic flow remain the same, but the extra abstraction-refinement machinery follows IC3 in spirit: it performs one-step incremental refinements in response to CTIs. This section presents CTIGAR within the known framework of IC3, first expanding IC3 concepts as necessary, then presenting CTIGAR's handling of extended proof obligations, and finally discussing when and how domain refinement is accomplished.

3.1   CTIGAR Extensions of IC3 Concepts

Concrete counterexample to induction (CTI). Central to IC3 is the evaluation of many consecution queries. Each has the form $F_i \wedge \neg s \wedge T \Rightarrow \neg s'$ and tests for the inductiveness of formula $\neg s$ relative to frame F_i. When the query is not valid, the counterexample reveals a predecessor, t, of s. CTI t explains why s is not inductive relative to F_i: t can reach s, and it is not known to be unreachable within i steps. A CTI can be expressed in any theory as a conjunction of equations between state variables and values. In CTIGAR, t is called a *concrete CTI* to distinguish it from an *abstract CTI*, introduced next.

Abstract CTI. As in standard predicate abstraction, the abstraction domain is a set of first-order atoms X over state variables V. An *abstract CTI* $\hat{s} = \alpha(s)$ corresponding to a given concrete CTI s is an over-approximation of s that is expressed as a Boolean combination of the predicates of the domain.

For a concrete state s that assigns values to every state variable in V, $\alpha(s)$ is a cube obtained by evaluating the atoms X over s, and it is the most precise abstraction. Expressing the most precise abstraction of a partial assignment requires, in general, a disjunction of cubes (obtained by an AllSAT query [34]). However, a "best effort" cube abstract CTI can be derived more simply by including only first-order literals that are equivalent to $\top$ under the partial assignment. The latter abstraction method is used in this work.[3]

For example, consider concrete CTI $s : x = 1 \wedge y = -1 \wedge z = 0$ and abstract domain $\{x < y,\ x < z\}$. The corresponding abstract CTI is $\hat{s} : \neg(x < y) \wedge \neg(x < z)$. If w were also a state variable, making s partial, and the domain were to include the predicate $y < w$, then the abstract CTI would remain the same: $y < w$ is equivalent to neither $\top$ nor $\bot$ under the partial assignment s.

Lifted CTI. A failed consecution query $F_i \wedge \neg t \wedge T \Rightarrow \neg t'$ reveals a concrete CTI s as well as an assignment z to the primary inputs. "Lifting" the full assignment s to a partial one is an important generalization mechanism in state-of-the-art IC3 implementations. In the original paper on IC3, static lifting was accomplished by considering the k-step cone of influence [10]; a dynamic approach

---

[3] Both methods were implemented, and the "best effort" cube-based one was found to be both simpler to implement and faster: experiments show that AllSAT-derived (DNF) abstract CTIs fare no better than "best effort" (cube) abstract CTIs.

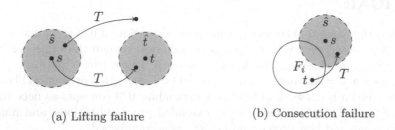

(a) Lifting failure   (b) Consecution failure

Fig. 1. Single-step abstraction failures

based on ternary simulation was then proposed [24]; and a SAT-based approach
was described in [15]. The SAT-based approach extends to the theory setting in
a straightforward manner and is thus appropriate for CTIGAR.

The lifting query takes the form $s \wedge z \wedge T \wedge \neg t'$, which asks whether an s-state
has a successor other than t under input assignment z. Since this is not the case
by construction, the query yields an unsatisfiable core that typically reveals a
significantly reduced partial assignment that can replace s.

Assuming that T is total, lifting the concrete CTI always succeeds. However, in
CTIGAR it is the *abstract CTI* rather than the concrete CTI that is important.
In the corresponding query $\hat{s} \wedge z \wedge T \wedge \neg t'$, the abstract state $\hat{s}$ replaces s.
If this query is unsatisfiable, both $\hat{s}$ and the lifted abstract state revealed by
the unsatisfiable core constitute an underapproximate preimage of the successor
CTI. The query, however, may be satisfiable, since $\hat{s}$ over-approximates s and
may therefore include states that transition to $\neg t$-states under input assignment
z in addition to those—s at minimum—that transition to t-states. Failed lifting
may eventually result in a *spurious* CTI, as discussed in Section 3.2 below.

3.2   The CTIGAR Flow

IC3 with CTIGAR is, as in propositional IC3, centered around the handling of
proof obligations in lowest-frame-first order. Recall from Sections 2.2 and 3.1
that two types of queries are performed in relation to proof obligation $\langle s, i \rangle$:

① A lifting query $u \wedge z \wedge T \Rightarrow t'$ is performed to eliminate non-essential symbols
   from the original predecessor cube u to obtain cube s.
② A consecution query $F_i \wedge \neg s \wedge T \Rightarrow \neg s'$ tests if $\neg s$ is inductive relative to F_i.
   - If it succeeds, the argument is generalized to produce a stronger clause
     $c \subseteq \neg s$ that is inductive relative to F_i.
   - If it fails, the assignment to unprimed state variables provides a CTI v,
     which is lifted to cube $t \subseteq v$ and enqueued as proof obligation $\langle t, i-1 \rangle$.

Abstraction failures. The presence of abstract states complicates the situation
in the sense that the following *abstraction failures* may arise:

① *Lifting Abstraction Failure* (LAF). The formula $\hat{s} \wedge z \wedge T \wedge \neg \hat{t}'$ is satisfiable, i.e., $\hat{s}$ contains at least one concrete state that has a successor outside of $\hat{t}$ under the inputs z, as indicated in Figure 1(a).

② *Consecution Abstraction Failure* (CAF). The formula $F_i \wedge \neg \hat{s} \wedge T \wedge \hat{s}'$ is satisfiable when $F_i \wedge \neg s \wedge T \wedge s'$ is not. In this setting, F_i contains at least one concrete state t outside $\hat{s}$ which has successor(s) in $\hat{s}$ that are not s, as illustrated in Figure 1(b). The transition from t to $\hat{s}$ is *spurious*: $\neg s$ is strong enough to be relatively inductive, while $\neg \hat{s}$ is not.

Proof Obligations. In CTIGAR, the components of a proof obligation reflect the possibility of abstraction failures. A proof obligation $\langle \hat{s}, [s,] \, i, \, n \rangle$ comprises:
- an abstract CTI $\hat{s}$ (reduced from $\alpha(s)$ if abstract lifting succeeded);
- an *optional* concrete CTI s present if an LAF occurred;
- the frame index i, as in propositional IC3;
- the number n of spurious transitions encountered along the trace.

A *trace* is a sequence of proof obligations in which the last element is a CTI to the property P; and for each two consecutive elements, the CTI of the first element stems from a failed consecution query of the second. In this context, t_a denotes a CTI derived from the unprimed state variables V of a failed *abstract* consecution query $F_i \wedge \neg \hat{s} \wedge T \wedge \hat{s}'$, and t_c a CTI derived from a failed *concrete* consecution query $F_i \wedge \neg s \wedge T \wedge s'$.

The concrete CTI s is not included if abstract lifting succeeds because the lifted abstract CTI $\hat{s}$ describes only states that transition into the successor. In other words, the lifted abstract cube $\hat{s}$ is *as good as s in a concrete counterexample trace* when abstract lifting succeeds.

Because of the possibility of abstraction failures when lifting (LAF) or testing consecution (CAF), the operations of lifting to construct a new proof obligation and of handling a proof obligation are tightly coupled:

① *Lifting in CTIGAR.* Let s be either the concrete CTI s_a, derived via a failed abstract consecution query, or s_c, derived via a failed concrete consecution query. The cube t ($\hat{t}$, respectively), represents the successor of s, and z describes the primary input assignment from the failed query. The new proof obligation is constructed as follows:

---

1. Construct the abstract CTI $\hat{s} = \alpha(s)$;
2. Perform abstract lifting via the query $\begin{cases} \hat{s} \wedge z \wedge T \Rightarrow t' & \text{if } s = s_c \\ \hat{s} \wedge z \wedge T \Rightarrow \hat{t}' & \text{if } s = s_a \end{cases}$:
   (a) if lifting succeeds, let $\hat{s}_\ell$ be the lifted abstract CTI and enqueue new obligation $\langle \hat{s}_\ell, i - 1, m \rangle$, where $m = n + 1$ if s is the result of a CAF (see ②) and therefore spurious, and $m = n$ otherwise;
   (b) if lifting fails, enqueue the new obligation $\langle \hat{s}, s, i - 1, m \rangle$, where the presence of s indicates an LAF and the value of m is as above.

Table 1. Overview of Lifting and Consecution in CTIGAR

① Lifting		② Consecution	
$\hat{s} \wedge z \wedge T \Rightarrow t'$ / $\hat{s} \wedge z \wedge T \not\Rightarrow t'$		$F_i \wedge \neg\hat{s} \wedge T \Rightarrow \neg\hat{s}'$	
succeeds:	fails (LAF):	succeeds:	fails for $\langle \hat{s}, i, n \rangle$:
Proof obligation	Proof obligation	generalize and	Extract and consider CTI t_a
$\langle \hat{s}_\ell, i-1, m \rangle$,	$\langle \hat{s}, s, i-1, m \rangle$,	add $c \subseteq \neg\hat{s}$	fails for $\langle \hat{s}, s, i, n \rangle$:
where $m = n+1$ in case of CAF		to $F_1, \ldots, F_{i+1}$	query $F_i \wedge \neg s \wedge T \Rightarrow \neg s'$
and $m = n$ otherwise		succeeds:	fails:
		Extract CTI t_c	CTI t_a (CAF)

Case 2b indicates the occurrence of an LAF, which will be discussed in Section 3.3. Analogously to propositional IC3, CTIGAR uses consecution queries to discharge proof obligations.

② *Consecution in CTIGAR.* Let $\langle \hat{s}, [s,] i, n \rangle$ be an extended proof obligation. A failure of consecution when $i = 0$ indicates a counterexample trace. This situation is addressed in Section 3.3. Consecution is checked as follows:

> *Abstract* consecution is checked via the query $F_i \wedge \neg\hat{s} \wedge T \Rightarrow \neg\hat{s}'$;
> 1. if consecution succeeds, an SMT solver is used to generalize $\hat{s}$ in standard IC3 fashion ([28,12]), resulting in a clause $c \subseteq \neg\hat{s}$ that is inductive relative to F_i.
> 2. if consecution fails, the CTI t_a is extracted;
>   (a) if concrete CTI s is present, then *concrete consecution* is checked via the query $F_i \wedge \neg s \wedge T \Rightarrow \neg s'$;
>   i. if concrete consecution succeeds, then t_a triggers a new proof obligation (see ①)—this situation constitutes a CAF;
>   ii. if concrete consecution fails, CTI t_c is extracted, and t_c triggers a new proof obligation (see ①).
>   (b) if s is absent, then t_a is not spurious, and t_a triggers a new proof obligation (see ①).

The CAF in step 2(a)i is addressed Section 3.3. Table 1 summarizes the scenarios that can arise in CTIGAR.

The following section addresses abstraction lifting (LAF) and consecution (CAF) failures and counterexample traces.

3.3   Refinement

During lifting and the handling of proof obligations in Section 3.2, abstraction failures of type LAF or CAF may occur. This section presents a range of refinement strategies to address these failures. CTIGAR can react to LAFs and CAFs *eagerly* (immediately when they occur), *lazily*, or on a spectrum in between. In the latter two cases, refinement is postponed until a possible counterexample trace is discovered (which cannot be ignored), or until the number of spurious transitions exceeds a threshold.

Refinement can take many forms depending on the abstract domain. In the context of predicate abstraction, Craig interpolation [21,36] (popularized by [29]) is widely used to obtain refinement predicates. An interpolant for a pair of formulas (A, B), where $A \Rightarrow B$ is valid, is a formula J whose uninterpreted symbols occur in both A and B, such that $A \Rightarrow J$ and $J \Rightarrow B$. Interpolants always exist in first-order logic, and efficient interpolating decision procedures are available for a wide range of theories (e.g., [13,22]).

① *Lifting refinement.* Recall from Section 3.2 (Figure 1(a)) that an LAF arises when the domain is too weak for abstract lifting. An LAF occurs when $s \wedge z \wedge T \Rightarrow t'$ holds, where t is the successor of s and z is the assignment to the inputs, while $\hat{s} \wedge z \wedge T \Rightarrow t'$ fails. Refinement ensures that the lifting query will succeed for the newly computed abstraction $\hat{s}$. When interpolation is possible, one can extract from the valid query $s \wedge z \wedge T \Rightarrow t'$ an interpolant R:

$$s \Rightarrow R \quad \text{and} \quad R \Rightarrow (z \wedge T \rightarrow t') \,.$$

The conjuncts of the formula R are added as first-order atoms to the abstract domain. Since $s \Rightarrow R$, the new precise abstraction of s is $\hat{s} \wedge R$, where $\hat{s}$ is the old abstraction of s. Furthermore, because $R \Rightarrow (z \wedge T \rightarrow t')$, the new abstract lifting query $(\hat{s} \wedge R) \wedge z \wedge T \Rightarrow t'$ is valid. Abstract lifting succeeds in the refined domain, thus eliminating this particular LAF.

② *Consecution refinement.* Recall from Section 3.2 that a CAF introduces a spurious transition (Figure 1(b)). In other words, the abstract domain is too weak for $\neg s$ to be relatively inductive even though $\neg s$ is. A CAF occurs when $F_i \wedge \neg s \wedge T \Rightarrow \neg s'$ holds but $F_i \wedge \neg \hat{s} \wedge T \Rightarrow \neg \hat{s}'$ fails. Refinement ensures that the abstract consecution query will succeed for the newly computed abstraction $\hat{s}$. When interpolation is possible, one can extract from the valid query $F_i \wedge \neg s \wedge T \Rightarrow \neg s'$ an interpolant R:

$$F_i \wedge \neg s \wedge T \Rightarrow R' \quad \text{and} \quad R' \Rightarrow \neg s' \,.$$

The formula $\neg R$ is added to the abstract domain. Since $R' \Rightarrow \neg s'$, $s \Rightarrow \neg R$, so that the new cube abstraction of s is $\hat{s} \wedge \neg R$, where $\hat{s}$ is the old abstraction of s. Furthermore, because $s \Rightarrow \hat{s} \wedge \neg R$,

$$F_i \wedge (\neg \hat{s} \vee R) \wedge T \ \Rightarrow \ F_i \wedge \neg s \wedge T \ \Rightarrow \ R'$$

so that the new abstract consecution query

$$F_i \wedge (\neg \hat{s} \vee R) \wedge T \Rightarrow (\neg \hat{s}' \vee R')$$

is valid. Under the refined domain, abstract consecution thus succeeds, eliminating this particular CAF.

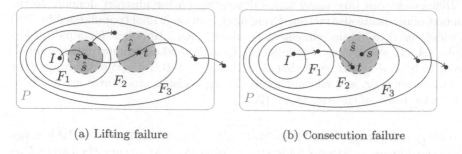

(a) Lifting failure   (b) Consecution failure

Fig. 2. Lazy refinement of abstraction failures

Eager and Lazy Refinement. In the flow described in Section 3.2, CAFs merely trigger an incrementation of the *spurious transition count (STC)*. When a potential new obligation's STC reaches some threshold controlling the degree of laziness, a *consecution refinement* is triggered. The STC indicates the number of spurious transitions on the trace rooted at that obligation. In this setting, a refinement can be triggered for four reasons:

- A counterexample trace is discovered, but the trace has at least one CAF anywhere (Figure 2(b)), triggering a *consecution refinement.*[4]
- A CTI s is disjoint from the initial states I, its abstraction $\hat{s}$ is not, and abstract lifting fails (a LAF). This situation triggers a *lifting refinement.*
- An obligation's STC reaches a threshold, triggering either a *consecution refinement* or a *lifting refinement.*[5]
- The trace rooted at an obligation has reached a threshold number of LAFs (Figure 2(a)), triggering a *lifting refinement.*[6]

Any (even multiple) CAF or LAF points can be analyzed during refinement. Addressing any one blocks the current arrangement of the obligation queue.

4   Implementation and Experimental Evaluation

4.1   Implementation

The experimental evaluation in this section is performed using a prototype of CTIGAR based on the IC3 reference implementation [8]. It uses linear integer arithmetic as the background theory and a combination of MATHSAT 5 [2] and Z3 [22] as SMT solvers. The implementation includes a simple ANTLR 4 [39] parser that does not perform any optimizations at all on the resulting control flow graphs.

---

[4] Otherwise, the trace is a witness to the failure of the property.
[5] CAFs only occur for obligations for which LAFs occurred, so both are useful.
[6] If lifting refinements are triggered eagerly, CAFs never occur.

Abstract Domain. The abstract domain is initialized with the the atom I (encoding the initial program location), and inequalities of the form $x < y$ for all pairs of program variables x, y; additionally, the initial domain is enriched according to the equations discovered by a Karr analysis [32,38] of the whole program.

Refinement predicates of the form $\sum_i b_i x_i = c$ are replaced by $\sum_i b_i x_i \leq c$ and $\sum_i b_i x_i \geq c$, and conjunctions are split into their arguments. Interpolants used for refinement are usually conjunctions in practice. Otherwise, the entire interpolant can be treated as a new predicate; additionally, atoms can be extracted and added as predicates as well.

Refinement State Mining. Orthogonal to interpolation-based refinement, refinement state mining (RSM) is a predicate discovery scheme deriving linear equalities from CTIs. The concrete cubes encountered in lifting and consecution queries are partitioned into sets S_l according to their program location l (represented by dedicated *program counter* variable pc). If the size of an S_l exceeds a threshold, a solver is deployed to discover a linear equality $\sum_k b_k x_k = c$ (where all b_k and c are coefficients, and x_k are program variables in S_l) covering as many states in S_l as possible while minimizing the number of coefficients that are zero. If the query succeeds, the covered states are removed from S_l and the resulting predicate is added to the abstract domain.

Similar to the DAIKON tool [25], the discovered predicates are not necessarily invariants or guaranteed to eliminate spurious CTIs. Alternatively, invariant finding algorithms such as the one described in [40] could be used.

4.2 Benchmarking

The prototype CTIGAR implementation was run on a collection of 110 linear integer arithmetic benchmarks from various sources: The InvGen benchmark suite as found in [27] , the Dagger benchmarks suite as found in [26], and the benchmark suite as found in [1]. Duplicates were only run once. Some benchmarks were omitted from this collection. The benchmarks crawl_cbomb.c, fragtest.c, linpack.c, SpamAssassin-loop*.c and p*-*.c contain pointers or other C constructs that the prototype does not handle. The benchmarks half.c, heapsort*.c, and id_trans.c contain truncating integer divisions, which the prototype does not handle. The benchmarks puzzle1.c, sort_instrumented.c, and test.c do not contain assert statements. The benchmarks spin*.c rely on functions that provide mutex functionality, which the prototype does not handle. All benchmarks are safe.

4.3 Evaluation Configurations

CTIGAR was run in multiple configurations. All configurations that use lazy refinement permit at most three spurious transitions in a single trace to the

Table 2. Runtime results for CTIGAR and CPAChecker. All times are in seconds.

Lifting refinement	LLE	LLL	LCE	LCL	CPAChecker
Number of solved benchmarks	87	86	83	87	64
Cumulative time	7061.68	7547.85	8516.06	7745.06	1170.85
# Solved — unsolved by CPA	29	31	30	34	
Cumulative time	1134.49	2702.17	5425.5	5113.44	
# Solved — faster than CPA	16	16	18	20	
Cumulative time (CTIGAR)	12.38	17.35	14.68	29.24	
Cumulative time (CPA)	53.34	848.99	59.14	860.31	
Consecution refinement	**CCE**	**CCL**	**CAE**	**CAL**	**CPAChecker**
Number of solved benchmarks	86	91	91	92	64
Cumulative time	5414.57	8150.29	6154.33	5880.74	1170.85
# Solved — unsolved by CPA	31	36	34	36	
Cumulative time	2010.26	5149.72	2033.03	2247.59	
# Solved — faster than CPA	19	20	20	20	
Cumulative time (CTIGAR)	18.03	34.34	18.92	21.06	
Cumulative time (CPA)	62.05	863.98	65.34	863.98	

error. We chose 3 based on a manual analysis: three spurious transitions seem sufficient for lazy refinement while avoiding long irrelevant trace postfixes.

① **Configurations using lifting refinement:**
   (a) **LLE**: Eager refinement, triggered by a LAF.
   (b) **LLL**: Lazy refinement, triggered by a LAF.
   (c) **LCE**: Eager refinement, triggered by a CAF.
   (d) **LCL**: Lazy refinement, triggered by a CAF.
② **Configurations using consecution refinement:**
   (a) **CCE**: Eager refinement. Refinement is triggered by every CAF, regardless of whether the abstract state is lifted or not.
   (b) **CCL**: Lazy refinement. Refinement is triggered as above.
   (c) **CAE**: Eager refinement. Refinement is triggered by a CAF only if the abstract state is unlifted.
   (d) **CAL**: Lazy refinement. Refinement is triggered as above.

These versions of the prototype implementation of CTIGAR were compared against CPAChecker [6], the winner of the second software verification competition. The last column in Table 2 refers to the performance of CPAChecker in its competition configuration:
`config/sv-comp13--combinations-predicate.properties`.

The measurements were performed on AMD Opteron(TM) 6272 CPUs at 2100 MHz. No memory threshold was set. The timeout set for the benchmarks was 1200 seconds, wall time. However, if CTIGAR or CPAChecker did not run into the timeout, the run time is reported in the operating systems's user mode used for the benchmark, which is more accurate than the wall time.

4.4   Discussion of Runtime Results

All configurations solved substantially more benchmarks than CPAChecker.[7] CPAChecker was typically faster on benchmarks that were solved by both the prototype CTIGAR implementation and CPAChecker. However, there were 16-20 benchmarks in each configuration that were solved faster by our prototype.

The consecution refinement strategies proved be be somewhat more successful and faster than the lifting refinement strategies. In general, lazy refinement strategies seem to be slightly more successful than eager refinement strategies.

Deploying the interpolation procedure presented in [1] increased the computational overhead of interpolation while not providing measurable improvement of the abstract domain.

Figure 3 to the right presents a comparison of the number of predicates in the abstraction domain vs. the runtime for all terminating instances across all configurations in a log-log-plot. It shows that performance only degrades polynomially with the number of predicates in the domain rather than exponentially.

Figure 4(a) depicts the percentage of successful abstract lifting calls across different configurations (both in consecution and lifting refinement). Abstract lifting succeeds in around 60% to 80% of all cases, providing CTIs that are underapproximate preimages.

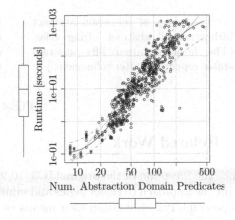

Fig. 3. Number of abstraction domain predicates vs. runtime for terminating instances.

As evident from Figure 4(b), the best configurations (notably CAL) do not immediately address lifting failures but instead lazily proceed with abstract CTIs that do not underapproximate preimages. Strictly using underapproximate preimages is, apparently, not essential. This observation contrasts with previous approaches [16,31]. The experiments also show that a large portion of abstract CTIs are not underapproximate preimages yet are successfully generalized and eliminated, avoiding the cost of computing non-trivial underapproximate preimages.

---

[7] CPAChecker returned UNSAFE on `MADWiFi-encode_ie_ok.c`, but it assigns non-integer values to some integer variables in its error path assignment. A manual inspection of the benchmark reveals that it is in fact safe; nonetheless, the benchmark is counted as solved by CPAChecker. In addition to the 64 solved benchmarks, CPAChecker returned with the message `Analysis incomplete: no errors found, but not everything could be checked.` on 16 benchmarks.

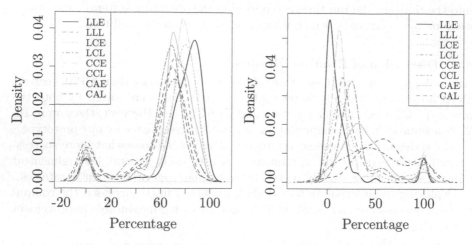

(a) Percentage of successful abstract liftings of all abstract lifting tries. (The implementation lifts abstract states repeatedly after refinement.)

(b) Percentage of abstract states that are still unlifted after having been successfully used for strengthening up to the frontier level.

Fig. 4

5   Related Work

Since the inception of the original IC3 [10,9] numerous attempts have been made to lift the approach to richer logics and infinite domains. Welp and Kühlmann [42] propose interval simulation as a means of generalizing proof obligations in the domain of bit-vectors. Refinement is not required in this setting, as intervals approximate values in the finite concrete domain conservatively. The same holds for region abstraction applied in the context of timed systems [33].

A more general approach applicable to infinite state transition systems and a wider set of theories is to replace the SAT engine underlying IC3 with an SMT solver. In an attempt to avoid a diverging sequence of proof obligations in the infinite concrete domain, Cimatti and Griggio [16] suggest a non-trivial under-approximation of the pre-image (an effort countermanded by the subsequent generalization step). To avert the overhead of the pre-image computation, the algorithm in [16] relies on the Lazy Abstraction with Interpolants (LAwI) refinement scheme [37] as long as the resulting interpolants can be converted into clausal form efficiently, effectively using IC3 as a fallback only.

An inherent drawback of the path-wise unwinding deployed in [16] is that the generalized clauses are not relatively inductive. A recent follow-up publication [17] therefore uses a monolithic transition relation (previously dismissed as inefficient in [16]), replacing the pre-image computation with (implicit) predicate abstraction. Unlike in CTIGAR, refinement is triggered by an abstract counterexample trace and based on an unwinding of the transition relation. Hoder and Bjørner [31] uses Horn clauses to represent recursive predicate transformers. Proof obligations are generalized using a specialized interpolation procedure for linear arithmetic. Effectively, this amounts to an eager refinement step potentially introducing new literals that are linear combinations of the atoms in the consecution query. Vizel et al. [41] implement lazy abstraction for finite state systems by projecting the frames to a sequence of variable sets (of monotonically increasing size), which are refined if a spurious counterexample trace is found.

The following discussion represents an attempt to put CTIGAR into a broader context. Unlike CTIGAR, conventional predicate abstraction tools [4,20] construct an explicit abstract transition relation. Most of these tools, however, use Cartesian abstraction rather than computing the most precise abstraction [5] and refine spurious abstract transitions using a focus operation [3]. SATABS [20] in particular prioritizes transition refinement (triggered by a spurious abstract counterexample trace) over refining the abstract domain, resulting in a succession of relatively simple single-step SAT queries. In contrast, CTIGAR, following IC3, strengthens frames (rather than the abstract transition relation) using single-step consecution queries triggered by single states, and only refines the domain in case of abstraction failures. CTIGAR as well as [17] deploy implicit predicate abstraction. Similarly, lazy abstraction [30,37] does not maintain an explicit abstract transition relation, but uses traces and sequence interpolation to refine the safely reachable states. The fact that CTIGAR derives interpolants from single transition steps instead may have advantages beyond the resulting simplicity of the SMT queries: Cabodi's work suggests that—at least in the propositional case—sequential interpolation is inferior to standard interpolation [14].

6   Conclusion

The impact of using abstract CTIs on lifting and consecution queries is inevitable: abstraction introduces spurious transitions. Focusing on that impact within the IC3 algorithm, rather than outside of it, naturally leads to a CTI-guided, rather than a counterexample trace-guided, abstraction-refinement scheme—CTIGAR rather than CEGAR. The potential benefits of CTIGAR over CEGAR are obvious: faster and more focused refinement triggers, explicit states for state-mining-based predicate synthesis, and one-step interpolation queries for interpolation-based refinement. More broadly, CTIGAR continues the trend started by IC3 of focusing on individual states and single-step queries instead of traces and multi-step queries (BMC and its derivatives).

The prototype implementation of CTIGAR performs competitively against a state-of-the-art CEGAR-based tool in terms of number of solved benchmarks, confirming its potential. Results vary but are robust across parameter settings: lazy vs. eager, lifting- vs. consecution-based refinement. It is expected that further experience with CTIGAR will reveal implementation techniques that close the performance gap between our CTIGAR prototype implementation and well-tuned checkers like CPAChecker.

References

1. Albarghouthi, A., McMillan, K.L.: Beautiful Interpolants. In: Sharygina, N., Veith, H. (eds.) CAV 2013. LNCS, vol. 8044, pp. 313–329. Springer, Heidelberg (2013)
2. Cimatti, A., Griggio, A., Schaafsma, B.J., Sebastiani, R.: The MathSAT5 SMT Solver. In: Piterman, N., Smolka, S.A. (eds.) TACAS 2013. LNCS, vol. 7795, pp. 93–107. Springer, Heidelberg (2013)
3. Ball, T., Cook, B., Das, S., Rajamani, S.K.: Refining Approximations in Software Predicate Abstraction. In: Jensen, K., Podelski, A. (eds.) TACAS 2004. LNCS, vol. 2988, pp. 388–403. Springer, Heidelberg (2004)
4. Ball, T., Cook, B., Levin, V., Rajamani, S.K.: SLAM and Static Driver Verifier: Technology Transfer of Formal Methods inside Microsoft. In: Boiten, E.A., Derrick, J., Smith, G.P. (eds.) IFM 2004. LNCS, vol. 2999, pp. 1–20. Springer, Heidelberg (2004)
5. Ball, T., Podelski, A., Rajamani, S.K.: Boolean and Cartesian abstraction for model checking C programs. Software Tools for Technology Transfer (STTT) 5(1), 49–58 (2003)
6. Beyer, D., Keremoglu, M.E.: CPACHECKER: A Tool for Configurable Software Verification. In: Gopalakrishnan, G., Qadeer, S. (eds.) CAV 2011. LNCS, vol. 6806, pp. 184–190. Springer, Heidelberg (2011)
7. Biere, A.: Bounded Model Checking. In: Handbook of Satisfiability, pp. 457–481. IOS Press (2009)
8. Bradley, A.R.: IC3 reference implementation, https://github.com/arbrad/IC3ref/
9. Bradley, A.R.: k-Step Relative Inductive Generalization. The Computing Research Repository, abs/1003.3649 (2010)
10. Bradley, A.R.: SAT-Based Model Checking Without Unrolling. In: Jhala, R., Schmidt, D. (eds.) VMCAI 2011. LNCS, vol. 6538, pp. 70–87. Springer, Heidelberg (2011)
11. Bradley, A.R.: Understanding IC3. In: Cimatti, A., Sebastiani, R. (eds.) SAT 2012. LNCS, vol. 7317, pp. 1–14. Springer, Heidelberg (2012)
12. Bradley, A.R., Manna, Z.: Checking Safety by Inductive Generalization of Counterexamples to Induction. In: Formal Methods in Computer-Aided Design (FMCAD), pp. 173–180. IEEE (2007)
13. Bruttomesso, R., Cimatti, A., Franzén, A., Griggio, A., Sebastiani, R.: The MATHSAT 4 SMT solver. In: Gupta, A., Malik, S. (eds.) CAV 2008. LNCS, vol. 5123, pp. 299–303. Springer, Heidelberg (2008)
14. Cabodi, G., Nocco, S., Quer, S.: Interpolation sequences revisited. In: Design Automation and Test in Europe (DATE), pp. 316–322. IEEE (2011)
15. Chockler, H., Ivrii, A., Matsliah, A., Moran, S., Nevo, Z.: Incremental Formal Verification of Hardware. In: Formal Methods in Computer-Aided Design (FMCAD), pp. 135–143. IEEE (2011)
16. Cimatti, A., Griggio, A.: Software Model Checking via IC3. In: Madhusudan, P., Seshia, S.A. (eds.) CAV 2012. LNCS, vol. 7358, pp. 277–293. Springer, Heidelberg (2012)
17. Cimatti, A., Griggio, A., Mover, S., Tonetta, S.: IC3 Modulo Theories via Implicit Predicate Abstraction. In: Ábrahám, E., Havelund, K. (eds.) TACAS 2014. LNCS, vol. 8413, pp. 46–61. Springer, Heidelberg (2014)

18. Clarke, E.M., Grumberg, O., Jha, S., Lu, Y., Veith, H.: Counterexample-Guided Abstraction Refinement. In: Emerson, E.A., Sistla, A.P. (eds.) CAV 2000. LNCS, vol. 1855, pp. 154–169. Springer, Heidelberg (2000)

19. Clarke, E.M., Grumberg, O., Jha, S., Lu, Y., Veith, H.: Counterexample-Guided Abstraction Refinement for Symbolic Model Checking. Journal of the ACM 50(5) (September 2003)

20. Clarke, E., Kroning, D., Lerda, F.: A Tool for Checking ANSI-C Programs. In: Jensen, K., Podelski, A. (eds.) TACAS 2004. LNCS, vol. 2988, pp. 168–176. Springer, Heidelberg (2004)

21. Craig, W.: Linear reasoning. A new form of the Herbrand-Gentzen theorem. Journal of Symbolic Logic 22(3), 250–268 (1957)

22. de Moura, L., Bjørner, N.: Z3: An efficient SMT solver. In: Ramakrishnan, C.R., Rehof, J. (eds.) TACAS 2008. LNCS, vol. 4963, pp. 337–340. Springer, Heidelberg (2008)

23. Donaldson, A.F., Haller, L., Kroening, D., Rümmer, P.: Software Verification Using k-Induction. In: Yahav, E. (ed.) SAS 2011. LNCS, vol. 6887, pp. 351–368. Springer, Heidelberg (2011)

24. Een, N., Mishchenko, A., Brayton, R.: Efficient Implementation of Property Directed Reachability. In: Formal Methods in Computer-Aided Design (FMCAD), pp. 125–134. IEEE (2011)

25. Ernst, M.D., Perkins, J.H., Guo, P.J., McCamant, S., Pacheco, C., Tschantz, M.S., Xiao, C.: The Daikon System for Dynamic Detection of Likely Invariants. Science of Computer Programming 69(1-3), 35–45 (2007)

26. Gulavani, B.S., Chakraborty, S., Nori, A.V., Rajamani, S.K.: Dagger Benchmarks Suite, http://www.cfdvs.iitb.ac.in/~bhargav/dagger.php

27. Gupta, A., Rybalchenko, A.: InvGen Benchmarks Suite, http://pub.ist.ac.at/~agupta/invgen/

28. Hassan, Z., Bradley, A.R., Somenzi, F.: Better Generalization in IC3. In: Formal Methods in Computer-Aided Design (FMCAD). IEEE (2013)

29. Henzinger, T.A., Jhala, R., Majumdar, R., McMillan, K.L.: Abstractions from Proofs. In: Principles of Programming Languages (POPL), pp. 232–244. ACM (2004)

30. Henzinger, T.A., Jhala, R., Majumdar, R., Sutre, G.: Lazy Abstraction. In: Principles of Programming Languages (POPL), pp. 58–70. ACM (2002)

31. Hoder, K., Bjørner, N.: Generalized Property Directed Reachability. In: Cimatti, A., Sebastiani, R. (eds.) SAT 2012. LNCS, vol. 7317, pp. 157–171. Springer, Heidelberg (2012)

32. Karr, M.: Affine Relationships Among Variables of a Program. Acta Informatica 6, 133–151 (1976)

33. Kindermann, R., Junttila, T., Niemelä, I.: SMT-Based Induction Methods for Timed Systems. In: Jurdziński, M., Ničković, D. (eds.) FORMATS 2012. LNCS, vol. 7595, pp. 171–187. Springer, Heidelberg (2012)

34. Lahiri, S.K., Nieuwenhuis, R., Oliveras, A.: SMT Techniques for Fast Predicate Abstraction. In: Ball, T., Jones, R.B. (eds.) CAV 2006. LNCS, vol. 4144, pp. 424–437. Springer, Heidelberg (2006)

35. McMillan, K.L.: Interpolation and SAT-Based Model Checking. In: Hunt Jr., W.A., Somenzi, F. (eds.) CAV 2003. LNCS, vol. 2725, pp. 1–13. Springer, Heidelberg (2003)

36. McMillan, K.L.: An Interpolating Theorem Prover. Theoretical Computer Science 345(1), 101–121 (2005)

37. McMillan, K.L.: Lazy Abstraction with Interpolants. In: Ball, T., Jones, R.B. (eds.) CAV 2006. LNCS, vol. 4144, pp. 123–136. Springer, Heidelberg (2006)
38. Müller-Olm, M., Seidl, H.: A Note on Karr's algorithm. In: Díaz, J., Karhumäki, J., Lepistö, A., Sannella, D. (eds.) ICALP 2004. LNCS, vol. 3142, pp. 1016–1028. Springer, Heidelberg (2004)
39. Terence Parr. ANTLR4, http://www.antlr.org/
40. Sharma, R., Gupta, S., Hariharan, B., Aiken, A., Liang, P., Nori, A.V.: A Data Driven Approach for Algebraic Loop Invariants. In: Felleisen, M., Gardner, P. (eds.) ESOP 2013. LNCS, vol. 7792, pp. 574–592. Springer, Heidelberg (2013)
41. Vizel, Y., Grumberg, O., Shoham, S.: Lazy Abstraction and SAT-Based Reachability in Hardware Model Checking. In: Formal Methods in Computer-Aided Design (FMCAD), pp. 173–181. IEEE (2012)
42. Welp, T., Kuehlmann, A.: QF_BV Model Checking with Property Directed Reachability. In: Design Automation and Test in Europe (DATE), pp. 791–796. EDA Consortium (2013)

Unbounded Scalable Verification Based on Approximate Property-Directed Reachability and Datapath Abstraction

Suho Lee and Karem A. Sakallah

University of Michigan and Qatar Computing Research Institute

Abstract. This paper introduces the Averroes formal verification system which exploits the power of two complementary approaches: counterexample-guided abstraction and refinement (CEGAR) of the design's datapath and the recently-introduced IC3 and PDR approximate reachability algorithms. Averroes is particularly suited to the class of hardware designs consisting of wide datapaths and complex control logic, a class that covers a wide spectrum of design styles that range from general-purpose microprocessors to special-purpose embedded controllers and accelerators. In most of these designs, the number of datapath state variables is orders of magnitude larger than the number of control state variables. Thus, for purposes of verifying the correctness of the control logic (where most design errors typically reside), datapath abstraction is particularly effective at pruning away most of a design's state space leaving a much reduced "control space" that can be efficiently explored by the IC3 and PDR method. Preliminary experimental results on a suite of industrial benchmarks show that Averroes significantly outperforms verification at the bit level. To our knowledge, this is the first empirical demonstration of the possibility of automatic scalable unbounded sequential verification.

1 Introduction

This paper explores the possibility of scaling formal verification of complex hardware systems beyond what is possible today by exploiting the power of two complementary approaches: counterexample-guided *datapath abstraction and refinement* and the recently-introduced IC3 [1] and PDR [2] approximate reachability algorithms. Our prototype implementation of this verification framework, which we call the Averroes system for sequential verification, is premised on the conjecture that the complexity of sequential verification can be reduced significantly by a) abstracting away irrelevant datapath "state" that basically clutters reachability analysis without providing any useful guidance for its convergence, and b) performing approximate reachability on this abstracted state space. The approach can be viewed as a "layering" of two CEGAR loops: an inner loop that performs approximate reachability on the datapath-abstracted state space, and an outer datapath refinement loop that tightens the abstraction based on the spurious counterexamples generated by the inner loop. Initial empirical evaluation of this approach shows that it significantly outperforms bit-level verification on a set of industrial RTL benchmarks and suggests that the combination of

A. Biere and R. Bloem (Eds.): CAV 2014, LNCS 8559, pp. 849–865, 2014.

datapath abstraction and approximate reachability makes it possible to perform automatic unbounded scalable verification on real-world industrial benchmarks.

The rest of the paper is organized in 9 sections. Sections 2 and 3 briefly review previous work and cover preliminaries. We then provide a high-level description of the IC3/PDR approach in Section 4 followed by an example, in Section 5, to motivate datapath abstraction. Sections 6 and 7 provide an overview and a detailed description of the Averroes algorithm. Preliminary experimental evaluation is covered in Section 8, and Section 9 ends the paper with some conclusions.

2   Previous Work

The recently introduced IC3 algorithm [1] and its re-implementation in PDR [2] represent a major milestone in the decades' long quest for scalable model checking (MC). Both can be described as SAT-based induction methods and both share some features of the earlier attempts at using induction [3,4]. In particular, assuming that a given safety property P holds but is not inductive (i.e., is not closed under the transition relation), induction methods can be viewed as ways of performing *approximate reachability* with the goal of finding an assertion that strengthens (i.e., restricts) P so that it becomes an *inductive invariant* [5]. Alternatively, such methods can be seen as an application of counterexample-guided abstraction refinement (CEGAR) [6,7,8] whereby overapproximations of the reachable states are *refined* iteratively until enough unreachable states have been eliminated to prove that P does in fact hold or to produce a counterexample trace. Eliminating the need to compute exact reachability makes it possible for induction methods to converge in a number of iterations that can be much smaller than the sequential depth of the transition relation. Additionally, induction methods can be applied without having to unroll the transition relation which allows them to have better scalability than the earlier memory-intensive BDD [9,10] or BMC [11,12] approaches.

Several extensions of the IC3/PDR approach have already been proposed. In [13], the authors describe an extension to PDR that enables reasoning about nonlinear predicate transformers and linear real arithmetic. In [14], IC3-style reachability is generalized to handle transition systems described by first-order formulas, combined with control flow graph (CFG) analysis, and used to verify safety properties of software. The work that is closest to ours is [15] where Kurshan's *visible variable abstraction* [6] is layered on top of IC3 to significantly scale performance, over just IC3, on a set of large industrial benchmarks.

The datapath/control dichotomy has been addressed by many authors. In [16], properties are classified as control, data, and data/control, and various degrees of data sensitivity are introduced and analyzed. A formal model of systems that can be decomposed into an interconnection of datapath and controller modules is described in [17] and used to automatically generate an abstraction by datapath reduction. In [18], datapath abstraction is shown to yield significant savings in both runtime and memory in a symbolic verification system. The Reveal verification system [19] performs automatic datapath abstraction from Verilog RTL models and iteratively refines them in a standard CEGAR flow. It is important to note that all of these approaches were limited to bounded verification that involved unrolling a design's transition relation a fixed number of times. To our knowledge, the approach described in this paper is the first to couple datapath abstraction and refinement with unbounded model checking.

3   Preliminaries

Our concern in this paper is to determine if a sequential hardware design satisfies a specified safety property. We assume that the design's behavior is encoded by a transition relation $T(X, X^+)$ where X and X^+ denote n-bit vectors of current- and next-state variables. In general, T is easily derivable from any suitable design description, e.g., a netlist or a model in a hardware description language such as Verilog. Furthermore, T may involve additional non-state variables including primary inputs and signals that model combinational blocks in the design. These extra variables are assumed to be part of the definition of T even when not explicitly listed. In the sequel, we will assume that T is available as a propositional formula in conjunctive normal form (CNF). We also assume the existence of two additional predicates (also available as CNF formulas) on the design's state variables: $I(X)$ denoting the design's initial (reset) state(s), and $P(X)$ denoting the set of states that satisfy the desired safety property. We will informally refer to the states that satisfy (resp. violate) $P(X)$ as good (resp. bad or error) states. Finally, we denote by $R(X)$ the design's set of reachable states, i.e., those states that can be reached from $I(X)$ in one or more transitions. A *trace* Π is a state sequence $\langle s_0(X), s_1(X), \cdots, s_{k-1}(X) \rangle$ such that each s_i is a set of states, $s_0(X) \in I(X)$, and $s_i(X) \wedge T(X, X^+) \to s_{i+1}(X^+)$ holds for $0 \le i \le k - 2$. The length of a trace with k states is $k - 1$. An empty trace is one whose state sequence (as a set) is empty; its length is undefined.

The verification task can now be stated as follows: prove that all states in R are good or derive a counterexample trace that starts in I and ends in $\neg P$. The algorithms we consider in this paper solve this task by induction. Using Bradley's terminology [5], these algorithms consist of two main steps:

- **Initiation**: prove that the initial states are good: $I \to P$.
- **Consecution**: derive a *strengthening* assertion $A(X)$ such that $A \wedge P \wedge T \to A^+ \wedge P^+$, where A^+ and P^+ are shorthand for $A(X^+)$ and $P(X^+)$.

What distinguishes these algorithms from earlier induction approaches is that the strengthening assertion A is derived incrementally rather than monolithically [1,2]. Furthermore, in contrast to methods that perform exact image computations (symbolically using BDDs or through SAT-based unrolling of the transition relation), these algorithms create and repeatedly tighten a sequence of approximate reachability frontiers without having to unroll the transition relation. Thus, they do not suffer from the memory explosion inherent in earlier approaches and are demonstrably more scalable. The first such algorithm in this category was Bradley's IC3 [1] which was subsequently re-implemented and enhanced by Een et al. [2] who dubbed it PDR. In the rest of this paper we will refer to this class of algorithms as IC3/PDR to emphasize their incremental inductive nature (the first two Is in IC3) and their property-directed slant (the PDR viewpoint).

```
1.  trace Reach-CEGAR(T,I,P){
2.    F₀ = I;
3.    if (F₀ & !P)
4.      then return CE trace;// len(CEX)=0
5.    if (F₀ & T & !P⁺)
6.      then return CE trace;// len(CEX)=1
7.    k = 1;
8.    Fₖ = P;
9.    while (true){
10.     Fₖ₊₁ = P;
11.     while (Fₖ & T & !P⁺)// CTI
12.       if Reachable(CTI,I)
13.         then return CEX trace;// len(CEX)≥k+1
14.         else Refine(1,k+1);
15.       if (Fᵢ = Fᵢ₋₁ for some 2≤i≤k+1)
16.         then return empty trace;// P holds
17.       k++;
18.   }
19. }
```

Fig. 1. High-Level Pseudo Code for CEGAR-Based Reachability

4   Reachability Approximation and Refinement

For our purposes we find it useful to view the IC3/PDR approach as a clever application of CEGAR whereby a series of reachability overapproximations are systematically refined based on counterexamples to induction (CTIs) [5] until either a) a feasible state sequence from the initial state to an error state (a counterexample trace) is found or b) the refinements become sufficient to render the property being checked inductive, i.e., an overapproximation of the reachable states that satisfies the property is found. A sketch of this approach, loosely mimicking IC3, is given in Fig. 1. The procedure, which we call **Reach-CEGAR**, takes as input T, I, and P, and returns a trace. An empty trace indicates that P holds; otherwise the returned trace represents a counterexample CEX demonstrating how P is violated.

Reach-CEGAR maintains an array of *frontiers* $F_0, F_1, \cdots, F_k, \cdots$ such that $F_0 = I$ and $F_j, j > 0$ is an overapproximation of what is reachable after j steps from I. After checking for 0- and 1-step counterexamples (lines 2 to 6), **Reach-CEGAR** enters its main loop (lines 9 to 18). At iteration $k > 0$, the goal is to check for the existence of CTIs that correspond to counterexample traces whose length is at least $k + 1$. Each satisfying assignment to the current-state variables in the query on line 11 is a CTI that is checked to determine if it is reachable from I (line 12). If unreachable, the CTI is used to tighten the approximations of frontiers 1 to $k + 1$ (line 14) by constraining them with appropriate *refinement clauses*. This process continues until either a reachable CTI is found (line 13) or all CTIs from the current frontier have been ruled out as unreachable. At that point **Reach-CEGAR** checks for convergence (line 15) which is indicated when two frontier approximations become equal. If converged, **Reach-CEGAR** returns an empty trace signaling that P is satisfied (line 16). Otherwise, it increments the iteration counter (line 17) and proceeds to check for the existence of CTIs that correspond to longer counterexample traces.

This sketch hides many details that are critical to the performance of the algorithm. Specifically, in IC3/PDR **Reachable** and **Refine** are not separate procedures. Instead, the reachability check implied by **Reachable** is decomposed into a collection of 1-step backward reachability checks that are queued and processed in some order. Each such check may spawn further checks and/or yield one or more refinements that are propagated backward and forward to tighten the frontier approximations. The checks and attendant refinements, which are performed through appropriate calls to an incremental SAT solver, are closely choreographed to improve the quality of the derived refinement clauses and speed up convergence. Different implementations will thus yield different refinements that can lead to drastically different performance.

There is, however, a critical detail in the implementation of **Reach-CEGAR** that deserves mention. Let ρ_j denote the CNF formula corresponding to the refinement clauses associated with frame j. With a slight abuse of notation, we will also view ρ_j as a set of clauses. At the beginning of each major iteration k, **Reach-CEGAR** insures that the sets of refinement clauses are distinct and subsumption-free, i.e., $\omega \nrightarrow \upsilon$ where $\omega \in \rho_j$ and $\upsilon \in \rho_i$ for $i \leqslant j$. The frontier overapproximations can now be expressed as:

$$F_j = P \wedge \bigwedge_{i=j}^{k+1} \rho_i, j \in [1, k+1]$$

which in turn implies that $F_1 \to F_2 \to \cdots \to F_{k+1}$, and reduces the convergence check on line 15 to checking that the set of refinement clauses at some frame j has become empty ($\rho_j = 1$). At that point, the refinement clauses at the last frontier serve as an inductive strengthening assertion [5] that helps prove the property: $\rho_{k+1} \wedge P \wedge T \to \rho_{k+1}^+ \wedge P^+$

5   Motivating Example

Fig. 2 gives the Verilog description and corresponding state transition graph (STG) of an example sequential circuit that will serve to demonstrate the potential benefits of combining datapath abstraction with approximate reachability. The circuit clearly satisfies the specified property $P(X, Y) = (Y \leq X)$ since, as can be seen from the STG, the reachable states satisfy $R(X, Y) = (Y = X)$.

When IC3 is run on this example it proves the property after eliminating two CTIs and generating three refinement clauses. At exit the refinement clauses and corresponding frontier approximations are:

$$\rho_1 = \neg x_1 \qquad\qquad F_1 = P \wedge \rho_1 \wedge \rho_2 \wedge \rho_3$$
$$\rho_2 = 1 \qquad\qquad F_2 = P \wedge \rho_2 \wedge \rho_3$$
$$\rho_3 = (\neg x_0 \vee y_0) \wedge (\neg x_1 \vee y_1) \quad F_3 = P \wedge \rho_3$$

Note that the clause set for frontier 2 is empty ($\rho_2 = 1$) implying that $F_3 = F_2$.

In contrast, PDR proves the property by eliminating 6 CTIs and learning 7 refinement clauses. The difference between the two programs is due to their particular choices for the initial frontier approximations (PDR sets $F_k = 1$ instead of $F_k = P$) and the manner in which they perform backward reachability and refinement. The difference becomes more pronounced when the bit width of the

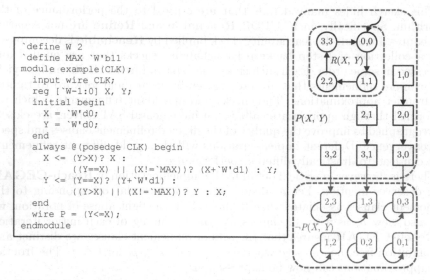

```
`define W 2
`define MAX `W'b11
module example(CLK);
  input wire CLK;
  reg [`W-1:0] X, Y;
  initial begin
    X = `W'd0;
    Y = `W'd0;
  end
  always @(posedge CLK) begin
    X <= (Y>X)? X :
         ((Y==X) || (X!=`MAX))? (X+`W'd1) : Y;
    Y <= (Y==X)? (Y+`W'd1) :
         ((Y>X) || (X!=`MAX))? Y : X;
  end
  wire P = (Y<=X);
endmodule
```

Fig. 2. Verilog description and corresponding STG of an example sequential circuit with a specified safety property. The state variables are 2-bit unsigned integers $X = x_1x_0$ and $Y = y_1y_0$ and their values are used to label the states (X followed by Y) in the STG. The good states are represented by circles (reachable states) and squares (unreachable states); squares with rounded corners correspond to bad states. Note that the circuit's sequential depth is exponential in the bit width W: $2^W = 2^2 = 4$.

state variables in the example is increased from 2 to 64. The results are shown in Table 1. For each bit width, the table compares five measures of performance for IC3 and PDR: runtime, number of frames, number of CTI checks, total and net number of refinement clauses, and total and net number of refinement literals. The number of net refinement clauses and literals reflects the effect of clause subsumption. With a time-out of 1500 seconds, both programs completed the verification up to a bit width of 8; neither program finished for larger bit widths. In most cases PDR outperformed IC3, carrying out many more CTI checks while learning fewer refinement clauses (after subsumption). However, for both programs the number of accumulated refinement clauses grows rapidly as the bit

Table 1. IC3 v. PDR on Example Circuit of Figure 2 for Different Bit Widths

Bit Width	Sequential Depth	Runtime, sec		Frames		CTI Checks		Refinement Clauses				Refinement Literals			
								Total		Net		Total		Net	
		IC3	PDR	IC3	PDR	IC3	PDR	IC3	PDR	IC3	PDR	IC3	PDR	IC3	PDR
2	4.00E+00	0.02	0.02	2	4	2	6	3	12	3	7	5	22	5	12
4	1.60E+01	0.07	0.05	15	15	16	71	84	114	34	32	258	328	87	69
8	2.56E+02	59.59	3.82	232	141	293	4782	31527	6503	740	195	178736	38364	3267	679
16	6.55E+04	T.O.	T.O.	311	1074	402	299511	179776	327581	1241	9576	2273502	4252418	13779	113497
32	4.29E+09	T.O.	T.O.	207	1080	200	313973	28018	327958	325	11431	724242	3932210	6786	126096
64	1.84E+19	T.O.	T.O.	200	923	241	244916	11470	259737	356	8922	636123	2857933	13744	97484

```
1.  trace DP-CEGAR(T,I,P){
2.    (T̂, Î, P̂) = DP-Abstract(T,I,P);
3.    Δ = 1; // Initialize datapath lemmas
4.    while (true){
5.      ACEX = Reach-CEGAR(T̂, Î, P̂, Δ);
6.      if empty(ACEX)
7.        then return empty trace;// P holds
8.      CEX = DP-Concretize(ACEX);
9.      if Feasible(CEX)
10.       then return CEX trace;// P fails
11.       else Δ = Δ && DP-Refine(ACEX);
12.   }
13. }
```

Fig. 3. High-Level Pseudo Code for CEGAR-Based Datapath Abstraction

width increases. The large gap between the total and net number of refinement clauses also indicates that both programs learn *weak* clauses that end up being subsumed by stronger ones in later iterations. This suggests that the refinement process gets mired in irrelevant bit-level details that miss the big picture about the property being checked.

6   Datapath Abstraction and Refinement

Our proposed procedure for integrating an IC3/PDR-style reachability computation within a datapath abstraction and refinement framework is summarized in Fig. 3. The initial datapath abstraction is performed by **DP-Abstract** which returns first-order logic (FOL) versions of the bit-level transition, initial, and property formulas (line 2) by, basically, replacing wide datapath signals with uninterpreted terms, and datapath operators and predicates with, respectively, uninterpreted functions and predicates. Single-bit control signals are not abstracted [19]. The abstract formulas are overapproximations of the bit-level versions and, thus, represent a sound abstraction. The procedure then initializes Δ (line 3) which serves as a database of derived datapath refinement lemmas. The reachability computation is carried out by calling a modified version of **Reach-CEGAR** (line 5) that operates on the abstract formulas. Note, in particular, that this version of **Reach-CEGAR** takes as a fourth argument a formula representing the learned datapath lemmas which it augments to all the queries it performs. If **Reach-CEGAR** returns an empty trace, **DP-CEGAR** terminates with the conclusion that the property holds (line 7). However, if **Reach-CEGAR** returns a non-empty abstract trace ACEX, a concrete bit-level version is constructed by **DP-Concretize** (line 8) and checked for feasibility (line 9). If found to be feasible, CEX is returned as a witness for the violation of the property (line 10). Otherwise, a datapath refinement procedure, similar to that in [20], is called to refute this spurious CEX by generating one or more datapath lemmas (line 11), and another round of abstract reachability is invoked. The hypothesis behind this architecture is that the approximate CEGAR-based reachability computation is now performed on an abstracted version of the design that eliminates irrelevant bit-level details and, thus, is more scalable. More specifically, the abstract CEGAR-based reachability procedure is now operating on approximate reachability frontiers in an abstract approximate state space. The combination of these two orthogonal approximations can lead to drastic pruning by generating two types of refinement lemmas: *reachability* refinement lemmas, and *datapath* refinement lemmas. The latter are "universal" in that they are invariants that tighten the datapath abstraction by relating the uninterpreted terms, functions, and predicates. The former are derived during the approximate reachability computation, except they are now in terms of the abstract state variables. They are, thus, expected to be much stronger than the bit-level refinement clauses derived by IC3 and PDR.

To illustrate the potential of this approach, consider its application to the example sequential design from Section 5. Datapath abstraction creates the following uninterpreted variables, constants, predicates, and functions from the corresponding bit-level equivalents[1]:

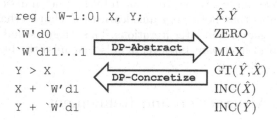

When **Reach-CEGAR** is applied to the abstract transition relation it returns the 0-step counterexample

$$ACEX = (\hat{X} = \text{ZERO}) \wedge (\hat{Y} = \text{ZERO}) \wedge (\text{GT}(\hat{Y}, \hat{X}))$$

since it does not know the semantics of the abstract constant ZERO and the abstract predicate GT. However, upon concretization and bit-level feasibility checking, **DP-CEGAR** concludes that this counterexample is spurious and derives the following datapath lemma

$$\delta_1 = \neg \text{GT}(\text{ZERO}, \hat{X})$$

to rule it out. The second call to **Reach-CEGAR** returns a 1-step abstract counterexample which is also found to be infeasible and is refuted by the datapath lemma

$$\delta_2 = \neg[(\hat{Y} = \hat{X}) \wedge (\hat{X}^+ = \text{INC}(\hat{X})) \wedge$$
$$(\hat{Y}^+ = \text{INC}(\hat{Y})) \wedge (\text{GT}(\hat{Y}^+, \hat{X}^+))]$$

This lemma is a constraint that relates the uninterpreted GT predicate and the uninterpreted INC function: in words, it states that applying INC to equal values

---

[1] Note that this abstraction is reversible; we just need to maintain the correspondence between the abstract entities and their bit-level counterparts.

cannot yield results in which one is greater than the other. The third, and final call, to **Reach-CEGAR** returns an empty trace after eliminating two CTIs and generating two abstract *single-literal* refinement clauses: $\neg GT(\hat{X}, \hat{Y})$ and $(\hat{Y} = \hat{X})$. Thus, after eliminating 0- and 1-step counterexamples with two datapath lemmas, **DP-CEGAR** is able to prove the property in just one reachability iteration *regardless of the bit width of the state variables.*

7   The Averroes Algorithm

In this section we describe the **Averroes** program, a prototype implementation of **DP-CEGAR**. Averroes[2] is written in C++ and accepts design descriptions in a variety of formats including RTL Verilog. It calls **DP-Abstract** to create an initial abstraction of T, I, and P, similar to that described in [19], and passes it on to **Reach-CEGAR**, an IC3/PDR approximate reachability procedure to be described shortly. Abstract counterexample traces returned by **Reach-CEGAR** are bit blasted and checked for feasibility one transition at a time. Each infeasible transition in a counterexample triggers the generation of one or more datapath refinement lemmas using a simplified version of the minimal unsatisfiable subset (MUS) extractor in [20]. Feasibility checking is done using the bit vector (BV) theory in the Yices (version 1.0.35) SMT solver [21].

Fig. 4 highlights the major steps of the approximate reachability computation in **Reach-CEGAR** (lines 9–18 in Fig. 1). The formulas processed by **Reach-CEGAR** are all in the first-order logic of equality with uninterpreted functions (EUF) and all reasoning is done using the Yices SMT solver. Satisfying solutions returned from the SMT solver are converted to a conjunction of literals which take several forms:

- positive or negated bit-level variables
- positive or negated uninterpreted predicates
- equalities or disequalities between uninterpreted constants, terms, and functions

The procedure utilizes a queue Q of proof obligations each of which is a pair $(c(X), k)$ where $c(X)$ is a conjunction of literals (a cube) and k is a frame number. The following numbered list corresponds to the numbered boxes in Fig. 4:

1. At the start of major iteration k, frame k is overapproximated to P ($F_k = P$). The iteration then repeatedly checks for CTIs using the function 1-step which calls the SMT solver with the query: $F_k \wedge T \wedge \Delta \wedge \neg P^+$
2. A satisfying solution $s(X) \in F_k(X)$ to this query indicates a CTI that must now be checked for reachability from $I(X)$. Before proceeding with that check, however, the solution is "expanded" to remove irrelevant literals using a) cone of influence (COI) reduction, and b) finding MUSes, if any exist, of the formula[3] $s \wedge P \wedge T \wedge \Delta \wedge P^+$[22]. The enlarged cube $\hat{s}$ is now added to

[2] The Averroes tool and some hand-crafted examples are available at
http://web.eecs.umich.edu/~suholee/AVERROES.html

[3] PDR does this at the bit level using 3-valued simulation. In our case, this formula may be satisfiable and not yield an expansion of the cube!

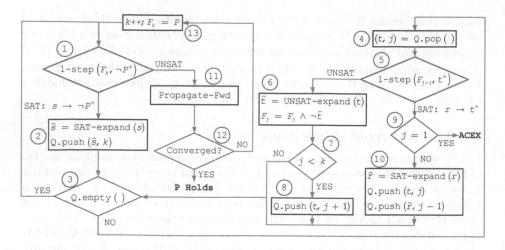

Fig. 4. Implementation of **Reach-CEGAR** in the Averroes Verifier. **Reach-CEGAR** performs approximate reachability computation on an EUF abstraction of the bit-level transition relation.

the Q as a proof obligation in frame k, meaning "can $\widehat{s}$ be eliminated from F_k by showing that it is unreachable from I along paths whose length is at least k?"

3. An empty queue signifies that the current CTI has been successfully eliminated and the algorithm proceeds to check for the existence of another CTI from the current frame.

4. The reachability computation starts here by retrieving a proof obligation (t, j) from the queue.

5. The 1-step function checks the formula $F_{j-1} \wedge T \wedge \Delta \wedge t^+ \wedge P^+$ to determine if t can be reached in one step from frame $j - 1$.

6. If t is not reachable from frame $j - 1$, it is enlarged to $\widehat{t}$ by extracting one or more MUSes from the UNSAT formula in step 5. The negation of $\widehat{t}$ is now added as a refinement clause to frame j (which means that all frames $1 \le i \le j$ are tightened as a result of the unreachability of t in frame j).

7. The processing of cube t terminates if we reach the last frontier k.

8. Otherwise, t is added as a proof obligation in frame $j + 1$. This step is optional but, as pointed out in [2], it helps to improve performance and to find counterexample traces that are longer than $k + 1$.

9. If the current proof obligation is $(t, 1)$ and t is found to be reachable from frame 0, then we have found an abstract counterexample trace ACEX and the procedure terminates.

10. If t in frame j is found to be reachable (in one step) from frame $j - 1$, the satisfying solution r to the query in step 5 is enlarged similarly to how s was enlarged in step 2. Specifically, irrelevant literals are removed from r by COI reduction and MUS extraction, if any exist, from $r \wedge P \wedge T \wedge \Delta \wedge \neg t^+ \wedge P^+$.

Processing continues by re-inserting (t, j) into the queue and adding $(\widehat{r}, j-1)$ as a new proof obligation.

Table 2. Statistics of the Large Industrial Benchmarks

Benchmark	Regs	FFs	State Bits	%Regs	%Reg Bits	AIG Size
mult_hold_1	6	2	258	75	99	24452
mult_hold_2	6	2	514	75	100	98052
mult_hold_3	6	2	1026	75	100	392708
mult_hold_4	6	10	266	38	96	24638
mult_viol_1	7	2	268	78	99	25008
mult_viol_2	7	2	524	78	100	99119
mult_viol_3	7	2	1036	78	100	394797
mult_viol_4	7	10	279	41	96	25193
mult_viol_5	7	10	279	41	96	25193
mult_viol_6	7	10	279	41	96	25190
mult_viol_7	7	10	279	41	96	25190
fifo_hold_2	28	10	474	74	98	6848
fifo_hold_3	44	10	866	81	99	17968
fifo_hold_4	76	10	1642	88	99	53904
M0+_hold	56	26	1306	68	98	41630

11. When all CTIs from the current frontier k have been eliminated, refinement clauses from earlier iterations are checked to see if they can be moved forward to tighten later frontiers. A refinement clause $\omega \in F_j$, $1 \leq j \leq k$ that causes the query $F_j \wedge T \wedge \Delta \wedge \neg\omega^+ \wedge P^+$ to be UNSAT indicates that cube $\neg\omega$ in frame $j + 1$ is unreachable in one step from frame j and can thus be eliminated from frame $j + 1$. This is accomplished by propagating clause ω forward: $F_{j+1} = F_{j+1} \wedge \omega$.

12. The procedure terminates proving that P holds if two successive frames become equal, i.e., if $F_j = F_{j+1}$ for some $1 \leqslant j \leqslant k$. This check is equivalent to finding the clause set associated with frame j has become empty.

13. Otherwise, a new frame is created and initialized to P and the procedure continues to check for CTIs corresponding to longer counterexample traces.

8   Experimental Evaluation

Anecdotally, abstracting a design's datapath is commonly believed to yield scalable verification of its control logic. However, unlike verification at the bit-level which enjoys a large corpus of benchmarks and published results, there is little documentation in the open literature of the effectiveness of datapath abstraction on a diverse set of word-level benchmarks. The dearth of publicly-available RTL benchmarks that preserve the word-level semantics of a design was one of the main challenges we faced when evaluating the effectiveness of Averroes. Realizing that reporting on hand-crafted synthetic benchmarks would not be convincing, we opted instead to evaluate performance on a set of 139 industrial Verilog benchmarks that we obtained under non-disclosure agreements.[4]

---

[4] Companies understandably want to protect the IP of their, or their customers', RTL designs. However, to spur further research in this space, it is important to find a way to make such RTL designs publicly available without compromising their owners' IP rights.

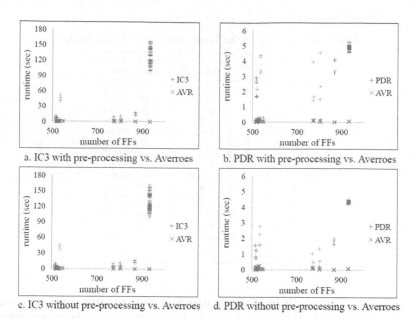

a. IC3 with pre-processing vs. Averroes   b. PDR with pre-processing vs. Averroes

c. IC3 without pre-processing vs. Averroes   d. PDR without pre-processing vs. Averroes

Fig. 5. Verification Results of the Generic Industrial Benchmarks

Of these, 124 were medium-sized "generic" benchmarks that were used for initial calibration. Their code sizes ranged between 298 and 805 lines; in terms of flip-flops, the smallest had 514 and the largest had 931. The remaining 15 benchmarks included 11 large multipliers, 3 FIFO designs, and the ARM Cortex-M0+ core [23]. The code sizes for these ranged from 116 to 10,226 lines. Table 2 lists additional statistics including the number of multi-bit registers (Regs), the number of single-bit flip-flops (FFs), the total number of state bits (FFs + the number of bits in the registers), the percentage of registers and register bits in the benchmark, and the number of AND nodes in the AIG representation [24] of its synthesized bit-level netlist. The multiplier benchmarks involved checking the sequential equivalence before and after clock gating optimizations; in four of these the property holds, and in the remaining seven it fails. The FIFO benchmarks check a "read-after-write" property for different FIFO depths. Finally, the M0+ experiment involved checking self-equivalence under partial initialization (i.e., when only a subset of the state bits are initialized on reset); this is sometimes referred to as self-equivalence with don't-cares or SEQX. In all cases, the verification involved an *unbounded check* to determine if the given safety property holds, on all, or is violated, by some, reachable states.

We compared the performance of Averroes to that of IC3 and PDR *with and without pre-processing*. In their default modes, IC3 and PDR simplify the input design before they start the approximate reachability loop: IC3 applies AIG sweeping [25]; PDR invokes the ABC dprove command [26]. Such pre-processing can greatly reduce the size of the input circuit which helps with the subsequent reachability computation. All experiments were run on a 3.2GHz Xeon desktop computer with a 16 GB memory. A time-out of 10,000 seconds was used for

Table 3. Verification Results of the Large Industrial Benchmarks

Benchmark	Runtime, sec			Frames			CTI Checks			Refinement Clauses			Solver Calls		
	IC3	PDR	AVR	IC3	PDR	AVR	IC3	PDR	AVR	IC3	PDR	AVR	IC3	PDR	AVR
mult_hold_1	T.O.	T.O.	0.02	1	3	1	41595	3	4	256	131720	3	776723	6331714	22
mult_hold_2	T.O.	T.O.	0.02	1	3	1	9559	3	4	512	13008	3	159978	1032718	22
mult_hold_3	ERR	T.O.	0.02	N/A	3	1	N/A	3	4	N/A	5986	3	N/A	546718	22
mult_hold_4	ERR	T.O.	0.04	N/A	2	2	N/A	2	8	N/A	1	8	N/A	10	56
mult_viol_1	ERR	116.15	0.05	N/A	2	1	N/A	2	5	N/A	3	3	N/A	21	15
mult_viol_2	ERR	256.32	0.18	N/A	2	1	N/A	2	5	N/A	2	3	N/A	16	15
mult_viol_3	ERR	1483.92	0.75	N/A	2	1	N/A	2	5	N/A	2	3	N/A	16	15
mult_viol_4	ERR	T.O.	0.54	N/A	2	7	N/A	2	30	N/A	262365	29	N/A	8177493	335
mult_viol_5	ERR	T.O.	11.88	N/A	2	22	N/A	2	47	N/A	252987	69	N/A	7961852	3040
mult_viol_6	ERR	T.O.	299.23	N/A	2	115	N/A	2	120	N/A	247035	275	N/A	8102702	55251
mult_viol_7	ERR	T.O.	1884.52	N/A	2	451	N/A	2	536	N/A	239809	754	N/A	7826919	425892
fifo_hold_2	13.79	14.87	1.35	9	12	8	1599	12	115	1691	4030	115	30060	94230	1574
fifo_hold_3	249.94	201.58	12.88	16	20	16	6455	20	355	6759	17772	317	306131	612147	9711
fifo_hold_4	5322.7	746.94	264.85	33	31	28	29898	36984	1804	25700	24609	1403	2602365	1611008	103590
M0+_hold	ERR	T.O.	917.76	N/A	8	17	N/A	5315	1154	N/A	3783	911	N/A	75898	45755

a. IC3 and PDR were run *with* pre-processing.

Benchmark	Runtime, sec			Frames			CTI Checks			Refinement Clauses			Solver Calls		
mult_hold_1	ERR	T.O.	0.02	N/A	2	1	N/A	134	4	N/A	217	3	N/A	1307	22
mult_hold_2	ERR	T.O.	0.02	N/A	2	1	N/A	257	4	N/A	512	3	N/A	3147	22
mult_hold_3	ERR	T.O.	0.02	N/A	2	1	N/A	521	4	N/A	612	3	N/A	2915	22
mult_hold_4	ERR	T.O.	0.04	N/A	2	2	N/A	189	8	N/A	250	8	N/A	1611	56
mult_viol_1	ERR	0.62	0.05	N/A	2	1	N/A	256	5	N/A	383	3	N/A	1439	15
mult_viol_2	ERR	10.86	0.18	N/A	2	1	N/A	386	5	N/A	532	3	N/A	2129	15
mult_viol_3	ERR	219.93	0.75	N/A	2	1	N/A	537	5	N/A	798	3	N/A	3396	15
mult_viol_4	ERR	T.O.	0.54	N/A	2	7	N/A	181	30	N/A	284	29	N/A	1821	335
mult_viol_5	ERR	T.O.	11.88	N/A	2	22	N/A	191	47	N/A	252	69	N/A	1596	3040
mult_viol_6	ERR	T.O.	299.23	N/A	2	115	N/A	177	120	N/A	273	275	N/A	1751	55251
mult_viol_7	ERR	T.O.	1884.52	N/A	2	451	N/A	179	536	N/A	260	754	N/A	1660	425892
fifo_hold_2	19.67	21.12	1.35	9	16	8	1944	7191	115	2090	5544	115	38000	192592	1574
fifo_hold_3	259.1	1252.89	12.88	17	29	16	6468	28402	355	8000	39937	317	273378	2525164	9711
fifo_hold_4	4715.67	10454.09	264.85	32	32	28	29359	98122	1804	42802	153114	1403	2453754	7618089	103590
M0+_hold	ERR	T.O.	917.76	N/A	8	17	N/A	5592	1154	N/A	4363	911	N/A	77808	45755

b. IC3 and PDR were run *without* pre-processing.

each verification run. Each of the 124 generic benchmarks was provided with a single specified safety property and were meant to calibrate the performance of Averroes against that of IC3 and PDR. Fig. 5 compares the runtime of Averroes against that of IC3 and PDR as a function of the number of flip-flops in these benchmarks. In almost all cases, Averroes is the fastest verifier and, unlike IC3 and PDR, its performance is largely independent of the number of flip-flops. This validates the hoped-for benefit of datapath abstraction. Oddly, the performance of IC3 and PDR with pre-processing was worse than without! This seems to be due to the fact that there was not much structural reduction due to pre-processing causing pre-processing overhead to outweigh its benefit.

Table 3 shows the results of our experiments on the 15 large benchmarks; time-outs are indicated as T.O., and ERR indicates that IC3 reported an error and was unable to process the benchmark[5]. As with the generic benchmarks, Averroes was the fastest verifier across this entire set of 15 benchmarks. IC3 and PDR had particular difficulty with the multiplier benchmarks. IC3 either

---

[5] We traced this error to an incorrect time-out exit that occurred before the specified time-out value!

Table 4. Runtimes (in Seconds) of FIFO on Various Depths

depth	State Bits	IC3	PDR	AVR	AVR_MA	AVR_MAA
2^2	474	13.79	14.87	1.35	1.8	8.28
2^3	866	249.94	201.58	12.88	10.92	20.57
2^4	1642	5322.7	746.94	264.85	120.51	21.93
2^5	3186	T.O.	T.O.	T.O.	2538.49	23.31
2^6	6266	T.O.	T.O.	T.O.	T.O.	19.17
2^7	12418	T.O.	T.O.	T.O.	T.O.	24.02
2^8	24714	T.O.	T.O.	T.O.	T.O.	20.58
2^9	49298	T.O.	T.O.	T.O.	T.O.	21.15
2^{10}	98458	T.O.	T.O.	T.O.	T.O.	27.9
2^{11}	196770	T.O.	T.O.	T.O.	T.O.	29.02
2^{12}	393386	T.O.	T.O.	T.O.	T.O.	23.57
2^{13}	786610	T.O.	T.O.	T.O.	T.O.	33.79
2^{14}	1573050	T.O.	T.O.	T.O.	T.O.	46.85
2^{15}	3145922	T.O.	T.O.	T.O.	T.O.	57.04
2^{16}	6291658	T.O.	T.O.	T.O.	T.O.	79.19

timed out or had an error exit. PDR timed out on eight out of the eleven cases. A possible explanation for this behavior is that the combinational logic in the multiplier benchmarks, which involves wide (32- to 256-bit) datapath signals, led to bit-level formulas that were too large and complicated for IC3 and PDR to handle effectively. An examination of the runtime per solver call for mult_hold_2 and fifo_hold_2 confirms this. These two benchmarks have similar sizes in terms of state bits, but mult_hold_2 leads to an AIG whose size is more than 14 times larger than that of fifo_hold_2. PDR made 3,147 solver calls in 10,000 seconds for the multiplier benchmark, averaging about 3.18 seconds per call. The corresponding data for the FIFO benchmark were 192,592 calls in 21.12 seconds, an average of 110 micro seconds per call which is more than four orders of magnitude faster. Additionally, the peculiarly low number of solver calls for mult_hold_4 in Table 3-a seemed too suspicious; on closer examination we found out that the first 10 calls were very quick, but the solver timed out on the 11th. This again suggests a difficult formula that thwarted the solver.

In contrast to PDR's performance, Averroes was able to solve all 11 cases, most in fractions of a second. Other performance metrics, such as the number of net refinement clauses and number of solver calls, are significantly less than those for PDR suggesting that datapath abstraction was effective in reducing the "size" of the reachability search space and that the abstract refinement clauses were much stronger than their bit-level counterparts in pruning the space. The cases requiring longer runtimes, about 30 minutes for mult_viol_7, were due to extremely long counterexample traces that require the traversal of many frames which, in turn, translate into many solver calls. For instance, the counterexample trace for mult_viol_7 consisted of 1002 transitions which required the traversal of 451 frames and making 425,892 solver calls.

The three FIFO benchmarks involved checking a "read-after-write" property for the FIFO entries. The FIFO depths (number of entries) ranged from 4 (for fifo_hold_2) to 16 (for fifo_hold_4) and each benchmark had two FIFOs whose width is 32 bits and two FIFOs whose width is 16 bits. Again, Averroes outperforms both IC3 and PDR on these benchmarks, on average being about 20 times faster. This is another indication of the effectiveness of datapath abstraction. To dramatize this, we carried out a parametric experiment by increasing the width of the FIFO entries. As expected, the runtime of Averroes did not change, whereas the runtimes of IC3 and PDR exhibited exponential behavior. However, all three verifiers exhibited exponential behavior as FIFO depths were increased! Upon reflection, this too should have been expected since FIFOs are basically "small" memories and datapath abstraction alone is insufficient to handle them. While memory abstraction is beyond the scope of this paper, we present in Table 4 data showing the performance of Averroes when it is augmented with the structural memory abstraction described in [27]. This type of abstraction can be layered on top of any model checking verifier and can certainly be added to IC3 and PDR. But as the column labeled AVR_MA in this table shows, memory abstraction scales the performance of Averroes only to a FIFO depth of 32. Further scaling requires integrating memory abstraction with datapath abstraction of the memory addresses. This is shown in column AVR_MAA. Clearly the combination of memory abstraction and memory *address* abstraction yields a verification flow that is largely independent of memory size. The linear increase in the runtime of Averroes is due to the bit-level feasibility checks on wider memory addresses as memory size increases.

The last benchmark in Table 3 is the SEQX instance of the Cortex-M0+. The verification goal here was to show that the M0+ core is self-equivalent when 41 of its state bits are left uninitialized on reset (i.e., their initial value is X or don't care). Specifically, SEQX holds when none of these don't-care values propagate to observable outputs. Effectively, the verifier is establishing the state equivalence of 2^{41} possible initial states. We should note that SEQX becomes quite trivial if the number of uninitialized state bits is small. In fact, bit-level verifiers can quickly solve such problems using structural hashing techniques. However, as the number of uninitialized state bits increases, structural hashing ceases to be effective (not very many equivalent signals to merge) and bit-level verifiers fail. This is clearly shown in Table 3: neither IC3 nor PDR was able to prove self-equivalence; Averroes required about 15 minutes to show that SEQX holds for M0+.

9   Conclusion

Many complex computational problems can be scalably handled by judicious elimination of irrelevant details. The Averroes verifier described in this paper integrates two orthogonal abstractions that, together, yield a scalable system for the verification of control-centric properties in hardware designs containing wide datapaths and complex control logic. To our knowledge, this is the first public demonstration of an automated verification flow for unbounded model checking of safety properties in industrial benchmarks. To be sure, there are many other abstraction approaches that have been shown to work well in different domains. However, for the particular control logic bugs targeted by our approach, datapath abstraction seems to provide the most scalability. Specifically, our preliminary evidence strongly suggests that scalability is quite achievable by augmenting bit-level reasoning with RTL word-level abstractions.

Acknowledgment. This work was funded in part by ARM, Ltd. Additional support was provided by the Qatar Computing Research Institute.

References

1. Bradley, A.R.: Sat-based model checking without unrolling. In: Jhala, R., Schmidt, D. (eds.) VMCAI 2011. LNCS, vol. 6538, pp. 70–87. Springer, Heidelberg (2011)
2. Een, N., Mishchenko, A., Brayton, R.: Efficient implementation of property directed reachability. In: FMCAD 2011, pp. 125–134. IEEE (2011)
3. Sheeran, M., Singh, S., Stålmarck, G.: Checking safety properties using induction and a sat-solver. In: Johnson, S.D., Hunt Jr., W.A. (eds.) FMCAD 2000. LNCS, vol. 1954, pp. 108–125. Springer, Heidelberg (2000)
4. Bjesse, P., Claessen, K.: Sat-based verification without state space traversal. In: Johnson, S.D., Hunt Jr., W.A. (eds.) FMCAD 2000. LNCS, vol. 1954, pp. 372–389. Springer, Heidelberg (2000)
5. Bradley, A.R., Manna, Z.: Checking safety by inductive generalization of counterexamples to induction. In: FMCAD 2007, pp. 173–180. IEEE (2007)
6. Kurshan, R.P.: Computer-Aided Verification of Coordinating Processes: The Automata-Theoretic Approach. Princeton University Press (1994)
7. Clarke, E., Grumberg, O., Jha, S., Lu, Y., Veith, H.: Counterexample-guided abstraction refinement. In: Emerson, E.A., Sistla, A.P. (eds.) CAV 2000. LNCS, vol. 1855, pp. 154–169. Springer, Heidelberg (2000)
8. Clarke, E., Grumberg, O., Jha, S., Lu, Y., Veith, H.: Counterexample-guided abstraction refinement for symbolic model checking. J. ACM 50(5), 752–794 (2003)
9. McMillan, K.L.: Symbolic Model Checking. Kluwer Academic Publishers (1993)
10. Cimatti, A., Clarke, E., Giunchiglia, F., Roveri, M.: Nusmv: A new symbolic model checker. STTT 2(4), 410–425 (2000)
11. Biere, A., Cimatti, A., Clarke, E.M., Zhu, Y.: Symbolic model checking without bdds. In: Cleaveland, W.R. (ed.) TACAS/ETA 1999. LNCS, vol. 1579, pp. 193–207. Springer, Heidelberg (1999)
12. Clarke, E., Biere, A., Raimi, R., Zhu, Y.: Bounded model checking using satisfiability solving. Formal Methods in System Design 19(1), 7–34 (2001)
13. Hoder, K., Bjørner, N.: Generalized property directed reachability. In: Cimatti, A., Sebastiani, R. (eds.) SAT 2012. LNCS, vol. 7317, pp. 157–171. Springer, Heidelberg (2012)
14. Cimatti, A., Griggio, A.: Software model checking via ic3. In: Madhusudan, P., Seshia, S.A. (eds.) CAV 2012. LNCS, vol. 7358, pp. 277–293. Springer, Heidelberg (2012)
15. Vizel, Y., Grumberg, O., Shoham, S.: Lazy abstraction and sat-based reachability in hardware model checking. In: FMCAD 2012, pp. 173–181 (2012)
16. Hojati, R., Brayton, R.K.: Automatic datapath abstraction in hardware systems. In: Wolper, P. (ed.) CAV 1995. LNCS, vol. 939, pp. 98–113. Springer, Heidelberg (1995)
17. Macii, E., Plessier, B., Somenzi, F.: Formal verification of digital systems by automatic reduction of data paths. IEEE Transactions on Computer-Aided Design of Integrated Circuits and Systems 16(10), 1136–1156 (1997)
18. Paruthi, V., Mansouri, N., Vemuri, R.: Automatic data path abstraction for verification of large scale designs. In: ICCD 1998, pp. 192–194. IEEE (1998)
19. Andraus, Z.S., Sakallah, K.A.: Automatic abstraction and verification of verilog models. In: DAC 2004, pp. 218–223 (2004)
20. Liffiton, M.H., Sakallah, K.A.: Algorithms for computing minimal unsatisfiable subsets of constraints. Journal of Automated Reasoning 40(1), 1–33 (2008)
21. Dutertre, B., De Moura, L.: The Yices SMT solver (2006) Tool paper at, http://yices.csl.sri.com/tool-paper.pdf

22. Chockler, H., Ivrii, A., Matsliah, A., Moran, S., Nevo, Z.: Incremental formal verification of hardware. In: FMCAD 2011, pp. 135–143 (2011)
23. ARM Cortex-M0+ Processor,
    http://www.arm.com/products/processors/cortex-m/cortex-m0plus.php
24. Biere, A.: The aiger and-inverter graph (aig) format (2007), fmv.jku.at/aiger
25. Een, N.: Cut sweeping. Cadence Design Systems, Tech. Rep. (2007)
26. Mishchenko, A., Case, M., Brayton, R., Jang, S.: Scalable and scalably-verifiable sequential synthesis. In: ICCAD 2008, pp. 234–241. IEEE (2008)
27. Bjesse, P.: Word-level sequential memory abstraction for model checking. In: FMCAD 2008, pp. 1–9 (November 2008)

QUICr: A Reusable Library for Parametric Abstraction of Sets and Numbers

Arlen Cox, Bor-Yuh Evan Chang, and Sriram Sankaranarayanan

University of Colorado Boulder

Abstract. This paper introduces QUICr, an abstract domain combinator library that lifts any domain for numbers into an efficient domain for numbers and *sets* of numbers. As a library, it is useful for inferring relational data invariants in programs that manipulate data structures. As a testbed, it allows easy extension of widening and join heuristics, enabling adaptations to new and varied applications. In this paper we present the architecture of the library, guidelines on how to select heuristics, and an example instantiation of the library using the APRON library to verify set-manipulating programs.

1   Introduction

Programs do not consist entirely of scalar variables. In nearly all programming languages, collections are either implemented as a library or built-in as a first-class type. Therefore, when verifying programs, it is vital to support containers as well as scalar values. In the decision procedures community, this is widely recognized with support for arrays, sets, and maps [1–3], but when invariant generation is concerned, such as in abstract interpretation [4], only arrays have been carefully considered [5–11], leaving other containers rarely explored [12–14]. Given that there is a plethora of abstract domains for reasoning about scalars [15, 16], it is necessary to build abstract domains that not only reason about containers, but also interact efficiently and precisely with existing domains for scalars. The best way to ensure interaction is, rather than building abstract domains for containers, building domain combinators that construct abstract domains for containers from existing abstract domains for numbers. Recently, such a domain for arrays was created [5], and a domain for sets was created [12]. This paper describes an implementation of the domain for sets called QUICr[1].

The implementation of the domain for sets is an OCaml functor that takes a numeric abstract domain and builds a domain for simultaneous reasoning about numbers and sets of numbers. It constructs a relational abstract domain such that without knowing the specific contents of a set, that set can be related to another set by equality or subset relationships. This kind of reasoning is useful for a variety of applications:

- *Whole-program verification of container-manipulating programs* – The QUICr library can reason about constants and known sets as well as unknown sets.

---

[1] Library available at http://pl.cs.colorado.edu/projects/quicgraphs

A. Biere and R. Bloem (Eds.): CAV 2014, LNCS 8559, pp. 866–873, 2014.

It does not conflate known parts with unknown parts unnecessarily and thus can keep track of sets that are partially known and partially unknown. Iteration over these sets as well as addition and removal from these sets is supported allowing the inference of a wide range of program properties.

- *Modular verification of container-manipulating programs* – If a whole program is not known, a precondition can be provided as a relational constraint between sets without knowing any contents. Inferred loop invariants and post-conditions will also be relational with respect to any existing sets. The QUICr library will automatically utilize any capabilities of the underlying numerical domain to express relationships between set variables.
- *Shape/data abstraction combinators* – Advanced domain combinators such as those provided by shape analyzers [17–19] typically cannot to incorporate collection data abstractions into their inductive definitions. To verify both shape and data properties of programs, current analyzers [20] rely on multiset abstractions. By adding relational domains, data can be related between multiple inductive definitions and thus more precisely represented.
- *Parametric abstraction combinators* – Effective reasoning about sets enables the construction of new domain combinators that do not yet exist today without relational set abstractions. When combining abstract domains [21, 22], it is often useful to be able to express relationships between an unbounded number of elements in each abstract domain. With a relational domain for sets it is possible to express these relationships efficiently and effectively.

The goal of this paper is to both document how to use the QUICr library as well as to inspire thinking about applications for set domains. Towards this goal we provide an overview of the underlying representation as it is implemented in the library (Section 2). This knowledge is sufficient to understand the heuristics currently employed in the library and how the heuristics can be extended to handle additional and different situations that may arise from as-of-yet unknown applications (Section 3). To demonstrate that the QUICr library is precise and efficient with the built-in heuristics, we also give results from some modular verification of container-manipulating programs (Section 4).

2   Overview of QUIC Graphs

The QUICr library provides an implementation of the QUIC graphs [12] abstract domain combinator for numeric domains. It is used as part of an abstract interpretation system (see inset) that not only proves properties of programs, but performs necessary invariant generation. QUICr represents, accumulates and manipulates set constraints, while sharing equality information with the numeric domain in a way similar to Nelson Oppen [23]. This combination allows representing and inferring constraints that consist of both

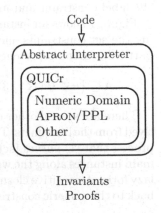

Code
↓
Abstract Interpreter

QUICr

Numeric Domain
APRON/PPL
Other

↓
Invariants
Proofs

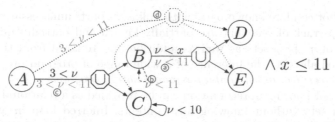

Fig. 1. Example QUIC graph and accompanying numeric domain instances, showing a sequence of inferences: ⓐ is derived by pushing the external numeric domain fact $x \leq 11$ and $\nu < x$; ⓑ is derived by inferring a new self-loop with $\top$ and pushing ⓐ; ⓒ is derived by pushing ⓑ $\sqcup \nu < 10$ and $3 < \nu$; and ⓓ is derived by inference/transitive closure of the graph

set constraints involving union, intersection, subset, and equality, along with numeric constraints that are dictated by the representations used by the underlying numeric domain.

For straight-line code, QUICr can be used to implement a decision procedure and can compute the validity of Hoare triples for set manipulating programs. For example, the inset shows a Hoare triple that can be validated using QUICr instantiated with an equivalence classes-based numeric domain. The QUICr library manipulates the formulas to learn that $A = B$ because they are both equal to C unioned with the same value. The problem that QUICr solves is not only how to efficiently represent and manipulate these formulas to construct a decision procedure, but how to do so to automatically infer loop invariants.

$$[x = y]$$
$$A := C \cup \{x\};$$
$$B := C \cup \{y\}$$
$$\left[\begin{array}{l} x = y \wedge A = B \\ \wedge A = C \cup \{x\} \end{array}\right]$$

QUICr represents set constraints using a constraint hypergraph where each vertex represents either the empty set, a singleton set, or a set variable, while each hyperedge represents a constraint between the linked vertexes. Each constraint is constructed of three parts: (1) a union of each edge target; (2) an intersection of each edge source; and (3) a numeric domain instance that labels the edge and represents a fact that holds on each element ν in the intersection. Each edge then represents the constraint that each element in the intersection must satisfy the label constraint and must also be in the union.

Figure 1 shows an instance of a QUIC graph. On the left is a graph representing the set constraints and on the right is a numerical domain constraint. This particular graph represents the following three basic facts:

$$A \subseteq \{\nu \in B \cup C \mid 3 < \nu\} \qquad B \subseteq \{\nu \in D \cup E \mid \nu < x\} \qquad x \leq 11$$

There are several other edges shown using lighter lines that represent facts derived from the basic facts. These derived facts come from a three-part lazy inference process that (1) *pushes* facts from one edge to another, strengthening numeric domain instances along the way, (2) *infers* new edges from the existing edges using a lazy form of transitive closure, and (3) *cycles* equalities found in the set constraints back to the numeric constraints as necessary. These three inference operations rely

Table 1. Heuristics refine the candidate generation strategy to both improve performance and increase precision over a naive candidate generation by providing hints [24] for join and widen operations

Name	Description	Effect
Empty Remove	Replace edges with empty set with equivalent edges without that empty set.	Improves performance by removing redundant edges.
Min Rewrite	Assign a total order to all vertexes in the graph and for each edge and add an edge using the identical edge using the minimum equivalent vertex for each vertex.	Increases use of empty sets and thus of Empty Remove; increases use of singleton sets and reductions associated with singletons; creates likely-common edges.
Patt Match	Pattern matching identifies certain subgraphs and eagerly adds derived facts based on those subgraphs.	Improves precision by adding additional candidates that correspond to likely edges in the join; often arise from specific code patterns (iteration over sets).

solely on basic domain operators provided by numeric domains, such as built-in meet, join, and widen operators. These inferred strengthenings are used to implement domain operations such as join, widen, and containment.

Because the graph representation can be exponential in number of variables, the QUICr implementation lazily derives facts, on demand. To implement this, QUICr uses a rewrite rules approach, which has two benefits: (1) it allows easy viewing of progress – each rule can print out status information to indicate where it is being applied and why; (2) it allows easy extension of the rules – adding new rules or reordering rule application is simply a matter adding new calls or reordering calls in the rule application function. This architecture can thus be easily extended to improve precision by identifying application-specific reductions or to increase performance by eliminating application of some rules.

To implement join and widen operations, QUICr employs a generator/checker strategy. A list of candidate edges is generated with unknown numeric domain constraints. The analyzer attempts to derive each of these edges in both inputs to join or widen. When the edge can be derived in both, it is added to the result using a computed numeric domain constraint. Otherwise, the candidate is ignored. Initially, the candidates are chosen to be all of the edges from both sides of the join. Unfortunately, this strategy suffers from a variety of problems. Edges that are derivable by lazy inference in both graphs, but are not directly in either graph will be lost. Additionally, there can be many edges that are redundant or nearly redundant, causing many extra checker invocations. To improve precision and performance, QUICr employs heuristics to refine the initial list of candidate edges. The implemented heuristics and their effects are detailed in Table 1.

3 QUICr Usage and Extension

QUICr is implemented as a functor in the OCaml language. A *functor* is a module constructor that takes a module as a parameter and produces another module.

In this case, it takes a numeric abstract domain as a parameter and produces an abstract domain for sets of numbers. The current requirements on the numeric abstract domain are that (1) it must be possible to add and remove fresh variables from the domain – this is used to add or remove the bound variable; (2) it must provide sound top, bottom, meet, join, widen, and containment operators – these are used when pushing facts; and (3) it must provide an interface to retrieve and add equality constraints in the numeric domain. If these conditions are met, any numerical abstract domain can be substituted.

Unlike the implementation in [12], QUICr is more general and comes with four numerical domains provided: (1) a simple equivalence class abstract domain, where variables can be equal to each other and numeric constants; and domains provided by APRON: (2) boxes; (3) octagons; and (4) polyhedra. Additionally, it can be instantiated with any numeric domain that meets the APRON interface (such as PPL [16]). Adapting other existing domains only requires developing a functor that behaves as an interface adapter.

While built-in heuristics that are described in Table 1 are sufficient for many applications (see Section 4), they might not be sufficient for every application. If this is the case, additional heuristics can be added. The easiest form of heuristic to add is additional pattern matches. QUICr provides a graph matching system that can match arbitrary subgraphs against a template pattern. These matches can trigger rewrites and refine candidate generation. This is especially useful if a particular pattern is not being discovered by the built-in heuristics. For example, patterns are provided to identify nested unions and to then unnest the unions. This situation arises frequently when iteratively copying and manipulating sets.

Once instantiated, QUICr provides pretty printers for set constraints. It can output to both the console as well as to HTML and LaTeX. The provided example application uses the HTML output to produce programs annotated with the standard mathematical representation of sets.

4   Instantiation

Provided with the library is an example analyzer that allows selecting from the command line among the three of the four included numeric domains. It uses a simple input language reminiscent of JavaScript to analyze set and number manipulating programs. To evaluate the effectiveness of the QUICr, it is instantiated with the APRON-provided polyhedra numeric domain [15]. Then, by hand translation of Python programs, the resulting abstract domain is applied to all of the set-manipulating programs in the Python test suite, attempting to validate the assertions specified in the test suite. For example, the copy test iteratively copies one set to another, producing a set identical to the original. The results are shown in Table 2.

The shown benchmarks are those that include loops over the contents of a set or multiple sets and therefore must infer loop invariants. The inference of these loop invariants is based on the widening operation and thus not guaranteed to be precise. However, it is nearly always fast and is able to prove a significant number of real properties automatically.

Table 2. Results on a set of small benchmarks. **#N**: # of numeric domain variables, **#S**: # of set variables, **#A**: # of assertions to be proved, **#P**: # of assertions automatically proved, **T(s)**: Time taken (seconds), **#I**: number of iterations of abstract interpreter before convergence. − represents a time out (600 seconds). Heuristics were selected based on the first four tests and validated on remaining tests.

	#N	#S	#A	#P	T(s)	#I
copy	1	6	2	2	0.2	2
filter	4	6	2	2	0.6	3
merge	2	14	2	1	0.6	4
partition	4	8	4	4	1.1	3
generic_max	3	8	6	3	0.9	6
b_filter	6	6	2	2	0.7	3
b_map	9	7	2	2	0.2	5
b_max_min	3	4	1	1	0.4	3

	#N	#S	#A	#P	T(s)	#I
b_reduce	7	4	1	0	0.4	3
iter_ind	20	12	1	1	84.4	39
mul_ret	9	2	2	2	0.2	6
nest_dep	5	7	1	0	2.2	12
resize1	15	5	5	4	1.7	18
simp_cond	11	5	4	3	4.6	12
simp_nest	9	10	2	0	−	1399
srange	6	2	2	2	0.1	6
Total			37	29	98.3	125

5 Ongoing Development

Not only is QUICr useful today, but it is useful as a platform for development of future set and multi-set domain combinators. The graph structure can be extended by adding additional edge types. For example, we are evaluating an edge type that utilizes an underapproximating numeric domain. With such an edge type, it is possible to infer equalities with set comprehensions and to support set complement operations.

Additionally, the graph structure can be extended to add additional bound variables. Currently there is one bound variable per edge, but this may be an unnecessary restriction. With multiple bound variables, more complex relationships can be represented in the base domain. For example, with multiple bound variables we could represent the constraint that a set consists of elements that are the sum of elements from two other sets. We want to exploit this to be able to infer functions that map one set onto another.

Despite our use of QUICr to perform verification of container-manipulating programs, we believe that sets can be used as part of many other analyses. It is our desire for the QUICr library to be integrated into new, innovative domain combinators that effectively use set relations to represent unbounded numbers of connections between domains. We also hope to see additional extensions beyond our own to support more advanced set operations including cardinality queries, Cartesian products, and multi-set operations.

References

1. de Moura, L.M., Bjørner, N.: Generalized, efficient array decision procedures. In: FMCAD, pp. 45–52 (2009)
2. Kuncak, V.: Modular Data Structure Verification. PhD thesis, EECS Department. Massachusetts Institute of Technology (2007)

3. Bradley, A.R., Manna, Z., Sipma, H.B.: What's decidable about arrays? In: Emerson, E.A., Namjoshi, K.S. (eds.) VMCAI 2006. LNCS, vol. 3855, pp. 427–442. Springer, Heidelberg (2006)
4. Cousot, P., Cousot, R.: Abstract interpretation: A unified lattice model for static analysis of programs by construction or approximation of fixpoints. In: POPL, pp. 238–252 (1977)
5. Cousot, P., Cousot, R., Logozzo, F.: A parametric segmentation functor for fully automatic and scalable array content analysis. In: POPL, pp. 105–118 (2011)
6. Dillig, I., Dillig, T., Aiken, A.: Fluid updates: Beyond strong vs. weak updates. In: Gordon, A.D. (ed.) ESOP 2010. LNCS, vol. 6012, pp. 246–266. Springer, Heidelberg (2010)
7. Seghir, M.N., Podelski, A., Wies, T.: Abstraction refinement for quantified array assertions. In: Palsberg, J., Su, Z. (eds.) SAS 2009. LNCS, vol. 5673, pp. 3–18. Springer, Heidelberg (2009)
8. Kovács, L., Voronkov, A.: Finding loop invariants for programs over arrays using a theorem prover. In: Chechik, M., Wirsing, M. (eds.) FASE 2009. LNCS, vol. 5503, pp. 470–485. Springer, Heidelberg (2009)
9. Halbwachs, N., Péron, M.: Discovering properties about arrays in simple programs. In: PLDI, pp. 339–348 (2008)
10. Jhala, R., McMillan, K.L.: Array abstractions from proofs. In: Damm, W., Hermanns, H. (eds.) CAV 2007. LNCS, vol. 4590, pp. 193–206. Springer, Heidelberg (2007)
11. Gopan, D., Reps, T.W., Sagiv, S.: A framework for numeric analysis of array operations. In: POPL, pp. 338–350 (2005)
12. Cox, A., Chang, B.-Y.E., Sankaranarayanan, S.: QUIC graphs: Relational invariant generation for containers. In: Castagna, G. (ed.) ECOOP 2013. LNCS, vol. 7920, pp. 401–425. Springer, Heidelberg (2013)
13. Pham, T.-H., Trinh, M.-T., Truong, A.-H., Chin, W.-N.: FixBag: A fixpoint calculator for quantified bag constraints. In: Gopalakrishnan, G., Qadeer, S. (eds.) CAV 2011. LNCS, vol. 6806, pp. 656–662. Springer, Heidelberg (2011)
14. Dillig, I., Dillig, T., Aiken, A.: Precise reasoning for programs using containers. In: POPL, pp. 187–200 (2011)
15. Jeannet, B., Miné, A.: Apron: A library of numerical abstract domains for static analysis. In: Bouajjani, A., Maler, O. (eds.) CAV 2009. LNCS, vol. 5643, pp. 661–667. Springer, Heidelberg (2009)
16. Bagnara, R., Hill, P.M., Zaffanella, E.: The parma polyhedra library: Toward a complete set of numerical abstractions for the analysis and verification of hardware and software systems. Sci. Comput. Program. 72(1-2), 3–21 (2008)
17. Berdine, J., Cook, B., Ishtiaq, S.: Slayer: Memory safety for systems-level code. In: Gopalakrishnan, G., Qadeer, S. (eds.) CAV 2011. LNCS, vol. 6806, pp. 178–183. Springer, Heidelberg (2011)
18. Chang, B.Y.E., Rival, X.: Modular construction of shape-numeric analyzers. In: Festschrift for Dave Schmidt, pp. 161–185 (2013)
19. Sagiv, S., Reps, T.W., Wilhelm, R.: Parametric shape analysis via 3-valued logic. In: POPL, pp. 105–118 (1999)
20. Bouajjani, A., Drăgoi, C., Enea, C., Rezine, A., Sighireanu, M.: Invariant synthesis for programs manipulating lists with unbounded data. In: Touili, T., Cook, B., Jackson, P. (eds.) CAV 2010. LNCS, vol. 6174, pp. 72–88. Springer, Heidelberg (2010)
21. Cousot, P., Cousot, R.: Systematic design of program analysis frameworks. In: POPL, pp. 269–282 (1979)

22. Toubhans, A., Chang, B.-Y.E., Rival, X.: Reduced product combination of abstract domains for shapes. In: Giacobazzi, R., Berdine, J., Mastroeni, I. (eds.) VMCAI 2013. LNCS, vol. 7737, pp. 375–395. Springer, Heidelberg (2013)
23. Nelson, G., Oppen, D.C.: Simplification by cooperating decision procedures. ACM Trans. Program. Lang. Syst. 1(2), 245–257 (1979)
24. Laviron, V., Logozzo, F.: Refining abstract interpretation-based static analyses with hints. In: Hu, Z. (ed.) APLAS 2009. LNCS, vol. 5904, pp. 343–358. Springer, Heidelberg (2009)

Author Index